DOSTOEVSKY
A Writer in His Time

JOSEPH FRANK

edited by
Mary Petrusewicz

PRINCETON UNIVERSITY PRESS *Princeton and Oxford*

Copyright © 2010 by Princeton University Press

Published by Princeton University Press, 41 William Street, Princeton, New Jersey 08540

In the United Kingdom: Princeton University Press, 6 Oxford Street, Woodstock,

Oxfordshire OX20 1TW

press.princeton.edu

Second printing, and first paperback printing, 2012

Paperback ISBN 978-0-691-15599-9

The Library of Congress has cataloged the cloth edition of this book as follows

Frank, Joseph, 1918–

    Dostoevsky : a writer in his time / Joseph Frank.

      p. cm.

    Abridged ed. of author's work in 5 v.: Dostoevsky. c1976–2002.

    Includes bibliographical references and index.

    ISBN 978-0-691-12819-1 (acid-free paper) 1. Dostoyevsky, Fyodor, 1821–1881. 2. Novelists,

Russian—19th century—Biography. 3. Russia—Intellectual life—1801–1917. I. Title.

    PG3328.F75 2010

    891.73'3—dc22

    [B]   2009001418

British Library Cataloging-in-Publication Data is available

This book has been composed in *Adobe Garamond*

Printed on acid-free paper. ∞

Printed in the United States of America

10 9 8 7

Frontispiece: The bust of Dostoevsky on his grave

Parched with the spirit's thirst, I crossed
An endless desert sunk in gloom,
And a six-winged seraph came
Where the tracks met and I stood lost.
Fingers light as dream he laid
Upon my lids; I opened wide
My eagle eyes, and gazed around.
He laid his fingers on my ears
And they were filled with roaring sound:
I heard the music of the spheres,
The flight of angels through the skies,
The beasts that crept beneath the sea,
The heady uprush of the vine;
And, like a lover kissing me,
He rooted out this tongue of mine
Fluent in lies and vanity;
He tore my fainting lips apart
And, with his right hand steeped in blood,
He armed me with a serpent's dart;
With his bright sword he split my breast;
My heart leapt to him with a bound;
A glowing livid coal he pressed
Into the hollow of the wound.
There in the desert I lay dead.
And God called out to me and said:
"Rise, prophet, rise, and hear, and see,
And let my words be seen and heard
By all who turn aside from me.
And burn them with my fiery word."

—A. S. Pushkin, "The Prophet"
    trans. D. M. Thomas

CONTENTS

PART I

The Seeds of Revolt, 1821–1849

PART II

The Years of Ordeal, 1850–1859

PART III

The Stir of Liberation, 1860–1865

PART IV

The Miraculous Years, 1865–1871

PART V

The Mantle of the Prophet, 1871–1881

ILLUSTRATIONS

Unless otherwise noted, all illustrations are from *Feodor Mikhailovich Dostoevsky v portretakh, illyustratsiyakh, dokumentakh*, ed. V. S. Nechaeva (Moscow, 1972).

PREFACE

Dostoevsky: A Writer in His Time

Since the present volume is a condensation of the five that I have already published on the life and works of Dostoevsky, I should like to acquaint my new readers with the point of view from which they were written. My approach arose primarily from a troubling sense that important aspects of Dostoevsky's work had been overlooked, or at least not accorded sufficient importance, in the considerable secondary literature devoted to his career. The major perspective of these studies derived from his personal history, and this had been so spectacular that it was almost irresistible for biographers to recount its peripeties at length. No other Russian writer of his stature could equal the range of his familiarity with both the depths and heights of Russian society—a range that included four years spent as a convict living side by side with peasant criminals, and then, at the end of his life, invitations to dine with younger members of the family of Tsar Alexander II, who, it was believed, might benefit from his conversation. It is quite understandable that such a life, in all its fascinating particularities, should have furnished the background against which Dostoevsky's works were initially viewed and interpreted.

The more I read Dostoevsky's novels and stories, however, not to mention his journalism, both literary and political (his *Diary of a Writer* was the most widely circulated monthly publication ever published in Russia), the more it seemed to me that a conventional biographical point of view could not do justice to the complexities of his creations. To be sure, while Dostoevsky's characters struggle with the psychological and sentimental problems that provide the substance of all novels, more important, his books are also inspired by the ideological doctrines of his time. Such doctrines, particularly in his major works, furnish the chief motivations for the often bizarre, eccentric, and occasionally murderous behavior of characters like Raskolnikov in *Crime and Punishment*, or both Stavrogin and Kirillov in *Demons*. The personal entanglements of the figures in the novels, though depicted with often melodramatic intensity, cannot really be understood unless we grasp how their actions are intertwined with ideological motivations.

It thus seemed to me, when I set out to write my own work on Dostoevsky, that its perspective should be shifted, and that the purely personal biography should no longer dominate the explanatory context in which he was creating. Much less space is thus given in my books to the details of Dostoevsky's private life and much more to the clash of various ideas prevailing during the period in which he lived. The most perceptive reader of my first four volumes, the much lamented and gifted novelist and critic David Foster Wallace, remarked that "Ellman's *James Joyce*, pretty much the standard by which most literary bios are measured, doesn't go into anything like Frank's detail on ideology or politics or social theory." This is not to say that I ignore Dostoevsky's private life, but it remains linked to other aspects of his era that provide it with a much larger significance. Indeed, one way of defining Dostoevsky's originality is to see in it this ability to integrate the personal with the major social-political and cultural issues of his day.

The above remarks about the shortcomings of the critical literature on Dostoevsky apply primarily to books in the various languages other than his own (mainly English, French, and German). It certainly cannot be said that the ideological and philosophical background of Dostoevsky's creations has not been explored in Russian scholarship and criticism. Indeed, my own analysis of this background is greatly indebted to several generations of Russian scholars and critics such as Dimitry Merezhkovsky, Vyacheslav Ivanov, and Leonid Grossman, as well as to philosophers such as Lev Shestov and Nikolay Berdyaev. But as a result of the Bolshevik Revolution, it became difficult for Russian scholars, up until very recently, to build on these initiators and to continue to study Dostoevsky impartially and objectively. His greatest works, after all, had been efforts to undermine the ideological foundations out of which that revolution had sprung, and it was thus necessary to highlight his deficiencies rather than his achievements. As for émigré scholars, with very few exceptions their works dwelt on the moral-philosophical implications of Dostoevsky's ideas rather than on the texts themselves. While utilizing all this interpretative effort with gratitude, I have tried to rectify what seemed to me its limitations, whether caused by ideological restrictions or by nonliterary concerns.

Placing Dostoevsky's writings in their social-political and ideological context, however, is only the first step toward an adequate comprehension of his works. For what is important about them is not that his characters engage in theoretical disputations. It is, rather, that their ideas become part of their personalities, to such an extent, indeed, that neither exists independently of the other. His unrivaled genius as an ideological novelist was this capacity to invent actions and situations in which ideas dominate behavior without the latter becoming allegorical. He possessed what I call an "eschatological imagination," one that could envision putting ideas into action and then following them out to their ultimate consequences. At the same time, his characters respond to such consequences according to the ordinary moral and social standards prevalent in their milieu, and it is the fusion of these two levels that provides Dostoevsky's novels with both their imaginative range and their realistic grounding in social life.

Dostoevsky's innate propensity to dramatize ideas in this way was noted in an extremely acute remark by one of his closest associates, the philosopher Nikolay Strakhov. "The most routine abstract thought," he wrote, "very often struck him with an uncommon force and would stir him up remarkably. He was, in any case, a person in the highest degree excitable and impressionable. A simple idea, sometimes very familiar and commonplace, would suddenly set him aflame and reveal itself to him in all its significance. He, so to speak, felt thought with un-usual liveliness. Then he would state it in various forms, sometimes giving it a very sharp, graphic expression, although not explaining it logically or develop-ing its content" (3: 42). It is this inborn tendency of Dostoevsky to "feel thought" that gives his best work its special stamp, and why it is so important to locate his writings in relation to the evolution of ideas in his lifetime.

He came to fame in the 1840s, when his first novel, *Poor Folk*, was hailed by Alexander Herzen as the foremost example of a genuinely Socialist creation in Russian literature. Indeed, all that Dostoevsky published during the 1840s bore the hallmark of his acceptance of the Utopian Socialist ideas then in vogue among a considerable portion of the intelligentsia—ideas that can be considered to have been inspired by Christianity, though recasting its ethos in terms of modern social problems. Nonetheless, although Utopian Socialism did not preach violence to attain its aims, and Dostoevsky's works are filled with the need for sympathy and compassion, he belonged to a secret group whose aim was to stir up a revolution against serfdom (the existence of this organization did not become known until long after his death). Before this underground cabal could take any action, however, its members were included in the arrest and sentencing of the innocuous discussion group known as the Petrashevsky Circle, to which they all belonged.

The members of this group were submitted to the ordeal of a mock execution before learning of their true sentences, in Dostoevsky's case imprisonment with hard labor in Siberia. As a result, Dostoevsky's previously "secular" Christianity underwent a crucial metamorphosis. Hitherto it had been dedicated to the im-provement of life on earth; now this aim, without being abandoned, became overshadowed by an awareness of the importance of the hope of eternity as a mainstay of moral existence. His period of imprisonment also convinced him that the need for freedom, particularly the sense of being able to exercise one's free will, was an ineradicable need of the human personality and could express itself even in apparently self-destructive forms if no other outlet were possible. Also, as Dostoevsky wrote himself, the four years he spent in the prison camp were responsible for "the regeneration of [his] convictions" on a more mundane level. This was a result of his growing awareness of the deep roots of traditional

Christianity in even the worst of peasant criminals, who bowed down during the Easter service, with a clanking of chains, when the priest read the words "accept me, O Lord, even as the thief." The basis of Dostoevsky's later faith in what he considered the ineradicable Christian essence of the Russian people arose from such experiences.

When he returned to Russia after a ten-year Siberian exile, he thus found it impossible to accept the reigning ideas of the new generation of the 1860s that had arisen during his absence. Promulgated by Nikolay Chernyshevsky and N. A. Dobrolyubov, these ideas were a peculiar Russian mixture of the atheism of Ludwig Feuerbach, the materialism and rationalism of eighteenth-century French thought, and the English Utilitarianism of Jeremy Bentham. Russian radicalism had acquired a new foundation, labeled "rational egoism" by Chernyshevsky, that the post-Siberian Dostoevsky found it impossible to accept. The first important work he launched against this new credo was *Notes from Underground*, in which the underground man's belief in the determinism of all human behavior—a determinism asserted by Chernyshevsky to be the final, definitive word of science—clashes irresistibly with the moral sensibilities that, despite his desire to do so, the tormented underground man cannot suppress.

Crime and Punishment was a response to the ideas of another radical thinker, Dimitry Pisarev, who drew a sharp distinction between the slumbering masses and those superior individuals like Raskolnikov who believed they had a moral right to commit crimes in the interest of humanity. In the end, however, Raskolnikov discovers that his true motive was to test (unsuccessfully) whether he could overcome his Christian conscience to achieve such a goal. The masterly novel *Demons*, still the best ever written about a revolutionary conspiracy, is based on the Nechaev affair, the murder of a young student belonging to an underground group led by Sergey Nechaev. This totally unscrupulous agitator with a will of iron composed a *Catechism of a Revolutionary* whose Utilitarian approval of any means to obtain presumably beneficial social ends makes Machiavelli look like a choirboy.

Aside from contesting the ideas he opposed, Dostoevsky also aspired to create a Christian moral image that would serve as a positive example for the new generation. *The Idiot* is an attempt to portray such a Christian ideal to counter the "rational egoism" that Dostoevsky was attacking; but it was finally impossible for him to have Prince Myshkin end in anything but disaster. Such a worldly failure is of course inherent in the paradigm of Christ's self-sacrifice; but Dostoevsky by this time had also come to believe that "to love man like oneself, according to the commandment of Christ, is impossible. The law of personality on earth binds. The ego stands in the way." It is only in the afterlife that "the law of personality" could be decisively overcome.

The 1870s marked a new phase in Dostoevsky's work because these years saw a mutation in radical ideology itself. Radical publicists such as N. K. Mikhailovsky and Peter Lavrov had now rejected the Western notion of "progress" as the only path of social evolution. Without surrendering their unrelenting opposition to the tsarist regime, these thinkers, in a criticism of capitalism influenced by Marx's denunciation of the "primitive accumulation" that turned peasants into proletarians, began to search in their homeland for alternatives to the relentless pauperization of the lower class they saw taking place in Europe. With the serfs having been liberated in 1861, it was feared that the same process would inevitably occur in Russia. Dostoevsky had observed the results of this social transformation during his first trip to Europe in 1862 and denounced it as the triumph of the flesh-god Baal.

The radicals thus began to reevaluate the merits of Russian peasant life, and this brought them much closer to Dostoevsky than in the past. Such a change of perspective is surely one reason why his next novel, *A Raw Youth*, was unexpectedly published in the radical journal, *Notes of the Fatherland*. It contains a brilliantly limned portrait of the main character, an intellectual caught between an unsatisfied need for religious faith and his attraction to the stabilities of such faith among the peasantry. It also includes the first (and only) important peasant character in any of Dostoevsky's novels, a figure who provides the book with a moral anchor amidst its all too complicated romantic intrigue.

The Russian radicals had now accepted the moral-social values of Russian peasant life, rooted in the Orthodox Christian faith, but they still refused to accept that faith themselves, the source of such values, and continued to cling to their atheism. Such an inner contradiction lies at the heart of Dostoevsky's last and greatest novel, *The Brothers Karamazov*, which bravely attempts to cope with this issue by employing the theme of theodicy. How could a God, presumably of love, have created a world in which evil existed? The radicals of the 1860s had simply denied the existence of God, but those of the 1870s, as Dostoevsky wrote in a letter, were rejecting not God "but the meaning of His creation."

No modern writer rivals Dostoevsky in the grandeur of his presentation of this eternal Christian dilemma—the fierceness of his attack on the presumed goodness of God, on the one hand, through Ivan Karamazov, and his attempt to counter it with the Legend of the Grand Inquisitor and the preaching of Father Zosima on the other. These pages bring Dostoevsky into the company of Greek and Elizabethan tragedy, and of Dante, Milton, and Shakespeare, rather than of fellow novelists, who rarely venture into such exalted territory. Each of his central figures is elaborated on a richly symbolic scale influenced by some of the greatest works of Western literature, among which his own novel now takes an undisputed place.

The power and pathos of Dostoevsky's novels and journalism, his impassioned wrestling with the deepest issues confronting Russian society, raised him above the bitter quarrels then taking place and that, just a month after his own death in 1881, led to the assassination of Tsar Alexander II. It is no accident that, when he read Pushkin's poem "The Prophet" in public, as he often did in the last ten years of his life, Dostoevsky was hailed as a prophet himself by enraptured listeners who found solace in his words preaching universal conciliation in the name of Christ. It was also a testimony to his stature that his funeral procession, almost a mile in length, included a vast array of organizations and groups of differing social-political orientations. All of them were united by their admiration for the writer whose works had so illuminated, in such moving and spellbinding forms, the problems assailing all literate Russians in his lifetime, and whose genius had raised their indigenous conflicts to universal heights.

One of Dostoevsky's dreams for his work had been to bring about the unity of Russian culture; and if he did not succeed during his lifetime, it may be said that he attained this goal with his death. Moreover, the unanimity of esteem felt by Russians at that moment has been continued in the worldwide reverence accorded to his major novels up through our own day.

ACKNOWLEDGMENTS

A few years after the publication of the fifth and final volume of my books on Dostoevsky (2002), the idea was broached of attempting to follow the model provided by Leon Edel with his five-volume work on Henry James. This multi-volumed text, shortened to one, has been highly praised and widely read; and it was suggested by Princeton University Press that perhaps a one-volume condensation of my five, if done properly, would be equally welcomed. At first I encountered such a prospect with some reluctance. The length of my treatment of Dostoevsky was the result of placing his life and writings in the context of a much larger social, historical, and ideological background than had previously been attempted; and I did not wish to lose the new insights that, as I was pleased to see widely acknowledged, this context provided. Moreover, my books contained independent analyses of both his literary and journalistic writings that I wished to remain intact as far as possible. In them I had tried to illuminate Dostoevsky's unique fusion of the issues of his own life and time with those both of Russian culture as a whole and of the religious-metaphysical "accursed questions" about the meaning of life that had always plagued Western mankind. Hence my hesitation about a one-volume edition; but this was overcome when I was assured that my original volumes would remain in print, and so would be easily available to new readers wishing for a wider horizon.

The decision thus was made to search for an editor to undertake the arduous and taxing task of composing the one-volume manuscript. The choice eventually fell on Mary Petrusewicz, an experienced writer and editor with a PhD degree in Russian literature who taught undergraduate and continuing education courses in the humanities (including courses on Dostoevsky) at Stanford University. Her editorial duties, performed in an exemplary manner after initial consultation for safeguarding what I considered essential, took two years to be completed. I then reviewed the resulting manuscript and made key authorial additions, adjustments, and textual revisions to ensure that this condensed book represented the best and smoothest adaptation of the five previous volumes. She has herself described the principles that guided her excellent work in the Editor's Note appended to the present book (p. 933) and that, as the reader will see, focuses on what seemed to me of greatest importance—to bring out, as she says, "the full power of Dostoevsky's texts."

Hanne Winarsky, the literary editor of Princeton University Press, kept a close eye on the enterprise as it was being carried out, and I should like to thank her most gratefully for her comments and suggestions. Robin Feuer Miller, whose own book on *The Idiot* is a major contribution to the comprehension of this most autobiographical of Dostoevsky's novels, also must be thanked most warmly. Her detailed comparison of the new one-volume version with the original five volumes was invaluable in scrutinizing the work of transformation, and I can only add my own voice to that of the appreciation equally expressed in the note of the editor herself.

My wife, Marguerite Frank, a professional and published mathematician and a discriminating and avid reader of literature as well, has been a sharp and discerning critic of all of my volumes. Through these many years she has helped me to maintain them as close as possible to the highest intellectual and literary standards. In this instance she was dissatisfied with my treatment of perhaps the most complex of all the female characters in Dostoevsky's novels, the beautiful and ill-fated Nastasya Filippovna of *The Idiot*. In the past, I had always used her comments to guide my own revisions. But now she so much altered and enriched my own initial view that I asked her to express them herself; and the pages devoted to Nastasya Filippovna in the present book thus come from her pen. Let me conclude by citing what I wrote in the Preface to my fifth volume: "Nothing I can say will adequately express what every one of my books owes to her participation."

TRANSLITERATION

For Russian words, I use the Library of Congress system without diacritics, and I use -*ya* instead of -*ia* and -*yu* instead of -*iu*, the adjectival endings -*yi* and -*ii* are rendered by -*y*: *yurodivy* instead of *yurodivyi*, *Dostoevsky* instead of *Dostoevskii*. The soft sign is omitted in proper names: *Gogol* rather than *Gogol'*.

Citations to Dostoevsky's texts and correspondence are made to the volumes of the great Academy of Sciences edition: F. M. Dostoevsky, *Polnoe sobranie sochinenii*, 30 vols. (Leningrad, 1972–1990). For the other texts cited here, I have used the translation of *Diary of a Writer* by Kenneth Lantz. For my quotations from Dostoevsky's early short stories and novels up to and including *Notes from Underground*, I have used the translations of Constance Garnett (altering her version where this seemed indicated). For the later novels, I have consulted various translations: those of Constance Garnett, Jessie Coulson, and Richard Pevear and Larissa Volokhonsky for *Crime and Punishment*; for *The Idiot*, Constance Garnett; for *The Gambler*, Victor Terras and Constance Garnett; for *The Eternal Husband*, Constance Garnett; for *Demons*, David Magarshack and Constance Garnett; for *A Raw Youth*, the translations of both Constance Garnett and Andrew McAndrew. For *The Brothers Karamazov*, I have used mainly the translation of Constance Garnett revised by Ralph Matlaw, but supplemented with the versions of Richard Pevear and Larissa Volokhonsky, as well as that of Ignat Avsey.

All citations have been checked with the Russian text and alterations made as necessary.

ABBREVIATIONS

Biografiya   Orest Miller and Nikolay Strakhov. *Biografiya, pis'ma i zametki iz zapisnoi knizhki F. M. Dostoevskogo* (St. Petersburg, 1863).

DMI   *F. M. Dostoevsky materialy i issledovaniya*, ed. A. S. Dolinin (Leningrad, 1935).

DRK   *F. M. Dostoevsky v Russkoi kritike* (Moscow, 1956).

DSiM   *F. M. Dostoevsky, stati i materialy*, ed. A. S. Dolinin, 2 vols. (Moscow–Leningrad, 1922–1924).

DVS   *F. M. Dostoevsky v vospominaniakh sovremennikov*, ed. K. Tyunkina, 2 vols. (Moscow, 1990).

DW   *A Writer's Diary, Feodor Dostoevsky*, trans. and annotated Kenneth Lantz, intro study Gary Saul Morson (Evanston, Ill, 1993). I cite Dostoevsky's *Dnevnik pisatelya* in this English version, though with numerous revisions of the translation.

DZhP   Leonid Grossman, *Dostoevsky na zhiznennom puti* (Moscow, 1928).

LN   *Literaturnoe Nasledstvo* (Moscow, 1934–1973).

Pis'ma   *F. M. Dostoevsky, Pis'ma*, ed. and annotated by A. S. Dolinin, 4 vols. (Moscow, 1928–1959).

PSS   *F. M. Dostoevsky, Polnoe sobranie sochinenii v tridtsati tomakh*, ed. and annotated by G. M. Fridlender et al., 30 vols. (Leningrad, 1972–1990). This definitive edition of Dostoevsky's writings contains his correspondence and provides an extensive scholarly apparatus.

PSSiP   *I. S. Turgenev, Polnoe sobranie sochinenii i pisem*, ed. P. Alekseev, 28 vols. (Moscow–Leningrad, 1960–1968).

ZT   Leonid Grossman, *Zhizn' i trudy Dostoevskogo* (Moscow–Leningrad, 1935).

PART I

The Seeds of Revolt, 1821–1849

CHAPTER 1

Prelude

The last years of the reign of Alexander I were a troubled, uncertain, and gloomy time in Russian history. Alexander had come to the throne as the result of a palace revolution against his father, Paul I, whose increasingly erratic and insensate rule led his entourage to suspect madness. The coup was carried out with at least the implicit consent of Alexander, whose accession to power, after his father's murder, at first aroused great hopes of liberal reform in the small, enlightened segment of Russian society. Alexander's tutor, selected by his grandmother Catherine the Great, had been a Swiss of advanced liberal views named La Harpe. This partisan of the Enlightenment imbued his royal pupil with republican and even democratic ideas; and during the first years of his reign, Alexander surrounded himself with a band of young aristocrats sharing his progressive persuasions. A good deal of work was done preparing plans for major social reforms, such as the abolition of serfdom and the granting of personal civil rights to all members of the population. Alexander's attention, however, was soon diverted from internal affairs by the great drama then proceeding on the European stage—the rise of Napoleon as a world-conqueror. Allied at first with Napoleon, and then becoming his implacable foe, Alexander I led his people in the great national upsurge that resulted in the defeat of the Grand Army and its hitherto invincible leader.

The triumph over Napoleon brought Russian armies to the shores of the Atlantic and exposed both officers and men (the majority of the troops were peasant serfs) to prolonged contact with the relative freedom and amenities of life in Western Europe. It was expected that, in reward for the loyalty of his people, Alexander would make some spectacular gesture consonant with his earlier intentions and institute the social reforms that had been put aside to meet the menace of Napoleon. But the passage of time, and the epochal events he had lived through, had not left Alexander unchanged. More and more he had come under the influence of the religious mysticism and irrationalism so prevalent in the immediate post-Napoleonic era. Instead of reforms, the period between 1820 and 1825 saw an intensification of reaction and the repression of any overt manifestation of liberal ideas and tendencies in Russia.

Meanwhile, secret societies—some moderate in their aims, others more radical—had begun to form among the most brilliant and cultivated cadres of the

Russian officers' corps. These societies, grouping the scions of some of the most important aristocratic families, sprang from impatience with Alexander's dilatoriness and a desire to transform Russia on the model of Western liberal and democratic ideas. Alexander died unexpectedly in November 1825, and the societies seized the opportunity a month later, at the time of the coronation of Nicholas I, to launch a pitifully abortive eight-hour uprising known to history as the Decembrist insurrection. An apocryphal story about this event has it that the mutinous troops, told to shout for "Constantine and *konstitutsiya*" (Constantine, the older brother of Nicholas, had renounced the throne and had a reputation as a liberal), believed that the second noun, whose gender in Russian is feminine, referred to Constantine's wife. Whether true or only a witticism, the story highlights the isolation of the aristocratic rebels; and their revolution was crushed with a few whiffs of grapeshot by the new tsar, who condemned five of the ringleaders to be hanged and thirty-one to be exiled to Siberia for life. Nicholas thus provided the nascent Russian intelligentsia with its first candidates for the new martyrology that would soon replace the saints of the Orthodox Church.

Feodor Mikhailovich Dostoevsky was born in Moscow on October 3, 1821, just a few years before this crucial event in Russian history, and these events were destined to be interwoven with his life in the most intimate fashion. The world in which Dostoevsky grew up lived in the shadow of the Decembrist insurrection and suffered from the harsh police-state atmosphere instituted by Nicholas I to ensure that nothing similar could occur again. The Decembrist insurrection marked the opening skirmish in the long and deadly duel between the Russian intelligentsia and the supreme aristocratic power that shaped the course of Russian history and culture in Dostoevsky's lifetime. And it was out of the inner moral and spiritual crises of this intelligentsia—out of its self-alienation and its desperate search for new values on which to found its life—that the child born in Moscow at the conclusion of the reign of Alexander I would one day produce his great novels.

CHAPTER 2

The Family

Of all the great Russian writers of the first part of the nineteenth century—Pushkin, Lermontov, Gogol, Herzen, Turgenev, Tolstoy, Nekrasov—Dostoevsky was the only one who did not come from a family belonging to the landed gentry. This is a fact of great importance, and influenced the view he took of his own position as a writer. Comparing himself with his great rival Tolstoy, as he did frequently in later life, Dostoevsky defined the latter's work as being that of a "historian," not a novelist. For, in his view, Tolstoy depicted the life "which existed in the tranquil and stable, long-established Moscow landowners' family of the middle-upper stratum." Such a life, with its settled traditions of culture and fixed moral-social norms, had become in the nineteenth century that of only a small "minority" of Russians; it was "the life of the exceptions." The life of the majority, on the other hand, was one of confusion and moral chaos. Dostoevsky felt that his own work was an attempt to grapple with the chaos of the present, while Tolstoy's *Childhood, Boyhood, Youth* and *War and Peace* (he had these specifically in mind) were pious efforts to enshrine for posterity the beauty of a gentry life already vanishing and doomed to extinction.[1]

Such a self-definition, made at a later stage of Dostoevsky's career, of course represents the distillation of many years of reflection on his literary position. But it also throws a sharp light back on Dostoevsky's past, and helps us to see that his earliest years were spent in an atmosphere that prepared him to become the chronicler of the moral consequences of flux and change, and of the breakup of the traditional forms of Russian life. The lack, during his early years, of a unified social tradition in which he could feel at home unquestionably shaped his imaginative vision, and we can also discern a rankling uncertainty about status that helps to explain his acute understanding of the psychological scars inflicted by social inequality.

On his father's side, the Dostoevskys had been a family belonging to the Lithuanian nobility. The family name came from a small village (Dostoevo, in

---

[1] *DW* (January 1877); see also, for the self-comparison with Tolstoy, F. M. Dostoevsky, *The Notebooks for* A Raw Youth, ed. Edward Wasiolek, trans. Victor Terras (Chicago, 1969), 425, 544–545.

the district of Pinsk) awarded to an ancestor in the sixteenth century. Falling on hard times, the Orthodox Dostoevskys sank into the lowly class of the non-monastic clergy. Dostoevsky's paternal great-grandfather was a Uniat archpriest in the Ukrainian town of Bratslava; his grandfather was a priest of the same persuasion; and this is where his father was born. The Uniat denomination was a compromise worked out by the Jesuits as a means of proselytizing among the predominantly Orthodox peasantry of the region: Uniats continued to celebrate the Orthodox rites, but accepted the supreme authority of the pope.

Since the non-monastic clergy in Russia form a caste rather than a profession or a calling, Dostoevsky's father was naturally destined to follow the same career as *his* father. But, after graduating from a seminary at the age of fifteen, he slipped away from home, made his way to Moscow, and there gained admittance to the Imperial Medical-Surgical Academy in 1809. Assigned to service in a Moscow hospital during the campaign of 1812, he continued to serve in various posts as a military doctor until 1821, when, aged thirty-two, he accepted a position at the Mariinsky Hospital for the Poor, located on the outskirts of Moscow. His official advancement in the service of the state was steady, and in April 1828, being awarded the order of St. Anna third class "for especially zealous service,"[2] he was promoted to the rank of collegiate assessor. This entitled him to the legal status of noble in the official Russian class system, and he hastened to establish his claim to its privileges. On June 28, 1828, he inscribed his own name and that of his two sons, Mikhail and Feodor (aged eight and seven, respectively), in the rolls of the hereditary nobility of Moscow.

Dr. Dostoevsky had thus succeeded, with a good deal of determination and tenacity, in pulling himself up by his bootstraps and rising from the despised priestly class to that of civil servant, member of a learned profession, and nobleman. It is clear from the memoirs of Dostoevsky's younger brother Andrey—our only reliable source for these early years—that the children had been informed about the family's ancient patent of nobility, and looked on their father's recent elevation as a just restoration of their rightful rank.[3] The Dostoevskys thought of themselves as belonging to the old gentry aristocracy rather than to the new service nobility created by Peter the Great—the class to which, in fact, their father had just acceded. Their actual place in society was in flagrant contradiction to this flattering self-image.

Medicine was an honorable but not very honorific profession in Russia, and Dr. Dostoevsky's salary, which he was forced to supplement with private practice, was barely enough for his needs. The Dostoevskys lived in a small, cramped apartment on the hospital grounds, and living space was always a problem.

---

[2] *ZT*, 21.

[3] A. M. Dostoevsky, *Vospominaniya* (Leningrad, 1930), 17–18.

Mikhail and Feodor slept in a windowless compartment separated by a partition from the antechamber; the oldest girl, Varvara, slept on a couch in the living room; the younger children spent the nights in the bedroom of the parents. It is true, as Andrey notes, that his family had a staff of six servants (a coachman, a so-called lackey, a cook, a housemaid, a laundress, and a *nyanya* or governess for the children), but this should not be taken as an indication of affluence. From Andrey's comment on the "lackey," who was really a *dvornik* or janitor, we see how eager the Dostoevskys were to keep up appearances and conform to the gentry style of life. His job was to supply the stoves with wood in winter and to bring water for tea from a fountain two versts distant from the hospital, but when Marya Feodorovna went to town on foot, he put on livery and a three-cornered hat and walked proudly behind his mistress. When she used the coach, the livery appeared again and the "lackey" stood impressively on the back foot-board. "This was the unbreakable rule of Moscow etiquette in those days,"[4] Andrey remarks wryly. Dostoevsky certainly remembered this rule, and his parents' adherence to its prescripts, when Mr. Golyadkin in *The Double* hires a carriage and a livery for his barefoot servant Petrushka in order to increase his social standing in the eyes of the world.

The Dostoevskys' pretensions to gentry status were wistfully incongruous with their true position in society. Dostoevsky would one day compare Alexander Herzen, born (even if out of wedlock) into the very highest stratum of the ruling class, with the critic Vissarion Belinsky, who was "not a *gentilhomme* at all! Oh no! (God knows from whom he descended! His father, it seems, was a military surgeon)."[5] So, of course, was Dostoevsky's, and the remark indicates what he learned to perceive as the reality of his family's situation. Dr. Dostoevsky and his offspring would never enjoy the consideration to which they felt entitled by right of descent from noble forebears.

—■—

While stationed at a Moscow hospital in 1819, the thirty-year-old Dr. Dostoevsky must have mentioned to a colleague that he was seeking a suitable bride. For he was then introduced to the family of Feodor Nechaev, a well-to-do Moscow merchant with an attractive nineteen-year-old daughter, Marya Feodorovna. Marriages in those days, especially in the merchant class, were not left to chance or inclination. Dr. Dostoevsky, after being approved by the parents, was probably allowed to catch a glimpse of his future bride in church, and then invited to meet her after he agreed to a betrothal; the introduction to the girl was the sign of consent, and the future bride had nothing to say about the matter.

[4] *DVS*, 1: 44.
[5] *DW* (1873, no. 1), 6.

1. Dr. M. A. Dostoevsky

2. Mme M. F. Dostoevsky

Both Dr. Dostoevsky and his new in-laws were similar in having risen from lowly origins to a higher position on the Russian social scale.

The older sister of Dostoevsky's mother, Alexandra Feodorovna, had married into a merchant family much like her own. Her husband, A. M. Kumanin, had risen to fill various official functions, and the Kumanins were among those merchant families whose wealth allowed them to compete with the gentry in the opulence of their lifestyle. The proud and touchy Dr. Dostoevsky, who probably felt superior to his brother-in-law both by birth and by education, had to swallow his pride and appeal to him for financial succor on several occasions. Dostoevsky's own attitude to his Kumanin relatives, whom he always regarded as vulgarians concerned only with money, no doubt reflected a view he had picked up from his father. In a letter to Mikhail just after hearing of his father's death, Dostoevsky tells him "to spit on those insignificant little souls"[6] (meaning their Moscow relatives), who were incapable of understanding higher things. Andrey speaks of the Kumanins warmly; they looked after the younger Dostoevsky orphans as if they had been their own children. But though Dostoevsky too later appealed to them for aid at critical moments in his life, he never referred to them in private without a tinge of contempt.

Dostoevsky always spoke of his mother with great warmth and affection; and the picture that emerges from the memoir material shows her to have been an engaging and attractive person. Like her husband, Marya Feodorovna had assimilated a good bit of the culture of the gentry. In a letter, she describes her character as being one of "natural gaiety,"[7] and this inborn sunniness, although sorely tried by the strains of domestic life, shines through everything that we know about her. She was not only a loving and cheerful mother but also an efficient manager of the affairs of the family. Three years after Dr. Dostoevsky became a nobleman, he used his newly acquired right to own land to purchase a small estate about 150 versts from Moscow called Darovoe. A year later, the Dostoevskys hastened to acquire an adjacent property—the hamlet of Cheremoshnia—whose purchase caused them to go heavily into debt. No doubt the acquisition of a landed estate with peasant serfs seemed to make good business sense to the doctor, and it was a place where his family could spend the summer in the open air. But in the back of his mind there was probably also the desire to give some concrete social embodiment to his dream of becoming a member of the landed gentry. It was Marya Feodorovna, however, who went to the country every spring to supervise the work; the doctor himself could get away from his practice only on flying visits.

Located on poor farming land, which did not even furnish enough fodder for the livestock, the Dostoevsky estate yielded only a miserable existence to its

[6] *Pis'ma*, 2: 549; August 16, 1839.

[7] V. S. Nechaeva, *V seme i usadbe Dostoevskikh* (Moscow, 1939), 109.

peasant population, but as long as Marya Feodorovna was in charge things did not go too badly. During the first summer she managed, by a system of canals, to bring water into the village from a nearby spring to feed a large pond, which she then stocked with fish sent from Moscow by her husband. The peasants could water their livestock more easily, the children could amuse themselves by fishing, and the food supply was augmented. She was also a humane and kindhearted proprietor who distributed grain for sowing to the poorest peasants in early spring when they had none of their own, even though this was considered to be bad estate management. Dr. Dostoevsky reprimands her several times in his letters for not being more severe. Almost a hundred years later, the legend of her leniency and compassion still persisted among the descendants of the peasants of Darovoe.[8] It was no doubt from Marya Feodorovna that Dostoevsky first learned to feel that sympathy for the unfortunate and deprived that became so important for his work.

—■—

Dostoevsky's father, Mikhail Andreevich, forms a strong contrast in character to his wife. His portrait shows him to have had coarse and heavy features. His dress uniform, with its high, stiff, gilded collar, gives an air of rigidity to the set of his head that is barely offset by the faintest of smiles; and the rigidity was much more typical of the man than was the trace of affability. He was a hardworking medical practitioner whose ability was so appreciated by his superiors that, when he decided to retire, he was offered a substantial promotion to change his mind. He was also a faithful husband, a responsible father, and a believing Christian. These qualities did not make him either a lovable or an appealing human being, but his virtues were as important as his defects in determining the environment in which Dostoevsky grew up.

Dr. Dostoevsky suffered from some sort of nervous affliction that strongly affected his character and disposition. Bad weather always brought on severe headaches and resulted in moods of gloom and melancholy; the return of good weather relieved his condition. Dostoevsky later traced the incidence of his own epileptic attacks to such climatic changes. If Dr. Dostoevsky was, as even Andrey is forced to concede, "very exacting and impatient, and, most of all, very irritable,"[9] this can be attributed to the extreme and unremitting state of nervous tension induced by his illness. Dostoevsky, who inherited this aspect of his father's character, constantly complained in later life about his own inability to master his nerves, and was also given to uncontrollable explosions of temper.

[8] Ibid., 5.
[9] *DVS*, I: 76.

Dr. Dostoevsky was thus a naggingly unhappy man whose depressive tendencies colored every aspect of his life. They made him suspicious and mistrustful, and unable to find satisfaction in either his career or his family. He suspected the household servants of cheating, and watched over them with a cranky surveillance characteristic of his attitude toward the world in general. He believed that he was being unfairly treated in the service and that his superiors were reaping the benefits of his unrewarded labors in the hospital. Even if both of these conjectures may have had some basis in fact, he brooded over them in a manner quite out of proportion to their real importance. His relations with the Kumanins were also a continual source of vexation, because his pride filled him with an impotent bitterness at his feelings of inferiority. This acute social sensitivity is another trait transmitted from father to son; many Dostoevsky characters will be tormented by the unflattering image of themselves that they see reflected in the eyes of others.

What sustained Mikhail Andreevich in the midst of his woes was, first and foremost, the unstinting and limitless devotion of his wife. But in his very darkest moments, when no earthly succor seemed available, he took refuge in the conviction of his own virtue and rectitude, and in the belief that God was on his side against a hostile or indifferent world. "In Moscow," he writes to his wife on returning from the country, "I found waiting for me only trouble and vexation; and I sit brooding with my head in my hands and grieve, there is no place to lay my head, not to mention anyone with whom I can share my sorrow; but God will judge them because of my misery." [10] This astonishing conviction that he was one of God's elect, this unshakable self-assurance that he was among the chosen, constituted the very core of Dr. Dostoevsky's being. It was this that made him so self-righteous and pharisaical, so intolerant of the smallest fault, so persuaded that only perfect obedience from his family to all his wishes could compensate for all his toil and labor on their behalf.

While Dr. Dostoevsky may have made his family pay a heavy psychic price for his virtues, these virtues did exist as a fact of their daily lives. He was a conscientious father who devoted an unusual amount of his time to educating his children. In the early nineteenth century, corporal punishment was accepted as an indispensable means of instilling discipline, and in Russia the flogging and beating of both children and the lower classes was accepted as a matter of course. Dr. Dostoevsky, however, never struck any of his children, despite his irritability and his temper; the only punishment they had to fear was a verbal rebuke. It was to avoid having his children beaten that, though he could scarcely afford to do so, Dr. Dostoevsky sent them all to private schools rather than to public institutions. And even after his two older sons had gone away to study at military

[10] Nechaeva, *V seme*, 77.

schools, Dr. Dostoevsky still continued to worry about them and to bombard them—as well as others, when his sons neglected to write—with inquiries about their welfare. If we disregard Dr. Dostoevsky's personality and look only at the way he fulfilled his paternal responsibilities, we can understand a remark that Dostoevsky made in the late 1870s to his brother Andrey that their parents had been "outstanding people," adding that "such family men, such fathers . . . we ourselves are quite incapable of being, brother!"[11]

■

Despite the diversity of their characters, Dr. Dostoevsky and his wife were a devoted and loving couple. Their twenty years of marriage produced a family of eight children, and nobody reading their letters without *parti pris* can doubt that they were deeply attached to each other. "Good-bye, my soul, my little dove, my happiness, joy of my life, I kiss you until I'm out of breath. Kiss the children for me."[12] So writes Dr. Dostoevsky to Marya Feodorovna after fourteen years of marriage, and while some allowances must be made for the florid rhetoric of the time, these words seem far in excess of what convention might require. Marya Feodorovna is equally lavish with her endearments. "Make the trip here soon, my sweetheart," she writes from Darovoe, "come my angel, my only wish is to have you visit me, you know that it's the greatest holiday for me, the greatest pleasure in my life is when you're with me."[13]

The letters of his parents reflect the image of a close-knit and united family, where concern for the children was in the foreground of the parents' preoccupations. Nonetheless, Dr. Dostoevsky's emotional insecurity was so great, his suspicion and mistrust of the world sometimes reached such a pathological pitch, that he could suspect his wife of infidelity. One such incident occurred in 1835, when he learned that she was pregnant. Andrey recalls seeing his mother break into hysterical weeping after having communicated some information to his father that surprised and vexed him. The scene, he explains, was probably caused by the announcement of his mother's pregnancy. The letters indicate, however, that Dr. Dostoevsky was tormented by doubts about his wife's faithfulness, although he made no direct accusations. Schooled by long experience, Marya Feodorovna was able to read his state of mind through the distraught tone of his letters and his deep mood of depression. "My friend," she writes, "thinking all this over, I wonder whether you are not tortured by that unjust suspicion, so deadly for us both, that I have been unfaithful to you."[14]

[11] *DVS*, 1: 87.
[12] Nechaeva, *V seme*, 81.
[13] Ibid., 99.
[14] Ibid., 106.

Her denial of any wrongdoing is written with an eloquence and expressiveness that even her second son might have envied. "I swear," she writes, "that my present pregnancy is the seventh and strongest bond of our mutual love, on my side a love that is pure, sacred, chaste and passionate, unaltered from the day of our marriage." There is also a fine sense of dignity in her explanation that she has never before deigned to reaffirm her marriage oath "because I was ashamed to lower myself by swearing to my faithfulness during our sixteen years of marriage."[15] Dr. Dostoevsky nonetheless remained adamant in his dark imaginings, accusing her of delaying her departure from the country so as to avoid returning to Moscow until it was too late to make the journey without risking a miscarriage. In reply, she writes sadly that "time and years flow by, creases and bitterness spread over the face; natural gaiety of character is turned into sorrowful melancholy, and that's my fate, that's the reward for my chaste, passionate love; and if I were not strengthened by the purity of my conscience and my hope in Providence, the end of my days would be pitiful indeed."[16]

One could easily imagine the life of the Dostoevsky family being torn apart and subject to constant emotional upheaval, but nothing dramatic seems to have occurred. In this very letter, the current of ordinary life flows on as placidly as before. Information about the affairs of the estate are exchanged, and the older boys in Moscow append the usual loving postscript to their mother; there is no break in the family routine, and both partners, in the midst of recriminations, continue to assure the other of their undying love and devotion. Dr. Dostoevsky went to the country in July to assist at the delivery of Alexandra, and then, on returning in August, writes affectionately to his wife: "Believe me, reading your letter, I tearfully thank God first of all, and you secondly, my dear. . . . I kiss your hand a million million times, and pray to God that you remain in good health for our happiness."[17] Not a word recalls the tensions of the previous month; Marya Feodorovna's soothing and loving presence seems to have worked wonders.

Displays of such extreme emotion between the parents were probably rare. Nothing was more important for the Dostoevskys than to present an image of well-bred propriety and gentry refinement to the world; it is impossible to imagine them in their cramped apartment, with a household staff in the kitchen and neighboring hospital families all around, indulging in the violent quarrels and scandalous outbursts that Dostoevsky later so often depicted in his novels. Dr. Dostoevsky probably alternated between a grim and ominous silence and endless censoriousness about the minutiae of daily life. His reluctance to speak

[15] Ibid.
[16] Ibid., 109.
[17] Ibid., 111.

out openly in the instance of Alexandra may be taken as typical, and when Marya Feodorovna stated the issue bluntly, he rebuked her for writing to him so directly and possibly revealing his secret suspicions to prying eyes. The impulse to cover and conceal is manifest, and was certainly operative in his personal behavior as well. It is therefore probable that the household in which Dostoevsky grew up was characterized far more by order, regularity, and routine, and by a deceptively calm surface of domestic tranquility, than by the familial chaos that so preoccupied him half a century later.

But we can hardly doubt that the gifted and perceptive boy would become aware of the stresses underlying the routine of his early years, and that he learned to feel it as beset with hidden antagonisms—as subject to extreme fluctuations between intimacy and withdrawal. Family life for Dostoevsky would always be a battleground and a struggle of wills, just as he had first learned to sense it from the secret life of his parents. And for a boy and youth destined to become famous for his understanding of the intricacies of human psychology, it was excellent training to have been reared in a household where the significance of behavior was kept hidden from view, and where his curiosity was stimulated to intuit and unravel its concealed meanings. One may perhaps see here the origin of Dostoevsky's profound sense of the *mystery* of personality and his tendency to explore it, as it were, from the outside in, always moving from the exterior to deeper and deeper subterranean levels that are only gradually brought to light.

———■———

Life in the Dostoevsky family was carefully organized around the pattern of Dr. Dostoevsky's daily routine. The family awakened promptly at six in the morning. At eight Dr. Dostoevsky went to the hospital and the children were put to their lessons. Dr. Dostoevsky returned around twelve and inquired about the work that had been accomplished, and lunch was served at one o'clock. After lunch a deathly silence was maintained for two hours while the *paterfamilias* napped on the couch in the living room before returning to the hospital. The evenings were spent in the living room, and each evening before dinner, if Dr. Dostoevsky was not too busy with his sick lists, he read aloud to the children. At nine in the evening the family had dinner, and the children, after saying their prayers in front of the icon, then went to bed. "The day was spent in our family," Andrey comments, "according to a routine established once and for all, and repeated day after day, very monotonously."[18] Feodor was also subjected to this routine from his earliest years—one that combined the physical discomfort of crowded and gloomy quarters ("low ceilings and cramped rooms crush the mind and the spirit," Raskolnikov tells Sonya) with the psychic discomfort of an

[18] *DVS*, I: 55, 57.

unrelaxing pressure to work under the eye of a stern paternal overseer. The children were rarely allowed outdoors during the frigid Moscow winters.

During the periods of mild weather, the Dostoevsky family went for walks in the early evening. Dr. Dostoevsky was in charge of these excursions, and the children were held in with a tight rein; any display of exuberance or animal spirits was out of the question. Andrey describes him taking the occasion to give them lessons in geometry, using the crazy-quilt pattern of the Moscow streets to illustrate the various types of angle. The importance of hard work and self-discipline was constantly drummed into their minds, and though their father did not terrorize them physically, his impatient vigilance constantly hung over their heads as a threat. It is probable that, when Dostoevsky spoke to his friend Dr. Yanovsky in the late 1840s about "the difficult and joyless circumstances of his childhood,"[19] he was thinking of circumstances such as these.

A great change occurred in the life of the Dostoevsky children when their parents acquired the small property at Darovoe in 1831. Feodor and Mikhail spent four months there with their mother every year for four years; after this time, because of their studies, they could come only for shorter stretches of a month or so. These were the sunniest periods in Dostoevsky's boyhood. If he later told his second wife that he had had a "happy and placid childhood,"[20] it was undoubtedly of these months in the country that he was thinking, free from the menace of paternal disapproval and from the oppressive confinement of life in the city. Evocations of a happy childhood are exceedingly rare in Dostoevsky's novels and the one or two that exist are set either in a village or on a country estate; no pleasant memories were linked in his sensibility with life in the city. "Not only that first voyage to the village," Andrey writes, "but all the following trips there always filled me with some kind of ecstatic excitement."[21] No doubt the high-spirited and impressionable Feodor experienced the same sensation even more intensely as the carriage to Darovoe pulled away every spring with bells tinkling on the horses' harness and as the at first unfamiliar (and then beloved) rural sights began to unroll before his eyes, until they finally arrived at the family's thatched-roof, three-room cottage sheltered by a grove of ancient linden trees.

These sojourns in the country also offered Dostoevsky his first opportunity to become acquainted with the Russian peasantry at close quarters (the house serfs had acquired the manners and habits of servants). The children were allowed to roam freely and to enlist the aid of serf children in their games. The children were also allowed to mingle freely with the older peasants in the fields. Feodor once ran back two versts to the village, according to Andrey, to bring

[19] Ibid., 57.
[20] *DZhP*, 33.
[21] *DVS*, 1: 64.

water to a peasant mother at work in the field who wished to give her baby a drink.[22] This untroubled boyhood relation with the peasants certainly contributed to shaping Dostoevsky's later social ideas; one may say that he aimed to bring about, on a national scale, the same harmonious unity between the educated classes and the peasantry that he remembered having known as a child. These childhood summers brought him—in the opinion of Dostoevsky's friend Count Peter Semenov—"closer to the peasantry, their way of life, and the entire moral physiognomy of the Russian people" than most scions of the landed gentry, "whose parents purposely kept them from any association with the peasants."[23]

The country around Darovoe was crisscrossed with numerous ravines that provided a haunt for snakes and wandering wolves. The children were warned to avoid them by their mother, but this did not stop Feodor from plunging into the nearby birchwood (called "Fedya's wood" by the family) with a delicious shudder of fear. He confided his sensations in a passage in the original version of *Poor Folk*, later eliminated. "I remember that at the back of our garden was a wood, thick, verdant, shadowy. . . . This wood was my favorite place to walk, but I was afraid to go into it very far . . . it seemed as if someone is calling there, as if someone is beckoning there . . . where the smooth stumps of trees are scattered about more blackly and thickly, where the ravine begins. . . . It becomes painful and terrifying, all around nothing but a dead silence; the heart shivers with some sort of obscure feeling, and you continue, you continue farther, carefully. . . . How sharply etched in my memory is that wood, those stealthly walks, and those feelings—a strange mixture of pleasure, childish curiosity and terror" (1: 443).

Dostoevsky never forgot his summers in Darovoe, and in 1877, shortly after returning there to visit for the first time since his childhood, he wrote of "that tiny and unimportant spot [which] left a very deep and strong impression on me for the remainder of my life."[24] Names of places, and of people he knew there, constantly turn up in his work, most abundantly in *The Brothers Karamazov*, which he was beginning to think of at the time of his belated return to the scenes of his youth. The village harbored a *durochka*, a female half-wit named Agrafena, who lived out of doors for most of the year and, in the dead of winter, was forcibly taken in by one peasant family or another. She is the prototype of

---

[22] Nechaeva, *V seme*, 83.

[23] *DVS*, 1: 209. Tolstoy's second son, Ilya, born in 1866, writes in his memoirs: "The world was divided into two parts, one composed of ourselves and the other of everyone else. We were special people and the others were not our equals. . . . It was mostly *maman*, of course, who was guilty of entertaining such notions, but *papa*, too, jealously guarded us from association with the village children. He was responsible to a considerable degree for the groundless arrogance and self-esteem that such an upbringing inculcated into us, and from which I found it so hard to free myself." Edward Crankshaw, *Tolstoy: The Making of a Novelist* (New York, 1974), 253.

[24] *DW* (July–August 1877), 752.

Lizaveta Smerdyakova, and suffered the same unhappy fate: despite her infirmity, she became pregnant and gave birth to a child who died shortly after birth. Andrey describes her as continually muttering something incomprehensible about her dead child in the cemetery, exactly like another Dostoevskian *durochka*, Marya Lebyadkina in *Demons*. Other echoes of these years appear in the dream sequence of Dimitry Karamazov of a village decimated by fire, like the one that broke out in Darovoe in the spring of 1833. "The whole estate," writes Andrey, "looked like a desert, with charred posts sticking up here and there."[25] Each family was given fifty rubles as a loan (a considerable sum in those days) to help in the work of reconstruction, and it is doubtful whether it was ever repaid.

———■———

In 1833, Mikhail and Feodor left home to go to Souchard's day school; a year later they were sent to Chermak's, the best boarding school in Moscow. The preparation for boarding school was tied up with a particularly trying experience for the two older boys. Mastery of Latin was required at Chermak's, but Souchard's had no such instruction, and Dr. Dostoevsky himself decided to fill in the deficiency. These lessons provide Andrey with the most graphic illustration of his father's hair-trigger temper. "At the slightest error of [my] brothers, father always became angry, flew into a passion, called them sluggards and fools; in the most extreme, though rarer, instances, he even broke off the lesson without finishing it, which was considered worse than any punishment."[26] Dr. Dostoevsky required his sons to stand stiffly at attention throughout the Latin drill. From this we may conclude that he had already decided to enroll them in a military establishment and was trying to accustom them to the rigors of martial discipline. No doubt, as Andrey remarks, his "brothers were very much afraid of these lessons."[27]

The transition from home to school, and particularly to boarding school, came as a rude shock to Feodor. Despite his father's flare-ups, home was still a comfortable and familiar place, and his mother a perpetual source of consolation. The words of the heroine of *Poor Folk* evoke what was probably Dostoevsky's reaction to the new world of the school. "I would sit over my French translation or vocabularies, not daring to move and dreaming all the while of our little home, of father, of mother, of our old nurse, of nurse's stories" (1: 28). Another reminiscence of this initiation may be contained in the image of Alyosha Karamazov surrounded by his schoolmates, who "forcibly held his hands from his ears, and shouted obscenities into them" (9: 23). The Dostoevsky

[25] *DVS*, 1: 72.
[26] Ibid., 76.
[27] Ibid.

children had lived in a peasant village and were certainly familiar with the facts of life, but they had been shielded from a knowledge of vice and perversity. Andrey remembers his own introduction to such matters by his schoolfellows with distaste. "There was no nastiness, no abominable vice, which was not taught to the innocent youngsters who had just left the paternal home."[28]

There is only one independent account that allows us to catch a glimpse of Dostoevsky in his school years. "On the first day I arrived," writes a slightly younger student, "I gave way to a surge of childish despair on finding myself . . . exposed to their taunts. During the recreation period, . . . Dostoevsky . . . chased away the mocking scamps, and began to console me. . . . He often visited me after that in class, guided me in my work, and lightened my sadness by his exciting stories during the recreation period."[29] This pattern of behavior illustrates aspects of Dostoevsky's character that remain constant: his staunch independence, and his willingness to intervene personally against a situation that offended his moral instincts. He was not afraid to spring to the defense of the helpless and persecuted. Dostoevsky's independence and self-assertiveness were exhibited at home as well. Andrey tells us that Feodor was sometimes so unrestrained in maintaining his own point of view that Dr. Dostoevsky would say, with the wisdom of experience, "Really, Fedya, control yourself, you'll get into trouble . . . and end up under the red cap,"[30] that is, wearing the headgear of the convict regiments of the Russian Army. Dostoevsky did serve in such a regiment after his release from prison camp in 1854.

The routine of these years of schooling was as invariable as those of early childhood. Every weekend the older boys returned home, and once the first excitement of reunion was over there was little else to do except read and supervise the assignments handed out the week before to their younger brothers and sisters. Visits were still restricted to the immediate family, nor were the older boys ever allowed to go out unaccompanied or given pocket money. Such restraints, however, were merely the custom of the times and the society.

——■——

The last four years of Dostoevsky's life in Moscow were darkened by his mother's illness, which took a sharp turn for the worse in the fall of 1836. Medical consultations were held every day by the doctor and his colleagues, and the visits of relatives succeeded each other in a never-ending and exhausting file. "This was the bitterest time in the childhood period of our lives," writes Andrey. "We were about to lose our mother any minute. . . . Father was totally destroyed." Just before the end, Marya Feodorovna regained consciousness, called for the icon of

[28] Ibid., 75.
[29] *DZhP*, 26.
[30] *DVS*, 1: 82.

the Savior, and then blessed her children and her husband. "It was a moving scene and we all wept," Andrey recalls.[31]

But it was not only the impending crisis in his family life that troubled Feodor during his last two years at home; he also knew that he was destined for a career repugnant to his deepest inclinations. Dr. Dostoevsky had decided that his two older sons were to be military engineers, and in the fall of 1836 he submitted a request through his hospital superior for their admission to the Academy of Military Engineers in St. Petersburg at government expense. Both Mikhail and Feodor were dreaming of literary fame and fortune, but once their father's request was granted, the die was cast. No doubt this decision stirred up a good deal of resentment and hostility, particularly in the fiery Feodor; but this was blunted by the lesson so often hammered home to the Dostoevsky children by their father. "He often repeated that he was a poor man," Andrey observes, "that his children, especially the younger ones, had to be ready to make their own way, that they would remain impoverished at his death, etc."[32] The post of military engineer offered solid financial advantages, and Dr. Dostoevsky believed he was doing the best he could for his offspring.

What little we know of Dostoevsky in these years makes it likely that he began to chafe very early under the restricting atmosphere of his home life and the necessity of knuckling under to a rigidly inflexible and emotionally unstable father who tended to identify his own wishes with the sacred dictates of God himself. Such feelings of disaffection, however, were certainly counterbalanced both by the natural inclination to accept and revere paternal authority and, as Feodor grew older, by his growing awareness of Dr. Dostoevsky's genuine dedication to the welfare of his family. For while the burdens that Dr. Dostoevsky imposed on his children were heavy indeed, their future, as they well knew, was at the center of his preoccupations; nor did he ever allow them to forget that his laborious life was devoted to their interests. Moreover, the adolescent Dostoevsky probably could sense his father's anxieties behind the stiff and official authoritarian façade.

Dostoevsky's only direct utterance about his father while the latter was still alive is made in a letter to Mikhail; and its mixture of pity with some impatience reveals Dostoevsky's ambivalence. "I feel sorry for our poor father," he writes. "A strange character! Oh, how much unhappiness he has had to bear! I could weep from bitterness that there is nothing to console him. But, do you know, Papa doesn't know the world at all. He has lived in it for 50 years and retains the same ideas about people as 30 years ago. Happy ignorance! But he is very disillusioned with it. That seems our common fate."[33] This was written after the death of

---

[31] Ibid., 83–84.
[32] Ibid., 84.
[33] *Pis'ma*, I: 52; October 31, 1838.

Marya Feodorovna had deprived Dr. Dostoevsky of his sole sustaining support in the midst of his woes; but it surely represents an opinion that his son had begun to form long before.

If we are to seek for some image of Dostoevsky's father in his works, it is useless to go to the creations of his maturity; whatever father figures we find there are too much intertwined with later experiences and ideological motifs to have any biographical value. But the picture given of Varvara's father in *Poor Folk* comes straight from Dostoevsky's still-fresh memories of his youth, and is steeped in the details of his daily life. "I tried my very utmost to learn and please father. I saw he was spending his last farthing on me and God knows what straits he was in. Every day he grew more gloomy, more ill-humored, more angry. . . . Father would begin saying that I was no joy, no comfort to them; that they were depriving themselves of everything for my sake and I could not speak French yet; in fact all his failures, all his misfortunes were vented on me and mother. . . . I was to blame for everything, I was responsible for everything! And this was not because father did not love me; he was devoted to mother and me, but it was just his character" (1: 29). It is likely that Dostoevsky had heard just such reproaches on numerous occasions, and had tried to excuse them in his heart in the same way. He depicts his father not as a brutal and heartless despot but as a harassed and finally pitiable figure driven to desperation by the difficulties of his situation.

Some of the traits of Dr. Dostoevsky, drawn at this time with a satirical rather than a pathetic pen, can also be found in the first version of another early work, *Netotchka Nezvanova*. A character named Feodor Ferapontovich, a minor civil service official, constantly reproaches his children for ingratitude. "Turning to his little children, he would ask them in a threatening and reproachful voice: 'What have they done for all the kindness he had shown them? Have they recompensed him, by assiduous study and impeccable pronunciation of French, for all his sleepless nights, all his labors, all his blood, for anything? for anything?' In other words, Feodor Ferapontovich . . . every evening turned his house into a little hell." The qualities in his character held up to ridicule are attributed to some sort of hidden suffering: "whether from the fact that he had been hurt, or cut down by somebody, some kind of secret enemy who constantly insulted his self-respect," and so forth (2: 444). One can imagine the young Dostoevsky speculating in much the same way about the sources of his father's more galling peculiarities.

Certain traits of Dostoevsky's character may be attributed to the effects of his relationship with his father. All the people who had any prolonged personal contact with Dostoevsky remark on the secretiveness and evasiveness of his personality; he was not someone who opened himself easily or willingly to others. There is scarcely a memoir about him that does not comment on this lack of expansiveness, and one suspects that this elusiveness may well have developed from the need to dissimulate as a means of coping with his father's combination of capriciousness and severity. The pathological shyness from which Dostoevsky suffered all his life can possibly also be attributed to an unwillingness to expose himself, a fear of being rebuffed and emotionally abused that had become second nature.

Most important of all, as Freud noted, is that Dostoevsky internalized as a child a highly developed sense of guilt. Instead of Oedipal sexual rivalry, however, it is more helpful, at this stage of Dostoevsky's life, to view his guilt feelings in the light of the paternal insistence on scholastic achievement as a moral obligation, and as the only defense against grinding poverty and loss of status. The importance given to this aspect of life in the family is well illustrated by a ceremony that took place every year on Dr. Dostoevsky's name day (and which later turns up in *The Village of Stepanchikovo*, performed for Colonel Rostanev, a father of ideal kindness). The two older boys and eventually the oldest girl prepared a morning greeting for their father on that joyous occasion. This meant memorizing a French poem, copying it on fine paper, presenting it to their father, and then reciting it by heart—with as good an accent as they could muster—while he followed with the written text. "Father was very touched," Andrey says, "and warmly kissed the purveyor of greetings";[34] clearly the most welcome present he could receive was this evidence of their progress in learning French.

Dostoevsky's genius first reveals itself by the creation of characters desperately eager to satisfy their bureaucratic superiors in some routine clerical task (not so far removed from schoolwork, after all); consumed with guilt at their velleities of rebellion; and oppressed by their sense of social inferiority. No wonder! All through his childhood, Dostoevsky had been placed psychically in exactly the same position by his father, and by the obvious social situation of his family.

The ambivalence of Dostoevsky's emotions about his father was also, unquestionably, of the greatest significance for his future. No doubt it was in the fluctuations of his own psyche between resentment and filial piety that he first glimpsed the psychological paradoxes whose exploration became the hallmark of his genius. And one can locate the emotive roots of his Christian ideal in the evident desire of the young Dostoevsky to resolve this ambivalence by an act of self-transcendence, a sacrifice of the ego through identification with the other (in this case, his father). Whether one calls such a sacrifice moral masochism, as Freud did, or, more traditionally, moral self-conquest, the fact remains that Dostoevsky as a boy and youth was not only hostile and inimical to his father

[34] *DVS*, 1: 59.

but also struggled to understand and to forgive him. This struggle then became fused with the Christian images and ideals that he was taught from the very first moment that he awoke consciously to life. All of Dostoevsky's later values can thus be seen as deriving from the synthesis of this early psychic need with the religious superstructure that gave it a universal and cosmic import, and elevated it to the stature of the fulfillment of man's destiny on earth.

CHAPTER 3

The Religious and Cultural Background

Dostoevsky's contemporary, Alexander Herzen, remarks in his memoirs that "nowhere does religion play so modest a role in education as in Russia."[1] Herzen was, of course, talking about the education of the male children of the landed or service aristocracy, whose parents had been raised for several generations on the culture of the French Enlightenment and for whom Voltaire had been a kind of patron saint. By the beginning of the nineteenth century, such parents had long since ceased to be concerned about Orthodox Christianity, even though they continued to baptize their children in the state religion and to structure their lives in accordance with its rituals. The war years and the post-Napoleonic period, in Russia as elsewhere, were marked by a wave of emotionalism and a revival of religion. But in Russia this stimulated the growth of Freemasonry and various revivalist sects rather than any massive return to the official faith. Most upper-class Russians would have shared the attitude exemplified in Herzen's anecdote about his host at a dinner party who, when asked whether he was serving Lenten dishes out of personal conviction, replied that it was "simply and solely for the sake of the servants."[2]

Parents with such ideas would scarcely consider it indispensable to provide their offspring with any kind of formal religious education. It was only at fifteen (after he had read Voltaire, as Herzen remarks) that Herzen's father "brought in a priest to give religious instruction so far as this was necessary for entrance into the University."[3] Tolstoy, though raised largely by devout female relatives, was also never given any religious education as a child. Turgenev's monstrous mother held the religion of the common people in such contempt that, instead of the usual prayers, she substituted each day at table the reading of a French translation of Thomas à Kempis.

Only against such a background can one appreciate the full force of Dostoevsky's quiet words: "I came from a pious Russian family. . . . In our family, we

[1] Alexander Herzen, *My Past and Thoughts*, trans. Constance Garnett, rev. Humphrey Higgens, 4 vols. (New York, 1968), 1: 42.

[2] Ibid., 2: 412.

[3] Ibid., 1: 42.

knew the Gospel almost from the cradle."[4] This is, as we know from Andrey, literally true: the children were all taught to read by their mother from a well-known eighteenth-century religious primer, translated from the German and titled *One Hundred and Four Sacred Stories from the Old and New Testaments.* Coarse lithographs accompanying the text depicted various episodes from the scriptures—the creation of the world, Adam and Eve in Paradise, the Flood, the raising of Lazarus, the rebellion of Job the just man against God. The very first impressions that awakened the consciousness of the child were those embodying the teachings of the Christian faith, and the world thereafter for Dostoevsky would always remain transfigured by the glow of this supernatural illumination. Dostoevsky was to say later that the problem of the existence of God had tormented him all his life; but this only confirms that it was always emotionally impossible for him to accept a world that had no relation to a God of any kind.

One of his earliest childhood memories was that of saying his prayers before the icons in the presence of admiring guests. "I put all my trust in Thee, O Lord!" the child intoned. "Mother of God, keep me and preserve me under Thy wing!"[5] In the Dostoevsky household, such a childish performance of a religious ritual was evidently a source of pride and social satisfaction. To reinforce the effect of this early religious initiation, a deacon came to the house regularly to give formal instruction. This clergyman also taught at the neighboring Catherine Institute for Girls, a fashionable school for daughters of the aristocracy; and this meant that, unlike the majority of the Russian non-monastic clergy, he would have been highly literate. "He possessed an uncommon verbal gift," writes Andrey, "and the entire lesson . . . was spent telling stories, or, as we called it, interpreting the Scriptures."[6] The children also were required to study the introduction to religion composed by the metropolitan Filaret, whose first sentence Andrey still remembers after more than half a century: "The One God, worshipped in the Holy Trinity, is eternal, that is, has no beginning nor end to his being, but always was, is, and will be."[7] The attempt of theologians to rationalize the mysteries of faith, it would appear, never held any appeal for Dostoevsky. What stirred his feelings to the depths was the story of the Advent as a divine-human narrative full of character and action—as an account of real people living and responding with passion and fervor to the word of God.

Religion not only loomed large because of its manifest status in the eyes of his parents and relatives, it was also involved quite naturally with the most exciting experiences of his earliest years, the events that stood out as joyful breaks in his monotonous and laborious routine. The name of Dostoevsky has become so

[4] *DW* (1873, no. 50), 152.
[5] Miller, *Biografiya*, 5–6.
[6] *DVS*, I: 75.
[7] Ibid.

inalterably associated with that of St. Petersburg that one tends to forget he was born in Moscow—"the city of innumerable churches, of everlasting bells, of endless processions, of palace and church combined," the city that the peasants called "our Holy Mother."[8] The beating heart of all this intense religious life was the Kremlin; and whenever the Dostoevsky family went for an outing in the city, they invariably directed their steps toward this sacred spot. "Every visit to the Kremlin and the Moscow cathedrals," Dostoevsky remembered later, "was, for me, something very solemn."[9] Time and again he wandered through its forest of bulbous cupolas, listened to the many-tongued harmony of its bell towers, contemplated its treasured relics and richly decorated cathedrals, from whose walls the Orthodox saints, as the much-traveled Théophile Gautier saw them, stared down with eyes that seemed "to menace, though their arms extended to bless."[10]

The stout walls and crenelated battlements of the Kremlin bore mute testimony to its function as a fortress as well as a religious sanctuary, and reminded the onlooker that it was not only a place of sacred worship but also a monument to Russia's historical grandeur. The God-anointed tsars were crowned in the Cathedral of the Assumption; another church contained the sepulchers of all the past rulers of Russia, who, clothed in flowing white robes and with a halo encircling their head, appeared on the wall above each tomb. In Russia, as a student of its ecclesiastical history reminds us, "the national and religious elements have been identified far more closely than in the West,"[11] and one of the great landmarks of this symbiosis is the Kremlin. The Russian struggle against foreign invaders—whether pagan Tartar, Mohammedan Turk, German or Polish Catholic, or Swedish Lutheran—has always been a struggle on behalf of the Orthodox faith. By the early nineteenth century the two powerful idea-feelings of religion and nationalism had been inseparable for Russians for a thousand years. One can well understand how they must have blended together in Dostoevsky's consciousness, during these childhood excursions, into an inextricable mélange of ardor and devotion that he later found it impossible to disentangle.

—■—

Up until the age of ten, when his parents acquired their small property in the country, Dostoevsky and his brothers and sisters left the city only once a year. Mme Dostoevsky always took the older children, accompanied by some relatives or friends, for an annual spring excursion to the monastery of the Trinity and St. Sergey about sixty miles from Moscow. This journey required several

---

[8] A. P. Stanley, *Lectures on the History of the Eastern Church* (London, 1924), 303.
[9] *DW* (1873, no. 50), 152.
[10] Théophile Gautier, *Voyage en Russie* (Paris, n.d.), 276.
[11] Stanley, *Lectures*, 279.

days by carriage and terminated in a vast fortress-like beehive of churches, monasteries, and hostelries that, over the centuries, had clustered around the spot where St. Sergey had first constructed a hut in the northern forests in the fourteenth century.

A famous hermit and ascetic, St. Sergey became the patron saint of Moscow when, after he had blessed the armies of Prince Dimitry and sent two of his priestly followers to accompany the troops, Dimitry's forces inflicted a crushing defeat on the hitherto invincible Tartar hordes. Since that time, the name of St. Sergey had become "at least as dear to every Russian heart as William Tell to a Swiss or as Joan of Arc to a Frenchman."[12] St. Sergey's humble dwelling in the woods grew into one of the main foci—more important even than the Kremlin—for the indigenous Russian amalgam of religious-patriotic sentiment. Its importance as such a symbol was reinforced in the seventeenth century, when it became the center of national resistance against the Polish invaders in the Time of Troubles.

Each year the Dostoevsky children visited this vast religious caravansary, swarming both with peasant pilgrims in bark shoes and elegant visitors in glittering uniforms and gowns in the very latest French mode. Each visit, as Andrey recalls, constituted an "epoch" in the lives of all the children;[13] for his brother Feodor they were unforgettable. One of the most famous stories in the canonical life of St. Sergey is that of the bear that emerged from the woods to come face-to-face with the saint. Subdued by the sanctity of the holy man, the animal peacefully accepted some of the bread and water that was St. Sergey's only nourishment, returning each subsequent day to share this frugal meal. This friendship between the beast and the saint is depicted among the frescoes on the entrance tower to the monastery, and Dostoevsky as a child must have seen it many times. In *The Brothers Karamazov*, when Father Zosima preaches to a young peasant about the innocence of animals and of all of nature, it is the story of St. Sergey and the bear that he uses to point the moral.

One can gauge from such details how completely Dostoevsky's childhood immersed him in the spiritual and cultural atmosphere of Old Russian piety and brought him emotively close to the beliefs and feelings of the illiterate peasantry still untouched by secular Western culture. For the Russian upper class, of course, religion and the people were inseparable, and it was by frequenting the servants' quarters that the offspring of the aristocracy first became acquainted with the sources of their native culture and the deep religious roots of Russian folk-feeling. The role that Pushkin assigned to his old nurse as a transmitter of folk tradition has immortalized this crucial encounter in the lives of so many

[12] Ibid., 319.
[13] A. M. Dostoevsky, *Vospominaniya* (Leningrad, 1930), 48–49.

educated Russians. Dostoevsky also went through a similar archetypal initiation, but for him the contrast between his home environment and that of the servants and the peasants was much less accentuated. One can scarcely imagine him hiding in a closet, like the young Tolstoy, to watch the exciting and unfamiliar spectacle of the saintly fool (*yurodivy*) who lived in the Tolstoy household saying his nightly prayers amid sobs and exclamations. There was nothing exotic about the people and their faith to Dostoevsky as a child, and both entered his world in a more natural fashion.

One of the recurring events that the Dostoevsky children looked forward to with the greatest eagerness was the visit of the wet nurses who had been employed to suckle them in infancy. These peasant women lived in villages close to Moscow, and once a year, during the winter lull in peasant life, they came to pay a ceremonial call on the family and spend two or three days as guests. Such visits always gave rise to an orgy of storytelling in the late afternoon, after the children had done their lessons and it was too cold to go outdoors. Andrey remembered these stories as being a mixture of fairy tales and Russian folk legends; but his four-year-older brother Feodor recalled another type of story.

"Who has read the *Acta Martyrum*?" Dostoevsky asks the readers of his *Diary of a Writer* (1877). "In the whole of Russia the knowledge of the *Acta Martyrum* is extremely widely diffused—of course, not of the book *in toto*, but of its spirit, at least. . . . In childhood I heard these narratives myself, before I even learned to read."[14] These stories of the lives of the saints were steeped in the special spirit of Russian kenoticism—the glorification of passive, completely nonheroic and nonresisting suffering, the suffering of the despised and humiliated Christ—that is so remarkable a feature of the Russian religious tradition.[15] Even a skeptical foreign observer like the French liberal Anatole Leroy-Beaulieu, who had vast personal acquaintance with Russian life and culture, was still struck toward the end of the nineteenth century by the admiration of the Russian common people for "the spirit of asceticism and renunciation, the love of poverty, the craving for self-sacrifice and self-mortification."[16] It was impressions such as these, garnered in earliest childhood from the lips of humble peasant storytellers, that nourished Dostoevsky's unshakable conviction that the soul of the Russian peasant was imbued with the Christian ethos of love and self-sacrifice.

Certain incidents vividly etched in Dostoevsky's boyish imagination what he came to regard as this ethos in action. One involved the housekeeper and *nyanya*, Alyona Frolovna, whose tall and corpulent personage loomed large in the lives of all the children. Alyona was a free Moscow townswoman, but she brought

---

[14] *DW* (July–August 1877), 803.
[15] See George P. Fedotov, *The Russian Religious Mind* (New York, 1960), chap. 4.
[16] A. Leroy-Beaulieu, *The Empire of the Tsars and the Russians*, 3 vols. (New York, 1902), 3: 48.

with her the pagan superstitions and the ritual formalism that the Russian lower classes blended so naturally with their Christianity. Alyona was charged with teaching the children manners; and she informed them solemnly that it would be a deadly sin to eat any food without first having taken a bite of bread, "for so God had ordained!" Suffering from frequent nightmares, she always attributed her outcries, which woke the entire family, to the nocturnal visits of the *domovoy*—the Russian house-demon or hobgoblin—who had been strangling her with his claws. Alyona had never been married, and called herself a "bride of Christ" (the phrase made a great impression on the children); her sister—a nun living in a cloister near Petersburg—came to visit her once a year, and always spent the day with the Dostoevsky family.[17]

The figure of Alyona was thus surrounded for the children with a certain sublime nimbus of the sacred, and this must have made the incident on which Dostoevsky reports even more symbolically striking. It occurred shortly after the Dostoevskys had purchased their country property and was only the first of the misfortunes destined to become linked with this unhappy spot for the family. Most of the peasant huts had been destroyed in the fire of 1833, and the loss, as well as the cost of replacement, was a staggering financial blow for the hard-pressed family. While they were still reeling under the shock of the news, Alyona's response was to offer the savings being accumulated for her old age: "Suddenly, she whispered to mother: 'If you should need money, take mine; I have no use for it; I don't need it.'"[18] This impulsive gesture remained in the memory of the twelve-year-old Feodor as typical of the capacity of the Russian people, in moments of moral stress, to live up to the Christian ideals they nominally revered but that, in the ordinary course of daily life, they so often violated or betrayed.

■

Dostoevsky's family, rooted in its clerical and merchant origins, had remained relatively untouched by the skepticism and religious incredulity so prevalent among the Russian gentry. As a child, he never felt any separation between the sacred and the profane, between the ordinary and the miraculous; religion was never for him a matter of ritual occasions. The texture of his everyday life was controlled by much the same supernatural forces that, in a more naïvely superstitious form, also dominated the mentality of the Russian common people.

"Every Sunday and every religious holiday," writes Andrey, "we unfailingly went to church for mass and, the evening before, to vespers."[19] More important was that the entire mental world of the parents was religiously oriented, and that

[17] *DVS*, I: 42–43.
[18] *DW* (April 1876), 284–285.
[19] *DVS*, I: 61.

God permeated every aspect of the young Dostoevsky's quotidian existence—much as he would have done centuries earlier in an English Puritan or German Pietist household. Andrey tells us that, after the conclusion of the purchase of their estate, his parents immediately went off to utter a prayer of thanksgiving at the chapel of the Iversky Madonna—the most revered icon in Moscow, which the people, in 1812, had wished to carry into battle against the French. The same reflex occurred when the family suddenly heard the news of the fire on their country estate. "I remember that my parents fell on their knees before the icons in the living room," writes Andrey, "and then left to pray to the Iversky Madonna." [20]

One has only to glance at the letters of Dostoevsky's parents to be struck by this piously devout aspect of their mentality and to observe them speaking of God with the same combination of sentimental unction and intense practicality that is so striking—and now seems so strange—in Defoe's novels, or in the sermons of English Puritan divines. For all his medical degree and scientific education, Dr. Dostoevsky never lost the clerical stamp of his early training, and the style of his letters is full of Church Slavonic expressions that reveal his thorough acquaintance with ecclesiastical literature. "How great is the divine mercy!" he writes to his oldest son Mikhail. "How unworthy are we to give thanks to the great and bountiful God for His inexpressible mercy to us! How unjustly have we grumbled, yes, let this serve as an admonitory example for the remainder of our lives, since the All-Highest sent us this transitory trial for our own good and our own welfare!" [21] The occasion for this edifying outburst was the acceptance of Mikhail (who had been refused admittance to the Academy of Military Engineers in 1837) into another school of the same kind.

The letters of Dostoevsky's mother are more personally expressive in tone, and influenced by the late eighteenth-century sentimental novel rather than by the lives of the saints. But here too the intermingling of the sublime and the trivial, the religious and the mundanely practical, is in evidence. Mme Dostoevsky writes her husband from the country: "I . . . have given thanks to God a hundredfold that He was gracious enough to hear my prayers and brought you safely to Moscow. Do not grumble against God, my friend, do not grieve for me. You know that we were punished by Him; but also granted His grace. With complete steadfastness and faith, let us rely on His sacred providence and He will not withhold His mercy from us." [22] What misfortune Mme Dostoevsky refers to here is unknown; in any case, the remainder of the letter is taken up with a lawsuit concerning Darovoe, and with other purely business matters relating to the crops and the peasants.

[20] Ibid.

[21] V. S. Nechaeva, *V seme i usadbe Dostoevskikh* (Moscow, 1939), 117–118; February 2, 1838.

[22] Ibid., 73; June 29, 1832.

It may be taken for granted that the children were continually being admonished and instructed in much the same style. And for the most gifted of them all, young Feodor, this habit of mind began to stir reflections very early on the most profound and insoluble of religious enigmas—that of God's relation to man, and the existence of evil, pain, and suffering in a world where the will of a beneficent God presumably prevails. Such reflections would surely have been stimulated by the continual discomfiture with life that his father never hesitated to voice and that, from time to time, take on a truly Job-like note. "True," he writes his wife, "I will not hide from you that there are sometimes minutes in which I anger my Creator by grumbling against the briefness of the days given me by my lot in life; but do not think anything of it; it will pass."[23] It is improbable that Dr. Dostoevsky, like the father of Kierkegaard, ever rose in revolt against God and cursed him because of the harshness of his fate, but the temptation to do so was continually there and, given his explosive irritability, would scarcely have been concealed.

Years later, when Dostoevsky was reading the book of Job once again, he wrote his wife that it put him into such a state of "unhealthy rapture" that he almost cried. "It's a strange thing, Anya, this book is one of the first in my life which made an impression on me; I was then still almost a child."[24] There is an allusion to this revelatory experience of the young boy in *The Brothers Karamazov*, where Zosima recalls being struck by a reading of the book of Job at the age of eight and feeling that "for the first time in my life I consciously received the seed of God's word in my heart" (9: 287). This seed was one day to flower into the magnificent growth of Ivan Karamazov's passionate protest against God's injustice and the Legend of the Grand Inquisitor, but it also grew into Alyosha's submission to the awesomeness of the infinite before which Job too had once bowed his head, and into Zosima's teaching of the necessity for an ultimate faith in the goodness of God's mysterious wisdom. It is Dostoevsky's genius as a writer to have been able to feel (and to express) both these extremes of rejection and acceptance. While the tension of this polarity may have developed out of the ambivalence of Dostoevsky's psychodynamic relationship with his father, what is more important is to see how early it was transposed and projected into the religious symbolism of the eternal problem of theodicy.

———■———

No less important than the children's religious instruction was their secular education. Dr. Dostoevsky knew that an open sesame to any sort of advancement in Russian society for his sons was fluency in French, and a language tutor named

---

[23] Ibid., 107; June 2, 1835.
[24] *Pisma*, 3: 177; June 10/22, 1875.

Souchard (whose day school they attended) was engaged simultaneously with the deacon who gave them religious instruction. The only text we know assigned by Monsieur Souchard was Voltaire's *La Henriade*—a heroic epic filled with the religious orthodoxy appropriate to the theme. Souchard, in addition, was so ardent a Russian patriot that he asked for (and received) special permission from Nicholas I to russify his name. Such a personage was not likely to imbue his pupils, as did so many of the tutors of aristocratic families, with dangerously subversive notions, whether in religion or in politics. Herzen, for example, was told by *his* French tutor that Louis XVI had been rightfully executed as a traitor to France.

The secular education of the Dostoevsky children was also carried on by the parents themselves in nightly reading sessions, and it is striking to see by how many threads this early ideological and artistic stimulation is tied to the maturer Dostoevsky. He remembered in 1863 how "I used to spend the long winter evenings before going to bed listening (for I could not yet read), agape with ecstasy and terror, as my parents read aloud to me from the novels of Ann Radcliffe. Then I would rave deliriously about them in my sleep" (5: 46). This was the unforgettable fashion in which he first became acquainted with the novelistic mode that transformed the art of narrative at the end of the eighteenth century. The main structural features of this mode are a plot based on mystery and suspense, characters who always find themselves in situations of extreme psychological and erotic tension, incidents of murder and mayhem, and an atmosphere calculated to impart a shiver of the demonic or supernatural. Dostoevsky would later take over such features of the Gothic technique and carry them to a peak of perfection that has never been surpassed.

Dr. Dostoevsky also read them Karamzin's *History of the Russian State*, the first work to disinter the Russian past from dusty monkish chronicles and poetic legend and to present it as a national epic appealing to a wide circle of cultivated readers: Karamzin, as Pushkin remarked, discovered the Russian past as Columbus had discovered America. Writing in the great eighteenth-century tradition of admiration for enlightened despotism, Karamzin stressed the importance of the autocratic power in maintaining Russian unity and preserving national independence once the Tartar yoke had been thrown off. Andrey tells us that Karamzin was his brother Feodor's bedside book, a work he read and reread continuously.

Second in importance only to his *History* was Karamzin's famous *Letters of a Russian Traveller*—a brilliant account of his *Wanderjahre* in Switzerland, Germany, France, and England; this book too was read aloud and discussed in the Dostoevsky family circle. Karamzin's work provided several generations of Russian readers with a splendid panorama of the mythical European world they tried so desperately to emulate from afar. The impression they derived from the book, however, would no doubt have been rather mixed. The early stages of the French Revolution coincided with Karamzin's first visit to France, and while, like so many others, the Masonic liberal Karamzin greeted the revolution with joy, its later phases also filled him with dismay and disillusion. By the time he published his *Letters*, he warned his countrymen against following the European path, insofar as this had led to subversion and social chaos. Karamzin's *Letters* thus helped to propagate the idea, so important for Russian thought in the nineteenth century, that Europe was a doomed and dying civilization.

The influence of Karamzin's *Letters* on Dostoevsky was profound. Early in the book, Karamzin drops in to pay a call on Kant, the sage of Königsberg, who expounds for his young Russian visitor's benefit the two main ideas of the *Critique of Practical Reason* (published just the year before). Kant explained that the consciousness of good and evil is innate to mankind, written indelibly into the human heart. Earthly life, however, reveals a glaring contradiction: the virtuous in this world, those who choose to live by the good and obey the moral law, are not always the ones who prosper and receive their just reward. But if, as we must assume, the Eternal Creative Mind is rational and beneficent, then we must also assume that this contradiction will not be left unresolved. Hence we postulate the existence of an immortal life after physical death in which the good receive their reward, even though this postulate can never be *proven* by human reason. "Here," Karamzin reports Kant as saying, "reason extinguishes her lamp and we are left in darkness. Only fancy can wander in this darkness and create fictions." Dostoevsky thus first came across these two ideas, both defying a strictly rational explanation—that moral consciousness (conscience) is an ineradicable part of human nature, and that immortality is a necessary condition of any world order claiming to make moral sense—when he read Karamzin as a boy. What he acquired subsequently only built on this foundation.[25]

Many other Russian works were also read in the family circle. Andrey mentions a whole series of recent historical novels by Russian imitators of Walter Scott, the newest literary products of Romantic Nationalism. The children became familiar with the poetry of Zhukovsky, the ballad poetry of the German Romantics, and the works of Derzhavin, whose famous ode to God, written in the tradition of philosophical Deism, powerfully evokes the immensity of the universe and the immeasurable majesty of God's creative power.

[25] In this interview, Kant also expounds on that human striving toward an ideal that Dostoevsky would vigorously uphold against the determinist and materialist tendency of his time: "Activity is man's lot, He can never be completely content with that which he has, but is always striving to obtain something more. Death surprises us on the road toward something we still desire. Give a man everything he desires and yet at that very moment he will feel that this *everything* is not *everything*. Failing to see the aim or purpose of our striving in this life, we assume there is a future where the knot must be untied." N. M. Karamzin, *Letters of a Russian Traveller, 1789–1790*, trans. and abridged by Florence Jonas (New York, 1957), 40–41.

The years of Dostoevsky's childhood and adolescence were thus a period of intense literary and intellectual assimilation. He became thoroughly familiar with all the styles and forms of Russian prose, beginning with Karamzin and the historical novel and ranging through such works as Begichev's family chronicle novel *The Kholmsky Family* (a precursor of *War and Peace*), and Dahl's colloquial sketches of peasant life, which foreshadow Turgenev. Among Russian novels, two were his particular favorites: Narezhny's *Bursak* (a picaresque tale in the tradition of Gil Blas), and *Serdtse i dumka* (*Heart and Head*), by one of the most original novelists of the 1830s, Alexander Veltman, who here uses the motif of the double for comic and satiric purposes.

It was thus Russian culture that loomed largest on Dostoevsky's horizon as a child and overshadowed all the others. Here too, as in the case of his religious education, the contrast with the majority of his contemporaries is marked. Russian parents of the upper class took little personal interest in the education of their children; they turned them over to foreign tutors and governesses as soon as they were out of swaddling bands to acquire the requisite polish of European manners. As a result, while the young Russian nobleman more often than not would be "at home in the literature and history of Western Europe," he was apt to be "quite ignorant of Russian letters and the past of his own homeland."[26] Herzen's first reading experiences, for example, were provided by his father's extensive library of eighteenth-century French literature; and he does not mention a single Russian book in *My Past and Thoughts* among those he loved as a child. Tolstoy immortalized his good-hearted German tutor in *Childhood*, but whereas he could recite some poems of Pushkin at the age of eight, he had stumbled on them himself and never received any tutoring in Russian literature or history before going to school a year later. Turgenev too had French and German tutors but only learned to read and write in Russian from his father's serf-valet; it was at the age of eight, after breaking into a room containing a moldering library, that the first Russian book he ever read (Kheraskov's hoary old epic, the *Rossiada*) came into his hands. Dostoevsky was thus taught at an early age to identify himself emotionally with Russia and its past.

———————■———————

Dr. Dostoevsky did not foresee that the type of education he gave them would inspire in both Mikhail and Feodor an all-exclusive love for literature that, as they matured, turned into dreams of pursuing literary careers. Such dreams were unquestionably stimulated by two decisive literary encounters whose echoes later resounded in Dostoevsky's writing. In 1831, Dr. Dostoevsky took his wife and older sons to a performance of Schiller's *The Robbers* (*Die Räuber*). His second son, then ten years old, remembered the evening all his life, and referred to it in a letter shortly before his death. "I can justly say," he writes, "that the tremendous impression I carried away from it then acted very richly on my spiritual side."[27]

This, presumably, was Dostoevsky's first encounter with the work of the German poet whose role in Russian culture of the early nineteenth century was perhaps more important than that of any other foreign writer.[28] In the *Diary of a Writer* for 1876, he remarks that "[Schiller] soaked into the Russian soul, left an impression on it, and almost marked an epoch in the history of our development."[29] Certain themes from Schiller's violent *Sturm-und-Drang* theatrics in *The Robbers* remained with Dostoevsky all his life. Near its end, when Dostoevsky came to write his own version of *The Robbers* in *The Brothers Karamazov*, the abundance of Schillerian references indicates to what extent Dostoevsky could still express his own deepest values in Schillerian terms. There is Karl Moor's stormy revolt against divine and human fatherhood, offset by his acknowledgment of a moral power stronger than his own will and to whom alone is reserved the task of meting out divine justice. There is also Franz Moor's use of the cynical doctrines of eighteenth-century materialism to justify his parricidal villainy, though despite his professed atheism he cannot overcome his terror of hell and eternal damnation. It finally proves impossible for him to eradicate that spark of conscience about which Kant had spoken.

Two years after this first decisive literary encounter, during one of the summers at Darovoe, Dostoevsky gobbled up all the novels of Walter Scott; Andrey depicts him as always carrying around a copy of *Quentin Durward* or *Waverley*. "As a result of this reading," Dostoevsky once wrote, "I carried with me into life so many beautiful and lofty impressions that, surely, they provided my soul with great strength in the fight against seductive, passionate, and corrupting impressions."[30] Some indication of what these impressions were is given in *Netotchka Nezvanova*, where the young orphan Netotchka finds consolation in her discovery of Scott's novels. "The feeling for the family portrayed so poetically in the novels of Scott . . . forced itself into my soul deliciously and powerfully as an answer to my memories and sufferings. This feeling for the family was the ideal in whose name Scott created his novels, a feeling to which they gave an exalted historical meaning, and which they depicted as the condition for the preservation of mankind" (2: 450–451).

---

[27] *Pis'ma*, 4: 196; August 18, 1880.

[28] For a useful summary of the material, see Edmund K. Kostka, *Schiller in Russian Literature* (Philadelphia, 1965); chap. 7 is devoted to Dostoevsky. See also D. Chizhevsky, "Schiller v Rossii," *Novy Zhurnal* 45 (1956), 109–135, and the spirited study by the Soviet Germanist N. Vilmont, "Dostoevsky i Schiller," in his *Velikie sputniki* (Moscow, 1966), 7–316.

[29] *DW* (June 1876), 343.

[30] *Pis'ma*, 4: 196; August 18, 1880.

Perhaps this aspect of Scott struck him so forcibly because it helped him accept his own familial situation with more equanimity. The budding consciousness of the youthful Dostoevsky may have vibrated to Scott's glorification of patriarchal relations between ruler and ruled as the surest anchor of social stability. If so, this is exactly the relation between the tsar-father and his "children"—his subjects—that Dostoevsky will later convince himself existed in Russia, and which served as a bulwark, in his view, against the disintegrating individualism of European society. He came to believe that the protection of this "feeling" was a necessary "condition for the preservation of mankind." And if *The Brothers Karamazov*, after *King Lear*, is the greatest work ever written to illustrate the moral horrors that ensue when family bonds disintegrate, it is partly because Dostoevsky had been mulling over this theme all his life.

Dr. Dostoevsky was a subscriber to the new periodical, *The Library for Reading (Biblioteka dlya chteniya)*, and it was probably in these pages that Dostoevsky first became aware of such writers as Victor Hugo, Balzac, and George Sand, who were soon to play so important a part in his spiritual and literary evolution. At the same time, Dostoevsky was also receiving his first important exposure to German Idealist and Romantic ideas in the classroom. His professor of literature during his senior year was I. I. Davydov, one of the small group of academics responsible for propagating Schelling's ideas in Russia. He thoroughly indoctrinated Dostoevsky with the whole tradition of German Romantic Idealist art and aesthetics that dominated Russian culture in the 1830s.

What affected Dostoevsky most profoundly was Schelling's view of art as an organ of metaphysical cognition—indeed, as *the* vehicle through which the mysteries of the highest transcendental truths are revealed to mankind. The entire generation of the 1840s became imbued with this belief in the exalted metaphysical mission of art; and no one was to defend it with more passion and brilliance than Dostoevsky. As we shall see, Dostoevsky was also influenced by Schelling's view that the highest truths were closed to discursive reason but accessible by a superior faculty of "intellectual intuition," as well as by his Idealist conception of nature as dynamic rather than static and mechanical—or, in other words, as exhibiting a spiritual meaning and purpose. Such ideas must have seemed to the young Dostoevsky a welcome confirmation, offered by the most up-to-date science and philosophy, of the religious convictions he had been taught as a child and had always accepted.

———■———

Of even greater importance for Dostoevsky than all the influences we have mentioned so far, however, was that of Alexander Pushkin. Some of Pushkin's prose was read in the family circle, but his reputation was as yet by no means established, and the juvenile enthusiasm of both Mikhail and Feodor for his work gives evidence of their serious literary propensities. Some of Pushkin's greatest works appeared during Dostoevsky's adolescence ("The Queen of Spades," "Songs of the Western Slavs," "The Covetous Knight," "The Bronze Horseman," "Egyptian Nights"), and, though greeted tepidly by the critics they were avidly read by the young Feodor.

On hearing of Pushkin's death in February 1837, Dostoevsky told the family that, if he were not already wearing mourning for his mother, he would have wished to do so for Pushkin. There is something impulsively right in this youthful desire; if it was his mother who had given birth to him in the flesh, it was Pushkin who had given birth to him in the world of the spirit. Pushkin dominates Dostoevsky's literary life from beginning to end, and the great writer of his youth is also the one to whom he devoted his last public utterance. In the famous speech he gave at the dedication of a Pushkin monument in 1880—a speech that caused a national sensation—Dostoevsky interpreted Pushkin's writing as the first (and still unsurpassed) utterance of Russia's deepest moral-national values. Pushkin's work provides the foundations and defines the horizon of Dostoevsky's own creative universe.

Dostoevsky read and reread Pushkin, meditated unceasingly on his works, and bequeathed to posterity a series of inspired interpretations of them that have permanently affected Russian criticism. Even more, Dostoevsky's own writings are impossible to imagine without taking Pushkin into account as a predecessor. Leonid Grossman has well said that "His greatest figures are linked to Pushkin's heroes, and often are manifestly deepenings of the original Pushkinian sketches that lift them to the level of tragic intensity."[31] The terrified clerks of the early stories could not have existed without "The Bronze Horseman" and "The Station Master"; Raskolnikov recreates the murderous folly of Pushkin's Hermann in "The Queen of Spades," who is equally obsessed with an *idée fixe* and equally ready to murder to obtain wealth and power; Stavrogin transforms the charming ne'er-do-well Evgeny Onegin into a terrifying demonic force. The theme of impostorship—so brilliantly dramatized in *Boris Godunov*, and so fateful and omnipresent in Russian history—also haunts Dostoevsky's pages from first to last, beginning with *The Double*, taken up again in *Demons*, and culminating majestically in the Legend of the Grand Inquisitor.

D. V. Grigorovich, who later became a novelist, was a fellow student with Dostoevsky at the Academy of Military Engineers. He remembers being impressed not only by Dostoevsky's thorough knowledge of Pushkin's works but also by the fact that only he, among all the other students, took Pushkin's death to heart. It is clear that Dostoevsky was living emotionally in a world quite dif-

---

[31] Leonid Grossman, *Biblioteka Dostoevskogo* (Odessa, 1919), 70; for more details, see A. L. Bem, *U istokov tvorchestva Dostoevskogo* (Prague, 1936), 37–123. Another good treatment is D. D. Blagoy, "Dostoevsky i Pushkin," in *Dostoevsky—khudoznik i myslitel'* (Moscow, 1972), 344–426.

ferent from that inhabited by most of his comrades, whose heads were filled with more immediately practical concerns. At the age of sixteen, it is the disastrous fate of his literary idol, as well as all that Pushkin's untimely death implied for Russian culture, that involves Dostoevsky's deepest feelings. And if we are to understand him properly, we should keep in mind this precocious capacity to pour the full intensity of his private emotions into what was, essentially, a matter of cultural and national concern.

CHAPTER 4

The Academy of Military Engineers

The death of Marya Feodorovna snapped the strongest emotional thread tying the young Dostoevsky to Moscow; but the inner conflict between his desire to leave and the bleakness of the prospect ahead may account for the mysterious illness that struck him down just before his departure for the Academy of Military Engineers. Without any apparent cause, he lost his voice and seemed to have contracted some throat or chest ailment whose diagnosis was uncertain. The impending trip to St. Petersburg had to be postponed until finally Dr. Dostoevsky was advised to begin the journey and trust to the revivifying effects of travel. Andrey remarks that his brother's voice, after that time, always retained a curious throaty quality that never appeared quite normal.

The advice was sound, and Feodor's illness passed away once the gates of Moscow were left behind. And no wonder! What Russian youth would not have felt a surge of strength and excitement at the prospect of going to St. Petersburg for the first time? For all young Russians, the journey was from past to present, from the city of monasteries and religious processions to that of severe government buildings and monstrous military parades, the journey to the spot where Peter the Great had broken "a window through to Europe." It was also, for Mikhail and Feodor, the journey from boyhood to manhood, the end of the protected family world they had known and the beginning of the insecurities of independence.

Years later, Dostoevsky wrote of this journey in *The Diary of a Writer*, evoking the state of mind in which both boys approached this new era in their lives. The brothers had their heads stuffed full of the mathematics that were necessary for their entrance examination into the academy, but both were secretly harboring literary ambitions. "We dreamt only of poetry and poets. My brother wrote verses, at least three poems a day even on the road, and I spent all my time composing in my head a novel of Venetian life."[1] The two young men planned immediately to visit the site of the duel in which Pushkin had been killed four months earlier and then "to see the room in which his soul expired."[2] Both were

[1] *DW* (January 1876), 184.
[2] Ibid., 185.

3. A government courier on a mission

possessed by a mood of vague yearning and expectancy to which the mature Dostoevsky gives both a moral and a cultural significance. "My brother and I were then longing for a new life, we dreamt about something enormous, about everything 'beautiful and sublime'; such touching words were then still fresh, and uttered without irony." [3]

It is against the background of this lofty moral idealism, so characteristic of the Russian culture of the 1830s, that one must gauge the shock of what then occurred. At a posting station along the road the Dostoevskys saw the whirlwind arrival of a government courier wearing the imposing full uniform of the time, crowned by the white, yellow, and green plumes of a three-cornered hat waving in the wind. The courier, a powerful and red-faced man, rushed into the station to drink a glass of vodka, emerged again rapidly, and leaped into a new troika. No sooner was he installed than he rose to his feet and began to beat the driver, a young peasant, on the back of the neck with his fist. The horses lurched forward as the driver frantically whipped them up, and the troika vanished from sight with the courier's fist moving mechanically up and down in relentless rhythm as the whip rose and fell in a corresponding tempo. [4] At the end of this account Dostoevsky imagines the young peasant, on returning to his village,

[3] Ibid., 184.

[4] Incidents of this kind were common in Dostoevsky's time. The marquis de Custine, in his *La Russie en 1839*, describes a similar scene. "A little further on I saw a mounted courier, a *feldjaeger* or some other infamous employee of the government, get out of his carriage, run up to one of the two polite coachmen and strike him brutally with his whip, with a stick, with his fists." Cited in George F. Kennan, *The Marquis de Custine and His Russia in 1839* (Princeton, NJ, 1971), 28.

beating his wife to revenge his own humiliation. "This sickening picture," he says, "remained in my memory all my life."[5]

These words appeared in 1876, and in the notebooks for *Crime and Punishment* he jots down "My first personal insult, the horse, the courier,"[6] thus confirming the primacy of the experience for Dostoevsky and the formative role that he assigns to it in his own self-development. For the courier became nothing less than a symbol of the brutal, oppressive government that he served—a government whose domination over an enslaved peasantry by naked force incited all the violence and harshness of peasant life. "Never was I able to forget the courier, and much that was shameful and cruel in the Russian people I was then inclined for a long while, and as it were involuntarily, to explain in an obviously much too one-sided fashion."[7] With these guarded phrases, Dostoevsky reveals the motivation of his radicalism of the 1840s, when nothing would obsess him more passionately than the issue of serfdom. "This little scene appeared to me, so to speak, as an emblem, as something very graphically demonstrating the link between cause and effect. Here every blow dealt to the animal leaped out of each blow dealt at the man. At the end of the 1840s, in the epoch of my most unrestrained and fervent dreams, it suddenly occurred to me that, if ever I were to found a philanthropic society [that is, radical or Socialist], I would without fail engrave this courier's troika on the seal of the society as its emblem and sign."[8] Dostoevsky is telling his readers that, in his youth, he had explained the vices of the peasantry solely in social-political terms, solely as a result of the clenched fist crashing down on the back of their necks. He had been convinced that these vices would vanish once the fist had been stayed.

It seems certain that the youth of sixteen had never observed such unimpassioned, systematic, and methodical brutality exercised on a perfectly blameless victim. The "official" nature of the inhumanity in this instance perhaps lit up in a flash the presumptive social source of the evil. And once again we note the capacity of his sensibility to be stirred at its deepest levels by a public and a social matter in which he was not personally involved at all.

Critical clichés persist in viewing the Romanticism of the early nineteenth century as a solipsistic and introspective movement turning its back on the turbulent social-political problems of "real life." The government of the time had quite a different opinion, as Benedetto Croce has pointed out. "The suffering of the world, the mystery of the universe, the impulse toward the sublime in love and heroism, the grief and despair over a dreamt-of but unattainable beatitude,

---

[5] *DW* (January 1876), 186.

[6] Fyodor Dostoevsky, *The Notebooks for* Crime and Punishment, ed. and trans. Edward Wasiolek (Chicago, 1967), 64.

[7] *DW* (January 1876), 186.

[8] Ibid.

the Hamlet-like visits to cemeteries, the romantic pallor, romantic beards, and romantic haircuts—all these and similar things gave evidence of restive spirits. It was expected and feared that they would join conspiratorial sects and rise with arms in their hands the moment they had the chance."[9] The young Dostoevsky was unquestionably a Romantic, but the impressions that he gleaned from literature reinforced and strengthened those offered by life. Dostoevsky would not have been so overcome by the beating of the peasant coachman if he had not read Karamzin and Pushkin, and had not already made his own some of Schiller's moral ideal of "the beautiful and sublime."

———■———

This shocking episode with the coachman was Dostoevsky's introduction to St. Petersburg and to all the sordid underside of the resplendent façade of the government in whose service he was about to enter. Indeed, his very first contact with officialdom brought him face-to-face with the hidden corruption that ran through all the institutions of Russian society. On arriving in St. Petersburg, Dr. Dostoevsky deposited his sons in a preparatory school, where the boys studied for their entrance examination into the academy. Even this important patronage, however, did not guarantee success. Mikhail was refused entrance on grounds of "ill health"; Feodor, though passing his exam brilliantly, did not receive one of the vacancies for entrance without payment of the admission fee. This had been promised when Dr. Dostoevsky had made application for his sons, but such places, it turned out, were reserved for those students able to make "gifts" to the examiners. "What rottenness!" Dostoevsky indignantly writes his father. "We, who struggle for every last ruble, have to pay, while others—the sons of rich fathers—are accepted without fee."[10] Luckily, the Kumanins came to the rescue by supplying the required amount. Mikhail was finally admitted to another school of army engineers and was transferred to the Baltic provinces.

From a purely worldly point of view, Dr. Dostoevsky had chosen well for his sons. The Academy of Military Engineers—housed in the imposing Mikhailovsky palace—was considered the finest establishment of its kind in Russia in the 1830s, and places in it were particularly sought because it enjoyed the patronage of Nicholas I. But Dostoevsky's life in the academy was one long torture, and he always looked back on the decision to send him there as a woeful mistake. The error consisted not only in overlooking the real bent of his interests but also in placing him in a milieu dominated by physical violence, military harshness, and iron discipline rather than by the relaxed democratic camaraderie that Herzen depicts as reigning among his fellow students at the University of Moscow

[9] Benedetto Croce, *Storia d'Europa nel secolo decimonono* (Bari, 1953), 55.
[10] *Pis'ma*, 4: 236; February 4, 1838.

4. The Academy of Military Engineers

during the same years. "What examples I saw before me!" Dostoevsky remi-
nisces twenty years later. "I saw children of thirteen already reckoning out their
entire lives: where they could attain to what rank, what is more profitable, how
to rake in cash (I was in the Engineers), and what was the fastest way to get a
cushy, independent command!"[11]

For the young man from Moscow whose head was filled with thoughts of "the
beautiful and sublime," the moral mediocrity of his comrades came as a withering disillusionment. And if he had been outraged by the incident of the government courier, one can well imagine his horror at the savagery of the upper classes
toward all those to whom they stood in a position of authority. The memoirs of
D. V. Grigorovich give a searing picture of this feature of academy life, and even
at a distance of sixty years, such memories brought back "a painful feeling."[12]
Merciless tormenting of the lower-classmen was one of the privileges enjoyed by
the older students. The authorities closed their eyes to this cruel sport so long as
external discipline was maintained, and any protest or resistance could bring on
a mass beating that frequently landed the offender in the hospital.

On finding himself thrown into this milieu, Dostoevsky's first reaction was
to feel himself a complete stranger and an outcast. Using the language of the

[11] Ibid., 4: 267.
[12] Ibid., 235.

Romantic literature that he was then absorbing, he writes to Mikhail just six months after his admission: "the atmosphere of [man's] soul is composed of the union of heaven and earth; what an unnatural child man is; the law of spiritual nature is broken. . . . It seems to me that the world has taken on a negative meaning, and that from a high, refined spirituality there has emerged a satire."[13] Dostoevsky was already beginning to think of human life as an eternal struggle between the material and the spiritual in man's nature; and he would always continue to regard the world as a "purgatory," whose trials and tribulations serve the supreme purpose of moral purification.

A younger fellow student whom Dostoevsky befriended, and who later became a noted artist, gives this picture of Feodor: "His uniform hung awkwardly, and his knapsack, shako, rifle—all those looked like some sort of fetters that he was obliged to wear temporarily and which weighed him down."[14] Grigorovich tells us that Dostoevsky "already then exhibited traits of unsociability, stayed to one side, did not participate in diversions, sat and buried himself in books, and sought a place to be alone."[15] A. I. Savelyev, a young officer then on duty in the academy, remarks that "he was very religious, and zealously performed all the obligations of the Orthodox Christian faith. He could be seen with the Bible, Zschokke's *Die Stunden der Andacht* [a famous collection of devotional essays with a strong emphasis on the necessity of giving Christian love a social application], etc. After the lectures on religion by Father Poluektov, Feodor would converse with him for a long while. All this struck his comrades so much that they dubbed him the monk Photius."[16] Nor did he content himself only with harboring social-Christian ideas in solitude; he tried courageously to put them into practice by opposing some of the abuses of academy life.

Savelyev recalls that Dostoevsky and his friend Ivan Berezhetsky stood out from the run of students by their "compassion for the poor, weak, and unprotected." They "employed every means to stop this customary violence, just as they tried to protect the watchmen and all those who looked after the services of the school."[17] Physical maltreatment of the teachers of foreign languages, especially Germans, was also a favorite indoor sport at the academy, and this too Dostoevsky fought against, though not always with success.

He was the editor of the lithographed student newspaper—which would indicate a certain amount of public authority and acceptance. And, even though known as solitary, he did have a small circle of like-minded friends, some of whom were destined to play an important role in his life. With Grigorovich he

[13] Ibid., 1: 46; August 9, 1838.
[14] *DVS*, 1: 106.
[15] Ibid., 127.
[16] Ibid., 97.
[17] Ibid., 99.

shared a passionate interest in literature and the arts; with A. N. Beketov, who was to become the center of a "progressive" circle in the 1840s, a deep social concern and moral passion; Berezhetsky, who vanishes from sight except for this brief moment of his friendship with Dostoevsky, may have attracted him by his mixture of humanitarianism, intellectual pretentiousness, and haughty elegance. It is Berezhetsky who is mentioned in all the memoirs as Dostoevsky's closest friend in the academy. Savelyev pictures them strolling through the ample rooms of the palace and talking of contemporary poetry (Zhukovsky, Pushkin, Vyazemsky) while the rest of the student body were at the regular Tuesday evening dance class or engaged in outdoor sports. Another memoirist depicts them arguing loudly about Schiller, with Dostoevsky running after Berezhetsky in the corridors to drive home the final word.

Writing to Mikhail at the beginning of 1840, Feodor says that, in the preceding year, he had had a friend for whom he had felt "the love of a brother"; "I had a companion at my side, the one creature I loved in that way." This could only have been Berezhetsky, with whom he communed over the works of Schiller. "I learned Schiller by heart, talked him, dreamed him. . . . Reading Schiller *with him*, I verified *in him* the noble, fiery Don Carlos and Marquis Posa and Mortimer. That friendship brought me so much sorrow and joy! . . . the name of Schiller has become near and dear to me, a kind of magic sound, evoking so many reveries; they are bitter, brother."[18] The temperature of male friendship in early nineteenth-century Russia was extremely high, and a passionate male attachment under the magical aegis of Schiller was a fairly common occurrence in the 1830s.[19] What it represented, in this instance, may be deduced from the names of the Schillerian characters whom Dostoevsky believed he saw embodied in his friend—all are young men inspired by high idealism, by love, or by friendship to serve the great social causes of freedom and justice.

Why the recollection of his friendship with Berezhetsky should have been "bitter" to Dostoevsky we do not know; some rift had occurred. Here the lucubrations of the underground man may help to fill us in. "Once indeed, I did have a friend. But I was already a tyrant at heart; I wanted to exercise unbounded sway over him. . . . I required of him a disdainful and complete break with [his] surroundings. . . . But when he devoted himself to me entirely I began to hate

[18] *Pis'ma*, 1: 57; January 1, 1840.

[19] As only one example, Herzen's *Memoirs of a Young Man* (1840) describes his friendship with Nikolay Ogarev with exactly the same throb of emotion. "By some incomprehensible force we gravitated toward each other; I had a presentiment of him as a brother, a close kinsman of my soul, and he felt the same about me. . . . [W]e were in love *à la lettre*, and we fell more and more in love with every day." Schiller was their ideal, and "we appropriated to ourselves the characters of all of his heroes. Life opened out before us triumphantly, majestically; we sincerely vowed to sacrifice our lives for the good of mankind," etc. In Alexander Herzen, *My Past and Thoughts*, trans. Constance Garnett, rev. Humphrey Higgens, 4 vols. (New York, 1968), 4: 1823.

him immediately and repulsed him—as though all I needed him for was to win a victory over him, to subjugate him and nothing else" (5: 140). This passage may represent Dostoevsky's mature self-judgment on the perversity of his own character—perversities that we shall soon have ample occasion to see him exhibiting. The difficulties of Dostoevsky's position in the academy no doubt led him to impose such great demands on his friend's sympathy and patience that they finally became intolerable. One may perhaps date the beginning of Dostoevsky's critical attitude toward "Schillerism" as a mode of behavior from such an experience.

———■———

The most important event in Dostoevsky's life during his years at the academy was the death (or the murder) of his father. At the time of the presumed murder, Dostoevsky had not laid eyes on his father for two years. After depositing his sons in St. Petersburg, Dr. Dostoevsky returned to Moscow and never saw them again. For reasons of health (his application for retirement complains of rheumatic attacks and failing eyesight), he resigned his post and went to live in Darovoe. Deprived of the support of Marya Feodorovna, and of his one or two friends on the hospital staff, he went to pieces morally in the solitude of the provinces. Alyona Frolovna, who continued in her post as housekeeper, heard him carrying on long conversations with his dead wife as if she were present, and it was at this time that he took to drinking heavily. One of the two young village girls who had served the Dostoevskys as housemaids in Moscow became his mistress and bore him an illegitimate child in 1838. Whether Feodor had any knowledge of what was happening to his father at the time is highly unlikely— one cannot imagine from where he would have obtained the information.

Freud, in his famous article "Dostoevsky and Parricide," built an elaborate construction on Dostoevsky's presumptive reaction to the news of the murder, which, according to psychoanalytic theory, fulfilled the parricidal impulses that he had been harboring because of Oedipal rivalry but suppressing all along. Overcome with guilt on hearing the news, which objectified his most secret and most unbearable wishes, he punished himself by means of his first true epileptic seizure. In fact, there is no source material at our disposal that shows any early evidence of the epilepsy from which Dostoevsky suffered in later life. The "facts" that Freud adduces can be shown to be extremely dubious at best, and at worst simply mistakes; the case history Freud constructed in the effort to "explain" him in psychoanalytic terms is purely fictitious.[20] There are, as we shall see, good reasons to accept Freud's *aperçu* that Dostoevsky felt implicated in the murder

[20] See Joseph Frank, "Freud's Case History of Dostoevsky," in *Dostoevsky: The Seeds of Revolt, 1821–1849* (Princeton, NJ, 1976), 379–392.

and emotionally assumed a large share of the guilt, but these reasons are quite other than the ones that Freud alleges.

The problems involved in launching his two sons properly on their future careers were a constant source of anxiety for Dr. Dostoevsky. Nothing seemed to go as planned, and unanticipated expenses kept mounting. There is a good deal of discussion in the correspondence about three hundred rubles that Dr. Dostoevsky had paid, in addition to the regular fee of the preparatory school, so that his sons could receive supplementary instruction in artillery and fortifications— only to learn from them finally that "the three hundred rubles were not at all necessary for [Kostomarov]."[21] The news of Mikhail's rejection by the academy was a great blow, and so was Feodor's failure to obtain free admission. Dr. Dostoevsky's letters are full of concern and trepidation; but though his own financial resources were being strained to the utmost, he tried to meet the demands of his sons. A joint letter from them in December 1837 thanks him for the receipt of seventy rubles, which they say is more than sufficient to satisfy their needs. "We have received your letter, and along with it seventy rubles, money soaked in the sweat of toil and your own deprivation. Oh, how that makes it precious to us now! We thank you, thank you from the bottom of our heart, which is fully aware of everything you are doing for us."[22] This is the somewhat exalté style— an imitation of the tone of their parents' letters—in which both Mikhail and Feodor write to their father. But both were aware that their sentiments were fully justified by the objective situation.

Dr. Dostoevsky's chagrins were by no means finished even after his sons had settled into the harness of their respective establishments. Feodor, for reasons that still remain obscure, failed to be promoted during his first year of study, and on receiving the letter announcing the unhappy news, Dr. Dostoevsky suffered a partial stroke. Dostoevsky explained the setback, in letters to both his father and Mikhail, as a result of the enmity of some professors, and he lists his course grades, which are excellent, as proof of the injustice. However, he neglected to list his grade in military drill, which was abysmally low and may have been the real cause of his failure. Since he knew that favoritism was rife in the academy, he may well have believed that his deficiencies in drill alone would not have been enough to cancel out all his other work. Whatever the explanation for his setback, there is no doubt that the whole affair left Dostoevsky with a very bad conscience so far as his father was concerned. And when he tells Mikhail that "I would regret nothing if the tears of our poor father did not burn my soul,"[23] at least the last part of this utterance may be taken at face value.

It is quite likely that Dostoevsky also felt troubled at the reiterated demands

[21] *Pisma*, 1: 57; January 1, 1840.
[22] Ibid., 4: 233; December 3, 1837.
[23] Ibid., 1: 49; October 31, 1838.

he made on his father for extra money. These requests were all couched in terms of necessity; but their real source was Dostoevsky's desire not to cut too sorry a figure among his more affluent comrades. Dostoevsky may have held most of his fellow students in contempt, but he could not endure the idea of being considered by them both personally odd *and* socially inferior, and the struggle to maintain his social status and self-esteem is naïvely evident in his letters. He writes his father in the spring of 1839 for money so that he can buy an extra pair of boots besides those issued, order his own tea in addition to the regular ration, and acquire a locker for his books. In justifying this request, he explains to his father that he is merely conforming to the "rules" of his present society. "Why be an exception?" he asks, revealing his own dilemma. "Such exceptions are sometimes exposed to the most awful unpleasantnesses." [24]

The "rules" he talks about, however, were imposed by the need to maintain a becoming social position in the eyes of his comrades. This is confirmed by the memoirs of Count Peter Semenov (who became a noted explorer and natural scientist). It so happened that Semenov shared the same bivouac at Peterhof with Dostoevsky. "I lived in the same camp with him, in the same linen tents . . . and I got along without my own tea (we received some in the morning and the evening), without any more boots than I was issued, and without a trunk for my books, though I read as much as F. M. Dostoevsky. As a result, all this was not actual need but simply a desire not to be different from other comrades who had their own tea and boots and trunk." [25]

So far as one can judge, Dostoevsky never wrote home for funds without receiving the sum requested. In March 1839, he wrote that he was fifty rubles in debt (without explaining why or for what), and asked for ten rubles in addition to pay for expenses at camp. In answer, he received bills that could be exchanged for ninety-four rubles. Two months later he made an additional request, and this drew a response in which Dr. Dostoevsky paints a somber picture of the state of affairs at Darovoe—a picture in accord with the known facts. He reminds his son that, for the last several years, there had been poor harvests, and predicts that this year will bring on total ruin. Even the previous year, he says, things had been so bad that the straw roofs of the peasant huts had been used for fodder; "but that was nothing compared to the present distress. From the beginning of spring not a drop of water, not even dew. Heat and terrible winds have ruined everything. What threatens is not only ruin but total starvation. After this can you continue to grumble at your father for not sending you money?" [26] All the same, the amount Dostoevsky had asked for was dispatched with the warning to use it sparingly. This letter was written on May 27, 1839; Dr. Dostoevsky died

[24] Ibid., 52; May 10, 1839.
[25] *DVS*, 1: 210.
[26] V. S. Nechaeva, *V seme i usadbe Dostoevskikh* (Moscow, 1939), 121.

sometime in early June, perhaps a week or two later. His despairing communication to his son was, literally, his last testament, and Dostoevsky must have received it almost simultaneously with the news of his father's death.

———■———

It is not necessary to inquire here into the conflicting versions that have been given of the presumed murder. Whether it was a spontaneous outburst of rage or carefully concerted in advance, whether the cause was the unbearable exactions and severity of Dr. Dostoevsky—who made the hapless peasants pay dearly for his own grief and desolation, or whether his fate was sealed by the notable restiveness of the peasants in that region during 1839 because of the burning drought—none of these questions can be answered conclusively. Death apparently came by suffocation, and no marks of foul play were visible on the body. Dr. Dostoevsky was reported to have died of an apoplectic stroke, and though murder was rumored throughout the district, the family decided to let the matter rest. The Kumanins had no great love for the irascible doctor; murder would have been almost impossible to prove and, even if proved, would have meant the exile of almost all the male serfs and the effective destruction of the children's patrimony. Andrey Dostoevsky surmises that his two older brothers were told that their father had been murdered almost from the start.[27]

From all of this, one can well surmise that Dostoevsky may have been overwhelmed by a shock of guilt and remorse on hearing of his father's death and learning its cause. The uneasiness he had felt all through this period—an

[27] According to Andrey, a week after the death, with Dr. Dostoevsky already buried, his mother-in-law arrived to gather up the younger children and look after affairs. She was told by neighbors—a retired Major Khotyaintsev and his wife—that the death had not been natural but a murder; they advised her to let the matter rest so as to guard the interests of the family. This was the version of Dr. Dostoevsky's end that she brought back to Moscow and that was accepted by the family.

A recent investigator who inspected the records of the district has uncovered facts apparently unknown to the family. A rumor about a possible murder was first brought to the attention of the authorities by another neighbor, A. I. Leybrekht, who, under investigation by the provincial court, revealed that Major Khotyaintsev had *asked* him specifically to alert the authorities to the possibility of murder. Khotyaintsev was involved in a lawsuit against the Dostoevskys over land demarcation and was a wealthier landowner with five hundred souls. If some of the Dostoevsky peasants had been deported to Siberia as murderers, he could have snapped up the adjacent property for a song. This may explain why he wished to spread the rumor of murder but at the same time appear to be a friend of the family concerned over their interests.

Dr. Dostoevsky's corpse was examined independently by two doctors, both of whom concurred on the cause of death as being apoplexy. The investigation continued for over a year by various provincial legal bodies. Several peasants considered to be among the murderers were called in for interrogation, but no evidence of foul play was discovered. None of this further investigation was apparently known to Dr. Dostoevsky's surviving children, and the story told to their grandmother by Khotyaintsev, entering into the family tradition, was given credence by Dostoevsky himself, with incalculable consequences for his moral and emotional equilibrium. *DVS* 1: 89–90; G. Fedorov, "K biografii F. M. Dostoevskomu," *Literaturnaya Gazeta* 25 (June 18, 1975), 7.

uneasiness caused both by his failure to gain promotion and by the awareness that he was exploiting his father's meager resources to appease his craving for social status—could have suddenly exploded in a frenzy of self-accusation. If his father had been mistreating the peasants abominably, was he not to blame? Was it not to satisfy his purely fanciful "needs" that his father had come to his horrible end?

If we assume that the turmoil of Dostoevsky's psyche can be described in some such terms, then we can come close to providing a *specific* explanation for Dostoevsky's behavior in the 1840s and for the character of his work. Nothing would have been more natural than for him to try to relieve his guilt by projecting it externally in social terms, where it assumed the particular humanitarian form of joining a conspiracy to spread propaganda against serfdom. The sensitive humanitarian had already been shocked at the beating of a peasant coachman. How much more would he have been overwhelmed by the scenes at Darovoe that his tortured imagination conjured up—scenes for which he could not avoid assuming some of the responsibility? And thus his sense of guilt became transformed into the burning hatred of serfdom. Only through the destruction of the monstrous system could the trauma of his guilt be assuaged, and it was for this goal that he ultimately embarked on the path that led him to Siberia.

To this extent, and for these far more self-evident reasons, one can accept Freud's view that Dostoevsky emotionally assumed a burden of parricidal guilt. But Freud's acceptance of the family tradition that the shock of the news brought on Dostoevsky's first epileptic seizure is contradicted by the letters of Dostoevsky himself in 1854, when he first mentions the disease; and it seems unlikely in view of all the other circumstances. None of the people who knew Dostoevsky in the academy and who left memoirs refer to any such attack. All were writing after Dostoevsky's death, when the existence of his epilepsy had long been public knowledge. Dostoevsky was then living in common quarters with a hundred other classmates and was constantly under surveillance; an epileptic attack would have been very hard to conceal.

Dostoevsky's only recorded response to the death of his father—a letter to Mikhail in mid-August 1839—makes no mention of any unusual perturbation on receipt of the news. "My dear brother! I have shed many tears over the death of father"—this is all that is said. What seems to trouble Dostoevsky most is the fate of his younger brothers and sisters, not so much practically as morally; he finds distasteful the idea that they will be educated by the Kumanins. Hence he fervently approves of Mikhail's plan—never put into practice—to retire to Darovoe after becoming an officer and devoting himself to their upbringing. "The harmonious organization of the soul in the midst of one's own family, the development of all tendencies on Christian principles, the pride of family virtues, the fear of sin and dishonor—this is the result of such an education. The bones of our parents will sleep tranquilly in the moist earth."[28] This is, clearly, the kind of upbringing and education that he felt he had been given, and that he now tends to idealize under the shock of his loss. There is a total sense of identification with his father in such words, which leads to the desire to perpetuate the values of the family tradition as Dostoevsky now sees them.

At the same time, the letter also expresses a sense of relief, as if a burden had been lifted off Dostoevsky's shoulders. He tells Mikhail that now, more often than in the past, he is able to look on everything that surrounds him in the academy more calmly. He speaks openly for the first time about his intention to abandon the army. "My one goal is to be free. I am sacrificing everything for that. But often, often I think, what will freedom bring me? . . . what will I be, alone in the crowd of the unknowns?"[29] Despite such nagging fears, Dostoevsky expresses confidence in himself and the future, and the firm conviction that his "sacred hopes" will one day be realized. Dostoevsky had never dared previously to acknowledge a defiance of his father's wishes—a defiance that could only have led to a heartbreaking clash of wills. The death of his father had cleared this major emotional obstacle from his path, and his sense of guilt was thus also accompanied by a sense of liberation.

It was, perhaps, an obscure awareness of some such feeling that now impels Dostoevsky to remark that his soul was "no longer accessible to its old stormy surges," and that it was "like the heart of a man concealing a profound enigma." Moreover, the aim of his life henceforth, he says, will be "to study 'the meaning of life and man.'" Professing a qualified satisfaction with the progress he has already made in this enterprise, he adds the revealing information that he pursues it by delving into the "characters in the writers with whom the best part of my life is spent freely and joyously." "Man is an enigma," he continues, a few sentences later. "This enigma must be solved, and if you spend all your life at it, don't say you have wasted your time; I occupy myself with this enigma because I wish to be a man."[30] It is no coincidence that these impressive words appear in the only letter commenting on the murder of his father. For no event could have driven home to him so intimately and starkly the enigma of human life—the enigma of the sudden irruption of irrational, uncontrollable, and destructive forces both within the world and in the human psyche; the enigma of the incalculable moral consequences even of such venial self-indulgence as his own demands on his father. It was this enigma that, indeed, he was to spend the rest of his life trying to solve; and no one can accuse him, while doing so, of having wasted his time.

[28] *Pis'ma*, 2: 549; August 16, 1839.
[29] Ibid., 550.
[30] Ibid.

CHAPTER 5

The Two Romanticisms

In addition to the mathematics and engineering requirements, the Academy of Military Engineers also provided a humanistic education for future officers of the Russian Army. For at least the first year or two of his studies Dostoevsky attended lectures on religion, history, civil architecture, Russian and French language and literature, and also lessons in German. The chair in Russian literature was held by V. T. Plaksin, who accepted Romanticism as the art of the modern world; he lectured on Pushkin and Lermontov, and on the Russian folk poet Koltsov. From Plaksin, Dostoevsky could not have acquired much more in the way of ideas about literature than German Romantic doctrines. His professor of French literature, however, Joseph Cournant, was something else entirely, and Dostoevsky's letters soon become studded with references not only to Racine, Corneille, and Pascal but also to such French Renaissance writers as Ronsard and Malherbe. Cournant included contemporary literature in his purview and introduced his students to Balzac, Hugo, George Sand, and Eugène Sue. Writing to his father in May 1839, Dostoevsky rather deceptively explains why it is "absolutely necessary" for him to subscribe to a French circulating library. "How many great works of genius there are—mathematical and military genius—in the French language." [1]

Dostoevsky's studies at the academy, however, provided only the minor part of his humanistic education. The major share was obtained in the company of a young man, Ivan Nikolaevich Shidlovsky, a chance acquaintance whom the Dostoevskys met on their arrival in St. Petersburg. In 1873 Dostoevsky told a writer, come to gather material about him for a biographical article, "Mention Shidlovsky . . . he was a very important person for me then, and he deserves not to have his name sink into oblivion." [2] Ivan Shidlovsky had come to Petersburg to take up a post in the Ministry of Finance; like the Dostoevsky brothers, however, his heart was in literature and not in service to the state. Tall and striking in appearance, eloquent and loquacious, the twenty-one-year-old Shidlovsky impressed everybody by the depth of his culture and the passion of his perorations on lofty topics. Naturally, he wrote poetry himself, and he soon succeeded

[1] *Pisma*, 4: 242; May 5, 1839.
[2] *DVS*, 2: 191.

not only in breaking into print, but also in gaining entrée into the outer fringes of the literary life of the capital. Shortly after arriving he called on N. A. Polevoy, the defender of French Romanticism, whose own magazine had been closed in 1839 because of what Pushkin called its "Jacobin" tendencies and who had joined the staff of another publication. One can well imagine the tremendous effect that Shidlovsky must have made on the budding author, and the aureole that soon surrounded him in the younger man's bedazzled eyes. Shidlovsky was the first person to take Dostoevsky's literary aspirations seriously and to encourage them with example, precept, and counsel.

Whenever Dostoevsky could get away from the academy for a free moment, he would spend it with Shidlovsky; and when his friend left Petersburg for good, probably sometime in late 1839, he was disconsolate. "I often sat together with him for whole evenings talking of God knows what!" he writes Mikhail. "Oh, what a pure and candid soul!"[3] They talked about the great writers whom Dostoevsky was reading under Shidlovsky's tutelage ("we spoke of Homer, Shakespeare, Schiller, Hoffmann"),[4] and it was largely through his eyes that Dostoevsky now began to view the great Romantic culture heroes whose very names filled him with awe.

A typical Russian Romantic of the 1830s, Shidlovsky was consumed, as they all were, with unappeasable desires that could not be satisfied within the bounds of earthly life. His few extant poems are all expressions of this Romantic malaise, which leads him to melancholy questionings about the meaning of human existence. No answer is ever given to these inquiries, but Shidlovsky is consoled by the belief that there is a God who sometimes vouchsafes his presence in nature and holds out hope of solace to unhappy humans. Dostoevsky was a great admirer of these poems. "Ah, soon, soon, I shall read the new poems of Ivan Nikolaevich," he writes Mikhail in the fall of 1838. "What poetry! What inspired ideas!"[5]

In a long letter that Shidlovsky wrote to Mikhail in February 1839, he writes equally freely and casually about his urge to go off on a drinking spree with Mikhail, and his flirtations with the wives of friends who aspire to be immortalized in his verse. Shidlovsky, evidently, was one of those "broad" Russian natures, oscillating between the most contradictory moral impulses, that Dostoevsky later so often portrayed. No doubt his complete freedom from any kind of stuffiness constituted one source of the magnetism he exercised on his younger friends. But Shidlovsky's ebullience did not prevent him from plunging into one severe spiritual crisis after another brought on by his torn and divided personality.

[3] *Pis'ma*, 1: 56; January 1, 1840.
[4] Ibid.
[5] Ibid., 51; October 31, 1838.

He tried, in but one example, to fight off a temptation to suicide by increased fervency in prayer; and on Christmas day, he tells Mikhail, the miracle occurred: "some sort of wonderful illumination shone before my eyes; tears gushed forth passionately—and I believed."[6] "We must believe," he writes in another passage, "that God is good, for otherwise He is not God; that the beauty of the Universe is this visible and tangible goodness. . . . This is the only true sign of the great poet, who is man at his highest peak; soil him with dirt, slander him, oppress him, torture him, his soul will nonetheless stand firm, true to itself, and the Angel of inspiration will guide him safely out of the dungeon of life into the world of immortality. . . . the body, a clay vessel, sooner or later is shattered, and all our past vices and occasional virtues vanish without a trace."[7] These ideas that Dostoevsky was eagerly absorbing from the lips of his master were a fine example both of the Romantic egoism and of the urge for pantheistic self-obliteration that had been stimulated by the influence of Schelling and was so widespread in the 1830s. In his famous *Literary Reveries*, the young critic V. G. Belinsky—soon to become the most important cultural force of his time—had written that man's "infinite, supreme felicity consists in the dissolution of *Self* in the feeling of love" for all of God's creation.[8]

How thoroughly Dostoevsky assimilated the values of this Romantic phase of Russian culture may be judged from his letter to Mikhail a year later. "One had only to look at [Shidlovsky] to see what he was: a martyr! He had become thin; his cheeks sunken; his sparkling eyes dry and burning; the moral beauty of his face heightened as the physical declined. He was suffering, cruelly suffering. My God, how he loved the young girl. . . . She had married someone else. Without this love he would not have been this priest of poetry, pure, noble, disinterested. . . . [H]e was a marvelous, exalted being, the true sketch of man as Shakespeare and Schiller have shown him; but he was just then on the point of falling into the dark madness of Byronic characters."[9] This last phrase probably alludes to Schidlovsky's struggle against the temptation of suicide.

Dostoevsky's wide-eyed hero worship is touchingly naïve in its expression, but what he saw in Shidlovsky was the living embodiment of the great Romantic conflict between man and his destiny by which his imagination had now become ignited. Shidlovsky brought him face-to-face with man as "a marvelous, exalted being," just as Dostoevsky had learned to apprehend him in Shakespeare and Schiller; no poring over texts could have conveyed with such vital immediacy the heights and depths of the Romantic experience. The supreme nobility of a

---

[6] Cited in G. Prochorov, "Die Brüder Dostojewski und Shidlovski," *Zeitschrift für Slavische Philologie* 7 (1930), 320.

[7] Ibid.

[8] Cited in V. G. Belinsky, *Selected Philosophical Works* (Moscow, 1948), 14.

[9] *Pisma*, 1: 56; January 1, 1840.

hopeless (and disinterested *because* hopeless) passion, the spiritual value of suffering for an unattainable ideal, the role of the poet as self-sacrificing "priest" of this Romantic dispensation, proclaiming his faith and his love of God in the midst of his travails—all this Dostoevsky now accepts as the very acme of sublimity.

M. H. Abrams has sharpened our awareness of how the "characteristic concepts and patterns of Romantic philosophy and literature are a displaced and reconstituted theology" and represent a return to Christian fashions of feeling.[10] "A conspicuous Romantic tendency, after the rationalism and decorum of the Enlightenment," he writes, "was a reversion to the stark drama and suprarational mysteries of the Christian story and doctrines and to the violent conflicts and abrupt reversals of the Christian inner life, turning on extremes of destruction and creation, hell and heaven, exile and reunion, death and rebirth, dejection and joy, paradise lost and paradise regained."[11] The Romantic values that Dostoevsky assimilated from Shidlovsky were thus a recasting, in early nineteenth-century terms, of the same religious agitations and questionings that had stirred him profoundly as a young boy in the book of Job. And here we can locate an even deeper reason, besides the ones already mentioned, for the importance that Dostoevsky assigned to Shidlovsky in his life: Shidlovsky's primary role was to have aided Dostoevsky in making the transition between his childhood faith and its sophisticated modern equivalents. No wonder Dostoevsky was everlastingly grateful to the man who had performed this crucial task!

Dostoevsky did not have to suffer any agonizing reevaluation of his old beliefs in adapting himself to the new world of Romantic culture that he was so eager to assimilate. Nor should one underestimate the future influence of Shidlovsky's living demonstration that intense religious commitment could be combined with a frank confession of the torments of doubt; genuine faith for Dostoevsky would never afterward be confused with a tranquil acceptance of dogma. Dostoevsky, it is true, soon left this Romantic phase behind, and often later parodied and satirized various types of Romantic egoism. But the Romantic dissatisfaction with the limits of earthly life and, in particular, its positive valuation of moral suffering always remained a feature of his own worldview.

Russian culture in the mid-1830s—during the period of Dostoevsky's most receptive adolescence—was in a period of transition between the predominant influence of German Romantic literature and Idealist philosophy, on the one hand, and the beginning of a turn toward that of French social Romanticism (which included a good deal of what came to be called social Realism or, in Rus-

---

[10] M. H. Abrams, *Natural Supernaturalism* (New York, 1971), 65.
[11] Ibid., 66.

sia, Naturalism), on the other. The generation of the 1820s had grown up in a time of great political turmoil and took a strong interest in social and political matters. As every reader of *Evgeny Onegin* will recall, the St. Petersburg dandy of the time considered an acquaintance with the doctrines of Adam Smith an indispensable part of his mental wardrobe.[12] The shock administered to Russian society by the Decembrist uprising and its sternly repressive aftermath, however, turned the thoughts of the next generation into other channels. The seeds of German Romantic influence had already been well planted before 1825, and they blossomed luxuriously in the sternly nonpolitical hothouse climate fostered by Nicholas I.

As a result, concern with the practical affairs of man and society was now scornfully rejected as unworthy of the true dignity of the human spirit. Only by striving to unriddle the secrets of the Absolute could man remain faithful to the high calling revealed to him by his own self-consciousness. Art and Idealist metaphysics replaced all other areas of life as the focus of cultural interest. Only one publication—Polevoy's *The Moscow Telegraph*—stood out against this current and strove, particularly after the French revolution of 1830, to put in a good word for the strong social and Socialist orientation of much of the new French literature. But Polevoy's own work as a novelist reveals the hybrid amalgam of influences so typical of the mid-1830s: his main emphasis is on the eternal disparity between the dreams of imagination and the limits of the real. Dostoevsky came to intellectual maturity during the mid-1830s, and he was profoundly affected by the disparate mixture of cultural tendencies prevalent in these years.

Dostoevsky's portrait of Shidlovsky is only one of the numerous passages in his letters in which we can observe him busily assimilating the tenets of what may be called metaphysical Romanticism, with its strong emphasis on man's relation to a world of supernatural or transcendental forces. During the summer of 1838, as Dostoevsky proudly informs Mikhail, he read "all of Hoffmann in Russian and in German (*Kater Murr* has not been translated)," as well as "the *Faust* of Goethe and his shorter poems."[13] This was exactly the moment when the young critic Belinsky was telling his friends that Hoffmann was as great as Shakespeare. Another young critic, P. V. Annenkov, whose reminiscences provide a penetrating and insightful portrait of this period, recalled that "the fantastic world of Hoffmann's stories seemed . . . a particle of revelation or disclosure of the omnific Absolute Idea."[14] It is again indicative of this era of cultural

---

[12] "From Adam Smith he sought his training / And was no mean economist; / That is, he could present the gist / Of how states prosper and stay healthy / Without the benefit of gold, / The secret being that, all told, the *basic staples* make them wealthy. / His father failed to understand, / And mortgaged the ancestral land" (1.7). Translation by Walter Arndt (New York, 1963).

[13] *Pis'ma*, I: 47; August 9, 1838.

[14] P. V. Annenkov, *The Extraordinary Decade*, ed. Arthur P. Mendel, trans. Irwin R. Titunik (Ann Arbor, MI, 1968), 13.

fluctuation that even Herzen, destined to become one of Russia's most influential social-political voices, and who had already come under the influence of Saint-Simonism, should have made his début as a writer in 1837 with a celebration of the metaphysical Romanticism of Hoffmann. Dostoevsky was thus in step with the time in his reading and catching up rapidly with the latest taste.

Dostoevsky probably learned a good deal from Hoffmann's genius for depicting pathological emotional states and subconscious criminal impulses, as well as for creating a unique poetic atmosphere—a blend of the realistically trivial with a richly imaginative and fantastic dream world. Many years later, in comparing Hoffmann with Poe, Dostoevsky expressed a preference for the German over what he considered the too practical and too down-to-earth American. Poe, he said, confined his fantasy only to the framework of his stories; once given the situation, everything else is presented with startling exactitude and verisimilitude. Hoffmann, on the other hand, "personifies the forces of nature in images," allows the supernatural to intrude overtly, and "even sometimes seeks his ideal outside the confines of the earthly." This, in Dostoevsky's view, makes Hoffmann "immeasurably superior to Poe as a poet" (13: 524). Despite this preference, Dostoevsky's own work is closer to Poe than to Hoffmann: he too has an uncanny ability to visualize and dramatize the extraordinary within the conventions of realism, and without any (overt) supernatural intrusion.

Dostoevsky's tendency now, whenever he wishes to describe his inner life, is to employ the categories of Romantic metaphysics—for example, he remarks in a letter to Mikhail on being a "foreign presence" in the academy, and on the world as a "purgatory of celestial spirits" (a phrase with a very Schillerian ring). As his letter continues, his mood of depression is replaced by one of stormy rebellion: "But just to see the harsh covering under which the universe languishes, to know that one explosion of the will is enough to shatter it and to fuse with the eternal, to know and to remain like the lowliest of mortals . . . that's terrible! How cowardly man is! Hamlet! Hamlet!" [15] Hamlet's failure becomes a sign of man's degradation: humanity is not strong enough to live up to its own exalted self-awareness.

Time and again, in leafing through Dostoevsky's letters, one sees how well-schooled he had become in this Romantic proclivity for casting his personal problems into cosmic terms. A passage in another letter is important as the first indication of Dostoevsky's acceptance of a philosophical irrationalism whose roots are to be found in the widespread vogue of Schelling in Russia. Mikhail had written to his brother that "to *know* more, one must *feel* less." Feodor's answer is a vehement assertion to the contrary. "What do you mean by the word *to know*?" he asked belligerently. "To know nature, the soul, god, love. . . . These

---

[15] *Pisma*, 1: 46; August 9, 1838.

are known by the heart, not the mind." Dostoevsky argues that thought cannot unriddle the mystery of creation because "mind is a material faculty," and as such is not in touch with transcendental truth. "Mind is an instrument, a machine, moved by the fire of the soul." It is the soul (Dostoevsky also uses the word "heart") that is the true medium for attaining the highest knowledge, for "if the goal of knowledge is love and nature, this opens up a clear field for *the heart*." Poetry is thus just as much a medium of knowledge as philosophy, because "the poet, in the transport of inspiration, unriddles God." [16]

If, along with these quotations, we recall Dostoevsky's absorption of the works of Schiller in communion with Berezhetsky, we can see how strongly he came under the influence of metaphysical Romanticism. And—from important motifs of the later Dostoevsky—it is clear how deep and longlasting this influence was to remain. It will require his long years of hardship and suffering, and the extraordinary experiences he was forced to undergo, before Dostoevsky would be able to transform these influences into the life-tempered genuineness of his tragic art. Dostoevsky's accusation of cowardice leveled against Hamlet will one day be critically recast in Raskolnikov's frenzied self-accusations over his inability to be a "Napoleon" and inwardly remaining one of "the lowliest of mortals." Nor would Dostoevsky forget the idea of suicide—of an "explosion of the will"—as a supreme gesture of metaphysical defiance when he creates the character of Kirillov in *Demons*. Despite his growing affinity for the new French social Romanticism, metaphysical Romanticism retained its significance for Dostoevsky because it was never spiritually rejected or overcome as a whole. It opened his sensibility to the early nineteenth-century forms in which man struggled to express his age-old religious questionings, and it provided some of the paradigms through which he would ultimately affirm his own genius.

———■———

Equally important in its effect on Dostoevsky, however, was the competing literary current of French social Romanticism. There is, it must be admitted, a certain artificiality in separating these two Romanticisms from each other too sharply. How, for example, is one to dissociate the metaphysical from the social in such a writer as Schiller? Auerbach has said of one of Schiller's plays, *Louise Millerin*, that it is "a dagger thrust to the heart of absolutism," [17] and the same phrase can well be applied to them all. Another German critic has written that "what Schiller furthered in his creations from *The Robbers* to *Don Carlos* was . . . what the French Revolution translated into fact." [18] The inflammatory effect of Schiller on the birth of more than one revolutionary vocation in Russia is

[16] Ibid., 50; October 31, 1838.
[17] Erich Auerbach, *Mimesis*, trans. Willard Trask (Princeton, NJ, 1968), 440.
[18] Cited in Benno von Wiese, *Friedrich Schiller* (Stuttgart, 1959), 448.

well-known, and if Dostoevsky and Berezhetsky took on themselves the chivalric task of protecting the weak and helpless in the academy, one may be sure that their reading of Schiller had aroused their social conscience. All this being true, however, a distinction can still usefully be drawn between those influences that taught Dostoevsky to view human life primarily in some absolute or transcendental perspective and those that sharpened his awareness of the concrete social issues of his contemporary world.

Such issues were being posed most luridly in the new French literature that Dostoevsky had been encouraged to read by Cournant's course. And Shidlovsky's friendship with Polevoy brought Dostoevsky, even if at one remove, into the orbit of the chief critical advocate of the political liberalism and moral humanitarianism of the French Romantic school. In the same letter in which he speaks of having read Hoffmann and Goethe, Dostoevsky also boasts to Mikhail of having gotten through "almost all of Balzac" and "all of Hugo except *Cromwell* and *Hernani*."[19] "Balzac is great," he writes enthusiastically. "His characters are the creations of universal mind! Not the spirit of a time but the struggle of thousands of years has prepared such a result in the soul of man."[20] This is Dostoevsky's first ecstatic response to a writer who, as Leonid Grossman has said, played Virgil to his Dante. No predecessor in the European novel was more important for Dostoevsky than Balzac, and such works as *Eugénie Grandet* and *Le père Goriot* were to serve as trailblazers clearing the path for his own productions.

It was Balzac who took over the historical novel of Scott and used it for the treatment of contemporary social life. It was Balzac who first spoke of Scott as having taught him that the modern novel was "*un drame dialogué*"—and no one would develop the form in this direction more brilliantly than Dostoevsky. Of all of Dostoevsky's contemporaries, only Balzac can compare with him in uniting a visionary social observation of astonishing exactitude with an inner drama of the soul that spans the entire range of moral experience from the satanic to the divine.

For Balzac, modern French society was nothing but the battleground of a ruthless struggle for power between the old aristocracy of birth and the new freebooters of high finance. In this conflict to the death, all the time-honored moral foundations of the human community were being destroyed. "The Golden Calf," as Harry Levin writes, "[had] indeed usurped the altar and the throne,"[21] and Europe was doomed because it could no longer muster any higher values to oppose the unrestricted reign of material interests. This vision of European society, blocked out in Balzac's monumental proportions, forms part of the background for Dostoevsky's later vision of the West. If Karamzin had given him a

[19] *Pisma*, 1: 47; August 9, 1838.
[20] Ibid.
[21] *The Gates of Horn* (New York, 1963), 191.

sense that Europe was moribund, it was Balzac who probably first persuaded him that Europe was totally in thrall to Baal, the flesh-god of materialism, and that it could not escape the catastrophe of a bloody class struggle—a conviction shared, after all, by his fellow Balzacians Marx and Engels. But Balzac's work also gave the young Dostoevsky what may have been his first glimpse of the doctrines of the Saint-Simonian school (in *L'Illustre Gaudissart*), which opposed the inhumanity of early capitalism and preached a "new Christianity," interpreting Jesus as the prophet of a "religion of equality."

Great as was Dostoevsky's admiration for Balzac, it was rivaled, if not surpassed, by his worship of Victor Hugo. To judge the significance of this admiration properly, we should remember that, by this time, Hugo and his writings had become a red flag—a symbol for the great wave of social humanitarianism released by the revolution of 1830. "La charité, c'est le socialisme," wrote Lamartine in 1834,[22] indicating the Christian sources of the new social movement, and it was as an expression of such Christian sentiments that Hugo spoke of his own work:

> J'ai, dans le livre, avec le drame, en prose, en vers,
> Plaidé pour les petits et pour les misérables;
> Suppliant les heureux et les inexorables;
> J'ai réhabilité le bouffon, l'histrion,
> Tous les damnés humains, Triboulet, Marion,
> Le laquais, le forçat, et la prostituée.[23]

More than thirty years later, Dostoevsky still considered Hugo's writings to be inspired by "a Christian and highly moral" idea. "It can be formulated as the regeneration of fallen mankind, crushed by the unjust weight of circumstances, the inertia of centuries and by social prejudices . . . [and as] the justification of the humiliated and of all the rejected pariahs of society" (13: 526).

Hugo's overriding importance for Dostoevsky is exhibited in a passage in a letter to Mikhail early in 1840, in which he compares Homer and Hugo: "Homer (a legendary figure perhaps like Christ, incarnated by God and sent to us) can be paralleled only with Christ. . . . You see, in *The Iliad* Homer gave the entire ancient world the organization of its spiritual and earthly life, exactly in the same sense as Christ to the new. . . . Victor Hugo as a lyric poet, with a pure angelic character, with a childlike Christian tendency in his poetry, and no one can compare with him in this. . . . Only Homer, with the same unshakable

---

[22] Cited in David Owen Evans, *Social Romanticism in France, 1830–1848* (Oxford, 1951), 81.

[23] "With book and play, in prose, in verse, I have / Taken up the cause of the weak and those in misery; / Pleading with the happy and the pitiless; / I have raised up the clown, the comedian, / All human beings who are damned, Triboulet, Marion, / The lackey, the convict, and the prostitute." Victor Hugo, *Oeuvres complètes* (Paris, 1882), 6: 91.

confidence in his mission, with his childlike faith in the god of poetry whom he serves, is similar in the tendency of the source of his poetry to Victor Hugo." [24]

Quite aside from its relation to Hugo, this passage demonstrates Dostoevsky's early acquaintance with ideas then considered quite "advanced." If he is willing to entertain the thought that Homer and Christ have both been sent by God, and that their status in relation to mankind is approximately the same, then the youthful Dostoevsky can hardly be accused of any simple-minded acceptance of conventional religious notions; his words smack much more of the Utopian Socialist doctrine of religion as "progressive revelation" [25] than of Christian orthodoxy. Moreover, it is highly significant that Victor Hugo, in the modern world, plays the same role of prophetic mouthpiece of God as is assigned to Homer in the ancient one. Dostoevsky's thought seems to be that Christ had proclaimed for modernity "the organization of its spiritual and earthly life," and that Hugo, inspired by this divine source, was expressing in his poetry the true meaning of Christ's teaching. This would indicate that Dostoevsky's Christianity had already become strongly social and humanitarian, and was practically identical with what was being called "Socialism" in France. During the summer of 1838, no doubt on Shidlovsky's recommendation, Dostoevsky plowed through Polevoy's six-volume *History of the Russian People*. This was the first Russian work utilizing the doctrines of the liberal French Romantic school of historians such as Thierry and Michelet, and it stressed the importance of the spirit of the people, rather than, as did Karamzin, that of the state and of morally enlightened despots.

One of the secrets of Dostoevsky's genius may well have been his refusal ever to decide emotively between the personal and literary tensions created by his equal devotion to the two Romanticisms. We see his commitment to the supernatural, otherworldly, and more traditionally Christian outlook of metaphysical Romanticism—Christian at least in spirit, and even though the artist is substituted for the priest and the saint. But we also have the strong tug of his feelings toward the practical application of the Christian values of pity and love— toward the "philanthropic" groundswell of the French social Romanticism flooding in ever more irresistibly after 1830. The one keeps its eyes devoutly fixed on the eternal, the other responds to the needs of the moment. The former concentrates on the inner struggle of the soul for purification, the latter combats the degrading influence of a brutalizing environment. The supreme value attributed to suffering comes into conflict with compassion for the weak and the oppressed; the need to justify God's ways to man clashes with the desire to refashion the world. Dostoevsky felt the competing pull of both these moral and religious imperatives, and the balance of their opposing pressures helps to account for the unremittingly tragic impact of his best work.

[24] *Pisʹma*, 1: 58; January 1, 1840.
[25] See D. G. Charlton, *Social Religions in France, 1815–1870* (London, 1963), 84.

CHAPTER 6

The Gogol Period

At the beginning of 1840, Dostoevsky was still an obscure student of military engineering with vague ambitions for a literary career but with nothing to show that such ambitions would ever be realized. By 1845, however, he was being hailed by Belinsky—the most powerful critical force in Russian literature—as the newest revelation on the Russian literary horizon. During these years, he went through a metamorphosis that set him firmly on the road he was to follow the rest of his life. "Brother," he writes Mikhail in the spring of 1845, "as regards literature *I am not as I was* two years ago. Then it was childishness, nonsense. Two years of study have brought much and taken much away."[1] What took place during these two years to bring about such a realization?

If we look for some answer in the events of Dostoevsky's life, there is little we find there that seems illuminating. His studies at the academy went forward without further incident, and he was promoted to the rank of ensign in August 1841. He continued in the higher classes for officers, but he was now entitled to live outside the school. At first he shared an apartment with a fellow engineer named E. I. Totleben, and this chance acquaintance later played an important role in Dostoevsky's life after his release from prison camp. Dostoevsky also shared an apartment in 1843 with a young medical student from Revel—a friend of Mikhail's—named Igor Riesenkampf.

Riesenkampf's reminiscences of Dostoevsky are the chief source of information about his life at this time, and they give us our first glimpse of the qualities in his character that were always to make relations with him so difficult and so mutable. "Feodor Mikhailovich was no less good-natured and no less courteous than his brother, but when not in a good mood he often looked at everything through dark glasses, became vexed, forgot good manners, and sometimes was carried away to the point of abusiveness and loss of self-awareness."[2] The inability to bridle his temper—a trait of character that he shared with his father—was to plague Dostoevsky all his life, and to place a heavy burden of tolerance on his friends. Dostoevsky once became exasperated at a social gathering made up

---

[1] *Pis'ma*, 1: 76; March (February) 24, 1845.
[2] A. I. Riesenkampf, "Vospominaniya o F. M. Dostoevskom," *LN* 86 (Moscow, 1973), 325.

largely of members of the foreign colony in Petersburg and, writes Riesenkampf, he "let fly with such a philippic against foreigners that the startled Swiss took him for some sort of *enragé* and thought it best to beat a retreat."[3] Dostoevsky's xenophobia, so disagreeably vehement later, went a long way back and could easily be aroused.

Riesenkampf attributes this extraordinary irascibility to the poor state of his friend's health. To his medical eye, Dostoevsky's sallow complexion indicated some blood deficiency, and he noted, too, a tendency to chronic infection of the respiratory organs. And this was not all—for Dostoevsky was continually prey to nervous disorders of various kinds. "He constantly complained to me that, during the night, it seemed that somebody near him was snoring; as a result . . . he was unable to settle down. At such times he got up and spent the rest of the night reading, or most often in working on various stories."[4] Such bouts of insomnia were always followed by periods of extreme irritability, when he would quarrel with everybody for little or no reason. To make matters worse, Dostoevsky was haunted by fears of falling into a lethargic sleep and being buried alive; to forestall such a mishap, he would leave notes asking not to be entombed before the lapse of a certain number of days. Nonetheless, Dostoevsky made great efforts to conceal his various discomfitures and bore them stoically; it was only because they lived together that Riesenkampf became aware of them at all. "In the circle of his friends he always seemed lively, untroubled, self-content."[5]

During his first several years of freedom from the academy, Dostoevsky began to lead the life of a young man about town and to savor some of the delights of a St. Petersburg resident. He assiduously attended the plays and ballets at the Alexandrinsky Theatre. He turned out when Franz Liszt and Ole Bull came to town, when the famed Italian tenor Rubini was performing for a Russian audience. Andrey—who came to live with his brother in the fall of 1841 for a year—mentions occasional card parties in the flat with his fellow officers.[6] From a remark to Mikhail on the inconveniences of living with Andrey ("Impossible to work or to amuse oneself—you understand"),[7] we surmise that, when the occasion arose, Dostoevsky did not deprive himself of the other pleasures readily available to young men in the capital.

All these amusements, of course, required a liberal supply of funds, and Dostoevsky was chronically short of cash. This was not so much poverty as a careless

[3] Ibid., 330.
[4] Ibid., 331.
[5] Ibid.
[6] *DVS*, 1: 95.
[7] *Pisma*, 1: 65; December 23, 1841.

prodigality, combined, perhaps, with a bad social conscience. For Dostoevsky received his salary as an officer as well as a large share of the income from the family estate—which was now administered by his brother-in-law, Peter Karepin, who, at the age of forty, had married Dostoevsky's seventeen-year-old sister Varvara. But he was always in debt nonetheless, and he fell into the self-defeating habit of drawing his salary in advance, as well as borrowing at murderous rates of interest. The thrifty Baltic German Riesenkampf, whom Mikhail had asked to keep an eye on Dostoevsky's expenses, was appalled by his total lack of the bourgeois virtues. Not only did he spend recklessly on amusements, but he allowed himself to be fleeced unmercifully by his soldier-servant, who supported a mistress and her family on the pickings garnered from Dostoevsky's expenditures.

Dostoevsky graduated from the academy in August 1843 and was placed on duty in the drafting department of the St. Petersburg Engineering Command. Relieved of the burden of his studies, he became involved in all sorts of translation schemes from which he hoped to realize a quick profit. A year later, announcing his long-cherished plan to retire from the service, he asked Karepin for the sum of a thousand silver rubles in return for surrendering his share in the family estate when it came to be divided among the heirs. Karepin at first refused this proposition as harmful to the interests of the rest of the family and, feeling called upon to give the young man some fatherly advice, urged him not to lose himself in "Shakespearean dreams."[8] This Philistine animadversion to Shakespeare threw Dostoevsky into a towering rage, and he replied with a series of bitter and insulting letters filled with resentment against the father figure who now blocked his path to freedom. Dostoevsky's demands were unquestionably inordinate under the circumstances, and he does not cut a favorable figure when he deliberately exaggerates the extent of his need or threatens to turn over his share of the estate to his creditors. But he was desperate to scrape together all he could so as to pay his debts before taking the plunge into independence.[9]

These are the major events of Dostoevsky's life during this five-year period, and what they show is that, beginning in 1843, he began seriously to try to carve out a place for himself in the St. Petersburg Grub Street. This date, as we know, marked the beginning of the major mutation in his literary ideas that extended over the next two years. Since these years coincide quite exactly with the movement of Russian literature from Romanticism to the "philanthropic"

[8] Ibid., 4: 450; September 5, 1844.
[9] It seems likely that Dostoevsky eventually got his thousand rubles. He told the commission investigating the Petrashevsky affair that he renounced his claim to his parents' estate in 1845 in return for the immediate payment of a sum of money. N. F. Belchikov, *Dostoevsky v protsesse Petrashevtsev* (Moscow, 1971), 123.

social realism of the Natural School, Dostoevsky's personal development can best be understood in the context of this more general evolution.

———■———

Mikhail arrived in St. Petersburg to take examinations in the winter of 1840–1841, and at his farewell party, in January, Dostoevsky regaled their assembled friends with readings from his works in progress. These were, according to Riesenkampf, two plays, entitled *Mary Stuart* and *Boris Godunov*—and that, unfortunately, is all that posterity knows about them. Like Stendhal and Balzac, Dostoevsky probably began with the ambition of writing for the stage for the same reasons given in their case by Victor Brombert: "The novel was simply not a road to quick or sensational success. The lure of the theater, with its promise of immediate glory, audible applause, money, and women, was far greater."[10] Tragedy was the form that enjoyed the most critical prestige at the height of the Romantic period, and it was then also being cultivated both by Shidlovsky and Mikhail.

In the early 1840s, Dostoevsky's mind and imagination were filled not only with the characters of Shakespeare and Schiller but also with those of Racine and Corneille. Responding indignantly to Mikhail's criticism of the classicist form of Racine and Corneille, Feodor springs to their defense by vaunting "the burning, passionate Racine, enraptured by his ideal," and he has special praise for *Phèdre*, whose struggle with her guilt-haunted conscience anticipates so many of Dostoevsky's characters. Indeed, with his subtle analysis of the secret recesses of a moral conscience divided against itself, no earlier writer is closer to Dostoevsky's psychology than the devoutly Christian Jansenist Racine.[11] Corneille also arouses Dostoevsky's enthusiasm, and he remarks that "with his gigantic characters and Romantic soul he is almost Shakespeare."[12] Such comments display Dostoevsky's admirable independence of judgment, his ability to appreciate the creative force wherever he finds it regardless of literary fashion.

Dostoevsky apparently gave up the effort to complete his two plays sometime in 1842, but if we are to judge by a reference a couple of years later to a work called *The Jew Yankel*, he did not cease to write for the stage. For in January 1844 he asks Mikhail for a loan and swears "by Olympus and by my Jew Yankel (my completed drama, and by what else? perhaps by my moustaches, which I hope will grow one day) that half of what I get . . . will be yours."[13] It is impossible to judge from this jesting promise whether the play was really completed or whether Dostoevsky

---

[10] Victor Brombert, *Stendhal: Fiction and the Themes of Freedom* (New York, 1968), 29.

[11] "The equivalence of love and hate, the one incessantly born from the other . . . is at the center of the Racinian psychology of love." Paul Bénichou, *Morales du grand siècle* (Paris, 1967), 223.

[12] *Pis'ma*, 1: 58–59; January 1, 1840.

[13] Ibid., 69; and half of January 1844.

merely hoped that, like the moustaches, it too would grow. The Jew Yankel is a minor character in Gogol's historical novel, *Taras Bulba*, and whether Dostoevsky finished the play or not, his name indicates that Dostoevsky has shifted his literary model from Pushkin and Schiller to Gogol. That he should even *think* of making such a character the central figure of a play, rather than Mary Stuart or Boris Godunov, clearly highlights the trend of the times. Tragedy in the grand Romantic style was dead, and the Gogol period of Russian literature—the period of tragicomic realism and social satire—had now begun to sweep all before it.

The confluence of a number of causes united, in 1843, to transform the Russian literary world. One factor was the publication in 1842 of Gogol's *Dead Souls* and of his short story, "The Overcoat." Another was the internal evolution of the critic Belinsky, who at that time was in charge of the critical section of the journal *Notes of the Fatherland* (*Otechestvennye zapiski*). A third was that Russian journalism, just at that moment, began to catch up with the new French vogue for what came to be called in Russian "the physiological sketch" (after the French *physiologie*)—that is, local color sketches of urban life and social types, a form that became popular after the revolution of 1830. The combined effect of all these events gave birth to the Natural School of Russian writers in the 1840s—a group in which, with the success of *Poor Folk*, Dostoevsky immediately took a prominent place.

Gogol, to be sure, was not unappreciated before 1842, and Belinsky had hailed him in 1835 as the rising young star of Russian literature. Everybody had been impressed with the vigor, freshness, and originality of Gogol's work, which earned him immediate personal acceptance by such luminaries as Pushkin and Zhukovsky, but the Russian critical establishment was far from being ready to accord him the status he had been given by Belinsky as "the leader of our literature."[14] The view of Gogol that Dostoevsky imbibed was thus scarcely such as to encourage an attitude of deference or a desire for emulation: the great figures of the Romantic pantheon were much more glamorous, and there was no disagreement about *their* stature. Dostoevsky had read Gogol by 1840, but there is no indication as yet of any serious literary influence.

Matters were to change drastically two years later, largely as the result of an epoch-making shift in Belinsky's ideas. We do not know exactly when Dostoevsky first began to read Belinsky and accept him as an authority. But from everything we already have learned, it is probable that he would have been indifferent to what he may have seen of Belinsky's work between 1838 and 1840. For these were the years when the young critic was going through his celebrated "reconciliation with reality." He was then under the influence of M. A. Bakunin, the future revolutionary anarchist, who at this point in his astonishing career

[14] V. G. Belinsky, *Izbrannye filosofskie sochineniya*, 2 vols. (Moscow, 1950), 1: 215.

was preaching an interpretation of Hegel as a doctrine of total political quietism and unquestioning acceptance of "reality." Belinsky, with his usual fervid extremism, accepted such ideas wholeheartedly and took them to lengths that caused even Bakunin to protest. The result was a series of articles whose thesis is well described in the memoirs of I. I. Panaev. "Carried away by Bakunin's interpretation of Hegel's philosophy . . . Belinsky . . . spoke with contempt of writers who showed the necessity for social reform. . . . He spoke with particular indignation of George Sand. Art represented for him some sort of higher, isolated world, enclosed in itself, occupied only with eternal truths and not having any link with the squabbles and trifles of our life."[15]

One of the first manifestations of Belinsky's dislike of contemporary French literature—including Hugo, Lamartine, de Vigny, and Balzac—was an attack, in the spring of 1839, on Polevoy, its chief critical advocate in Russia. Shidlovsky and his young friend Feodor Dostoevsky certainly discussed this jeremiad. About the same time, Shidlovsky attended a benefit for Polevoy that included a vaudeville skit about a young student, Vissarion Glupinsky (*glupy* means stupid or silly), who "explains Hegelian philosophy and objective individuality to everybody, etc."[16] The author of this work remained anonymous (but was probably Polevoy); and it indicates the opinion about Belinsky that Dostoevsky would have gathered from his own literary circle.

Belinsky moved from Moscow to Petersburg in the winter of 1839 and, partly under the stimulus of a new milieu and a new group of friends, began to change his ideas quickly. Also, he was deeply troubled by the opposition of such Moscow luminaries as A. I. Herzen and T. N. Granovsky, whose opinions he could not help respecting, to his uncritical adulation of Russian "reality." During the winter of 1841, his new circle gathered at the home of Panaev once a week for conversation and conviviality, and here Belinsky became acquainted for the first time with the newest French thought. Panaev translated the articles of Pierre Leroux from the *Revue Indépendante*, just then beginning to appear; the conclusion of George Sand's *Spiridion* was put into Russian especially for Belinsky's benefit; Thiers's *Histoire de la révolution en 1789* was read, as well as Louis Blanc's vehemently socialist *Histoire des dix ans*. "His [Belinsky's] previous indignation against George Sand," Panaev writes, "was replaced by the most passionate enthusiasm for her. All his previous literary authorities and idols—Goethe, Walter Scott, Schiller, Hoffmann—faded before her. . . . He would only speak of George Sand and [Pierre] Leroux."[17]

[15] I. I. Panaev, *Sobranie sochinenii*, 6 vols. (Moscow, 1912), 6: 212.
[16] Cited in Yu. Oksman, *Letopis zhizn' i tvorchestvo V. G. Belinskogo* (Moscow, 1958), 195.
[17] Panaev, *SS*, 6: 273.

The result of all this, in a little more than a year, was to transform Belinsky from his previous disdain for social-political concerns into a violent partisan of the new French social doctrines. In the fall of 1841, he writes to his friend V. P. Botkin that "the idea of Socialism" had become for him "the idea of ideas, the being of beings, the question of questions, the alpha and omega of belief and knowledge. . . . It has (for me) engulfed history and religion and philosophy."[18] It is clear that, whatever "Socialism" may mean to Belinsky, it is infinitely more than the adoption of a new set of social-political ideas. And when he tries to speak about it in more detail, we see that what has impressed him most is the apocalyptic and messianic aspect of all the Utopian Socialist tenets—the idea, particularly strong in the Sand-Leroux preachments, that Socialism is the final realization on earth of the true teachings of Christ. For the last chapters of George Sand's novel *Spiridion* reveal that the unsullied doctrine of Christ, shamefully travestied by the despotic Roman Catholic Church, is the same as that proclaimed by the French Revolution. The great Christian heretics of the past have always upheld the eternal evangel of liberty, equality, and fraternity, which is nothing but the modern social-political translation of the original meaning of the Christian doctrine of love.

The influence of such ideas, intermingled with other Sandian notions bearing on the relations between the sexes, is perceptible in Belinsky's exposition of his new credo. "And there will come a time—I fervently believe it—when no one will be burned, no one will be decapitated, when the criminal will plead for death . . . and death will be denied him . . . when there will be no senseless forms and rites, no contracts and stipulations on feeling, no duty and obligation, and we shall not yield to will but to love alone; when there will be no husbands and wives, but lovers and mistresses, and when the mistress comes to the lover saying: 'I love another,' the lover will answer: 'I cannot be happy without you, I shall suffer all my life, but go to him whom you love,' and will not accept her sacrifice, . . . but like God will say to her: I want blessings, not sacrifices. . . . There will be neither rich nor poor, neither kings nor subjects, there will be brethren, there will be men, and, at the word of the Apostle Paul, Christ will pass his power to the Father, and Father-Reason will hold sway once more, but this time in a new heaven and above a new world."[19] This will be the realization, as Belinsky rightly says himself, of the dream of "the Golden Age," and this dream is what Belinsky refers to as "Socialism."

Belinsky's conversion to this kind of Socialism initiated a new phase in Russian culture of the 1840s. Annenkov, who had left Russia in the midst of Belinsky's Hegelian period, returned to Petersburg in 1843 to find, much to his

---

[18] V. G. Belinsky, *Selected Philosophical Works* (Moscow, 1948), 159.
[19] Ibid., 164–165.

surprise, that the Petersburg literati were enthralled by the very same works he had heard about in Paris. "Proudhon's book, *De la propriété*, then almost out of date, Cabet's *Icarie*, little read in France itself except by a small circle of poor worker-dreamers, the far more widespread and popular system of Charles Fourier—all these served as objects of study, of impassioned discussions, of questions and expectations of every sort, and understandably so. . . . Whole phalanxes of Russians . . . were overjoyed at the chance to change over from abstract, speculative thought without real content to just the same kind of abstract thought but now with a seemingly real content. . . . The books of the authors already named were in everybody's hands in those days; they were subjected to thoroughgoing study and discussion; they produced, as Schelling and Hegel had done earlier, their spokesmen, commentators, interpreters, and even, somewhat later—something that had not occurred in connection with earlier theories—their martyrs, too." [20]

------◼------

All this intellectual agitation at first went on only in the closed small circle of Belinsky's friends—the nucleus of what later came to be called his Pléiade. [21] But this circle was composed, at the same time, of the core of his staff of *Notes of the Fatherland*, and the ideas that were stirring them soon began to find their way into its pages. There was, for example, a renewed flurry of interest in George Sand, whose novels now began to be translated almost as soon as they appeared in Paris. Much more notice was also given to the new French literature, and attention was discreetly called to its subversive social message. Most important of all, however, was the providential publication of *Dead Souls*—a true godsend for Belinsky. For this gave him a new Russian work of major artistic stature through which he could translate his ardent social concerns into immediately relevant Russian terms.

The intrigue of Gogol's *Dead Souls* deals directly with serfdom as his chief protagonist Chichikov travels through the Russian provinces purchasing "dead souls," serfs who have died but whose names are still on the tax list and retain some economic value. His provincial landowners are a remarkable gallery of mindless grotesques, limned by the hand of a master and totally appalling in the complacent sloth, triviality, and sordidness of their lives. Belinsky eagerly seized on the book as an exposure of the grim horrors of Russian reality, which, after his Hegelian debauch, he now found even more unbearable. Naturally, one

---

[20] P. V. Annenkov, *The Extraordinary Decade*, ed. Arthur P. Mendel, trans. Irwin R. Titunik (Ann Arbor, MI, 1968), 112.

[21] The best-known names of the Pléiade were Panaev himself and K. D. Kavelin. Between 1843 and 1848, it blossomed to include Nekrasov, Turgenev, Dostoevsky, Goncharov, and Saltykov-Shchedrin. Herzen and Ogarev were also occasional participants when they came to Petersburg.

could not speak about such matters too openly in public print; but Belinsky was a master at conveying his ideas in Aesopian language. There was no mistaking what Belinsky meant when he called *Dead Souls* "a purely Russian and national creation . . . pitilessly tearing the cover off reality and filled with a passionate, impatient, urgent love for the fruitful core of Russian life" (read: the enslaved Russian peasant).[22]

Between 1843 and 1845, one spoke of little else in Russian literary journalism except *Dead Souls*. "It seemed as if [Belinsky] considered it the mission of his life," Annenkov writes, "to make the content of *Dead Souls* immune to any supposition that it harbored in it anything other than a true picture, artistically, spiritually, and ethnographically speaking, of the contemporary position of Russian society. . . . He tirelessly pointed out, both by word of mouth and in print, what the right attitudes toward it were, urging his auditors and readers at every opportunity to think over, but to do so seriously and sincerely, the question as to why types of such repulsiveness as were brought out in the novel . . . exist in Russia without horrifying anyone."[23]

Belinsky's critical campaign was accompanied by general exhortations to Russian writers to follow Gogol's example. Literature, he now maintained, should turn to contemporary society for its material; and he declared George Sand the greatest of all moderns because he found in her the "vital convictions"[24] lacking in Hugo and Balzac. By 1844, in a survey of Russian literature of the previous year, Belinsky was already hailing the appearance of a new school that "deals with the most vital problems of life, destroys the old inveterate prejudices and raises its voice in indignation against the deplorable aspects of contemporary morals and manners, laying bare in all its stark and grim reality 'all that is constantly before the gaze, but which unseeing eyes heed not, all the frightful appalling mass of trivialities in which our life is steeped, all the depth of cold, disintegrated everyday characters with which our earth teems.'"[25]

Belinsky here is talking about the young writers of the Natural School who had just begun to loom on the horizon and whose works were being published in *Notes of the Fatherland*. This group (not yet baptized) had emerged in response to Belinsky's call for a new literature of social realism, but instead of taking the provincial world of *Dead Souls* as their model, its members were far more influenced by the Petersburg setting of "The Overcoat," which coincided opportunely with the latest foreign literary fashion of the physiological sketch. D. V. Grigorovich, Dostoevsky's erstwhile fellow student at the academy, recalls that "[i]mitators immediately began to appear in Russia. . . . Nekrasov, whose practical

---

[22] See *N. V. Gogol v Russkoi kritike* (Moscow, 1953), 122.
[23] Annenkov, *Decade*, 112.
[24] Belinsky, *IFS*, 1: 432.
[25] A citation from *Dead Souls*. Belinsky, *Works*, 192–193.

mind was always on the lookout, . . . imagined a publication in several small volumes: *The Physiology of Petersburg*."[26] Invited to write one of these sketches, and deciding to concentrate on the life of the Italian organ-grinders in Petersburg, Grigorovich began to haunt their performances and take notes. "I had . . . then already begun to feel . . . the desire to depict reality as it genuinely is, as Gogol depicts it in "The Overcoat"."[27] In the early autumn of 1844, running into Dostoevsky on the street, Grigorovich dragged him home to get his opinion of this new work.

———■———

By the time he chanced upon Grigorovich, Dostoevsky had already begun to go through a similar literary evolution. Until 1842, and despite his sympathy for the compassionate humanitarianism of the French social Romantics, it is clear that Dostoevsky was still laboring in the literary traces of the dominant taste of the 1830s. There had been, after all, no current of critical opinion in Russia indicating any other direction to follow for a young aspirant to literary fame. Belinsky's campaign on behalf of Gogol, however, and the transformation of *Notes of the Fatherland* into a Russian outpost of the French "Socialist" tendency, changed the entire picture at one stroke. And since Dostoevsky had become emotionally committed to the moral ideals of this movement a good while before Belinsky, it is not difficult to understand the alacrity with which he climbed aboard the new cultural bandwagon.

Beginning in 1843, we find the first references to his intense and enthusiastic preoccupation with Gogol. Of all Russian writers, Riesenkampf tells us, Dostoevsky "was particularly fond of reading Gogol, and loved to declaim pages of *Dead Souls* by heart."[28] If *The Jew Yankel* was finished by the latter part of January 1844, then it must have been written sometime in the autumn and winter of 1843, and it would represent Dostoevsky's first response to the changed climate of Russian literature created by the joint efforts of Gogol and Belinsky.

Most of the other information about Dostoevsky's literary activities depicts him as totally absorbed in the new trend. He was, for example, an assiduous reader of the French *roman-feuilleton*, which, in the early 1840s, had become a staple of French journalism and was one of the most effective means by which humanitarian and Socialist ideas were being propagated. He proposed to Mikhail in late 1843 a joint venture to translate and publish Eugène Sue's *Mathilde*—the first novel in which Sue addressed social problems. (The project was abandoned for lack of funds.) Dostoevsky also read the muckraking *Les mystères de Paris* (in which Sue popularized certain Fourierist ideas), which, when it appeared in

---

[26] *DVS*, 1: 129.
[27] D. V. Grigorovich, *Polnoe sobranie sochinenii*, 12 vols. (St. Petersburg, 1896), 12: 266.
[28] *DVS*, 1: 114.

Russia in 1844, was enthusiastically promoted by Belinsky. "The author," he wrote, "wished to present to a depraved and egoistic society worshipping the golden calf the spectacle of the sufferings of wretched people . . . condemned by ignorance and poverty to vice and crime."[29]

At the same time that he was reading Sue, Dostoevsky was also impressed, according to both Riesenkampf and Grigorovich, by Frédéric Soulié's *Mémoires du diable*. Exploiting the tradition of Romantic satanism, Soulié combined it with a bitter social satire and wildly melodramatic intrigue. The aim of the book was to show that, under the Restoration and the July Monarchy, "virtue was normally persecuted and exploited, and vice, cunningly masked as virtue, was triumphant."[30] Dostoevsky was also interested in Émile Souvestre, who specialized in novels with parallel plot lines contrasting the fortunes of noble, self-sacrificing characters devoted to the welfare of humanity with those of cold, ambitious careerists who reach the highest rungs of the ladder in a depraved and unjust society. It is no surprise to see Dostoevsky working during the latter half of 1844 on a translation of George Sand's *La dernière Aldini*: any work of Sand's was an eminently marketable commodity. Here she exhibits the moral superiority of a true son of the people—the offspring of humble fisher-folk—to the spineless and decadent aristocracy of his native country. The book is filled with flashes of the revolutionary social Christianity now making its appearance in Sand's incredibly voluminous production. "Liberalism," proclaims the hero, "is a religion which should ennoble its followers, and, like Christianity in its early days, make the slave a freeman, the freeman a saint or a martyr."[31] Dostoevsky no doubt toiled over such pages with reverence, but having almost completed the job, he discovered to his dismay that the work had already appeared in Russian.

Dostoevsky read widely in the numerous novels of George Sand and, as with the entire generation of the 1840s, such works greatly enriched his acquaintance with progressive and revolutionary ideas. In the moving obituary that he wrote forty years later, George Sand, he says, was more important in Russia than Dickens or Balzac because her readers "managed to extract even from novels everything against which [they] were being guarded."[32] The great satirist Saltykov-Shchedrin is even more explicit. "From the France of Saint-Simon, Cabet, Fourier, and Louis Blanc and, in particular, George Sand . . . flowed to us [in the 1840s] a faith in mankind; from there gleamed for us the certainty that the Golden Age was to be found not in the past but in the future."[33] George Sand had helped to

[29] Belinsky, *Works*, 323.

[30] Harold March, *Frédéric Soulié* (New Haven, 1931), 177.

[31] George Sand, *The Last of the Aldinis*, trans. George Burnham Ives (Philadelphia, 1900), 359–360.

[32] *DW* (June 1876), 346.

[33] Cited in M. Polyakov, *Vissarion Belinsky* (Moscow, 1960), 325.

inspire such a faith in Belinsky, and the novelist whom Renan once called an Aeolian harp, resounding to all the ideological currents blowing in the tempestuous 1840s, also performed the same signal service for Dostoevky.

There are intriguing resemblances between Sand's remarkable novel *Spiridion* (a combination of Gothic mystery story and spiritual autobiography) and certain features of *The Brothers Karamazov*.[34] Both are set in a monastery; both involve the transmission of an ancient and semiheretical religious tradition; both stress that true religion should depend only on free moral choice, not on the tyranny of dogma or institutions; both contain as central characters an old and dying monk—the inheritor of this tradition, who is hated by his fellow monks— and an ardent young disciple inspired by his doctrine and his example; both dramatize the struggle between skeptical reason and true faith. In both novels, the struggle is resolved through a mystical vision that restores a selfless love for all of God's creation and revives belief in the existence of conscience and the immortality of the soul; in each, the dying guardian of the tradition sends his young follower into the world to apply the doctrine of Christian love to the ills of social life.[35] In 1876, Dostoevsky was certain that George Sand had "died a Deist with a firm belief in God and immortal life," and he pointed out that her Socialism, based as it was "upon the spiritual thirst of mankind for perfection and purity," coincides with Christianity in its view of human personality as morally responsible.[36] Whether or not such comments were directly inspired by recollections of *Spiridion*, they well illustrate the sort of moral-religious Christian Socialism that George Sand helped to instill in Dostoevsky himself in the early 1840s.

With the collapse of his hopes for *La dernière Aldini*, all of Dostoevsky's plans for obtaining extra funds by translation went glimmering. Nor was he any more successful with another project that seemed promising—a complete Russian version of Schiller's plays, with Mikhail as translator and himself as editor and publisher. Mikhail did put *The Robbers* and *Don Carlos* into Russian, and both were published in periodicals, but the expectation of a complete edition, with substantial profits, once again proved a will-o'-the-wisp. The only enterprise of Dostoevsky's that succeeded was a translation of *Eugénie Grandet*, prompted by Balzac's triumphal presence in Petersburg in the winter of 1843. Translated over the Christmas and New Year's holidays, it was published in the *Repertoire and Pantheon* in 1844, and this was the manner in which Dostoevsky's name, prophetically linked to that of Balzac, first appeared in print. By this time he was

---

[34] Dostoevsky read *L'Uscoque*, which was published in the *Revue des Deux Mondes* in 1838. *Spiridion* began to appear in the same publication the same year, and the eminently respectable journal was available in the French library to which Dostoevsky was a subscriber.

[35] *DVS*, I: 112–113.

[36] *DW* (June 1876), 349.

already sharing a flat with Grigorovich, who, through his acquaintance with
Nekrasov, had begun to gravitate toward the orbit of the Belinsky Circle.

———■———

The idea for *Poor Folk* was conceived in the midst of this abundance of literary
activity, all prompted by Dostoevsky's acute awareness of the new literary temper of the times. "I am finishing a novel about the size of *Eugénie Grandet*," he
writes to Mikhail in the early fall of 1844. "A rather original novel. . . . I will give
it to the *Notes of the Fatherland*."[37] Dostoevsky was obviously writing to satisfy
the new exigencies for Russian literature laid down by Belinsky; but nothing else
is really known about the gestation of the novel, except for a remark that he
made while hard at work on the book. "I read like a fiend," he says to Mikhail
in the spring of 1845, just as he was putting the finishing touches to his manuscript, "and reading has a strange effect on me. I reread some book I've read
before, and it's as if new strength began to stir in me. I penetrate into everything, I understand with precision, and I myself draw from this the ability to
create."[38]

It is thus primarily to literature that we should turn for the "sources" of *Poor
Folk*. The title, as well as the style of the diary of the chief female character,
Varvara, links her to Karamzin's sentimental idyll *Poor Liza*, which laments tearfully over the sad fate of a beauteous and virtuous peasant maiden, seduced and
betrayed by a weak-willed young aristocrat.[39] Gogol's "The Overcoat" and Pushkin's "The Station Master" also played a role in the conception of the work and
are referred to in the text. Less visible but perhaps no less crucial was *Eugénie
Grandet*, which celebrates the unselfconscious heroism of a plain country girl
who proves capable of true moral grandeur. According to Balzac, this obscure
family drama was no less cruel and fateful than that of "the princely House of
Atreus."[40] Balzac's example may well have shown Dostoevsky the way to effect-
ing a similar elevation in the human stature of his own humble protagonists.

It is precisely the lofty moral stature of Dosotevsky's humble and humiliated
characters that distinguishes them from Gogol's brilliant caricatures. Indeed, in
a journalistic *feuilleton* written twenty years later, when Dostoevsky views his
own literary evolution from the days of his early Romanticism up to his discovery of the theme of his first novel, he makes this very distinction between himself and Gogol. The feuilleton, titled "Petersburg Visions in Verse and Prose," is

[37] *Pis'ma*, 1: 73; September 30, 1844.

[38] Ibid., 76; March (February) 24, 1845.

[39] This view has been advanced by K. K. Istomin and A. I. Bem. For further discussion, see Bem's
suggestive article, "Pervye shagi Dostoevskogo," *Slavia* 12 (1933–1934), 134–161.

[40] Honoré de Balzac, "Eugénie Grandet," *La comédie humaine*, ed. Marcel Bouteron (Paris,
1947), 3: 599.

written by Dostoevsky's fictive alter ego, a "romantic dreamer," and relates a "vision" he experiences while hurrying home one January evening and pausing on the banks of the Neva. There, his eyes open to "something new, to a completely new world" (13: 158). He begins to see "some strange figures, entirely prosaic, . . . just titular councilors, and yet, at the same time, fantastic titular councilors." Behind them there was someone "who made faces before me, concealed behind all that fantastic crowd, and pulled some kind of strings or springs and all these puppets moved and laughed and everybody laughed!" Then the narrator catches a glimpse of another story that was no laughing matter—"some titular heart, honorable and pure, moral and devoted to the authorities, and together with him some young girl, humiliated and sorrowing, and all their story tore deeply at my heart" (13: 158–159). This story, of course, is the one that Dostoevsky tells in *Poor Folk*.

The very text of the vision makes clear that Dostoevsky is talking about literature: the new world that swims into his ken is that of the master puppeteer Gogol—this is a discovery of Gogol. But Gogol is the first step; the second is the discovery of the situation of *Poor Folk* and of Dostoevsky's approach to his characters ("honorable and pure," "humiliated and sorrowing"). After the "vision," Gogol's characters, who normally arouse laughter, are seen in such a way that their story "tears deeply at the heart."

In another variant of the "vision" used thirty years later in *A Raw Youth* (1875), the narrator imagines Petersburg vanishing into the sky like smoke. He exclaims: "What if this [Petersburg] fog should part and float away? Would not all this rotten and slimy town go with it . . . and the old Finnish marsh be left as before, and in the midst of it . . . a bronze horseman on a panting, overdriven steed?" (8: 116). The image of Petersburg is associated here with Pushkin's poem "The Bronze Horseman," and the bronze horseman is Peter the Great as cast in the famous statue by Falconet. Pushkin's protagonist Evgeny, whose fiancée has just been swept away in the flood of 1824 evoked in the poem, shakes his fist at the statue because it is Peter who is responsible for the ruin of Evgeny's life. But once the bereaved Evgeny commits his impetuous act of *lèse-majesté*, he is so terrified and guilt-stricken that he goes out of his mind, imagining that he hears the ringing hoofs of the bronze horseman pursuing him; and his body is finally washed ashore in a hut on a lonely island devastated by the storm.

Pushkin thus dramatizes the immense power of Petersburg to crush the lives of all those lowly and helpless folk who live in the shadow of its splendors, but, even more important, Pushkin treats the fate of poor Evgeny with sympathy and compassion rather than with the ridicule that Gogol employs for similar types. After the vision, this is exactly the attitude that Dostoevsky himself will adopt toward such characters. Pushkin, in other words, pointed the way for Dostoevsky to overcome his Romanticism without turning into a mere imitator of

Gogol; the vision symbolizes the moment when Dostoevsky became aware of how, by following the example of Pushkin, he could join the new Gogolian trend and affirm his artistic originality at the same time. If, after the vision, Gogol's characters are seen freshly—and in such a way that their story "tears deeply at the heart"—it is because they are now being viewed through the prism of Pushkin. In short, the "completely new world" that the vision revealed to Dostoevsky was that of his own style of sentimental Naturalism, a synthesis of Gogol, Pushkin—and Dostoevsky.

CHAPTER 7

Poor Folk

No début in Russian literature has been described more vividly than that of Dostoevsky, and few, in truth, created so widespread and sensational a stir. Dostoevsky's account is well-known, though he considerably exaggerated and sentimentalized his own innocence and naïveté. "Early in the winter [of 1845], suddenly, I began to write *Poor Folk* [*Bednye lyudi*], my first novel; before that I had never written anything. Having finished the novel, I did not know what to do with it, and to whom it should be submitted."[1] Dostoevsky knew very well what he wished to do with his novel, and there is also evidence that Grigorovich was pushing him to give his work to *Notes of the Fatherland*.[2]

There can be no doubt, however, about what occurred when the novel was ready. Grigorovich was profoundly moved by the work; he took it to Nekrasov; and both young literati shed tears over the sad plight of Dostoevsky's characters. Acting on impulse, they rushed to Dostoevsky's apartment at four o'clock in the morning—it was a St. Petersburg "white night," bright and luminous as day—to convey their emotion. The next day Nekrasov brought it to Belinsky, who greeted it with equal warmth and appreciation. Annenkov visited Belinsky while the critic was plunged in Dostoevsky's manuscript, and he has left a graphic account of Belinsky's enthusiasm at his discovery. "You see this manuscript? . . . I haven't been able to tear myself away from it for almost two days now. It's a novel by a beginner, a new talent . . . his novel reveals such secrets of life and characters in Russia as no one before him even dreamed of. Just think of it—it's the first attempt at a social novel we've had. . . . The matter in it is simple: it concerns some good-hearted simpletons who assume that to love the whole world is an extraordinary pleasure and duty for every one. They cannot comprehend a thing when the wheel of life with all its rules and regulations runs over them and fractures their limbs and bones without a word. That's all there is—but what drama, what types! I forgot to tell you, the artist's name is Dostoevsky."[3]

---

[1] *DW* (January 1877), 584.

[2] *Pis'ma*, 1: 75; March (February) 24, 1845.

[3] P. V. Annenkov, *The Extraordinary Decade*, ed. Arthur P. Mendel, trans. Irwin R. Titunik (Ann Arbor, MI, 1968), 150.

Belinsky's response, aside from the proclivity of his excitable temperament to extreme reactions, is only explicable in terms of his struggle against the Russian epigones of Romanticism and his single-minded attempt to create a new movement of social Realism in Russian literature. While urban, lower-class Russian life had now begun to be depicted in all its forms and diversities in the physiological sketch, the emphasis was on description of externals rather than on narration, on photographic accuracy (the sketches were called "daguerrotypes" and were accompanied by illustrations) rather than on imaginative penetration and inner identification. Dostoevsky was the first writer who, having chosen this material within the thematic range of the Natural School, had managed to produce more than a series of physiological sketches. "I am very often at Belinsky's," he writes Mikhail in the fall of 1845. "He is as well-disposed to me as one possibly could be, and seriously sees in me *a public proof* and justification of his opinions."[4] Dostoevsky *had* succeeded in producing the work that Belinsky had been waiting for; and the immense stir created by *Poor Folk* among contemporaries is to a large degree attributable to the controversy over the new orientation that Belinaky had given to Russian literature.

■

Poor Folk is cast in the form of an epistolary novel between two correspondents—the lowly titular councillor Makar Devushkin, a middle-aged copying clerk employed in one of the vast offices of the St. Petersburg bureaucracy, and a young girl just barely out of her teens, Varvara Dobroselova.[5] Both are tender, lonely, fragile souls whose solicitation for each other brings a ray of warmth into their otherwise bleak lives. But the innocent idyll is soon ended by the pressure of the sordid forces against which they struggle. The hopelessness of Varvara's position and the chance to reestablish her social situation compel her to accept an offer of marriage, and the book ends on Devushkin's wail of anguish as Varvara vanishes forever into the steppes with her callous bridegroom Bykov (whose name evokes the Russian word for bull).

Nothing is more impressive in *Poor Folk* than the deftness with which Dostoevsky uses the epistolary form to reveal the hidden, unspoken thoughts of his characters; what one reads between the lines of their letters is more important than what appears on the surface—or rather, it is the tension between the spoken and unspoken that gives us the true access to their consciousness. Devushkin, so simple and uncomplicated at first glance, is a character constantly

---

[4] *Pis'ma*, 1: 82; October 8, 1845.

[5] Both names have allegorical echoes. Devushkin evokes *devushka*, the word for a young girl or maiden. The incongruity of this appellation is touchingly humorous, and yet indicates some of the quality of Devushkin's character. Dobroselova is a combination of the Russian word for "good" and for "country village."

struggling with himself. He reduces himself to abject poverty for the sake of Varvara, showering her with little gifts of candy and fruit that he can ill afford, and he suffers agonies of humiliation, which he tries to conceal, because of the difficulties caused by his destitution. Above all, there is his "ideological" struggle—the wrestle with the rebellious thoughts that surge up in him unexpectedly under the pressure of his emotional involvement with Varvara and that are so much at variance with the unquestioned credo of obedience he has always accepted up to that time.

Dostoevsky surrounds this simple tale of his characters' brief encounter with a number of accessories that enlarge the story to the dimensions of a true social novel. Varvara's inset diary takes us back into her innocent rustic girlhood, and it also contains the portrait of the tubercular student Pokrovsky—Dostoevsky's first brief description of the new *raznochinets* intellectual who would later evolve into Raskolnikov. His nominal father—a hopeless drunkard, married off to a girl made pregnant by Bykov—is depicted by Dostoevsky with a tragicomic pathos worthy of Dickens, particularly in the scenes in which the broken old man follows the hearse of his adored educated son to his final resting place. "The old man seemed not to feel the cold and wet and ran wailing from one side of the cart to the other, the skirts of his old coat fluttering in the wind like wings. Books were sticking out from all his pockets; in his hands was a huge volume which he held tightly. . . . The books kept falling out of his pockets into the mud. People stopped him and pointed to what he had lost, he picked them up and fell to racing after the coffin again" (1: 45).

Another such inset story is that of the starving clerk Gorshkov and his family, come from the provinces to clear his name of a charge of embezzlement while in government service. This is the archetypal family in the lowest depths of poverty that will appear again and again in Dostoevsky—and here characterized by a terrible and unnatural silence, as of a suffering too deep for lamentation. There is no sound even of the children, Devushkin tells Varvara: "One evening I happened to pass their door; it was unusually quiet in the house at the time; I heard a sobbing again as though they were crying so quietly, so pitifully, that it was heartrending, and the thought of those poor creatures haunted me all night so that I could not get to sleep properly" (1: 24).

All these narrative lines interweave to build up an image of the same unavailing struggle to keep afloat humanly in the face of crushing circumstances, the same treasures of sensibility, sensitivity, and moral refinement appearing in the most unlikely places—unlikely, at least, from the point of view of previous Russian literature. Everywhere poverty and humiliation, the exploitation of the weak and the helpless by the rich, powerful, and unscrupulous—all this in the midst of crowded St. Petersburg slum life, with its nauseating odors and debris-littered dwellings. *Poor Folk* combined these picturesque merits of the best of the physiological sketches with a new and unerring insight into the tortures of the humiliated sensibility. The world as seen from below rather than above constitutes the major innovation of Dostoevsky vis-à-vis Gogol, whose sympathy with his humble protagonists is never strong enough to overcome the condescension implicit in his narrative stance. The situations and psychology of *Poor Folk* speak for themselves against class pride and class prejudice, and against the presumed superiority of the upper over the lower. But the book also contains a much more outspoken protest that, although not mentioned by Belinsky, could certainly not have left him indifferent.

—■—

Devushkin undergoes a distinct evolution in the course of the book. The early letters reveal him accepting his lowly place in life without a murmur of protest, and even taking pride in performing his unassuming tasks conscientiously. At the very lowest point of Devushkin's misery, though, he loses heart and takes to drink. Never had he felt so degraded and worthless; and this is the moment when a faint spark of rebellion flares even in his docile and submissive breast. Emerging onto one of the fashionable Petersburg streets, filled with luxurious shops and smartly dressed people, he is struck by the difference from the sullen and unhappy crowds of his own slum district, and he suddenly begins to wonder why he and Varvara should be condemned to poverty while others are born into the lap of luxury.

"I know, I know, my dear that it is wrong to think that, that it is free-thinking; but to speak honestly, to speak the whole truth, why is it fate, like a raven, croaks good fortune for one still unborn, while another begins life in the orphan asylum?" (1: 86). Fortune seems to have no relation to personal merit; nor is this revolutionary idea the full extent of Devushkin's "freethinking." As he continues, we find him emitting the distinctively Saint-Simonian idea that the humblest worker is more entitled to respect, because more useful to society, than the wealthiest and most aristocratic social parasite. All this leads Devushkin to a piercing vision of the contrasted lives of the rich and the poor—a vision that, as in one of the feuilleton-novels of Sue or Soulié, strips away the façade beyond which both classes live concealed so that one sees them simultaneously:

There, in some smoky corner, in some damp hole, which, through poverty, passes as a lodging, some workman wakes up from his sleep; and all night he has been dreaming of boots, for instance, which he had accidentally slit the day before, as though a man ought to dream of such nonsense! . . . His children are crying and his wife is hungry; and it's not only shoemakers who get up in the morning like that . . . but this is the point, Varinka, close by in the same house . . . a wealthy man in his gilded apartments dreams at night, it may be, of those same boots . . . in a different sense, but still boots, for in the sense I am using the word, Varinka, every one of us is a bit of a shoemaker, my darling; . . . it's a pity there is no one at that wealthy person's side, no man who would whisper in his ear: "Come, give over thinking of such things, thinking of nothing but yourself, living for nothing but yourself; your children are healthy, your wife is not begging for food. Look about you, can't you see some object more noble to worry about than your boots?" (1: 88–89)

The indifference of the rich and mighty to the misery all around them fills Devushkin with indignation—to such an extent, indeed, that he even feels for a moment that his own sense of inferiority is misplaced. "Get to the bottom of that," he says, "and then judge whether one was right to abuse oneself for no reason and to be reduced to undignified mortification" (1: 89).

This passage contains the central social theme of the book, which is Dostoevsky's variant of the same plea one finds in the French social novel of the 1830s and in Dickens—the plea addressed to the wealthy and powerful to assume some moral responsibility for their less fortunate brothers. This theme comes to a climax in the famous scene with Devushkin's Civil Service superior, when the poor clerk, who has been careless in copying some urgently needed document, is called in for a reprimand. His feelings are described as follows: "My heart began shuddering within me, and I don't know myself why I was so frightened; I only know that I was panic-stricken as I had never been before in all my life. I sat rooted to my chair—as though there was nothing the matter, as though it were not I" (1: 92). By this time his appearance is little better than that of a scarecrow, and his last remaining button falls off and noisily bounces along the floor as he is trying to mumble some excuse. Moved by his obvious misery, the kindhearted General privately gives Devushkin a hundred-ruble note. When the latter tries to kiss his hand in gratitude, he flushes, avoids the self-debasing gesture, and gives Devushkin an equalitarian handshake instead. "I swear that however cast down I was and afflicted in the bitterest days of our misfortune," he tells Varvara, "looking at you, at your poverty, and at myself, my degradation and my uselessness, in spite of all that, I swear that the hundred rubles is not as much to me as that His Excellency deigned to shake hands with me, a straw, a worthless drunkard" (1: 93). The General could feel not only with Devushkin's pitiful economic distress but also with his longing to preserve his self-respect: this is what saves the charitable impulse from being still another humiliation.

Belinsky was deeply struck by this scene, and Dostoevsky reports him exclaiming over it at their first meeting. "And that torn-off button! That moment of kissing the General's hand!—why, this is no longer compassion for that unhappy man, but horror, horror! In that very gratitude is horror!"[6] The delicacy of feeling displayed in the handshake, the implicit recognition of a human equality with the lowly Devushkin, is a symbolic point made twice over. Devushkin resents that, before being given charity, the affairs of his destitute drinking companion Emelyan Ilyich are investigated, which he takes as an affront to Emelyan's dignity ("nowadays, my dear soul, benevolence is practiced in a very queer way"). Similarly, when Gorshkov, after winning his lawsuit, goes around muttering that his "honor" has been restored, the cynical hack writer Ratazyaev says that, with nothing to eat, money is more important than honor. "It seemed to me," Devushkin observes, "that Gorshkov was offended" (1: 69, 98).

Dostoevsky was acutely aware that the spiritual is of equal importance with the material in alleviating the lot of the unfortunate—even, perhaps, of greater importance, since poverty only heightens the need for self-esteem and self-respect to the point of morbidity. Indeed, the prominence of this motif in *Poor Folk* already reveals a tension in Dostoevsky's work that will have important consequences later. In *Poor Folk*, this tension between the spiritual and the material is still latent and in a state of equilibrium; the emphasis accorded the spiritual (or, if one prefers, the moral-psychological) dimension of human experience only heightens the pathos of the material injustices that Dostoevsky's characters have to suffer. But when, beginning in the early 1860s, an aggressive and blinkered materialism became the ideology of Russian radicalism, Dostoevsky broke with the radicals in defense of the "spiritual" in a broad sense. This opposition between the satisfaction of man's material needs and his innate moral-psychic needs will one day, of course, culminate in the Legend of the Grand Inquisitor.

It turns out that the assistance of the General, though it allows Devushkin to cope with his most pressing necessities, does not solve his human problem. The beginning of the end for Devushkin occurs when the book shifts from the theme of poverty to that of the impossibility of retaining Varvara. That the General's charitable gesture did not solve *all* of Devushkin's problems for good indicates that Dostoevsky was projecting his theme in a wider context, where the social is only one component of a still more complex human imbroglio. And the fate of Gorshkov, who dies on the very day he is fully vindicated and restored to honor and security, again illustrates Dostoevsky's awareness of human problems for which, properly speaking, there is no social solution at all.

One other motif also suggests that Dostoevsky intended a widening of the thematic horizon at this point. For while earlier Devushkin revolts explicitly only against the injustices of the social hierarchy, at the very end of the book there is the timid beginning of a revolt against the wisdom of God himself.

---

[6] Belinsky's article is reprinted in *DRK*, 24.

When Varvara announces her acceptance of the marriage proposal and places her fate in God's "holy, inscrutable power," Devushkin replies, "Of course, everything is according to God's will; that is so, that certainly must be so, that is, it certainly must be God's will in this; and the Providence of the Heavenly Creator is blessed, of course, and inscrutable, and it is fate too and they are the same. . . . Only Varinka, how can it be so soon? . . . I . . . I will be left alone" (1: 101–102). One catches here a glimpse of the future metaphysical Dostoevsky moving out beyond the confines of the question of social justice, or rather taking it only as his point of departure.

Poor Folk, as well as being at its core a moving plea for social commiseration, is also a highly self-conscious and complex little creation. All through the eighteenth century, the sentimental epistolary novel had been the form in which models of virtue and sensibility, such as Richardson's Clarissa Harlowe and Rousseau's Julie, or poetic and exalted souls, such as Goethe's Werther, had poured forth their lofty feelings and noble thoughts. The epistolary novel had thus become a vehicle for high-flown romantic sentiment, and its central characters were always exemplary figures from the point of view of education and breeding. Indeed, the underlying social thrust of the form was to demonstrate the moral and spiritual superiority of its largely bourgeois protagonists to the corrupt world of aristocratic class privilege in which they lived. Dostoevsky uses the form for much the same purpose in relation to a much lower social class. But, since the sentimental epistolary novel had traditionally become identified with highly cultivated and emotionally exalted characters, he took a considerable artistic risk in doing so.

To portray the abortive romance of an elderly copy clerk and a dishonored maiden in this sentimental pattern was to violate the hitherto accepted conventions of narrative, but we can see that Dostoevsky did so very self-consciously. In the slum boardinghouse where Devushkin has rented a corner of the kitchen, the two servants are called Teresa and Faldoni (not their real names, of course, but presumably an invention of the caustic littérateur Ratazyaev). Not only had Karamzin's *Letters* made the names of these two heroic lovers famous in Russia, their story had also furnished the subject for a French epistolary novel translated into Russian at the beginning of the century. Devushkin himself is dubbed a "Lovelace" by Ratazyaev, that is, identified with the aristocratic libertine who rapes Clarissa Harlowe. The incongruity of all these appellations illustrates the effect that Dostoevsky wishes to obtain. By elevating his Devushkin and Varvara to the stature of epistolary protagonists while demoting Teresa and Faldoni to the level of comic caricatures (Teresa is "a plucked, dried-up chicken," Faldoni "a red-haired, foul-tongued Finn, with only one eye and a snub nose") (1: 23),

Dostoevsky implicitly claims for his lowly characters the respect and attention hitherto accorded the much more highly placed sentimental heroes and heroines. And by inviting the reader mentally to compare Devushkin and Lovelace, Dostoevsky exhibits the moral preeminence of the humble clerk over the brilliant but selfish and destructive aristocrat.

The originality of Dostoevsky's use of the sentimental epistolary form, as V. V. Vinogradov has remarked, stands out against the background of the considerable literary tradition already existing for the portrayal of the St. Petersburg bureaucratic scribe (or *chinovnik*, as he is known in Russian). This tradition, which goes back to the 1830s, treated such a character only as material for the burlesque anecdote and satirical sketch; and one finds protests as early as 1842 against the unfair caricatures of the *chinovnik* that had become so popular a literary fashion.[7] Gogol's "The Overcoat" derives from this tradition, and keeps much of its jeering, jocular, clubroom-anecdotal tone. Even though Gogol interjects a sentimental plea for pity in the midst of the burlesque anecdote, this plea is still made from a point of view outside of and superior to the character. The unexpected passage thus clashes with the contemptuous tone and treatment accorded Akaky Akakievich[8] in the rest of the story and produces rather the effect of a tacked-on moral. Dostoevsky, on the other hand, by casting the theme of the shabby and ridiculous *chinovnik*—hitherto only a comic butt—in the form of the sentimental epistolary novel, breaks the satirical pattern and integrates his "philanthropic" theme with his form.

Dostoevsky's contemporaries saw him primarily as a follower of Gogol; recent critics have focused on his "parodistic" transformation of Gogolian characters and motifs, which he converts from the tonality of grotesque, fantastic comedy into that of sentimental tragicomedy. These points of view, however, are not mutually exclusive. Dostoevsky does reverse those *stylistic* features of "The Overcoat" that tend to ridicule Akaky Akakievich. The effect of this reversal, though, is not to *undermine* the significance of Gogol but rather to *strengthen* his overt "humanitarian" theme. Gogol's narrative technique works to create a comic distance between character and reader that defeats emotional identification; Dostoevsky counteracts the purely satirical features of the model by taking over its elements and, through his use of the sentimental epistolary form, reshaping them to accentuate Devushkin's humanity and sensibility. There is no term known to me that quite fits this process of formal parody placed in the service of thematic reinforcement. Far from being the antagonistic relation of a parodist to his model, it more resembles that of a sympathetic critic endowed with the creative ability to reshape a work so as to bring its form into harmony with its

---

[7] V. V. Vinogradov, *Evolutsiya Russkogo naturalizma* (Leningrad, 1929), 311–338. This is part 2 of Vinogradov's classic study of *Poor Folk*.

[8] His very name is derived from the Russian word for "doo-doo" (shit), *kaki*.

content. Both *Poor Folk* and "The Overcoat" contain the same Gogolian mixture of "laughter through tears," but in different proportions; laughter is uppermost for Gogol, while for Dostoevsky it is tears that predominate.[9]

———■———

Dostoevsky's novel also incorporates hints as to the more immediate literary ancestry of the new treatment he now accords the *chinovnik*. Indeed, one of the most striking features of *Poor Folk*, as A. Beletsky remarked long ago, is precisely its "literariness," the numerous references and reflections on the current literary scene that Dostoevsky manages to work into its pages.[10] Devushkin and Varvara send each other books to read and comment on their impressions—Devushkin even dreams at one point of publishing a volume of his own poetry and becomes self-conscious about his "style." Their remarks add up to nothing less than a self-commentary on the work provided by the author—a commentary that climaxes in Devushkin's reaction to two stories, Pushkin's "The Station Master" and Gogol's "The Overcoat."

Varvara lends Devushkin a copy of Pushkin's *Tales of Belkin*, and the story "The Station Master" particularly stirs him. "You know I feel exactly the same as in the book," he informs her, "and I have been at times in exactly the same position as, for instance, Samson Vyrin, poor fellow" (1: 59). Vyrin is the stationmaster who, out of his good nature and his respectful docility to his betters, allows a young nobleman to run off with his beautiful daughter. The old man drowns his despair in drink and dies of a broken heart, and the story is delineated by Pushkin with genuine sympathy for his suffering. Devushkin weeps profusely over this sentimental tale, which prefigures what he foresees for Varvara and himself, and he says prophetically: "Yes, it's natural. . . . It's living! I've seen it myself; it's all about me."

"The Overcoat," however, arouses Devushkin to a violently antagonistic outburst. What particularly incenses him is Gogol's supercilious depiction of Akaky Akakievich's life and character traits in a fashion that Devushkin finds personally insulting and profoundly untrue. By what right, he asks indignantly, "here under your very nose . . . [does] someone make a caricature of you?" (1: 62). Nor is he impressed by the one passage containing the plea to treat Akaky as a brother. What the author *should* have added, he asserts, is that he was "kindhearted, a good citizen, that he did not deserve such treatment from his fellow clerks, obeyed his superiors . . . believed in God and died (if one insists that he abso-

---

[9] Victor Terras, *The Young Dostoevsky, 1846–1849* (The Hague, 1969), 14–15; for discussions of parody, see Wido Hempel, "Parodie, travestie und pastiche," *Germanische-Romanische Monatsschrift* 46 (April 1965), 150–175, and Yu. Tynyanov, "Dostoevsky i Gogol (K teorii parodii)," in *Texte der Russischen Formalisten*, ed. Jurij Striedter (Munich, 1969): 1: 301–371.

[10] Cited in V. I. Kuleshov, *Naturalnaya shkola v literature XIX veka* (Moscow, 1965), 256.

lutely has to die), mourned by all" (1: 62–63). Devushkin also thinks the story would be improved if it had a happy ending.

While Dostoevsky does not conform to this demand of Devushkin's uncultivated taste for a sentimental tale with an edifying moral at the end, he does move in that direction. For he depicts the sad story of Devushkin's life in the tenderhearted fashion of Pushkin's sentimentalism in "The Station Master." Retaining the "naturalism" of detail and décor associated with the comic tradition of the portrayal of the *chinovnik*, Dostoevsky unites it with the tearful strain of Russian sentimentalism that goes back to Karamzin; and this fusion created an original artistic current within the Natural School—the current of sentimental naturalism—which quickly found imitators and became an independent, if minor, literary movement.[11]

Dostoevsky also carried on a running polemic with the Romantic enemies of the Natural School and with those literary jobbers who exploited the latest fashions solely out of pecuniary motives. Ratazyaev is the first of Dostoevsky's many unflattering portraits of the literary tribe, and it is interesting to see how early this deep-seated antipathy to his fellow writers set in. Ratazyaev is a versatile hack who knocks out works in various genres, and Devushkin, terribly impressed, transcribes sample passages for Varvara's edification from such masterpieces as *Italian Passions* or *Yermak and Zuleika*. These give Dostoevsky the opportunity to parody Romantic novels in the high-society style of Marlinsky, and to poke fun at the dime-a-dozen imitators of Scott: "What is the poor maiden [Zuleika], nurtured amid the snows of Siberia in her father's *yurta* to do in your cold, icy, soulless, selfish world?" (1: 52–53). Ratazyaev, naturally, does not think much of "The Station Master" because now, he tells Devushkin, all that is "old-fashioned," and physiological sketches are all the rage (1: 60).

These parodies serve by contrast to deepen the characterization of Devushkin; and they serve also as a background to heighten the moral elevation of his own life. For Devushkin is *in fact* living the life of love and is *really* engaged in the struggle against "a cold, icy, soulless, selfish world" that these bombastic exaggerations merely counterfeit. Dostoevsky thus uses the implicit relation of his form to the literary tradition, the direct comment of his characters, and satirical parody to endow his pathetic-sentimental story with an "ideological" dimension that defines his strikingly independent position among the social-literary currents of the 1840s.

---

[11] Vinogradov, *Evolutsiya*, 390.

CHAPTER 8

Dostoevsky and the Pléiade

Belinsky's excitement over the manuscript of *Poor Folk* quickly made Dostoevsky's name a byword among his circle, and the fame of the new young author spread throughout the literary community even before the publication of the novel in January 1846. Panaev, who paid Dostoevsky the compliment of immediately beginning to imitate his manner, wrote several years later: "We carried him in our arms through the streets of the city, and, exhibiting him to the public, cried: 'Here is a little genius just born, and whose works in time will kill off all the rest of the literature past and present. Bow down! Bow down!' We trumpeted his name everywhere, in the streets and in the salons."[1] The ironic tone of this passage reflects the later attitude of the Belinsky Pléiade to Dostoevsky, but it also confirms the enormous acclaim that he received even before his first novel appeared in the *Petersburg Almanac*, a collection of writing of the Natural School edited by Nekrasov.

With his usual impetuosity and wholeheartedness, Belinsky immediately adopted the young author as an intimate and spoke of him to others with unconstrained affection. "'Yes,' [Belinsky] used to say proudly," recalls Turgenev, "as though he had himself been responsible for some terrific achievement, 'yes, my dear fellow, let me tell you it may be a tiny bird,' and he would put his hand about a foot from the floor to show how tiny it was, 'but it's got sharp claws.' . . . in his access of paternal tenderness to a newly discovered talent, Belinsky treated him like a son, just as if he were his own 'little boy.'"[2]

Dostoevsky thus became—for an all-too-brief season—the literary lion of cultivated Petersburg society, and the newfound glory of his position, the flattering adulation he received on all sides, would have turned the head even of a more balanced personality. In Dostoevsky's case, it opened the floodgates of a boundless vanity that, up to this point, he had kept tightly closed. His letters are now filled with a manic exuberance and self-glorification quite comprehensible under the circumstances. "Everywhere," he tells Mikhail, "an unbelievable esteem, a passionate curiosity about me. . . . Everybody considers me some sort of prodigy. I can't even open my mouth without it being repeated in all quarters

[1] Cited in *DZhP*, 121.

[2] Ivan Turgenev, *Literary Reminiscences*, trans. David Magarshack (New York, 1958), 148.

that Dostoevsky said this or Dostoevsky thinks of doing that. . . . Really, brother, if I began to recount all my successes, there would not be enough paper for them. . . . I tell you quite frankly that I am now almost drunk with my own glory."[3]

He reports to Mikhail that two aristocratic *littérateurs*, Count Odoevsky and Count Sollogub, have been asking about him, and that A. A. Kraevsky, the powerful proprietor of *Notes of the Fatherland*, had bluntly told Sollogub, "Dostoevsky will not honor you with the pleasure of his company." "This is really so; and now this petty little aristocrat has mounted his high horse and thinks he will crush me with the magnificence of his condescension."[4] Face-to-face with Sollogub, though, who called on him unexpectedly one day, Dostoevsky was nervous, confused, and frightened.

More important for Dostoevsky than such casual acquaintance with celebrity-hunters was his acceptance into the charmed inner circle of the Belinsky Pléiade. At first everything went perfectly with the Pléiade—or so it seemed to the eager young initiate, who had lived a solitary life lacking any true intimacy except with Shidlovsky and with his brother Mikhail. "Recently the poet Turgenev came back from Paris," he tells Mikhail, "and he attached himself to me at first sight with such devotion that Belinsky explains it by saying he has fallen in love with me! And what a man, brother! I have all but fallen in love with him myself. A poet, an aristocrat, talented, handsome, rich, intelligent, well-educated, and twenty-five years old. And, to conclude, a noble character, infinitely direct and open, formed in a good school. Read his story 'Andrey Kolosov' in *Notes of the Fatherland*. It's the man himself, though he was not thinking of self-portrayal."[5] There is a good deal of vanity in this passage, but also a touching innocence and an obvious need for genuine friendship—a need that caused him to mistake Turgenev's well-known but casual affability for a sincere inclination.

The passage was written the day after Dostoevsky had paid his first visit to the salon of the Panaevs, which had become the favorite rendezvous for Belinsky and his group. Weak-willed, good-natured, dissipated, with a knack for writing amusing satirical sketches of fashionable Petersburg life, the amiable Panaev was everybody's friend. His wife Avdotya was not only a famous beauty but also the most notable bluestocking of her time, who had achieved some notoriety as a novelist. Already, or soon to become, Nekrasov's mistress (he lived with the Panaevs in a peaceful *ménage à trois* for ten years), she was at the center of mid-nineteenth-century Russian literary life, and her *Memoirs* gives one of the best behind-the-scenes portraits of the period. "Dostoevsky visited us for the first time in the evening with Nekrasov and Grigorovich," she writes, "who had just

[3] *Pis'ma*, I: 84–85; November 16, 1845.
[4] Ibid.
[5] Ibid., 84.

begun their literary careers. It was evident, from only one glance at Dostoevsky, that he was a terribly nervous and impressionable person. He was slender, short, fair-haired, with a sickly complexion; his small gray eyes darted somewhat uneasily from object to object, and his colorless lips were nervously contorted. He already knew almost all of our guests, but, clearly, he was disconcerted and did not take part in the general conversation. Everyone tried to involve him, so as to overcome his shyness, and to make him feel that he was a member of the circle."[6]

Once Dostoevsky's original diffidence had worn off his manner changed completely, and he began to display in public the same uncontrollable vanity so noticeable in his letters. "Because of his youth and nervousness," Mme Panaev observes, "he did not know how to conduct himself, and he would only too clearly express his conceit as an author and his high opinion of his own literary talent. Stunned by the unexpected brilliance of his first step in his literary career, showered with the praises of competent literary judges, he could not, as an impressionable person, conceal his pride vis-à-vis other young writers whose first works had started them modestly on the same career. With the appearance of new young writers in the circle, trouble could be caused if they were rubbed the wrong way by his irritability and his haughty tone, implying that he was immeasurably superior to them in talent."[7]

All the evidence agrees that Dostoevsky's behavior with the Pléiade would have caused difficulties with a group of saints, not to speak of a circle of young and not-so-young writers competing for public attention and each with his own vanity to coddle. The result, only to be expected, was that they turned on Dostoevsky after a certain point and made him the butt of a veritable campaign of persecution. To make matters worse, the leader of the pack, alas, was the same Turgenev whom Dostoevsky had believed to be his devoted friend. "They began to pick him to pieces," Mme Panaev tells us, "to exasperate his pride by pinpricks in conversation; Turgenev was a past master at this—he purposely drew Dostoevsky into argument and drove him to the farthest limits of irritability. Dostoevsky, pushed to the wall, sometimes defended with passion the most ridiculous views, which he had blurted out in the heat of argument and which Turgenev pounced on and laughed at."[8]

It was clear to an observer like Mme Panaev, who felt genuinely sorry for Dostoevsky, that he was an abnormally high-strung personality whose irritability and susceptibility should be discounted as the symptom of some affliction. This was apparently the view of Belinsky as well. When Turgenev would gleefully relate some of Dostoevsky's latest enormities to the critic, his response was,

[6] *DVS*, I: 140.
[7] Ibid., 141.
[8] Ibid.

"Well, you're a fine one! You latch on to a sick man, you egg him on, as if you didn't know that when he gets worked up he doesn't know what he's saying."[9] The situation was only envenomed by Grigorovich, a notorious purveyor of gossip, who reported to Dostoevsky everything said about him in his absence; and so Dostoevsky usually arrived at the reunions already boiling with rage.

Matters came to a head one day sometime in the fall of 1846, when Turgenev went too far in his mockery. Mme Panaev describes the scene: "Once, while Dostoevsky was present, Turgenev depicted his meeting in the provinces with a person who imagined himself a genius, and painted the ridiculous side of this individual in a masterly fashion. Dostoevsky, white as a sheet and quivering from head to foot, took flight, not waiting to hear the rest of Turgenev's story. I remarked to them all: why drive Dostoevsky out of his mind like that? But Turgenev was in the very highest spirits and carried away the others, so that nobody paid any attention to Dostoevsky's sudden exit. . . . From that evening, Dostoevsky no longer visited us, and even avoided meeting any member of the circle in the street. . . . He saw only [Grigorovich], who reported that Dostoevsky abused us vehemently . . . that he had become disenchanted with all of us, that all [of us] were envious, heartless, and worthless people."[10] By November 1846 Dostoevsky writes to Mikhail, "They [the Pléiade] are all scoundrels eaten up with envy."[11]

———■———

The persecution of the Pléiade turned Dostoevsky's life into sheer torture. His physical and nervous equilibrium had already shown signs of fragility, and it buckled completely under the new strain. In the spring of 1846 Dostoevsky suffered what he describes as "a severe shock to the whole nervous system."[12] This shock, according to the diagnosis of the time, had caused an excessive influx of blood to the heart and resulted in an inflammation of that organ; it was checked by the application of leeches and two bloodlettings. Dostoevsky was declared out of danger after this treatment but was advised to follow a severe diet, to avoid strong emotions, and to lead an orderly and regular life—advice more easily given, in his case, than followed. In the late spring Dostoevsky's friend Valerian Maikov suggested that he consult Dr. Stepan Yanovsky, a young medical man just then establishing his practice. Much interested in literature, Yanovsky struck up a friendship with Dostoevsy that lasted for the remainder of their lives. His reminiscences of Dostoevsky in the mid-1840s contain details about his health, although, unfortunately, Yanovsky refers specifically only to a "local

---

[9] Ibid., 142.
[10] Ibid., 142–143.
[11] *Pis'ma*, I: 102; November 26, 1846.
[12] Ibid., 90; April 26, 1846.

5. F. M. Dostoevsky in 1847

ailment" that took several months to cure.[13] (Such discretion leads one to suspect that the ailment might have been venereal.)

After a few weeks the two young men became fast friends; and Dostoevsky also consulted Yanovsky about the nervous disorders that continued to plague his life. These had grown worse since the days when he believed that someone was snoring beside him at night; now they took the form of veritable "hallucinations," which he was afraid heralded the onset of what he called a "*kondrashka*" (apoplexy), that is, one of his fainting fits. While reassuring Dostoevsky that his "hallucinations" were the result of nerves, Yanovsky does report one severe attack of "apoplexy" during the summer of 1847.

So far as Dostoevsky's hallucinations are concerned, there is nothing but the report of their existence to be gleaned from Yanovsky's pages. It is likely, though, that Dostoevsky describes them in *The Insulted and Injured* (1861), a novel that contains many autobiographical details about his life during the mid-1840s. The narrator, an impoverished young author, writes: "I gradually began at dusk to sink into that condition which is so common with me now at night in my

[13] See *DVS*, I: 154–157.

illness, and which I call *mystic terror*. It is a most oppressive, agonizing state of terror of something that I cannot define, something ungraspable and outside the natural order of things, but which may yet take shape this very minute, as though in mockery of all the conclusions of reason, and come to me and stand before me as an undeniable fact, hideous, horrible, and relentless. . . . [I]n spite of all the protests of reason, . . . the mind . . . loses all power of resistance. It is unheeded, it becomes useless, and this inward division intensifies the agony of suspense. It seems to me something like the anguish of people who are afraid of the dead" (3: 208).

Dostoevsky later described the same symptoms in conversation with Vsevolod Solovyev, the famous historical novelist. "Two years before Siberia," he said, "at the time of my various literary difficulties and quarrels, I was the victim of some sort of strange and unbearably torturing nervous illness. I cannot tell you what these hideous sensations were; but I remember them vividly; it often seemed to me that I was dying, and the truth is—real death came and then went away again." [14] His hallucinations contributed to undermine his psychic balance and to make it impossible for him to control his emotions in the face of opposition or hostility.

———■———

All sorts of rumors and stories ridiculing Dostoevsky now began to make the rounds in Petersburg literary circles. At the end of 1846 a satirical poem about Dostoevsky, jointly written by Turgenev and Nekrasov, circulated in manuscript. Called "The Knight of the Rueful Countenance," it labels Dostoevsky a "pimple" on the face of Russian literature, jeers at his inflated opinion of his literary prowess, and ridicules him for having fainted dead away on being presented to a beautiful, aristocratic society belle who wanted to meet the author of *Poor Folk*.[15] This humiliating incident actually occurred at a ball given by Count Vielgorsky at the beginning of 1846.

If Dostoevsky displays such a remarkable ability to portray feelings and states of suspicion, persecution, and exasperation reaching the pitch of hysteria, and if he has a tendency to see human relations in terms of a struggle for psychic domination, the reason is surely that he was all too familiar with such phenomena in his own psyche. The combination of excessive vainglory and egoism with an equal desire for acceptance and love is one that he often depicted, and these same incompatibles are manifest in his disastrous relations with the Pléiade.

These unhappy occurrences led to some critical self-scrutiny. One of the most poignant letters contains an apology for Dostoevsky's behavior during a holiday

[14] *DVS*, 2: 191.
[15] It is reprinted in *DZhP*, 121–122.

6. Feodor's older brother,
M. M. Dostoevsky, in 1847

at Revel with his brother, and reveals his inability—which he would later embody in so many of his characters—to harmonize his true inner sentiments with
his outward behavior. "I remember that you once told me," he writes Mikhail,
"that my behavior with you excluded mutual equality. My dear fellow. This was
totally unjust. But I have such an awful, repulsive character. . . . I am ready to
give my life for you and yours, but sometimes, when my heart is full of love,
you can't get a kind word out of me. My nerves don't obey me at such moments. I am ridiculous and disgusting, and I always suffer from the unjust conclusions drawn about me. People say that I am callous and without a heart. . . .
I can show that I am a man with a heart and with love only when *external
circumstances themselves, accidents*, jolt me forcibly out of my usual nastiness.
Otherwise I am disgusting. I attribute this lack of balance to illness."[16] Such
self-analysis goes a long way to explain Dostoevsky's genius for portraying the
contradictory fluctuations of love-hate emotions in his characters, and his limitless tolerance for the gap between deeply felt intention and actual behavior in
human affairs.

[16] *Pisʹma*, 1: 107–108; January–February 1847.

Dostoevsky had a stormy interview with Nekrasov prompted by reports that Nekrasov was reading the satirical poem about him aloud at various Petersburg gatherings, and in fact these malicious attacks remained a constant in the stormy relations beween the members of the Pléiade and Dostoevsky. Dostoevsky's entire attitude to the generation of the 1840s, as he later depicted it in his works, was profoundly affected by his misadventures with the Belinsky Pléiade. For he never tired of satirizing the discrepancy between the moral posturings of members of this generation and the petty sordidness of their lives and conduct. And if he felt particularly qualified to undertake the task of unmasking their evasions and hypocrisies, it was because he could always draw on his unhappy memories to confirm his brilliantly devastating exposures.

CHAPTER 9

Belinsky and Dostoevsky: I

Belinsky's age, as well as his authoritative position, excluded the intimate rivalry that pitted Dostoevsky against his contemporaries; and Dostoevsky, quite naturally, also felt an immense gratitude toward the man who had catapulted him to fame. Belinsky never joined in the persecution and openly expressed his disapproval; but despite all the good will on both sides, the acquaintance that began so promisingly in the late spring of 1845 ended in a quarrel in the first half of 1847. This short span of time remained one of the most important and memorable in Dostoevsky's life.

Belinsky was a powerful and passionate personality who stood squarely at the center of the Russian culture of his time; and the memoir literature concerning him is enormous. But the most heartfelt and moving tribute he ever received was the one written by Dostoevsky, remembering, almost thirty years later, the exalted state of rapture in which he had emerged after his first interview with the great critic. "I left in a state of ecstasy. I stopped at the corner of his house, looked up at the sky, at the luminous day, at the passersby, and with my whole being I felt that a solemn moment had occurred in my life, a decisive cleavage; something entirely new had begun, but something that I had not anticipated even in my most impassioned dreams. . . . 'Oh, I will be worthy of that praise; and what people, what people! . . . such men are only to be found in Russia; they are alone, but they alone have the truth, and . . . the good and the true, always conquer and triumph over vice and evil. We shall win; oh, to be of them, with them!' . . . That was the most wonderful moment in all my life."[1]

Dostoevsky's period of elation, however, ended with the publication of *Poor Folk*. The book was attacked vehemently from many sides, the main criticisms being that it was terribly long-winded, tedious, and its language too obviously an imitation of Gogol's stylistic mannerisms. He was cheered by the prospect of an impending critical campaign in his favor led by Belinsky, which would include lengthy articles by Odoevsky and Sollogub (he now called the latter "my friend"). "In me," he had told Mikhail just before the novel was published, "they find a new original current (Belinsky and others) . . . I go deep and search for

---

[1] *DW* (January 1877), 587–588.

7. V. G. Belinsky in 1843

the whole by examining the atoms, while Gogol grasps the whole directly and thus is not as profound as I am."[2]

But the critical campaign in his favor never materialized; and the essay that Belinsky published a few weeks later in *Notes of the Fatherland* must have proved a bitter disappointment. Even before the publication of this article, Belinsky had begun to nourish reservations about Dostoevsky that he had tried (tactfully but unsuccessfully) to communicate to the young author. During the summer and fall of 1845, Dostoevsky was hard at work on his next important novel, *The Double (Dvoinik)*, and parts were read at Belinsky's. Annenkov remembers that Belinsky "constantly drew Dostoevsky's attention to the necessity of . . . acquiring a facility in rendering one's thoughts, ridding oneself of the complexities of exposition."[3] Belinsky apparently could not accustom himself to the author's then still diffuse manner of narration with its incessant returns to what had already been said. Dostoevsky, according to Annenkov, "heard the critic's recommendations out in a mood of affable indifference."[4] But while he may have been self-confidently indifferent to such tentative suggestions, made in the still friendly and private atmosphere of the Pléiade, the same advice had an entirely different edge

[2] *Pisma*, 1: 86–87; October 8, 1845.
[3] P. V. Annenkov, *The Extraordinary Decade*, ed. Arthur P. Mendel, trans. Irwin R. Titunik (Ann Arbor, MI, 1968), 151.
[4] Ibid.

when confronted in cold print. Every word of qualification struck a mortal blow at Dostoevsky's boundless vanity and overweening sense of self-importance.

The Double was published in *Notes of the Fatherland* early in February 1846, and Belinsky's article on Dostoevsky discusses both of his works. The general view of *The Double*, like his view of *Poor Folk*, is highly favorable. "For everyone initiated into the secrets of art, it is clear at a glance that, in *The Double*, there is even more creative talent and depth of thought than in *Poor Folk*."[5] But the negative criticism is equally unequivocal. "It is obvious that the author of *The Double* has not yet acquired the tact of measure and harmony, and, as a result, many criticize even *Poor Folk* not without reason for prolixity, though this criticism is less applicable here than to *The Double*."[6] Such remarks were instantly snapped up by the Pléiade and gleefully repeated. This was the moment that Dostoevsky suffered the severe nervous illness referred to earlier, and the shock of his disappointment obviously contributed to his malady. "All this," he tells Mikhail, "was hell for me for a time, and I fell sick from chagrin."[7] Dostoevsky managed to survive this blow, however, and his friendship with Belinsky apparently remained unimpaired.

Then, during the early fall of 1846, Dostoevsky unwittingly became involved in a rivalry that rocked all of Petersburg literary life and placed an additional strain on his relations with Belinsky. For the critic had broken with Kraevsky, the powerful proprietor of *Notes of the Fatherland*, and joined his friends Nekrasov and Panaev, who had obtained editorial control of *The Contemporary* (*Sovremennik*)—the famous periodical founded by Pushkin. All of Kraevsky's contributors were now summoned to choose between their old affiliation and their loyalty to Belinsky's literary and moral ideals.

Dostoevsky had already begun his customary system of taking advances for unwritten work and was heavily in debt to Kraevsky. Moreover, despite his reverence for Belinsky, his personal feud with the Pléiade had been getting worse, and he had now become friendly with another coterie of lively intellectuals, one of whose members, the talented young Valerian Maikov, had replaced Belinsky at the key post of chief critic of *Notes of the Fatherland*. Dostoevsky refused to align himself entirely on the side of *The Contemporary*, and the consequences of his effort to stay above the battle soon made themselves felt. "I have had the unpleasantness of quarreling definitively with *The Contemporary* in the person of Nekrasov," he writes Mikhail in November 1846. "He became annoyed because I continue to give stories to Kraevsky, to whom I am in debt, and because I would not declare publicly that I do not belong to *Notes of the Fatherland*."[8]

[5] *DRK*, 27.
[6] Ibid., 28.
[7] *Pisma*, 1: 89; April 1, 1846.
[8] Ibid., 102; November 26, 1846.

The very next month, Belinsky spoke of Dostoevsky again in a survey of Russian literature for 1846, and the terms in which he criticizes him are now much sharper and much less apologetic. Reading between the lines, we can glimpse Belinsky's suspicion that Dostoevsky's work was moving in a direction opposed to the one he would have wished him to follow. Though he does not renounce his protégé, the effect of his soaring compliments is considerably modified by a more serious objection. *The Double*, he says, also "suffers from another important defect: its fantastic setting. In our days the fantastic can have a place only in madhouses, but not in literature, being the business of doctors, not poets."[9] Such remarks, from the erstwhile ecstatic admirer of Hoffmann, are enough to justify Dostoevsky's charge that Belinsky "is such a weak person that even in literary matters he keeps continually changing his mind."[10]

As for Dostoevsky's next story, "Mr. Prokharchin," published in the October 1846 issue of *Notes of the Fatherland*, Belinsky shows no mercy. He finds it "affected, *maniéré*, and incomprehensible." As if accepting the personal accusations of the Pléiade against Dostoevsky, he writes that "this strange story" seems to have been "begotten" by "something in the nature of—how shall we say?—ostentation and pretension."[11] Nothing could have been more wounding to Dostoevsky, under the circumstances, than such a thrust from the man whose moral authority still remained for him unimpaired.

The final break between the two occurred sometime in the months immediately following the publication of this article. Belinsky's letters contain allusions to Dostoevsky that repeat the gossip making the rounds and express dissatisfaction with his work. Dostoevsky's stock, quite evidently, was rapidly falling to a new low, and the reports that he may have given Belinsky about his work in progress would hardly have restored him to the critic's esteem. For Dostoevsky abandoned the two stories he had intended to write for Belinsky's proposed almanac, which would have remained within the accustomed range of the Natural School, and had now surrendered to a new source of inspiration. "All that is nothing but a stale repetition of what I have long since said," he writes Mikhail at the end of October 1846. "Now more original, living, and luminous ideas are begging to be put on paper. . . . I am writing another story, and the work goes, as it once did for *Poor Folk*, freshly, easily, and successfully."[12] This work was "The Landlady" (*Khozyaika*), of which he speaks again enthusiastically three months later.

Belinsky could only have accepted the new departure Dostoevsky's work was taking as confirmation that the hopes he had once placed in the promising young

---

[9] V. G. Belinsky, *Selected Philosophical Works* (Moscow, 1948), 385.
[10] *Pisma*, 1: 103; November 26, 1846.
[11] Belinsky, *Works*, 385.
[12] *Pisma*, 1: 100; end of October, 1846.

writer had been illusory. For "The Landlady" was evidently a return to the style of Russian Hoffmannism that Belinsky now loathed with all the fury of his previous adoration. Writing of "The Landlady" in early 1848, Belinsky could not have been more crushing. "Throughout the whole of this story," he says, "there is not a single simple or living word or expression: everything is far-fetched, exaggerated, stilted, spurious and false."[13] The whole attitude toward art of the two erstwhile friends had now become diametrically opposed.

Dostoevsky no doubt seemed to Belinsky to be betraying everything that the critic had fought so hard to attain, and the literary ideals they supposedly shared. But Dostoevsky had never been as exclusively committed to the poetics of the Natural School as Belinsky probably believed on the basis of his impression of *Poor Folk*. At the very moment Dostoevsky was finishing up this work in 1845, he was also writing Mikhail, "Have you read *Emelya* of Veltman in the last *Library for Reading?*—what a charming thing!"[14] In this new work by Dostoevsky's old favorite, Veltman shuttles back and forth between the real and the imaginary in a Romantic style rejected in the 1840s as completely out-of-date. Dostoevsky had also chosen the epigraph for *Poor Folk* from Odoevsky's volume, *Russian Nights* (1844), whose stories and dialogues are the literary quintessence of the Romantic Schellingian spirit of the Russian 1830s.

———■———

It is clear to us now that Dostoevsky was experimenting with styles and character types that he was later to fuse together superbly. But it was difficult at the time not to conclude that, compared with the other young writers on the rise, he had simply lost his way. Between 1846 and 1848 Turgenev published a good many of the stories included in *A Sportsman's Sketches*; Herzen produced his novel *Who Is To Blame?* and a series of brilliant short stories; Goncharov made his impressive début with *A Common Story* and followed it with a chapter from his novel in progress, "Oblomov's Dream"—not to mention either Grigorovich's two novels of peasant life, *Anton Goremyka* and *The Village*, or A. V. Druzhinin's *Polinka Sachs*, which raised the banner of female emancipation. Compared to the array of such works, Dostoevsky's publications seemed relatively insignificant indeed.

The Double was attacked on two fronts, one stylistic and the other thematic. Decades later, even the Russian Symbolist Andrey Bely, both a connoisseur of Gogol and an admirer of Dostoevsky, wrote that "The *Double* recalls a patchwork quilt stitched togther from the subjects, gestures, and verbal procedures of Gogol."[15] Belinsky's remark about its chief character belonging in a madhouse,

---

[13] Belinsky, *Works*, 478.
[14] *Pis'ma*, 1: 78; May 4, 1845.
[15] Cited in A. L. Bem, *U istokov tvorchestva Dostoevskogo* (Prague, 1936), 143.

taken up by others, saw Dostoevsky as an imitative, sensational depicter of pathological states of mind. There is external evidence that Dostoevsky himself (as
well as others) thought of *The Double* primarily in relation to *Dead Souls*. "They
[Belinsky and the Pléiade] say," he writes Mikhail jubilantly on the day his new
work was published, "that after *Dead Souls* nothing like it has been seen in Russia. . . . You will like it even better than *Dead Souls*."[16] In revising the novel
nineteen years later, Dostoevsky eliminated most of the traces pointing from
one to the other; but the best way to understand *The Double* is to see it as Dostoevsky's effort to rework *Dead Souls* in his own artistic terms, just as he had already done in *Poor Folk* with Gogol's "The Overcoat."

Both *Poor Folk* and *The Double* are part of the same artistic endeavor to penetrate into the psychology of Gogol's characters and depict them from within.
Golyadkin, the protagonist of *The Double*, may be described as a composite of
the timidity and pusillanimity of Poprishchin in Gogol's "Diary of a Madman"
imbued with the "ambition" of Chichikov in *Dead Souls*, but the closeness of vision, the descent into his inner life, hardly creates any feeling of sympathy. The
mock-heroic tonality taken over from *Dead Souls*, which Gogol used for purposes of broad social satire, is now applied to a world shrunk to the level of
slightly off-color vaudeville farce; the picaresque adventure involves the search
not even for a large fortune but for a slightly higher office post and acceptance
into the charmed circle of a corrupt bureaucratic hierarchy. Dostoevsky thus
once again takes his departure from a Gogolian model and intensifies its effect,
but this time his aim is not to bring out more unequivocally the "humanitarian"
component of the original. Rather, it is to reinforce Gogol's acute perception of
the grotesque effects of moral stagnation and social immobility on character.
The result is a new synthesis of Gogolian elements, transformed and recast not
by sentimentalism but by a deepening Hoffmannian fantasy into a genuine exploration of encroaching madness. In this way, Dostoevsky accentuates the humanly tragic aspect of Gogol's still relatively debonair portrayal of social-psychic
frustrations.

Breaking the connection maintained in *Poor Folk* between Devushkin's poverty and his struggle for self-respect, Dostoevsky now emphasizes the latter
motif. His focus, becoming internal and psychological, concentrates on the effort of Golyadkin to assert himself, but this inevitably brings Golyadkin into
opposition with the existing rigidities of the social order. And Dostoevsky's
theme now becomes the crippling inner effects of this system on the individual—the fact that Golyadkin "goes mad out of *ambition*, while at the same time

---

[16] *Pisma*, 1: 81; February 1, 1846. Dostoevsky evokes this linkage in his original subtitle, *The Adventures of Mr. Golyadkin*, which recalls Gogol's subtitle, *The Adventures of Chichikov*. Just as Gogol
had written a mock-heroic account of Chichikov's "adventures" in trying to rise in the world, so
Dostoevsky was doing the same for Mr. Golyadkin.

fully despising ambition and even suffering from the fact that he happens to suffer from such nonsense as ambition" (13: 31).

———■———

The first several chapters of *The Double* give a brilliant picture of Golyadkin's split personality before it has disintegrated entirely into two independent entities. There is Golyadkin's evident desire to pretend to a higher social station and a more flattering image of himself—hence the carriage, the livery, the simulated shopping spree for elegant furniture as if he were a new bridegroom, even the marvelous detail of changing his banknotes into smaller denominations to have a fatter pocketbook. His pretensions to the favors of his imaginary beloved Klara Olsufyevna is only an expression of this urge for upward mobility and ego gratification, not its cause. During the first part, Golyadkin's "ambition" dominates his feelings of inferiority and guilt and manages to keep them in check. The movement of the action shows him, however unsuccessfully, still trying to impose himself on the world despite its rebuffs. Once the double appears, however, the process is reversed, and we find Golyadkin striving by every means possible to prove himself a docile and obedient subordinate who accepts the dictates of the authorities ruling over his life as, literally, the word of God.

It is in this latter part of the work that Dostoevsky's social-psychological thrusts become the sharpest. Golyadkin struggles against becoming confused with his double, who behaves in a fashion that the initial Golyadkin would dearly like to emulate but that he has been taught to believe is morally inadmissible. The double is of course "a rascal," but the *real* Golyadkin is "honest, virtuous, mild, free from malice, always to be relied on in the service, and worthy of promotion . . . but what if . . . what if they get us mixed up" (1: 172)! The possibility of substitution leads Golyadkin to accuse his double of being "Grishka Otrepeev"—the famous false pretender to the throne of the true tsars in the seventeenth century—and introduces the theme of impostorship, so important for Dostoevsky later and (with its evocation of *Boris Godunov*) so incongruous in this context.

The more threatened Golyadkin feels because of the machinations of his double, the more he is ready to surrender, give way, step aside, throw himself on the mercy of the authorities and look to them for aid and protection. He is ready to admit that he may even truly be "a nasty, filthy rag"—though, to be sure, "a rag possessed of ambition . . . a rag possessed of feelings and sentiments" (1: 168–169). The inchoate phrases that tumble off his tongue are filled with the mottoes of the official morality of unquestioning and absolute obedience encouraged by the paternal autocracy. "I as much as to say look upon my benevolent superior as a father and blindly trust my fate to him," he tells his superior Andrey Filippovich, in his desperate efforts to "unmask the impostor and scoundrel" who is taking his place. "At this point," says the narrator, "Mr. Golyadkin's voice trembled and two tears ran down his eyelashes" (1: 196). As the double, "with an unseemly little smile," had told Golyadkin in the important dream sequence of the preceding Chapter 10: "What's the use of strength of character! How could you and I, Yakov Petrovich, have strength of character?" (1: 185).

Some of the most genuinely amusing moments in the novel occur as Golyadkin, believing that he has received a letter from his beloved Klara setting a rendezvous for an elopement, sits waiting in the courtyard of Klara's house (taking shelter from the pouring rain under a pile of logs) for her to keep their supposed assignation—and at the same time, inwardly protests against such an unforgivable breach of the proprieties. "Good behavior, madame"—these are his ruminations—"means staying at home, honoring your father and not thinking about suitors prematurely. Suitors will come in good time, madame, that's so. . . . But, to begin with, allow me to tell you, as a friend, that things are not done like that, and in the second place I would have given you and your parents, too, a good thrashing for letting you read French books; for French books teach you no good," and so on (1: 221). The original version of *The Double* concludes shortly thereafter as Golyadkin is driven off in a carriage by his doctor, who suddenly becomes a demonic figure, and—but we are left hanging in the air! The work is abruptly cut short at this point on a note of Gogolian flippancy and irresolution: "But here, gentlemen, ends the history of the adventures of Mr. Golyadkin" (1: 431).

The haunting brilliance of Dostoevsky's portrayal of a consciousness pursued by obsessions of guilt and ultimately foundering in madness has never been disputed, yet it is genuinely difficult to pinpoint Dostoevsky's moral focus. One way of doing so is to see that for all his taunts at Golyadkin, Dostoevsky is even more sarcastic about the exalted eminences of the bureaucratic realm that glimmer before Golyadkin as his unattainable ideal. *They* are clearly corrupt to the core, and lack even that minimum of moral self-awareness responsible for Golyadkin's plight.[17] Golyadkin at least *believes* in the pious official morality to which everybody else gives lip service, and his struggle with the double is an effort to defend that morality from being betrayed. In fighting off the double, Golyadkin is really fighting off his own impulses to subvert the values presumably shared by his official superiors. This is probably what Valerian Maikov meant when he said that Golyadkin perishes "from the consciousness of the disparity of particular interests in a well-ordered society," that is, from his realization of the impossibility of asserting himself as an individual without violating the morality that has been bred into his bones and that keeps him in submission.

---

[17] This point is well brought out in F. Evnin, "Ob odnoi istoriko-literaturnoi legendy," *Russkaya Literatura* 2 (1965), 3–26.

Yet Dostoevsky's genuine indignation at the crippling conditions of Russian life, which offered no outlet for the ego to assert itself normally, did not turn him into a moral determinist willing to absolve the victims of all responsibility for their conduct. His very portrayal of a figure like Devushkin implied that debasing social conditions were far from being able entirely to shape character. As a result, Dostoevsky's work of this period often contains a puzzling ambiguity of tone because a character is shown *simultaneously* both as socially oppressed and yet as reprehensible and morally unsavory precisely because he has surrendered too abjectly to the pressure of his environment.

The Double suffered from being too imitative of Gogol, but it was also too original to be fully appreciated. For the complexities of Dostoevsky's narrative technique also posed a special problem for his readers. *The Double* is narrated by an outside observer who gradually identifies himself with Golyadkin's consciousness and carries on the narrative in the speech-style of the character. Its verbal texture thus contains a large admixture of stock phrases, clichés, mottoes, polite social formulas, and meaningless exclamations, which are obsessively repeated as a means of portraying the agitations and insecurities of Golyadkin's bewildered psyche. This is a remarkable anticipation, unprecedented in its time, of Joyce's experiments with cliché in the Gerty McDowell chapter of *Ulysses*, and of what Sartre so much admired in John Dos Passos—the portrayal of a consciousness totally saturated with the formulas and slogans of its society. The effect in *The Double*, however, was a tediousness and monotony that Dostoevsky's critics, and readers, were not yet prepared to put up with either for the sake of social-psychological verisimilitude or artistic experimentation.

And even though Dostoevsky's narrative technique per se no longer creates any barrier for the modern reader, the complexity of Dostoevsky's attitude still creates problems of comprehension. In isolating Golyadkin's imbroglio from any overt social pressure, and by treating both Golyadkin *and* the world he lives in with devastating irony, Dostoevsky tends to give the impression that Golyadkin is simply a pathological personality who has only himself to blame for his troubles. Even Belinsky, who might have been expected to grasp the social implications of Golyadkin's psychology, remarked that his life would not really have been unbearable except "for the unhealthy susceptibility and suspiciousness of his character" which was "the black demon" of his life.[18] In other words, Dostoevsky was simply portraying a case of paranoia and mental breakdown with no larger significance than that of a case history. And from Belinsky's remark to Annenkov that, like Rousseau, Dostoevsky was "firmly convinced that all of mankind envies and persecutes him,"[19] we can surmise how closely Belinsky associates the protagonist of *The Double* with his erstwhile protégé.

[18] V. G. Belinsky, "Petersburgsky sbornik," in *DRK*, 27.
[19] V. G. Belinsky, *Izbrannye pis'ma*, 2 vols. (Moscow, 1955), 2: 388.

This judgment set the pattern for a view of Dostoevsky's work that dominated Russian criticism until the end of the nineteenth century. In 1849 Annenkov, echoing Belinsky, accused Dostoevsky of being the leader of a new literary school (that included his brother Mikhail and Yakov Butkov, Dostoevsky's competitor as a portrayer of Petersburg slum life) specializing in the portrayal of "madness for the sake of madness."[20] Annenkov severely criticized this unhealthy taste for rather sensational and grotesque tragicomedy, in which he could not discern any more serious or elevated artistic aim. Such an accusation was of course unfair to Dostoevsky, whose "abnormal" and "pathological" characters can all be seen, on closer examination, to make a social-cultural point. But Dostoevsky perhaps relied too much on the reader to grasp the ideological implications of his psychology and to understand that the "abnormalities" of his characters derived from the pressure of the Russian social situation on personality. The result was an artistic lack of balance that led to a good deal of misunderstanding and has caused unceasing critical disagreement.

The "idea" embodied in *The Double*—the internal split between self-image and truth, between what a person wishes to believe about himself and what he really is—constitutes Dostoevsky's first grasp of a character type that became his hallmark as a writer. Golyadkin is the ancestor of all of Dostoevsky's great split personalities, who are always confronted with their quasi-doubles or doubles (whether in the form of other "real" characters or as hallucinations) in the memorable scenes of the great novels—such as the underground man, Raskolnikov, Stavrogin, and Ivan Karamazov—although the frame of reference in *The Double* is still purely social-psychological. In this early phase of Dostoevsky's work, Golyadkin's intolerable guilt feelings at his own modest aspirations primarily disclose the stifling and maiming of personality under a despotic tyranny.

Several short stories that Dostoevsky produced at this time are written from the same perspective as *The Double* and raise much the same critical issues. In each, Dostoevsky continued to explore the pathological effects on personality of the Petersburg world of giant chancelleries and terrified *chinovniki*, but without portraying this environment as in any way *specifically* responsible for the abnormalities he depicts. The result was a continuation of the confusion that had been caused by *The Double*, and an increasing dissatisfaction with Dostoevsky's works by the critics and, presumably, by most of the reading public as well.

[20] P. V. Annenkov, *Vospominaniya i kriticheskie ocherki*, 3 vols. (St. Petersburg, 1879), 2: 23.

CHAPTER 10

Feuilletons and Experiments

Despite the wounding criticism from Belinsky and others, the besieged and struggling Dostoevsky nonetheless continued along his own path. Weary with the narrow stylistic range of the Natural School, he felt his shift to a new style and subject matter as an inner release. "I am writing my *Landlady*," he tells Mikhail at the end of January 1847. "My pen is guided by a source of inspiration rising directly from the soul. Not like *Prokharchin*, over which I agonized all summer."[1] Even as inspiration coursed through him, however, and even as he had already begun to block out another major novel (*Netotchka Nezvanova*), Dostoevsky's chronic indebtedness forced him to keep a sharp eye on the literary marketplace and to snap up any assignments that could bring in a little extra cash. While rushing the completion of "The Landlady," he picked up an assignment from the *St. Petersburg Gazette*. The writer who supplied the feuilletons for this newspaper died unexpectedly, and the editor hastily filled the gap by appealing to some of the young St. Petersburg literati to furnish him with copy. Four feuilletons, signed F. D., were written by Dostoevsky.

All the up-and-coming young talents of the Natural School—Grigorovich, Panaev, Turgenev, Goncharov, Sollogub, Pleshcheev—wrote feuilletons, and Dostoevsky was simply joining a general literary trend that had originated in France. Starting out as a medium of publicity, this type of newspaper column branched out to describe urban types and social life, giving birth to the physiological sketch. Once the taste for such sketches had caught on, it occurred to Frédéric Soulié to unite them week by week with a loose narrative line, and this was the origin of the feuilleton-novel. The feuilleton allows the writer to roam wherever his fancy pleases and to display his personality. Indeed, as we learn from Belinsky, he is essentially "a chatterer, apparently good-natured and sincere, but in truth often malicious and evil-tongued, someone who knows everything, sees everything, keeps quiet about a good deal but definitely manages to express everything, stings with epigrams and insinuations, and amuses with a lively and clever word as well as a childish joke."[2] These words fit the personality

---

[1] *Pis'ma*, 1: 108; January–February 1847.
[2] Cited in V. S. Nechaeva, *V. G. Belinsky*, 4 vols. (Leningrad, 1949–1967), 4: 298.

assumed by the young Dostoevsky to the life.[3] With all their sly evasions, the feuilletons do express a good deal of what was preoccupying Dostoevsky—and many others like him—in the spring of 1847.

The first three of these articles display Dostoevsky's skill at slipping past the censorship and depicting educated society chafing at the tight reins by which they were being held by Nicholas I. His fourth feuilleton furnishes insight into a new vein of his production that begins in 1847 with "The Landlady"—a vein that no longer focuses on a *chinovnik* of limited mental capacities but rather on a character type of the intelligentsia, "the dreamer." Dostoevsky's dreamer emerges exactly at the moment when a general campaign was being carried on against the dangers of *mechtatelnost'* (dreaming, reverie) as a congenital malady of the Russian intelligentsia. Everywhere one turns in Russian culture of the mid-1840s, one finds evidence of this campaign. High-flown Romantic ideals and attitudes are denounced as leading to a debilitating withdrawal from the world and the cultivation of a self-satisfied attitude of exalted contemplation. Belinsky inveighed against those who, modeling themselves on Schiller's ideal of "the beautiful soul," believed they could transcend the conflicts of ordinary life.[4]

Belinsky was in effect denouncing Russian fiction of the 1830s, which, influenced by Hoffmann and German Romanticism, is filled with the dissonance between the ideal and the real. In those days, this lack of adjustment was felt to be a crushing indictment of the narrowness and limitations of the quotidian. And since it was only artists (and philosophers) who, according to the metaphysics of Romantic Idealism, were in inspired contact with the realm of transcendental truth, artists invariably turned up as the heroes of such creations. The classic expression of this theme in Russian literature is Gogol's "Nevsky Prospect" (1835).

However, Gogol's story stands at the borderline between the purely Romantic delineations of this clash between the ideal and the real and its later development in the 1840s. For Gogol does not weigh the values of the story heavily in

---

[3] Dostoevsky evidently found that the easy manner of the feuilletonist fitted him like a glove, and one never finds him later, even when presumably expounding ideas, writing anything that can be considered ordinary expository prose. His stance is always personal and intimate; his points are made not by logical persuasion but through sketching character types, dramatizing attitudes, narrating experiences and observations. The whimsical tone of the feuilletonist of the 1840s, though never abandoned completely, is replaced by that of the serious and sometimes choleric social observer, but his use of irony and persiflage remains the same, and so does the identification with the reader, who becomes an implicit partner in a dialogue. From this point of view, Dostoevsky's five-finger exercises in the 1840s mark the début of an essential aspect of his career. Among the most striking features of *Notes from Underground* is its artistic singularity; it seems to come, formally speaking, from nowhere, but it probably comes from the feuilleton. Such an origin would account for all of the original formal features of the novella, which are so baffling otherwise—the first-person narrator who takes us into his confidence to the point of embarrassment; the direct address to the reader, who is treated as an interlocutor; the apparent fortuitousness and haphazardness of the narrative sequence; the blend of irony and pathos.

[4] Cited in A. G. Tseitlin, *I. A. Goncharov* (Moscow, 1950), 62.

favor of the young artist Piskarev; there is something pathetic, rather than sublimely tragic, about his ignorance of the ways of the world. Only a short step separates Gogol's portrayal of the artist-dreamer from Dostoevsky's own portrait of the type in his Petersburg feuilletons of this period. In the interval between the two portrayals, though, came Belinsky's attack on Romanticism, which led to a complete reversal of the original Romantic relation between the ideal and the real. Now the dreamer (an abortive or inauthentic artist) becomes a symbol of the failure to grapple with and master the demands of life. This is the context in which, along with Goncharov, Herzen, the early Turgenev, and many others, Dostoevsky offers his own unique version of the dreamer character type and his conflicts.

In Dostoevsky's feuilleton, everything serves to nourish the dreamer's capacity for living in an artificial universe of his own creation. "Sometimes entire nights pass imperceptibly in indescribable pleasures; often in a few hours he experiences the heavenly joys of love or of a whole life, gigantic, unheard of, wonderful as a dream, grandiosely beautiful" (13: 30). The Petersburg chronicler, throughout his seemingly casual *causerie*, skillfully conveys all the smoldering frustration undoubtedly felt by the progressive intelligentsia. But nowhere else is the tempting siren song of *mechtatelnost'* rejected with more inner awareness of its delights and dangers! Although the cultivation of such delights brings with it an increasing incapacity to tolerate reality, and the chronicler ends by labeling such a life a tragedy, a sin, a caricature, he nevertheless asks, "are we not all more or less dreamers?" (13: 31).

———■———

Dostoevsky's apparent empathy for, and even identification with, the figure of the dreamer is what distinguishes his creations from the typical character type of the 1840s. The new turn taken by Dostoevsky's work in "The Landlady" is thus in the somewhat dated tradition of Gogol's "Nevsky Prospect." The style and plot-motifs, moreover, have been traced to an even earlier work of Gogol's, "A Terrible Vengeance." This story is part of *Evenings on a Farm near Dikanka* (1831–1832), where Gogol was still drawing inspiration from Ukrainian folklore and imitating the epic-ballad style of Cossack folk-tales. "A Terrible Vengeance" has a heroine with the same name as the heroine of "The Landlady" (Katerina); she too is loved incestuously by her father—a sorcerer and magician—who murders her mother; he exercises a mysterious and irresistible power over her that drives her to madness; and the story is composed in the highly stylized language of folk poetry.

There can be no doubt that "The Landlady" attempts to revitalize this Romantic folktale tradition. The dreamer character of the story, Vasily Ordynov, is supplied with all the essential traits of this type. The last survivor of an aristocratic family, he has inherited a small sum of money, allowing him to live a lonely and secluded life devoted to study. He is an old-fashioned Romantic Idealist dreamer, for whom art and philosophy provide equal and eventually converging paths to discovery of the highest truths. Dostoevsky stresses his isolation and sense of estrangement from other people and from the throbbing life of the Petersburg in which he lives, nourishing in proud solitude the flattering belief that he has been singled out for great creative achievement. Like the unhappy Piskarev in "Nevsky Prospect," a chance encounter has the most fateful consequences for Ordynov. He falls under the spell of the beautiful young Katerina, whom he first sees praying fervently in a church and in whose face he discerns "traces of childlike fear and mysterious horror." Accompanying her is her father, Murin, the mysteriously enthralling central figure, whose "fiery, feverishly glowing eyes flashed a haughty, prolonged stare" (1: 267–268).

Moved by an irresistible impulse, Ordynov rents a room in their flat, and from this point on the story becomes a string of incidents, one more incredible and sensational than the last. Ordynov falls ill and lies in a constant state of delirium; when not out of his mind with fever, he is swooning with sensual ecstasy from Katerina's caresses. She alternates between passionate embraces with Ordynov and enraptured attention to Murin as he reads from the heretical books of the *raskolniki* or tells wild tales of bandit exploits on the Volga. Murin tries to shoot Ordynov and falls into an epileptic fit. Ordynov, spurred on by Katerina, is on the point of killing the unconscious Murin, but fails when "he fancied that the old man's whole face began laughing and that a diabolical, soul-freezing chuckle resounded at last through the room" (1: 310). His failure to carry out this deed and free Katerina from Murin's spell marks the dreamer's defeat by the malignant power that also holds his beauteous landlady in thrall. Much of what occurs is so extravagant that Ordynov himself wonders repeatedly if he is not living through some sort of hallucination.

———■———

Dostoevsky definitely overdoes the use of Gothic and Romantic accessories in "The Landlady," and one can understand Belinsky's violent antipathy to the story. "Murin's eyes," he jibes, "hold so much electicity, galvanism, and magnetism that he might have commanded a good price from a physiologist to supply the latter ... with their lightening-charged crackling glances for scientific ... experiments."[5] "The Landlady" does not really succeed because Dostoevsky failed to endow his out-of-date Romantic framework with the same new significance that he had managed to give the sentimentalism in *Poor Folk* and the equally Romantic *Doppelgänger* motif in *The Double*. Nonetheless, the story is

[5] V. G. Belinsky, *Selected Philosophical Works* (Moscow, 1948), 478.

much more than the overheated Romantic phantasmagoria that Belinsky and all the others took it for. The passage of time has revealed this story to be among the richest of Dostoevsky's early works in anticipation of the future. For Dostoevsky was struggling here to give the basic theme of his *chinovnik* stories—the crushing of human personality in the Russian world of despotism and unconditional subordination—a much wider symbolic resonance in terms of Russian history and folklore.

Katerina's psyche has become crippled and distorted by her belief in Murin's occult powers, and these are presented not only as purely magical and pagan but are intertwined with the Christian symbols of Russian Orthodoxy. What ties Katerina to Murin is the fear and horror he has managed to instill in her through these mysterious powers, and which have now become transformed into a strange kind of "enjoyment." Murin himself is perfectly aware of what he has done to Katerina, and generalizes it, for the benefit of Ordynov, into a universal law. "Let me tell you, sir," he explains to the thunderstruck Ordynov, "a weak man cannot stand alone. Give him everything, he will come of himself and return it all. . . . Give a weak man his freedom—he will bind it himself and give it back to you. To a foolish heart freedom is no use!" (1: 317).

It is thus the theme of "freedom" that emerges at the center of "The Landlady" and that links the story firmly, on this level, with Dostoevsky's other works of the same period. Just as he has dramatized the fashion in which Devushkin and Golyadkin have been psychically crippled by the prevailing conditions of Russian society, so he now explores the same subject in a different style and manner. And to drive the point home even more decisively, he provides Ordynov, at the conclusion of the story, with the following reflections:

> He had constant visions of an immense, overpowering despotism over a poor, defenseless creature, and his heart raged and trembled in impotent indignation. He fancied that before the frightened eyes of her suddenly awakening soul the idea of its degradation had been craftily presented, that the poor *weak* heart had been craftily tortured, that the truth had been twisted and contorted to her, . . . and by degrees the free soul had been clipped of its wings till it was incapable at last of insurrection or of a free movement toward real life. (1: 319)

Seen in this light, the folklore aspect of the story and its evocation of the Old Russian past is significant. For it is the dark superstitions of this past—its religion of fear and eternal damnation—that have inculcated in Katerina a crushing sense of guilt and furnished the arms by which Murin has subdued and broken her spirit. What Dostoevsky seems to be suggesting here is the opposition between a religion of light and hope and faith in man and one, more traditional, of mysticism and fatalism—the same contrast, as we shall see, being made by

Belinsky at this time. From this point of view, it seems likely that Dostoevsky meant "The Landlady" as a symbolic critique not only of Slavophilism but also of Orthodoxy, so far as he, like Belinsky, then saw the latter as a religion of fear or terror.

"The Landlady" is thus of considerable interest in Dostoevsky's laudable (if artistically unsuccessful) attempt to transpose into another key and tonality the major theme of his works written according to the poetics of the Natural School. It is of even greater interest when we become aware that this story marks a decisive moment of transition in Dostoevsky's artistic maturation. The character of Katerina is the first in which Dostoevsky focuses on the psychology of masochism and begins to explore the unhealthy "enjoyment" that can be derived from self-laceration. Katerina is still a victim of Murin and all the dark forces that he represents, but she is also a victim of her inability to conquer the "pleasure" that she derives from her enslavement and degradation. A new dimension is thus added to Dostoevsky's portrayal of personality, which now moves in the direction of transferring to the individual some of the moral responsibility for his or her own plight.

Of crucial importance in the Dostoevsky canon as the first hint of this evolution from a social-psychological to a moral-psychological grasp of character, "The Landlady" also contains more limited anticipations of things to come. Dostoevsky never again tried to write so extensively in an epic-ballad style, but a similar haunting note of folk poetry occasionally appears, most notably in the lyrical accents of the crippled Marya Lebyadkina in *Demons*. And there is, indeed, a certain similarity in situation between Katerina and Marya that explains the stylistic echo. Katerina hopes that Ordynov has come to rescue her, just as Marya waits for Stavrogin and imagines him to be her "deliverer," but in neither case is the Russian folk-maiden delivered from the enchantment of evil by her "false" swain from the intelligentsia. In addition, Murin's contemptuous opinion about mankind's inability to endure "freedom," and his symbolic role as the representative of a religion of tyranny, clearly prefigures the awesome majesty of the Grand Inquisitor.

———■———

"The Landlady" is the first of Dostoevsky's fictional works in which the figure of the dreamer makes his appearance. One expects Ordynov to come into contact or conflict with the "real," but instead, his first, faltering emergence from isolation leads into a realm far more fantastic than anything he had ever imagined. To be sure, the world that Ordynov encounters is intended to represent the *psychic* "reality" of the Russian past impinging on the present. But Dostoevsky was not yet master of the artistic means that could have made this "reality" seem anything more than what Belinsky called it—an attempt "to reconcile Marlinsky and Hoffmann," in which everything was "far-fetched, exaggerated, stilted, spurious, and false." Dostoevsky's next effort in the same direction, however, happily corrects these two defects of "The Landlady." Romantic folklore is dropped entirely and the psychology of the dreamer is now placed squarely at the center of the artistic perspective.

The result is that charming little story, "White Nights" (*Belye nochi*), one of the two minor masterpieces (the other is *The Double*) that Dostoevsky wrote after *Poor Folk*. Charm is not a literary attribute that one ordinarily associates with Dostoevsky, but he was versatile enough to capture this elusive quality on the one or two occasions when he tried for it. "White Nights" stands out from the tragicomic and satirical universe of his early creations by the beautiful lightness and delicacy of its tone, its atmosphere of springtime adolescent emotionality, and the grace and wit of its good-natured parodies.

Both Ordynov and this new dreamer are similar in their sense of isolation and loneliness, but the dreamer in "White Nights" looks with friendly curiosity and benevolent interest on the rest of humanity. Just as in "The Landlady," the dreamer in "White Nights" makes his contact with reality by meeting a young girl—not, however, a pain-racked beauty like Katerina but a pert little miss of seventeen named Nastenka, betrothed to a young man who had gone to Moscow to establish himself. For one dazzling moment, encouraged by Nastenka, the dreamer obtains a glimpse of "real" happiness, but she flies to the arms of her intended when he returns from Moscow, and the dreamer is left to mull over this last of his dreams. The wistfully humorous lyrical extrapolations of the dreamer are, in part, taken over word for word from the portrait of this type in the fourth Petersburg feuilleton, and Dostoevsky conjures up once again, with even more detail, all the enchantments and fascinations of the extraordinary world in which he lives.

The most famous passage in his lengthy tirade is one that Dostoevsky added in 1860, when he revised the story and decided to give the dreamer a specific cultural genealogy. "You ask, perhaps, what is he dreaming of? . . . of friendship with Hoffmann, St. Bartholomew's Night, of Diana Vernon, of playing the hero at the taking of Kazan by Ivan Vasilevich, of Clara Mowbray, of Effie Deans, of the council of the prelates and Huss before them, of the rising of the dead in *Robert the Devil* (do you remember the music, it smells of the churchyard!), of Minna and Brenda, of the battle of Berezina, of the reading of a poem at Countess V. D.'s, of Danton, of *Cleopatra ei suoi amanti*, of a little house in Kolomna . . ." (1: 115–116). The passage contains allusions, so far as they can be identified, to Hoffmann, Mérimée, Scott, Karamzin, George Sand (perhaps!), Meyerbeer, Zhukovsky, and Pushkin.

Dostoevsky inserted this kaleidoscope of Romantic influences into "White Nights," and its sparkle now tends to conceal what probably stood out more in the original text—the parody of Romantic novels depicting desperate and undying love in high society and exotic climes. Hitherto, the narrator's inflamed imagination has battened on such enticing fare, and while his declamation for the benefit of the open-mouthed Nastenka is too extended to quote in full, one extract is indispensable to give the flavor of Dostoevsky's witty deflation:

> Surely they must have spent years hand in hand together—alone the two of them, casting off all the world and each uniting his or her life with the other's? Surely when the hour of parting came she must have lain sobbing and grieving on his bosom, heedless of the tempest raging under the sullen sky, heedless of the wind which snatches and bears away the tears from her black eyelashes? . . . And, good Heavens!, surely he met her afterwards, far from their native shores, under alien skies, in the hot south in the divinely eternal city, in the dazzling splendor of the ball to the crash of music, in a *palazzo* (it must be in a *palazzo*), drowned in a sea of lights, on the balcony, wreathed in myrtle and roses, where, recognizing him, she hurriedly removes her mask and whispering "I am free," flings herself trembling into his arms, and with a cry of rapture, clinging to one another, in one instant they forget their sorrow and their parting and all their agonies, and the gloomy house and the distant garden in that distant land, and the seat on which with a last passionate kiss she tore herself away from his arms numb with anguish and despair . . . (1: 117).

By the time he meets Nastenka, the bloom of such imaginary romances has long since begun to fade, and the dreamer has become aware of the insubstantiality of their deceptive delights. The meetings with Nastenka finally provide him with that one day (or rather, several "white nights") of real life, and he knows that as a result his own existence will be changed forever. The dreamer's love for Nastenka is untainted by selfishness, and he even tries to help her make contact with her elusive fiancé. When the latter appears at last, there is not a trace of jealousy or resentment in his response, even though he knows he is condemned once again to the gloom of his lonely chamber. "May your sky be clear, may your sweet smile be bright and untroubled, and may you be blessed for that moment of blissful happiness which you gave to another, lonely and grateful heart! My God, a whole moment of happiness! Is that too little for the whole of a man's life?" (1: 141).

"White Nights" thus terminates on a note of benediction for the one moment of "real" happiness that the dreamer has been vouchsafed. The splendors of the ideal and the imaginary fade into insignificance before the reality of love for a sprightly snip of a girl of glowing flesh and blood. This is Dostoevsky's vibrantly poetic contribution to the attack on Romantic *mechtatelnost'* so common in Russian literature of the late 1840s; and though his little story cannot compete with the novels of Herzen and Goncharov on the same theme, nowhere in Russian literature is it expressed with more sensitivity and lyrical grace. "White Nights" was the only one of Dostoevsky's minor stories to be greeted favorably by the critics, but it also provided the occasion for a friendly polemic with Aleksey Pleshcheev, who in response wrote his own "Friendly Advice," dedicated to Dostoevsky.

Pleshcheev's main character, also a dreamer, sounds very much like Dostoevsky's and even echoes some of his phrases. But he attains the object of his heart's desire, marries a wealthy and ordinary young lady—and then settles down to lead the most Philistine existence imaginable! For Pleshcheev, the dreamer's passion for Nastenka is itself only a less grandiose, more commonplace form of Romantic self-delusion. The Soviet critic who makes this point also remarks that the enticements of *mechtatelnost'*, even though thematically condemned, are nonetheless painted by Dostoevsky in the most glowing colors.[6] The power of imagination is glorified in the very act of seeming to censure its effects, and a good deal of the story's appeal certainly derives from this ambiguity. Indeed, Dostoevsky pronounces his negative judgment with such elegiac tenderness that one cannot help suspecting a greater sentimental attachment to the richness of Romantic culture than he would perhaps have been willing to acknowledge.

Indeed, Dostoevsky was tied to Romanticism by too many emotional fibers of his being to detach himself from it entirely. If he was always ready to satirize and parody the fatuity of Romantic attitudes, or their use as a screen for egoistic impulses ("in the foreground is of course himself, our dreamer, in his precious person"), he would nonetheless always continue to believe in the importance of maintaining the capacity to be stirred by the imaginative and the ideal. During the 1860s, the theme of Dostoevsky's early story would become one of the main issues at stake in the battle between the generations. And no matter how much Dostoevsky later belabored the pretensions and the moral vacuity of the Romantic generation of the "fathers," he would always prefer the latter to their offspring, who fanatically insisted on reducing "real life" exclusively to the matter-of-fact, prosaic, and even grossly material.

———■———

Discouraged with turning out copy for Kraevsky, and longing to write in peace and at leisure, Dostoevsky complains to Mikhail in 1846 that what he yearns for is "at last [to] work for Holy Art, a holy work carried out in purity and simplicity of heart—a heart which has never yet so trembled and been stirred as now by

[6] Yu. M. Proskurina, "Povestvovatel'-rasskazchik v romane F. M. Dostoevskogo *Belye nochi*," *Filologicheskie Nauki* 9 (1966), 133.

all the new images being created in my soul."[7] Dostoevsky has thus by no means abandoned the Romantic Idealist conception of art as only distinguishable in form, but not in substance, from religion, nor would he ever do so in the future.

At about the same time, though, Belinsky was expressing a preference for a socially didactic art as the only kind he could now endure. In December 1847 he writes to Botkin, "I no longer require any more poetry and artistry than necessary to keep the story true; . . . the chief thing is that it should . . . have a moral effect upon society. If it achieves that goal even entirely without poetry and artistry, for me it is *nonetheless* interesting, and I do not read it, I devour it. . . . I know that I take a one-sided position, but I do not wish to change it and I feel sorrow and pity for those who do not share my opinion."[8]

Dostoevsky and Belinsky had broken off relations sometime between January and April of 1847, and Belinsky's final judgment on his erstwhile disciple was a totally negative one. "I don't know if I've informed you," the critic wrote to Annenkov early in 1848, "that Dostoevsky has written a story, *The Landlady*—what terrible rubbish! . . . each work of his is a new decline. . . . I really puffed him up, my friend, in considering Dostoevsky—a genius! . . . I, the leading critic, behaved like an ass to the nth degree."[9] Nor, as we know, did the usually generous and warm-hearted Belinsky find any more favorable words to say about Dostoevsky as a person. "Of Rousseau, I have only read *The Confessions* and, judging by it . . . I have conceived a powerful dislike of that gentleman. He is so much like Dostoevsky, who is profoundly convinced that all of mankind envies and persecutes him."[10]

Even during his darkest days of despair over the poor reception of his works, Dostoevsky still clung to the hope that he could reverse the process of his downfall. He had begun to block out a new major novel probably as early as October 1846, and in December he writes Mikhail that he has agreed to give Kraevsky "the first part of my novel *Netotchka Nezvanova*."[11] Dostoevsky, we know, was repeatedly forced to break off work on both this novel and "The Landlady" in 1847 for journalistic assignments that brought in much-needed extra cash, though doing so with great reluctance. He knew that only a substantial literary success could halt his precipitous decline in public favor, and he was well aware that a new group of literary competitors was looming on the horizon. "A whole host of new writers have begun to appear," he had remarked uneasily to Mikhail in April 1846. "Some are my rivals. Herzen (Iskander) and Goncharov stand out

[7] *Pisma*, 1: 103; November 26, 1846.
[8] V. G. Belinsky, *Izbrannye pisma*, 2 vols. (Moscow, 1955), 2: 369–370.
[9] Ibid., 388.
[10] Ibid.
[11] *Pisma*, 1: 104; December 17, 1846.

the most among them." [12] In the December letter, he confesses to Mikhail, "I can't help feeling that I've begun a campaign against all our literature, journals, and critics, and that with the three parts of my novel in *Notes of the Fatherland* this year I will again affirm my superiority in the teeth of all who wish me bad luck." [13] It would take over a year, however, before the first installments of *Netotchka Nezvanova* began to appear at the beginning of 1849.

The unfinished state of *Netotchka Nezvanova* makes it difficult to obtain any overall sense of what Dostoevsky was trying to do; but it seems clear that the work was designed as a *Bildungsroman*, depicting the life history of Netotchka as written by her in maturity and reflecting the experiences that shaped her life. The direct influence of George Sand is felt in this novel fragment more strongly than anywhere else in Dostoevsky, and his young heroine was probably intended as a Russian analogue to Lucrezia Floriani, or to Sand's even more famous Venetian *cantatrice* Consuelo (in the novel by that name). The book would have been the Romantic autobiography of an artist, so beloved of novelists in the 1830s, and in choosing this old-fashioned genre as a model, Dostoevsky was following the same stylistic impulse that had led him to the sentimental epistolary novel in *Poor Folk*, the *Doppelgänger* technique in *The Double*, and the Romantic folktale in "The Landlady." In each case, he took a form that had become outmoded and attempted to revitalize it with a new, contemporary significance.

Judging by the three episodes that Dostoevsky completed, this significance would have centered on an immediate cultural issue. As a result of the concerted attack on Romantic values, doubts about the function and the status of art had begun to be expressed everywhere in Russian literature of the late 1840s. Dostoevsky wished to portray a character that unites a dedication to art with an equally firm commitment to the highest moral-social ideals. Netotchka's life begins in the shadow of an artistic obsession that disorients her moral sensibility. But, triumphantly overcoming this initial handicap, her love of art would go hand in hand with a sensitive and fearless moral-social conscience. With this work, then, Dostoevsky was endeavoring to steer a middle way between the discredited Romantic glorification of art and the temptation, so easily succumbed to by Belinsky, to discard the values of art entirely in favor of the utilitarian and the practical.

The question of the supreme moral-spiritual significance of art was one that concerned Dostoevsky deeply. He firmly believed that in following his own literary path he was not betraying the humane outlook that he fully shared wth the Natural School. The subtitle of the novel—*The History of a Woman*—makes clear that Dostoevsky, like George Sand, intended to emphasize motifs involving

[12] Ibid., 89; April 1, 1846.
[13] Ibid., 104; December 17, 1846.

the status of the female sex. Moreover, Netotchka's success in becoming a great artist in the face of her miserable origins would reveal all the wealth of neglected talent in the socially outcast and despised, as well as in her supposedly inferior biological status.

In all these ways, Dostoevsky was endeavoring to tap some of the interest in "the woman question" then so prominent on the Russian literary scene and that had already been utilized in such novels as *Polinka Sachs* and in Herzen's story "The Thieving Magpie." Herzen anticipates Dostoevsky in also having taken a female artist (a gifted serf actress) as the heroine of his tale, but he shows her destruction when she rejects the sexual advances of her owner and patron. Dostoevsky's aim, unprecedented in the Russian novel of his time, was to depict a talented and strong-willed woman who refuses to allow herself to be crushed— who becomes the main *positive* heroine of a major novel. In doing so he hoped once again, as with *Poor Folk*, to reestablish his independent position on the Russian social-cultural scene and offer an alternative both to Herzen's bleakness and despair and to Goncharov's unappealing submission to *meshchantsvo* (bourgeois practicality) in *A Common Story*.

Netotchka's earliest notions of art are colored by the egoistic cruelty of her stepfather, the artist Yefimov; and she remembers that "the idea became instantly established in my imagination that an artist was a special kind of person not like other people" (2: 62). This first part of Dostoevsky's novel contains one of the bitterest indictments of Romantic egoism in its "artistic" variety that can be found in the literature of the time. Only Dickens's Harold Skimpole in *Bleak House* (published four years later) can compare with the character Yefimov as a moral condemnation of the heartlessness of Romantic aestheticism. The second sequence of *Netotchka Nezvanova* whisks the heroine, by a miracle of fate, into that very world she had dreamed about under the influence of Yefimov's obsession. Here, Netotchka learns to understand the significance of her own twisted psychic history. She absorbs the moral that those who have suffered because of the egoism of others should not become oppressors in their turn, and various characters in her new family struggle with and manage to conquer the temptation of egoistic resentment.

The relations between Princess Katya and Netotchka are of particular interest, since they develop into the type of psychological duel that Dostoevsky would later use in so many variations. The impressionable Netotchka, starved for affection, falls passionately in love with the beautiful Katya in a fashion whose erotic overtones are perfectly explicit. Katya is aware of Netotchka's infatuation, but she refuses to respond to it because her fierce pride resents Netotchka's intrusion into a world over which Katya had herself reigned supreme. Katya is thus the first of Dostoevsky's "infernal women" whose wounded pride stands in the way of their acceptance of love and generates, rather, hatred and persecution of the lover; but in this early phase, where the drama is played out between children, the wound is not yet so deep that it can no longer be healed.

It is evident from Dostoevsky's portrayal of Katya that he was already a master of the love-hate dialectic that was to become so important a feature of his major works. In Katya for the first time it becomes completely self-conscious. When asked about her past behavior by Netotchka, she replies, "Well, I always loved you, always! But then, I was not able to bear it; I thought, I'll devour her with kisses, or I'll pinch her to death" (2: 220). This is the naïve form in which Katya explains her ambiguous feelings, which stem from the unwillingness of the prideful ego to surrender its own autonomy to the infringement represented by the temptation of love. In *Netotchka Nezvanova*, this conflict is still presented purely in moral-psychological terms, but the self-sacrifice of Netotchka (who takes the blame on herself for Katya's misbehavior), and Katya's response of love in return, already contain the emotive-experiential basis of Dostoevsky's Christianity. Salvation for Dostoevsky would always depend on the capacity of the prideful ego (which later becomes identified with the prideful intellect) to surrender to the free self-sacrifice of love made on its behalf by Christ.

The unfinished *Netotchka Nezvanova* is primarily of interest because it sheds so much light on Dostoevsky's internal evolution as a writer. Here he moves decisively beyond the limits of the Natural School and already stands at the threshold of the world of his major novels. The setting of his action is no longer confined to the slums of Petersburg or to the world of the bureaucratic chancelleries and their inhabitants, nor can his characters any longer be classified in the well-defined and by this time fairly conventional social-ideological categories of his earlier stories (the downtrodden people, the dreamer). For the first time Dostoevsky's horizon embraces the higher social sphere of the enlightened, cultivated aristocracy, and his people are now complex individuals grasped primarily in terms of their own quality of personality and in the light of Dostoevsky's fully elaborated and original psychology of sadomasochism. The significance of *Netotchka Nezvanova* is that it enables us to pinpoint this pivotal moment in Dostoevsky's literary career.

———■———

Starting out as a member of the Natural School and as a disciple of Gogol, Dostoevsky distinguished himself immediately by his psychological handling of social themes in *Poor Folk*. More and more, though, he became concerned with the psychic distortions suffered in the struggle of the personality to assert itself and to satisfy the natural human need for dignity and self-respect in a world of rigid class barriers and political despotism. But so long as Dostoevsky's stories continued to use the familiar iconography of the Natural School, a social causation was always at least implied for the psychic malformation of his characters—even if not stressed sufficiently to satisfy Belinsky. In "The Landlady," however, Dostoevsky suggested strongly for the first time that such malformations can lead to a masochistic "enjoyment" of self-degradation that reinforces the bonds enslaving personality and makes its captivity partially self-imposed. Nonetheless, the symbolism of the story still attributes the "cause" of Katerina's emotional imprisonment to a malevolent external force.

It is only with *Netotchka Nezvanova* that we can see how Dostoevsky's explorations of personality gradually led him not only to reverse the hierarchy between the psychological and the social assumed by the Natural School but also to entirely disengage his psychology from its earlier direct dependence on social conditioning. For here Dostoevsky brings the theme of sadomasochistic "sensuality" to the foreground as the major source of cruelty and oppression in human relations, and the conquest of such "sensuality" now becomes *the* overriding moral-social imperative. Even though the social position and relations of the characters serve to frame and motivate the action, Dostoevsky's focus is no longer on external social conditions and their reflection in the consciousness and in behavior (as with Devushkin or Golyadkin). Rather, it is on the personal qualities that the characters display in the battle against the instinctive tendency of the injured ego to hit back for whatever social-psychic traumas it has been forced to endure. The world of *Netotchka Nezvanova* is thus no longer exclusively social-psychological but has already become the moral-psychological universe of his later fiction. For the capacity to overcome the sadomasochistic dialectic of a wounded egoism—the capacity to conquer hatred and replace it by love—has now emerged as the ideal center of Dostoevsky's moral-artistic cosmos.

But all this exists as yet only in germ, as yet contained within the limits of a world where the conflicts have not been driven to the extreme and where nothing (except death) is irreparable. The truly tragic dimension of the later Dostoevsky is still lacking, the sense of the immitigable and the irreconcilable, the clash of contending values, each with its claim to absolute hegemony—love and justice, faith and reason, the God-man and the Man-god—which Dostoevsky alone among all the great novelists has known how to convey with such unrivaled force.

The last installment of *Netotchka Nezvanova* was published in the May 1849 issue of *Notes of the Fatherland* without the name of Dostoevsky as author. He had been arrested on April 23, and Kraevsky was forced to obtain special permission to use the manuscript he had already received from the political suspect now under lock and key. No more of the book was written, and Dostoevsky did not take it up again when he began to think of resuming his literary career six or seven years later. His name vanished from sight after his arrest, and what remained predominant until he returned was the negative verdict of Belinsky on everything he had written after *Poor Folk*. Belinsky had died a year earlier, on

May 28, 1848, and Dostoevsky's reaction reveals how deeply attached he still was, for all their disagreements, to the combative, volatile, and lovable figure of "furious Vissarion." Visiting Dr. Yanovsky the same day, Dostoevsky made his entrance with the words, "Old fellow, something really terrible has happened—Belinsky is dead!"[14] Dostoevsky remained to spend the night, and at three in the morning he suffered an attack of convulsions similar to that of his "*kondrashka*."

[14] Cited in *ZT*, 52.

CHAPTER 11

Belinsky and Dostoevsky: II

To the public and literary aspects of their involvement must be added the asserted direct influence of the renowned critic on the formation of the young man's convictions and beliefs. Thirty years later, Dostoevsky published two articles about Belinsky in his *Diary of a Writer*, and their burden is that Belinsky was the ideological mentor responsible for having placed Dostoevsky's feet on the path leading to Siberia.

Dostoevsky's account provides an irresistibly hagiographic version of the great drama of his conscience. Before meeting Belinsky, he had been a young, pure-hearted, idealistic, naïvely devout believer in the God and Christ of his childhood faith. It was Belinsky, the revered idol of Russian radical youth, who had succeeded in converting him to Socialism and atheism. The result had been his participation in subversive activity, and then his arrest, conviction, and exile to Siberia. There he rediscovered God and Christ through the Russian people, and came to realize that atheism could lead only to personal and social destruction. Dostoevsky's articles of 1873, however, do not quite jibe with what we know of his life.

Belinsky's name had become a slogan and a banner to successive generations of Russian radicals, and it is about this mythical or symbolic Belinsky that Dostoevsky was really writing in the 1870s. In a letter of 1871 to Nikolay Strakhov, who had objected to the violence of Dostoevsky's language about Belinsky, Dostoevsky replies: "I insulted Belinsky more as a phenomenon of Russian life than as a personality."[1] The portrait Dostoevsky sketched of him two years later is dominated by this impersonal perspective, and the result, as we shall see, is that he integrates his own personal history—even when the facts do not quite fit—into the general image he wishes to create of Belinsky's baneful effect on Russian culture as a whole.

———————— ■ ————————

By the time the critic and the young writer met in 1845, Belinsky's point of view had evolved in a manner that took Dostoevsky by surprise. When Belinsky

[1] *Pisma*, 2: 364; May 18/30, 1871.

converted to French Utopian Socialism in 1841–1842, he accepted a doctrine strongly informed by Christian moral-religious values. Saint-Simon had entitled the last work he wrote *Le nouveau Christianisme*, and all of French Utopian Socialism may be summed up under the same title. The Utopian Socialists directed their attention to the morality of the Gospels, and they saw Christ (much as Dostoevsky had done in 1838) as a divine figure come to prescribe the laws governing earthly life in the modern world and whose teachings, freed from centuries of perversion, were at last to be put into practice.

The "new Christianity" of Utopian Socialism was based on an opposition between the true religion of Jesus Christ—a religion of hope and light, of faith in the powers of man as well as in the beneficence of God—and a false religion of fear and eternal damnation that distorted Christ's teaching. Victor Considérant makes this contrast explicit in his *La destinée sociale*, one of the most widely read of all Socialist treatises in Russia during the 1840s. "Take care!" he warns the supporters of the old religion of fear, "you who condemn God to desire the humiliation and misery of man here on earth, . . . man in his strength and intelligence . . . will know that he has nothing to fear from [God], but everything to hope for."[2] A devout adherence to the new Christianity went hand in hand with fierce opposition to the established Church as a source of ignorance and obscurantism and as an ally of political reaction. Hence, in the same letter to V. P. Botkin announcing his conversion to a Socialism in which "Christ will pass His power to the Father, and Father-Reason will hold sway once more, but this time . . . above a new world," Belinsky scoffs at a friend who retains "his warm faith in the *muzhik* with the little beard who, sitting belching on a soft cloud surrounded by a multitude of seraphs and cherubims, considers that his might is right and his thunders and lightnings rational demonstrations."[3]

Meanwhile, however, the ideas of the German Left Hegelians had begun to penetrate into Russia almost simultaneously with those of the Utopian Socialists. Left Hegelianism was primarily a critique of religion, and the effect of its influence was to call into question the religious foundation of Utopian Socialist convictions. D. F. Strauss's *Life of Jesus* considered the New Testament to be not divine revelation but a mythopoetic expression of the historical aspirations of the Jewish community of the time. It was only a historical accident, Strauss maintained, that these myths had crystallized around the figure of Jesus Christ, who was merely one of the many self-proclaimed prophets of the period. Feuerbach's *The Essence of Christianity* was even more radical in its secularization of the divine, and argued that, instead of God having created man in his own image, exactly the opposite was true. The human species had divinized its high-

---

[2] Victor Considérant, *La destinée sociale*, 3 vols. (Paris, 1851), 2: 38.
[3] V. G. Belinsky, *Selected Philosophical Works* (Moscow, 1948), 165–166.

est attributes by projecting them onto supernatural beings and, in doing so, had alienated its own essence. The task of mankind was now to reclaim from the transcendent all the qualities that rightfully belonged to humanity, and to realize them on earth by incorporating them into social life.

Such ideas burst like a bombshell among the Russian Westernizers, already well schooled to appreciate them from their previous training in Hegel's thought. A copy of Feuerbach arrived in Russia in January 1842, and Annenkov remembers this book as having been "in everybody's hands" in the mid-1840s. "Feuerbach's book," he writes, "nowhere produced so powerful an impression as in our 'Western' circle, and nowhere did it so rapidly obliterate the remnants of all preceding outlooks. Herzen, needless to say, was a fervent expositor of its propositions and conclusions."[4] Belinsky, however, was not won over as quickly as Annenkov implies. He had, as he confessed himself, a congenital need for religion, and he was still arguing about God with Turgenev—just freshly returned from the philosophical Mecca of Berlin—in the spring of 1843.

Reporting on one such interminable colloquy, the novelist recalls Belinsky saying reproachfully to him, "We haven't yet decided the question of the existence of God . . . and you want to eat!"[5] By 1845, though, just a few months before meeting Dostoevsky, Belinsky had come to the conclusion, as he writes Herzen, that "in the words *God* and *religion* I see darkness, gloom, chains and the knout, and now I like these two words as much as the four following them."[6] These phrases mark the moment when atheism and Socialism fused together in Russia into an alliance never afterward to be completely dissolved. Not all the Russian Westernizers, to be sure, were willing to accept atheism as a new obligatory credo. T. N. Granovsky—a famous liberal historian at the University of Moscow, who was one day to sit for the portrait of Stepan Trofimovich Verkhovensky in *Demons*—refused to give up his belief in the immortality of the soul, and in the summer of 1846 he broke with Herzen over the issue—a rift that occurred almost simultaneously with Dostoevsky's first meeting with Belinsky.

—■—

Even though Left Hegelianism was militantly antireligious, at first it attacked only the historicity and divinity of God and Christ; the moral-religious values that Christ had proclaimed to the world were left untouched. Feuerbach in particular declared Christian moral-religious values to be the true essence of human nature; his aim was not to replace such values by others but to see them realized in the love of man for man rather than for the God-man. Soon, however, the

[4] P. V. Annenkov, *The Extraordinary Decade*, ed. Arthur P. Mendel, trans. Irwin R. Titunik (Ann Arbor, MI, 1968), 35.

[5] Ivan Turgenev, *Literary Reminiscences*, trans. David Magarshack (New York, 1958), 123.

[6] V. G. Belinsky, *Izbrannye pis'ma*, 2 vols. (Moscow, 1955), 2: 259.

rejection of the divinity of Christ led to a questioning of the moral-religious ideals that Christ had proclaimed, and this was greatly aided by the appearance of the last and most sensational of the Left Hegelian treatises, Max Stirner's *The Ego and His Own*. Stirner argued that the acceptance of *any* abstract or general moral value was an impediment to man's freedom and alienated the human personality as much as a belief in supernatural beings did. Of no group was he more scornful, no antagonist did he attack more mercilessly, than the Socialists and liberals still clinging to their general ideal of "humanity." What is fundamental for the individual ego, according to Stirner, is simply the satisfaction of its *own* needs, whatever these may be; his philosophy is that of a totally subjective and totally amoral self-aggrandizement.

From Annenkov we know that Belinsky was quite concerned with Stirner's book during the summer of 1847. "It has been proved," Annenkov reports him as saying, "that a man feels and thinks and acts invariably according to the law of egotistical urges, and indeed, he cannot have any others." To be sure, Belinsky did not take the word "egoism" in Stirner's narrowly selfish sense, and believed that individuals could eventually be made to realize that their own "egotistical interests are identical with that of mankind as a whole." [7] What is important, though, is Belinsky's evident willingness to accept Stirner's nonidealistic view of the roots of human behavior, the critic's desire to search for a new, more "practical" and "rational" foundation for his values. We find the same impulse at work in his attraction for the physiological Materialism of Emile Littré, and he now refers privately to the starry-eyed Utopian Socialists, with contemptuous obscenity, as "those insects hatched from the manure heaped up from the backside of Rousseau." [8]

Belinsky's important manifesto in the first issue of *The Contemporary*, defining the ideological line of the rejuvenated periodical, bears unmistakable evidence of the change in his ideas. "Psychology which is not based on physiology," he announces, under the influence of Littré, "is as unsubstantial as physiology that knows not the existence of anatomy." He foresees the day when "chemical analysis" will "penetrate the mysterious laboratory of nature" and will "by observations of the embryo . . . trace the *physical* process of *moral* evolution." [9] The Soviet historian of the journal, Evgenyev-Maksimov, remarks that "the recipes proposed by Utopian Socialism had already (1847) lost credit in the eyes of the majority of the contributors to *The Contemporary*. Skeptical and even contemptuous utterances concerning this tendency in Western European social thought are by no means rare." [10] These influential articles ridiculed such pillars of Utopianism as Pierre

---

[7] Annenkov, *Decade*, 211–213.

[8] Belinsky, *IP*, 2: 286.

[9] Belinsky, *Works*, 369.

[10] V. Evgenyev-Maksimov, *Sovremennik v 40–50 godakh* (Leningrad, 1934), 143–144.

Leroux, Cabet, and Victor Considérant and praised Proudhon's just-published *Système des contradictions èconomiques* for having abandoned fantasy and devoted itself to the study of economic laws governing existing society. In the last three years of his life, Annenkov observes, Belinsky "was concerned . . . with the new truths proclaimed by economic doctrines which was liquidating all notions of the old, displaced truth about the moral, the good and the noble on earth, and was putting in their place formulas and theses of a purely rational character."[11]

A feature of Utopian Socialist "religion" had been, as Maxime Leroy writes, "a divinization of the people,"[12] who were considered morally superior to their upper-class oppressors; and Belinsky also quickly abandoned this idealization of the oppressed masses. At the beginning of 1848 he defends Voltaire in a letter to Annenkov, even though the great Frenchman had "sometimes called the people 'vile populace.'" Belinsky justifies this insulting phrase "because the people are uncultivated, superstitious, fanatic, bloodthirsty, and love torture and execution." He adds that Bakunin (now an ardent revolutionary) and the Slavophils, by their excessive idealization of the people, have "greatly helped me to throw off a mystical faith in the people."[13] Such is the atmosphere of the last period of Belinsky's thought, which began shortly after Dostoevsky met him in 1845 and was certainly apparent in 1846. There is every reason to believe that Dostoevsky was familiar with its manifestations.

———■———

During the span of Dostoevsky's friendship with Belinsky, the critic was thus oscillating between a Feuerbachian "humanism" with moral-religious overtones and the acceptance of a more "rational" viewpoint shading toward mechanistic materialism and moral determinism. We should remember, however, that Belinsky had little use for intellectual consistency as such, and the quick portrait of Belinsky sketched by Dostoevsky in his two articles of 1873 coincides with the image that emerges from a study of all the other materials. "Valuing science, and realism above everything," Dostoevsky writes in his second article, "at the same time he [Belinsky] understood more deeply than anyone else that reason, science, and realism alone could construct only an anthill and not a social 'harmony' within which it would be possible for mankind to live. He knew that, at the foundation of everything, were moral principles,"[14] and he knew that in attacking Christianity, which was based on the moral responsibility of the individual, he was not only undermining the foundations of the society he wished to destroy but also denying human liberty. But Belinsky also believed, in Dostoevsky's view,

[11] Annenkov, *Decade*, 208.
[12] Maxime Leroy, *Histoire des idées sociales en France*, 3 vols. (Paris, 1946–1954), 2: 442.
[13] Belinsky, *IP*, 2: 389.
[14] *DW* (no. 1, 1873), 6–7.

that Socialism would restore the freedom of the personality and raise it to hitherto undreamed-of heights.

It is this Utopian Socialist Belinsky (perhaps still intermittently a "new Christian"), passionately concerned with the freedom of the individual personality,
who dominates in the second article, which includes the only direct public testimony that Dostoevsky ever gave about his participation in the Petrashevsky affair, which led to his imprisonment and Siberian exile, and the motives inspiring
him. His aim was to convince his readers of the 1870s that radicals were not
stirred to action by dishonorable motives: "the Socialism then . . . was regarded
merely as a corrective to, and improvement of [Christianity]. . . . All these new
ideas seemed in the highest degree holy and moral and, most important, universal, the future law for all mankind without exception. . . . By 1846 I had already
been consecrated into all the *truth* of this 'future regeneration of the world' and
into all the *holiness* of the future Communistic society by Belinsky."[15]

What is distorted here is simply Dostoevsky's assertion that it was Belinsky
who had indoctrinated *him* with such ideas. We know very well that Dostoevsky
had become converted to this sort of moral-religious Socialism at least several
years before he met Belinsky. As a novelist, though, Dostoevsky instinctively
reached after dramatic concentration, and he cast his own life here in its most
effective form. Belinsky, after all, *had* played the role assigned to him by Dostoevsky in *Russian culture* of the 1840s. Why confuse the reader with the insignificant details of his own personal history?

Dostoevsky's strategy becomes clearer if we examine the first article—written
a month or two earlier—in which he aimed to convince his readers that Socialism and Christianity are fundamentally incompatible, notwithstanding the
honorable and idealistic motives of its youthful adherents. He appeals to his
own experience of the later phase of Belinsky to prove the point, and once again
he dresses up his recollections to convey an impression that is not autobio-
graphically accurate. For he implies that Belinsky had converted him to atheism,
and to that *rejection* of Christian moral-religious values that usually accompanied such a conversion in the late 1840s. The polemical intent is clear: Socialism
in Russia had been atheistic and anti-Christian from the start, and it was impossible to maintain any connection between it and Christian morality. "As a Socialist," Dostoevsky writes, "[Belinsky] was duty bound to destroy the teachings
of Christ, to call it a deceptive and ignorant philanthropy [*chelovekolyubie*], condemned by modern science and economic doctrines."[16]

The core of Dostoevsky's portrait of Belinsky is concentrated in an argument
between the young writer and the critic concerning the problem of the moral

[15] Ibid., 148.
[16] Ibid., 7.

responsibility of the individual (a fundamental Christian moral value) and hence the issue of free will. This issue was of such epochal importance for the later Dostoevsky that one might be inclined to think he had smuggled it back anachronistically into the 1840s. Valerian Maikov, however, attacked Belinsky on this very subject in the winter of 1846–1847, and his attack was launched from a Utopian Socialist position appealing to the figure of Jesus Christ as the great symbol of man's moral freedom from material determination.

As Dostoevsky presents it, the dialogue begins with Belinsky's denial that the suffering and oppressed lower classes had any personal moral responsibility for their actions. "'But, do you know,' he [Belinsky] screamed one evening (sometimes in a state of great excitement he used to scream), 'do you know that it is impossible to charge man with sins, and to burden him with debts and turning the other cheek, when society is organized so vilely that man cannot help committing crimes, when he is economically pushed into crime, and that it is stupid and cruel to demand from men what, by the very laws of nature, they cannot accomplish even if they wanted to.'" [17] The Belinsky speaking here is no longer the old "humanist" who responded to the emotive appeal of Christian moral-religious values; this is the voice of the admirer of Littré, and perhaps also the reader of Max Stirner, who would see the moral will as helpless or nonexistent and the criminal acts of the oppressed only as a natural and legitimate expression of their "egoistic" needs.

The conversation turns to the personality of Christ; and it is revelatory of the time that no discussion of social problems could avoid taking a position about Christianity. Dostoevsky continues: "'I'm really touched to look at him,' said Belinsky, interrupting his furious exclamations, turning to his friend [also present] and pointing at me [Dostoevsky]. 'Every time I mention Christ his face changes expression as if he were ready to start weeping. Yes, believe me, you naïve person'—he turned again to me abruptly—'believe me that your Christ, if he were born in our day, would simply vanish in the face of contemporary science and of the contemporary movers of mankind.'" [18]

If Dostoevsky's face registered such extreme emotion, it was because Belinsky's words about Christ were of a coarseness of which Belinsky was fully capable. "That man [Belinsky]," Dostoevsky writes in 1871 to Strakhov, "reviled Christ to me in the most obscene and abusive way." [19] Moreover, Belinsky's comments betray the manifest Left Hegelian influence of Strauss, who had attributed Christ's charismatic powers to the fact that he lived in a pre-rational world. The reply to this Left Hegelian thrust is uttered by Belinsky's unnamed friend and is appropriately Utopian Socialist: "'Well, no: if Christ appeared now,

[17] Ibid.
[18] Ibid.
[19] *Pisma*, 2: 364; May 18/30, 1871.

He would join the movement and would lead it. . . .' 'All right, all right,' Belinsky agreed with surprising suddenness—'He would, as you say, join the Socialists and follow them.'"[20] Belinsky's uncertainty on this crucial point reveals his own transitional state of mind, although at the end of 1846, Belinsky had not long to go before calling the Utopian Socialists "social and virtuous asses."[21]

Dostoevsky's comment on the interchange leaves no doubt about the ideological crosscurrents that were really involved. "Those movers of mankind whom Christ was destined to join were the French: George Sand above all, the now totally forgotten Cabet, Pierre Leroux, and Proudhon, then only just having begun his career. . . . There was also a German before whom [Belinsky] bowed to with deference then—Feuerbach. Strauss was spoken of with reverence."[22] Christ would thus have, quite accurately, joined the movement of the preponderantly Utopian Socialist and moral-religious French; the Left Hegelian Germans that are mentioned had rejected all claims to the supernatural but had not rejected Christian moral values. Dostoevsky's judicious phrasing leaves those like Stirner, who *had* rejected such values, out of the group that Belinsky believed "Christ was destined to join." In fact, the argument on which he reports—the argument not only of Belinsky with Dostoevsky, but also of Belinsky with himself—was really being carried on between the two competing doctrines then disputing for the ideological mastery of the Left throughout the world.[23]

"In the last year of [Belinsky's] life," concludes Dostoevsky, "I no longer went to visit him. He had taken a dislike to me, but I was then passionately following all his teaching."[24] Just what Dostoevsky means by "all his teaching" is terribly vague. Is it the teaching of moral-religious Utopian Socialism? Is it the teaching of Belinsky's insulting Left Hegelian tirade against Christ, and his denial of free will and responsibility because of the overwhelming weight of "the laws of nature"? Dostoevsky wants the reader (who was now inclined, after a decade's infatuation with scientific materialism, to revere Christian moral values) to understand that he *was* converted to Belinsky's atheism and materialism; but there is good reason to doubt this, and not only from Dostoevsky's works of this time. Dostoevsky's closest friends in the next several years refused to surrender the

[20] *DW* (no. 1, 1873), 8.

[21] Evgenyev-Maksimov, *Sovremennik*, 117.

[22] *DW* (no. 1, 1873), 8.

[23] When Arnold Ruge, the editorial impresario of the Left Hegelians, arrived in Paris in August 1843 to recruit contributors for the *Deutsch-Französische Jahrbücher*, the atheism of the Left Hegelians proved a major obstacle. "Almost without exception they [the French] were believers and held to Robespierre's anathema of godless philosophy." David McLellan, *The Young Hegelians and Karl Marx* (London, 1969), 37–38. Writing to Feuerbach from Paris in May 1844, Ruge says disgustedly, "All parties base themselves directly on Christianity." Cited in Werner Sombart, *Der proletarische Sozialismus*, 2 vols. (Jena, 1924), 1: 119.

[24] *DW* (no. 1, 1873), 9.

moral-religious inspiration of Utopian Socialism and were critical of Belinsky and of his intellectual heirs who soon appeared on the literary scene.

■

The enormous importance of the encounter between the powerful critic and the young novelist is more symbolic than historical, more literary than literal. Dostoevsky's verbal skirmishes with Belinsky were of crucial significance for him as the future novelist of the spiritual crises of the Russian intelligentsia, but they did not lead to any decisive change in his ideas and values. The force of Belinsky's impact, though, no doubt explains why Dostoevsky was so determined to tidy up his biography and to give to life the artistic symmetry that, according to his final view of Russian culture, it should rightly have had. For if Belinsky had not really introduced Dostoevsky to Socialism, he *had* introduced him to *atheistic* Socialism—the only kind that the Dostoevsky of the 1870s believed to be intellectually honest and self-consistent.

The mechanical "scientific" materialism that Belinsky admired in Littré did succeed in becoming the philosophical dogma of the Russian Left for much of Dostoevsky's life. And moral values were derived from a Utilitarian egoism that, if it stemmed more directly from Bentham than from Max Stirner, fully shared the latter's supreme contempt for all sentimental humanitarianism. Dostoevsky thus had good reason to regard his disputes with Belinsky as having foreshadowed the later development of Russian social-political and cultural life, and his encounter with Belinsky certainly colored his own reaction to such changes. For his Christianity always retained the strongly altruistic and social-humanitarian cast of the 1840s, and it was always pitted against a "rationalism" that served to justify a totally amoral egoism.

There can be no question either that the religious theme of Dostoevsky's great novels was profoundly affected by the challenge of Belinsky. Not that atheism, or doubts about the beneficence of God, first loomed on his mental and emotional horizon in 1845. It would be naïve to imagine that the little boy whose consciousness had been stirred by the book of Job, or the young man who had participated in Shidlovsky's tormented soul searchings, should have needed Belinsky to introduce him to such matters; but it was Belinsky who first acquainted Dostoevsky with the new—and much more intellectually sophisticated—arguments of Strauss, Feuerbach, and probably Stirner. And though his religious faith ultimately emerged unshaken—even strengthened—from the encounter, these doctrines did present him with an acute spiritual dilemma. Traces of this inner crisis can certainly be found in the wrestlings of Dostoevsky's own characters with the problems of faith and Christ.

Feuerbach had argued that God—and Christ—were merely fictions representing the alienated essence of mankind's highest values. The task of mankind was thus to reappropriate its own essence by reassuming the powers and prerogatives alienated to the divine. The Left Hegelians, to be sure, did not recommend this as a task for any particular individual to undertake—it was only mankind as a whole that could recoup this great human treasure, but Stirner comes very close to urging everyone immediately to embark on their own personal deification. The effect of all this on the young Dostoevsky is not difficult to foresee. Nobody has portrayed more brilliantly the tragic inner dialectic of this movement of *atheist* humanism, and if Dostoevsky had no effective answer to Belinsky in 1845, he amply made up for it later by the creation of his negative heroes. For when such characters reject God and Christ, they invariably engage in the impossible and self-destructive attempt to transcend the human condition, and to incarnate the Left Hegelian dream of replacing the God-man by the Man-god.[25]

The long-range effect of this crisis was probably to sharpen Dostoevsky's sense of the absolute incompatibility between reason and faith. This paved the way for his later commitment to an irrationalism for which he had been prepared both by his religious and philosophical education and by the psychic experience he called "mystic terror." Like Kierkegaard, with whom he has so often been compared in the last half-century, Dostoevsky also later indicated that a paradoxical "leap of faith" was the only source of religious certainty. And the similarity of solution derives from the identity of the point of departure: Kierkegaard greatly admired Feuerbach for stressing how impossible it was to combine religion with the scientific and rational character of modern life. "Feuerbach," writes Karl Löwith, "perceived this contrast in exactly the same way that Kierkegaard did; but the latter drew the equally logical, but exactly opposite, conclusion: that science, and natural science in particular, is simply irrelevant to the religious situation."[26] Dostoevsky too finally chose to take his stand with the existential irrational of the "leap of faith" against Feuerbach's demand that religion be brought down to earth and submit to the criterion of human reason.

It would require many years, however, before Dostoevsky would begin to draw such conclusions. For the moment, he sought a more congenial atmosphere than he had found in the Pléiade or with Belinsky personally. A new group of friends, the little-known Beketov Circle, provided the emotional support he was looking for as his literary reputation declined and relations with Belinsky became tense.

[25] See Henri de Lubac, *Le drame de l'humanisme Athée* (Paris, 1950), esp. part 3, and also the penetrating remarks, based on a wide knowledge of the sources, in Andrzej Walicki, *W kręgu konserwatywnej utopi* (Warsaw, 1964), chap. 14.

[26] Karl Löwith, *From Hegel to Nietzsche* (New York, 1967), 334–335.

CHAPTER 12

The Beketov and Petrashevsky Circles

The first mention of Dostoevsky's new acquaintances occurs in mid-September 1846—after the crisis induced by the failure of *The Double.* "I take my dinner with a group," he writes Mikhail. "Six people . . . including Grigorovich and myself, have gotten together at Beketovs."[1] These were months when Dostoevsky was "almost in a panic of fear about my health,"[2] but the psychological aid provided by his friends seems to have restored him completely. "Brother," he writes two months later, "I am reborn, not only morally but also physically. Never have I felt in myself so much abundance and clarity, so much equanimity of character, so much physical health. I am indebted for much of this to my good friends . . . with whom I live; they are sensible and intelligent people, with hearts of gold, of nobility and character. They cured me by their company."[3] The security supplied by his new milieu was of great importance in helping him to weather the perturbations brought on by Belinsky's rejection.

The center of the group was Aleksey N. Beketov, who had been one of Dostoevsky's intimates at the Academy of Military Engineers, and the group included his two brothers, then still students, Nikolay and Andrey. Grigorovich spoke of Beketov as "the embodiment of goodness and straightforwardness," around whom people unfailingly clustered because of his outstanding moral qualities. He was the sort of person who "became indignant at every sort of injustice and was responsive to every noble and honorable endeavor," and it was he who set the dominating tone, which was strongly social-political. "But whoever spoke, and whatever was spoken about . . . everywhere one could hear indignant, noble outbursts against oppression and injustice."[4]

Nothing more is known about the Beketov Circle, which came to an end when the two younger brothers left for the University of Kazan early in 1847. N. Flerovsky, a student at Kazan in 1847, remembered that "They propagated the teaching of Fourier, and here the results were the same as in Petersburg"; presumably he

---

[1] *Pisma,* 1: 95; September 17, 1846.
[2] Ibid., October 7, 1846.
[3] Ibid., 103; November 26, 1846.
[4] D. V. Grigorovich, *Polnoe sobranie sochinenii,* 12 vols. (St. Petersburg, 1896), 12: 277.

meant that they attracted others and formed a circle.[5] The Beketovs were evidently Fourierists; and Dostoevsky's reference to "the benefits of association" points to the Utopian Socialist orientation of the group. Dostoevsky preferred not to call attention to this new affiliation in his later writing, for his connection with them calls into question the portrait he painted of himself as he was supposed to have been in the 1840s. Far from being a political innocent, abruptly baptized into Socialism, atheism, and materialism all at once by the great intellectual agitator Belinsky, Dostoevsky was a committed moral-religious progressive who stoutly maintained his convictions in the face of Belinsky's attacks and then allied himself with others of the same persuasion.

It was at the Beketovs that he became acquainted with the well-known poet, then still a student, Aleksey Pleshcheev, who has already been mentioned and whose name turns up everywhere in the annals of the progressive intelligentsia during the 1840s. The attractive and well-bred scion of an aristocratic family— gentle, tenderhearted, cloudily rhapsodic—Pleshcheev became a close friend of Dostoevsky. During the 1840s, the two young men were inseparable, and, as public evidence of this amity, they dedicated stories to each other. The ethos of Pleshcheev's work, which constantly evokes the image of the Utopian Socialist Christ, was close to Dostoevsky's heart. Even in a poem that became "the hymn of several generations of revolutionaries,"[6] the poet enjoins his comrades, condemned like himself to torture and execution, to pardon "our senseless executioners"[7] with Christian forgiveness.

It was also through the Beketovs that Dostoevsky struck up an equally close friendship with Valerian Maikov. Two years younger than Dostoevsky, Maikov had a brief but meteoric career in Russian letters beginning in 1845 and ending with his untimely death by a stroke in the summer of 1847. During this short span, however, he made a considerable splash by taking over the post of chief critic on *Notes of the Fatherland* from Belinsky, turning the journal into an organ of the Utopian Socialist Beketov tendency and setting himself up as rival of the powerful reigning arbiter of taste and ideas. Not only did Maikov visit the Beketovs', he was also among the early members of the circle gathered around Mikhail Butashevich-Petrashevsky, whose Friday evenings also attracted Pleshcheev and were soon to become the rallying place for the progressive intelligentsia in Petersburg.

Maikov praised Dostoevsky fervently and was the only voice raised to defend him against Belinsky's criticisms. The death of his friend a few months later was a terrible blow to Dostoevsky, depriving him of the one person in the Petersburg literary world thoroughly in tune with the writing he had been producing after

[5] Cited from the memoirs of Flerovsky in *Sorokovye gody XIX veka* (Moscow, 1959), 191.

[6] V. I. Kuleshov, *Naturalnaya shkola v literature XIX veka* (Moscow, 1965), 145.

[7] A. N. Pleshcheev, *Polnoe sobranie stikhotvorenii* (Leningrad, 1964), 83.

Poor Folk, but the memory of Valerian Maikov was kept alive by the close ties Dostoevsky had established with the Maikov family. Their home was the center of a literary-artistic salon at which Dostoevsky, despite his notorious explosiveness, was a frequent and welcome guest. His affection for Valerian was transferred to Apollon, a slightly older brother who had already acquired some reputation as a poet and who was to remain the most loyal of Dostoevsky's few intimates in later years.

———■———

Valerian Maikov's vigorous defense of his friend's literary talent also represented an effort to advance beyond Belinsky as a cultural critic. Hostile to the remnants of German Romantic and Idealistic thought still lurking in the background of Belinsky's criticism, Maikov proposed to replace them with an empirical foundation drawn from psychology. Art, he said, was grounded in what he called "the law of sympathy," according to which man understands everything by comparison with himself; he absorbs the world and domesticates it to his feeling (in art) and his understanding (in science and philosophy).[8] Psychology—the study of the inner life of man—thus becomes the key offering access to the secrets of the universe. Maikov shared Fourier's preoccupation with the human psyche as an all-important realm that had never been adequately explored.

It is likely that Maikov's friendship with the famous and slightly older Dostoevsky had something to do with the formulation of such a critical program, and it is no accident that Maikov's essays contain the most perceptive comments about Dostoevsky made by any of his contemporaries. "Both Gogol and Dostoevsky depict existing society," he writes. "But Gogol is preeminently a social poet, while Dostoevsky is preeminently a psychological one. For the first, the individual is important as the representative of a certain society or a certain group; for the second, society itself is interesting because of its influence on the personality of the individual. . . . Dostoevsky gives us a strikingly artistic depiction of Russian society, but with him this provides only the background of the picture, and is . . . completely swallowed up by the importance of the psychological interest."[9]

After *Poor Folk*, society appears largely as it is refracted through the consciousness of Dostoevsky's characters; and while Belinsky disapproved of such internalization, Maikov welcomed it not only as the natural flowering of Dostoevsky's gifts but also as an epistemological insight into the nature of reality. "In *The Double*," writes Maikov, "he penetrates so deeply into the human soul, he looks so fearlessly and passionately into the secret machinations of human

[8] Valerian Maikov, *Kriticheskie opyty* (St. Petersburg, 1891), 25–31.
[9] Ibid., 325.

feeling, thought, and action, that the impression created by *The Double* may be compared only with that of an inquisitive person penetrating into the chemical composition of matter." Such a "chemical view of society," he continues, goes so deep that it seems to be "suffused with some sort of mystical light," but there is nothing "mystical" here at all, and the depiction of reality is as "positive" as can be.[10] Flatly rejecting any prescriptive function for criticism, Maikov declares that "fidelity to reality constitutes such an essential condition for every work of art that a person gifted with artistic talent never produces anything contrary to this condition." Hence, it is superfluous to impose restrictions and demands on artistic creation in the name of "reality."[11]

The quarrel with Belinsky that Maikov initiated actually went to the heart of the ideological split between those who still clung to the moral-religious inspiration of Utopian Socialism and those who, like Belinsky, were searching for a more "positive" foundation for their social-political convictions. Maikov's position comes out explicitly in the major article in *Notes of the Fatherland* that announced his literary program and launched the attack against Belinsky. One quotation from Maikov's argument about free will and moral responsibility—the same question that Dostoevsky recalled arguing about with Belinsky at just that moment—will illustrate the social-cultural significance of the debate. To clinch his point that man cannot simply be seen as a creature of his conditioning, Maikov appeals to the example of Jesus Christ: "Christ reveals himself as the most perfect image of what we call a great personality. His true doctrine stands in such radical opposition to the ideas of the ancient world, and contains such an immeasurable independence from phenomena fateful for millions of beings called free and reasonable—in a word, they are elevated to such a degree above the laws of historical phenomena, that mankind even to this day . . . has not yet grown up even to half of that independence of thought without which it is impossible to comprehend and to realize them. Such independence, in an incomparably lesser degree, is shown in the ideas of all those truly great people who are responsible for moral revolutions of lesser scope."[12]

To consider Christ the greatest moral revolutionary of all times—a sublime paradigm for all the lesser ones who follow in his wake—was of course to flaunt the banner of moral-religious Socialism in the face of those rallying to another standard. The idea of Christ as revolutionary was standard in the 1840s, but to view Christ as the divine harbinger of man's (moral-psychological) freedom from the shackles of historical determinism was much less conventional. There can be little doubt that Dostoevsky's own idea of Christ was profoundly affected by Maikov's Utopian Socialist icon, and that Christ for him would always

[10] Ibid., 327.
[11] Ibid., 342.
[12] Ibid., 68.

remain not only the traditional Savior from the bonds of sin and death but also the sacred pledge of the possibility of moral freedom.

Maikov's article also reveals how insistently the issue of free will and moral responsibility had already begun to gnaw at those who, like Dostoevsky, refused to surrender the moral-religious basis of their progressivism. For it was by no means a simple matter to believe in the moral power of the personality as the appalling evidence piled up of the human ravages of early capitalism. Even Maikov could not help admitting that it was "stupid and vile" to preach morality to the exploited lower classes. But this did not lead him to deny the *possibility* of free will and moral responsibility, even though he agreed that "only heroism can unite moral worth with poverty." [13] Such "heroism," nonetheless, exists; the human personality will never allow itself to be completely subjugated by material conditions. The same inner debate already adumbrated in Maikov's essays will later be passionately argued in Dostoevsky's pages. Twenty years later, when Dostoevsky began to break with radicalism entirely, the tendencies evident in the later Belinsky had hardened into dogma, and it was impossible any longer to be a radical and to continue to affirm the existence of free will.

Still another side of Maikov's thought helps to throw additional light on Dostoevsky. Man, Maikov writes, using Fourier's terminology, "is endowed with virtues, that is, needs and capabilities that make up his vitality . . . [and] the source of everything vicious . . . [is] . . . the clash between his . . . powers and external circumstances, which create a disharmony between them." [14] Human nature is thus essentially good, and evil is the result of the arrangements of society that do not allow mankind properly to satisfy its needs and capabilities. Maikov, however, uses this Fourierist view of human nature to undermine the assumption that "nationality" is a positive value. National traits of character, Maikov argues, are the product of the drives built into the human psyche as they objectify themselves in one direction or another under the influence of material conditions (climate, geography, race, history). But the universal human ideal is "the harmonious development of all human needs and their corresponding capacities." [15] Judged by this ideal, all national attributes—even those ordinarily considered to be virtues—are really defects or vices: they are one-sided and unbalanced, and distort human nature in its full plenitude. Such a forthright rejection of nationality was by no means uncommon as a by-product of progressive Western Utopian Socialist influence.

---■---

Belinsky thrived on polemics and was at his best when aroused to a fighting fury. He replied to Maikov's onslaught in the winter of 1846 with his famous *A View*

[13] Ibid., 295.
[14] Ibid., 66.
[15] Ibid., 64.

of Russian Literature of 1846, which contained the fateful article that certified the total shipwreck of Dostoevsky's literary reputation and his public repudiation by the critic who had raised him to fame. One suspects that Dostoevsky's well-known friendship with Maikov may have had something to do with the new severity of Belinsky's judgment. For it was not Dostoevsky alone who received the back of Belinsky's hand; anyone else known to have been allied with Maikov, or whose work Maikov had praised, is also treated harshly. Poor, inoffensive Pleshcheev was caught in the cross fire and contemptuously dismissed as vainly pretending to a nonexistent literary talent; although not a major poet, his humanitarian themes would have elicited a word of sympathy under other circumstances.

Belinsky's answer to Maikov is a curious and contradictory mixture of Littré and Hegel, which never really grapples with the moral-religious basis of Maikov's progressive Westernism. What is new, however, is Belinsky's vehement affirmation and defense of nationality against Maikov's deprecation. Up to this time, it was Belinsky who had led the assault against the Slavophil idealization of Russian national virtues *as embodied in the backward and illiterate peasantry*. But now, as if in deliberate opposition to Maikov, Belinsky declares that "on this subject [nationality] I am rather inclined to side with the Slavophils rather than to remain on the side of the humanistic cosmopolitans."[16] And Belinsky's sensational about-face acted as a catalyst to spur on the ideological fusion between the two camps—the "backward-looking" Slavophils and the progressive Westernizers—begun a few years earlier, and soon to produce the various varieties of Russian Populism that dominated Russian culture until the last decade of the nineteenth century.

Indeed, much of what Belinsky says about nationality in this article turns up in the later journalism of Dostoevsky almost word for word. Like Belinsky, and in opposition to the Slavophils, Dostoevsy would always refuse to glamorize the Russian past or to dream of the restoration of some sort of Arcadian, pre-Petrine world, but like Belinsky again he wholeheartedly shared the Slavophil criticism of "Russian Europeanism." Belinsky noted that this automatic and demeaning aping of European civilization had created "a sort of duality in Russian life, consequently a lack of moral unity." Would Dostoevsky not later see himself precisely as the chronicler of this "lack of moral unity" in Russian life? Moreover, for Dostoevsky too the remedy would be not to reject Europe and return to the past (an impossible task in any case) but to realize that "Russia had fully outlived the epoch of reformation, that the reforms had done their business . . . and that the time had come for Russia to develop independently from out of herself."[17]

[16] V. G. Belinsky, *Selected Philosophical Works* (Moscow, 1948), 371.
[17] Ibid., 359–360.

Belinsky here is talking about the reforms of Peter the Great, and Dostoevsky would repeat exactly the same argument about those instituted by Alexander II in the early 1860s.

Russian nationality is no longer to be disparaged; on the contrary, as the Slavophils argued, it was to become the principle on which the Russia of the future was to be founded. But this made the task of defining such a principle all the more pressing. The Slavophils believed that Russia differed from Europe because its own history had been marked by peaceful Christian concord rather than by the egoistic struggles for power between classes and nations so typical of Western rivalries. But Belinsky disdainfully sweeps aside the idea that Russian nationality can be identified with the principle of love and humility. Instead, the "versatility" of the Russian character, its seeming amorphousness and unprecedented ability to assimilate and absorb alien cultures, plays a predominant role. This capacity may seem like weakness at first sight, but to a mind schooled in Schelling and Hegel and nurtured on the messianic speculations of Romantic nationalism, it is child's play to extract the positive from the negative. For the extreme malleability of the Russian folk-psyche may be "ascribed to natural giftedness," and may be the source of future strength. It may mean that "the Russian nationality is foreordained to express the richest and most many-sided essence in its nationality."[18]

Such ideas would have been familiar to Dostoevsky from the violent nationalism of Belinsky's essays during his Hegelian phase; and the vision of Russia as charged with a world-historical mission to synthesize the conflicting national cultures of Europe had been much in the air since the 1820s. But such ideas were given a new vitality when Belinsky used them to rebut Maikov's "cosmopolitanism" in the 1840s. For in freeing the idea of "nationality" from the negative and limiting connotations given it by Maikov, he adroitly turned it toward a universalism that rescued patriotic emotion from the Slavophils and reconciled them with progressive Westernism. This is the same vision of Russia as the future creator of a pan-human world culture that we shall find evoked so eloquently by Dostoevsky, and it will be supported by exactly the same arguments—the ease with which Russians learn foreign languages, their ability to identify with alien cultures, the role of Russian literature as a precursor of the new world synthesis. To these, of course, Dostoevsky will add the Russian Christ as the divine warrant of moral freedom and the triumph of human liberty over the laws of nature. In such a perspective, his post-Siberian "Slavophil" ideology may thus be seen as an amalgam of ideas whose roots go back both to Belinsky and to Valerian Maikov.

Such lines of continuity help to restore the true historical picture that Dostoevsky himself did so much to blur. For the moment, though, let us note only

[18] Ibid., 363.

the general tenor of Belinsky's article. "Europe today is engrossed with great new problems . . . but . . . it would be quite futile to treat these problems as our own. . . . We ourselves, in ourselves, and around ourselves—that is where we should seek both the problems and their solutions."[19] These words translate the mood of Belinsky's disillusionment with Utopian Socialism, but even those who still clung to some remnant of Utopian Socialist hopes now began to reinterpret and to readapt them in terms of Russian social problems.

■

The spring of 1847 was an extremely difficult period in Dostoevsky's life. The final split between him and Belinsky occurred sometime between the beginning of the year and early spring. What he himself called "the dissolution of my fame in the journals" was proceeding apace, and he informs Mikhail that his funds are so low that "if there had not been some kind people, I would have gone under."[20] Only Valerian Maikov was left to afford him some comfort, but the young Maikov lacked Belinsky's authority, and his praise could not offset the older critic's condemnation.

Dostoevsky moved to new quarters in the early spring of 1847 and began to live a lonely, bachelor existence. It must have been about this time that he organized dinners on a cooperative basis for the people he knew best—Pleshcheev, the two Maikov brothers, Dr. Yanovsky, the minor writer Yakov Butkov; somewhat later, the schoolteacher and critic Alexander Milyukov, whose memoirs of Dostoevsky are quite valuable. These dinners were held in the Hôtel de France, reputed for its cuisine and located on the avenue where Dostoevsky now lived, and he took a great deal of pleasure, according to Yanovsky, in arranging such convivial occasions. He knew the importance of maintaining a psychic balance between the external and the internal, and was fearful of "nerves and fantasy" obtaining the upper hand in his own life. No doubt it was partly to counteract his new isolation that he now began to frequent the gatherings of the Petrashevsky Circle.

This was Dostoevsky's first encounter with the figure whose eccentricities had already made his name a byword in Petersburg. In 1847, Mikhail Butashevich-Petrashevsky was a young man of twenty-six, the same age as Dostoevsky. Educated in the Alexander Lyceum at Tsarskoe-Selo—the most exclusive school in Russia for children of the nobility—he had acquired a reputation even there for refractoriness and opposition to authority. Barely managing to graduate, he obtained a post in the Ministry of Foreign Affairs as a translator, and continued his studies by acquiring a diploma in law at the University of St. Petersburg. Petra-

<hr>

[19] Ibid., 375.
[20] *Pisma*, 1: 106; January–February, 1847.

8. M. V. Butashevich-Petrashevsky
in 1840

shevsky, however, also attended the courses in political economy given by V. S. Poroshin, who lectured on the various new Socialist systems. This initiation into Socialist ideas influenced him strongly, just as it had influenced others—Valerian Maikov among them—who had sat in Poroshin's classroom. Fourierism in particular made a great impression on Petrashevsky, and he devoted himself to propagating his new faith.

Sometime in the early 1840s, Petrashevsky began to invite his immediate friends to drop in for conversation; and this was the nucleus of what became his "circle." An indefatigable reader and book collector, he acquired a sizable library of "forbidden" books dealing with the most important historical, economic, and social-political issues of the day. Indeed, one of the greatest attractions at Petrashevsky's was his extensive library, which he was only too eager to make accessible to others. By 1845 the circle had extended much beyond the bounds of Petrashevsky's old schoolfellows, and he had become a well-known figure in Petersburg social life. Petrashevsky by now had dropped all of Fourier's fantastic cosmology and natural history, nor did he share the religiosity either of Fourier or of his successor as the head of the movement, Victor Considérant. What impressed Petrashevsky in Fourierism was "the organization of the phalanstery."[21] He was persuaded that the establishment of such a Utopian dwelling, and the application of Fourier's theory of human nature to the organization of its work, would transform human labor from a burden to a joyous, self-fulfilling activity.

---

[21] Cited in V. I. Semevsky, *M. V. Butashevich–Petrashevsky i Petrashevtsy* (Moscow, 1922), 153.

Indeed, he was so convinced of the feasibility of Fourier's Utopia that in 1847 he tried to realize it on his own small estate. Enlisting the support of his peasants, who obligingly agreed to all his proposals (or so he believed), he proceeded to build a fully equipped phalanstery for them. The great day arrived, the forty-odd peasant families left their miserable *izbas* for their new residence, but the next morning the ideal dwelling, with all its comforts and amenities, had been burned to the ground.

Far from disillusioning Petrashevsky, this episode only convinced him that a preparatory period of intellectual enlightenment was essential for social progress; and so he devoted himself even more fervently to spreading enlightenment everywhere he could, not only at his open-house "Fridays" but also at various clubs and organizations that he joined (such as a dancing class for tradesmen and shopkeepers) specifically to meet as many people as possible and spread the ferment of dissatisfaction.

Despite his wide range of acquaintances, Petrashevsky had no close friends. Always courteous with members of his circle, there was yet something grating about his personality that perhaps sprang from his self-appointed role as an intellectual *agent provocateur*. Dostoevsky, under questioning by the investigation commission after the mass roundup and arrest of the Petrashevsky Circle, denied any intimacy with him, but added, "To be sure, I always respected [him] as an honorable and noble human being."[22] Most of the visitors who came to Petrashevsky's, moreover, could not help harboring mixed feelings about him because of his reputation as a capricious eccentric. There were endless anecdotes about his hassles with bureaucratic officials, whom he constantly provoked by insisting that they obey to the letter the prescriptions of the Russian legal code. Some of the stories about him derive simply from the striking individuality of his personal appearance. He was alleged to have gone to church dressed as a woman; on another occasion, having been ordered to cut his hair, he arrived at the office with luxuriant locks that turned out to be a wig! How many reports of this kind are apocryphal is impossible to say. But they all obviously derive from his mockery of the innumerable petty regulations governing every aspect of ordinary life in Russia and his stiff-necked and courageous refusal to submit to them tamely. The result was, nonetheless, that he acquired the reputation of being a jester rather than a person of sense and responsibility, and it was difficult even for most of the members of his circle to accept him without inner reservations.

This was the already notorious personality whom Dostoevsky began to visit in the spring of 1847. He went to Petrashevsky's as he would have gone to any other social gathering. There was nothing secret or conspiratorial about Petra-

---

[22] N. F. Belchikov, *Dostoevsky v protsesse Petrashevtsev* (Moscow, 1971), 153. This volume, first published in 1936, reproduces all the official documents concerning Dostoevsky's involvement in the Petrashevsky affair, along with excellent editorial comments and clarification.

shevsky's Fridays any more than there had been about the reunions of the Belinsky Pléiade or the Beketov Circle. After all, people came together to talk a little more freely about the same matters that were being broached in the literary journals. It was generally believed that, as long as such conversation was carried on behind closed doors, there was nothing to fear from the government. A lively young Petersburger, in a letter dating from the beginning of 1848, lists among the attractions of the city "the sermons of Nilson, the propaganda of Petrashevsky, and the public lectures and feuilletons of Pleshcheev"[23]—all seemed to him to exist on the same level of tolerated public diversion and expression of opinion. This belief, as we shall soon see, was mistaken.

———■———

By the late spring of 1848, with increasing membership that fluctuated from week to week, the meetings turned into a sort of debating club, and a small bell, with a handle suspiciously carved in the figure of a statue of liberty, was used to regulate the ebb and flow of talk. D. D. Akhsharumov, who later became a doctor and a pioneer in Russian social hygiene, writes that the gatherings were "an interesting kaleidoscope of the most diversified opinions about contemporary events, the decisions of the government, . . . contemporary literature . . . happenings in the city were brought up, everything was talked about at the top of one's voice, without the slightest restraint. . . . Because of the . . . conversations touching primarily on social-political questions, these Petrashevsky evenings interested us enormously; they were the only ones of their kind in Petersburg. The gatherings usually continued far into the night, until two or three in the morning, and ended with a modest supper."[24]

Dostoevsky did not frequent the Petrashevsky meetings assiduously during the first year and a half, and Yanovsky says that he spoke of the gatherings contemptuously, attributing their popularity both to the free refreshments and to a desire "to play at liberalism, because, you see, which of us mortals does not enjoy playing that game."[25] The Petrashevsky milieu could hardly have replaced either the Pléiade or the Beketov Circle in his affections. Both of these had been small groups bound together by ties of personal friendship and common aims, while Dostoevsky and Petrashevsky did not even get on well together. Dostoevsky would certainly have disliked Petrashevsky's rampant Left Hegelian atheism as much as he had disliked that of Belinsky, and we can imagine him disliking it a good deal more. Belinsky's tempestuous explosions were at least indicative of a genuine emotional concern for the dilemmas of religious faith, and the warmth and good-heartedness of his character, as well as his genius as a critic, no doubt

[23] Semevsky, *Butashevich–Petrashevsky*, 108.
[24] Ibid.
[25] *DVS*, 1: 169.

made up for a good deal. Petrashevsky was of an entirely different temperament and always spoke of religion with coldly hostile sarcasm or scornfully mocking irreverence. After Dostoevsky's death, Nikolay Speshnev—about whom we shall soon be hearing a good deal—told Mme Dostoevsky that "Petrashevsky had produced a repulsive impression on [Dostoevsky] because he was an atheist and mocked at faith."[26]

Like all of the intelligentsia, Dostoevsky was oppressed by the general lack of freedom in Russian social life; but the most insufferable injustice—the issue that stirred his deepest emotional responses—was the enslavement of the peasantry. On May 18, 1847, however, Nicholas I insisted, in a speech to a delegation of nobles, that peasants could not be considered "as private property, and even more as goods,"[27] and he asked for the aid of the nobility in helping him to convert the status of the peasants from serfs to that of tenants. News of this pronouncement, spreading like wildfire through the capital, aroused the highest hopes; even Belinsky became convinced that Nicholas was at least determined to cut out the deadly cancer threatening the life of Russian society. There was, as a result, very little sense of political urgency in the talk at Petrashevsky's before the fall of 1848. Articles were read and views exchanged on every conceivable subject; the advantages of one or another Socialist system were pondered and weighed; the rigors of the censorship were condemned; the malfeasance of various highly placed bureaucratic officials exposed. But the final effect must have been that sense of exasperated impotence that, we may assume, Dostoevsky could tolerate only in small and intermittent doses.

This atmosphere of stagnation was swept away by the outbreak of the revolutions of 1848 in Europe, which caused panic in Russian ruling circles and a wild excitement among the intelligentsia. The tsar himself, when the news arrived, was supposed to have erupted in the midst of a ball clutching at the telegraphic dispatch and ordered his dancing officers to saddle their horses. Herzen has left a picture of frenzied Petersburgers snatching the newspapers from each other's hands at cafés until, finally, someone clambered on a table and read to all the others at the top of his voice. Alexander Milyukov conveys the rebellious mood that swept over the intelligentsia as the astonishing news kept pouring in from abroad. "From the first day of the February revolution, the most incredible events succeeded one another in Europe. The unheard-of reforms of Pius IX provoked uprisings in Milan, Venice, Naples; the surge of liberal ideas in Germany provoked revolutions in Berlin and Vienna. . . . The rotten foundations of the old reaction were falling, and a new life was beginning for all of Europe. But, at the same time, the most oppressive stagnation reigned in Russia; thought and

[26] Miller and Strakhov, *Biografiya*, 91.
[27] Yu. Oksman, *Letopis zhizn' i tvorchestvo V. G. Belinskogo* (Moscow, 1958), 501.

the press were confined more and more, and no activity appeared anywhere since social life had been crushed. . . . Practically with every mail delivery from abroad, we heard about new rights granted to the people, whether willingly or not, while in Russian society we heard only rumors of more limitations and constraints. Whoever remembers that period knows how all this worked on the minds of the youthful intelligentsia." [28]

The first effect of this mutinous restlessness was to swell the ranks of the Petrashevtsy with an influx of new members. Never before had the gatherings been so well attended and so lively, and beginning in the fall of 1848 Dostoevsky began to show up at Petrashevsky's Fridays with some regularity. In the back of everyone's mind, of course, was the question of whether the Russian regime itself could indefinitely escape the fate that had overtaken the absolute monarchs of Europe, and the talk at Petrashevsky's began to focus more directly on Russian social-political problems. All the more because, as Herzen noted, "all the rumors about the intention of the Tsar to declare the liberation of the peasants, which had become very widespread . . . instantly ceased." [29] It was at this time that the Petrashevsky gatherings were organized on a more formal basis, and a "president" was chosen each Friday to take charge of the animated arguments.

With the crisis atmosphere in the country brought on by the revolutions in Europe, it was inevitable that the meetings at Petrashevsky's would arouse suspicion. His escapades had already called him to the notice of the secret police, and he had been placed under discreet observation in 1844. At the beginning of 1848 he incautiously circulated a petition among the St. Petersburg nobility calling for a revision of the law governing the sale of estates. The purpose of this proposal was to raise the value of such property by making it available to non-noble buyers, but such a buyer would be required to change the status of peasants, after purchase, from serf to tenant. Petrashevsky thought this a very clever maneuver to enlist the greed of the landowners on the side of the peasant emancipation. The only result, however, was to alert the authorities once again to his irritating, gadfly existence.

Deciding to investigate him more carefully, both the secret police and the Ministry of Internal Affairs placed Petrashevsky under secret surveillance. Agents of the ministry reported, after ten months, that meetings were taking place in his home every Friday lasting until three or four in the morning. "They [the guests] . . . read, spoke, and disputed; but what exactly they spoke about it was impossible to determine because of the caution and secrecy with which Petrashevsky surrounded himself." [30] Accordingly, a secret agent named Antonelli

[28] *DVS*, 1: 181.

[29] P. S. Schegolev, ed., *Petrashevtsy*, 3 vols. (Moscow–Leningrad, 1926–1928), 1: 92.

[30] V. R. Leikina, E. A. Korolchuk, and V. A. Desnitsky, eds., *Delo Petrashevtsev*, 3 vols. (Moscow–Leningrad, 1937–1951), 3: 3–4.

turned up as a fellow employee of Petrashevsky at the ministry in January 1849. Antonelli furnished his superiors with regular reports of his conversations with the suspect; and though Petrashevsky was suspicious of his efforts to ingratiate himself, Antonelli was present at the last seven meetings of the circle between March 11 and April 22.

The information regarding Dostoevsky's participation in the debates of the Petrashevsky Circle is scanty. Denying to the investigation commission that he had ever held forth at Petrashevsky's about social or political matters, Dostoevsky admitted that he took the floor twice on other subjects. "*Once about literature*, . . . and the other time *about personality and egoism*."[31] There are, indeed, few traces of Dostoevsky as an active presence in the ample material about the circle that has become available since the 1920s. Only in the very last weeks of its existence does his name figure at all among those who took a leading part in discussion.

Dostoevsky's reluctance to participate more vigorously in their debates could not have sprung from ignorance. Count Semenov knew Dostoevsky intimately (the lonely young writer frequently visited his apartment) and remembers him as one of the most erudite people he knew; according to Semenov, he had read extensively in the history of the French Revolution (Thiers, Mignet, Louis Blanc), as well as in Socialist theory (Saint-Simon, Fourier).[32] The list of the works that Dostoevsky withdrew from Petrashevsky's collection shows that the range of the material he consulted spans the gamut of problems that were being discussed at the meetings. For a firsthand contact with Left Hegelian thought, Dostoevsky took out Strauss's *Life of Jesus*. Blanc's three-volume *Histoire des dix ans* covered recent French history and brought him up-to-date on the social-political conditions that had led to the creation of Utopian Socialism. He also withdrew several works of Proudhon (titles unknown), and Paget's *Introduction à l'étude de la science sociale*—one of the best popularizations of Fourierism then available. In Étienne Cabet's *Le vrai Christianisme suivant J. Christ*, Dostoevsky came across the argument that total communist egalitarianism was the only true Christianity.

If Dostoevsky did not throw himself more wholeheartedly into the fray at Petrashevsky's, it was because he was uninterested in the interminable debates over the merits of one or another Socialist system. He was in accord with the moral impulse inspiring them, but he was not persuaded that any of their panaceas could be put into practice. "Socialism offers a thousand methods of social organization," he commented in his deposition, "and since all of these books are written intelligently, fervently, and often with genuine love for mankind, I read

---

[31] Belchikov, *Dostoevsky v protsesse Petrashevtsev*, 106.
[32] *DVS*, 1: 209.

them with curiosity. But . . . I do not adhere to any of the social systems, . . . and . . . I am convinced that the application of any of them would bring with it inescapable ruin, and I am not talking about us but even in France." [33]

Although this declaration was made under duress, it expresses an attitude that Dostoevsky shared with many of his contemporaries. Valerian Maikov too had been sympathetic to Socialist ideals but skeptical about the feasibility of any of the specific programs advanced by the various schools, and the same position inspired an important series of articles published in *The Contemporary* in 1847 by Vladimir Milyutin, a brilliant young economist who was an intimate of Maikov and who also turned up at Petrashevsky's.

Milyutin saw Socialist theories as inspired by an admirably humanitarian aim, but concerned, like Maikov—and Dostoevsky—with the freedom of the individual, he criticized the "new schools" for limiting this freedom drastically. The Utopias of the Socialists are still in what Milyutin calls their mythological-metaphysical phase. Exactly the same idea is expressed in Dostoevsky's deposition. "Socialism is a science in ferment," he explained to his judges. "It seems to me, however, that out of the present chaos something consistent, logical, and beneficial will be worked out for the common good." [34] In contrast to these pieties, Dostoevsky was already thinking along more concrete and down-to-earth lines, linking Socialist ideas with existing Russian conditions. Alexander Milyukov, who belonged to one of the several satellite groups that had now formed around the Petrashevsky Circle, writes in his memoirs that Dostoevsky especially insisted "that all these theories had no importance for us, that we should [look to] the life and age-old historical organizations of our people, where in the *obshchina* [communal ownership of land], *artel* [worker's wage-sharing cooperative], and in the principles of mutual village responsibility [for the payment of taxes] there have long since existed much more solid and normal foundations than in all the dreams of Saint-Simon and his school. He said that life in an Icarian commune or phalanstery seemed to him more terrible and repugnant than any prison." [35]

More important, however, is that we see another idea emerging in Milyukov's account. Since "true" or "natural" Socialism is *already* contained in the social institutions of the Russian peasantry, these furnish a basis for the construction of a new social order superior to the artificial Utopias of the Western Socialists. Because this idea is at the heart of the later Russian Populism and was to prove of such tremendous importance for Dostoevsky, Milyukov has been accused of smuggling the opinions of the post-Siberian Dostoevsky back into the 1840s. [36]

[33] Belchikov, *Dostoevsky v protsesse Petrashevtsev,* 146.

[34] Ibid., P. N. Sakulin, *Russkaya literatura i sotsializm* (Moscow, 1922), 174–175.

[35] *DVS,* 1: 185.

[36] See A. S. Dolinin, "Dostoevsky sredi Petrashevtsev," *Zvenya* 6 (Moscow–Leningrad, 1936), 528–529.

The evidence, though, tends to confirm Milyukov's words. Franco Venturi, in his magisterial history of Russian Populism, notes the existence of an embryonic "Populist" wing among the Petrashevtsy.[37] It is within this group—who were following Belinsky's recent injunction to work out the solution to Russian social problems in Russian terms—that Dostoevsky must be placed.

Dostoevsky's thoughts, as we see, were thus immovably riveted on Russia and Russian problems. These subjects were rarely discussed at Petrashevsky's in terms he thought sensible, and so he took the floor only to expound some idea important for his literary work. But if Dostoevsky was known for his indifference whenever the talk revolved around the fine points of Socialist doctrine, he was equally notorious for his impassioned intensity whenever it focused on the problem of serfdom. For there is one overwhelming impression that emerges from all the accounts of Dostoevsky given in the memoirs: he was, literally, someone who found it impossible to control himself whenever he spoke about the mistreatment of the enslaved peasantry.

Count Semenov, present on one such occasion, diagnoses the emotive source of Dostoevsky's radicalism in the 1840s. "Dostoevsky," he writes, "was never, and could never be, a *revolutionary*; but, as a man of feeling, he could be carried away by a wave of indignation and even hatred at the sight of violence being perpetrated on the insulted and injured. This happened, for example, when he saw or heard about the sergeant of the Finnish regiment having had to run the gauntlet. Only in such moments of outrage was he capable of rushing into the street with a red flag."[38]

Dostoevsky spoke with uncontrollable fervor at such moments. "I remember very well," writes Milyukov, "that he was particularly outraged at the mistreatment from which both the lowest class and the youth in school suffered."[39] These horrors inspired Dostoevsky to sudden outbursts of blazing eloquence. Some members of the circle even felt him to have the makings of a born agitator. It was perhaps Dostoevsky's volcanic eruptiveness, whenever he spoke about serfdom, that brought him to the attention of the enigmatic and fascinating Nikolay Speshnev. For within the amorphous agglomeration of the Petrashevsky Circle, the iron-willed Speshnev was one of the few ruthlessly determined to turn words into deeds, and he was on the watch for people he might recruit for this purpose. He formed a little circle that was the only true secret society to emerge from the Petrashevsky Fridays, and Dostoevsky was among its members. Not Belinsky or Petrashevsky but Speshnev was Dostoevsky's mentor in revolutionary radicalism; it was Speshnev who shaped Dostoevsky's conception of what underground conspiracy meant in practice.

[37] Franco Venturi, *Roots of Revolution*, trans. Frances Haskell (New York, 1960), 85.
[38] *DVS*, 1: 211.
[39] Ibid., 186.

CHAPTER 13

Dostoevsky and Speshnev

Nikolay Speshnev—who unquestionably furnished Dostoevsky, twenty years later, with some of the inspiration for the character of Nikolay Stavrogin in *Demons*, stood out among the rather drab personages clustering around Petrashevsky as a bird of a more brilliant plumage. He was, in the first place, a very wealthy landowner. Like Petrashevsky, he had attended the Alexander Lyceum, and the two had known each other as students, but with an arrogant off-handedness typical of his character, Speshnev had not bothered to graduate. He was the only member of the circle who did not have to earn a living, and he was the only one who had traveled to Europe and had enjoyed the cultural advantages of the cosmopolitan life of the Russian gentry.

Bakunin—a product of the same milieu, and who knew a fellow aristocrat when he saw one—was much impressed with Speshnev when they met in Siberia in 1860. "Speshnev," he wrote to Herzen, "is a remarkable man in many ways: intelligent, cultivated, handsome, aristocratic in bearing, not at all standoffish though quietly cold, inspiring confidence—like every one possessing a quiet strength—a gentleman from head to foot."[1] The wife of Nikolay Ogarev, who met him just before his arrest in 1849, describes him as being tall, with finely chiseled features and dark brown hair flowing in waves down to his shoulders; his large blue-gray eyes were, she thought, shadowed by a look of gentle melancholy.[2]

Speshnev had lived in Europe between 1842 and 1847, and, when he returned to Petersburg in December of that year, was surrounded with the aureole both of a romantic and a revolutionary legend. Women, as Bakunin notes somewhat enviously, found Speshnev irresistible. "Women are not opposed to a bit of charlatanry," he sagely informs Herzen, "and Speshnev creates quite an effect: he is particularly good at wrapping himself in the mantle of a deeply pensive and quiet impenetrability."[3] If we are to believe Bakunin, Speshnev cut a wide swath during 1846 in the Russian-Polish society of Dresden. Whether old or young,

---

[1] P. S. Schegolev, ed., *Petrashevtsy*, 3 vols. (Moscow–Leningrad, 1926–1928), 1: 134.
[2] Ibid., 75.
[3] Ibid., 135.

9. N. A. Speshnev

whether mother or daughter, all the women were mad about him. Even more dazzling than this Byronic reputation as a Don Juan was the report that he had taken part in the *Sonderbund* war, which had broken out in 1843 between the liberal and Catholic cantons in Switzerland over the expulsion of the Jesuits. Speshnev was said to have fought as a volunteer with the army of the liberal cantons.

Whether true or not, this rumor is enough to indicate the complexion of Speshnev's politics. He began, under the influence of his reading of the French Romantic historians, as a political liberal. Steeping himself in the literature both of orthodox economy and its Socialist critics, he soon passed through Utopian Socialism to egalitarian communism. His contact with Polish émigré circles in Germany and France had acquainted him with the methods of underground conspiracy, and, becoming fascinated with the history of secret societies, he read everything he could find on the subject. He was familiar with Buonarotti's *La conspiration de Babeuf* (which served as a handbook on conspiratorial tactics for all the French secret societies up to 1848), as well as with the compendious tome of the Abbé Barruel, *Mémoires pour servir à l'histoire du Jacobinisme, de l'impiété et de l'anarchie*, which described the supposed success of the Masons and Jacobins in secretly engineering the French Revolution. Everywhere he went, Speshnev moved in left-wing or (as in the case of the Poles) oppositional political circles. In Paris he became acquainted with the group around the *Revue Indépendante* and was invited to furnish articles about Russia.

Unlike Belinsky, however, Speshnev seems never to have been strongly influenced by the sentimental humanitarianism and the religious-philosophical messianism of the Sand-Leroux school. He was attracted instead by the doctrines rampant among the extreme French secret societies that preached the necessity of violence, and whose communism was combined with a philosophy of materialism, atheism, and Utilitarian self-interest. One of the most articulate spokesmen for this position, who received an approving nod from Karl Marx in *The Holy Family*, was Theodore Dézamy.[4] Dézamy was as committed as Cabet to a totally egalitarian and leveling communism of the crudest kind, but he believed that it could be realized only by the ruthless application of terror to crush all the enemies of the new ideal order. One of Dézamy's books, *Le Jésuitisme vaincu par les socialistes*, was found in the search of Speshnev's quarters after his arrest.

There is also reason to believe that Speshnev, during his sojourn in Paris, was influenced by the fathers of Marxism themselves (not yet Marxists, to be sure). In the fall of 1844, Engels wrote a letter to the *New Moral World*, an Owenite-communist journal, proudly claiming that "we are having much success among the Russians living in Paris. There are three or four Russian nobles and landowners here who are declared radical Communists and atheists." V. I. Semevsky, a historian with an unrivaled knowledge of Russian radicalism, thinks "we can scarcely doubt that one of these Russians was Speshnev."[5]

What we know about Speshnev comes largely through the testimony of others and the summary of his case made for Nicholas I, as well as the drafts of two letters written by him sometime in 1847. They are presumed to have been addressed to his Polish friend, Edmond Chojecki; and they furnish striking confirmation of the qualities in Speshnev that so impressed his contemporaries. One cannot help admiring his easy erudition in philosophical and social-economic matters and the lucid, ironic, coldly incisive quality of his mind. The most important remarks are those that show how strongly he had come under the influence of Max Stirner. Rejecting all attempts to establish any sort of metaphysical system, Speshnev writes: "Anthropotheism [the position of Feuerbach] . . . divinizes a new and different object, but there is nothing new about the fact of divinization. . . . Is the difference between a God-man and a Man-god really so great?" Both, he says, are abstractions, which do not concern the existing individual of flesh-and-blood. "Am I, writing to you now, really identical with humanity or 'the human'? . . . If not, then 'humanity' and 'the human' are . . . alien authorities." Speshnev concludes that "such categories as beauty and ugliness, good and bad, noble and base, always were and always will remain a matter of taste."[6]

[4] Karl Marx, *Frühe Schriften*, ed. Hans-Joachim Lieber and Peter Furth, 2 vols. (Darmstadt, 1971), 1: 828.

[5] V. I. Semevsky, *M. V. Butashevich–Petrashevsky i Petrashevtsy* (Moscow, 1922), 192.

[6] V. I. Evgrafova, ed., *Proizvedeniya Petrashevtsev* (Moscow, 1953), 496–497.

The affinities between Speshnev's views and the ideas that motivate the character Stavrogin in *Demons* are striking. Speshnev lectured on religion from a "philosophical" point of view during one of the evenings at Petrashevsky's when Dostoevsky may well have been present. But even if we assume that Dostoevsky invented the ideological motivation of Stavrogin, this merely verifies the astonishing capacity of his imagination, at what may seem to be its wildest flights, to intersect with some of the historical reality of Russian culture. For Stavrogin's "Confession" contains the following passage, which offers the rationale for his behavior: "I have neither the feeling nor the knowledge of good and evil, and not only have I lost the sense of good and evil, but good and evil really do not exist (and this pleased me) and are but a prejudice; I can be free of all prejudices . . ." (12: 113).

Speshnev's appearance at the Petrashevsky Fridays early in 1848 naturally stirred interest and excitement, if only because the widely traveled visitor could provide firsthand information about Socialist circles in Europe. But his striking personality also produced its effect, greatly aided by his posture of reticence and the air of mystery that he assumed—the air of a man perfectly poised, who knew much more than he was willing to disclose to the uninitiated. He rarely entered into the current of the conversations at Petrashevsky's, spent most of his time in the host's study consulting his library, and would only condescend now and then to drop a laconic word. From what Speshnev said about himself during the investigation, we see that he deliberately cultivated such a stance to increase his authority and prestige. He "was sometimes very sharp in speech, to prevent others from hiding from him, and succeeded in recognizing all hidden thoughts so as to know with whom he was dealing."[7] The manner in which Speshnev was treated by Petrashevsky suggests that he was suspected of being the emissary of some European revolutionary organization. Speshnev was of a totally different moral temper than Petrashevsky, and the two men were, ideologically, poles apart. Petrashevsky pinned his hopes to a gradual evolution, decried precipitous political action, and rejected egalitarian communism as economic barbarism. Speshnev openly called himself a communist, believed in the nationalization of all means of production in the hands of a strong central power, and felt that the initial and most important step should be the seizure of such power by the revolutionaries at the first opportunity.

Whenever Speshnev *did* speak, he injected a new note of steely decisiveness into the desultory atmosphere of the meetings; no one had ever expressed himself there with such brutality and frankness. In the talk on religion, he remarked that in Russia, it was possible to propagandize ideas only by word of mouth.

---

[7] Schegolev, *Petrashevtsy*, 3: 60.

"And therefore, gentlemen, since only the spoken word remains to us, I intend to use it without any shame or conscience, with no sense of dishonor, in order to propagandize for Socialism, atheism, terrorism, everything, everything that is good in the world. And I advise you to do the same."[8]

During the winter of 1848–1849, a number of incidents occurred in the Petrashevsky Circle that betrayed an increasing radicalism among some of the participants. Speshnev was either directly involved in all these incidents or was suspected by others to be working in the background, and he seized whatever possibilities he could sense to move beyond the cautiousness of Petrashevsky.

The most curious episode of this kind involved the flamboyant figure of Rafael Chernosvitov, a Siberian gold prospector who floated into the Petrashevsky orbit one day in November 1848. An ex-army officer, he had knocked about a good deal, been decorated for bravery, and was the proud possessor of a wooden leg replacing the one lost in battle. A garrulous personality, he evidently enjoyed bedazzling his young and gullible audience with portentous hints about his enormous influence over the wild and unruly population of his Siberian district and his contacts with the governor-general. Dostoevsky, who enjoyed the pithiness of Chernosvitov's language, compared his racy Russian to that of Gogol, but he also remarked to Speshnev that the colorful newcomer was probably a police spy. Speshnev thought he was the agent of a revolutionary organization in Siberia sent to feel out the ground in the heartland of the empire; so, perhaps, did Petrashevsky. At the same time, Chernosvitov suspected *them* of being the leaders of a movement preparing an uprising in European Russia.

It is indicative of Speshnev's status that Petrashevsky invited him to participate in a series of private conversations with Chernosvitov. Each of the three tried to feel out the other as the talk turned on the possibility of a revolution. Chernosvitov assured his interlocutors that, beyond the Urals, the free Siberian peasants all possessed arms and were ready to massacre any invading army. Speshnev pointed out that, if the bulk of the Russian Army could be decoyed into Siberia, and if this could be coordinated with uprisings in the two major cities, the fate of tsarism would be sealed. Declaring his readiness to participate in such an undertaking, Chernosvitov tried to elicit admissions from the other two that they were indeed organizing for such a revolt. Speshnev was willing to play along in the hope of extracting more information from Chernosvitov, but Petrashevsky flatly refused to participate in outright deception. The talks broke down as a result of this refusal.

[8] Semevsky, *Butashevich–Petrashevsky*, 194.

Nonetheless, Chernosvitov's speech served as a catalyst to bring into the open half-formulated thoughts that were fermenting among the group. Another person who took them up was a young army lieutenant named Nikolay Mombelli, who spoke privately to Petrashevsky about the formation of a secret mutual assistance society, with the aim of infiltrating the bureaucracy to bring about reforms and to counter the oppression of the authorities. This led to another series of private conversations, again with Speshnev and Petrashevsky as the main participants.

Mombelli, as we now know, was a member of Speshnev's secret organization, and Speshnev immediately seized the opportunity to outline his own idea of what a secret society should be. He explained that "there are three illegal methods of action—Jesuitical [i.e., infiltration], propaganda, and revolt; that neither of these is certain, and thus there is a better chance if all three roads are taken, and for this a central committee [is] necessary whose function would be to form auxiliary ones: a committee of brotherhood to set up a school of Fourierist, Communist, and Liberal propaganda, and, finally, a committee to form, behind all this, a secret society for revolt."[9] Mombelli suggested that all members of the proposed organization begin by writing their biography (perhaps for purposes of pressure and blackmail) and that traitors were to be executed. But Petrashevsky engaged in delaying tactics, constantly urged prudence, and said that, even though he did not approve of violent revolution, he still believed he would live in a phalanstery during his lifetime. Speshnev finally lost patience, refused to attend any more such futile meetings, and temporarily broke off relations with Petrashevsky sometime in December 1848.

It is against the background of these various attempts by Speshnev to form a secret society, all frustrated and thwarted by Petrashevsky, that we must place what we know of Dostoevsky at this time. For it was shortly after these abortive efforts that, one evening in January 1849, he visited the flat of Apollon Maikov and told his friend that he had been delegated to make him a proposal to join in a new secret group. "Petrashevsky," Dostoevsky said, "well, he's a fool, a play-actor and a chatterbox; nothing sensible would ever come out of him." More practical people had thought up "a plan of action" without telling Petrashevsky. The idea was "to set up a secret printing press"; seven others had joined, and Maikov was invited to be the eighth. "I remember Dostoevsky," Maikov writes, "like the dying Socrates before his friends, sitting in his nightshirt with an unbuttoned collar and lavishing all his eloquence on the sanctity of this action, on our obligation to save the fatherland, etc.—so that I finally began to laugh and crack jokes."[10] Maikov warned Dostoevsky that he was heading for certain ruin,

[9] Schegolev, *Petrashevtsy*, 3: 63.

[10] N. F. Belchikov, *Dostoevsky v protsesse Petrashevtsev* (Moscow, 1971), 265.

but he promised not to breathe a word of the proposal to anyone, and he remained true to his pledge during Dostoevsky's lifetime.

This attempt to enlist Maikov was first revealed in a letter written by Maikov after Dostoevsky's death (but never sent) and published only in 1922; it contains the names of Speshnev and Pavel Filippov as two other members of this secret group (Dostoevsky listed Filippov, along with Golovinsky, as among his closest friends at this time). Maikov told the same story to a friend, who transcribed it in a diary that came to light in 1956. The other members of the secret society were Nikolay Mordvinov, Mombelli, Nikolay Grigoryev, and the economist Vladimir Milyutin, and the purpose of the organization was to produce "a revolution in Russia."[11] In his letter, Maikov also mentions having learned later that the parts for a handpress had been gathered together and assembled shortly before the arrest of all the Petrashevtsy.

Nothing further has been unearthed for certain about this Speshnev faction, although its existence was not a secret from the more penetrating observers who came to Petrashevsky's. Years later, Dostoevsky gave some additional information to his friend and official biographer, Orest Miller. "For [Dostoevsky]," Miller writes, "the memory evidently remained that a conspiracy *in intent* had . . . existed for the future. The aim [of 'the society for propaganda'] was to spread discontent with the existing order everywhere, beginning with the schools: to establish connections with everybody who was already discontented—with the religious dissidents (*raskolniki*) and the peasant serfs."[12]

Some further light on the organization is cast by an oath of allegiance found among Speshnev's papers after his arrest. The signer pledged himself to obey the orders of the central committee whenever this executive body decided that the time for a revolution had arrived. He promised to take part in the battle at the appointed time and place; to come equipped with firearms, or cold steel, or both; and to fight "without sparing himself" for the success of the cause.[13] The dossier about Speshnev compiled in 1849 for the investigating commission has unfortunately been lost, and what we know about him comes largely at secondhand through the testimony of others and the summary of his case made for Nicholas I. Of all the Petrashevtsy arrested, only Speshnev was threatened with the use of more severe methods of extracting information. Under the threat, Speshnev disclosed the existence of the smaller group that had grown out of the Petrashevsky Fridays, and also the secret conversations with Chernosvitov and Mombelli. These new leads succeeded in throwing the commission off the scent of the secret society, but the oath gives us a lurid glimpse into the kind of society

---

[11] Ibid., 271–274.
[12] *Biografiya*, 90.
[13] Evgrafova, *Proizvedeniya Petrashevtsev*, 503–504.

that Speshnev would have formed, and allows us to imagine some of the atmosphere of its deliberations.

———■———

Dr. Yanovsky, whom Dostoevsky had refused even to take to Petrashevsky's, became aware of a notable change in the character of his friend between the end of 1848 and the time of his arrest three months later. "He became somewhat melancholy, more irritable, more touchy, ready to quarrel over the merest trifle, and very often complained of giddiness."[14] Yanovsky reassured his patient that there was no organic cause for these symptoms, and predicted that his gloomy state of mind would probably soon pass away. To which Dostoevsky replied, "'No, it will not, and it will torture me for a long time. For I have taken money from Speshnev' (he named a sum of about five hundred rubles) 'and now I am *with him* and *his*. I'll never be able to pay back such a sum, yes, and he wouldn't take the money back; that's the kind of man he is.'" And Dostoevsky repeated several times, so that the sentence engraved itself in Yanovsky's memory: "Do you understand, from now on I have a Mephistopheles of my own!"[15]

Long before his nightime conversation with Maikov, Dostoevsky had been continually anxious over the perils of his Petrashevsky involvement; and he became increasingly perturbed about the unknowns who crowded into Petrashevsky's flat week after week. Haunted by the possibility of betrayal and arrest even for assisting at these relatively innocent Petrashevsky gatherings tolerated by the authorities, how much more would he have been agitated, how much more a prey to extreme fluctuations of emotion, because of his relations with the Speshnev group! He later told his second wife that, if not for the providential accident of his arrest, he would certainly have gone mad.[16]

The sudden increase in the size of the Petrashevsky Fridays led to the formation of several satellite groups organized to take account of differing interests. Beginning in March 1848, some members decided to hold regular meetings, usually on Saturday, in the spacious apartment shared by Alexander Palm and Sergey Durov. The first was a lieutenant of the Life Guards, who also contributed to literary journals; the second was a freelance writer and translator. After his arrest, Dostoevsky told the authorities, with seeming ingenuousness, that the Palm-Durov Circle arose out of a plan to publish a literary almanac, which required all the literati to meet often for discussion.[17]

Much of what went on in the Palm-Durov Circle is still obscure. Some facts,

---

[14] *DVS*, 1: 172.

[15] Ibid.

[16] Cited by A. S. Dolinin, "Dostoevsky sredi Petrashevtsev," *Zvenya* 6 (Moscow–Leningrad, 1936), 533.

[17] Belchikov, *Dostoevsky v protsesse Petrashevtsev*, 129.

however, are indisputable. The circle included all the members of Speshnev's secret society (there is some doubt about Milyutin). The Speshnevites, as will appear, tried to mobilize the circle for the purposes of reproducing and distributing
revolutionary propaganda (the plan outlined by Dostoevsky during his midnight
visit to Maikov), but they never succeeded in doing so. Sometime toward the end
of March, Pavel Filippov, a Speshnevite, suggested that it was time for the members of the circle to share their social-political ideas with others. He proposed
that "they undertake, as a united effort, the composition of articles in a spirit of
liberalism [i.e., "revolutionary"]." It was necessary, Filippov explained, to strip
bare "all the injustice of the laws . . . [and] all the corruption and deficiencies in
the organization of our administration." [18] The articles on juridical and administrative issues could be reproduced on a home lithograph and distributed.

This proposal, enthusiastically supported by Grigoryev, Mombelli, and
Speshnev, seems to have been accepted. Topics were taken by each of the members of the circle. None of the promised articles were forthcoming, but several
manuscripts did appear that seemed suitable for propaganda purposes, and the
question of the lithograph was debated in connection with their reproduction
and distribution. The first manuscript of this kind to surface was written by
Grigoryev, a lieutenant in the horse grenadiers and a member of the Speshnev
secret society. Called "A Soldier's Conversation," this sketch concerns a peasant
shipped off to the army as punishment for attacking a landowner who had
abused his sister. A soldier in 1812, he speaks wonderingly of what he had seen in
France, where the people had thrown out a king and "now they do not want
tsars and run things for themselves, just like we do in the villages." [19] An early
example of agit-prop literature, the sketch is full of pseudo-naïve social protest,
couched in terms that peasants would presumably understand and calculated to
appeal to their mentality and values. Mikhail Dostoevsky advised Grigoryev to
destroy it, but others urged him to make it even more forceful. The only copy of
the work unearthed by the investigating commission was found among Speshnev's papers, and by Grigoryev's account, Speshnev had asked his permission to
read "A Soldier's Conversation" "practically in the public street." [20]

A manuscript by Filippov is of the same character: a new, revolutionary version of the Ten Commandments, written in a combination of Church Slavonic
and modern Russian. Each commandment is interpreted in a manner to persuade the reader that a revolt against oppression and social injustice is in conformity with the will of God. The authorities were particularly disturbed by Filippov's comments on the sixth commandment, which "said that if peasants kill

[18] Schegolev, *Petrashevtsy*, 3: 124.

[19] "A Soldier's Conversation" is reprinted in V. R. Leikina, E. A. Korolchuk, and V. A. Desnitsky,
eds., *Delo Petrashevtsev*, 3 vols. (Moscow–Leningrad, 1937–1951), 3: 233–237.

[20] Ibid., 250.

their master, they are obeying the will of God; that whoever goes to war is sinful, and the tsar in particular sins when he leads his people to commit murder."[21] Such material could only have been intended for circulation among the peasantry, and particularly, perhaps, the *raskolniki*. Dostoevsky was surely aware of its existence and may well have taken a hand in its composition.

There is still another work that the members of the Palm-Durov Circle spoke about reproducing and distributing. Pleshcheev told a group of students at the University of Moscow that "it is necessary to stir up self-consciousness in the people, and that the best means to do this would be to translate foreign works into Russian, adapting them to the speech-style of the simple people and distributing them in manuscript. And who knows, maybe some way will be found to print them. A society in Petersburg had been formed for this purpose, and . . . if we [the students] wished to cooperate with it we could begin with Lamennais's *Paroles d'un croyant.*"[22] Lamennais's work is a powerful "new Christian" attack on social injustice, and Milyukov had promised to send a copy of his translation to Moscow. Milyukov used a stately Church Slavonic for his rendering and gave it a homespun Russian title—*The New Revelations of the Metropolitan Antonio.* The work that Harold Laski once called "a lyrical version of the *Communist Manifesto*"[23] was felt to be well suited to stir up the latent dissatisfactions of the Russian peasant by its appeal to the egalitarian roots of primitive Christianity. Milyukov's translation was read at a meeting of the Palm-Durov Circle in early April.

Over the course of several weeks of discussions, however, the initial excitement over the articles gave way to second thoughts. Opposition came to the fore and was voiced most vigorously by Mikhail Dostoevsky. It is remarkable that, under arrest during the long months of investigation, Dostoevsky never states anywhere that *he personally disapproved of Filippov's idea* to print and distribute revolutionary propaganda. Instead, he reports on the disapproval of others—particularly his brother—and then associates himself with this disapproval *so that the entire Palm-Durov circle should not break up entirely*: "my brother told me that he would no longer go to Durov's if Filippov did not withdraw his proposal. . . . I noticed . . . that many would act in the same way as my brother. . . . Finally, when we met the next time, I asked for the floor and talked them all out of it, assuming a tone of light mockery and sparing as much as possible everyone's susceptibilities."[24]

If we assume that the plan for the lithograph sprang from the attempt of the Speshnev secret society to manipulate the Palm-Durov Circle, whose literary-

[21] Schegolev, *Petrashevtsy*, 3: 200.

[22] E. M. Feoktistov, *Vospominaniya* (Leningrad, 1929), 164; cited in V. R. Leikina-Svirskaya, "Revolutionaya praktika Petrashevtsev," *Istoricheskie Zapiski* 47 (1954), 210–211. Feoktistov, later a powerful bureaucrat, was one of the students to whom Pleshcheev spoke.

[23] Cited in D. O. Evans, *Social Romanticism in France, 1830–1848* (Oxford, 1951), 39.

[24] Belchikov, *Dostoevsky v protsesse Petrashevtsev*, 141.

musical character it was using as a screen for its activities, then Dostoevsky's testimony and behavior take on a distinct meaning. When the Speshnevites became aware that the Palm-Durov Circle might dissolve entirely, Dostoevsky was assigned (or took on himself) the job of smoothing matters over so that the circle could continue to be used as a cover. The investigating commission distinguished sharply between the two brothers. Mikhail was freed two months after the investigation began, and was indemnified for his loss of income (though other radicals were indignant at the miserliness of the sum awarded).[25]

Despite Dostoevsky's effort to calm the agitation, the Filippov proposal marked a turning point in the history of the Palm-Durov Circle. Both hosts became increasingly uneasy about continuing the gatherings, and when Durov asked impatiently if they could not be held elsewhere, Mombelli, probably from an impulse to keep the circle together at all costs, suggested Speshnev's. For the Palm-Durov Circle to have met at Speshnev's, however, would have negated its usefulness to his secret society, and Speshnev refused. Two or three further meetings were held at the Palm-Durov apartment, but both men were anxious to terminate them. Just before the roundup of the Petrashevtsy on April 22, 1849, Palm wrote to all members canceling the next date, and Durov made sure not to be home that evening.

It was after the plan for a lithograph was defeated that, we may infer, the Speshnevites decided to act alone. Filippov, with funds provided by Speshnev, began to order the parts for a handpress in various establishments in Petersburg. The authorities learned about the handpress from both Filippov and Speshnev, each of whom tried to shield the other by taking the blame for the idea. Dostoevsky adroitly evaded the issue. "The question speaks of a *home printing press*. I never heard from anybody at Durov's about *printing*; yes, or anywhere else. . . . Filippov suggested a *lithograph*."[26] Not finding any trace of the handpress, and unable to establish that others were involved in attempting to set it up, the commission made no further effort to pursue this line of inquiry. The existence of the Speshnev secret society was never discovered; and Dostoevsky later told Orest Miller that "many circumstances [of the case] completely slipped from view; *an entire conspiracy vanished.*"[27]

———————— ∎ ————————

Petrashevsky had perhaps gotten wind of the plan for propaganda being discussed among the Palm-Durov Circle. This may explain why, at the April 1

[25] Schegolev, *Petrashevtsy*, 3: 385. For the documents and other relevant references, see "Sledstvennoe delo M. M. Dostoevskogo—Petrashevtsa," in *Dostoevsky: materialy i issledovaniya*, ed. G. M. Fridlender, 1: 254–265.

[26] Belchikov, *Dostoevsky v protsesse Petrashevtsev*, 144.

[27] *Biografiya*, 90.

meeting of the Petrashevsky Circle, he launched a full-scale attack against the hotheads dreaming of a putsch. Outlining three problems as being of paramount social-political importance—the abolition of censorship, the reform of the judicial system, and the liberation of the serfs—Petrashevsky argued that the reform of the judicial system should be ranked as the first and most pressing goal. A reform of the courts so as to ensure public hearings and trial by jury would have a happy effect on the destinies of sixty million people, and it stood the best chance of being implemented.

The fiery twenty-year-old Golovinsky, whom Dostoevsky had brought along that evening for a first visit to Petrashevsky's, bounded to his feet and launched into a passionate refutation. Even the police spy Antonelli was impressed: "Golovinsky spoke with heat, with conviction, with genuine eloquence, and it was evident that his words came straight from the heart." He said that "it was sinful and a shame against humanity to look on indifferently at the sufferings of twelve million unhappy souls. . . . they . . . were striving for freedom themselves in every way." [28] It was impossible for the government to liberate the serfs, Golovinsky maintained, without stirring up opposition in one or another class, and without thus acting against its own political stability. The liberation of the serfs could only come "from below."

Profiting from Golovinsky's tirade, Petrashevsky took the floor to argue that the liberation of the serfs would probably lead to a class conflict that might result in a military or a clerical despotism. "To bring about the improvement of the judicial system," Petrashevsky concluded, "was much less dangerous and more realizable." [29] Golovinsky, replying to Petrashevsky's remark about class war, observed that a dictatorship would probably be necessary during the period of transition. Outraged at talk of dictatorship, and a declared admirer of the republican institutions of the United States, Petrashevsky retorted that he would be the first to raise his hand against any dictator.

This heated exchange brought into the open the conflict between the activists around Speshnev and the Fourierists or moderates for whom Petrashevsky spoke. In general, the activities of Dostoevsky and his friends (whether or not known to be members of the Speshnev society) were dedicated to radicalizing the sluggish Petrashevsky meetings and stirring their members to address themselves to the immediate revolutionary issue: the liberation of the serfs. The exchange also uncovers some of the agitated atmosphere and extreme political conclusions being drawn in Dostoevsky's immediate circle. Political democracy was a secondary consideration in their ideology, and they contemplated the idea of a revolutionary dictatorship—no doubt exercised by a body similar to Speshnev's

[28] Leikina et al., *Delo Petrashevtsev*, 426.
[29] Ibid., 427.

secret central committee—without repugnance. Where Dostoevsky stood is perfectly clear: Antonelli records that he intervened to support Golovinsky.

Two weeks later, the same argument was resumed during the famous session of the Petrashevsky Circle at which Dostoevsky read Belinsky's *Letter to Gogol*, which he had already read twice at the Palm-Durov apartment. Dostoevsky could not have found a more propitious moment to introduce the weight of Belinsky's *Letter* in the controversy already raging over tactics. Belinsky's epistle, written in the summer of 1847 as an answer to Gogol's *Selected Passages* (more accurately, as an answer to a letter of Gogol's about Belinsky's unfavorable reaction to the book), is the most powerful indictment against serfdom ever penned in Russian, and Dostoevsky and his friends used it effectively to reinforce their argument that serfdom was too morally intolerable to be endured a moment longer.

Dostoevsky read two of Gogol's letters, as well as Belinsky's text, and the effect of his rendition, as described by Antonelli, was sensational. "This letter [of Belinsky] produced a general uproar of approval. Yastrzhemsky shouted, at all the passages that struck him: 'That's it! That's it!' Balosoglo went into hysterics, and in a word, the whole group was electrified."[30] Dostoevsky then took the copies back and asked Filippov "to keep [the matter] a secret."[31] Dostoevsky also passed the text to Mombelli, who, with incredible rashness, gave it to his regimental scribe and asked him to make several more copies. This evidence that Dostoevsky was actively circulating and propagandizing Belinsky's *Letter* weighed heavily against him.

Gogol's *Selected Passages* is a curious book that continues to baffle and irritate admirers of his work. Here the erstwhile pitiless satirist of Russian life displays his conversion to a religious pietism that, if it remains aware of social injustice, nonetheless sees the only remedy in the inner striving of each Christian soul for moral self-improvement and self-perfection. The work was an abrupt slap in the face for all those who believed (as did many Slavophils, not to mention the progressive Westernizers) that serfdom was incompatible with genuine Christianity. Belinsky was outraged by the book, not only because of its possible social repercussions but also as a personal insult—a betrayal of everything he had fought for under the banner of Gogol's name. He could not, of course, attack the book too violently in public print; but when he received a private letter from Gogol expressing surprise at his unfavorable reaction, his anger burst forth in a raging flood of invective. Herzen called this white-hot torrent of words Belinsky's last "testament," and even Lenin, in the late nineteenth century, admired the fiery ardor of its indignation.[32]

[30] Ibid., 435.
[31] Schegolev, *Petrashevtsy*, 3: 201.
[32] Both are cited in V. G. Belinsky, *Selected Philosophical Works* (Moscow, 1948), 529.

Despite its reputation as a revolutionary manifesto, however, Belinsky's *Letter to Gogol* is relatively moderate in its concrete demands. Moreover, Belinsky responds to Gogol in the accents of a Utopian Socialist new Christian, even though he had presumably by this time abandoned the "sentimental" values of this credo for a more "rational" ideology. "That you [Gogol] base your teaching on the Orthodox Church," Belinsky writes, "I can understand: it has always served as the prop of the knout and the servant of despotism; but why have you mixed Christ up in this? What in common have you found between Him and any church, least of all the Orthodox Church? He was the first to bring the people the teaching of freedom, equality, and brotherhood and set the seal of truth to that teaching by Martyrdom."[33] Belinsky flatly contradicts Gogol's assertion that "the Russian people are the most religious in the world" and calls them, on the contrary, "profoundly atheistic," but he means only that their religion is one of superstition and ritual rather than of true inward faith. "Superstition" (the purely external and mechanical performance of religious ritual) is barbarous and backward, but Belinsky makes clear that genuine "religiousness" can well go hand-in-hand with progress and enlightenment.[34]

Nor is Belinsky's *Letter* revolutionary in any Socialist sense at all; there is nothing in it calling for a fundamental transformation of society on new principles. It is a fervent democratic protest against despotism and serfdom that does not go beyond political liberalism in its demands. What Russia needs, Belinsky tells Gogol, "is not sermons (she has had enough of them!), or prayers (she has repeated them too often!), but the awakening in the people of a sense of their human dignity lost for so many centuries amid the dirt and the refuse; she needs rights and laws conforming not with the preaching of the Church but with common sense and justice. Instead of which she presents the dire spectacle of a country where men traffic in men, without even having the excuse so insidiously exploited by the American plantation owners who claim that the Negro is not a man." Hence, for Belinsky, "the most vital national problems in Russia today are the abolition of serfdom and corporal punishment, and the strictest possible observance of at least those laws that already exist."[35] This is the "minimal program" that Belinsky advocated in the very last year of his life.

Even though placed at a disadvantage by the wave of excitement caused by Dostoevsky's reading, Petrashevsky valiantly took the floor and tried to counter its heady effects. He argued once more that a change in the judicial system should take preeminence over all other issues. Antonelli summed up his reasoning: "a reform of the judicial system could be achieved in the most legal fashion, by demanding from the government those things it could not refuse, being

---

[33] Ibid., 506.
[34] Ibid., 506–507.
[35] Ibid., 504.

aware that they were just."[36] Golovinsky, taking a conciliatory line, pointed out that the liberation of the serfs might perhaps be obtained through the courts, particularly in the Western provinces; and he asked permission to pursue this topic at the next two meetings. "In general," writes Antonelli with a flourish, "the meeting of the 15th, as the foreign newspapers express it, was *très orageuse.*"[37]

Thrones were toppling everywhere in Europe in 1848; new rights were being obtained, new liberties being clamored for. The arrest of Dostoevsky and the entire Petrashevsky Circle occurred as part of the tsar's endeavor to suppress the slightest manifestation of independent thought that, sympathizing with the revolutions erupting elsewhere, might perhaps lead to similar convulsions closer to home. The last years of Nicholas's reign froze Russian society into a terrified immobility, and whatever few traces of independent intellectual and cultural life had been allowed to exist earlier were simply wiped away. To take only one example, the new minister of education, Prince Shirinsky-Shakhmatov, eliminated the teaching of philosophy and metaphysics in the universities. "It drives one insane," Granovsky wrote to a friend in 1850. "Good for Belinsky who died in time."[38]

On April 22, the date of the last meeting at Petrashevsky's, Dostoevsky spent the evening at Grigoryev's, perhaps talking over plans with him and others for the operation of the handpress. At four in the morning he returned home and went to bed, but shortly thereafter was awakened by a faint metallic sound in the room. Opening his eyes sleepily, he saw standing before him the local police official, and a lieutenant-colonel dressed in the light blue uniform of an officer of the Third Section—the dreaded secret police. Told politely by the officer to rise and dress, he did so while his room was searched and his papers sealed. Finally, Dostoevsky was conducted to a waiting carriage, accompanied by the local police official, the officer, his frightened landlady, and her servant Ivan, who "looked around with an air of stupid solemnity appropriate to the occasion."[39] When Dostoevsky left the room and entered the carriage, he stepped out of the relatively normal life he had been living up to that time—with the exception of his brief apprenticeship as an underground conspirator—and into an extraordinary new and alien world.

This new world would strain Dostoevsky's emotional and spiritual capacities to the utmost and immeasurably widen the range of his moral and psychological experience. What he had only read about previously in the most extravagant

[36] Leikina et al., *Delo Petrashevtsev*, 3: 435.
[37] Ibid., 436.
[38] Quoted in V. I. Cheshikhin, *T. N. Granovsky i ego vremya* (St. Petersburg, 1905), 317.
[39] *DVS,* 1: 193.

creations of the Romantics would now become for him the very flesh and blood of his existence. He would know the chilling despair of solitude in prison; he would feel the desperate anguish of the hunted; he would live through the terrifying agony of the condemned clinging desperately to the last precious moment of life; he would sink to the lowest depths of society, live with outcasts and criminals, and listen to the talk of sadists and murderers for whom the very notion of morality was a farce; and he would have instants of sublime inner harmony, moments of fusion with the divine principle ruling the universe, in the ecstatic "aura" preceding an epileptic attack. When he returns to society again and begins to rediscover himself as a writer, the horizon of his creations will now be defined by this new world and its overwhelming revelations. And this will enable him to create works of incomparably more profound imaginative scope than had been possible in the 1840s, when his only approach to such a world had been through its Romantic stereotypes.

PART II

The Years of Ordeal, 1850–1859

CHAPTER 14

The Peter-and-Paul Fortress

"The whole city," wrote Senator K. N. Lebedev in his diary, "is preoccupied with the detention of some young people (Petrashevsky, Golovinsky, Dostoevsky, Palm, Lamansky, Grigoryev, Mikhailov, and many others), who, it is said, reach the number of 60, and this number will no doubt increase with the uncovering of links with Moscow and other cities."[1] Senator Lebedev, who was well connected and personally acquainted with some of the young men under arrest, spoke to I. P. Liprandi, a seasoned official in the Ministry of Internal Affairs, "about our child-conspirators," and received one reply: "The affair, in his opinion, is exceedingly important, and should terminate with capital punishment."[2]

At the notorious headquarters of the Third Section, close to the Summer Gardens, Dostoevsky found a good deal of bustle and stir: "light-blue gentlemen kept on arriving uninterruptedly with various victims."[3] The prisoners clustered around the official checking the identity of those brought in and could see, marked on the documents he was consulting, the name of the secret agent—P. D. Antonelli. Someone whispered in Dostoevsky's ear, using a peasant idiom, "Here, grandmother, is your St. George's Day."[4] April 23 was the spring St. George's Day in the Russian calendar of saints, but this folk expression was peculiarly appropriate in a deeper sense. It has been traced back to the decree of Boris Godunov in 1597 that abolished the right of peasants to change masters on the fall St. George's Day.[5] This was the effective beginning in Russian history of the total enslavement of the peasantry; and the idiom enshrines in folk speech the woebegone reaction of the Russian people to their loss of any liberty. The arrested Petrashevtsy were now indeed in "a fine fix" for having wished to make permanent the emancipation once enjoyed by the Russian peasant only on St. George's Day in the fall.

Dostoevsky's consternation was only heightened when he saw his younger brother, Andrey, brought in among other prisoners.[6] All spent the first day,

[1] Quoted in P. S. Schegolev, ed., *Petrashevtsy*, 3 vols. (Moscow–Leningrad, 1926–1928), 1: 127.
[2] Ibid.
[3] *DVS*, 1: 193.
[4] Ibid.
[5] I. Pawlowski, *Russisch-Deutsches Wörterbuch*, 2 vols. (Leipzig, 1974), 2: 1766.
[6] A. M. Dostoevsky, *Vospominaniya* (Leningrad, 1930), 192–193.

10. The Peter-and-Paul Fortress

April 23, scattered through various rooms of the headquarters of the Third Section. At midday, Count A. I. Orlov, the head of the secret police, made the rounds of his "guests" and favored them with a little speech. Those assembled had unfortunately not known how to use the rights and freedoms accorded to them as Russian citizens, and their behavior had forced the government to deprive them of the said freedoms. After investigation of their crimes they would be judged, and the final decision as to their lot would depend on the mercy of the tsar. No accusations were made or other information offered; nor were the prisoners allowed to converse with each other.

At about eleven in the evening, each name was called, and one by one the prisoners were taken by carriage to the ill-famed Peter-and-Paul Fortress. Built on an island in the Neva, this formidable citadel had been one of the first buildings to rise in the new city of Sankt Pieter Burkh. Here Peter the Great installed his headquarters while a vast army of serf laborers toiled and died to realize his vaulting dream of a great modern metropolis arising in the midst of the Finnish swamps, and for a few years this miniscule tuft of land became the effective capital of the Russian Empire. Deciding that the island would continue to serve as the bastion of the royal house of the Romanovs and the final resting place of its members, Peter ordered his Swiss-Italian architect, Trezzini, to erect a cathedral within the fortress grounds. Soon a Baroque church began to rise on the spot—a church whose tall and elegant bell tower, crowned with a golden cupola and spire, could be seen from every part of the city.

Less conspicuous but no less essential was a small maximum-security prison within the fortress complex, which Peter used for the seclusion, torture, and, finally, execution of his son, the Tsarevich Ivan. Later tsars also found it convenient for the detention of highly placed personages who had incurred the royal displeasure. It was here that Catherine the Great, before shipping him off to Siberia, had imprisoned Alexander Radishchev, who had dared to expose the horrors of serfdom in his *Journey from St. Petersburg to Moscow*. It was here that the Decembrists had languished after their bungled uprising, while each awaited his turn to be taken to the Winter Palace and personally interrogated by the tsar. The prison very early acquired an evil reputation, and its ill repute only increased with time. No one had ever escaped over its wall, and it was reserved for inmates whose misdeeds were considered a danger to the state.

Even though Dostoevsky did not leave any description of the physical conditions of his incarceration, the memoirs of Andrey, as well as those of other prisoners, allow us to reconstruct them. The cells were ample for one person; most had vaulted ceilings, and all had windows (behind an iron grill) whose glass was smeared over, except at the very top, with a paste that allowed only a diffuse light to filter through. At night, each cell was lit by a small oil lamp, set high on the wall in a window embrasure, whose cotton wick often sputtered and fumed instead of giving off light. The lamp in Andrey's cell smoked so much that it stung his eyes, but when, during his first night, he made a motion to snuff it out, a voice instantly told him to desist.

All cells had a small judas in the door, and the prisoners were constantly under surveillance by guards walking silently in the corridors. The furniture consisted of a cot, a stove of Dutch tiles, a table, a stool, and, in one corner, what Andrey calls "a necessary piece of furniture,"[7] probably a basin and a close-stool. The cot was covered with a straw mattress and a pillow of sacking material without sheets or pillowcase; the only covering was a blanket made of the coarse and heavy woolen cloth used for army overcoats. The walls of Andrey's cell had recently been scraped to remove the graffiti of previous occupants; other cells still retained traces of the marks made on them by those struggling against apathy and numb dejection.

Most of the accounts of the fortress complain of its dampness, and Andrey writes that "one felt the cold piercing through to the very bones. I never took off the warm overcoat in which I slept."[8] Other prisoners were not so appreciative of the prison garb they were forced to wear. "Cold shivers run all through me," writes the gently nurtured P. A. Kuzmin, an officer of the General Staff, "when I remember the sensation I felt in putting on my convict's clothes"—made of the roughest material and stained by previous usage—whose contact with his flesh filled him with uncontrollable repulsion.[9] Besides the cold, Andrey was also bothered by the appearance of good-sized rats the moment darkness came on, and he slept only during the daytime for fear of being attacked.

[7] Ibid., 196.
[8] Ibid.
[9] M. N. Gernet, *Istoriya tsarskoi tyurmy*, 5 vols. (Moscow, 1961), 2: 220.

Andrey's cell was in the Zotov bastion, more dilapidated than other sections of the prison. For he recalled the commandant of the fortress, General I. A. Nabokov (the great-great-uncle of the author of *Lolita*), looking round him with distaste on his first visit and muttering, "Yes, it's bad here, very bad, and we've got to hurry"—meaning to build new quarters for prisoners.[10] Dostoevsky was placed in the Alekseevsky Ravelin, which was reserved for the most important prisoners. We may assume that his living conditions were much the same as those that I. F. Jastrzembski praises ("all the hygienic conditions there were satisfactory; fresh air, cleanliness, good food, etc., everything was fine")[11] and superior to those afforded his brother. Those prisoners who had a little money could have tea brought to them twice a day and could buy cigars, cigarettes, and tobacco. But "no book, not a sheet of paper," writes Andrey, "was allowed. One could only dream and mull over what might lie ahead."[12]

Most trying for the imprisoned was the silence, the isolation, and the sense of being continually under secret observation. "The very thought that I was being held *au secret*," writes Jastrzembski, "brought on nervous attacks, fainting, and palpitations of the heart."[13] Akhsharumov, who could hear deep sighs, and sometimes the sound of weeping, from neighboring cells and from the corridor, remarked that these, along with "the silence, the stuffy air, total inactivity . . . exercised a dispiriting effect, which took away courage."[14] Petrashevsky complained that he was being tortured and deprived of sleep by mysterious tappings on the wall and by whispering voices also coming from the wall, which disconcertingly substituted themselves for his own thoughts.

———■———

The Commission of Inquiry was headed by General Nabokov and included General P. P. Gagarin, Count V. A. Dolgorukov, General Ya. I. Rostovtsev, and General Dubelt. When it became clear to the commission that the young student Andrey Dostoevsky had been arrested by error, the other members were willing to allow him to languish in his cell until the formalities for his release had been completed, but Nabokov protested and installed Andrey in his own quarters. Both Feodor Dostoevsky and Durov spoke to Milyukov "with particular warmth . . . of the commandant [Nabokov], who had continually concerned himself with them and, so far as he could, eased their condition."[15]

[10] A. M. Dostoevsky, *Vospominaniya*, 197.
[11] Schlegolev, *Petrashevtsy*, I: 149.
[12] A. M. Dostoevsky, *Vospominaniya*, 197.
[13] Schlegolev, *Petrashevtsy*, I: 149.
[14] N. F. Belchikov, *Dostoevsky v protsesse Petrashevtsev* (Moscow, 1971), 244.
[15] *DVS*, I: 191.

Dubelt, representing the Third Section, was sharply attentive to the proceedings and intervened frequently in barbed and sarcastic tones. He had been greatly upset on learning that the surveillance of the Petrashevsky Circle had been carried on for over a year without his knowledge, and he regarded this concealment as a personal insult. It was to satisfy a private vendetta, as well as to protect his bureaucratic interests, that he undertook, at every opportunity, to undermine the importance given to the case by the Ministry of Internal Affairs and by his ex-army comrade Liprandi. Jastrzembski, so severe for everyone else, remarks: "I know several instances in which he did as much as he could to help those accused of political crimes, and I do not know of a single instance in which he destroyed anybody."[16]

The commission interviewed the prisoners individually and questioned them on the basis of the information supplied by Antonelli; they were also asked to answer questions in writing touching on their associations with Petrashevsky and other members of the circle. Additional information was being continuously supplied by the group set up to study the papers and documents confiscated at the time of the arrest, and these of course provided some of the crucial evidence. Dostoevsky was called for questioning several times between April 26 and May 16, and later he told only one rather dubious story to Orest Miller about his treatment: that Rostovtsev had offered him a pardon in exchange for telling about "the whole business."[17] Whether true or not, the story indicates that Dostoevsky recalled the interrogation as far more nerve-racking than terrifying.

"When I found myself in the fortress," Dostoevsky told Vsevolod Solovyev in 1873, "I thought that the end had come, that I would not last three days, and—suddenly I calmed down. Look, what did I do there? I wrote "A Little Hero"—read it, is there any sign of bitterness or torment in it? I dreamed peaceful, fine, good dreams, and then, the longer it lasted, the better it was."[18] Dostoevsky's state of mind, not to mention the state of his health, was much more precarious than he later recalled. But he did find unexpected reserves of inner strength that enabled him to endure the trials of captivity without losing heart, and it was this sense of mastery that dominated in his recollection of the event.

In his first letter from the fortress, written on June 20, Dostoevsky tells Andrey to write the Kumanins in Moscow requesting help for himself and for Mikhail's family. Most important, though, he wanted to see the latest issue of *Notes of the Fatherland.* "The third part of my novel is appearing, but . . . I didn't even see the galleys . . . haven't they disfigured my novel?"[19] Dostoevsky seems more concerned with this problem than about his personal predicament, and

---

[16] Schlegolev, *Petrashevtsy,* 1: 160–161.
[17] *Biografiya,* 106–107.
[18] *DVS,* 2: 199.
[19] *Pisma,* 4: 258–259; June 20, 1849.

there is as yet no sign of any emotional perturbation. Some of the other Petrashevtsy began to go to pieces in captivity as the months wore on and the interrogations continued.

At the beginning of July, the prisoners were given permission to receive books and to correspond with the outside world. By this time Mikhail had been released, and Dostoevsky's letters to him inform us about his physical condition and state of mind. "My health is good," he writes on July 18, "except for the hemorrhoids and my nervous troubles, which go *crescendo*. I have begun to have nervous spasms as before, my appetite is poor, and I sleep very little, with painful dreams when I do. I sleep about five hours of the twenty-four, and wake up about four times every night."[20] A month later, he writes: "I have been living on castor oil for a whole month now and it is all that keeps me alive. My hemorrhoids are terribly inflamed and I have a pain in my chest I never had before. Moreover, my impressionability increases, especially at night; I have long, ugly dreams, and to top it all, I have recently felt all the time as though the floor were heaving under me, and I sit in my room literally as if in a ship's cabin. From all this, I conclude that my nerves are giving way."[21] In mid-September, he writes Mikhail that his health has not improved and that he is anticipating the advent of autumn with misgiving, but that he refuses to lose heart: "I only wish to remain healthy," he writes, "and anyhow, *a good disposition depends on myself alone.* Man has infinite reserves of toughness and vitality; I really did not think there was so much, but now I know it from experience."[22]

The moment Dostoevsky was given access to reading material, he threw himself on whatever was available with indiscriminate eagerness, but what he comments on, in his letters to Mikhail, are the new works appearing in *Notes of the Fatherland*—mostly translations. In this period (known as "the era of censorship terror"), Russian literature was muzzled by a censorship fiercer than any it had known for a long time, and few Russian writers were willing to say anything that might be considered in the least provocative. The notoriously obscurantist Count Buturlin, who headed a special commission to tighten the censorship, was reputed to have said that "if the Gospel were not as widespread as it was, it would be necessary to ban it on account of the democratic spirit it disseminated."[23] Nonetheless, Dostoevsky tried to write. "I have," he tells Mikhail in his first letter, "thought out three stories and two novels; one of them I am now writing, but I am afraid to work too much."[24] In the next letter, he explains why:

[20] Ibid., 1: 124; July 18, 1849.

[21] Ibid., 126; August 27, 1849.

[22] Ibid., 127; September 14, 1849.

[23] P. V. Annenkov, *The Extraordinary Decade*, ed. Arthur P. Mendel, trans. Irwin R. Titunik (Ann Arbor, MI, 1968), 243.

[24] *Pisma*, 1: 124; July 18, 1849.

"When I was attacked by similar nervous states in the past, I made use of them to write—I can always do more and better writing in this condition—but now I have to hold back, so as not to finish myself off for good."[25]

In prison, the only project Dostoevsky completed was the charming story now called "A Little Hero." It was given to Mikhail after Dostoevsky had been sent to Siberia, and eight years later it was printed anonymously in *Notes of the Fatherland*. Taking place in a world that Dostoevsky rarely touches: the world of wealthy landowners living on their country estates—the world of Turgenev and Tolstoy—the story is purely personal, a deft psychological sketch notable in Dostoevsky's work only for the "normalcy" of the youthful passions it depicts. Nevertheless, the main intrigue—the boy's worshipful adoration of his beloved—is noteworthy, because his love consists in an act of self-sacrifice to aid a suffering soul and in keeping a secret. Might not Dostoevsky have seen himself precisely in some such terms at this particular moment?

As one scrutinizes what Dostoevsky wrote and said—in answer to unspecified accusations, and attempting to parry the suspicions of his interrogators—it is clear that he tried to protect himself as best he could; and he made the same effort on behalf of others. "When I went off to Siberia," he later wrote, "I took with me at least the consolation of having behaved honorably in the investigation, not imputing my guilt to others, and even sacrificing my own interests if I saw the possibility of protecting others from trouble in my deposition. But I held myself in check. I did not confess everything, and for this I was punished more severely."[26] The mixed military-civil court that sentenced Dostoevsky gauged the severity of its punishment according to whether the accused had exhibited any repentance or had freely revealed facts otherwise unknown. Dostoevsky did neither.

■

The most important document that Dostoevsky wrote for the Commission of Inquiry was an "Explanation," which he was asked to submit immediately after the preliminary questioning on May 6. Even though no formal accusations were ever made, the questions put to him indicated the grounds on which he had been taken into custody. Accordingly, he attempted to clarify his actions so as to justify whatever about them might be considered suspicious or subversive. He gives an image of Petrashevsky as a strange and eccentric character, constantly and fussily occupied with futilities, a person hardly to be taken seriously from any practical point of view and of no possible danger to the state. By inference, Dostoevsky's participation in such activity was equally innocuous.

[25] Ibid., 126; August 27, 1849.
[26] Ibid., 178; March 24, 1856.

Dostoevsky said nothing about the Palm-Durov group because their existence had not yet been discovered. Claiming he had spoken only three times at Petrashevsky's and only on nonpolitical topics, he attempts to justify what could be considered his "freethinking" and "liberalism." In the most bizarre vindication recorded in the entire annals of the Petrashevsky proceedings, he maintains that, far from proving any hostility to the régime, whatever inflammatory words he may have uttered should be taken as an exhibition of his trust in the government as the guardian of the rights enjoyed by the citizens of a civilized state! "I was always offended by this fear of speech, much more apt to be offensive to the government than agreeable to it. . . . This means that one assumes the law does not adequately protect the individual, and that it is possible to be destroyed because of an empty word, an incautious phrase."[27] It is impossible to imagine Dostoevsky advancing such an argument except with bitter irony; no one could believe that the government of Nicholas I was *insulted* by the terrified silence of its citizens and wished them to utter their opinions on social-political topics more vociferously!

Dostoevsky also tried to answer the more concrete charges that he could conceive being leveled against him, and in doing so he discusses his views in a manner that reveals certain patterns of thought whose constancy entitles us to accept them as his genuine convictions. "In the West," he writes, "a terrible spectacle is taking place. . . . The age-old order of things is cracking and falling to pieces."[28] In his view "the Western revolution" is "*a historical necessity* of the contemporary crisis in that part of the world."[29] Dostoevsky has thus already developed his apocalyptic view of Europe on the brink of crisis and collapse, and he also draws the same sharp line between Europe and Russia that was to remain a permanent feature of his thought. Vigorously denying that he considered any such revolution "a historical necessity" for his fatherland, he writes, "In my eyes, nothing could be more nonsensical than the idea of a republican government in Russia."[30] Dostoevsky had no theoretical objections to autocratic rule; nor, it might be recalled, had most of the early Utopian Socialists, such as Fourier, who appealed unsuccessfully to several monarchs to finance the establishment of phalansteries in their countries. If Dostoevsky was willing to participate in a conspiracy against the autocracy now, it was only because his hatred of serfdom had reached a pitch of intensity that swept aside all ancillary considerations.

Relying on an image popularized in Walter Scott's *Ivanhoe* and given authority by the Romantic historian Augustin Thierry, Dostoevsky describes European history as a more than one-thousand-year-old "stubborn struggle between soci-

[27] Belchikov, *Dostoevsky v protsesse Petrashevtsev*, 98.
[28] Ibid., 100.
[29] Ibid., 101.
[30] Ibid., 100.

ety and an authority deriving from a foreign civilization of conquest, force, and repression."[31] No such problem existed in Russia, where it had been the native autocracy that time and again had saved the country from enslavement and chaos. Russia had twice been rescued, Dostoevsky writes, "solely by the efforts of the autocracy: first from the Tartars, and second in the reforms of Peter the Great, when solely a warmly childlike faith in its great pilot made it possible for Russia to endure such a sharp swerve into a new life."[32] The same view of the providential role of the reigning tsars will crop up again and again in his later utterances.

Indeed, Dostoevsky would have welcomed a tsar willing to save the country again by eliminating the intolerable blight of serfdom. "If reforms are pending," he writes, "such reforms must come from an authority even much more reinforced during this period; otherwise, the matter will have to be dispatched in a revolutionary fashion. I do not think that admirers of a Russian revolt can be found in Russia. Well-known examples are recalled to this day, though they occurred long ago."[33] This menacing reference to the bloody uprisings of Pugachev and Stenka Razin, prefiguring the kind of revolts that might be provoked again unless liberating changes were made, was hardly calculated to reassure Dostoevsky's judges. But when all hope of such reforms "from above" had been crushed after 1848, it was such reasoning that had persuaded Dostoevsky to participate in the desperate venture organized by Speshnev. Dostoevsky writes in conclusion: "I recall my words, repeated by me at various times, that everything of any value in Russia, beginning with Peter the Great, invariably came from above, from the throne; while from below, up to the present, nothing had been manifested except obstinacy and ignorance. This opinion of mine is well known to my acquaintances."[34]

The gravest charge that Dostoevsky knew had been made against him was that he had read aloud Belinsky's *Letter to Gogol*, which is equally violent against all those institutions of throne, state, and church that the erstwhile satirist had taken under his wing. Dostoevsky claimed that he had read the exchange of letters in a perfectly neutral manner, and he blocks in a picture of his personal relations with the most notorious radical of his time as a way of justifying his interest in the explosive missive. "I criticized him for striving to give literature a partial significance unworthy of it," he writes, "degrading it to the description . . . *solely*

---

[31] Ibid., 101.

[32] Ibid.

[33] Ibid.

[34] Ibid. Annenkov writes of the 1840s: "Literature and our cultivated minds had long ago relinquished the notion of the people as a human entity ordained to live without rights of citizenship and to serve the interests of others only, but they had not relinquished the notion of the people as a brutish mass without any ideas and with never a thought in its head." Annenkov, *Decade*, 134.

of journalistic facts or scandalous occurrences. . . . [You] only bore everybody to death when you clutch at everyone coming and going in the street . . . and begin to preach at him forcibly and teach him reason. Belinsky became angry with me, and finally from coolness it came to a formal quarrel, so that we did not see each other all through the last year of his life."[35]

Regarding the *Letter* itself, Dostoevsky explains: "I [was] firmly convinced that it could not lead anyone into temptation, although it is not lacking in some sort of literary value. . . . I do not agree exactly with a single one of the exaggerations that it contains."[36] This rather feeble disclaimer is as far as Dostoevsky could go in concealing his fundamental agreement with Belinsky's powerful assault. Dostoevsky at this point makes his one and only concession to the perils of the situation and expresses regret at his lack of caution: "I have only now understood that I made a mistake and that I should not have read that work aloud."[37]

To conclude his "Explanation," Dostoevsky returns to the question of his relations with Petrashevsky ("I know absolutely nothing of the secrets of Petrashevsky"),[38] and he proceeds to discuss Fourierism in general for the benefit of the commission. "Fourierism, and along with it every Western system, is so unsuited to our soil, so unrelated to our conditions, so alien to the character of our nation—while, on the other hand, it is so much a product of the situation of things there in the West, where the proletarian question is being solved at any cost—that Fourierism, with its relentless necessity, at the present time, among us who have no proletariat, would be killingly funny."[39] What he writes corresponds, as we have seen, exactly with utterances that he had made freely in the Palm-Durov Circle. And Dostoevsky had already found the *tone* in which he would later depict the Utopian Socialists: he would never portray them except in a satirical and parodistic manner.

■

By June, the commission had learned a good deal about what had gone on in the Petrashevsky Circle, discovered the existence of the Palm-Durov group, and got wind of the plan discussed there to lithograph prohibited texts for illegal circulation. Called in four more times for interrogation and presented with a further list of questions, Dostoevsky had to pick his way carefully among dangerous pitfalls, and we can watch him trying not to be trapped in an outright lie, or seeming to hold back information, while guarding against any utterance that

[35] Belchikov, *Dostoevsky v protsesse Petrashevtsev*, 105.
[36] Ibid., 105–106.
[37] Ibid., 106.
[38] Ibid., 109.
[39] Ibid., 111–112.

might prove injurious to himself or to others. He denied that his youthful friend Golovinsky had advocated a revolution in order to obtain the liberation of the serfs or had envisaged "a revolutionary dictatorship" during the period of turmoil and transition to a new government. His replies to all such questions were evasive or consisted of elaborate circumlocutions intended to confuse the issue entirely. No wonder General Rostovtsev commented that, as a witness, Dostoevsky had been "clever, independent, cunning, stubborn."[40]

The final examination of all the defendants took place before the mixed military-civil court appointed to pass sentence on the accused. Each was summoned into its presence in mid-October, told he was to be judged according to military law (much more severe than the civil code), and asked to submit in writing anything further he wished to add to his testimony. Some of the Petrashevtsy took this opportunity to throw themselves on the mercy of the authorities in a humiliating fashion. To cite one instance, Akhsharumov wrote: "I repent everything and ask for pardon, and I write this not because I wish to be spared the punishment I deserve, but out of remorse, with a pure heart; feeling myself gravely guilty toward thee, as my Sovereign, I consider it my duty as a Christian and a subject to plead for pardon. Forgive me, Sire, if it is possible, because of my remorse and in memory of the service of my father."[41]

Dostoevsky, however, maintained his reserve and dignity to the end, and replied in quite another style. "I can add nothing new to my defense," he says, "except perhaps this—that I never acted with an evil and premeditated intention against the government—what I did was done thoughtlessly and much almost accidentally, as for example my reading of Belinsky's letter."[42] It was not the government of Nicholas I that he abhorred but the horrifying institution of serfdom, which he detested with an implacable hatred.

The Commission of Inquiry completed its work on September 17, 1849. The decision of the mixed military-civil court, handed down on November 16, condemned fifteen of the accused, including Dostoevsky, to execution by firing squad; others were given lesser sentences to hard labor and exile. This judgment was then sent for review to the highest military court, the General-Auditoriat, which declared that a judicial error had been committed and ruled more harshly than the military-civil court. It pointed out that, under the law used for field courts-martial, all the prisoners should have been equally condemned to death by execution. Dostoevsky's dossier was also revised by the higher court. Originally, he had been sentenced for having read aloud and circulated Belinsky's *Letter*, and also for having failed to denounce Grigoryev's "A Soldier's Conversation" to the authorities. A third charge was now added: he had "taken part in

---

[40] Ibid., 86.
[41] Schlegolev, *Petrashevtsy*, 3: 164.
[42] Belchikov, *Dostoevsky v protsesse Petrashevtsev*, 176.

deliberations about printing and distributing works against the government by means of a home lithograph."[43]

Once having asserted the full rigor of the law, the General-Auditoriat asked the tsar to show mercy. Instead of death, a list of lesser sentences was appended and submitted for the tsar's scrutiny, and he accepted the plea for mercy. It was known that Nicholas enjoyed playing the role of all-powerful but clement ruler, and Senator Lebedev confided to his journal that the General-Auditoriat had probably increased the severity of the recommended sentences in order to allow Nicholas more amply to exhibit his forbearance.[44] No mercy, however, was shown to Petrashevsky, whose sentence—exile and hard labor in the mines for life—was simply confirmed. For most of the others (though not all), Nicholas shortened the length of the sentences.

Dostoevsky, initially condemned to eight years of hard labor instead of outright execution, enjoyed a reduction in his period of penal servitude to four years, after which he was ordered to serve in the Russian Army for an indeterminate time. Dostoevsky regarded this latter provision as a special dispensation personally granted in his favor by the tsar (the same sentence was given to Durov). A convict sentenced to hard labor lost all his civil rights and did not regain them even after having completed his sentence, but Dostoevsky's civil rights would automatically be restored by military service. He believed this to have been the first time that a convict had been allowed to regain his civil rights, and that it "occurred according to the will of the Emperor Nicholas I, taking pity on his youth and talent."[45] Whether justified or not, this conviction nonetheless helps to explain some of Dostoevsky's later favorable utterances about Nicholas.

Final disposition of the case was made on December 21. The law called for a mock execution to be staged when a sentence of death had been commuted by an act of imperial grace, but this ceremony was usually just a ritual formality. In this case, however, explicit instructions came from the tsar that only after all the preparations had been completed for putting them to death were the prisoners to be told that their lives had been spared. Nicholas carefully orchestrated events to produce the maximum impact on the unsuspecting victims of his regal solicitude. And Dostoevsky thus underwent the extraordinary emotional adventure of believing himself to have been only a few moments away from certain death, and then of being miraculously resurrected from the grave.

———■———

Once their interrogation had been completed in October, the prisoners learned nothing more about the deliberations concerning their case. The dreary days

[43] *PSS*, 11: 189–190.
[44] V. I. Semevsky, "Sledstvie i sud po delu Petrashevtsev," *Russkie Zapiski*, 9–11 (1916), 11: 31.
[45] Miller, *Biografiya*, 115.

rolled by with deadening monotony. "My incarceration had already gone on for eight months," writes Akhsharumov in his memoirs, "I had ceased talking to myself, moved about the room somewhat mechanically, or lay on my cot in apathy."[46] On the morning of December 22, though, the prisoners became aware of an unusual animation in the corridors of the fortress, whose deathly stillness had been broken only by the peal of the church bells. Looking out of the window of his cell, Akhsharumov noticed a number of carriages lining up in the courtyard—so many of them, indeed, that it seemed the line would never end. Suddenly, he saw them being surrounded by squadrons of mounted police. Only then did it occur to him that the bustle and stir might have something to do with the Petrashevsky case, and that he had lived to see the day when the tedium of his imprisonment was finally to be relieved.

Meanwhile, he could also hear within the prison the sound of guards noisily opening the cells. His turn came at last, and he was handed the clothing in which he had been seized—light spring clothing—as well as some warm, thick socks. He was told to dress, but he received only an evasive answer to his excited questions and was ordered to hurry. Escorted out of the cell and along the corridor to an outside porch, he was placed in the two-seater closed carriage that quickly drew up, and a soldier clambered in as escort. Unable to see through the frost-covered window, he scratched at the pane with his fingernail to clear a view as the carriage began to move, but could catch only dim glimpses of the awakening city as the carriage rolled through the early morning streets.

There is no account of Dostoevsky's feelings during this seemingly interminable journey, but they must have been similar to those recorded by others. The excitement of the departure, and all it might portend, produced an invigorating and exhilarating effect. The evidence indicates that not a single one of the Petrashevtsy imagined they could possibly be condemned to death; even the cynical Speshnev, who had recommended the use of terror as a revolutionary weapon, told Orest Miller that the idea of being driven to meet a firing squad never crossed his mind.[47]

Akhsharumov calculated that the trip lasted about thirty minutes before the carriage stopped and he was told to step outside. "Looking around, I saw . . . the Semenovsky Square. It was covered with newly fallen snow and surrounded by troops formed into a square. On the edges far away stood a crowd of people looking at us; everything was silent; it was the morning of a clear wintry day, and the sun, just having risen, shone like a bright, beautiful globe on the horizon through the haze of the thick clouds."[48] The sight of the sun, which he had not seen for eight months, overwhelmed Akhsharumov with a sense of well-being,

[46] *DVS*, I: 223.
[47] *Biografiya*, 117.
[48] *DVS*, I: 226.

and for a moment he forgot where he was. But he came to himself when, roughly seized by the elbow, he was shoved forward and told in which direction to move. Only then did he become aware that he was standing in a foot of deep snow and that, dressed in his light clothing, he was bitterly cold.

It was only then, too, that he became aware of a construction, slightly to his left, that had been built in the middle of the square—a four-sided scaffolding, twenty to thirty feet high, hung round with black crêpe, and with a staircase leading up from the ground. But he was more interested in the sight of a group of his old comrades crowding together in the snow and exchanging excited greetings after their long separation. What struck him, as he came closer, was the terrible change that had taken place in the features of those he knew best: "Their faces were emaciated, exhausted, pale, drawn, several had untrimmed beards and uncut hair. I was especially struck by the face of Speshnev; he had always stood out from the others because of his notable handsomeness, vigor, and flourishing good health. His face, once circular, had become longer; it was sickly, pale yellow, with gaunt cheeks, eyes as if sunken and with great blue rings underneath, framed by long hair and a large overgrown beard."[49]

The joyous moment of reunion was quickly interrupted by the loud voice of a general, who rode up and ordered them to remain silent. A Civil Service official then had the prisoners lined up according to the order in which he called their names, Petrashevsky and Speshnev being first on the list. A priest carrying a cross succeeded the official and declared to the assembled prisoners: "Today you will bear the just decision of your case—follow me."[50] And he led the procession to the scaffolding, but only after passing in front of the entire array of troops. Several of the Petrashevtsy had been officers in the Petersburg regiments lining the square, and the purpose of the maneuver was to display to the soldiers the degradation of their disloyal superiors. Conversation resumed again as the prisoners stumbled through the snow, and their attention was attracted by some gray stakes rising from the ground on one side of the scaffold. What were they for? Would they be tied to them and shot? Surely not, though it was impossible to tell what might happen—probably they would all be sent to penal servitude. So ran the snatches of talk that Akhsharumov heard while the group was led to the staircase.[51]

Once having ascended the platform, the prisoners were separated again and arranged in two files on each side. Standing beside Mombelli, Dostoevsky quickly and incongruously, in a state of febrile agitation, told him the plan of a story he had written in prison. Suddenly the square resounded with the crisp, metallic sound of soldiers snapping to attention, and the accused were ordered

[49] Ibid., 226–227.
[50] Ibid.
[51] Ibid.

to remove their headgear while their sentences were being read. Most hesitated to obey the order in the biting cold, and the soldiers standing behind them were ordered to rip off their hats. Another Civil Service official, in full dress uniform, then moved along the line so as to face each man while reading to him the list of his imputed crimes and the punishment. It was impossible, according to Akhsharumov, to catch what he said because he spoke so rapidly and indistinctly. But, during the half-hour or so that he was performing his function, one sentence echoed and re-echoed like the tolling of a funeral bell: "The Field Criminal Court has condemned all to death before a firing squad."[52]

As the meaning of these words began to sink in, the sun suddenly appeared again through the clouds, and Dostoevsky, turning to Durov, said, "It's not possible that we'll be executed."[53] In reply, Durov gestured to a peasant cart standing beside the scaffolding, in which were piled up, as he mistakenly imagined, coffins covered with straw matting. From that moment, as Dostoevsky recalled, he was convinced that he was doomed, and he could never afterward forget the words thrown out so matter-of-factly: "condemned to death by a firing squad." After the official finished, the prisoners were given long white peasant blouses and nightcaps—their funeral shrouds—and helped into them by their military escort. The same priest, now with Bible as well as cross in hand, appeared on the scaffolding again and uttered the following appeal: "Brothers! Before dying one must repent. . . . The Savior forgives the sins of those who repent. . . . I call you to confession."[54]

In 1873, Dostoevsky wrote that many of the Petrashevtsy who heard this entreaty may have been troubled by lapses they wished to confess ("those which every man, throughout his life, conceals in his conscience"). "But that action for which we were being condemned," writes Dostoevsky, "those thoughts, those ideas, which ruled our souls—they seemed to us not only not to require repentance, but even to be something purifying, a martyrdom for which much could be forgiven!"[55] Akhsharumov reports that none of the Petrashevtsy responded to the priest's repeated call to repent. But if the Petrashevtsy refused to lend themselves to a public act of contrition, they did not exhibit any hostility to the sacred symbol of the Christian faith in which all had been raised. When the priest moved down the row and held up the cross to their lips, they unanimously—including such confirmed atheists as Petrashevsky and Speshnev—kissed it. Much later, in *The Idiot*, Dostoevsky depicted such a scene, and suggested that the kiss, without containing anything specifically "religious," helped the condemned man to sustain the ordeal.

[52] Ibid., 229.
[53] Miller, *Biografiya*, 118.
[54] *DVS*, 1: 229.
[55] *DW*, 152.

11. The mock execution of the Petrashevtsy

What occurred next was the most terrifying of all: the first three men in one of the rows—Petrashevsky, Mombelli, and Grigoryev—were seized by the arm, taken off the platform, and tied to the stakes standing just beside it. In one account—that of F. N. Lvov, which tends to glorify Petrashevsky—the impenitent agitator is supposed to have quipped in going from the platform to the stakes: "Mombelli, lift your legs higher, otherwise you'll go to the kingdom of heaven with a cold."[56] The order was given to pull the caps of the bound men over their heads, but Petrashevsky defiantly pushed his back and stared straight at a firing squad taking aim. Dostoevsky was among the next three in the row from which the first group had been selected, and he fully expected that his turn would come in a few moments.

What was he feeling at this time? Quite late in life, he told Orest Miller that "he felt only a mystic terror, and was completely dominated by the thought that in perhaps five minutes he would be going to another, unknown life."[57] He describes his emotions in the famous passage from *The Idiot* in which Prince Myshkin tells the Epanchin ladies what he heard from a man who believed he had just five minutes to live before being executed: "His uncertainty and his repulsion

[56] F. N. Lvov, "Zapiska o dele Petrashevtsev," *LN* 63 (Moscow, 1956), 188.
[57] *Biografiya*, 119.

before the unknown, which was going to overtake him immediately, was terrible" (8: 52). *The Idiot*, of course, was written twenty years after the gruesome charade on Semenovsky Square. However Lvov, who stood with him on the scaffold, wrote between 1859 and 1861, "Dostoevsky was quite excited, he recalled *Le dernier jour d'un condamné* of Victor Hugo, and, going up to Speshnev, said: '*Nous serons avec le Christ*' [We shall be with Christ]. '*Un peu de poussière*' [A bit of dust]—the latter answered with a twisted smile."[58] Nothing could better illustrate the difference between Dostoevsky's tormented and uncertain faith and the stoicism of a confirmed atheist like Speshnev. It is precisely because Dostoevsky could not help believing in some sort of life after death that he was so tormented by its impenetrable mystery.

The suspense of waiting for the firing squad to pull the trigger—Akhsharumov recalls it as having been "terrible, repulsive, frightening"[59]—lasted about a minute, and then the roll of the drums was heard beating retreat. Not having served in the army, Akhsharumov did not understand the meaning of the signal and thought it would coincide with a volley from the rifles; the ex-officer Dostoevsky knew immediately that his life had been spared. The next moment the firing squad had lowered their rifles and were no longer taking aim; the three men at the stake were untied and returned to their places. One of them, Grigoryev, was white as a sheet, all the blood having drained from his face; he had already shown signs of mental derangement in prison, and the mock execution ceremony finished him off entirely. Never recovering his senses, he remained a helpless mental invalid for the rest of his days. Meanwhile, an aide-de-camp arrived on the scene at a gallop carrying the tsar's pardon and the real sentences. These were read to the astonished prisoners, some of whom greeted the news with relief and joy, others with confusion and resentment. The peasant blouses and the nightcaps were taken off, and two men—looking like executioners, and dressed in worn, multicolored caftans—climbed the scaffolding. Their assigned task was to break swords over the heads of the prisoners, who were compelled to kneel for this part of the ceremony; the snapping of the sword signaled exclusion from civilian life, and they were then given convict headgear, soiled sheepskin coats, and boots.

Now outfitted in the garb appropriate to their lowly status, the condemned men were still lacking one essential item—their shackles. These were dumped in the middle of the platform with a grinding crash that made the planking vibrate, but only Petrashevsky was led forward by two blacksmiths, who, fastening the chains on his legs, began to close them with a large hammer. At first standing patiently while the work was going on, Petrashevsky finally seized one of the

[58] Lvov, "Zapiska," 188.
[59] *DVS*, 1: 230.

heavy hammers and, sitting on the floor, began to rivet the shackles with his own hands. "What impelled him to do violence to himself, what he wished to express in this fashion, is difficult to say," writes Akhsharumov, "but we were all in an unhealthy frame of mind or in a state of exaltation."[60] Such a scene would have been much more understandable to Dostoevsky, with his intuitive comprehension of masochism as the self-assertion of a personality driven to desperation by helplessness and humiliation. A peasant cart then pulled up with a troika of horses and a gendarme perched beside the driver as an escort, ready to transport Petrashevsky on the first leg of his journey into exile; but he protested that he wished to say good-bye to his friends before departing. Petrashevsky then embraced each in turn and bowed deeply to them all. The unaccustomed weight of his shackles impeded him from climbing into the cart, and he had to be aided before sinking heavily into his seat and being driven away. His sentence provided that he be dispatched to Siberia immediately; the others were to follow in the course of the next several days.

———■———

The remaining prisoners were taken back to the fortress in the carriages that had brought them. On returning to his cell, Dostoevsky seized pen and paper to write Mikhail—and this moving letter allows us to grasp the moral-spiritual consequences of the ordeal he had just sustained. It is from this instant that the primarily secular perspective from which Dostoevsky had previously viewed human life sinks to the background, and what comes forward to absorb it are the agonizing "accursed questions" that have always plagued mankind—the questions whose answers can be given, if at all, only by religious faith. Dostoevsky's novels would later create a remarkable fusion between these two dimensions of human awareness. Indeed, it is this union of uncommon social sensitivity with agonized religious probings that gives his work its properly tragic character and its unique place in the history of the novel.

Poured out in the fever of the moment, Dostoevsky's letter mingles penetrating glimpses into the recesses of his soul with requests for aid, last-minute instructions, and a sober factual account of what had just occurred. Notable is the deep love it exhibits for his older brother and his family; they were, he assures Mikhail, in his thoughts during his (presumed) last moments, "and only then did I know how much I loved you, my dear brother!"[61] The agonizing question of the future preoccupies him, and he oscillates between fear and hope while wondering whether he will ever be able to resume his literary career. "Can it be that I will never again take my pen in hand? I think it will be possi-

[60] Ibid., 231.
[61] Pis'ma, 1: 128; December 22, 1849.

ble in four years. . . . My God! How many forms, still alive and created by me anew, will perish, extinguished in my brain or dissolved like poison in my bloodstream. Yes, if it's impossible to write I will die. Better fifteen years' imprisonment with pen in hand!" But Dostoevsky clings desperately to the lifeline provided by service in the army and tells Mikhail, "Don't grieve over me. Know that I am not downhearted, remember that I have not given up hope. In four years my lot will be easier. I will be a soldier—and that's different from a convict." [62]

What Dostoevsky dreads most is that his health will break down under the physical strain of the trials he is about to face: "Will my body hold out? I don't know. I am leaving in ill health. I have scrofula. But maybe it will!" Despite such concerns, Dostoevsky assures Mikhail that he has never been in a better emotional state: "Never before have I felt welling up in me such abundant and healthy reserves of spiritual life as I do now." [63] "My life in prison," he added, "has already sufficiently destroyed in me those fleshly demands that are not entirely pure; I did not spare myself before. Now, deprivation means nothing to me, and this is why I am not afraid that any kind of material hardship will destroy me. . . . Oh, only let me be healthy!" [64]

"I cannot recall when I was ever as happy as on that day," Dostoevsky told his second wife many years later. "I walked up and down my cell in the Alekseevsky Ravelin and sang the whole time, sang at the top of my voice, so happy was I at being given back my life." [65] Such happiness overwhelmed Dostoevsky with the impact of a revelation. "But I still have my heart and the same flesh and blood," he assures Mikhail, "and these too can live, suffer, desire and remember, and that, after all, is also life. *On voit le soleil!*" [66] This last phrase ("One sees the sun") is a slightly altered snatch of Hugo's *Le dernier jour d'un condamné*, whose details had surged back into Dostoevsky's memory as he stared death in the face. The citation forms part of the frantic reflections of Hugo's "condemned man" as he awaits execution by the guillotine and desperately tells himself that life under any conditions is preferable to extinction. At least—*on voit le soleil!*

Everything in his previous life is judged as he turns back to contemplate it from, as it were, the edge of eternity: "When I look back on my past and think how much time I wasted on nothing, how much time has been lost in futilities, errors, laziness, incapacity to live; how little I appreciated it, how many times I sinned against my heart and soul—then my heart bleeds. Life is a gift, life is

[62] Ibid., 130.
[63] Ibid., 129.
[64] Ibid., 131.
[65] Anna Dostoevsky, *Reminiscences*, trans. and ed. Beatrice Stillman (New York, 1975), 22.
[66] *Pis'ma*, 1: 129; December 22, 1849.

happiness, every minute can be an eternity of happiness! *Si jeunesse savait* [If youth only knew]! Now, in changing my life, I am reborn in a new form, Brother! I swear that I will not lose hope and will keep my soul and heart pure. I will be reborn for the better. That's all my hope, all my consolation!"[67]

"Life is life everywhere," Dostoevsky reassures Mikhail, "life is in ourselves, not in the exterior. I shall have human beings around me [in Siberia], and to be a *man* among men and to remain one always, not to lose heart and not to give in no matter what misfortune may occur—that is what life is, that is its task, I have come to be aware of this. This idea has entered into my flesh and blood."[68] Such words try to convey some of the blinding truth that Dostoevsky now understood for the first time—the truth that life itself is the greatest of all goods and blessings, and that man has the power to turn each moment into an "eternity of happiness." Dostoevsky had always refused to accept the increasingly prevalent dismissal of individual moral obligation, but what had been only a theoretical preference now entered into "his flesh and blood"; it had become an "idea-feeling," so deeply interwined with his emotions that no argument would ever be able to shake it in the future.

No passage in Dostoevsky's letter is more poignant than his description of the morally purifying effects of what he believed would be his last moments on earth. "If anyone remembers me as nasty," Dostoevsky tells Mikhail, "or if I quarreled with anybody, if I produced an unpleasant impression on anyone—ask them to forget, if you happen to meet them. There is no gall and no rancor in my soul; I should so much like at this moment to love and to embrace just someone from among those I knew. This is a consolation, I experienced it today, saying good-bye to those dear to me before death."[69] If the values of expiation, forgiveness, and love were destined to take precedence over all others in Dostoevsky's artistic universe, it was surely because he had encountered them as a truth responding to the most anguished predicament of his own life.

Indeed, it is Dostoevsky's piercing sense of the awful fragility and transiency of human existence that will soon enable him to depict, with a powerful urgency unrivaled by any other modern writer, the unconditional and absolute Christian commandment of mutual, all-forgiving, and all-embracing love. For Dostoevsky's morality is similar to what some theologians, speaking of the early Christians, have called an "interim ethics," that is, an ethics whose uncompromising extremism springs from the lurking imminence of the Day of Judgment and the Final Reckoning: there is no time for anything but the last kiss of reconciliation because, quite literally, there *is* no "time." The strength (as well as some of the

[67] Ibid., 130–131.
[68] Ibid., 129.
[69] Ibid., 130.

weakness) of Dostoevsky's work may ultimately be traced to the stabbing acuity with which, above all, he wished to communicate the saving power of this eschatological core of the Christian faith.[70]

——————■——————

On December 24, 1849, two days after the grisly pageant enacted in Semenovsky Square, Mikhail was informed that his brother would begin his long and hazardous journey to Siberia that very night. Mikhail hastened to convey the information to Alexander Milyukov, and both went to the fortress to say farewell. When Dostoevsky, accompanied by Durov, was ushered into the room where Mikhail and Milyukov were waiting, the latter was struck by Dostoevsky's unshakable conviction of his ability to survive. "Looking at the farewell of the brothers Dostoevsky," he observes, "everyone would have remarked that the one suffering the most was remaining in freedom in Petersburg, not the one who was just on the point of traveling to Siberian *katorga*. Tears rose in the eyes of the older brother, his lips trembled, but Feodor Mikhailovich remained calm and consoled him."[71]

"Stop, brother," Dostoevsky said at one point, "you know me, I am not going to my grave, you are not accompanying my burial—and there are not wild beasts in *katorga* but people, perhaps better than I am, perhaps worthier than I am."[72] Such words are the only documentation we have so far as Dosoevsky is concerned; but other evidence throws light on the question of what he, as well as the other Petrashevtsy, expected to encounter among the people with whom they would share their captivity. In the documents that Petrashevsky wrote for the Commission of Inquiry, we find the following remarkable and touching reverie:

> Perhaps fate . . . will place me side by side with a hardened evildoer, who has ten murders on his soul. . . . Resting at a way station and dining on a piece of stale bread . . . we begin to talk—I tell him how, and for what reason, I suffered misfortune. . . . I tell him about Fourier . . . about the phalanstery—what and why things are that way there, and so forth. . . . I explain why people become evildoers . . . and he, sighing deeply, tells me about his life. . . . From his story I see that circumstances crushed much that was good in this man, a strong soul fell under the weight of misfortune. . . . Perhaps, at the end of the story, he will say: 'Yes, if things were

[70] The eschatological importance of the presumably brief "interim" between the First and Second Coming for the interpretation of the ethics of Jesus was brought into prominence by Albert Schweitzer in *The Quest of the Historical Jesus*. For a penetrating discussion of its thesis, see Reinhold Niebuhr, *The Nature and Destiny of Man*, 2 vols. in 1 (New York, 1955), 2: 47–52.

[71] *DVS*, 1: 191.

[72] Ibid., 192.

arranged your way, if people lived like that, I would not be an evildoer' . . . and I, if the weight of my shackles allows me, extend a hand to him—and I say—'let's be brothers'—and, breaking my piece of bread, I give it to him, saying: 'I am not used to eating very much, you need it more, take it and eat.' With this, a tear appears on his roughened cheek and . . . before me appears . . . not an evildoer, but my equal in misfortune, perhaps also in the beginning a person badly misunderstood. . . . The act of humanization is completed, and the evildoer no longer exists.[73]

Such "philanthropic, Utopian dreams of Petrashevsky," as a Soviet Russian critic has remarked, "expressed the general state of mind and convictions of the circle. And Dostoevsky . . . too, despite instinctive doubts and forebodings, must have imagined something similar."[74] All the more so since Dostoevsky's early writings had led to the rise of "sentimental Naturalism," whose creations stressed the human worth hidden in the lives of the most downtrodden elements of society.

Dostoevsky's farewell may thus be taken as a more laconic expression of the same roseate fantasies articulated by Petrashevsky, a reaffirmation of the philanthropic aspect of his moral-social conviction of the time. Nonetheless, in the suggestion that the convicts might even perhaps be "worthier" than himself, Dostoevsky was unconsciously speaking better than he knew. For what was uttered only as a consolatory possibility in 1849, and was surely not accepted literally either by Dostoevsky or by those he was attempting to reassure, would one day become the basis of a view of the Russian people that he would not hesitate to proclaim to the entire world.

[73] V. R. Leikina, E. A. Korolchuk, and V. A. Desnitsky, eds., *Delo Petrashevtsev*, 3 vols. (Moscow–Leningrad, 1937–1951), 1: 84–85.

[74] V. A. Tunimanov, *Tvorchestvo Dostoevskogo*, 1854–1862 (Leningrad, 1980), 149–150.

CHAPTER 15

Katorga

In the four years he spent in prison camp, Dostoevsky had not received a single word from his family, and the complete loss of contact inspired him to compose a lengthy letter to Mikhail on February 22, 1854, just a week after being released. Picking up the thread of his life at the moment of departure for Siberia, it begins by recounting the impressions gathered on the eighteen-day journey and the major incidents marking his arrival at the first way station, Tobolsk. "It was a sad moment when we crossed the Urals," Dostoevsky recalls. "The horses and sledges had foundered in the drifts. A snowstorm was raging. We got out of the sledges— it was night—and stood waiting while they were dragged out. All around us was the snow and storm; it was the frontier of Europe; ahead was Siberia and our unknown fate, while all the past lay behind us—it was so depressing that I was moved to tears."[1]

On January 9, the party reached Tobolsk, once the capital city of Western Siberia and, at that time, the main distribution center in which prisoners arriving from European Russia were sorted out and dispatched to their final destinations. The prison was set inside a fortress complex, and as Dostoevsky's party climbed the road up to it, one of the first sights to greet their eyes was the town's most ancient and notorious exile, the famous Uglich bell, located just off the road along which they were proceeding. Its story was known to all: At the discovery of the death of Crown Prince Dimitry, suspected of having been murdered by his guardian, Boris Godunov, the bell had rung to summon the inhabitants of Uglich to avenge the boy's death. The new tsar, Boris, later ordered the offending bell to be publicly flogged and mutilated, and it was exiled to Siberia in perpetuity with the injunction that it never ring again. But the people of Tobolsk had long since housed the Uglich bell in a small belfry, and its deep-voiced sonority called them to prayer. There it stood along the roadside, a constant reminder to later exiles of the despotic, capricious, and all-encompassing authority of the Russian tsars, as well as of the ultimate futility of many of their sternest *ukazy*.

Dostoevsky's reception in Tobolsk illustrates some of the moral incorporated in the subversive survival of the Uglich bell. "I will only say," Dostoevsky writes

---

[1] *Pisma*, 1: 134; February 22, 1854.

to Mikhail, "that the sympathy and lively concern we met with blessed us with almost complete happiness. The exiles of the old days (that is, not they themselves but their wives) looked after us as though we were their own flesh and blood. What wonderful people, tried by twenty-five years of sorrow and self-sacrifice! We had only a glimpse of them, for we were strictly confined. But they sent us food and clothing, they consoled us and gave us courage."[2]

Jastrzembski also left a description of their arrival in Tobolsk and of his first glimpse of convict clerks, branded on cheeks and forehead. "We were taken into a room. A narrow, dark, cold dirty room. . . . Here there were plank beds, and on them three sacks filled with straw instead of mattresses and three pillows of the same kind. It was pitch-black. Outside the door, on the threshold, could be heard the heavy tread of the sentinel, walking back and forth in a 40 degree frost." Their room was separated only by a partition from another, which held other prisoners awaiting trial, and they could hear "the exclamations of people playing cards and other games, and what insults, what curses."[3]

All three travelers were in a lamentable state after their weeks on the road. "Durov's fingers and toes were frostbitten," recalls Jastrzembski, "and his feet had been badly damaged by the shackles. Dostoevsky, moreover, had broken out with scrofulous sores on his face and in his mouth while still in the Alekseevsky Ravelin."[4] Utterly dejected by the prospect of even further suffering looming ahead, Jastrzembski decided to commit suicide—a decision, he says, for which his solitary imprisonment in the Ravelin had been an excellent preparation. As it turned out, one of the officers of gendarmes at Tobolsk was an old acquaintance, who provided him and his friends with a candle, matches, and some hot tea, "which seemed to us sweeter than nectar. Some excellent cigars suddenly turned up in Dostoevsky's possession. . . . We spent a good part of the remainder of the night in friendly conversation. The sympathetic, gentle voice of Dostoevsky, his tenderness and delicacy of feeling, even some of his capricious sallies, quite like a woman, had a soothing effect on me. I gave up any extreme decision. Dostoevsky, Durov, and I were separated in the Tobolsk prison, we wept, embraced, and never saw each other again."[5]

———■———

If Dostoevsky was instrumental in bringing solace to Jastrzembski, the same function was performed for Dostoevsky by the wives of "the exiles of the old days," who helped so much to ease the lot of political prisoners, whether Russian or Polish, during the last years of the regime of Nicholas I. One hundred and

[2] Ibid., 135.
[3] Miller, *Biografiya*, 126.
[4] Ibid.
[5] Ibid., 126–127.

twenty Decembrists, all of good (and some of the very best) families, had been sent into exile in 1825. All had long since served their sentences at hard labor. Not allowed to reside in European Russia, they had remained in Siberia and formed part of the very small educated and cultivated society composed of the higher ranks in the army and the bureaucracy. Many of them had relations at court, some were independently wealthy, and all were treated with marked consideration by the officials coming from Petersburg. New arrivals were only too happy to mix with people of their own class and breeding in this still wild frontier territory, otherwise peopled only by uncouth and enterprising freebooters out to make a fortune and by a mixture of Asiatic nomads, still living their age-old tribal existence. The Decembrists, through their connections, were thus able to exercise a considerable influence despite their suspect status as ex-rebels, and their wives and children were unceasingly active in charitable work among the convicts.

On the last day that Dostoevsky and Durov spent in Tobolsk, three Decembrist wives arranged to visit them in the quarters of one of the officers. It was a moment he was to remember all his life, and one that he refers to again, in the same grateful and reverential tone, years later in his *Diary of a Writer* (1873): "We saw these sublime sufferers, who had voluntarily followed their husbands to Siberia. They gave up everything, position, wealth, family ties, sacrificed everything for the highest moral duty, a duty which nothing could impose on them except themselves. Completely innocent, during twenty-five years they bore everything to which their husbands had been condemned. The meeting lasted an hour. They blessed us as we entered on a new life, made the sign of the cross, and gave us a New Testament—the only book allowed in prison. It lay under my pillow for four years during penal servitude. I read it sometimes, and read it to others. With it, I taught one convict to read."[6] Each copy of the holy book contained, in its binding, ten rubles in bank notes.

The three women who came in to talk with Dostoevsky were Mme Muravyeva, Mme Annenkova, and Mme Fonvizina. The only native Russian of the three, and the most important of all for Dostoevsky, was Natalya Fonvizina, a remarkable woman of considerable intellectual culture and profound religious faith. Mme Fonvizina was related to Count Gorchakov, the governor-general of Siberia, and promised to speak to him on Dostoevsky's behalf. Letters were sent to the three daughters of Count Gorchakov, then on a visit to their father, enlisting their intercession on behalf of the Petrashevtsy. It was also during this hour-long meeting that Dostoevsky first heard about the terrible Major Krivtsov, the commandant of the prison camp at Omsk, and was warned to be on his guard against him.

[6] *DW* (1873), 9.

On the morning of the departure of Dostoevsky and Durov for Omsk, Natalya Fonvizina and another Decembrist wife, Marie Frantseva, rode out in advance to meet them on the way. "Having gone out in a sledge very early," writes the latter in her memoirs, "we got out of our vehicle and walked ahead on purpose up the road for a verst because we did not want the coachman to be a witness to our farewells; particularly since I had to give in secret to the gendarme a letter for my close friend, Lieutenant Colonel Zhdan-Pushkin, in which I asked him to look after Dostoevsky and Durov. . . . At last we heard the distant tinkle of bells. Quickly, a troika appeared out of the edge of the forest [and] . . . Dostoevsky and Durov leaped out of their Siberian sledge. The first was a thin, not very tall, not very good-looking young man. . . . They were dressed in convict half-coats and fur hats with earflaps; heavy shackles made a resounding noise on their feet. We . . . had time only to tell them not to lose heart, and that kind people would look after them even where they were going. I gave the letter I had ready for Pushkin to the gendarme, who conscientiously delivered it to him in Omsk."[7]

Unfortunately, the gendarme also carried another letter, which he delivered just as conscientiously—a secret letter from the commandant at Tobolsk to the one at Omsk. It contained instructions, originating from the tsar himself, that the two deportees were to be treated as "prisoners in the full sense of the word; according to their sentence, the improvement of their condition in the future should depend on their conduct, on the clemency of the monarch, and by no means on the indulgence of those in immediate authority over them; a trustworthy official should be appointed to maintain a strict and unceasing vigilance."[8] In these faraway outposts of the Russian Empire, such instructions were more apt to be honored in the breach than in the observance, and there is no evidence that any such petty bureaucrat was ever appointed. All the same, such orders made it more difficult to come to the aid of the political prisoners; there was always the chance that some zealous underling, eager to gain advancement, would denounce any favoritism to the headquarters of the governor-general.

———————◼———————

Dostoevsky's letter to Mikhail contains an unvarnished description of his years in prison:

> I had already become acquainted with convicts in Tobolsk, and here in Omsk I settled down to living with them for four years. They were coarse, ill-natured, cross-grained people. Their hatred for the gentry knew no bounds, and therefore they received us, the gentlemen, with hostility and

[7] M. D. Frantseva, "Vospominaniya," *Istorichesky Vestnik* 6 (1886), 628–629.
[8] *ZT*, 66.

malicious joy in our troubles. They would have eaten us alive, given the chance. Judge, moreover, how much protection we had, having to live, to eat and drink and sleep with these men for several years, without even the chance of complaining of the innumerable affronts of every possible kind. 'You are noblemen, iron beaks that used to peck us to death. Before, the master used to torment the people, but now he is lower than the lowest, has become one of us'—that's the theme on which they played variations for four years. One hundred and fifty enemies never tired of persecuting us; it was a pleasure for them, an amusement, something to do, and if anything at all saved us, it was indifference, moral superiority (which they could not but recognize and respect), and unyielding resistance to their will. They always acknowledged that we were superior to them. They had no understanding of our crime. We ourselves were silent on the subject, and so we could not understand each other, and we had to endure all the persecution and vindictiveness toward the gentry class for which they lived and breathed.

Things were very bad for us. A military prison is much worse than a civilian one. I spent the whole four years in the prison behind walls and never went out except to work. The work they found for us was heavy (not always, of course), and I was sometimes completely exhausted in foul weather, in damp and rain and sleet, and in the unendurable cold of winter. Once I spent four hours on urgent work, when the mercury froze and there was perhaps about 40 degrees of frost. My foot became frostbitten.

We lived on top of each other, all together in one barrack. Imagine an old, dilapidated, wooden construction, which was supposed to have been pulled down long ago, and which was no longer fit for use. In summer, intolerable closeness; in winter, unendurable cold. All the floors were rotten. Filth on the floors an inch thick; one could slip and fall. The little windows were so covered with frost that it was almost impossible to read at any time of the day. An inch of ice on the panes. Drips from the ceiling, draughts everywhere. We were packed like herrings in a barrel. The stove took six logs at once, but there was no warmth (the ice in the room barely thawed), only unendurable fumes—and this, all winter long. There in the barracks the convicts washed their clothes and the whole space was splashed with water. There was no room to turn around. From dusk to dawn it was impossible not to behave like pigs, for after all, 'we're live human beings.' We slept on bare boards and were allowed only a pillow. We spread our sheepskin coats over us, and our feet were always uncovered all night. We shivered all night. Fleas, lice, and black beetles by the bushel. In winter we wore short sheepskin coats, often of the most wretched quality, which hardly gave any warmth, and on our feet half-boots—just try to walk around with them in the freezing cold.

The food they gave us was bread and cabbage soup with a quarter of a pound of beef in it; but the meat was minced up and I never saw any of it. On holidays, thin porridge almost without fat. On fast days, boiled cabbage and hardly anything else. I suffered unbearably from indigestion and was ill several times. You may judge whether we could have lived without money, and if I had had none I should certainly have died; and nobody, no convict, whoever he was, could have borne such a life without it. But everybody worked at something, sold it, and thus had a kopek or two. I drank tea and sometimes bought a piece of meat to eat, and this was my salvation. It was impossible not to smoke tobacco as well, for one might have choked in that atmosphere. All this was done by stealth.

I often lay ill in the hospital. Disordered nerves have given me epilepsy, but the fits occur only rarely. I have rheumatism in the legs besides. Apart from this I feel fairly well. Add to all theses amenities the almost complete impossibility of possessing a book (and if you get one you read it on the sly), the eternal hostility and quarreling around one, the wrangling, shouting, uproar, din, always under escort, never alone, and all this for four years without change—really, one may be pardoned for saying that things were bad. Besides all this, the eternal threat of punishment hanging over one, shackles, the total stifling of the soul, there you have an image of my existence.[9]

Dostoevsky then gives a greatly modified version of the convicts who had initially appeared to him as hateful creatures almost of another species.

Men, however, are everywhere men. In four years in prison I came at last to distinguish men among criminals. Believe me, there are deep, strong, beautiful characters among them, and what a joy it was to discover the gold under the coarse, hard surface. And not one, not two, but several. It is impossible not to respect some of them, and some are positively splendid. I taught a young Circassian (sent to hard labor for highway robbery) reading and writing in Russian. What gratitude he heaped on me! Another convict wept at parting from me. I used to give him money—but was it very much? His gratitude, on the other hand, was unbounded. And meanwhile my own character became worse; I was capricious and impatient with them. They respected the condition of my soul and bore all without a murmur. And by the way: What a store of types and characters

[9] *Pis'ma*, 1: 135–137.

from the people I have carried out of the prison camp! . . . Enough for whole volumes! What a wonderful people.[10]

Dostoevsky's letter evokes the physical conditions of his imprisonment more honestly than he would be allowed to do later by the censorship in *House of the Dead*, the book that directly emerged from his prison-camp days. And the seeming contradiction between the two views of his fellow convicts illustrates the process of discovery that took place between the beginning of his imprisonment and the end—by which time he had succeeded in penetrating beneath the shocking and abhorrent surface to an understanding of the psychic and moral depths. Indeed, the transition from one to the other view already furnishes the ground plan that he will later use to structure his prison memoirs.

———■———

On arriving in Omsk, Dostoevsky obtained his first glimpse of the fearsome Major Krivtsov. "He began by roundly abusing the two of us," he says in his letter, "Durov and myself, as fools because of our crimes, and promised . . . corporal punishment at the first offense."[11] This incident is later recounted in *House of the Dead*: "His spiteful, purple, pimply face made a very depressing impression: it was as though a malicious spider had run out to pounce on some poor fly that had fallen into its web." After ordering the heads of the newly arrived prisoners to be shaved and confiscating all their property and personal clothing (except, for some reason, white underlinen), he concluded with the threat: "Mind you behave yourselves! Don't let me hear of you! Or . . . corporal punishment. For the least misdemeanor—the lash!" (4: 214).

Whether Dostoevsky ever was flogged as a convict has been a subject of unceasing speculation. Dostoevsky himself says of Krivtsov: "God saved me from him."[12] According to an incident recounted in the memoirs of P. K. Martyanov, one of the few reliable sources of information about Dostoevsky's prison years, Krivtsov did issue an order for Dostoevsky to be punished by the lash. Making one of his impromptu inspections of the prison (he was nicknamed "eight-eyes" by the convicts, because he seemed to see and know everything that went on), Krivtsov discovered Dostoevsky lying on a pallet in the barracks at a time when he should have been at work. Dostoevsky had been excused because of illness and allowed a day of rest; this was explained to Krivtsov by the noncommissioned officer on guard duty, one of a group of ex-naval cadets, all of good family, who had been demoted because of minor acts of insubordination and exiled to Siberia as punishment. But the furious Krivstov, livid with rage, shouted that

[10] Ibid., 138–139.
[11] Ibid., 135.
[12] Ibid.

Dostoevsky was being protected and commanded that he be flogged immedi-ately.[13] Preparations were being made to carry out the order when the comman-dant of the fortress, General de Grave, hurriedly arrived. He had been sum-moned by a messenger from the ex-naval cadet, who, like his fellows, was lenient toward the convicts in general and the political prisoners in particular. Not only did the general countermand Krivtsov's order on the spot, he also gave him a dressing down in public for having illegally tried to punish a sick convict.

The entire sequence of events beginning with Dostoevsky's mock execution, followed by the exposure to prison camp conditions and the constant terror of being at the mercy of Krivtsov's drunken rages, certainly contributed to the out-break of Dostoevsky's epilepsy. The first genuine attack, as far as can be deter-mined, occurred sometime in 1850, and was characterized seven years later in a medical report as having been marked by shrieks, loss of consciousness, convul-sive movements of the face and limbs, foam at the mouth, raucous breathing, and a feeble, rapid, and irregular pulse. The same report states that a similar at-tack recurred in 1853; since then, the seizures had continued on the average of once a month. Dostoevsky's letter to Mikhail is the only firsthand document available, and he speaks of his epilepsy as an entirely *new* phase of his old ail-ment ("disordered nerves")—the worsening of a condition whose initial symp-toms may have shown up in Petersburg but only became epileptic in Siberia. Dostoevsky always alludes to his Siberian seizures as an affliction of which he had had no previous experience.

Major Krivtsov unquestionably enjoyed torturing the convicts simply to dis-play his authority. As Dostoevsky recounts and as his Polish fellow prisoner, Szymon Tokarzewski, confirms, he frequently invaded the barracks at night and awoke the convicts, exhausted after a day of hard labor, because they were lying on their right sides or their backs and he decreed that the only permissible sleep-ing position was on the left side. "Whoever . . . slept on the right side was flogged," writes Tokarzewski. "[Krivtsov] justified this punishment by saying that Christ always slept on his left side, consequently everybody was required to follow his example."[14] His savage anger at what he considered Dostoevsky's ma-lingering was strengthened by his awareness that Dostoevsky *was* being "pro-tected." Konstantin Ivanov, son-in-law of Mme Annenkova, and adjutant to the general of the Engineering Corps, arranged for Dostoevsky, so far as possible, to be assigned only the lightest kind of labor—painting, turning the wheel of a lathe, pounding alabaster, shoveling snow.

Dostoevsky, however, felt that taxing labor outdoors was necessary to combat the noxious effects of the pestilential atmosphere in the barracks, and he sought

[13] P. K. Martyanov, "V perelome veka," *Istorichesky Vestnik* 10–11 (1895), 11: 453.
[14] Szymon Tokarzewski, *Siedem lat katorgi* (Warsaw, 1907), 127.

it out after a time. "Being constantly in the open air, working every day until I was tired, learning to carry heavy weights—at any rate I shall save myself," he writes in *House of the Dead.* "I thought: I shall make myself strong, I shall leave the prison healthy, vigorous, hearty and not old. I was not mistaken; the work and exercise were very good for me" (4: 80). Sergey Durov, on the other hand, apparently avoided manual labor; and though scarcely older than Dostoevsky, he emerged four years later an ailing and broken old man barely able to stand on his feet.

All the same, Dostoevsky's health would probably have suffered more if not for the kindness of the head of the fortress hospital, Dr. Troitsky, toward the political prisoners. Dostoevsky's first stay in the hospital may have been caused by his epileptic attack, or because he collapsed from exhaustion while clearing snow, but he returned there frequently, even when not ailing from any specific complaint. Dr. Troitsky would pass the word along through the ex-naval cadets that space was available. Dostoevsky would then show up to be entered on the books as "convalescing," and take a respite from the incessant noise and turmoil of the barracks. The hospital afforded him relative quiet, the luxury of a bed, and nourishing food, tea, and wine supplied either from hospital rations or from the doctor's own kitchen. Krivtsov certainly knew about Troitsky's favors to the "politicals," but since the hospital was an army installation, not part of the prison, there was little he could do. And while both the general of engineers and General de Grave were well aware that the doctor was playing fast and loose with the application of the sentence passed on the Petrashevtsy, they preferred to close their eyes to such infractions, with a warning to the doctor to be careful.

Such a warning was by no means superfluous; one of the physicians in the hospital finally denounced his superior's favoritism toward the political prisoners in a letter to Petersburg. An investigation was ordered, and an official dispatched from Tobolsk to carry on the inquiry. But since he received no cooperation from the local authorities, the informer could not produce any witnesses to substantiate the charges he had made. In desperation, the investigator decided to search the convicts' quarters. Since this required the permission of the commandant, General de Grave had time secretly to pass the word along to the prisoners, who, hastening to remove everything illegal and forbidden, obligingly left a few items to reward the searcher. He turned up a pot of pomade, a bottle of eau de cologne, women's stockings, and some children's toys. The prize, however, consisted of a few sheets of writing paper, on which he pounced in the hope of having at last unearthed some incriminating evidence of forbidden literary composition. The sheets did, in fact, contain a literary work—but not of a kind he had anticipated. It turned out to be a prayer, addressed to the Almighty, pleading for divine intercession to exorcise the presence of Satan, who had, it would appear, returned to earth from the nether world in the shape of Major

Krivtsov. Dostoevsky's literary talents would hardly have gone unused in this bit of gallows humor.

As a matter of fact, Dostoevsky kept a notebook in the hospital in which he jotted down phrases and expressions typical of the convict's salty and picturesque peasant language. These precious pages he confided to the care of the medical assistant, A. I. Ivanov, and Dostoevsky kept the scribbled sheets, sewn together by hand into a little notebook, until his dying day. Besides noting phrases and proverbs, he also preserved the texts of songs. Dostoevsky made ample use of all this material in the book that directly emerged from his prison-camp days, as well as in many of his novels, where locutions first noted in Siberia are incorporated to enliven the text.

The existence of the *Siberian Notebooks* reveals Dostoevsky's grim determination to one day resume his literary career. "I cannot find the expression to tell you," he wrote his friend Apollon Maikov after his release from prison camp, "what torture I suffered because I was not able to write." [15] In the one encounter during these years where he could speak freely to someone from the metropolis, what he inquired about most eagerly was the literary scene from which he had been so forcibly torn away. This conversation took place in the winter of 1853 with Evgeny Yakushkin, the son of an exiled Decembrist family who, after completing his studies in Russia, had returned on a mission to Siberia as a land surveyor.

Passing through Omsk, Yakushkin asked an officer friend to arrange a meeting with Dostoevsky. "I remember," Yakushkin writes many years later, "that Dostoevsky's appearance made a terribly painful impression on me when he walked into the room in his convict clothes, wearing shackles, and with his sickly face bearing the traces of a serious illness." Relations were quickly established after the first moment, and the two eagerly spoke "of what was going on in Russia, of current Russian literature. He asked me about some of the new writers who had just appeared and spoke of his difficult situation in a convict battalion." [16] Pressing a small sum of money on Dostoevsky, Yakushkin also willingly agreed to take a letter back to Mikhail that was written on the spot, and he was delighted when Dostoevsky said that the meeting had brought him back to life. This manifestation of interest and sympathy reassured the erstwhile writer that he was still remembered, and had not, like the heroine of his own *Poor Folk*, vanished into the steppe without leaving a trace.

Dostoevsky's last two years in prison camp were painful enough, but less of a hardship than those preceding. Major Krivtsov was arrested, tried for miscon-

---

[15] *Pis'ma*, 1: 166; January 13, 1856.

[16] The letter is included in the article by V. Lyubimova-Dorotovskaya, "Dostoevsky v Siberii," *Ogonek* 46–47 (1946), 27–28.

duct, and forced to resign from government service; with him went the reign of terror he had established. Dostoevsky had the satisfaction of seeing the ex-major in town, "a civilian wearing a shabby coat and a cap with a cockade in it" (4: 218). Once Krivtsov was gone, "everyone seemed to breathe more freely and to be more confident" (4: 219). Governor-General Gorchakov too, whose mistress (the wife of a well-rewarded army general) shamelessly collected graft hand over fist, also fell from favor and was replaced. "I enjoyed more privileges toward the last than in the early years of my life in prison," he notes in *House of the Dead*. "I discovered among the officers serving in the town some acquaintances and even old schoolfellows of mine . . . through their good offices I was able to obtain even larger supplies of money, and even to have books" (4: 229). Except for two titles—Russian versions of *The Pickwick Papers* and *David Copperfield*— we do not know the books to which Dostoevsky finally had access. Years later he would see Mr. Pickwick as one of the precursors of his own Prince Myshkin, "a perfectly good man," the embodiment of a Christian moral ideal mocked in the world. Most important, Dostoevsky had at last established friendly relations with some of the peasant convicts, and this provided a welcome relief from his oppressive sense of living in a world surrounded only by enmity and hatred.

He was released from prison in February 1854—to serve as a lowly private in the Russian Army for an indeterminate period. All the same, the presentiment of the difficulties lying ahead could not suppress the immense joy of his long-awaited delivery. For years he had paced in solitude every evening around the stockade of the prison camp, counting another paling each day to mark the gradual expiration of his sentence; at last the great moment had arrived! "The fetters fell off," he writes in *House of the Dead*, "I picked them up, I wanted to hold them in my hand, to look at them for the last time. I seemed already to be wondering that they could have been on my feet a minute before. 'Well, with God's blessing, with God's blessing!' said the convicts in coarse, abrupt voices, in which, however, there was a note of pleasure. Yes, with God's blessing! Freedom, new life, resurrection from the dead. . . . What a glorious moment!" (4: 232).

CHAPTER 16

"Monsters in Their Misery"

Dostoevsky's views of his fellow convicts changed dramatically between his first days in prison camp and his last. Dostoevsky, the great psychologist, never analyzes his inner state of mind, never discusses the specific modality of his ideological evolution, his transformation from a philanthropic radical with Christian socialist leanings into a resolute believer in the Russian people as the unique national embodiment of the moral ideals he had found so appealing in Utopian Socialism. Reminiscing, in his *Diary of a Writer* (1873), "on the regeneration of my convictions," Dostoevsky simply remarks, "It did not occur so quickly, but gradually—and after a long, long time."[1] He thus did not emerge from prison camp with a firmly defined set of new convictions to replace those he had abandoned. Rather, he tried to make sense out of his exposure to a range of new impressions that had clashed with his preconceived notions, and only subsequently came to understand in a more self-conscious fashion how this experience had changed his ideas. Such "ideas" would have begun to take shape when Dostoevsky, making contact once again with Russian life in the mid-1850s and early 1860s, found it necessary to define an ideological position amid the abrupt transformations of these agitated years.

Notes from the House of the Dead (*Zapiski iz mertvogo doma*) first appeared in the pages of Dostoevsky's journal *Time* during 1861–1862, and it is one of the anomalies of the text that it does not include an account of his conversion experience. However, since the focus of the text is impersonal and collective rather than confessional and personal, the process of re-education is never depicted directly. It must be inferred from suggestions and side remarks—such as reactions of surprise on the part of the narrator, and his occasional injunctions to the reader to pay special attention to one or another observation. It was only twenty-six years later, in an article in the February 1876 issue of his *Diary of a Writer* entitled "The Peasant Marey," that Dostoevsky supplied the missing pages from his prison memoirs that help to pierce the enigma of "the regeneration of [his] convictions."

The importance of this article has long been recognized, but no one has examined it in the light of our knowledge of the psychology of conversion to ex-

---

[1] *DW* (1873), 152.

plore all the physical, mental, and emotive pressures that converged on Dostoevsky at this critical time. Only by doing so, however, may we hope to supplement his own reticence and advance a step further in understanding this mysterious and decisive episode. Here we shall take up *House of the Dead* and "The Peasant Marey" as documents that record the experiences of his prison-camp years. Reference to this text will be made again later, corresponding to the time of composition and publication.

---■---

To begin with, Dostoevsky rearranged his experiences in *House of the Dead* in order to communicate the objective correlatives of what he knew to be the inner "truth" of his own moral-spiritual mutation. No matter how much Dostoevsky may have embellished his memories of the past, such "improvements" all went in the direction of imparting as much artistic and symbolic pregnancy as possible to this profound alteration of his sensibility. And he provides clues that help us to grasp the underlying motives of his regeneration.

It was not, Dostoevsky asserted years later, the hardships of exile and forced labor that had altered his ideas: "No, something different . . . changed our outlook, our convictions and our hearts . . . the direct contact with the people, the brotherly merger with them in a common misfortune, the realization that [we had] become even as they, that we had been made equal to them, and even to their lowest stratum." [2] Such words idealize a "merger" that was far from having been as "brotherly" as Dostoevsky wished his readers to believe, but he is pointing to something crucial in the process of his transformation all the same. For he highlights the *end product* of the process he went through, stressing that it was only when forced to live cheek-by-jowl with the peasant convicts that he came to realize to what extent he had been a dupe of illusions about the Russian peasant and the nature of Russian social-political reality. It was this encounter with the Russian people that led to the collapse of his entire psychic-emotive equilibrium and called for a desperate effort to adjust to the unsettling truths that assailed him on every side. Dostoevsky's remarkable response to this challenge constitutes the hinge on which his regeneration turned, and once this response was made, his convictions were gradually altered to conform to the new vision he had acquired of his companions in misfortune.

The first period of Dostoevsky's life in *katorga*, extending perhaps for over a year or longer, plunged him into a mood that may be considered one of traumatic shock. And, despite Dostoevsky's denial, the physical rigors of the prison regime could hardly have failed to affect his general psychic state. Nor should one forget either the constant terror of Major Krivtsov in which Dostoevsky

[2] Ibid.

lived. This constant anxiety accounts for the morbid curiosity with which he questioned others about their sensations on being flogged. "I wanted to know with precision in certain cases," he writes, "how great it [the pain] was, to what, finally, it could be compared. I do not really know why I wanted so much to know. I recall only one thing: it was not a vain curiosity. I repeat, I was terribly upset and shaken." And he could not listen to the information he solicited without "my heart leaping into my throat, and beating strongly and violently" (4: 153–154). The specter of being subjected to such indignity, and the gnawing doubt as to whether he would be capable of conducting himself bravely, is enough to account for the symptoms of nervous excitement invariably stimulated by such conversations. Dostoevsky was now living under the frightening shadow of what he had always found so intolerable for others, and of what, in the past, he could never even hear spoken of without an outburst of rage.

One of the first incidents that Dostoevsky records in *House of the Dead* proved to him that it was not only Krivtsov who might do violence to his person. He and Durov, having arrived the day before, had gone into the prison kitchen to buy a glass of tea. As the two sipped their tea, surrounded by others busily eating what they too had bought, they pretended not to notice the baleful glances cast in their direction by the peasant convicts. Suddenly, they were accosted by the drunken Tartar Gazin. A giant of a man, he sneeringly asked the two "gentlemen" whether they had been sent to Siberia to enjoy themselves by drinking tea. When both remained silent, Gazin seized a huge bread tray and held it menacingly over their heads. It might have come crashing down at the next moment, but whether by accident or design someone rushed in to tell Gazin, a large-scale vodka smuggler, that his stock had been stolen, and the Tartar hurried off with no damage being done.

The menace to life and limb was always palpable; and Dostoevsky was given ample proof, in the way the prisoners treated each other, that the menace could turn into mayhem at any moment. He writes that beatings were customary when convicts became drunk and unruly to a degree that might have provoked "eight-eyes" to discipline the barracks as a whole. Gazin was a serious offender of this kind, and sometimes lunged at people with a knife when inflamed by vodka. What would happen next was witnessed by Dostoevsky many times: "A dozen men from his barracks rush at him all together and begin to beat him. One cannot imagine anything more terrible than this rain of blows: he is beaten tirelessly and brutally, and one stops only when he is unconscious and resembles a corpse" (4: 41). It seemed to him—from the oaths, insults, menaces, and threats that flew back and forth—as if some bloody brawl was always about to break loose, though in most cases, to his initial surprise, matters would end after a volley of the most scurrilous abuse. All the same, there was no escape, as he wrote in his letter, from "the eternal hostility and quarreling around one, the wrangling, shouting, uproar, din." A flight to the hospital carried the risk of infection and meant confinement in a fetid ward, but we have already seen that this was one of Dostoevsky's places of refuge. "I was fleeing from the prison. Life was unbearable there; more unbearable than the hospital, morally unbearable" (4: 164–165).

Such moral revulsion was increased by what Dostoevsky quickly learned of the appalling depravity that reigned among the convicts. "I was astonished and upset, as if until then I had not suspected or heard anything about all that, and yet I knew it and had learned about it. But the reality makes quite a different impression than what one learns from books and hearsay" (4: 65). Censorship would not permit him, of course, to speak too plainly about the mores of the convicts, but there is little that he does not manage to convey. The drunken sprees on illegal vodka are described in detail. Prostitution, both female and male, is clearly alluded to, explicitly in the case of the former (women were available in Omsk, and guards could be bribed to overlook absences from work parties in town), more circuitously, though still unmistakably, for the latter. Nothing astonished Dostoevsky more, however, than the universal prevalence of thievery. And no wonder he was astonished, having written a touching little story, "An Honest Thief," in which a hopeless drunkard, to obtain a bit of vodka, steals a pair of breeches from a friend almost as destitute as himself, and dies of remorse for having done so. No such remorse could be observed in the prison camp. "They began making up to me at once," he writes, "got me—for money, of course—a box with a lock on it for me to put away precious belongings . . . as well as some underclothes I had brought with me to prison. Next day they stole it from me and sold it for drink" (4: 25). "In the course of several years," Dostoevsky observes, "I never saw a sign of repentance among these people; not a trace of despondent brooding over their crimes, and the majority of them inwardly considered themselves absolutely in the right. This is a fact" (4: 15).

In a passage describing the long winter evenings, when the convicts were locked in early and had several hours to spend together before being overcome by sleep, he gives vent to the bitter misanthropy that assailed him in these early days: "noise, uproar, laughter, swearing, the clank of chains, smoke and grime, shaven heads, branded faces, ragged clothes, everything defiled and degraded. . . . Man is a creature that can become accustomed to anything, and I think this is the best definition of him" (4: 10). Even aside from all this, matters were made much worse because of the ingrained hostility displayed by the peasant convicts against "gentlemen" like Dostoevsky.

———■———

One of the first things that Dostoevsky was told, by a prisoner who had once been an army officer, was that the peasant convicts "do not like the gentlemen, especially political prisoners, they will eat them alive, and that's understandable. First of all, you are another breed, different from what they are, and then, they were all serfs or soldiers. Judge for yourself if they can like you" (4: 28). Elsewhere, Dostoevsky remarks that "If I had begun to try and win their good-will by making up to them, being familiar with them . . . they would at once have supposed that I did it out of fear and cowardice and would have treated me with contempt" (4: 77). Dostoevsky did not seek any closer contact with the peasant convicts and decided to remain aloof; but nothing appears to have taken him more by surprise than the discovery of their innate and instinctive hostility.

Like other members of his class, Dostoevsky had probably thought that, while the peasant would certainly strike back at personal injury, he was too primitive and intellectually undeveloped to take any conscious objection to his own status and condition. In a famous article on Peter the Great, which may be considered a manifesto of the ideology of the Russian Westernizers, Belinsky had written in 1841 that "the Russian *muzhik* is still semi-Asiatic. . . . For men in their natural state, apart from satisfying their hunger and similar wants, are incapable of thinking."[3] If Dostoevsky held some such opinion of the *muzhik*, we can understand why the evidence of a certain social-political consciousness among them should have come as such a jolt. What affected him most was the reflection of this self-consciousness in the implacable enmity of the peasant convicts toward the nobles in general, and himself in particular.

"Not one word in our defense!" Dostoevsky observes about the incident in the prison kitchen with Gazin. "Not one shout at Gazin, so intense was their hatred of us!" This is only the first of many occasions when Dostoevsky learned the truth of the words uttered by one of the Polish political prisoners, whom Dostoevsky had naïvely asked why peasant convicts seemed to resent his tea even though many of them were eating their own food. The prison-hardened Polish noble replied, "It is not because of your tea. They are ill-disposed to you because you were once gentlemen and not like them. Many of them would dearly like to insult you, to humiliate you. You will meet with a lot of unpleasantness here" (4: 32).

Such predictions were borne out a few days later, when Dostoevsky was sent on his first assignment with a work party. He found that "everywhere I was pushed aside almost with abuse. The lowest ragamuffin, himself a wretched workman, . . . thought himself entitled to shout at me on the pretext that I hindered him if I stood beside him. At last one of the smarter ones said to me plainly and coarsely: 'Where are you shoving? Get away! Why do you poke yourself in where you are not wanted!'" As a result, Dostoevsky continues, "I had to stand apart, and to stand apart when all are working makes one feel

[3] V. G. Belinsky, *Selected Philosophical Works* (Moscow, 1948), 125.

ashamed. But when it happened that I did walk away and stood at the end of the barge, they shouted at once: 'Fine workmen they've given us; what can one get done with them?'" (4: 76). The thin-skinned and excruciatingly vulnerable Dostoevsky, ready to flare up at the slightest pinprick to his self-esteem, was now caught in a nightmare of humiliation from which there was no escape, and which he simply had to learn how to endure.

Over and over again in *House of the Dead* he returns to confirm the heartache inflicted by this relentless class hatred. Indeed, he came to consider, as the most agonizing of all the torments of camp life, this awareness of being eternally ringed by enemies, eternally alienated from the vast majority by a wall of animosity that nothing he could do would ever cause to crumble. An ordinary peasant convict, he explains, "within two hours after his arrival . . . is on the same footing as all the rest, is *at home*, has the same rights in the community as the rest, is understood by everyone, and is looked on by everyone as a comrade. It is very different with *the gentleman*, the man of a different class. However straightforward, good-natured and clever he is, he will for years be hated and despised" (4: 198).

A peasant convict named Petrov, an ex-soldier reputed to be the most dangerous man in prison, was one of the few men of his class to seek an acquaintance with Dostoevsky. He pumped Dostoevsky for all sorts of information—sometimes concerning French politics, sometimes whether the people in the antipodes really walked on their heads. "But," writes Dostoevsky, "I had the impression that in general he considered me . . . almost as a new-born baby, incapable of understanding the simplest matters. . . . [H]e had decided . . . that outside of books I understood nothing and was even incapable of understanding anything" (4: 86). Dostoevsky was certain that, even when stealing from him, Petrov pitied him because he was not able to defend his own belongings. "He said to me himself one day," Dostoevsky recalls, "that I was 'a man with a good heart,' and 'so simple, so simple, that it makes one feel sorry for you'" (4: 87).

An outside observer portrays Dostoevsky, during the first year in prison camp, as looking like "a wolf in a trap." "His cap was pulled down over his forehead to his eyebrows; he looked fierce, withdrawn, unfriendly; his head drooped and his eyes remained fixed on the ground."[4] This time of withdrawal marked the beginning of a searching revision of all his earlier ideas and convictions. "In my spiritual solitude," Dostoevsky writes, "I reviewed all my past life, went over it all to the smallest detail, . . . judged myself sternly and relentlessly, and even sometimes blessed fate for sending me this solitude, without which I would not have judged myself like this, nor viewed my past so sternly" (4: 220). Dostoevsky tells us nothing about the contents of these self-accusatory musings, but some

---

[4] P. K. Martyanov, "V perelome veka," *Istorichesky Vestnik* 10–11 (1895), 11: 448.

pages in his prison memoirs hardly can be read except as an Aesopian exposure of his folly as an apprentice revolutionary conspirator.

One day, Dostoevsky noticed that the other convicts had assembled in the courtyard of the prison at an unusual time. He immediately fell in as if for a roll call, but was jeered at and told to leave the group. Hesitating to obey the shouts coming at him from all directions, he was finally taken by the arm and led away to the camp kitchen. There, looking on at the rumpus, were gathered a handful of peasant convicts and all the other gentlemen, who told him that a "complaint" had been organized against Major Krivtsov because of the quality of the food. What had happened then became clear: the peasant convicts had spontaneously and unanimously refused to let a gentleman join their protest.

The complaint was easily crushed by the infuriated major, who ordered some of the protestors to be flogged at random, but the treatment that Dostoevsky had received remained as a rankling and admonitory recollection. "I had never before been so insulted in prison," he writes, despite all the humiliations inflicted upon him otherwise, "and this time I felt it very bitterly" (4: 203). That very afternoon, he spoke about it to Petrov:

"Tell me, Petrov," said I, "are they angry with us?"
"Why angry?" he asked as though waking up. . . .
"Because we did not take part in the complaint."
"But why should you make a complaint?" he asked, as though trying to understand me. "You buy your own food."
"Good heavens! But some of you who joined in it buy your own food too. We ought to have done the same—as comrades."
"But . . . but how can you be our comrades?" he asked in perplexity (4: 207).

The social-political implications of this interchange finally sank into the consciousness of the erstwhile revolutionary conspirator who had once hoped to stir up a peasant revolution. The notion that peasants would have accepted the leadership of gentlemen in any struggle to obtain freedom, as he now realized, had been the sheerest delusion.

Elsewhere in the book, Petrov is depicted as a natural revolutionary, exactly the type of peasant to whom the Speshnevites had wished to appeal—those who, as Dostoevsky writes, "are the first to surmount the worst obstacles, facing every danger without reflection, without fear" (4: 87). Such a man, as he now became aware, found it impossible to understand how a gentleman could unite with the peasants as a comrade in a social protest. Never again would Dostoevsky believe that the efforts of the radical intelligentsia could have the slightest effect in stirring the broad masses of the Russian people, and history was to prove him right during his lifetime—if not, to be sure, half a century after his death.

The people would never follow the intelligentsia, and their own leaders can only charge ahead on the road to self-destruction. For such "agitators and ring-leaders . . . are too ardent to be shrewd and calculating; [and] . . . almost always fail, and are sent to prison and penal servitude in consequence" (4: 201). These are surely some of the melancholy conclusions that Dostoevsky began to draw as he judged his own past "sternly and relentlessly." Everything that his readers believe they know about the peasants, Dostoevsky tells them, is woefully mis-taken. "You may have to do with peasants all your life, you may associate with them every day for forty years . . . you will never know them really. It will all be an optical illusion and nothing more. . . . I have reached this conviction . . . from reality, and I have had plenty of time to verify it" (4: 198–199). He could well have recalled, in these moments of self-judgment, the famous concluding lines of Pushkin's *The Captain's Daughter*, a novel set in the midst of the bloody Pugachev uprising in the eighteenth century. Pushkin's words express the point of view to which Dostoevsky had now come around himself: "God save us from seeing a Russian revolt, senseless and merciless. Those who plot impossible up-heavals among us are either young and do not know our people, or are hard-hearted men who do not care a straw either about their own lives or those of others."[5]

Dostoevsky's previous sympathetic attitude toward the peasants in the role of benefactor had now been replaced by a loathing of everything around him, but most of all of his fellow prisoners. "There were moments," he confesses in a let-ter to Mme Fonvizina, "when I hated everybody I came across, innocent or guilty, and looked at them as thieves who were robbing me of my life with im-punity. The most unbearable misfortune is when you yourself become unjust, malignant, vile; you realize it, you even reproach yourself—but you just can't help it."[6] It is hardly possible to exaggerate the importance of this destruction of Dostoevsky's humanitarian faith in the prison camp, but Dostoevsky *did* man-age to find a way out of his torturing psychic entrapment, and, as we shall see a bit later, he went through an experience exhibiting all the characteristics noted in cases of conversion—whether religious or involving questions of political allegiance.

———————■———————

There were twelve other prisoners of the noble class in the Omsk camp while Dostoevsky was serving his sentence. In addition to Durov, three others were Russian, and what Dostoevsky tells us about them indicates abundantly, if obliquely, why he took so little comfort in their presence. One was an ex-officer

[5] Alexander Pushkin, *The Captain's Daughter*, trans. Natalie Duddington, reprinted in *The Poems, Prose and Plays of Pushkin*, ed. Avrahm Yarmolinsky (New York, 1936), 741.

[6] *Pisma*, 1: 143; February 20, 1854.

of the Russian Army whom Dostoevsky calls Akim Akimich—a person so conditioned to subordination that obedience with him had become inclination and second nature. He dwelt on the routine of army life with loving devotion, "and all in the same even, decorous voice like the dripping of water." At times, Dostoevsky admits, "I . . . cursed the fate which had put me with my head next to his own on the common bed" (4: 208–209).

The second convict is referred to only as a "parricide." His real name was D. I. Ilyinsky, and he is a figure of some importance in Dostoevsky's career: his history later furnished the novelist with the main plot of *The Brothers Karamazov*, and his personality probably also provided some of the character traits for Dimitry Karamazov. Ilyinsky was an ex-officer convicted (but only on circumstantial evidence) of having killed his father to obtain his inheritance. Always "in the liveliest, merriest spirits," he steadfastly denied his guilt, and Dostoevsky did not give entire credence to his conviction, remarking that "such savage insensibility seems impossible" (4: 16). Years later, while writing the final draft of his prison book, Dostoevsky learned that Ilyinsky had been released: a criminal had confessed to the murder. So Dostoevsky's psychological intuition, based solely on his observation of Ilyinsky's character, had been vindicated.

The third Russian noble, mentioned only by the initial A., was Pavel Aristov, "the most revolting example of the depths to which a man can sink and degenerate, and the extent to which he can destroy all moral feeling in himself without difficulty or repentance" (4: 62). Seventy entirely innocent people had been arrested as a result of Aristov's denunciations while the latter was engaging in riotous orgies with the money furnished by the Third Section, and he continued turning up more "subversive political conspirators" so long as he was supplied with payment. After a certain period, however, even the Third Section became suspicious, and Aristov was eventually sent to prison camp for embezzlement and false denunciations. There he had ingratiated himself with Major Krivtsov and served as a spy and informer on the peasant convicts. Dostoevsky was literally aghast at encountering in the flesh someone of Aristov's ilk, who surpassed his most livid fantasies of the evil that a human being could knowingly tolerate and perpetrate. "All the while I was in prison," he declares, "A. seemed to me a lump of flesh with teeth and a stomach and an insatiable thirst for the most sensual and brutish pleasures" (4: 63).

To make matters worse, he was "cunning and clever, good-looking, even rather well educated." What made Aristov's presence literally intolerable for Dostoevsky was his manner of glorying in his own infamy: "And how revolting it was to me to look on his everlasting mocking smile! He was a monster; a moral Quasimodo" (4: 63). And just as Dostoevsky did not forget Ilyinsky, so too Aristov remained an ineradicable memory. The first references in Dostoevsky's notebooks to the character of Svidrigailov, the cynically derisive aristocratic debauchee in *Crime and Punishment*, are entered under the name of Aristov.[7] More immediately, Dostoevsky held Aristov responsible for deepening the crisis of values brought on by prison-camp life. "He poisoned my first days in prison," Dostoevsky explains, "and made them even more miserable. I was terrified at the awful baseness and degradation into which I had been cast. . . . I imagined that everything here was as base and degraded. But I was mistaken, I judged all by A" (4: 64).

Indeed, Dostoevsky looked on the peasant convicts as simply cruder replicas of Aristov; having lost any sense of the distinction between good and evil, they seemed to belong to another species. Another appalling individual was a bandit chief named Orlov, about whom Dostoevsky had heard "marvelous stories" before he turned up in the army hospital during one of Dostoevsky's stays. Orlov "was a criminal such as there are few, who had murdered old people and children in cold blood—a man of terrible strength of will and proud consciousness of his strength." Far from having lost his humanity, like Aristov, because of subjugation by the lusts of the flesh, Orlov for Dostoevsky was "unmistakably the case of a complete triumph over the flesh. It was evident that the man's power of control was unlimited, that he despised every sort of punishment and torture, and was afraid of nothing in the world." He was, clearly, a person of extraordinary self-possession, and Dostoevsky notes being "struck by his strange haughtiness. He looked down on everything with incredible disdain, though he made no effort to maintain his lofty attitude—it was somehow natural" (4: 47).

Tremendously excited by *House of the Dead* when he first came across it, Nietzsche could well have seen Orlov as one of the incarnations of his Superman, and what Dostoevsky tells us of his own conversations with the famous brigand remarkably anticipates the Nietzschean distinction between master and slave morality.[8] For when Dostoevsky began to question Orlov about his "adventures," the latter became aware that his interlocutor "was trying to get at his conscience and to discover some sign of penitence in him." Orlov's only response was to glance at Dostoevsky "with great contempt and haughtiness, as though I had suddenly in his eyes become a foolish little boy, with whom it was impossible to discuss things as you would with a grown-up person. There was even a sort of pity for me to be seen on his face. A moment later he burst out laughing at me, a perfectly open-hearted laugh free from any hint of irony." Dostoevsky concludes that "he could not really help despising me, and must

[7] *PSS*, 7: 315, 408.

[8] Georg Brandes told Nietzsche himself that Dostoevsky represented the very slave morality against which the German thinker was philosophizing with a hammer. Nietzsche agreed, and replied in a letter (November 20, 1888): "I treasure him, all the same, as the most valuable psychological material I know—I am exceedingly grateful to him, however much he always grates against my deepest instincts." Cited in Wolfgang Gesemann, "Nietzsche's Verhältnis zu Dostoevsky auf dem europäischen Hintergrund der 80er Jahre," *Die Welt der Slaven* 2 (July 1961), 142.

have looked upon me as a weak, pitiful, submissive creature, inferior to him in every respect" (4: 48). It is impossible to read these words without thinking of Raskolnikov's impassioned dialectic in *Crime and Punishment*, which, although nourished by ideologies that had not yet made their appearance on the Russian social-cultural scene, certainly draws much of its vitality from such a recollection. And Raskolnikov may well be seen as a conscience-stricken member of the intelligentsia—exactly like Dostoevsky himself at this moment—who had tried to whip himself up into behaving like an Orlov, but who ultimately finds it morally impossible to sustain the awful consequences of his deeds.

The Omsk stockade also contained eight Polish nobles, all sent to Siberia for having participated in plots to gain independence for their homeland from the Russian crown. Few other inmates of the *House of the Dead* are described in the laudatory terms that Dostoevsky lavishes on the Polish prisoners with whom he became friendly. "I never ceased to love him," Dostoevsky says of B. (Joszef Boguslawski), and these words stand out as a sudden splotch of radiant color in the surrounding darkness. It was largely disagreements over politics that led to their rift with Dostoevsky, for they refused to tolerate the virulent Russian nationalism that Dostoevsky displayed when the talk turned, as it obviously did, to the sacred cause for which the Polish prisoners were suffering their cruel punishment. Tokarzewski records, "How painful it was to listen to this conspirator, this man sentenced to prison for the cause of freedom and progress, when he confessed that he would be happy only when all the nations would fall under Russian rule. . . . He affirmed that [Ukraine, Volynia, Podolia, Lithuania, and Poland] had forever been the property of Russia; that the divine hand of justice had put these provinces and countries under the scepter of the Russian tsar because they would [otherwise] have remained in a state of dark illiteracy, barbarism, and abject poverty. . . . Listening to these arguments we acquired the conviction that Feodor Mikhailovich Dostoevsky was affected by insanity."[9]

Dostoevsky keeps silent about such political arguments in *House of the Dead* because of censorship, but he writes that he was greatly upset by the Polish abhorrence of the Russian peasant convicts, whom they looked down on with supreme contempt. "They . . . were elaborately, offensively polite and exceedingly uncommunicative with them. They never could conceal from the convicts their aversion for them, and the latter saw it very clearly and paid the Poles back in the same coin" (4: 26). Tokarzewski relates how he first entered the barracks where Dostoevsky was to join him later: "And these shapes of men or of the damned approached us and extended their hands, hands so many times covered with blood, so many times soiled by offense and crime. . . . I pulled away my

---

[9] Waclaw Lednicki, *Russia, Poland and the West* (New York, 1954), 275. Lednicki's book contains a translation of most of the chapter that Tokarzewski devotes to Dostoevsky in his *Siedem lat katorgi* (Warsaw, 1907).

hand and, pushing everyone aside, I entered the barracks with my head held proudly aloft."[10]

Such was the Polish attitude, and Dostoevsky would have had to be considerably more obtuse than he was not to have realized that it resembled his very own. Yet the intensely patriotic Dostoevsky soon found himself defending his country, and presumably the majority of its inhabitants, against the only educated people in the prison camp whom he personally liked and who had helped to relieve his numbing loneliness. But how could he argue on behalf of Russia without overcoming his violent repugnance for that portion of the Russian people existing all around him in flesh and blood? His disputes with the Polish exiles only intensified his inner crisis—the crisis initially caused by the destruction of his humanitarian faith in the people—to an unbearable pitch of psychic malaise. Nothing was more emotionally necessary for Dostoevsky than to find some way of reconciling his ineradicable love for his native land with his violently negative reactions to the loathsome denizens of the camp.

———■———

In the article entitled "The Peasant Marey," Dostoevsky supplies the missing pages from his prison memoirs that help to pierce the enigma of "the regeneration of [his] convictions." To counter the disillusion created by a previous article in *Diary of a Writer* in which he had depicted the people as "coarse and ignorant, addicted to drunkenness and debauch," and as "barbarians awaiting the light," he dredges up from memory an incident in the prison camp that had once rescued him from despair under the weight of the same disillusioning impressions.

The incident that Dostoevsky describes took place during "the second day of Easter Week"[11] and was motivated by his memory of the peasant Marey, one of his father's serfs whom he had known as a boy. During Lent the prisoners, relieved of work for one week, went to church two or three times a day. "I very much liked the week of the preparation for the sacrament," Dostoevsky confirms in *House of the Dead*. "The Lenten service so familiar to me from the faraway days of my childhood in my father's house, the solemn prayers, the prostrations—all this stirred in my heart the far, far-away past, bringing back the days of my childhood." The convicts stood at the back of the church, as the peasants had done in Dostoevsky's youth, and he remembered how he, from his privileged position, had once watched them "slavishly parting to make way for a thickly epauletted officer, a stout gentleman, or an overdressed but pious lady. . . . I used to fancy then that at the church door they did not pray as we

———

[10] Ibid., 272–273.
[11] *DW* (1876), 206.

did, but they prayed humbly, zealously, abasing themselves and fully conscious of their humble state" (4: 176).

The Easter preparations thus naturally evoked memories of the days when his faith had been untroubled—and of his sense even then that the peasants were more truly Christian in their devotions than the arrogant ruling class. "The convicts prayed very earnestly and every one of them brought his poor farthing to the church every time to buy a candle, or to put it in the collection. 'I, too, am a man,' he thought, and felt perhaps as he gave it, 'in God's eyes we are all equal.' We took the sacrament at the early mass. When with the chalice in his hands the priest read the words 'accept me, O Lord, even as the thief,' almost all of them bowed down to the ground with the clanking of chains, apparently applying the words literally to themselves" (4: 177). Such impressions certainly began to weaken Dostoevsky's notion that the convicts were so many cruder replicas of Aristov; nor should we overlook the possible effects of the Orthodox Easter service itself, which, in celebrating the central mystery of the resurrection of Christ, places strong emphasis on the brotherly love and mutual forgiveness that should unite all the faithful in joy at the miraculous event.

By the second day of Easter week, then, Dostoevsky had gone through a long period in which his most exalted feelings had repeatedly been aroused, and it was thus all the more infuriating to witness the appalling spectacle that he saw all around him. "It was the second day of the 'holiday' in the camp; the prisoners were not taken out to work, many were drunk, cursing and quarreling flared up from one moment to the next on every side. Ugly, filthy songs; gambling groups squatting underneath the plank bed; convicts beaten half to death, by common consent, because of having been too rowdy, and lying on the plank bed covered with sheepskins until they revive and wake up; knives already drawn several times—all this, on the second day of the holiday, tormented me to the point of illness."[12] What finally impelled him "to run out of [the barracks] like a madman" was that "six robust peasants, all together, threw themselves on the drunken Tartar Gazin, in order to subdue him; they beat him furiously—a camel could have been killed with such blows, but they knew that it was difficult to kill this Hercules, so they beat him without fear."[13]

Unable to bear this horrifying sight a moment longer, Dostoevsky rushed outside into the bright, sunlit day, the blue sky radiant overhead. He began to walk, as he often did, in the open space between the stockade and the buildings; but the beauty of the day could not calm the indignation raging in his breast. "Finally," he recalls, "my heart was inflamed with rancor"; and just at this instant he happened to meet one of the Polish prisoners, Mirecki, strolling in the same

[12] Ibid.
[13] Ibid.

isolated walkway and evidently for the same reasons. "He looked at me gloomily, his eyes flashed and his lips began to tremble: '*Je hais ces brigands* [I hate those bandits]!'—he muttered through his clenched teeth, in a half-strangled voice, and passed by."[14]

The effect of these words was to make Dostoevsky abruptly turn on his heel and go back to the barracks. Mirecki had voiced the very poisonous thoughts, had exhibited the same anger seething within Dostoevsky himself; and this had given him a terrible jolt. It raised to the surface the extent of his alignment with the Poles against his fellow Russians; and he returned to the barracks as a gesture of solidarity with his countrymen. All the same, still finding it impossible to support the sight of the pandemonium indoors, Dostoevsky lay down on his few inches of plank bed and pretended to be asleep. "But now I could not dream: my heart was beating agitatedly, and I could hear Mirecki's words ringing in my ears: '*Je hais ces brigands!*'"[15]

The severity of his inner conflict was reaching a peak; this was why he found it so difficult to blot out the present, as he had so often been accustomed to do, and allow his subconscious to wander freely in the past via involuntary associations. "I used to analyze these impressions, adding new touches to things long ago outlived, and—what is more important—I used to correct, continually to correct them."[16] What emerged now was the memory of an incident of his childhood—a period of his life just revived in his subconscious by the Easter preparations and ceremonies. And the experience had involved the same emotions of shock, fright, and fear that had been aroused by the prison-camp orgy. Wandering through the forest one day on his father's scruffy little "estate," the nine-year-old Dostoevsky suddenly thought he heard a shout that a wolf was roaming in the vicinity. The wood was criss-crossed with ravines, in which wolves sometimes appeared, and Dostoevsky's mother had warned him to be careful. The frightened boy ran out of the wood and toward a peasant plowing in a nearby field, one of his father's serfs, whom he knew only as "Marey." The surprised Marey halted work to soothe the white-faced and trembling child, and assured him that no one had shouted and no wolf was near. Dostoevsky recalled Marey smiling at him gently "like a mother," blessing him with the sign of the cross and crossing himself, and then sending him home with the reassurance that he would be kept in sight. "All this came back suddenly, I do not know why," Dostoevsky writes, "with surprising clarity and in full detail. I suddenly opened my eyes, straightened up on the plank bed and, I recall, my face still retained its gentle smile of recollection."[17]

[14] Ibid.
[15] Ibid., 206–207.
[16] Ibid., 207.
[17] Ibid., 209.

Dostoevsky never spoke to Marey again after this single contact, and he insists that he had completely lost consciousness of the incident. "And suddenly now—twenty years later, in Siberia—I was recalling that meeting so distinctly, in every detail." He is certain that "[Marey] could not have looked at me with an expression gleaming with more genuine love if I had been his only son. And who forced him to do so? He was our peasant serf, and I, after all, the son of his owner; no one would know how kind he had been and reward him for it. . . . The encounter was isolated, in an empty field, and only God, perhaps, saw from above what deep and enlightened human feeling, what delicate, almost womanly tenderness, could fill the heart of a coarse, bestially ignorant Russian peasant serf not yet expecting, nor even suspecting, that he might be free."[18]

And abruptly, as a result of this comforting memory, Dostoevsky finds that his whole attitude toward his fellow convicts has undergone a transformation. "I remember, when I got off the plank bed and gazed around, that I suddenly felt I could look on these unfortunates with quite different eyes, and suddenly, as if by a miracle, all hatred and rancor had vanished from my heart. I walked around, looking attentively at the faces that I met. That despised peasant with shaven head and brand marks on his face, reeling with drink, bawling out his hoarse, drunken song—why, he may be that very Marey; after all, I am not able to look into his heart." The same evening Dostoevsky met Mirecki again; and by this time he felt inwardly secure, capable now of facing the earlier indictment with a twinge of superior pity for the poor, unhappy Pole. "He could not have had any memories of any Mareys, and any other opinions about these people other than: '*Je hais ces brigands.*' No, these Poles had much more to endure than we did!"[19]

In his still unsurpassed *Varieties of Religious Experience*,[20] William James speaks of the inner peace, harmony, and tranquility that result from a conversion experience. Even though nothing is changed externally, the subject distinctly has the sense of perceiving a truth that, if perhaps glimpsed dimly before, had never been so lucid and so momentous. The memory of the peasant Marey had this effect on Dostoevsky, who believed he could at last see through the abhorrent surface of the world to a beauty hitherto concealed from the eyes of his moral sensibility. "Owing to circumstances," he writes, "almost throughout the whole history of Russia, the people have been . . . subjected to so much depravity and seduction, to so much torture, that it is really surprising how they have managed to succeed in preserving the human image, not to speak of its beauty. Yet they did preserve also the beauty of their image." It was this "beautiful image" that Dostoevsky could now discern; he had finally learned how to

[18] Ibid., 210.
[19] Ibid.
[20] William James, *The Varieties of Religious Experience* (New York, 1929), 172.

separate "[its] beauty from the alluvial barbarism" and "to discover diamonds in this filth."[21]

What occurred to Dostoevsky, then, bears all the earmarks of a genuine conversion experience; it also involves, as we see, a recovery of faith in the Russian common people as, in some sense, the human image of Christ. And this aspect of Dostoevsky's regeneration—that it centers primarily on his relations with the people—must be stressed. It was only from the people that Dostoevsky sought absolution, both because of the immediate sense of guilt engendered by the complexities of his prison-camp sentiments and, further back, because of his acceptance of a share of the guilt in his father's presumed murder. Since it was against the people that Dostoevsky had doubly sinned, it is by them that he wished to be forgiven, and the memory of the peasant Marey fulfilled this precise function.

In this way, under conditions of nervous tension, psychic division, and physical exhaustion similar to those in which sudden alterations of belief frequently occur, Dostoevsky underwent a striking change of heart. His recovery of faith in the people was also a rediscovery of Orthodoxy, or at least an estrangement from his previous "progressive" Christianity, whose doctrines he could well castigate as the fatal source of all his old illusions. An essential feature of such doctrines had been a naïvely optimistic glorification of the people as an inexhaustible fount of moral virtue, but such an image could hardly be valid for Dostoevsky in its old sentimental, idyllic, quasi-Rousseauian form. Yet Dostoevsky persisted in believing in the sterling moral essence of precisely *this* peasant, in violation of the evidence of his senses and rational faculties. And to sustain this belief required the support of a faith that did not shrink back from the paradoxical, the irrational, the impossible; a faith that was willing unblinkingly to accept both the ugliness and the savagery and, at the same time, to search for—and find— the saving mark of humanity concealed beneath the hideous exterior. One might say that, just as Dostoevsky's faith in the miracle of the Resurrection had been quickened and revived by the Easter ceremonies, so his faith in the Russian people had been renewed by the "miracle" of Marey's resurrection in his consciousness. No doubt the leap required to accept Christ's triumph over death played its part in stimulating the similar leap that transformed his vision of the peasant convicts. The feature of the two, in any case, would remain blended together forever in Dostoevsky's sensibility and eventually lead to that literal "divinization" of the Russian people he was one day to proclaim.

———■———

In *House of the Dead*, Dostoevsky continually offers examples of how the Christian faith, pervading camp life, helped to mitigate some of its inhumanity.

---

[21] *DW* (1876), 202.

Of Christmas, Dostoevsky writes: "The great festivals of the church make a vivid impression on the minds of the peasants from childhood upwards. . . . Respect for the solemn day had passed into a custom strictly observed among the convicts; very few caroused, all . . . tried to keep up a certain dignity" (4: 105). The religious holidays usually brought forth an outpouring of moral solidarity with the convicts in the form of charity. "An immense quantity of provisions were brought, such as rolls, cheesecakes, pastries, scones, and similar good things. I believe there was not a housewife of the middle and lower class of the town who did not send something of her baking by way of Christmas greetings to the 'unfortunates' and the captives" (4: 108). Dostoevsky excludes the upper, educated class from such participation in the Christmas spirit, and he remarks elsewhere that "the higher classes in Russia have no idea how deeply our merchants, tradespeople and peasants concern themselves about 'the unfortunates'" (4: 18).

Dostoevsky stresses the mollifying effect on the behavior of the peasant convicts of their acceptance of the Christian moral code. "All [the gifts] were accepted with equal gratitude. . . . The convicts took off their caps as they received them, bowed, gave their Christmas greetings and took the offering into the kitchen. When the offerings were piled up in heaps, the senior convicts were sent for, and they divided all equally among the wards. There was no scolding or quarreling; it was honestly and equitably done" (4: 108). What a contrast with the usual bickering and perpetual pilfering of each other's belongings!

Alms-giving from the population reached a peak during the religious holidays, but it was continual all through the year, and sometimes took the form of money handed to the convicts as they shuffled through the streets of Omsk in a work convoy. The first time Dostoevsky received alms in this way was "soon after my arrival in prison." A ten-year-old girl passed him walking under escort and ran back to give him a coin. "'There, poor unfortunate, take a kopek, for Christ's sake,' she cried, overtaking me and thrusting the coin in my hand. . . . I treasured that kopek for a long time" (4: 19). What this incident came to mean to him may be seen in *Crime and Punishment*, where Raskolnikov cuts off his ties with humanity, and indicates his rejection of all impulses of sympathy and pity by the symbolic gesture of throwing into the Neva a twenty-kopek piece given to him as charity by a little girl.

These Christian aspects of Russian lower-class life suggested that the humanitarian, philanthropic ideals of his earlier work, which he had once attributed to the progressive ideology of the Russian Westernizers, were actually embodied in the instinctive moral reflexes of the much-despised and denigrated Russian peasant. It is little wonder that Dostoevsky was later to become such a virulent opponent of all those who aspired to replace Christian values with other notions of morality. To do so, he was passionately convinced, would undermine the basic moral foundations of Russian life as he had come to know them—under circumstances where the survival of *any* kind of morality could only be considered a miracle! The most vicious man in the camp was the well-educated Aristov, who was entirely free of any trace of the traditional moral restraints.

One episode in particular took on a crucial symbolic significance for Dostoevsky as he leaned on his faith to penetrate to the moral essence of the peasant convict. During the Christmas theatricals, on entering the military ward that served as a theater, Dostoevsky was astonished by the respect and even deference he received; a front-row seat was immediately provided, although the crush in the small space was "incredible." Interpreting the subconscious behavior of the convicts, Dostoevsky attributes it to the fact that he had helped in the staging. "They looked upon me as to some extent a theatre-goer, a connoisseur . . . so on this occasion I had the honor of a front place" (4: 121–122).

This incident reveals the ability of the peasant convicts to overcome their instinctive vindictiveness against their former masters for the sake of a higher value. And the moral drawn by Dostoevsky was that "the highest and most striking characteristic of our people is just their sense of justice and their eagerness for it. There is no trace in the common people of the desire to be the cock of the walk on all occasions and at all costs, whether they deserve to be or not. One has but to take off the outer superimposed husk and look at the kernel more closely, more attentively and without prejudice. . . . There is not much our wise men could teach them. On the contrary, I think it is the wise men who ought to learn from the people" (4: 122).

Once again we are at the source of what was to become one of the most deeply held convictions of the post-Siberian Dostoevsky. For was he not later to proclaim, with accents of prophetic passion, that the Russian peasantry was imbued with a sense of moral rectitude that could serve as a shining example to its "betters"? And while such an idea was often ridiculed by his opponents, it was too firmly rooted in the redemptive emotions of these prison years for Dostoevsky ever to question its validity.

———■———

All this was added to the growing awareness that, the more Dostoevsky came to know some of his fellow convicts, the more he came to understand that some crimes had been prompted by reasons he could not fully condemn. One daring passage in *House of the Dead* even contains a general exculpation of prisoners whose personal histories he does not spell out in detail: "There are men who commit crimes on purpose to be sent to penal servitude, in order to escape from a far more penal life of labor outside. There he lived in the deepest degradation, never had enough to eat and worked from morning to night for his exploiter" (4: 43). Dostoevsky says nothing to indicate any disapproval of such a choice.

Dostoevsky's increasingly acute awareness of the moral difference between one crime and another also became the cause of a "thought which haunted me persistently all the time I was in prison, a difficulty that cannot be fully solved." Identical crimes, under the law, received much the same punishment; yet the reasons for which they had been committed, morally speaking, were infinitely varied. "One may have committed a murder for nothing, for an onion; he murdered a peasant on the high road, who turned out to have nothing but an onion." (As the prison proverb had it, "A hundred murders and a hundred onions [each worth a kopek] and you've got a ruble.") "Another murders a sensual tyrant in defense of the honor of his betrothed, his sister or his child. Another is a fugitive [a runaway serf], hemmed in by a regiment of trackers, who commits a murder in defense of his freedom, his life, often dying of hunger; and another murders little children for the pleasure of killing, of feeling their warm blood on his hands, of enjoying their terror, and their last dove-like flutter under the knife. Yet all of these are sent to penal servitude." Variations in the length of sentences do not cope with the problem because "there are as many shades of differences as there are characters," and Dostoevsky, admitting defeat, finally resigns himself to the impossibility of an answer: "It is in its own way an insoluble problem, like squaring the circle" (4: 42–43).

Such words anticipate Dostoevsky's later pronounced distaste for legal formalities of any kind, which stick to the letter of the law and rarely leave room for any probing of the heart and mind of the individual criminal. He was eventually to pour all his anguish over this issue into the portrayal of the investigation of the putative crime of Dimitry Karamazov, with its regard only for the "facts" and its total neglect of Dimitry's own responses. This growing apprehension of human diversity among his fellow convicts enormously increased the range of Dostoevsky's philanthropic convictions of the 1840s—but without causing him to blur the distinction between good and evil. What had been a pitying sentimentalism toward weak and basically unassertive characters now took on a tragic complexity as Dostoevsky's sympathies with the unsubjugated peasant convicts stretched the boundaries of official morality to the breaking point. More important than the crime itself were the motives, the human situation, from which it emerged. It is in the context of such considerations that we must place one of the most famous passages in the book. "After all," Dostoevsky declares, "one must tell the whole truth; these men were exceptional men. Perhaps they were the most gifted, the strongest of our people" (4: 231). Their crimes sprang from a strength of character and, frequently, a defense of instinctive moral principles, exhibited under circumstances where others would have been completely crushed.

———■———

Dostoevsky's years in the house of the dead exposed him to an extraordinary range of personalities, among whom genuine saintliness rubbed elbows with the basest depravity. Nearly everyone had, at some crucial instant, stepped outside the bounds of normal social life to commit a violent act that had decided his destiny once and for all. The effect of such exposure on Dostoevsky's imaginative grasp of human experience was considerable, and his portrayal of character was later to take a qualitative leap in depth and scale that may be directly attributed to this cause.

There was one particular aspect of camp life that became the most distinctive hallmark of his genius. *House of the Dead* contains a remarkable series of analyses that, focusing on the unconscious urges of the human psyche, describe its irresistible need to assert itself and affirm its native dignity. This need was so imperious that, unable to find normal outlets under the repressive conditions of the prison camp, it burst forth in all sorts of irrational, absurd, and even self-destructive forms. Always preoccupied with the deformations of character caused by lack of freedom, Dostoevsky had explored this theme in his early stories, but there he had barely scratched the surface. Life in prison camp gave him the unique vantage point from which to study human beings living under extreme psychic pressure, and responding to such pressure with the most frenzied behavior. Once Dostoevsky had mastered himself sufficiently to be able to contemplate his environment with lucidity, he began to understand even such sense-defying conduct as the product of a genuine human need—no longer as the monstrous perversities of a collection of moral Quasimodos wholly beyond the human pale.

We cannot truly understand Dostoevsky's later worldview if we separate his perceptions and values too sharply from the context of psychic constraint in which they were remolded. For Dostoevsky was persuaded that no human order could ultimately prove viable unless it acknowledged—and offered some relief for—these irrepressible demands of the human spirit. *House of the Dead* is so rich in illustrations of this power of the irrational, and they are so varied in their nature and importance, that one scarcely knows where to begin. But let us start with Dostoevsky's remarks on the psychically unsettling effects of the communal life imposed on the convicts. He was convinced that this closeness contributed to their excessive restlessness and irritability. "I am certain," he affirms, "that every convict felt this torture, though of course in most cases unconsciously." As for himself, perhaps the worst "torture in prison life, almost more terrible than any other . . . [was] *compulsory life in common*" (4: 20–22). Elsewhere, he repeats: "I could never have imagined, for instance, how terrible and agonizing it would be never once for a single minute to be alone for the [four] years of my imprisonment" (4: 11).

The truth of these words is proven by a letter that Dostoevsky wrote, almost immediately after his release, to Mme Fonvizina: "It is now almost five years that I have been under guard among a crowd of people, and I never had a single hour alone. To be alone is a normal need, like eating and drinking; otherwise, in this enforced communism one turns into a hater of mankind. The society of other people becomes an unbearable torture, and it was from this that I suffered most during those four years."[22] It is striking to see how early Dostoevsky identifies his prison-camp existence with life in one of those ideal Socialist Utopias (Fourier, Cabet) that so many of his friends in the Petrashevsky Circle had once admired. He had, to be sure, never fully accepted such Utopias himself, but his rejection had now become viscerally rooted in this overwhelming sense of the need for the personality to defend itself against psychic encroachment.

A much more dramatic illustration of the power of irrational impulse over human behavior is provided by Dostoevsky's remarks about prisoners awaiting punishment by flogging or beating. "To defer the moment of punishment . . . convicts sometimes resorted to terrible expedients; by stabbing one of the officials or a fellow convict they would get a new trial, and their punishment would be deferred for some two months and their aim would be attained. It was nothing to them that their punishment, when it did come, two months later, would be twice or three times as severe" (4: 144). One of the patients in the hospital had drunk a jug of vodka mixed with snuff to delay his punishment, and died from the effects. Commonplace prudence, as we see, was swept away by a fear too elemental to master.

The irrational component of such examples is still motivated by comprehensible causes. This is not the case with other types of behavior, where the cause is so slight as to be entirely incommensurate with the effect, or where no immediate cause is perceptible. Dostoevsky's true genius reveals itself when he turns to explore these aberrant extremes, and intuits the deep human significance of what looks like madness. A peculiar feature of peasant convict life, for example, was the general attitude toward money. It was, Dostoevsky points out, "of vast and overwhelming importance" in prison, allowing the convict to obtain all sorts of forbidden luxuries—extra food, tobacco, vodka, sex—which helped make life more endurable. One would thus assume that the convicts hung on to their money for dear life and used it sparingly, but exactly the opposite turned out to be the case. Every convict who managed to scrape together a sufficient sum would invariably squander it gloriously on a drunken fling. And so, after

---

[22] *Pisma*, 1: 143; February 20, 1854.

amassing the money "with cruel effort, or making use of extraordinary cunning, often in conjunction with theft and cheating," the convict threw it away with what Dostoevsky calls "childish senselessness" (4: 65–66).

But, he hastens to explain, "if he throws it away like so much rubbish, he throws it away on what he considers of even more value." And what is more precious for the convict than all the material benefits he can obtain from money? "Freedom or the dream of freedom," Dostoevsky replies. For one must realize that "the word convict means nothing else but a man with no will of his own, and in spending money he is showing a will of his own." By drinking and carousing, by breaking the rules of prison discipline and bullying his companions in misery, the convict is "pretending to his companions and even persuading himself, *if only for a time*, that he has infinitely more power and freedom than is supposed" (4: 66). Nothing is more important for the convict than to *feel* that he can assert his will and thus exercise his freedom; there is no risk he will refuse to run, no punishment he will not endure, for the sake of his temporary (and illusory) but infinitely precious satisfaction.

Here Dostoevsky is no longer simply stressing the dominating role of irrational elements in human behavior; now the need of the human personality to exercise its will, and hence to experience a sense of autonomy while doing so, is seen as the strongest drive of the psyche. The inability to fulfill this drive can be disastrous. Even, Dostoevsky observes, "this sudden outbreak in the man from whom one would least have expected it, is simply the poignant hysterical craving for self-expression, the unconscious yearning for himself, the desire to assert himself, to assert his crushed personality, a desire which suddenly takes possession of him and reaches the pitch of fury, or spite, of mental aberration, of fits and nervous convulsions. So perhaps a man buried alive and awakening in his coffin might beat upon its lid and struggle to fling it off, though of course reason might convince him that all his efforts would be useless; but the trouble is that it is not a question of reason, it is a question of nervous convulsions" (4: 66–67).

Similar conditions exist outside, and many of the convicts had landed in the camp precisely for having revolted against them. Each had been a peasant, house serf, soldier, or workman who had long led a quiet and peaceable life, bearing the burdens of his lot with patience and resignation. "Suddenly something in him seems to snap; his patience gives way and he sticks a knife into his enemy and oppressor" (4: 87–88). Such descriptions of personalities oppressed beyond endurance, who break out in hysterical frenzy and revolt against their subjugation, are among the most impressive passages in the book. Here we are at the source of what was one day to become the revolt of the underground man, but this work could be written only after Dostoevsky had become convinced that, in the world envisaged by the radical ideology of the 1860s, the situation of the human personality would become identical with what he had seen and felt in the prison camp.

———■———

Many details of *House of the Dead* help us understand how the peasant convicts maintained their psychic equilibrium, and here again emphasis is placed on the prevalence of irrational components over other aspects of convict behavior. The convicts preferred to be given a "task" rather than simply to work the regulation number of hours; the assignment would incite them to work harder so as to gain a little extra free time and acquire some slight degree of control over their lives. For this very reason, everyone hated the *forced* labor and found it particularly burdensome, even though Dostoevsky was surprised to find it so relatively light. Many peasant convicts had worked much harder in civilian life, and Dostoevsky admits to realizing "only long afterwards . . . that the hardness, the penal character of the work lay not in its being difficult and uninterrupted but in its being *compulsory*, obligatory, enforced" (4: 20).

Most of the convicts were skilled craftsmen who earned a little money by selling their products to the local population. All the convicts possessed forbidden tools, and Dostoevsky surmised that "the authorities shut their eyes" to this infraction of the rules because they understood intuitively that such work was a safety valve for the prisoners. "If it were not for his own private work to which he was devoted with his whole mind, his whole interest," Dostoevsky writes, "a man could not live in prison." More important than the extra money were the psychic benefits of this self-imposed task, freely performed and which guarantees the individual a sense of self-possession and moral autonomy. "Without labor, without lawful normal property man cannot live; he becomes depraved and is transformed into a beast. . . . Work saved them from crime; without [private] work the convicts would have devoured one another like spiders in a glass jar" (4: 16–17). The social-political implications of this assertion constitute a flat rejection of the moral basis of Utopian Socialism (or any other kind), which views private property as the root of all evil.

But just as the human personality could be driven to irrational crime and self-destruction, so too it had an irrational inner self-defense against reaching such a state. And this self-defense is the human capacity to hope. "From the very first day of my life in prison," Dostoevsky says, "I began to dream of freedom." In the case of many other convicts, "the amazing audacity of their hopes impressed me from the beginning." It was as if prison life was not part of a convict's existence, and he was emotionally unable to accept it as such. "Every convict . . . looks at twenty years as though they were two, and is fully convinced that when he leaves prison at fifty-five he will be as full of life and energy as he is now at thirty-five" (4: 79). Even convicts condemned to life sentences continued to hope for a change of luck, and, writes Dostoevsky, "*this strange impatient and intense hope*, which sometimes found involuntary utterance, at times so wild as to be almost like delirium, and what was most striking of all, often persisted in by men of apparently the greatest common sense—gave a special aspect and character to the place" (4: 196).

One of Dostoevsky's most hallucinatory evocations is his recollection of having seen convicts chained to the wall in the Tobolsk prison and kept like that, unable to move more than a distance of seven feet, for five and sometimes ten years. And yet all were well-behaved and quiet, and "everyone is intensely anxious for the end of the sentence. Why, one wonders? I will tell you why: he will get out of the stifling dark room with its low vaulted roof of brick, and will walk in the prison yard . . . and that is all. He will never be allowed out of the prison. . . . He knows that and yet he is desperately eager for the end of his time on the chain. But for that longing how could he remain five or six years on the chain without dying or going out of his mind? Some of them would not endure it at all" (4: 79–80).

It is the capacity to hope, then, that keeps men alive and sane even under the most ghastly conditions. "When he has lost all hope, all object in life," Dostoevsky writes, in a piercing phrase, "man often becomes a monster in his misery" (4: 197). The vast majority of the convicts, wrapped in their incessant dream of freedom, fortunately never reached such a state of total despair. All the same, Dostoevsky's imagination at this point could not resist taking the eschatological leap that was to become so characteristic for him—the leap to the end condition of whatever empirical situation he is considering—and so, in order to dramatize the supreme importance of hope for human life, he deliberately *invents* a situation in which it is systematically destroyed. Such a passage, the most haunting in the book, appears in the midst of his analysis of the differing reactions to free and to forced labor.

> The idea has occurred to me that if one wanted to crush, to annihilate a man utterly, . . . one need only give him work of an absolutely, completely useless and irrational character. . . . [I]f he had to pour water from one vessel into another and back, over and over again, to pound sand, to move a heap of earth from one place to another and back again—I believe the convict would hang himself in a few days or would commit a thousand crimes, preferring rather to die than to endure such humiliation, shame and torture. (4: 20)

One has only to transpose the terms of this passage slightly in order to see its metaphysical implications. Not to believe in God and immortality, for the later Dostoevsky, is to be condemned to live in an ultimately senseless universe, and the characters in his great novels who reach this level of self-awareness inevitably destroy themselves because, refusing to endure the torment of living without hope, they have become monsters in their misery.

———■———

The matrix of the later Dostoevsky is already contained in the deceptively objective and noncommittal pages of *House of the Dead,* and this work provides the proper context within which to gloss one of the most disputed passages Dostoevsky ever wrote. Contained in his frank and moving letter to Mme Fonvizina shortly after being released, this passage offers a revealing glimpse into Dostoevsky's wrestlings with the problem of faith. By this time his erstwhile benefactress had returned to Russia, and Dostoevsky has gathered from her letter that the homecoming has overwhelmed her with feelings far more of sadness than of joy. "I understand that," Dostoevsky assures her, "and I have sometimes thought that if I returned to my country one day my impressions would contain more of suffering than of gladness. I think that on returning to his country each exile has to live over again, in his consciousness and memory, all of his past misfortune. It resembles a scale on which one weighs and gauges the true weight of everything one has suffered, endured, lost, and what the virtuous people have taken from us."

After thus linking the sadness of return with the exile's rankling animosity toward "the virtuous people," Dostoevsky offers Mme Fonvizina the consolation against such bitterness that he has found himself in his religious faith. What he is about to say, his words suggest, has helped him master the surges of his own moods of melancholy and anger. "I have heard many people say that you are a believer, N. D. . . . It's not because you are a believer, but because I myself have lived and felt that [her mood of dejection] that I will tell you that at such moments one thirsts for faith as 'the parched grass,' and one finds it at last because truth becomes evident in unhappiness. I will tell you that I am a child of the century, a child of disbelief and doubt, I am that today and (I know it) will remain so until the grave. How much terrible torture this thirst for faith has cost me and costs me even now, which is all the stronger in my soul the more arguments I can find against it. And yet, God sends me sometimes instants when I am completely calm; at those instants I love and feel loved by others, and it is at these instants that I have shaped for myself a *Credo* where everything is clear and sacred for me. This *Credo* is very simple, here it is: to believe that nothing is more beautiful, profound, sympathetic, reasonable, manly, and more perfect than Christ; and I tell myself with a jealous love not only that there is nothing but that there cannot be anything. Even more, if someone proved to me that Christ is outside the truth, and that *in reality* the truth were outside of Christ, then I should prefer to remain with Christ rather than with the truth."[23]

[23] Ibid., 142.

Dostoevsky's answers, as first revealed in this crucial letter, originate in the two most momentous experiences of his prison years. One is the peasant Marey vision, whose inspiration helped him to achieve those moments of inner tranquility and loving identification with others during which he could formulate his credo. The other, contained in his new grasp of the centrality and power of the irrational as a force in human life, resulted in his unambiguous choice of Christ over "the truth." The ideal and the message of Christ had now come to mean something far more intimate and personal than a doctrine of social transformation; something far more deeply intertwined with the most anguishing needs of his own sensibility. Faith in Christ had supported him at the moment he had confronted death, it had proven to be a crucial link between himself and his fellow Russians, and it had rescued him from the ghastly prospect of living in a universe without hope. All of Dostoevsky's doubts as "a child of the century"—and he had been familiar with them long before meeting Belinsky—had simply been overpowered by his new comprehension of the psychic-emotive demands of the human spirit. Such doubts could no longer shake his faith, because everything in the house of the dead had spoken against them and had proclaimed the feebleness and paltriness of reason when confronted by the crisis situations of human existence.

It has often been questioned whether Dostoevsky's credo should be taken at face value. Can a person with such an admittedly ineradicable skepticism truly be considered a believing Christian? But the clash between reason and faith has been a constant of the Christian tradition ever since St. Paul (who knew that his faith was "foolishness to the Greeks"), and a line of Christian thinkers running from Tertullian and St. Augustine to Luther, Pascal, and Kierkegaard has dwelt on the opposition between reason and revelation. Dostoevsky is closest of all to the great Danish defender of the faith, who, confronting the full impact of the Left Hegelian critique of religion as the self-alienation of the human spirit, chose to *accept* this critique and to separate faith off entirely from human reason.

Like Dostoevsky, and even more rigorously, Kierkegaard decided to take his stand with the irrational of faith against reason and to push the opposition between the two to the point of paradox. Faith, he said, is "subjective certainty," which he defined as "objective uncertainty . . . grasped with the apprehension of the most passionate inwardness."[24] Some words in Kierkegaard's notebooks further help to illuminate the subjective, existential aspect of that "most passionate inwardness" on which Dostoevsky also fell back to compensate for the "objective uncertainty" of his own belief in Christ. "Whether I have faith," Kierkegaard wrote, "can never be ascertained by me with immediate certainty—for faith is precisely this dialectical hovering, which is unceasingly in fear and trembling

[24] Walter Lowrie, *Kierkegaard*, 2 vols. (New York, 1962), 2: 138.

but never in despair; faith is exactly this never-ending worry about oneself, which keeps one alert and ready to risk everything, this worry about oneself as to whether one truly has faith—and look! precisely this worry about oneself is faith."[25] No better description can be given of the ever-unstable balancing point of Dostoevsky's own faith, which, as we see it spontaneously expressed in his credo, will always remain perilously poised in "dialectical hovering" above the abyss of doubt.

[25] Cited in Walter Ruttenbeck, *Sören Kierkegaard, der Christliche Denker und sein Werk* (Berlin, 1929), 225.

CHAPTER 17

Private Dostoevsky

Dostoevsky was released from the Omsk stockade on February 15, 1854, but the freedom for which he had waited so long was still minimal. As he remarked in his letter to Mme Fonvizina, "In the overcoat of a soldier, I am just as much of a prisoner as before."[1] For reasons of health he was allowed to remain in Omsk for a month, and both he and Durov lived at the home of the hospitable Konstantin Ivanov and his wife.

Dostoevsky's letters give us a graphic picture of his plight as a lowly soldier. Completely dependent on the good will and even charity of others, he was forced to continually plead for help. What made his situation even worse was the conviction that he had emerged from prison camp with new powers as a writer and that, if he were only allowed to utilize his talents, all his problems could be solved at one stroke. In his letter to Mikhail written during his recuperation in Omsk, Dostoevsky makes no effort to conceal his personal agenda when he asks for a full report on all his relatives and on the exact state of Mikhail's finances. (Mikhail had opened a small cigarette factory with his share of the distribution of the Dostoevsky family property.) Dostoevsky is determined to fight his way back into Russian literature and he knows this will involve a long campaign, during which his survival will depend on the help he can muster from family and friends. "I need money," he tells Mikhail bluntly. "*I have to live, brother. These years will not have passed without bearing their fruits.* . . . What you spend for me—will not be lost. If I manage to live, I will return it with interest . . . and now I will no longer write trifles. You will hear of me being talked about."[2]

A further request to Mikhail, made in even more pressing terms, was for the dispatch of books. Even after Major Krivtsov had been toppled, Dostoevsky's relation to literature had been too emotionally charged to allow him to pick up a book lightly. He recalls "the strange and agitating impression of the first book I read in prison"—one of the Russian "thick" periodicals containing literary works, criticism, and social commentary. "My former life rose up before me full of light and color and I tried from what I had read to conjecture how far I had

[1] *Pisma*, I: 143; between February 20, 1854, and the end of the month.
[2] Ibid., 138. February 22, 1854.

dropped behind. . . . What emotions were agitating people now? What questions were occupying their minds? I pored over every word, tried to read between the lines and to find secret meanings and allusions to the past; I looked for traces of what had agitated us in my time. And how sad it was for me to realize how remote I was from this new life, how cut off I was from it all. I should have to get used to everything afresh, to make acquaintance with a new generation again" (4: 229).

He thus begs Mikhail to send him what would constitute the contents of a small research library. As one might expect, he asks for the dispatch of "the magazines of this year, at least *Notes of the Fatherland*," yet he seems even more anxious to plunge back into the past: "I need (badly need) ancient historians (in French translation) and the moderns—that is, Vico, Guizot, Thierry, Thiers, Ranke, etc., the economists, and the Church Fathers."[3] "Send me the Carus," he continues, "Kant's *Critique of Pure Reason*, and if you are able to send things clandestinely, slip Hegel in without fail, especially Hegel's *History of Philosophy*. My entire future is tied up with that."[4] Dostoevsky warns Mikhail to burn his letter; but so great is his desire for books that he is willing to run the risk of violating regulations in order to obtain them. More than a year later, no books had yet arrived from Mikhail, although the latter had turned over a consignment to a mutual friend for shipment. Some may have reached their destination in the late spring of 1855, when Mikhail is thanked for the receipt of a package. But Dostoevsky could hardly have obtained everything he asked for: at that time he was sharing a cottage with Baron Wrangel, who refers to "the pitiful stock of our books" and pictures Dostoevsky rereading each of them a countless number of times.[5]

Dostoevsky was mulling over several projects that he hoped would speed his rehabilitation. One was concerned, he writes, "with the mission of Christianity in art." He intended to call this work *Letters on Art* and to dedicate it to Her Highness Maria Nikolaevna, the daughter of Nicholas I, who was then president of the Academy of Fine Arts. "I wish to demand the authorization to dedicate my article to her," he explains, "and to publish it without signature."[6] The works of the Church Fathers would have supplied him with information on both theology and the attitude of the early Church toward art, while Kant and Hegel involved another plan to unobtrusively break into print again by translating. In a letter written in November 1854, the young Wrangel tells his father that he and his new-found friend intend "to translate Hegel's *Philosophy* [?] and the *Psyche* of Carus."[7] Dostoevsky had asked for Carus's once-famous treatise on psychology,

[3] Ibid.
[4] Ibid., 139.
[5] A. E. Wrangel, *Vospominaniya o F. M. Dostoevskom v Siberii* (St. Petersburg, 1912), 66.
[6] *Pis'ma*, 1: 183–184; April 13, 1856.
[7] Wrangel, *Vospominaniya*, 34.

sometimes considered a precursor of psychoanalysis, *Psyche zur Entwicklungsge-schichte der Seele* (1846). Wrangel writes his father that Dostoevsky "did not know German";[8] no doubt this is why he enlisted the aid of someone for whom German would have been as much of a native tongue as Russian.

What Dostoevsky would have admired in Carus, whose scientific credentials were impeccable, was a mind totally abreast of the very latest theories of biology and physiology but who interpreted them in the old-fashioned terms of Schelling's *Naturphilosophie*. Carus saw both nature and human life as originating in a Divine Idea and considered the individual soul to be immortal because it shared in the eternity of this divine creative principle. In the mid-1840s, in opposition to Belinsky's "scientific" arguments in favor of atheism, materialism, and determinism, Dostoevsky would have eagerly seized on Carus's book as proof that one could be up-to-date and "scientific," without abandoning a belief in some sort of supernatural principle or in the precepts of Christian morality. For he could find in Carus a glowing tribute to the fundamental tenet of this morality—the law of love—supported by a quotation from the New Testament. It is the law of love, running through all of nature and beginning with sexual differentiation, that for Carus first stirs in mankind the impulse of devotion and self-sacrifice, and hence leads to the ultimate conquest of egoism ("the unconditional surrender to the godly that hovers above all consciousness, in a word, to *the love of God*").[9]

Dostoevsky's deepened awareness of the power of the irrational in human existence would only have confirmed what he was now learning from Carus about the strength of the irrational and the unconscious: "The key to the understanding of the essence of the conscious life of the soul lies in the region of the unconscious."[10] By "unconscious," though, Carus refers not only to psychic life but to all of nature, which he considers to be endowed with soul-life and to differ from the psyche only in degrees of consciousness and self-consciousness. Carus emphasizes that the higher forms of consciousness must be kept in equilibrium with the unconscious forces of existence if they are not to become unbalanced. One can see in this proto-Jungian schema some analogy to, and certainly an encouragement for, Dostoevsky's ideology of *pochvennichestvo*, elaborated a few years later. This called for the fusion of an intelligentsia inspired by Western ideas of rationalism and enlightenment with the unconscious moral forces slumbering in the still uncorrupted bosom of the Russian people.

Carus compares moral evil to a state of physical illness; both are deviations from the normal condition of the unconscious forces that regulate the health of an organism. But, just as nature has means of restoring its own equilibrium in

[8] Ibid., 21.
[9] Carl Gustav Carus, *Psyche zur Entwick-Lungsgeschichte der Seele* (Pforzheim, 1846), 297–298.
[10] Ibid., 1.

the case of physical illness, so the moral consciousness has its own "unconscious" means—the human "conscience"—that works to restore the moral health of the personality.[11] This image of conscience as a natural and instinctive regulator of the human psyche, whose distortion or perversion leads to a literal "sickness" of the self, was to become one of the major themes of the great works of Dostoevsky that lay ahead.

Whatever plans Dostoevsky may have had for literary activity, however, had to be abandoned in the face of the grim necessities of his existence. His leisure ended when he left the Ivanovs, whose kindness he praises to his brother with heartfelt words. "I would have died for good if I had not found people here," he confesses. "K. I. I[vanov] has been a veritable brother to me. . . . And he was not alone. Brother, there are many noble people in the world."[12] In mid-March he made the journey to Semipalatinsk and joined the ranks of the Seventh Line Battalion of the Siberian Army Corps.

———◾———

Semipalatinsk turned out to be, as Baron Wrangel describes it, "a half-city, half-village,"[13] sprawling amidst the ruins of an ancient Mongol town located on the steep right slope of the Irtish River. Most of the houses were unpainted, one-story constructions of wood; only the single Orthodox Church, forced to compete with seven mosques, was built of stone, and a huge covered marketplace sheltered the caravans of camels and packhorses that conducted the flourishing trade between Russia and Central Asia. On the opposite bank of the river could be seen the large felt tent dwellings of the half-nomad Khirghizes. Loose, drifting sand filled the streets, and Russian officers called the place "the Devil's Sandbox."[14] Semipalatinsk was still part of a border region on the edge of the steppe, and incursions by raiding parties of Mongols and hostile Khirghizes into the area were by no means uncommon, although a garrison town would not have been directly threatened.

Through some friends of the indefatigably charitable Ivanovs, Dostoevsky was given permission to live by himself in town. At last he would be able to snatch a few hours of that solitude he had so desperately craved in the prison camp! He found a one-room cottage near the barracks, owned by an elderly widow. The furnishings were of the simplest, and hordes of cockroaches, according to the fastidious Wrangel, roamed freely over the table, bed, and walls. The housekeeping was done by the elder daughter of the family, twenty-two years old and the widow of a soldier, who looked after him lovingly, and seemed to be

[11] Ibid., 93.
[12] *Pisma*, I: 137: February 22, 1854.
[13] Wrangel, *Vospominaniya*, 15.
[14] George Kennan, *Siberia and the Exile System*, 2 vols. (New York, 1891), I: 158.

constantly in his quarters. Wrangel recalls taking tea with Dostoevsky out-of-doors one day and being casually joined, as he puts it discreetly, by the house-keeper *en grand négligé* (just a smock tied at the waist with a red sash). After four years in the prison camp, could Dostoevsky have resisted such readily available female charms? Nothing would have been more natural, and we know that he exhibited a personal interest in the affairs of the family. For he tried, unsuccessfully, to persuade the mother not to allow the attractive younger daughter, sixteen years old, to supplement the family income by occasional prostitution with the army garrison.

Gradually, the presence of an ex-convict named Dostoevsky, who had formerly enjoyed some literary notoriety, began to be known among the more literate members of the Russian community in Semipalatinsk. Educated men were at a premium in that part of the world, and exiles of all kinds (mostly Poles) were employed as tutors to supplement or even replace the scanty public education available to Russian children. Dostoevsky was soon approached to tutor the offspring of various families, and in this fashion he began to strike up closer relations with various households. He became acquainted with the commander of his battalion, the good-natured and knockabout Lieutenant-Colonel Belikhov, who had worked his way up from the ranks. This worthy officer found reading a chore, so he invited Dostoevsky to come and read to him from newspapers and magazines. It was at the home of Belikhov one evening that Dostoevsky first met Alexander Ivanovich Isaev and his wife, Marya Dimitrievna.

Isaev was another of those incorrigible and appealing Russian drunkards whom Dostoevsky had already portrayed and whom he was to immortalize in the elder Marmeladov in *Crime and Punishment*. Isaev had come to Semipalatinsk as a customs official, but for some reason—perhaps the exacerbated pride of a drunkard—he had resigned his post. The Isaev family, which included a seven-year-old son, Pasha, was thus living in hand-to-mouth fashion while the breadwinner nominally sought other employment. Meanwhile, what little money he and his wife could scrape together was squandered by Isaev in drinking bouts with his cronies among the riffraff of the town. Dostoevsky, Wrangel tells us, was infinitely charitable with regard to human foibles and fallibilities. Writing to Mikhail, Dostoevsky remarks that Isaev "was, despite all the dirt, exceptionally noble." [15] It was not, however, the husband who soon drew Dostoevsky to spend all his time at the Isaevs but the wife, destined to become the first great love of his life.

Marya Dimitrievna's father was at that time head of the quarantine for travelers arriving in Astrakhan, a port city on the Caspian Sea. All of his daughters had been educated in a private *pension*, and Mme Isaeva's intellectual and spiritual

---

[15] *Pisma*, 2: 560; January 13, 1856.

capacities were unmistakably a cut above those of the average Semipalatinsk army or bureaucratic spouse. "Marya Dimitrievna was about thirty years old," writes Wrangel, "a quite pretty blonde of medium height, very slim, with a passionate nature given to exalted feeling. Even then an ill-omened flush played on her pale face, and several years later tuberculosis took her to the grave. She was well-read, quite cultivated, eager for knowledge, kind, and unusually vivacious and impressionable. She took a great interest in Dostoevsky and treated him kindly, not, I think, because she valued him deeply, but rather because she felt sorry for an unhappy human being beaten down by fate. It is possible that she was even attached to him, but there was no question of being in love."[16]

Certainly, like everyone else in town, she was aware that he had an "illness," but he himself was as yet uncertain about its diagnosis. "I have already spoken to you of my illness," he writes Mikhail. "Bizarre attacks, resembling epilepsy and yet not being epilepsy."[17] She saw him as being "direly in need of resources, and . . . said he was a man 'without a future,'" writes Wrangel. "Feodor Mikhailovich took the feeling of pity and sympathy as mutual love, and fell head over heels in love with all the fire of youth."[18] He became a close "friend of the family," assumed the function of tutor to their son, and, as Wrangel puts it, "spent entire days at the Isaevs."[19] This was the situation when Wrangel appeared on the scene in November 1854 to provide Dostoevsky with closer friendship, and more powerful patronage, than any he had been able to acquire so far.

———■———

During the agonizing minutes that Dostoevsky stood on the scaffolding in Semenovsky Square, his eyes may well have turned to the massed crowds surrounding the spectacle. If Dostoevsky had been able to distinguish one person from another, he would surely have been struck by one young man—just barely seventeen years of age, and wearing the three-cornered hat and uniform overcoat of the elite Alexander Lyceum located at Tsarskoe Selo—who was watching the proceedings with a sorrowful air of concern. The name of this young man was Baron Alexander Yegorovich Wrangel, and he belonged to one of those Russian-German aristocratic families of Baltic origin that, under Nicholas I, staffed the higher echelons of the bureaucracy and the army.

The young Wrangel had heard conversations about the case at home—and he pricked up his ears, because he had just read *Poor Folk* and was reading *Netotchka Nezvanova* with great admiration. Any information concerning the fate of the gifted and unfortunate Dostoevsky aroused his curiosity, although he took care

[16] Wrangel, *Vospominaniya*, 38.
[17] *Pis'ma*, 1: 146; July 30, 1854.
[18] Wrangel, *Vospominaniya*, 39.
[19] Ibid.

not to reveal in public a literary taste that would have been considered politically suspect in his milieu. On the day of the mock execution, despite reprimands from a relative to leave the square, Wrangel stayed to the very end of the macabre comedy and only left when the crowd dissolved, "crossing themselves and blessing the mercifulness of the Tsar."[20]

After graduating from the lyceum and dying of boredom in the Ministry of Justice, Wrangel decided to join a number of his classmates in applying for a post in Siberia. Just twenty-one years old, he was appointed public prosecutor of the region that included Semipalatinsk. He had met Mikhail Dostoevsky on some occasion in Petersburg and was happy to call on him before beginning his journey and to receive from him letters for Dostoevsky, some clothes, books, and fifty rubles. Arriving in Semipalatinsk on November 20, 1854, he immediately sent a message inviting Private Dostoevsky to take tea with him the very next day. "Dostoevsky did not know who had summoned him and why," Wrangel recalls, "and when he came in, was extremely reserved. He was in his gray soldier's overcoat, with a stiff red collar and red epaulettes, morose, his face pale and sickly. . . . Intently looking at me with his sharp, gray-blue eyes, it seemed that he was trying to peer into my very soul—now what sort of a man is he?"[21]

Dostoevsky buried himself in the letters that Wrangel had brought, beginning to sob quietly while reading those written by his brother and sister. Wrangel too had a packet of correspondence awaiting him, and he too began to sob uncontrollably as memories of his family and friends rose before his eyes. "We both stood there face to face, forgotten by fate, solitary. . . . I felt so distressed that, despite my exalted rank . . . as it were involuntarily, without thinking, I threw myself on the neck of Feodor Mikhailovich, who stood opposite looking at me with a sad and pensive expression."[22] The older man comforted the younger, and the two promised to see each other frequently.

Dostoevsky and Wrangel became fast friends. "He is," Dostoevsky explains to Mikhail, "very gentle, although with a strongly developed *point d'honneur*, incredibly kind . . . what irritates and enrages others distresses him—the sign of an excellent heart. *Très comme il faut.*"[23] The two began to spend so much time together that tongues started to wag among what Wrangel calls "the bribetaking bureaucrats,"[24] and he noticed that his mail began to arrive four days later than its distribution to others. The military governor, considering Wrangel's tender years, felt called upon to warn him about falling under the influence of such a notorious revolutionary. Taking matters into his own hands, Wrangel asked the

[20] Ibid., 8.
[21] Ibid., 17.
[22] Ibid., 18.
[23] *Pisma*, 2: 538; January 13, 1856.
[24] Wrangel, *Vospominaniya*, 25.

official to invite Dostoevsky to his home and judge for himself. As it turned out, the visit was a great success; the invitation was repeated; and from this moment Dostoevsky was received, through Wrangel's good offices, in whatever good society could be found in Semipalatinsk.

Three months after Wrangel set foot in Semipalatinsk, an event occurred that opened up a more promising perspective on Dostoevsky's future. Nicholas I died suddenly, on February 18, 1855, struck down while the Russian Army in the Caucasus was still engaged in battle against Turkey, and almost a month later the news finally arrived in the distant Siberian outpost. The thoughts of the many political exiles at once turned to the prospects of amnesty, which traditionally accompanied the installation of a new regime. Moreover, "rumors of the gentleness of character, humaneness, and kindliness of the new tsar had long since penetrated to Siberia." [25] Dostoevsky shared such general expectations; and now, with the influential Wrangel at his side, whose family had connections with the highest court circles, he had every reason to believe they would be fulfilled.

Less than a month later, Wrangel wrote a letter to his father in which he spoke of Dostoevsky for the first time. "Fate has brought me together with a rare person as regards both qualities of heart and mind," he says; "he is our young and unfortunate writer Dostoevsky. I am much obliged to him, and his words, advice, and ideas will strengthen me for my entire life." And then he arrived at the real issue: "Do you know, dear father, whether there will be an amnesty? So many unfortunates are waiting and hoping, as a drowning person clutches at a straw." Two weeks later he sent a letter to his sister, urging her to question their father on the prospects of an amnesty for political prisoners and suggesting that a word might be uttered on Dostoevsky's behalf to General Dubelt or to Prince Orlov. "Can it be that this remarkable man will perish here as a soldier? . . . I am sad and sick about him—I love him like a brother, and honor him like a father." [26]

By the time these letters were written, Dostoevsky and Wrangel had taken up residence together in a dacha, affectionately called "Cossack Garden," on the outskirts of town. The climate of Semipalatinsk during the summer months was unbearably hot, and Wrangel decided to escape at the beginning of spring the moment the steppe began to blossom and turn green. He found an empty house on a bank of the river in the midst of luxuriant vegetation, and, since the summer encampment of Dostoevsky's regiment was close by, it was easily arranged for the latter to share his quarters. The picture Wrangel gives of their life together has an idyllic quality that Dostoevsky was not to know again for many years. Wrangel, an enthusiastic and versatile gardener, had determined to show the natives that all sorts of flowers and fruits unknown to the region could be

[25] Ibid., 39.
[26] Ibid., 34–35.

cultivated there, and the work connected with this project "very much pleased and occupied Dostoevsky, [who] more than once recalled his childhood and the farmhouse of his family."[27]

■

By this time, Dostoevsky's illicit romance with Marya Dimitrievna had become more and more absorbing, and the need to possess her completely soon drove all other thoughts out of his mind. Much to everyone's astonishment, Alexander Isaev succeeded in finding another post—in the small town of Kuznetsk, a miserable backwater lost in the depths of the Siberian wilderness. The news struck Dostoevsky like a blow, and suddenly shattered the fragile world of relative contentment he had so laboriously managed to construct. "And look, she agrees," he tells Wrangel bitterly, "she doesn't object, that's what's so shocking."[28]

Since the Isaevs were destitute, the impoverished Dostoevsky, borrowing money from the obliging Wrangel, helped them scrape together what they needed for the journey. The departure took place on a soft May night, bathed in moonlight, and Wrangel and Dostoevsky, according to the Russian custom, accompanied the party on the first leg of the journey after they had paused for a final visit at Cossack Garden. Wrangel plied Isaev with champagne until he lapsed into a drunken stupor, then deposited him in a separate carriage so as to give the two lovers a period of privacy at parting. When the time came to say farewell, Dostoevsky and Marya Dimitrievna embraced, wiped away their tears, and the befuddled *paterfamilias* was placed back in the open *tarantas* in which the Isaevs were forced to make the journey. "The horses started up," recalls Wrangel, "puffs of dust rose from the road, already the cart and its passengers could scarcely be seen, the post bell grew fainter and fainter . . . and Dostoevsky still stood as if rooted to the spot, silent, his head lowered, tears coursing down his cheeks. I went up to him, took his hand—he seemed to wake up after a long sleep, and, not saying a word, got into the carriage. We returned home at daybreak."[29]

Letters immediately began to fly between Semipalatinsk and Kuznetsk at a weekly rhythm, and thanks to one that survived we can obtain some firsthand impression of Dostoevsky's feelings for his first great love. "I have never considered our meeting as an ordinary one," he writes, "and now, deprived of you, I have understood many things. I lived for five years deprived of human beings, alone, having nobody, in the full sense of the word, to whom I could pour out my heart. . . . The simple fact that a woman held out her hand to me has constituted a new epoch in my life. In certain moments, even the best of men, if I may say so, is nothing more or less than a blockhead. The heart of a woman, her

[27] Ibid., 43.
[28] Ibid., 50.
[29] Ibid., 51.

12. Marya Dimitrievna Isaeva

compassion, her interest, the infinite goodness of which we do not have an idea, and which often, through stupidity, we do not even notice, is irreplaceable. I found all that in you." [30]

Their relationship had already seen some stormy moments, and its tempestuous past hardly augured well for the future. But Dostoevsky took most of the blame himself ("in the first place I was an ungrateful swine"), and attributed Marya Dimitrievna's outbursts to a noble nature "offended by the fact that a filthy society did not value or understand you, and for a person with your force of character it is impossible not to rebel against injustice; that is an honest and noble trait. It is the foundation of your character. Life and trouble have of course exaggerated and irritated much in you; but, good God! all this is redeemed with interest, a hundred times over." [31] Dostoevsky would always see Marya Dimitrievna in a flattering light, as a person whose violent indignation and explosions of temper expressed a noble rage against the injustices of life. One day he would immortalize this aspect of her personality in the tragically wrathful Katerina Ivanovna Marmeladova of *Crime and Punishment*.

Dostoevsky's separation from Marya Dimitrievna marked the beginning of an agitated and torturing relationship. The arrival of each weekly letter, filled with accounts of the illness of his beloved, the tedium and loneliness of her existence, the burdens of caring for her alcoholic husband (whose health was now

[30] *Pisma*, I: 152–153; June 4, 1855.
[31] Ibid., 153.

failing badly) and of trying to bring up Pasha decently—all this drove Dostoevsky into a frenzy of despair. Nor was his anxiety lessened by the increasingly frequent references to a sympathetic young schoolteacher who had begun to play the role in her life formerly assumed by Dostoevsky. "With each letter," writes Wrangel, "the utterances about him became more and more enthusiastic, praising his kindness, devotion, and nobility of soul. Dostoevsky was torn apart by jealousy; it was pitiful to observe his gloomy state of mind, which affected his health."[32] His mood became so downcast that the alarmed Wrangel arranged a meeting between the erstwhile lovers at a town midway between the two localities. But when the friends arrived after some very hard riding, they found, instead of Marya Dimitrievna, a letter explaining that she could not keep the rendezvous because her husband's condition had worsened.

In August 1855, Isaev drew his last breath, leaving Marya Dimitrievna alone, ailing and penniless, to struggle along in the quagmire of Kuznetsk. Frantic on receiving the news, Dostoevsky wrote to Wrangel, then traveling on business, to send the destitute woman some money, and to do so with particular tact and care; the obligation of gratitude would only make her more sensitive to any undue negligence of tone. No one understood better than the creator of Devushkin in *Poor Folk* the agonies of a cultivated sensibility humiliated by poverty and an inferior social position.

The demise of Isaev made it possible for Dostoevsky to dream at last of possessing, legally and publicly, the lady of his heart; but it was unthinkable to ask for her hand while remaining in his lowly status as a soldier. All this time, to be sure, he had been pulling whatever strings he could to obtain promotion. Upon joining the Siberian Army Corps he had asked Mikhail to approach the authorities in St. Petersburg and persuade them to transfer him to a corps on active service in the Caucasus. Dostoevsky believed that his chances of obtaining a full pardon in the future might be enhanced if he were to exhibit his loyalty by serving in a combat zone. In addition, Wrangel now asked Governor-General Gasfort to send Dostoevsky's poem "On the First of July, 1855" to the recently widowed empress. In this work, Dostoevsky urges her to take comfort in the great deeds of her vanished spouse at the same time that he asks pardon for himself:

Forgive, forgive me, forgive my wish;
Forgive that I dare to speak with you.
Forgive that I dare nourish the senseless dream
Of consoling your sadness, lightening your suffering.
Forgive that I, a mournful outcast, dare
Raise his voice at this hallowed grave. (2: 407)

[32] Wrangel, *Vospominaniya*, 64.

The poem did finally reach the empress. Dostoevsky was promoted to the rank of *unter-ofitser* (a noncommissioned grade) in November 1855, and could hope for more important signs of favor in the future. Wrangel left Semipalatinsk a month later for St. Petersburg, and while in the capital he intended to devote himself to advancing Dostoevsky's cause. A long delay thus occurred between the date Wrangel set foot in the capital and the first letter in which he could give some hope to Dostoevsky, waiting on tenterhooks in his dreary exile for the news that would decide his future. Meanwhile, rumors reached him that Marya Dimitrievna had accepted another suitor. The distraught Dostoevsky sat down to pour out his anguish in a letter but was interrupted by the arrival of one from her, which lacked, as he tells Wrangel, even "a trace of our future hopes, as if that thought had been completely put aside." And then, finally, came the question he had long feared: what should she do if she received an offer of marriage from a man "of a certain age with good qualities, in the service, and with an assured future?"[33]

Dostoevsky's reaction to this missive, with its request for brotherly advice, reveals the melodramatic intensity that will so often mark the love entanglements of his fictional characters. "I was as if struck by lightning, I staggered, fainted, and wept all night. . . . In all my life I have never suffered so much. . . . My heart is consumed by deathly despair, at night there are dreams, shrieks, spasms in my throat choke me, tears sometimes stubbornly refuse to flow, sometimes come in torrents." One can understand why Dostoevsky should exclaim, "Oh! Let God preserve everyone from this terrible, dreadful emotion! Great is the joy of love, but the sufferings are so frightful that it would be better never to be in love."[34]

Worst of all, though, was the moral conflict in which he was plunged. Did he have the right to stand in the way of her making a reasonable marriage when his own prospects were so uncertain? But when he imagined Marya Dimitrievna, "ill, nervous, so refined in heart, cultivated, intelligent," burying herself in Kuznetsk forever, and with a husband who perhaps "for his part might consider blows as being perfectly legal in marriage"—this simply drove him out of his mind! He had the eerie sense of living through the pathetic finale of his own first novel, with Marya Dimitrievna cast "in the situation of my heroine of *Poor Folk*, who marries [the brutal] Bykov (how prophetic I was!)." And he was certain that she did love him and was thinking of another only out of the direst necessity. "*Mais elle m'aime, elle m'aime*, I know that, I see it—by her sadness, her anguish, her melancholy, by the continual outbursts in her letters, and by much else that I will not write about."[35]

---

[33] *Pisma*, 1: 168–176; March 23, 1856.
[34] Ibid.
[35] Ibid.

Dostoevsky appealed to Wrangel, with an urgency verging on hysteria, to redouble his efforts in Petersburg so as to obtain for him a transfer to the Civil Service or a promotion to commissioned rank. Most important, he needed permission to publish (Dostoevsky claimed he would have a "novel" and an article completed in September). He also sent Wrangel, in violation of army regulations, a personal letter addressed to General E. I. Totleben, an old acquaintance from his days in the Academy of Military Engineers and now a national hero because of the brilliant fortifications he had devised for the defense of Sevastopol during the Crimean War. Wrangel had already paid him a visit on Dostoevsky's behalf, but it was Dostoevsky's idea, as a last resort, to appeal directly to the man of the hour and enlist his enormous prestige to accelerate a favorable decision.

"I was guilty," he admits to Totleben after briefly outlining the facts of his arrest, trial, and conviction. "I was condemned legally and justly; a long tribulation, torturing and cruel, sobered me up and changed my ideas in many ways. But then—then I was blind, believed in theories and utopias." And here, for the first time, Dostoevsky attributes his earlier belief in "theories and utopias" to the nervous illness from which he had suffered beginning in the spring of 1846 up to his arrest two years later. "I had been ill for two years running, with a strange, moral sickness. I was a hypochondriac. There were even times when I lost my reason. I was excessively irritable, impressionable to the point of sickness, and with the ability to deform the most ordinary facts and give them another aspect and dimension. But I felt that, even though this sickness exercised a strong and evil influence on my fate, it would have been a very pitiful and even humiliating justification."[36] Mental illness now becomes associated for Dostoevsky—both as a cause and as symptom—with ideological delusions that exercise "a strong and evil influence" on the destiny of those susceptible to their pernicious appeal.

———■———

As Dostoevsky's dossier tortuously wound its way through the Byzantine labyrinth of the Russian bureaucracy, matters went from bad to worse for the two separated lovers. To Mikhail, Dostoevsky tries to justify his decision to marry— a decision that, as he is well aware, seemed madness in the eyes of his family, given the precariousness of his situation—and solicits his aid in reassuring Marya Dimitrievna that, if she were to become his wife, the family would give her a warm welcome. With Wrangel, Dostoevsky is more frank about the difficulties of his sentimental imbroglio. The specter of "a man of a certain age" had vanished because this worthy gentleman had been invented only to test Dostoevsky's affections. "If I had answered with indifference," explains Dostoevsky,

[36] Ibid., 178; March 24, 1856.

"she would have had proof that I had really forgotten her. When I received that letter I wrote a desperate one, terrible, which tore her apart, and then another. She had been ill these last days; my letter really finished her off. But it seems that my despair was sweet to her, although she suffered for me." "I understand her: her heart is noble and proud," he assures Wrangel.[37]

Wrangel's visit to the magnanimous General Totleben, and Dostoevsky's skillful letter to his erstwhile fellow cadet, at last succeeded in overcoming the first obstacle to his union. The powerful and influential hero agreed to intervene on Dostoevsky's behalf and to ask the Ministry of War either to promote him to ensign or to release him to the Civil Service at the lowest rank. In either case, Dostoevsky would also be accorded the right to publish his literary work under the normal conditions of the law. It was this information that evoked Dostoevsky's ecstatic reply of May 23, 1856, to the first affirmative word he had so far obtained from Petersburg, and the belief that "The affair, if I understand correctly, is on the right path."[38]

Notable too is Dostoevsky's enthusiastic response to what he hears from Wrangel about the new monarch. "God grant happiness to the magnanimous sovereign! And so, it's all true, what everyone has said about the ardent love that all feel for him! How happy this makes me! More faith, more unity, and if there is love as well—then everything can be done!"[39] This last sentence can almost be taken as a statement of the political ideal to which Dostoevsky was to dedicate his life—the ideal of rallying Russia to faith, unity, and love in support of the rule of Alexander II. For in March 1856, speaking before the gentry of Moscow, Alexander II had made his famous declaration: "It is better to begin the abolition of serfdom from above, than wait until it begins to abolish itself from below."[40] Dostoevsky had become a revolutionary *only* to abolish serfdom and *only* after the seeming dissolution of all hope that it would be ended, to quote Pushkin, "by the hand of the Tsar." But now the glorious day had dawned of which Pushkin could only dream, and the tsar whom Dostoevsky was to support so fervently for the rest of his life was the Tsar-Liberator who had finally decided to eradicate this intolerable moral blight from the Russian consciousness.

Despite the good news that Dostoevsky had received, his state of mind soon returned to its unalterable gloom. The plan had been for Marya Dimitrievna to move to Barnaul, the center of the mining district of the Altai region, where Dostoevsky hoped to be employed, but she now refused to go. Even worse, her letters also suggested, as he tells Wrangel, "that she could not make me happy,

[37] Ibid., 184–185; April 13, 1856.
[38] Ibid., 183; April 13, 1856.
[39] Ibid., 187; May 23, 1856.
[40] W. E. Mosse, *Alexander II and the Modernization of Russia* (New York, 1962), 42.

that we are both too unhappy, and that it would be better for us . . ." (at this point, two pages have been ripped from the manuscript of the letter by the vengeful hand of Dostoevsky's second wife). When the letter resumes, we learn that Dostoevsky had decided to go to Kuznetsk and investigate matters for himself. "I am ready to go to jail if only I can see *her*. My situation is critical. We must talk it over and decide everything at one stroke!"[41]

Once on the spot, Dostoevsky's suspicions of having been replaced were amply confirmed. "What a noble, what an angelic soul!" he writes to Wrangel. "She cried, she kissed my hands, but she loves another."[42] The other was the young schoolmaster, Nikolay Vergunov, who had befriended the Isaevs on their arrival and whose relations with Marya Dimitrievna had become close. No doubt Marya Dimitrievna had begun to lose patience with the slow improvement of Dostoevsky's prospects; perhaps she had lost faith in them entirely. A young schoolmaster in hand, even with a pitiable income, was preferable to an even more penurious writer whose glowing anticipations of fame and fortune might never be realized. Dostoevsky himself refuses to utter one word of blame about what he might well have considered a betrayal.

What occurred between the threesome, during Dostoevsky's two days in Kuznetsk, rivals the stormiest scenes of a three-decker novel and was transposed by Dostoevsky a few years later in the pages of *The Insulted and Injured*. He depicts himself (or his fictional hero, a young writer who is the author of *Poor Folk*) as retreating helplessly before the infatuation of his beloved for another; but in real life Dostoevsky played a different role. He was far from willing to abandon the field without a struggle, and his best weapon turned out to be his imagination as a novelist. For he sketched in, with all the resources of his art, the appalling problems that might arise in the future because of incompatibilities in age and character between Marya Dimitrievna and her young lover, aged twenty-four. Dostoevsky became so agitated, even in recounting these events to Wrangel, that his handwriting is barely legible.

"And [gap in text] will he not later," he told Marya Dimitrievna and now repeats for Wrangel, "in several years, when she is still [gap in text], will he not wish for her death? . . . Might he not later reproach her with having calculated on his youth and taken over his life solely to satisfy her voluptuous demands?" Naturally, all these agitated premonitions had not been put so bluntly in face-to-face conversation; Dostoevsky had been more subtle, sketching his menacing visions as conjectures while maintaining that Vergunov could not possibly behave in such a fashion. "I didn't convince her of anything" he estimates, "but I spread some doubt; she wept and was tormented."[43]

[41] *Pisʹma*, 1: 188; May 23, 1856.
[42] Ibid., 189; July 14, 1856.
[43] Ibid., 190.

At this point, a peripety occurred that reminds us of those sudden climactic moments in Dostoevsky's work when mutual hostility turns to love. "I felt pity for her, and then she completely came back to me—she felt pity for me! If you know what an angel she is, my friend! You never knew her; at every instant something original, sensible, clever but also paradoxical, infinitely good, truly noble (a knight in female clothing), she has the heart of a knight; she will be her own ruination. She doesn't know herself, but I know her!" Dostoevsky also met Vergunov, who broke down and wept in his presence. "I met him; he cried, but only knows how to cry," he remarks, with a touch of disdain.[44] At Marya Dimitrievna's suggestion, Dostoevsky wrote a letter to Vergunov summing up all the weighty reasons he had advanced against the approaching union of the pair. She kept spinning like a weathervane and told Dostoevsky before his departure, "'Don't cry, don't grieve, everything is not decided; you and I and nobody else!' These are her exact words," he assures Wrangel. "I don't know how I spent those two days. It was bliss and unbearable torture! At the end of the second day, I left *full of hope*."[45]

Meanwhile, Dostoevsky was continuing efforts to obtain admission for Pasha Isaev to the Corps of Cadets in Siberia, and he asks Wrangel to see if General Gasfort cannot be persuaded to use his influence to help the young petitioner find a place. He also pleads with Wrangel for still another favor involving the Isaevs. "For God's sake, for the sake of heaven's radiance, don't refuse. *She* should not have to suffer. If she marries him, at least let them have some money." And so Dostoevsky urges Wrangel to speak about Vergunnov to Gasfort "as a worthy young man with first-rate abilities; praise him to the skies, say that you know him; that it wouldn't be a bad thing to give him a higher post. . . . All this for *her*, for her *alone*. Just so she won't end in misery, that's all!"[46] Dostoevsky, who had such an acute personal and literary sense of the aching miseries of genteel poverty, was genuinely moved by the possible future plight of the woman he loved with passion and toward whom he felt an immense debt of gratitude. "She came at the saddest moment of my life," he told Wrangel a few months later, "and she resuscitated my soul."[47]

———■———

In the early fall of 1856, Dostoevsky's promotion was at last officially confirmed, and he became a commissioned officer with a respectable social status and a regular income. His first and only thought on receiving the news was that it would enable him to visit Marya Dimitrievna. Dostoevsky makes no attempt to con-

[44] Ibid., 191.
[45] Ibid., 189.
[46] Ibid., 192.
[47] Ibid., 198; November 9, 1856.

ceal the ravages of what, as he knew, was a pathological fixation. "Don't shake your head, don't condemn me," he begs Wrangel. "I know that in many ways I am behaving irrationally in my relations with her, that there is almost no hope for me—but whether there is or is not hope is all the same. I can't think of anything else! Only to see her, to hear her! I am a poor madman. A love of this kind is an illness. I feel it."[48] He was hoping against hope that another visit would have the same rekindling effect as his first. Consumed with guilt at squandering the money he had begged for so urgently from his brother, he asks Wrangel not to tell Mikhail about his proposed project for a new trip to win over his reluctant amorata.

At the same time, Dostoevsky urges Wrangel to inquire whether it would be possible for him, now that he is an officer, to seek retirement from the army for reasons of health. This is the first reference in Dostoevsky's correspondence to what had become an increasingly worried concern with his physical and mental condition. "If I wish to return to Russia," he says, "It would be solely to embrace those I love, and to see qualified doctors so as to know what my illness is (epilepsy), what these attacks are which always keep recurring, and which each time weaken my memory and all my faculties and which, I fear, may one day lead me to madness. What kind of an officer am I?"[49]

In December 1856, undertaking the long journey to Kuznetsk again, he finally succeeded in obtaining Marya Dimitrievna's consent. All of Dostoevsky's energies were now turned to the task of raising the money for the wedding, which involved a staggering sum for someone who, already up to his ears in debt, could count only on his small salary as an officer. Dostoevsky would have to finance not only another trip to Kuznetsk for himself, but also a return with his new wife and stepson in a closed carriage (it was midwinter), the transport of their household goods, and the purchase of whatever was necessary to set up housekeeping. On top of all this were the expenses occasioned by his promotion, which required that he outfit himself from head to foot with equipment literally worth its weight in gold in remote Siberia. Luckily, a friendly captain of engineers attached to one of the mining establishments had offered to advance him six hundred rubles as a long-term loan, and one of his sisters had recently sent him two hundred rubles as a gift. Since he had unpublished manuscripts worth, by his estimate, about a thousand rubles, he was sure that once he received permission to publish, his troubles would be over. "But if they forbid me to publish for still another year—I am lost." Dostoevsky accordingly renews his plea to Wrangel to communicate to him immediately "the slightest *news concerning permission to publish*."[50] He was so desperate that he affirmed

[48] Ibid., 197–198.
[49] Ibid., 198.
[50] Ibid., 1: 205–206; December 21, 1856.

13. Dostoevsky in uniform, 1858

his willingness to publish, if necessary forever, without a signature or under a pseudonym.

Two months elapsed before Dostoevsky could complete preparations for the wedding, during which time he wrote a carefully worded letter to his wealthy uncle in Moscow asking for the amount of his loan as a gift. He then departed for a two-week stay at Kuznetsk, and on February 7, 1857, the ceremony was performed in the presence of various local worthies, including Vergunov, who makes his last appearance as a witness at the wedding of the woman he had once loved and the man who had thwarted his suit. The honeymoon couple then embarked on the exhausting trip back to Semipalatinsk, breaking the journey at Barnaul to accept the hospitality of Dostoevsky's old friend Count Peter Semenov. What occurred during this stopover cast a pall on Dostoevsky's ill-starred marriage from the very beginning. "On the road home," Dostoevsky writes to Mikhail, "misfortune came my way: totally unexpectedly, I had an attack of epilepsy, which frightened my wife to death, and filled me with sadness and dejection."[51]

Marya Dimitrievna had never before been exposed to the unearthly shriek, the fainting fit, the convulsive movements of the face and limbs, the foaming at the mouth, the involuntary loss of urine that marked Dostoevsky's acute seizures; and she was terrified at discovering that she had unwittingly linked her fate to a husband ravaged by such an illness. Even worse, Dostoevsky now learned, for the first time, the true nature of his malady. "The doctor . . . told me, contrary to everything said previously by doctors, that I had *genuine epilepsy*, and that I could expect, in one of these seizures, to suffocate because of throat spasms and would die from this cause. I myself entreated and admonished the doctor, by his reputation as an honest man, to be detailed and frank. In general, he advised me to be careful at the time of a new moon."[52]

If there is reason to suspect that Marya Dimitrievna regretted her recent marriage vows, there is no ambiguity about Dostoevsky's own sentiments. "In marrying," he admits to Mikhail, "I completely trusted the doctors who told me they were only nervous seizures, which would pass with a change in the circumstances of my life. If I had known as a fact that I had genuine epilepsy, I would not have married. For my peace of mind and in order to consult with *genuine* doctors and *take measures*, it is *necessary* to obtain my retirement as quickly as possible and return to Russia, but how can this be done?"[53] Marya Dimitrievna had arrived back in Semipalatinsk quite ill herself; and Dostoevsky began now to better understand the precariousness of both her physical and emotional equilibrium. "She is a good and tender creature, somewhat quick, excitable, extremely impressionable; her past life has left painful traces in her soul. Her impressions change with incredible rapidity, but she never ceases to be noble and good. I love her very much, she loves me, and for the moment everything is going along in good order."[54]

Once settled in Semipalatinsk, where the newlyweds rented a comfortable four-room apartment, Dostoevsky could at last devote himself, in the time left over from military duties, to his literary career (though uncertainty continued to hang over his right to publish). He manfully acquitted himself of his new responsibilities, placed Pasha in the Siberian Cadet Corps, and wrote dutiful letters to his new father-in-law and his wife's sisters (whom he had never met). In one such letter to an invisible sister-in-law, almost a year after his marriage, Dostoevsky expresses a weariness stemming from a profound sense of disappointment with his life. "Do you know," he remarks strangely, "I have a sort of

[51] Ibid., 2: 579–580; March 9, 1857.
[52] Ibid., 580.
[53] Ibid.
[54] Ibid.

presentiment, I think I shall die quite soon . . . and it is quite calmly that I am certain of an imminent death. It seems to me that I have already lived through all that one is required to live through in this world, and that there is nothing to which I can aspire."[55] Such words unquestionably have something to do with the fears induced by his epilepsy—in mid-January 1858, Dostoevsky applied officially for permission to retire from the army on grounds of disability and in order to consult competent doctors in St. Petersburg—but they also express an inner lassitude whose most probable explanation is a desire to escape from the burdens of life in common with Marya Dimitrievna.

References to her disappear almost entirely from the correspondence as time goes on, except for brief remarks that allow us to infer a background of bickering and recriminations. The most overt reference may be found in a letter to Wrangel, from whom Dostoevsky had no secrets regarding his wife, and who, as he knew, had always looked on the older man's infatuation as an unfortunate mishap. Writing two years after his marriage, Dostoevsky says, "If you wish to know what is up with me, what can I tell you? I have burdened myself with the cares of a family and I pull them along. But I believe that my life is not yet finished and do not want to die."[56] As it happened, it was Marya Dimitrievna who, five years later, was to die of tuberculosis, and the growing ravages of her illness only increased the irritability and irascibility of a character that had so seduced Dostoevsky by its capacity for righteous indignation. And, in all fairness, we must recognize that she herself had good reason to harbor emotions of resentment and betrayal against her second husband, whose promised recapture of fame remained maddeningly problematic and whose epilepsy kept recurring with alarming frequency.

[55] Ibid., 1: 228; November 30, 1857.
[56] Ibid., 253–255; September 22, 1859.

CHAPTER 18

A Russian Heart

Thanks to the kindness of new friends like Wrangel and Yakushkin, who oblig-ingly conveyed letters between Dostoevsky and his family and old circle of friends in Petersburg and Moscow, the novelist, though far removed from the centers of Russian social and cultural life, could still gain some sense of the ideas and tendencies now stirring the intelligentsia. The outbreak of the Crimean War in 1853 (news of which had barely managed to seep into the prison camp) had stirred all the latent patriotic ardor of Dostoevsky's old friend Apollon Maikov, a progressive Westernizer, and his open letter, published in the *St. Petersburg Gazette* in 1854 as a cultural-political manifesto, records the upsurge of chauvin-istic nationalism that swept over much of literate Russian society at the begin-ning of hostilities. In this open letter the critic urges writers, as Russians, to honor the "sacred feeling of love for the fatherland" and to "illuminate [in their work] that ideal of Russia which is perceptible to everybody."[1]

"I have read your letter," Dostoevsky responds approvingly in January 1856, "and have not understood the essential. I mean about patriotism, the Russian idea, the feeling of duty, national honor . . . my friend! . . . I have always shared exactly these same sentiments and convictions. . . . What is really new in this movement that you have seen come to birth and of which you speak as a new tendency?" "I entirely share your patriotic sentiments about the *moral* liberation of the Slavs," he continues, "I agree with you that Europe and her mission will be realized by Russia. This has been clear to me for a long time."[2] Dostoevsky asserts repeatedly that both he and Maikov have remained the same men on the level of "the heart," whatever alterations may have taken place in the "ideas" they profess; and these assertions serve as a prelude to the important profession of faith that Dostoevsky makes and his disclosure of how he now interprets his past.

"Perhaps a little while ago," writes Dostoevsky, "you were still troubled by the influx of French ideas into that class of society which thinks, feels, and stud-ies. . . . But you will agree yourself that all right-thinking people, that is, those who gave the tone to everything, regarded French ideas from a scientific point

---

[1] Cited in Leonid Grossman, "Grazhdanskaya smert F. M. Dostoevskogo," *LN* 22–24 (Moscow, 1935), 688–689.

[2] *Pis'ma*, 1: 165; January 18, 1856.

of view—no more, and remained Russian even while devoting themselves to the exceptional. In what do you see anything new?"[3] By "French ideas," of course, Dostoevsky was referring to the radical and Utopian Socialist currents of the 1840s, which he denies had had the power to change the Russian character. Dostoevsky's self-interpretation feeds into and anticipates his later creations: time and again he will show in his major characters the persistence of something he considers "Russian," even in those who are most powerfully and corrosively affected by Western European ideas. For Dostoevsky was passionately persuaded (and he accepted his own experience as irrefutable evidence of its truth) that the instinctive sentiments and loyalties of Russians would always break through in some way, no matter how impenetrable might seem to be the overlay of Western European culture in the makeup of their personalities. Referring to his years in *katorga*, he adds: "I learned . . . that I had always been a Russian at heart. One may be mistaken in ideas, but it is impossible to be mistaken with one's heart."[4]

To be a Russian, then, means to be united with other Russians by a bond that evokes a sense of mutual moral responsiveness; and this bond, stemming from the heart, goes deeper and is more primary than all the false ideas that may distort Russian vision or blunt Russian moral sensitivity. Many Dostoevsky characters, in a few years, will be caught precisely in such an inner struggle between their Russian heart and the evil, corrupting, and amoral power of non-Russian ideas. As Dostoevsky explores and contemplates his past for the benefit of Maikov, what emerges is the first faint outlines of the rational/irrational dichotomy so characteristic of his post-Siberian creations. And this dichotomy has already begun to take on many of the specific moral, psychological, and ideological connotations to which Dostoevsky will later give such brilliant expression.

———■———

Dostoevsky's letter to Maikov is precious as a source for the analysis of his own personal and artistic evolution. But how much truth is there in his belief that the Russian intelligentsia as a whole had been only superficially affected by "French ideas"? So far as Dostoevsky himself is personally concerned, he had always lived in uneasy tension with the subversive impulses (inspired primarily by hatred of serfdom) that had led him into the ranks of a revolutionary conspiracy. With regard to the Russian Westernizers, whom Dostoevsky naturally tended to interpret by analogy with himself, the situation is much more complex. One has the impression that Dostoevsky believed them all, or at least a sizable portion of them, to have also rallied behind the tsarist regime during the war. And if this is what he *did* mean, then he was woefully mistaken. For not only the Westernizers

[3] Ibid., 166.
[4] Ibid.

but the patriotic Slavophils as well had been appalled by the corruption, disorder, and incompetence revealed by the regime of Nicholas I in the Crimean struggle. The majority of the intelligentsia, of whatever political stripe, shared the feelings expressed in the diary of A. I. Koshelev, a relatively liberal Slavophil, who wrote that Russian defeats in the Crimean War "did not distress us too much because we were convinced that even the defeat of Russia would be more bearable and more useful than the condition in which it had found itself in recent years. The mood of society and even of the people, if in part unconscious, was of the same nature."[5] Removed as he was from the centers of Russian social and cultural life, and living in a predominantly military milieu hostile to any independent thinking, Dostoevsky was evidently unaware of such subversive stirrings.

Still, if we look at Russian culture as a whole, we can see an evolution similar to Dostoevsky's own taking place among the Russian Westernizers in the years covered precisely by his arrest and exile. This massive shift of Russian social-cultural attitudes may be dated from a famous article of Belinsky's, published in 1847, in which he lauded the world-historical role of the Russian people, and Dostoevsky certainly had it in mind when assuring Maikov that the influence of French ideas on educated Russians had been only a momentary deviation from the true Russian path. During the 1850s, the most significant development in Russian thought was the gradual assimilation of Slavophil ideas by educated opinion as a whole, and the amalgamation of such ideas into a new synthesis with those of the former Westernizer party. Since the most important publications in which this synthesis had been worked out were all issued abroad, Dostoevsky could have had no knowledge of them in his Siberian banishment.

To a great extent, this new synthesis of ideas was devised and propagated by Alexander Herzen, who now occupied the dominating place in Russian culture formerly held by Belinsky in the 1840s. Herzen, who had gone to live in Europe in 1847, had been stirred by the intoxicating hopes of the French revolution of 1848, and had also been horrified at the pitiless repression of the French working-class uprising during the notorious June Days of 1848, when it was crushed by the National Guard at the orders of the bourgeois government of the new French Republic. Herzen poured all his anguish and his disgusted disillusionment with Western political ideals into his deeply moving *From the Other Shore*—a work that still retains its force as a profound meditation on the historical destiny of modern Western civilization. His conclusion was that Western Europe would never make the inevitable transition to the new Socialist millennium because the principles of private property, monarchical centralism (ultimately deriving from Roman Catholicism), and obedience to civic authority were too strongly

[5] Cited in A. A. Kornilov, *Obshchestvenoe dvizhenie pri Aleksandre II* (Moscow, 1909), 6.

ingrained in the European character to permit a decisive break with the centuries-old past of its tradition.

From the Other Shore is a piercing cry of despair, uttered by Herzen as he saw his old ideals as a Russian Westernizer shot to pieces in the fusillades marking the end of the 1848 uprisings all over the Continent. But in a series of important utterances in the next few years (in *The Russian People and Socialism, On the Development of Revolutionary Ideas in Russia*, and many other publications less well known), Herzen went from negation to affirmation, and what he now affirmed stood in the sharpest contrast to what he had formerly believed. For he prophesied that backward Russia, precisely because it had remained outside the main current of European social-historical development, was the chosen instrument of history to lead the world into the new Socialist era. Taking up some of the ideas of the Slavophils and uniting them with those of the Westernizers, Herzen produced a grandiose amalgam that inflamed the Russian imagination and decisively affected the course of Russian social-cultural thought throughout the remainder of the century.

"From the Slavophils," writes Andrzej Walicki, "Herzen took over the view of the village commune as the embryonic stage of a new and higher form of society and the conviction that collectivism (which he called the 'socialist element' or even 'communism') was a national characteristic of the Russian people. . . . Like the Slavophils, Herzen valued the self-government principle of the communes and the unaffected spontaneity of relations between its members, which were not governed by contracts or codified laws. Finally, like the Slavophils, Herzen believed that the Orthodox faith in Russia was 'more faithful to the teaching of the Gospels than Catholicism,' that religious isolation had fortunately enabled the Russian people to . . . remain apart from the 'sick' civilization of Europe."[6]

When there were rumors of the coming conflict between Russia and Turkey in 1849, Herzen wrote to the Italian revolutionist Giuseppe Mazzini that Russia would probably succeed in taking Constantinople (he did not foresee the intervention of the Western powers) and that this conquest would be the signal for the future worldwide revolution. He imagined that the peasant soldiers of Nicholas's army, once victory had been gained, would refuse to return home to serfdom. Calling instead on the other Slavs freed from the Turks to join them, they would lead a general Slav uprising, with Russia at the head of a new Slavic democratic and social federation. "For Russia is the Slavic world organized, the Slavic state. To her belongs the hegemony."[7] Such words illustrate the convergence between Dostoevsky's new convictions and the dominating trend of Russian culture at the time.

Herzen went to live in London in 1852, and established there the first Free

[6] Andrzej Walicki, *The Slavophile Controversy* (London, 1975), 587.
[7] See Raoul Labry, *Alexandre Ivanovic Herzen*, 1812–1870 (Paris, 1928), 356.

Russian Press in exile. In the next few years he began to issue his own writings, as well as to found a number of new publications. Among these was an almanac, issued at irregular intervals, called *The Polar Star* (*Polyarnaya Zvezda*, the title of a similar almanac once edited by the Decembrist poet Ryleev), and, most important, his famous weekly, *The Bell* (*Kolokol*). Herzen's ideas, after a few years, began to receive the widest diffusion inside Russia, and *The Bell* was read everywhere (even, rumor had it, in the Imperial Palace itself), despite being banned from the country and available only in copies smuggled across the frontier. By the late 1850s and early 1860s, the basic tenets of Herzen's "Russian Socialism"—with its strong overtones of messianic nationalism and its positive reevaluation of peasant life and institutions—had become the general ideology of the Russian Left, despite the increasingly vehement quarrels over how they should be applied to the existing Russian social-political situation.

——■——

Dostoevsky's letter to Apollon Maikov thus provides us with a rewarding glimpse into that psychological-ideological matrix, still in its formative stage, out of which Dostoevsky's future works would emerge, and it also reveals his literary plans. Dostoevsky confides to Maikov that he had thought out during his years in camp what he calls "my grand, definitive story." But he had not begun to write it on his release because of his love affair with Marya Dimitrievna, "which distracted and absorbed me completely," and instead had begun "a comic novel, but so far have only written individual adventures of which I have enough; now I am *sewing up the whole*."[8] Whether these words refer to *Uncle's Dream* or *The Village of Stepanchikovo* is not clear. In any case, Dostoevsky was convinced, as he wrote to Wrangel a few months later, that only a novel "will make me a name and attract attention to myself,"[9] but he was also persuaded that permission would not be given him to publish a work of fiction.

What he now pinned his hopes on, above all, was his *Letters on Art*, the work he intended to write (or had partially written) devoted to "the mission of Christianity in art"[10] and dedicated to the daughter of Nicholas I. Unfortunately, no trace of any such text has turned up among Dostoevsky's papers, although his literary journalism of the early 1860s unquestionably reflects the ideas he was pondering over at this time—the relation of art to a transcendental or supernatural ideal. Continuing his efforts to prove his loyalty to the throne, Dostoevsky also wrote another poem, "On the Coronation and Conclusion of Peace"—an invocation of the blessings of God on the new tsar and savior of Russia—which he dispatched through General Gasfort to Wrangel.

[8] *Pisma*, 1: 166–167.
[9] Ibid., 167.
[10] Ibid.

At the exact moment that he was racking his brains over the best way to bring his name back into literary circulation, the task of reminding the cultural world of his existence was accomplished for him with no special effort on his part. In the issue of *The Contemporary* dated December 1855, a sketch by Panaev contains a section obviously alluding to the critical excitement caused by *Poor Folk* as a result of Belinsky's praise, and then, with the ensuing collapse of the author's momentary fame, his abandonment by all those who had previously trumpeted his glory. "Poor fellow!" writes Panaev. "We killed him, we made him ridiculous. It was not his fault. He could not maintain himself at the height on which we had placed him."[11] Although no names were mentioned, all of the people who counted for Dostoevsky—all the former members of the Belinsky Pléiade with whom he had once been friendly, and all his literary colleagues and rivals—would have been perfectly well aware at whom Panaev was poking fun.

Panaev's attack, aimed at a man who had spent four long years in prison camp for a political crime and was still serving out his sentence in the Russian Army, was a distinctly vicious blow. But in the narrow little world of St. Petersburg journalism, where editors and writers rubbed elbows every day with high officials of the bureaucracy, rumors about Dostoevsky's two poems had filtered down and led to a revival of all the antipathy against him that had once been so widespread. Dostoevsky read this insulting lampoon, and we can deduce his outrage from Aleksey Pleshcheev's letter to him in April 1859. "I told [Nekrasov] frankly that you had decided not to turn to [his journal] except in case of extreme need because they treated you badly; Nekrasov, after hearing me out, said that if . . . *The Contemporary* spoke shamefully of you while you were in exile, then that was very disgusting."[12]

Nekrasov's uneasiness could well have been caused by a work of his own that Dostoevsky never saw. This mysterious text, finally published in 1917, is a satirical account of how Nekrasov had brought the manuscript of *Poor Folk* to Belinsky. The withering depiction of Dostoevsky it contains was another response to Dostoevsky's efforts to achieve rehabilitation. The best part of the fragment is the image of the genuine tortures caused Dostoevsky by his mixture of excruciating shyness and inordinate vanity. The same comedy, so reminiscent of *The Double*, is repeated here: Dostoevsky has not the strength to ring Belinsky's doorbell and retreats back down the staircase, but when Nekrasov remarks that Belinsky might be displeased, he returns in a flash and the two enter.

Chudov [Nekrasov] only then understood all the irresolution of Glazhievsky [Dostoevsky] when he saw to what an astonishing degree the

[11] I. I. Panaev, *Sobranie sochinenii*, 6 vols. (Moscow, 1912), 5: 1–11.
[12] "Pis'ma A. N. Pleshcheeva k F. M. Dostoevskomu," in *DMI*.

author of "A Stony Heart" quailed before the threatening eyes of the critic. At moments of intense timidity he had the habit of squeezing himself together, of retreating into himself to such an extent that ordinary shyness cannot convey the slightest idea of his condition. It could only be characterized by the very word he had invented himself, *stushevat'sya*, to vanish, disappear, efface oneself, which now came into Chudov's head.[13] Glazhievsky's entire face suddenly became crestfallen, his eyes vanished under his brows, his head went into his shoulders, his voice, always muffled, lost all its clarity and freedom, sounding as if the man of genius had found himself in an empty cask inadequately supplied with air; and meanwhile his gestures, disconnected words, glances, and the continuing trembling of the lips, expressing suspicion and fear, had something so tragic about them that it was not possible to laugh.[14]

The mixture of sympathy and derision with which Nekrasov regards his erstwhile friend is the most vivid evocation we have of some of the impressions Dostoevsky created on others in the 1840s. But Nekrasov could not know that the figure he described no longer existed. For Dostoevsky had sloughed off completely his crippling insecurity and hypochondria in the prison camp. "If you believe there is still anything remaining in me of that nervousness, that apprehensiveness, that tendency to suspect that I had every conceivable illness, as in Petersburg," he tells Mikhail, "please change your mind, there is not a trace of that, as of many other things."[15] Dostoevsky had been steeled by suffering. And when, on returning from exile, he began to take up the polemical cudgels against *The Contemporary* a few years later, the once ridiculous and timorous "little idol" whom it had been so easy to sneer at proved to be a redoubtable antagonist.

—■—

Dostoevsky's prowess as a polemicist soon became evident in his vehement opposition to the ideas now being propounded in *The Contemporary* by its most notable and influential critic, N. G. Chernyshevsky. More than anyone, Chernyshevsky formulated the ideals and aims of the radical "generation of the 1860s" against which Dostoevsky would unleash the full force of his considerable combative skills.

[13] In the definitive dictionary of the Russian literary language, the first reference given for this word in the sense of "slipping away unobserved, to disappear" is a citation from Dostoevsky's *The Double*. *Slovar sovremennogo Russkogo literaturnogo yazika*, 17 vols. (Moscow–Leningrad, 1950–1965), 14: 1116.

[14] K. Chukovsky, "Dostoevsky i Pleyada Belinskogo," in *N. A. Nekrasov: stati i materialy* (Leningrad, 1926), 352.

[15] *Pisma*, 1: 159; August 21, 1855.

The son of an obscure priest, and educated in a seminary, Chernyshevsky entered the University of St. Petersburg in 1846, and there he met people who brought him into contact with the ideas current in the Petrashevsky Circle and became converted to Socialism. It was only a matter of chance, as he noted in his *Diary*, that he had not begun to frequent the Petrashevsky Circle himself and had escaped the roundup. Chernyshevsky's opinions about literature had been formed on the essays of Belinsky's last period, and the young publicist thus discusses writing mainly in terms of social content, evaluating it in the light of his own preference for a literature continuing the Gogolian tradition (as interpreted by Belinsky) of denunciation and exposure of the evils of society. These articles ruffled the sensibilities of the gentry literati grouped around *The Contemporary*, the representatives of the older generation of the 1840s, who did not appreciate either his unceremonious handling of their own works or his sarcastic jeering tone, which struck them as a breach of good taste.

Chernyshevsky had been educated in a provincial seminary, as had the young Nikolay Dobrolyubov, whom he soon recruited to aid him; so had a good many others who became well-known as writers, journalists, and publicists giving voice to the sentiments of a new generation. They were the first of the *raznochintsy*, the men without official rank or status, who play so dominant a role in Russian culture throughout the remainder of the century. The differences that quickly surfaced between the two generations can be traced to the gulf created by their class backgrounds and the dissimilarities in their education.

The gentry literati looked down on the "seminarians," as they were called contemptuously, because of their coarseness and lack of breeding. For their part, the seminarians abhorred culture and the reverence for art as a source of wisdom that distinguished the slightly older generation of the 1840s. For Chernyshevsky and Dobrolyubov, such reverence still smacked of religion. As the scions of clerical families, both had been intensely religious in their youth, but they had converted to atheism with equal zeal under the influence of Feuerbach and his Russian Left Hegelian followers such as Belinsky and, more specifically, Herzen. All the same, the stubborn streak of fanaticism in their makeup, and their supreme contempt for the amenities of culture as shameful frivolities, can plausibly be attributed to the heritage of their clerical ancestry.[16] In any case, they were—or

---

[16] Abbott Gleason applies to Chernyshevsky and Dobrolyubov the words used by Nicolas Berdyaev to characterize Russian Nihilism in general. Nihilism, Berdyaev wrote, "grew up on the spiritual soil of Orthodoxy; it could appear only in a soul which was cast in an Orthodox mold. It was Orthodox asceticism turned inside out, and asceticism without Grace. At the base of Russian Nihilism, when grasped in its purity and depth, lies the Orthodox rejection of the world, its sense of the truth that 'the whole world lieth in wickedness,' the acknowledgement of the sinfulness of all riches and luxury, of all creative profusion in art and thought. . . . Nihilism considers as sinful luxury not only art, metaphysics and spiritual values, but religion also." See Nicholas Berdyaev, *The Origins of Russian Communism* (Ann Arbor, MI, 1960), 45, cited in Abbott Gleason, *Young Russia* (New York, 1980), 103.

wished to be—hard-headed materialists and positivists, whose energies were devoted to bringing about those radical social changes in which they saw the only hope for the future. The social-cultural influence of the earlier generation, in their view, was one of the major obstacles to a reshaping of the Russian personality along more virile and energetic lines, and such remolding was a necessary precondition for any further progress. A good dose of class antipathy thus envenomed with personal distaste the clashes of opinion that soon began to occur between the two groups.

What had been, at the beginning, only a low murmur of discontent from the gentry literati turned into a cry of outrage when Chernyshevsky published his doctoral thesis, *The Aesthetic Relation of Art to Reality*, and then reviewed it himself (anonymously) in the pages of *The Contemporary*. Even earlier, Chernyshevsky's public defense of this work, in the amphitheater of the University of St. Petersburg, had taken on the character of a deliberate defiance of the authorities with distinct social-political overtones. For in rejecting the principles of German Idealist aesthetics, he was in effect attacking all attempts to entice mankind into living in a world of imaginary pleasures and satisfactions when the real material needs of the vast majority still remained to be satisfied. Naturally, no such argument could be made explicitly, but all of Chernyshevsky's readers knew what was involved when, as Marx had already done with Hegel for much the same reasons, he rejected the Idealist point of view and, as it were, brought art back to earth.

Idealist aestheticians (Hegel and F. T. Vischer) viewed art as a function of man's desire to improve the imperfections of nature in the name of the ideal. Chernyshevsky, taking the opposite view, flatly affirmed that "Beauty is Life" and that nature, far from being less perfect than art, was the sole source of true pleasure and infinitely superior to art in every respect. Indeed, art exists only because it is impossible for man always to satisfy his real needs; hence, art is useful, but solely as a surrogate until the genuine article comes along. "The imagination builds castles in the air," Chernyshevsky writes sarcastically, "when the dreamer lacks not only a good house, but even a tolerable hut." [17] By making art subordinate to life and its real demands, Chernyshevsky was telling the artist that his task is to fulfill the social needs of the moment—whatever these needs happen to be in the opinion of the critic. It is also clear that, if Chernyshevsky's ideas are accepted, art is left without any independent value or stature.

The publication of Chernyshevsky's thesis blew up a storm in the Russian periodical press, and a torrent of criticism hailed down on the head of the audacious young iconoclast. Even the mild-mannered and temperate Turgenev was incensed, and his letters show how disturbed he was at this heavy-handed assault

[17] N. G. Chernyshevsky, *Selected Philosophical Essays* (Moscow, 1953), 318.

on his artistic pieties. "I have not read anything for a long time that so upset me," he writes to Kraevsky, who had printed a critical onslaught against the book in *Notes of the Fatherland*. "*It is worse than an evil book; it is—an evil deed.*"[18] Dostoevsky would have been as much opposed to Chernyshevsky's ideas, if not more so, than Turgenev, Tolstoy, and all the others who had spoken up with indignation. For Dostoevsky's defense of the role of Christianity in art in his planned *Letters on Art* would also have met head-on the atheistic implications of Chernyshevsky's rejection of "imagination." This will indeed be an important thrust of the attack he will launch, in just a few years, on the Utilitarian aesthetics of the radicals.

It was against this background that Dostoevsky and his old friend Aleksey Pleshcheev began their exchange of letters just as the latter was on the point of departing for his first visit home from exile. "I will visit Nekrasov," Pleshcheev remarks. "But if even one of them [the circle of *The Contemporary*] addresses me in a high-handed fashion—I will never set foot across his threshold again. Enough! The time is past when one bowed down to great men, who in fact turn out to be complete trash."[19] Nekrasov, he soon hastens to write to his friend, "spoke of you with much sympathy; and in general—he is a person, so it seems to me—really good." Pleshcheev had written earlier that "Turgenev speaks of you with warm concern."[20]

■

Dostoevsky soon learned, through his correspondence, of a new phase of Chernyshevsky's campaign to undermine the prestige and spiritual authority of the gentry liberal intelligentsia. In this case, he singled out an unpretentious little story of Turgenev's, "Asya," and used it to launch a full-scale onslaught against the weakness of character displayed by the "superfluous man"—the cultivated, educated, Russian gentry liberal, filled with Western humanitarian ideas and dreaming of beneficence for mankind as a whole, but who invariably went down in defeat before the immense stagnation, inertia, and backwardness of Russian life. Such a character had been a favorite of Russian writers at least since Pushkin's *Evgeny Onegin,* and the main figure of "Asya," a Russian dilettante idling in Europe, is a minor offshoot of this line.

Chernyshevsky's article, entitled "A Russian at a Rendezvous," is more a political diatribe than literary criticism. It dwells on the hesitations of Turgenev's protagonist, the utter lack of resolution that Chernyshevsky sees as typical of a whole group of characters belonging to the gentry liberal intelligentsia portrayed

[18] Cited in V. Evgeniyev-Maximov, Sovremennik *pri Chernyshevskom i Dobrolyubove* (Leningrad, 1936), 21.
[19] *DMI*, 440–441; May 30, 1858.
[20] Ibid., 439; April 10, 1858.

by the same author. Although, writes Chernyshevsky, he was educated to believe that such people are the source of enlightenment in Russian society, "we are gradually beginning to come round to thinking that this opinion about him is an empty dream; we sense that we shall not long remain under its influence; that there are people better than he is, namely, those whom he wrongs" (all the other, socially inferior classes of Russian society, especially the *raznochintsy*).[21]

This gauntlet flung in the face of the moral-spiritual hegemony of the gentry liberal intelligentsia began a polemic that raged all through the 1860s and to which most of the important representatives of Russian literature made significant contributions. Turgenev's *On the Eve* and *Fathers and Children*, Herzen's *The Superfluous Men and the Bilious*, Chernyshevsky's *What Is To Be Done?*, Dostoevsky's *Notes from Underground*, Tolstoy's little-known comedy *An Infected Family*—all were products of this battle royal, whose opening round was signaled by Chernyshevsky's article. At the end of the decade, the debate was magisterially terminated by Dostoevsky's *Demons*.

All these works, however, remained to be written, and the only notable reply to Chernyshevsky was offered by Turgenev's inseparable companion and alter ego, the critic Annenkov. In an article titled "The Weak Person as a Literary Type," Annenkov did not attempt to argue with Chernyshevsky; rather, he analyzed the problem of why the weak person had become such an important figure in Russian literature. The so-called solid (*tsel'ny*) characters in Russia, he writes— those who act instinctively and spontaneously—always seem to give free rein to the worst and most egoistic aspects of human nature. The weak person in Russian culture, Annenkov argues, has been made so because he is burdened with the enlightened values of humanity and civilization and is morally torn by the problem of attempting to live up to them. "Education endowed him with the capacity promptly to understand suffering in all its aspects, and to experience within himself the misfortune and unhappiness of others. Hence his role as the representative of the deprived, unjustly offended, and the downtrodden; this requires even more than the simple feeling of compassion, it requires a sharp-sighted and humane intuition."[22]

It may be assumed that Dostoevsky was familiar with this exchange, whose numerous echoes filled the pages of the literary journals of the time, and all the more so since it involved an issue in which he had a keen personal interest. Had he not, in "The Landlady," portrayed the relation between "strong" and "weak" characters and given it a wide-ranging significance for Russian culture? Dostoevsky's weak characters can be considered a plebeian variation of the same literary type, and their inner impotence illustrates the same dilemma. It may well

[21] N. G. Chernyshevsky, *Izbrannye filosofskie sochineniya*, 3 vols. (Leningrad, 1950–1951), 2: 235–236.

[22] P. V. Annenkov, *Vospominaniya i kriticheskie ocherki*, 3 vols. (St. Petersburg, 1879), 2: 164, 167.

have been Annenkov's article that helped Dostoevsky understand some of the larger implications of his own earlier writings. For we find him, approximately a year later, stressing the importance of *The Double* in terms that indicate a new awareness of its social-cultural ramifications. One of his projects for raising money was to revise this novella for a republication. "Why lose a remarkable idea," he writes Mikhail, "whose social value is considerable, that I was the first to discover and of which I was the herald."[23] Evidently, Dostoevsky now viewed himself as having created a character type (the weak and indecisive Golyadkin) whose importance as a symbolic figure in Russian culture had only recently begun to be fully appreciated.

[23] *Pisma*, 1: 257; October 1, 1859.

CHAPTER 19

The Siberian Novellas

Once Dostoevsky had received his commission as an officer in March 1857, and once his rights as a nobleman had been restored in May 1857, we hear no more about his *Letters on Art*. Instead, all his energies are now concentrated on the various projects for novels and stories on which he had never ceased to work in the three years since his release from the prison camp, despite the demands of his military duties and the stultifying aftermaths of his epileptic seizures. He still did not know whether he had regained the right to publish, but his correspondents assured him that such a right was implicitly included in those he had been accorded. Since other returning Petrashevtsy had begun to appear in print, Dostoevsky decided to publish, at first without signature, and to see whether this would provoke any reaction from the authorities.

The only work immediately available was the story he had completed in the Peter-and-Paul Fortress, "A Little Hero," which was published in the August 1857 issue of *Notes of the Fatherland*. That summer, Dostoevsky's literary efforts were concentrated on work that, as he tells Evgeny Yakushkin, was "as bulky as a novel of Dickens" and had occupied him for about a year and a half. Dostoevsky speaks of a plan containing three books, but "only the first book has been written in 5 parts" and he promises to now "start to polish it by sections and send the sections to you."[1] He asks Yakushkin to inquire among editors in Petersburg if they would be interested in the first volume and how much they would pay.

From a letter to Mikhail a few months later, it is clear that Dostoevsky had hoped to publish in installments as these were completed, but that Mikhail advised him to hurry up and complete whatever he was then writing. "Seeing that my novel is taking on huge proportions," Dostoevsky writes, "that it was turning out excellently, and that it was necessary, absolutely necessary (for money) to terminate it quickly—I began to hesitate. Nothing is sadder than such hesitation in the midst of work. Eagerness, will, energy—all sputter out." As a result, Dostoevsky informs his brother that "the whole novel with all its material is now packed in the trunk."[2]

---

[1] *Pisma* 1: 221–222; June 1, 1857.
[2] Ibid., 2: 585–586; November 3, 1857.

All notions of writing a novel of *any* kind had been abandoned by the beginning of the new year because Dostoevsky decided to write shorter works that would bring immediate returns. He had received an advance from a planned new journal, *The Russian Word* (*Russkoe Slovo*), for such a short work. Encouraged, Dostoevsky then wrote to Mikhail Katkov, the editor of a relatively new journal, *The Russian Messenger* (*Russky Vestnik*), asking for an advance and proposing his major novel as bait. Although he had no intention of writing this novel, he considered that a substantial story would satisfy his obligations. Katkov promptly sent the money, accompanied by an encouraging letter, and Dostoevsky was now committed to writing two shorter works in the immediate future. "As for my novel," he writes his brother several months later, "I will only get down to it on my return to Russia. . . . It contains . . . a new character . . . without doubt actually very common in Russia in real life. . . . [I]f one is to judge by the tendency and ideas everybody is filled with, I am certain that, once back in Russia, I will enrich my new novel with new observations."[3]

The words "idea" and "character" are inseparable for Dostoevsky, and he uses them interchangeably. Such a character would incarnate the social-cultural tendencies of this period of ferment in Russian life, just on the eve of the liberation of the serfs, and as the country was emerging from its long stagnation under Nicholas I. Dostoevsky had thus already begun to adopt the explicitly "ideological" orientation of all his best post-Siberian creations, and to envisage his creative aim as being the embodiment of character types representative of these burgeoning tendencies and currents. His early work had also been conceived in terms of the dominating ideas of the 1840s, but such ideas had already been embodied in a standard repertory of Gogolian figures (the *chinovnik*, the romantic dreamer), which Dostoevsky simply took over and used for his own purposes. Henceforth he would see his creative task as the depiction of types not yet observed by others or still in the process of formation.

Although Dostoevsky put aside his plans for a major novel, he did write his two shorter works—the Siberian novellas *Uncle's Dream* (*Dyadyushkin son*) and *The Village of Stepanchikovo* (*Selo Stepanchikovo*). Dostoevsky had hoped to send *Uncle's Dream* to *The Russian Word* by September 1858, and he apologizes to his brother, who had negotiated the advance, with the explanation that his illness had kept him from his desk. "Last month I had four attacks, which had never happened before—and I almost did not work at all. After my attacks I . . . feel completely crushed."[4] Also, work on *Uncle's Dream* was difficult because Dostoevsky wrote it with inner distaste. "I don't like it, and it saddens me that I am forced to appear in public again so miserably. . . . You can't write what you want

---

[3] Ibid., 1: 236; May 31, 1858.
[4] Ibid., 2: 593; September 13, 1858.

to write, and you write something that you wouldn't even want to think about if you didn't need money. . . . Being a needy writer is a filthy trade."[5] *Uncle's Dream* had probably been part of the "comic novel" that he had worked on with so much pleasure, but which now had become a burden. "I would be happy to do better," he writes Mikhail, "but all the ideas in my head are for large works."[6] Nevertheless, it was sent off in mid-December and published in the spring (March 1859) in *The Russian Word*.

At first, Dostoevsky's attitude toward *The Village of Stepanchikovo* was as resentful as toward *Uncle's Dream*. "The story that I am writing for Katkov," he tells Mikhail, "displeases me very much and goes against the grain. But I have . . . to pay back a debt."[7] By the time he had sent off three-quarters of the manuscript, though, his opinion had swung round full circle. "Listen, Misha!" he admonishes his brother, "the novel, of course, has very great defects, . . . but what I am as sure of as an axiom is that, at the same time, it has the greatest qualities and is *my best work*. . . . I base all my hopes on it, and, even more, the consolidation of my literary reputation."[8] To his dismay, Katkov flatly rejected the work and asked the author to return his advance payment; but Dostoevsky did not lose faith in his creation. "There are," he tells his brother, "scenes of high comedy that Gogol would have signed without hesitation."[9]

The two brothers offered the work to Nekrasov, who had earlier offered through Mikhail to send Dostoevsky an advance if he were in financial straits. Even though Dostoevsky was still smarting from the wounds inflicted by *The Contemporary*, Katkov's rejection left him no recourse but to seize on what seemed the most likely chance to obtain funds immediately. Nekrasov was handed the manuscript in the first days of September 1859 and hesitated over a month before coming to a decision—a month during which Dostoevsky, on tenterhooks in Semipalatinsk, kept urging his brother to prod the editor. "Note all the particulars and all his words, and, I implore you for God's sake, write me about it in as much detail as you can."[10]

Dostoevsky's novella contained parodistic thrusts against the Natural School of the 1840s—and thus implicitly against Belinsky—which Nekrasov (not to mention Chernyshevsky and Dobrolyubov) would have found offensive. No wonder he waited on tenterhooks! To make matters worse, these thrusts included a reference to one of Nekrasov's own poems, "When from dark error's subjugation," which Dostoevsky will use at greater length in the epigraph to

[5] Ibid., 594–595; December 13, 1858.
[6] Ibid., 594.
[7] Ibid., 593.
[8] Ibid., 1: 246.
[9] Ibid., 251; September 13, 1858.
[10] Ibid., 252; September 19, 1859.

Notes from Underground. In *The Village of Stepanchikovo*, he cites the poem ironically, using it to criticize the humanitarianism of the Natural School as containing a latent self-complacency, an implicit posture of superiority to and patronage of the "fallen," who must be "sought out and raised up."

Nekrasov did not like the novella at all. "Dostoevsky is finished," he is reported to have said. "He will no longer write anything important."[11] But Nekrasov was not one of the most successful editors of his time for nothing, and,
rather than reject the story outright, he accepted it—but offered to pay so little
that no self-respecting author could accept his terms. Dostoevsky thought at
first that he was bargaining. "If Nekrasov bargains and becomes more *reasonable,*
the priority is his whatever happens," he instructs Mikhail. "You see, it is very
important that the novel be published in *The Contemporary.* This journal once
sent me packing, and now maneuvers to have my text. This is very important for
my literary situation."[12]

Dostoevsky, however, was woefully deceiving himself, and Mikhail soon became aware of the true state of affairs. He offered the work next to Kraevsky
for *Notes of the Fatherland,* where it was finally accepted after some negotiations
and at a higher price per sheet. "That's what it means not to derogate one's dignity," Mikhail writes triumphantly. He also conveys some literary comments
of Kraevsky, whose rather negative remark is valuable all the same in helping
to define the new tonality observable in Dostoevsky's Siberian novellas. "You
surrender yourself sometimes to the influence of humor and wish to arouse
laughter. The strength of F. M. . . . lies in feeling, in pathos, here perhaps he has
no equals, and so it's a pity that he neglects this gift."[13] Kraevsky was right in de-
tecting a new and much sharper satirical edge replacing Dostoevsky's earlier
pathos.

———————————— ■ ————————————

From his exile in Semipalatinsk, Dostoevsky asked his brother to send him any
press comments that might appear after *Uncle's Dream* and *The Village of Stepanchikovo* were published, but Mikhail, probably to spare Feodor's sensibilities, remarked that literary journals were no longer reporting on each other to the same
extent as in the 1840s. The truth was that *no* reference of any kind appeared in
the literary press about either of Dostoevsky's works; they were passed over in
complete silence.

This is hardly suprising because, in these very same years, Turgenev was producing much of his best work and turning out a novel almost annually; Tolstoy
had just burst on the scene with his *Childhood, Boyhood, Youth* and *Sevastopol*

[11] *DVS,* 1: 323.

[12] *Pis'ma,* 1: 264; October 11, 1859.

[13] "Pis'ma M. M. Dostoevskogo k F. M. Dostoevskomu," in *DMI,* 525; October 21, 1859.

Stories; Pisemsky's *A Thousand Souls* was the literary sensation of 1858 and was followed by the drama *A Bitter Fate*; and Saltykov-Shchedrin had stirred up a furor with his caustic *Provincial Sketches*, which created a new genre of literary muckraking in Russian writing. Moreover, the whole country was in a fever of anticipation over the forthcoming liberation of the serfs, and the mood of the moment demanded literature with solid social-cultural substance. The only glimpse of social reality in *Uncle's Dream* was, as the prince recalls, a lady whose daughter "killed one of her serf girls in a rage and was tried for it" (2: 315), and this snip of reality was easily overlooked in the comic context. The time-worn plots of Dostoevsky's novellas appeared to involve nothing more momentous than a marriage decision. Even worse, *The Village of Stepanchikovo* depicted life on a country estate in which idyllic relations prevailed between the peasants and their landlowner. The only conflicts were caused by the excessive good na-ture of this exemplary proprietor and gave rise to comic situations that Dos-toevsky's socially conscious readers, preoccupied as never before with the abuses and injustice of serfdom, could hardly take as anything worthy of serious attention.[14]

Even someone as well disposed toward Dostoevsky as Pleshcheev spoke of *Uncle's Dream* as "too farcical," and his concluding estimate of *The Village of Stepanchikovo*, which he asked Alexander Milyukov not to convey to Dos-toevsky, was that "all this is fabricated, contrived; terribly stilted."[15] These crit-icisms are of literary form and they occurred, in my view, because the tech-nique Dostoevsky used clashed radically with the norms then prevailing in Russian prose, which, growing from the physiological sketch, continued to emphasize character description and the portrayal of milieu rather than narra-tive movement. Most important Russian novelists of the mid-nineteenth cen-tury began with such sketches; later, their own novels would continue to have the simplest of plot lines and to retain the emphasis on the portrayal of charac-ter through incidents linked together by the commonplace events of ordinary social existence.

Dostoevsky's readers could hardly have realized that his technique, derived from the elaborate plots of 1830s' dramatic farce, marks a new departure in his work. For all of Dostoevsky's major novels (with the exception of *House of the Dead*) will display the essential features deriving from such a form: a rapid and condensed plot action, unexpected turns of events that pile up fast and furi-ously, characters who are presented in terms of dialogue and dramatic move-ment rather than through analytic portraiture or lengthy depiction of conscious-ness, and climaxes usually taking place amid the tumultuous group scenes that

[14] L. P. Grossman, "Derevnya Dostoevskogo," in *F. M. Dostoevsky, Selo Stepanchikovo i ego obi-tateli* (Moscow, 1935), 28.

[15] Cited in *PSS*, 3: 505.

have been labeled "conclaves" and compared with the celebrated finale of Gogol's *The Inspector-General*.[16]

Even though Dostoevsky's two novellas have a distinctly comic surface, this
should not be taken to mean that they are entirely devoid of serious substance.
A close reading—one focusing on the allusions embedded in the prose and on
the parodistic subtext—discloses as much satire in Dostoevsky's pages as lighthearted tomfoolery. We see as well a notable increase in the range and variety of
Dostoevsky's character types compared with his protagonists of the 1840s, and
they are projected with a boldness of contour and a loquacity of self-expression
that somehow make them seem to have grown almost physically in size and stature. It is difficult to imagine the Dostoevsky of the early stories writing the later
novels, but the author of these Siberian novellas already gives indications of
being able to do so. Finally, whatever the strained high jinks made necessary by
his "comic" plots, Dostoevsky has nonetheless already begun to adumbrate the
great new theme—it may be called "the critique of ideology," or the conflict defined in his letters as that between "ideas" and "the heart"—that will dominate
all his post-Siberian writings.

Uncle's Dream

The plot intrigue of *Uncle's Dream* may be set down in a few words. "Uncle" is a
decrepit but wealthy Russian prince, almost in his dotage, who accidentally arrives in the town of Mordasov one fine day and is immediately taken in tow by
the powerful "leading lady" of the environs, Marya Alexandrovna Moskaleva.
She conceives the scheme of marrying him to her still unwed twenty-three-year-
old daughter, Zina, a proud beauty, and expends treasures of ingenuity in carrying out her plan. But it is finally defeated, to the immense joy of her numerous
rivals for social supremacy, by the jealousy of the rejected suitor for Zina's hand,
a young Petersburg bureaucrat named Mozglyakov, who persuades his distant
relative the prince, quite unable to distinguish between his waking and sleeping
states, that the marriage proposal he had made to Zina in a drunken stupor had
only been "a dream."

Dostoevsky dresses up this anecdote in a faintly mock-heroic style and presents it, in an obvious parody of the title of Balzac's *César Birotteau*, as "the full
and remarkable history of the exaltation, glory and solemn downfall of Marya
Alexandrovna and all her family" (2: 516). The story is also subtitled "From the
Annals of Mordasov" (2: 296)—and such epic accents, of course, only underline

---

[16] L. P. Grossman, "Dostoevsky—khudozhnik," in *Tvorchestvo F. M. Dostoevskogo* (Moscow,
1959), 344–348.

the insignificance of the events (just a year or two earlier Saltykov-Shchedrin had used the same device in his *Provincial Sketches*, also recounted by a local busybody serving as narrator). This new type of Dostoevskian narrator is a gossip chronicler, as much (if not more) interested in rumor and slander as in what he is able to verify with his own eyes and ears; nor is he ever really certain how to interpret even what he witnesses firsthand. A narrator of this kind is later used by Dostoevsky for other works also set in the Russian provinces, such as *Demons* and *The Brothers Karamazov*, and he develops this device into a subtle instrument for controlling his narrative perspective. It is particularly valuable in allowing him to portray his main figures against a background of rumor, opinion, and scandal-mongering that serves somewhat the function of a Greek chorus in relation to the central action.[17]

The image given here of provincial life, with its eternal gossip, backbiting, and ruthless struggles for power over trifles, provides the background against which the major figures of the story stand out in sharp relief. And no figure in Mordasov is more major than Marya Alexandrovna—who is even compared to Napoleon and is said to be actually superior to the all-conquering emperor. Marya Alexandrovna openly exhibits a will to domination that she is hardly entitled to exercise by rank or fortune, and she is the first Dostoevsky character of this type to appear in a work in which the conventions of realism are scrupulously observed. The only previous character of this kind had been the fantastic and mesmeric Murin, who rules over all the others in the highly symbolic "The Landlady." Dostoevsky had earlier been able to conceive the psychology of such a figure only in terms of Romantic hyperbole. Now, however, he places such a "strong" personality within the most humdrum of Russian provincial settings, thereby taking his first step toward that reassimilation of the scope and grandeur of Romantic thematics, and its fusion with Russian social reality, that will distinguish his later work. Indeed, no matter how petty the form taken by such "grandeur" in this instance, the name of Napoleon is enough to alert us to what Dostoevsky will make of such an urge for domination in the future.

Marya Alexandrovna's manifest superiority emerges when she is faced with the task of persuading the proud and high-principled Zina, who has only contempt

---

[17] Traces of the original play form are still evident in *Uncle's Dream*, especially at the beginning of Chapter 3, which describes the characters as part of the stage scenery. "Ten o'clock in the morning. We are in Marya Alexandrovna's house in the main street, in the very room which the lady of the house calls her *salon*. . . . In this *salon* there are well-painted floors, and rather nice wall-papers that were ordered expressly for the walls. In the rather clumsy furniture red is the predominating color. There is an open fireplace, over the mantelpiece a mirror, before the looking-glass a bronze clock with a Cupid on it in very bad taste" (2: 303). What we have are probably the remains of an intermediate draft halfway between stage directions and narrative. The chapter begins in the present tense and then shifts, with no explanation, into the narrative past, as if Dostoevsky at this point were uncertain exactly how to handle the transition from the dramatic present of the play form to narrative.

for her mother's ambitions and machinations, to agree to marry the decrepit prince. Zina, it should be explained, is in love with an impoverished young schoolmaster dying of tuberculosis, and her mother knows that she has pledged not to marry while he is in the throes of his death-agony. To accomplish her aim, Marya Alexandrovna realizes that she must offer some truly tempting prospect, and after some forceful but ineffectual preliminary maneuvers, she is forced to unlimber weapons of a heavier caliber. A marriage with the prince, she tells her daugher, would not be a true marriage at all ("he is not capable of requiring such a love"), and in any case "the Prince will live for a year or two at the utmost." The young schoolmaster could not possibly be jealous of the prince, and hence Zina is told to "reflect that you will give him fresh courage and relieve his mind by marrying the Prince!" But Zina sees through her mother's sophistries and pinpoints her strategy with exasperated precision: "I understand you, Mamma, I quite understand you! You can never resist a display of noble sentiments even in the nastiest action" (2: 325). These "noble sentiments" are Marya Alexandrovna's "ideology," and she draws them from the storehouse of commonplaces piled up by the Romantic literature of the 1820s and 1830s both in Russia and in Europe.

Realizing that any appeal to enlightened self-interest is doomed to failure, Marya Alexandrovna strikes a higher note—self-sacrifice. Why not think of marriage with the prince as an act of devotion? "Where is the egoism, where is the baseness?" Dostoevsky, as he will so often do in the future, is not afraid to mock ideas and ideals in which he believes himself when, as in this instance, they are only being used as a screen for selfishness and egoism. Marya Alexandrovna concludes by telling Zina that, if the prince's wealth bothers her, she can renounce it, give away to the poor all but the barest necessity, and "help him, for instance, that luckless boy lying now on his death-bed" (2:326).

There is no need to detail here all of Marya Alexandrovna's sophistries, but finally she strikes a vein of pure gold. As the narrator comments, "An inspiration, a genuine inspiration, dawned on her," and she realizes that she has found a way of appealing to Zina's authentic idealism: let Zina sacrifice herself by a degrading marriage so as to help her dying beloved. At this point, Marya Alexandrovna pulls out all the stops: "He [the local doctor] told me, in fact, that under different circumstances, especially with a change of climate and surroundings, the patient might recover. He told me that . . . in Spain there is some extraordinary island, I believe it is called Malaga—like some wine, in fact—where not only persons with weak lungs, but consumptives recover simply from the climate, and that people go there on purpose to be treated." Once cured—and the prince conveniently deceased—the lovers could be properly united, or, if not, the schoolmaster will die happily, "trusting in your love, forgiven by you, in the shade of the myrtles and lemons, under the azure exotic sky!" (2: 327). This lengthy tirade, of which only a few samples have been given, is more than Zina can resist; she breaks down and gives her reluctant consent.

Much the same tactic is used with the gullible Mozglyakov, who is persuaded that, although ready to marry the prince, Zina is actually madly in love with *him* and only testing his character by her decision. If he behaves nobly, thinking only of *her* happiness, and the great advantages of such a marriage, his rewards in the future will surpass his most fervid dreams: "For the Prince's health Zina will go abroad, to Italy, to Spain. . . . You will follow her there . . . there your love will begin with irresistible force; love, youth! Spain—my God. Your love of course is untainted, holy. . . . You understand me, *mon ami!*" (2: 354). And then, the prince dead, the wealthy widow Zina will of course marry the man who has proven worthy of her love. Mozglyakov, however, sobers up quickly; and it is he who finally ruins the grand design and engineers Marya Alexandrovna's defeat. But even his momentary acceptance of her intoxicating harangue shows the power of her personality and the power of ideology (in this case literary Romanticism) to impose its cloud-capped visions as a substitute for the awful truth.

———■———

Dostoevsky, we know, did not think much of *Uncle's Dream*; fifteen years later, replying to a correspondent who wished to turn it into a play, Dostoevsky explains that he wrote it "solely with the aim of commencing my literary career and in terrible fear of the censorship (as an ex-convict). And hence I wrote a little thing of sky-blue mildness and remarkable innocence."[18] It hardly, he surmises, contains enough substance even to make it a "comedy," although it does include the prince, who is "the single serious figure in the entire story." Dostoevsky's remark indicates the importance that he continues to attach to the ideological connotations that he gave to the figure of old Prince K., who tries to conceal his true age with the aid of false hair, false teeth, a false mustache, a glass eye, and other such creations of the cosmetician's art. Indeed, writes Dostoevsky, it was "only on closer inspection that you discerned . . . he was a sort of corpse worked by mechanisms," and "was entirely made up of different little bits" (2: 310, 300).

What gives Prince K. his special stamp is the consistent satire of a certain kind of Russian Westernizer that Dostoevsky works into his depiction. One of the earliest touches of this kind, which sets the tone, occurs in a few sentences that describe the prince taking a little fresh air. "He was sometimes seen also on foot, wearing an overcoat and wide-brimmed straw hat, with a lady's pink neckerchief round his neck, with an eyeglass in his eye and a wicker-basket for mushrooms, cornflowers and other wild flowers. . . . When he was met by a peasant,

[18] *Pisma*, 3: 85–86; September 14, 1873.

who stepped aside, took off his hat, bowed low and said: 'Good-day, Prince, your Excellency, our sunshine,' the Prince promptly turned his lorgnette upon him, nodded graciously and said to him affably: '*Bonjour, mon ami, bonjour!*'" (2: 302). The prince's pastoral get-up and French salutation reveal just how distant he was from the realities of Russian peasant life, but for all his giddiness, he is not unaware of what is going on in the world. He arrives in Mordasov originally because of an accident to his coach, and he assures everyone that the peasant coachman "was trying to take my life. . . . Only fancy, he has got hold of some new ideas, you know! There is a sort of skepticism in him . . . in short, he is a communist in the fullest sense of the word!" (2: 312).

The prince's rambling reminiscences are filled with allusions to the Congress of Vienna and Lord Byron, as well as references to his romance with an enchanting French *vicomtesse* whom he lost to a German baron "when I was abroad in the Twenties" (2: 315). The prince is thus a product of the same period of literary Romanticism whose productions supply Marya Alexandrovna with her rhetorical arsenal. And even though the addlepated prince is a figure of comedy, Dostoevsky could not resist evoking, if only for an instant, the grim background against which the cultured Russian of that time was pursuing his carefree European existence. For the prince recalls "a very poetical [Moscow] lady" he had once met while taking the waters abroad, who had a daughter of fifty, and "she, too, almost talked in verse. Afterwards she had a very unfortunate mishap: she killed one of her serf-girls in a fit of rage and was tried for it" (ibid.).

Apropos of this attack on "naïve Romanticism," a word must be devoted to the epilogue of the novella, which, as Russian criticism has long been aware, contains a parody of the famous ball scene in the last book of *Evgeny Onegin*. It is the scene in which Evgeny and Tatyana meet again after many years, she no longer the simple country lass but the queen of Petersburg society, he now hopelessly in love with the girl he had once scorned. Marya Alexandrovna had used this scene earlier to bewitch the bewildered Mozglyakov, holding up before him the vision of a similar encounter with Zina, the wealthy widow of Prince K., who falls into his arms in gratitude for his nobility of soul. Three years later, sent to a remote part of the Russian Empire, Mozglyakov meets the Governor-General ("an old military man") and is invited to his wife's name-day ball that very evening. Of course, his wife turns out to be the beautiful and imperious Zina, who snubs the bewildered Mozglyakov entirely. Mozglyakov stands around "with a biting Mephistophelean smile" and in a picturesque attitude, leaning against a column for several hours; but "his disillusioned air and all the rest of it were thrown away. Zina completely failed to observe him" (2: 397). At last, hungry and tired, he beats a retreat and leaves town the next morning.

On the level of the theme, Dostoevsky's parody of Pushkin supplies a suitable conclusion to the attack on literary Romanticism that runs through the work as a subtext. By revealing so glaringly the triumph of "real life," with its necessary limitations and compromises, over an inflated and unworldly idealism nourished on literary stereotypes, Dostoevsky is making a point that he will return to again and again in the future—of course, in relation to other ideologies with far graver consequences when put into practice.

The Village of Stepanchikovo

The Village of Stepanchikovo is more ambitious than *Uncle's Dream*, although pitched at the same level and written in the same key of farcical comedy. Considering it his best work up to that time, Dostoevsky spoke of it as an authentic personal expression of his own point of view. "I have put into it my soul, my flesh and blood," he tells his brother. "I do not wish to say that I have expressed myself completely in it; that would be nonsense! . . . but it contains two immensely typical characters, created and noted down over a five-year-period, worked out flawlessly (in my opinion)—characters entirely Russian and only badly presented up to now in Russian literature."[19] Dostoevsky is obviously referring to his two main figures, Foma Fomich Opiskin and Colonel Rostanev, whose strange relationship constitutes the heart of his story.

For at least the first of these characters, Foma Fomich (his last name, Opiskin, means a mistake in writing or a slip of the pen), the passage of time has verified Dostoevsky's conviction that he had produced an "immensely typical" figure; no less a judge than Thomas Mann has called him "a comic creation of the first rank, irresistible, rivaling Shakespeare and Molière."[20] Indeed, the name Foma Fomich has since become a byword in Russian for any kind of insolent and impertinent hypocrite, toady, and sponger and is used much as the names of Uriah Heep and Pecksniff are used in English. As Mann's mention of Molière suggests, the role Foma Fomich plays in the household of Colonel Rostanev reminds one strongly of Tartuffe in Molière's famous play, unquestionably one of Dostoevsky's sources. Others of lesser importance have been unearthed; and important as they may be, it is more illuminating to view Foma as a new version of a type that Dostoevsky had often depicted in the 1840s. Like most of the protagonists of these early works, Foma is (or had been) one of the downtrodden, with just enough education to make him feel his obscure social status as a wounding humiliation. In the past, we learn, Foma had tried his hand at everything, at last finding employment as a reader and paid companion to a vicious general,

[19] Ibid., 1: 246; May 9, 1859.
[20] See Thomas Mann, "Dostoevsky—in Moderation," published as the preface to *The Short Novels of Dostoevsky*, trans. Constance Garnett (New York, 1945), xvii. The German text is included in Thomas Mann, *Neue Studien* (Stockholm, 1948).

an invalid who enjoys degrading his flunky for amusement: "there was no igno-miny which he had not to endure in return for eating the General's bread" (3: 8).

Previously, Dostoevsky had treated such characters with sympathy, if occa-sionally also, as in *The Double*, mixed with ironic condescension; but in his very last work before Siberia, *Netotchka Nezvanova*, where he emphasizes the lack of any *social* cause for the failed musician Yefimov's resentment against the world, he was moving toward the placement of moral responsibility squarely on the person himself for the consequences of his actions. Now, with Foma Fomich, Dostoevsky firmly and finally confronts the philanthropic moral assumptions of the Natural School—within whose ranks he had begun his own career and whose values he had once accepted—and rejects them out-of-hand. There is no mistaking the indictment that Dostoevsky levels against Foma's conduct when his fortunes are reversed and *he* achieves a position of power: "He paid us out for his past! A base soul escaping from oppression becomes an oppressor" (3: 13). Not even the most extreme humiliations that Foma endured because of his so-cial inferiority can absolve him from the onus of being "a base soul," whose defi-nition is precisely the inability to overcome a need to dominate and humiliate others as revenge for one's own humiliation and sufferings.

Foma Fomich is framed in the story by two other characters, who serve as "quasi-doubles" to highlight this authorial judgment of his baseness. The per-sonal history of the wealthy heiress Tatyana Ivanovna, a guest in the hospitable home of Colonel Rostanev, is an exact parallel to that of Foma's. All the same, the native sweetness and kindness of her nature remain unaltered when her posi-tion changes overnight. Closer in character to Foma is the clerk Yezhevikin, the impoverished father of the young governess Nastenka with whom Colonel Ros-tanev is in love. Like Foma, Yezhevikin has a rankling envy of his betters and, while pretending to be "the most abject, groveling flatterer" (3: 166), clearly is mocking and sneering at those before whom he is verbally subservient. At the same time, though, he is genuinely honest, possessing a sense of dignity that does not allow him to exploit others in his own interest or even to accept any but the most essential financial aid offered out of kindness by the Colonel.

That *The Village of Stepanchikovo* explicitly involves a critical revision by Dos-toevsky of his own past is also clearly indicated by the narrative perspective. For the story is told by a young man, a nephew of the Colonel, brought up by him and a recent graduate of the University of St. Petersburg. What happens in Ste-panchikovo is recounted through his startled and disbelieving eyes, and the change he undergoes is of first-rate thematic importance. Before meeting Foma Fomich in the flesh, the narrator responds to all the rumors about him in accor-dance with the humanitarian principles inculcated by his progressive university education. And these principles turn out to be, in a simplified and parodistic form, precisely those that had inspired Dostoevsky's own works in the 1840s.

Perhaps, says the young narrator fumblingly, Foma is "a gifted nature" who "has been wounded, crushed by sufferings," and so is avenging himself on humanity ("and perhaps if he could be reconciled to humanity . . . he would turn out to be a rare nature, perhaps even a very remarkable one") (3: 29). This point of view is abandoned instantly by the narrator once he sees Foma in action; and his change of heart reveals to what extent Dostoevsky was conscious of having broken with the ideology of his earlier work. From this time on, the social-psychological perspective he had largely maintained throughout the 1840s will be replaced by one in which the moral responsibility of the person takes precedence over all other considerations.

As the narrator rightly observes, Foma Fomich could not have achieved the "insolent domination" he exercises at Stepanchikovo if not for the equally remarkable character of the owner of that estate, Colonel Rostanev. No single Dostoevskian character anticipates Colonel Rostanev as clearly as Yefimov does Foma Fomich, but the Colonel may nonetheless be linked to a thematic tendency already observable in *Netotchka Nezvanova*. Just as in the case of Yefimov, that is, without overtly clashing with the social-psychological framework, Dostoevsky stressed the need to overcome the instinctive impulse of the humiliated ego to hit back; each important episode illustrates in some way the nefarious moral consequences of a failure to conquer resentment and the ravages of an egoism so self-absorbed as to be incapable of forgiveness or even of mercy. Now, in *The Village of Stepanchikovo*, Dostoevsky essays his first positive embodiment of this thematic motif in a single character, his first attempt to create that ideal of a "perfectly good man" to which he will return repeatedly throughout the remainder of his life. And the juxtaposition and pairing of Foma and the Colonel—the face-to-face opposition of an egomaniacal member of the Russian intelligentsia with a simple Russian soul, overflowing with charity and love—anticipates a similar pattern in many later works.

Dostoevsky presents his first ideal figure in the unlikely guise of an officer, now retired to run his estate. While appearing the very image of presumably self-assertive masculine health and strength, Colonel Rostanev possesses a moral disposition seraphic in its mildness, amiability, and lack of self-regard. "He was a perfect child at forty, open-hearted in the extreme, always good-humored, imagining everybody an angel. . . . He was one of those very generous and pure-hearted men who are positively ashamed to assume any harm of another . . . and in that way always live in an ideal world, and when anything goes wrong always blame themselves first. To sacrifice themselves in the interests of others is their natural vocation" (3: 13–14). Colonel Rostanev is thus a "weak" character in the best sense of that word; and one has the distinct impression that in dealing with his qualities, Dostoevsky is doing so with a side-glance at the Chernyshevsky-Annenkov controversy. Why otherwise should the narrator have felt called on to meet the following objection: "Some people would have called him cowardly, weak-willed and feeble. Of course he was weak, and indeed he was of too soft a disposition; but it was not from lack of will, but from fear of wounding, of behaving cruelly, from excess of respect for others. . . . He was, however, weak-willed and cowardly only when nothing was at stake but his own interests, which he completely disregarded, and for this he was continually an object of derision, and often with the very people for whom he was sacrificing his own advantage" (3: 14).

Foma Fomich obtains his initial hold over the Colonel when he arrives in the retinue of the Colonel's mother, the widow of the general who had used (and abused) Foma as his buffoon. Foma has succeeded in gaining control over this credulous and superstitious woman, who rivals him in selfishness and self-indulgence while lacking his cunning and intelligence. "He (Foma) read aloud to them [*Madame le générale* and her repulsive hangers-on] works of spiritual edification; held forth with eloquent tears on the Christian virtues; told stories of his life and heroic doings; went to mass and even to matins; at times foretold the future; had a peculiar faculty for interpreting dreams, and was a great hand at throwing blame on his neighbors" (3: 8). As the narrator bitingly remarks: "And this idiot woman my uncle thought it his duty to revere, simply because she was his mother" (3: 14). As a result, the Colonel's reverence for his mother is transferred to Foma, and Foma exploits this filial devotion to turn the Colonel into a plaything at the mercy of the whims of a malicious underling. It is the consummate moral imposter Foma who displays all the sins he imputes to the Colonel, but the latter, incapable of finding fault with others and only too ready to accuse himself, is tremendously impressed by Foma's high-minded regurgitations of snippets from Gogol's *Selected Passages* (and his earlier *Testament*).

A good many of the ideas uttered by Foma Fomich unquestionably contain injunctions and exhortations that speak for Dostoevsky's own moral ideals. "Be softer, more attentive, more loving to others," Foma admonishes the Colonel, "forget yourself for the sake of others. . . . Suffer, labor, pray and hope" (3: 89). Dostoevsky does not satirize the literal sense of such perfectly respectable Christian counsels, which he had no intention of undermining *in themselves*, but rather their perversion to obtain and justify domination over others. The target of Dostoevsky's attack is Foma's pose of self-glorification and almost self-deification. He repudiates Foma, after all, by juxtaposing him with Colonel Rostanev, who is the authentic embodiment of all the moral values that Foma is eternally proclaiming in words and totally ignoring in deeds. A remark made years later by Dostoevsky reflects his unchanging negative attitude toward the *Selected Passages*. "The ideal of Gogol is strange," he wrote; "inwardly it is Christianity, but his Christianity is not Christianity." [21] Dostoevsky created Colonel Rostanev as his first "outward" image of what it meant to be a genuine Christian.

Most of the action is taken up with the various devices invented by Foma, with ingenious nastiness, to harass and mortify the Colonel—all being calculated, at the same time, to exalt the insatiable vanity of the erstwhile flunky. A serious level of intrigue involves the plan, concocted by Foma and the Colonel's mother, to force the Colonel into marriage with Tatyana Ivanovna. Actually, he is in love with Nastenka, the poor young governess of his two children by his first marriage. Aware of the Colonel's inclination, Foma and *Madame le générale* persecute Nastenka unmercifully with the aim of driving her away, and the Colonel initially invites his young nephew to Stepanchikovo as a prospective suitor for Nastenka if he can win her consent. Once he is on the scene, however, the situation becomes clear, and the narrator urges his uncle to defy the plotters and marry Nastenka himself.

The dénouement occurs when Foma finally goes too far, accusing the Colonel in public of having seduced and depraved the young woman. This is too much even for the long-suffering Colonel, who, enraged at the slur on Nastenka's reputation, physically pitches Foma Fomich through a glass door and out of the house. The unbeatable Foma soon returns, bruised and battered, but chastened enough now to realize that he must change his tune. So he blesses the marriage, pretending to have been in favor of it all along, and lives happily ever after in clover with the grateful pair, posing, preaching, and carrying on much as before, but careful not to overstep the line that finally had been drawn: "She (Nastenka) would not see her husband humiliated and insisted on her wishes being respected" (3: 164).

───■───

Dostoevsky was speaking truthfully when he declared that *The Village of Stepanchikovo* had been written with "his flesh and blood," and one can already see reflected in its pages some of the important artistic consequences of his Siberian years. These consequences are most evident in Foma Fomich, who illustrates Dostoevsky's deepened understanding of the explosive power of resentment and frustration simmering in the irrational depths of the human personality. For what had been suggested in Yefimov only as an aberration of the Romantic ego is now presented as a widespread human potentiality. Foma's immeasurable vanity, the narrator remarks, may seem a special case, but in fact, "who knows, perhaps in some of these degraded victims of fate, your fools and buffoons, vanity far from being dispelled by humiliation is even aggravated by that very humiliation . . . and being forever forced to submission and self-suppression" (3: 12).

[21] See "Neizdanny Dostoevsky," *LN* 83 (Moscow, 1971), 607.

Such a comment springs directly from Dostoevsky's indelible recollections of the prison camp, where he had seen the need of the personality to assert itself in some way at all costs.

Indeed, it is possible—though probably a trifle premature—to regard Foma Fomich as a first sketch of the underground man. In general, Foma acts in a perfectly rational manner. Even though his behavior as a whole can hardly be compared with the willful self-destructiveness of the underground man, there is one scene in which he does exhibit a willingness to sacrifice immediate self-interest for the sake of an "irrational" ego satisfaction. When the Colonel offers Foma a large sum of money to leave Stepanchikovo and settle in the nearby town, proposing to buy him a house there as well, Foma rejects the inducement with monumental scorn and squeals of outrage that his "honor" is being insulted. Another character comments, on hearing of the incident, "I doubt whether Foma had any mercenary design on it [the refusal]. He is not a practical man; he is a sort of poet, too, in his own way. . . . He would have taken the money, do you see, but he couldn't resist the temptation to strike an attitude and give himself airs" (3: 93–94). Such a predominance of emotive impulse over economic calculation is only a momentary velleity in Foma's case, but it does point the way to the future elaboration of his psychology into that of the underground man.[22]

We have already commented on the deflation of the narrator's philanthropic sentiments once he catches sight of Foma in the flesh, and Dostoevsky reinforces this key motif at the conclusion, where he also adds another important touch to the characterization of the Colonel. For just after Foma has been tamed and placated, the Foma motif is reiterated in relation to another "great man" and "light of learning," Korovkin, whom the Colonel has met by chance one day and invited to Stepanchikovo. This worthy gentleman turns up at the climax, amid the general rejoicing, attired in greasy rags and dead drunk. The Colonel begins to apologize for him in words almost identical with those earlier used by the narrator about Foma: "You know, he may be an excellent man, but fate. . . . He has had misfortunes. . . ." At which point the affectionate narrator, to comfort his embarrassed uncle, pretends to agree with him: "And I began fervently declaring that even in the creature who has fallen lowest there may still survive the finest human feelings; that the depths of the human soul are unfathomable; that we must not despise the fallen but on the contrary ought to seek them out and raise them up; that the commonly accepted standard of goodness and morality was

---

[22] Besides the underground man and, in Colonel Rostanev, the future idiot, we also catch a prefiguration of Raskolnikov in one of the subplots. A seedy young fortune hunter, a cultivated but more craven variation of the Foma type, persuades Tatyana Ivanovna into a runaway elopement. When caught red-handed and stopped in the nick of time, the culprit turns out to be a Raskolnikov *avant la lettre*, who pleads that he was not inspired by "mercenary motives." "I should have used the money usefully," he babbles. "I should have helped the poor. I wanted to support the movement for enlightenment, too, and even dreamed of endowing a university scholarship" (2: 123).

not infallible, and so on, and so on; in fact, I warmed up to the subject, and even began talking about the Natural School. In conclusion, I even repeated the verses: 'When from dark error's subjugation . . .'" (3: 160–161).

The verse, taken from a poem by Nekrasov, celebrates the magnanimity of a high-minded "progressive" lover who, having risen above social prejudice, "redeems" a prostitute by making her his wife. By this time, the narrator regards the words of Colonel Rostanev as typical of the indiscriminately benevolent attitude represented by the poem—the very same attitude he has just managed to slough off himself. He thus cites the poem ironically, as a notorious expression of such well-meant but naïve illusions. The Colonel, though, in his entire innocence, takes the narrator's words at face value; but what he says, in supposed agreement, differs significantly from the narrator's progressive litany. "'My dear, my dear,' he said, much touched, 'you understand me fully, and have said much better than I could what I wanted to express: Yes, yes! Good heaven! Why is it man is wicked? Why is it I am so often wicked when it is so splendid, so fine to be good'" (3: 161).

Dostoevsky, it seems to me, wishes the reader now to feel a distinct difference between the effusions of the Colonel and the narrator's tongue-in-cheek recital of his benevolent commonplaces, which have already been exploded in the main action involving Foma. What separates the two attitudes is that, in the Colonel's case, his spontaneous sympathy with his fellow man immediately involves a sense of his own weakness and human fallibility. Nothing of the kind can be seen in the humanitarianism of the Natural School, which contains, on the contrary, a latent self-complacency, an implicit posture of superiority to and patronage of the "fallen," who must of course be "sought out and raised up."

In the brief epilogue, Dostoevsky comments on the same altruistic position as exhibited by Nastenka. It is she who keeps Foma in check after her marriage with the Colonel, but the narrator remarks that she nonetheless forgave Foma because of her happiness, "and what is more, I believe she seriously with all her heart entered into my uncle's idea that too much must not be expected from a 'victim' who had once been a buffoon, but on the contrary, balm must be poured on his wounded heart. Poor Nastenka had herself been one of the *humiliated*, she had suffered and she remembered it" (3: 164). Once again Dostoevsky emphasizes the personal sense of identification with the victim or sufferer—a compassion springing not from any theoretical doctrine of social pity, with its implied sense of distance and hierarchy, but out of a frame of mind and heart placing the forgiver on exactly the same moral-human level as the forgiven.

Erich Auerbach has remarked that Russian Realism, unlike the other European literatures of the nineteenth century, "is based on a Christian and traditionally patriarchal concept of the creatural dignity of every human individual regardless of social rank and position" and "is fundamentally related to old-Christian rather than to modern occidental realism."[23] In *The Village of Stepanchikovo*, we can catch Dostoevsky in the process of discarding his Western-oriented beliefs of the 1840s or, more exactly, transforming the predominantly social emphasis of his earlier commitments to Christian values into one inclining toward a more traditional Christian sense of universal moral culpability and responsibility for evil and sin. It is only a love for one's fellow man springing from such a sense, we may interpret him as saying, that can escape the onus of pharisaical pride and insulting condescension and both judges and pardons at the same time.

[23] Erich Auerbach, *Mimesis*, trans. Willard Trask (Princeton, NJ, 1968), 521.

CHAPTER 20

Homecoming

The publication of Dostoevsky's two Siberian novellas marks the end of his artistic exile and the beginning of his return to the center of Russian cultural life. These works appeared in print during 1859, and at the very end of this year, in mid-December, Dostoevsky finally realized his long-awaited dream of returning to St. Petersburg. This homecoming, however, did not take place all at once; even after arriving in European Russia, he was forced to stagnate for a few months in Tver, a city on the railroad line between Petersburg and Moscow. The Ministry of War had denied him the right to live in either of the two cities where he could obtain competent medical treatment, advising him to ask for authorization from the tsar through the Third Section.

Early in July 1859, Dostoevsky began the journey from Siberia to European Russia, which took about a month and a half and again involved a huge sum of money, which he scraped together with the help of a loan from Pleshcheev. The party paused at Omsk for a few days to pick up Pasha Isaev, who had been withdrawn from the Siberian Cadet Corps. A moving moment occurred when Dostoevsky's *tarantas*, rolling through the Ural Mountains, reached the frontier between Asia and Europe. Ten years before, a prisoner in shackles, Dostoevsky had passed this frontier in the midst of a howling snowstorm; now it was a fine summer afternoon when they stumbled on "the handsome column with an inscription, and beside it, in an *izba*, an invalid [a wounded veteran acting as caretaker]. We got out of the *tarantas*, and I crossed myself; God, at last, had led me to see the Promised Land. Then we took out our plated flask full of a tangy wild-orange brandy . . . and we drank our good-bye to Asia with the invalid; Nikolaev [the guide] also drank and the coachman too (and how he drove afterwards)."[1]

Much of Dostoevsky's energies during the months passed in Tver were taken up with negotiations over his permission to move to Petersburg, but as a self-described "literary proletarian"[2] whose only source of livelihood was his pen, he was constantly turning over ideas for new works and calculating the possibilities

---

[1] *Pis'ma*, I: 270; October 23, 1859.
[2] Ibid., 2: 603.

of squeezing a little more out of his past publications. Although Mikhail supplied him with funds, and even with indispensable clothing (not to mention a new fur hat for Marya Dimitrievna), Dostoevsky was painfully aware that his brother could not long continue to support such a financial burden.

Dostoevsky, however, had no intention of resting on his laurels, especially since he was aware that those he had acquired in the past had become almost invisible in the eyes of a new generation of readers. Now that his two novellas were out of the way, we find him juggling with a baffling variety of literary projects whose relation to what he actually wrote remains, except in a few instances, extremely conjectural. From Dostoevsky's letters, we gather that he was worried about the lack of "the passionate element" in *The Village of Stepanchikovo* (as compared with Turgenev's *A Nest of Gentlefolk*), but his ambition to emulate Turgenev was soon swept aside by other plans that he excitedly announces to Mikhail as "definitive," only to sweep them away a few days later for still others. What he wished to hit upon, and desperately needed to find, was an idea that would be certain to create a genuine literary sensation and to attract the public attention that would raise his prestige and financial value.

On October 9, he announces to Mikhail that he has firmly decided to undertake writing the future *House of the Dead* at once—a project that would allow him to take advantage of the sympathy inspired in the reading public by a returning political exile. Dostoevsky writes of "the depiction of characters *unheard of* previously in literature, and the touching, and finally the most important—my name. Remember that Pleshcheev attributed the success of his poems to his name (do you understand?). I am convinced that the public will read this with avidity."[3]

Dostoevsky's letters also disclose a dialogue being carried on between the two brothers over a joint literary venture. So far, we have seen Mikhail Dostoevsky only as an ex-journalist and minor short-story writer turned cigarette manufacturer, who, out of the goodness of his heart, had supplied his more gifted brother with funds and acted as his literary agent. His cigarette business, however, was a very small affair, largely dependent on the labor of his family. Mikhail had given up literature only as a result of the direst necessity and had never abandoned the idea of returning to it one day. The new atmosphere in Russia now enabled Mikhail to realize his dream. "Here in Petersburg," the liberal historian K. D. Kavelin wrote at the beginning of 1856, "it is impossible any longer to recognize the [previous] caravansary of militarism, the cudgel, and benightedness. Everything is talked about, . . . sometimes stupidly, but all the same discussed and, as a result of this, studied."[4] Under the impetus of this heady sense of freedom, 150 new newspapers and journals were started in Russia between 1856 and 1860, and

[3] Ibid., 605; October 9, 1859.
[4] A. A. Kornilov, *Obshchestvennoe dvizhenie pri Alexander II* (Moscow, 1909), 31.

on June 19, 1858, Mikhail submitted to the St. Petersburg Censorship Committee a plan for a weekly "political and literary" periodical to be entitled *Time* (*Vremya*). Permission to publish such a journal was granted at the end of October 1858, and the censor appointed to oversee it was none other than the novelist Ivan Goncharov.

A month after Mikhail submitted his proposal, he explained what he had in mind to his brother; and Feodor replied with enthusiasm: "Most important: a literary feuilleton, a critical review of the journals . . . enmity toward the *mutual back-scratching* now so widespread, more energy, fire, sharpness of mind, firmness—that's what we need now! . . . I have written down and sketched out several literary essays along these lines: for instance, *on contemporary poets*, on the *statistical tendency* in literature, on the uselessness of *tendencies* in art—essays written heatedly and even cuttingly, but, most important, readably." [5]

Several more years were to pass, however, before Dostoevsky had the opportunity to express such opinions in print. Nothing was done by Mikhail, probably for financial reasons, to get his new publication under way in 1858, and 1859 found it still in the planning stage. "Look at others, neither talents nor abilities, and yet they rise in the world, amass a capital," Dostoevsky writes disconsolately in November 1859. "I am convinced . . . that you and I are much cleverer, more capable, and knowledgeable about affairs than Kraevsky and Nekrasov. Why, they are just peasants about literature. And yet they get rich, and we are strapped for cash. . . . No brother . . . it's necessary to take a risk and engage in some literary enterprise—a journal, for example." [6] Dostoevsky was now thinking not of a weekly periodical (*gazeta*) but of a monthly "thick" journal (*zhurnal*) that would compete with those of Kraevsky and Nekrasov.

Nothing had been decided when, in December 1859, Dostoevsky arrived in St. Petersburg. His family had rented an apartment for him and his new wife and stepson, furnished it as best they could, and even hired a cook, who eagerly awaited their appearance because it frightened her to live there alone. Other people, more discreetly, were also watching for the arrival of the Dostoevskys. The military governor-general of Petersburg wrote the Petersburg chief of police on December 2 that, by order of the tsar, the secret surveillance under which ex-ensign Dostoevsky had been kept in Tver was to be continued on his homecoming to the capital.

———◼———

Dostoevsky's return to the scene of his early literary triumphs was celebrated only in the small circle of his intimates. Dr. Yanovsky recalled that "in Petersburg

[5] *Pis'ma*, 2: 593; September 13, 1858.
[6] Ibid., 1: 286; November 12, 1859.

we all . . . were at his housewarming: there were Apollon Maikov, Alexander Milyukov, his brother Mikhail with his family, many others, and also Speshnev, who had gotten into Petersburg that very day."[7] Dostoevsky was thus again unexpectedly brought face-to-face with the man he had once called his "Mephistopheles" and who, in the entourage of the governor-general of Eastern Siberia, Nikolay Muravyev, had himself just returned from exile. Muravyev was an energetic administrator with liberal pretensions who enjoyed rubbing elbows with such political exiles as his second cousin Mikhail Bakunin. He had appointed Speshnev editor of a local, government-sponsored journal in Irkutsk, and attached him to his personal staff. During his sojourn in St. Petersburg, Muravyev succeeded in having Speshnev's rights as a nobleman restored. Bakunin, who by this time had escaped from Siberia largely as a result of Muravyev's laxity, had also been much impressed with Speshnev, who had come to Petersburg to examine personally the leaders of the new radical generation. As Pleshcheev writes to Dobrolyubov: "Today, on my name day, I was overjoyed not only by your letter, but also by the visit of a man very close to my heart— Speshnev; he is traveling from Siberia with Muravyev and will unfailingly be at Chernyshevsky's, whom he wants to meet. I also gave him your address. I recommend him as a person. . . . He is in the highest degree an upright character with a will of iron. It can absolutely be said that, among us all—he was the most remarkable figure."[8]

There is, regrettably, no word from Dostoevsky of his impressions of Speshnev after their long years of separation. We must be content to imagine Dostoevsky's thoughts as he greeted the man who had once lured him along the dangerous path of revolutionary adventure. Both would have been able to rejoice, at any rate, that their great dream of the liberation of the serfs was on the point of being realized; both could congratulate each other that their sacrifices had not been in vain. Whether they would have agreed on anything else is highly questionable, but in those days of rapturous expectation, when all Russia was poised on the edge of the great new challenge of freedom, it made very little difference.

Everything seemed possible then, and for a few years—a very few—all shades of social-political opinion were united as never before by the prospect of impending change. It was not a government sycophant but the intransigent Chernyshevsky himself who had recently declared in *The Contemporary* (February 1858) that "the new life, which now begins for us, will be as much more beautiful, prosperous, brilliant, and happy, in comparison with our former life, as the last one hundred and fifty years were superior to the seventeenth century in

---

[7] See the fragment of Yanovsky's unpublished letter to A. G. Dostoevsky in *LN* 86 (1973), 377.

[8] *DMI*, 490–491.

Russia."[9] It may be doubted whether Chernyshevsky himself meant such words to be taken with entire literalness, but no matter—they reflect and express a mood prevalent among all sections of the Russian intelligentsia in those glorious days when "bliss was it in that dawn to be alive."

All were joined together in favor of liberation and reform and against the hardened and selfish reactionaries who opposed the beneficent measures proposed by the tsar to ameliorate the body politic. The little group who came to celebrate Dostoevsky's return all shared in this celebratory mood, and there was no sense as yet that the ally of Chernyshevsky and Dobrolyubov could not also, at the same time, remain the friend of Dostoevsky and Maikov. It would take a few short years to bring matters to a head and to make personal relations of this kind, or at least the old cordiality, forever impossible. But tensions had not yet gone that far, and it should be said that Dostoevsky would honestly try in the future, even if unsuccessfully, to keep them from reaching this point of rupture.

A feeling of celebration was thus everywhere in the air at that moment of Russian history, and Dostoevsky had ample reasons of his own for a sense of buoyancy and jubilation. The Siberian cycle of his life, which began when he left St. Petersburg in shackles, had now been completed. Despite his epilepsy and the disappointments of his marriage, he had managed to survive, and even to thrive, in the onerous years he had just lived through, emerging from his worst ordeal—the four years in the prison camp—with the conviction that he had acquired new powers there both as a writer and as a man.

He knew he would no longer write "trifles" and that he could face whatever fate had in store for him, if not with serenity, then at least with unflinching courage: he had been tried and not found wanting. He had begun to publish again and never doubted for a moment, whatever the relative failure of his fledgling efforts, that he would once again regain his literary eminence. His head and his notebooks were full of plans for new stories, novels, and essays, and he was certain that his unique experiences had given him invaluable insights into the soul of the Russian people that only he could communicate. As the prospective editor of a monthly journal, he was about to throw himself into the fray at the most exciting and tumultuous moment of Russian culture during the nineteenth century. A new life was just beginning for him—the life of literature, for which he had longed so desperately as a convict and a soldier—and he could hardly wait to get to work.

And work he would, in the next five years, as literary editor and chief contributor to his own journals—reading manuscripts, interviewing and writing to contributors, correcting proof, and, all the while, turning out a flow of copy

[9] Cited in William F. Woehrlin, *Chernyshevskii: The Man and the Journalist* (Cambridge, MA, 1971), 193.

with a fecundity, a prolificity, an abundance little short of astonishing if we remember that he was incapacitated for days at a time by the constant recurrence of his epilepsy. These were the years in which he wrote two major books (*The Insulted and Injured* and *House of the Dead*), three short works of fiction (including *Notes from Underground*), a lively series of travel sketches of Europe (*Winter Notes on Summer Impressions*), and produced, in addition, a continual flow of literary essays and polemical journalism.

—But all this takes us into the thick of the next part, and we should not encroach on it any further. Let us end the narrative of this portion of Dostoevsky's life at the joyous moment when his old friends have gathered round to greet the returning exile and drink his health and happiness. Let us take leave of him before the spontaneous conviviality of this reunion has been fractured by ideological enmity, before the burdens he is about to assume have begun to weigh him down, and while he is still basking in the heady exuberance of his homecoming.

PART III

The Stir of Liberation, 1860–1865

CHAPTER 21

Into the Fray

Dostoevsky's presence in St. Petersburg was soon noticed by the larger literary fraternity in which he was so eager to resume his place. Just a few days after establishing residence, he was elected a member of the newly founded Society for Aid to Needy Writers and Scholars, usually called the Literary Fund. Dostoevsky lent his support to the activities of the fund, and not only through his participation in the numerous readings and events that the society organized to fill its coffer. Difficult as it is to imagine, he also performed the tasks of an efficient and conscientious administrator. Elected secretary of the fund's administrative committee in 1863, he kept the records of the meetings and handled the considerable correspondence of this organization with skill and dispatch.

The very first benefit organized by the Literary Fund took place on January 10, 1860, and Dostoevsky would certainly have been attracted by the program, which announced a reading by Turgenev of his newly written, deeply meditative, and highly controversial essay, "Hamlet and Don Quixote," a work that marked an important moment in the social-cultural debate of the early 1860s. An amicable exchange of notes between the two a few months after the benefit reveals that the rancorous breakup of their friendship in 1845 had been, at least for the moment, forgotten. Dostoevsky thoroughly absorbed the essay, whose ideas left significant traces on his own thinking and on his image of the self-sacrificing Don Quixote type in Prince Myshkin. For Turgenev's famous pages proved to be a panegyric of the man of faith, Don Quixote, who is held up for admiration in preference to the worldly, skeptical, disillusioned Hamlet, "sicklied o'er by the pale cast of thought." Don Quixote is inspired by an ideal greater than himself (even if a comically deluded one), and this elevates him to a moral superiority that towers over the indecisive Hamlet.

Turgenev pretended to be dissecting two eternal psychological types that always had existed in human nature; but everyone knew that the Hamlets of Russian literature were the "superfluous men," the well-meaning but powerless and hopelessly impractical members of the gentry liberal intelligentsia. The Don Quixotes, on the other hand, were those who had died on the European barricades in 1848 (like the protagonist of Turgenev's own *Rudin*) and those members of the younger generation in Russia ready once again to sacrifice themselves for the cause of the people. So as not to leave any doubt concerning the implications of his categories, Turgenev mentions both the Utopian Socialist Charles Fourier and, for good measure, Jesus Christ as examples of the Don Quixote type. Perhaps intending to mollify the hostility of the younger radical publicists like Chernyshevsky and Dobrolyubov, Turgenev now indicates agreement with much of their indictment of the Russian Hamlets. But, as we shall see, their antagonism to his work was too deeply rooted in the social-cultural situation to be so easily overcome.

In April 1860, Dostoevsky himself came into public view as a participant in some amateur theatricals organized by the Literary Fund. Pisemsky had hit on the idea of presenting plays with celebrated literary figures filling the roles, and Dostoevsky was invited to join the fun in the role of the postmaster Shpekin in Gogol's *The Inspector-General*. The evening was a howling success; all cultivated Petersburg turned out to see the notorious lions of literature disporting themselves behind the footlights. So much laughter was provoked by the appearance of Turgenev, Kraevsky, and Maikov—arrived to present their "gifts" to the supposed inspector-general and to complain about the depredations of the governor—that those who wished to enjoy the play protested publicly against the unseemly uproar. Among these indignant spectators was the Grand Prince Konstantin Nikolaevich, the brother of the tsar, who was known to have worked behind the scenes in favor of the abolition of serfdom, and who had also come to catch a glimpse of the literary luminaries. "I do not believe," writes the journalist Peter Weinberg (with whom Dostoevsky would soon cross swords), "that anyone familiar with Feodor Mikhailovich in the last years of his life could possibly imagine him as a comic . . . knowing how to stimulate a pure Gogolian laughter; but it was really so, and Dostoevsky-Shpekin was . . . faultless."[1]

———■———

The distractions of his renewed social life notwithstanding, Dostoevsky's energies were focused on reestablishing his literary reputation. All of his time in the spring of 1860 went into planning and drafting two new books, a major novel and the sketches that were to become *Notes from the House of the Dead*. By this time, the planned novel had become essential to fill the obligatory slot reserved for the installment of a major fictional work in every issue of a Russian "thick" monthly. On June 18, Mikhail asked permission of the St. Petersburg Censorship Committee to publish a journal on the basis of the title and program already approved but as a monthly instead of a weekly. The request was approved, and the remainder of the year was occupied by the preparations for publication.

[1] G. M. Fridlender, *F. M. Dostoevsky—materialy i issledovaniya*, 6 vols. (Leningrad, 1974–1983), 4: 243.

Even aside from the question of a regular income, Dostoevsky was eager to join the journalistic fray. Just a few months earlier, *The Contemporary* had printed Chernyshevsky's *The Anthropological Principle in Philosophy*, a work destined to become the philosophical bible of the radical generation of the 1860s, and its appearance had blown up a fierce journalistic storm. Chernyshevsky propounds a simple-minded materialism that sees man as being subservient to the laws of nature (as defined in terms of the sciences of the day, particularly chemistry and physiology), a materialism that—as even a commentator sympathetic to the general thrust of his position admits—"left no room for the irreducible and irrational in human behavior, for all those facts where we deal not with things and objects, but with willing and choosing human beings and their relationships. The problem of freedom was Chernyshevsky's greatest stumbling block, and he would have swept it away into unreality had he not let it reappear by the backstairs in his idea of man as the creator as well as the creature of his environment."[2]

The problem of freedom was indeed one that Chernyshevsky attempted to eradicate, since he did not hesitate to proclaim that nothing such as free will exists, or can exist, as an objective datum. The notion of will or "wanting," he writes, "is only the subjective impression which accompanies in our minds the rise of thoughts and actions from preceding thoughts, actions or external facts."[3] As for ethics and morality, Chernyshevsky adopted a form of Benthamite Utilitarianism that rejects all appeal to any kind of traditional (Christian) moral values. Good and evil are defined in terms of "utility," and man seeks primarily what gives him pleasure and satisfies his egoistic self-interest, but since he is a rational creature, man eventually learns through enlightenment that the most lasting "utility" lies in identifying his own self-interest with that of the majority of his fellows. Once this realization has dawned, the enlightened individual attains the level of a selfishly unselfish "rational egoism," which, according to Chernyshevsky, is the highest form of human development.

Such conceptions, which spread quickly among the younger generation, provided the philosophical underpinnings for the new morality preached by the radical ideology of the 1860s, and no ideas could have set Dostoevsky's teeth more on edge. For if he had acquired any new convictions at all during the searing experiences of his last ten years, it was to convince him of two ineluctable truths. One was that the human psyche would never, under any conditions, surrender its desire to assert its freedom; the other was that a Christian morality of love and self-sacrifice was a supreme necessity for both the individual and society. Without these inherited moral values, life among the peasant convicts would have been a literal hell for Dostoevsky, and he shuddered at the thought that it

---

[2] Strakhov, *Biografiya*, 204.
[3] Ibid.

was precisely *these* values the radicals had now set out to undermine and destroy. An eventual clash with Chernyshevsky and his followers among the generation of the 1860s was thus sooner or later inevitable. This fateful moment, however, did not arrive until several years later, and only after a great deal of social turbulence had ended all hope of accommodation.

Meanwhile, in the fall of 1860, the first two chapters of *House of the Dead* appeared in *The Russian Word*. Difficulties with the censorship then delayed the publication of further installments. In January 1861 the journal reprinted the introduction and first chapter; three more chapters followed at weekly intervals. At the end of January, a continuation of the work was announced, but this promise was never kept, and Dostoevsky's name abruptly vanished from the list of contributors assembled by the resourceful editor, A. Gieroglifov. The reason, of course, was that the first issue of *Time* appeared at the beginning of the year, and Dostoevsky had no intention of allowing so valuable a literary property to benefit a rival publication.

The announcement of the program of *Time* was sent out in September, and while Dostoevsky's name could not be displayed because he was an ex-convict, the characteristic stamp of the writer's fiery temperament would have been immediately apparent in its apocalyptic accents. "We live," declares the first sentence, "in an epoch in the highest degree remarkable and critical." Russia is in the midst of a great transformation, and the important social-political changes being awaited, which will finally resolve "the great peasant question," are only the external symptoms of a more fundamental mutation: "This transformation consists in the fusion of enlightenment, and those who represent it, with the principle of the people's life, . . . the people who, 170 years ago, recoiled from the Petrine reforms, and since that time, torn away from the educated class, have been living their own separate, isolated, and independent existence" (18: 35).[4]

Dostoevsky carefully separates his own position from that of both the Slavophils and Westernizers. The people's rejection of the Petrine reforms, he asserts, was not merely a negation of change and development, as implied by the Slavophils; rather, it had led them to seek change in their own way and on their own terms. Dostoevsky goes back even farther than the reforms of Peter the Great in search of their creativity and finds it in the religious fermentation of the *Raskol*—the refusal of a substantial portion of the population to accept the Greek-inspired reforms of the Russian liturgy—which had led to a schism (*raskol*)

---

[4] Wherever possible, references to Dostoevsky's notebooks will be keyed to the texts included in the Academy of Sciences edition (*PSS*) of his works. The translations into English are indebted to those in *The Unpublished Dostoevsky*, ed. Carl Proffer, trans. by various hands, 3 vols. (Ann Arbor, MI, 1973–1976). Individual page references to the English text, however, will not be given.

within the Russian Church in the seventeenth century and the proliferation of various dissenting sects of Old Believers. Even though, as Dostoevsky concedes, the results of the schism were "sometimes monstrous" (18: 36), the *raskolniki* nonetheless represented an attempt to create an indigenous Russian culture independent of European influence, and he intimates that the positive values of Russian life for which the upper class was seeking so eagerly could perhaps be found among the dissident sects.

Meanwhile, with equal extremism, the upper class had been assimilating European culture through every pore and moving in exactly the opposite direction. This does not mean, writes Dostoevsky, that in striving to create a truly national culture the upper class will simply renounce everything it has acquired. Indeed, such acquisitions have laid the foundation for the great world-historical role that Russia will be called on to play in the future: "We . . . foresee with reverence . . . that the Russian idea, perhaps, will be the synthesis of all those ideas which Europe had developed, with such persistence and courage, in each of its nationalities; that perhaps everything antagonistic in these ideas will find reconciliation and further development in Russian nationality [*narodnost'*]" (18: 37).

Dostoevsky's famous doctrine of Russian "pan-humanism" is already expressed here in 1861 in *Time*, and though his views will later take on a more pronounced Slavophil cast, he evaluates even the Russian Westernizers positively, rather than, as the Slavophils were wont to do, as irredeemably corrupted by European influence. Such a comprehensive attitude toward those whom Dostoevsky would later call the "Russian Europeans" will always separate him from the pure Slavophils. The precise lineaments of the Russian culture of the future that Dostoevsky envisages remain obscure; nor will they gain more clarity in his later pronouncements. The emphasis is on the *necessity* of fusion, which Dostoevsky urges in accents that vibrate with the pain of the still-aching scars of his prison years. These memories now lead him to insist that the upper class must undertake "the spread of enlightenment, energetically, quickly, and at whatever cost—this is the major problem of our time, the first step toward every activity" (18: 37).

———■———

The journals of the Dostoevsky brothers, first *Time* and then its successor *Epoch* (*Epokha*), have thus taken their place in Russian literature as the mouthpieces of an independent social-cultural tendency called *pochvennichestvo*.[5] The *pochvenniki* believed in the primacy of helping to forward a new Russian cultural synthesis from the fusion of the people and their cultivated superiors. For the

[5] The word *pochva*, whose literal meaning is "soil," also has the accessory sense of "foundation" or "support."

radical intelligentsia, on the other hand, all other issues were secondary to that of improving the lot of the peasantry in the manner they considered most consistent with social justice. The program of *Time* was broad enough and vague enough, however, to appeal to a large spectrum of opinion among the intelligentsia; and the slogan of *pochvennichestvo*, given the influence of Herzen's ideas, did not have any particularly compromising connotations in the eyes of the radicals at that moment. *Time* was initially considered to be just another progressive journal, with what would be called, at the end of the decade, a pronounced Populist (*narodny*) slant.

However, Dostoevsky had also recruited Nikolay Strakhov and Apollon Grigoryev as his two leading contributors, knowing that both were firmly opposed to many aspects of the radical ideology of the 1860s. Strakhov, who was to become an intimate friend of Tolstoy as well as Dostoevsky, was then at the start of a notable career as critic and publicist—a career during which he would advocate philosophical Idealism and defend a moderately Slavophil and eventually pan-Slavic social-political position. Like many of the radicals he was to confront in print, Strakhov was the son of a priestly family and had been educated in a seminary. Unlike his opponents, he had later studied mathematics and natural science and had taken an advanced university degree in biology. Such qualifications gave him a scientific competence far superior to that of the average Russian publicist, and he combined these credentials with a devotion to Hegel and German Idealism that made him acutely aware of the limitations of scientific knowledge when confronted with the eternal "accursed questions" of human existence.

Strakhov first attracted Dostoevsky's attention through articles he had printed in the journal *The Torch*: a series on science called *Letters about Life* and a review of P. L. Lavrov's recent *Studies on the Question of Practical Philosophy*. Lavrov, who would soon emerge as a leading spokesman for the ideology of the Russian Populists, had been attacked by Chernyshevsky for not being a vigorous enough materialist, and Lavrov's book had then been used as the pretext to develop his own ideas in *The Anthropological Principle in Philosophy*. Strakhov, on the contrary, found Lavrov too much of a materialist for his taste, and launched a counterattack in defense of human freedom and moral autonomy against all attempts to make them subservient to material conditions. "The will," Strakhov declared, "is subordinate, in an essential and necessary fashion, to one thing only—the idea of its own freedom, the idea of its independent, original and conscious self-determination."[6]

Strakhov possessed an impressive culture and professional mastery to which Dostoevsky could not pretend, and their daily conversations sharpened the nov-

[6] Cited in A. S. Dolinin, "F. M. Dostoevsky i N. N. Strakhov," in *Shestidesiatye gody*, ed. N. K. Piksanov and O. V. Tsekhnovitser (Moscow, 1940), 240.

14. Nikolay Strakhov in the 1850s

elist's awareness of the implications of his own views. "Our conversations were endless," Strakhov writes, "and they were the best conversations I was ever lucky enough to have in my life." What captivated him about Dostoevsky was "his unusual mind, the speed with which he seized on every idea after just a simple word or allusion." Strakhov also noted another trait of Dostoevsky's intellectual physiognomy that has particular relevance for the ideological character of his great creations. "He was . . . a person in the highest degree excitable and impressionable. A simple idea, sometimes very familiar and commonplace, would suddenly set him aflame and reveal itself to him in all its significance. He, so to speak, *felt thought* with unusual liveliness. Then he would state it in various forms, sometimes giving it a very sharp, graphic expression, although not explaining it logically or developing its content. Above all, he was an artist, he thought in images and was guided by feeling."[7]

[7] *Biografiya*, 225, 195.

If Dostoevsky received a certain intellectual schooling from Strakhov, what he derived from Apollon Grigoryev stirred much deeper levels of his personality. Grigoryev had long been a well-known man of letters and by 1861 was near the end of a stormy existence as a poet, critic, and occasional writer of prose fiction. He was a charismatic presence who exercised his fascination on a whole group of young contributors, including Strakhov, who later collected and published his critical essays, and the daily editorial meetings of *Time* provided ample opportunity for the exchange of ideas. Dostoevsky would certainly have found the tempestuous Grigoryev more to his taste as a human being than the prudish, finicky Strakhov. For Grigoryev was one of those "broad" Russian natures— much like the young poet Shidlovsky, the friend and inspirer of Dostoevsky in his youth—who combined the most refined and exalted artistic and spiritual aspirations with drink-sodden and disorderly lives.

"Mystic, atheist, Freemason, member of the Petrashevsky circle, artist, poet, editor, critic, dramatist, journalist, singer, guitarist, orator"—these are some of the disparate aspects of Grigoryev as seen through the eyes of his contemporaries.[8] Dostoevsky wrote that Grigoryev "was, perhaps, of all his contemporaries . . . the most Russian of men as a temperament (I am not saying—as an ideal, that is understood)" (20: 136). His poetry and criticism were held in great esteem by some of the best judges of his time, but he would disappear for weeks on end to indulge in drunken sprees and riotous debauches among the Gypsies, and many of his best essays were written in debtors' prisons. "I remember him," writes one of his closest friends, the poet Polonsky, "believing neither in God nor the Devil—and on his knees in church, praying to the last drop of his blood. I remember him as a skeptic and as a mystic, I remember him as a friend and enemy, fighting with people and flattering Count Kushelev [the owner of a periodical] about his infantile compositions."[9] It has been suggested that traits of Grigoryev, who liked to call himself "the last Romantic," were later embodied in the equally tumultuous and surprisingly poetic Dimitry Karamazov.[10]

For Grigoryev, the true values of Russian life were to be found not in a chimerical and idealized Eden before Peter or in the downtrodden peasantry but rather among those surviving groups—like the Moscow merchant class depicted in Ostrovsky's plays, often staunch Old Believers—who had managed to flourish while zealously clinging to their own mode of existence. He was himself a great connoisseur of Russian folk culture and of the Gypsy music he found so irresistible. Some of his best poems, rediscovered and collected at the beginning

[8] In B. F. Egorov, "Apollon Grigoryev—kritik," *Uchenie Zapiski Tartuskogo Gosudarstvennogo Universiteta* 98 (1960), 194.

[9] Cited in A. L. Volynsky, *Russkie kritiki* (St. Petersburg, 1896), 684.

[10] V. G. Selitrennikova and I. G. Yakushkin, "Apollon Grigoryev i Mitya Karamazov," *Filologicheskie Nauki* 1 (1969), 13–24.

15. Apollon Grigoryev
in the 1850s

of the present century by Alexander Blok, attempt to translate the fiery passion and despairing poignancy of his Gypsy revels into words.

Grigoryev's mature essays sketch an original philosophy of Russian culture whose major theses certainly affected Dostoevsky's own opinions. The central figure in this history is Pushkin, whose work, as Grigoryev interprets it, marks a watershed in Russian cultural self-consciousness. Before Pushkin, foreign influences had been accepted, assimilated, and revered, but in Pushkin, for the first time, one can observe a struggle between the "predatory" types that imitated Western paradigms—the egoistic Romantic and Byronic heroes of his early poetry—and the gently ironical Ivan Petrovich Belkin or the youthfully pure-hearted narrator of *The Captain's Daughter* by whom they are replaced. These are purely Russian characters in their mildness, unaffectedness, and simplicity; and they indicate Pushkin's desire to return to his native soil, with its "truly human, i.e., Christian"[11] values, after succumbing to the seduction of foreign ideals. Grigoryev sees all of post-Pushkin Russian literature in terms of this struggle between "predatory" (*khishchny*) and Russian "meek" (*smirenny*) types, and he

[11] Apollon Grigoryev, *Sochineniya*, ed. N. N. Strakhov (St. Petersburg, 1876), 247.

works out his cultural typology in a whimsically breathless and involuted style reminiscent of his beloved Thomas Carlyle. His essays contain both broadly impressive generalizations and penetrating observations on a host of writers up to and including contemporaries such as Turgenev, Tolstoy, and Pisemsky, and he is now generally acknowledged to be the greatest literary critic of mid-nineteenth-century Russia.

Grigoryev's ideas helped to give a concrete literary-cultural content to Dostoevsky's own most intimate experiences. The "return to one's native soil," whose necessity had presented itself to him so agonizingly in the prison camp, now proved to be the path taken by the greatest of all Russian writers—and it was the one destined to be followed by all Russian literature! For Dostoevsky, Grigoryev's contention that "meek" types are the true carriers of Russian moral-social values would have been taken as precious confirmation of his own artistic premonitions. Much of Dostoevsky's later works may indeed be seen as a dramatization of the conflict between Grigoryev's "predatory" Western (or Western-influenced) types and genuinely Russian "meek" ones—a conflict whose clash of values, portrayed as a duel between moral-spiritual absolutes, he would one day succeed in raising to the level of high tragedy.

Grigoryev also shared with Dostoevsky a view of art as a means of metaphysical cognition—the chosen vehicle by which the secrets of the Absolute reveal themselves in time and history. Both men defended the status of art against the mocking onslaught of the radical Utilitarians. Grigoryev drew the same conclusion as his Danish predecessor, Kierkegaard, that life could not be contained within rational categories of any kind. "To me 'life' is truly something mysterious," he writes Dostoevsky, "it is something inexhaustible, 'an abyss which swallows all finite reason,' to use an expression from an old mystic book, a boundless space in which the logical conclusions of the cleverest mind will often get lost, like a wave in the ocean; [life is] even something ironic, but at the same time full of love, in spite of this irony." [12]

One passage from a letter of Grigoryev to Apollon Maikov, written while Dostoevsky was still in Siberia and hence before the two men could have exchanged ideas, will illustrate this similarity in fundamental outlook: "I do not know what I find more repulsive: Petersburgian progress . . . the dilettantism of orthodoxy, or finally the cynical atheism of Herzen. All these amount to the same thing and have the same value, and 'these three' all come equally from one cause: from a lack of faith in life, the ideal and art. All this results from the *utilitarian* Utopia of sensual felicity or spiritual slavery and Chinese stagnation under the pressure of *external* unity in the absence of inner unity, i.e., Christ, i.e., the Ideal, i.e., *Measure*, Beauty, in which alone truth is contained and which

---

[12] Ibid., 618.

alone can bring truth to man's soul."[13] The identification of Christ in this passage with the Ideal and with Beauty could not be more Dostoevskian.

Most striking of all, perhaps, is the temperamental affinity revealed by Grigoryev's reference, in a line of his poetry, to "the mad happiness of suffering," and by his reiteration, in a letter, that "there are sufferings of the soul capable of passing over into a sense of beatitude." How can one not think of Dostoevsky, asks the Italian Slavist Wolf Giusti, after reading such utterances?[14] Both men share a common devotion to the Christian faith as it had developed in their homeland, and just as Dostoevsky had recently declared, with reference to the Christian Crusades, that "Europe and its task will be completed by Russia,"[15] so Grigoryev believed that the historical life of Europe was "exhausted, and another is beginning; it will come out of Orthodoxy, a new world lies in this force."[16] But, again like Dostoevsky, he was too much a product of Romanticism and too much a modern to accept either his Christian faith or Orthodoxy without a struggle. "From wherever I begin," he acknowledges, "I always arrive at the same single point: at this deep and sorrowful need to believe in the ideal and the *Jenseits* [the supernatural]."[17] No Russian contemporary of Dostoevsky comes closer than Grigoryev to sharing the same tangled complexity of impulses and attitudes.

It was with such comrades-in-arms that Dostoevsky sallied forth to participate in the journalistic wars of the 1860s. Victory certainly cannot be said to have attended his banner, but while the *pochvenniki* were in the field, they furnished a respectable opposition to the triumph of what has been called (inaccurately, so far as Chernyshevsky and Dobrolyubov are concerned) Russian Nihilism. Moreover, these wars served to provide Dostoevsky with the materials that he was soon to transmute and elevate, by the power of his genius and personal vision, into the artistic-ideological synthesis of the great novels of the middle and later 1860s.

———■———

With the launching of *Time*, the routine of Dostoevsky's life was established for the next five years. All of his energies were absorbed by his work both as editor and contributor, and it is impossible to dissociate his private existence from the quotidian task of running the magazine. Its editorial offices were located in the

---

[13] January 9/21, 1858; in Apollon Grigoryev, *Materialy dlya biografii*, ed. Vlad Knyazhnin (Petrograd, 1917), 217.

[14] W. Giusti, "Annotazioni su A. A. Grigorev," *Annali* (Istituto Universitario Orientale, Sezione Slava), 1 (1958), 66. This is an extremely perceptive evaluation of the work and personality of Grigoryev.

[15] *Pis'ma*, 1: 165; January 18, 1856.

[16] Cited in V. V. Zenkovsky, *A History of Russian Philosophy*, trans. George L. Kline, 2 vols. (New York, 1953), 1: 405.

[17] Ibid., 403.

16. Mikhail Dostoevsky's
home and the offices of
Time

residence of Mikhail Dostoevsky, and both Feodor and Strakhov lived close by,
the latter having moved from another apartment specifically to be nearer at
hand. This section of the city was a busy and populous lower-class district, whose
grimy and muddy streets, always swarming with hordes of merchants, tradesmen, and laborers, Dostoevsky later portrayed in *Crime and Punishment*. And,
as Strakhov recalls nostalgically, "amid these surroundings, which filled us with
sadness and repulsion, we all lived through very happy years." [18]

Strakhov's memoirs describe a life of unremitting literary labor, with Dostoevsky working round-the-clock and quitting his desk only to sleep. Dostoevsky
wrote at night, starting about midnight and continuing until five or six in the
morning; he then slept until two or three, and began his day around that time.
The staff of the journal convened at three in the afternoon, "and there [in the of-
fices] we leafed through the newspapers and journals, caught up with everything
new, and often then went to dinner together." [19] Very often too Dostoevsky vis-

[18] *Biografiya*, 223.
[19] Ibid., 224.

17. F. M. Dostoevsky, 1861

ited Strakhov's daily tea in the early evening, when a group of friends would gather for talk and conviviality.

Strakhov also stresses the complete absorption of Dostoevsky and his collaborators in the internecine warfare which, at that agitated moment, imparted so much unaccustomed animation to the Russian periodical press. To be an editor then was an invigorating endeavor. A journal like *Time* was invariably in the center of a cross fire, and nothing was more important than to know who was a friend and who a foe. "Dostoevsky, Apollon Grigoryev, and I could be certain that, in each new issue of a journal, we would invariably come across our names. The rivalry between various journals, the intense attention given to their tendency, the polemics—all this turned the job of journalism into such an interesting game that, once having experienced it, you could not help but feel a great desire to plunge into it again."[20]

[20] Ibid.

Despite his own career as a publicist, Strakhov harbored an unconquerable disdain for the rough-and-tumble of journalistic infighting. He had, as he remarks proudly, belonged to a literary circle of the 1840s for which "the very summit of culture would have been *to understand Hegel and to know Goethe by heart.*"[21] These two names (especially the latter) had become symbols for a social-cultural attitude *au-dessus de la mêlée*, of a concern with "eternal" issues far removed from the petty disputes of day-by-day social existence; and Strakhov was shocked, on his first contact with the Milyukov Circle, to find himself exposed to a wholly different point of view. The tendency in this circle, which Dostoevsky had joined soon after his return from exile, "had been formed under the influence of French literature. Political and social questions were thus in the foreground, and swallowed up purely artistic interests. The artist, according to this view, should investigate the evolution of society and bring to consciousness the good and evil coming to birth in its midst; he should, as a result, be a teacher, denouncer, guide. Hence it almost directly followed that eternal and general interests had to be subordinated to transient and political ones. Feodor Mikhailovich was totally steeped in this publicist tendency and remained faithful to it until the end of his life."[22]

Dostoevsky's passion for journalism derived from the desire to remain in touch with the burgeoning social-cultural issues of his time and to use them for artistic purposes. He made no distinction, unlike the more pretentious Strakhov, between what Goethe called "the demands of the day" and those of his literary career. "I rather looked at journalism cross-eyed," Strakhov admits, "and approached it with some haughtiness."[23] Precisely because Dostoevsky made no distinction between "eternal" issues and those of the current scene—because he could sense the permanently significant in and through the immediate and seemingly ephemeral—he was ultimately capable of writing those ideological novels that constitute his chief claim to glory.

Dostoevsky effortlessy came into close personal contact during these years with a wide range of Russian social-cultural opinion. Indeed, he could see all its nuances embodied in the flesh as he spoke to the youthful members of the younger generation who swarmed into the editorial offices of his journal and who, if they were lucky, were invited to attend editorial meetings where manuscripts were read aloud and final decisions taken. *Time* was constantly on the lookout for new young writers and remained unusually receptive to their fledgling efforts. Many names later well known, some in the annals of the extreme left wing (such as P. N. Tkachev), published their first work under Dostoevsky's aegis. "Perhaps never again in his life," remarks V. S. Nechaeva, "would Dos-

[21] Ibid., 173.
[22] Ibid., 172.
[23] Ibid., 200.

toevsky have the same chance to come into contact with young people of such diverse backgrounds and situations, but united by an interest in social and literary questions, as when he was at the head of *Time* and *Epoch*." [24]

Dostoevsky's editorial policy attempted to combine a sympathy for the aspirations of the predominantly radical youth for social justice and political reform with an unremitting hostility to the aesthetic, ethical, and metaphysical tenets of radical ideology. This effort to reconcile the irreconcilable led to inevitable tensions between the various groups of contributors to *Time,* who made up two opposing factions. At the center of one was the tempestuous Grigoryev, with Strakhov as a fellow-traveler, "though," writes Strakhov, "his emotions were not at all stirred by the search for *pochva*, but rather by an implacable hatred of materialism." [25] On the other side, most of the young radicals gathered around A. E. Razin, the self-educated son of a peasant serf family and the author of a popular introduction to a scientific view of the universe for schoolchildren entitled *God's World*, who was, in addition, a close friend of Dobrolyubov. Between the two was a group composed of the Dostoevsky brothers and the survivors of the gentry liberal circles of the 1840s—Milyukov, Pleshcheev, Apollon Maikov, and others less well-known. [26]

Grigoryev left Petersburg in the spring of 1861 in part because of dissatisfaction with the editorial policy of *Time*; in particular with Dostoevsky's refusal to attack more vigorously the radicals on *The Contemporary*—Chernyshevsky and Dobrolyubov. Dissatisfied as well with Dostoevsky's relatively mild rebuttal of Dobrolyubov's views on art, Strakhov admits, "I could not contain myself and I wished to come as quickly as possible into a straightforward and decisive relationship with Nihilist doctrines. . . . I regarded its appearance in literature with great indignation." [27] Dostoevsky did not share the same animus, and his observations of the current scene reveal the extremely unstable synthesis he was trying to work out between a sympathetic and a critical attitude toward the radicals. Much attention is given by Dostoevsky to the relative freedom of the press that had permitted the rise of an "accusatory literature" (for example, Saltykov-Shchedrin's *Provincial Sketches*) exposing abuses. Such writing had recently come under attack from both the Right (which did not relish the criticism of existing conditions) and the Left (which believed that such criticism did not go far enough). *The Contemporary*, in the person of Dobrolyubov, had made a point of ridiculing complacent liberal journalists who, while pillorying minor bureaucratic misdeeds, refused to utter a word about the system as a whole or to suggest that a total transformation of society was necessary to remedy the outrages they

[24] V. S. Nechaeva, *Zhurnal M. M. i F. M. Dostoevskikh*, Vremya, *1861–1863* (Moscow, 1973), 65.
[25] Ibid., 68.
[26] Ibid., 68–69.
[27] *Biografiya*, 220.

reported. Dostoevsky tries to steer prudently through these dangerous shoals, indicating his approval of what he calls "beneficent publicity" on the one hand but without expressing any indignation at the jibes of the radicals on the other. While keeping his distance on all matters of substance, he thus displays in this discreet and allusive fashion at least a sympathetic tolerance for the radical position in the social-cultural skirmishes of the early 1860s.

Only in the last two sections of the first number of *Time*, however, do the limits of Dostoevsky's agreement with the radicals begin to emerge more conspicuously. On the issue of literacy, Dostoevsky insists that it is the obligation of the upper class to take the lead in making such literacy accessible, and this duty leads him into some reflections on the "superfluous men"—members of the gentry liberal intelligentsia—who were then under heavy attack from the radicals. Not content with their sarcastic sallies against the characters of Turgenev's stories and novels, the attack had been continued, with mounting ferocity, by Dobrolyubov, and had recently reached a crescendo in his sensational article, "What Is Oblomovism?" (the term coined by Goncharov to describe the lethargy of his protagonist, Oblomov). Listing the most famous examples of superfluous men in Russian literature, all the greatest creations of the best-known writers—Pushkin's Onegin, Lermontov's Pechorin, Herzen's Beltov, Turgenev's Rudin—Dobrolyubov had described them without exception as blood brothers of the supine Oblomov.[28]

The complaint made by the superfluous men had always been that conditions in Russia offered no arena for the employment of their abilities. But with the liberation of the serfs in 1862, a life of honorable action inside Russia was possible, and indeed had become a task devolving on all men of good will. Even Herzen was ready to agree that "the day of the Onegins and the Pechorins is over. . . . One who does not find work now has no one else to blame for it."[29] Dobrolyubov had insisted that the entire class of gentry liberals should be thrown into the discard, but Herzen had argued that they could still be useful. Essentially, this was also Dostoevsky's opinion; where the two men differed was in their notion of what "work" and "usefulness" implied in the new post-liberation Russia.

Herzen always remained a radical revolutionary, and "work" for him did not mean the end of his hostility to a regime that he opposed on principle in the name of democratic Socialism. For Dostoevsky, on the other hand, the time had come for the superfluous men, those fine flowers of the Russian intelligentsia

[28] N. A. Dobrolyubov, *Selected Philosophical Essays*, trans. J. Fineberg (Moscow, 1956), 199.
[29] Alexander Herzen, *My Past and Thoughts*, trans. Constance Garnett, rev. Humphrey Higgens, 4 vols. (New York, 1968), 4: 154.

(among whom he would later number Herzen himself), to devote themselves to the humdrum task of bettering the lot of their fellow Russians. Suppose, Dostoevsky writes mockingly, each of these gentlemen undertakes to teach just one child how to read. Such a proposal, of course, would shock their pretensions, and Dostoevsky conveys their horrified response in his ironically dialogic manner: "Is that an activity for people like us! . . . we who conceal titanic powers in our breast! We wish to, and can, move mountains; from our hearts flows the purest well-spring of love for all humanity. . . . It's impossible to take a five-inch step when we wish to walk in seven-league boots! Can a giant teach a child to read?" To which Dostoevsky replies in his own voice: "There it is: sacrifice all your titanism to the general good; take a five-inch step instead of a seven-league one; accept wholeheartedly the idea that if you are unable to advance further, five inches is all the same worth more than nothing. Sacrifice everything, even your grandeur and your great ideas, for the general good; stoop down, stoop down, as low as the level of a child" (18: 68).

The intelligentsia is thus enjoined to subdue its pretensions and to do what it can within the limits of a possibility bounded by the existing (but greatly transformed) social-political situation. Such an injunction will determine Dostoevsky's immitigable opposition to all attempts to stir up what he firmly believed could only be futile and self-destructive revolutionary unrest.

CHAPTER 22

An Aesthetics of Transcendence

It was rare for an issue of *Time* to appear without one of Dostoevsky's articles or an installment from one of his works in progress, and his presence was also constantly felt in the form of introductions to translations, as well as editorial notes appended to the articles of other contributors. Understandably concerned over the impression that would be created by the first issue of the journal, Dostoevsky rewrote almost entirely an article originally assigned to the poet D. D. Minaev. The result was the feuilleton "Petersburg Visions in Verse and Prose," a unique mixture of Dostoevsky's prose text with Minaev's verse.

The piece has been recognized as a work of rare autobiographical value, containing a precious account of how Dostoevsky viewed the process of his own literary maturation from the days of his early Romanticism up to his discovery of the theme of his first novel. One immediate aim of the feuilleton was certainly to reintroduce himself to the Russian reading public by this evocative résumé of his literary past, but when he returns to the present, we catch a first glimpse of the changes that are already faintly discernible in his artistic outlook. In the revelatory passage that has come to be known as "the vision on the Neva," the writer recalls how, at the beginning of his career, he had once walked across a bridge over the Neva during a bitterly cold winter day, looking at the frozen expanse sparkling and gleaming in the rays of the setting sun "so that it seemed as if . . . a new town was taking shape in the air":

> It seemed as if all that world, with all its inhabitants, strong and weak, with all their habitations, the refuges of the poor, or the gilded palaces for the comfort of the powerful of this world, was at that twilight hour like a fantastic vision of fairyland, like a dream which in its turn would vanish and pass away like vapor in the dark blue sky. . . . I seemed to have understood something in that minute which had till then been only stirring in me, but was still uninterpreted. . . . I suppose that my existence began from just that minute. . . . (19: 69)

Dostoevsky attributes an extraordinary importance to this imaginary transformation of the majestic city of Peter the Great into a dissolving phantasmagoria that might have been a waking dream. And this fusion of the fantastic and the real, he affirms, marked the beginning of his self-discovery as an artist. Using literary imagery, and still speaking in the fictional disguise of the feuilletonist, he recalls how he had once been in thrall to Romantic influences (Schiller, Hoffmann, Scott), which had given wings to his imagination and lifted him far above his immediate surroundings. Never deigning to cast even a glance at the world around him, he had desired to live "with all my heart and soul in those golden and passionate dreams exactly as if from opium." But then, the revelatory impact of the vision made him aware of all those people he had hardly noticed before, "all those . . . strange, astonishing figures, totally prosaic . . . titular councillors [lower-level bureaucrats] and at the same time, as it were, some sort of fantastic titular councillors" (19: 70). As they emerged into view, they all appeared to be puppets moved by strings; and behind them was the puppet master (Gogol), laughing uproariously himself and provoking everyone else to laughter as well.

But the youthful Dostoevsky did not wish, like the puppet master of genius, to laugh at all the humble creatures surrounding him; instead, he invented another story about them that "tore deeply at my heart" (19: 70). This story, of course, was the sentimental tale *Poor Folk*. Dostoevsky's characters became "fantastic" not because of the comic distortions provided by the oblique prism of Gogolian humor but through the unexpected delicacy of their feelings and responses. Here, then, was his own literary point of departure—the infatuation with Romanticism, the turn to Gogol, the realization that reality too contained its own kind of visionary strangeness, and the invention of a new variety of such bestrangement.

—■—

The vision on the Neva provides a penetrating glimpse into Dostoevsky's preSiberian literary evolution, and he insists that the same vision, even if in slightly different forms, has continued to nourish his imagination ever since. "My dreams, if you like, are the same, but with other faces, although old acquaintances also sometimes knock at my door." Dostoevsky thus continues to view the ordinary world around him as filled with the strange and the uncanny; in the horde of Christmas shoppers flowing through the Petersburg streets, he suddenly sees "just in front of me . . . some sort of figure, not real but fantastic. I, you see, am in no way able to shake off a state of mind disposed to the fantastic. Already in the 1840s they called me a fantasist and ridiculed me for it. Then, all the same, I did not crawl into a hole. Now, it's understood—gray hair, the experience of life, etc., etc., and all the same I still remain a fantasist" (19: 73).

These words are a belated reply to Belinsky's devastating criticism of *The Double* in 1846, and a defiant affirmation of Dostoevsky's refusal to abandon his own particular mode of apprehending reality; but Dostoevsky is doing more here than simply defending his past. As an unrepentant "fantasist," as a "mystic" and a "dreamer," he also sees "other faces" that have begun to impinge among his old acquaintances. One is that of a poor impoverished clerk, totally beaten down and subdued by life, so meek that he does not even turn his head when he is lashed by a coachman's whip on the Nevsky Prospect. But one day, he suddenly breaks his silence to confess—something totally unimaginable! That he is really Garibaldi, the notorious bandit and "destroyer of the natural order of things" (19: 71–72). The Russian newspapers and journals, including *Time*, were in those days full of stories about Garibaldi's heroic struggle for Italian independence against Austria, and the Italian patriot had become the darling of the progressive press. Like Poprishchin in Gogol's "Diary of a Madman" (Dostoevsky makes the comparison himself), who landed in a madhouse believing himself to be the king of Spain after reading in the newspapers about the vacancy of the throne, Dostoevsky's clerk becomes obsessed with the idea that he and the great rebel Garibaldi are one and the same person.

To imagine such velleities of insurrection simmering in the breast of the humblest and most resigned of titular councillors is, of course, the very acme of "the fantastic." "And when I dreamed this dream," Dostoevsky admits, "I began to laugh at myself and the eccentricity of my dream" (19: 72). But then the dream turned out to be "true"—or at least confirmed as a possibility by a newspaper story about a similar clerk, retired and living in the direst poverty, who was found at his death to be worth a half-million rubles. An autopsy was to be performed on the corpse, but "it seems to me that no autopsy will elucidate mysteries like this one" (19: 75). "The prosaic" is shown once again to contain the most extravagant possibilities and the most baffling psychological enigmas.

Nonetheless, Dostoevsky takes a stab at elucidating the "mystery" with the aid of two alternative psychologies. One is derived from Pushkin's "The Covetous Knight," and in its light "my Solovyev [the name of the millionaire derelict] suddenly appeared to me as a colossal figure." Like Pushkin's nobleman, he enjoys the secret sense of power given by his boundless wealth—"he has only to whistle, and everything he needs will crawl to him obediently." But he does not even whistle; it is power, not satisfaction, that he inwardly craves: "he needs nothing . . . he is above all desires." Dostoevsky, however, decides not "to steal from Pushkin" in this instance (though he will not hesitate to do so in both *The Idiot* and *A Raw Youth*), and he invents another motivation for Solovyev. In his youth, the clerk had been quite normal, but then something occurred—"perhaps one of those moments . . . when he suddenly caught a glimpse of something, and that something frightened him" (19: 73–74). From that moment he began to save, in a manner that gradually became deranged, and his niggardliness was an aberrant manner of responding to the terror of whatever existential crisis had abruptly undermined his being.

What is striking about these two figures at first sight—and quite contrary to Dostoevsky's emphasis—is their pronounced resemblance to his characters of the 1840s. Why should he have considered them "other faces" in relation to his early work? In their initial incarnation, any deviation from the path of perfect submission and absolute obedience was enough to plunge his characters into psychic derangement; nothing could have been further from their own thoughts than any impulse of willful insubordination. Although Dostoevsky's downtrodden clerk resembles his earlier characters in every external feature, the obsession with being Garibaldi reveals something dramatically new—an acknowledgment of an urge to destroy the entire world as revenge for his frustrations. Now, in some hidden and suppressed corner of his psyche, the character himself internalizes the full social-political implications of his resentments, and his consciousness thus contains an explicit, ideologically subversive dimension.

Evidences of such a subversive change can also be found in Dostoevsky's notes (1860–1861) for his proposed rewriting of *The Double*. Golyadkin realizes that his invitation to the daughter of his superior, at a party he had crashed, was really "a revolt against society"; the motif is enlarged so that a trivial event, pathetically comic in its original form, now becomes a threatening social-political gesture. Similarly, Golyadkin anticipates the underground man in his fantasies of political power, which swing back and forth between revolution and reaction: "Alone with *Junior*, dreams of becoming a Napoleon, a Pericles, a leader of the Russian revolt. Liberalism and revolution, restoring Louis XI with tears" (1: 434).

What was only potential in the earlier work is now developed in a fashion that converts the original comic pathos into a movement of despairing rebellion and a perverted will to power. Golyadkin's psychology, the split in his personality between "ambition" and fear of the authorities, takes on a new ideological richness, and the same change of scale can be noted in the case of the millionaire derelict. With him we seem to be back in the world of "Mr. Prokharchin" (1846), who dies in misery while concealing a small fortune and whose avarice had been the result of having "caught a glimpse of something, and that something frightened him." [1] But here too Dostoevsky begins to conceive such a figure as analogous to Pushkin's "The Covetous Knight," and to portray his miserliness as another manifestation of a perverted will-to-power not unlike that of the clerk whose dreams are haunted by Garibaldi.

Even though this psychology is far from being fully developed as yet, Dostoevsky is moving toward viewing his early characters as endowed with some of the same elevation of thought and feeling as Pushkin's great Romantic creations. After first rejecting Romanticism and shrinking its themes and motifs to the level

---

[1] For an analysis of "Mr. Prokharchin," see Joseph Frank, *Dostoevsky: The Seeds of Revolt, 1821–1849* (Princeton, NJ, 1976), 133–136.

of "the prosaic" in the 1840s, Dostoevsky thus reverses direction to enlarge his "sentimental Naturalism" with some of the grandeur that had once inflamed his youthful literary imagination. He is already beginning to feel his way toward the synthesis of his great novels, where a scrupulous depiction of "the prosaic" will be combined with "the fantastic" of psychological extremism, world-consuming ambition, and complex ideological ratiocination.

———■———

Part of *Time*'s considerable success was attributable to Dostoevsky's flair for providing his readers with exciting literary sustenance from a great range of sources. At the same time, what he chose to print bears the inevitable mark of his own preoccupations, and his editorial comments often foreshadow his later works or illuminate the manner in which everything he read became grist for his creative mill.

During 1861, *Time* ran a series of accounts of famous recent murder trials in France. These are recommended as irresistible reading, "more exciting than all possible novels because they light up the dark sides of the human soul that art does not like to approach, or which it approaches only glancingly and in passing" (19: 89). What interests Dostoevsky are the psychological motives and behavior of those who kill. With such words, Dostoevsky is anticipatorily staking out the novelistic domain in which he will soon achieve his greatest triumphs. For he will raise the novel of mystery and criminal adventures to new heights by shifting the focus from such external plot action to the psychology (which for him will be inseparable from the ideology) of the criminal.

A lengthy preface in the first issue preceded three stories by Edgar Allen Poe, and both Dostoevsky's text and the translations can be linked closely with his creations in the next few years. Dostoevsky's preface, in the words of a Soviet Russian scholar, contains "the first serious and penetrating evaluation of the American writer made in Russia" (19: 282). Indeed, according to an American specialist, Dostoevsky's preface of 1860 includes "the most perceptive observations yet made in any language specifically on Poe's artistic technique."[2]

What struck Dostoevsky in Poe was "the vigor of his imagination," which he defines as "the power of specific detail": Poe will invent the most extraordinary and even impossible situations, but in his stories "you will so clearly see all the details of the form of the existence presented to you" that the reader is absolutely convinced of their verisimilitude. Unlike Baudelaire, whose translations of Poe (including the prefatory essays) Dostoevsky had certainly read, he does not view him as a *poète maudit* condemned by the reigning vulgarity of American life; rather, he suggests quite brilliantly that the outstanding feature of Poe's imagina-

[2] Jane Delaney Grossman, *Edgar Allen Poe in Russia* (Wurzberg, 1973), 34.

tion is typically American. Materialism was presumed to be the dominating aspect of American civilization, and "if there is the fantastic in Poe, it has, so to
speak, something material about it. Clearly, he is fully an American even in his
most fantastic stories" (19: 88–89).

The stories of Poe that Dostoevsky printed can all be related to the two great
works he will write in just a few years—*Notes from Underground* and *Crime and
Punishment.* Even the least of Poe's stories in *Time*—"The Devil in the Belfry,"
hardly more than a broad comic anecdote—is an allegory of the intrusion of the
irrational into an orderly world that has always run in accordance with its immutable laws. When the devil gets into the belfry of the sleepy town of Vonder-
votteimittis, the lives of the sedate burghers are thrown completely out of kilter
because the belfry clock at noontime does not stop at twelve but goes on to
chime thirteen. The two other stories, "The Tell-Tale Heart" and "The Black
Cat," contain features that can be linked even more concretely with Dostoevsky's
artistic future.

Both are written in a first-person mode by a narrator unable to suppress a
sense of guilt about his crimes and whose conscience finally bursts forth in self-
betrayal. Both also illustrate the same irresistible pressure of the irrational to
thwart the best-laid and most cunning calculations of the rational mind. The
narrator of "The Tell-Tale Heart," a motiveless murderer who kills because of a
pathological obsession, believes he has committed the perfect crime, but he finally confesses because he thinks that others as well as himself hear the thunderous noise of the victim's heart continuing to beat through the floor under which
the corpse lies buried.

"The Black Cat" is also the story of a crime executed in secret and ultimately
discovered because of an oversight caused by panic and terror. Above all, "The
Black Cat" contains the narrator's comment on his inexplicable sadism toward
the cat he supposedly loves. Such behavior is attributable to "the spirit of PER-
VERSENESS. Of this spirit philosophy takes no account. Yet I am not more
sure that my soul lives, than I am that perverseness is one of the primitive impulses of the human heart—one of the indivisible primary faculties, or sentiments, which gives direction to the character of Man. Who has not, a hundred
times, found himself committing a vile or stupid action, for no other reason
than because he knows he should *not*? Have we not a perpetual inclination, in
the teeth of our best judgment, to violate that which is Law, merely because we
understand it to be such?"[3] This passage may surely be seen as one of the sources
leading to the philosophical-psychological dialectic of the first part of *Notes from
Underground.*

[3] E. A. Poe, "The Black Cat," in *Complete Works*, ed. James A. Harrison, 17 vols. (New York,
1902; rpt. 1965), 4: 146.

Yet, for all his admiration of Poe's talent, Dostoevsky does not consider him the equal of another "fantasist," E.T.A. Hoffmann, whom Dostoevsky had read as an adolescent with reverence. What gives Hoffmann the upper hand, he maintains, is that the supernatural and unearthly interpenetrate and fuse in his work with the commonplace and the verisimilar. Sometimes Hoffmann "even seeks his ideal outside the earthly, in some sort of extraordinary world that he accepts as superior, as if he himself believed in the existence of this mysterious enchanted world." Poe is inferior to Hoffmann as a "poet," since the German Romantic constantly infuses his work with aspiration toward "an ideal"—and in such aspiration Dostoevsky locates "the purity, and the real, true beauty inherent in man" (19: 88–89). Dostoevsky's own best post-Siberian creations attempt to strike a balance between the two writers, rivaling Poe for vividness and verisimilitude but never losing Hoffmann's sense of the unearthly and the transcendent as a controlling force in human life.

Dostoevsky thus tried to be both a writer like Poe and a poet like Hoffmann; for him these two aspects of literature should not ever be separated. Indeed, the necessity of keeping the two united was an issue very much on his mind precisely at this moment, and it was one that continued to preoccupy his thinking about art and life. For the most important function of art, he believed, was to inspire man by providing him with an ideal of transcendence toward which he could eternally aspire. This was the very position he asserted when, in the second number of *Time*, he launched his first open attack against the radical camp.

——————— ∎ ———————

At first sight, Dostoevsky's article, "Mr.—bov and the Question of Art," appears to be only a response to a recent article of Dobrolyubov devoted to the stories of the Ukrainian-Russian author Maria Markovich, who wrote under the pseudonym of Marco Vovchok. In reality, however, Dostoevsky's article contains the results of long meditations on the question of art that extend from the beginning of his literary career through his Siberian years.

During the mid-1840s, Dostoevsky had disagreed with Belinsky over the social function of art and had argued that the artist should be accorded absolute freedom. Several years later, exactly the position that Dostoevsky had rejected as a young writer was codified into an influential theory by Chernyshevsky in *The Aesthetic Relation of Art to Reality*. Artists, insisted the radical critic, had the obligation to subordinate their inspiration to "life," and "life" was defined essentially in terms of the immediate task of obtaining social justice. Chernyshevsky's ideas stirred up a huge controversy in Russian criticism, which then became stylized into an opposition between Gogol and Pushkin. The first was elevated by the radicals into an exemplar of what they wished literature to be, an accusation and exposé of the evils of Russian society; the second was celebrated by their opponents as the image of the serene Olympian dedicating his divine gifts to the "eternal" entanglements of the human condition. Both were praised and denounced with equal fervor and equal lack of discrimination, and Dobrolyubov particularly enjoyed heaping scorn on what he called Pushkin's "anthology-pieces" and "toy rattles."[4]

All this began during Dostoevsky's years in prison camp, but he caught up with the polemic once he emerged and began to read the periodicals. Indeed, since he then started to work on a series of essays titled *Letters on Art*, whose subject would have been "the significance of Christianity in art,"[5] there is evidence that he wished to add his own voice to the raging debate. This work, if ever written, has not survived; but some glimpse of its ideas may surely be obtained in the article "Mr.—bov and the Question of Art."

In line with the general policy of *Time*, Dostoevsky tries to dissociate his polemic from any invidious personal connotations, and he praises Dobrolyubov as being "almost the only one of our critics who is now being read" (18: 72). At the same time, Dostoevsky also tries to cover his flanks with a broadside against one of the bulwarks of the "Pushkinian" camp, the *Notes of the Fatherland*, and by defending the importance of Belinsky against a deprecating reference to the critic as not having given enough importance to the "historical" study of Russian literature. "In two pages of Belinsky," Dostoevsky retorts, ". . . more is said about the historical aspect of Russian literature than in all the pages of the *Notes of the Fatherland* from 1848 up to the present" (18: 71). No quarter is given to the critic of that journal, S. S. Dudyshkin, who might have been considered one of his allies against Dobrolyubov. Dostoevsky thus publicly aligns himself with the radicals, for whom Belinsky was an unsurpassable master, and establishes his credentials as a nonpartisan commentator who, even if picking a quarrel with Dobrolyubov, can hardly be considered to belong to the party of the enemy.

To begin, Dostoevsky sets the two extreme positions in confrontation with each other and demonstrates that both are self-contradictory. The partisans of the freedom of art, who do not tolerate constraints and directives, at the same time object to "accusatory" literature and its themes. As a result, they infringe the very principle of the freedom of art they presumably wish to defend. The radical Utilitarians demand that art be useful, but, since they are indifferent to artistic quality, they too find themselves in contradiction with their own leading principle: "A work without artistic value can never and in no way attain its goal; moreover, it does more harm than good to its cause; hence the Utilitarians, in neglecting artistic value, are the first to harm their own cause" (18: 79).

[4] *PSS*, 18: 280–281.
[5] *Pisma*, 1: 183–184; April 13, 1856.

Even though both poles are thus rejected as being internally inconsistent, it is obvious that Dostoevsky believes the mistake of the partisans of art to be only a venial sin, while that of the Utilitarians implies a denial of the very right of art to exist. It is true, Dostoevsky acknowledges, that Dobrolyubov does not specifically go to such lengths, but Chernyshevsky *had*, after all, compared art to school texts whose "purpose is to prepare the student for reading the original sources and later to serve as reference books from time to time."[6] And even if the Utilitarians do not openly reject art, they not only hold it in very low esteem but seem to resent artistic quality as such; if not, why do they "detest Pushkin, and label all his inspiration as affectations, grimaces, hocus-pocus and grace-notes, while his poems are considered trifles fit only for anthologies?" (18: 79).

As proof of the ultimate contempt of the Utilitarians for art, Dostoevsky singles out Dobrolyubov's praise of Marco Vovchok. Dostoevsky concentrates his fire on one of her stories, "Masha," which portrays the inner resistance of a young serf girl to her enslaved condition. For Dobrolyubov, this story illustrated the depth of the Russian common people's longing for freedom; it stood as a lesson for all those who believed that the Russian peasant was too undeveloped as an individual to harbor any desire for emancipation. In words that startlingly anticipate those Dostoevsky will soon use in *House of the Dead*, he writes: "the strength which lies in them [the Russian common people], finding no free and proper outlet, is compelled to force an unconventional way for itself . . . often in a way fatal to itself."[7]

The tendency of Marco Vovchok's work, Dostoevsky declares, is worthy of the highest praise, "and we are ready to rejoice in [her] activity" (18: 92). But it is one thing to approve of her intentions; it is quite another to overlook the glaring artistic deficiencies of her stories, which, in Dostoevsky's opinion, ruin whatever persuasive power the worthy ideas embodied in them might have exercised. To prove his point, Dostoevsky simply reprints the extracts from the story given by Dobrolyubov himself; he does not think it necessary to argue the case in detail, allowing the stilted sentiments and casebook reactions to speak for themselves. Masha, he comments, is "a tent-show heroine, some sort of bookish creature of the study, not a woman" (18: 90). And if Dobrolyubov thinks that reading "Masha" will cause supporters of serfdom to change their minds, then he is woefully mistaken. How can an author prove that a particular sentiment (for example, a hatred of serfdom) exists among the Russian common people when she lacks the artistic ability to portray characters who resemble Russians at all? The characters of "Masha" are "some sort of supernumeraries out of a ballet dressed up in Russian *caftans* and *sarafans*; they are *paysans* and *paysannes*, not

[6] N. G. Chernyshevsky, *Selected Philosophical Essays* (Moscow, 1953), 376.

[7] N. A. Dobrolyubov, *Selected Philosophical Essays*, trans. J. Fineberg (Moscow, 1956), 542.

Russian peasant men and women." Hence, Dostoevsky informs Dobrolyubov, "artistic form is in the highest degree useful, and useful precisely from *your* point of view" (18: 92–93). For the falsity of "Masha" will only persuade those who already hold a contemptuous opinion of the Russian peasant that, since no alternative image can be convincingly projected, the time-honored one they still cling to must be accurate.

———■———

If Dostoevsky had been concerned merely to indict the absurdities of both the partisans of art and the radical Utilitarians, and to establish his own independent position in this literary controversy, then he might have terminated his article after disposing of Marco Vovchok. But he was hunting for bigger game, and his real quarry was Chernyshevsky's Feuerbachian aesthetics, with its devaluation of the whole realm of the supernatural and the transcendent and its aim of exposing art as a substitute religion. No more than Chernyshevsky could he make his argument in any explicit form; but the drift of his words is unmistakable when placed in this context.

For Chernyshevsky, art was merely a deceptive alternative for the material satisfactions of real life and served as an imaginary surrogate just so long as these satisfactions are withheld. "If a man is obliged to live in the tundras of Siberia . . . ," Chernyshevsky had written, "he may dream of magic gardens with unearthly trees with coral branches, emerald leaves, and ruby fruit, but on transferring his residence to, say, the Kursk province, and being able to roam to his heart's content in a modest but tolerable orchard with apple, cherry, and pear trees. . . . The dreamer will forget not only about *The Arabian Nights* but also about the orange groves in Spain."[8] Dostoevsky, however, rejects the notion that art exists only as an imaginary replacement for the lacks of man's material needs. Man has other needs as well, and, Dostoevsky affirms, "art is for man just as much a need as eating or drinking. The need for beauty, and the creations embodying it, are inseparable from man, and without it man would perhaps have no wish to live. Man thirsts for [beauty] . . . and it is perhaps in this that lies the greatest mystery of artistic creation, that the image of beauty which emerges from its hands immediately becomes an idol *without any conditions*" (18: 94).

It is clear from his use of the word "idol" that Dostoevsky is touching on the relations of art and religion. The images of art have traditionally provided the objects of religious reverence because man has a need to worship something entirely transcending the bounds of human life as he knows it. Man has always displayed an unconditional need for beauty inseparable from his history; without it, as Dostoevsky poignantly suggests, he would perhaps not wish to go on living

[8] Chernyshevsky, *Essays*, 317–318.

at all. The creations of art thus immediately become "idols," objects of worship, "because the need for beauty develops most strongly when man is in disaccord with reality, in discordance, in struggle, that is *when he lives most fully*, for the moment at which man lives most fully is when he is seeking something, . . . it is then that he displays the most natural desire for everything that is harmonious and serene, and in beauty there is harmony and serenity" (18: 94). For Dostoevsky, as well as for Chernyshevsky, this quest is the result of a lack in the real world of human struggle and deprivation; but there can be no question for Dostoevsky of bridging the gap between the real and the ideal merely by material means. Since man "lives most fully" in Dostoevsky's universe only when he is in *disaccord* with reality, it is evident that the novelist's vision of what is ultimately important in human life totally differs from that of Chernyshevsky.

Indeed, the idea that man could ever attain total contentment with his life on earth is linked by Dostoevsky with images of the death of the spirit and of moral decadence. At such moments, Dostoevsky writes, "it is as if life slowed down, and we have even seen examples of how man, having attained the ideal of his desires, not knowing what to strive for any longer, satisfied to the gills, fell into some kind of melancholy, even provoking such melancholy in himself; how he sought for another ideal in his life, and, satiated beyond measure, not only failed to value what he enjoyed but even consciously diverged from the proper path, stimulating in himself tastes that were eccentric, unhealthy, stinging, discordant, sometimes monstrous, losing the feel for, and the aesthetic sense of, healthy beauty and demanding the exceptional in its stead." To adopt, as an ideal for mankind, the aim of the fullest material satisfaction is thus the equivalent of encouraging moral perversity and corruption. For this reason, a genuine "beauty" embodying the "eternal ideals" of mankind—ideals of harmony and serenity far transcending the human realm—is "an indispensable exigence of the human organism" (18: 94). Only such ideals, which man continually struggles to attain and to realize in his own existence, can prevent him from sinking into apathy and despair.

This conception of beauty as some form of transcendent expression of mankind's eternal ideals provides Dostoevsky with a vantage point from which to combat the narrow definition of "usefulness" in Utilitarian aesthetics. For if art is entrusted with the task of expressing mankind's eternal ideals, then to prescribe a particular role for it in terms of "utility" implies that one knows in advance the outcome of the entire historical destiny of the human race. But such knowledge, of course, is outside the human ken: "How, indeed, can one determine clearly and independently exactly what must be done to arrive at the ideal of all our desires, to achieve everything that humanity wishes and toward which it aspires?" Since we cannot do this, "how [can we] determine in full certainty what is harmful and useful"; indeed, we cannot even tell how, and in what degree, art has been "useful" to humanity in the past.

Who would have predicted, for example, that the works of two "old fogies" such as Corneille and Racine could play "a decisive and unexpected part in the circumstances of the historical life of a whole people" (that is, during the French Revolution) (18: 78)? The manifold ways in which art interacts with society are impossible to foresee; works that seem to have no direct social relevance at all may well, under certain circumstances, exercise the most powerful and direct influence on the life of action. But if we are not able to understand exactly how this comes about, "it is very possible that we also delude ourselves too when we strictly and imperatively dictate mankind's occupations and show art the normal path of its usefulness and its genuine mission." The Utilitarians wish to limit art to the social needs of the present, and regard any concern with the past—such as an admiration for *The Iliad*—as shameful escapism, a retreat into self-indulgent enjoyment and idle dilettantism. Dostoevsky recognizes the moral concern motivating such an erroneous position, and says that "this is why we feel so much sympathy for them [the radicals] and wish them to be respected" (18: 95–96).

In any case, since Russian culture has now become part of European civilization as a whole, it is only natural for Russian writers to draw freely on the common treasures of "the historical and universally human" (18: 99). Moreover, a contemporary writer can use the past to express the most burning issues of the present—a point Dostoevsky illustrates with a brilliant analysis of the poem "Diana," written by the bête noire of the radical critics, the lyricist A. A. Fet. This finely chiseled little work, quite Parnassian in feeling, describes a moment of disappointed expectation: the poet suddenly imagines that a statue of the goddess Diana will come to life and descend from her pedestal to walk through the streets of Rome. But, alas! "the motionless marble / whitely gleamed before me with unfathomable beauty" (18: 97).

Dostoevsky interprets the poem, especially these last two lines, as "a passionate appeal, a prayer before the perfection of past beauty, and a hidden inner nostalgia for that same perfection which the soul is seeking, but which it must long continue to seek, while long continuing to be tormented with birth-pangs before it is found" (18: 97). The "hidden inner nostalgia" that Dostoevsky discerns in this text is surely a longing for a new theogony, a new apparition of the sacred that would come to replace the beautiful, though lifeless, pagan idol; it is a longing for the birth of Christ, for the God-man who was indeed one day to walk on earth and supplant the immobile and distant Roman goddess. And since Dostoevsky has described his own time as one of "striving, struggle, uncertainty, and faith (because our time is a time of faith)," he interprets Fet's poem as expressing the most urgent of contemporary themes.[9]

[9] Dostoevsky's imaginative reading of this poem receives some indirect confirmation from the remarks of Roman Jakobson about the symbolic meaning attributed to sculpture in the Russian tradition. "It is important to see," he writes, "that in his poems [those of Pushkin] the statue is most

These reflections on art conclude with a single sentence that, Dostoevsky believes, resolves the conflict between the two entrenched misunderstandings, and which he prints as an independent paragraph in italics: "*Art is always actual and real; has never existed in any other way, and, most important, cannot exist in any other way*" (18: 98). This idea was first expressed in Russian criticism by Valerian Maikov, Dostoevsky's close friend in the 1840s; and he now reiterates it as the cornerstone of his own doctrine. If it sometimes seems that art deviates from reality and is not "useful," this is only because we do not yet know all the ways through which art serves mankind and because we are, even if for the most laudable reasons, too narrowly focused on the immediate and the common good. Of course, artists themselves sometimes stray from the proper path, and in such cases the efforts of Dobrolyubov and his brethren to call them to order are quite legitimate. But Dostoevsky makes a sharp distinction between criticism, admonition, exhortation, persuasion, and the issuance of what are in effect dictates and *ukazy* as to how artists should create.

All such efforts to regiment art are in any case doomed to futility; no true artist will obey them, and art will go its own way regardless of attempts to bridle its creative caprices. Such attempts are based on a total misunderstanding of the nature of art, which always has responded to, and has never separated itself from, the needs and interests of humankind. Dostoevsky thus defends the liberty of art not because he rejects the criterion of "utility," but precisely with the certainty that the freer art will be in its development, the more useful it will be to the interests of humanity" (18: 102). Once again he takes up a totally original position, arguing both for the liberty and the utility of art, but—most important of all—defining such "utility" in terms of man's eternal striving to incorporate within his life the inspiration of a supernatural religious ideal.

This crucial aspect of Dostoevsky's argument is of fundamental importance for an understanding of his own evolving view of life. It is significant, for example, that the instances of sane and healthy "beauty" he refers to—*The Iliad*, the

---

often called *idol*, something which had greatly surprised Tsar Nicholas I in *The Bronze Horseman.* Whether it is Pushkin the atheist, Blok the heretic, or the antireligious poetry of Mayakovsky, Russian poets had been raised in the world of Orthodox customs, and their work, whether intentionally or not, is steeped in *the symbolism of the Eastern Church.* It is the Orthodox tradition, which vehemently forbade sculpture, did not allow it inside churches, and considered it a pagan or diabolic sin (the two notions were the same for the Church), which suggested to Pushkin *the close link uniting statues and idolatry, diabolism and magic.*"

Jakobson then quotes Gogol to prove that, "from the Russian point of view, sculpture and the image of paganism" are inseparable. "It [sculpture] was born at the same time as the finite pagan world," Gogol had written, "it expressed [that world] and died at the same time. . . . It was, in the same degree as pagan belief, separated from Christianity by a frontier." Jakobson's article, originally published in Czech, is here quoted from the French translation of his selected criticism. Roman Jakobson, "La statue dans la symbolique de Pouchkine," in *Questions de poétique,* ed. Tzvetan Todorov, trans. by several hands (Paris, 1973), 186–187.

Apollo of Belvedere, the poem of Fet—all have religious connotations, if only pagan ones, and he even goes out of his way to stress this point. "This marble is a god," he says, speaking of the *Apollo*, "and spit at it as much as you like, you will not rob it of its divinity" (18: 78).[10] Even though Dostoevsky limits himself to examples from classical antiquity, this line of reasoning could easily culminate in an affirmation of the importance of "Christianity in art." Shortly after leaving prison camp in 1854, Dostoevsky had written that nothing in the world was "more beautiful" than the figure of Christ;[11] and it was this beauty that provided moral inspiration for the modern world, just as the gods of Greek and Roman mythology had done for antiquity. Perhaps for reasons of ideological strategy, he deliberately underplays this Christian aspect of his argument and takes refuge in the Greco-Roman past; but it was not from the religion of the Greeks and Romans that Dostoevsky expected any answer to the anguishing questions confronting both modern Russia and modern man.

———— ■ ————

What Dostoevsky says only by implication in this article is expressed openly in another essay written several months later, in which he offers a striking analysis of Pushkin's poem, "Egyptian Nights." The poem, one of his old favorites, describes Cleopatra offering to spend a night with any male who will agree to forfeit his life at dawn in return. Pushkin paints her challenge in voluptuous detail as she dwells on the delights awaiting the man who accepts her fatal invitation, and Katkov, that staunch pillar of the regime and the editor of *The Russian Messenger*, had spoken censoriously of the work as brazenly uncovering a secret that "should never see the light of day" (19: 134). Dostoevsky undertakes to enlighten Katkov as to the real significance of the poem, and one has the distinct impression that this reading is another fragment of his lost treatise on the role of Christianity in art.

Far from being immoral, Dostoevsky interprets the poem as an expression of "frightful terror . . . the illustration of a perversion of human nature reaching such a degree of horror . . . that the impression left by it is no longer scabrous but frightening." The poem vividly embodies the moral-psychic disorder induced by satiation—by the absence of any spiritual ideal. Cleopatra's world is one in which "all faith has been lost," and since "the future offers nothing . . . life must be nourished only by what exists" (19: 135–136). This is manifestly the universe as Chernyshevsky would have wished it to be, existence shorn of the splendors of the imaginary transcendent.

[10] Dostoevsky is here paraphrasing a famous poem of Pushkin, "The Poet and the Crowd," in which the poet scornfully tells the benighted mob, "The Apollo Belvedere is for you an idol. / In him no usefulness—usefulness—do you discern." *PSS*, 18: 289.

[11] *Pisma*, 1: 142; February 20, 1854.

Cleopatra is "the representative of this type of society," and the poet depicts her in a moment of boredom when only a "violent sensation" can relieve her tedium. She has already exhausted all the byways of eroticism; now something extra is needed, and what stirs in her soul is "a fierce and ferocious" irony—spiced with the dreadful joy of anticipation as she mingles sensuality with the cruelty of an executioner. Never had she known anything so savagely exciting, and her soul gloats with the repulsive delight of the female spider "who, it is said, devours the male at the instant of sexual union." "You understand much more clearly now," Dostoevsky explains to his readers, "what sort of people it was to which our divine redeemer descended. And you understand much more clearly the meaning of the word: redeemer" (19: 136–137).

If we transpose this remarkable reading from the classical past to mid-nineteenth-century Russia, we immediately obtain the outlines of much of Dostoevsky's own world, with some of his major themes and his entire psychology of decadence. Indeed, in the novel he was then writing, *The Insulted and Injured*, Dostoevsky was in the course of making this transposition himself. His villain, Prince Valkovsky, is the first Russian embodiment of the psychology of the Cleopatra type, which will reappear in such figures as Svidrigailov, Stavrogin, and the elder Karamazov (who says of himself, "I've got quite the countenance of an ancient Roman patrician of the decadent period") (14: 22). It is no accident that, three years later, Cleopatra turns up in *Notes from Underground* sticking gold pins into her slave girls for amusement.

The late Greco-Roman world had just then taken on a symbolic contemporary meaning as a result of the ongoing social-cultural debate. All through the 1850s, Herzen had compared the state of Western Europe after 1848 with that of Rome in its decline, and he spoke of Europe's revitalization by the impending Russian social revolution as parallel to the moral rejuvenation provided for the ancient world by the arrival of Christianity. Dostoevsky and Herzen thus shared much the same historical-philosophical vision of a declining European civilization destined to be redeemed by Russian Christianity. But while Herzen was simply using a historical analogy, Dostoevsky accepted this historical imagery as containing a literal truth. The loss of a religious ideal in the West had turned Europe into a society similar to that of Rome in its decadence, where various forms of moral disorder and perverted sensuality pullulated uncontrollably, and the Western ideas now being propagated by the radicals, Dostoevsky believed, would have exactly the same effect in Russia.

Despite the attack on Dobrolyubov and the efforts of Strakhov and Grigorev, *Time* generally managed to preserve its progressive reputation during the first year of publication. *Time* highlighted the plight of the proletariat in Europe and strongly defended Engels's *Condition of the Working Class in England*, with its terrible pictures of proletarian misery, against the criticisms of the German economist Bruno Hildebrand. In one of the earliest references to Engels's work in the Russian press, the writer of the *Time* article calls him "the most gifted and learned of all German Socialists," and Socialism as an economic theory (euphemistically called "association") was unambiguously championed in *Time* against laissez-faire doctrines. Proudhon, known to be close to Herzen, was always referred to with great respect.[12]

Dostoevsky's "progressivism," with all its hesitations and reservations, was in evidence in the many subjects hotly disputed between him and the powerful Katkov, a bitter enemy of the radicals, whose journal *The Russian Messenger* then proceeded to pillory *Time* and its collaborators all through 1861. *The Russian Messenger* at this period was the organ of a moderate liberalism within the Russian social-political spectrum. Katkov greatly admired Tocqueville, praised the English political system as a model, and supported laissez-faire economics in the name of individual freedom. Whatever Dostoevsky's reservations about *The Contemporary*, his instinctive democratic Populism made him far more hostile to Katkov's advocacy of Western bourgeois liberalism than to the Socialism of the radicals, who at least were defenders of the Russian commune, along with the Slavophils. Even though Dostoevsky, as a supporter of the regime, was a political ally of Katkov, his social sympathies were much closer to those of Chernyshevsky. The social-economic articles of *Time* thus resembled those in *The Contemporary* far more than they did those in Katkov's journal. The powerful editor of *The Russian Messenger* tended to look with supreme disdain at a Russian culture in which the stupidities of *The Contemporary* could gain so wide a following, and his disabused reflections about the so-called achievements of Russian culture and the wonders of Russian nationality stirred Dostoevsky to a fighting fury.

Even while springing to the defense of the radicals, Dostoevsky always does so from his own position and never conceals his disagreement with their theories. But he also never loses sight, at least at this stage of his career, of what he believed to be the purity of their dominating aim of bettering the lot of the downtrodden Russian peasant. Dostoevsky could not endure seeing the radicals maligned by those who, like Katkov, had never shared their passionate revulsion against injustice and yet now read them lessons in morality. "We see there," Dostoevsky tells Katkov, "suffering and torments without relief. . . . In the painful search for a way out, [such a person] stumbles, falls. . . . But why blacken them with the epithet of dishonest?" (19: 173). In Dostoevsky's refusal to accept

---

[12] For more information on these matters, see V. S. Nechaeva, *Zhurnal M. M. i F. M. Dostoevskikh*, Vremya, *1861–1863* (Moscow, 1973), 155–210, esp. 183, 188.

such insults, we can already catch a glimpse of how he will treat some of his erring characters misled by radical ideologies.

The Russian Messenger was not the only nonradical journal with which Dostoevsky exchanged potshots during 1861. A favorite target for his ire was *Notes of the Fatherland*, whose literary critic, S. S. Dudyshkin, had had the temerity to declare that Pushkin was not really a "national" poet. For Dostoevsky, such an opinion was equivalent to sacrilege, and he set out to destroy it in a slashing article that contains a brilliant reading of *Evgeny Onegin*. Dostoevsky interprets Pushkin much as Grigoryev was just then doing in an important series of articles published by *Time* on the development of the idea of nationality in Russian literature. Pushkin incarnated the moment when Russian culture, having assimilated Europeanism through every pore, became conscious that it could never be truly European and was confronted with the problem of its historical destiny. "This was the first beginning of the epoch," Dostoevsky writes, "when our leading people brutally separated into two parties, then entered into a furious civil war. For the Slavophils and Westernizers are also a historical phenomenon and in the highest degree national" (19: 10). This vision of the history of Russian culture would later furnish the novelist with part of the social-cultural ground plan of *Demons*, in which Stavrogin, a reincarnation of the Onegin type, inspires both Slavophil (Shatov) and Westernizer (Kirillov) ideological offshoots.

Indeed, some traits of Stavrogin begin to emerge as Dostoevsky transforms Grigoryev's sweeping panorama—the history of the coming-to-consciousness of the Russian national psyche—into a complex drama of inner self-discovery. "Onegin's skepticism carries something tragic in its very principle," he writes, "and sometimes sounds with a ferocious irony." He is caught, like Matthew Arnold's traveler in "Stanzas from the Grande Chartreuse," "Wandering between two worlds, one dead, / The other powerless to be born, / With nowhere yet to rest [his] head,"[13] in search of a new ideal to replace the old European one in which, like the entire highly civilized society to which he belongs, "he is no longer able fully to believe" (19: 11).

Onegin's existential anguish, writes Dostoevsky, is composed of both "bitter irony" and a total lack of self-respect because "his conscience murmurs to him that he is a hollow man," and yet he knows that he is not: "is one hollow when one can suffer?" (19: 11). He represents "an entire epoch which *for the first time* looks at itself." This Onegin type, becoming part of the consciousness of Russian society, has been reborn and reelaborated in each new generation: "In the personage of Pechorin [the protagonist of Lermontov's *A Hero of Our Time*] it reached a state of insatiable, bilious malice, and of a strange contrast, in the highest degree original and Russian, of a contradiction between two heteroge-

---

[13] Matthew Arnold, *Poems* (London, 1888), 214.

neous elements: an egoism extending to self-adoration, and at the same time a malicious self-contempt" (19: 12).

Dostoevsky sees "the jeering mask of Gogol" as revealing the same dilemma, and implies that Gogol "allowed himself to die, powerless to create and precisely to determine an ideal at which he would not be able to laugh." The final stage of the process is found in Turgenev's Rudin and the Hamlet of the Shchigrovsky District, who "no longer laugh at their own activity and their own convictions: they believe, and are saved by this faith." Both figures, in other words, are inspired by the humanitarian ideals of the 1840s, particularly by a deep compassion for the people, and hence have been rescued from despair: "they are almost no longer egoists" (19: 12). In this impassioned sketch of the history of the superfluous man in Russian literature, the intricacies of Dostoevskian psychology begin to merge with the course of Russian social-cultural development, and the conquest of egoism and the search for faith and an ideal become identified with a rediscovery of the values of the Russian common people.

Indeed, as we shall soon see, these very ideas were being presented to an avid reading public in regular installments of *The Insulted and Injured*. The treacherous Prince Valkovsky claims that moral obligations are a sham because, "What isn't nonsense is personality—myself. . . . I only recognize obligations when I see I have something to gain by them. . . . [W]hat can I do if I know for a fact that at the root of all human virtue lies the completest egoism. And the more virtuous anything is, the more egoism there is in it. Love yourself, that's the one rule I recognize" (3: 365). Valkovsky is Dostoevsky's first artistic reaction to the radical doctrines of the 1860s.[14] For Dostoevsky uses Valkovsky to follow out the logic of Chernyshevsky's position of "rational egoism" to the end—without accepting the proviso that egoism would miraculously convert itself into beneficence through rational calculation.

———■———

During 1861, Dostoevsky made a clean polemical sweep of the existing social-political ideologies in Russia. Not only did he take on the radical left (*The Contemporary*), the liberal left (*Notes of the Fatherland*), and the liberal center (*The Russian Messenger*), but he also had his word to say about the new Slavophil publication *Day* (*Den'*). Despite his efforts at nonpartisan commentary, however,

---

[14] In her preface to an edition of *The Insulted and Injured*, L. M. Rosenblyum remarks: "Although, in the uncovering of Valkovsky's views, no direct association is visible with the materialism of [the generation of] the 1860s, one may, all the same, assume that they contain, of course in a covert form, an onslaught against Chernyshevsky's *The Anthropological Principle in Philosophy*—the work in which the ethical principles of the radical democrats are set forth. *The Anthropological Principle* was published a year before *The Insulted and Injured*." See F. M. Dostoevsky, *Unizhennye i oskorblennye*, ed. L. M. Rosenblyum (Moscow, 1955), 25; *PSS*, 3: 527–528.

Time acquired the reputation, during its first year, of belonging to the camp of *The Contemporary*, and Strakhov and Grigoryev were chafing at the bit.

Doing what he could to right the balance, Strakhov kept up a steady sniping fire against the radicals in articles written as letters addressed to the editor. Shrewd in spotting significant social-political trends, in June 1861 he singles out the explosive début of a new young radical publicist, Dimitry Pisarev, who had excitedly announced in *The Russian Word* that all the philosophy of the past was just "useless scholasticism." Strakhov comments that "Pisarev has gone further than all" his fellow radicals on the path of negation: "He rejects everything . . . in the name of life, and life he obviously understands as the alluring variety of lively and unlimited pleasures."[15] In this acute observation, Strakhov picks out an important turn of radical ideology toward an unrestrained individualism that, in the very next year, would lead to a schism among the radical intelligentsia of decisive importance for Russian culture in the 1860s.

Dostoevsky regularly appended footnotes to articles to dissociate himself from Strakhov's condemnation of radicals. What he reproached the radicals for, more openly in his notebooks than in public print, was their hastiness and impatience, their desire to leap over history and to bring about changes that could be realized only at a much later stage of Russian social development. "Where are you hurrying?" he asks Chernyshevsky in one note. "Our society is positively not ready for anything. The questions stand before us. They have ripened, they are ready, but our society is not ready in the least. It is disunited" (20: 153). Dostoevsky's tolerance for the radicals was already beginning to stretch a bit thin, and it snapped the following year, when the contributors and readers of *The Contemporary* turned from intellectual disaffection to active political agitation.

The basis for all further progress in Russia, as Dostoevsky saw it, was to work peacefully in favor of the advances made possible by the liberation of the serfs and the further impending reforms that Alexander II had announced. *Time* printed the full text of the manifesto announcing the liberation and referred to it as a "sublime event" initiating a glorious new phase of Russian history. *The Contemporary*, on the other hand, let the occasion pass without uttering a single word: the radicals had been bitterly disappointed by the terms of the liberation, which they considered imposed too great a tax burden on the peasantry in favor of the idle and undeserving landowners.

[15] Nikolay Strakhov, *Iz istorii literaturnago nigilizma* (St. Petersburg, 1890; rpt. The Hague, 1967), 34.

CHAPTER 23

The Insulted and Injured

Dostoevsky's novel *The Insulted and Injured* (*Unizhennye i oskorblennye*), began to appear as a serial in the first issue of *Time* and ran through seven numbers of the journal. The work encountered a mixed critical reception, but it was read with avid attention and achieved its purpose of making readers impatient for the next installment. Dobrolyubov devoted his very last essay, "Downtrodden People" (*Zabitye lyudi*), a classic of Russian criticism, to a penetrating survey of the entire corpus of Dostoevsky's writings up to and including this latest product of his pen. In an obvious reply to Dostoevsky's attack some months earlier, he remarked that the book was "beneath aesthetic criticism," but, he acknowledged, everyone had been reading what stood out as the most interesting Russian novel published in 1861.[1]

Our contemporary view of Dostoevsky can hardly be that of Dobrolyubov, but there is no reason to disagree with his verdict: *The Insulted and Injured* is by far the weakest of Dostoevsky's six major post-Siberian novels. Nor did Dostoevsky himself have any illusions about the quality of his own creation. "I recognize fully," he publicly admitted several years later, "that in my novel there are many characters who are puppets and not human beings, perambulating books and not characters who have taken on artistic form (this really requires time and a gestation of ideas in the mind and the soul)" (20: 134). Whatever its manifest flaws, however, *The Insulted and Injured* allows us to catch the author in a stage of transition, trying his hand for the first time at mastering the technique of the roman-feuilleton and also giving new character-types, themes, and motifs their initial, inchoate expression.

———■———

The Insulted and Injured is composed of two interweaving plot lines, which at first seem to have little to do with each other but then gradually draw together as the story unfolds. The first, typical of the sentimental Romantic novel, concerns an impoverished gentry family, the Ikhmenyevs. Their daughter, Natasha, falls in love with Alyosha, the son of a wealthy neighbor, Prince Valkovsky; and

[1] A. A. Belkin, ed., *F. M. Dostoevsky v Russkoi kritike* (Moscow, 1956), 42.

when the prince frowns on their romance because he has destined Alyosha for a wealthy heiress, the two young people run away and live together out of wedlock. As a result, Natasha is renounced by her outraged father, Nikolay Sergeevich Ikhmenyev, not only for having disgraced the family escutcheon but also because Prince Valkovsky, once a friend and supposed benefactor, has now become his deadly enemy. The crux of this plot line is the mutual unhappiness of Natasha and her father, who love each other deeply despite her lethal blow to the family pride and his furious condemnation of her scandalous behavior.

The second plot line introduces the roman-feuilleton Gothic element of mystery, secret intrigue, and venal betrayal. It focuses on the figure of little Nellie, a thirteen-year-old Petersburg waif, whom the narrator, a young novelist named Ivan Petrovich—a foster-son of the Ikhmenyevs, and once engaged to to Natasha—meets by chance. Intrigued by the eccentric appearance of an old man in a coffeehouse, the young observer of life follows him into the street and, when the oldster collapses and dies on the spot, moves into his dingy room. The deceased man was the grandfather of little Nellie, who comes to visit him and finds Ivan Petrovich occupying his quarters. Little Nellie is rescued from the clutches of a procuress by her new acquaintance and his friend Masloboev, an ex-schoolteacher leading a shady existence on the edge of the Petersburg underworld but still retaining some traces of the moral idealism of his youth. Ivan Petrovich takes Nellie in to live with him, looks after her welfare, and gradually pieces together the pathetic story of her appalling existence.

By a coincidence typical of the roman-feuilleton, she turns out to be—as we learn at the very end of the book—the prince's abandoned daughter. Valkovsky had seduced her mother, persuaded his infatuated young wife to rob her wealthy father, Jeremy Smith, and then had discarded her and their child once he had obtained possession of the money. The two plots finally come together when, in order to reconcile Natasha with *her* father, and at the prompting of Ivan Petrovich, Nellie tells the heart-rending story of her life. Painting in dismal colors the refusal of her grandfather to forgive her mother even as she lay destitute and dying on the floor of a dank Petersburg hovel, Nellie's piteous tale brings about the forgiveness of Natasha and defeats the plan of the villainous Valkovsky to throw the unprotected girl into the arms of the lecherous old Count Nainsky.

All the events are seen through the eyes of Ivan Petrovich, who is an obvious physical link between the two plots, just as Valkovsky is a more covert one. Ivan Petrovich is writing about a year after the events have taken place, and an additional element of pathos is provided by the situation in which he finds himself as he takes pen in hand to tell his story. "It has all ended in my being here in the hospital," he explains, "and I believe I am soon going to die. . . . I want to write it all down, and if I had not found this occupation I believe I should have died of misery" (3: 177). The tale recounts the shipwreck of his own life, and he is about to perish with a sense of waste and despair. But he has nonetheless succeeded in rescuing others (the Ikhmenyevs), in surrounding the last days of Nellie with loving tenderness, and in remaining true to himself and the values of kindness and compassion in which he believes.

This brief sketch of the cumbrous intrigue shows Dostoevsky making use of the tritest material—the wrath of a loving but angry and heartbroken father against an erring daughter; a rich, powerful aristocrat, cynical and corrupt to the core, who wreaks his will on the innocent and pure-hearted; a virtuous young man (the narrator) in love with the heroine and ready to sacrifice himself unstintingly on her behalf; and a poor waif exposed to the unspeakable evils of the Petersburg underworld, snatched from perdition by a generous rescuer, and who carries the secret of Valkovsky's scandalous past. All these motifs are the most threadbare ingredients of the roman-feuilleton, and Dostoevsky exploits them unashamedly for their maximum capacity to pluck at the heartstrings.

Here, for example, is part of a passage about Nellie's mother, inserted at the conclusion of Part II to whet the appetite for what lies ahead: "It is the story of a woman driven to despair, wandering through the cold, filthy streets of St. Petersburg, begging alms with the little girl whom she regarded as a baby. . . . It was a gloomy story, one of those gloomy and distressing dramas which are so often played out unseen, almost mysterious, under the lowering sky of Petersburg, in the dark corners of the vast town, in the midst of the giddy ferment of life, of dull egoism, of clashing interests, of gloomy vice and secret crimes, in the lowest hell of senseless and abnormal life . . ." (3: 299–300). Dostoevsky thickens the atmosphere with as heavy a hand and as murky a palette as Eugène Sue or Frédéric Soulié, and his overwrought sentimentality of tone conveys much of what provoked the contemptuous references of its first critics to the book's lack of artistic quality.

Even though Dostoevsky had never before used the ingredients and technique of the roman-feuilleton, this type of novel had long been identified with the propagation of "progressive" and Socialist ideas (*Les mystères de Paris* had dramatized a number of Fourierist notions). Dostoevsky's use of the form was thus considered by the critics as perfectly congruent with his subversive past and, even more, as indicating a reinforcement of the social humanitarian principles for which he had suffered hard labor and exile. This was the opinion of Dobrolyubov, who saw no marked difference between the Dostoevsky of the past and the present, and even attacked the novelist precisely for this reason. Dostoevsky, the critic pointed out, continued to depict "weak" characters unable to assert themselves, and while these are not superfluous men, Dobrolyubov nevertheless chides him, as both he and Chernyshevsky had done in the case of

Turgenev, for failing to realize that Russian life has entered a new phase in which literature is called upon to depict protagonists with more strength of will.[2]

This impression of continuity with Dostoevsky's early work was augmented by the repeated evocation of *Poor Folk* throughout the new text. In one scene, Dostoevsky describes the proud young author Ivan Petrovich, his first novel hot off the press, reading it aloud to his admiring foster family, the Ikhmenyevs. Natasha is moved to tears: "all at once she snatched my hand, kissed it, and ran out of the room" (3: 189). *Poor Folk* is used throughout as a touchstone of moral sensibility; all the "good" characters respond to it in an appropriately compassionate fashion, and even the disreputable and hard-drinking Masloboev confesses that "when I read it, I almost became a respectable man again" (3: 265). The scoundrelly Prince Valkovsky reacts with an outburst of scorn at the literary mode of which it was a product and whose inspiration had been revived and intensified in the more recent "accusatory" literature. "Poverty is all the fashion with you now," he says contemptuously to Ivan Petrovich, and he admonishes the young writer, for the benefit of his career, to move in "higher" circles.

Prince Valkovsky is so stagey and melodramatic an aristocratic villain that it is difficult for us now to take him at all seriously, but our reaction is not that of Dostoevsky's initial readers, who considered the prince a plausible and familiar social type. Even as severe a judge as the novelist Evgenia Tur, who declared bluntly that *The Insulted and Injured* "could not sustain the slightest criticism as art,"[3] wrote, without blinking an eyelash, that "everyone having some acquaintance with the world has met many such people, but happily, that is, happily for our society, such people as Prince Ivan [Valkovsky] are dying out year by year and are no longer being born."[4] Dostoevsky's portrayal of the prince was accepted as a searing exposé of the depravity of an entire social class. Moreover, the author's "sympathy with the weak and the oppressed" was clearly indicated—just as it had been during the 1840s—by the presentation of his humble folk as infinitely superior to the prince from a moral point of view and, indeed, as the living refutation of his witheringly contemptuous view of his fellow humans.

For a Russian reader of the time, accustomed to regard "weak" characters as doomed to inevitable defeat by the very excess of their moral merits, the prince was a thoroughly unmitigated scoundrel, while the battered but unblemished Ikhmenyevs—not to mention the all-suffering Ivan Petrovich—were exemplars of sterling worth and integrity. No power at the prince's command could shatter the indestructible bonds of their love and devotion to each other, as becomes

[2] I. I. Zamotin, *Dostoevsky v Russkoi kritike, 1848–1881* (Warsaw, 1913), 36–37.
[3] Cited in *PSS*, 3: 529.
[4] Belkin, *Dostoevsky v Russkoi kritike*, 94–95.

clear in Ikhmenyev's ecstatic but badly overstrained declaration terminating the climactic reconciliation scene:

> Oh Lord, I thank Thee for all, for all, for Thy wrath and for Thy mercy! . . . And for Thy sun which is shining upon us again after the storm! . . . Oh, we may be insulted and injured, but we're together again, and now the proud and haughty who have insulted and injured us may triumph! Let them throw stones at us! Have no fear, Natasha. . . . We will go hand in hand and I will say to them, "This is my darling, this is my beloved daughter, my innocent daughter whom you have insulted and injured, but whom I love and bless for ever and ever." (3: 422)

Without the benefit of hindsight, it was impossible for Dostoevsky's readers to see the future novelist germinating amid the clichés of *The Insulted and Injured*. One or two critics were uneasily aware of something "new" in the book; but this awareness took the form of negative criticism. One critic objected to the title because it had led him to expect a genuine social novel. In fact, as he rightly points out, the characters behave in such a bizarre fashion that most of their difficulties are caused by their own folly. The intrigues of Prince Valkovsky play only an accessory part in their dilemmas, and Dostoevsky handles his characters so as continually to *undercut* the supposed social humanitarian significance of the book. What determines their fate are the traits of their own personalities, not the external mechanism of the roman-feuilleton plot. Within the social humanitarian thematic of his hackneyed plot, Dostoevsky was perceptibly beginning to grope his way toward his later novel-tragedy of ideas. What we can glimpse in *The Insulted and Injured*, through the interstices of the clichés, is a premature novel about a young writer named Ivan Petrovich (the narrator and Dostoevsky's alter ego) who represents the "philanthropic" ideology of the 1840s, and whose world and life are shattered because his convictions prove inadequate to cope with the deeper forces of human passion and egoism that overwhelm his well-meaning innocence and Romantic idealism.

This theme of innocence and its self-deceptions is struck early by some semi-ironic remarks about Ikhmenyev, whose relation to Valkovsky derives from a warm-hearted self-delusion analogous to that of the unselfish Colonel Rostanev toward the malevolent Foma Fomich in *The Village of Stepanchikovo*. Ikhmenyev refuses to believe any of the discreditable rumors circulating about the prince and declares that "he was incapable of a mean action" (3: 182). Ikhmenyev prefers to live in a world where moral imperfection does not exist, and he takes much the same attitude toward his daughter Natasha, whom he steadfastly continues to regard as an angelic child even though she has reached marriageable age. Another example of such "naïve Romanticism," less instinctive and more literary in character, is found in Nellie's mother, who ran off with Valkovsky because "from the very beginning she dreamed of something like a heaven upon earth, of angels; her love was boundless, her faith limitless, and, I am convinced, she went mad not because he ceased to love her and threw her over, but because she had been deceived by him, *he was capable of deceiving* and had thrown her over, because her angel had turned into dirt, had spat on and humiliated her" (3: 437).

When, as invariably occurs, Romantics of this type are betrayed by life, their response is to fall back on outraged pride, regardless of the suffering this may cause to those they presumably love the most. Just as Ikhmenyev execrates his beloved daughter when she publicly dishonors his name by becoming the mistress of Valkovsky's son, so Nellie's mother condemns her daughter to a life of terrible misery and torment because "in her horror and, above all, her pride, she drew back from him [Valkovsky] with infinite contempt" (3: 438) and refused to use the documents in her possession proving their marriage. The proud and hence egoistic reaction of such frustrated Romantics leads to a masochistic intensification of their own misery and a certain sadism with regard to others (Natasha, Nellie). In the case of Ikhmenyev, this inner conflict is finally overcome by a movement of love that vanquishes pride and conquers the rankling resentment created by betrayal. It also involves the acceptance of a world where good and evil are inextricably intermingled, and where "the shattering of idealism" (to use K. Mochulsky's apt phrase)[5] is an unavoidable and even salutary precondition for forgiveness and reconciliation.

Much the same conflict occurs in the Natasha-Alyosha relationship, even though Natasha is not specifically a Romantic. She is described as having "that characteristic of good-natured people, perhaps inherited from her father—the habit of thinking highly of people, of persistently thinking them better than they really are, warmly exaggerating everything good in them" (3: 270). What she feels for Alyosha, however, destroys her "innocence" and reveals aspects of her character that bewilder and frighten her by their unexpected complexity.

Natasha is very far from being the innocent victim of a typical aristocratic seducer; on the contrary, it is she who forces the issue and decides to live openly with her lover. Indeed, her passion for the weak-willed, frivolous, and inconstant Alyosha has reached such a pitch that she is willing to submit to any degradation so as to cling to him and "to be his slave, his willing slave" (3: 200). But she is fully aware that her infatuation is "abject" and abnormal, springing more from a desire for domination than from a genuine love between equals. It is her pride that has been wounded by Alyosha's philandering, and her pride impels

---

[5] K. Mochulsky, *Dostoevsky: His Life and Work*, trans. Michael A. Minihan (Princeton, NJ, 1967), 210.

her not only to humiliate her father but also to plunge herself into an abyss of masochistic abasement and self-torment. Once again her conflict is resolved as the result of a successful inner struggle: Natasha conquers her egoism and regains her self-respect by voluntarily surrendering Alyosha to her far more suitable rival, the young heiress Katya.

In the case of little Nellie, Dostoevsky brings this type of moral-psychological conflict, with its characteristic swing from wounded sensibility to masochistic self-laceration and sadism, into its sharpest focus. Among all the "insulted and injured," Nellie has the most right to claim such a designation, and she has acquired a savage pride and a mistrust of humanity initially encouraged by her mother's fierce intransigence. Nellie's personality thus combines a youthful need for affection and love with suspicion and hatred, and she refuses at first to respond even to generosity or kindness. Dostoevsky's depiction of her shifting moods, and of the gradual softening and taming of her spirit, are among the best sections of the book. The self-tormenting depths of Nellie's psychology are brought out in one crucial scene, when all the embittered memories of her past have surged back in a flood and she rushes out of Ivan Petrovich's sheltering room to beg in the streets as a gesture of defiance. Tears come to Ivan Petrovich's eyes when he chances upon her:

> Yes, tears for poor Nellie . . . she was not begging through need; she was not forsaken, not abandoned by someone to the caprice of destiny. She was not escaping from cruel oppressors, but from friends who loved and cherished her . . . she had been ill-treated; her hurt could not be healed, and she seemed purposely trying to aggravate her wound by this mysterious behavior, this mistrustfulness of us all; as though she enjoyed her own pain, by this *egoism of suffering*, if I may so express it. This aggravation of suffering and this reveling in it I could understand; it is the enjoyment of many of the insulted and injured, oppressed by destiny and smarting under the sense of injustice. (3: 385–386)

It is Dostoevsky himself who italicizes the phrase "egoism of suffering," highlighting its importance because it contains the internal thematic link uniting three main centers of action: Natasha–Ikhmenyev, Natasha–Alyosha–Katya, Nellie–Ivan Petrovich. In each case, one or more of the characters respond in this fashion to some indignity or humiliation; in each the conflict is resolved when, in an act of outgoing love, the egoism of suffering is overcome.

——■——

Even though Dostoevsky had not yet decisively abandoned his old philanthropic ideals and values in *The Insulted and Injured*, there are still definite indications that he was continuing that revision of his past already initiated in *Petersburg*

Visions. Such a revision is the explicit purpose of the finest scene in the book, in which Dostoevsky underscores the ineffectuality of Ivan Petrovich when openly challenged by the treacherously villainous Prince Valkovsky. This scene, for the first time, allows us to catch a glimpse of the great Dostoevsky to come. Elevating the theme of egoism to its full metaphysical dimension, Dostoevsky here momentarily lifts his soap opera plot to a new height of dignity by covertly fusing the theme of egoism with that of radical ideology, at last striking the vein that will soon provide him with a new source of inspiration.

Valkovsky's long and gloating "confession" to Ivan Petrovich amply confirms the earlier suggestions that he is a shameless libertine; not only does he harbor a taste for the usual forms of vice, but he particularly enjoys the self-conscious desecration of the moral norms of society. Valkovsky unmasks himself for the sheer pleasure of shocking his idealistic young interlocutor, and he compares his pleasure in doing so to that of a sexual pervert exhibiting himself in public (manifestly referring to Rousseau's *Confessions*). Much of this self-exposure, of course, was calculated to discredit Valkovsky in the eyes of the reader, but it also functions to disclose some of the "irrational" depths of personality equally exhibited in the behavior of the other characters. Nothing gives Valkovsky more delight, he explains, than deliberately to provoke "some ever-young Schiller," first by pretending to take seriously "all those vulgar and worthless naïvetés and idyllic nonsense," and then "suddenly distorting my ecstatic countenance into a grimace, putting out my tongue at him when he is least of all expecting such a surprise" (3: 360).

Valkovsky, as we see, thus criticizes Ivan Petrovich in much the same terms as the young author himself uses for Ikhmenyev and Nellie's mother. The actual creator of *Poor Folk* is now placing his previous artistic self, and the values inspiring his early work, among the manifestations of that "naïve Romanticism" whose shortcomings his new novel sets out to expose. And this debunking of Ivan Petrovich becomes even more pointed when Prince Valkovsky displays his familiarity with the idea-feelings of his interlocutor. For it turns out that the Prince is not simply an inveterate blackguard but is himself a disillusioned idealist who "ages ago, in the golden days of my youth," as he sardonically explains, once too had had "a fancy to become a metaphysician and philanthropist, and came round almost to the same idea as you." He too had "wanted to be a benefactor of humanity, to found a philanthropic society," and had even constructed a model hospital on his estate. But boredom had finally got the better of him—boredom, and a sense of the ultimate futility of existence. "We shall die—and what comes then!" he exclaims; and "well, so I took to dangling after the girls." Alas, the protesting husband of "one little shepherdess" was flogged so badly that he died in the model hospital (3: 361).

Face-to-face with metaphysical ennui and the ineluctability of extinction,

Prince Valkovsky discovers that the "pleasures" of philanthropy are hardly powerful enough to compensate for the vacuity of existence, and, like Cleopatra, he begins to search for stronger stimulants. Besides, the ideology of social humanitarianism was now terribly out of date, and what had replaced it, Valkovsky appreciatively informs Ivan Petrovich, comes very pat to the prince's purposes. On being reproached for his "beastliness" by the indignant narrator, the Prince retorts that all such estimable remonstrances are "nonsense." Moral obligations are a sham because, "What isn't nonsense is personality—myself." For his own part, he proclaims, "I . . . have long since freed myself from all shackles, and even moral obligations. I only recognize obligations when I see I have something to gain by them. . . . You long for the ideal, for virtue. Well, my dear fellow, I am ready to admit anything you tell me to, but what can I do if I know for a fact that at the root of all human virtue lies the completest egoism. And the more virtuous anything is, the more egoism there is in it. Love yourself, that's the one rule I recognize" (3: 365).

By asserting a doctrine of absolute egoism against Ivan Petrovich's "philanthropic" self-abnegation, Valkovsky thus objectifies and justifies, as a sinister philosophy of evil, the very same drives and impulses against which the "good" characters have been carrying on a moral struggle. Dostoevsky is parodying Chernyshevsky's "rational egoism," and Valkovsky is Dostoevsky's first artistic reaction to the radical doctrines of the 1860s. For Dostoevsky uses Valkovsky to follow out the logic of Chernyshevsky's position to the end—without accepting the proviso that reason and self-interest would ultimately coincide, and that egoism would miraculously convert itself into beneficence through rational calculation. Dostoevsky remembered the irrational frenzies of frustrated egoism that he had witnessed in the prison camp, and he had read Choderlos de Laclos and the Marquis de Sade. Like them, he was persuaded that to base morality on egoism was to risk unleashing forces in the human personality over which Utilitarian reason had little control. Indeed, Dostoevsky's allusions to these two writers indicates his awareness of an indebtedness to the libertine tradition of the French eighteenth-century novel, in which characters similar to Prince Valkovsky also dramatize, whether with approval or dismay, the possible consequences of putting into practice the logic of an egoism unrestrained by moral inhibitions.

Like his eighteenth-century prototypes, when Prince Valkovsky yields to the temptations of sensuality and the sadistic pleasures of desecration and domination, he finds it convenient to have a doctrine of egoistic self-interest at hand providing a philosophical rationale for his worst instincts. Since everyone possesses such instincts, even the "good" characters, who believe in a morality of love and self-sacrifice, can easily become prey to the passions of "egoism," and Valkovsky illustrates what might happen if "egoism" were to be taken seriously as the prevailing norm of behavior. Valkovsky, as has long been accepted, is the prefiguration of such later characters as Svidrigailov and Stavrogin; he is also Dostoevsky's first attempt, inspired by the radical ideology of the 1860s, to portray the futility of "reason" to control the entire gamut of possibilities contained in the human psyche.

Other aspects of the novel also suggest that Dostoevsky had now come to regard his past moral-political attitudes as lamentably and unforgivably naïve. There is talk of a "circle," again linked with the *Poor Folk* world, that meets once a week and to which the hare-brained Alyosha has been attracted. "They all know you, Ivan Petrovich," he burbles. "That is, they have read your works and expect great things of you in the future" (3: 308–309). What Alyosha reports of their discussions brings the group within the orbit of the "progressive" ideas of the 1840s (with a little updating). They converse, he confides, "of everything in general that leads to progress, to humanity, to love, it's all in relation to contemporary questions. We talk of the need of a free press, of the reforms that are beginning, of the love of humanity, of the leaders of today, we read and discuss them" (3: 310). It is generally accepted that Dostoevsky is here drawing, more or less amiably, on his own experiences in the Petrashevsky Circle, handling all this as part of the same universe of illusory innocence represented by Ivan Petrovich and, at a further extreme, by Alyosha.

Since the report of the circle is conveyed by the giddy and flighty Alyosha, his words immediately characterize it as just another of his evanescent enthusiasms, engagingly youthful and refreshing and filled with the exuberance of adolescent inexperience. "We all talked of our present," he says, "of our future, of science and literature, and talked as well, so frankly and simply. . . . There's a high-school boy that comes too" (3: 309). The implications of this last bit of information are not lost on Prince Valkovsky, who listens to his son "with a malignant sneer; there was malice in his face," and the prince breaks into convulsive laughter "simply to wound and to humiliate his son as deeply as possible." But Alyosha, for the only time in the book, manages to stand up to his father and to answer him "with extreme sincerity and a sort of severe dignity." "Yes," he replies, "I am enthusiastic over lofty ideas. They may be mistaken, but what they rest upon is holy" (3: 311).

Such words, we may surmise, indicate the complex ambiguity that Dostoevsky himself felt about the ideals of his radical past—the ideals he had just brought back to life again in the pages of *The Insulted and Injured*. There was no question that they had been "mistaken," or at least lamentably shortsighted in their view of the human condition; but he still continued to believe that what they had rested upon—the values of compassion and love—were sacred. What now prevented such values from being realized, however, was no longer primarily the deformations of character caused by an oppressive and unjust social system and a crushing political tyranny. It was, rather, the hidden forces of egoism and pride slumbering in every human breast.[6]

---■---

All through *The Insulted and Injured*, then, we can see Dostoevsky poised on the brink of a new phase of creation. Time and again in this novel we can catch suggestions of character types and motifs that serve as unmistakable harbingers of the masterpieces to come. Dostoevsky's characters often bear a family resemblance in their psychology, and it is not too far-fetched to point out a connection between the ragged little waif Nellie in *The Insulted and Injured* and the beautiful Nastasya Filippovna in *The Idiot*. Both are consumed by the "egoism of suffering." Both exhibit a fierce pride, a drive toward masochistic self-abasement, and an undying hatred of their persecutors and oppressors. Nellie finally overcomes her egoism at the cost of her life; so does Nastasya by offering herself as a victim to Rogozhin's knife. What is only tearful in the early novel becomes tragic in the later one.

The same difference of level can be noted in the case of Alyosha Valkovsky, who turns out to be a first draft of Dostoevsky's most touching effort to portray his moral ideal in the figure of Prince Myshkin. The yawning gap between the impressions produced by the two characters illustrates how Dostoevsky can employ almost identical traits to obtain very different types of significance, for while the lineaments of Myshkin are faintly profiled in Alyosha, there is no trace in him as yet of Myshkin's supreme saintliness. The most striking attribute of Alyosha, and one that most clearly stamps him as Myshkin's predecessor, is his capacity for living so totally in each moment of time, or in each experience and encounter, that he lacks any sense of continuity or consequence. It is thus impossible to hold him responsible for anything, or even to take offense at the chaos in other people's lives that he unwittingly creates; he behaves completely like a child and is characterized as being one: "he was too simple for his age and had no notion of real life" (3: 202).

Alyosha is thus a pure *naif*, existing outside the categories of good and evil and of social responsibility. He is genuinely unable to choose between Natasha and Katya, just as Myshkin will be unable to decide between Nastasya Filippovna

---

[6] Nietzsche read *The Insulted and Injured* with great appreciation. Indeed, according to an account given by a friend, he told her that he had perused it with "his eyes overflowing" with tears. The formidable Nietzsche surrendered completely to Dostoevsky's efforts to pluck the heartstrings of his readers. As Wolfgang Gesemann has suggested, the German philosopher may also have been intrigued by Dostoevsky's attack against the sentimental idealism of the "schöne Seele," as well as "the excitement of the encounter with the creatively genial refinement of Stirnerism" in Prince Valkovsky. See Gesemann, "Nietzsche's Verhältnnis zu Dostoevsky auf dem europäischen Hintergrund der 80er Jahre," *Die Welt der Slaven* 2 (July 1961), 135, 147–150.

and Aglaya Epanchin, and the two women also meet here to decide the future of the indecisive love object. But the conflict between love as passion and love as compassion, which is one day to tear Prince Myshkin apart, is totally absent in the case of Alyosha, who flits lightly from girl to girl and is in love with them all. Alyosha is a Myshkin, as it were, still lacking a religious aura and motivated solely by ordinary human drives and instincts—a Myshkin whose childlike purity is mixed with so much self-indulgence that Dostoevsky has trouble projecting him as favorably as his role in the plot requires.

The Insulted and Injured also contains the first use of a thematic motif indissolubly connected with Dostoevsky's major novels. "We shall have to work out our future happiness by suffering," says Natasha, referring to her relations with her father, "pay for it somehow by fresh miseries. Everything is purified by suffering" (3: 230). Nothing is more important for a proper understanding of Dostoevsky than an accurate grasp of these words. Natasha here is responding to a question put by Ivan Petrovich: Why doesn't she simply return home to her father and throw herself on his mercy? Her reply is that he will insist on an "impossible atonement," will require her to renounce her past and her love for Alyosha—and to this she will not submit. Her father is still consumed by his wounded resentment, and only the prolongation of his unhappiness may ultimately soften his heart to genuine forgiveness. Natasha is not referring to material hardship or physical deprivation but rather to the process by which the ramparts of pride, egoism, and wounded self-esteem are battered down and the way left open for forgiveness and love. It is only in this sense that Dostoevsky will ever hold "suffering" to be a good.

Indeed, as if to obviate any misunderstanding, he pointedly makes clear that nothing is more despicable than to exhibit insensibility or indifference to the suffering of others, or worse, callously to impose suffering for the sake of self-advantage. For Dostoevsky, the nadir of human perversity is to justify a base or vicious act on the ground that the suffering it causes is "good" for the unwilling victim. Prince Valkovsky takes exactly this line in cynically accounting for his behavior toward Nellie's mother: "I reflected that by giving her back [her] money I should perhaps make her unhappy. I should have deprived her of the enjoyment of being miserable *entirely owing to me*, and cursing me for it all her life. . . . This ecstasy of suffering can be found in Schilleresque natures, of course; perhaps she will have nothing to eat, but I am convinced that she was happy. I did not want to deprive her of that happiness and did not send her back her money" (3: 367). The underground man, with somewhat less conviction, will use exactly the same reasoning to justify his odious humiliation of the repentant prostitute Liza in the closing scene of *Notes from Underground*.

These brief considerations should illustrate the anticipatory interest of Dostoevsky's first major post-Siberian novel. Its deficiencies will only be surmounted when, a few years later, he places the theme of egoism squarely at the center of his action and portrays the radical ideologies of both the 1860s and the 1840s as having encouraged the growth and spread in Russia of this noxious moral plague. Dostoevsky will continue to employ the roman-feuilleton plot, the technique of this kind of melodramatic thriller derived from the Gothic novel by way of Scott, Dickens, and Balzac (the "urban Gothic," as George Steiner has called it),[7] and rely on its effects of suspense and dramatic surprise to rivet the attention of his reader. But he will recast it completely to eliminate its usual motivation, or better, to subordinate such motivation firmly to his own creative explorations of the ultimate moral consequences of radical belief.

[7] George Steiner, *Tolstoy or Dostoevsky* (New York, 1961), 197.

CHAPTER 24

The Era of Proclamations

The one or two years following the liberation of the serfs on February 16, 1861 are known by Russian historians as "the era of proclamations." For the first time since the Decembrist uprising in 1825, open agitation was carried on against the regime in the streets of Petersburg and Moscow. Inflammatory leaflets turned up everywhere—not only on doorhandles and in mailboxes but also lying scattered along main streets such as the Nevsky Prospect. The sheer fact of their appearance was a highly significant and unprecedented event—not to mention the boldness of those who wrote and distributed them. The sudden explosion of this propaganda campaign revealed the rancorous discontent of the radical intelligentsia with the tsar whom, just a few years before, they had been hailing in adulatory terms for his intention to bring an end to serfdom.

Even before the issuance of the liberation decree, the radical progressives had become convinced that the economic terms proposed would, in the long run, lead to the impoverishment of the peasantry. The peasants themselves were simply bewildered by the complicated terms of the manifesto, which, of course, most of them could not read, and rumors swept the vast countryside that the "true liberation" supposedly proclaimed by the tsar was being concealed by the rapacious landed gentry. Literate peasants, who set up as "interpreters" (in the sense desired by the people) of the floridly written and ambiguous liberation decree, gained a wide following among credulous listeners only too willing to believe in the treachery and mendacity of their overlords. Such a "true liberation" had long been cherished in the apocalyptic imagination of the Russian peasants, who dreamed that they would be granted, without repayment, *all* the land they deemed to be their own—"mainly," writes Franco Venturi, "the complete separation of their community from the landlord, the breaking of all ties between them, and hence the *obshchina* closing in on itself." [1]

Refusal to obey the local authorities occurred in several districts, and the most widespread disorder took place in the small village of Bezdna in the province of Kazan. Here, a *raskolnik* named Anton Petrov acquired an immense authority over the peasantry of the region when, on the basis of an aberrant read-

[1] Franco Venturi, *The Roots of Revolution*, trans. Frances Haskell (New York, 1966), 218.

ing of the manifesto supposedly inspired by divine illumination, he proclaimed the "true liberation," which pretended to disclose the genuine intentions of the holy tsar. Troops were finally sent in during April 1861 to arrest the agitator, who was telling the peasants not to comply with any of their obligations to the landowners, and when his followers refused to surrender him, several salvos were fired into the unarmed and peaceful mass. The official casualty figures listed fifty-one dead and seventy-seven wounded, but word-of-mouth reports spoke of several hundred casualties. A requiem mass for the peasants killed at Bezdna was organized in nearby Kazan by the students of the university and the Ecclesiastical Academy, and a popular young clergyman who taught history at the academy made a speech declaring Anton Petrov to have been "a new prophet . . . and he too has proclaimed liberty in the name of God."[2]

This clergyman, Afanasy Prokofievich Shchapov by name, had already achieved some notoriety for a Slavophil interpretation of the religious schism in the Russian Church. He depicted the schismatics as a native form of defiance against the imposition of foreign customs and ideas; and when the *raskolniki* rejected the alien state reforms imposed by Peter the Great, even declaring the tsar himself to be nothing less than the dreaded Antichrist, Shchapov considered such a reaction to be a struggle for cultural independence. Tried for his subversive speech at the Kazan service, he was sentenced to confinement in a monastery, but Alexander II intervened and ordered Shchapov to be given a post in the branch of the Ministry of Internal Affairs dealing with relations with the Old Believers.

A year later he issued his most important work, *The Land and the Schism*, the second part of which was published in *Time*. Much of this text was devoted to the sect of the *Beguny* ("Runners" or "Wanderers"), whose beliefs Shchapov interpreted as a form of social protest. The *Beguny* refused to carry an internal passport, as required by law, because they believed the world to be ruled by Antichrist, and they wandered through the Russian land as wayfarers, stubbornly rejecting all the obligations imposed on them by the godless state. Shchapov's theories certainly contributed their share to Dostoevsky's own assessment of the dissenting sects, and he sought in their heretical theology an insight into the indigenous essence of the Russian folk character. A bill from a bookstore dated August 1862 shows him to have ordered, among many other works, five books on the *Raskol*, including the major historical study by Shchapov.[3]

Three months after the fusillade at Bezdna, the first leaflet of what was to become a veritable blizzard made its appearance in Petersburg and then in Moscow. Called *The Great Russian* and moderate in tone, it was inspired by the fears

[2] Ibid., 199.
[3] *ZT*, 116.

aroused by events in Bezdna and elsewhere in the countryside and was addressed to the educated classes. "The government is bringing Russia to a Pugachev revolt," declared the first issue.[4] The government, it was suggested, should pay the redemption fees for the land allotted to the peasants, and at the same time free the nationalities of the Russian Empire. A national assembly should also be convened to help the tsar come into more direct contact with the nation as a whole. The authors of *The Great Russian* remain unknown, but the suspects all belong to the circle of students and young army officers grouped around Chernyshevsky and *The Contemporary*. V. A. Obruchev, an ex-officer who had joined the staff of *The Contemporary*, was caught distributing the leaflet and was sent to Siberia for a number of years.

Simultaneously with the second and third numbers of *The Great Russian*, which circulated in the fall of 1861, another proclamation appeared, entitled *To the Young Generation*. Its author is now known to be N. V. Shelgunov, who also contributed social-economic articles to *The Contemporary*. The leaflet was revised by M. L. Mikhailov, who had gained fame as a defender of woman's rights in the pages of *The Contemporary*, and Herzen printed it in London, with considerable reluctance and foreboding, at his Free Russian Press. Mikhailov, already under surveillance, was arrested on September 14, 1861, and his sentence to Siberia for six years produced a widespread wave of indignation.

To the Young Generation was only one of a series of leaflets written by Mikhailov, Shelgunov, and perhaps Chernyshevsky (the others, addressed to peasants and soldiers, were never printed), and it took a much harsher line than the moderate *The Great Russian*. No question now remained that a political change was envisaged, and that the authors had broken with tsarism once and for all: "We do not need a power that oppresses us; we do not need a power that prevents the mental, civic, and economic development of the country; we do not need a power that raises corruption and self-seeking as its banner." What Russia needs is "an elected leader receiving a salary for his services," and Alexander II should be told that the greatest achievement of his reign—the liberation of the serfs—had created a new order in which he had become superfluous: "If Alexander does not understand this and does not wish voluntarily to make way for the people—so much the worse for him." The general dissatisfaction can still be kept within bounds if the tsar gives up the throne; but "if to achieve our ends, by dividing the land among the people, we have to kill a hundred thousand of the gentry, even that will not deter us."[5]

Noticeable in *To the Young Generation* is the strong influence of Herzen's "Russian Socialism," with its messianic vision of a social-political future for

---

[4] Venturi, *Roots of Revolution*, 237.
[5] N. V. Shelgunov, *Vospominaniya*, 2 vols. (Moscow, 1967), 1: 333–334.

Russia without precedent in the history of Europe. "We believe in the forces of Russia because we believe that we have been destined to bring a new principle into history, to hand on our own message and not to haunt the old gardens of Europe."[6] A full democracy was envisaged; all land belonging to the nation would be divided into *obshchinas*; everyone would be a member of a self-administered commune, and whether a state of any kind would continue to exist is left unclear. The leaflet attacks "constitutionalism" and "economists" who desire "to turn Russia into England and impregnate us with English maturity." "We have aped," the leaflet declares, "the French and Germans quite enough. Do we need to ape the English as well?"[7] Dostoevsky mentions *To the Young Generation* by name and was certainly familiar with its contents.

———■———

After the events at Bezdna and their aftermaths, the government tightened restrictions in all areas where they had been relaxed in recent years. Nowhere had they been more liberal than in the universities, where limitations on admission had been lifted and lectures were thrown open to all who wished to attend. Students had also acquired the right to set up their own libraries, establish mutual-aid funds, publish newspapers, and run their own affairs. New regulations drawn up for the universities abolished all the corporate liberties of the students and reimposed fees that had been eliminated for the poorer ones just a few years earlier. These regulations were installed at the beginning of the fall term; but the students refused to accept them, and, to the unfeigned delight of a large crowd of onlookers, organized a protest march through the streets despite the presence of police and army troops. Many were arrested the same night, other arrests followed later, and, when agitation continued, the universities were closed for a full year. A number of the students who participated in these events later became well-known in the ranks of the Russian revolutionary movement.

The sympathies of most of the intelligentsia, including Feodor and Mikhail Dostoevsky, were on the side of the students. When those arrested were incarcerated in the Peter-and-Paul Fortress, Dostoevsky surely recalled his own long months of solitary confinement in the same forbidding prison. But the students were not suspected of any criminal political conspiracy, visitors could come and go, and gifts from well-wishers poured in to make their lot more comfortable. A large slab of beef was grilled in the apartment of Mikhail Dostoevsky and sent, along with bottles of cognac and red wine, in the name of "the editorial bureau of *Time*," thus giving a public declaration of the liberalism of the periodical.[8]

[6] Ibid., 338–339.
[7] Ibid., 336.
[8] Strakhov, *Biografiya*, 232.

By the fall of 1861, Dostoevsky had already published several installments of *House of the Dead*, and these sketches provided the Russian public with its first terrifying image of what lay ahead for those sentenced for a political crime. "At that time we knew about Siberia through *Notes from the House of the Dead*," wrote Shelgunov years later, "and this, of course, was quite enough to make us fear for the fate of Mikhailov."[9] No writer was now more celebrated than Dostoevsky, whose name was surrounded with the halo of his former suffering and whose sketches only served to enhance his prestige as a precursor on the path of political martyrdom that so many members of the younger generation might be forced to tread themselves. He was often asked to read from his works by student groups and for the benefit of worthy causes, and he invariably accepted such invitations because he believed it of first importance to keep in touch with his potential readers. As his fame increased, he also hoped that it might be possible to exercise some influence on public opinion.

Nothing untoward occurred at the various benefits in which Dostoevsky participated up through the spring of 1862; but matters took a different turn at a sensational "literary-musical evening" on March 2, which took place before an excitable crowd of three thousand people. The event, which Dostoevsky later enshrined in the masterly fête scene of *Demons*, was organized on behalf of the Literary Fund to help needy students. However, everyone knew, as Shelgunov wrote in his memoirs, that among the "needy students" for whom the flower of the cultured public wished to raise money were Mikhailov and Obruchev,[10] and the social-political character of the evening was accentuated by other details.

The literati invited to participate were all of a progressive or radical complexion: Dostoevsky, Chernyshevsky, Nekrasov, V. S. Kurochkin, editor of the radical satirical journal *The Spark* (*Iskra*)—and a Professor Pavlov, initiator of the Sunday-school movement, whose favorite slogan, "La révolution par l'école," was being taken quite literally by some teachers, who used the classroom to indoctrinate their pupils in favor of atheism and subversion. Henrik Wienawski, Anton Rubinstein, and the leading soprano of the Italian opera had agreed to take charge of the musical interludes—and if Rubinstein played his piano transcription of Beethoven's *The Ruins of Athens* (1811) it was because this work, as was well known, had been composed in honor of the Greek revolt against the Turkish Empire.

Dostoevsky opened the program, and he read from some still unpublished chapters of *House of the Dead* describing the death of a soldier from consumption in the prison hospital. The name of this soldier also turned out to be Mikhailov, and the death scene is embellished with those Dickensian details that

---

[9] Shelgunov, *Vospominaniya*, 1: 164.
[10] Ibid., 186.

Dostoevsky loved to employ. He dwelled on the emaciated body of the twenty-five-year-old, and the iron fetters that prison regulations would not allow to be removed. The grizzled sentry summoned to carry out the corpse is so moved by the piteous sight that he takes off his helmet and sword belt and crosses himself. One can well imagine the moving effect of this passage, with its constant repetition of the name, on those many people who knew the other Mikhailov well and were filled with ominous premonitions about his future.

Yet the audience response to Dostoevsky was as nothing compared to the veritable hurricane aroused by the intervention of Professor Pavlov, who had announced a lecture titled "A Thousand Years of Russian History." The millennium of Russia had been celebrated that very year with a great display of official pomp, and Pavlov's speech, duly submitted to the censorship, had been approved for delivery. But the nervous and highly volatile Pavlov, who is mentioned in the memoirs of the left-wing L. F. Panteleev as "not a completely normal person,"[11] whipped the audience into hysteria by his manner of delivery. Speaking in a quavering voice that sometimes rose to a shriek, he accentuated the words of his text so as to turn them into an implacable indictment of Russian history under its thousand years of autocratic rule. Shelgunov provides his firsthand report: "In the hall one could hear a growing rumble, there were shouts of furious exhilaration, seats were rattled, heels were pounded. I was sitting on the platform with others, among them Nekrasov, awaiting his turn. The agitated E. P. Kovalevsky [the president of the Literary Fund] ran up, and, turning to us, said: 'Stop him! Stop him! Tomorrow he'll be sent away!' But it was impossible to get Pavlov off the platform; more and more carried away, he finished his talk amidst the deafening shouts of the public and left the platform."[12] The audience had been worked up to an indescribable pitch of enthusiasm, and the applause was not only ear-shattering but climaxed by a ringing chorus of the *Marsellaise*. Kovalevsky's prediction proved correct: the next day Pavlov was sent into provincial exile and allowed to return to the capital only several years later.

Unlike Dostoevsky's fête scene, which terminates in pandemonium, the audience in the hall eventually calmed down, and the evening ended with a rousing version of Glinka's "Kamarinskaya," a symbol of peasant earthiness and self-assertion. So many encores were requested that a well-bred agent of the secret police, in his report, indignantly commented on the "indelicacy" of dragging out the evening for so long that ladies had been pinned to their seats for seven hours.[13]

[11] L. F. Panteleev, *Vospominaniya*, ed. S. A. Reiser (Leningrad, 1958), 228.
[12] Shelgunov, *Vospominaniya*, 1: 187.
[13] These details are taken from the article of G. V. Krasnov, "Vystuplenie N. G. Chernyshevskogo s vospominaniyami o N. A. Dobrolyubove 2 Marta 1862 g. kak obshchestvennoe sobytie," in *Revolutsionnoe situatsiya v Rossii v 1858–1861*, ed. M. V. Nechkina, vol. 4 (Moscow, 1965), 148.

As a protest against Pavlov's exile, Petersburg students now boycotted the in-formal courses organized by faculty to replace the regular classes. Professors were asked to join the movement by canceling their lectures, and those who refused were mercilessly harassed. The authorities themselves finally decided to termi-nate the de facto university, which had been given permission to use certain offi-cial buildings for its courses. "The reason for the destruction of the [free] univer-sity," Strakhov wrote nineteen years later, "was the famous 'literary-musical evening.' . . . The noise and enthusiasm were enormous, and it has always seemed to me since that the evening was the highest point reached by the liberal move-ment of our society, as well as the culmination of our cloud-castle revolution."[14] After this scandalous demonstration, Strakhov explains, it became clear that "every liberal measure aroused a movement in society that used such a measure for its own ends, which were not liberal at all but entirely radical."[15] This is the conclusion that Dostoevsky also began to draw, but rather than joining in the hue and cry against the radicals, he urgently tried to warn them against the con-sequences of their own folly.

———■———

Historians do not agree with Strakhov's judgment that the literary-musical eve-ning was the highest crest reached by the pounding wave of social-political un-rest during the spring of 1862. The true peak of the era of proclamations arrived two months later, in mid-May, when a leaflet entitled *Young Russia* was circu-lated. It is this remarkable document that brought the revolutionary ferment of the time to its convulsive climax.

The tsarist authorities never discovered that its author was a twenty-year-old youth, P. G. Zaichnevsky, who already had acquired a considerable underground past despite his tender years. On entering the University of Moscow in 1859, his first move had been to set up a clandestine printing press and publish works by Herzen, Ogarev, Feuerbach (*The Essence of Christianity*), and Büchner (*Force and Matter*). Making no secret of his radical sympathies, he attempted to orga-nize peasant resistance to the terms of the liberation during the summer of 1861, and he was arrested after proclaiming his revolutionary ideas in a letter inter-cepted by the secret police. All the same, Zaichnevsky enjoyed the same aston-ishingly lax conditions of imprisonment in Moscow as had been accorded the Petersburg students. Friends could bring books, magazines, and newspapers (some of them illegal) to keep him in touch with the political scene. Zaich-nevsky wrote the proclamation in his cell with the help of a small group of friends, all regular visitors, who had taken part in Moscow student demonstra-

[14] *Biografiya*, 232–233.
[15] Ibid., 233–234.

tions in the autumn of 1861. The manuscript, smuggled out with the help of a guard, was printed by Zaichnevsky's comrades on their own press, and they made Petersburg the center of distribution so as to divert attention from the real source.

Young Russia minced no words in declaring its aims, and exhibited none of the reluctance to go to extremes still discernible in the other two proclamations. It demanded "a revolution, a bloody and pitiless revolution, a revolution which must change everything down to the very roots, utterly overthrowing all the foundations of present society and bringing about the ruin of all who support the present order." [16] This would mean the total transformation of a system in which "a small number of people who own capital control the fate of the rest" and in which, consequently, "everything is false, everything is stupid, from religion . . . to the family." [17] Accordingly, the leaflet demanded the total emancipation of women, the abolition of marriage (as "immoral"), the suppression of the family (as a barrier to the full development of the individual), the dissolution of convents and monasteries (as "centers of debauchery"), and the secularization of all church property. [18]

The ultimate objective of *Young Russia* was a democratic republic, but Zaichnevsky was less interested in the future than in the immediate task of preparing the revolution, which, like so many others, he was convinced was on the point of breaking out because of the peasant's discontent with the terms of liberation. The first step was thus to attack all those, such as Herzen and the authors of *The Great Russian*, who advocated some sort of liberal compromise, and in his critical analysis of the policy advocated by Herzen in *The Bell* Zaichnevsky joins forces with the polemic against the superfluous men of the 1840s initiated by Chernyshevsky and Dobrolyubov. All thought of compromise is rejected because, *Young Russia* declares, revolutions in the past had failed through lack of determination, and "we will go further, not only than the poor revolutionaries of 1848, but also than the great terrorists of the 1790s [in France]." [19] The ultimate aim, of course, was to give power to the people, who would eventually rule themselves in a perfect democratic fashion, but such a transfer of sovereignty could occur only after the triumph of the revolution. Till then, it would be necessary to place all power in the hands of a revolutionary dictatorship, which would "stop at nothing" to establish "new foundations of society and the economy." [20] Well-read in the history of revolutions, Zaichnevsky himself gave the appropriate label to his own political outlook: Russian Jacobinism.

---

[16] Cited in Venturi, *Roots of Revolution*, 292.
[17] Ibid.
[18] B. P. Kozmin, *Iz istorii revolyutsionnoi mysli v Rossii* (Moscow, 1961, 252).
[19] Venturi, *Roots of Revolution*, 293.
[20] Ibid.

Such generalities pale into insignificance, however, beside the description of what might occur if the victorious revolution encountered any resistance. "The day will soon come when we will unfurl the great banner of the future, the red banner. And with a mighty cry of 'long live the Russian Social and Democratic Republic,' we will move against the Winter Palace to wipe out all those who dwell there." Bloodshed would, so far as possible, be restricted to the tsar and his immediate entourage, but if the "whole imperial party" rose in defense of the royal family, then "we will cry 'To your axes' and then we will . . . destroy them in the squares, if the cowardly swine dare to go there. We will destroy them in their houses, in the narrow streets of the towns, in the broad avenues of the capital, and in the villages. Remember that, when this happens, anyone who is not with us is against us and an enemy, and that every method is used to destroy the enemy."[21] Such fantasies of mass carnage and extermination, coupled with a direct threat against the royal family, imparted a sinister aura to *Young Russia* that horrified most of its readers and caused Dostoevsky to despair of the mental capacities of its authors.

A vivid sense of the first reactions caused by *Young Russia* may be given in Dostoevsky's own words, written eleven years after he found a copy wedged into the door handle of his apartment: "And here I, who heart and soul disagreed with these people, and with the meaning of their movement—I became suddenly vexed and almost ashamed, as it were, of their incompetence: 'Why is everything so stupid and ignorant about them?'" He found himself greatly upset "by the educational, mental level, and the lack of even a minimal comprehension of reality—this, to me, was terribly oppressive" (21: 25). While such a proclamation might once have seem justified as a desperate last resort in a period of black reaction, its bold disclosure at the present time, *after* the liberation of the serfs, could only have struck Dostoevsky as catastrophic. Its effect on society, as he must have instantly foreseen, would inevitably be to precipitate a general revulsion against the radicals and *all* their objectives.

Bloodcurdling passages from the text of *Young Russia* provided grounds for the suspicion that its authors and their friends (the proclamation spoke in the name of a "Central Revolutionary Committee") were responsible for the series of fires that began in Petersburg almost simultaneously with the pamphlet's circulation. Whole areas of the city were devastated, including many of the poorer districts; thousands of the victims were left homeless. The Petersburg fires in the spring of 1862 surpassed anything known till then in the extent of damage and the mysterious inability to control the blazes. Public opinion, which the authorities did nothing to counteract, immediately connected the catastrophe with the call for total destruction trumpeted in *Young Russia*, and such an association was

[21] Ibid., 295–296.

all the more inevitable because fire, called by peasants the Red Rooster, had always been one of their traditional weapons against the landowners.

An atmosphere of gloom and apprehension reigned throughout the city. Some notion of the frightened anecdotes that were circulating may be gleamed from a letter of Ivan Aksakov to another prominent Slavophil, Yury Samarin. Every store clerk, Aksakov tells him, had read *Young Russia*, and "this proclamation (even before the fires) had filled the people with *horror* in the literal sense of the word. . . . It made even more suspicious, in the eyes of the people, literacy, science, enlightenment—gifts coming from our hands, those of the gentry."[22] The tsar was reported to have told the lower ranks of the army and the noncommissioned officers of a plot against his life, and explained that he relied on them but not on the officers, because the upper ranks no longer believed in God. Aksakov continues: "The people, of course, did not understand the proclamation, but made out only that it preaches impiety, disrespect for '*one's father and mother*,' holds marriage in contempt and wishes to slit the throats of the royal family. . . . Turgenev told me (he was at the fire in the Shchukin Market)—that he heard with his own ears how the most ordinary grizzled *muzhik* shouted: 'The *professors* burned this down.' 'Professors, students'—these words have already become known to the people!"[23]

Young Russia thus brought on a rising tide of resentment against the educated class and everything it represented. More than any other of his contemporaries, Dostoevsky had suffered at first hand from the split between the mentality of the people and that of the educated class and had dedicated his journal to the task of creating the unified Russian culture made possible at last by the liberation. Nothing would have seemed to him more ominous for the future, more of a setback for everything he hoped to advance, than the intensifying enmity that he saw swelling all around him between the two groups.

Dostoevsky or Mikhail (probably both in collaboration) wrote an article for *Time* asserting that there was not a scrap of evidence to link the blazes with *Young Russia* or to imagine that the students as a body sympathized with the gory ideas advocated in the proclamation. When this article was rejected by the censorship, the Dostoevskys wrote another, with no better success. Neither article could be published, but the proof sheets, which contain an annotation in the hand of the tsar, were extracted years ago from the cavernous files of the Ministry of Internal Affairs. "Three scrofulous schoolboys, of whom the oldest is in fact not more than thirteen," jeers the first suppressed article, "printed and distributed the stupidest leaflet, not even being able to cope very well with the

---

[22] Cited in N. G. Rosenblyum, "Peterburgskie pozhary 1862 g. i Dostoevsky," *LN* 86 (Moscow, 1973), 30.

[23] Ibid.

foreign books from which they stole everything and of which they made a mockery. This stupid leaflet should have been greeted with a salvo of laughter."[24] Instead, the text continued, various decrepit gentlemen with the mentality of old peasant women were thrown into a panicky, paralytic fear and immediately started a campaign of wild tittle-tattle that has now infected everybody.

In view of the lynch mob mentality of the moment, these articles represent a considerable act of political courage. Indeed, after being forbidden by the censorship, the articles were sent, by special order of the tsar, to the secret police and then to the commission set up to investigate the cause of the fires. One phrase that attracted attention was the reference to "three scrofulous schoolboys," and when Mikhail Dostoevsky was called in for questioning on June 8, as the responsible editor of *Time*, he was asked to identify them by name. Poor Mikhail had to explain laboriously that the reference was only a "literary expression" and did not refer to actual schoolboys known to the editors of *Time*. "I have nothing at all to do with people who write such things as *Young Russia*," he declared with firm dignity.[25] This ended the matter so far as the Dostoevsky brothers were aware, although in fact *Time* narrowly escaped being prohibited. A decision to this effect was taken secretly and then withdrawn, with the proviso that *Time* should be kept under close observation. The sword of Damocles had thus already begun to swing invisibly over the heads of the hapless Dostoevskys, and it was to fall exactly a year later.

Others were spared the wait. Encouraged by the popular outrage directed against the suspected revolutionary destroyers of the capital, the government decided to strike while the city was still smoldering. On June 15 the Petersburg censorship committee suspended publication of both *The Contemporary* and the equally left-wing *Russian Word* for eight months. On July 7 Chernyshevsky was taken into custody along with an important member of the new revolutionary organization Land and Liberty (Zemlya i Volya), Nikolay Serno-Solovievich. By this time Dostoevsky was far away, embarked on his first trip to Europe during the summer of 1862, but we shall see that his thoughts turned constantly to home, and that the situation there filled him with anxiety and dismay.

[24] Ibid., 49–54.
[25] *ZT*, 114.

CHAPTER 25

Portrait of a Nihilist

Despite the overheated expectations of the young radicals, there is no reliable evidence that the stability of the regime was ever seriously threatened. Peasant discontent with the terms of the liberation, at Bezdna and elsewhere, was remarkably peaceful, nonviolent except for a few isolated cases, and inspired by unbroken loyalty to the tsar; the violence came entirely from the government. Dostoevsky's opinion on how the authorities behaved at this critical juncture may be surmised from a scene in *Demons* that can be read as a comment on their lack of judgment. When a loyal delegation of factory workers comes to protest, on behalf of their comrades, against a rascally overseer who had swindled them of their wages, Governor-General von Lembke is terrified out of his wits and orders them flogged. Mistakenly assuming their appeal for justice to be a revolutionary uprising, von Lembke responds with force, and his deluded severity only serves to unleash all the social chaos that then breaks loose.

Even if no revolution was imminent in Russia during the early 1860s, however, the events we have been chronicling signify the sensational advent on the Russian historical scene, in full force and as a dominating group, of a new generation of the intelligentsia largely different in social composition from the previous one and bringing with it a whole new set of ideas and values. Everyone was aware of the change, and it was stated in telling words at the beginning of the next decade by N. K. Mikhailovsky, who now occupied the place of Belinsky and Chernyshevsky as the leading radical publicist: "What happened?—the *raznochintsy* arrived. Nothing further happened. Nonetheless this event . . . created an epoch in Russian literature."[1] Mikhailovsky confines his remarks to literature, because to speak openly of politics in this connection would have been dangerous, but of course his readers would easily take his meaning.

Who and what were the *raznochintsy*? They were the sons of priests, petty officials, impoverished landowners, sometimes serfs, enfranchised or not, all of whom had managed to acquire an education and to exist in the interstices of the Russian caste system. They had been nourished on the writings of the older

---

[1] Cited in *Istoriya Russkoi literatury XIX v.*, ed. N. D. Ovsyaniko-Kulikovsky, 5 vols. (Moscow, 1915), 3: 45.

generation of gentry liberals and gentry radicals such as Herzen, Ogarev, Granovsky, and Turgenev but recognized as their only real ancestor and predecessor the stormy figure of "furious Vissarion" Belinsky, a *raznochinets* like themselves, who had assimilated the rich literary and philosophical culture of the gentry but whose intransigent social behavior both shocked and delighted his noble friends by its defiance of hypocritical convention. The young Count Tolstoy, an impenitent upholder of gentry values, instantly objected in 1856 to the tone of Chernyshevsky's criticism in a letter to Nekrasov, and he accurately traces the degeneration of literary manners back to its source: "All this is Belinsky! He spoke at the top of his voice, and spoke in an angry tone . . . and . . . this one [Chernyshevsky] thinks that to speak well one has to speak insolently, and to do so one has to stir oneself up."[2]

At first, this new generation had vented their anger against existing conditions in the pages of literary journals; now they had moved on not only to distributing violent proclamations but also, it was widely thought, had set Petersburg ablaze. And just at this very instant, by an extraordinary stroke of historical fortune, a great novel appeared portraying a *raznochinets* hero in all his self-proclaimed rebelliousness and irresistible strength. Turgenev's *Fathers and Children*, written during the previous two years and dedicated to the memory of Belinsky, was printed by Katkov's *Russian Messenger* in March 1862, just between the first two proclamations and *Young Russia* and simultaneously with the literary-musical evening. Tugenev's central figure, Bazarov, the son of a humble army doctor like Belinsky, was immediately accepted as a verisimilar literary image of the new social type of the 1860s. Turgenev wrote seven years later that "when I returned to Petersburg on the very day of the notorious fires in the Apraksin Marketplace, the word 'Nihilist' had been caught up by thousands of people, and the first exclamation that escaped from the lips of the first aquaintance I met on the Nevsky Prospect was: 'Look what *your* Nihilists are doing! They are setting Petersburg on fire!'"[3]

Turgenev's novel immediately became the exclusive storm center of social-cultural controversy; and the debates over the character of Bazarov, who personified the split between the gentry liberal intelligentsia of the 1840s and the radical *raznochintsy* of the 1860s, led to a *new* rift between two factions within the radical camp itself. These debates set the terms that dominated Russian social-cultural and literary life for the remainder of the decade, and they form an indispensable background for understanding some of Dostoevsky's most important thematic concerns.

Herzen's *The Superfluous and the Bilious* (1860), written after a secret visit by

[2] B. Eikhenbaum, *Lev Tolstoy*, vol. 1 (Leningrad, 1928), 223–224.
[3] I. S. Turgenev, *Literary Reminiscences*, trans. David Magarshack (New York, 1958), 194.

Chernyshevsky to London in the summer of 1859, reveals two of the traits that will invariably be attributed to the *raznochintsy* type: an offensive and aggressive tone, and a deprecation of art. Herzen sharply conveyed the attitude of the new generation toward the superfluous gentry liberals. His "bilious" interlocutor, he says, "looked on us as on the fine skeleton of a mammoth, as at an interesting bone that had been dug up and belonged with a different sun and different trees."[4] For his part, Herzen comments acidly on "the depressing faces of the Daniels of the Neva, who gloomily reproach men for dining without gnashing their teeth, and for enjoying pictures or music without remembering the misfortunes of the world." And he professes himself rather frightened by "the ease with which they [the bilious] despaired of everything, the vindictive pleasure of their renunciation, *and their terrible ruthlessness*." For Herzen believed that "the denial of every personal right, the insults, the humiliations they had endured" had left all of "the bilious" with "a devouring, irritable and distorted vanity."[5] These pages are a preliminary sketch for Turgenev's fuller and less ironically hostile treatment of the same type, whom he called, in a letter to Katkov, "the real hero of our time," adding, "What a hero and what a time—you will say. . . . But that is how things are."[6]

Turgenev had carefully studied the writings in which the new generation expressed its contemptuous rejection of the old, and he drew on the ideas he found there with remarkable precision. All the social-cultural issues of the day are reflected so accurately in the book that one Soviet Russian critic has rightly called it "a lapidary artistic chronicle of contemporary life."[7] Nonetheless, the shading that Turgenev gave to these issues was determined by his own artistic aims and ambiguous attitudes; like Dostoevsky, he could simultaneously sympathize with the ardent moral fervor of the young, deplore their intemperance, detest their ideas, and lament over their fate. Many of the positions that Bazarov advocates are not so much echoes of *The Contemporary* as subtle deformations and exaggerations calculated to reveal their ultimate implications and thus their dangerous potentialities. It is hardly surprising that partisans of these ideas should have found Turgenev's rendition unacceptable; much more unexpected is that even one radical spokesman should have proclaimed Bazarov to be the beacon lighting up the path to the future.

———■———

Fathers and Children inaugurates what will become the dominant theme of the Russian novel of the 1860s: the conflict between the narrow rationalism and

[4] Alexander Herzen, *My Past and Thoughts*, trans. Constance Garnett, rev. Humphrey Higgins, 4 vols. (New York, 1968), 4: 1574–1584.

[5] Ibid.

[6] I. S. Turgenev, *Pis'ma*, 13 vols. (Moscow–Leningrad, 1961), 4: 303.

[7] G. M. Fridlender et al., *Istoriya Russkogo romana*, 2 vols. (Moscow–Leningrad, 1962), 1: 501.

18. I. S. Turgenev, ca. 1865. From Turgenev, *Polnoe sobranie sochinenii*, vol. 9 (Moscow–Leningrad, 1965)

materialism upheld by this new generation and all those "irrational" feelings and values whose reality they refuse to acknowledge. But if Turgenev exposes the shortcomings of the worldview of the *raznochintsy* in this way, he nonetheless delineates Bazarov as someone far superior in energy, force of character, and promise for the future to any of the gentry characters by whom he is surrounded. Both of the older Kirsanovs (the father and uncle of Arkady, Bazarov's gentry liberal friend) are clearly relics of the past. Unable to cope with the new Russian society on the point of bursting its old bounds, Arkady and his father flourish in contented mediocrity on their estate, but the towering image of the rebellious Bazarov definitely places their "family happiness" (to use a Tolstoyan tag) in the shade. "Your sort, you gentry," Bazarov tells Arkady, when the two friends come to the parting of the ways, "can never get beyond refined submission or refined indignation, and that's a mere trifle. You won't fight . . . but we mean to fight . . . we want to smash other people!" (8: 380)

All through the novel, Turgenev's portrait of the relations between the two generations deftly captures the full range of the opposition that had been building up both in personal contacts and in journalistic exchanges, and his delineation of this conflict sets the ideological terms in which the polemics of the immediate future would be carried on. The obsolescence of the older generation is revealed by Nikolay Kirsanov's fondness for Pushkin and his amateur efforts on the violoncello. "It's time to throw up that rubbish," Bazarov says, referring to Pushkin, and he counsels Arkady to give his father "something sensible to read." The two friends condescendingly decide that Büchner's *Force and Matter* would be suitable as an introduction to more serious intellectual fare because it "is written in popular language" (8: 239).

Bazarov's attack against art is carried on vigorously and, for an informed reader of that time, with obvious reference to Chernyshevsky's thesis. But while Chernyshevsky had merely argued that art should be subordinate to life, and had not denied it a certain secondary usefulness, Turgenev pushes the opposition between the "aesthetic" and the "useful" into a total negation. When Arkady's uncle Pavel Petrovich complains that young Russian artists regard "Raphael as a fool," Bazarov retorts, "To my mind, Raphael's not worth a brass farthing; and they are no better than he" (8: 247). No distinction is made between different kinds of art as more or less useful, and another remark of Bazarov illustrates the point with epigrammatic terseness: "A good chemist is twenty times as useful as any poet" (8: 219).

Bazarov evidently exemplifies Chernyshevsky's conviction that the physical sciences, with their theory of a universal material determinism, furnish the basis for a solution to all problems, including those of a moral-social nature. But this faith in science, which still implies a belief in general principles of some sort, is then splintered by Bazarov into particular sciences. "There are sciences," he declares, "as there are trades and vocations; but abstract science doesn't exist at all" (8: 219). Ultimately, even science itself becomes reduced to "sensations," and it is these, in all their infinite variety, that have the last word. "There are no general principles—you've not made even that out as yet!" Bazarov exclaims to Arkady with some astonishment. "There are feelings. . . . Why do I like chemistry? Why do you like apples?—also by virtue of our sensations." The "feelings" referred to by Bazarov are purely physical sensations, not psychic or emotive ones, and Bazarov insists that "men will never penetrate deeper than that" (8: 325). Chernyshevsky's scientism thus ends up as a solipsistic empiricism or sensationalism in which all general principles or values are dissolved (much as in Max Stirner) into a matter of individual taste or preference.

It is this attack on *all* general principles that forms the basis of what Turgenev labels Bazarov's "Nihilism"—a term that had just come into usage in connection with the radicals and was destined, as a result of Turgenev's novel, to a great career. A Nihilist, Arkady eagerly explains, "is a man who does not bow before any authority, who does not take any principle on faith, whatever reverence for that principle may be enshrined in" (8: 216). In the most famous passage in the book, Bazarov explains the universal scope of this rejection to the incredulous elder Kirsanovs:

> "Allow me though," began Nikolay Petrovich. "You deny everything, or, speaking more precisely, you destroy everything. . . . But one must construct too, you know?"
> "That's not our business now. . . . The ground has to be cleared first" (8: 243).

To be sure, Arkady immediately leaps in to say that "the present condition of the people requires it"—thus linking such negation with the aim of a revolutionary social transformation. But this distant aim, so far as Bazarov is concerned, remains clearly subordinate to the work of negation and destruction, to a personal emancipation from all inherited principles and prejudices and the encouragement of such emancipation among others. Turgenev here thus reverses the actual order of priorities among the followers of *The Contemporary*, whose goals were much more social-political than personal. Very probably, though, he had already become aware of another radical current in the essays of Pisarev and other contributors to the *Russian Word*, who, as Strakhov had noted, put a much stronger accent on self-assertion and self-liberation and whose philosophical preferences were in fact quite close to Bazarov's "sensationalistic" empiricism.

Bazarov's attitude toward "the people" is also a mixture of conflicting ideas that, without representing any single prevalent point of view, finally again puts the emphasis on a solitary individualism. On the one hand, he is proud of his plebian origins, and when Pavel Petrovich, shocked at his utterances, accuses him of not being "Russian," he replies, "My grandfather ploughed the land" (8: 244), and points out that the peasants feel more at home with him than with the gentry. But he is also an inflexible Westernizer who refuses to idealize the peasants and ridicules their backwardness and superstition. Even that holy of holies, the village *obshchina*, does not escape the lash of Bazarov's iconoclasm, and in this he reflects not only the opinion of his creator, the Western liberal Turgenev, but also a viewpoint just beginning to make its appearance in *The Russian Word*.[8]

No scene in *Fathers and Children* is more prophetic than the one in which Turgenev brilliantly dramatizes all the ambiguities of Bazarov's love-hate rela-

---

[8] See, for example, the remark in Pisarev's essay "Nineteenth-Century Scholasticism" (1861) that "the Russian peasant has perhaps not yet acquired sufficient stature to realize his own personality and rise to a reasonable egoism and respect for his own individuality" (or, more literally, his own *I*). Dimitry Pisarev, *Selected Philosophical, Social and Political Essays* (Moscow, 1958), 77.

tion to the people—the internal clash between his self-assertive ideas, which express an aching need for personal self-fulfillment, and the obligation imposed by history on his generation to devote their lives to bettering the lot of the backward peasantry. Bazarov recalls that once, while walking past the *izba* of a prosperous peasant, Arkady had piously remarked that Russia would "attain perfection when the poorest peasant had a [clean and comfortable] hut" and that "every one of us ought to work to bring [that] about." Such an obligation impels Bazarov to confess to a feeling of intense "hatred for this poorest peasant, this Philip or Sidor, for whom I'm ready to jump out of my skin, and who won't even thank me for it . . . and what do I need his thanks for? Why, suppose he does live in a clean hut, while nettles are growing out of me—well, what then?" (8: 325).

Turgenev penetrates here, with consummate insight, to the anguishing dilemma of the young Russian radical of the 1860s, heart and soul dedicated to serving a people from whom he is totally alienated by his culture—a people on whose behalf he must surrender all claims to happiness, and yet who cannot even understand the nature or meaning of his self-sacrifice. Such an awareness of the tragic isolation of the intelligentsia—an isolation that had been one of Dostoevsky's most shocking discoveries during his years in the Siberian prison camp—had hardly been fully grasped yet as an objective datum of the Russian social-cultural situation. It was to become much more widespread in the next few years, partly because the people did not behave in the manner that the intelligentsia had anticipated, partly because Turgenev had raised the issue to the level of consciousness. As a result, Bazarov's sense of indomitable will and strength as an *individual,* as well as his realization that he stands alone above and beyond the people, will come to the foreground and shape the guiding attitudes of the *raznochintsy* intelligentsia throughout the remainder of the 1860s.

———■———

Even before the publication of *Fathers and Children,* rumors had been making the rounds in Petersburg that Turgenev's new novel was a revengeful lampoon of Dobrolyubov. Chernyshevsky continued to believe this to his dying day and repeated the accusation as late as 1884.[9] Depending on how the text was read, it could be taken either as an "apotheosis" of Bazarov (to cite the scandalized reaction of Katkov)[10] or as a condemnation and exposure of the type he incarnated. The second view was that of a majority of readers, and is echoed in a report of the secret police surveying the cultural scene in 1862 with a good deal of

[9] Cited in V. E. Evgenyev-Maximov, Sovremennik *pri Chernyshevskom i Dobrolyubove* (Leningrad, 1936), 514.

[10] P. V. Annenkov, *Literaturnye vospominaniya* (St. Petersburg, 1909), 549–550.

perspicacity: "With this work . . . Turgenev branded our adolescent revolutionaries with the caustic name of 'Nihilists,' and shook the doctrine of materialism
and its representatives."[11] To make certain that Turgenev would receive the
proper chastisement for his audacity, Chernyshevsky entrusted the review of the
novel to the twenty-two-year-old M. A. Antonovich, a protégé of Dobrolyubov
known for his belligerence.

Antonovich's essay, "The Asmodeus of Our Time," is not so much an article
about Turgenev's novel as a headlong onslaught intended to destroy whatever
credit it might be given as a picture of the aims and ideal of the young generation. Most of the article is devoted to defaming Turgenev by every possible
means. Whatever the justice of some of his remarks concerning Bazarov, they are
drowned in the flood of abuse that made Antonovich's article a synonym for
critical malpractice.

Quite opposite was the reaction of Dimitry Pisarev, the chief critic of *The
Russian Word*, a journal that had been considered a staunch ally of *The Contemporary*. Strakhov noted in the young critic a tendency to draw the most extreme
conclusions from the lessons of Chernyshevsky—the very same "Nihilist" conclusions that Bazarov would soon be proclaiming in Turgenev's pages. Pisarev
naturally found Turgenev's hero completely to his taste, and he welcomed precisely those aspects of Bazarov considered defamatory by Antonovich as distinctive of the new "hero of our time." Pavel Petrovich once refers to Bazarov as possessing a "satanic pride," and Pisarev hastens to agree that "this expression is very
felicitously chosen and is a perfect characterization of our hero."[12] Bazarov also
trumpets a worldview based on an "empiricism" that reduces all matters of principle to individual preference, and Pisarev blithely accepts such a doctrine as the
very last word of "science." "Thus Bazarov everywhere and in everything does
only what he wishes, or what seems to him useful and attractive. He is governed
only by personal caprice or personal calculation. Neither over him, nor outside
him, nor inside him does he recognize any regulator, any moral law, any principle. . . . Nothing except personal taste prevents him from murdering and robbing, and nothing except personal taste stirs people of this stripe to make discoveries in the field of science and social existence."[13] Three years later, Raskolnikov
in *Crime and Punishment* will show what might occur when this interpretation
of the Bazarov type is admiringly put to the test.

All through Pisarev's article, particular stress is placed on Bazarov's grandeur
as an *individual*, who towers not only above all other member of the educated
class but even more above the people. As a result, Pisarev is sensitive to

[11] Evgenyev-Maximov, *Sovremennik*, 548.
[12] D. I. Pisarev, *Sochineniya*, 4 vols. (Moscow, 1955), 2: 8–9, 10–11.
[13] Ibid., II, 10.

Bazarov's moral-spiritual isolation and even casts it in the form of a universal social law:

> The masses, in every period, have lived contentedly, and with their inherent placidity have been satisfied with what was at hand. . . . This mass does not make discoveries or commit crimes; other people think and suffer, search and find, struggle and err on its behalf—other people eternally alien to it, eternally regarding it with contempt, and at the same time eternally working to increase the amenities of its life.[14]

Nothing similar can be found in *The Contemporary*, where the intelligentsia and the people were invariably considered to be united in the attainment of a common social-political goal. The image of the transcendent *raznochinets* hero who acts alone and who cannot help but feel *contempt* for the people whose lives he wishes to ameliorate and elevate was something genuinely new on the Russian social-cultural scene. Whatever the satisfaction afforded by Pisarev's praise, Turgenev could hardly have recognized his own complex conception in this celebration of a Bazarov beyond good and evil, a type that had become glorified almost to the dimensions of a Nietzschean superman. And there can be little doubt that it set Dostoevsky's imagination working along the lines eventually leading to Raskolnikov and his article "On Crime," which also separates the world into "ordinary" and "extraordinary" people and claims for the second category the *right* to "step over" the moral law.

Dostoevsky read *Fathers and Children* on its magazine publication, at the beginning of March, and conveyed his admiration to Turgenev without delay. He received a reply before the month was out expressing Turgenev's gratitude and satisfaction: "You have so fully and sensitively grasped what I wished to express in Bazarov. . . . It is as if you had slipped into my soul and intuited even what I did not think necessary to utter. I hope to God . . . everyone sees even a part of what you have seen!"[15] A month later, he writes to Dostoevsky again: "no one, it seems, suspected that I tried to present him [Bazarov] as a tragic figure—and everyone says: why is he so bad?—or—why is he so good?"[16]

Dostoevsky's original letter has been lost, but a hint of what Dostoevsky had written Turgenev is given in a few sentences that he set down a year later in *Winter Notes on Summer Impressions*, when he refers to Turgenev's "restless and tormented Bazarov (the mark of a great heart) in spite of all his Nihilism" (5: 59). Bazarov here is grasped precisely as the kind of tragic figure that Turgenev had

[14] Ibid., 15.
[15] Turgenev, *Pis'ma*, 4: 358–359.
[16] Ibid., 385.

wished to portray, a hero whose tragedy lies in the conflict between his Western ideas (his ideology) and "the great heart," whose impulses and longings he could not suppress or deny.

It may be assumed that Dostoevsky discussed Turgenev's novel with Strakhov when assigning him to review it for *Time*, and Strakhov's analysis, one of the finest contemporary reactions to the book, undoubtedly conveys a good deal of Dostoevsky's own ideas. Appearing in the April issue, Strakhov's article takes into account the responses of both Antonovich and Pisarev, but, in his view, both the enthusiasm of Pisarev and the hostility of Antonovich are equally mistaken for the very reason given by Turgenev himself: each poses the problem of the book in terms of whether the author was really a partisan of the fathers or the children, the past or the future. Its real meaning lies much deeper and is concerned with a far different problem.

"Never," Strakhov writes, "has the disaccord between life and thought been felt as intensely as at the present time."[17] It is this disaccord that Turgenev dramatizes, and it is here, rather than in the conflict of generations, that the book's ultimate moral lesson can be located. Bazarov, as Pisarev had rightly said, is manifestly superior as an individual to all the other people in the book, fathers included. But it turns out that he is not superior to the forces of life that they embody, no matter in how paltry a form; he is not superior to the forces that he vainly tries to suppress in himself because they do not jibe with the theory about life that he accepts. Bazarov disapproves of responding to the blandishments of nature, and Turgenev depicts nature in all its beauty; Bazarov does not value friendship or romantic love, and Turgenev shows how real both are in his heart; Bazarov rejects family sentiment, and Turgenev portrays the unselfish, anguished love of his doting parents; Bazarov scorns the appeal of art, and Turgenev delineates him with all the resources of a great poetic talent. "Bazarov is a Titan revolting against his mother earth,"[18] Strakhov writes; but no Titan is powerful enough to triumph over the forces that, because they are immutably rooted in man's emotional nature, provide the eternal foundation of human life.

Shortly after Strakhov's article appeared, Turgenev arrived in Petersburg from Paris and hastened to pay a visit to the editorial offices of *Time*. "He found us assembled," Strakhov recalls, "and invited Mikhail Mikhailovich, Feodor Mikhailovich, and myself to dine with him in the Hotel Clea. The storm that had blown up against him obviously upset him."[19] Lionized by the reactionaries, vilified by the majority of the radicals, praised by Pisarev for having glorified Nihilism—it was only among the editors of *Time*, and nowhere else in Russia,

---

[17] Nikolay Strakhov, *Kriticheskiya stat'i*, 2 vols. (Kiev, 1902–1908), 1: 201.
[18] Ibid., 37.
[19] *Biografiya*, 237.

that he had found any informed sympathy with and comprehension of the
greatest novel of his literary career.

———■———

Turgenev was famous for his affability as a conversationalist, and during the animated dinner-table talk at the Hotel Clea, he amused the company by recounting the dangers that awaited Russians who innocently entrusted themselves to
the delights of European residence. Probably some mention had been made of
Dostoevsky's impending first trip abroad. Such a trip was a great event in the life
of any educated Russian, and Dostoevsky had recently expressed his own yearnings in a letter to the poet Polonsky. "How many times . . . have I dreamt of
being in Italy. Ever since the novels of Ann Radcliffe, which I read when I was
eight years old, all sorts of Catarinas, Alfonsos, and Lucias have been running
around in my head. . . . Then it was the turn of Shakespeare—Verona, Romeo
and Juliet—the devil only knows what magic was there! Italy! Italy! But instead
of Italy I landed in Semipalatinsk, and before that in the Dead House. Will I
never succeed in getting to Europe while I still have the strength, the passion,
and the poetry?"[20]

The financial situation of *Time* was now promising enough to allow him to
realize this long-cherished dream; and he also desired to consult specialists in
Europe about his epilepsy. He writes to his brother Andrey that he is traveling
without his wife, partly for lack of funds, partly because Marya Dimitrievna
wished to supervise Pasha's preparation for the entrance examinations to the
gymnasium. The plan was for Dostoevsky to join up with Strakhov, also making
a first trip to Europe, in mid-July. On June 7, 1862, he left for the first of what
were to be many *Wanderjahren* in Europe.

The first leg of Dostoevsky's trip took him from Russia through Germany,
Belgium, and France to Paris, where he planned to spend a month. Some of the
observations he garnered along the way can be found in his *Winter Notes on
Summer Impressions*, written the following year and published in *Time*. This series of articles, despite its title, is filled with the most serious cultural and social-
political reflections, even though such ideas appear in the midst of casual travel
sketches whose lighthearted tone communicates a deceptive air of frivolity. For
all his attempts to amuse and distract, these sketches nonetheless help us to understand important aspects of Dostoevsky's first reactions to the spectacle of European life.

His initial impressions of Berlin, Dresden, and Cologne were all disillusioning, and after the requisite sightseeing he rushed on to Paris "in the hope that
the French would be kinder and more interesting" (5: 48–49). Before arriving in

[20] *Pisma*, 1: 302; July 31, 1861.

Paris, however, he paused along the way—very probably at Wiesbaden, with its inviting roulette casino—to try his luck at gambling. What happened on this first fling remains obscure; but Strakhov believes that Dostoevsky quickly acquired eleven thousand francs, and suggests that this easy win pushed him along the path to perdition.[21] A later letter from Mikhail, informing his brother that he was forwarding some money from a publisher, indicates that Dostoevsky was again short of cash. "For God's sake, don't gamble any more," his brother pleads. "How can you gamble considering our luck?"[22] This episode was the first symptom of Dostoevsky's addiction to roulette, which was to grip him so strongly in the future.

Paris was the Mecca for all Russian tourists—whether those, like Herzen and Bakunin, who came to worship at the hallowed shrine of revolutionary upheaval or those, more numerous, who hastened to kick up their heels at the Bal Mabille and chase *grisettes* in the Latin Quarter. It was mid-June when he reached Paris—after first catching a disturbing whiff of the political climate in the Second Empire when four French police spies, with the assignment of inspecting all entering foreigners and telegraphing descriptions to the proper authorities, boarded the train and took seats in his compartment. He remained in Paris for two weeks, long enough to soak up the atmosphere of order and propriety, and he labels the city—jestingly, of course—"the most moral and virtuous city on the face of the earth" (5: 68). "The Parisian loves to do business, but it seems that even in doing business and in skinning you alive in his shop like a chicken, he skins you not, as in the old days, for the sake of profit, but out of virtue, in the name of some sacred necessity" (5: 76).

Following in the footsteps of Herzen, who had diagnosed the French bourgeoisie as reflected in the plays of Eugene Scribe, Dostoevsky hastened to the theater to investigate how this image has evolved. In all of the plays by Dumas *fils*, Augier, Sardou, and the indefatigable Scribe, Dostoevsky found characters of unutterable nobility and impeccable virtue; all concern a young man who, in the first act, renounces a fortune for the highest motives, only to end in the last act by invariably marrying a poor girl who suddenly inherits incalculable wealth—unless it finally turns out that he, instead of being a penniless orphan, is really the legitimate son of a Rothschild. After seeing the sights, and consulting various medical authorities about his epilepsy, Dostoevsky summed up his impressions of the French in a letter to Strakhov a day before leaving for London. "By God!" he wrote. "The French are a nauseating people. . . . The Frenchman is pleasant, honest, polite, but false, and money for him is everything. No trace of any ideal."[23] Since Dostoevsky's words coincide so perfectly with the

[21] *Biografiya*, 259.
[22] *DMI*, 536.
[23] Ibid., 310; June 6/July 8, 1862.

portrait of the French given by the much more urbane and cosmopolitan Herzen in his sparkling *Letters from France and Italy*, we may view them as just another example of a recurring Russian reaction to bourgeois French life.[24]

If what absorbed Dostoevsky in Paris was the stifling sense of bourgeois order and propriety, what overwhelmed him in London was the clamorous vitality of the city in all the nakedness of its clashing discords: "Even externally, what a contrast with Paris! This city day and night going about its business, enormous as the ocean, with the roaring and rumbling of machines, the railroad line constructed above the houses (and soon underneath the houses), that boldness in enterprise, this apparent disorder which is, in essence, a bourgeois order to the highest degree, this polluted Thames, this air filled with coal dust; these magnificent parks and squares and those terrifying streets of a section like Whitechapel, with its half-naked, wild and starving population. The City with its millions and the commerce of the universe, the Crystal Palace, the World's Fair" (5: 69).

For a socially conscious Russian, London was the capital city of the classic land of the dispossessed proletariat, and Dostoevsky's attention was riveted by this aspect of lower-class life. Someone had described to him (and who could it have been if not the London resident Herzen?) how every Saturday night a half-million workers, with their wives and children, swarmed through the downtown streets to celebrate the beginning of their one day of leisure: "All of them bring their weekly savings, what they have earned by hard labor and amidst curses." Everything remains open, all the butcher shops and the eating places continue to do business, and night is transformed into day as the streets are lit by powerful gas lamps: "It is as if a ball had been organized for these white negroes. The crowd pushes into the open taverns and in the streets. They eat and drink. The beer halls are decorated like palaces. Everybody is drunk, but without gaiety, with a sad drunkenness, sullen, gloomy, strangely silent. Only sometimes an exchange of insults and a bloody quarrel breaks the suspicious silence, which fills one with melancholy. Everyone hurries to get dead drunk as quickly as possible, so as to lose consciousness." Dostoevsky wandered among such a crowd at two o'clock one Saturday night, and, he says, "the impression of what I had seen tormented me for three whole days" (5: 70–71).

On another evening he strolled among the thousands of prostitutes plying their trade in the Haymarket; and he marveled both at the luxuriousness of the cafés, where accommodations could be rented for the night, and at the attractiveness of some of the women. He saw several that had "faces truly fit for a keepsake" (5: 71–72). Dostoevsky was accosted not only by prostitutes but also by women engaged in the charitable labor of trying to redeem these lost souls.

---

[24] "The bourgeois," writes Herzen, "weeps in the theatre, moved by his own virtue as portrayed by Scribe, moved by his mercantile heroism and the poetry of shopkeeping." Cited in A. S. Dolinin, "Dostoevsky i Gertsen," *Poslednie romany Dostoevskogo* (Moscow–Leningrad, 1963), 220–221.

Their black dresses suggest some early volunteers of the Salvation Army, which formally organized three years later, but Dostoevsky seized the opportunity to nourish his anti-Catholic prejudices. "It is a subtle and well-thought-out propaganda," he writes. "The Catholic priest himself searches out some miserable worker's family. . . . He feeds them all, gives them clothes, provides heating, looks after the sick, buys medicine, becomes the friend of the family, and finally converts them all to Catholicism" (5: 73). The idea of Roman Catholicism has already become identified for Dostoevsky with that of a betrayal of the true spirit of the Christian faith, which substitutes for Christ's message of charity and love the temptation of worldly goods and comforts.

———■———

The most important event of Dostoevsky's stay in London was his meeting with Herzen, whom he probably visited several times during the eight or so days of his English sojourn. Herzen's masterly *On the Development of Revolutionary Ideas in Russia* (1851) had listed Dostoevsky among "the most noble and outstanding" people who had been condemned to Siberia for their political idealism. *Poor Folk* was singled out as evidence of the Socialist turn taken by Russian literature during the 1840s, and more recently Herzen had exhibited the liveliest interest in *House of the Dead*. On the pamphlet *Young Russia*, the two men also saw eye-to-eye. In an article printed in the July 15 issue of *The Bell*, just a few days after Dostoevsky's first visit, Herzen, sounding for all the world like a *pochvennik*, writes of the pamphlet's authors, "their fearless logic is one of the most characteristic traits of the Russian genius *estranged from the people*. . . . As a result of the slavery in which we lived, the alienation from ourselves, our break with the people, our impotence to act, there remained for us a painful consolation . . .—the nakedness of our negation, our logical ruthlessness, and it was with some sort of joy that we pronounced those final, *extreme* words which the lips of our teachers have barely whispered, turning white as they did so and looking around uneasily."[25]

Dostoevsky was a great admirer of Herzen's brilliant part essay, part dialogue, *From the Other Shore*, and he praised it to its author. Indeed, few others writings of Herzen would have been as close to Dostoevsky's heart as this bitter indictment of the illusions of Utopian Socialism, this denunciation of European civilization as hidebound to the social-political forms of the past and incapable of going beyond their limits, this torrent of scorn poured on the radical European intelligentsia for imagining that the masses would really pay attention to their high-flown lucubrations.

Herzen had then developed his theory of Russian Socialism, in which his disillusionment with the European working class and its leaders gave way to a hope

[25] A. I. Gertsen, *Polnoe sobranie sochinenii*, 30 vols. (Moscow, 1954–1966), 26: 203–204.

for the future founded on the traditional egalitarian Socialism of the Russian peasant and his native *obshchina*. Would not Dostoevsky have indicated his agreement with Herzen on *this* point—and to such a degree that the skeptical Herzen even recoiled somewhat from the fervency of Dostoevsky's words? Such would seem to be the sense of Herzen's own reference to their conversation in a letter to Ogarev, whom Dostoevsky had probably met a day or so earlier. "Dostoevsky was here yesterday—he is a naïve, not entirely lucid, but very nice person," he writes. "He believes with enthusiasm in the Russian people." [26]

Dostoevsky must surely have been aware that in visiting Herzen, he was taking a step that might place him in danger. The Third Section kept a sharp eye on the activities of the Herzen household, and Chernyshevsky had been arrested after spies reported that Herzen was imprudently offering to print *The Contemporary* in London. Dostoevsky's presence did not escape the vigilant operatives who kept Herzen under surveillance, and information was sent back to Russia that in London, Dostoevsky "had struck up a friendship with the exiles Herzen and Bakunin." [27] The flamboyant Bakunin, then also living in London, had recently made a sensational escape from Siberian exile by way of the United States.

L. P. Grossman has argued that Bakunin was the direct prototype for Stavrogin in *Demons*, and a good deal of ink has been spilled over the question of their actual meeting. [28] Dostoevsky's imagination, however, though it certainly worked from prototypes, invariably fused all sorts of suggestions into a representative image; he never took only a single personage as an exclusive source of inspiration. Whether the two men ever met thus becomes a minor question so far as Dostoevsky the artist is concerned, though it may well have occurred because Bakunin so assiduously attended Herzen's Sunday afternoon receptions. In any event, Dostoevsky's name was placed on the list of those persons who visited Herzen not simply out of curiosity but because they sympathized "more or less with his criminal intentions." [29] A special command was issued to search his luggage on his way home.

———■———

Dostoevsky and Strakhov joined forces in Geneva in late July and traveled together through Switzerland and the north of Italy by way of Turin, Geneva, and Livorno to Florence. In Florence they spent a week in a modest *pensione* on the

[26] Ibid., 27: 247.

[27] G. F. Kogan, "Razyskaniya o Dostoevskom," *LN* 86 (Moscow, 1973), 596.

[28] L. P. Grossman and Vyacheslav Polonsky, *Spor o Bakunine i Dostoevskom* (Moscow, 1926). For a witty summing up of the opposing arguments, which concludes that Grossman's thesis is a myth, see Jacques Catteau, "Bakounine et Dostoevski," in *Bakounine: Combats et débats* (Paris, 1979), 97–105.

[29] Kogan, "Razyskaniya," 596.

Via Tornebuoni. The two Russians were inseparable, and Strakhov has left an engaging image of Dostoevsky in his unaccustomed role as tourist: "all his attention was focused on people, on grasping their nature and character, and on the general impression of life going on around him in the streets."[30] This account agrees with Dostoevsky's own remarks in *Winter Notes*, but one wonders whether he was as little interested in the Uffizi as Strakhov pretends (casting himself, of course, in the role of civilized art lover). The two men read Hugo's *Les misérables* (just then coming out), with Dostoevsky eagerly buying volume after volume and passing them on to Strakhov. Most of all they walked and talked, and Strakhov paints an idyllic image of these leisurely conversations.

His amicable portrait, however, has been challenged by an unfinished draft of an article entitled "Observations" found in the Strakhov archives, which uncovers some of the tensions that eventually led Strakhov, shortly after Dostoevsky's death, to denounce his erstwhile friend in a scurrilous letter to Tolstoy. Dedicated to Dostoevsky, it seems to have been composed in Florence or shortly thereafter, and it begins by recalling one of those dialogues that its author later depicted with such accents of nostalgia. "In one of our walks through Florence," he writes, "you declared to me very heatedly that there was in the tendency of my thought a defect that you hated, despised, and would persecute until your dying day. Then we shook hands firmly and parted."[31] So much for the cameo of unruffled concord that Strakhov later offered to a gullible world!

Why should Dostoevsky have reacted so heatedly and insultingly? Strakhov had always been in favor of a hard line with the radicals, and his remarks seem to refer to this position. No one, he argued, should be permitted to escape the logical consequences of his convictions and actions; no excuses should be made on the ground that people did not understand the full implications of their own ideas. "You found unbearable and repugnant," writes Strakhov, "that I often led our reasoning to the conclusion which, in the simplest fashion, can be expressed as: 'but really, it is impossible that 2 plus 2 does not equal 4.'"[32]

Strakhov was thus insisting that the radicals be made to assume the full onus of their beliefs. Dostoevsky, on the other hand, did not as yet wish to pin them against the wall, and he had replied to Strakhov that their seeming inconsistency should be given a more charitable interpretation: "obviously the people who say *2 plus 2 does not equal 4* do not at all intend to say this, but, without question, think and wish to express something else."[33] For Dostoevsky, illogicality is not a proof of error but the indication of a conflict between what is said and what is actually meant; the error is a clue to something hidden and concealed under the

[30] *Biografiya*, 243–244.
[31] L. P. Lansky, ed. "N. N. Strakov o Dostoevskom," *LN* 86 (Moscow, 1973), 560.
[32] Ibid.
[33] Ibid., 560–561.

idea that must be understood as its *real* meaning. These words reveal the basis on which, so far, Dostoevsky had refused to condemn the radicals in toto, no matter how hostile he was to their expressed ideas. For underneath these he continued to sense a desire for the good that should be recognized and acknowledged.

Another passage in Strakhov's allusive text takes a sudden leap from the realm of social politics to that of the ultimate basis of morality. "Is man really good?" Strakhov asks abruptly. "Are we really able boldly to deny his rottenness?" His answer to this question is emphatically negative, and he supports his conclusion by an appeal to the testimony of the Christian faith: "The ideal of the perfect man, shown us by Christianity, is not dead and cannot die in our souls; it has grown together with it forever. And thus, when the picture of contemporary humanity is unrolled before us and we are asked: Is man good? we immediately find in ourselves the decisive answer: 'No, rotten to the core!'"[34] The fragment contains enough for us to understand why Dostoevsky could have been stirred to such anger and hostility against his presumed "friend."

Despite a widely held belief to the contrary, Dostoevsky did not share Strakhov's "Christian" view that man is "rotten to the core" (which represents the opinion only of an extreme Augustinian or Reformation Christianity). Dostoevsky believed that since man, and Russian man in particular, was capable of remorse and repentance, the hope of his redemption should never be abandoned. No doubt Strakhov understood this to be the root cause of Dostoevsky's refusal to renounce all sympathy with the radicals once and for all, and his response that he "would hate, despise, and persecute" such a cast of mind for the remainder of his days. Strakhov was indeed striking here at Dostoevsky's deepest pieties, at his fundamental faith in the treasures of Christian love concealed in the soul of the ignorant Russian people; and such a sacrilege Dostoevsky could not forgive.

After their week in Florence together the two men parted company, Strakhov going on to Paris and Dostoevsky intending to journey south to Rome and Naples. For unknown reasons he changed his mind and by the beginning of September was back in Petersburg ready to take up his post again as de facto editor and chief contributor to *Time*.

[34] Ibid., 562.

CHAPTER 26

Time: The Final Months

On returning to Petersburg in the fall of 1862, both Dostoevsky and Strakhov took up their work on *Time* again with renewed vigor. Grigoryev had also returned from self-imposed exile in Orenburg and was once again a rallying presence. By mid-year, *Time*'s subscription list had gone over the four thousand mark, thus reaching the level of such long-established publications as *Notes of the Fatherland*. Financial security was at last in sight for the hard-pressed Dostoevskys, who had worked like galley slaves to establish their publication on a sound economic footing. Even more encouraging, their editorial portfolio was overflowing with manuscripts that kept pouring in from all corners of Russia and testified to the growing prestige acquired by *Time* in the brief span of two years.

The editors of *Time*, however, found themselves in an increasingly awkward predicament. The government ban of *The Contemporary* in July 1862, along with the simultaneous arrest of Chernyshevsky, had caused a sharp shift in the social-cultural climate. It was no longer possible to criticize radical ideas—no matter how respectfully, or with how many qualifications—without seeming to support the repressive measures of the regime. To cease to argue with the radicals would have meant to abandon *Time*'s very reason for being, but to continue with the same editorial policy was to court disaster and even execration.

Some notion of the tense and suspicious atmosphere then reigning in literary circles may be gathered from Nekrasov's astonishing frankness in his letter to Dostoevsky explaining why another promised contribution would not be forthcoming. Rumors were circulating, he admitted, "that I betrayed Chernyshevsky [to the authorities] and walk around freely in the open air in Petersburg. . . . In view of all this, I must not, for the time being, give any further cause for ambiguous rumors."[1] Dostoevsky was upset by the implications of this letter and had every reason to take umbrage at Nekrasov's insinuation that *Time* might be considered reactionary. Even though his articles during 1862–1863 reveal his growing disenchantment with the radicals and an increasing tilt toward Slavophilism, *Time* had not become conservative in any sense that would have gained favor

---

[1] N. S. Nekrasov, *Polnoe sobranie sochinenii i pisem*, 12 vols. (Moscow, 1948–1953), 10: 479–480.

with the authorities. It continued to refer to the *Raskol*, which was officially illegal and rejected the whole apparatus of the Russian state, as proof of the capacity
of the Russian people to create their own indigenous forms of culture; and Dostoevsky repeatedly adduces the communal system of landholding as additional
evidence of such capacity. Indeed, he could hardly have been clearer in his agreement with the basic tenets of Herzen's Russian Socialism.

The reappearance of *The Contemporary* at the end of February 1863 brought
into the field against *Time* a new and exceedingly formidable foe, the scathing
satirist Saltykov-Shchedrin, who had now joined the editorial staff of the revived
journal; and he was promptly assigned the task, formerly entrusted to the bellicose but inept Antonovich, of carrying on the fight against the *pochvenniki*.
Saltykov-Shchedrin, whose *Provincial Sketches* had appeared in Katkov's *The
Russian Messenger*, and some of whose sketches had also graced the pages of
Time, had not previously been known as a flaming radical. Since Dostoevsky
had frequently expressed great admiration for his talents, his sudden intervention as a prominent antagonist was bitterly resented.

Although the argument was carried on anonymously, each recognized the in-
imitable stamp of the other's style and tone. Saltykov-Shchedrin labeled *Time*'s
contributors as "meek little birds," constantly living in fear and trembling even
though "no one has injured you. No one opposes you, no one even thinks about
you." There was much more in this condescending vein, including the prediction that *Time* would soon "Katkovize," that is, wholly join the anti-radical
camp; but meanwhile, it is trying to maintain an impossible position. "What is
the guiding thought of your journal? None. What have you said? Nothing. You
have continuously striven to utter some sort of truth on the order of 'soft-boiled
boots' [a Russian expression for nonsense], you always have sat between two
stools, and your naïveté extends so far that you have not wished to notice that
you have tumbled to the ground."[2] This was only the beginning of an increasingly fierce exchange between these two major figures that, a year later, would
culminate in a brilliant burst of parodistic dialogue skits on both sides. Nor did
Dostoevsky forget to include two satirical barbs against Saltykov-Shchedrin in
his very next work, *Notes from Underground*.

Russia, however, was then occupied by events far surpassing in immediate
importance the internal squabbles of its native intelligentsia. January 1863 marked
the outbreak of still another Polish revolt against Russian hegemony. If Russian
opinion had been favorable to the Polish desire for more local independence,
feelings quickly shifted after the uprising began with a massacre of sleeping Russian soldiers in their barracks. The Poles also demanded, in addition to independence, a restoration of the Polish borders of 1772, which included Lithuania,

[2] M. E. Saltykov-Shchedrin, *Sobranie sochinenii*, 20 vols. (Moscow, 1965–1977), 6: 46.

White Russia, and much of the Ukraine. The pressure exerted by France and England on behalf of these claims only succeeded in whipping up Russian nationalism to a fever pitch, and the support of the radicals for the Polish cause (some young Russian officers even deserted and fought with the Poles) ended whatever influence the extreme left still may have had in society at large. Herzen's support for the Poles, assumed much against his better judgment (he was won over by the volatile Bakunin, always spoiling for a revolution), dealt a deathblow to *The Bell*.

The radicals within the country could hardly express support for the Polish cause in the Russian press. Of course, an event of such gravity did not pass unnoticed; but coverage was limited—as in the case of *Time*—to a neutral summary of official dispatches and an account of the international diplomatic maneuverings. In Moscow, however, Katkov was carrying on a blistering campaign against the Poles and the Russian radicals, whom he threw together into one unsavory heap, and he became the much-applauded man of the hour, the admired voice of Russian patriotic indignation. The failure of the Petersburg press to raise its voice with equal vehemence was bitterly resented in Moscow. The Muscovites were all too ready to take the relative silence as a sign of treason, and they did not hesitate to hurl such an accusation against the first available target offering itself to their fury. Unfortunately for *Time*, this target turned out to be an article by Strakhov that, although intended as a public avowal in favor of the Russian cause, was written in such tortuous and elusive terms that it could be misread as a justification of the desperate Polish revolt.

Time was suppressed by the government in May 1863; and it is a sad irony that Dostoevsky's journal should have been shut down at the very moment it was battling most ferociously with *The Contemporary*. Dostoevsky explains what happened in a letter to Turgenev a month after the axe had fallen. "The idea of the article (Strakhov wrote it) was as follows: that the Poles despise us as barbarians to such a degree, are so boastful to us of their 'European' civilization, that one can scarcely foresee for a long time any moral peace (the only durable kind) with us. But, as the exposition of the article was not understood, it was interpreted as follows: that we affirmed, *of ourselves*, that the Poles have a civilization so superior to ours, and we are so inferior, that obviously they are right and we are wrong."[3]

Such a charge was indeed instantly made by a writer in the *Moscow Gazette*—a newspaper edited by Katkov—and it was echoed elsewhere. When Dostoevsky wrote a reply, the censorship banned its publication, and, as he indignantly reports to Turgenev, "certain journals (the *Day*, among others) have seriously undertaken to prove to us that Polish civilization is only a surface civilization, aristocratic and Jesuitical, thus not at all superior to ours,"[4] when this was the very point of Strakhov's article. The tsar, already ill-disposed toward *Time*, decided that the moment had come to put an end to this persistent journalistic nuisance once and for all. The order to ban the publication, handed down on May 24, 1863, was justified not only on the basis of Strakhov's article but also because of "the harmful tendency of the journal."[5]

So ended the life of *Time*, and its demise left Mikhail saddled with a huge load of debt. The event was disastrous from every point of view and produced a further strain in the relations between Strakhov and Dostoevsky. To be sure, Strakhov could not be held entirely to blame because, as editor in charge, Dostoevsky had read and approved his essay. The two remained on ostensibly friendly terms, although the whole disaster left a festering resentment that came out much later in mutually hostile private remarks.

———■———

The suppression of *Time* dealt a severe blow to Dostoevsky's personal fortunes and deprived him of his sole regular source of income. Luckily, he was not left completely without resources for the future, because the various major works published in its pages had managed to reestablish his literary reputation. The *Insulted and Injured* had brought him back to public attention, and his *Notes from the House of the Dead* had raised him to a fame far surpassing the transient glory he had achieved with *Poor Folk* in 1845. We examined *House of the Dead* earlier for its documentary value; let us now take up the text as a work of art.

Prison memoirs have become so familiar to us (and Russian literature is now, alas, so rich in examples of them) that one tends to forget it was Dostoevsky who gave his country the first masterpiece of this kind. But so it was: his *House of the Dead* created the genre in Russia, thus responding to an immense curiosity concerning the conditions of life of those "unfortunates" who ran afoul of the state, especially those convicted of political crimes. The politicals usually came from the ranks of the educated, and any public allusion to *their* fate was certain to excite the liveliest interest. "My figure will disappear," Dostoevsky had written to Mikhail in October 1859. "These are the notes of an unknown, but I guarantee their interest. There will be . . . the depiction of characters *unheard* of previously in literature, and . . . finally, the most important, my name. . . . I am convinced that the public will read this with avidity."[6] Dostoevsky counted on his readers

[4] Ibid., 318.
[5] Cited in V. S. Nechaeva, *Zhurnal M. M. i F. M. Dostoevskikh, Vremya, 1861–1863* (Moscow, 1973), 308.
[6] *Pis'ma*, 2: 605; October 9, 1859.

to accept the work as an accurate report of his prison years, and so they did.[7] But his presence as a political convict would pervade the book as a whole rather than being placed in the foreground. This double perspective is carefully maintained, and must be kept in mind if we are to avoid the error of taking the work as either an unadorned memoir or a purely fictional construct; in fact, it is a unique combination of both.

House of the Dead obviously owes its origins to the accidents of Dostoevsky's existence, but it also fits quite neatly into a genre much cultivated in Russian literature at that moment. Many accounts of personal experience written in a loose, sketchlike form and tied together in a seemingly haphazard fashion were then being produced; and Dostoevsky was familiar with them all. On leaving prison camp, he had read Turgenev's *A Sportsman's Sketches* and the popular vignettes by S. T. Aksakov about hunting and fishing. Tolstoy's *Sevastopol Stories* were also published shortly after Dostoevsky's release, and he hastened to read these too, as well as everything else that came from Tolstoy's pen. Herzen's masterly memoirs, *My Past and Thoughts*, had begun to appear during the mid-1850s in *The Bell*, and new installments were published throughout the remainder of the decade.

The sudden emergence of this semi-journalistic literary mode may be attributed partly to a temporary relaxation of the censorship, which encouraged writers to speak more freely than they had done in the past without the protective disguise of "fiction" (Herzen, living in exile, did not have to worry about the censorship at all). Writers thus instinctively turned back to the form of the physiological sketch, much favored during the 1840s—another period of relative literary freedom—which had emphasized the accurate observation of social types embedded in their environment, and aimed at depicting people in the routine of their everyday existence. Most early sketches of this type had focused on urban characters and city life, but the renaissance of the form in the 1850s extended its thematic range to take in the life of the peasantry.

Since the aim of such sketches was to convey an impression of truthfulness, they were not linked together by any sort of novelistic intrigue that might arouse suspicion concerning the verisimilitude of the life being portrayed. Such relative plotlessness then became a distinctive feature of the Russian novel when writers like Turgenev and Tolstoy went on to more complex genres than the sketch and

---

[7] According to his intention, Dostoevsky's sketches were generally accepted as a reliable account of documentary value, and later researches in the central historical archives of the Russian Army have tended to confirm this instinctive assessment, although there are some discrepancies between the documents and Dostoevsky's version. A tendency has been noted to make the crimes of his compatriots more severe than the record indicates, and, it has been suggested, he did so in order implicitly to justify the extreme harshness of the punishments. But since he had no way of knowing what the facts really were, relying only on what he was told, he may not knowingly have distorted at all. It is possible that what Dostoevsky learned came closer to the truth than what the authorities had been able to verify from the testimony of sullenly hostile peasant informants.

the short story. Dostoevsky stands out as the great exception to this tendency of Russian nineteenth-century prose and had already begun to experiment with the elaborately plotted roman-feuilleton technique, which he would soon raise to new heights. But *House of the Dead*, among many other things, is also a tribute to his literary versatility and proves that he could adapt his technique to his material and to whatever artistic purpose he chose. It was important, above all, that the reader have no doubts about the veracity of his account, and so Dostoevsky, eschewing all "novelistic" effects, developed his own original variation of the larger sketch forms used by the Russian writers he admired.

Unlike those of either Turgenev or Tolstoy, Dostoevsky's sketches reach the reader through the interposition of two frame narrators. The first is the presumed editor of the book, who appears in the introduction and gives the impression of being a well-educated, curious, and observant person; not a native of Siberia, he has spent a considerable time there—probably in some administrative capacity, like Dostoevsky's friend Baron Wrangel. This first narrator supplies a tongue-in-cheek picture of life in that remote region ("the inhabitants are simple folk and not of liberal views; everything goes on according to the old-fashioned, solid, time-honored traditions") that drips with polite sarcasm and indicates to the Russian reader that the region was really a sink of iniquity (4: 5). His words are also an invitation to look carefully beneath the surface of the prose for hidden meanings, and this signal was surely meant to alert the reader not to take completely at face value the information provided by the first narrator about the second. The nominal author of the sketches is a former landowner, Alexander Petrovich Goryanchikov (the name suggests someone who has suffered greatly: *gore* in Russian means "grief" or "misfortune"), who has served a ten-year sentence for murdering his wife in a fit of jealous rage during their first year of marriage. Goryanchikov lives in complete seclusion, earns his scant living by giving lessons to local children, and shuns all contact with the world, presumably unable to adjust to normal life after his years in penal servitude.

When Goryanchikov dies suddenly, the first narrator manages to rescue some of the dead man's papers from being thrown away. One bundle contains a "disconnected description of the ten years spent by Alexander Petrovich in the prison camp." These pages break off occasionally and are interspersed with passages from another story, "some strange and terrible reminiscences"—a probable reference to the murder, which haunts Goryanchikov. Hence this portion of the posthumous text is not reproduced, and the editor decides that only Goryanchikov's account of his prison years is "not devoid of interest." For since Goryanchikov reveals "an absolutely new, till then unknown world," the editor decides to offer his sketches for public scrutiny (4: 8).

Just how seriously this second narrator should be taken has been a continual matter of dispute. Some critics are disposed to take him very seriously indeed, and the ever-iconoclastic Victor Shklovsky has tried to make out a case for giving the fate of Goryanchikov a central place in the interpretation of the book.[8] But if we regard him as the genuine narrator of *House of the Dead*, rather than Dostoevsky himself, then it is impossible not to charge the author with unforgivable carelessness. In Chapter 2, for example, when Akim Akimich tells the convict narrator that the peasant inmates "are not fond of gentlemen . . . especially politicals," he is clearly addressing someone included in this latter category; and there are other allusions to the same status of the narrator scattered throughout the book (4: 28). Moreover, if we are to accept Goryanchikov as more than a convention, then Dostoevsky can be accused of allowing a disturbing clash to occur between his theme as a whole and the frame narration in which it is contained. For none of the consoling truths that the narrator has learned in the house of the dead, none of the exuberance, the sense of hope, the possibility of beginning a new life that he felt on his release—none of these events are in accord with the character and fate of the Goryanchikov who is presumed to have written the manuscript we read.[9]

The more convincing accepted view is that Dostoevsky introduced Goryanchikov primarily as a means of avoiding trouble with the censorship, and that he did not expect his readers to take him as more than a convenient device. Nor, in fact, did they do so: the book was universally accepted as a more or less faithful account of Dostoevsky's own past as a political prisoner, even though, as he remarked much later with a touch of humor, he still came across people who believed he had been sent to *katorga* for having murdered his wife (22: 47). Such a device was practically obligatory for a book of this kind under Russian conditions, and was also employed by another survivor of the Petrashevsky Circle, F. N. Lvov, who published his souvenirs of Siberia almost simultaneously. A later exile, P. F. Yakubovich—whose memoirs, published at the end of the century, betray Dostoevsky's influence—explained in a letter how important it still was to adopt a "disguise" while making it as transparent as possible ("the author does not try to make his disguise more successful: on the contrary, he wishes to use an obvious and well-worn stereotype").[10] It is thus preferable to allow for the pressure of external circumstances, and not to impose more of an "artistic" pattern on the narrative structure of *House of the Dead* than the evidence supports; there is artistry enough, but of a different kind.

Even if we agree, however, that Goryanchikov is more of a device than a

---

[8] Victor Shklovsky, *Za i protiv* (Moscow, 1957), 101.

[9] Moreover, as V. A. Tunimanov has written, for the reader "it is not Goryanchikov who emerges from prison but the author-narrator, that is, Dostoevsky. The 'conclusion' of the book is not at all despairing, and one should not, evidently, exaggerate the pessimism of the *Notes*. . . ." See Tunimanov, *Tvorchestvo Dostoevskogo, 1854–1862* (Leningrad, 1980), 80.

[10] Ibid., 75.

narrator, and that it is Dostoevsky himself who unmistakably speaks in the body of the book, R. L. Jackson has perceptively suggested that the invention of this figure may have had a deeper significance all the same. The image we receive of Goryanchikov, who shuns almost all human contact and seems to be living in a state of shock—as if under the effect of a traumatic experience too severe to be overcome—certainly represents one aspect of Dostoevsky's own reaction to his prison-camp encounters. Very little reflection of such an attitude can be seen in the book itself—or rather, we detect its gradual transmutation into feelings of comprehension and friendliness, although there is no portrayal of the inner process through which this change occurs. Jackson believes that, by placing the distraught Goryanchikov at the threshold of the work, Dostoevsky was in a sense eliminating him from the remainder, and in so doing "freed *Notes from the House of the Dead* from the tyranny of a deeply personal, misanthropic subjectivity, a tormented ego driven to the limits of malice and despair, to almost complete moral exhaustion by years of forced existence in the 'human herd.'"[11] Such a conjecture seems to me quite plausible, and Goryanchikov could well have served some such cathartic function during the course of creation.

———■———

While *House of the Dead* has no plot in the obvious sense, it is, all the same, carefully organized, and its overarching pattern reflects the narrator's gradual penetration into the strange and disorienting world of the prison camp—his attainment, as he slowly overcomes his prejudices and preconceptions, of a new understanding of the intense humanity and particular moral quality of those he had at first regarded only with loathing and dismay. The plan of the work, shaped by this process of discovery, is thus "dynamic" in character, and reproduces the movement of moral-psychological assimilation and reevaluation that Dostoevsky himself underwent.

The first six chapters depict his first disorienting impressions of this strange new world to which he had been exposed. Only after this initiation, when he has overcome his bewilderment at the appalling spectacle he sees before him, do individuals begin to stand out with any clarity, and it is then that the names of persons appear in the chapter titles. This aspect of the form has been well defined by K. Mochulsky, who remarks that, in the beginning, Dostoevsky "is an external observer, grasping only the most glaring and striking features"; it is only later that "he penetrates into the mysterious depths of this world" and "perceives anew that which had been seen, re-evaluates his first impressions, deepens his

---

[11] R. L. Jackson, "The Narrator in Dostoevsky's *Notes from the House of the Dead*," in *Studies in Russian and Polish Literature, in Honor of Waclaw Lednicki* (The Hague, 1962), 197.

conclusions."[12] Jacques Catteau has also sensitively remarked on the significant shift in the principles of the organization of chapters between Parts One and Two. At first, what is accentuated is the shock of initial contact ("First Impressions"), or the sudden perception of individual character ("Petrov"), while the second part spreads out into chapters held together by spatial contiguity ("The Hospital") or by loose subject groupings ("Prison Animals," "Comrades").[13] In other words, the personality of the narrator, quite prominent in the earlier chapters, fades into the background as he merges into the everyday life of the community.

The repetitions of the book, the continual returns of character and motif, form part of the structure by which the negative first impressions are deepened and transformed. Such repetitions also act on the reader to reinforce the sense of living in an enclosed world of immutable routine, a world in which people, and time itself, constantly revolve in an endless cycle allowing for no real change. Indeed, Dostoevsky's handling of time is particularly subtle and unobtrusive, and works to shape the perceptions of the reader underneath the seeming artlessness of the sketch form; he thus anticipates many of the experiments of our own day in correlating the shape of narrative time to accord with subjective experience. Time literally comes to a stop in the early chapters as the narrator concentrates gropingly on the unfamiliar perceptions that he is forced to cope with; but it speeds up gradually until, at the end, we find it hard to believe that ten years have actually elapsed. Much of the book is also structured around the cycle of the seasons (essentially the cycle of the first year of imprisonment, although Dostoevsky plays fast and loose with the literal sequence of events.)

It is probably this greater sense of unity achieved by Dostoevsky that has led to so much speculation regarding the genre to which *House of the Dead* should be assigned. Is it a series of sketches, a personal memoir, or, as Victor Shklovsky has insisted, "a novel of a special type,"[14] a documentary novel about a collectivity rather than about a single individual or family? The reasonable conclusion is that it is a mixed form combining aspects of all three types, and that it is less important to classify it properly than to understand the unique amalgam that Dostoevsky created. The basis is unquestionably that of the sketch form, as in Turgenev; there is also a strong element of the personal memoir, as in Tolstoy (the history of an encounter with and adaptation to a strange, bewildering, and frightening milieu), but Shklovsky is also right in calling attention to the importance accorded the collectivity. For what distinguishes *House of the Dead* from all

---

[12] K. Mochulsky, *Dostoevsky: His Life and Work*, trans. Michael A. Minihan (Princeton, NJ, 1967), 186.

[13] Jacques Catteau, "De la structure de la *Maison des morts* de F. M. Dostoevskij," *Revue des Etudes Slaves* 54 (1982), 63–72.

[14] Shklovsky, *Za i protiv*, 107.

works of a similar kind is this unprecedented effort by an educated Russian to grasp and portray the moral-spiritual essence of a peasant world that he has been forced to *accept* provisionally as his own.

Dostoevsky conveys this apprehension of group life, the sense of living in a contained and unified world, by, among other means, reshaping the Russian sketch form to strengthen the atmosphere of self-enclosure. In his classic study of the young Tolstoy, B. M. Eikhenbaum has pointed out that, in the typical sketch, "a characteristic compositional device" was to use "a lyrical landscape as a frame." This device, "especially canonized by Turgenev" in *A Sportsman's Sketches*, is also used by Tolstoy in his *Sevastopol Stories*, and in both writers the lyrical evocation of nature provides a welcome release from the oppressive limits of the central situation.[15] Nature offers an escape into an innocent world of peace and serenity by contrast with the routine brutality of the treatment of peasant serfs or the unending slaughter at Sevastopol. An occasional poignant release of this kind can also be observed in Dostoevsky's sketches as he turns his eyes to the sky overhead, feels the quickening effects of spring freshness, or gazes at the steppe fading into the distance through the slats of the prison stockade. But since such instances rarely if ever are used to frame and punctuate a sequence, they never function implicitly to offer some alternative to the world being portrayed.

Much more often the frame in Dostoevsky's sketches is provided by the constraints of prison life—the life he shares with the collectivity. Time and again in *House of the Dead*, after the description of some holiday or other event (such as the prison theatricals) that has broken the stifling tedium of routine, this enclosing and constricting type of frame terminates the chapter. "But why describe this Bedlam! The oppressive day came to an end at last. The convicts fell asleep on the plank bed. . . . The holiday so long looked forward to was over. Tomorrow the daily round, tomorrow work again" (4: 116). Here we have the "nature" of the prison world, which does not allow man to dissolve his heartache in its limitless and consoling expanse; rather, it only sinks the individual, who may have felt a momentary upsurge of liberation, more despairingly back into the imprisonment of his mass fate.

Still another aspect of *House of the Dead* distinguishes it markedly from the similar works of Turgenev and Tolstoy. All three writers share the same overriding theme—the encounter of a member of the upper, educated class with the Russian people—and each treats it in his own distinctive way. Turgenev stresses the spiritual beauty and richness of Russian peasant life, the poetry of its superstitions and customs, and by doing so makes the serf status of the peasant and the casual cruelty of his treatment all the more unforgivable. Tolstoy discovers the Russian peasantry amid the besieged bastions of Sevastopol and is astonished

---

[15] B. M. Eikhenbaum, *The Young Tolstoy*, trans. Gary Kern (Ann Arbor, MI, 1972), 77.

at the calm tranquility of its unassuming heroism—so much at variance with the vanity occupying the consciousness of upper-class officers dreaming of decorations and promotions, and this understanding inspires Tolstoy with "a joyous conviction of the strength of the Russian people."[16] Such strength, however, is demonstrated exclusively by their imperturbable and almost cheerful acceptance of death out of instinctive loyalty to God, the tsar, and Mother Russia.

Only Dostoevsky depicts the Russian people *in revolt* against their enslaved condition, implacably hating the gentlemen who have oppressed them and ready to use their knives and axes to strike back when mistreatment becomes unbearable. Even more, it is precisely such peasants—whose crimes, for the most part, were a violent protest against the refusal to consider them as fully sentient human beings—whom Dostoevsky singles out as the finest specimens of the Russian people: "After all, one must tell the whole truth; these men were exceptional men. Perhaps they were the most gifted, the strongest of our people. But their mighty energies were vainly wasted, wasted abnormally, unjustly, hopelessly. And who was to blame, whose fault was it?" (4: 231). There can be no doubt of the answer: the abhorrent institution of serfdom, and the whole complex of social customs that had led to the treatment of serfs as members of an inferior species. No wonder that Dostoevsky's portrait of the Russian peasantry—his image of them as indomitable and unyielding in their ceaseless struggle against the most brutal subjugation—became, above all others, a favorite of the Russian radicals in the midst of the revolutionary aspirations of the early 1860s.

■

From a purely artistic point of view, *House of the Dead* is probably the most unusual book that Dostoevsky ever produced. One would be hard put to recognize the prison memoirs and his purely creative work as coming from the same pen. The intense dramatism of the fiction is here replaced by a calm objectivity of presentation; there is little close analysis of interior states of mind, and there are marvelous descriptive passages that reveal Dostoevsky's ability as an observer of the external world. These "non-Dostoevskian" qualities of *House of the Dead*, as it were, are one reason why a number of his great contemporaries preferred his prison memoirs to all those other works to which we now assign a much greater value. In a letter to Fet, Turgenev spoke of the "smelly self-laceration" of *Crime and Punishment*, but he called the bath scene in *House of the Dead* "simply Dantesque."[17] Herzen made the same comparison with Dante, and added that Dostoevsky "had created out of the description of the customs of a Siberian prison a fresco in the spirit of Michelangelo."[18] Tolstoy considered the book one of the

[16] L. N. Tolstoy, *Tales from Army Life*, trans. Louise and Aylmer Maude (London, 1951), 105.
[17] I. S. Turgenev, *Pis'ma*, 13 vols. (Moscow–Leningrad, 1961), 6: 66.
[18] Cited in *PSS*, 4: 296.

most original works of Russian prose; in *What Is Art?* he placed it among the few works in world literature that could be taken as models of a "lofty religious art, inspired by love of God and one's neighbor." [19]

The bath scene singled out for praise by Turgenev is indeed an impressive example of Dostoevsky's ability to present a mass tableau with broad strokes:

> There was not a spot on the floor as big as the palm of your hand where there was not a convict squatting, splashing from his bucket. . . . On the top shelf and on all the steps leading up to it men were crouched, huddled together washing themselves. But they did not wash themselves much. Men of the peasant class don't wash much with soap and hot water; they only steam themselves terribly and then douche themselves with cold water—that is their idea of a bath. Fifty birches were rising and falling rhythmically on the shelves; they all thrashed themselves into a state of stupefaction. . . . As a rule the steaming backs of the convicts show distinctly the scars of the blows or lashes they have received in the past, so that all those backs looked now as though freshly wounded. The scars were horrible! A shiver ran down me at the sight of them. They pour more boiling water on the hot bricks and clouds of thick, hot steam fill the whole bathhouse; they all laugh and shout. Through the clouds of steam one gets glimpses of scarred backs, shaven heads, bent arms and legs. . . . It occurred to me that if one day we would all be in hell together it would be very much like this place. (4: 98)

Even in what seems a purely descriptive passage, Dostoevsky selects the symbolic detail ("all those backs looked now as though freshly wounded") that reinforces one of his main motifs—the terrible inhumanity of flogging, with its degradation of the human spirit and its devilish temptation to unleash the sadistic instincts. Dostoevsky skillfully weaves together all the seemingly casual events and accidents of prison life through this type of symbolic accentuation, and the book contains a number of such famous episodes greatly admired by his contemporaries.

———————■———————

Since there are several allusions in *House of the Dead* to recent changes for the better in prison-camp conditions, every reader would understand, even though no dates are given, that the work deals with events that took place during the reign of Nicholas I. The first narrator writes as someone who, in the early 1860s, is looking back at a recent but by now almost legendary past, and several passages, such as the dramatic episode involving "the parricide Ilyinsky," introduce

---

[19] Ibid., 297.

the point of view of the present. Other indications of the time of writing evidently reflect Dostoevsky's response to the social-cultural situation of the early 1860s. Indeed, it can be argued that the entire book was written as a response to this situation, and that Dostoevsky's portrayal of the instinctive Christianity of the peasant convicts, as well as of their hostile alienation from the educated class, was intended to reveal the patent futility of revolutionary hopes inspired by a radical ideology that the peasants would reject with abhorrence if they understood it at all.

A few passages can hardly be read except as manifest thrusts against some of the notions, strenuously propagated by Chernyshevsky, that had now attained the status of irrefutable truth among the younger generation. There was a firm belief, for example, in the overwhelming power of environment to determine human behavior—a theory that Dostoevsky rejects. "It is high time," he declares, "we gave up apathetic complaints of being corrupted by our environment. It is true no doubt that it does destroy a great deal in us, but not everything, and often a crafty and knowing rogue, especially if he is an eloquent speaker or writer, will cover up not simply weakness but often real baseness, justifying it by the influence of 'environment'" (4: 142). Dostoevsky is thus perfectly willing to acknowledge the pressure of environment, but not to eliminate individual moral responsibility altogether.

In an even more overt sally against Chernyshevsky, a selfless widow is evoked who lives in the vicinity of the prison camp and devotes her life to helping the convicts. "There are in Siberia, and practically always have been," he remarks, "some people who seem to make it the object of their lives to look after the 'unfortunates,' to show pure and disinterested sympathy and compassion for them, as though they were their own children." Nastasya Ivanovna had nothing remarkable about her: "All that one could see in her was an infinite kindness, an irresistible desire to please one, to comfort one, to do something nice for one." Dostoevsky recalls her modest present of a cigarette case of cardboard, covered with colored paper trimmed with gilt around the edges; she knew he smoked cigarettes and thought the case might give him pleasure. "Some people maintain (I have heard it and read it)," Dostoevsky continues, "that the purest love for one's neighbor is at the same time the greatest egoism. What egoism there could be in this instance, I can't understand" (4: 68).

Dostoevsky could hardly have rejected with more firmness the attempt of Chernyshevsky to establish a new ethics on the foundation of egoism. But while such passages are a clear challenge to the intention of recasting the moral code in Utilitarian terms, a more subtle and powerful rejection—one that will soon provide the inspiration for *Notes from Underground*—can be found in the pages describing the frenzied desire of the convicts to express the freedom of their personalities, even if in doing so they sacrifice all self-interest in the usual sense to attain only the momentary, irrational illusion of moral-psychic autonomy. What the prisoners value more than anything else, as Dostoevsky unforgettably shows, is "freedom or the dream of freedom," and to keep this dream alive they will sometimes go to lengths that seem like madness.

So-called model convicts will sometimes suddenly break out in a self-destructive fashion. "And all the while," Dostoevsky explains, "possibly the cause . . . is simply the poignant hysterical craving for self-expression, the unconscious yearning for himself, the desire to assert himself, to assert his crushed personality, a desire which suddenly takes possession of him and reaches the pitch of fury, of spite, of mental aberration, of fits and nervous convulsions. So perhaps a man buried alive and awakening in his coffin might beat upon the lid and struggle to fling it off, though of course reason might convince him that all his efforts would be useless; but the trouble is that it is not a question of reason, it is a question of nervous convulsions" (4: 66–67).

The man who had watched such explosions of stifled humanity erupting before his very eyes, and who was capable of analyzing them with such anguished penetration, could hardly accept Chernyshevsky's "rational egoism" as the ultimate word of human wisdom. And we shall see that Dostoevsky had already begun symbolically to pit this ineradicable human need—the need for man to assert the freedom of his personality—against the Socialist ideal of the generation of the 1860s, with its peculiarly Russian attempt to integrate such an ideal with material determinism and a Utilitarian moral code.

CHAPTER 27

Winter Notes on Summer Impressions

The last important work that Dostoevsky published in *Time* was *Winter Notes on Summer Impressions* (*Zimnie zametki o letnikh vpechatleniyakh*), a series of articles in which he launches a full-scale assault on the major pieties of the radical credo. Dostoevsky seizes the occasion of his first journey through Europe to explore the whole tangled history of the relationship between educated Russians and European culture. Within this framework he also discusses the larger issues then being posed by radical ideology: the basis of a new moral-social order; the question of Socialism; the future destiny of mankind. By the time he finishes he will have discovered both the literary and the ideological stance that will lead within two years to the composition of his first post-Siberian masterpiece, *Notes from Underground*.

———————◼———————

Much like Americans such as Hawthorne, Emerson, and Henry James, cultivated Russians felt a need to define their own national individuality by comparing themselves with Europe, and Dostoevsky's *Winter Notes* takes its place in a long line of works through which Russians have examined the roots of their own culture as it had evolved, since Peter the Great, under the successive waves of European influence. Only by making the prescribed pilgrimage to the West, only by ceasing to regard Europe through the haze of distance as some enchanted land, could a Russian discover what aspects of European influence in his homeland he might wish to preserve and what discard. As a result, the travel diary has always been one of the chief means by which Russian self-consciousness has been sharpened and affirmed; and Dostoevsky's *Winter Notes*, true to type, thus gives us a fuller and franker expression of his convictions than any so far encountered in public print.

Like the vast majority of travelers to a foreign land, much of what Dostoevsky saw and felt corresponded gratifyingly to the expectations he had entertained before leaving. Roman Jakobson has amusingly pointed out the similarity in the reaction to Europe, and particularly to France, that can be observed over the time span of a century and a half in the writings of the most diverse variety of Russian visitors. Whether in 1800 or 1900, whether a Socialist radical, a patri-

otic Slavophil, a diehard reactionary, a moderate liberal, or a completely apolitical Symbolist aesthete—Russians have invariably responded to a homogeneous
"myth of France" well represented in one of the letters by Dostoevsky already
quoted.[1] "Ours are simply carnivorous scoundrels," he remarks to Strakhov,
"and, most of the time, know it, but here they are completely convinced that
this is how it must be. The Frenchman is pleasant, decent, polite, but false, and
money for him is everything."[2]

Long before he departed on his journey, Dostoevsky had been persuaded that
Europe was a dying culture that had lost its spiritual bond of unity. It was thus a
simple matter for him to pierce through the illusions of the glittering European
surface and instantly to detect the corruption lying concealed underneath. True,
some manifestations of this corruption might appear to be similar in Paris and
Petersburg; rogues and scoundrels existed as surely in the one place as in the
other. But Dostoevsky's letter shows the tactic that he will use in *Winter Notes* to
evade the consequences of such awkwardly impartial reflections. Russians are
conscious of their moral delinquency; they feel it as such; and hence they have
preserved the indispensable basis of morality. Europeans have become so depraved
that the very meaning of their own conduct escapes them and they complacently
take evil for good. This insistence on the moral stultification of Europe runs as a
leitmotif all through *Winter Notes* and emerges as its ultimate conclusion. But
such a generalization, hardly unexpected for the regular readers of *Time*, is of less
interest at the moment than the manner and means by which it is expressed.

Written in the first person, *Winter Notes* is a continuous dialogue with those
whom Dostoevsky addresses as "my friends" (5: 49). They have been urging him
to communicate his impressions of Europe. Very well! The "winter notes" are his
answer to their demands. Dostoevsky determines to dedicate himself to conveying his "sincere observations," though he is certain that his friends will have a
predetermined attitude toward Europe—one of awe—that does not surge up in
his own reactions. His first contacts with European life in Germany had violated
all the rules and regulations of the "renowned authorities." Nothing—neither
Unter den Linden nor the Cologne cathedral—had aroused the proper desire to
genuflect! All this was terribly disturbing, even inexplicable, until he returned to
his hotel room one day feeling ill and examined his symptoms: "My tongue was
yellow and malignant. . . . I thought, 'Can it be, can it really be that man, this
lord of all creation, is dependent to such a degree on his liver? What baseness!'"
(5: 48).

If for no other reason, this reference to the liver inevitably recalls the opening
sentences of *Notes from Underground*; and while the anatomical allusion may

[1] Roman Jakobson, "Der Russische Frankreich-Mythus," *Slavische Rundschau* 3 (1931),
636–642.
[2] *Pisma*, 1: 310; June 26/July 8, 1862.

seem at first glance only a casual coincidence, closer scrutiny reveals a deeper relation. Indeed, the rhetorical strategy used here is an anticipation of the one so masterfully deployed in the fictional work, where the author, again writing in the first person, also dramatizes a split in his consciousness between a pattern of behavior that might be considered normal and reasonable and an unexpected emotive reaction that surges up from some instinctive and visceral level of the personality. Both works, in addition, maintain the same close "dialogical" relation with the reader ("my friends"), who becomes an implicit and invoked presence *within* the text and is constantly appealed to as an interlocutor.

In this first chapter of *Winter Notes*, precisely the same situation exists between Dostoevsky and his readers as he will later recreate for the underground man. These readers anticipate an attitude of wide-eyed reverence before the glories of Europe, and the author shares this expectation sufficiently so that, when his own involuntary responses fail to correspond, he can only laugh at himself for his incapacity. But at the same time, he feels his irreverence to be a more authentic reaction than the automatic obeisance that his readers expect. Hence, his irony cuts two ways, being directed both against himself (for having somehow failed to measure up to Europe) and against the reader (for being unable to tolerate any but a hackneyed and conventional point of view). Such an "inverted irony," which turns back on the writer as a means of turning *against* an imagined judge and critic in the person of the reader, is precisely the one that will be used in *Notes from Underground*.

Dostoevsky wishes the reader to understand that his reaction is by no means as aberrant as may appear. Quite the contrary, it springs directly from the whole ambivalent relation of the Russian psyche to European culture. It expresses the adoration of Europe induced by education, the self-hatred provoked by such adoration, and then the irrepressible need to assert independence even if only in a self-mocking manner. The Russian refusal to acknowledge the secret of its ambivalent relation to Europe is reflected by Dostoevsky's inverted irony, which jestingly anticipates such outraged reactions and overcomes them at the same time.

His meditations on the anomalies of the Russian attitude toward Europe naturally led Dostoevsky to think back on the origins of his fateful relationship, and he sketches its history in a chapter that, though labeled "completely superfluous," contains the very heart of the matter. "I began to ponder," he says, "on this theme: how Europe has, at various times, been reflected in us and constantly broken in on us with its civilization, and . . . how many of us now are really civilized through and through?" (5: 55). In the past, despite the brilliant French surface of the court of Catherine the Great, the Russian landowner and apprentice courtier had still kept his old habits and feelings. These were admittedly brutal, barbarous, and revolting, but they were still his own, they were still

Russian; and the people felt more at home with this generation than with their more "humane" offspring. Then came Chatsky, the hero of Griboyedov's comedy *Woe from Wit*, who had assimilated the culture of Europe and, on returning home to Russia, found life there unbearable. The first of the superfluous men, Chatsky flees back to Europe, lamenting that there is no longer any place for him in his homeland. "One thing I cannot understand," writes Dostoevsky. "Chatsky was after all a very intelligent man. How could it happen that an intelligent man could find nothing here to do? All of them found nothing to do, for a period of two or three generations" (5: 62).

As for the latest Russian type, the progressive and radical, he neither acts out a farce like Catherine's courtier nor is troubled by self-doubt; he has become completely and complacently European. "For how self-assured we are now in our civilizing mission. . . . There is no such thing as a native soil, as a people. Nationality?—only a certain system of paying taxes! The soul?—a *tabula rasa*, a bit of wax, out of which you can paste together on the spot a real man, a universal general man, a homuncule—all that's necessary is to apply the fruits of European civilization, and read two or three books!" (5: 59). One can already hear the jeering, provocative voice of the underground man in these sentences, which contain exactly the inflections of his tone: a partial identification ("we") with ideas he really abhors and implicitly rejects through the very sarcasm by which they are affirmed. Visibly, Dostoevsky's meditations on the manner in which Europe has been assimilated into the Russian psyche, and his attempt to dramatize this symbiosis through his own reactions as a *representative* figure, have led him stylistically to the very threshold of his next creation.

---■---

With the fourth chapter of *Winter Notes*, Dostoevsky finally crosses the French border and, as we recall, discovers that his railroad compartment has been invaded by police spies. No doubt he wished his Russian readers to feel the proper shudder of horror at such surveillance, and to conclude that the vaunted liberties of the West were simply so many shams: Russians had no reason to be envious of European "liberty." But Dostoevsky could not let the matter rest, and reinforces this exposure of European hypocrisy by contrasting the presumed Russian reaction with the European violation of the norms of political decency. The elderly couple who ran one of the hotels at which he stayed in Paris, and who requested information about him for the police, anxiously explained that all this documentation was absolutely "ne-cess-ary"—and a very respectable and worthy couple they were, the essence of bourgeois propriety. "But the word 'ne-cess-ary,' far from being pronounced in any apologetic or derogatory tone, was uttered, rather, precisely in the sense of the completest necessity to the point of being identical with their own personal convictions" (5: 67–68).

Such, presumably, would not have been the case in Russia, where people bowed to force and the pressure of historical necessity without allowing it to obliterate their moral awareness.

Dostoevsky then quickly moves on to London, the city in which the soulless-ness and heartlessness of Western life—its crass materialism, its unashamed con-tempt for anything other than the sordid pursuit of worldly gain—was mirrored in the most arrogantly brazen fashion. The chapter on London bears as its title the single, flamboyant name of the false god of the flesh execrated in the Old Testament, "Baal." It is this god, transposed into a symbol of modern material-ism, before whom all of Western civilization now bows down in prostrate wor-ship; and the results can be seen in the canvas that Dostoevsky brushes in with a palette even darker in hue than that of Dickens, the inspired native poet of the city's sordidness and mass misery. London is nothing but a pitiless wilderness of wild, half-naked, besotted proletarians, gloomily drowning their despair in de-bauchery and gin. And over all this chaos of restless, preoccupied crowds, of whistling and roaring machinery, of heart-rending scenes of brutalized degrada-tion, reigns the great idol to whom all render homage—the spirit of Baal em-bodied in the resplendent and majestic London World's Fair.

During his eight days in London, Dostoevsky paid an obligatory visit to the famous Crystal Palace to see the second London World's Fair, which had opened in May 1862 and was dedicated to exhibiting the latest triumphs of science and technology. A monument of modern architecture originally constructed for the first London World's Fair in 1851 by Sir Joseph Paxton, the huge cast-iron and glass building, covering nineteen acres and located on high ground just outside the city, had since been transformed into a museum. The Crystal Palace thus became for Dostoevsky an image of the unholy spirit of modernity that brooded malevolently over London; and in his imagination this spirit takes on the form of the monstrous Beast whose coming was prophesied in the Apocalypse:

> Can this really be the accomplished ideal?—you think;—is not this the end? is not this really the "one herd." Will we not have to accept this really as the whole truth and remain silent once and for all? All this is so majes-tic, victorious, and proud that it takes your breath away. You observe these hundreds of thousands, these millions of people, obediently flowing here from all over the world—people coming with one thought, peacefully, unceasingly, and silently crowding into this colossal palace; and you feel that something has been finally completed and terminated. This is some sort of Biblical illustration, some prophesy of the Apocalypse fulfilled be-fore your eyes. You feel that one must have perpetual spiritual resistance and negation so as not to surrender, not to submit to the impression, not

19. Main hall of the Crystal Palace. From *Scientific American*, March 19, 1851.

to bow before the fact and deify Baal, that is, not to accept the existing as one's ideal (5: 69–70).[3]

Dostoevsky thus acknowledges the power of this idol by his awe-struck description of its shrine, but his words are equally plangent when he portrays the

[3] Walter Houghton remarks that the World's Fair of 1851 was generally greeted by "the identification of progress with the spirit of God," and he cites a passage from Charles Kingsley, who wrote that "he was moved to tears; to him [entering the Crystal Palace] was like going into a sacred place." A few days later, Kingsley preached a sermon in which he saw everything that the Palace symbolized as "proofs of the Kingdom of God, realization of the gifts which Christ received for men, vaster than any of which they [our forefathers] had dreamed." Walter E. Houghton, *The Victorian Frame of Mind, 1830–1870* (New Haven, 1957), 43.

fate of its victims and sacrifices. Any vestiges of human feeling among them seemed to have been obliterated; all he could detect was a frantic search for sensual pleasure and for oblivion. "The people are always the people," Dostoevsky observes after sketching some London street scenes, "but here everything was so colossal, so striking, that you seemed to grasp tangibly what up to now you had only imagined. Here you no longer see a people, but the systematic, submissive and induced lack of consciousness" (5: 71). What lay at the bottom of all this external splendor, attained at the price of so much human misery, was "the same stubborn, dumb, deep-rooted struggle, the struggle to the death between the general Western principle of individuality and the necessity of somehow living together, of somehow establishing a society and organizing an ant-heap. Even turning into an ant-heap just so as to organize something, just so as not to eat each other up—otherwise, one turns into a cannibal!" (5: 69).[4]

English (Western) society was thus dominated by the war of all against all, which at best, since some form of social order had to be created, could lead only to the "ant-heap"—to the total, unthinking compliance of human volition with the commands of the social Moloch. How different, we can well imagine Dostoevsky thinking, with the spirit that ruled in the Russian village, no matter how backward and meager in resources! Had he himself not written, just a year before, that the West was incapable of putting the principle of communality into practice because there it "has not fused with life," while in Russia it already existed as an accepted social fact and only awaited further favorable development?

Shortly after his meeting with Dostoevsky, Herzen once again stated much the same conclusion more sweepingly in a series of open letters addressed to Turgenev entitled *Ends and Beginnings* (Europe was at the end of its historical life, Russia at the beginning). "Petty-bourgeoisiedom," Herzen states bluntly, "is the final word of the civilization based on the unconditioned rule of property," and Russia would be able to utter a new "word" in world history because it had never accepted this principle of property as sacrosanct.[5] The radical Russian

---

[4] It is striking to observe the similarity of Dostoevsky's remarks about London with those of Friedrich Engels in his *The Condition of the Working Class in England*. "Hundreds of thousands of people from all classes and ranks of society crowd by each other [on the streets]. . . . Meanwhile it occurs to no one that others are worth even a glance. The brutal indifference, the unfeeling isolation of each individual person in his private interest becomes the more repulsive and offensive the more these individuals are pushed into a tiny space. We know well enough that this isolation of the individual, this narrow-minded self-seeking—is everywhere the fundamental principle of modern society. . . . From this it follows that the social war—the war of all against all—has been openly declared. As in Stirner, men here regard each other only as useful objects." Cited in Steven Marcus, *Engels, Manchester and the Working Class* (New York, 1975), 147. Geoffrey C. Kabat makes a detailed comparison between this work of Engels and *Winter Notes* in his *Ideology and Imagination* (New York, 1978), 74–91.

[5] Herzen, *My Past and Thoughts*, trans. Constance Garnett, rev. Humphrey Higgins, 4 vols. (New York, 1968), 4: 1688–1689. My translation differs slightly from that given in this text.

Socialist Herzen and the *pochvennik* Dostoevsky thus shared the same aversion to Western society and placed the same hopes in the presumed Socialist proclivities of the Russian peasant. But for Dostoevsky these Socialist proclivities were rooted in an exalted conception of Christian self-sacrifice that the enlightened atheist and liberated man of the world Herzen would hardly have been willing to accept as an ideal.

∎

The last three chapters of *Winter Notes* are devoted to Paris, and these pages come closest to giving Dostoevsky's readers some of the ordinary fare contained in Russian accounts of Europe. All his impressions are highly stylized in the manner of the famous French satirist of the bourgeoisie, Henri Monnier, whom Dostoevsky had read with appreciation as a young man. Monnier's most famous phrase—*ma femme et mon parapluie!*—had been cited by Dostoevsky in a letter seventeen years earlier,[6] and the image of the complacent, self-satisfied, pompously ridiculous French bourgeois whom Monnier pilloried reappears in Dostoevsky's pages, sketched even more acidly by a pen dipped in caustic contempt.

In general, the image that Dostoevsky conveys is of a society rotten to the core with greed for gold yet consumed with vanity at its own moral perfection. All of French life under Napoleon III is seen as a sinister comedy, staged exclusively for the purpose of allowing the bourgeoisie to enjoy *both* their continual accumulation of wealth and the spectacle of their ineffable virtue. Dostoevsky writes that "all their [the workers] ideal is to become property owners and to possess as many things as possible" (5: 78). While the bourgeoisie fears everyone—the working class, the communists, the Socialists—all such apprehensions are the result of a ludicrous mistake. No group in the West really represents any threat to the hegemony of the *spiritual* principle embodied in the bourgeoisie.

What, after all, has become of the ideals of the French Revolution under the Second Empire, the ideals of *liberté*, *égalité*, and *fraternité*? In momentary accord with Karl Marx and the Socialists, Dostoevsky views political freedom and legal equality, unaccompanied by economic equality, simply as repulsive fictions invented by the bourgeoisie to delude the proletariat. As for *fraternité*, this, Dostoevsky says, is in the most curious position of all. Europe is always talking about brotherhood and has even raised it to the status of a universal ideal, yet brotherhood is the very antithesis of the European character:

> In the French nature, indeed, in the Western European nature in general, brotherhood is not present. Instead, we find the personal principle, the principle of isolation, a vigorous self-concern, self-assertion, self-determination, within the bounds of one's own ego. This ego sets itself in

[6] *Pis'ma*, 1: 78; May 4, 1845.

opposition, as a separate, self-justifying principle, against all of nature and all other humans; it claims equality and equal value with whatever exists outside itself. (5: 79)

Dostoevsky then goes on to describe what brotherhood *really* is; and though he speaks in purely moral terms, every Russian reader would instantly know that the social reality to which he was referring is the Russian peasant *obshchina*, with its land held in common and its democratic administration for the good of all. True brotherhood, as in the *obshchina*, is an instinctive mutual relation between the individual and the community in which each desires only the welfare of the other. The individual does not, as in the West, insist on his exclusive rights as an isolated ego; he freely brings these rights to the community in sacrifice without even being asked to do so. Reciprocally, the community, without making any demands or *imposing* any conditions on the individual, guarantees him equal protection and status with all.

Dostoevsky illustrates this ideal situation in the form of a dialogue between the individual and the community. "My greatest joy," the individual says, "is to sacrifice everything to you, without hurting you by so doing." But the community, as Dostoevsky sees it, then responds: "You offer us too much. . . . Take everything that is ours too. Constantly and with all our might, we shall struggle to increase your personal freedom and your individual fulfillment. . . . We are all behind you; we guarantee your safety; we watch eternally over you." And then, turning back to the skeptical reader once more, Dostoevsky falls into the jeering tone of the underground man: "There's a Utopia for you, gentlemen! Everything is based on feelings, on nature, not on reason. Why, this actually humbles reason. What do you think? Is this a Utopia or not?" If by Utopia one means a not yet realized ideal, then for Dostoevsky the exchange he had just sketched was not Utopian at all; he firmly believed that such a ballet of moral sublimity actually *existed*—though in forms that were often imperfect and distorted—at the heart of Russian peasant life. And this state of social harmony was not only impossible for, but even incomprehensible to, the European personality, which could not conceive of obtaining anything for itself without a struggle against others. "Its demands are made belligerently, it insists on its rights, requires an equal status—and that is the end of brotherhood" (5: 80–81).

Dostoevsky insists that brotherhood requires a much higher development of personality than has been attained in the West: "Understand me: a voluntary, totally conscious sacrifice of oneself in the interests of all, made under no sort of compulsion, is in my opinion a sign of the highest development of the personality. Voluntarily to sacrifice one's life for all, to die on the cross or at the stake, is possible only with the very strongest development of personality" (5: 79). This sacrifice, moreover, must be made without the slightest suggestion or thought of recompense; if such an idea is present, then it ruins everything by destroying the underlying moral nature of the act of self-sacrifice and turning it into a Utilitarian calculation. "One must make the sacrifice," Dostoevsky explains, "so as to give all and even desire that nothing can be given in return, so that nobody is deprived of anything on your behalf." From which it follows that true brotherhood cannot be artificially established or created: "it must live unconsciously in the nature of the entire race, in a word: to have the brotherly principle of love—one must love. One must instinctively be drawn to brotherhood . . . despite the age-old sufferings of a nation, despite the barbarous crudity and ignorance that has taken root there, despite age-old slavery and the invasion of foreign races—in a word, the need for brotherly communication must be in the nature of a people, must be born with them or have been assimilated as a way of life from time immemorial" (5: 80). It is thus only the Russian people who are capable of brotherhood; all attempts to establish this principle in the West, as an alternative to the horrors of the war of all against all, are doomed to failure.

This is the context in which Dostoevsky raises the question of Socialism, which had just then ceased to have much importance in Europe but was still crucial in Russia. It was the Socialists, Dostoevsky concedes, who really took the ideal of *fraternité* seriously and tried to find ways of putting it into practice. They proclaim: "All for one and one for all!"—and nothing better than such an ideal, Dostoevsky agrees, can possibly be imagined. But when the Socialists confront as their major obstacle the nature of European man, to whom the principle of brotherhood is spiritually alien, they appeal to his reason, and try to convince him that brotherhood will be to everyone's advantage once it is established. The Socialists argue, preach, explain, draw up plans and projects, and point out with great specificity just what benefits will accrue and "just how much each must freely contribute, at the detriment of his personality, to the commune" (5: 81).

Dostoevsky, to do him justice, does not accuse the Socialist ideal of involving any compulsion. On the contrary, he explicitly recognizes that the Socialists desire a voluntary acceptance of their goals, yet he accepts as axiomatic that Socialism—the Utopian Socialism of the mid-nineteenth century, with its endeavor to establish ideal communities and to transform human relations—involves an encroachment on the rights of personality. This postulate, so self-evident for Dostoevsky that he does not take the trouble to explain it, must be understood in the perspective of his implicit comparison with the Russian commune. The Russian, for whom brotherhood is a vital instinct, experiences no inner conflict as the results of the self-sacrifices demanded by life in his village. But the European, whose primary instinct is egoistic self-interest, can only feel the demands of the Socialist commune as an infringement of the complete autonomy of his individual personality. For this reason, the rational motive of self-interest—the motive that the Russian radicals, following Chernyshevsky, were making the cornerstone of their worldview—is the "hair" that will destroy the innate Russian instinct of true brotherhood once it gets into the machinery.

To buttress this conclusion, Dostoevsky mentions a few incidents from the checkered history of Socialist communities (those of Cabet and Victor Considérant), about which he was well informed. Most such attempts quickly fell apart as a result of internal bickering, and Dostoevsky draws what seems to him the pertinent lesson:

> Naturally there is something very tempting about living, if not fraternally, then at least on a purely rational basis, i.e., it is fine when all protect you and require of you only work and agreement. But here a mystery arises: it seems that man is completely protected, promised food, drink, and work, and for all this he is asked in return only a small drop of his personal freedom for the good of all, the tiniest, tiniest drop. But no, man does not like to live by such calculations, even this tiny drop is burdensome. It seems to him, stupidly, that this is prison and that he is better off by himself because—he is completely free. And, you know, even though he is flayed alive for this freedom, obtains no work, starves to death, and his free will is equal to nothing—all the same, it seems to this eccentric fellow that his free will is better. (5: 81)

In this momentous passage, we can observe the bitter lessons of Dostoevsky's prison years, with their nightmarish proof of man's ineradicable need to *feel* free, combining with his reflections on Socialism, on the Russian commune, and on the relations of Russia with Europe, to create the outlines of the underground man. For the "eccentric fellow" (*chudak*) who materializes in this quotation, and refuses to give up the tiniest drop of his freedom as the price for joining the Socialist commune, unmistakably provides the first glimpse of this memorable character.

Faced with the choice of preserving the full autonomy of personality or surrendering part of it in order to obtain some self-advantage, mankind, Dostoevsky firmly believed, would instinctively choose suffering and hardship for the sake of freedom. This is why rationalist Socialist communes are doomed to failure, and why the acceptance of European ideas by Russian radicals—ideas that accentuate the self-regarding elements of the human psyche—is so disastrous. Dostoevsky thus considers the revolt of the *chudak*, under such circumstances, as inevitable and even salutary (which explains his seeming identification with the similar revolt of the underground man against the laws of nature). In both instances, we have a defense and assertion of the positive value of moral-psychic freedom. But, as Dostoevsky also indicates, the consequences of such behavior *without* any possibility of reconciliation between the individual and society will inevitably be self-destructive; and only a world governed by the Christian moral-social ideals still alive in the Russian commune can thus ward off chaos. Only in such a world will the freedom of the personality be respected; only here will the individual be inspired by the spirit of love to surrender his personality, not for a Utilitarian doctrine of self-interest but for the good of all. From Dostoevsky's point of view, then, whatever we may think of its plausibility, his opposition to the philosophy of "rational egoism" was a defense of the Russian commune; and this commune was the destined foundation, singled out by the hand of Providence, on which the Christian Socialist society of the future would be built. He was convinced that, once realized in Russia, it would blossom into a new and glorious phase of world history.

Dostoevsky's *Winter Notes* thus brings us right to the threshold of his great creative period, which begins with the composition of *Notes from Underground* two years later. It is not so much that *Winter Notes* contains some of the major symbols and motifs of *Notes from Underground*—the liver complaint, the ant-heap, the Crystal Palace, the "stupid" recalcitrance of the "eccentric fellow" to surrender even the tiniest drop of his freedom to the artificial and rational Socialist community. Even more important is the rhetoric of inverted irony, which the underground man will simply internalize at a much higher level of philosophical and psychological self-awareness. For he will concentrate within himself *all* the contradictions arising from the ambivalent Russian attitude toward Europe as represented by the two radical ideologies that Dostoevsky had so far encountered in his lifetime: the rational egoism and materialism of the 1860s and the philanthropic and Romantic Utopian Socialism of the 1840s.

CHAPTER 28

An Emancipated Woman, A Tormented Lover

Despite the severity of the permanent interdiction of *Time*, its editors and contributors could not believe that the misunderstanding on which it was based would long continue. Strakhov, whose reputation was at stake, hurriedly wrote letters to Katkov and Ivan Aksakov explaining his loyalty to the Russian cause. The censorship would not allow Strakhov's letters to be printed, but Katkov, magnanimous to a repentant foe, replied that he would clarify the matter in an article. Hopes thus revived, as Dostoevsky wrote to Turgenev in mid-June, that the decision of the authorities could be reversed. A week or two later, Katkov's article lifted the dire accusation of pro-Polonism from *Time*'s shoulders, but he continued to object to the principles of *pochvennichestvo*, whose cloudiness he decried as being at the root of the trouble. Still, this article paved the way for the authorities to change their mind, although they took longer to do so than Dostoevsky had anticipated.

Meanwhile, he had decided to travel abroad again during the summer months, although funds were now tight. According to Strakhov, Dostoevsky believed that his first trip abroad had greatly improved his health. Dostoevsky himself told Turgenev that he was coming to Paris and Berlin primarily to consult specialists in epilepsy (he gave the names of two doctors). "If you knew the depression I have after my attacks," he writes despairingly, "and which sometimes last for weeks!"[1] Dostoevsky was also eager to go abroad for another motive that he could scarcely avow in public. Waiting for him in Paris would be his new traveling companion, like Strakhov a contributor to *Time* but in this instance a female, and an attractive one: twenty-three-year-old Apollinaria Suslova, who became the second great love of Dostoevsky's life.

Very little is known about Dostoevsky's conjugal existence with Marya Dimitrievna after his return to Petersburg from exile. But the very absence of information, the lack of any but the most fleeting references to her in Dostoevsky's letters and in memoirs of the period, suggests that she lived largely in seclusion, and she often spent long periods of time in other cities with a milder climate than Petersburg. It is possible that Dostoevsky had relations with other women

---

[1] *Pis'ma*, 1: 318; June 17, 1863.

of which we know nothing; he was not at all averse to such casual encounters when the occasion made them feasible. There are some supercilious remarks by Strakhov—a perennial bachelor, apparently terrified of women—that may be taken as referring to such indulgences, although they are prudently extended to characterize the attitude of the Milyukov Circle as a whole. "People who were extremely sensitive in moral relations, who nourished the most exalted kind of thought," he writes, "and who, for the most part, were far removed from any sort of physical dissolution, nonetheless looked quite calmly on all disorders of this kind and spoke of them as amusing trifles, which it was quite permissible to surrender to in moments of leisure." [2]

All the same, Dostoevsky had been attracted to Marya Dimitrievna not only physically but also because of her qualities of mind and the nobility of her character, and he sought a similar combination in other women. A story by Suslova was published in the tenth issue of *Time* (October 1861), and she would hardly have missed the chance to visit the editorial bureau of the journal: the intrepid Miss Suslova, then all of twenty-one, was not someone to hesitate taking a step then considered bold for a respectable young lady. Her story, "For the Time Being," depicts a young woman who runs away from an unloved husband and earns her own meager living by giving lessons. The story is a typical product of the Russian movement for female emancipation in the 1860s, and Suslova intended her own life to be a living incarnation of such a protest.

What little we know about Apollinaria Suslova—Dostoevsky's beloved Polina—is due largely to her remarkable younger sister Nadezhda, who became the first Russian woman to obtain a medical degree and whose life has thus been investigated as a pioneer of women's liberation. Both girls came from a family of peasant serf stock, and their history illustrates the rise of the *raznochintsy* intelligentsia. Their father, an enterprising serf of Count Sheremetev, had bought his freedom even before the liberation, and then became one of the managers of the count's estates. Apollinaria spent her early years in the countryside growing up among the peasantry, and prideful references to her closeness to the *muzhiki* appear in her diary. The family moved to Petersburg when she was fifteen, and the sisters were sent to a private school, where they learned foreign languages but apparently little else. They soon took advantage of the opening of the University of St. Petersburg to the public and attended the lecture courses offered there by various noted professors. Both girls also tried their hand at literary composition, Apollinaria leading the way by her contributions to *Time*.

Most likely she and Dostoevsky became lovers during the winter of 1862–1863. Nothing reliable is known about the intimate details of their relationship, but there is ample evidence that the Dostoevsky-Suslova liaison did not go

20. Apollinaria Suslova.
From Dominique Arban
et al., *Dostoïevski* (Paris,
1971)

smoothly after the first excitement of possession and novelty had worn off. There was a twenty-year difference of age between the two; and Dostoevsky was weighed down by worry over Marya Dimitrievna, drained by his crushing editorial and literary obligations, and compelled to cope with the depressing and enervating effects of epileptic attacks recurring at this time with shorter intervals of respite. It is difficult to imagine that he could have made a satisfactory lover for an ardent and inexperienced young girl, and one suspects that he aroused Suslova's sensuality without being able to satisfy it entirely. When she was offhandedly seduced a few months later by a young and handsome Spanish medical student seeking some diversion in the Latin Quarter, she responded to his caresses with a rapturous intensity that argues a previous sense of dissatisfaction.

Another source of conflict between the two soon cast a pall over the idyll of their romance. Suslova was a young Russian feminist of the 1860s who despised conventional public opinion regarding the relations between the sexes. "All my friends are kind people," she notes in her diary, "but weak and poor in spirit; they are abundant in their words, but poor in their deeds. I haven't met a single one among them who would not be afraid of the truth, or who wouldn't have retreated before the conventions of life. . . . I cannot respect such people. I consider it a crime to talk one way and act another."[3]

These words are contained in the draft of a letter to her Spanish lover, Salvador, and Dostoevsky is certainly included among the "friends" that Suslova mentions here with such disdain. Dostoevsky's romance was no secret from his brother Mikhail, but he made strenuous efforts to keep it hidden from others. He was terrified that gossip might get back to Marya Dimitrievna and make their common life together even stormier than it was. More generously, we may also assume that he did not wish to cause the consumptive invalid any extra suffering. He was thus forced to meet Suslova on the sly and to hide their love affair from the prying eyes of the world—exactly the sort of kowtowing to social bigotry that would have revolted her to the core. Inevitably too, with all his other pressing duties and responsibilities, he was compelled to see her only during those brief periods he could snatch from more urgent concerns. Such a demeaning situation would have upset even an ordinary young girl involved in the first great love affair of her life. With the high-spirited and mettlesome Suslova, the result could only have been to create a sense of resentment against the man she had surrendered to and idolized, and who, she could not help feeling, had betrayed her trust.

Among her papers was found the undated draft of a letter intended for Dostoevsky but never sent: "I was never ashamed of my love for you: it was beautiful, even grandiose. . . . You behaved like a serious, busy man [who] understood his obligations after his own [fashion], but would not miss his pleasures either; on the contrary, perhaps even found it necessary to have some pleasure, on the grounds that some great doctor or philosopher once said that it was necessary to get drunk every month."[4] Such words surely suggest a malaise deriving from a sense of occupying a distinctly secondary place in Dostoevsky's life—of having become part of a routine that included the physical release provided by their liaison. What inspires her sarcasm is a suspicion of being "used" for Dostoevsky's convenience, his failure to reciprocate her own "beautiful" and "grandiose" sentiments in an appropriate manner.

Twenty years later, Suslova's second husband, the noted philosophical essayist V. V. Rozanov (whose first important book was a classic study of Dostoevsky), once asked her why she and Dostoevsky had become estranged. He reports their conversation in a letter to a third party: "Because he would not get a divorce. . . .

---

[3] F. M. Dostoevsky, *The Gambler, with Polina Suslova's Diary*, trans. Victor Terras, ed. Edward Wasiolek (Chicago, 1972), 365. The Russian source for Suslova's diary and letters is A. S. Dolinin, *Gody blizosti s Dostoevskim* (Moscow, 1928).

[4] Ibid., 364.

I gave myself to him, out of love, without asking anything. He should have behaved in the same way! He behaved otherwise and I left him."[5] To make matters worse, when quarrels began to break out between them, Dostoevsky could do little more than wring his hands in anguish and guilt. In an entry in her diary made a year later, while mulling over her previous relations with her ex-lover Salvador, she writes, "And what is it I want of him now? That he should confess his guilt, be remorseful, that is, be a Feodor Mikhailovich?"[6] Dostoevsky's name took on the deprecating stamp of someone who can do nothing but cravenly acknowledge his contrition.

■

Such was the mood in which Suslova preceded Dostoevsky to Paris in the early spring of 1863, there to await his arrival. Dostoevsky attempted to raise funds by offering his next work to another journal (*The Library for Reading*) and, when this failed, obtaining a loan of fifteen hundred rubles from the Literary Fund. In return, and as guarantee, he offered the rights to all his already published works in perpetuity if he failed to repay his debt by February 1864. The risks involved in such a guarantee were of course enormous and indicate how determined he was, at whatever price, to manage what would be a honeymoon trip with his adored Polina through France and Italy.

When Dostoevsky finally left Petersburg in August, one might have thought he would hasten to Paris by the fastest route. Instead, he delayed his trip to make a four-day stopover in Wiesbaden for a fling at the gaming tables. He began by winning 10,400 francs, and he had enough self-control to take his windfall away, put the money in his suitcase, and make a vow not to return to the casino. But, as was so often to happen in the future, he returned to the hypnotic lure of the spinning wheel and lost half his winnings. In a letter to his wife's sister, V. D. Constant, written shortly thereafter from Paris, Dostoevsky explains that he is keeping part of what is left for himself, sending part to Mikhail for safekeeping, and enclosing another part to her for the expenses of Marya Dimitrievna.[7] The latter was spending the summer in Vladimir and taking a cure that might call for extra outlays.

This pause at Wiesbaden may be considered the true beginning of the gambling mania that invariably swept over Dostoevsky whenever he came to Europe during the 1860s. The immediate cause of Dostoevsky's gambling, as he explained it to his intimates, was always the hope of winning enough money to rescue him, and though he usually ended by losing every penny it cannot be said that his aim was entirely unreasonable. He frequently did win large sums, which

---

[5] L. P. Grossman, *Put' Dostoevskogo* (Leningrad, 1929), 154.
[6] *The Gambler, with Polina Suslova's Diary*, 257.
[7] *Pis'ma*, I: 323–326; September 1 (new style), 1863.

he then proceeded to lose because he could never stop in time. All the same, his winnings always convinced him that success—and a solution to all his material worries—lay within tantalizing reach. Telling Mikhail how he had quickly racked up gains of three thousand francs at Wiesbaden, he writes: "Tell me: after that how is it possible not to be carried away, why should I not believe that happiness is in my grasp if I stick rigorously to my system? And I need money, for myself, for you, for my wife, to write a novel. . . . Yes, I have come here in order to save you all and to save myself."[8]

Whatever the psychic origins of Dostoevsky's gambling mania, its most interesting feature was the theory he developed about it. What Dostoevsky calls his "system," in the letter to Mikhail, is merely the conviction that, if he could impose an iron self-control on his feelings—if he could suppress the whole irrational part of his psyche—why, then he would certainly win! "This secret," he tells V. D. Constant, "I really know it; it's terribly stupid and simple and consists in holding oneself in at every moment and not to get excited, no matter what the play. And that's all; it's then absolutely impossible to lose, and one is sure of winning."[9]

As Dostoevsky above all should have been in a position to know, human beings are not exclusively creatures of reason and self-control; to dominate oneself to the extent demanded by his theory is an extremely arduous task. The letter to Constant goes on, "however clever you may be, with a will of iron, you will succumb all the same. Even Strakhov the philosopher would succumb."[10] Gambling for Dostoevsky thus implicitly involved an attempt to raise himself above the level of human fallibility, and in these unpretentious and apologetic remarks Dostoevsky approaches one of the great themes of Western literature that will soon appear in his own creations. For one cannot help thinking here of Marlowe's *Dr. Faustus*, as well as of the Machiavellian villains of Elizabethan tragedy, who pit a cold and calculating reason against all the moral dictates of conscience standing in the way of an unbridled pursuit of self-interest. In the tradition of European literature, such attempts to put into practice this dream of the icy self-domination of reason have invariably been depicted as a source of sacrilege and of monstrous moral disorder. They signify mankind's attempt to set itself up as a rival of the will of the Christian God, who had endowed the human species with a middling rank and an ambiguous status in that great chain of being that ruled the imagination of Western man for so many centuries. Something of this traditional view still persists in Dostoevsky, and in *Crime and Punishment* he will soon portray the consequences of a similar belief in the supremacy of the power of naked human reason to replace the workings of conscience.

[8] Ibid., 330; September 8/20, 1863.
[9] Ibid., 324; September 1 (new style), 1863.
[10] Ibid.

In the long run, as Dostoevsky learned to his cost, he was doomed to gamble away his winnings in uncontrollable excitement. For by doing so he was paradoxically affirming his acceptance of the proper order of the universe as he conceived of it, and learning the same lesson as the underground man and all of his great negative heroes, beginning with Raskolnikov, who deludedly believe they can master and suppress the irrational promptings of their inherited Christian values. After each such episode, in any case, Dostoevsky always returned to his writing desk with renewed vigor and a sense of deliverance.

———■———

By the time Dostoevsky arrived in Paris, on August 14, 1863, the unhappy fate of his romance with Suslova had already been sealed. Just a few days before, she had fallen into the masterful Spanish arms of the irresistible Salvador; and since her diary begins at this very moment, we can follow the course of events. She broke the news in a letter that she confides to her notebook; it begins brutally:

> You are coming too late. . . . Only very recently I was dreaming of going to Italy with you, . . . everything has changed within a few days. You told me one day that I would never surrender my heart easily. I have surrendered it within a week's time, at the first call, without a struggle, without assurance, almost without hope that I was being loved. . . . Don't think that I am shaming you, but I want to tell you that you did not know me, nor did I know myself. Good-bye, dear![11]

Such words were certainly meant to wound to the quick, and they convey the impression that Suslova's easy acquiescence may have been partly prompted by a desire to take revenge on Dostoevsky. In any case, her attitude toward him as a person, if not as a lover, is ambivalent and will remain so. The text in her diary continues, "How generous, how high-minded he is. What an intellect! What a soul!"[12]

Whether or not Suslova had really abandoned herself to Salvador so easily, she was already aware that his flaming Latin passion had cooled considerably after conquest. Dostoevsky turned up in the midst of this drama between Polina and her Latin lover, calling on her before her letter arrived. On seeing her emerge to meet him, trembling and upset, he asked what was wrong, and she blurted out that he should not have come, "because it's too late." Dostoevsky then "hung his head," almost as if having expected the blow, and said, "I must know everything, let's go somewhere, and tell me, or I'll die." The two left in a carriage for Dostoevsky's hotel, and, she writes, he "kept hold of my hand all the way, press-

---

[11] *The Gambler, with Polina Suslova's Diary,* 202.
[12] Ibid.

ing it hard from time to time and making some sort of convulsive movements."[13] Once in Dostoevsky's room, a scene occurred that Suslova later used verbatim in a short story: "He fell at my feet, and, putting his arms around my knees, clasping them and sobbing, he exclaimed between sobs: 'I have lost you, I knew it!' Then, having regained his composure, he began to ask me about the man. 'Perhaps he is handsome, young, and glib. But you will never find a heart such as mine!'"[14] Dostoevsky had all along feared losing her to a younger and handsomer rival, and his worst forebodings had now been realized.

She finally broke down and began to weep herself, explaining that her own love was unrequited. Probably encouraged by what must have been Suslova's unflattering picture of her seducer, he told her, Suslova's account continues, "that he was happy to have met a human being such as I was in the world. He begged me to remain his friend. . . . Then he suggested that we travel to Italy together, while remaining like brother and sister." The conversation concluded with a promise of further meetings, and an acknowledgment by Suslova of Dostoevsky's continued hold over her affections. "I felt relieved after I had talked with him. He understands me."[15]

For the next week, matters remained in this indecisive stage. Suslova saw Dostoevsky regularly while at the same time writing letters, both proud and pleading, to Salvador, unable to make up her mind to send them. In September, finding out that Salvador's excuses not to see her were ruses to quit her company as rapidly as possible and for good, she writes: "I became hysterical. I screamed that I was going to kill him. . . . I made everything ready, burned some of my notebooks and letters. . . . I felt wonderfully well." Not having slept all night, Suslova rushed to Dostoevsky at seven in the morning the next day. Opening the door for her in his nightclothes, the startled Dostoevsky then "went back to bed wrapping himself up in his blanket. He looked at me with astonishment and apprehension. . . . I told him that he should come to my place right away. I wanted to tell him everything and ask him to be my judge."[16]

By the time Dostoevsky arrived, Suslova's mood had changed completely: she came to meet him munching a piece of toast, and declared with a laugh that she was now much calmer. "Yes," he said, "and I am very glad about that, but who can tell anything for sure when it concerns you?" Now for the first time Suslova told him the whole story, concealing nothing, and Dostoevsky advised her to forget about the unhappy betrayal. "I had, of course, sullied myself, but . . . it had only been an accident. . . . Salvador, being a young man, needed a mistress, and I happened to be available so he took advantage of me, and why shouldn't

[13] Ibid., 203.
[14] Ibid., 206.
[15] Ibid., 207.
[16] Ibid., 209–210.

he have done so?" Suslova now admits that "F. M. was right. I understood perfectly well, but how hard it was for me!"[17]

Dostoevsky was still afraid that Suslova might "come up with some foolishness," and warned her against doing anything rash. Her reply tells us a good deal about herself, as well as about her future relations with Dostoevsky and the portrait he was to paint of her later in *The Gambler*. "'I would not like to kill him' I said, 'but I would like to torture him for a very long time.'" A passage in her diary elaborates on this impulse: "right now I suddenly feel a desire to avenge myself, but how? By what means?" Suslova finally decided to send Salvador a sum of money in payment for the "service" he had rendered her, hoping by this gesture to wound the *hidalgo* dignity that had previously impressed her in his character.[18] The insulting letter was sent, but it elicited no more reply than all the others.

A few days later, Suslova and Dostoevsky departed on their long-planned trip to Italy. He would have been less than human if he had not hoped that his role of friend and counselor would eventually return again to being that of lover, but Suslova was seething with an unappeased desire for vengeance, and in the absence of Salvador she turned on the hapless Dostoevsky instead. He too, after all, was an ex-lover who had betrayed her expectations, and while grateful for his continued sympathy and solicitude, she also took a sadistic pleasure in treating him as she no doubt imagined herself treating Salvador had he been within her reach.

In a diary entry for September 5, made on their first stop in Baden-Baden, Suslova confesses, "A thirst for revenge burned in my soul for a long time after, and I decided that, if I do not become distracted in Italy, I will return to Paris and do as I had planned" (presumably kill Salvador).[19] Other diary entries reveal her ego in the process of obtaining satisfaction for the painful wounds inflicted by the unhappy past: "While we were enroute there, he [Dostoevsky] told me he had some hope. . . . I did not say anything to this, but I knew it was not going to happen."[20] Suslova's behavior continued to inflame his passion while frustrating its satisfaction. Certainly she derived some consolation from the ardency of Dostoevsky's wooing. She describes lying on her bed, summoning Dostoevsky to hold her hand. "I felt good," she notes. "I took his hand and for a long time held it in mine. . . . I told him that I had been unfair and unkind to him in Paris, that it may have seemed as though I had been thinking only of myself, yet I had been thinking of him, too, but did not want to say it, so as not to hurt him."[21]

[17] Ibid., 211.
[18] Ibid., 211–212.
[19] Ibid., 213.
[20] Ibid., 214.
[21] Ibid.

No wonder Dostoevsky suddenly leaped to his feet, stumbled, explained that he wished to close the window, but then admitted, "with a strange expression" on his face, that he had just been on the point of bending to kiss her foot. Desiring then to undress and go to bed, Suslova indicated as much indirectly, but Dostoevsky invented excuses for not leaving the room immediately and then came back several times on one pretext or another (the two had adjoining rooms). The next day he apologized for his behavior and "said that I must probably find it unpleasant, the way he was annoying me. I answered that I didn't mind, and refused to be drawn into a discussion of the subject, so that he could neither cherish hope nor be quite without it." [22] Suslova later excerpted this scene from her notebook and used it, dialogue and all, in a short story.

Although Suslova's evasiveness was surely a major factor in the darkening of his disposition, his severe losses at roulette contributed their share as well. At the start, he tells Mikhail, "I came to the table [at Baden] and in *a quarter of an hour* had won 600 francs. That fired me up. Suddenly, I began to lose, I couldn't stop, and I lost everything, down to the last kopek." [23] His letters home plead with Mikhail to scrape together whatever he can and send it immediately, and he asks his sister-in-law to retrieve for him one hundred rubles from the amount dispatched earlier for Marya Dimitrievna. The diplomatic maneuvers involved in such a task were extremely intricate, and Dostoevsky takes several pages to explain how the feat might be accomplished without arousing Marya Dimitrievna's stormy susceptibilities.

As if all this were not enough, Dostoevsky's agitated stay in Baden-Baden was complicated by the obligation to call on Turgenev, who had settled there recently in a *ménage à trois* with Pauline Viardot, her husband, and family. Turgenev would have been offended if he had heard of Dostoevsky's passage by accident, but Dostoevsky also knew that, if he caught sight of Suslova, tongues would immediately start to wag in Petersburg. "At Baden I saw Turgenev," Dostoevsky reports to Mikhail. "I visited him twice and he came to see me once in return. He did not see A. P. I did not want him to know. . . . He spoke to me of all his moral torments and his doubts. Philosophic doubts, but which undermine life. A bit fatuous. I did not hide from him that I gambled. He gave me *Phantoms* to read, but gambling prevented me from reading and I returned it unread. He said that he wrote it for our journal and that if, once in Rome, I asked him for it, he will send it there. But what do I know of the journal?" [24]

The sensitive Turgenev was still suffering from the uproar caused by *Fathers and Children*, especially from the unrelenting hostility of that portion of the radical press (*The Contemporary* and *The Spark*) that considered the work a defamation of

[22] Ibid., 215.
[23] *Pisma*, 1: 330; September 8/20, 1863.
[24] Ibid., 331.

the younger generation. The failure to read *Phantoms*, destined for *Time* or whatever journal replaced it, was of course a terrible faux pas, and Mikhail's cry of anguish when he read the above passage can be heard in his response: "Do you know what Turgenev means for us *now*?"[25] Nothing could have been a greater affront to Turgenev's considerable literary vanity, especially at this troubled moment of his career.

Dostoevsky had asked that the money he so urgently requested be forwarded to Turin, where it would await them once the ill-matched pair, alternating between tenderness and tantrums, had crossed the Alps by way of Switzerland. On arrival, however, they found nothing, and both lived in constant fear of being summoned to pay their hotel bill and dragged to the police. "Here, that's how things are done," Dostoevsky informs Mikhail, "no arrangement is possible . . . and I am not alone here. It's horrible!" But the eagerly awaited funds finally came to the rescue. Meanwhile, Dostoevsky had tried to do some writing—perhaps a travel article, perhaps some notes for *The Gambler*, but, he tells Mikhail, "I tore up everything I had written in Turin. I have had enough of writing on order."[26]

After a stormy sea voyage from Genoa, with a stopover in Livorno, the two arrived in Rome. "Yesterday morning," he wrote to Strakhov, "I visited St. Peter's! The impression is very strong, Nikolay Nikolaevich, and gives one a shiver up the spine."[27] The shiver, one presumes, was not caused by aesthetic appreciation but rather by the mighty power for evil that Dostoevsky always associated with the Roman church. Despite the harassments attendant on his wanderings, and prompted by Strakhov, Dostoevsky had found time to further his education. "Tell Strakhov that I am carefully reading the Slavophils," he had instructed Mikhail, "and that I have found something new."[28]

What he could not have discovered through Belinsky and Herzen was the systematic *theological* basis that the Slavophils had provided for their ideas. Slavophil theology was bitterly anti-Catholic and traced all the evils of mankind, past and present, back to the Roman Catholic pope's assumption of the temporal power once possessed by the Roman emperors.[29] St. Peter's, in Dos-

[25] *DMI*, 543.

[26] *Pisma*, I: 329–331; September 8/20, 1863.

[27] Ibid., 335.

[28] Ibid., 331.

[29] In an article that has had a major influence on the history of Russian thought, Ivan Kireevsky declared that "the classical world of ancient paganism, which Russia lacked in her inheritance, represented in its essence a triumph of formal human reason," which led, among other disasters, to "the pope [becoming] the head of the church instead of Jesus Christ . . . the whole totality of faith was supported by syllogistic scholasticism; the Inquisition, Jesuitry, in one word, all the peculiarities of Catholicism developed through the power of the same formal process of reasoning, so that Protestantism itself, which the Catholics reproach with rationalism, developed directly out of the

toevsky's eyes, could only have been seen as the living embodiment of such un-Christian claims to worldly grandeur, and his visit to Rome thus coincided with an important phase in the evolution of his ideas. Slavophil thought now gave his personal prejudices a wide-ranging conceptual foundation, and it was only after this second trip to Europe that Dostoevsky begins to express the opposition between Russia and Europe in primarily religious terms. "The Polish War," he confides to his notebook during the winter of 1863–1864, "is a war of two Christianities—it is the beginning of the future war between Orthodoxy and Catholicism, in other words—of the Slavic genius with European civilization" (20: 170).

∎

The fluctuations of Dostoevsky's affair with Suslova seemed to have reached a new phase in Rome, and her diary entries, which reveal the strange duel in which the pair now engaged, already prefigure some of the situations of *The Gambler*. Dostoevsky now openly begins to protest against Suslova's attitude toward him, and bluntly accuses her of moral sadism. "Yesterday F. M. was importunate again," she writes during their Roman stay. "'You know,' he said, 'that you can't torture a man this long, for he will eventually quit trying.'" A little while later, he dropped the game of jocosity and admitted "I am unhappy"—at which, she writes, "I embraced him with ardor," and the merry-go-round began once again. That evening, leaving Suslova's room at one in the morning, with his temptress lying fetchingly undressed in bed, Dostoevsky said "that it was humiliating for him to leave in this fashion. . . . 'For the Russians never did retreat.'"[30] The serio-comic flavor of the contest between the two is close to the tonality of *The Gambler*.

It was in the midst of such scenes that *The Gambler* was originally conceived, and its first mention occurs in a letter to Strakhov from Rome. Dostoevsky remained critically short of funds, and tried to raise some by asking his friend to offer magazine editors a new story idea in return for an advance.

---

rationalism of Catholicism. A perspicacious mind could see in advance, in this final triumph of formal reason over faith and tradition, the entire present fate of Europe, as a result of a fallacious principle: Strauss and the new philosophy in all of its aspects; industrialism as the mainspring of social life; philanthropy based on calculated self-interest; the system of education accelerated by the power of aroused jealousy; Goethe, the crown of German poesy, the literary Tallyrand, who changes his beauty as the other changes his governments; Napoleon, the hero of our time, the ideal of soulless calculation; the numerical majority, a fruit of rationalistic politics; and Louis Philippe, the latest result of such hopes and such expensive experiments!" These words illustrate the suggestive sweep of Slavophil thought, which coincides with Dostoevsky's ideas. See Nicholas V. Riasanovsky, *Russia and the West in the Teaching of the Slavophils* (rpt. Gloucester, MA, 1965), 96.

[30] *The Gambler, with Polina Suslova's Diary*, 218–220.

What Dostoevsky outlines is the first version of *The Gambler*, which at this stage was more ambitious thematically than the final redaction:

> The subject of this story is the following: a type of Russian man living abroad. . . . It will be the mirror of the national reality, so far as possible. . . . I imagine an impulsive character, but a man very cultivated nonetheless, incomplete in all things, having lost his faith *but not daring not to believe*, in revolt against the authorities and fearing them. . . . The essential is that all his vital powers of life, his violences, his audacity are devoted to *roulette*. He is a gambler, but not an ordinary gambler—just as the Covetous Knight of Pushkin is not a simple merchant. . . . He is a poet in his fashion, but he is ashamed of that poetry because he profoundly feels its *baseness*, although the need of risk ennobles him in his own eyes. The story retraces how, for three years, he drags himself through the gambling houses and plays *roulette*.[31]

The outline contains a motif manifestly pointing toward *Notes from Underground* that will be appropriated for this earlier work. The conception of a character who has lost his faith but does not dare *not* to believe recalls the Golyadkin type of *The Double*, terrified at his own audacity in stepping over the divinely sanctioned boundaries of the Russian caste system. Dostoevsky had continued to make notes for a revised version of this text all through 1860–1864, and a year after his letter to Strakhov about *The Gambler* he turned this Golyadkin type into the underground man, who also suffers from not daring *not* to believe in certain ideas that he finds incompatible with his moral sensibility. These ideas are no longer those that prop up the Russian bureaucratic system but rather the essential tenets of the Western European ideologies that have invaded and reshaped the Russian moral-social psyche. What remained then for *The Gambler* was the national theme, the delights and dangers of the "poetry of risk," and the emotional difficulties of Dostoevsky's tortuous involvement with Suslova.

The peregrinations of the pair next took them to Naples. By this time he was becoming thoroughly sick of the whole escapade, and longed to be back in Russia. Apologizing for not having provided a forwarding address to which *Phantoms* could be mailed, Dostoevsky explains to Turgenev that "I remained everywhere only for a brief time, and it generally happened that, leaving one city, I scarcely knew in the evening where I would be the following day. Certain circumstances caused all these movements not always to depend on me; it was rather I who depended on circumstances."[32] Dostoevsky probably felt himself to have become a plaything of Suslova's whims, since the couple's destination was

---

[31] *Pis'ma*, I: 333.
[32] Ibid., 337; October 18, 1863.

decided by her changing moods. He thus decided in Rome that Naples was to be the last stop on their swing southward; from there he planned to go north again and return home via Turin and Geneva. While no longer under any illusion as to her character, Dostoevsky's passion for Suslova had not abated, and it was painful for him to give her up entirely. The two travelers parted on a note of reconciliation, and the alluring image of the tempting Apollinaria, who had never *completely* excluded the possibility of a resumption of their love affair— who always seemed to remain just ever so slightly, but not entirely, beyond his grasp—haunted Dostoevsky for several more years to come.

By the time he reached Turin, Dostoevsky's thoughts were fortunately preoccupied with other concerns, and he sketches for the benefit of Turgenev the discouraging prospect that he foresees awaiting him but that, all the same, he is eager to rejoin: "A difficult task awaits me in Petersburg. Although my health has infinitely improved, in two or three months it will, without doubt, be entirely destroyed. Nothing can be done about it. The journal has to be remade from scratch. It must be more up-to-date, more interesting, and at the same time it must respect literature—incompatible aims according to a number of Petersburg thinkers. But we have the intention of fighting fiercely against this contempt leveled at literature. . . . Support us I beg of you [by sending *Phantoms*], join us."[33] *Phantoms* did appear in the first number of *Epoch*, thus testifying to the good will Turgenev nourished for the defenders of *Fathers and Children*.

The same letter also contains an apology for Dostoevsky's impossible behavior at their last meeting in Baden, which he vaguely attributes to "the tumult of passions" in which he was then caught. "If I had not the hope of doing something more intelligent in the future," he writes wryly, "really, I would be very ashamed now. But after all! Am I going to ask pardon of myself?"[34] Far from doing so, Dostoevsky gambled once more in Hamburg, once more was stranded without a penny, and was forced to appeal to Suslova in Paris for help. A loyal friend, she raised three hundred francs. Dostoevsky limped home in early November to find matters still undecided so far as the journal was concerned, and his personal affairs in more disarray than he had anticipated.

Passing through Petersburg very rapidly, by November 10 Dostoevsky was in Vladimir with Marya Dimitrievna, whose condition gave him a shock. "The health of Marya Dimitrievna is *very* bad," he wrote her sister in Petersburg. "She has been terribly ill for two months now. . . . She has been particularly worn out, for these past two months, by a continual fever."[35] Her situation was so grave that Dostoevsky decided not to return with her to the harsh climate of

[33] Ibid., 338.
[34] Ibid.
[35] Ibid., 339; November 10, 1863.

Petersburg and planned to live in Moscow, renting a small apartment in the northern capital where he could stay when looking after the affairs of the journal. Dostoevsky punctiliously introduced his wife to his Moscow relatives, hoping they would look after her during his absences, and the financial pressures on him eased for the moment because his wealthy Moscow uncle, who had recently died, left him a bequest in his will. But this windfall provided the only bright spot in a situation that rapidly became more and more tormenting.

CHAPTER 29

The Prison of Utopia

All during the summer and fall, Mikhail had been writing endless petitions to the authorities for permission to resume publication, and in mid-November permission was given, not to revive *Time*, but to publish a new journal—on condition that it maintain an "irreproachable tendency."[1] The loss of the previous name of the journal meant that the new publication could not benefit from the prestige already acquired by *Time* in the past two years and would have to begin anew to establish itself. Dostoevsky took as active a part as he could in the preparations, and there was a steady flow of correspondence between the two cities. The title *Epoch* was finally hit upon, and the first announcement asking for subscriptions was placed at the end of January 1864, which meant that most potential subscribers had already sent their money elsewhere. Also, the first issue (a double one) came off the presses only in April, creating an impression of editorial disorganization and unreliability. Strakhov uncharitably blames Mikhail Dostoevsky for lacking energy at this crucial moment, forgetting to mention that Mikhail's youngest daughter Varya died of scarlet fever in February and that the poor father was prostrate with grief.

Dostoevsky mentions to Mikhail that he would write a lead article establishing the position of the journal, and he mentions two others as well: "A critique of the novel of Chernyshevsky and the one of Pisemsky would create a considerable effect. . . . Two opposed ideas and both demolished. As a result, the truth."[2] Pisemsky's *The Unruly Sea* (1863), which had been published in *The Russian Messenger*, was among the first of the important so-called anti-Nihilist novels that form a subcategory in Russian prose fiction of the nineteenth century. Such books differ from Turgenev's *Fathers and Children*, or Dostoevsky's *Crime and Punishment*, by depicting the Nihilists as outright scoundrels moved only by the basest personal motives. On the opposing side, Chernyshevsky's Utopian novel, *What Is To Be Done?* (1863), gave a glowing picture of the extraordinary moral virtues of the "new people" whom Turgenev had maligned with the label of Nihilist, and it also includes an enticing tableau of their future Utopian Socialist

[1] *DMI*, 543.
[2] *Pisma*, 1: 341; November 19, 1863.

paradise. Just as he had done in the past, Dostoevsky wished to steer a middle ideological course between the slanders of the reactionaries and the daydreams of the radicals, aiming at a "truth" independent of both while doing justice to each at the same time.

Chernyshevsky had been arrested on July 7, 1862, and it may cause some confusion to see him mentioned now as the author of a novel published in 1863—a novel, moreover, whose subversive content is plain. But the book did appear with the official imprimatur of the censorship while Chernyshevsky was tightly under lock and key, and its publication is perhaps the most spectacular example of bureaucratic bungling in the cultural realm during the reign of Alexander II. It may also seem surprising that the literary essayist, philosophical commentator, historian, and economist Chernyshevsky should have turned his hand to fiction. But when imprisonment cut him off from his usual literary labors, he decided, with undaunted determination, to take a leaf from two writers he admired, William Godwin and Harriet Beecher Stowe, and carry on his work as ideological mentor of the radicals by means of the novel. The result was *What Is To Be Done?*, which, for all its obvious artistic weaknesses, ranks as one of the most successful works of propaganda ever written in fictional form. Few books have had so effective an impact on the lives of so wide a mass of people, beginning with the efforts of Chernyshevsky's immediate disciples to form Socialist cooperative communes similar to those he depicted and continuing up to V. I. Lenin, for whom it was a source of personal inspiration.[3]

Printed in three issues of *The Contemporary* beginning in March 1863 (and partly overlapping with the publication of *Winter Notes* in *Time*), the work created an indescribable commotion, much of which derived from its polemical relation to *Fathers and Children*. Chernyshevsky staunchly believed that Turgenev's masterpiece was nothing but a dastardly caricature of Dobrolyubov (who died of tuberculosis in 1861), and his own book undertakes to present a more accurate image of the "new people" (as Dobrolyubov first called the young radicals) whom Turgenev had supposedly defamed. The two chief male characters, Lopukhov and Kirsanov, are both *raznochintsy* and medical students when the book opens—perfect analogues of Bazarov. Both are part of a romantic triangle involving the heroine, Vera Pavlovna, but whereas Bazarov is destroyed when his fatal attraction to Mme Odintsova proves stronger than his will, the opposite occurs to Chernyshevsky's characters. Since they follow the precepts of "rational

---

[3] "The issues of *The Contemporary* in which it had been printed," writes Andrzej Walicki, "were preserved with immense piety, as though they were family heirlooms. For many members of the younger generation the novel became a true 'encyclopedia of life and knowledge.' Plekhanov declared that 'no printed work has had such a great success in Russia as Chernyshevsky's *What Is To Be Done?*'" Andrzej Walicki, *A History of Russian Thought*, trans. Hilda Andrews-Rusiecka (Oxford, 1975), 190.

egoism," they are able to untie the woefully tangled love knot without a quiver of the outdated romantic *Weltschmerz* that undoes Bazarov, or even a trace of such primitive emotions as resentment or jealousy.

This refutation of Turgenev would have been enough to guarantee the book its enormous success, but it gripped the imagination of its young readers even more strongly by offering solutions to the whole range of problems that preoccupied the radical intelligentsia in the 1860s—solutions that, it reassured them, could be put into practice with miraculous ease. Rational egoism was the wonder-working talisman that provided the final key to all human complexities—whether the relations between the sexes, the establishment of new social institutions, the attainment of success in private life, the hoodwinking of the stupid tsarist authorities, or the transformation of mankind both physically and spiritually in the future earthly paradise. All one had to do was accept a rigorous egoism as the norm of one's behavior, and then believe that a "rational" egoism compels one, by the silent force of logic, always to identify self-interest with that of the greatest good of the greatest number.

It is hardly possible to suppress a smile as Chernyshevsky's virtuosos of virtue solemnly argue themselves into the conviction that a strict egoism alone determines all their actions. In reality, although ridiculing the ethics of self-sacrifice at every opportunity, they behave in perfect accordance with its precepts. But such behavior is not *felt* by them as self-sacrifice because, according to Chernyshevsky's image of human nature, once the principles of rational egoism are internalized, obsolescent reactions of "nonrational egoism" simply cease to exist. The passions and the emotions will thus *always* respond in a manner compatible with the injunctions of enlightened reason, which has proven once and for all that to benefit others is in reality the highest degree of self-concern. Nothing more self-renunciatory could be imagined, but this display of the purest virtue is masked as the most arrant and egregious selfishness.

As an example, we may take Lopukhov's decision to marry Vera Pavlovna immediately, and so rescue her from familial oppression rather than waiting, as had been planned, until he obtained his medical degree; he thus throws up for Vera's sake the chance of a brilliant academic and medical career. Chernyshevsky is aware that a corrupt and cynical "average" reader may consider this to be strange behavior for an "egoist." And he hastens to explain that Lopukhov had "made up his mind, conscientiously and resolutely, to renounce all material advantages and honors, so as to work for the benefit of others, finding that the pleasure of such work was the best utility for him." Armed with this conviction, Lopukhov now finds it easy to give up everything he had striven all his life to attain. What worries him is only whether he is being perfectly consistent. Might he really be giving in to the enemy and making a sacrifice? Instead of interpreting his own actions as a sacrifice, he uses them, on the contrary, to prove the omnipresence of egoism. "What a hypocrite!" he says of himself. "Why should I take a degree? . . . Perhaps, with lessons and translations, I'll make even more than a doctor."[4] On the basis of such reasoning, the troubled Lopukhov quiets his fears that he might be infringing on the miraculous tenets of rational egoism.

The most finished illustration of this control of the will by reason is the revolutionary superman Rakhmetov, whose underground activity as an organizer is skillfully conveyed by euphemisms. Rakhmetov is a monster of efficiency and self-mastery. Toughening himself by sleeping on a bed of nails, he subordinates all concern about other people to the attainment of his great unnamed purpose: revolution. Rakhmetov is a Bazarov wholeheartedly absorbed in his cause, unshakable and unconquerable in his strength, and deprived even of the few remaining traits of self-doubt and emotional responsiveness that make his predecessor humanly sympathetic. This ideal of the steel-nerved rationalist-revolutionary who destroys all vestiges of personal sympathies and inclinations so as to comply with the icy logic of social utility forms an intermediate link in the line leading from Bazarov to Raskolnikov.

For the Dostoevsky who had just written *House of the Dead* and *Winter Notes*, Chernyshevsky's novel, with its touchingly naïve faith in Utilitarian reason, could hardly have been felt except as a direct challenge. And the challenge was all the more provoking because, in the famous fourth dream of Vera Pavlovna, Chernyshevsky brushes in a tableau of the evolution of humanity in the pseudoepical style used by the French Social Romantics like Ballanche and Lamennais at the beginning of the century—an evolution that culminates in the advent of the Socialist Utopia. Not surprisingly, this utopia turns out to resemble the life that Fourier had imagined for his ideal phalanstery, and it would have brought back for Dostoevsky memories of his days in the Petrashevsky Circle, where Fourier's ideas had been passionately debated in an atmosphere of candid exaltation. Fourteen years later—and what years for Dostoevsky and Russia!—the resurgence of such fantasies could only have appeared to him as the height of absurdity. Once again he was confronted with this dream image of a future in which man had conquered nature and established a way of life allowing all desires to be freely and completely satisfied. All conflict, all unhappiness, all inner striving and spiritual agitation have vanished. This is the literal end of history, whose attainment marks the final stasis of mankind in an unending round of pleasure and gratification. For Dostoevsky, the ideal of such a world called up images of Greco-Roman decadence and the inevitable growth of the most perverse passions in an effort to escape from the sheer boredom of satiation.

To make matters worse, Chernyshevsky had selected as an icon of this glorious world of fulfillment the Crystal Palace of the London World's Fair—

[4] N. G. Chernyshevsky, *Chto delat'?* (Moscow, 1955), 129, 135.

precisely the same edifice that Dostoevsky had seen as the monstrous incarnation of modern materialism, the contemporary version of the flesh-god Baal. But, to Chernyshevsky's bedazzled eyes, this structure represented the first hint of what would become the gleaming visual embodiment of the Socialist Utopia of the future, the manifest goal of all human aspirations. In Chernyshevsky's pages, then, Dostoevsky once again encountered all the old Utopian dreams of the 1840s with which he was so familiar, now allied with the new faith in Utilitarian reason that ran so squarely counter to the sense of human life he had so painfully acquired. One can see why, when it became necessary to supply an artistic text for *Epoch*, his initial intention of writing an article partly devoted to Chernyshevsky's novel should have blossomed into the idea of providing a more imaginative and artistic response.

Turgenev's *Phantoms* was secured for *Epoch*, but the journal still needed more prose fiction. Pressed by editorial necessity, Dostoevsky decided to supply a new artistic work for the February deadline, even though the conditions of his life were anything but propitious for artistic creation. "At every instant," Dostoevsky wrote in January from Moscow, "Marya Dimitrievna sees death before her eyes: she is afflicted and becomes desperate. . . . Her nerves are completely worn out. Her chest is very bad, and she is thin as a nail. It's terrible! It's awful to see this!"[5]

Pasha Isaev had been dispatched to console his mother, but his presence only stirred the agonizing realization that her condition was hopeless, and he was sent home. A rare outside glimpse of the Dostoevskys appears in a letter of Apollon Maikov, who dropped in for a visit in January on a trip to Moscow. "It is terrible," he tells his wife, "to see how much worse Marya Dimitrievna looks: yellow, nothing but skin and bones, the very image of death. She was very, very happy to see me, asked after you, but her coughing placed a limit on her talkativeness. Feodor Mikhailovich diverts her with various trifles, little handbags, piggybanks, etc., and she seems very pleased with them. They both present a very sad picture: she with tuberculosis, and he with epilepsy."[6]

Nevertheless, Dostoevsky tried as best he could to work on a story that, though unnamed, was manifestly the first part of *Notes from Underground*. Yet his own health was also badly deteriorating, and he tells Mikhail at the beginning of February that he has been ill for the past two weeks, not only with epilepsy ("that would not be important," he remarks) but also with an infection of the bladder that has prevented him from either sitting or lying down comfortably. "I won't hide from you that my work is going badly. My novella, suddenly, has begun to displease me. However, it's my own fault. I have messed up

[5] *Pis'ma*, 1: 345; January 10, 1864.
[6] L. P. Lansky, "Dostoevsky v neizdanoi perepiske sovremennikov (1837–1881)," *LN* 86 (Moscow, 1973), 393; January 1864.

something in it."[7] His failure to meet his deadline, even after pushing it ahead to March, depressed him terribly, and he was also worried that he might have written himself out.

———■———

In mid-February, Dostoevsky traveled to Petersburg (Mikhail's little Varya died during his stay there), and on his return to Moscow on February 29 he wrote both to console his bereaved brother and to outline further plans and projects for *Epoch*. He mentions "the idea for a magnificent article on the theoreticism and the fantastic among the theoreticians (of *The Contemporary*)."[8] Although never developed as such, this idea probably became absorbed into *Notes from Underground*, the first part of which was completed sometime around the end of February. Approved by the censorship on March 20, it appeared in the first double number of *Epoch* several weeks later.

It is likely that, in setting out to write his article on *What Is To Be Done?*, Dostoevsky had begun to compose in the familiar first-person style of *Winter Notes* and using the same sort of persona—a Russian accepting Western ideas, but emotionally and subconsciously in revolt against them. In this case, the "Western" ideas would be those of the radicals of the 1860s, as exemplified not only by *What Is To Be Done?* but also, more theoretically, by *The Anthropological Principle in Philosophy*, with its outright denial of free will. When confronted a bit later with the need for a "story," Dostoevsky retained the original form but gave the "I" of the narrative more social specificity by drawing on his plans for the revision of *The Double*. The conception of Golyadkin, as we know from Dostoevsky's notebooks, had been evolving steadily in the direction of an inner assimilation of radical ideology; and the narrator of Dostoevsky's new work thus becomes a development of the Golyadkin type. This supposition—the fusion of the underground man with Golyadkin at a certain stage—is supported by a small detail in the work: both men serve under the same bureau chief, Anton Antonovich Setotchkin.

There is some indication, too, that Dostoevsky intended to write a series of episodes with the underground man as central figure, but he never developed the plan beyond the two parts of the existing text of *Notes from Underground*.[9] And just as Part I grew out of an article about *What Is To Be Done?*, absorbing along the way some of the material for a rewriting of *The Double*, so Part II probably emerged from Dostoevsky's intention to write a work called *A Confession*

[7] *Pis'ma*, 1: 347; February 9, 1864.

[8] Ibid., 349; February 29, 1864.

[9] In the magazine, a footnote appended to the title of the work announced that the first installment "should count as an introduction to a whole book, almost a preface." This phrase was eliminated on republication. See the commentary and textual variants in *PSS*, 5: 375; 342.

(the title had been announced in *Time* at the beginning of 1863 as Dostoevsky's next contribution). First mentioned in October 1859, this project is described in a letter to Mikhail as "a *confession*—a novel that I wished to write after everything, so to say, I have had to live through myself. . . . I conceived it in *katorga* . . . in painful moments of sorrow and self-criticism."[10] This confession would have contained a disillusioned contemplation of Dostoevsky's ideological past in the 1840s. Since this is precisely what we find in Part II, we can assume that this scheme was also embodied in *Notes from Underground*, nor would such an amalgamation have been entirely fortuitous. Despite all its coldly calculating terminology of egoism and Utilitarianism, Chernyshevsky's novel had revived much of the sentimental, idealistic atmosphere of the 1840s and shared its philanthropic reveries of a redeemed and purified humanity. Dostoevsky could thus easily integrate such material from his own past, both ideological and personal, into his new creation, and it is surely no coincidence that the underground man in Part II is exactly the same age as Dostoevsky at the time of his success with *Poor Folk* in 1845. Whatever autobiographical elements are contained in this second part, however, all are assimilated into the overriding artistic thrust of the text as a whole.

On March 20, 1864, Dostoevsky wrote to Mikhail that he was following a severe regimen, taking innumerable precautions with his diet, and that his infectious condition was on the mend. Marya Dimitrievna's sister had also providentially arrived from Petersburg to take charge of the household. "Without her," he comments, "I don't know what would have become of us."[11] Marya Dimitrievna was growing weaker every day, and Dostoevsky was told that her death might occur at any moment; but she continued desperately to cling to life, and was still pathetically making plans for the summer months and choosing her place of residence in future years. The emotional drain of this heart-rending situation must surely have been enormous; but Dostoevsky assures Mikhail that "I have gone back to my work on my novella [Part II of *Notes from Underground*]. . . . [I]t's absolutely necessary that it be successful; it is necessary *for me*. It has an extremely bizarre tone, brutal and violent; it may displease; poetry will have to soften it all through and make it bearable. But I hope that this will get better."[12]

One week later Dostoevsky was sent the first issue of *Epoch* containing Part I of *Notes from Underground*, and could scarcely recognize what he saw before him. His conception had been mutilated by the censorship. "It would have been better," he says, "not to have published the next-to-last chapter at all (where the essential, the very idea of the work is expressed) than to publish it like that, that is, with phrases that are garbled and contradict each other. Alas! What is to be

[10] *Pis'ma*, 2: 608; October 9, 1859.
[11] Ibid., 612; March 20, 1864.
[12] Ibid.

done? Those swinish censors: in passages where I mocked at everything and sometimes blasphemed for the sake of appearances—that is let by, and where I concluded with the need for faith and Christ—that is censored. What are the censors doing? Are they conspiring against the government or what?"[13] These comments are of major importance for the interpretation of Part I, and we shall return to the problems that they pose.

Meanwhile, Dostoevsky was working away at the second part valiantly, but finding it increasingly difficult to surmount the crushing burden of his almost impossible circumstances. "My friend," he writes Mikhail at the beginning of April, "I have been ill a good part of the month, then convalescent, and even now I am not yet entirely well. My nerves are shot and I have not been able to get back my strength. I am so grimly tormented by *so many things* that I don't even wish to speak of them. My wife is dying, *literally*. There is not a day when, at such and such a moment, we do not believe that we see her going. Her sufferings are terrible and this works on me because. . . ." The sentence trails off in this fashion, and Dostoevsky evidently assumes that Mikhail will understand what he leaves unsaid; perhaps he was thinking of his affair with Suslova, whose secret only Mikhail was supposed to have known. Yet, Dostoevsky continues, "I write and write, every morning, . . . [and] the story is getting longer. Sometimes I imagine that it is worth nothing, and yet I write with enthusiasm; I do not know what it will give."[14] Dostoevsky hopes that he can send half of the second part soon to be set up in type, but insists that it can only be published as a whole and not in installments.

———■———

Several other letters to Mikhail in early April contain urgent requests for money; and he also outlines an elaborate strategy for extracting a loan on behalf of *Epoch* from their wealthy and pious Moscow aunt. On April 13, Dostoevsky again describes his lamentable condition ("I am in a frightening state, nervous, morally ill"),[15] but provides additional information about his story. He now sees it comprising three chapters: the first is almost finished; the second is drafted but chaotic; the third is not yet begun. Dostoevsky wonders whether the first chapter could not be published by itself, though convinced it would injure the effect of the whole: "deprived of the sequel (the two others are essential) it loses all its juice. You know what a *transition* is in music. This is exactly the same. The first chapter seems to be nothing but chatter; but suddenly this chatter in the last two chapters is resolved by a sudden catastrophe."[16] These

[13] Ibid., 2: 353; March 26, 1864.
[14] Ibid., 355; April 2, 1864.
[15] Ibid., 362; April 13, 1864.
[16] Ibid., 365.

words, the last in Dostoevsky's correspondence referring to the composition of *Notes from Underground*, were written six days before Marya Dimitrievna breathed her last.

Over the course of the next several days, other, more ruminative, thoughts occupied Dostoevsky. "Will I ever see Masha again?" Dostoevsky asks in a notebook fragment (20: 172). Keeping a vigil at the bier of his dead wife, Dostoevsky pored over their life together as he sat beside her corpse, and such thoughts led him on to ponder as well great issues of life on earth and its meaning, and of the possibility of an eternity beyond the grave. In such a severe and solemn moment of self-scrutiny, he tried to unriddle his own answers to these perennial enigmas. Nowhere else does he tell us so unequivocally what he really thought about God, immortality, the role of Christ in human existence, and the meaning of human life on earth.

He endeavors not only to persuade himself that immortality exists, but also to explain why it *must* exist as a necessary completion of terrestrial human life. After asking the poignant question, Dostoevsky turns aside from eternity and shifts his gaze to the vicissitudes of the human condition. "To love man like *oneself*, according to the commandment of Christ," he declares peremptorily, "is impossible. The law of personality on earth binds. The *Ego* stands in the way" (20: 172). These words were set down just after Dostoevsky had completed the first part of *Notes from Underground*, where he had portrayed the refusal of the human ego to surrender its right to self-assertion—in its rejection, even at the price of madness and self-destruction, of any philosophy that denied this irrepressible human need.

It may appear as if Dostoevsky were inclined to agree with Strakhov—and Christian doctrine—that human nature was incurably rotten, incapable of fulfilling the law of Christ except if strengthened by God's grace. But Eastern Orthodoxy has always placed more emphasis on man's free will than on grace; and in the very next sentences of his notebook entry, Dostoevsky makes clear that he does not consider any special gift of grace to be necessary: the incarnation of Christ has been sufficient to spur mankind into eternal struggle against its own limitations:

> Christ alone could love man as himself, but Christ was a perpetual eternal ideal to which man strives and, according to the law of nature, should strive. Meanwhile, since the appearance of Christ as *the ideal of man in the flesh*, it has become as clear as day that the . . . highest use a man can make of his personality, of the full development of his *Ego*—is, as it were, to annihilate that *Ego*, to give it totally and to everyone undividedly and unselfishly. In this way, the law of the *Ego* fuses with the law of humanism, and in this fusion both the *Ego* and the all (apparently two extreme opposites)

mutually annihilate themselves one for the other, and at the same time each attains separately, and to the highest degree, their own individual development. (20: 172)

Dostoevsky declares it a "law of nature" that mankind struggle to follow the example of Christ. This belief had been the sole ray of hope piercing the moral darkness by which he had been surrounded in the prison camp; and if its light had not been obscured even by the blackness of prison life, then its radiance could be assumed to continue to glimmer in every Christian breast. This is surely one reason why Dostoevsky had declared, in the heartfelt letter he wrote to Mme Fonvizina shortly after quitting the camp, that "if someone proved to me that Christ is outside the truth, and that *in reality* the truth were outside of Christ, then I should prefer to remain with Christ rather than with the truth." [17] Dostoevsky is affirming here the depth and strength of his existential commitment to Christ—which meant, concretely, to the moral message of love and self-sacrifice that Christ had brought to the world.

Indeed, the sole significance of Christ, as Dostoevsky now speaks of him, is to serve as the divine enunciator of this morality; he fulfills no other purpose, not even the traditional one of redeeming mankind from the wages of sin and death. There is, in fact, not much difference between the Christ of the notebook entry and the Utopian Socialist Christ whom Dostoevsky had defended against Belinsky in 1845–1846, or the Christ he had described earlier as having been sent by God to the modern world, just as Homer had been dispatched to the ancient one, in order to provide "the organization of its spiritual and earthly life." [18] But, in the intervening years, Dostoevsky had acquired a new realization of all the obstacles that prevented Christ's message from being embodied in such an "organization"—the chief one being the human ego itself, with its raging demand for the recognition of its rights.

Five years later, Dostoevsky sketched the plan for what he considered the most important project of his creative career—a series of novels to be called *The Life of a Great Sinner*; and the origins of this conception are in the words just quoted. For it is only when the egoism of personality has been expanded to its fullest stretch, only when someone has indeed become a "great sinner," that the full sublimity of the *imitatio Christi*—the full grandeur of the voluntary self-sacrifice of the personality out of love—can be most effectively presented. Such a self-sacrifice, in Dostoevsky's view, would unite the law of personality with that of "humanism," and the use of this term, which had been employed twenty years earlier by Feuerbach and the Left Hegelians to denote the secular and social realization of the Christian law of love, testifies that Dostoevsky, without

---

[17] Ibid., 1: 142; February 20, 1854.
[18] Ibid., 58; January 1, 1840.

abandoning his earlier ideals, was now striving to integrate them with his more recently acquired convictions. But what had once been conceived as a worldly possibility has now receded into the infinite future, and he goes on to declare that "all history, whether of humanity in part or of each man separately, is only the development, struggle, and attainment of this goal [the fusion of egoism and humanism]." Once having reached it, however, mankind would then truly have arrived at "the Paradise of Christ" (20: 172).

In a movement typical of his imaginative manipulation of ideas, Dostoevsky thinks them through to the end and envisages the situation resulting from their completion. "But if that is the final goal of all humanity," he reasons, "(having attained which it would no longer be necessary to develop, that is, . . . eternally strive toward it)—therefore, it would no longer be necessary to live—then, consequently, when man achieves this, he terminates his earthly existence. Therefore, man on earth is only a creature in development, consequently, someone not finished but transitional." Earthly human nature, with its necessarily unresolved conflict between egoism and the law of love, is not, then, the final state of mankind, and this conviction enables Dostoevsky to answer the question posed at the beginning of his meditations. "It is completely senseless to attain such a great goal if upon attaining it everything is extinguished and disappears, that is, if man will no longer have life when he attains the goal. Consequently, there is a future paradisial life" (20: 172–173).

Here we have Dostoevsky's argument for the necessity of immortality—without such a belief, the endless struggle of humanity on earth to fulfill the law of Christ would simply have no point. What motivates Dostoevsky's reflections above all—what he cannot bear to contemplate as a possibility—is the dire prospect that all the toils and turmoils of human life should turn out to be entirely meaningless. Like another doubt-filled Christian who was also a child of *his* century, Blaise Pascal, nothing terrified Dostoevsky more than the specter of living in a senseless universe. *House of the Dead* provides a chilling imaginative evocation of this terror in one of the most self-revealing passages that Dostoevsky ever wrote. Here he describes forced labor "at a task whose character was absolutely useless and absurd" (4: 20), and intuits the suicidal self-destruction that would be the inevitable result. The question of immortality is not raised directly in that book, but it contains a haunting depiction of mankind's unquenchable desire to exist in a universe whose infinite spaces, instead of remaining silent, would respond to the longings contained in every human soul. Although Dostoevsky illustrates the point in connection with compulsory labor, his conclusions apply with equal if not greater force to the problem of whether human life has any ultimate value or is just "a tale told by an idiot, signifying nothing." It would be an intolerable insult to human dignity for man to live in a world totally deprived of sense, and such a world, in

Dostoevsky's view, would be one in which death simply meant extinction—a world in which the travails of human life would receive no satisfactory explanation. Here we penetrate to the heart of that intimate connection between psychology and religious metaphysics so typical of Dostoevsky, and this connection explains the rather unexpected nature of his argument in favor of immortality.

Dostoevsky then faces those whom he calls the "Antichrists," who think they can refute Christianity by pointing to its failure to transform earthly life. "It will be," Dostoevsky begins, alluding to such a transformation, "but it will be after the attainment of the goal, when man is finally reborn according to the laws of nature into another form which neither marries nor is given in marriage" (20: 173–174). No passage in Dostoevsky so clearly illuminates why his novels almost always present human life as inextricably embroiled in tragic conflicts. Ordinary human desires, even the most legitimate ones, even the duty, through marriage and the family, to fulfill society's most sacrosanct obligations, must inevitably clash with the imperatives of the Christian law of love. Whatever else Dostoevsky may have been, he was not an uncritical defender of existing institutions, and these words show how continually he was reaching out in imagination beyond the bounds of *all* earthly establishments.

A summarizing passage of the utmost importance then returns to Dostoevsky's point of departure and simultaneously offers a poignant glimpse into the personal roots of these touchingly tentative reflections:

> And thus man strives on earth toward an ideal *opposed* to his nature. When a man has not fulfilled the law of striving toward the ideal, that is, has not *through love* sacrificed his *Ego* to people or to another person (Masha and myself) he suffers and calls this condition a sin. And so, man must unceasingly feel suffering, which is compensated for by the heavenly joy of fulfilling the law, that is, by sacrifice. Here is the earthly equilibrium. Otherwise, the earth would be senseless. (20: 174)

These pages reveal Dostoevsky inwardly striving to accept the essential dogmas of the divinity of Christ, personal immortality, the Second Coming, and the Resurrection. The highest aim of Dostoevsky's Christianity, though, is not personal salvation but the fusion of the individual ego with the community in a symbiosis of love, and the only sin that Dostoevsky appears to recognize is the failure to fulfill this law of love. Suffering arises from the consciousness of such a failure, and Dostoevsky's words help us to grasp not only why suffering plays such a prominent role in his works, but also why it is misleading to infer that he believes *any* kind of suffering to be necessarily good. Only that suffering is valuable which, by testifying to an awareness of insufficiency in responding to the example of Christ, also proclaims the moral autonomy of the human personality; and since human egoism will *always* prevent the ideal of Christ from being fully realized on earth, this type of suffering will not (and cannot) cease before the end of time.

In his artistic works, the fetters of the law of personality are in most cases felt impartially as an inescapable element of the human condition. For Dostoevsky never portrays the Christian ideal as a positively beneficent force in human life by which these fetters can be thrown off; sometimes this ideal even has the contrary effect. The appearance of a Christ-like figure in *The Idiot*, for example, only leads to a worsening of conflicts instead of aiding in their appeasement or resolution. But, as we have seen, the major significance that Dostoevsky ascribes to the Incarnation was precisely to exercise such an awakening and quickening function: Christ was sent by God not to give mankind the peace of absolution but to stir it to struggle against the law of personality. Dostoevsky points out that "Christ himself prophesied his teachings only as an ideal, predicted himself that strife and development will continue to the end of the world (the teaching about the sword)" [St. Mark quotes Christ as having said "Not peace I bring but a sword"] (20: 173–174). Life for Dostoevsky was, as it had been for Keats, "a vale of soul-making," into which Christ had come to call mankind to battle against the death of immersion in matter and to inspire the struggle toward the ultimate victory over egoism.

Eastern Orthodoxy, unlike the Augustinian tradition of the West, has always regarded man not as having fallen into irredeemable sin from a state of perfection before the Fall but rather as having emerged into earthly life still imperfect and unformed; man contains the "image" of God but not his "likeness," which John of Damascus defined as the "assimilation to God through virtue." [19] St. Irenaeus compares man on earth to a child required to grow and develop. For Dostoevsky, human life was the anvil on which souls were being forged by the human blows of fate, and it was only in eternity that this endless process would come to a halt. Only in eternity would the law of personality finally be overcome, and this is surely why Dostoevsky could never effectively imagine such a triumph within the realistic conventions of the nineteenth-century novel to which he remained faithful.

All of Dostoevsky's major works will henceforth be controlled by the framework of values expressed in this notebook entry, and they will dramatize the fateful opposition between the law of Christ and the law of personality as Dostoevsky understood it. Yet to say this tells us little that would not be equally true of every great writer in the tradition of European literature beginning with Dante, Shakespeare, and Milton. To understand Dostoevsky, we must try to grasp his *particular* understanding of this great theme, which he fills in, fleshes out, and dramatizes in terms of the social-cultural issues and conflicts of his own

[19] Timothy Ware, *The Orthodox Church* (Baltimore, 1963), 224–225.

day. These conflicts provide him with the living substance of his works; it is through them that he rises to the heights of the great argument that possessed his spirit and inflamed his creative imagination; and his genius consists precisely in the ability to unite these two (at first sight) so very dissimilar levels. But the time has come to illustrate how he did so in *Notes from Underground*, whose second part, completed in May 1864, was published two months after Marya Dimitrievna's demise.

CHAPTER 30

Notes from Underground

> If philosophy among other vagaries were also to have the notion that it
> could occur to a man to act in accordance with its teaching, one might
> make out of this a queer comedy.
>
> —Søren Kierkegaard, *Fear and Trembling*

Few works in modern literature are more widely read than Dostoevsky's *Notes from Underground* (*Zapiski iz podpol'ya*) or so often cited as a key text revelatory of the hidden depths of the sensibility of our time. The term "underground man" has become part of the vocabulary of contemporary culture, and this character has now achieved—like Hamlet, Don Quixote, Don Juan, and Faust—the stature of one of the great archetypal literary creations. Most important cultural developments of the present century—Nietzscheanism, Freudianism, expressionism, surrealism, crisis theology, existentialism—have claimed the underground man as their own or have been linked with him by zealous interpreters; and when the underground man has not been hailed as a prophetic anticipation, he has been held up to exhibition as a luridly repulsive warning. The underground man has thus entered into the very warp and woof of modern culture in a fashion testifying to the philosophical suggestiveness and hypnotic power of this first great creation of Dostoevsky's post-Siberian years.

Notes from Underground attracted little attention when first published (no critical notice was taken of it in any Russian journal). In 1883, N. K. Mikhailovsky wrote his all-too-influential article, "A Cruel Talent," citing some of its more sadistic passages and arguing that the utterances and actions of the character illustrated Dostoevsky's own "tendencies to torture."[1] Eight years later, writing from an opposed ideological perspective, V. V. Rozanov interpreted the work as essentially inspired by Dostoevsky's awareness of the irrational depths of the human soul, with all its conflicting impulses for evil as well as for good. No world order based on reason and rationality could possibly contain this seething

---

[1] N. K. Mikhailovsky, "Zhestoky talant," in *F. M. Dostoevsky v Russkoi kritike*, ed. A. A. Belkin (Moscow, 1956), 306–384.

chaos of the human psyche; only religion (Eastern Orthodoxy) could aid man to overcome his capricious and destructive propensities.[2]

It was evident from the day of publication that Dostoevsky's *Notes from Underground* was an attack, particularly in Part I, on Chernyshevsky's philosophy of "rational egoism," but up to the early 1920s interpreters paid little attention to this ancient quarrel, which was considered only incidental and of no artistic importance. It was assumed that Dostoevsky had been aroused by opposition to Chernyshevsky but had used radical ideas only as a foil. Chernyshevsky had believed that man was innately good and amenable to reason, and that, once enlightened as to his true interests, he would be able, with the help of reason and science, to construct a perfect society. Dostoevsky may have also believed man to be capable of good, but he considered him equally full of evil, irrational, capricious, and destructive inclinations, and, or so interpreters argued, it was *this* disturbing truth that he presented through the underground man as an answer to Chernyshevsky's naïve optimism.

Such a simplistic reading can hardly be sustained after a little reflection, for it would require us to consider Dostoevsky as just about the worst polemicist in all of literary history. He was, after all, supposedly writing to dissuade readers from accepting Chernyshevsky's ideas. Could he really have imagined that anyone in his right mind would *prefer* the life of the underground man to the radiant happiness of Chernyshevsky's denizens of Utopia? Obviously not, and since Dostoevsky was anything but a fool, it may be assumed that the invention of the underground man was not inspired by any such self-defeating notion. In reality, as another line of interpretation soon began to make clear, his attack on Chernyshevsky and the radicals is far more intricate and cunning than had previously been suspected.

The first true glimpse into the artistic logic of *Notes from Underground* appears in an article by V. L. Komarovich, who in 1921 pointed out that Dostoevsky's novella was structurally dependent on *What Is To Be Done?*[3] Whole sections of the work in the second part—the attempt of the underground man to bump into an officer on the Nevsky Prospect, for example, or the famous encounter with the prostitute Liza—are modeled on episodes in Chernyshevsky's book, and are obvious *parodies* that inverted the meaning of those episodes in their original context. But Komarovich continued to regard the imprecations of the underground man against "reason" in the first part simply as a straightforward argument with Utilitarianism. The underground man was

[2] V. V. Rozanov, *Dostoevsky and the Legend of the Grand Inquisitor*, trans. Spencer E. Roberts (Ithaca, NY, 1972), 35.

[3] V. L. Komarovich, "'Mirovaya garmoniya,' Dostoevskogo," in *O Dostoevskom*, ed. Donad Fanger (Providence, RI, 1966), 119–149.

still speaking for Dostoevsky and could be identified with the author's own position.

A further decisive advance was made a few years later by A. Skaftymov, who, without raising the issue of parody, argued that the negative views of the underground man could in no way be taken to represent Dostoevsky's own position, because such an identification would constitute a flagrant repudiation of all the moral ideals that he was upholding in his journalism. "The underground man in *Notes*," wrote Skaftymov, "is not only the accuser but also one of the accused," whose insults are as much (if not more) directed against himself as against others, and whose self-destructive existence by no means represents anything that Dostoevsky was approving. Skaftymov also perceptively remarks that Dostoevsky's strategy is that of destroying his opponents "from within, carrying their logical presuppositions and possibilities to their consistent conclusion and arriving at a destructively helpless blind alley."[4]

These words provide an essential insight into one of the main features of Dostoevsky's technique as an ideological novelist, but although fully aware that the novella is "a polemical work," Skaftymov fails to see how this polemical intent enters into the very creation of the character of the underground man. Skaftymov's analysis of the text thus remains on the level of moral-psychological generalities and does not penetrate to the heart of Dostoesky's conception. This can be reached, in my view, only by combining and extending Komarovich's remarks on the parodistic element in *Notes from Underground* with Skaftymov's perception of how the underground man dramatizes within himself the ultimate consequences of the position that Dostoevsky was opposing. In other words, the underground man is not only a moral-psychological type whose egoism Dostoevsky wishes to expose, he is also a social-ideological one, whose psychology must be seen as intimately interconnected with the ideas he accepts and by which he tries to live.

Dostoevsky overtly pointed to this aspect of the character in the footnote appended to the title of the novella. "Both the author of the *Notes* and the *Notes* themselves," he writes, "are of course fictitious. Nonetheless, such persons as the author of such memoirs not only may, but must, exist in our society, if we take into consideration the circumstances that led to the formation of our society. . . . He is one of the representatives of a generation that is still with us" (5: 99). Dostoevsky here is obviously referring to the formation of Russian society, which, as he could expect all readers of *Epoch* to know—had he not explained this endlessly in his articles in *Time*?—had been formed by the successive waves of

---

[4] Originally published in a Czech periodical, the essay has been reprinted in A. Skaftymov, *Nravstvennie iskaniya Russkikh pisatelei* (Moscow, 1972), 70, 96.

European influence that had washed over Russia since the time of Peter the Great. The underground man *must* exist as a type because he is the inevitable product of such a cultural formation, and his character does in fact embody and reflect two phases of this historical evolution. He is, in short, conceived as a parodistic persona whose life exemplifies the tragic-comic impasses resulting from the effects of such influences on the Russian national psyche.

His diatribes in the first part thus do not arise, as has commonly been thought, because of his rejection of reason; on the contrary, they result from his acceptance of *all* the implications of reason in its then-current Russian incarnation—and particularly, all those consequences that advocates of reason such as Chernyshevsky blithely chose to disregard. In the second part, Dostoevsky extends the same technique to those more sentimental-humanitarian elements of Chernyshevsky's ideology that had resuscitated some of the atmosphere of the 1840s.

Dostoevsky's footnote thus attempted to alert his audience to the satirical and parodistic nature of his conceptions, but it was too oblique to serve its purpose. Like many other examples of first-person satirical parody, *Notes from Underground* has usually been misunderstood and taken straight. Indeed, the intrinsic danger of such a form, used for such a purpose, is that it tends to wipe out any critical distance between the narrator and reader and makes it difficult to *see through* the character to the target of the satire. This danger can be avoided only if, as in *Gulliver's Travels*, the reader is disoriented from the start by the incongruity of the situation, or if in other ways—linguistic exaggerations or manifestly grotesque behavior—he is made aware that the I-narrator is as much a literary convention as a genuine character. Although Dostoevsky makes some attempt to supplement his footnote in this direction, these efforts were not sufficient to balance the overwhelming psychological presence of the underground man and the force of his imprecations and anathemas against some of the most cherished dogmas of modern civilization. As a result, the parodistic function of his character has always been obscured by the immense vitality of its artistic embodiment, and it has, paradoxically, been Dostoevsky's very genius for the creation of character that has most interfered with the proper understanding of *Notes from Underground*.

If we are interested in grasping Dostoevsky's own point of view, as far as this can be reconstructed, then we must take *Notes from Underground* for what it was initially meant to be—a brilliantly Swiftian satire, remarkable for the finesse of its conception and the brio of its execution, which dramatizes the dilemmas of a representative Russian personality attempting to live by the two European codes whose unhappy effects Dostoevsky explores. And though the sections have a loose narrative link, the novella is above all a diptych depicting two episodes of a symbolic history of the Russian intelligentsia.

Part I

1. The Dialectic of Determinism

The first segment of *Notes from Underground* extends from Chapter 1 through Chapter 6, and its famous opening tirade gives us an unforgettable picture of the underground man stewing in his Petersburg "corner" and mulling over the peculiarities of his character and his life: "I am a sick man. . . . I am a spiteful man. I am an unpleasant man. I think my liver is diseased." He is ill but refuses to see a doctor, though he respects medicine: "Besides, I am extremely superstitious, let's say sufficiently so to respect medicine." Medicine of course had become *the* science after Bazarov, Lopukhov, and Kirsanov, but the underground man sarcastically labels excessive respect for medicine as itself just an irrational superstition. He knows he should visit a doctor, but somehow—really for no good reason, simply out of spite—he prefers to stay home, untreated. Why? "You probably will not understand that," he says. "Well, I understand it" (5: 99). Whatever the explanation, there is a clear conflict between a rational course of behavior and some obscure feeling labeled "spite."

We then learn that the underground man is an ex-civil servant, now retired, who in the past had engaged in incessant battles to tyrannize the humble petitioners that came his way in the course of business. But while he had enjoyed this sop to his ego, he confesses that "I might foam at the mouth, but bring me some kind of toy, give me a cup of tea with sugar, and I would be appeased." The underground man's nature is by no means vicious and evil; he is more than ordinarily responsive to any manifestation of friendliness, but such responses are carefully kept bottled up no matter how strongly he might feel them: "Every moment I was conscious in myself of many, many elements completely opposed to that [spite]. . . . I knew that they had been teeming in me all my life, begging to be let out, but I would not let them, would not let them, purposely would not let them" (5: 100).

The underground man is shown as being caught in a conflict between the egoistic aspects of his character and the sympathetic, outgoing ones that he also possesses, but these latter are continually suppressed in favor of the former. We see him torn apart by an inner dissonance that prevents him from behaving in what might be considered a "normal" fashion—that is, acting in terms of self-interest and "reason" in Part I, where the underground man talks to himself or to an imaginary interlocutor, or giving unhindered expression to his altruistic (or at least amiably social) impulses in Part II, where he is living in society in relation to others. What prevents him from doing so is precisely what Dostoevsky wishes to illuminate and explore.

The nature of these impediments becomes clear only gradually in Part I as the underground man continues to expose all his defects to the scornful contemplation of his assumed reader. For it turns out that the contradictory impulses struggling within him have literally paralyzed his character. "Not only could I not become spiteful," he says, "I could not even become anything neither spiteful nor kind, neither a rascal nor an honest man, neither a hero nor an insect." The underground man's only consolation is that "an intelligent man in the nineteenth-century must and morally ought to be pre-eminently a limited creature," and he boastfully attributes his characterlessness to the fact that he is "hyperconscious." As a result of this "hyperconsciousness," he was "most capable of recognizing every refinement of 'all the sublime and the beautiful,' as we used to say at one time" (the 1840s). But "the more deeply I sank into my mire the more capable I became of sinking into it completely" (5: 100, 102).

This strange state of moral impotence, which the underground man both defends and despises, is complicated by the further admission that he positively *enjoys* the experience of his own degradation. "I reached the point," he confesses, "of feeling a sort of secret, abnormal, despicable enjoyment in returning home to my corner on some disgusting Petersburg night, and being acutely conscious that that day I had again done something loathsome, that what was done could never be undone, and secretly, inwardly gnaw, gnaw at myself for it, nagging and consuming myself till at last the bitterness turned into a sort of shameful accursed sweetness, and finally into real positive enjoyment" (5: 102).

The underground man frankly admits to being an unashamed masochist, and all too many commentators are happy to accept this admission as a sufficient explanation of his behavior. To do so, however, simply disregards the relation of the underground man's psychology to his social-cultural formation. For he goes on to explain that his sense of enjoyment is derived from "the hyperconsciousness of [his] own degradation," a hyperconsciousness that persuaded him of the impossibility of becoming anything else or of behaving in any other way even if he had wished to do so. "For the root of it all," he says, "was that it all proceeded according to the normal and fundamental laws of hyperconsciousness, and with the inertia that was the direct result of those laws, and that consequently one was not only unable to change but could do absolutely nothing" (5: 102).

This passage has often been taken as a reference to the underground man's "Hamletism," which links him with such figures as the protagonists of Turgenev's "Hamlet of the Shchigrovsky District" and "Diary of a Superfluous Man," both of whom are destroyed by an excess of consciousness that unfits them for the possibilities offered by their lives. Such thematic resemblances need not be denied, but this pervasive motif in Russian literature of the 1850s and 1860s is given a special twist by Dostoevsky and shown as the unexpected consequence of the doctrines advanced by the very people who had attacked the "Hamlets" most violently—the radicals of the 1860s themselves. For the pseudo-scientific terms of the underground man's claim of "hyperconsciousness" are a parody of Chernyshevsky, and the statement is a paraphrase of Chernyshevsky's assertion, in *The Anthropological Principle in Philosophy*, that no such capacity as free will exists or can exist, since whatever actions man attributes to his own initiative are really a result of the "laws of nature." The underground man reveals the effects on his character of the "hyperconsciousness" derived from a knowledge of such "laws," and thus mockingly exemplifies what such a doctrine really means in practice.

He imagines, for instance, that he wishes to forgive someone magnanimously for having slapped him in the face, but the more he thinks about it, the more impossible such an intention becomes. "After all, I would probably never have been able to do anything with my magnanimity—neither to forgive, for my assailant may have slapped me because of the laws of nature, and one cannot forgive the laws of nature; nor to forget, for even if it were the laws of nature, it is insulting all the same." Or suppose he wishes to act the other way round—not to forgive magnanimously, but to take revenge. How can one take revenge when no one is to blame for anything? "You look into it, the object flies off into air, your reasons evaporate, the criminal is not to be found, the insult becomes fate rather than an insult, something like a toothache, for which no one is to blame." This is why, as the underground man asserts, "the direct, legitimate, immediate fruit of consciousness is inertia—that is, conscious sitting on one's hands." Or, if one does not sit on one's hands but acts—say on the matter of revenge—then "it would only be out of spite" (5: 103, 108–109). Spite is not a *valid* cause for any kind of action, and hence it is the only one left when the laws of nature make any justified response impossible.

In such passages, the moral vacuum created by the thoroughgoing acceptance of determinism is depicted with masterly psychological insight. As a well-trained member of the intelligentsia, the underground man intellectually accepts such determinism, but it is impossible for him really to live with its conclusions. "Thus it would follow, as the result of hyperconsciousness, that one is not to blame for being a scoundrel, as though that were any consolation to the scoundrel once he himself has come to realize that he actually is a scoundrel." Or, as regards the slap in the face, it is impossible to forget because "even if it were the laws of nature, it is insulting all the same" (5: 102–103). Dostoevsky thus juxtaposes a *total* human reaction—a sense of self-revulsion at being a scoundrel, an upsurge of anger at the insult of being slapped—against a scientific rationale that dissolves all such moral-emotive feelings and hence the very possibility of a human response. Reason tells the underground man that guilt or indignation is totally irrational and meaningless, but conscience and a sense of dignity continue to exist all the same as ineradicable components of the human psyche.

Here, then, is the explanation for the so-called masochism of the underground man. Why does he refuse to see a doctor about his liver or insist that one may enjoy moaning needlessly and pointlessly about a toothache? It is because, in both instances, some mysterious, impersonal power—the laws of nature—has reduced the individual to complete helplessness, and his only method of expressing a *human* reaction to this power is to refuse to submit silently to its despotism, to protest against its pressure no matter in how ridiculous a fashion. The refusal to be treated is such a protest, self-defeating though it may be; and the moans over a toothache, says the underground man, express "all the aimlessness of your pain, which is so humiliating to your consciousness; all the system of the laws of nature on which you spit disdainfully, of course, but from which you suffer all the same while it does not" (5: 106).

Both these situations are analogous to the shameful "pleasure" that the underground man confesses at keeping alive the sense of his own degradation after his debauches. He refuses to be consoled by the alibi that the laws of nature are to blame, and his dubious enjoyment translates the moral-emotive response of his *human nature* to the blank nullity of the *laws of nature*. Far from being a sign of psychic abnormality, this sensation is in reality—given the topsy-turvy world in which he lives—a proof of the underground man's paradoxical spiritual health. For it indicates that, despite the convictions of his reason, he refuses to surrender his right to possess a conscience or an ability to feel outraged and insulted.

2. The Man of Action

Only by recognizing this ironic displacement of the normal moral-psychic horizon can we accurately grasp the underground man's relation to his imaginary interlocutor. This interlocutor is obviously a follower of Chernyshevsky, a man of action, who believes himself to be nothing less than *l'homme de la nature et de la vérité*. The underground man *agrees* with this gentleman's theory that all human conduct is nothing but a mechanical product of the laws of nature, but he also knows what the man of action does not—that this theory makes all human behavior impossible, or at least meaningless. "I envy such a man till my bile overflows," says the underground man. "He is stupid, I am not disputing that, but perhaps the normal man should be stupid—how do you know?" The normal man, the man of action, happily lacks hyperconsciousness, and when impelled by a desire to obtain revenge, for example, he "simply rushes straight toward his goal like an infuriated bull with its horns down, and nothing but a wall will stop him" (5: 103–104). He is unaware that whatever he may consider to be the basis for his headlong charge—for example, the need for justice—is a ludicrously old-fashioned and unscientific prejudice that has been replaced by the laws of nature. Only his stupidity allows him to maintain his complacent normality, and to remain so completely free from the paralyzing dilemmas of the underground man.

Confronted by the so-called tenets of natural science—such as, for example, "that in reality one drop of your own fat must be dearer to you than a hundred thousand of your fellow creatures, and that this conclusion is the final solution of all so-called virtues and duties and all such ravings and prejudices"—the men of action stop all their questionings and reasonings. The hyperconscious underground man, who lacks this saving grace of stupidity, still cannot help behaving *as if* some sort of free human response were still possible and meaningful; "consequently there is only the same outlet left again—that is, to beat the wall as hard as you can" (5: 103–105). He knows that the idea of guilt, along with all other moral ideas, has been wiped off the slate by the laws of nature, yet he irrationally persists in having moral responses. And since there is nowhere else for him to assign moral responsibility, by the most irrefutable process of deduction he and he alone is to blame for everything. But at the same time, he knows very well that he is *not* to blame, and he wishes it were possible to forget about the laws of nature long enough to convince himself that he could freely choose to become *anything*—a loafer, a glutton, or a person who spends his life drinking toasts to the health of everything "sublime and beautiful."

Every self-contradictory response of the underground man in these chapters derives from this dialectic of determinism, driven by the contradiction between the underground man's intellectual acceptance of Chernyshevsky's determinism and his simultaneous rejection of it with the entire intuitive-emotional level of personality identified with moral conscience. As a result, his self-derision and self-abuse are not meant to be taken literally. The rhetoric of the underground man contains an inverted irony similar to that of *Winter Notes*, which turns back on itself as a means of ridiculing his scornful interlocutor, the man of action. For the life of the underground man is the *reductio ad absurdum* of that of the man of action, and the more repulsive and obnoxious he portrays himself as being, the more he reveals the *true* meaning of what his self-confident judge so blindly holds dear. It is only the impenetrable obtuseness of the radical men of action that prevents them from seeing the underground man as their mirror image, and from acknowledging the greeting he might have given them (in Baudelaire's words): "*hypocrite lecteur, mon semblable, mon frère!*"

3. The Most Advantageous Advantage

After showing the inherent inability of the human psyche to accommodate itself to the "rational" world of Chernyshevsky's philosophy, the underground man turns more directly to demolish the arguments that Chernyshevsky and the men of action use to defend their position. His acceptance of Chernyshevsky's philosophy has always included a sardonic realization of the incongruity of its basic precepts with the norms of human experience, and this incongruity is now formulated more explicitly in the arguments developed throughout Chapters 7–9.

"Oh, tell me," the underground man asks incredulously, "who first proclaimed, that man only does nasty things because he does not know his real interests; and that if he were enlightened, if his eyes were opened to his real, normal interests . . . he would see his own advantage in the good and nothing else, and since we all know that not a single man can knowingly act to his own disadvantage, consequently, so to say, he would begin doing good through necessity" (5: 110). This was indeed the essence of Chernyshevsky's position—that "rational egoism," once accepted, would so enlighten man that the very possibility of his behaving irrationally, that is, contrary to his interests, would disappear. But this argument, as the underground man points out caustically, has one flaw: it overlooks that man has, and always will have, a supreme interest, which he will never surrender, in being able to exercise his free will.

The underground man's discourse in these chapters is composed of several strands. One is the repeated presentation of the way in which "statisticians, sages, and lovers of humanity" frequently end up by acting contrary to all their oft-proclaimed and solemnly high-minded principles of rationality. Another is to look at human history and to ask whether man ever was, or wished to be, totally rational. "In short, one may say anything about the history of the world— anything that might enter the most disordered imagination. The only thing one cannot say is that it is rational. The very word sticks in one's throat." A third comes much closer to the present and, in passing, takes a sideswipe at the British historian Henry Thomas Buckle, then popular with the Russian radicals, who believed that the laws of history could be worked out according to those of the natural sciences. The underground man simply cannot control his merriment over Buckle's assertion that "through civilization mankind becomes softer, and consequently less bloodthirsty, and less fitted for warfare," and he appeals to the reader: "Take the whole of the nineteenth century in which Buckle lived. Take Napoleon—both the Great and the present one. Take North America—the eternal union [then racked by the Civil War]" (5: 111, 116, 112).

These examples show to what extent rationalists and logicians are apt to shut their eyes to the most obvious facts for the sake of their systems, and all these systems, for some reason, always define "human advantages" exclusively "from the average of statistical figures and scientific-economic formulas. Now then, your advantages are prosperity, wealth, freedom, peace—etc., etc. So that a man who, for instance, would openly and knowingly oppose the whole list would be, according to you, and of course to me as well, an obscurantist or an absolute madman, no?" (5: 110). But while the underground man does not reject prosperity, wealth, freedom, and peace in themselves, he rejects the view that the only way to attain them is by the sacrifice of man's freedom and personality.

"There it is, gentlemen," he says commiseratingly, "does it not seem that something really exists that is dearer to almost every man than his greatest advantage (the very one omitted, about which we spoke of just now) for which, if necessary, a man is ready to go against all laws, that is, against reason, honor, peace, prosperity—in short, against all those wonderful and useful things if only he can attain that fundamental, most advantageous advantage dearer to him than everything else?" (5: 111). The answer to this question, whose parentheses parody some of the more laborious passages in *The Anthropological Principle*, has been given in the first six chapters. The one "most advantageous advantage" for man is the preservation of his free will, which may or may not be exercised in harmony with reason but which always wishes to preserve the right to *choose*, and this primary "advantage" cannot be included in the systems of the lovers of humanity because it makes forever impossible their dream of transforming human nature to desire *only* the rational.

4. The Crystal Palace

Chernyshevsky embodied this dream of transformation, as we know, in his vision of the Crystal Palace, and Dostoevsky picks up this symbol to present it from the underground man's point of view. In this future Utopia of plentitude, man will have been completely reeducated, "science itself will have taught man . . . that he does not really have either will or caprice and that he never has had them, and that he himself is nothing more than some sort of piano key or organ stop; . . . so that everything he does is not at all done by his will but by itself, according to the laws of nature" (5: 112).

The musical imagery here derives directly from Fourier, who believed he had discovered a "law of social harmony" and whose disciples liked to depict the organization of the passions in the phalanstery by analogy with the organization of keys on a clavier. Also, when the underground man comments that in the Crystal Palace "all human action will . . . be tabulated according to these laws [of nature], mathematically, like tables of logarithms up to 108,000 and entered in a table" (5: 113), he is not exaggerating. Fourier had worked out an exhaustive table of the passions that constituted, in his view, the immutable laws of (human) nature, and whose needs would have to be satisfied in any model social order. Dostoevsky thus combines Fourier's table of passions with Chernyshevsky's material determinism in his attack on the ideal of the Crystal Palace as involving the total elimination of the personality. For the empirical manifestation of personality consists in the right to *choose* a course of action whatever it may be, and no choice is involved when one is good, reasonable, satisfied, and happy by conformity with laws of nature that exclude the very possibility of their negation.

Luckily, though, the underground man assures us, the Crystal Palace is *not* possible because "man is so phenomenally ungrateful . . . shower upon him every earthly blessing, . . . give him such economic prosperity that he has nothing else to do but sleep, eat cakes, and busy himself with ensuring the continuation of world history—even then man, out of sheer ingratitude" will "even risk his cakes and deliberately desire the most fatal rubbish, the most uneconomical absurdity, simply in order to prove to himself (as if this were so necessary) that men are still men and not piano keys" (5: 116–117). For if the world of the Crystal Palace really existed, "even if man really were nothing but a piano key, even if this were proved to him by natural science and mathematics—he will devise destruction and chaos, will devise sufferings of all sorts, and will insist on getting his way!" And if all this suffering and chaos can also be calculated and tabulated in advance, "then man would purposely go mad in order to be rid of reason and to insist on getting his way!" In both cases, the cause of this chaos is the same: the revolt of the personality against a world in which free will (and hence moral categories of any kind) has no further reason for being. The clear sense of the text is that the self-destructive revolt of freedom is not a value in itself; it is envisaged *only* as a last-ditch defense against the hypothetical accomplishment of the Crystal Palace ideal. As the underground man writes in relief, "And after this how is one not to sin by rejoicing that this is not yet, and that for the time being desire still depends on the devil alone knows what!" (5: 117).

Such is the terrible prospect of the proposed completion of the Crystal Palace ideal, and the underground man continues to question the buoyant assurance of Chernyshevsky and his followers that such an ideal is man's true desire. He denies that humanity is longing to achieve the static, secular apocalypse of the Crystal Palace, which would signify the end of history and the cessation of all further striving, aspiration and hope. "May it not be that . . . he only likes that edifice from a distance, not from close up; perhaps he only likes to build it and not to live in it, leaving it *aux animaux domestiques* such as ants, sheep, etc., etc. Now the ants have an entirely different taste. They have an astonishing edifice of this kind eternally indestructible—the ant-hill" (5: 118).

Although this comparison of the Socialist ideal to an ant-hill was a commonplace in the Russian journalism of the period, Dostoevsky may have used this image in connection with the end of history as an allusion to Herzen. "If humanity went straight to some goal," Herzen had written in *From the Other Shore*," there would be no history, only logic; humanity would stop in some finished form, in a spontaneous *status quo* like the animals. . . . Besides, if the libretto existed, history would lose all interest, it would become futile, boring, ridiculous."[5] The obvious similarity of these texts shows how much Dostoevsky

---

[5] A. I. Gertsen, *Polnoe sobranie sochinenii*, 30 vols. (Moscow, 1954–1966), 6: 36.

had absorbed from the work he admired so greatly; it also reveals how accurately he was thematizing a profound ideological contrast between his own generation and that of the 1860s. For the intellectual and ideological physiognomy of the generation of the 1840s, nourished on Romantic literature and German Idealist philosophy, formed a sharp contrast to that of the 1860s. Herzen, like Dostoevsky, always staunchly refused to accept Chernyshevsky's material determinism and denial of free will.[6] It is thus appropriate that the underground man later attributes his opposition to the ideal of the Crystal Palace at least partly to having come of age when he did.

All these arguments are then focused in a final rejection of the Crystal Palace as leaving no room for "suffering." "After all," the underground man says, "I do not really insist on suffering or on any prosperity either, I insist . . . on my caprice, and that it be guaranteed to me when it's necessary." Suffering is no more an end in itself than madness or chaos, and remains subordinate to the supreme value of the assertion of moral autonomy, but it serves as a prod to keep alive this sense of moral autonomy in a world deprived of human significance by determinism: "In the Crystal Palace it [suffering] is even unthinkable: suffering is doubt, negation, and what kind of a Crystal Palace would that be in which doubts can be harbored?" The ability to doubt means that man is not yet transformed into a rational-ethical machine that can behave *only* in conformity with reason. This is why the underground man declares that "suffering is the sole origin of consciousness" (5: 119); suffering and consciousness are inseparable because the latter is not only a psychological but primarily a moral attribute of the human personality.

5. The Palatial Chicken Coop

Chapter 10 of *Notes from Underground* poses a special problem because it was so badly mutilated by the censorship. In this chapter, as we know, Dostoevsky claimed to have expressed "the essential ideal" of his work, which he defined as

[6] Very close to the end of his life, Herzen wrote a telling letter to his son, Alexander Jr., in which he made the point perfectly clear. The younger Herzen, by this time a noted physiologist, had published a lecture course in which all animal and human activity was interpreted as a function of the nervous reflex system; and he thus concluded, like Chernyshevsky, that free will was an illusion. His father replied: "At all periods, man seeks his autonomy, his liberty and, though pulled along by necessity, *he does not wish to act except according to his own will*; he does not wish to be a passive gravedigger of the past or an unconscious midwife of the future; he considers history as his free and indispensable work. He believes in his liberty as he believes in the existence of the external world as it presents itself to him because he trusts his eyes, and because, without that confidence, he could not take a step. Moral liberty is thus a psychological or, if one wishes, an anthropological reality." No more expressive statement could be given of Dostoevsky's own existential conception of liberty and moral freedom. See A. I. Gertsen, *Izbrannye filosofskie proizvedeniya*, 2 vols. (Moscow, 1946), 2: 283.

"the necessity of faith and Christ," but the passages in which he did so were suppressed and never restored in later reprintings. At no period of his life, it should be noted, would Dostoevsky have relished the dangerous and time-consuming prospect of attempting to persuade the censors to reverse an earlier ruling. To have tried to do so would only have imperiled and delayed the publication of the reprints and collected editions of his work on which he counted for badly needed income.

Despite its mutilation, let us examine this "garbled" chapter to see what can still be found that may help us to come closer to Dostoevsky's "essential idea." We learn that the underground man rejects the Crystal Palace because it is impossible to be irreverent about it, but, he says, "I did not at all say [this] because I am so fond of putting out my tongue. . . . On the contrary, I would let my tongue be cut off out of sheer gratitude if things could be so arranged that I myself would lose all desire to put it out" (5: 120–121). Dostoevsky thus intimates that the underground man, far from rejecting all moral ideals in favor of an illimitable egoism, is desperately searching for one that, rather than spurring the personality to revolt in rabid frenzy, would instead lead to a willing surrender in its favor. Such an alternative ideal would thus be required to recognize the autonomy of the will and the freedom of the personality, and would appeal to the moral nature of man rather than to his reason and self-interest conceived as working in harmony with the laws of nature. For Dostoevsky, this alternative ideal could be found in the teachings of Christ, and from a confusion that still exists in the text, we can catch a glimpse of how he may have tried to integrate this alternative into the framework of his imagery.

This confusion arises in the course of a comparison between the Crystal Palace and a chicken coop. "You see," says the underground man, "if it were not a palace but a chicken coop, and it started to rain, I might creep into the chicken coop to avoid getting wet, but all the same I would not take the chicken coop for a palace out of gratitude that it sheltered me from the rain. You laugh, you even say that, in such circumstances, a chicken coop and a mansion—it's all the same. Yes, I answer, if one has to live simply to avoid getting wet." It is not the usefulness of the chicken coop that is impugned by the underground man but the fact that, in return for its practical advantages, it has been elevated into mankind's ideal. "But what is to be done if I have taken it into my head that this [not to get wet; utility] is not the only object in life, and that if one must live, it may as well be in a mansion? That is my choice, my desire. You will only eradicate it when you have changed my desire. Well, do change it, tempt me with something else, give me another ideal" (5: 120).

The underground man thus opens up the possibility of "another ideal," and, as the text goes along, he seems to envisage a different sort of Crystal Palace— one that would be a genuine mansion rather than a chicken coop satisfying purely material needs. For he then continues: "And meanwhile, I will not take a chicken coop for a palace. Let the Crystal edifice even be an idle dream, say it is inconsistent with the laws of nature, and I have invented it only as a result of my own stupidity, as a result of some old-fashioned, irrational habits of my generation. But what do I care if it is inconsistent? Isn't it all the same if it exists in my desires, or better, exists as long as my desires exist?" (5: 120). At this point, we observe a shift to a "Crystal edifice" based on the very *opposite* principles from those represented by the Crystal Palace throughout the rest of the text; this new Crystal edifice is *inconsistent* with the laws of nature (while the Crystal Palace is their embodiment) and owes its existence to desire rather than to reason. The change is so abrupt, and so incompatible with what has gone before, that one can only assume some material leading from one type of Crystal building to the other has been excised from the manuscript.

Dostoevsky, we may speculate, must have attempted here to indicate the nature of a true Crystal Palace, or mansion, or edifice (his terminology is not consistent), and to contrast it to the false one that was really a chicken coop. From his letter, we know that he did so in a way to identify a true Crystal Palace with the "need for faith and Christ," but such an attempt may well have confused and frightened the censors, still terrified out of their wits by the recent blunder over *What Is To Be Done?* and now accustomed to view the Crystal Palace as the abhorrent image of atheistic Socialism. Hence, they would have excised the sentences in which Dostoevsky tried to give his own Christian significance to this symbol, perhaps considering them to be both subversive and blasphemous. These suppositions would explain the strange history of Dostoevsky's text and would account for the flagrant contradiction, clearly evident on close reading, that provoked his indignant outcry that his entire meaning had been distorted.

Although this alternative ideal may have originally been indicated more clearly, Dostoevsky's conception still requires the underground man to remain trapped in the negative phase of his revolt. An alternative is suggested only as a remote and, for the underground man, unattainable possibility. Each episode in the original text was meant to have its own type of climax, and there would have been a distinct gradation between the first and the second ideal. What appears in the underground man's thoughts only as an impossible dream in the first part becomes a living reality in the second, strongly presented in terms of dramatic action. For the underground man in this first part longs for another ideal; he knows it must exist; but he is so committed to a belief in material determinism and the laws of nature that he cannot imagine what it could be. "I know, anyway, that I will not be appeased with a compromise, with an endlessly recurring zero, simply because it exists according to the laws of nature and *actually* exists. I will not take as the crown of all my desires—a block of buildings with apartments for the poor on a lease for a thousand years, and, for any contingency, a dentist's sign hanging out" (5: 120). What that something else is, and why the underground man cannot find it, provides the substance for the second part of Dostoevsky's novella.

Part II

1. "Apropos of the Wet Snow"

The underground man is forty years old in 1864 when he begins to write his *Notes*; he is twenty-four when the events in Part II take place, which would locate them in 1848—the very year that Dostoevsky first assiduously began to attend the meetings of the Petrashevsky Circle. The underground man is still primarily a social-cultural type, but in the second part, where he becomes a parody of the attitudes of the 1840s, he was certainly nourished by Dostoevsky's judgment of himself as a member of that generation. Evaluating his state of mind at that time, Dostoevsky had written to General Totleben in 1856: "I believed in theories and Utopias. . . . I was a hypochondriac. . . . I was excessively irritable with an unhealthy susceptibility. I deformed the simplest facts, endowing them with another aspect and other dimensions."[7] This description applies, word for word, to the portrait we are given of the underground man's psychology in his youth.

The subtitle, "Apropos of the Wet Snow," also helps to set the action firmly in a symbolic setting. Annenkov had noted in 1849 that the writers of the Natural School were all fond of employing "wet snow" as a typical feature of the dreary Petersburg landscape, and Dostoevsky thus uses his subtitle to bring back an image of Petersburg in the 1840s—an image of what, in the first part, Dostoevsky had called "the most abstract and premeditated city in the world" (5: 101), a city whose very existence (ever since Pushkin's "The Bronze Horseman") had become emblematic in Russian literature for the violence and inhuman cost of the Russian adaptation to Western culture.

The atmosphere of the 1840s, with all its social humanitarian exaltations, is also evoked explicitly by the quotation from a poem of Nekrasov appended as an epigraph to the second part. This is the same poem, dating from 1846, that had already been mentioned ironically in *The Village of Stepanchikovo*, the first work in which Dostoevsky explicitly dissociated himself from what he now considered the naïve illusions of the Natural School and of his own past. Written from the point of view of the (male) benefactor of a repentant prostitute who

[7] *Pis'ma*, 1: 178; March 24, 1856.

has saved her from a life of sin by his ardent and unprejudiced love, the poem describes her torments of conscience:

When from the murk of corruption
I delivered your fallen soul
With the ardent speech of conviction;
And, full of profound torment,
Wringing your hands, you cursed
The vice that had ensnared you;
When, with memories punishing
Forgetful conscience
You told me the tale
Of all that happened before me,
And suddenly, covering your face,
Full of shame and horror,
You tearfully resolved,
Outraged, shocked . . .
Etc., etc., etc. (5: 124)

By cutting this passage short with three et ceteras, Dostoevsky manifestly indicates that the philanthropic lucubrations of the speaker are just so much banal and conventional platitudes. The redemption of a prostitute theme had indeed become a commonplace by the 1860s. It figures as a minor episode in *What Is To Be Done?*, where one of the heroes salvages a fallen woman from a life of debauchery, lives with her for a time, and turns her into a model member of Vera Pavlovna's cooperative until she dies of tuberculosis. The climactic episode in the second part of *Notes from Underground*—the encounter between the underground man and the prostitute Liza—is an ironic parody and reversal of this Social Romantic cliché.

Part II of *Notes from Underground*, then, satirizes the sentimental Social Romanticism of the 1840s just as Part I satirized the metaphysics and ethics of the 1860s, and Dostoevsky draws for this purpose on the image of the 1840s he had already sketched in the pages of *Time*. The superfluous men of the gentry liberal intelligentsia lived in a dream world of "universal beneficence" while neglecting the simplest and most obvious moral obligations. It was incumbent on them, he had made clear, to live up to their own pretensions and to turn their abstract love of humanity into a concrete act directed toward a flesh-and-blood individual. This is precisely the theme of the second part of *Notes from Underground*, which has been transposed into the bureaucratic world of Dostoevsky's early work and embodied in a character who is the lowly but supremely self-conscious equivalent of the superfluous man.

This shift of theme is reflected in Part II by a noticeable change of tone. Ultimate issues were at stake in the first part, where the final argument against the world of the "false" Crystal Palace could only be the rage of madness and self-destruction, and Dostoevsky's irony is accordingly bitter and twisted, his tonality harsh and abrasive. No such ultimate issues are involved in the misadventures of the underground man's early manhood, which are all provoked by that standard comic source—overweening vanity. Hence the second part is written in a lighter tone of burlesque and caricature, and whole sections are nothing but an extended mockery of the underground man's stilted and pedantic responses to the simplest human situations.

2. The Dialectic of Vanity

The opening pages of the second part recall the beginning of the first. The conflict between the impulse to dominate and the desire to enter into a more amicable relation with others was not developed at all earlier, but it now comes to the fore and provides a more intimate background to the relative abstractions of Part I. The underground man, consumed by boundless vanity, is so acutely self-conscious that he cannot enter into normal social relations with anyone: "All my fellow clerks I, of course, hated from first to last, and I despised them all, and yet at the same time I was, as it were, afraid of them. . . . Somehow it then turned out this way quite suddenly: one moment I despised them, the next I placed them much above me" (5: 125). The underground man's vanity convinces him of his own superiority and he despises everyone, but since he desires such superiority to be *recognized* by others, he hates the world for its indifference and falls into self-loathing at his own humiliating dependence. This is the psychological dialectic of a self-conscious egoism that seeks to conquer recognition from the world and only arouses dislike and hostility in return. Such a dialectic of vanity parallels the dialectic of determinism in the first part and has the same effect of immuring the ego in a world alienated from any human contact. Just as determinism dissolves the possibility of human response in the first part, so vanity blocks all social fraternity in the second.

Besides portraying this dialectic of vanity in action, Dostoevsky also traces it back to the general cultural atmosphere of the 1840s, which fostered a forced and artificial Romantic egoism and a sense of superiority to ordinary Russian life that the underground man absorbed through every pore. Indeed, what distinguishes him from the very earliest years is his marked intellectual prowess. "Moreover, they [his school fellows] all began to grasp slowly," he writes, "that I was already reading books none of them could read, and understood things . . . of which they had not even heard." Describing his later life, he says: "at home I spent most of my time reading. . . . I tried to stifle all that was continually seething within me by . . . reading. Reading, of course, was a great help" (5: 140, 127). Books are thus responsible for keeping the *real* feelings of the underground man bottled up—the feelings opposed to his vanity and desire to dominate. Books interpose a network of acquired and artificial responses between himself and other people, and, since we are in the world of the Russian intelligentsia of the 1840s, these books could only have been the works of the French Utopian Socialists and the Social Romantics and their Russian disciples on which Dostoevsky himself had then battened.

Over and over again Dostoevsky stresses the connection between the dialectic of vanity in which the underground man is caught and his intellectual culture. "A cultivated and decent man cannot be vain," he remarks, "without setting an inordinately high standard for himself, and without despising himself at certain moments to the point of hatred." Comparing his features with those of other clerks in his office, he thinks, "Let my face even be ugly . . . but let it be noble, expressive, and, above all, *extremely* intelligent" (5: 125, 124). As a result of imbibing the European culture popular in Russia in the 1840s, the underground man has lost any capacity for simple and direct human feeling in relation to others. Instead, his vanity and sense of self-importance have become inflated to a degree out of all proportion to his actual social situation, and the conflicts engendered by this discrepancy provide a comic analogue to the fratricidal war of all against all arising in Western European society from the dominance of the principle of egoistic individualism.

Dostoevsky is a master at portraying the psychology of pride and humiliation, and when the humiliation springs from some genuine oppression or suffering, he knows how to make it intensely moving, but it would be a flagrant misreading to take the underground man as such a victim. For he lives in a purely imaginary world and distorts and exaggerates everything with which he comes into contact. "It is perfectly clear to me now," he says, "that, owing to my unbounded vanity and, probably, to the high standard I set for myself, I very often looked at myself with furious discontent, which verged on loathing, and so I inwardly attributed the same view to everyone" (5: 141).

Even if his humiliations are entirely self-caused, their effect on him is no less distressing. His inability to enter into human contact with other people plunges him into a savage isolation, and he is acutely aware that his behavior is debasing and degrading: "I indulged my vice in solitude at night, furtively, timidly, filthily, with a feeling of shame that never deserted me, even at the most loathsome moments, and which at such moments drove me to curses. Even then I already had the underground in my soul" (5: 128). The reference to vice at this point foreshadows the all-important Liza episode, but in these earlier chapters, filled with comic grotesquerie, the emphasis falls on the underground man's efforts to break out of his solitude through purely social (rather than sexual) intercourse.

All these episodes display the torments of the underground man as he attempts to assert his existence as an ego who desires above all that someone— anyone—recognize him in a fashion compatible with his absurdly inflated self-image. It is for this reason that he becomes involved in the slapstick, mock-heroic farce of trying to summon up enough courage to bump into an officer on the Nevsky Prospect. His preoccupation with this ridiculous problem merely illustrates the picayune obsessiveness of his vanity; but the episode is also a parody of an incident in *What Is To Be Done?* One of the heroes of that book takes a solemn resolution not to yield the right of way in the street to "dignitaries," and when an outraged gentleman begins to berate the poorly dressed student for bumping into *him*, the dignitary promptly ends up with his face in the mud.

Ironically reversing the scale of values manifested by this democratic protest against the public humiliations of inequality, Dostoevsky depicts the frantic desire of the underground man to assert his "equality" as ludicrous vanity rather than staunchly independent self-respect. The parody of Chernyshevsky is coupled with an allusion to Gogol's "The Overcoat," which Dostoevsky slips in at the point where the underground man, feverishly preparing the proper costume for his epical encounter, decides to replace the hideous raccoon collar on his overcoat with a more dignified one of beaver. Not only does this detail thicken the period atmosphere (Gogol's story was published in 1842), it also enriches the ideological implications of the incident, since Gogol's work provided the initial inspiration for the philanthropic thematics of the Natural School of young writers to which Dostoevsky had once belonged.

The theme of masochism, so prominent in Part I, reappears again in this first chapter of the second part. For as he walks along the Nevsky Prospect, the underground man experiences "a regular martyrdom, a continual, intolerable humiliation at the thought, which passed into an incessant and direct sensation, that I was a fly in the eyes of this whole world, a nasty, disgusting fly—more intelligent, more cultured, more noble than any of them, of course, but a fly that was continually making way for everyone, insulted and humiliated by everyone. . . . Already then I began to experience a rush of the enjoyment of which I spoke in the first chapter [of the first part]" (5: 130). Once again, however, we must be careful not to take this psychological characterization as self-explanatory. The underground man's masochism is a part of the dialectic of vanity, and it has a more complex function than merely to illustrate a taste for self-abasement.

Masochism is assigned much the same function in both parts of the work— just as it had led to suffering in Part I, and kept alive the faculty of conscience, so in Part II it also acquires a positive significance. The seemingly pathological cultivation of masochistic "enjoyment" by the underground man ultimately buttresses his ego, which refuses to submit docilely to the judgment of the world. Such self-assertion is precisely what enables the underground man, twenty years later, to resist the temptations of a Crystal Palace in which the laws of nature have simply abolished the human personality altogether. Hence, in both parts of the work, Dostoevsky assigns a *relative* value—the value of protecting the autonomy of the personality—to the ideology of the 1840s, regardless of its weaknesses and shortcomings in other respects.

3. Manfred at a Party

Chapter 2 of Part II finally brings into relief the true target of Dostoevsky's satire. At last we discover—of course, in the form of a carefully distorted caricature—what the underground man has been reading in the books that have shaped his vision. For here he takes on the features of the Romantic dreamer whom Dostoevsky had depicted in his early works and whose literary fantasies had been contrasted with the moral-social claims of "real life" from which he had taken refuge. In the second part of *Notes from Underground*, the dreamer is manhandled very harshly indeed. He is no longer a purely literary Romantic lost in exotic fantasies of erotic gratification and artistic glory, as in Dostoevsky's pre-Siberian works; he has become a Social Romantic filled with grandiose plans for transforming the world. But his new social mission has not succeeded in altering the dreamer's endemic self-preoccupation, and his failure to meet the moral demands of real life becomes all the more unforgivable in view of the social conscience by which he believes himself to be inspired.

In this chapter, we observe what occurs when, exhausted by the seesaws of the dialectic of vanity, the underground man has recourse "to a means of escape that reconciled everything," that is, when he finds "a refuge in 'the sublime and the beautiful,' in dreams":

> I, for instance, was triumphant over everyone; everyone, of course, lay in the dust and was forced to recognize my superiority voluntarily, and I forgave them all. I, a famous poet and court official, fell in love; I inherited countless millions and immediately sacrificed them for humanity; and at the same time I confessed before all the people my shameful deeds, which, of course, were not completely shameful but also contained an enormous amount of "the sublime and the beautiful," something in the Manfred style. Everyone would weep and kiss me (what idiots they would be if they didn't), while I would go barefoot and hungry preaching new ideas and routing the reactionaries at Austerlitz. (5:133)[8]

---

[8] The main character of Cabet's *Voyage en Icarie*, a reformer philanthropist, also defeats a coalition of crowned reactionaries at Austerlitz. Dostoevsky is already suggesting here the tendency of radical social reformers to identify themselves with Napoleon. See *PSS*, 5: 386.

During such delightful interludes, the underground man felt "that suddenly a vista of suitable activity—the beneficial, good, and above all *ready-made* (what sort of activity I had no idea, but the great thing was that it should all be ready for me)—would rise up before me, and I should come into the light of day, almost riding a white horse and crowned with laurel." These dreams, of course, replace any actual moral effort on his part; even more, they stifle any awareness that such effort could exist otherwise than in hackneyed, "ready-made" forms. At such moments the underground man felt an overwhelming love for humanity, and, "though it was never applied to anything human in reality, yet there was so much of this love that afterward one did not even feel the impulse to apply it in reality; that would have been a superfluous luxury." Also, these lofty visions of magnanimity happily served as a sop to the stirrings of conscience, because to "an ordinary man, say, it is shameful to defile himself . . . [while] a hero is too noble to be utterly defiled, and so he is permitted to defile himself." The underground man, as he himself remarks, "had a noble loophole for everything" (5: 133).

Yet he cannot long remain content with these delectations of his solitude; inevitably he feels the need to exhibit them (and himself) to the admiring eyes of humanity. After three months of dreaming, his dreams invariably "reached such a state of bliss that it became essential to embrace my fellows and all mankind immediately. And for that purpose I needed one human being at hand who actually existed" (5: 134). These words prelude the grotesquely amusing episode (Chapters 3 and 4) relating the encounter of the underground man with his old schoolfellows. The moment he catches sight of real people, of course, the underground man's exorbitant demands for esteem invariably lead to a rebuff. Only too ready to embrace mankind, he discovers that mankind would rather shake hands and keep a polite distance; and this rejection brings on the dialectics of vanity, with its accompanying duel for domination. The surrealistic comedy of the underground man's meeting with his erstwhile comrades derives from his hopeless yet irresistible impulse to "subjugate them all." After forcing himself on their friendly little party, he insults Zverkov, the guest of honor, simply out of resentment and envy, and then parades up and down the room for three solid hours while the others disregard him entirely and continue their festivities.

The whole group of celebrating schoolfellows eventually departs for a brothel to finish off the evening, leaving the underground man in solitary possession of the debris of the feast. By this time, he has gotten it into his head that only a duel will satisfy his injured honor—and besides, a duel can be the occasion for all sorts of noble reconciliations! "Either they'll all fall down on their knees to beg for my friendship—or I will give Zverkov a slap in the face!" (5: 148). The mention of a duel at once unleashes a flood of literary references (Russian literature is filled with famous duels), and the underground man pursues his companions in a mood that parodies Pushkin's story "The Shot."

Imagining what might happen if he carries out his plan to insult Zverkov, the underground man muses:

> I will be arrested. I will be tried, I will be dismissed from the service, thrown in prison, sent to Siberia, deported. Never mind! In fifteen years when they let me out of prison I will trudge off to him, a beggar in rags, I shall find him in some provincial city. He will be married and happy. He will have a grown-up daughter. . . . I will say to him: 'Look, monster, at my hollow cheeks and my rags! I've lost everything—my career, my happiness, art, science, the woman I loved, and all through you. Here are pistols. I have come to discharge my pistol and—and I . . . forgive you.' Then I will fire into the air and he will never hear from me again. . . . I was actually on the point of tears, though I knew perfectly well at that very moment that all this was out of Pushkin's *Silvio* [Silvio is the hero of "The Shot"] and Lermontov's *Masquerade*. (5: 150)

As might have been expected, these shopworn heroics remain purely imaginary, and everyone has vanished from sight by the time the underground man enters the salon of the "dressmaking establishment."

4. Liza

It is at this point, when the underground man finally encounters another human being more vulnerable than himself, that the comedy changes into tragedy. Dostoevsky was well aware of this shift in tonality, and we have earlier quoted his allusion to it as similar to "a transition in music": "in the first chapter, seemingly, there's only chatter; but suddenly this chatter, in the last two chapters, is resolved by a catastrophe."[9] The final text was subsequently broken up into smaller chapters, and the catastrophe beginning with Chapter 5 runs through Chapter 10. No part of *Notes from Underground* has been more wrenched out of context to support one or another theory about Dostoevsky, even though the function of this section is surely to drive home the contrast between imaginary, self-indulgent, self-glorifying, sentimental Social Romanticism and a genuine act of love—a love springing from that total forgetfulness of self that had now become Dostoevsky's highest value. By his ironic reversal both of Nekrasov's poem and of the incident in *What Is To Be Done?*, Dostoevsky wished to expose all the petty vainglory lying concealed in the intelligentsia's "ideals," and to set this off against the triumph over egoism that he saw embodied in the spontaneous Christian instincts of a simple Russian soul.

[9] *Pisma*, 1: 353; March 26, 1864.

When the underground man arrives in the brothel, the madam, treating him like the old patron that he is, summons a girl. As he goes out with her, he catches sight of himself in a mirror: "My harassed face struck me as extremely revolting, pale, spiteful, nasty, with disheveled hair. 'No matter, I am glad of it,' I thought; 'I am glad that I shall seem revolting to her; I like that'" (5: 151). Not having been able to subdue his companions or to insult them sufficiently to be taken seriously, the underground man typically anticipates revenging himself on the helpless girl; the more repulsive he is to her, the more his egoism will be satisfied by forcing her to submit to his desires. It is not by physical submission alone, however, that the underground man attains a triumph over Liza. For when, after having sex, he becomes aware of her hostility and silent resentment, "a grim idea came into my brain and passed all over my body, like some nasty sensation, such as one feels when going into a damp and moldy underground" (5: 152). This idea takes the form of playing on Liza's feelings, with the intention of triumphing over her not only physically but spiritually as well.

The underground man thus proceeds very skillfully to break down the armor of feigned indifference and cynicism by which Liza protects herself against the debasing circumstances of her life. "I began to feel myself what I was saying," he explains, "and warmed to the subject. I longed to expound the cherished *little ideas* I had brooded over in my corner." Mingling horrible details of degradation with images of fidelity, whose banality makes them all the more poignant (Balzac's *Le père Goriot* is parodied in the process), the underground man succeeds in bringing to the surface Liza's true feelings of shame about herself and precipitating her complete emotional breakdown. None of his apparent concern, of course, had been meant seriously; the underground man simply had been carried away by the power of his eloquence and because "the sport in it attracted me most." But Liza is too young, naïve, and helpless to see through his perversity, which sounded like truth and was, in fact, even half-true. "I worked myself up to such pathos that I began to have a lump in my throat myself, and . . . suddenly I stopped, sat up in dismay, and bending over apprehensively, began to listen with a beating heart." For Liza had lost control of herself and "her youthful body was shuddering all over as though in convulsions" (5: 155, 156, 161, 162).

The underground man, carried away by his victory, cannot resist attempting to live up to the exalted role of hero and benefactor that he had so often played in his fantasies. When he leaves, he gives Liza his address with a lordly magnanimity, urging her to come and visit him and quit her life of shame. It is this gesture that undoes him and provides Dostoevsky with his dénouement. For the moment the underground man emerges from the self-adulatory haze of his charlatanism, he is stricken with terror. He cannot bear the thought that Liza might see him as he really is—wrapped in his shabby dressing gown, living in his squalid "underground," completely under the thumb of his manservant, the impassive, dignified, Bible-reading peasant Apollon. Never for a moment does it occur to him that he might really try to help her all the same; he is so worried about how *he* will look in *her* eyes that the reality of her situation entirely vanishes from view. Or not entirely: "Something was not dead within me, in the depths of my heart and conscience it refused to die, and it expressed itself as a burning anguish" (5: 165).

After a few days pass and Liza fails to appear, the underground man becomes more cheerful; as usual, "I even began sometimes to dream, and rather sweetly." These dreams all revolved around the process of Liza's reeducation, her confession of love for him, and his own confession that "I did not dare to approach you first, because I had an influence over you and was afraid that you would force yourself, out of gratitude, to respond to my love, would try to rouse in your heart a feeling which was perhaps absent, and I did not wish that because it would be . . . tyranny. . . . It would be indelicate (in short, I launch off at this point into European, George-Sandian inexplicably lofty subtleties), but now, now you are mine, you are my creation, you are pure, you are beautiful, you are my beautiful wife" (5: 166–167). And here Dostoevsky throws in two more lines from Nekrasov's poem.

Interspersed with these intoxicating reveries is the low comedy of the underground man's efforts to bend the stubborn and intractable Apollon to his will. Dostoevsky interweaves these two situations adroitly by coordinating Liza's entry with a moment at which the underground man, enraged by the imperturbable Apollon, is giving vent to all his weakly hysterical fury. By this time, he has reached an uncontrollable pitch of frustration and nervous exasperation; at the sight of the bewildered Liza he loses control, sobbing and complaining that he is being "tortured" by Apollon. All this is so humiliating that he turns on her in spiteful rage when, by stammering that she wishes to leave the brothel, she reminds him of all that came before. His reply is a vicious tirade, in which he tells her the truth about their earlier relation: "I vented my spleen on you and laughed at you. I had been humiliated, so I wanted to humiliate; I had been treated like a rag, so I wanted to show my power." With the typical inversion of his egoist's logic, he shouts: "And I shall never forgive you for the tears I could not help shedding before you just now, I shall never forgive *you*, either!" (5: 173–174).

But now an unprecedented event occurs—unprecedented, at least, in the underground man's experience; instead of flaring up herself and hitting back, Liza throws herself into his arms to console *him*. Both forget themselves entirely and break into tears, but the unconquerable vanity of the underground man, which incapacitates him from responding selflessly and spontaneously to others, soon regains the upper hand: "In my overwrought brain the thought also occurred that our parts were after all completely reversed now, that she was now the heroine, while I was just such a crushed and humiliated creature as she had been before me that night—four days before." And then, not out of love but hate, the underground man takes her on the spot to revenge himself on *her* for having dared to try to console him. To make his revenge more complete and crush her entirely, he slips a five-ruble note into her hand when their embraces are finished. "But I can say this for certain: though I did that cruel thing purposely," he admits, "it was not an impulse from the heart, but came from my evil brain. This cruelty was so affected, so purposely made up, so completely a product of the brain, of *books*, that I could not keep it up for a minute" (5: 175, 177). Dostoevsky could not have stated more explicitly that the heart of the underground man, the emotive core of his nature, had not lost its moral sensitivity. It was his brain, nourished by the education he had so thoroughly absorbed—an education based on Western prototypes, and on the images of such prototypes assimilated into Russian literature—that had perverted his character and was responsible for his despicable act.

Liza, however, manages to leave the money on the table unobserved before leaving. Noticing the crumpled bill, the underground man is filled with remorse and runs after Liza into the silent, snow-filled street to kneel at her feet and beg forgiveness. But then, pulling himself up short, he realizes the futility of all this agitation: "'But—what for?' I thought. 'Would I not begin to hate her, perhaps, even tomorrow, just because I kissed her feet today?'" And later at home, "stifling the living pang of [his] heart with fantastic dreams," he conceives the most diabolic rationalization of all for his villainy. "Will it not be better that she carry the outrage with her forever?" he thinks. "Outrage—why, after all, that is purification: it is the most stinging and painful consciousness! Tomorrow I would have defiled her soul and have exhausted her heart, while now the feeling of humiliation will never die in her, and however loathsome the filth awaiting her, that outrage will elevate and purify her—by hatred—h'm—perhaps by forgiveness also. But will all that make things easier for her, though? . . . And, indeed, I will at this point ask an idle question on my account: which is better—cheap happiness or exalted suffering? Well, which is better?" (5: 177–178).

With this final, stabbing irony, Dostoevsky allows the underground man to use the very idea of purification through suffering as an excuse for his moral-spiritual sadism. In so doing, Dostoevsky returns to the main theme of the first part and places it in a new light. Consciousness and suffering had been affirmed as values when the underground man, struggling to preserve his human identity, wished to suffer *himself* rather than to surrender to the laws of nature. But so long as this struggle springs only from the negative revolt of egoism to affirm its existence, so long as it is not oriented by anything positive, it inevitably runs the risk of a diabolic reversal; there is always the danger that the egoist, concerned only with himself, will cause *others* to suffer with the excuse of helping to purify *their* souls. Such a possibility, broached here in passing at the end of *Notes from*

Underground, will be brilliantly developed in *Crime and Punishment*, when Raskolnikov tries to convince Sonya that his sacrifice of *another* for a noble end is
morally equivalent to *her* self-sacrifice for the same purpose.

5. Conclusion

As the second part of *Notes from Underground* comes to a close, the underground
man again returns to the frustrations of his solitude. For one moment he had
caught a glimpse of how to escape from the dialectic of vanity: Liza's disregard
of her own humiliation, her whole-souled identification with *his* torments—in
short, her capacity for selfless love—is the only way to break the sorcerer's spell
of egocentrism. When she rushes into his arms, thinking not of herself but of
him, she illustrates that "something else" which his egoism will never allow him
to attain—the ideal of the voluntary self-sacrifice of the personality out of love.
In his encounter with Liza, the underground man had met this ideal in the flesh,
and his inability to respond to its appeal dooms him irrevocably for the future.
Nonetheless, as we look at *Notes from Underground* as a whole, we see that the
egoistic Social Romanticism of the 1840s, with its cultivation of a sense of spiritual noblesse and its emphasis on individual moral responsibility, does not have
a totally negative value. Egocentric though it may be, such sentimental Social
Romanticism still stressed the importance of free will and preserved a sense of
the inner autonomy of the personality, and without such a sense no truly human
life is possible at all.

The underground man, hyperconscious as always, knows exactly where the
source of the trouble is located: "Leave us alone without books and we shall at
once get lost and be confused—we will not know what to join, what to cling to
and what to hate, what to respect and what to despise. We are even oppressed by
being men—men with *real, our own* flesh and blood, we are ashamed of it,
we think it a disgrace and try to be some sort of impossible generalized man"
(5: 178–179). It may be inferred, then, that the only hope is to reject all these
bookish, foreign, artificial Western ideologies and to return to the Russian "soil"
with its spontaneous incorporation of the Christian ideal of unselfish love.

So ends this remarkable little work, certainly the most powerful and concentrated expression that Dostoevsky ever gave to his genius as a satirist. *Notes from
Underground*, it has often been said, is the prelude to the great period in which
Dostoevsky's talent finally came to maturity, and there is no question that with
it he attains a new artistic level. For the first time, he motivates an action *entirely*
in terms of a psychology shaped by radical ideology; every feature of the text
serves to bring out the consequences in personal behavior of certain ideas, and
the world that Dostoevsky creates is entirely conceived as a function of this purpose. Psychology has now become strictly subordinate to ideology; there is no

longer a disturbing tug-of-war, as in *The Insulted and Injured*, between the moral-psychological and the ideological elements of the structure.

Dostoevsky has also at last found the great theme of his later novels, which will all be inspired by the same ambition to counter the moral-spiritual authority of the ideology of the radical Russian intelligentsia (depending on whatever nuance of that ideology was prominent at the time of writing). In this respect, the nucleus of Dostoevsky's novels may be compared to that of an eighteenth-century *conte philosophique*, whose characters were also largely embodiments of ideas; but instead of remaining bloodless abstractions like Candide or Zadig, they will be fleshed out with all the verisimilitude and psychological density of the nineteenth-century novel of Social Realism and all the dramatic tension of the urban-Gothic roman-feuilleton. It is Dostoevsky's genius for blending these seemingly antithetical narrative styles that constitute the originality of his art as a novelist.

Dostoevsky, though, never again attempted anything as hermetic and allusive as *Notes from Underground*. It is very likely that he considered the work a failure—as indeed it was, if we use as a measure its total lack of effectiveness as a polemic. No one really understood what Dostoevsky had been trying to do (with the exception, as we shall see, of Saltykov-Shchedrin), and even though Grigoryev, with his artistic flair, praised the novella and told his friend to continue writing in this vein, the silence of the remainder of the literary world was positively deafening. Suslova's letter, which contains references to Dostoevsky's "scandalous novella" and the "cynical things" he was producing, conveys the general reaction. Since she had not yet read the text, her words report what she had heard in the literary salon of the novelist Evgenia Tur (which she was then frequenting in Paris), and whose habitués were only repeating the latest literary gossip from Petersburg. Such reactions probably persuaded Dostoevsky that he had perhaps counted too much on the perspicacity of his readers to discern his meaning. He would never again place them before so difficult a challenge to their literary and ideological acumen.

CHAPTER 31

The End of *Epoch*

After the interment of Marya Dimitrievna, Dostoevsky returned to Petersburg at the end of April and once again began to take an active part in the editorial affairs of *Epoch*. To tide himself over financially, he obtained a loan from the Literary Fund, and, as if to signal the beginning of a new era in his life, he also ran up a substantial bill at a fashionable Petersburg tailor for a new suit of clothes and a summer overcoat. But if the death of his first wife might be considered a blessing in disguise, whatever the pangs of conscience and the disruptions provoked by her long death agony, he was soon to be confronted with another personal loss that was an unmitigated disaster.

Mikhail Dostoevsky and his family had taken up residence for the summer at a dacha in Pavlovsk, the fashionable watering place not far from Petersburg. Dostoevsky was living in Petersburg with his stepson Pasha and making preparations to go abroad again for his health, certainly with the tempting image of a reunion with Suslova never out of his mind. Just before his departure, however, he was so struck by his brother's ailing appearance that he decided to delay his voyage. And, in the first week of July, he scribbled a quick note to his stepson from Pavlovsk: "Dear Pasha, send me some linen. My brother is dying. Don't tell anyone about this."[1]

Mikhail had been overtaxed by the strain of publishing *Epoch* singlehanded, and by the burden of financial obligations that he could meet only by incurring others still more onerous. Not sparing himself physically, and suffering from an intermittent liver ailment, he collapsed on July 6 after hearing that an article on which he had counted could not pass the censorship; three days later he was dead. "How much I have lost with him," Dostoevsky wrote to his brother Andrey some weeks later, "That man loved me more than anything in the world, even more than his wife and family, whom he adored. . . . All the affairs of brother's family are terribly disorganized. The affairs of the journal (an enormous and complicated affair)—all this I will take on myself. There are many debts. Not a penny left for the family, and they are all minors. . . . Naturally,

[1] *Pisma*, 1: 375; first week of July 1864.

I am at their service. For a brother such as he was, I will cut off my head and sacrifice my own health."[2]

Mikhail was buried in the Pavlovsk cemetery on July 13, and Dostoevsky then faced an extremely difficult decision. *Epoch* was saddled with a huge deficit—both long-term debts and more urgent ones, which demanded immediate payment. In a letter written eight months later to his old friend Baron Wrangel, Dostoevsky explained: "I had to choose between two roads: abandon the journal, turn it over to the creditors . . . along with all the furniture and belongings, and take in the family. Then get to work, pursue my literary career, write novels, and provide for the needs of the widow and orphans. Another possibility: find the money and carry on the publication at whatever cost. What a pity that I did not choose the first!"[3]

Dostoevsky obtained ten thousand rubles from his wealthy Kumanin aunt in Moscow, the sum that would have been left him in her will, and scraped together additional funds wherever he could. He was convinced that, if he could keep publishing until the end of the year, and bring the monthly numbers approximately up to schedule, he would attract enough subscribers to cover expenses and to pay off his debts. His plan was to whip the journal into shape, establish it on a sound financial footing, and then turn it over to Mikhail's family as a source of income when—as he was determined to do in the future—he would withdraw to write his novels. The rapid rise of *Time* had convinced him that he was capable of turning *Epoch* into a flourishing enterprise.

If hard work and grim determination had been enough to guarantee success, then Dostoevsky would certainly have succeeded. As it turned out, there were too many obstacles to be overcome, even though he literally drove himself to the edge of collapse. "It was necessary to take matters in hand with energy," he explains to Wrangel. "I printed on three presses at the same time, without regard for my health and strength; I alone took on the work of chief editor and the reading of proofs; alone I negotiated with authors and the censorship, corrected articles, raised money, stayed awake until 6 o'clock in the morning, slept five hours a night, and I put the journal on its feet; but it was already too late."[4]

Despite Dostoevsky's heroic efforts, the needed subscriptions did not flow into the coffers of *Epoch*, and it became financially impossible to continue publication after the first two issues of 1865. In his letter to Wrangel, Dostoevsky blames the situation on the general fall in subscriptions that had affected all Russian publications, coupled with an economic crisis in the country that made it difficult to obtain credit. But there were, as Dostoevsky knew, more particular causes for the failure of *Epoch*. Completely drained by his labors as editor and

[2] Ibid., 4: 272–273; July 29, 1864.
[3] Ibid., 1: 399; April 5, 1865.
[4] Ibid., 400; April 14, 1865.

publisher, he was hardly able, after *Notes from Underground*, to do more than write a few articles and one unfinished satirical story ("The Crocodile"). The journal thus was deprived of the cohesion and ideological force given to *Time* by his vigorous contributions on matters of current interest, and it published nothing to match the mass appeal of such works as *The Insulted and Injured* and *House of the Dead* (though it did publish Turgenev's *Phantoms*, Leskov's *Lady Macbeth of Mtsensk*, and Grigoryev's splendid memoirs, *My Literary and Spiritual Wanderings*). Many people were not even aware that the noted writer Feodor Dostoevsky had any connection with the new journal. Others were confused by the new editor-in-chief, an unknown named A. Y. Poretsky (as an ex-convict, Dostoevsky still could not officially be named as responsible editor), who took charge of the publication in the name of "the family of Mikhail Dostoevsky." It was clearly impossible for Dostoevsky to explain to every potential subscriber, or even to state publicly, that Poretsky was only a straw man whose chief asset was a high rank in the Civil Service.

Born under an unlucky star, *Epoch's* brief career had a disastrous effect on the future course of Dostoevsky's life. When the journal went bankrupt, he was saddled with the crushing load of debt he had contracted to keep it afloat, and he struggled for most of the remainder of his life to satisfy his creditors. "Oh, my friend!" he exclaims to Wrangel. "I would voluntarily again go to prison camp, and for the same number of years, in order to pay off all my debts and feel free again."[5] With the failure of *Epoch*, preceded by the death of his first wife and then of his brother, another period of Dostoevsky's life comes to a close. The two people to whom he had been closest in the world were now gone; he was left bereft and alone, and his hopes of establishing himself as an editor with a regular income from a monthly periodical had finally gone glimmering. Dostoevsky knew that he had reached a watershed in his life, and he marked the occasion in a letter to Wrangel.

"You pity me," Dostoevsky writes, "because of my fatal loss, the death of my angel, my brother Misha, but you do not know to what extent destiny has crushed me! Another person who loved me, and whom I loved immeasurably, my wife, died of tuberculosis in Moscow, where she had gone to live last year."[6] Dostoevsky evokes an image of their conjugal life that reveals what complex emotional fibers had united these two beings throughout their mutual torments. "She died on April 16 of last year. . . . Oh! my friend, she loved me immeasurably, and I also loved her the same way, but we were not happy together. I will tell you everything when we see each other—now I will only say that, despite being positively unhappy together (because of her strange, suspicious, and

[5] Ibid., 401.
[6] Ibid., 396; March 31, 1865.

unhealthy fantastic character)—we could not cease loving each other; the unhappier we were, the more we became attached to each other. No matter how strange, that is how it was. She was the most honorable, the noblest and the most magnanimous woman of all those I have ever known in my life."[7]

At the death of his wife and brother, Dostoevsky continues, he suddenly became aware that the life he had been trying to build, both personally and professionally, had been shattered. "I could not possibly have imagined to what an extent my life would become empty and painful when they scattered earth on her grave. And now a year has passed, and my feeling is the same, not lessening at all. . . . After burying her, I flew to Petersburg, to my brother—only he was left to me, and in three months he died as well, having been slightly ill a whole month so that the crisis resulting in his death occurred almost unexpectedly in three days. And thus I suddenly found myself alone and simply terrified. My entire life at one stroke broke into two. In one half, which I had lived through, was everything I had lived for, and in the other, still unknown half everything was strange and new, and there was not a single heart that could replace those two. . . . Literally—I had nothing left for which to live. To establish new relations, to plan out a new life! The very thought of doing so was repellent to me. I, *for the first time*, felt to the marrow of my bones that no one could replace *them*, that it was only *them* that I loved in the world and that a new love not only could not be acquired but should not be. Everything around me became cold and empty. And thus, when I received your warm and kind letter three months ago, filled with previous memories, I became so depressed that I cannot tell you how I felt."[8]

More than a week later, Dostoevsky continues: "Nine days have passed since I began this letter and in these nine days I have not literally had a moment to finish it."[9] Continuing his account of the problems of *Epoch*, Dostoevsky stops again after two paragraphs, resuming only five days later, on April 14. As a result of having tried to keep *Epoch* afloat, Dostoevsky was now in desperate economic straits: "I owe 10,000 rubles in signed contracts, and 5,000 on my word; 3,000 have to be paid immediately, come what may. In addition, 2,000 are necessary in order to purchase the right to publish my works, a right now held as a guarantee on a loan, so that I can begin to edit myself." Dostoevsky's plan was to write a new novel and issue it in separate installments, "as is done in England"; he also wished to re-edit *House of the Dead* "with illustrations, in a luxury edition," and then, the following year, an edition of his complete works. But the prospect of writing under such desperate pressure, solely to meet his debts, fills him with anguish: "Now I am going to begin writing a novel under the lash,

[7] Ibid., 397–398.
[8] Ibid., 398.
[9] Ibid., April 9, 1865.

i.e., out of necessity. It will produce an effect, but is that what I need? To work out of necessity, just for money, crushes and destroys me." [10]

Returning to the immediate situation, Dostoevsky sees his position as hopeless: "But in order to begin I need, and right away, at least 3,000 rubles. I am beating the bushes trying to get it—otherwise, I am done for. I feel that only an accident can save me. What remains from all the reserve of strength and energy in my soul is something troubled and disturbed, something close to despair. Worry, bitterness, a complete cold industriousness, the most abnormal state for me to be in, and in addition loneliness—of all my past forty years, nothing remains to me. And yet it still seems to me that I am just now preparing to live. Funny, isn't it? The vitality of a cat." [11]

Nothing could have been more unexpected than this last remark, and yet nothing is more characteristic of the man who had not allowed himself to be crushed by the house of the dead and who, no matter how desperate his situation, had never given way to a paralyzing despondency. Dostoevsky, after all, believed in the freedom of the will, and in his case this conviction sprang from the deepest resources of his personality. There is never a moment in Dostoevsky's life when we can catch him giving up entirely, never a moment when—in the wreckage of whatever hopes he may have been building on, or whatever disaster has overtaken him—he is not making plans for the future and feeling the same surge of energy and expectation to which he so surprisingly gives expression here.

Time had already proceeded with its healing work, and just a month or two before his letter to Wrangel, Dostoevsky had probably struck up a liaison—for how long it is hard to say—with a worldly-wise and emotionally battered woman by the name of Martha Brown. Also, in that very month of April, just as he was completing his letter to Wrangel, Dostoevsky proposed marriage to the beautiful and rebellious young daughter of a wealthy, highly placed family, Anna Korvin-Krukovskaya, whose short stories he had printed in *Epoch* and whose talent he had encouraged. The sudden shift so noticeable in the letter—the abrupt transition from past to present—may be attributed to such events, when a resurgence of faith in the future suddenly intruded on the melancholy past that he was recalling. Indeed, an entirely new life for Dostoevsky was to begin in a little more than a year, when he would marry another young woman and then flee to Europe for a prolonged exile in order to escape his creditors.

——■——

Dostoevsky first heard of Martha Brown from the man with whom she was then living, a minor contributor to *Epoch* named Peter Gorsky. He was one of the numerous denizens of St. Petersburg's literary Grub Street who clustered around

[10] Ibid., 401; April 14, 1865.
[11] Ibid., 401–402.

the various publications, eking out a beggarly existence on the edge of destitution and often supplementing their literary labors with manual work. All that we know of the relations between Dostoevsky and Martha Brown is contained in a handful of letters written by her between November 1864 and January 1865, which raises the possibility that the two became lovers.

Her real name, which Dostoevsky may never have learned, was Elizaveta Andreyevna Chlebnikova, and she was the wayward daughter of a landowning family (her maiden name had been Panina) who had received some education and could write a literary Russian. An adventurous existence had taken her over most of Western Europe in the company of various men—a Hungarian, an Englishman, and a Frenchman, among others. On first setting foot in England, without a penny and ignorant of the language, she had tried to take her life in despair and was saved by the police. For some weeks she lived under the bridges of the Thames among other vagabonds. Thanks to the zeal of various missionaries concerned to save her soul, she acquired English rapidly; and a charitable Methodist pastor, impressed by her knowledge of the Bible and ability to recite the Lord's Prayer in English, took her to live with his family on the Isle of Guernsey. With the blessing of her patron, she married a sailor named Brown, and she then lived (one assumes as Mrs. Brown) in Weymouth, Brighton, and London. When or why the marriage ended is unknown; equally obscure is what brought Martha Brown back to Russia, where, as she remarks, many people no longer thought she was Russian at all.

Her first letter to Dostoevsky is a formal reply to an offer of work as a translator; the others are an appeal to Dostoevsky, as someone with position and moral authority, to intervene with Gorsky and attempt to bring him to his senses. By this time she was occupying a bed in the Peter and Paul Hospital, where Gorsky had shown up to exhibit his displeasure and make a drunken scene. Two letters indicate that, although now fully recovered, she preferred to remain in the disease-ridden hospital rather than lapse back into a life of misery and abuse with Gorsky. The last letter, dated sometime in the second half of January 1865, reveals a new state of affairs. Brown, living in the city, is no longer with Gorsky. The letter suggests some previous conversation between the pair about Martha Brown coming to stay with Dostoevsky as his mistress. "In any case," she goes on, "whether I can succeed or not in satisfying you in a physical sense, and whether there will exist between us that spiritual harmony on which will depend the continuance of our acquaintance, believe me when I say that I shall always remain grateful that you favored me with your friendship. . . . I swear to you that I have never, until now, resolved to be as frank with anyone as I have ventured to be with you."[12]

---

[12] The letters of Martha Panina were published by G. Prokhorov in "Nerazvernuvshiisya roman F. M. Dostoevskogo," *Zvenya* 5 (1936), 582–598; the citation is on 600.

"Forgive me for this egoistic admission," she continues, "but so much grief, despair, and hopelessness has accumulated in my soul during these past two years, which I have spent in Russia as in a prison, that, as God is my witness, I am happy, I am fortunate, to have met a man possessing such calmness of soul, such patience, such good sense and righteousness as could be found neither in Flemming [an earlier lover] nor in Gorsky. I am absolutely indifferent at present as to whether our relation will be long or short. But I swear to you that what I value, incomparably more than any material gain, is that you were not squeamish about the fallen side of my personality, that you placed me higher than I stand in my own estimation."[13] Whether this letter led to the love affair she so obviously desired, or whether such an affair had already begun, cannot be determined.

At the same time as this final letter from Brown, Dostoevsky also received another from a young woman with whom he was soon to fall in love. Her name was Anna Korvin-Krukovskaya, and two of her stories had been printed in *Epoch* during the previous months, but both had appeared under a pseudonym. For Miss Korvin-Krukovskaya, who had sent the stories in secret to the magazine, was the elder daughter of a retired lieutenant-general with strict principles about the behavior of his female folk. A gentleman of the old school, strongly imbued with the sense of his own importance and the dignity of his family, he lived with his much younger wife and two daughters on his estate at Palibino in the depths of the countryside near Vitebsk on the Polish-Russian border. Young Anna, then all of twenty-two, had hidden her literary exploits from her father, if not from her sister Sofya—later to become famous under the name of Kovalevskaya as the first woman to hold a chair of mathematics in Europe—and dispatched them with the conspiratorial aid of the estate steward. Sofya's memoirs allow us to peer into the recesses of this isolated nest of gentlefolk in the Russian provinces, out of which would emerge two extraordinary women with whom Dostoevsky maintained cordial relations throughout the remainder of his life.

General Korvin-Krukovsky had little taste for the social frivolities of Petersburg. But, in deference to the desires of his more convivial spouse, and also to introduce his daughters to a wider range of suitors, he allowed them to plunge into the fashionable Petersburg whirl each year for a period of a month. The letter Dostoevsky received from Anna on February 28 signified that one of these annual descents on Petersburg relatives was impending, and informed him that the Korvin-Krukovskys would be glad to receive a visit if notified in advance of his intention to call. Since Dostoevsky was a noted author who had accepted the fledgling literary efforts of their daughter, such an invitation would seem the least that might be expected. In fact, however, permission to extend it had been

[13] Ibid.

granted to Anna only after a long struggle against the deeply rooted prejudices of her suspicious and disgruntled father.

The general had met one Russian literary lady as a young man, the then reigning society belle Countess Rostopchina, and he had chanced on her again years later at the gambling tables of Baden-Baden behaving in a distinctly unladylike manner. Such was the inevitable fate of all Russian authoresses, and when he discovered by accident that his own Anyuta was glorifying in this dubious appellation, he flew into such a rage that his frightened family feared he would be felled by a stroke. To make matters worse, the encouraging letter from Dostoevsky that he read also contained payment for Anna's contributions to *Epoch*. "Anything can be expected from young ladies who are capable, unbeknownst to their father and mother, of entering into correspondence with an unknown man and receiving money from him!" he thundered. "Now you are selling your stories, but the time may come, perhaps, when you will sell yourself!"[14]

After this first paroxysm of wrath, the general relapsed into sullen silence. Permission was given to Anna to meet Dostoevsky on the next trip to Petersburg only after much maneuvering on the part of the women. But the general, though kindhearted enough under his forbidding exterior, still felt uneasy, and prudently admonished his wife to be on her guard. "Remember, Lisa, that you have a great responsibility," he told her before departure. "Dostoevsky is not a person of our society. What do we know about him? Only that he is a journalist and former convict. Quite a recommendation! To be sure! We must be very careful with him."[15] Such were the origins of the letter that Dostoevsky received inviting him to call on the family in Petersburg.

Shortly after their arrival in Petersburg, in the early spring of 1865, the Korvin-Krukovskys received Dostoevsky for the first time; and the long-awaited visit, anticipated by Anna with such eagerness and trepidation, turned out to be a catastrophe. Strictly conforming to her husband's parting injunctions, Anna's mother insisted on being present; Sofya too, consumed with curiosity, had received permission to remain in the living room; two elderly Russian-German aunts, finding one pretext or another to enter and catch a glimpse of the famous author, finally installed themselves there for good. Furious at this solemn assemblage, Anna exhibited her displeasure by silence. Dostoevsky too, taken aback at being forced to confront such a forbidding gathering, failed to respond to Mme Korvin-Krukovskaya's polite conversation. "He seemed old and sickly that day," Sofya recalled, "as was always the case, incidentally, when he was in low spirits."[16] After half an hour of this slow torture, Dostoevsky seized his hat and hastily departed. Anna ran into her room, uncontrollably burst into

---

[14] S. V. Kovalevskaya, *Vospominaniya* (Moscow, 1974), 70.

[15] Ibid., 73.

[16] Ibid., 50.

tears, and her reproaches soon reduced her mother to the same lachrymose condition.

Five days later, Dostoevsky called again unexpectedly and found only the two girls at home. He and Anna immediately engaged in eager conversation, as if they had been old friends, and matters could not have gone more swimmingly. He seemed to Sofya to be quite another person, much younger than before and marvelously kind and clever; she could hardly believe that he was all of forty-four years old! When their mother returned home, she was startled and a little frightened to find Dostoevsky ensconced there alone with her daughters, but the two were so radiantly happy that she promptly invited him to stay for dinner. The ice was finally broken, and Dostoevsky now began to call on the Korvin-Krukovskys two or three times a week.

Dostoevsky, however, was a guest who sometimes shocked the strait-laced household, concerned to guard against any improprieties in the conduct of the unexpected friend of their daughters. According to Sofya, Dostoevsky once told his spellbound female audience about a novel he had intended to write in the days of his youth. He had wished, he said, to depict an educated and cultivated gentleman who, traveling abroad, wakes one morning in his sunny hotel room filled with a sense of physical contentment and self-satisfaction. But he suddenly begins to feel uneasy, and as he concentrates his thoughts, he recalls an incident from the distant past. Once, after a riotous night, and spurred on by drunk companions, he had violated a ten-year-old girl . . . But at this moment Mme Korvin-Krukovskaya broke in with a horrified shriek: "Feodor Mikhailovich! For pity's sake! There are children present!" [17]

To what extent Dostoevsky's referral of this literary idea to the days of his "youth" should be taken as literally true can only remain a matter for speculation; the juxtaposition of refined aestheticism and lustful depravity emerges in his works sharply only after his return from Siberia in the 1860s. Yet his lifelong preoccupation, and what some have considered his pathological obsession, with this scabrous theme can hardly be doubted. Sometime in the late 1870s Dostoevsky was sitting in another drawing room when the question arose of what should be considered the greatest crime on earth.

> Dostoevsky spoke quickly, agitatedly and stumblingly. . . . The most frightful, the most terrible sin—was to violate a child. To take a life—that is horrible, Dostoevsky said, but to take away faith in the beauty of love— that is the most terrible crime. And Dostoevsky recounted an episode from his childhood. When I lived in Moscow as a child in a hospital for the poor, Dostoevsky said, where my father was a doctor, I played with a little girl (the daughter of a coachman or a cook). She was a delicate,

---

[17] Ibid., 77.

graceful child of nine. . . . And some disgraceful wretch violated the girl when drunk and she died, pouring out blood. I recall, Dostoevsky said, being sent for my father in the other wing of the hospital, but it was too late. All my life this memory has haunted me as the most frightful crime, the most terrible sin, for which there is not, and cannot be, any forgiveness, and I punished Stavrogin in *Demons* with this very same terrible crime.[18]

As can be seen from Sofya's recollections, Dostoevsky's verbal comportment may have led Anna's mother to regret having admitted him into the intimacy of the family circle. Another occasion when she undoubtedly had second thoughts about her tolerance occurred during a farewell party consisting of mostly Russian-Germans, very staid, official, and stuffy—exactly the sort of group in which Dostoevsky felt most uncomfortable. He resented that Anna, as elder daughter, shared the obligations of receiving with her mother and was not allowed to confine her attentions exclusively to himself. Even worse, he conceived a furious jealousy for a handsome young officer present, who was obviously attracted to Anna and to whom, he convinced himself, Anna would be forced to become engaged against her will. He expressed his displeasure and created a scandal by unpleasant remarks uttered in a loud voice (for example, that the Bible had not been written for society women to read) and by a generally boorish behavior. It was after this evening, according to Sofya, that Anna's previous reverence for Dostoevsky sharply altered. The private conversations between the two changed in tone; now they seemed to be disputing, sometimes acrimoniously, rather than engaging in a friendly exchange of ideas.

As the moment approached for Anna's return to Palibino, Dostoevsky became more censorious and despotic, and Anna less docile and more assertive. "The continual and very burning subject of their argument," writes Sofya, "was Nihilism. The debate over this question continued sometimes long after midnight." "'All of contemporary youth is stupid and backward!' Dostoevsky once shouted. 'Shiny boots are more valuable for them than Pushkin!' To which Anna retorted coolly that 'Pushkin has in fact become out of date in our time,' knowing that nothing could drive Dostoevsky into more of a fury than a lack of respect for Pushkin."[19]

All the same, one evening when Sofya was bravely struggling with Beethoven's *Sonate Pathétique*, which she knew to be among Dostoevsky's favorites, he and Anna treacherously slipped away to another room unobserved. And when the disconsolate pianist went to find her lost audience, she burst in on a proposal of marriage. There is some uncertainty whether Anna accepted, in the emotion of

[18] S. V. Belov, "Z. A. Trubetskaya, Dostoevsky i A. P. Filosofova," *Russkaya Literatura* 3 (Moscow, 1973), 117.
[19] Kovalevskaya, *Vospominaniya*, 81.

the moment, and then was freed from her pledge by Dostoevsky (that is the story he told his second wife), or whether she ever gave any reply at all. Sofya does not mention an engagement, and one assumes that, if it had existed, Anna's family would have been informed. Whatever the truth, Anna told Sofya: "I do not love Dostoevsky in such a way as to marry him." Besides the difference in age and ideas, Anna realized, with salutary insight, that Dostoevsky needed a wife entirely submissive to his will. "Look," she told her younger sister, "I am sometimes surprised at myself that I cannot love him! He is such a good man! . . . But he does not at all need someone like myself! Besides, he is so nervous, so demanding!"[20] Dostoevsky would find exactly the sort of wife he needed a year later, but he always maintained cordial relations with Anna and her sister.

He saw a good deal of Anna in the mid-1870s, even though, in the interim, she had married a well-known French radical named Charles Victor Jaclard and committed herself wholeheartedly to a life of revolutionary activity. Not only was she the first translator of parts of Karl Marx's *Das Kapital* into French, but she also established warm personal relations with Marx and played a leading role among the women (they included a surprising number of Russians) who participated courageously in the defense of the Paris Commune of 1870. It is likely that Dostoevsky drew on his courtship of her for the portrait of Aglaya Epanchina in *The Idiot*, whose engagement to Prince Myshkin upset her respectable family as much as Anna's friendship with Dostoevsky had initially done with hers. Once more, however, after his attempt to win Anna's hand had come to an amicable but irreversible end, Dostoevsky was thrown back on the isolation from which he so achingly longed to escape.

Meanwhile, whatever Dostoevsky's gloom over the failure of *Epoch*, the end of his impossible labors must nonetheless have come as something of a relief. Even when he still believed that *Epoch* could be a success, he had looked forward to the moment when he could return to his essential creative task as a novelist. Now he was being forced to do so, and for us it is evident that his failure as an editor and journalist was his salvation as an artist. During the next five years, under the pressure of necessity but never at the cost of artistic integrity, he would write three of his greatest novels—*Crime and Punishment*, *The Idiot*, and *Demons*—and establish his reputation once and for all as belonging to the very front rank of Russian literature. As these works were to prove, it was in the fierce give-and-take of argument and polemic that he had gradually hammered out his own position and found the great theme that was to occupy him throughout the remainder of his life—the moral-psychic dangers involved in the desire of the radical Russian intelligentsia to establish human life on new, "rational" foundations that would replace the God-given order still alive in the Russian moral sensibility.

[20] Ibid., 88.

PART IV

The Miraculous Years, 1865–1871

CHAPTER 32

Khlestakov in Wiesbaden

Dostoevsky was again eager to travel abroad because it was there that he could hope to meet his ex-mistress Apollinaria Suslova, the young feminist writer who had never been entirely out of his mind during the past two years and with whom he had carried on a secret correspondence even as his wife was dying. Suslova had remained in Europe when Dostoevsky returned to Russia, and letters between the pair constantly went back and forth. Unfortunately, all of this correspondence has been lost (except for the draft of one letter preserved in Suslova's diary). That Dostoevsky still dreamed of renewing his relations with Suslova is evident from a letter he sent her younger sister, Nadezhda (who later became a close friend of Anna Korvin-Krukovskaya). Nadezhda Suslova was then pursuing her medical studies in Zurich, and since Apollinaria, living in Montpellier, was to join her there, Dostoevsky wrote letters to both addresses.

Nadezhda herself, whom Dostoevsky admired and often visited in Petersburg, had criticized him harshly for his supposed ill treatment of her sister; and he appeals to Nadezhda's firsthand knowledge of his character to counter the damaging effect of Apollinaria's complaints. For the past several years, he reminds her, "I have come to seek in your company some peace for my soul during all the times of trial, and recently it was only to you that I came when my heart was too full of grief. You have seen me in my sincerest moments and you can judge: do I feed on the sufferings of others, am I brutal, (inwardly), am I cruel?"[1] Apollinaria, he tells her sister, is herself "a great egoist. Her egoism and her vanity are colossal. She demands *everything* of other people, all the perfections, and does not pardon the slightest imperfection in the light of other qualities that one may possess." Dostoevsky predicts that she will always be unhappy, because "the person who demands everything of others but recognizes no obligation can never be happy." What little we know of Apollinaria Suslova's later life would seem to bear out this prophecy.[2]

---

[1] *PSS*, 28/Bk. 2: 121–122; April 19, 1865.

[2] What information there is of Suslova (1839–1918) comes from her husband, V. V. Rozanov, a morally dubious figure who sometimes advocated a vicious anti-Semitism and wrote simultaneously for both progressive and reactionary newspapers under different pseudonyms. Rozanov and Suslova were married when he was twenty and she forty. After six years, she ran away with a Jewish

"I still love her," Dostoevsky confesses, "I love her very much, but already I wish not to love her. She *does not deserve* such a love." Dostoevsky insists that what Suslova finds insulting in his letter "is that I have dared to oppose her, dared to tell her I was suffering. . . . She has no humanity at all in her relations with me. She knows that I still love her. Why then does she torture me? Don't love me, but also don't torture me." If Dostoevsky's behavior patterns exhibit a strong masochistic component, such words illustrate that there was a limit to his presumed enjoyment of suffering; but neither could he forget that Suslova had once loved him, nor relinquish the tantalizing hope that she might surrender herself again. For all his misgivings, he could not let slip what seemed his last chance for personal happiness, and the pursuit of Apollinaria was certainly among the reasons why he determined, at whatever cost, to return to Europe during the summer of 1865.

■

The major obstacle to such a plan was a lack of funds, and just how hard-pressed Dostoevsky was at this time can be seen from a notice he received from the local police warning him to pay his creditors six hundred rubles. In case of default, he could expect a visit from the police to make an inventory of his personal belongings preparatory to their sale at auction. Dostoevsky turned for help to the Literary Fund, which granted him the loan of six hundred rubles, thus rescuing him from the loss of all his household effects.

Continuously subjected to such harassment, Dostoevsky was all the more eager to leave the country for a time. On June 8 he wrote to Kraevsky, his old editor of the 1840s and still at the head of *Notes of the Fatherland*, to offer him the plan for a new work and to request an advance of three thousand rubles. "My novel is called *The Drunkards*," Dostoevsky explains, "and will deal with the present problem of alcoholism."[3] Dostoevsky promised to have the first

---

lover of good family and education working in the book trade. Rozanov refused to give her a legal separation in the hope that she would return; she then refused to grant him a divorce even when he later fathered several children by a woman he wished to marry. When Rozanov appealed to her father, with whom she was then living, the old man replied that "the enemy of the human race has moved in with me now, and it [has become] impossible for me to live here." One of Rozanov's friends, who went to plead with Suslova when she was past sixty, mentioned the fierce implacability of her hatred.

In a letter written in 1902, Rozanov describes their first meeting when he was seventeen and she thirty-seven. She was, he writes, "sublime . . . I have never yet seen such a Russian woman, and if Russian, then . . . a Mother of God of the flagellants." (A Mother of God of the flagellant sect exercised absolute autocratic power over those belonging to her group.) See Leonid Grossman, *Put' Dostoevskogo* (Moscow, 1928), 134–137, and Anatole Leroy-Beaulieu, *L'Empire des tsars et les Russes* (Paris, 1990), 1197.

[3] *PSS*, 28/Bk. 2: 127; June 8, 1865.

chapters ready by October 1865; in case of death, or if he failed to meet the deadline, he offered as guarantee the right in perpetuity to all his previous works. But Kraevsky declined the proposal, even though Dostoevsky specified other conditions protecting the rights of the publisher. In any event, Dostoevsky's plan for *The Drunkards* came to little more than the idea he mentioned in his letters. Totally hemmed in by the affairs of *Epoch*, he would hardly have had time to work out ideas for a new novel. *The Drunkards* was never written, but it did provide the subplot involving the Marmeladov family in *Crime and Punishment*.

As a last resort, Dostoevsky turned to a publisher named Stellovsky, ill famed for driving hard bargains. Stellovsky had already approached Dostoevsky with an offer of two thousand rubles in return for the right to publish a single edition of his works with no royalties accruing. Dostoevsky had turned down this miserly proposition, but, driven back to Stellovsky by necessity, he now agreed to accept even more severe conditions. The publisher would advance three thousand rubles in exchange for the right to print an edition of Dostoevsky's complete works. In addition, Dostoevsky agreed to furnish a new novel of specified format by November 1, 1866, and in case of failure, Stellovsky would have the right to publish *all* of Dostoevsky's future works without compensation to the author for a period of nine years. Despite the risks of entering into such a contract, Dostoevsky accepted. After revising his works for Stellovsky's new edition and obtaining a provisional promise from the journal *The Library for Reading* to forward him an advance in return for a story or some travel articles, he left for Europe at the end of July.

Each time Dostoevsky had gone abroad in the past, he had hurried to the roulette tables, and the same pattern was repeated now. By the time he arrived in Wiesbaden on the twenty-ninth of July to try his luck, the three thousand rubles obtained from Stellovsky had been distributed among his most pressing creditors and also parceled out to meet the needs of Mikhail's family and Dostoevsky's stepson Pasha; only one hundred seventy-five silver rubles had been retained for the voyage. Five days later, however, he lost everything down to his last penny, and was even forced to pawn his watch. For help he turned first to Turgenev in Baden-Baden, whom he had seen just the month previous in Petersburg and with whom he was on the friendliest footing.

Writing from Wiesbaden, Dostoevsky first explained his unfortunate circumstances and then apologetically added that, while feeling "aversion and shame" at disturbing his fellow novelist, he had nowhere else to appeal for help. And "since you are more intelligent than the others, it is morally easier to turn to you. Here is what is involved: I appeal to you as one human being to another, and I ask for one hundred thalers." Dostoevsky promised to repay within a month out of funds he expected to receive from *The Library for Reading* and also from "someone who *must* help me"[4] (perhaps Apollinaria Suslova, who shortly afterward arrived in Wiesbaden for a visit).

Turgenev rapidly sent fifty thalers, which was all he could afford at the moment. Dostoevsky gratefully acknowledged the loan: "although [it] has not entirely cleared me, all the same it is of great help. I hope to pay you back very soon."[5] In addition to Turgenev, Dostoevsky also appealed to Herzen in Geneva, with whom his relations in the recent past had been cordial, but he received no immediate reply. Meanwhile, Suslova appeared on the scene to spend a few days with her still amorous ex-lover, whose circumstances were hardly propitious for renewing his efforts to regain her affections. During the intervening two years, Suslova's desultory and wandering life in France and Switzerland had been unhappy and frustrating. Her first and deepest amorous relation had been with Dostoevsky, and she tended to blame him for her inability to establish more satisfactory ones with other men.

Dostoevsky could hardly have anticipated that his eagerly awaited rendezvous with Suslova would occur under such inglorious circumstances, reduced as he was to utter destitution and living in fear of being expelled from his hotel at any moment and taken to the police. Dostoevsky's letters to Suslova after her departure are filled with concern over her welfare, and it is likely that, leaving herself with barely enough to continue her journey, she aided Dostoevsky with whatever funds she had available. "Dear Polya," he writes, "in the first place I do not understand how you managed to arrive [in Paris]. To my disgusting anguish about myself has been added the anguish about you. . . . At Cologne the hotel, the carriages, the voyage—even if you had enough for the train, you were probably hungry. All this hammers in my head and gives me no rest."[6]

Dostoevsky had no secrets from Suslova, and it is from his letters to her that we obtain the most graphic image of the debasing conditions under which he was living and which cut his pride to the quick. "Meanwhile," his letter continues, "my situation has gotten so bad that it is unbelievable. Scarcely had you left when on the next day, early in the morning, the hotel declared to me that they would no longer give me any meals, neither tea nor coffee. I went for an explanation and the stout German owner explained to me that I did not 'deserve' the meals and that he would send me tea. So that since yesterday I no longer eat and only drink tea. Yes, and . . . all the staff treat me with an inexpressible, totally German contempt. There is no greater crime for a German than to be without any money and not pay on time."[7]

[4] Ibid., 128; August 3/15, 1865.
[5] Ibid., 129; August 20 1865.
[6] Ibid., 129–130; August 10/22, 1865.
[7] Ibid.

Two days later, Dostoevsky adds some new details in another letter sent without postage. "My affairs are terrible *nec plus ultra*; it is impossible to go any further. Beyond, there must be another zone of misfortunes and filthiness of which I still have no knowledge. . . . I am still living without meals, and this is already the third day that I live on morning and evening tea—and it's curious: I do not at all really wish to eat. The worst is that they hem me in and sometimes refuse me a candle in the evening [especially] when some bit of the previous one is left over, even the smallest fragment. But I leave the hotel every day at three o'clock and only return at six, so as not to give the impression that I do not dine at all. How much like a Khlestakov [a character in Gogol's *The Inspector-General*]!" Dostoevsky concludes with a plea to Suslova to raise some money for him from her friends in Paris if possible, and adds, as a despairing postscript: "now I no longer see at all what will become of me."[8]

To the distress induced by his circumstances was added the humiliation of failing to receive any answer from Herzen. "Herzen torments me," he admits to Suslova. "If he received my letter and *does not wish* to respond—what a humiliation and what behavior! really, did I deserve this, and for what reason?"[9] A postscript to this letter announces with relief that Herzen had finally replied, and though he could not spare the full amount requested, he had offered to send a lesser sum if this would help. Dostoevsky wonders why Herzen has not simply dispatched the smaller sum and decides forgivingly that he was probably short of funds, but now, he tells Suslova, it is impossible to bring himself to answer with another pleading entreaty.

Despite the bleak picture of solitary misery that emerges from Dostoevsky's letters, he was not as isolated as might be assumed. There were other Russians in Wiesbaden with whom he struck up an acquaintance, and they played a crucial part in helping him escape from the debasement of his penury. Of particular importance was the priest in charge of the Russian Orthodox Church, Father I. L. Yanishev. A man of unusual culture, Father Yanishev became well-known in Orthodox theological circles because of his endeavors to ground moral theology on the psychological analysis of human character, and in one book he paid special attention to a problem of vital concern to Dostoevsky, the freedom of the will. Father George Florovsky, in his great work on the history of Russian theology, writes about him with a shade of disapproval, because his teachings were "above all, a justification of the world. 'Earthly blessings' are accepted as the *necessary* milieu *outside of which moral awakening is impossible*—'without which virtue is impossible.' . . . In the contemplative mysticism of the ascetics, Yanishev found only quietism."[10]

---

[8] Ibid., 130–132; August 12/24, 1865.

[9] Ibid.

[10] Father Georgy Florovsky, *Puti Russkogo bogosloviya* (Paris, 1983), 390.

Instead of such "quietism," Yanishev favored a Christianity understood as charitable love for others—a love that he called "the center and crown of the Christian faith." [11] The novelist certainly did not need Yanishev to teach *him*, the erstwhile Christian Socialist, that Christianity was primarily "charitable love," but if the two talked of such matters Dostoevsky would certainly have been pleased to find such a conception defended by so eminent a clergyman. And when the young novice Alyosha Karamazov is told by his mentor Father Zosima to quit the monastery and test his Christianity in the hurly-burly of everyday life, he is being instructed to follow one of the chief tenets of Father Yanishev's teachings. Dostoevsky remained in contact with Father Yanishev even after Wiesbaden, and two years later wrote of him to Apollon Maikov: "He is a rare person, worthy, meek, with a sense of his own dignity, of an angelic purity of soul and a *passionate* believer." [12] More immediately pressing issues than theological ones were naturally on Dostoevsky's mind when the two men first met, and Father Yanishev aided the distraught man of letters not only with spiritual counsel but also with a down-to-earth loan.

It was during this period of protracted mortification that Dostoevsky, while strolling one day among the linden trees at Wiesbaden, poured some of his troubles into the sympathetic ears of Princess Shalikova, a distinguished lady who also frequented the company of Father Yanishev and was herself an author under various pseudonyms. At it turned out, she was also a distant relative of Katkov, the powerful anti-radical editor of *The Russian Messenger*, and she encouraged Dostoevsky to apply to him as a possible publisher. Princess Shalikova may also have conveyed some indication of Katkov's recent appreciation of Dostoevsky *as a writer*. Whatever was said, the result is well-known: Dostoevsky wrote to Katkov sometime during the first two weeks in September with the first outline of the conception of what became *Crime and Punishment*. At this stage, Dostoevsky was thinking not of a novel but of a story or novella, which he had been working on "for two months" and was on the point of completing. He promised Katkov that it would be finished in one or two weeks, at most a month, and then outlined its central theme, which, he assured the editor, "in no way contradicts [the policy] of your journal; rather the contrary":

> It is the psychological report of a crime. . . . A young man, expelled from
> the university, . . . living in the direst poverty . . . falling under the influ-
> ence of the strange "unfinished" ideas afloat . . . decides to break out of his
> disgusting position at one stroke. He has made up his mind to kill an old
> woman . . . who lends money at interest. The old woman is stupid, stupid

---

[11] N. N. Glubokovsky, *Russkaya bogoslovskiya nauka v eya istoricheskom razvitii i noveishem sostoyanii* (Warsaw, 1928), 17.

[12] *PSS*, 28/Bk. 2: 259; February 18/March 1, 1868.

and ailing, greedy, takes as high a rate of interest as a Yid, is evil and eats up other lives. . . . 'She is good for nothing. Why should she live?' . . . These questions befuddle the young man. He decides to kill her in order to bring happiness to his mother living in the provinces, rescue his sister, . . . finish his studies, go abroad, and then all his life be upright, staunch, unbend-able in fulfilling his 'humane obligation to mankind,' which would ulti-mately 'smooth out' his crime, if one can really call a crime this action against a deaf, stupid, evil, sickly old woman . . . He spends a month after that until the final catastrophe . . . unsuspected and unexpected feelings torment his heart. Heavenly truth, earthly law, take their toll and he fin-ishes by *being forced* to denounce himself. Forced because, even though he perishes in *katorga*, at least he will be reunited with the people; the feeling of isolation and separation from mankind, which he felt right after com-pleting the crime, has tortured him. The law of truth and human nature took its [text illegible]. . . . The criminal himself decides to accept suffer-ing in order to atone for his deed.[13]

In conclusion, Dostoevsky asked to be paid the modest sum of one hundred twenty-five rubles per folio sheet, although it was well-known that writers like Turgenev and Tolstoy received a good deal more, and he pleadingly requested an immediate advance of three hundred rubles to rescue him from his present diffi-culties, whose details he left unspecified. No reply arrived immediately, and with the help of Father Yanishev (and Wrangel) Dostoevsky managed to pay his bills and return to Russia. When Katkov finally sent the advance to Wiesbaden, Dos-toevsky was already back in his native land. Father Yanishev forwarded the money, and this was the beginning of Dostoevsky's long relationship with *The Russian Messenger*, which published all his major novels except *A Raw Youth*. It was also the beginning of a much more prolonged period of literary labor than Dostoevsky had imagined when he promised to complete his "story" in a few more weeks.

———■———

Dostoevsky's return to Petersburg in mid-October immediately plunged him back into the swarm of menacing creditors from whose persecution he had fled to Europe. To make matters worse, Dostoevsky's epileptic attacks increased in frequency shortly after his return (as if, he remarked to Wrangel bitterly, to make up for the three months' respite afforded him in Europe). All this misery was further aggravated by "family disagreements, the countless troubles connected with the affairs of my late brother, of his family, and of our deceased journal."[14]

[13] Ibid., 136–138; September 15/27, 1865.
[14] Ibid., 150; February 18, 1866.

Mikhail's widow and her children held Dostoevsky responsible for their strait-ened economic situation, and he was deeply aggrieved at their hostility.

Dostoevsky complains about the difficulties of literary composition under such nerve-racking conditions, and it might be thought that he would have avoided complicating them further. Instead, even though most of the story he had proposed to Katkov already existed in a next-to-final draft, he decided to re-cast his plan. "At the end of November," he explained to Wrangel two months later, "a good part (of the initial plan) had been written and was ready; but I burned it all; I can confess this to you now. I didn't like it myself. A new form, a new plan carried me away, and I started afresh." [15] This new plan involved writ-ing a much longer work, a novel in six parts whose title would be *Crime and Punishment*.

It would be an exaggeration to speak of Dostoevsky as maintaining any nor-mal social life during the second half of 1865, and he remarked himself that "I have not visited anyone all winter." [16] In fact, however, Apollinaria Suslova was now living in Petersburg, and he continued to pursue her, though with results that hardly alleviated his loneliness. On November 2, 1865, Suslova confided to her diary: "Today F M was here and we argued and contradicted each other all the time. For a long time now he has been offering me his hand and his heart, and he only makes me angry doing so. Speaking of my character, he once said: 'If you were to get married, you'd begin to hate your husband three days later, and leave him.'" [17] Their relationship ended when his offers of marriage were persistently refused. But Dostoevsky would soon recreate the strained intensity of their love-hate bickering in *The Gambler*—where, however, he acquires imag-inatively what he had failed to achieve in reality. For there the beautiful and contemptuous Polina is in love with the feckless and self-destructive gambler.

The first and second parts of *Crime and Punishment* were serialized in the January and February issues of *The Russian Messenger*. Despite predictable reac-tions from the radicals on *The Contemporary* (its critic G. Z. Eliseev wrote of "this new 'fantasy' of Mr. Dostoevsky, a fantasy according to which the entire student body is accused without exception of attempting murder and rob-bery"), [18] the book's installments were a sensational success with the reading pub-lic. "Only *Crime and Punishment* was read during 1866," Strakhov recalled, "only it was spoken about by lovers of literature, who often complained about the sti-fling power of the novel and the painful impression it left, which caused people with strong nerves almost to become ill and forced those with weak ones to give

---

[15] Ibid.

[16] Ibid., 151.

[17] Dostoevsky, *The Gambler, with Polina Suslova's Diary*, trans. Victor Terras, ed. Edward Wa-siolek (Chicago, 1972), 301–302.

[18] Cited in *PSS*, 7: 346.

up reading it altogether."[19] Strakhov also remembered "most striking of all," the coincidence "with reality." On January 12, 1866, a student named A. M. Danilov killed a moneylender and his manservant in order to loot their apartment, and the crime instantly recalled Raskolnikov's deed.

Despite the furor aroused by these early chapters, which, as Dostoevsky later learned from Katkov, had brought *The Russian Messenger* at least five hundred new subscribers, as the manuscript increased in length there were disturbing indications that the journal editors hoped to lower the price so as to decrease their overall outlay. Dostoevsky believed it would be necessary to travel to Moscow and talk to Katkov personally, but he did not wish to make a move before at least half the work had been published. "With the help of God," he remarked fervently to Wrangel, "this novel can be the most splendid thing."[20] Dostoevsky thus continued to live on the very edge of poverty, haunted by the fear that his creditors would press him to the wall and ruin everything. In response to some friendly advice from Wrangel counseling him to enter government service, and thus assure himself of a guaranteed income, Dostoevsky sketched for Wrangel's benefit his hopes for a substantial economic return. "But here's the trouble," he added sadly: "If I am locked up in prison for debt, then I will certainly spoil it and maybe not even complete it at all; everything will then go to pieces."[21]

By mid-March, Dostoevsky made the trip to Moscow and was promised a further advance of a thousand rubles. He also visited the family of his second sister, Vera, whose husband, A. P. Ivanov, served as a physician in the Konstantinovsky Land Surveying Institute. The hospitable Ivanovs always had a houseful of guests, and one of them was an attractive twenty-year-old by the name of Marya Sergeevna Ivanchina-Pisareva, a friend of one of the Ivanov daughters. Just a month before, Dostoevsky had written gloomily to Wrangel that "at least you, my good friend, are happy with your family; while fate has so far denied me this great and *sole* human happiness."[22] Dostoevsky had, all this time, been eagerly seeking some remedy for his emotional solitude, and he was very much taken with Marya Sergeevna. One morning, when the family had gone to Easter matins, he remained at home with her and formally proposed marriage, but in view of the difference in their ages (Dostoevsky was then forty-five), the sprightly young lady turned him off with an unmistakably discouraging quotation from Pushkin's "Poltava": "Okameneloe godami / Pylaet serdtse starika" (Petrified by the years / The heart of the old man flames up).[23]

---

[19] Ibid., 349.
[20] *PSS*, 28/Bk. 2: 150; February 18, 1866.
[21] Ibid., 151.
[22] Ibid., 152.
[23] The incident is recounted in the memoirs of Dostoevsky's niece Marya Ivanova. See *DVS*, 2: 48.

It was just a day or two after Dostoevsky's return from Moscow that the shattering event occurred that left all of Russia aghast. The tsar's habit, well-known to his adoring subjects, was to walk his dog every day in the Summer Gardens adjacent to the Winter Palace, and a small crowd was watching on April 4, 1866, as he was about to enter his carriage. At that moment a pale and desperately poor ex-student pushed his way through the spectators, took aim with a pistol, and fired. Whether Dimitry Karakozov was a faulty marksman or whether someone—a tradesman named Osip Kommissarov, who became a national hero overnight—had jostled his arm, the shot went wild, and Karakozov was overpowered by the crowd. Saved by the police from a lynching at the hands of the outraged mob, he was dragged to Alexander II, who personally took his pistol from him and asked if he were a Pole. It seemed inconceivable to the tsar that an attempt on his life would be made by anyone but a foreigner, yet Karakozov, who came from a family of small, impoverished landowners and who had been expelled from the university, like Raskolnikov, for failing to pay his fees, replied: "Pure Russian."

News of Karakozov's attempt stunned all of Russia and produced a spontaneous outpouring of devotion to the monarch rivaling the manifestations of patriotism exhibited during major historical catastrophes such as the Napoleonic invasion. Like many others, Dostoevsky was shocked into a state of near hysteria by the unbelievable report, and he rushed to the home of his oldest friend, Apollon Maikov, to share his agitated feelings. Peter Weinberg, who was visiting Maikov, left this image of Dostoevsky:

> Feodor Mikhailovich Dostoevsky ran headlong into the room. He was terribly pale, looked in an awful fright, and he was shaking all over as if in a fever.
>
> "The tsar has been shot at," he shrieked, not greeting us, in a voice breaking with emotion.
>
> "Killed?" Maikov cried out in some sort of strange inhuman voice.
>
> "No . . . He was saved . . . Fortunately . . . But shot at . . . shot at . . . shot at."
>
> We gave him a little something to quiet himself—though Maikov too was close to fainting—and we all three ran into the street.[24]

Dostoevsky was horrified at the news itself, but he must also have been filled with foreboding at the severe consequences that he knew would now ensue. Herzen, who strongly repudiated Karakozov's action, wrote forebodingly in *The Bell* that "we expect only calamity from it, and are dumbfounded at the thought

[24] See the reminiscences of Z. K. Ralli, who knew the Ishutin group and Karakozov himself, and cites this passage of Weinberg in his own recollections. "Iz vospominaniya Z. K. Ralli," in *Revolyutsionnoe dvizhenie 1860–godov*, ed. B. I. Gorev and B. P. Kozmin (Moscow, 1932), 143.

of the responsibility that this fanatic has taken upon himself."[25] Turgenev hastened to write Annenkov that "one cannot but shudder at the thought of what
would have happened in Russia if the dastardly deed had succeeded."[26]

What *did* happen was bad enough: Count N. M. Muraviev, who had suppressed the Polish rebellion of 1863 with bloody ferocity, was appointed head of
a commission to investigate the assassination attempt and given virtually the
powers of a dictator. Simultaneously, Katkov launched a ferocious press campaign against all liberal and radical organs of opinion whose nefarious influence
had led to the horrendous crime. As Herzen accurately foresaw, the government,
aided by the demagogic jeremiads of Katkov, now would "mow down everything right and left, . . . mow down the freedom of speech that has not yet fully
emerged, mow down independent thought, . . . mow down 'the people' who at
present are being so flattered, and all this under the name of saving the Tsar and
avenging him."[27] The reigning atmosphere of terror is conveyed in the memoirs
of Eliseev, who had criticized the early chapters of *Crime and Punishment* in the
pages of *The Contemporary*. "Every day," he recalled, "news arrived that during
the night this or that literary man had been taken, and the next morning they
took so-and-so and so-and-so. Little by little half of the literary men I knew had
been taken. . . . All of these rumors, the constantly growing apprehension and
the sleepless nights had so enervated me and brought me so near the point of
complete prostration that I considered going and asking them to lock me up in
the fortress."[28]

Another editor of *The Contemporary*, Dostoevsky's erstwhile friend Nekrasov, behaved under these nerve-shattering circumstances in a manner that has
always been considered especially reprehensible. As a man of letters and a poet,
Nekrasov had been personally associated with all the eminent representatives of
Russian radical opinion beginning with Belinsky, and it was Nekrasov who had
entrusted the editorial fate of his journal to Chernyshevsky and Dobrolyubov.
His own poems had been filled with "civic themes," those social-humanitarian
motifs expressing the convictions of the radical intelligentsia. Despite all this,
in a desperate effort to preserve *The Contemporary* from extinction, he read a
poem in honor of Muraviev at a banquet given for the count at the exclusive
English Club. His eulogy concluded with the threatening words, "Spare not the
guilty ones!" And to heighten the disgrace, Nekrasov also composed a poem in
honor of the pitiable and drink-sodden Kommissarov, who was everywhere

[25] Cited in A. A. Kornilov, *Obshchestvennoe dvizhenie pri Alexander II, 1835–1881* (Moscow, 1909),
175.

[26] Cited in Henri Granjard, *Ivan Tourguénev et les courants politiques et sociaux de son temps* (Paris,
1954), 336.

[27] Cited in Kornei Chukovsky, *The Poet and the Hangman*, trans. R. W. Rotsel (Ann Arbor, MI,
1977), 40.

[28] Ibid., 40–41.

being celebrated as "the instrument of God" chosen to avert a great calamity from the Russian people. All these demeaning efforts, which severely tarnished Nekrasov's reputation and poisoned the remainder of his days, proved to be futile. The implacable Muraviev, after the public obeisance of the poem, is reported to have told Nekrasov with condescending contempt: "I would like to protect you from collective responsibility for the evil we are combating, but that is hardly within my power."[29] And he promptly closed down *The Contemporary* for good and all.

Dostoevsky too may well have felt a shudder of fear during these frightening days of grim repression. As an ex-convict, he was still under police surveillance; he was also the ex-editor of a journal that had been banned for political unreliability. Nor did Dostoevsky have any illusions about the authorities' powers of discernment; he knew they were too obtuse to distinguish between various shades of social-political opinion, and that he would be lumped in the same suspicious category as the radicals he had been polemically combating in *Epoch*. Nothing untoward occurred to him personally, however, though he blamed his difficulty in obtaining a passport to go abroad "on the present circumstances."

This remark is made in an important letter (April 1866) to Katkov, which contains a lengthy appraisal of the situation in the country brought on by the measures taken in the wake of Karakozov's fateful shot. One should remember that Dostoevsky was writing to the leader of the violent assault against all shades of liberal and radical opinion, and that he was now financially dependent on Katkov for his very sustenance. It is thus all the more praiseworthy that he felt impelled to speak out against the wave of repression sweeping the country. Dostoevsky frankly confides that "I am, and probably always will be, an authentic Slavophil by conviction."[30] The Slavophils had always insisted that the Russian people were God-fearing and obedient subjects of the tsar, and that there was no necessity for the authorities to regard them with suspicion.

If the Nihilists have been successful in influencing Russian youth, Dostoevsky insists, it is for reasons that can hardly be considered evil. "All those high school pupils, those students, of whom I have seen so many, have become Nihilists so purely, so unselfishly, in the name of honor, truth, and genuine usefulness! You know they are helpless against these stupidities, and take them for perfection." The captive Karakozov was being interrogated and tried in secret, and little information was available about what those doctrines ("these stupidities") may have been; but Dostoevsky would have been surprised to discover how accurately he had intuited the consequences of that "unsteadiness" of moral convictions he was then portraying in Raskolnikov. Karakozov was a member of a

---

[29] Ibid., 18–19.
[30] *PSS*, 28/Bk. 2: 154; April 25, 1866.

small underground group of radicals headed by Nikolay Ishutin, all students or ex-students and all inspired by the extremism of the revolutionary ideas of the 1860s as Dostoevsky had just described them—including the desire for self-sacrifice. "One member of the group," writes Franco Venturi, "thought of poisoning [his father] so as to be able to give his legacy to the cause."[31] It was out of such a milieu that Karakozov had emerged.[32]

Dostoevsky insists that "the innocents are convinced that Nihilism—gives them the most complete chance to exhibit their civic and social activity and freedom."[33] The only possible answer, implied though not stated, is to provide more freedom for the idealism of youth to express itself in some socially permitted fashion. "Do you know what the people are saying?" he asks. "They say that April 4th has proven mathematically the powerful, extraordinary, sacred union of the tsar with the people. And such union should allow certain governmental personalities to show more faith in the people and in society. Meanwhile, everybody now awaits with fear more constraints on speech and thought. . . . But how can Nihilism be fought without freedom of speech? Even if they, the Nihilists, were given freedom of speech . . . they would make all Russia laugh by the *positive* explanation of their teachings. While now they are given the appearance of sphinxes, an enigma, wisdom, secrecy, and this fascinates the unexperienced."[34]

This remarkable letter, written at a moment when the clamor for more severity against the radicals was resounding on all sides, throws light on the state of mind in which Dostoevsky was composing his novel. During the next few months, straining himself to the limits of his endurance, Dostoevsky worked without respite, even though harassed by his creditors. To Father Yanishev, whose loan he repaid out of the thousand rubles obtained from Katkov, he wrote at the end of April: "My epilepsy has worsened so much that if I work for

[31] Franco Venturi, *The Roots of Revolution*, trans. Francis Haskell (New York, 1966), 332–334.

[32] Ishutin's group prepared the way for Sergey Nechaev a few years later, and many of the people Nechaev recruited had been initiated into revolutionary activity by Ishutin. This earlier group was organized in two sections: one, called the "Organization," was devoted to agitation and propaganda; the second, called "Hell," was dedicated to terrorism against the landowning classes and government, and the final aim was the assassination of the tsar. "A member of 'Hell,'" according to Ishutin, "must live under a false name and break all family ties; he must not marry; he must give up his friends; and in general he must live with one single exclusive aim: an infinite love and devotion for his country and its good."

Ishutin and those like him were implacably opposed to the liberation of the serfs and to any attempt to promote or implement democratic reforms because they would prevent a more thoroughgoing revolution. Venturi remarks, "this violent opposition to reforms inevitably coincided with the opinion of the most reactionary nobles who always opposed the emancipation of the serfs and who now continued to criticize it." (Ibid., 334–338) We shall see Dostoevsky making the same equation between left and right extremes in his letters and in *Demons*.

[33] *PSS*, 28/Bk. 2: 154–155; April 25, 1866.

[34] Ibid., 155.

a week without interruption I have an attack, and the next week cannot work because the result of two or three attacks will be—apoplexy. And yet I must finish. That's my situation."[35]

———■———

In a letter to Anna Korvin-Krukovskaya—who had, with the approval of her father, invited him to vacation in Palibino—Dostoevsky explained that his novel would probably keep him pinned to Petersburg throughout the summer. "In truth," he added a bit later, "the melancholy, sleazy and foul-smelling Petersburg of summer time fits with my mood and may even provide me with some pseudo-inspiration for my novel; but it's too oppressive."[36] As the spring wore on, Dostoevsky finally decided to give Moscow a try, but then, finding the heat and the loneliness unbearable after a few days, he moved to the nearby village of Lublino, a summer resort about three miles from Moscow, where the Ivanovs had rented a dacha. The Ivanovs' ten children had all brought along friends, and there were other young people whom the benevolent Dr. Ivanov had taken under his wing. Since Dostoevsky needed peace and quiet in order to work, a spacious room was found nearby to which he could retire in tranquility. He and Pasha installed themselves in Lublino at the beginning of July.

Two memoirs have been left of this relatively blithe summer of 1866: one by Dostoevsky's niece Marya Alexandrovna Ivanova, then eighteen years old and already displaying outstanding musical talent (she later became a brilliant pianist), the other by the then fifteen-year-old N. Von-Voght (or Fon-Fokht, to use the Russian spelling), a student at the Konstantinovsky Institute whom the Ivanovs had befriended. Both depict the lighthearted, untroubled atmosphere of those carefree days, when much time was spent in long walks to neighboring villages during the soft, moonlit evenings, on word games and amateur theatricals to while away the hours after dinner, and on the inevitable good-humored chaffing and jesting of high-spirited youth. The usually gloomy and care-worn Dostoevsky evidently blossomed in this rejuvenating atmosphere, and, despite his age and forbidding reputation (everyone there had some knowledge of his early works and knew of his legendary aura as a Siberian survivor), he is depicted as playing the part of master of the revels with great relish.

"Although he was forty-five years old," writes his niece, "he behaved with surprising unaffectedness toward the young company, and was the initial organizer of all the distractions and pranks. . . . Always elegantly dressed, with starched collars, gray trousers and a dark-blue, loose-fitting jacket, Dostoevsky carefully looked after his appearance and was very unhappy, for instance, that

[35] Ibid., 156; April 29, 1866.
[36] Ibid., 157; May 9, 1866.

his small beard was so scanty."[37] Much diversion was afforded by Dostoevsky's ability to turn out reams of mocking light verse, most of it directed against a young nephew of the Ivanovs, Dr. Alexander Karepin, who was also the butt of impromptu skits equally flowing from Dostoevsky's pen. Still unmarried, Dr. Karepin was an opponent of the new ideas about women's emancipation advocated by Chernyshevsky in *What Is To Be Done?*, and Dostoevsky once worked him into a fury by asserting that the government had set up an organization to encourage women to desert their husbands and come to Petersburg to learn how to operate sewing machines (an allusion to the dressmaking establishment organized by the heroine of the novel). Dr. Karepin took all this with solemn literalness and flew into a rage against such interference with family stability until reassured that it was only a joke.

Despite all the amusements, Dostoevsky could hardly forget about his novel or about the new work that he had promised Stellovsky by the beginning of the year. His plan, as he confided to Anna Korvin-Krukovskaya, had been "to do an unheard of and eccentric thing: write 30 signatures [sixteen pages] in 4 months of two different novels, one in the morning and the other in the evening, and to finish on schedule."[38] His morning labors were presumably spent in sketching ideas for *The Gambler*, which he completed only several months later. According to one anecdote, the late evening hours were indisputably reserved for pressing ahead with *Crime and Punishment*. A lackey of the Ivanovs, assigned to sleep in Dostoevsky's dacha so as to aid him in case of an epileptic attack, announced after a few days that he refused to reside with the author any longer. Dostoevsky, he explained, was planning to kill somebody—"all through the night he paced up and down in his room and spoke about this aloud."[39]

Dostoevsky made weekly visits to Moscow for consultation with the editors of *The Russian Messenger*, and "always returned dissatisfied and upset. He explained this as the result of being forced to correct his text, or even to throw out parts because of censorship pressure."[40] Dostoevsky mentions in a mid-July letter to Milyukov that the worst "censorship pressure" came not only from the legal authorities but also from Katkov and his assistant editor Lyubimov, who were insisting that he rewrite the chapter containing the scene in which Sonya reads to Raskolnikov the passage from the Gospels concerning the raising of Lazarus. "I wrote," Dostoevsky confides, "with genuine inspiration, but perhaps it's no good; but for them the question is not its literary worth, they are worried about its morality. Here I was in the right—nothing was against morality, and *even quite the contrary*, but they saw otherwise and, what's more, saw traces of

---

[37] M. A. Ivanova, "Vospominaniya," *DVS*, 2: 41.

[38] *PSS*, 28/Bk. 2: 160; June 17, 1866.

[39] Ivanova, *DVS*, 2: 41.

[40] N. Fon-Fokht, "K biografiya F. M. Dostoevskogo," *DVS*, 2: 56.

Nihilism. . . . I took it back, and this revision of a large chapter cost me at least three new chapters of work, judging by the effort and the weariness; but I corrected it and gave it back." [41]

This time-consuming task was one reason why Dostoevsky's hope of writing his novel for Stellovsky during the summer, while forging ahead with *Crime and Punishment*, proved to be overly optimistic. Dostoevsky admitted to Milyukov that "I have not yet tackled the novel for Stellovsky, but I will. I have worked out a plan—a quite satisfactory little novel." "Stellovsky," he adds, "upsets me to the point of torture, and I even see him in my dreams." [42] However, Dostoevsky made no further progress that would enable him to fulfill the terms of the threatening contract.

Since the original manuscript of *Crime and Punishment* has been lost, it is difficult to determine just what the editors had objected to in the text. The only other information available is a remark made in 1889 by the editors of *The Russian Messenger*, who, in publishing Dostoevsky's letter, commented that "it was not easy for him to give up his intentionally exaggerated idealization of Sonya as a woman who carried self-sacrifice to the point of sacrificing her body. Feodor Mikhailovich substantially shortened the conversation during the reading of the Gospel, which in the original version was much longer than what remains in the printed text." [43] It seems clear, then, that Dostoevsky had initially given Sonya a more affirmative role in this scene, and this led to what Katkov considered her unacceptably "exaggerated idealization."

What Katkov found inadmissible may perhaps be clarified by a passage in Dostoevsky's notebooks, where Sonya *is* presented occasionally as the spokeswoman for the morality that Dostoevsky wished to advocate. In one scene, she explains to Raskolnikov that "in comfort, in wealth, you would perhaps have seen nothing of human happiness. The person God loves, the person on whom He really counts, is the one to whom He sends much suffering, so that he sees better and recognizes through himself why in unhappiness the suffering of people is more visible than in happiness." Immediately following this speech, Raskolnikov retorts bitterly: "And perhaps God does not exist" (7: 150). This reply is included in the Gospel-reading chapter, and we may assume that Sonya's words were meant for the same context. It is possible that similar speeches in the notes were also included in the rejected version.

If so, it is not difficult to understand why the worthy editors of *The Russian Messenger* might have been upset. For Dostoevsky is depicting a fallen woman as the inspired interpreter of the Gospels, the expositor of the inscrutable purposes of divine will. Moreover, if the logic of Sonya's words is taken literally, it would

[41] *PSS*, 28/Bk. 2: 166; July 10–15, 1866.
[42] Ibid.
[43] Cited in *PSS*, 7: 326.

mean that God had ultimately brought about, for his own ends, her degradation and Raskolnikov's crime. Such a bold reversal of the ordinary tenets of social morality could well have been seen by the editors as being tainted with "Nihilism," since it could provide an opening for an implicit accusation against God himself. Exactly such an accusation will soon be made by the death-stricken Ippolit Terentyev in *The Idiot* and later by Ivan Karamazov.

If these speculations have any validity, they may help to clarify why Dostoevsky was accused by the editors of blurring the boundaries between good and evil. "*Evil* and *good* are sharply separated," he assures Lyubimov, "and it will be impossible to confuse or misinterpret them. . . . Everything you spoke about has been done, everything is separated, demarcated and clear. *The reading of the Gospel* is given a different coloring."[44] Katkov probably improved Dostoevsky's text by insisting that he shorten Sonya's preachings, and the novelist may well in the end have recognized this himself. As he returned the proofs in mid-July, he remarked: "For 20 years I have painfully felt, and seen more clearly than anyone, that my literary vice is: *prolixity*, but I can't seem to shake it off."[45] There is, however, nothing prolix about *Crime and Punishment*, whose every word, as we shall soon see, stems from acute artistic self-awareness.

On October 1, shortly after Dostoevsky's return to Petersburg, Milyukov called and found his friend walking up and down his study in terrible agitation. It was then that Dostoevsky revealed to him the terms of the Stellovsky agreement and confessed that he was hopelessly entrapped. Just a month was left to satisfy his part of the bargain and nothing had yet been written. Even if he managed to write a first draft, it would be almost physically impossible to transcribe and correct it in time to meet the deadline. Milyukov, horrified at what might occur, advised him to find a stenographer and dictate the novel (*The Gambler*). Luckily, Milyukov had contact with a professor of stenography who had recently established the first such course for women in Russia. A day or two later, one of his star pupils, Anna Grigoryevna Snitkina, turned up in Dostoevsky's flat with newly sharpened pencils and a portfolio especially purchased for this epochal occasion, ready to assume her duties. This businesslike visit of the outwardly cool young lady proved to have a decisive effect on Dostoevsky's entire life.

[44] *PSS*, 28/Bk. 2: 164; July 8, 1866.
[45] Ibid., 167; July 19, 1866.

CHAPTER 33

From Novella to Novel

The main outlines of Dostoevsky's conception of *Crime and Punishment* were set early, but it was only as the work developed and expanded under his hands that it took on its multifaceted richness. In the splendid complete edition of Dostoevsky's writings published by the Academy of Sciences of the former Soviet Union, the editors have reassembled the disorderly confusion of the notebooks that Dostoevsky kept while working on *Crime and Punishment* and printed them in a sequence roughly corresponding to the various stages of composition. Dostoevsky, as we know, was in the habit of casually flipping open his notebooks and writing on the first blank space that presented itself to his pen, and since he also used the same pages to record all sorts of memorabilia, the extraction of this material was by no means a simple task. Thanks to these meritorious labors, however, we now possess a working draft of the story or novella as originally conceived, as well as two other versions of the text. These have been distinguished as the Wiesbaden version, the Petersburg version, and the final plan embodying the change from a first-person narrator to the indigenous variety of third-person form invented by Dostoevsky for his purposes.

—■—

The Wiesbaden version coincides roughly with the story that Dostoevsky described in his letter to Katkov, and a draft of six short chapters has been reconstructed from his notes. Written in the form of a diary or journal, the events it records correspond to what eventually became the conclusion of Part I and Chapters 1–6 of Part II in the definitive redaction. (The action of this part of the novel begins with Raskolnikov's return to his room after the murder, and it ends as he reads a newspaper account of the crime and encounters the police clerk Zametov.) What strikes one about the six Wiesbaden chapters is how much of the later text they already contain. Here are almost all of the secondary characters in their final form; details suggesting a bloody criminal deed are given and the terror of the narrator vividly conveyed; but it is not indisputable that the missing first chapter contained a depiction of the murder itself. It is possible that the story began *after* the crime, whose events would be gradually disclosed retrospectively through the narrator's account of its unbearable effects on his emotions.[1]

This first draft concentrates entirely on the moral-psychic reactions of the narrator after the murder—his panic, his terror, his desperate attempts to control his nerves and pretend to behave rationally while consumed by a raging fever and constantly at the mercy of his wildly agitated emotions. What continually haunts him, in moments of lucidity, is his total estrangement from his former self and from the entire universe of his accustomed thoughts and feelings. And it gradually dawns on him that he has been severed from all this by one stroke—the stroke that killed the repulsive pawnbroker and, by a horrible mischance, her long-suffering and entirely blameless sister Lizaveta, who, to make matters worse, is said to have been pregnant. This emphasis, of course, corresponds to the original motivation that Dostoevsky gave Katkov for the criminal's surrender: "The feelings of isolation and separation from humanity, which he felt right after completing the crime, has tortured him."

This theme dominates in the early draft and is expressed in three scenes of a growing order of magnitude. The first takes place at the police station, when the narrator responds to official insolence with anger, oblivious of the total change in his relations to others, and then, weighed down as he was by the terrible burden of the crime he had committed, gradually realizes that no longer could he morally assert a right to be treated with respect. This realization comes to the narrator only in hindsight, but a more instant recognition occurs when, after concealing the spoils of the crime, he decides to pay a visit to his friend, Razumikhin. As the narrator climbs the stairs, he feels a sensation that "if there is (now) for me on earth something (especially) hard (and impossible) then it is to talk and have relations . . . with other (people . . .). And (the consciousness of all that) was my instant of the most oppressive anguish for perhaps all that month, in which I went through so much endless torture" (7: 35–36). The words printed in parentheses are corrections and additions that Dostoevsky made in the various drafts of his text. These words indicate the moment at which the narrator realizes that even the simplest and most ordinary human relations have now become impossible for him, and Dostoevsky drew a circle around the paragraph to indicate its importance. The final epiphany of this experience occurs in a

---

[1] The question remains open, though the second hypothesis seems to me more plausible. It is difficult to imagine Dostoevsky beginning with an unmotivated murder. Gary Rosenshield, whose perceptive analysis of the techniques of narration is one of the best studies devoted to *Crime and Punishment*, writes that "the narrator's preoccupation with his present memory of the past perhaps indicates that *Crime and Punishment* was originally a psychological study of a criminal only after the murder." See Gary Rosenshield, *Crime and Punishment* (Lisse, 1978), 15, 17.

The lost first chapter was probably contained in a notebook that Dostoevsky mislaid. There is a reference to this missing notebook in *PSS*, 28/Bk. 2: 157; May 9, 1866.

sequence that begins when the narrator, quitting Razumikhin and walking through the busy streets on the way home, is lashed by the whip of a passing coachman whose path he is blocking. Just as in the police station, his first reaction is one of outraged pride, but he realizes almost at once how inappropriate such a response was in his present predicament. "The thought came to me immediately that it would have been a lot better (perhaps even good) if the carriage had crushed me (completely)" (7: 38).

Among the onlookers were a merchant's wife and her little daughter, who slip a twenty-kopek piece into the narrator's hand because "the blow had awakened their pity for me." Clutching the coin, the narrator walks toward the Neva in the direction of the Winter Palace while gazing at the cupola of St. Isaacs's Cathedral and "all that splendid panorama." As a student, he had walked by the same vista many times. Now, as he stands in the same place that he knew so well, "suddenly the same (painful) sensation which oppressed my chest at Razumikhin's half an hour ago, the same sensation oppressed my heart here." He realizes that "there was no reason for me (any longer) to stop here (or anywhere). . . . [A]ll those former sensations and interests and people were far away from me as if from another planet" (7: 39–40). As he leans over the railing of a canal, the narrator lets the twenty-kopek piece slip into the water, thus symbolizing his break with all these emotions and values of the past.

Although the effects of estrangement are clearly intended to dominate in the resolution of the action, they are reinforced by other episodes. One such is the narrator's half-dream, half-hallucination, kept almost unchanged in the novel, which reveals both his self-revulsion at the crime and his fear of pursuit. Lying in bed, he suddenly hears "a terrible cry" and opens his eyes; slowly he realizes that it is one of the police officials he has just met who is beating the landlady on the staircase. "I had never heard such unnatural sounds, such yelling, grinding of teeth, curses, and blows. . . . What is it all about, I thought, why (is he beating her), why? Fear like ice penetrated me to the core . . . (soon they will come for me (also) I thought). . . ." Imagining all this to be real, the narrator asks Nastasya about the frightening occurrence; but he is told that nothing of the sort had happened—it had all been a delusion, despite the narrator's conviction that he had been fully awake. "A yet greater tremor seized me," he writes, presumably at this evidence of his derangement. When Nastasya tells him "(that) is the blood in you crying out" (7: 41–43), she takes this bit of folk wisdom literally, while to the narrator the word "blood" immediately evokes the crime. Such an experience, added to his estrangement, was surely meant to provide further incentive for the narrator's eventual confession.

Why Dostoevsky abandoned this story can only remain a matter for speculation, but one possibility is that his protagonist began to develop beyond the boundaries in which he had first been conceived. All through the extant text, the narrator is crushed and overcome by the moral-psychic consequences of his murderous deed, but just as the manuscript breaks off, he begins to display other traits of character. Instead of fear and anguish, he now exhibits rage and hatred against all those who have been looking after him in his illness and decides to slip away from their oppressive care. The conversation about the murder at his bedside, he explains, "made me feel unbearable malice . . . and what is more remarkable still is that during these agonies, this terror, I never thought a single time with the slightest compassion about the murder I had committed" (7: 73). Here is a character entirely different from the one previously portrayed, and Dostoevsky may have stopped writing at this point because this figure had begun to evolve beyond his initial conception. In some notes for the immediate continuation of this version, he jots down: "Recovered. Cold fury, calculation. Why so much nerves?" (7: 76). This last phrase is obviously a scornful question of the narrator addressed to himself.

Once Dostoevsky had begun to see his character in this light, alternating between despair and "cold fury," it became increasingly difficult to imagine a purely internal motivation for his self-surrender, and this may have led Dostoevsky to fuse the story with his previous idea for the novel called *The Drunkards*. References to "Marmeladov's daughter" now appear in all the outlines of the action. "Like a prostitute. . . . The daughter helps the mother. Takes the money. Pity for the children" (7: 80). After the narrator has committed the crime, it is he who feels a need for pity, which he cannot imagine being offered except by a Sonya capable of loving and forgiving even her ignominious father. What is explicitly articulated in these notes will remain implicit, though perfectly discernible, in the final text and underlies Raskolnikov's irresistible impulse to turn to her with his confession.

As Sonya Marmeladova now becomes linked with the narrator's decision to give himself up, though, Dostoevsky has great difficulty imagining how this action will be motivated. One alternative envisages the narrator invoking a "picture of the golden age" and then asking: "But what right have I, a vile killer, to desire happiness for people and to dream of a golden age. I want to have that right. *And following this* (this chapter) he goes and gives himself up. He stops by only to say good-bye to her, then he bows down to the people and—confession" (7: 91). Such edifying resolutions, however, clashed with the manner in which the narrator had begun to evolve. His denigration of mankind as a whole, not only its more "useless" specimens, now begins to appear frequently. For example: "(The misfortunes of his father, mother). How nasty people are! Are they worth having me repent before them? No, no. I'm going to remain silent" (7: 82). Most important of all, Dostoevsky now links such misanthropy with the motif of power.

All these notes portray the character's own thoughts and feelings. In others, Dostoevsky sets down instructions for himself, and these suggest that he has begun to see how these two divergent aspects of his protagonist might be portrayed as more than a simple alteration. "N.B. *Important.* After the sickness, a kind of cruelty and complete justification of himself" (7: 78). There is a significant character shift after the murder and the resulting illness. Now an aspect of personality, previously hidden, unexpectedly emerges. Another note reveals all the weight that Dostoevsky attributed to this discovery. "So that there is then a *coup de maître*," he writes with pardonable pride. "At first there was danger, then fear and illness, and his whole character did not show itself, and then suddenly his (whole) character showed itself in its full demonic strength and all the reasons and motives for the crime become clear" (7: 90). The handling of the character is thus conceived not so much in terms of any deep-seated modification but rather as the bringing to light of potentialities always present but hitherto only lying dormant in the background.

———■———

The notebooks reveal how carefully Dostoevsky worked over every detail of his text, and how he always refused to sacrifice artistic integrity to editorial pressure; indeed, nowhere is this care more evident than in how Dostoevsky manipulates the coming to consciousness—in both Raskolnikov and the reader—of the true motive for Raskolnikov's crime. At first his crime appears to be the result of his Utilitarian logic, set in motion by his own economic straits, the desperate plight of his family, and a desire to aid others with the spoils of the murder. A good bit later, we learn about the article in which he has justified the right of "extraordinary people" to step over the moral law in order to bring benefits to humanity as a whole. In the confession scene with Sonya, however, Raskolnikov gives as his motive simply the desire to obtain power for himself alone, solely to test whether he is entitled to take his place among those superior individuals who possess the innate right to overstep the moral law. The notes we have been citing, as we shall show in the next chapter, suggest that the differing explanations offered by Raskolnikov represent different phases of the inner metamorphosis that results from his gradually dawning *grasp* of the full implications of what he has done. Not only does his horrified conscience continue to operate on the moral-psychological level, but he also comes to understand the inner contradictions in the ideas in which he has believed. As Dostoevsky writes in another note: "N.B. His moral development begins from the crime itself; the possibility of such questions arise which would not then have existed previously" (7: 140).

Whether the novel actually answers the questions that arise for Raskolnikov has often been doubted. Another note, entitled "the chief anatomy of the novel," is frequently cited to prove Dostoevsky's indecisiveness on this crucial question, but in my view it proves just the opposite: "After the illness, etc. It is absolutely necessary to establish the course of things firmly and clearly and to eliminate what is vague, that is, explain the whole murder one way or another, and make its character and relations clear." A marginal jotting, keyed to the word "murder," reads: "pride, personality, and insolence" (7: 141–142). Here we have the forces unleashed in Raskolnikov by the unholy amalgam then typical of Russian radical ideology—an altruistic desire to alleviate social injustice and suffering, thrown together with a supremely Bazarovian contempt for the masses. It is the danger of self-delusion and moral-psychic tragedy lurking in this perversely contradictory mixture that Dostoevsky was trying to reveal through Raskolnikov's fate.

Dostoevsky, as we have seen, speaks of Raskolnikov's character as suddenly exhibiting "its full demonic strength"; other references change this significantly to "satanical pride" (7: 149). Pisarev used exactly the same expression for Bazarov three years earlier in his article in *The Russian Word*, and though the notes are regrettably sparse with information about the ideological context within which Dostoevsky was working, his use of this phrase is far from accidental. It reveals that Dostoevsky's character was being created in relation to Pisarev's deification of the new *raznochinets* "hero of our time," and that the ideas attributed to Raskolnikov can be traced primarily to the famous article of the radical critic. Moreover, the course of radical ideology itself, evolving from the relative humanitarianism of *The Contemporary* (represented in Dostoevsky's novel by the ridiculous, obtuse, but good-hearted Lebezyatnikov) to the contemptuous elitism and worship of the superior individual exhibited by Pisarev and Zaitsev, duplicates precisely the mutation in Raskolnikov on which Dostoevsky was now basing the portrayal of his character. Psychology and ideology thus fuse together once again into the seamless unity that Dostoevsky called "idea-feelings," and his ability to intuit these syntheses of emotion and ideology constitutes much of his particular genius as a novelist.

There is a specific allusion to Pisarev's ideas in the early version of a speech by Luzhin, the unscrupulous businessman who wishes to marry Raskolnikov's sister, Dunya. In this note he is still called Chebalov, but his words are identical with those of the preening suitor in Part II, Chapter 5; and this homily, it should be noted, is recognized by Raskolnikov as expressing the identical pattern of ideas that had led him to the murder. "Chebalov says to Raskolnikov. *Tant que* I've put my affairs in good order, I am useful to others, and therefore, the more I am an egoist, the better it is for others. As for the old beliefs: you loved, you thought of others, and you let your own affairs go down the drain, and you ended up being a weight around the neck of your neighbors. It's simply a matter of arithmetic. No, you know, I like the realists of the new generation, the shoemaker and Pushkin; and although I do not agree with them in part, still the general tendency" (7: 151). This last, unfinished sentence unmistakably refers to Pisarev, who had launched the slogan of "Realism" as a social doctrine in 1864 and, following Bazarov, had resoundingly declared a shoemaker to be more useful than Pushkin. It was manifestly within this specific ideological framework that Dostoevsky was now conceiving the tormented course of Raskolnikov's career and interweaving these ideas with his psychology.

———■———

Crime and Punishment came to birth only when, in November 1865, Dostoevsky shifted from a first-person to a third-person narrator. This was the culmination of a long struggle whose vestiges can be traced all through the early stages of composition. Some of the problems of using the first person are already apparent from the earliest version, whose first chapter is supposedly written five days after the murder (committed on June 9). The narrator dates the beginning of his diary as June 14 because, as he explains, to have written anything earlier would have been impossible in view of his mental and emotional confusion. Indeed, Dostoevsky reminds himself that "in all these six chapters (the narrator) must write, speak, and appear to the reader in part as if not in possession of his senses" (7: 83).

Dostoevsky thus wished to convey the narrator's partial derangement while, at the same time, using him as a focus on the external world and portraying the reactions induced by his crime as the action proceeds. All this posed serious difficulties, and the manuscript version shows Dostoevsky's constant uncertainty about how to hold the balance between the narrator's psychic disarray and the needs of his story. This problem of time perspective bothered Dostoevsky from the very start, and he moves the second chapter back several more days, to June 16, in order to give his narrator more time to come to his senses; but the distance between past and present was still not great enough, and this led to an inevitable clash between the situation in which the narrator was immersed and his function as narrator. As Edward Wasiolek has pointed out, "Raskolnikov is supposed to be . . . fixed wholly on his determination to elude his imaginary pursuers. But the 'I' point of view forces him to provide his own interpretations, and, even worse, his own stylistic refinements. Every stylistic refinement wars against the realism of the dramatic action."[2] Moreover, there would be serious doubts about the verisimilitude of a narrator who presumably is in a state of semihysteria and yet is able to remember and analyze, to report long scenes as well as lengthy dialogues, and in general to function as a reliable observer. This problem was only made more acute when the Marmeladovs entered the picture and fragments of the drunkard's extensive monologues began to appear among the notes.

Dostoevsky was acutely aware of this issue, and the first expedient he thought of is indicated by a brief note: "The *story* ends and the *diary* begins" (7: 81).

---

[2] See *The Notebooks for Crime and Punishment*, ed. and trans. Edward Wasiolek (Chicago, 1967), 101. My citations of the notebooks are taken from this indispensable work, with some slight alterations.

Since no trace of such a dual form can be found, this idea was probably abandoned very quickly; but one understands how Dostoevsky's mind was working. He wished to separate a recital of events, set down by the narrator after they had been completed, from another account of the same events written by someone still caught in their flux. This would have eliminated the disturbing clash between one and the other so noticeable in the Wiesbaden version. The same purpose inspires the next alternative, the Petersburg version, which is entitled "On Trial" and whose author is now in the custody of the legal authorities.

In this text, the narrator begins: "(I was on trial and) I will tell everything. . . . I am writing this for myself, but let others and all my judges read it" (7: 96). This draft continues with Marmeladov's monologic recital of his woes (presented almost verbatim in the novel), and by this time the schema of events has been recast so that this scene clearly precedes the murder. Most important, though, the position of the narrator, sitting in jail and contemplating his errors, allows him both to respond and to reflect without unduly straining credibility. But even in this plan, the time gap between the termination of all the events and the composition of the narrative is very small (roughly a week), and Dostoevsky continued to remain uneasy. After all, the narrator can hardly be completely tranquil, for the trial has not yet taken place.

The notebooks thus contain a third possibility, which is attached to a near-definitive outline of the action concerning Raskolnikov during the first two-thirds of the novel. "A New Plan," Dostoevsky announces. "The Story of a Criminal. Eight years before (in order to keep it completely at a distance)!" (7: 144). The phrase in parentheses indicates just how preoccupied Dostoevsky was with this issue of narrative distance, and how clearly he saw all of the problems involved. In this new plan, the narrator would be writing after the conclusion of his prison term (eight years), and what was probably the subtitle would indicate the profound moral alteration induced by the passage of time: the narrator now calls himself a criminal, no longer maintaining that the murder could not be considered a "crime" at all. The narrator is now so far removed from his previous self that it would require only a short step to shift from an I-narrator to the third person.

This narrative shift, however, did not occur all at once, and Dostoevsky debates the reasons for it in pages that, lying in close proximity to those just cited, were probably written at about the same time. "If it is to be a confession," he muses, "then everything must be made overly clear to the *utter extreme*." The recognition of this necessity leads Dostoevsky to some second thoughts: "If a confession, then in parts it will not be chaste (*tselomudrenno*) and it will be difficult to imagine why it was written." The use of the term "chaste" (which can also be translated broadly as "proper") in this context probably refers to the question of why the narrator should have wished to engage in so painful an act of self-exposure. At this point, Dostoevsky comes to the conclusion that his narrative technique must be altered.[3]

"But the subject is like this. The story from oneself [the author], and not from *him* [the character]" (7: 148–149). By "subject" Dostoevsky may be thinking about his conception of a main character who, after the crime, reveals unexpected aspects of himself—aspects of which, previously, he had not been fully aware. If, in a first-person narration, "everything must be made clear *to the utter extreme*" at every instant, then it would be difficult to obtain such an effect of self-surprise; at best, the revelations could be referred to and explained, but they could hardly be presented with full dramatic force. Taken in conjunction with the problem of justifying his narrative, such considerations would explain why Dostoevsky, despite his desperate economic straits, could not resist making a fresh start and transferring to a third-person narrator.

But there still remained the question of exactly what kind of narrator this should be. Contemporary narratologists have long known that authorial narrators are not just loose, amorphous presences who know how to spin a yarn; they are, rather, "implied authors," with distinct profiles and attitudes that decisively shape the novelistic perspective. Dostoevsky was fully conscious of this important truth and tried to define exactly the stance that his authorial narrator would adopt. No such problem had arisen earlier because the narrator was the central character. Everything had been presented from his own point of view, which meant that, though guilty of a terrible crime, he would inevitably arouse a certain sympathy because of his altruistic impulses, his inner sufferings, and his final repentance. What sort of third-person narrator could play the same role in relation to the reader? As Dostoevsky pondered the choice between the first and third person, he wrote, "But from *the author*. Too much naïveté and frankness are needed." Why this should be so is hardly self-evident; but the context suggests that Dostoevsky may still have been thinking of some sort of confessional novel, which, even if cast in the third person, would involve the total identification of the narrator with the main protagonist. Such an assumption would help explain the emphasis of the next sentence, which insists on the separation of the author from the character: "It is necessary to assume *as author someone omniscient and faultless*, who holds up to the view of all one of the members of the new generation" (7: 149).

---

[3] L. M. Rosenblyum believes that Dostoevsky employs the term *tselomudrenno* to stress the impropriety of a first-person narrator depicting the murder in all its repulsive naturalistic crudity. It may also, in her view, apply to the *rapidity* with which Raskolnikov, as originally sketched, resolves the moral problem caused by the murder through his repentence. See Rosenblyum, *Tvorcheskie dnevniki* (Moscow, 1981), 272–273.

The narrator will thus be undertaking a specific historical task: to exhibit for scrutiny an example of the very latest Russian type, the successor to Bazarov and the other "new men" of Russian literature. But Dostoevsky may have felt that such a narrator would be too coolly detached, too "omniscient and faultless" to serve his purposes ("faultless" translates the Russian *ne pogreshayushim*, which literally means "sinless" and can be taken to imply an accusatory or condemnatory posture). He therefore alters his narrator, in another notation, merely to a "sort of invisible and omniscient being, who doesn't leave his hero for a moment, even with the words: 'all that was done completely by chance'" (7: 146). By attaching the narrator as closely as possible to the protagonist's point of view, Dostoevsky retains the advantages of I-narration, which automatically generates the effect of sympathy created by all inside views of a character; and he reminds himself to maintain such inside views, as far as possible, even when moving from the direct portrayal of consciousness into summary and report. At the same time, he retains the freedom of omniscience necessary to dramatize the process of Raskolnikov's self-discovery, to reveal the character gradually, to comment on him from the outside when this becomes necessary, and to leave him entirely when the plot-action widens out.

This narrative technique fuses the narrator very closely with the consciousness and point of view of the central character as well as other important figures (though without, as Mikhail Bakhtin was inclined to maintain, eliminating him entirely as a controlling perspective).[4] Dostoevsky had used a similar narrative approach earlier in *The Double*, and such a fusion was by no means unprecedented in the history of the novel (in Jane Austen, among others). But in *Crime and Punishment* this identification begins to approximate, through Dostoevsky's own use of time shifts of memory and his remarkable manipulation of temporal sequence, the experiments of Henry James, Joseph Conrad, and later stream-of-consciousness writers such as Virginia Woolf and James Joyce. Brilliantly original for its period, this technique gives us the gripping masterpiece we know, whose intricate construction and artistic sophistication can only cause us to wonder at the persistence of the legend that Dostoevsky was an untidy and negligent craftsman. Some light on this legend may be cast by the remark of E. M. de Vogüé, a novelist himself, who wrote of *Crime and Punishment* with some surprise in 1886 that "a word . . . one does not even notice, a small fact that takes up only a line, have their reverberations fifty pages later . . . [so that] the continuity becomes unintelligible if one skips a couple of pages."[5] This acute observation, which expresses all the disarray of a late nineteenth-century reader accustomed

---

[4] For a discussion of Bakhtin's views, see my essay "The Voices of Mikhail Bakhtin," in *Through the Russian Prism* (Princeton, NJ, 1990), 18–33.

[5] See E. M. de Vogüé, *Le roman Russe* (Paris, 1910), 253.

to the more orderly and linear types of expository narration, helps to account for the tenacity of such a critical misjudgment, but we have now begun to attain a more accurate appreciation of Dostoevsky's pathbreaking originality. Even so, *Crime and Punishment* still has not yet been read with sufficiently close attention to the interweaving of those "reverberations" on whose connections its meaning depends.

CHAPTER 34

Crime and Punishment

> This was the time, when, all things tending fast
> To depravation, speculative schemes—
> That promised to abstract the hopes of Man
> Out of his feelings, to be fixed thenceforth
> For ever in a purer element—
> Found ready welcome. Tempting region that
> For Zeal to enter and refresh herself,
> Where passions had the privilege to work,
> And never hear the sound of their own names.
>
> —William Wordsworth, *The Prelude*

Crime and Punishment (*Prestuplenie i nakazanie*) is the first of the truly great novels of Dostoevsky's mature period. The psychology of Raskolnikov is placed squarely at the center of the work and is carefully interwoven with the ideas ultimately responsible for his fatal transgression. Every other feature as well illuminates the agonizing dilemma in which Raskolnikov is caught, with its inextricable mixture of tormenting passions and lofty rationalizations. The main character is surrounded by others who serve as oblique reflectors of his inner conflicts, and even the subplots serve as implicit thematic commentary. The development of the plot-action is organized to guide the reader toward a proper grasp of the significance of Raskolnikov's crime. Every element of the book thus contributes to an enrichment of its theme and to a resolution of the deepest issues that are posed. At the center of the plot-action is the suspense created by Raskolnikov's inner oscillations and the duel between him and Porfiry Petrovich, but this must be placed in the context of all those "reverberations" generated by the novel's extraordinarily tight-knit ideological-thematic texture. No detail or event seems casual or irrelevant.

It is not surprising that the radicals refused to recognize themselves in his pages, since Dostoevsky portrayed Nihilist ideas not on the level at which they were ordinarily advocated, but rather as they were refashioned by his eschatological imagination and taken to their most extreme consequences. The aim of these ideas, as he knew, was altruistic and humanitarian, inspired by pity and compassion for human suffering. But these aims were to be achieved by suppressing entirely the spontaneous outflow of such feelings, relying on reason (understood in Chernyshevskian terms as Utilitarian calculation) to master all the contradictory and irrational potentialities of the human personality, and, in its latest variety of Bazarovism, encouraging the growth of a proto-Nietzschean egoism among an elite of superior individuals to whom the hopes for the future were to be entrusted.

Raskolnikov (from the Russian *raskolnik,* "dissenter") was created to exemplify all the potentially dangerous hazards contained in such an ideal, and the moral-psychological traits of his character incorporate this antinomy between instinctive kindness, sympathy, and pity, on the one hand, and on the other, a proud and idealistic egoism that has become perverted into a contemptuous disdain for the submissive herd. All the other major figures in the book are equally integrated with Raskolnikov's fluctuations between these two poles; each is a "quasi-double" who embodies, in a more sharply accentuated incarnation, one or another of the clashing oppositions within Raskolnikov's character and ideas. Bakhtin aptly remarks that each character Raskolnikov encounters becomes "for him instantly an embodied solution to his own personal question, a solution different from the one at which he himself had arrived; therefore every person touches a sore spot in him and assumes a firm role in his inner speech."[1] Such characters structure the novel not only through "inner speech" but more centrally through the unrolling sequence of encounters generated by the plot-action. These encounters, which present Raskolnikov with one or another aspect of himself, work to motivate that process of self-understanding so crucial for Dostoevsky's artistic purposes.

Crime and Punishment is focused on the solution of an enigma: the mystery of Raskolnikov's motivation. For Raskolnikov himself, as it turns out, discovers that he does not understand *why* he killed; or rather, he becomes aware that the moral purpose supposedly inspiring him cannot really explain his behavior. Dostoevsky thus internalizes and psychologizes the usual quest for the murderer in the detective story plot and transfers this quest to the character himself; it is now Raskolnikov who searches for *his own* motivation. This search provides a suspense that is similar to, though of course much deeper and more morally complex than, the conventional search for the criminal. To be sure, there is an investigating magistrate, Porfiry Petrovich, whose task it is to bring Raskolnikov to justice, but this purely legal function is subordinate to his role of spurring on the course of Raskolnikov's own self-questionings and self-comprehension.

---

[1] Mikhail Bakhtin, *Problems of Dostoevsky's Poetics,* trans. and ed. Caryl Emerson (Minneapolis, MN, 1984), 258.

Dostoevsky also brilliantly adapts another feature of the detective story. Such a narrative always contains clues, some pointing to the real criminal, others to perfectly innocent characters who are falsely suspected and are meant to mislead the reader temporarily. Since the central mystery is that of Raskolnikov's motivation, he uses such blunders to plant clues to *this* enigma that both guide and misguide the reader. The guiding ones, carefully woven into the background of the action from the very start (but so unobtrusively that they are easy to overlook, especially on first reading), point to what Raskolnikov will finally discover about himself—that he killed not for the altruistic-humanitarian motives he believed he was acting upon but solely because of a purely selfish need to test his own strength. The false clues, particularly prominent in Part I, are suggestions that Raskolnikov was acting in response to material, social, or purely psychopathic causes, but such a deterministic point of view is openly combated in the book itself.

These clues are false in the sense that they lead away from the true answer to the question of Raskolnikov's motivation, but the motivations they suggest are not false in any absolute sense. On the contrary, such imputed possibilities exert a strong pressure on Raskolnikov and add greatly to the sympathy he evokes in the reader. Clues of this kind should thus perhaps not be called false, but accessory or ancillary rather than primary; and their validity is constantly challenged both dramatically and, through such characters as Razumikhin, Zosimov, and Porfiry Petrovich, directly and discursively. Built into the narrative of *Crime and Punishment* is thus a view of how it should be read, a hermeneutic of its interpretation, which is an integral part of its anti-radical theme and incorporates Dostoevsky's oft-expressed belief in the importance of ideas and their power to influence human behavior.

———■———

Crime and Punishment begins *in media res*, two and one-half days before Raskolnikov commits the crime, and continues through a duration estimated to be approximately two weeks. Time in the novel, so far as it is felt through Raskolnikov's consciousness, contracts and expands freely according to the importance for him of the events being depicted. It thus seems to lack any objective dimension, and it is also manipulated freely to obtain thematic effects by what Ian Watt, writing about Conrad, has called "thematic apposition," that is, the juxtaposition of events occurring at different times in order to establish connections between them without explanatory authorial intrusion.[2] The objective chronology of events (the time sequence of what has occurred *before* it has been reshaped for the artistic purposes of the novel) plays a crucial part in illuminating the

[2] Ian Watt, *Conrad in the Nineteenth Century* (Berkeley and Los Angeles, 1979), 280.

mystery of Raskolnikov's motivation. It is this chronology that is gradually uncovered, with all its psychic-ideological implications, as the double time structure of the mystery plot (the time of the action in the present disclosing what
occurred in the past) proceeds on its way.

The famous opening section of *Crime and Punishment* is also a subtle construction whose various thematic strands it is important to disentangle. At the
center is the inner conflict of Raskolnikov, torn between his intention to commit a crime in the interests of humanity and the resistance of his moral conscience against the taking of human life. He is a sensitive young intellectual
whose fineness of sensibility is conveyed both through his instinctive impulses
of compassion for the suffering he sees all around him and through the intensity
of his self-revulsion at his own intentions. He has, when we first encounter him,
been brooding over the crime for six weeks, and though he lives in appalling
poverty, it is clear that he would not have thought of committing it for purely
selfish reasons. It is the fate of suffering humanity that concerns him, as revealed
in the tavern scene, where the Utilitarian-altruistic justification for the proposed
crime is clearly expressed for the first time.

Why not kill a wretched, rapacious, and "useless" old moneylender and employ the funds to alleviate the human misery so omnipresent in Raskolnikov's
world? This is the thought that was dawning in his mind when he enters the tavern and hears it uttered simultaneously by a student and a young officer. Dostoevsky does everything in his artistic powers to accentuate the squalor and
human wretchedness that stream past Raskolnikov's eyes or filter through his
sensibility, as he walks through the streets filled with pothouses, brothels, and
reeling drunks. His encounter with the hopeless drunkard Marmeladov, abject
and guilt-stricken at his own degradation, embodies for Raskolnikov everything
in the world that he finds intolerable, especially when Marmeladov explains to
all and sundry that he and the rest of his starving family are being kept alive by
the self-sacrifice of his prostitute daughter, Sonya. On the level of plot, Marmeladov thus seems only to strengthen Raskolnikov's desire to take action against
the horrifying misery that surrounds him, but on the level of ideological theme
Dostoevsky uses the encounter to uncover in advance both the heartlessness of
Raskolnikov's own convictions (not yet specifically introduced) and the alternative set of values to be posed against them.

When Marmeladov describes going to a moneylender for a loan he would
never repay, he understands that his failure to obtain one is in accord with
"modern" views. Should the moneylender give him the loan out of "compassion?" "But Mr. Lebezyatnikov, who keeps up with modern ideas, explained the
other day that compassion is forbidden nowadays by science itself, and this is
what is done in England, where there is political economy" (6: 14). Raskolnikov's
own reasoning is based on exactly the same Utilitarian notions of "political

economy," which exclude any feeling of compassion for the "useless" individual marked out as the sacrificial victim. By contrast, the ecstatic self-impaling alternative provided by Marmeladov before he collapses provides the starkest antithesis to the inhuman tenor of the ideas that Raskolnikov is dreaming of putting into practice. For here Marmeladov, in a mixture of freely altered citations from the Gospels, envisions Christ returning at the Last Judgment and pardoning even the "children of shame" like himself, because "not one of them believed himself worthy of this" (6: 21). It is certainly not accidental that Christ's all-forgiving love is opposed "by the wise ones and those of understanding" (this last word translates *razumnie*; the Russian word for "reason" is *razum*), whereby Dostoevsky ingeniously turns the Pharisees of the New Testament into precursors of the Russian radicals of the 1860s.

The symbolic weight of this Petersburg setting reinforces the social-humanitarian motivation that is the nominal justification for Raskolnikov's crime. This motivation is unforgettably expressed in the important tavern-scene with its conversation between the officer and the student playing billiards. Dostoevsky indicates here how widespread was the reasoning which they discuss to improve society by a humanitarian assassination. But Dostoevsky then increases the weight of this impersonal incitation ("One death, and a hundred lives in exchange—it's simple arithmetic") (6: 54) with a more intimate motive: the letter from Raskolnikov's mother. Here he learns about the desperate circumstances of his own family and his sister Dunya's decision to marry the tight-fisted and domineering lawyer Luzhin solely to help her adored brother. Dunya's resolve thus places Raskolnikov, as he realizes only too piercingly, in a comparably debasing (though outwardly more respectable) position as the drunken Marmeladov living off Sonya's earnings.

Dostoevsky's portrayal of the agonies of a conscience wrestling with itself, as Raskolnikov struggles to suppress his moral scruples and steel himself for murder, has no equal this side of *Macbeth*. His horrified recoil after the trial visit to the pawnbroker's flat, so as to spy out the ground in advance, is only the first of several reactions that increase in severity: "Oh God! how loathsome it all is. . . . And how could such an atrocious thing come into my head?" (6: 10). The unforgettable dream sequence in Chapter 5, which evokes a childhood recollection of the savagely sadistic beating and killing of a "useless" old mare by the drunken peasant Mikolka, epitomizes Raskolnikov's lacerating conflict. On the one side, there is the little boy who "loved that church, the old-fashioned icons for the most part without frames, and the old priest with his trembling head" (6: 46). This little boy, who still exists in the depths of Raskolnikov's psyche, furiously breaks away from his father's grasp, puts his arms around the head of the dead horse to kiss her lips and wounded eyes, and finally flies "in a frenzy with his little fists out at Mikolka" (6: 49). On the other, there is the grown Raskolnikov dreaming this dream, who now plans to behave exactly like Mikolka—and not in a drunken rage, but according to a carefully thought out, "rational" theory. The combat within Raskolnikov between these two aspects of himself is so rending that he wakes in a state of terror and self-loathing, believing (mistakenly) that he has at last conquered the obsessive temptation to kill.

The reader remains immersed in Raskolnikov's consciousness all through Part I and tends to identify with his point of view. But interwoven with the major episodes of Raskolnikov's inner struggle are background incidents whose purpose can only be to indicate that, in reality, Raskolnikov is purblind to the subconscious psychic-emotive forces that have been stirred up in his personality. In all such incidents, Raskolnikov behaves in a fashion that shows his emotions being mobilized *against* the feelings that inspire his Utilitarian-altruistic aims. Here, for example, we see a Raskolnikov who, just after springing to the aid of someone in distress, becomes a coldly unconcerned and contemptuous egoist in the next moment, indifferent to the misfortunes that had stirred his pity.

Egoism as an ingredient of Raskolnikov's character is indicated early in the "expression of profoundest disgust" that passes over his face as he walks through "the revolting misery" of the stinking streets (6: 43). For Dostoevsky, psychology and ideology were now inseparable, and each precipitous shift of behavior is correlated with some reference to radical doctrine. Just after his trial visit to the pawnbroker, reeling both with fever and self-disgust, he stops at the pothouse, where he meets Marmeladov and drinks a glass of beer. Instantly feeling better, he attributes his previous moral discomposure to lack of nourishment, and shrugs it off; Chernyshevsky had taught that morality was just a product of physiology.

Raskolnikov also has second thoughts about the kopeks he had charitably left with the Marmeladovs on his first visit, out of compassion for their misery. "What a stupid thing I have done," he reflects. "They have Sonya, and I need the money myself" (6: 25). This Utilitarian consideration checks the spontaneous outflow of pity, and with "a malignant laugh" he ponders on the infinite capacity of mankind to adapt itself to the most degrading circumstances. Much the same happens when, after calling the policeman to help the tipsy girl being followed by a lecherous fat "dandy," he unexpectedly turns away in disgust. Suddenly "something seemed to sting Raskolnikov; in an instant a complete revulsion of feeling came over him," and he swings to the other extreme: "Let them devour each other alive—what is it to me?," he mutters to himself (6: 42). What "stings" Raskolnikov is the bite of these Darwinian reflections, which view the triumph of the stronger as right and just and any help to the weaker as a violation of the laws of nature. This scene is then duplicated internally as Raskolnikov first imagines the girl's probable future of prostitution, venereal disease, and ruin at eighteen or nineteen, but then caustically dismisses this resurgence of pity because "a certain percentage, they tell us, must every year . . . go that way . . .

somewhere . . . to the devil, it must be, so as to freshen up the rest and leave them in peace" (6: 43).

Radical ideas, identical in their Utilitarian logic to those expressed in the tavern scene, thus continually act to reinforce the innate egoism of Raskolnikov's character and to turn him into a hater rather than a lover of his fellow humans. It is not only that his *ideas* run counter to the instinctive promptings of his moral-emotive sensibility; these ideas momentarily transform him into someone for whom moral conscience ceases to operate as part of his personality. Not that his moral aim is insincere, but in steeling himself to accomplish his purpose, we become aware, Raskolnikov must suppress in himself the very moral-emotive feelings from which this aim had originally sprung. What occurs in these scenes thus illustrates the manner in which Raskolnikov's ideas have been affecting his personality, and they cast an important light on what has been taking place within him emotively ever since he fell under their influence.

————■————

If we examine the objective chronology of the novel, disregarding for the moment the *artistic* manipulation of narrative structure, that is, the order in which this structure unfolds for the reader, we realize that radical notions began to influence Raskolnikov approximately six months before the events of the novel begin. It was then that he wrote his fateful article "On Crime," which recasts and extends Pisarev's reflections on Bazarov and divides people into two categories, the "ordinary" and the "extraordinary." The first group, the masses, docilely accepts whatever established order exists; the second, a small elite, is composed of individuals who "seek in various ways the destruction of the present for the sake of the better" (examples given are Newton and Kepler, Lycurgus, Solon, Muhammad, and Napoleon). Such "extraordinary" people invariably commit crimes, if judged by the old moral codes they are striving to replace, but because they work "for the sake of the better," their aim is ultimately the improvement of mankind's lot, and they are thus in the long run benefactors rather than destroyers. So that, Raskolnikov argued, "if such a one is forced for the sake of his idea to step over a corpse or wade through blood, he can find in himself, in his conscience, a sanction for wading through blood" (6: 199–200). Since writing that article, Raskolnikov had become fascinated with the majestic image of such a Napoleonic personality who, in the interests of a higher social good, believes that he possesses a moral right to kill.

Five months later, Raskolnikov makes his first visit to the pawnbroker, and then overhears the conversation in the tavern between the student and the young officer. This marks the moment of the appearance of his "strange idea" that murder can be sanctioned by conscience in the name of a higher social good. And looming behind the sudden birth of Raskolnikov's intention ("pecking at his brain like a chicken in the egg") are thus the long months of gestation during which he had dreamed of becoming such a Napoleonic personality and acquiring homicidal privileges (6: 53). His encounter with the pawnbroker simply concretized the possibility of applying this ambition, which had been germinating in his subconscious, to the local Petersburg conditions of his own life.

Dostoevsky's handling of his narrative, his mystery story technique of gradual disclosure, orchestrates the process of Raskolnikov's piecemeal self-discovery. Raskolnikov comes to understand how the temptation of incarnating a Napoleonic personality has run athwart of his supposedly unselfish purposes. The first allusion to Raskolnikov's article occurs during the tavern conversation. The narrator indicates the need for a Napoleonic personality to put into practice the ideas being discussed. For when the young officer objects that the injustice of the pawnbroker's existence is simply "nature," the student retorts vehemently, "we have to correct and direct nature, and but for that we should drown in a sea of prejudice. But for that there would never have been a single great man" (6: 54).

The notion of a "great man," who possesses the moral right to give a new meaning to "duty" and "conscience," is thus involved from the very first in Raskolnikov's "strange idea," and there is even an allusion to this grandiose ambition on the opening page, as Raskolnikov slips past his landlady's door, afraid of being confronted with his failure to pay the rent. "I want to attempt such a thing, and at the same time am frightened by such trifles. . . . Taking a new step, uttering their own word is what [men] fear most" (6: 6). Raskolnikov will later define his "extraordinary" people precisely by their ability to utter a "new word"; he is already placing the drably scruffy crime he intends to commit in such an exalted perspective.

Another more extended reference to the article is inserted as Raskolnikov frantically makes his final preparations for the killing. Long ago, we are told, he had been concerned about the "psychology of the criminal" (which is how the subject of his article is later described) and why run-of-the-mill lawbreakers were invariably overcome by "a failure of reason and willpower" just before committing their offense. Raskolnikov was convinced that "his reason and will would remain unimpaired at the time of carrying out his design, for the simple reason that his design was 'not a crime'" (6: 58–59). This reasoning is manifestly contained in Raskolnikov's article, whose "extraordinary" people did not commit "crimes" precisely because they had a *moral right* to disregard existing laws; "ordinary" criminals were perturbed by conscience and thus gave themselves away. Raskolnikov's belief that he would be immune to such agitations indicates his long-held self-classification as one of the "extraordinary" elite.

Raskolnikov is thus shown falling more and more into the grip of his monomania, and this means into the grip of his desire to prove to *himself* that he truly belongs to the "extraordinary" category. At the same time, he remains unaware of the deadly dialectic taking place in his personality, which requires him to muster a pitiless egoism in order to bring about a humanitarian and morally beneficent end. This lack of awareness is of course essential for Dostoevsky's artistic strategy, and it is emphasized by the manner in which Raskolnikov's inner struggle is finally resolved. Just at the moment when, after the mare-killing dream, Raskolnikov believes that his conscience has won and that he has at last shaken off "that spell, that sorcery, that fascination, that obsession" (6: 50) (the choice of words indicates to what extent he felt in the power of a subliminal psychic compulsion), he accidentally overhears a conversation revealing that his intended victim, Alyona Ivanovna, who lives with her younger sister Lizaveta, will be alone at a certain hour the next day. On learning of this miraculous opportunity, Raskolnikov "felt suddenly in his whole being that he had no more freedom of thought, no will. . . . It was as if a part of his clothing had been caught in the cogs of a machine and he was being dragged into it" (6: 52, 58). Fate thus takes a hand, but it is fate acting on a pathological psychic predisposition to kill conditioned by ideological self-intoxication.

The thematic function of this surrender of Raskolnikov to the grip of fatality is to obviate any possibility that Raskolnikov will be understood to have acted on the basis of a conscious, willed, rational decision. Rather, he is controlled by the psychic forces released through the struggle to overcome the moral resistance of his conscience. Raskolnikov is thus portrayed as being governed by compulsions he does not understand (though the reader has been afforded a glimpse of what they amount to in *practice*), and whose true meaning it will take him the remainder of the book to unravel. Moreover, the gap between Raskolnikov's self-deception and the perspective of the reader is further widened by Dostoevsky's masterly manipulation of time sequence in the chapter just preceding the murder.

The all-important tavern scene is placed at Chapter 6 of the narrative even though this event occurred six weeks earlier in the objective chronology. The reader thus receives the strongest impression of the enormous gap between Raskolnikov's nominally humanitarian-altruistic aim, which has just been enunciated for the first time, and the blood-soaked horror that will be depicted a few pages later. The discrepancy between abstract idea and concrete human reality is then reinforced by another time shift that soon follows, which refers to matters antedating the murder even farther back in the chronology—six months instead of six weeks. For an intercalation contains the references already mentioned in Raskolnikov's article, on the basis of which he believes in his own invulnerability to "irrational" agitations because, as the narrator rather mockingly notes, "as regards the moral question . . . his analysis was now complete; his casuistry had become as sharp as a razor, and he could not find any conscious objections in himself" (6: 58). Both his original theory and its Petersburg embodiment are thus brought into close "thematic apposition" to the crime itself.

These time shifts create a profound effect of dramatic irony that works both backward and forward in the text. All through the past six weeks, it becomes clear, Raskolnikov himself had been prey to the symptoms of the "ordinary" criminal, assailed by the same "eclipse of reason and failure of willpower . . . that reached [its] highest point just before the perpetration of the crime" (6: 58). His high fever augments the "failure of willpower" to which he had believed himself immune. The extent to which he had been self-deluded in the past thus becomes manifest, and since he has by no means succeeded in vanquishing his "ordinary" moral conscience, he will obviously not succeed either in attaining the nerveless self-mastery that theoretically flows from his doctrine.

The dramatic irony employed in this chapter receives sensational confirmation in the murder scene, which shocked Dostoevsky's contemporaries by the crudity and unsparing realism of its depiction. Nothing goes according to the few plans made in advance, and the unexpected necessity of also killing the meek and good-hearted Lizaveta glaringly illustrates the contingency of human reality that Raskolnikov had imagined he could so easily dominate. He acts in a state of terrorized panic, though behaving with the cunning and seeming consequentiality of a monomaniac. But there is no doubt that Raskolnikov's reasoning faculties were in complete abeyance. Only at the last moment, after killing Lizaveta, does he realize that he had failed to latch the door!

In most of this brutal murder scene, the narrator remains close to Raskolnikov's point of view and conveys the almost hypnotic nature of his behavior. But he notes at one point that "fear gained more and more mastery over him," and adds that Raskolnikov would have given himself up if he could have realized all the "hopelessness" and "hideousness" of his position. Not from fear, however, "but from the simple horror and loathing of what he had done. This feeling of loathing especially surged up in him and grew stronger every minute" (6: 65). Once more Raskolnikov's moral conscience rises up in revolt, but he is no longer able to suppress it, as he had in the past, by the casuistry of his Utilitarian logic; the crime itself is what this logic has brought him to in reality. What emerges instead is the rampant egoism justified by such logic, and now fully released in his monomania. As the two men who had come to visit Alyona Ivanovna rattle at the locked door behind which Raskolnikov stands, axe in hand, he was "tempted to swear at them, to jeer at them, while they could not open the door!" (6: 68).

This moment behind the door, when Raskolnikov's egoism reaches a self-destructive pitch of hatred for and defiance of everyone, will be used again as a flashback, and becomes a leitmotif. It represents all those emotive forces that, stirred up by his theory and then unleashed in the crime, have now become detached from their previous moral mooring. The two antithetical parts of Raskolnikov's personality, held together earlier by the razor-sharp dialectic of his casuistry, had persuaded him that it was possible to reconcile murder and morality. No longer is such a belief tenable, and he will continue to fluctuate between

these two poles for the remainder of the book, with only the faint glimpse of a possible resolution at the end.

———■———

Raskolnikov's point of view and that of the reader do not coincide in Part I—or at least were not meant to coincide. And while readers may not be able to detach themselves sufficiently from Raskolnikov to pick up all the foreshadowings, they nonetheless cannot avoid receiving the stunning impact of the discrepancy between events and his declared aims and expectations. In Part II of the novel, which runs from the immediate aftermath of the crime to the arrival of Raskolnikov's family in Petersburg, Dostoevsky will begin to close the gap between Raskolnikov's awareness and that already imparted to the reader by the narrator.

Most important in the first two chapters of Part II is what occurs when, summoned to the police station, Raskolnikov suddenly realizes that his entire relation to the normal moral-social world has irremediably changed. "A gloomy sensation of agonizing everlasting solitude and estrangement took conscious form in his soul . . . he felt clearly that . . . he could never appeal to these people . . . even if they had been his own brothers and sisters" (6: 81–82). He feels an overwhelming impulse to confess to the humane police officer Nikodim Fomich, and this involuntary need to overcome his glacial sense of alienation, which will continue to war with his vanity and egoistic pride, is what will soon cause him to seek the solace of human companionship through Sonya. But when Nikodim Fomich plunges into a conversation with his subordinate, the explosive but easily pacified Lieutenant Gunpowder, about the murder of Alyona Ivanovna, Raskolnikov collapses into a dead faint.

Raskolnikov will gradually learn about his own behavior by overhearing Nikodim Fomich's conversation with his subordinate concerning the two men who had come to visit the pawnbroker and who had been arrested as suspects. The events at the police station lead Raskolnikov to begin the process of exploring his own motivation, which the crime has shown him could hardly be the one he had previously imagined. "If really all this was done *consciously* [*soznatel'no*]," he thinks, "and not like a fool, if you really had a definite and unwavering goal, how is it that you never even looked at the purse, and have no idea of what you gained, or why you shouldered all this torment and consciously embarked on such a base, vile, and ignoble business?" (6: 86). And this query is the first step toward undermining the humanitarian-altruistic rationale given so much prominence in the tavern scene. What sweeps over Raskolnikov in response to this uncertainty is "a new and irresistible sensation of boundless, almost physical repulsion for everything around him. . . . He loathed everyone he met" (6: 87). This "irresistible sensation" contains much of the answer he was seeking, though he was not yet conscious of what it signified.

The entirely new moral-psychic situation in which Raskolnikov finds himself is then underlined by the visit to his only friend, the warmhearted, generous, ebullient Razumikhin. Their social-economic circumstances were exactly the same, but Razumikhin "was straining every nerve to improve his circumstances in order to continue his studies" (6: 44). Despite Razumikhin's lively banter and offer of aid to a friend who, as he quickly realizes, is "delirious," the visit only increases Raskolnikov's tormenting sense of irremediable solitude. He now feels even more alienated from the "magnificent spectacle" of Petersburg than before (6: 90). He unthinkingly throws into a canal the twenty-kopek piece given him as charity by a little girl "in Christ's name," indicating how little he can identify himself any longer with the compassionate aims expressed in the tavern scene. What remains is the raw terror of the dream that follows, when he imagines hearing the volatile Lieutenant Gunpowder mercilessly beating the landlady on the staircase.

At this juncture, there is a hiatus of three days, during which Raskolnikov lies in a semiconscious delirium, only confusedly aware of his surroundings and awakening once the peak of his illness has passed. The climax of this sequence is the visit of Peter Petrovich Luzhin—the fiancé whom Dunya had accepted only after a sleepless night spent praying on her knees fervently before an icon—to Raskolnikov's dingy and squalid room. Luzhin himself is a self-made man, a lawyer with a high rank in the Civil Service, filled with an overwhelming sense of his own importance. He is also a petty tyrant who looks forward to bending the proud Dunya to his will. Luzhin nonetheless likes to consider himself as "sharing the convictions of the younger generation" (6: 31). Raskolnikov thus finds himself confronted with someone who is not only personally hateful but who also reveals the moral dubiousness of exactly the same Utilitarian logic to which he had become so ruinously committed.

The elegantly attired Luzhin tries to impress the ragged but insouciant Razumikhin, distressingly unawed by the visitor's imposing hauteur, by declaring his sympathy with "the younger generation" and his approval of "the new, valuable ideas . . . circulating instead of the old dreamy and bookish ones." Progress, he declares sententiously, is being made "in the name of science and economic truth." For example, in the past the ideal of "love thy neighbor" had been accepted, and the chief result was that "it came to tearing my coat in half to share with my neighbor and we both were left half-naked." Now, on the contrary, science had shown that "everything in the world rests on self-interest," and "therefore in acquiring wealth solely and exclusively for myself, I am acquiring, so to speak, for all, and helping to bring to pass my neighbor's getting a little more than a coat; and that not from private, isolated liberality, but as a consequence of the general advance" (6: 115–116). One understands why the radicals resented seeing their ideas placed in the mouth of so unsavory a character as Luzhin, but

Dostoevsky accurately captures their reliance on Utilitarian egoism, their aversion to private charity (as demeaning to the receiver), and their rejection of the Christian morality of love and self-sacrifice (in theory if not in practice). Luzhin is so evidently hypocritical in pretending to be concerned about "my neighbor" that Raskolnikov is forced to confront the possibility that his own cherished beliefs could also have concealed such purely self-serving ends.

Luzhin's unctuousness is interwoven with a renewed discussion of the crime, during which Raskolnikov learns even more humiliating details about his blunders and his blindness. Under the pressure of the emotions produced by such glimpses of his failure, he finally intervenes in the conversation about the increase of crime among the educated class in particular. When Luzhin, seeking for an explanation, begins to speak of "morality . . . and so to speak principles," Raskolnikov cuts him short: "But why do you worry about it. . . . It's in accordance with your theory—carry out logically the theory you were advocating just now and it follows that people may be slaughtered" (6: 118). Raskolnikov himself, of course, had carried out the theory logically, and when he implicitly recognizes himself in Luzhin's words, he indicates his awareness that the ideas he had adopted so pure-heartedly could equally well (and even better) justify arrant selfishness, a greedy desire for personal gain, and a bent for sadistic domination. This encounter with Luzhin finally breaks the thread linking Raskolnikov's Utilitarian reasoning with its supposedly altruistic-humanitarian goals.

Raskolnikov plunges into the streets with a frenzied, inchoate feeling "that all *this* must be ended today . . . he *would not go on living like that*" (6: 120–121). A series of street encounters duplicate those of Part I but reveal the change in Raskolnikov, his need to seek relief from the solitude of his guilt and reestablish links with humanity. He pauses to listen to a street singer, and he gives her a five-kopek piece with no Utilitarian afterthoughts. The climax of this sequence is the meeting with the prostitute Duclida, who asks for six kopeks without offering him her favors in return. Another prostitute rebukes her for descending to beggary, and this grotesque assertion of self-respect recalls to Raskolnikov a book (Hugo's *Notre Dame de Paris*) in which a condemned man imagines he would prefer to live on a small ledge for a thousand years rather than die within a few hours. "No matter how—only to live! . . . What scoundrels men are!" (6: 123), he thinks, in words similar to his reaction on leaving the Marmeladovs and regretting his instinctive charity. But he is no longer the same person, and such a reaction is transformed into an all-embracing pity for humankind and a twinge of guilt: "'And he is a scoundrel who for this reason calls them scoundrels'—he added a moment later" (6: 123).

Raskolnikov's sensibility has thus now thrown off the grip of the Utilitarian dialectic, which had transformed all his impulses of compassion into an attitude of contempt. At the same time, the egoistic component of Raskolnikov's character is no longer held in check by the mirage of serving any moral cause; it operates solely to aid his self-defense and becomes a naked defiance of the law. This is the moment in the book when Dostoevsky brings into play his *coup de maître*—the master stroke of which he had spoken in his notes—and begins to develop Raskolnikov's "satanical pride" (7: 149), kept subordinate up to this point by his poverty, the initial accentuation of his predominantly altruistic purposes, and the desperate situation of his family: "And then suddenly his character showed itself in its full demonic strength, and all the reasons and motives for the crime become clear" (7: 90).

In the café, ironically called the "Palais de Cristal," where Raskolnikov goes to consult the newspapers in his quest for self-knowledge, he stumbles upon the mistrustful police clerk Zametov, who suspects him, and this menace drives him into a towering rage. He cannot resist taunting and baiting Zametov in words calculated to fuel his suspicions even further. For Raskolnikov, his dangerous game with Zametov allows him to relive the crime in miniature. The narrator compares the challenge to Zametov and the murder by describing Raskolnikov as breaking "into nervous laughter. . . . And in a flash he remembered . . . when he had stood behind a door with an axe, while the bolt rattled, and outside the door people were swearing and trying to force a way in, and he was suddenly filled with a desire to shriek at them, and laugh, laugh, laugh" (6: 126). This momentary flashback starkly illuminates the fierce and self-absorbed egoism that had driven Raskolnikov and lights up the true nature of his motivation.

Raskolnikov, however, can sustain such a bellicose attitude only when confronted by a concrete threat to his freedom. Left to himself, and painfully aware of his self-deception, he plunges back into total despair. Overcome by the same sense of icy desolation that had assailed him in the police station, he decides to settle for "the square yard of space," the life of ignominy he had refused to condemn a little while before. Turning his steps toward the police station to confess, he realizes he is passing the tenement in which the crime took place, and his eerily somnambulistic return to the scene of the murder climaxes his compelling need to play detective toward the confused tangle of his own deed. He is "terribly annoyed" that the old wallpaper is being replaced and that "everything was so altered." It is as if he wished to reverse time, or at least arrest its flow, and return to the beginning of what had gone so badly awry (6: 133). His odd behavior arouses suspicion, and he challenges those who question him to come with him to the police station. Finally, he sets off alone for the last step, but while still hesitating, in the midst of a world in which "all was dead and silent like the stones on which he walked, dead to him, to him alone" (6: 135), another masterly plot twist occurs, which again reverses the course of the action. His attention is caught by the commotion of an accident, and he rushes toward it to find the dying Marmeladov crushed by the wheels of a passing carriage.

Raskolnikov leaps to Marmeladov's aid and suddenly finds himself thrust into a world in which his aching need to establish bonds of emotive solidarity can be amply gratified. His crime, intended to benefit humanity, had cut him off from others by an invisible wall, but now he pours all his altruism, unhindered by Utilitarian reconsiderations, into easing the terrible lot of the Marmeladovs, whose misery Dostoevsky depicts with laconic, almost unbearable power. A sharp contrast is also drawn between Raskolnikov's impulse to give them his last penny and the pious platitudes of the priest summoned to perform the rites for the dying, whose ritually consoling words drive the half-crazed and tubercular Katerina Ivanovna into a despairing rage. The gratitude and affection lavished upon Raskolnikov open the floodgates of all his previously suppressed Christian sentiments, and he asks little Polechka, Sonya's half-sister, to "pray for me sometimes: 'and Thy servant, Rodion'—just that" (6: 147). The need for absolution, which he will soon seek through Sonya, is already evident here. This direct release of Raskolnikov's pent-up Christian emotions leads to a remarkable recovery from hopelessness, and he is filled with "a strange, new feeling of boundlessly full and powerful life—a feeling which might be compared with that of a man condemned to death and unexpectedly reprieved" (6: 146). The arrival in Petersburg of Raskolnikov's mother and sister, however, plunges him back into the agonizing awareness that his horrible secret has cut him off from those he loves the most.

■

Dostoevsky now, as a preparation for the full disclosure of the article "On Crime," begins to fill in those aspects of Raskolnikov's past that help to illuminate his self-identification with the "extraordinary" people. His mother, going farther back into the pre-radical past, recalls his plan to marry the landlady's daughter, despite, she says, "my tears, my entreaties, my illness, my possibly death from grief, from poverty" (6: 166). His concern for his family had thus always been subordinate to an immutable egoism of personal self-affirmation. This egoism had previously been combined with a whole-souled acceptance of Christian values quite the opposite of callous inhumanity; still, the innate extremism of Raskolnikov's temperament had been evident even in this commitment. The girl, Razumikhin remarks with some perplexity, was "positively ugly . . . and such an invalid . . . and strange" (6: 166). Raskolnikov explains that "'she was fond of giving alms to the poor, and was always dreaming of a nunnery. . . . I believe I would have liked her better still if she had been lame or a hunchback' (he smiled dreamily)" (6: 177). These disturbing words indicate a desire to embrace what others would find repellent, and suggest a desire for self-sacrifice bordering on martyrdom; it is as if Raskolnikov looked on his proposed marriage as some sort of self-exalting as well as morally heroic deed. His conversion to radicalism involved no change in the moral aims of these ambitions and supplied a similar outlet for his egoism, but it inspired a heroism in terms of Utilitarian principles. Six months after burying his fiancée, with whom, as he tells Dunya, he had argued about his new convictions, he wrote the article expressing this new self-image.

It is against this background that Raskolnikov comes for his first meeting with Porfiry Petrovich. Porfiry is highly cultivated, and, since he has come across Raskolnikov's article and made inquiries about the author, he has been closely following the movement of contemporary ideas. He thus has an understanding of Raskolnikov's cast of mind, which, taken along with everything he has learned from Zametov and others, convinces him that Raskolnikov is the murderer. Even though Razumikhin considers Porfiry to be employing the "old, material method" of criminal investigation, the very opposite is true: he understands that the cause of Raskolnikov's crime is ultimately "psychological" (that is, ideological) and cannot be understood in "material" terms.

The impossibility of amalgamating the qualms of Christian conscience with Raskolnikov's previous image of "greatness" is brought to the fore when, already upset by Porfiry's questioning, Raskolnikov is suddenly called a "murderer" by a workman in the street. This blunt accusation strikes the final blow to his tottering self-control. The thoughts that now race through his mind in a seemingly disconnected torrent climax the process of self-confrontation that has been occurring all along, and Raskolnikov's eyes are finally opened to the tragic antinomy on which he has become impaled—not only how far he had fallen short of his expectations, but even more, how foolish it had been for him to believe he could succeed when he continued to cling to the *moral purpose* of his intended deed. True great men like Napoleon cared not a whit about any such purpose, and acted solely out of a supreme conviction in their right to do whatever they pleased. "No, these men are not made so. The real *Master* to whom all is permitted storms Toulon, carries out a massacre in Paris, *forgets* an army in Egypt, *wastes* half a million men in the Moscow expedition and gets off with a jest at Vilna. And altars are set up to him after his death, and so *all* is permitted. No, such people it seems are not of flesh but of bronze!" (6: 211).

Raskolnikov now calls himself a "louse" because of the "aesthetic" incongruity between the pettiness of his own deed ("a vile, withered old woman, a money-lender") and the grandeur of the figure whose name and destiny had hung before him like a lodestar ("Napoleon, the pyramids, Waterloo"). But it is the realization that "I have been importuning Providence for a whole month, calling on it to witness that it was not for my own, so to speak, flesh and lust that I proposed to act but for a noble and worthy end"—it is *this* incongruity that makes him exclaim: "I killed a principle, but as for surmounting the barriers, I did not do that, I remained on this side" (6: 211). Raskolnikov had killed the "principle" of the old moral law against taking human life, but this very purpose and choice of victim showed that he had not been able "to surmount the barriers." He had attached a moral aim to his desire to achieve "greatness"; he had remained a man of flesh, who had failed to become one of bronze.

But Raskolnikov—even though he exclaims to himself, "Ah, how I hate the old woman now! I feel I should kill her again if she came to life!"—cannot sustain this hostility for very long, and his thoughts modulate into recollections of Lizaveta and Sonya ("poor, gentle things, with gentle eyes"). His inner struggle then terminates in the dream that ends Part III, in which he unsuccessfully tries to rid himself of the ghost of his victim. Fearfully reliving the moment of the murder, he tries to kill Alyona Ivanovna again, but finds her impervious to his blows. Huddled in a chair, with her head drooping and face concealed, she was "overcome with noiseless laughter" and simply "shook with mirth" (6: 213) as he redoubled his blows. He had murdered her in the flesh but not in his spirit, and she continues to haunt his conscience. He had failed to become one of the "great men" who had gone beyond good and evil altogether.

——■——

Svidrigailov emerges from the shadows at the beginning of Part IV, when Raskolnikov has finally glimpsed the incongruity of attempting to place an all-powerful egoism into the service of moral ends. Materializing in Raskolnikov's room almost as if part of the dream repetition of the murder, Svidrigailov seems to be an apparition; and Raskolnikov asks Razumikhin whether the latter had actually *seen* Svidrigailov in the flesh. Nothing similar had occurred in the case of Luzhin, and Svidrigailov's emergence from, as it were, Raskolnikov's subconscious suggests that he stems from a more deeply rooted level of Raskolnikov's personality than Luzhin, who embodies his ideas. Svidrigailov mirrors the elemental thrust of that egoism, concentrated in Raskolnikov's monomania, which had ultimately led to the murders. He now confronts Raskolnikov as someone who has *accepted* the thoroughgoing egoistic amorality that, as Raskolnikov now has begun to realize, he had unwittingly been striving to incarnate himself.

One of Dostoevsky's most strangely appealing characters, a sort of monster à la Quasimodo longing for redemption to normalcy, Svidrigailov's Byronic world-weariness signifies a certain spiritual depth, and the contradictions of his personality, swinging between the blackest evil and the most benevolent good, perhaps can best be understood in Byronic terms. Is he not similar to such a figure as Byron's Lara, "who at last confounded good and ill," and whose supreme indifference to their distinction made him equally capable of both? One can well say of Svidrigailov,

Too high for common selfishness, he could
At times resign his own for other's good,

But not in pity, not because he ought,
But in some strange perversity of thought,
That sway'd him onward with a secret pride
To do what few or more would do beside;
And thus some impulse would, in tempting time,
Mislead his spirit equally to crime.[3]

Svidrigailov thus embodies the same mixture of moral-psychic opposites as Raskolnikov, but arranged in a different order of dominance. What rules within the
older man is the conscious acceptance of an unrestrained egoism acting solely
in the pursuit of personal and sensual pleasure, but his enjoyments are tarnished
by self-disgust. What dominates in Raskolnikov are the pangs and power of
conscience even in the midst of a fiercely egoistic struggle to maintain his
freedom.

Svidrigailov arrives in Petersburg in hot pursuit of Dunya, but though he
pretends to be driven only by the pleasure of sensual passion, his desire for
Dunya has now become a quest for personal salvation. The plot parallelism with
Raskolnikov-Sonya is obvious and could hardly have been carried through if
Svidrigailov had been a less complex character. The disabling workings of *his*
self-disgust may be gathered from his picture of eternity as a little room, "something like a bathhouse in the country, black with soot, with spiders in every corner. . . . I sometimes imagine it like that, you know," he confesses to Raskolnikov. When the latter, "with a feeling of anguish," protests that he might
imagine something "juster and more comforting than that," Svidrigailov only
responds that perhaps this would be just, "and, do you know, it's what I would
certainly have made it deliberately!" (6: 221). For all his assumed moral insensibility, Svidrigailov is unable to escape a sense of self-revulsion, which he wishes
to extend to humanity as a whole.

Dostoevsky, however, reserves the full deployment of the Raskolnikov-
Svidrigailov relation for a later thematic stage. As yet, Raskolnikov sees himself
as someone who, like Sonya, has taken on the burden of suffering to aid a humanity trapped in helpless misery, and he thus tries to bring her round to regarding *his* crime as identical with *her* pathetic infringement of conventional
morality. Dostoevsky manages to capture Sonya's innocence in the midst of degradation, her gaucherie and burning purity of religious faith. What she offers to
Raskolnikov is an unsullied image of the self-sacrificing Christian love that had
once also stirred him to his depths. She is the *existential reality* of that love for
suffering mankind which, when amalgamated with the Utilitarian reason of
radical ideology, had become perverted into the monstrosities of his crime.

In the scenes between the two, Raskolnikov reveals his desire to embellish his

[3] Lord Byron, *Complete Poetical Works* (Cambridge, MA, 1905), 371.

own deed with the halo of Christian self-sacrifice. This is what makes him so susceptible to "the sort of *insatiable* compassion . . . reflected in every feature of her face"; it is what throws him on his knees to kiss her feet "because of your great suffering" (6: 243, 246). But even as he yields in this way to her example, the unalloyed faith of Sonya does not fail to arouse his educated scorn. When he learns that she and his victim Lizaveta had met to read the New Testament together, he calls them *yurodivy* (holy fools, usually considered simple-minded, if not demented), but finds himself irresistibly drawn to their unshakable faith in God's ultimate goodness—the faith that, against all reason, miraculously supports Sonya in the midst of vice as she struggles to help the deranged Katerina Ivanovna and the starving children.

Under the effect of this emotion, he commands Sonya to read from the copy of the New Testament given her by Lizaveta. He wishes to hear the passage from the Gospel of Saint John narrating the resurrection of Lazarus, which symbolically holds out the possibility of his own moral resurrection. In pages that have evoked a mountain of commentary, Dostoevsky depicts, with the bleakly reverential simplicity of a Rembrandt etching, "the candle end [that] had long since burnt low in the twisted candlestick, dimly lighting the poverty-stricken room and the murderer and the harlot [*bludnitsa*], who had come together so strangely to read the eternal book" (6: 251–252). Dostoevsky uses the Church Slavonic word *bludnitsa*, rather than a more colloquial one, and thus associates Sonya with Mary Magdalene as Raskolnikov blends with Lazarus. Nowhere perhaps do we come closer to Dostoevsky's own tortuously anguished relation to religious faith than in the mixture of involuntary awe and self-conscious skepticism with which Raskolnikov reacts to Sonya. But the moment he shakes off the emotions stirred by the Gospel reading, the clash of values between the two recommences.

Rakolnikov appeals to Sonya because it is only she to whom he can reveal the truth—because she too is a flagrant sinner and has become an outcast in the eyes of society. It is she, and not his virtuous family, who might be able to accept him without shock and horror, and even sympathize with his purpose, if not its results. "You too have stepped over the barriers . . . you were able to overstep!" he says to Sonya (6: 252). But exactly the opposite is true: Raskolnikov had wished to "step over" but had been unable to because he had been undermined by the remains of his moral conscience. Sonya had not wished to "step over" at all, and had violated the moral law against her will and desire. For all her debasement, Sonya is not inwardly torn because her sin has been redeemed by the purity of her *self*-sacrifice. It is this difference that Raskolnikov desperately tries to wipe away when he says, with flagrant sophistry, "you have laid hands on yourself, you destroyed a life . . . *your own* (it's all the same)!" On the one side, there is the ethic of Christian *agape*, the total, immediate, and unconditional sacrifice of self that is the law of Sonya's being (and Dostoevsky's own highest value); on the other, there is Raskolnikov's rational Utilitarian ethic, which justifies the sacrifice of *others* for the sake of a greater social good.[4]

Raskolnikov's attitude in this scene, in which he asks Sonya to link her fate with his ("so we must go together, by the same path!"), is an inconsistent admixture reflecting a new phase of his moral-psychic struggle. After undermining Sonya's hope that God will protect little Polechka from Sonya's fate ("'but, perhaps, there is no God at all,' Raskolnikov had said with a sort of malignance"), he illustrates the awfulness of this prospect by referring to children as "the image of Christ" and citing the Gospels: "Theirs is the Kingdom of Heaven." When the hysterically weeping Sonya, wringing her hands, asks, "What then must we do?" he replies, "Demolish what must be demolished, once and for all, and take the suffering on ourselves." This assumption of suffering, however, is immediately countered by a more despotic assertion of egoism than any he has yet consciously uttered so far: "What? Don't you understand? . . . Freedom and power, but above all, power! Power over all trembling creatures, over the ant-heap . . . that's the goal!" he tells the bewildered Sonya (6: 252–253). He thus involuntarily reveals the truth about himself that has begun to pierce through to his consciousness.

The culmination of the scandal scene at the wake following Marmeladov's funeral prepares the way for an intensification of the moral confrontation between Sonya and Raskolnikov at their next meeting, which follows hard on the rowdy commemoration. Luzhin, attempting to frame Sonya by secretly slipping money into her pocket, had accused her of theft, and Raskolnikov seizes on this incident as an additional self-justification. If Sonya had the choice, would she, he asks, decide that "Luzhin should live and commit abominations," even if this meant "the ruin of Katerina Ivanovna and the children"? To which the distraught Sonya can only reply, with the instinctive penetration of uncorrupted moral feeling: "But I can't know God's intentions. . . . [H]ow could it depend on my decision. . . . Who made me a judge of who shall live and who shall not?" (6: 313). Without a false note, Dostoevsky portrays the uneducated Sonya countering Raskolnikov with the argument that no human could arrogate to herself the power over human life traditionally exercised solely by God.

This reply is the prelude to Raskolnikov's final confession, which he makes to Sonya while alternating between feelings of hatred and love—and when she finally comprehends the truth, which he is unable to bring out in words, she

---

[4] Sonya, who provides the moral standard of the novel, never blames herself for being a prostitute, which is her only way of practicing *agape* in relation to her family, but she bitterly regrets having failed to give Katerina Ivanovna some cuffs that she had bought to adorn herself. Katerina had asked to be given them, but Sonya refused with the chilling Utilitarian question, "What use are they to you, Katerina Ivanovna?" and had never forgiven herself for this betrayal of *agape*, this chance to give the dying woman a moment of happiness (6: 245).

throws herself into his arms and exclaims, with total identification: "What have you done . . . to yourself? . . . There is no one, no one, unhappier than you in the whole world" (6: 376). But when Sonya promises to follow him to prison he recoils, and his egoism, the "satanic pride" released in his personality first by his ideas and then through the crime and its aftermath, resurfaces.

Raskolnikov's struggle to explain the cause of his crime not only to Sonya but, more important, to himself, equals in poetic force some of the final soliloquies of Shakespeare. Raskolnikov knows by this time that all the reasons for the crime he had previously given himself are false, and he finally admits, "I am lying, Sonya. . . . I've been lying for a long time. . . . There are quite different reasons here, quite, quite different!" (6: 320). He now knows that this "credo" that might alone could make right had not been his point of departure, and so he shifts, with self-tormenting sarcasm, to a description of the inner struggle with his conscience, whose values he still believed he was obeying even as he contemplated murder. It was just because he was assailed by the question of whether "I had the right to gain power—I certainly hadn't the right," or "whether a human being is a louse," that his failure became inevitable. "If I worried myself all those days, wondering whether Napoleon would have done it or not, it means I must have felt clearly that I wasn't Napoleon" (6: 311).

It was "the agony of that battle of ideas" that impelled Raskolnikov finally to throw it off entirely. With the wisdom of hindsight, he breaks through to a comprehension of the compulsion that had been at work in and through his monomania. "I wanted to murder without casuistry, to murder for my own sake, for myself alone!" Raskolnikov's real aim was solely to test "whether I was a louse like everyone else or a man. . . . Whether I am a trembling creature or whether I have the *right*." And Raskolnikov then sweeps away any and every motivation except the testing of his own strength: "I didn't murder either to gain wealth or to become a benefactor of mankind. Nonsense! I just murdered . . . and whether I became a benefactor to others, or spent my life like a spider catching everyone in my web and sucking the life out of others, must have been of no concern to me at that moment . . . I know it all now." Raskolnikov's real aim was solely to test "whether I have the *right*" (6: 321–322). With these climactic words, Raskolnikov's understanding finally coincides with what has long since been dramatically conveyed by Dostoevsky.

This act of self-recognition, however, does not persuade Raskolnikov to accept Sonya's injunction to "go at once, this very minute, stand at the crossroads, bow down, first kiss the earth which you have defiled and then bow down to all the world and say to all men aloud, 'I have killed!'" (6: 322). Quite the contrary, even though acknowledging the pure egoism that had motivated him "at that moment," he refuses to imagine surrendering to the legal authorities, who themselves represent for him the same amoral egoism operating on a vastly larger scale.

The very self-contradictory nature of the forces motivating Raskolnikov, of which he has only just become fully aware, would humiliate him further in the eyes of the law. "'And what should I say to them—that I murdered her, but did not dare to take the money and hid it under a stone?' he added with a bitter smile. 'Why, they would laugh at me, and would call me a fool for not getting it. A coward and a fool!'" (6: 323). Raskolnikov thus decides to continue to fight for his freedom.

———■———

Raskolnikov's confession to Sonya climaxes his quest for knowledge about himself. From this point on the action of the novel is oriented toward the future rather than toward uncovering the meaning of the past, and its thematic structure is well defined in Dostoevsky's notebooks: "Svidrigailov—the most desperate cynicism. Sonya—the most unrealizable hope. . . . [Raskolnikov] has passionately attached himself to both" (7: 204). These are the two alternatives between which he oscillates, knowing that Svidrigailov, who eavesdropped on his confession to Sonya, is privy to his secret. Both are aware that he is a murderer, and each, in effect, indicates an opposing path along which he can choose to decide his fate.

Sonya, while waiting to share his destiny, can only imagine the future as being his voluntary acceptance of punishment. Her pleas are reinforced by Porfiry Petrovich, who speaks frankly in his final interview with Raskolnikov. Porfiry's speech serves to bring out both the social-cultural contrast and the similarity in extremism between the radical intellectual Raskolnikov and the peasant sectarian Nikolay (the workman falsely suspected of the murder), who comes from a family of *Beguny* and who, under the spiritual guidance of an elder (*starets*) for two years, "was full of fervor, prayed at night, read the old books, the 'true ones,' and read himself crazy" (6: 347). Raskolnikov, too, had "read himself crazy," but Nikolay is ready to accept suffering to atone for his own sinfulness and that of the world, while Raskolnikov, though enduring agonies of conscience, still cannot bring himself to follow its injunctions. This is why, as Porfiry declares, his crime "is a fantastic, gloomy business, a modern case, an incident of today when the heart of man is troubled. . . . Here we have bookish dreams, a heart unhinged by theories." Here we have "a murderer [who] looks upon himself as an honest man, despises others, poses as a pale angel" (6: 348). Raskolnikov himself is the murderer, Porfiry affirms softly, and urges him to confess voluntarily under the best possible conditions—that is, so as to free an innocent man and thus obtain the goodwill and leniency of the court. Besides, Porfiry informs Raskolnikov, he has found a piece of material evidence and plans to arrest him in a few days.

In this final section, Raskolnikov's attention turns toward Svidrigailov. Svidrigailov's past is wrapped in a cloud of atrocious rumors, and he was, as Raskolnikov concludes, "evidently depraved, undoubtedly cunning and deceitful, possibly malignant." Raskolnikov refuses to see any connection between Svidrigailov's sinister past and his own crimes, and believes—what is of course true—that "their very evil-doing is not of the same kind." All the same, we see him "hastening to Svidrigailov" and somehow "expecting something *new* from him, directions, a way out" (6: 354). Svidrigailov, after all, is the only person who knows that Raskolnikov is guilty and has not urged him to confess; indeed, he seems completely unconcerned, amused rather than shocked, and it is through this cynicism that Raskolnikov feels he might perhaps offer "a way out." For all his assumed indifference to morality, however, Svidrigailov's rebuff at the hands of Dunya snaps the last thread attaching him to existence, and this scene is followed by the last hours before his suicide, during which the "cellar rats" (6: 392) of his own past swim out of his subconscious in various dreams. For him there is no natural innocence left in the world; everything he touches turns into the corruption of unashamed vice. With this awareness of his living damnation, Svidrigailov shoots himself.

Svidrigailov's mockingly provocative account of his sexual philanderings had revolted Raskolnikov, and his well-aimed sneers at Raskolnikov's reproaches had brought home to the murderer that he had lost any right to distinguish himself morally from his shameless interlocutor. Raskolnikov thus decides to yield to Sonya's entreaties and take Porfiry's advice. He goes to his mother for a last farewell and, when she blesses him with the sign of the cross, "for the first time after all these awful months his heart was softened. He fell down before her, he kissed her feet, and both wept, embracing" (6: 397). With Dunya, however, there is a last flare-up of Raskolnikov's pride, and he rebels against acknowledging that he has committed any "crime" at all. What he has learned from his failure is only his own weakness, his own inability to subdue his conscience *completely* and place it in the service of his "idea." But his own failure was not a refutation of this "idea," in which he still could not see any logical flaw; there was no great reason why a true "great man," untroubled and secure in his absolute right to overstep existing moral bounds, could not *also* be a "benefactor of mankind." "I too wished to do good and would have done hundreds, thousands of good deeds to make up for this one piece of stupidity." His failure was a purely personal one: "but I . . . I couldn't carry out even the first step, because I am contemptible, that's what's the matter" (6: 400). He had placed himself in the wrong category, and this tragic misjudgment about himself has nothing to do with the validity or justice of his unshaken belief.

In the final chapter, Raskolnikov bows down and kisses the earth at the Haymarket, as Sonya had admonished, in a gesture of repentance typical of the *raskolniki*, only to be met with the laughter and jeers of people who think he is either drunk or about to embark as a pilgrim for the Holy Land. Then he goes to confess to Lieutenant Gunpowder, unwilling to accept the humiliation of surrendering to Porfiry, and hears, in the midst of a friendly flow of chatter about various radical fads, that Svidrigailov had killed himself the night before. Raskolnikov is so overcome that he stumbles out into the courtyard without saying a word, but there stood Sonya, on her face "a look of poignant agony, of despair" (6: 409), and he returns to make the confession. His fate and that of Svidrigailov thus form a continuous parallel up to the very end.

———■———

In accordance with the tradition of the nineteenth-century novel, Dostoevsky provides an epilogue in which the lives of his main characters are followed beyond the limits of the plot action. The main aim of the epilogue is to offer an authorial perspective on the major thematic issues that, Dostoevsky felt, required either reinforcement or completion. One such issue is the decisive role that must be ascribed to the effect of Raskolnikov's ideas on his psyche. These ideas, in bringing on his monomania, had ultimately provided the motivating force for the crime; and the epilogue points once again to their centrality. Another issue is the gap that still exists between the moral-psychic emotions that led Raskolnikov to confess and his continued belief that his ideas, whatever his own personal defeat, have not been invalidated.

The reader knows that Raskolnikov's so-called "heartfelt repentance" is really a crushing sense of defeat, and the depression that marks his behavior in the Siberian prison camp, where he even rebuffs Sonya's effort to comfort him, is the result not of the hardship of his lot but of the collapse of belief in himself. He falls ill for a long time, and "it was wounded pride that made him ill." What tortures him is that he cannot see any flaw in his theory but finds it only in himself: "his exasperated conscience found no particular terrible fault in his past, except a single blunder which might happen to anyone. Not being able to find any flaw in his ideas, he could thus see no value in the 'continual sacrifice leading to nothing' that he had accepted. Of course he had committed a crime, but 'what is meant by crime? My conscience is at rest. . . . Well, punish me for the letter of the law . . . and that's enough. Of course in that case many benefactors of mankind who snatched power for themselves instead of inheriting it ought to have been punished at their first steps. But those men succeeded and so they were right, and I didn't, and so I had no right to have taken that first step'" (6: 416–417). Raskolnikov thus believes that there is nothing *inherently* incompatible between the ruthless acquisition of power by an "extraordinary person," who never questions for a moment that his ego is superior to all moral laws, and the possibility of that person then becoming a "benefactor of mankind."

To resolve this thematic crux Dostoevsky has recourse to the famous final dream of Raskolnikov, the dream in which he sees "the whole world . . .

condemned to a terrible new strange plague that had come to Europe from the depths of Asia." This dream, like all the others in the book, emerges from the depths of his moral-emotive psyche, and like them is the response of his conscience to his ideas. His logic is answered not by any sort of rational refutation but by the vision of his horrified subconscious (which in Dostoevsky is usually moral, as it also is in Shakespeare). The dream represents nothing less than the universalization of Raskolnikov's doctrine of the "extraordinary people" in which *all* attempt to put this belief into practice. Those attacked by the plague became "mad and furious" while believing they had reached new heights of wisdom and self-understanding. "Never had men considered themselves so intellectual, and so completely in possession of the truth as these sufferers. Never had they considered their decisions, their scientific conclusions, their moral convictions so infallible." The disease allows each person to preserve "moral convictions" and inspires a desire to enlighten others with the truth of such convictions so as to become a benefactor of humanity. "Each thought that he alone had the truth and was wretched looking at the others" (6: 419–420).

But the certainty of each ego in its own infallibility, and the absolute assurance and authority imparted by such certainty, leads to the breakdown of all common norms and values. "They did not know how to judge and could not agree what to consider evil and what good" (6: 420). No form of social cohesion could resist the contagion of the plague; the plague thus removes the implicit basis of consensus on which human society is based, and the final result is total social chaos. Here we see Dostoevsky destroying the last shreds of Raskolnikov's conviction that a supreme egoism could be combined with socially benevolent consequences. Let all presume they were "extraordinary people," and the result would be the Hobbesian world of Raskolnikov's feverish nightmare, the war of all against all. This is the world of Western society as Dostoevsky had described it in *Winter Notes*, the world in which "the ego sets itself in opposition, as a separate, self-justifying principle, against all of nature and all other humans; it claims equality and equal value with whatever exists outside of itself" (5: 79). It is not only equality that each ego now claims, but also absolute superiority; and this is the plague that has come to Russia from Europe to infect the radical intelligentsia, the plague of a moral amorality based on egoism and culminating in a form of self-deification. Dostoevsky thus uses the typical technique of his eschatological imagination to dramatize all the implicit dangers of the new radical ideology.

Raskolnikov's dream provides an impressive climax to the main ideological theme of the book and is, in effect, its proper ending. Also effective is the growing need for Sonya that Raskolnikov feels after the desolation of his dream; she offers him not only a means of renewing his life personally but also, perhaps, a way of achieving some sort of assimilation to the people (the peasant convicts refuse to accept him as a genuine Christian). In the final pages, though, just before Raskolnikov flings himself at Sonya's feet to embrace her and weep, he is sitting on the riverbank, gazing at the steppe, where he sees the tents of nomads in the distance. It seemed as if time had stood still, and he was back in the "age of Abraham and his flocks" (6: 421), the age of untroubled faith. It is only after this comparison occurs to him that he turns to Sonya, but Dostoevsky knew that Raskolnikov could not become another Sonya or return to "the age of Abraham," and that it would be a daunting task to find an adequate artistic image of a possible new Raskolnikov. This task could hardly be undertaken in his brief concluding pages, and so the epilogue, if not a failure as a whole, invariably leaves readers with a sense of dissatisfaction. It was a sense evidently felt by Dostoevsky, whose narrator speaks of Raskolnikov's "gradual regeneration" as being "the theme of a new story" (7: 422), and it would be a story that continued to preoccupy Dostoevsky throughout the remainder of his life. For time and again we shall see him returning to the challenge of creating a regenerated Raskolnikov—of creating, that is, a highly educated and spiritually developed member of Russian society who conquers his egoism and undergoes a genuine conversion to a Christian morality of love.

CHAPTER 35

"A Little Diamond"

The publication of *Crime and Punishment*, which created even more of a sensation than had *House of the Dead* five years earlier, marked a new era in Dostoevsky's literary career. Once again he was in the forefront of Russian literature, and it was now clear that he, Turgenev, and Tolstoy were in competition for the palm as the greatest Russian novelist. The final chapters of the novel had been completed with the aid of Anna Grigoryevna Snitkina, the stenographer who had worked with him on *The Gambler*, and by this time a major change had also occurred in his personal life. He had proposed marriage to Anna and been accepted.

The charming story of their meeting and courtship, recounted in the *Reminiscences* that were edited and published after her death, is one of the most luminous episodes in a life otherwise filled with gloom and misfortune.[1] Difficulties and hardships aplenty would continue to plague Dostoevsky and his new bride, particularly in the early years of their marriage when they lived abroad. But thanks to the sterling moral qualities and sturdy good sense of Anna Grigoryevna, the erratic and turbulent Dostoevsky would finally attain that relatively tranquil family existence he so much envied in others.

■

The reserved and attractive young lady who turned up at Dostoevsky's flat at half-past eleven on the morning of October 4, 1866, prepared to take dictation, came from a comfortable family of mixed Ukrainian and Swedish origin. Anna was raised in a strict but, according to her own account, harmonious family atmosphere in which the children (she had an older sister and younger brother) were well treated. "Life in our family was quiet, measured and serene, without

---

[1] The so-called memoirs of Anna Grigoryevna, *Vospominaniya*, were never completed by her, and a selection of the manuscript was first published in 1925 by L. P. Grossman. A revised version appeared in 1971, edited by S. V. Belov and V. A. Tunimanov, which was translated into English under the title of *Reminiscences*. In 1973, a volume of the literary-historical annual *Literaturnoe Nasledstvo* published a hitherto undeciphered portion of Anna's shorthand diary of the courtship period. This account fills out, as well as sometimes diverges from, what she included in the memoirs written in the later years of her life.

21. Anna Grigoryevna
Dostoevsky, ca. 1863

quarrels, dramas or catastrophes."[2] Between the ages of nine and twelve she was
sent to a school in which, except for the lessons in religion, all instruction was
given in German, and her fluency in that language stood the Dostoevskys in
good stead when they lived in Germany during the years just after their marriage. Anna was also growing up in the period when higher education began to
become available for Russian women. The first secondary school had been
opened for them in Petersburg in 1858, and Anna entered in the fall of that year,
graduating in 1864 with honors. The first Pedagogical Institute for women
opened in 1863, and Anna eagerly entered in the fall of 1864. "At that time," she
writes, "a passionate interest in the natural sciences had arisen in Russian society,
and I too succumbed to the trend. . . . I registered in the school's department of
mathematics and physics."[3] But she soon found that the sciences were not her
forte. What she enjoyed most were the brilliant lectures on Russian literature by
a Professor V. V. Nikolsky, which she attended assiduously.

[2] Anna Dostoevsky, *Reminiscences*, trans. and ed. Beatrice Stillman (New York, 1975), 10.
[3] Ibid., 4.

By this time, Anna's father had fallen ill, and it was clear he would not recover. Dropping out of school to help with his care, she exhibited a sense of duty and capacity for self-subordination that was to mark her conduct as Dostoevsky's spouse. When she came across the announcement of a course in stenography given in the evening after her father's usual bedtime, she enrolled with his encouragement, but found the work difficult and continued only because her father insisted. His death was such a wracking event that she interrupted her attendance, but the kindly Professor Olkhin continued to work with her by correspondence. When Olkhin was asked to find a stenographer to aid the noted writer Dostoevsky, he immediately thought of the young and determined Anna.

Anna was naturally excited at embarking on her first job, which for a woman in those days was an important event. Her first assignment, marking "my transformation from a school-girl into an independent practitioner of my chosen profession,"[4] would be to work with a writer whose books she admired and by whom she had been deeply affected. Anna and her sister disputed the issues of *Time* that were bought every month, and at the age of fifteen she tearfully pored over installments of *The Insulted and Injured*. The narrator, the tenderhearted but hapless Ivan Petrovich, particularly appealed to her, and she identified his deplorable fate with that of the author. Later she told her husband that she had been in love with him in that guise ever since those early years. More recently, she had been reading *Crime and Punishment*, and as she entered the apartment house in which Dostoevsky resided, "I was immediately reminded of the house . . . where . . . Raskolnikov had lived."[5]

The flat that Anna entered was modestly furnished, except for two large and beautiful Chinese vases in Dostoevsky's study (some remains from his Siberian years). The study itself she found "dim and hushed; and you felt a kind of depression in that dimness and silence." The first person she saw, beside the maidservant, was a half-dressed young man "with hair disheveled and shirt open at the chest," who emerged from a side room and rapidly vanished when he caught sight of her.[6] Anna, much to her sorrow, was to get to know Pavel Isaev all too well when she replaced his mother as Dostoevsky's spouse. Dostoevsky himself soon appeared, but also quickly quit the room to order tea, leaving Anna to mull over her impressions. He had seemed quite old at first sight, but when he returned and began to speak, he suddenly "grew younger at once." "His chestnut-colored hair, faintly tinged with red, was heavily pomaded and carefully smoothed. But it was his eyes that really struck me. They weren't alike—one was dark-brown, while the other had a pupil so dilated that you couldn't see the iris

[4] Ibid., 15.
[5] Ibid., 16.
[6] Ibid., 16–17.

at all. [Dostoevsky had recently fallen during an epileptic attack and had temporarily injured his right eye—J.F.] This dissimilarity gave his face an enigmatic expression. His face [was] pale and sick-looking. . . . He was dressed in a blue cotton jacket, rather worn, but with snow-white collar and cuffs."[7]

Dostoevsky, who had agreed to work with a stenographer only as a last resort, was nervous and distraught, obviously at a loss on how to treat this newly intrusive presence. He smoked continuously, stubbing out one cigarette and lighting another even before the first was finished; at one point he offered Anna a cigarette. Ladies, of course, did not smoke in the mid-nineteenth century—at least not in public—but neither did ladies hire themselves out as stenographers and visit the apartments of strangers unattended. By inviting Anna to take a cigarette, Dostoevsky thus indicated that he thought she might be a completely emancipated Nihilist à la Kukshina, a character in Turgenev's *Fathers and Children* who was always puffing away at a cigarette. When Anna refused, he inquired whether she was merely doing so out of politeness. "I was quick to assure him," she writes, "that I not only didn't smoke, but didn't even like to see other women smoke."[8] A bit later, he told Anna that "he had been pleasantly surprised by my knowledge of correct behavior. He was used to meeting Nihilist women socially and observing their behavior, which roused him to indignation."[9]

Once this uncomfortable moment had passed, Dostoevsky continued to converse, but in a dispirited fashion. "He looked exhausted and ill" to the observant Anna, and had difficulty in collecting his thoughts; he kept asking her name and then forgetting it a moment later. Such lapses in memory were frequent after his epileptic seizures, and with a frankness that astonished Anna he informed her that he suffered from epilepsy and had undergone an attack just a few days before. At last remembering why she had come, he read her a passage from *The Russian Messenger*, which she took down and transcribed, and he corrected two minor errors rather sharply. After the first stab at dictation, however, he walked around the room for some time sunk in thought, "as if unaware of [Anna's] presence," and then gave up the attempt to concentrate altogether. Telling Anna he was in no condition to work, he asked her to return in the evening at eight o'clock, when he would begin to dictate his novel.[10]

On her return that evening, Dostoevsky began by offering her tea and cakes, as he had done before, asked her name again and proffered a cigarette, apparently totally forgetful of what had occurred just a few hours earlier. As often

---

[7] Ibid., 18.
[8] A. G. Dostoevskaya, "Dnevniki i vospominaniya," *LN* 86 (Moscow, 1973), 222.
[9] *Reminiscences*, 21.
[10] Ibid., 19.

happened when Dostoevsky wished to establish some intimacy with others, he began to reminisce about his past, vividly evoking his arrest and mock execution. While the youthfully impressionable Anna listened with reverential rapture, he described all the details then still wrapped in legend, and he dwelt on some of his emotions at the time. "How precious my life seemed to me, how much that was fine and good I might have accomplished!" It was only later that Anna came to understand the reasons for such disconcerting frankness. "At that time Feodor Mikhailovich was utterly alone and surrounded by persons who were hostile to him. He felt too keenly the need to share his thoughts with those whom he sensed as kind and interested in him."[11]

Dostoevsky finally began to dictate the opening paragraphs of *The Gambler* but stopped very soon, and Anna left for home to transcribe the text. The next day she arrived a half-hour late to find Dostoevsky in great agitation. He had thought she might not return, and he would have lost not only a stenographer but also the small fragment of manuscript he had managed to compose! Every page was precious to him because, as he explained, he had agreed to provide a novel by the first of November, "and I haven't even worked out a plan for it." This was Anna's first knowledge of Dostoevsky's perilous dilemma. "Stellovsky's behavior," she writes, "made my blood boil," and she determined to do everything within her power to rescue the intended victim from his clutches. Learning the menacing details of Dostoevsky's precarious practical situation only reinforced the feeling he had inspired in Anna the night before. "This was the first time I had ever known such a man; wise, good, and yet unhappy; apparently abandoned by everyone. And a feeling of deep pity and commiseration was born in me."[12]

On the second day, Dostoevsky began dictating with more determination, but "it was obviously difficult for him to get into the work. He stopped often, thought things over and asked me to reread what he had already dictated."[13] After an hour he felt tired, decided to rest, and began to chat with Anna again. Once more forgetting her name, and absentmindedly offering her another cigarette, he brightened up considerably when she began to question him about contemporary Russian writers. Nekrasov "he bluntly called a cheat, a terrible gambler, someone who talks about the sufferings of mankind, but who drives around himself in a carriage with trotters." He mentioned Turgenev "as a first-rate talent, but regretted that as a result of his long residence abroad he had lost some of his understanding of Russia and the Russian people."[14] This opinion

[11] Ibid., 22.
[12] Ibid., 24–26.
[13] Ibid., 26.
[14] "Dnevniki," 225.

would be confirmed for Dostoevsky a year later by the publication of *Smoke*, the most bitterly condemnatory of all Turgenev's novels about his native land.

———■———

Encouraged by Anna's cool determination, Dostoevsky settled down to a regular routine. Anna arrived at his house every day at twelve and stayed until four. "During that time we would have three dictating sessions of a half-hour or more, and between dictations we would drink tea and talk."[15] Dostoevsky, as Anna noticed, now was much calmer when she arrived, and became more and more cheerful as the pages piled up and she estimated that the manuscript would be ready for submission by the appointed date.

Dostoevsky's mood also lightened as, in the midst of total isolation, he began to pour out his heart to an avid, attentive, and devotedly sympathetic listener. "Each day, chatting with me like a friend, he would lay bare some unhappy scene from his past. I could not help being deeply touched at his accounts of the difficulties from which he had never extricated himself, and indeed could not." Each day, as well, his attitude toward Anna, whose name he no longer forgot, became kindlier, warmer, more personal. "He often addressed me as '*golubchik*'" (or 'little dove,' his favorite affectionate expression), and in response to Anna's inquiries recounted many of the details of his past life.[16] Their conversations thus began to turn more and more to questions concerning his present trying situation and depressed state of mind, saddled as he was with debts and struggling to make ends meet. Anna noted how bad things were when the Chinese vases suddenly vanished and the silver spoons of the dining set were replaced on the table by wooden ones. Dostoevsky explained that both had been pawned to pay some pressing creditors who could no longer be put off.

Dostoevsky now also began to acquaint Anna with some of the details of his more recent sentimental life—such as his attraction to, and presumed engagement with, Anna Korvin-Krukovskaya. He embellished the story by making their engagement a fact; no doubt he wished to intimate that a highly desirable young woman *could* agree to link her life with his own. He had, according to this version of events, released the other Anna from her promise only because the sharp divergence of their social-political views excluded the possibility of happiness. Nothing is said in the *Reminiscences* about Suslova, but the diaries reveal that Dostoevsky showed her portrait to Anna, and when Anna called her a "remarkable beauty," Dostoevsky disparagingly observed that she had changed a good deal in the past six years.[17]

[15] *Reminiscences*, 27.
[16] Ibid., 27, 28.
[17] "Dnevniki," 262.

As the talk between the two dwelt more and more on Dostoevsky's present circumstances, he depicted himself, with all his skill in melodrama, as having reached a crucially decisive moment in his life that would soon decide his future fate for good and all. With more than a touch of Romantic Byronism, he told Anna that "he was standing at a crossroad and three paths lay open before him." He could go to the East—Constantinople and Jerusalem—and remain there, "perhaps forever"; he could "go abroad to play roulette," and "immolate himself in the game he found so utterly engrossing"; or he could "marry again and seek joy and happiness in family life."[18] Since Anna had already shown so much friendliness for him, would she give him the benefit of her advice? Which path should he follow?

Dostoevsky was evidently testing the temperature of the water into which he planned to plunge, and the reply he received from the sturdily commonsensical Anna was the one he had hoped for. Anna assured her anxious questioner that marriage and family happiness were what he needed. At which Dostoevsky instantly responded with a further question; since Anna had indicated that he might still be able to find a wife, should he seek for an intelligent one or a kind companion? Anna came down on the side of intelligence, but Dostoevsky, knowing himself far better than she did at this point, replied that he would prefer "a kind one, so that she'll take pity on me and love me."[19] Anna little knew then how much pity and love she would be required to lavish on Dostoevsky in the future!

"Even then," Anna confided to her diary, "it seemed to me that he would certainly propose, and I really did not know whether I would accept or not. He pleases me very much, but all the same frightens me because of his irascibility and illness." She noticed how often he shouted at the maidservant Fedosya, though adding that the rebukes were on the whole well deserved. The daily meetings with Dostoevsky now became the center of Anna's life, and everything she had previously known seemed to her uninteresting and insipid by comparison. "I rarely saw my friends," she writes, "and concentrated wholly on work and on those utterly fascinating conversations we used to have while we were relaxing after our dictation sessions. I couldn't help comparing Dostoevsky with young men I used to meet in my own social circle. How empty and trivial their talk seemed to me in comparison with the ever fresh and original views of my favorite writer. . . . Leaving his house still under the influence of ideas new to me, I would miss him when I was at home and lived only in the expectation of the next day's meeting with him. I realized with sorrow that the work was nearing its end and that our acquaintance must break off."[20]

[18] *Reminiscences*, 30.
[19] Ibid.
[20] "Dnevniki," 243.

The deadline of November 1 was fast approaching, and since Dostoevsky too was feeling the same sense of impending loss, he put into words what both had been mulling over in their minds. Confessing how much he enjoyed Anna's companionship and "our lively talks together," he remarked on what a pity it would be if all this were now to end. Why did not Anna invite him to meet her family? Such a request was certainly a harbinger of serious amatory intentions, and Anna agreed on the spot, but she would set the time for such a visit only after work on the manuscript had been terminated.[21]

There now remained no doubt that *The Gambler* would be completed by the due date, but Dostoevsky "began to be afraid that Stellovsky . . . would find a pretext for refusing to accept the manuscript."[22] The resourceful Anna consulted a lawyer, who advised registering the manuscript with a notary or with the police officer of the district in which Stellovsky lived. The same advice was given by a lawyer Dostoevsky went to see, perhaps at Anna's urging, and the instructions stood him in good stead. Meanwhile, elated at having been able to complete the novella at all, Dostoevsky planned a victory dinner for his friends in a restaurant and of course invited Anna, without whom, as he justly said, his triumph would not have been possible. But she refused because she had never been to a restaurant in her life, and she was afraid her shyness and awkwardness would impede the general merriment.

Stellovsky, true to his reputation, attempted by every possible means to prevent Dostoevsky from delivering the manuscript on time. The dictation was finished on October 29, and Anna brought the manuscript to Dostoevsky on the thirtieth, which happened to be his birthday; he was to make the final corrections on the thirty-first and hand in the work on the following day. Arriving on the thirtieth, Anna was confronted with Emilya Feodorovna, the widow of Dostoevsky's brother Mikhail, come with birthday greetings; and the lady snubbed the employee Anna unmercifully, even though Dostoevsky was warm in his praise of Anna's indispensable aid. This was only the first of Anna's many unhappy experiences with this dependent relative, who had also been cordially disliked by Dostoevsky's first wife, Marya Dimitrievna. Upset by his sister-in-law's haughty rudeness, Dostoevsky insisted, as he said good-bye to Anna at the door, that she now set the date for his visit to her home. The diary records that he spoke to her in an impassioned manner during this leave-taking and even jestingly suggested that they run away together to Europe; from which Anna concluded that "he loves me very much."[23]

Two days later, Dostoevsky tried to deliver the manuscript to Stellovsky's home but was told that he had left for the provinces, nor would the manager of

---

[21] *Reminiscences*, 32.
[22] Ibid.
[23] "Dnevniki," 263.

his publishing firm accept it, on the pretext that he had not received specific authority to do so. By this time it was too late for a notary, and the police officer of the district would not be returning to his office until ten o'clock in the evening. The frantic Dostoevsky, watching the precious hours slip away, just managed to meet his deadline two hours before its expiration. At last, however, he held the all-important receipt in his hands, and the ordeal was over.

———■———

The few days between the end of her employment and Dostoevsky's promised visit on November 3 were a stretch of dreariness and anxiety for Anna. The tedious days passed, however, and despite her anxieties the visit went well. Dostoevsky gallantly kissed the hand of Mme Snitkina, who surely needed no explanation of his intentions, and immediately plunged into an account of his adventures with Stellovsky. Once that theme had been exhausted, he proposed that Anna continue to work with him on the completion of *Crime and Punishment*. She agreed, if Professor Olkhin, who might wish to recommend another pupil, would give his consent. Dostoevsky took this proviso badly and remarked, "perhaps the truth is you don't want to work with me any longer?"[24]

Anna certainly knew that he was talking about more than stenography; and an unannounced visit from Dostoevsky three days later left no doubt on that score. He had not been able to spend more than one or two days without her company; and though he had firmly decided not to give way to his impulse to call, realizing that it might seem "strange" to Anna and her mother, once having "resolved not to come under any circumstances . . . as you see, here I am!"[25] Dostoevsky's inability to resist the promptings of his emotions could hardly have seemed, in this instance, anything other than charming and eminently excusable to Anna, but she would soon encounter other evidence of the same trait of character that drove her to the brink of despair.

The day following this impromptu visit, November 8, had nominally been set as the time when Anna and Dostoevsky would fix a schedule for the completion of *Crime and Punishment*, but Dostoevsky himself had other plans. On her arrival, Anna noticed that the expression on his face was "heightened, fervid, almost ecstatic." The exuberance of his mood he ascribed to a happy dream. Pointing to a rosewood box given him by a Siberian friend, Dostoevsky explained that he had dreamed he was rearranging his papers there (in other words, attempting to reorder his past), when he came across, buried in the midst of the heap, "a little diamond, a tiny one, but very sparkling and brilliant." This discovery had cheered him immensely, since he attributed "great meaning" to dreams and

[24] *Reminiscences*, 36.
[25] Ibid., 40.

believed firmly that "my dreams are always prophetic." Whenever he dreamed of his father or his brother Misha, he knew that some catastrophe was impending, but his dream of "the little diamond" seemed to foreshadow some happy change in the present grimness of his circumstances.[26]

Just what Dostoevsky hoped that his dream foretold (assuming it had not been invented to prepare Anna for what lay ahead) was soon revealed. Dostoevsky had had the idea for a new novel, one in which "the psychology of a young girl" played a crucial part, and he found it difficult to work out the ending; he needed some help, and appealed to Anna. The hero of Dostoevsky's novel turned out to be "a man grown old before his time, sick with an incurable disease (a paralyzed hand), gloomy, suspicious; possessed of a tender heart, it is true, but a failure who had not once in his life succeeded in embodying his ideas in the forms he dreamed of, and who never ceased to torment himself over this fact." Just at this critical period of his life, the writer meets a young girl roughly of Anna's age, named Anya, who was "gentle, wise, kind, bubbling with life and possessed of great tact in personal relationships." Dostoevsky's unhappy author naturally fell in love with this irresistible young girl, and began to be tormented by whether she could possibly respond to his own feelings. "What could this elderly, sick, debt-ridden man give a young, alive, exuberant girl?" Would not the very idea of uniting her fate with his be asking her to make a "terrible sacrifice?" Here was the point at which Dostoevsky wanted Anna to give him the benefit of her feminine counsel. Would she consider it psychologically plausible for such a young girl to fall in love with the artist?[27]

Anna replied to the query with the full emotional force of her own passionate longings. "But why would it be impossible? . . . Where is the sacrifice on her part, anyway? If she really loves him she'll be happy, too, and she'll never have to regret anything!" These were the words he had used all his literary skill to bring to her lips; once having heard them, he came to the dénouement. "'Imagine,' he said, 'that the artist is—me; that I have confessed my love for you and asked you to be my wife. Tell me, what would you answer?'" Anna understood, from the inner torment manifest in Dostoevsky's countenance, that "if I gave him an evasive answer I would deal a deathblow to his self-esteem and pride. I looked at his troubled face, which had become so dear to me, and said 'I would answer that I love you and will love you all my life.'"[28] Anna's refusal to hesitate even for a moment, to ask for a little time to reflect on what would be, after all, a momentous and risky decision, reveals both the firm resoluteness of her character and her overriding concern to spare Dostoevsky any further anguish. His welfare, under conditions that few other women would have borne so resiliently, would

[26] Ibid., 41–42.
[27] Ibid., 44–45.
[28] Ibid., 46.

always be her major preoccupation; and she remained unstintingly faithful to her pledge that she would love Dostoevsky for the remainder of her life.

——————■——————

The newly engaged couple, once the joyful excitement of the moment had passed, decided to keep their decision secret for a time, except from Anna's mother. The pair had decided on secrecy ostensibly because Dostoevsky's circumstances could not as yet allow them to fix a date for the wedding ceremony; but Dostoevsky also wished to keep the news from his various Petersburg relatives for as long as possible. If so, his purpose was foiled by his uncontrollable need to communicate his happiness to someone, anyone, in lieu of those who ordinarily should have shared his rejoicing. The cab driver who drove him to and from Anna's house every day became his confidant, to whom he chattered about his future marriage, and this information quickly reached the ears of Fedosya, the servant in Dostoevsky's home, before a week had gone by. The supposed secret was thus disclosed quickly and caused a great deal of displeasure among those who had become accustomed to counting on Dostoevsky's earnings for their own support.

Anna had known that Dostoevsky was in dire financial straits, but it was only after their engagement that she fully realized to what extent his indigence was caused by the demands made on him by others. He wholly supported his stepson Pasha, then twenty-one years of age and content to allow this situation to continue indefinitely; he provided in good part for his brother Mikhail's widow, Emilya Feodorovna, who had four grown children; and he also helped his younger brother Nikolay, a trained architect but a confirmed alcoholic who was often on his uppers.[29] The results of their combined extractions was vividly illustrated for Anna one cold evening in late November when Dostoevsky arrived at her home chilled to the bone and, after imbibing large quantities of tea, also took several glasses of sherry. He had worn his light fall overcoat instead of the fur greatcoat necessary for winter weather, and he confessed to having pawned his greatcoat for a few days when all three dependents converged with pleas for help at the same time. Anna was so outraged that she broke into tears "and talked like a madwoman, without choosing my words."[30] Dostoevsky calmed her by promising not to leave his house until the greatcoat was redeemed. This was only the beginning of Anna's struggle to wrest Dostoevsky free from those who, she believed, were unduly exploiting his generosity and sense of obligation.

[29] Mikhail Dostoevsky had kept a mistress named Praskovya Petrovna Anikieva, by whom he had a son, and Dostoevsky contributed to their support as well. There is a reference to her in A. G. Dostoevsky, *Dnevnik A. G. Dostoevskoi 1867 g.* (Moscow, 1923), 111.

[30] *Reminiscences*, 65.

Anna realized to her dismay that "the moment Feodor Mikhailovich got hold of any money, all his relatives . . . would instantly put forward their sudden but urgent needs; and out of the three or four hundred rubles received from Moscow for *Crime and Punishment* no more than thirty or forty would remain to Feodor Mikhailovich by the next day. Of this sum, moreover, nothing would be paid off on his promissory notes except the interest." [31] It would be impossible, if this pattern continued, for Dostoevsky ever to discharge his debts, no matter how much he wrote and how successful his works might be. Once she became his wife, Anna decided, she would take their finances into her own hands and put a brake on this self-defeating beneficence, but for the moment there was little she could do except remonstrate.

For the marriage to take place, a considerable sum would be required over and above the payments accruing from *Crime and Punishment*. Since literature was Dostoevsky's only source of income, he decided to travel to Moscow over Christmas and offer his next novel to Katkov in return for an advance sufficient to provide for the ceremony and a new establishment. *Crime and Punishment*, still in the course of publication, continued to hold readers riveted to the pages of *The Russian Messenger*, and Katkov readily acceded to Dostoevsky's request and promised two thousand rubles, which would start arriving in installments in January. The date of the wedding was thus set for mid-February. But the first installment of seven hundred rubles instantly vanished in the usual fashion, and after estimating that the wedding would cost between four and five hundred rubles, Dostoevsky prudently entrusted this part of the second installment to Anna for safekeeping.

Dostoevsky's first marriage had taken place in a miserable little Siberian village, in the most humble circumstances, among people he scarcely knew, and with the ex-lover of his bride as one of the witnesses. His second was celebrated amidst the splendors of the Izmailovsky Cathedral, brilliantly illuminated for the occasion and resounding with the voices of a superb choir, surrounded by his family and closest friends and, at his side, a radiant young bride who revered him as a man and as an artist. He could hardly believe his good fortune, and when introducing Anna to his friends at the wedding reception in her mother's home, he kept repeating, "Look at that charming girl of mine! She's a marvelous person, that girl of mine! She has a heart of gold!" [32] There are few moments in Dostoevsky's life when we catch him enjoying unalloyed happiness, and this is certainly one of those rare occasions. But Anna, as perhaps Dostoevsky was even then uneasily aware, would indeed need "a heart of gold" to cope with and surmount what lay ahead for her.

[31] Ibid., 69.
[32] Ibid., 76.

CHAPTER 36

The Gambler

The first mention of gambling as a theme for a novella, we know, goes back to the summer of 1863, when Dostoevsky was traveling in Europe with his erstwhile mistress Apollinaria Suslova. Dostoevsky was gambling furiously all during this trip, and he thought of recouping his losses by turning them into literature. While in Rome he wrote to Strakhov outlining a work for which he hoped Strakhov could obtain an advance. "I have in mind," he wrote, "a man who is straightforward, highly cultured, and yet in every respect unfinished, a man who has lost his faith but *who does not dare not to believe*, and who rebels against the established order and yet fears it." The letter then continues:

> The main thing, though, is that all his vital sap, his energies, rebellion, daring, have been channeled into *roulette*. He is a gambler, and not merely an ordinary gambler, just as Pushkin's Covetous Knight is not an ordinary miser. . . . He is a poet in his own way, but the fact is that he himself is ashamed of the poetic element in him, because deep down he feels it is despicable, although the need to take risks ennobles him in his own eyes. The whole story is the tale of his playing *roulette* in various gambling houses for over two years.[1]

By the time Dostoevsky came around to using the idea outlined in his letter, the religious motif had dropped by the wayside, and instead he developed what had been mentioned only as an afterthought—that the gambling of Russian expatriates "has some (perhaps not unimportant) significance." In the novella, this significance becomes linked to the remark about the gambler being "a poet in his own way." Dostoevsky explains this idiosyncratic notion of "poetry" by a reference to Pushkin's Covetous Knight, who amasses a fortune not for the sake of the money itself but solely for the psychological sense of power it enables him to acquire over others. "Poetry" in this Dostoevskian sense means acting not for immediate self-interest or for the gratification of any fleshly material desire, but solely to satisfy a powerful psychic craving of the human personality, whether for good or evil.

[1] *PSS*, 28/Bk. 2: 50–51.

Dostoevsky believed that the Russian character was peculiarly susceptible to this kind of "poetry," and much of the story—whose tone is jaunty, bouncy, and full of a certain youthful high spirits—is taken up with illustrating the contrasts between the Russian national character and others (French, English, German). It makes *The Gambler* (*Igrok*) the only work of Dostoevsky's that is "international" in the sense of that word made familiar by, for example, the fiction of Henry James. It is a story in which the psychology and conflicts of the characters not only arise from their individual temperaments and personal qualities but also reflect an interiorization of various national values and ways of life. In Russian literature, there is the German-Russian contrast in *Oblomov*, the French-Russian contrast in *War and Peace*, and the Caucasian-Russian contrast in *The Cossacks*. Dostoevsky's *The Gambler* belongs with such books as a spirited but by no means uncritical meditation on the waywardness of the Russian national temperament as manifested abroad.

---■---

Written in the form of a first-person confession or diary, like *Notes from Underground*, *The Gambler* recounts a decisive series of events in the life of the narrator, Aleksey Ivanovich. This cultivated and highly intelligent young Russian nobleman is serving as a tutor in the entourage of a Russian General Zagoryansky, who is temporarily living abroad. He imagines himself to be in love with the general's stepdaughter, Praskovya (Polina), and their romance constitutes the central plot line. Commentators have been so bemused by the biographical overlappings that they have simply identified Aleksey with Dostoevsky and taken Polina as the supposedly "demonic" Suslova. In fact, however, Aleksey is an unreliable narrator, and the picture he gives of Polina is woefully distorted by his own frustrations and grievances. The two characters who serve as moral yardsticks—Auntie, a wealthy Russian matriarch who erupts on the scene as large as life, and the English lord and prosperous manufacturer Mr. Astley—both speak of Polina in the highest terms. Their view of her character is totally different from that of the presumably love-struck and embittered Aleksey, who cannot overcome his conviction that she looks down on him, from the height of her superior social position, with the utmost indifference.

The characters in *The Gambler* break down easily into two groups—the Russians and the Europeans—and they are contrasted along lines that may be described, to use Dostoevsky's own category, as "poetic" and "prosaic." Among the Europeans are the fake (or exceedingly dubious) Count or Marquis de Grieux and his supposed cousin, Mlle Blanche de Cominges; her presumably noble origins are patently sham, and she is in fact a high-priced *cocotte*. Both of these French figures are linked with the family of the widowed general, who is residing in grand patriarchal style at a German gambling spa called Roulettenberg and squandering money right and left. The general has given promissory notes to de Grieux on all his Russian estates in return for loans and is completely in the Frenchman's power. The sensual and provocative Mlle Blanche would also dearly love to improve her social position by becoming *madame la générale*, and as long as the smitten general is in funds, she allows him to pay his court. All the hopes of the general depend on Auntie, whose momentarily expected demise will pour a considerable fortune into the general's lap. Even after paying off his debts, he would still remain an extremely wealthy Russian *barin*; and what de Grieux has not taken will be left to Mlle Blanche.

Both de Grieux and Mlle Blanche are thus moved by exclusively mercenary motives, and Mlle Blanche's relation to the general is paralleled by that of de Grieux to Polina. He had seduced her earlier in the belief that she was a wealthy heiress, but he becomes increasingly cool as the general's financial prospects grow dimmer. Unlike the aging general, who is deeply smitten with Mlle Blanche (this is *his* way of being a "poet"), Polina no longer has any illusions about de Grieux. "The moment he finds out that I, too, have inherited something from her [Auntie]," she tells Aleksey, "he will immediately propose to me" (5: 213). The only other important foreign character is Mr. Astley, an exemplar, it is true, of all the gentlemanly virtues, but also a partner in a sugar refining firm and thus limited by his English world of practicality and common sense.

The Russian characters, on the other hand, are all moved by feelings whose consequences may be practically disastrous but in every case involve some passion transcending the financial. Both the general and Polina have been stirred by love, and Polina has now transferred her affections to Aleksey—though he is too self-preoccupied to understand that her presumed coldness would dissolve in an instant if he did not continually insist on his slavish subservience to her supposed tyranny. What obsesses Aleksey is the sense of his own social inferiority as a humble tutor in the general's household, where, despite his culture, education, and status as a Russian nobleman, he is treated little better than a servant. He is *in fact* treated outrightly as a servant by the de Grieux–Mlle Blanche tandem, as well as by the hotel staff, and he totally misunderstands Polina because he believes that she disdains him for the same reasons. He cannot imagine that she might favor him over two other much more imposing suitors, de Grieux and Mr. Astley, and he exhibits a rankling acrimony to which she responds in kind. The dialogues between the two crackle with the tension of this love-hate relationship, though the supposed "hate" is really caused by Aleksey's wrongheaded view of Polina's feelings.

Even before arriving, Aleksey had been convinced that roulette would "affect my destiny radically and definitively" (5: 215); and he explains to Polina, when she inquires what transformation would occur in his life, that "with money I'll be a different man, even for you, not a slave" (5: 229). Aleksey begins to gamble, presumably as a means of winning Polina, but more from a need for egoistic self-affirmation than a genuine desire for love. When Polina rightly accuses him of counting on "buying me with money," he indignantly rejects the charge, but her reply hits the nail on the head. "If you aren't thinking of buying me, you certainly think you can buy my respect with money" (5: 230). Polina already knows that de Grieux's "love" waxes and wanes depending on his estimate of her presumably future wealth, and she is wounded to the quick by Aleksey's assumption that *her* feelings toward him could be swayed for the same reason. At the climax of the plot action, Aleksey's behavior toward Polina in fact comes to parallel that of de Grieux.

Aleksey's conduct, however, will not be the result of the same acquisitive motives displayed by the suavely elegant Frenchman. For when Aleksey begins to gamble, the excitement of the play causes him to lose sight entirely of his presumed goal of winning the funds necessary to change his life and gain Polina. Far from stopping when luck is in his favor, he continues to gamble, because "some kind of strange sensation built up in me, a kind of challenge to fate, a kind of desire to give it a flick on the nose, or stick out my tongue at it" (5: 224). The thrill of this "strange sensation," which may be taken as his means of overcoming his perpetual sense of abasement, overpowers every other consideration; and he invariably continues to gamble until he is entirely wiped out.

Those who win, on the other hand, behave like the emblematic Frenchwoman who, in one scene, places "her bets quietly, coolly and calculatingly; taking notes with a pencil and sheet of paper of the numbers that were coming up and trying to find the patterns according to which the chances fell at a given moment. . . . Every day she would win a thousand, two thousand, or at most three thousand francs . . . and . . . she would immediately walk away" (5: 262). But once Aleksey experiences the excitement of gambling "poetically," that is, the excitement of his "challenge to fate," he finds the sensation so exhilarating that he never wishes it to end, and so he becomes not only an incorrigible gambler but also an inveterate loser.

Aleksey has been shown to be an ardent Russian patriot who vehemently defends his country's unpopular policies against foreign critics. When de Grieux remarks "caustically and spitefully," referring to the tutor's losses, that "Russians were . . . lacking in talent even in gambling," Aleksey turns the insulting observation around into an encomium of the Russians' refusal to dedicate their lives entirely to the accumulation of wealth. "Roulette is simply made for Russians," he declares, because "the faculty of amassing capital has become, through a historical process, virtually the main point in the catechism of the virtues and qualities of civilized Western man." Russians have never learned to revere such amassing of capital as an end in itself, but they need money too, and so "are very fond of, and susceptible to, methods such as, for example, roulette, allowing one to get rich suddenly in two hours, and without work. And since we gamble to no purpose, and also without real effort, we tend to be losers!" (5: 223).

Aleksey's peroration is not merely a clever riposte to de Grieux's disdain; its wider application becomes evident in the diverting episode involving Auntie (also called Grandmother), who, instead of expiring on schedule in Moscow, explodes unexpectedly on the Roulettenberg scene and sends all the hopes pinned on acquiring her fortune flying out the window. The blunt old matriarch, despotic but fundamentally humane and kindhearted, represents the traditional down-to-earth virtues of the Russian gentry unspoiled by any truckling to foreign tastes and fashions. Her commanding presence inspires immediate respect and deference.

Auntie's behavior provides a textbook illustration of Aleksey's view concerning the Russian attraction to roulette. Instantly tempted by such a miraculous and seemingly effortless enrichment, she pays no attention to Aleksey's warnings and promptly begins to play. What possesses Auntie is the imperious pride of someone used to issuing commands and being obeyed, the pride of a Russian landowner all-powerful on her estates. "'There, look at it,' Grandmother said angrily, 'how long will I have to wait until the miserable little zero comes up'" (5: 263). It finally does, and she is hooked. Unwilling to stop until she imposes her will on the velleities of the wheel, she loses heavily, stubbornly cashes all her securities at a ruinous rate to continue to play, and loses every penny. A loan from Mr. Astley enables her to limp home contritely to Russia, where she plans to rebuild the local parish church in penance for her gambling sins.

One other aspect of this Auntie episode provides an important foreshadowing of the dénouement of the Aleksey-Polina romance. On her first visit to the casino, Auntie embarrasses everyone by insisting on entering its august precincts accompanied by her majordomo Potapych and her peasant maid Marfa. "So she is a servant, so I have to leave her behind!" she retorts to the general's warnings about propriety. "She is a human being too, isn't she? . . . How could she go anywhere, except with me?" (5: 259). Later, when gambling has taken over, she loses all concern for Marfa and snappishly dismisses the maid when she devotedly begins to escort her mistress again. Once the passion for gambling has gained the upper hand, all other human feelings and relations cease to exist.

———■———

The arrival and departure of Auntie creates a crisis in the lives of the other characters, since it is clear that she will not give a cent to the general and that her funeral mass will hardly be intoned tomorrow. De Grieux thus announces his intention to leave for Russia and claim the general's property. Before departing, he sends a letter to Polina explaining ceremoniously that he must renounce all further hopes for *their* future, but that, as a man of honor, he would turn over fifty thousand francs to the general on her behalf. Aleksey finds her sitting in his room that night and realizes that her presence could only mean one thing. "Why that meant that she loved me! . . . she had compromised herself before everybody, and I, I was just standing there, refusing to understand it!" (5: 291). How he might have behaved is indicated the next day by Mr. Astley, who remarks acidly that Polina "was on her way here yesterday, and I should have taken her to a lady relative of mine, but as she was ill, she made a mistake and went to you" (5: 300). Far from thinking of how best to protect the reputation of his alleged beloved, Aleksey rushes off to play roulette and win the fifty thousand francs needed to wipe out de Grieux's insult. Nothing had changed in their relations, and he still behaved as though it were necessary to "buy her respect."

At the casino, Aleksey hits a sensational winning streak, playing frantically and frenziedly in the "Russian" style—"haphazard, at random, quite without thought." His luck continues to hold, and "now I felt like a winner and was afraid of nothing, of nothing in the world, as I plunked down four thousand on black" (5: 293). Staking on impossible odds, his usually crushed personality is freed from its crippling limits; he is aware of nothing except the intoxication of this release, and he breaks off play only accidentally, when he hears the voices of onlookers marveling at his winnings. "I don't remember," he remarks, "whether I thought of Polina even once during all this time" (5: 294).

Just as he had forgotten Polina while gambling, so he becomes aware, on the way back, that what he now feels has little to do with her plight. What dominates his emotions is "a tremendous feeling of exhilaration—success, triumph, power—I don't know how to express it. Polina's image flitted through my mind also. . . . Yet I could hardly remember what she had told me earlier, and why I had gone to the casino." When his first remark to her is about the best place to conceal the money, she breaks "into the sarcastic laughter I had heard so often . . . every time I made one of my passionate declarations to her." Polina had sensed the falsity of his declamations in the past, and now she sees its bogusness confirmed even more glaringly. It is at this moment, when she realizes that Aleksey's attitude is not really different from that of de Grieux—both men gauge her most intimate sentiments only in terms of money—that her ulcerated pride and dignity bring on a hysterical crisis. Turning on Aleksey with detestation, she says bitterly: "I won't take your money. . . . You are giving too much. . . . De Grieux's mistress is not worth fifty thousand francs" (5: 295). But the true pathos of her condition is then revealed when she breaks down completely, caresses Aleksey in delirium, and keeps repeating: "You love me . . . love me . . . will you love me?" (5: 297).

Aleksey spends the night with Polina in his room, and when she awakens "with infinite loathing," she flings the fifty thousand francs in his face as she had wished to do with de Grieux. Aleksey is still puzzling over this event while composing his manuscript a month later, and his pretended lack of comprehension (really a guilty self-deception) is reminiscent of the underground man's self-excuses for the mistreatment of the prostitute Liza, who had come to him for aid. "To be sure," Aleksey is honest enough to admit, "it all happened in a delirious state, and I knew it too well, and . . . yet I refused to take that fact into consideration." But then he tries to reassure himself that "she wasn't all that delirious and ill. . . . So it must be she knew what she was doing" (5: 298–299). What Polina did know was that Aleksey's love had not been genuine enough, nonegoistic enough, to resist taking sexual advantage of her deranged and helpless condition.

———■———

Still under the spell of the psychic afflatus provided by his gambling exploit, Aleksey now goes off with his winnings to Paris in the company of Mlle Blanche. Mlle Blanche is honest enough in her own way and, while spending Aleksey's money hand over fist, she introduces him to a friend, Hortense, who keeps him occupied in a manner suggested by her nickname, *Thérèse-philosophe*—the title of a well-known eighteenth-century pornographic novel. He becomes terribly bored at Mlle Blanche's parties, however, where he is forced to play host to the dullest businessmen with newly minted fortunes and "a bunch of wretched minor authors and journalistic insects" with "a vanity and conceit of such proportions as would be unthinkable even back home in Petersburg—and that is saying a great deal!" (5: 304). The entire escapade comes to an end, and Aleksey is sent on his way, once all his money—to which he displays a total indifference ("un vrai Russe, un calmouk!" Mlle Blanche says admiringly)—has been dissipated, much to the benefit of Mlle Blanche's social prestige (5: 308).

Although the main story of *The Gambler* ends with this episode, a final chapter, dating from a year and eight months later, provides a pointed commentary. Aleksey has now become an addicted gambler, traveling around Europe and picking up odd jobs as a flunkey until he can scrape together enough money to return to the tables. He is completely dependent on the "strange sensation" afforded by gambling, the thrill that enables him to affirm his identity and triumph momentarily over his gnawing sense of inferiority. "No, it wasn't the money I craved. . . . I only wanted that the next day all these Hinzes [another employer], all these Oberkellners, all these magnificent Baden ladies, should all be talking about me, tell each other my story, wonder at me, admire me and bow before my new winnings." Nonetheless, he also feels that "I have grown numb, somehow, as though I were buried in some sort of mire" (5: 312). This feeling is particularly aroused by a meeting with Mr. Astley, supposedly accidental but in fact carefully arranged at the instigation of Polina.

Auntie had died meanwhile, leaving Polina a comfortable inheritance, and she has been keeping a concealed but protective eye on Aleksey all this while. Mr. Astley, covertly sent to see if Aleksey has changed in any way, discovers that he is much the same—if not worse. Mr. Astley reveals that he has come to see Aleksey expressly on Polina's behalf; it is really Aleksey that she has loved all along. "What's worse, even if I were to tell you that she still loves you, why, you would stay here just the same! Yes, you have destroyed yourself. You had some abilities, a lively disposition, and you are not a bad man. In fact, you might have been of service to your country, which needs men so badly. . . . It seems to me that all Russians are like that, or are disposed to be like that. If it isn't roulette, it's something else but similar to it. . . . You are not the first who does not understand what work is (I'm not talking about your plain people). Roulette is preeminently a Russian game" (5: 317). Mr. Astley is merely repeating Aleksey's earlier remark about the "poetic" nature of Russians, but now he shows the obverse side of this refusal to discipline the personality and harness it to achieve a desired result. The "poetic" character of the Russian personality, if left to operate unchecked, can lead both to personal disaster and to the obliteration of all sense of civic or moral obligation.

·

Read in such ethnic-psychological terms, *The Gambler* may be seen as Dostoevsky's brilliantly ambivalent commentary, inspired by his own misadventures in the casino, on the Russian national character. Disorderly and "unseemly" though the Russian character may be, it still has human potentialities closed to the narrow, inhuman, and Philistine penny-pinching of the Germans, the worldly, elegant, and totally perfidious patina of the French, and even the solidly helpful but unattractively stodgy virtues of the English. "For the most part," as Aleksey remarks to Polina, "we Russians are so richly endowed that we need genius to evolve our own code of manners. And genius is most often absent, for, indeed, it's a rarity at all times. It's only among the French and perhaps some other Europeans that the code of manners is so well defined that one may have an air of dignity and yet be a man of no moral dignity whatsoever" (5: 230).

But if Russians have not yet worked out their own code of manners, and if the dangers of such a lack have become obvious, they can only demean themselves by attempting to imitate any of the European models. For all his weaknesses, Aleksey arouses sympathy both because of his honesty about himself (except in the case of his night with Polina, which she has presumably forgiven) and because of his unerring eye and refreshing disrespect for the hypocrisies, pretensions, and falsities by which the Europeans cover up their shortcomings. There is an engaging brashness and sincerity about him that wins the friendship of all the "positive" characters (Polina, Auntie, Mr. Astley), and Dostoevsky certainly hoped the reader would share some of their sentiment. Nor was Aleksey meant to be perceived as *entirely* a lost man, if we judge by his reaction upon learning that Mr. Astley had been sent by Polina: "'Really, Really!,' I exclaimed, as tears came gushing from my eyes. I just could not hold them back . . ." (5: 317). Such tears may presage something for the future, and they surely indicate an access of undistorted feeling of which the earlier Aleksey had been incapable.

■

While *The Gambler* should not be read in simple biographical terms, it nonetheless allows us to catch a glimpse of how Dostoevsky may have rationalized his gambling addiction to himself. From this angle, the work may be considered both a self-condemnation and an apologia. No doubt it must have been some consolation to believe, as Dostoevsky probably did, that his own losses, which almost always resulted from a failure to stop playing when he was ahead, were the consequence of a positive national Russian trait carried to excess, and not merely a personal defect of character. He was, after all, a "poet" in both the literal and symbolic senses of that word; and his "poetry" was proof that he found it impossible to subordinate his personality to the flesh-god of money, before whom, as he had written in *Winter Notes*, all of Western civilization was now prostrate. He lost materially, but in some sense he gained a certain reaffirmation of national identity from his very losses. One should also keep in mind that, at the time Dostoevsky wrote *The Gambler*, his yielding to this weakness had so far injured no one but himself, and could still be referred to with a certain bravado. It was only after his second marriage that the addiction began to elicit feelings of acute guilt and remorse.

The Gambler, in any case, is a sparkling little work, whose style and technique are in the vein of satirical social comedy familiar from Dostoevsky's Siberian novellas. The relation of Aleksey and Polina, and the portrayal of the treacherous allurements of gambling, strike a deeper note than these earlier productions; but while Aleksey's gambling may be a "challenge to fate," this challenge is not developed into the moral-religious questionings of the major novels. Not the least interesting aspect of *The Gambler*, finally, is that it points both backward and forward in Dostoevsky's artistic development. Aleksey's obsession with winning somewhat resembles Raskolnikov's fascination with his theory of crime, and neither character can maintain the total, rational self-control of the emotions that is the prerequisite of success. Pointing to the future is the figure of Polina, the pure-souled woman degraded and almost driven mad by the violation of her deepest feelings when she finds herself in the position of being bought and sold. The outlines of the queenly Nastasya Filippovna in *The Idiot*, consumed with pathological hatred of herself and others for the same reasons, are already visible here; so, more faintly, is Aglaya Epanchina in Aleksey's remarks about "young

Russian ladies" and their sentimental illusions about Europeans. In the tenaciously long-lived Auntie, the warm and lovable matriarchal tyrant, we can see a first sketch for the similarly sympathetic and choleric Mme Epanchina. Dostoevsky was thus already feeling his way toward some of the characters of his next great novel, but when he wrote *The Gambler*, he had not yet the faintest idea of what this new major undertaking would turn out to be.

CHAPTER 37

Escape and Exile

The days immediately following the wedding were filled with postnuptial celebrations, and Anna remarks that "I drank more goblets of champagne during
those ten days than I did all the rest of my life." So too did her husband, and
those celebratory libations brought on Anna's first encounter with the frightening physical manifestations of Dostoevsky's dread disease. It overtook him at the
home of her sister, just as Dostoevsky, "extremely animated," was telling some
story. Suddenly, "there was a horrible, inhuman scream, or more precisely a
howl—and he began to topple forward."[1] Although her sister became hysterical
and fled from the room with a "piercing scream," Anna seized Dostoevsky firmly
by the shoulders, tried to place him on the couch, and, when this failed, pushed
aside the obstructing furniture and slid his body to the floor. There she sat holding his head in her lap until his convulsions ceased and he began to regain consciousness. The attack was so severe that he could hardly speak, and the words
he succeeded in uttering were gibberish. An hour later he suffered another onslaught, "this time with such intensity that for two hours after regaining consciousness he screamed in pain at the top of his voice. It was horrible."[2] Such repeated attacks were mercifully infrequent, and Anna attributes the one she
describes to the nervous strain, as well as the obligatory overindulgence in drink,
of the postnuptial visits.

Anna proved capable of coping with such severe tests of her equilibrium and
did not allow them to dampen her joy at being Dostoevsky's bride. But she
found herself initially helpless before a more insidious and covert threat—one
that arose partly from the circumstances of Dostoevsky's life, partly from her
bruising contacts with other members of Dostoevsky's family, most notably his
stepson, Pasha. Dostoevsky's routine made it almost impossible for her to spend
any time with him alone. He wrote or read at night, slept through most of the
morning, and rose in the early afternoon. An early riser, Anna busied herself
with household matters while he slept, but found that it was usual for his young
nieces and nephews to drop in during the late morning and stay for lunch.

---

[1] Anna Dostoevsky, *Reminiscences*, trans. and ed. Beatrice Stillman (New York, 1975), 6, 79.
[2] Ibid., 80.

In the afternoon, other friends and relatives arrived, and often remained for dinner. Anna, with no experience in managing a household, found this unceasing round of hospitality wearisome. The only people she found interesting and enjoyed entertaining were Dostoevsky's literary friends, but Anna, closer in age to the young, was asked to take them to another room and look after their amusement.

The irksomeness of Dostoevsky's sister-in-law, who spared no occasion to comment on Anna's shortcomings as a housekeeper—of course only to help her to improve!—was nothing compared to the machinations of Pasha, who carried on a veritable campaign designed to undermine the marriage and protect his hitherto unchallenged power over the Dostoevsky household management. Anna quickly came to feel that the daily aggravations were part of a larger purpose of "embroiling my husband and myself in quarrels and forcing us to separate."[3] Worst of all, while Dostoevsky was present, Pasha concealed his hostility under a surface of amiability; but he did not restrain himself from coarsely expressing his resentment to Anna's face once they were alone. Dostoevsky, who was infinitely patient with his stepson's shortcomings, was completely hoodwinked, and even commented happily on the improvement of his manners as a result of Anna's influence.

All these tensions led Anna to question the viability of her marriage. There was also anger that "he, 'the great master of the heart,' failed so see how difficult my life was and kept pressing his boring relatives on me and defending Paul, who was so hostile to me."[4] The very nature of their relationship made her sense of estrangement important. On her part, as Anna explains, this was more "cerebral" than physical; her passion for Dostoevsky was "not a passion which might have existed between persons of equal age." It was, rather, "an idea existing in my head . . . it was more like adoration and reverence for a man of such talent and such noble qualities of spirit," and "a searing pity for a man who had suffered so much without ever knowing joy and happiness, and who was so neglected by all his near ones."[5] The very basis of Anna's love for Dostoevsky was threatened by the conditions of their life together.

Matters came to a head about a month after the wedding, when Anna felt too tired and upset to accompany Dostoevsky to an evening party at the Maikovs. The moment his stepfather had left, Pasha assailed her with more than his usual vehemence, accusing her of spending too much of "the funds intended for all of us."[6] The beleaguered Anna broke down completely, retreated to her room in tears, and was still sobbing inconsolably in the darkened chamber when Dos-

[3] Ibid., 86.
[4] Ibid., 91.
[5] Ibid., 90.
[6] Ibid., 92.

toevsky returned. In reply to his anxious inquiry, Anna finally poured out all her griefs, to which he listened in astonishment. When Anna expressed fears that he had ceased to love her, he was quick with reassurances and proposed a trip to Moscow to allow them to escape from the pressures of their Petersburg routine.

Dostoevsky had been thinking of just such a trip to see Katkov and obtain an advance that would allow them to travel abroad in the summer. The reunited pair left the very next day, and on their arrival Anna was introduced to the Ivanovs, who were pleasantly surprised that he had married a respectable young woman and not "a Nihilist, with bobbed hair and spectacles" (the information that Anna was a stenographer had led to such suspicions).[7] One incident during their visit taught Anna a lesson she was never to forget. Taking part in a card game one evening, she was seated next to a lively young man to whom she responded with animation. Dostoevsky, playing in a different room, looked in frequently to see how Anna was faring; and his mood as the evening wore on became gloomier and gloomier. On returning to their hotel, in response to Anna's attempts to cheer him up, he turned on her furiously with the accusation of being a "heartless coquette" who had flirted with a younger man all evening solely to torment her husband.[8] This little scene ended with Dostoevsky comforting Anna and begging forgiveness for his accusations; but it revealed the bottomless depths of his anxieties, and she resolved to be more careful in the future.

Katkov readily accorded Dostoevsky another advance of a thousand rubles. It seemed that the hope of going abroad would finally be realized, and Anna returned to Petersburg glowing with a secret sense of satisfaction and triumph. Nothing was said as yet about their plan, but matters came to a head quickly when Emilya Feodorovna suggested renting a large house for the summer in Pavlovsk. To this proposal, Dostoevsky replied that he and Anna would be abroad at that time. Conversation stopped instantly, Emilya Feodorovna went to speak with Dostoevsky privately in his study, and a furious Pasha flatly told Anna that *he* would not tolerate such a trip. His remonstrances with Dostoevsky proved unavailing, however, and the family finally fell back on *demanding* that advance sums for their expenses be left before the couple's departure.

By the time these sums were totaled up, the amount far exceeded the thousand rubles that Katkov had promised. Matters were made worse when one of Dostoevsky's creditors insisted on at least partial payment of a debt under the threat of seizing and selling Dostoevsky's belongings. The financial obstacles to a trip seemed insuperable, and Dostoevsky was willing to abandon it and accept Pavlovsk. Anna, however, was convinced that "if we were to save our love, we

---

[7] Ibid., 97.
[8] Ibid., 100.

needed to be alone together if only for two or three months . . . then the two of us would come together for the rest of our lives, and no one could separate us again." With the determination that always marked her actions, she decided to raise the travel money herself by pawning her dowry. "Possessions—furniture, fancy clothes—have great importance when one is young," remembers the elderly Anna looking back on that time. "I was extremely fond of my piano, my charming little tables and whatnots, all my lovely things so newly acquired."[9] But she was convinced that the future happiness of her marriage was at stake, and this belief crowded out every other sentiment in guiding her course of action.

Anna immediately went to consult her mother, who agreed that such a radical step was necessary to ensure the future of the union. "She was a Swede," Anna comments, "and she feared that the good habits inculcated by my upbringing would vanish thanks to our Russian style of living, with its disorderly hospitality."[10] Dostoevsky had always refused to take a penny of Anna's belongings and was harder to persuade; it was only after she broke down and began to sob in the street, imploring him to "save our love, our happiness," that he hastily agreed.[11] Acquainted with the waverings of his will, Anna insisted that they go straightaway to apply for a foreign passport. Luckily, the clerk was an admirer of Dostoevsky and promised that the document would be ready in a few days. Anna's mother gathered up the jewelry, silver, and other valuables the very same evening, and an appraiser came a day later for the furniture.

Dostoevsky then announced that he and Anna were going abroad after all— and no later than two days hence! Pasha's objections were cut short, and Dostoevsky told his dependents that they would receive the sums asked for but not a kopek more; the extra money was Anna's. The pair packed quickly, entrusting all future financial arrangements to Anna's mother, and took along only a necessary minimum, since they expected to be gone for no longer than three months. In fact, they were not to return for four years. Although Anna was later able to write that "I shall be eternally grateful to God for giving me strength in my decision to go abroad," this gratitude was often tempered by bitter afterthoughts in the years closer to the event.[12] Anna's devotion and moral stamina were tested to the uttermost, and it was her ability to measure up to the challenge that, in the long run, forged an unshakable foundation for her marriage.

——— ∎ ———

The Dostoevskys left for their European "vacation" on April 12/26, 1867, taking the train from Petersburg to Berlin, and then moved on to Dresden, where they

[9] Ibid., 109.
[10] Ibid., 110.
[11] Ibid., 112.
[12] Ibid., 114.

rented three rooms in a private home and apparently intended to settle. Dostoevsky, heavily in debt to Katkov, planned to work there on his next novel, and to write an article on Belinsky for which he had received an advance from another editor. But the distractions entailed by their first weeks of living abroad, and particularly by a disastrous ten-day expedition to the roulette tables at Hombourg just a month after arriving, prevented him from progressing at all on the novel.

Anna had promised her mother to keep an account of the trip, and this shorthand diary, which she kept until the birth of her first child a little over a year later, provides an account of day-to-day events in Dostoevsky's life. Unfortunately, if we are to judge from her pages, Dostoevsky hardly spoke to her at all about his work; even when she had some knowledge of it—he dictated his lost article on Belinsky to her, for example—she simply records the fact and says not a word about its content. What preoccupied her—and not without good reason—was the straitened circumstances in which they lived, the problem of adjusting to Dostoevsky's continually changing moods, and the difficulties of living in a foreign environment where they did not know a soul and were constantly thrown back on themselves for companionship.

Dostoevsky was not an easy person to get along with even under the best conditions, and his continually recurring epilepsy invariably made him irritable, intolerant, and quarrelsome. Nor was his temper improved by his rabid xenophobia, which manifested itself in an intense dislike of the Germans among whom he lived and whose language he spoke brokenly. Anna was much more peaceable and less bigoted, but she joined Dostoevsky in denouncing the congenital "stupidity" of Germans or fretting bitterly about the petty cheating from which they suffered at the hands of waiters, landlords, and tradespeople. What Anna called Dostoevsky's "irritable, volcanic nature" also led to continual disagreements between the two. Dostoevsky was vexed at having his utterances challenged, and often upbraided Anna harshly when she differed with him. On one such occasion, when he was railing against the Germans, "I only contradicted for the sake of something to say . . . but Feodor . . . told me if I was as stupid as that I had better hold my tongue." Another time, they quarreled about a "sunset"! One dispute often led to another, and Anna jotted down, dispiritedly, "What does it all mean, this perpetual quarreling between us?"[13]

Anna nonetheless was infinitely tolerant of her husband's bad-tempered reactions and never forgot—how could she, being a pityingly pained witness to his

---

[13] *Dnevnik A. G. Dostoevskoi, 1867 g.* (Moscow, 1923), 173, 33–35, 59. This work was translated into English, from a German rendering, as *The Diary of Dostoevsky's Wife*, ed. Rene Fülöp-Miller and Dr. Fr. Eckstein, trans. Madge Pemberton (New York, 1928). I have used this translation as the basis for my own quotations from the original text.

frequent epileptic convulsions—that much of his irascibility was caused by the deranged state of his nerves. She never really took such abuse seriously, and writes, "I simply can't be cross with him; sometimes I show a severe face, but I've only to look at him for all my wrath to melt away." Dostoevsky's rages, as she depicts them, were all on the surface. It was Dostoevsky's habit to wake her and say good-night before going to bed (she retired earlier), and then "we talk together for ages, and he says pretty things to me and we joke and laugh, and that is the time we seem to come nearest together and is most precious to me of all the hours of the day."[14] All of their disputations, so far as can be judged from Anna's diary, ended with such renewed pledges of affection.

Anna was doggedly determined to make her marriage a success. What she feared most, rather than the hardships arising from their poverty or Dostoevsky's mercurial personality, was that she might lose him to his earlier passion for Suslova. Anna kept a watchful eye on her husband and knew that he was corresponding with his ex-mistress. Just before leaving for Dresden, Dostoevsky had received a letter from Suslova, to which he replied shortly after arriving there. Suslova had been living abroad for a year, and he brings her up to date. Of Anna, he writes that she has "a remarkably good and open character. . . . The difference in age is terrible (20 and 44), but I am more and more convinced that she will be happy. She has a heart and knows how to love." Dostoevsky responded to Suslova's complaints about her own sadness with an implicit reproach: "you consider people to be either infinitely radiant, or the next moment scoundrels and vulgarians."[15] Dostoevsky knew that Anna would not evaluate him in such exacting terms, and that inexhaustible tolerance was what he required most of all.

When Dostoevsky was absent—he spent a good deal of time alone in cafés reading French and Russian newspapers—Anna did not scruple to look through his letters. "It isn't the thing, I know, to read one's husband's letters behind his back," she remarks guiltily, "but I couldn't help it. The letter was from S[uslova]. After I had read it, I felt cold all over, and shivered and wept with emotion. I was so afraid the old inclination was going to revive and swamp his love for me. Dear God, do not send me this miserable fate! Just to think of it makes my heart stand still."[16] Suslova's letter has regrettably been lost, along with a later one that Anna picked up at the post office just after seeing Dostoevsky off for Hombourg. Carefully opening the flap so that it could be resealed, she decided that "it was a very stupid, clumsy letter and says but little for the understanding of the writer. I am quite sure she is furious about Feodor's marriage. . . . I went over to the looking-glass and saw how my face was covered with little red spots from

[14] Ibid., 35.
[15] PSS, 28/Bk. 2: 182.
[16] Dnevnik A. G. Dostoevskoi, 28.

excitement."[17] Such a possible challenge to her marriage certainly fortified Anna's resolve to endure all the onerous burdens that it entailed.

◼

The romance of Dostoevsky and Anna had blossomed in the course of their work together on *The Gambler*, and there is a certain irony in their future union being inaugurated under the auspices of this creation. Nothing placed more of a strain on Anna than the renewed onset of Dostoevsky's gambling obsession once they began living abroad. Three weeks after settling in Dresden, Dostoevsky began to speak of making a trip to Hombourg to try his luck, and Anna, though dreading the prospect ("when I think of his going away and leaving me here alone, cold shivers run down my spine"), raised no objection. Instead, she assured him that she could look after herself satisfactorily, and confided in her diary: "I see how this place begins to weary him and put him in a bad temper. . . . And, as the thought of this trip fills his mind to the extinction of everything else, why not let him indulge in it?"[18]

For Dostoevsky, the passion and excitement of the play, which he conveys so vividly in *The Gambler*, was obviously the lure, but there were always objective reasons allowing him to rationalize his desire, and these reasons had just recently acquired a new urgency. Just before leaving, two of his creditors filed charges that could have led to his arrest and incarceration in debtor's prison. As he wrote a bit later to Apollon Maikov, "it was touch and go that I wasn't seized."[19] Dostoevsky could thus no longer return to Russia without risking imprisonment, and his only chance of regaining his homeland was to obtain enough money to pay his debts. In addition, there was his hope of establishing a family, with all the new expenses that this would entail (for Anna had become pregnant shortly after their departure from Russia). Never had Dostoevsky been under greater psychic pressure to obtain funds quickly, and he was haunted by the image of others easily doing so at the roulette tables.

Dostoevsky took the train to Hombourg on May 4/16, filled more with trepidation and remorse than excitement as he left Anna in tears at the station. He wrote her a day later: "I am acting stupidly, stupidly, even more, badly and out of weakness, but there is just a miniscule chance and . . . to hell with it, that's enough."[20] Even though planning just a four-day interval, Dostoevsky remained in Hombourg for ten days, winning and losing, and finally being wiped out entirely. He pawned his watch, and so, as Anna remarks on his return, she never knew what time of the day or night it was.

[17] Ibid., 48.
[18] Ibid., 40.
[19] *PSS*, 28/Bk. 2: 204; August 16/28, 1867.
[20] Ibid., 184–185; May 5/17, 1867.

The agitated letters he wrote her daily are painful to read, and continually os-
cillate between self-castigation for yielding to temptation and frantic reassertions
of the possibility of winning if one could manifest the self-control so antithetical
to the Russian national character. "Here is my definitive observation, Anya: if
one is prudent, that is, if one is as though made of marble, cold, and *inhumanly*
cautious, then definitely *without any doubt*, one can win *as much as one wishes.*"
Someone in the casino was always performing such a feat; this time it was a Jew
who played "with horrible, *inhuman* composure" and "rake[d] in the money,"
leaving every day with a thousand gulden. Dostoevsky reports that he has short
stretches of such composure, and always wins while they last, but very soon he
loses control and is carried away into disastrous recklessness. Like Aleksey Ivanovich in *The Gambler*, he finds the whole business morally repugnant, and im-
plores his wife: "Anna, promise me never to show these letters to anyone. I do
not want tongues to wag about this abominable situation of mine. 'A poet remains a poet.'"[21]

What is so striking about these letters, aside from their pathetic disclosure of
Dostoevsky's weakness and capacity for self-delusion, is the depth of the guilt-
feelings they express. Dostoevsky had berated himself in the past because of
gambling losses he could ill afford, but he had never given way to such extreme
self-flagellations. Never before, to be sure, had anyone been so helplessly dependent on him as Anna, and never before had he felt so morally reprehensible in
sacrificing her to his compulsion. As he remarks, after confessing to gambling
away the money she had sent for his return fare: "Oh, if only the matter concerned just me, . . . I would have laughed, given it up as a bad job, and left. One
thing and *one thing only* horrifies me: what will you say, what will you think
about me? And what is love without respect? After all, because of this our marriage has been shaken. Oh, my dear, don't blame me permanently!" Entreating
Anna to send him the fare again, he pleads with her not to come herself out of
mistrust. "Don't even think of *coming here yourself* because of not trusting me.
Such a lack of trust—that I will not come back—will kill me."[22]

As his losses mounted and the hopelessness of his situation became self-
evident, what appeared to be the only means of salvation was the panacea of
getting back to work. "My darling, we will have very little money left," he writes,
"but don't grumble, don't be downcast, and don't reproach me. . . . I'll write
Katkov right away and ask him to send me another 500 rubles to Dresden. . . .
As for me, I'll get down to work on the article about Belinsky and while waiting
for a reply from Katkov will finish it. My angel, perhaps this is even all for the
best; I'll be rid of that cursed thought, the monomania, about gambling. Now

---

[21] Ibid., 186; May 6/18, 1867.
[22] Ibid., 196–198; May 12/24, 1867.

again, just as the year before last (before *Crime and Punishment*), I'll triumph through work."[23] Such resolutions were invariably the result of Dostoevsky's gambling misfortunes.

Dostoevsky at last returned to a long-suffering and lonely Anna, who had valiantly tried not to give way to despair in his absence. He wrote his promised letter to Katkov requesting another advance, and life resumed its ordinary round while the pair waited for a reply and lived frugally on some money (much less than they had expected) sent by Anna's mother. One of the few amusements of the Dostoevskys in Dresden, aside from listening to concerts in the public parks, was to visit the Dresden art museum, the Gemäldegalerie. Anna remarks that Dostoevsky would hurry "from one room to another . . . and never will stand except in front of his favorite pictures."[24] These pictures were all—with the exception of Claude Lorrain's *Acis and Galatea*—representations of Christ or of Christ and the Madonna. Just a few months before he began to struggle with creating a new novel, Dostoevsky was thus immersing himself in the emotions derived from contemplating the images of Christ and the Mother of God painted by some of the greatest artists of the Western Renaissance tradition. These were no longer the highly formalized iconic images he would have seen in Russian churches but depictions of Christ as a flesh-and-blood human being, existing in and interacting with a real world in which money existed and tribute had to be paid. Never before had he been exposed so abundantly to such imagery; and one can hardly gauge the impact it may have had on his sensibility at this moment. Can it be simply coincidence that his next novel came into being only when he discovered a character called "Prince Christ" in his notes and when, in effect, he set out to provide a Russian literary counterpart to the pictures he had so much admired in the Dresden Gemäldegalerie?

Dostoevsky's intention had been to move to Switzerland after receiving the funds from Katkov, but in planning the trip, the alluring idea of a stopover at Baden-Baden to recoup his gambling losses tempted him once again—especially since, in his letters to Anna from Hombourg, he had complained that his concern over her welfare was a source of emotional disturbance that prevented him from putting his infallible "method" for winning into practice. It had been a mistake not to have brought her along; but if they were together in Baden, this obstacle to success would be eliminated. As Anna writes sadly in her memoirs, "he spoke so persuasively, cited so many examples in proof of his theory, that he convinced me too," and she agreed to spend two weeks in Baden-Baden, "counting on the

[23] Ibid., 192; May 9/21, 1867.
[24] *Dnevnik A. G. Dostoevskoi*, 116.

fact that my presence during his play would provide a certain restraining influence. Once this decision was made, Feodor Mikhailovich calmed down and began to rewrite and finish the article he was having trouble with," the piece on Belinsky.[25]

The pair left Dresden for Baden-Baden on June 21/July 3 and arrived a day later—with so little money that they rented two rooms over a smithy in which work began at four in the morning. Anna, suffering some of the symptoms of her pregnancy, often felt weak and queasy, and was subject to accesses of depression and apathy. For the most part, however, she gallantly concealed her fears and misgivings from her husband and exhibited an extraordinary staunchness in coping with the nerve-racking demands placed on her by Dostoevsky's shortcomings.

He began to gamble immediately, with the usual results, but occasionally winning sums large enough to give them a certain security for the moment while allowing him to continue gambling for smaller stakes. This was what he intended to do, and he turned over the amounts he gained to Anna for safekeeping; but after losing the allotted amount he always returned and begged for more. Anna found his pleadings impossible to withstand because he was so tormented by the conflict between his remorseful sense of baseness and his irresistible obsession. A typical scene occurred on their third day, when half their money had vanished; after losing five more gold pieces, Dostoevsky "was terribly excited, begging me not to think him a rogue to have robbed me of my last crust of bread only to lose it, while I implored him only to keep calm, and that of course I did not think all those things of him, and that he should have as much money as he liked. Then he went away and I cried bitterly, being so cast down with sufferings and self-tormentings."[26]

In the midst of her own worries about the future (she worked to improve her shorthand skills, and began to practice translating from French as a possible source of family income), Anna found herself continually called on to calm Dostoevsky's own despondency and self-castigations. Once he went out to gamble, promising to return home quickly, and came back only seven hours later, without a penny and "utterly distracted." Anna tried to quiet him, "but he would spare me none of his self-reproaches, calling himself stupidly weak, and begging me, Heaven knows why, for forgiveness, saying that he was not worthy of me, he was a swine and I an angel, and a lot of other foolish things of the same kind . . . and to try and distract him I sent him on an errand to buy candles, sugar and coffee for me. . . . I was terribly disturbed by the state he was in, being afraid it may lead to another fit."[27]

[25] *Reminiscences*, 127–128.
[26] *Dnevnik A. G. Dostoevskoi*, 185.
[27] Ibid., 184.

One such attack is described, and helps us to understand why Anna felt that almost anything—even yielding without protest to Dostoevsky's mania—was better than risking the possibility of provoking an epileptic seizure. "I wiped the sweat from his forehead and the foam from his lips, and the fit only lasted a short while and was, I thought, not a severe one. His eyes were not starting out of his head, though the convulsions were bad. . . . As, bit by bit, he regained consciousness, he kissed my hands and then embraced me. . . . He pressed me passionately to his heart, saying he loved me like mad, and simply adored me. After the fits he is always seized with a fear of death. He says he is afraid they will end in his death, and that I must look after him." Dostoevsky also asked Anna to make sure, when she awoke the next morning, to check whether he was still alive.[28]

Dostoevsky himself was astonished at Anna's extraordinary tolerance of his failings, even when this meant pawning not only their wedding rings but the earrings and brooch he had given her as a present and, as a last resort, Dostoevsky's overcoat and Anna's lace shawl and spare frock. He even commented to her that, "if I had been older . . . I should have behaved quite differently and told him . . . that if my husband was trying to do some stupid things, I, as his wife, must not allow anything of the kind." On another occasion, when she had given way once more to his entreaties, he said, perhaps half-seriously, that "it would have been better for him to have a grumbling wife who would be . . . nagging instead of comforting him, and that it was positively painful to him the way I was so sweet."[29] Anna's refusal to blame or berate Dostoevsky could have increased his sense of guilt by blocking the possibility of turning against an accusatory judge, but such a surge of guilt never led to more than a momentary access of moral self-scrutiny.

Anna's forbearance, whatever prodigies of self-command it may have cost her, was amply compensated for (in her eyes) by Dostoevsky's immense gratitude and growing attachment. When Anna remarked once that she may have affected his luck adversely, Dostoevsky replied, "'Anna, my little blessing, whenever I die remember only how I blessed you for the luck you brought me,' adding that no greater good fortune had ever come his way, that God had been lavish indeed in bestowing me upon him, and that every day he prayed for me and only feared one day all this might alter, that to-day I both loved and pitied him, but once my love were to cease, then nothing would be the same." "That, however," Anna hastens to write, "will never happen, and I am quite certain we shall always love one another as passionately as we do now."[30]

"One had to come to terms with it," she wrote in her memoirs many years later, "to look at his gambling passion as a disease for which there was no

[28] Ibid., 311.
[29] Ibid., 189, 186.
[30] Ibid., 188.

cure."[31] Such a conclusion merely extended to gambling the same attitude she took toward Dostoevsky's personal irritability. Although this trait often led to an abusive treatment of herself as well as others, she blamed Dostoevsky's epilepsy and refused to accept it as his genuine nature. On the morning after the seizure mentioned, she noted, "Poor Feodor, he does suffer so much after his attacks and is always so irritable, and liable to fly out about trifles, so that I have to bear a good deal in these days of illness. It's of no consequence, because the other days are very good, when he is so sweet and gentle. Besides, I can see that when he screams at me it is from illness, not from bad temper."[32]

As the nerve-racking days passed without noticeable change, so that no end seemed in sight, even Anna's apparently infinite indulgence began to wear thin. Just after Dostoevsky had gone to pawn her brooch and earrings, she writes, "I could no longer control myself and began to cry bitterly. It was no ordinary weeping, but a dreadful convulsive sort of sobbing, that brought on a terrible pain in my breast, and relieved me not in the slightest. . . . I began to envy all the other people in the world, who all seemed to me to be happy, and only ourselves—or so it seemed to me—completely miserable."[33] Anna confesses to herself that she wished Dostoevsky to stay away as long as possible; but when he returned that day to tell her he had lost the money obtained for her jewelry, and wept as he said "Now I have stolen your last things from you and played them away!" she sank on her knees before his chair to try and calm his wretchedness. "Do what I might to comfort him, I couldn't stop him from crying."[34]

There are only a few instances in which she openly criticizes her husband; and these outbursts are always motivated by his incessant concern for the family of his dead brother. None of the torments of her present situation would bother her at all, Anna insisted, "if I knew that all this misery was unavoidable, but that we should have to suffer so that an Emilya Feodorovna and her lot can live in clover, and that I should have to pawn my coat so that she can have one, arouses a feeling within me the reverse of nice, and it hurts me to find such thoughtlessness and so little understanding and human kindness in anyone I love and prize so much." This is the most extreme upsurge of revolt in the Baden pages of her diary, and just a few sentences later, Anna shrinks back from her own audacity: "I am furious with myself for harboring such horrid thoughts against my dear, sweet, kind husband, I am a horrid creature, surely."[35]

[31] *Reminiscences*, 132.
[32] *Dnevnik A. G. Dostoevskoi*, 322.
[33] Ibid., 223–224.
[34] Ibid.
[35] Ibid., 269–270.

Dostoevsky had written Katkov again for another advance, though he had hesitated doing so from Baden-Baden, whose reputation as a gambling spa would make the reason for this new appeal evident; but he swallowed his pride in the face of dire necessity. Meanwhile, scenes of the kind already described were repeated daily, and when their last resource—her mother—seemed to be exhausted, Anna began to display her dissatisfaction more openly. "I told him . . . for a whole month I had borne it and said not a word, even when there was nothing else left to us, for still I could hope from some help from Mama, but that now everything was finished, it is impossible to ask Mama for any more, and I would be, moreover, ashamed to do it."[36]

She turned on Dostoevsky just after receiving a letter from her mother and learning that their furniture might be lost. "When Feodor began to speak of 'the damned furniture,' it hurt me so that I began to weep bitterly, and he was quite unable to calm me down. . . . I simply could not control myself, and said the very idea of winning a fortune through roulette was utterly ridiculous, and in my anger I jibed at him, calling him a 'benefactor of humanity.' . . . I am quite convinced that, even if we did win, it would only be to the benefit of all those horrid people, and we should not profit one jot or tittle." Hurt by Anna's phrase, Dostoevsky accused her the next day of being "harsh"; and this charge led to an explosion in the diary, where she lists all her many grievances and regretfully compares her own forbearance with the abusiveness of Dostoevsky's first wife. "It isn't worthwhile controlling oneself," she writes. "Marya Dimitrievna never hesitated to call him a rogue and a rascal and a criminal, and to her he was like an obedient dog."[37]

On July 21/August 2, Anna received another money order from her mother, and with this amount, combined with Dostoevsky's recent winnings, they at last had enough to pay their debts, redeem everything in pawn, cover their fare to Geneva, and live there until Katkov's next advance arrived. Anna mentions beginning to pack and making "various preparations for the journey."[38] Dostoevsky promptly began to gamble furiously on the very day these entries were made; and Anna, who was feeling unwell, flared up with indignation as he returned home with the usual litany and demands. Luckily he managed to win that evening and replenish their treasury.

The next day, having gone off to reclaim Anna's jewelry and wedding ring in the morning, Dostoevsky returned at eight in the evening and "at once turned on me in an outburst of wrath and tears, informing me that he had lost every single penny of the money I had given him to redeem our things with. . . . Feodor called himself an unutterable scoundrel, saying that he was unworthy of

[36] Ibid., 280.
[37] Ibid., 322–323, 326.
[38] Ibid., 339, 342.

me, that I had no business to forgive him, and all the time he never stopped crying. At last I succeeded in calming him down, and we resolved to go away from here tomorrow."[39] She then accompanied him to the pawnbroker, fearing to entrust him with another sum, after which they both went to the station to inquire about schedules.

Dostoevsky continued to gamble on their very last day and lost fifty francs that Anna had given him, as well as twenty more obtained from pawning a ring. Now short of funds for the trip, they pawned Anna's earrings again, redeemed the wedding ring, and bought their tickets. Just an hour and a half before departure, Dostoevsky returned to the casino with twenty francs for a last fling—of course to no avail. Anna jots down laconically: "I told him not to be hysterical, but to help me fasten the trunks and pay the landlady."[40] After settling accounts, which turned out to be an unpleasant affair, they finally left for the station. Nobody—not even the servant girls, whom Anna thought she had treated with consideration, and whose ingratitude she censures—bothered to bid them farewell.

◼

In the opening pages of his novel *Smoke*, Turgenev vividly sketches the fashionable crowd thronging about the Konversationshaus in Baden-Baden. This was the name of the main building of the spa; it contained the notorious gambling rooms in its central portion, a reading room in the right wing, and a famous restaurant and café on the left. The ladies in their glittering frocks recalled for Turgenev "the intensified brilliance and light fluttering of birds in the spring, with their rainbow-tinted wings."[41] Poor Anna disliked going there because of the shabbiness of her one black dress, though she was driven by sheer tedium to visit the reading room stacked with French, German, and Russian journals.

Not far from the café was a spot known as the "Russian tree," where the numerous Russian visitors were accustomed to assemble, exchange the latest gossip, and perhaps also to catch a glimpse of the most distinguished Russian inhabitant of the city, Turgenev. Dostoevsky never frequented the "Russian tree," and he was perhaps the only Russian who had no interest whatever in seeing or being seen by Turgenev—indeed, who hoped fervently that neither he nor Turgenev would catch sight of the other at all. Turgenev was one of the few people to whom Dostoevsky had turned while trapped in Wiesbaden and the debt hung over him. As luck would have it, just a few days after arriving in Baden-Baden, Dostoevsky was strolling with Anna when he ran into Ivan Goncharov, the author of *Oblomov*, whom he once described as a person with "the soul of a petty official . . . and the eyes of a steamed fish, whom God, as if for a joke, has

[39] Ibid., 345–346.
[40] Ibid., 352.
[41] *PSSiP*, 9: 143.

endowed with a brilliant talent."[42] Goncharov told the Dostoevskys how "Turgenev had caught sight of Feodor yesterday; but had said nothing to him knowing how gamblers do not like to be spoken to."[43] It was now incumbent on Dostoevsky to pay a call on Turgenev. "As Feodor owes Turgenev fifty rubles, he must make a point of going to see him, or otherwise Turgenev will think Feodor stays away from him for fear of being asked for money."[44]

Badly bruised by the altercation over *Fathers and Children*, Turgenev had retired to Baden-Baden to lick his wounds. Even an old friend and natural ally such as Herzen had turned against Turgenev's moderate pro-Western liberalism, which shrank back before the specter of revolution. A brilliant series of articles, *Ends and Beginnings*, published by Herzen in *The Bell* during 1862–1863, constituted a direct onslaught on Turgenev's most cherished convictions—and brought forth an equally famous reply. One cannot live without a God, Turgenev bitingly wrote in a personal letter, and Herzen "has raised [his] altar at the feet of the sheepskin [the Russian peasant], the mysterious God of whom one knows practically nothing."[45] This sharp divergence of political ideals was further envenomed by a nasty reference in *The Bell* that described Turgenev (without mentioning his name) as "losing sleep, appetite, his white hair and teeth" because of fear that the tsar did not know of his repentance.[46] This was an allusion to a letter from Turgenev to the tsar, written when his name became involved in an investigation, futilely requesting that he not be recalled to Russia to testify, and untruthfully disclaiming any connection with the revolutionary propaganda emanating from London through Herzen's Free Russian Press.

Echoes of this fierce quarrel resound all through *Smoke* and are responsible for some of its harshest passages, aimed at the Slavophilism of both the right and the left. Turgenev's sharpest barbs are reserved for those of whatever political stripe who harbor any hope of a special destiny reserved for Russia and its people. Turgenev's spokesman is a minor character named Potugin, who declares that if Russia were suddenly to disappear from the face of the earth, with everything it had created, the event would occur "without disarranging a single nail in the place . . . for even the *samovar*, the woven bast shoes, the yoke-bridle and the knout—these are our most famous products—were not invented by us."[47]

The publication of Turgenev's novel in April 1867 blew up a storm even more furious than the one attending *Fathers and Children*, and this time the novelist was assailed from all sides and by everybody. Annenkov wrote him, just after its

[42] *PSS* 28/Bk. 1: 244; November 9, 1856.
[43] *Dnevnik A. G. Dostoevskoi*, 185.
[44] Ibid., 223.
[45] *PSSiP*, 5: 67.
[46] Ibid., 628.
[47] Ibid., 232–233.

appearance in the pages of *The Russian Messenger*, that "The majority are frightened by a novel inviting them to believe that all of the Russian aristocracy, yes, and all of Russian life, is an abomination."[48] So outraged was good society, to which Turgenev belonged by birth and breeding, that the members of the exclusive English Club were on the point of writing him a collective letter excluding him from their midst (the letter was never sent, but a zealous "friend" informed Turgenev of the incident). Writing to Dostoevsky in late May 1867, Maikov brought him up to date on the Russian reaction: "The admirers of *Smoke*," he says, "are found only among the Polonophils."[49] Dostoevsky's reaction to the novel, which he had read before leaving Russia, was much the same; and the quarrel between the two men thus contained a social-cultural dimension as well as a purely personal and temperamental one.

The account of their meeting and quarrel in Baden-Baden is contained in a letter from Dostoevsky to Maikov, written a month later in Geneva. "I'll tell you candidly," Dostoevsky begins. "Even before that [the visit] I disliked the man personally." Dostoevsky's discomfiture, he admits, was made worse because of his unpaid debt; but "I also dislike the aristocratically farcical embrace of his with which he starts to kiss you but offers his cheek. The horrible airs of a general." Turgenev's upper-class manners always had rasped on Dostoevsky's nerves, and he will use this very detail in his withering portrait of the famous author Karmazinov (a deadly caricature of Turgenev) in *Demons*. It was not so much Turgenev's manners, though, that now accounted for Dostoevsky's hostility; "most important, his book *Smoke* put me out."[50] "He criticized Russia and the Russians monstrously, horribly," Dostoevsky writes. "Turgenev said we ought to crawl before the Germans, and that all attempts at Russianness and independence are swinishness and stupidity." When Turgenev remarked that "he was writing a long article against Russophils and Slavophils," Dostoevsky replied with the most quoted retort in their exchange: "I advised him, for the sake of convenience, to order a telescope from Paris. 'What for?' he asked. 'It's far from here,' I replied. 'Train your telescope on Russia and examine us, because otherwise it is really hard to make us out.'"[51]

Taken aback by Dostoevsky's sarcasm, Turgenev "got horribly angry"; and Dostoevsky then, with an air of "extraordinarily successful naïveté" momentarily abandoned his antagonistic stance and slipped into the role of reassuring fellow author: "But I really didn't expect that all this criticism of you and the failure of *Smoke* would irritate you so much; honest to God, *it isn't worth it*, forget about it all." This advice only increased Turgenev's exacerbation, and,

[48] *PSS* 28/Bk. 2: 450n.31.
[49] "Pis'ma Maikova k Dostoevskomu," in *DSiM*, 2: 338–339.
[50] *PSS* 28/Bk. 2: 210; August 16/28, 1867.
[51] Ibid., 211.

"turning red, he replied: 'But I'm not at all irritated! What do you mean?'" Dostoevsky then finally took up his hat; but before going, "somehow, absolutely without intention," he assures Maikov, "said what had accumulated in my soul about the Germans in three months." As we know from Anna's shorthand diary, this accumulation was one of undiluted bile; and Dostoevsky launched forth on a denunciation of the German people as "rogues and swindlers . . . much worse and more dishonest than ours."[52]

"Well here you go on talking about civilization," continues Dostoevsky, "well what has civilization done for them and what can they boast of so very much as superior to us?" These words drove Turgenev into a paroxysm of rage: "He turned pale (literally: I'm not exaggerating a bit, not a bit!) and said to me: 'In talking like that you offend me *personally*. You should know that I have settled here permanently, that I consider myself a German, not a Russian, and I'm proud of it!' I replied: 'I couldn't at all have expected you would say that, and therefore please forgive me for having offended you.' Then we parted quite politely and I vowed to myself never again to set foot at Turgenev's."[53] Turgenev presumably also resolved never again to set eyes on Dostoevsky, calling on him the next day at ten in the morning and leaving a card because Dostoevsky had made a point of informing him that he was never available before noon.

One other passage in the letter to Maikov is of great importance, because it leads Dostoevsky into remarks foreshadowing *The Idiot*. "And these people," Dostoevsky declares, "boast of the fact, by the way, that they are *atheists*! He [Turgenev] declared to me that he is an atheist through and through."[54] Whatever its origin, Turgenev's declaration caused Dostoevsky to explode to Maikov: "But my God, Deism gave us Christ, that is, such a lofty notion of man that it cannot be comprehended without reverence, and one cannot help believing that this ideal of humanity is everlasting! And what have they, the Turgenevs, Herzens, Utins, and Chernyshevskys presented us with? Instead of the loftiest, divine beauty, which they spit on, they are so disgustingly selfish, so shamelessly irritable, flippantly proud, that it's simply incomprehensible what they're hoping for and who will follow them."[55] One can see here the burgeoning impulse in Dostoevsky to present an image of the "loftiest, divine beauty" in the face of the jeering, mocking unbelievers, whose names somewhat indiscriminately represent all shades of opinion and two generations of the godless Westernized intelligentsia.

This encounter between Turgenev and Dostoevsky soon became public knowledge, at least in literary circles, because the portions of Dostoevsky's letter

[52] Ibid., 203–204.
[53] Ibid.
[54] *Dnevnik A. G. Dostoevskoi*, 214.
[55] *PSS* 28/Bk. 2: 211.

concerning Turgenev were sent by Maikov to the editor of a journal called *Russian Archives* (*Russky Arkhiv*), who was requested to preserve the information "for posterity" but not allow its publication before 1890. Learning of this document through his informal literary factotum Annenkov, Turgenev promptly sent a disclaimer to the same editor through Annenkov, authorizing his intermediary to deny the views attributed to him. Referring to "the shocking and absurd opinions about Russia and the Russians that he attributes to me . . . which are supposed to constitute my convictions," Turgenev denies that he ever would have expressed his "intimate convictions" before Dostoevsky. "I consider him," he writes, "a person who, as a consequence of morbid seizures and other causes, is not in full control of his own rational capacities; and this opinion of mine is shared by many others." During Dostoevsky's visit, Turgenev urbanely explains, "he relieved his heart by brutal abuse against the Germans, against me and my last book, and then departed; I hardly had the time or desire to contradict him; I repeat that I treated him as somebody who was ill. Probably his disordered imagination produced those arguments that he attributed to me, and on whose basis he composed against me his . . . message to posterity."[56] The editor responded reassuringly to Turgenev, noting as well that the document did not bear Dostoevsky's name, and the matter ended there. Whether Dostoevsky's "disordered imagination" did or did not invent the utterances ascribed to Turgenev can only remain an open question.

[56] *PSSiP*, 7: 17–18.

CHAPTER 38

In Search of a Novel

The Dostoevskys arrived in Geneva on August 13/25, spending a day en route in Basel. In the short time afforded them, they hurried out to take in the sights, of which the Basel Museum alone merited Dostoevsky's regard, or more precisely, two of the paintings displayed in the museum. Anna writes:

> There are only two really priceless pictures in the whole Museum, one of them being the Dead Savior, a marvelous work that horrified me, and so deeply impressed Feodor that he pronounced Holbein the Younger a painter and creator of the first rank. . . . [T]he whole form [of Christ] is emaciated, the ribs and bones plain to see, hands and feet riddled with wounds, all blue and swollen, like a corpse on the point of decomposition. The face too is fearfully agonized, the eyes half open still, but with no expression in them, and giving no idea of *seeing*. Nose, mouth and chin are all blue; the whole thing bears such a strong resemblance to a real dead body. . . . Feodor, nonetheless, was completely carried away by it, and in his desire to look at it closer got on to a chair, so that I was in a terrible state lest he should have to pay a fine, like one is always liable to here.[1]

This chance visit to the Basel Museum was to have momentous consequences for the creation of *The Idiot*, in which the canvas of Holbein the Younger plays an important symbolic role. No greater challenge could be offered to Dostoevsky's own faith in Christ the God-man than such a vision of a tortured and decaying human being, whose face bore not a trace of the "extraordinary beauty" with which, as Dostoevsky was to write in the novel, Christ is usually painted. Instead, this picture expresses the subjection of the supernatural Christ to the physical order of nature, conceived "in the form of a huge machine of the most modern construction which, dull and insensible, has clutched, crushed, and swallowed up a great priceless Being, a Being worth all nature and its laws, worth the whole earth, which was perhaps created solely for the appearance of that Being" (8: 339).

[1] *Dnevnik A. G. Dostoevskoi, 1867 g.* (Moscow, 1923), 361–366.

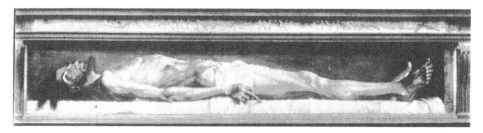

22. Hans Holbein the Younger, *Dead Christ* (1521–1522)

Holbein the Younger thus had created a work that relentlessly probed the basis of Christian belief with unflinching honesty, while presumably remaining loyal to its supernatural tenets. Dostoevsky's excitement at encountering such a painting may be attributed to having discovered a fellow artist whose underlying inspiration was so close to his own. For Holbein the Younger—the friend of Erasmus and Sir Thomas More, who left portraits of both these illustrious humanists—had been afflicted like them by the new currents of ideas flowing from the world of classical learning, and he had struggled to reconcile such secular influences, so contrary to the irrational dogmas of the Christian faith, with the renewal of such faith inspired by the iconoclastic fervors of the Reformation. In Holbein the Younger, Dostoevsky sensed an impulse, so similar to his own, to confront Christian faith with everything that negated it, and yet to surmount this confrontation with a rekindled (even if humanly tragic) affirmation.

■

Once in Geneva, Dostoevsky wasted no time in writing a letter to his staunchest friend, Apollon Maikov, asking for a loan. He had already received three advances from Katkov, whose generosity he found astonishing ("What a heart the man has!"),[2] and he now owed the editor four thousand rubles. This debt he planned to repay with his novel; meanwhile, it was necessary to survive before he could begin to supply Katkov with copy in January. Disclosing Anna's pregnancy, which he asks Maikov to keep secret for the time from Dostoevsky's relatives, he asks for one hundred and fifty rubles for two months, which would be repaid directly by *The Russian Messenger*. Fully aware that Maikov's means were limited, Dostoevsky writes piteously: "But really, I'm drowning, have utterly drowned. In two or three weeks I'll be absolutely without a kopek, and a drowning man extends a hand without consulting reason . . . except for you—I don't have *anyone*, and if you don't help me I'll perish, utterly perish."[3] Describing his passion for gambling as a moral-psychological flaw of character, he remarks:

[2] *PSS*, 28/Bk. 2: 207; August 16/28, 1867.
[3] Ibid., 208, 214.

23. Apollon Maikov, ca. 1861

"And worst of all is that my nature is vile and very passionate; everywhere and in everything I go to the last limit; I've been going over the line my whole life."[4]

Not having been in touch with Maikov for a protracted period of time, Dostoevsky urges him to write regularly; such letters "will take the place of Russia for me and will give me strength." Dostoevsky's intense nostalgia for his homeland and his despair over the impossibility of returning reflect now a gnawing fear that a prolonged residence in Europe would cripple his creative capacities: "And I need Russia, need it for my *writing* . . . and how badly I need it! It's just like a fish being out of water; you lose your strength and means. . . . I had wanted to set immediately to work and sensed that I absolutely couldn't work, that the impression was absolutely the wrong one. . . . The Germans upset my nerves, and the life of our Russian upper stratum and its faith in Europe and *civilization* did too!"[5]

Never had Dostoevsky's love for his native land reached such a pitch of fanaticism as during these years of involuntary expatriation. And never, as a result, did Russia appear to him, with the beguiling eyes of distance, more radiant and

[4] Ibid., 207.
[5] Ibid., 203, 204, 206.

more full of hope for the future. "Honest to God," he writes to Maikov, "the present time, with its changes and reforms, is almost more important than that of Peter the Great's. . . . [T]here will be *true justice* everywhere, and then what a great renewal!"[6] In the same letter Dostoevsky excoriates Turgenev and the Russian "atheists," whose ideal of man, presumably modeled on themselves, cannot stand comparison with the "lofty notion of man" given by Christ. Here we can observe how Dostoevsky's belief in the impending moral-social regeneration of the Russian people—a belief greatly nourished by his exile—blends with his religious convictions and his abhorrence of those who worship before the alien god of Western civilization. Just a few months later, such feelings will contribute to his creation of a specifically Russian image of the highest type of moral beauty possible to humankind.

At the time he wrote to Maikov, Dostoevsky was working on the essay on Belinsky. Anna remarks that dictation of the piece resumed at the beginning of September, and it was soon dispatched to Maikov with the request to transmit it to the editor of the almanac. But although Maikov followed Dostoevsky's instructions, the almanac never appeared and Dostoevsky's pages were lost. Just what the essay contained can only be inferred, but Dostoevsky surely would have tried to include some of the reminiscences later incorporated in his *Diary of a Writer* (1873). There he evokes the image of Belinsky when the critic had just been converted to Left Hegelian atheism. Responding to the question of whether Christ still had any role to play in the modern world, Belinsky retreats from his initial position that Christ would "simply vanish in the face of contemporary science," and hastens to agree with an opinion expressed by someone else that "He would, as you say, join the Socialists and follow them" (21: 11).

Such memories would have flooded back to Dostoevsky as he was writing his article, and if so, then the image of a returning Christ, that is, a Christ reentering the modern world and required to adjust himself to its new moral-social challenges, would have been insistently hovering before him in the period immediately before he began work on his new novel. It is not implausible to imagine that Prince Myshkin's attempt to live by the highest Christian values in the modern world, and to cope with young Nihilists who considered him as ludicrously outmoded as Belinsky had considered Christ himself, is linked in some subconscious fashion with Dostoevsky's struggles to tell the truth about "My Acquaintance with Belinsky."

◾

Dostoevsky's epileptic attacks became more frequent in Geneva, and he thought of moving elsewhere, but with barely enough resources to cover their room and

[6] Ibid., 206.

meals (they were constantly in arrears and forced to pawn belongings in order to get through a bad stretch), they could not think of leaving. Moreover, Anna would be giving birth in a few months, and Dostoevsky wanted to stay in a large, French-speaking city where medical care would be easily available and he could count on his command of the language.

Geneva was filled with a large number of Russians living abroad as political exiles, and they frequented the same cafés where Dostoevsky would have gone to read the Russian newspapers, but the only fellow exile with whom Dostoevsky struck up any sustained relation was Nikolay P. Ogarev, a distant cousin and boon companion of Herzen, who was himself prominent in radical circles. Just a few years earlier, in a famous chapter of *My Past and Thoughts*, Herzen had portrayed the two young men, still in their teens, climbing to the heights of the Sparrow Hills outside Moscow and "suddenly embracing . . . vow[ing] in the sight of all Moscow to sacrifice our lives to the struggle we had chosen."[7] This struggle involved a declaration of war against tyranny and despotism, and Herzen and Ogarev had remained faithful to their youthful oath by becoming leaders of the Russian revolutionary movement.

The son of a wealthy landowning family, Ogarev was a gentle, softhearted soul whose life had been passed in the shadow of Herzen's more vital and vigorous personality. A good part of his considerable fortune had been dissipated by his pleasure-loving first wife, whose infidelities, however, had never caused him to renounce her completely. His second wife, when the pair moved to London, became the mistress of his best friend, the recently widowed Herzen, to whom she bore three children. But this matrimonial reshuffling did not disturb the intimacy and close collaboration between the two men—which tells us a good deal about the gentleness of Ogarev's character. When his father died and he became master of the considerable estate, what part of his fortune had not been squandered by his first wife was further diminished because he freed his serfs on terms so advantageous to them and so economically disastrous for himself. By the time he met Dostoevsky in Geneva, Ogarev was almost as poor as the indigent novelist and lived with his devoted companion (an English ex-prostitute) and her son on a small stipend provided by the affluent Herzen, whose money had always received the most careful supervision.

Ogarev worked zealously for the cause he had pledged to advance on the Sparrow Hills. He had become co-editor with Herzen of *The Bell*, and he also edited a special journal, *The Common Assembly* (*Obschee Veche*), whose purpose was to stir up discontent among the Old Believers, the lower orders of the clergy, and peasants and soldiers unlikely to pay attention to propaganda cast in a more

[7] Alexander Herzen, *My Past and Thoughts*, trans. Constance Garnett, rev. Humphrey Higgins, 4 vols. (New York, 1968), 169.

modern linguistic and ideological idiom. Ogarev was thus publicly linked with the revolutionary agitation of the intelligentsia that Dostoevsky had come to abhor, but he was a highly cultivated, Romantic Idealist man of letters of the 1840s, with a refinement of taste and sensibility that Dostoevsky could respect independently of the partisan enmities of politics. Politically, Ogarev advocated the convening of a *zemsky sobor* (an assembly of representatives of *all* the people, including the peasantry) to cope with the problems created by the liberation of the serfs. The call for such an assembly would later become a mainstay of Dostoevsky's own political articles in his *Diary of a Writer*.

The two men had probably met during Dostoevsky's visit to London in 1863, when he called on Herzen several times and was introduced to his entourage; and the amiable Ogarev now visited the Dostoevskys at home. "I have just been at the house of the dead," he informs Herzen on September 3.[8] It was because of Ogarev that the Dostoevskys attended one session of the Congress that took place in Geneva a week later under the auspices of a group of progressives and radicals calling themselves the League of Peace and Freedom, who had appointed Bakunin, Ogarev, and another more obscure Russian émigré to represent their native land.

Bakunin was scheduled to speak at the second session of the Congress, and it was long thought that the Dostoevskys had been present when the celebrated revolutionary warrior—whose leonine personality made him an electrifying platform presence, further heightened by his exotic garb of a Cossack freebooter—made a stirring impromptu speech in French calling for the breakup of the Russian Empire and expressing the hope that its armies would be defeated in the future. He also called for the destruction of all "centralized states" to make way for the formation of a United States of Europe organized freely on the basis of new groupings once the old state frameworks had been demolished.

In her *Reminiscences*, Anna mistakenly writes that she and Dostoevsky attended the second session of the Congress. In fact, as her diary proves, the Dostoevskys attended the *third* session, and so could not have heard Bakunin's impassioned denunciation of everything Dostoevsky held dear. However, the sessions were covered thoroughly in the local and international press, which Dostoevsky read with great diligence, and he was thus well informed about what Bakunin had so thunderously advocated at the second meeting. Not all of the delegates had been in agreement, as Dostoevsky knew, with Bakunin's vision of total destruction as a necessary prelude to the advent of a new anarchist Utopia; but it was this vision that dominated the impression left by the Congress on his imagination. Several of his letters at this time contain references to the Congress, and they all ridicule its confusion and absurdity, as well as the self-contradiction

---

[8] Cited in the notes to A. G. Dostoevskaya, "Dnevniki i vospominaniya," *LN* 86 (Moscow, 1973), 284n.26.

of its presumably Bakunian goals.[9] In a letter to his favorite niece, Sofya Ivanova, he sets down the most detailed evocation:

> They began with the fact that in order to achieve peace on earth the Christian faith has to be exterminated; large states destroyed and turned into small ones; all capital be done away with, so that everything be in common, by order, and so on. All this without the slightest proof, all of this was memorized twenty years ago and that's just how it has remained. And most importantly, fire and sword—and after everything has been annihilated, then, in their opinion, there will in fact be peace.[10]

Three years later, such reactions will be poured into *Demons*, where Dostoevsky also stresses the self-contradictions in which the radicals became involved as they try to think through the consequences of their cherished ideas. The theoretician of the revolutionary group in that novel will be reduced to despair because his "conclusion is in direct contradiction to the original idea with which I start. Starting from unlimited freedom, I arrived at unlimited despotism" (10: 311).

◼

Once having sent off his ill-fated Belinsky article, Dostoevsky settled into his larger task, and in mid-September Anna jotted down, "today Fedya began to sketch the program of the new novel."[11] Dostoevsky's most immediate problem was, as usual, the financial one, and he wrote to everyone who might be willing to lend a helping hand. Maikov sent one hundred twenty-five rubles, and Dostoevsky also appealed to his old friend Dr. Yanovsky, requesting a loan of seventy-five rubles. The reply, happily containing one hundred rubles, arrived on a day when Anna was particularly gloomy because the pair had no money left at all. "I would certainly have to go to that dressmaker and pawn my lace mantilla. God! How much I wish I didn't have to go," she writes, adding that she would rather remain hungry for three more days than bow humbly before the condescending dressmaker.[12]

Matters were not always arranged so conveniently, and more than once both Anna and Dostoevsky were forced to pawn their clothing like paupers under the gaze of the impassive Swiss. Letters from both Pasha and Emilya Feodorovna complained that *they* were short of funds, thus driving Anna into her usual rage at their exigencies. They had just returned to Petersburg from the summer dacha at Lublino and had moved into Dostoevsky's old apartment, for whose rent he

---

[9] *PSS*, 28/Bk. 2: 217; September 3/15, 1867.
[10] Ibid., 224–225; September 29/October 11, 1867.
[11] "Dnevniki," 197.
[12] Ibid., 247.

made himself responsible. Anna was incensed at finding listed among her sister-in-law's grievances a lack of money to redeem her pawned best overcoat. "That is really killing, my overcoat has also been pawned, for more than six months, and before hers mine must be redeemed."[13] Katkov again exhibited his usual generosity, and the Dostoevskys finally had a regular but pitifully small income to tide them over until the novel could be gotten under way. Dostoevsky estimated, with his usual overoptimism, that once writing began he would complete it in five months.

Despite the pressure of his impending deadline, Dostoevsky nonetheless found time to make two short trips to Saxon-les-Bains for another fling at roulette. The lure of winning a large amount revived once more, and Anna could only mark its appearance with incredulity and stoic resignation. On September 17, she noted, "what a strange man. It would seem that fate has punished him so strongly, and showed him so many times that he cannot get rich by roulette. . . . [H]e still is convinced all the same . . . that he will certainly become rich, will certainly win, and then will be able to help his wretches."[14] The usual results occurred, and after the second catastrophe, in a letter filled with the familiar frantic apologies and self-flagellations, he sketched a plan to ask Ogarev for a loan of three hundred francs (unaware of the veteran radical's own circumstances). "After all, he's a poet, a writer, he has a heart, and in addition he himself comes to me and seeks me, which means he respects me."[15] When Dostoevsky put the question to Ogarev, the mention of such a large sum "almost frightened him,"[16] according to Anna, but he thought he might scrape together sixty francs. Two days later, the unfailingly generous Ogarev visited the Dostoevskys and brought the smaller amount, which they promised to return in two weeks (whether they kept their word remains unknown).

Dostoevsky's entire future, of course, depended on the success of his next novel, which only increased the tension under which he was working. The notebooks for *The Idiot* illustrate how persistently Dostoevsky struggled to find his artistic path through the maze of incidents that he piles up in such profusion. What he counted on, as he wrote to Maikov, was the sudden flash of inspiration that would enable him to discover, among the swarming multiplicity of his scenarios, the one that he could most profitably develop. All through the fall and winter months Dostoevsky sought this moment and tried to provoke its appearance—with so little success, however, that he feared his capacities might be fading because of the frequency of his epileptic attacks. Writing to Dr. Yanovsky in a moment of depression, he complains that "this epilepsy will end up by carrying me

---

[13] Ibid., 227.
[14] Ibid., 184.
[15] *PSS*, 28/Bk. 2: 235; November 6/18, 1867.
[16] "Dnevniki," 276.

off. My star is fading—I realize that. My memory has grown completely dim (completely!). I don't recognize people anymore. I forget what I read the day before. I'm afraid of going mad or falling into idiocy." [17]

Nonetheless, work stubbornly went on, though without the necessary spark of insight flashing forth from his notebook pages he became more and more discouraged. At the end of October, Anna awoke one night to find him lying on the floor in prayer, and while there were many blessings for which he might have been imploring God, inspiration for his next novel may well have been one of them. Above all, though, he had determined that he would not compromise his artistic integrity, whatever the cost. Explaining to Maikov why he had abandoned a considerable first draft, he declares, "I said to hell with it all. I assure you that the novel could have been satisfactory, but I got incredibly fed up with it precisely because of the fact that it was satisfactory and not *absolutely good*." [18] Rather than produce a satisfactory mediocrity, Dostoevsky instead chose to launch himself, almost unprepared, into the writing of one of the most extraordinary and thematically unprecedented novels in the history of the genre.

———■———

Dostoevsky read the newspapers every day, particularly the Russian ones, and perhaps even more attentively now than in the past. "Read them, please," he admonishes his niece Sofya Ivanova, "because the visible connection among all matters, general and private, is becoming stronger and . . . more obvious." [19] It is not surprising then, to find that for *The Idiot*, at least in its initial stages, Dostoevsky drew extensively on material from the newspapers. His early notes were affected by what he read of a court case involving the Umetsky family, whose fourteen-year-old daughter Olga had tried to burn down the family house four times and was then brought to trial. Investigation uncovered an unspeakable picture of family tyranny, cruelty, and revolting neglect on the part of the parents. Their inhumanity had led the poor child to attempt to take her own life several times before turning to arson as a last resort. "I'm just dying to get back to Russia," he tells Maikov in mid-October. "I wouldn't let the Umetsky case go by without having my word; I'd publish it." [20] Eventually, Olga Umetskaya would inspire the creation of Nastasya Filippovna, the most genuinely tragic and enchanting of all Dostoevsky's heroines.

The harrowing fate of Olga Umetskaya was not the only case that left its traces on *The Idiot*. It is likely that the character of Rogozhin, not mentioned in the early notes, is linked to the trial of a Moscow merchant named V. E. Mazurin,

[17] *PSS*, 28/Bk. 2: 358; November 1/13, 1867.
[18] Ibid., 239n.10
[19] Ibid., 222n.13
[20] Ibid., 228; October 9/21, 1867.

who murdered a jeweler. The corpse, concealed in the house, was covered with an American oilskin; it was also surrounded, exactly as would be the corpse of Nastasya Filippovna, by two containers of something called Zhdanov fluid, used in Russia as a disinfectant and deodorant. Two other crimes culled from the newspapers are also referred to frequently in *The Idiot*. One is the murder of six people by an eighteen-year-old student named Gorsky, who came from a noble family. Hired as a tutor by the Zhemarin family, he carefully prepared for his crime before carrying it out, killing a doorman and a cook as well as four family members, including his pupil. In *The Idiot*, Lebedyev speaks of his young Nihilist nephew as being capable of committing a similar deed, and Dostoevsky thus brings this mass murder into the orbit of his conviction that Nihilist ideas were weakening the power and moral conscience in the younger generation.

The second crime that found its way into *The Idiot* involved the murder of a servant by an acquaintance for the sake of a silver watch. Just before slitting the throat of the watch's owner, with whom he had been chatting peacefully, the criminal uttered a prayer: "Bless me, O Lord, and forgive for the sake of Christ." The murderer's motive in real life was to pawn the watch and return to his starving family in a village. But Dostoevsky uses the incident rather to indicate the deep, instinctive religiosity of the Russian people even in the midst of their worst excesses. Myshkin remarks, in what for Dostoevsky is a self-referential allusion, that if such a detail had been invented by a novelist, critics would have taxed it for being "improbable; but reading it in the newspapers as a fact, you feel that in such facts you are studying the reality of Russian life" (8: 412–413).

To supplement his devoted scrutiny of the newspapers, he was dependent on letters from friends like Maikov and from his immediate family, and his responses to these letters reveal, on the one hand, a growing antipathy toward European life in all its aspects, and on the other a compensating idealization of Russia that increased in proportion to his hostility. When Maikov wrote that he was translating *The Tale of Igor's Campaign*, the famous twelfth-century epic, into modern Russian, Dostoevsky became excited at the news. This task was, as Maikov explained, his "small *monumentum*, an offering on the 'altar of the fatherland,'"[21] and Dostoevsky's headlong decision to write *The Idiot* may well have been at least partly inspired by the same impulse to celebrate the highest values of Russian culture as he conceived them. Otherwise, the field would be left to those whom Dostoevsky rails against in a choleric outburst ("just recall our best liberals, recall Belinsky; wasn't he really a quite conscious enemy of the fatherland, wasn't he really retrograde?").[22] This view will soon find its way into

---

[21] *DSiM*, 2: 343; November 3, 1867.
[22] *PSS*, 28/Bk. 2: 259n.23.

The Idiot, where it is expounded by the highly intelligent Evgeny Pavlovich Radomsky, and he is seconded by Prince Myshkin.

Dostoevsky grasped at every indication he could find to justify his belief that Russian life—however much appearances might seem to indicate the contrary—was, at its moral core, superior to the much-vaunted European civilization. A striking example of such superiority, for him as well as for Maikov, was furnished by the vicissitudes of V. I. Kelsiev, the former associate of Ogarev, about whom Dostoevsky was informed in a letter from his friend. Maikov recounts how Kelsiev, after years of unbelievable hardship and self-sacrifice—years spent trying to enlist various denominations of the Old Believers for the revolutionary cause—had appeared at the Russian border one day, declared himself a political criminal, and surrendered to the authorities. Taken to Petersburg, he was brought before a special commission and his case was then sent to the tsar, who, after reading Kelsiev's confession and other documents, ordered him to be pardoned unconditionally. "You know," Maikov continues, "all this moves me to tears. How Russian this is! How much far and away higher and better this is than all that humanistic bedlam in Geneva." What carried the day, according to Maikov, was Kelsiev's autobiographical confession, in which he explained that "only in the Slavic question and in the role of Russia in Slavdom" was he able to discover a resolution for "all his own ideal, deracinated strivings for liberty and activity."[23]

Dostoevsky was ecstatic at such news and replied: "That's the way, that's the truth, that's the way to do things. . . . [A]ll our trashy little liberals of a seminarian-socialist hue . . . will fall on him like wild beasts . . . now they'll be saying of Kelsiev that he denounced everyone."[24] Dostoevsky will depict his young Nihilists in *The Idiot* as more ridiculous than menacing, and the abused Prince Myshkin treats them with the same magnanimity that the tsar displayed toward the hapless and remorseful Kelsiev (who honorably refrained from denouncing anybody, and defended his collaboration with Herzen and Ogarev). If Dostoevsky's reaction to the history of Kelsiev may have influenced his handling of the young Nihilists, there is no question that the figure of Kelsiev himself served as one of the sources for Shatov, the passionately honest and repentant revolutionary-turned-nationalist in *Demons*.

Dostoevsky's fanatical belief in the moral elevation of the Russian spirit, and the messianic destiny marked out for it in the future, is unabashedly proclaimed in an important letter to Maikov written just after sending off the first chapters of *The Idiot*. He mentions the admiration of their mutual friend Strakhov for the achievements of German culture, and he objects because "that's the way their life has worked out! And we at that time were putting together a great nation, had

[23] *DSiM*, 2: 341; September 20, 1867.
[24] *PSS*, 28/Bk. 2: 227n.8.

stopped Asia forever, endured endless suffering, *were able* to endure it all, did not lose the Russian idea, which will renew the world. . . . Our people are infinitely higher, more noble, more honest, more naïve, more capable, and full of a different, very lofty Christian idea, which Europe, with her sickly Catholicism and stupidly contradictory Lutheranism, does not even understand."[25] Dostoevsky had just taken the decision to embody this "lofty [Russian] Christian idea" in the character of Prince Myshkin, and some of the thoughts in this letter, especially the contrast between "the Russian idea" and Roman Catholicism, will appear in the Prince's harangue during his engagement party.

Dostoevsky reiterates his faith that "Russian thought is preparing a grandiose renovation for the entire world (you are right, it is closely linked with Russian Orthodoxy), and this will occur in about a century—that's my passionate belief." But for such a renovation to take place, the *rights* of the Great Russians over the other Slav nationalities must be definitively and unquestionably affirmed. Dostoevsky's messianism, then, in one context stresses what Reinhold Niebuhr would call its "ethical-universalistic" component—the notion that Russia was destined to install a Christian reign of goodness and justice on earth—and in another becomes "egoistic-imperialistic" and emphasizes the importance of extending Russian political power.[26] For Dostoevsky the two were identical: he viewed the second as the precondition of the first and, unlike many later critics, refused to see any insoluble conflict between them. When it came to individual human life, however, Dostoevsky's nationalistic hubris was tempered by an acute sense of human fallibility and of the impossibility, which he would dramatize in Prince Myshkin, for any terrestrial being fully to realize the Christian ideal. Only the God-man Christ had been capable of doing so, and the Incarnation had set before mankind a goal toward which it must eternally aspire.

For Dostoevsky, it was only in the afterlife of immortality that a perfect accomplishment of the Christian ideal of love could be realized, and his letters at this time contain several strong affirmations of his belief in such an afterlife. He consoles his sister and his niece Sofya Ivanova on the death of his brother-in-law, Dr. Ivanov: "lament and shed tears, but don't give way, in the name of Christ, to despair. . . . Look, you believe in a future life . . . none of you has been infected by the rotten and stupid atheism. Remember that he really knows now about you; never lose the hope of reunion and believe that this future life is a necessity, not only a consolation."[27]

---

[25] Ibid., 243n.14.

[26] For this distinction, see Reinhold Niebuhr, *The Nature and Destiny of Man*, 2 vols. (New York, 1964), 2: 15–34. This profound discussion stresses how deeply rooted the messianic dream is in all cultures that believe God's purpose will be realized in and through history. Niebuhr also points out how inevitably those two types become entangled with each other.

[27] *PSS*, 28/Bk. 2: 254; February 1/13, 1868.

This theme of immortality hovers in the background of *The Idiot* as an accompaniment to the theme of atheism—with which, as we see here, it is intimately related in Dostoevsky's sensibility. The plight of the dying young atheist Ippolit as he contemplates Holbein's *Dead Christ*, with its suggestion of the triumph of blind nature over Christ, is deepened into irremediable torment precisely because of this lack of religious faith and thus of the hope of immortality. Prince Myshkin, on the other hand, experiences a sense of "the universal fusion of all"—a foretaste of immortality, as it were, though not designated as such—in the moment of aura just preceding the onset of an epileptic seizure. But Dostoevsky had then only begun to create his novel, and it is doubtful whether the thematic use he would make of Prince Myshkin's epilepsy, or the scenes involving Ippolit, were as yet very clear in his mind.

———■———

Dostoevsky's notes for *The Idiot* are extremely complicated and detailed, and there is a learned dispute, into which we need not enter, over the exact number of his separate plans. Nor is it necessary to spend time on all the twists and turns of the plot situations that he envisaged. Some general sense of their nature is well conveyed in the remarks of Edward Wasiolek, who has done so much to clarify these notes and, indeed, to make all of the notebooks for Dostoevsky's novels accessible to English readers:

> The relationship between characters fluctuates from plan to plan: sisters are and are not sisters, nephews become sons, fathers become uncles. The Idiot is sometimes the son of the Uncle, sometimes the nephew, sometimes the foster son, sometimes illegitimate, and sometimes legitimate; acts are committed and die abortively in the next plan, or even a few lines later; people hang themselves but then perhaps don't hang themselves; the same people die by hanging, poisoning, broken hearts or drowning. It is not always clear who is who, where they come from, and where they are going. Characters appear and disappear, crowd on the periphery, nudge their way into the author's consciousness for a time and then melt away; some appear without names and personalities, take on flesh, then waste away. Some persist to the very threshold of publication and immortality, only to find no place in the final conception.[28]

"I spent the entire summer and autumn working on various ideas (some were very entangled)," Dostoevsky writes to Maikov at the end of December. "Finally, I fixed on one of these ideas . . . and wrote a great deal. But then, on December 4

---

[28] Fyodor Dostoevsky, *The Notebooks for* The Idiot, trans. Katherine Strelsky, ed. with intro. by Edward Wasiolek (Chicago, 1967), 7–8. My quotations are taken from this translation.

(New Style) I threw it all out." As we know, the prospect of writing a "mediocre" novel repelled him. "Then (since my entire future depended on it), I set about the painful task of inventing a *new novel*. Nothing in the world could have made me continue with the first one. I simply could not. I turned things over in my mind from December 4 through December 18. I would say that on the average I came up with six plans a day (at least that). My head was in a whirl. It's a wonder I didn't go out of my mind. At last, on December 18, I sat down and started writing a new novel."[29] The first five chapters of the final text were mailed on January 5, and two more followed on the eleventh.

Just having emerged from this intense spurt of creativity, Dostoevsky confesses to Maikov: "I have no idea myself of what the thing I have sent them is like." But he explains that it finally emerged from a long cherished ambition: "For a long time already, there was an idea that had been bothering me, but I was afraid to make a novel out of it because it was a very difficult idea and I was not ready to tackle it, although it is a fascinating idea and one that I am in love with. The idea is—*to portray a perfectly beautiful man.* . . . It was only the desperate situation in which I found myself that made me embark upon an idea that had not yet reached full maturity. I took a chance, as at roulette: 'Maybe it will develop as I write it!' This is unforgivable."[30]

Dostoevsky concealed from Maikov that his "main hero" was still only a nebulous outline in his mind. But some further comments on the novel, which show how deeply Dostoevsky had been thinking about Prince Myshkin's relation to previous literary types, were made to his niece Sofya Ivanova at the very beginning of his work on *The Idiot*, sometime in mid-October. Repeating what he had written to Maikov, he explains that "the main idea of the novel is to portray a positively beautiful man. There is nothing more difficult in the world, and this is especially true today. All writers . . . who have ever attempted to portray the *positively* beautiful have always given up. . . . The beautiful is an ideal. . . . There is only one positively beautiful figure in the world—Christ—so that the phenomenon of that boundlessly infinitely good figure is already in itself an infinite miracle. (The whole of the Gospel of St. John is a statement to that effect; he finds the whole miracle in the Incarnation alone, in the manifestation of the beautiful alone.)"[31] It is precisely this "manifestation of the beautiful alone" that Dostoevsky will find himself attempting to recreate within a human rather than a divine-human perspective, and the letter shows him to be fully aware of some of the problems he would necessarily be called on to confront in doing so.

"I will mention only," he continues, "that, of the beautiful figures in Christian literature, the most complete is that of Don Quixote. But he is good only

[29] *PSS*, 28/Bk. 2: 240; December 31, 1867/January 12, 1868.
[30] Ibid., 240–241.
[31] Ibid., 251.

because at the same time he is ridiculous. The figure of Dickens's Pickwick (a conception infinitely weaker than that of Don Quixote, but still a tremendous one) is also ridiculous, and that's the only reason it succeeds. Compassion for the beautiful man who is ridiculed and who is unaware of his own worth generates sympathy in the reader. And this ability to arouse compassion is the very secret of humor. Jean Valjean is another powerful attempt, but he engenders sympathy because of his terrible misfortune and society's injustice toward him. But there is nothing of this sort in my novel, absolutely nothing, and that is why I am terribly afraid it will be a positive failure." [32] The response of Dostoevsky's contemporaries, as we shall see, confirmed his worst fears. But though *The Idiot* is the most uneven of Dostoevsky's four best novels, it is the one in which his personal vision of life, in all its tragic complexity, is expressed with the greatest intimacy, with the most poignancy, and with a lyrical pathos that touches on sublimity.

[32] Ibid.

CHAPTER 39

An Inconsolable Father

The publication of the first seven chapters of *The Idiot* in *The Russian Messenger* (January 1868) successfully crowned the months of torturing gestation that Dostoevsky had just lived through. But his uncertainties about the novel's continuation were far from over. Dostoevsky was forced to create *both* a scenario and a final text for each new installment, remaining in continual uncertainty until the very last stage of composition. And he changed residences five times while the novel was under way. Twice the Dostoevskys were forced to change quarters in Geneva, and then they shifted from Geneva to Vevey, on the other side of the lake, which supposedly had a milder climate. Three months later the Dostoevskys went to Italy, living for two months in Milan and then for the remainder of the year in Florence, where the final chapters were completed.

Work was also interrupted by the birth of their first child, a joyful event then followed by the tragedy of her death—a terrible blow to the couple, whose anguish is movingly expressed in Dostoevsky's letters. Dostoevsky was continually plagued by worry over the wayward conduct of his stepson Pasha, as well as by the indigence of his late brother's family. All these and other matters constantly distracted him, and it is not difficult for an observer to share the admiring astonishment expressed by Maikov: "Anna Grigoryevna in her condition, poverty, exile, no close friends or family nearby, how do you bear all this, yes, and while bearing it, to write a novel into the bargain!"[1] These were the circumstances under which Dostoevsky toiled away at *The Idiot*; and he had ample justification for claiming that no major Russian novelist of his time had worked under such disheartening impediments.

———■———

Dostoevsky's most pressing concern during the remainder of January was to furnish the copy promised to Katkov, and he sat at his desk day and night, struggling to embody his artistic intuitions in living figures on the page. To Sofya Ivanova he provides an image of his working routine: "I get up late, light the fire in the fireplace (it's awfully cold here), and we drink our coffee; then I get down

---

[1] "Pis'ma Maikova," *DSiM*, 2: 343.

to work. At four o'clock I go out for dinner in a restaurant, where I eat for 2 francs, wine included. Anna Grigoryevna prefers to eat at home [because of the advanced state of her pregnancy]. After that I go to a café, where I drink coffee and read the *Moscow Gazette* and *The Voice* down to the last syllable. When I am through I take a walk for half an hour or so to get some exercise and then return home and go back to work. Later I stoke the fire again, we drink tea, then I get back to work again. Anna Grigoryevna says that she is frightfully happy." [2]

Whether Dostoevsky gave complete credence to Anna's reassurances may be left undecided, though he was much concerned over the state of her health and spirits. Six weeks later, he informs Maikov, "Anna Grigoryevna is waiting in awe, loves our future guest with all her heart, and bears up bravely and staunchly, although of late her nerves have given way a bit. She is occasionally assailed by somber thoughts, worries that she may die, etc. This makes things rather depressing and wearisome." [3] "I wish you knew, my dear friend," he continues, "with what joy I read and re-read, again and again, every letter I get from you!" It was only with Maikov that he could exchange literary ideas and impressions, and of course the ardent nationalism of Maikov's letters provoked a similar statement of Dostoevsky's own patriotic sentiments. "Here abroad," Dostoevsky tells Maikov, "I have definitely become an uncompromising monarchist when it comes to Russia." Dostoevsky had supported tsarism in the past, but largely because, as he writes, "if anyone has accomplished anything in Russia, it has certainly been he [Alexander II] alone." Now, however, he sees something more deeply rooted at work: "In our country, people have given and continue to give their love to every one of our tsars, and it is only in him that they finally believe. For the people this is a mystery, a sacrament, and anointment. The Westernizers understand nothing of this, and they, who pride themselves on basing their theories on facts, have overlooked the primary, the greatest fact of our history." [4]

Dostoevsky had now reached such a pitch of exasperation with *all* opponents of the tsarist regime that even a modicum of genuine affability was excluded in chance encounters with old friends. "It makes me sick when I run into our

---

[2] *PSS*, 28/Bk. 2: 252; January 1/13, 1868.

[3] Ibid., 258; February 18/March 1, 1868.

[4] Ibid., 281; March 21–22/April 2–3, 1868. Compare this passage with what one of the shrewdest Western analysts of Russian culture, Anatole Leroy-Beaulieu, wrote about the attitude of the Russian people toward the tsar just two years after Dostoevsky's death (1883). He was talking about the relations between church and state in the Russian Empire: "If the Tsar remains a secular layman, and if, in religious as well as in civic matters the Emperor acts in his capacity as head of state, it is not as head of a secular state in the modern or occidental sense. If he has no ecclesiastical status, the Tsar, for the mass of the people, has a religious one. He is the anointed of the Lord, established by the divine hand to safeguard and lead the Christian people. His anointment under the narrow cupola of the Uspensky Cathedral has endowed him with the virtue of the sacred. His dignity has no equal under Heaven. His subjects of all classes have, collectively and individually, taken an oath of fidelity to him on the Gospel." Anatole Leroy-Beaulieu, *L'Empire des tsars et les Russes* (Paris, 1990), 1033.

know-it-alls," he explodes to Maikov. "Oh, the poor wretches, oh, the nonentities, oh, the garbage swollen with vanity, oh, the turds. Disgusting! I met Herzen by chance in the street, and for ten minutes we spoke to each other in politely hostile tones, made a few digs at each other, and parted. No, I can't take them anymore. . . . The extent to which they understand nothing! And you should see how puffed up they have become, so very puffed up!"[5]

By the time this letter was written, in mid-March, Dostoevsky had already sent off the remaining nine chapters of Part I. The second batch of chapters, printed in the February issue of the journal, was accompanied by a note from the editors explaining that no further installment would appear until the April issue. In view of his wife's impending childbirth, Dostoevsky was granted a temporary respite from the obligation of uninterrupted publication.

———■———

The most important event in the lives of the Dostoevskys during their Geneva sojourn was the birth of their daughter Sofya on March 5, 1868. There are many references to this welcome baby in Anna's Geneva diary, and the couple often spoke affectionately with each other about little Sonya or Misha who was on the way. Dostoevsky insisted that Anna consult a leading gynecologist, recommended by Ogarev, and the doctor gave them the name of a reliable midwife, to whose care Anna was entrusted. Ever since arriving in Geneva the couple had lived in one room, and they now began to search for a two-room apartment, which was no easy task, given their limited means. Luckily, they found suitable quarters, and though Dostoevsky had engaged a nurse to look after Anna until her complete recovery, he also invited Anna's mother to join them (she came several months later) to help her daughter in the early period after birth.

After several false alarms the great event finally arrived, unfortunately on the very night that Dostoevsky suffered a severe epileptic attack and was completely incapacitated. Anna remained silent all through the succeeding hours of labor pain, praying to God for strength and succor and awakening Dostoevsky only at seven in the morning. Refreshed by his sleep, he rushed to summon the midwife, who displayed an indifferent stolidity that both the frantic father and the apprehensive mother found infuriating. Anna's delivery was extremely prolonged, partly, according to the midwife, because Dostoevsky's own agitation and transparent fears so much upset his wife. Anna recalls that "at times I saw him sobbing, and I myself began to fear that I might be on the threshold of death."[6] He was finally denied access to her room, and in the midst of her contractions Anna would ask either the nurse or the midwife to peek outside and report on the

---

[5] *PSS*, 28/Bk. 2; 282n.12.

[6] Anna Dostoevsky, *Reminiscences*, trans. and ed. Beatrice Stillman (New York, 1975), 142.

state of her husband. At last Dostoevsky heard the whimpering cry of a child among Anna's moans, broke into the room, though the door had been locked against him, and knelt at her bedside to kiss her hands with overflowing joy.

Dostoevsky announced the birth of Sofya in letters to his family and friends, contenting himself with reassuring and conventional phrases in all except the one to Maikov, from which a more worrisome picture emerges: "On February 22 (our style) my wife (after terrible sufferings that lasted thirty hours) gave birth to a daughter and is still quite ill; you know how nerves become disordered in this situation. . . . Sonya, my daughter, is a healthy, robust, lovable, marvelous child, and I spend practically half the day kissing her and can't tear myself away."[7] The exuberant parade of adjectives about Sonya confirms Anna's testimony that Dostoevsky was "the tenderest possible father," who helped with the baby's bath and "would sit by her crib for hours on end, now singing songs to her, now talking to her, and was convinced that she recognized him in her third month."[8]

For the moment, though, Dostoevsky was terrified that Anna might suffer a relapse and that he would be unable to pay for a doctor and medicines. Even though the Dostoevskys were not in dire want, thanks to the regular payments received from Katkov, they lived from month to month without a penny to spare and were often forced to pawn belongings to meet an unexpected expense. Dostoevsky was also greatly upset by a report—unfounded, and spread by Anna's mother—that Pasha Isaev had gone to Moscow to importune Katkov for some of the allowance sent his stepfather. Dostoevsky could not establish whether his information was true or false, but he wrote a humbly apologetic letter to Katkov nonetheless, on the deceptive assurance of his mother-in-law that the incident had occurred. The machinations of Anna's mother, determined to stop at nothing to end Dostoevsky's support of his stepson, added to his vexations at this trying juncture. He was feverishly working on plans for the next several sections of *The Idiot*, and the unremitting strain increased the frequency of his epileptic crises.

Despite all these tribulations, Dostoevsky's next letter to Maikov was somewhat less harried (no doubt because the new advance had arrived in the interim). Dostoevsky frequently, and with a touching wonder, mentions as "amusing" and almost "ridiculous" the extent to which Sonya resembles her father. "The child is only a month old, and she already absolutely has my expression, my physiognomy even to the wrinkles on my forehead—when she is lying down—it's exactly as if she were writing a novel!"[9] It was Maikov whom Dostoevsky had asked to look after the distribution of part of his new advance to Emilya

[7] *PSS*, 28/Bk. 2: 272–273; March 2/14, 1868.

[8] *Reminiscences*, 146.

[9] *PSS*, 28/Bk. 2: 277–278n.12; March 21–22/April 2–3, 1868.

Feodorovna and Pasha, and Maikov responded, "you, Feodor Mikhailovich, busy yourself about yours here with *unpardonable* zeal. So that I dislike going and handing out your money. You, I believe, look through spectacles that are too kindly and make things seem worse." [10] Maikov advised Dostoevsky to make a will so that, in case of his death, there would be no ambiguity about who would inherit the right to the income from his works. Apparently he had heard rumors that Mikhail's family and Pasha had been pleased that Anna had given birth to a girl; with a son they would have had no legal claim to any of Dostoevsky's property.

Dostoevsky followed his advice and in the same month wrote a "declaration" unambiguously assigning the rights of all his works to his wife. So far as his other dependents were concerned, however, he explained to Maikov why his obligations to them during his lifetime would remain sacred. "In Pasha's case, he was entrusted to my care by poor Marya Dimitrievna on her deathbed. . . . If I leave an impression of goodness and kindness on his heart now, it will stand him in good stead, as he matures." As for Emilya and her children, "there again, my late brother Misha is involved. Surely I don't have to tell you what that man was to me from my first moments of consciousness." [11]

———■———

The respite of a month accorded Dostoevsky by *The Russian Messenger* was a godsend, but he still had only twenty days before a continuation had to be dispatched and, he confesses to Maikov, "I still have not written a single line! . . . But what can I do. . . . There were nights on end when I couldn't get to sleep, not only because of mental strain, but because I actually had no other choice. That is a horrible thing for a man suffering from epilepsy. My nerves are now unstrung in the extreme." [12] Nonetheless, Dostoevsky's notebooks reveal that, with whatever time he had available during March and April (aside from a brief excursion to gamble), he sketched out various possibilities contained in the action already initiated by his first sixteen chapters. Nothing could be clearer, on the evidence of these notes, than Dostoevsky's complete uncertainty about the future direction of his story. Edward Wasiolek once again well describes Dostoevsky's artistic perplexity:

> He is not even sure of how much time elapses between the end of the action of the first part and the beginning of the second part. In the notes, he gives variously three weeks, five weeks, five days, one and one-half months, three months and six months. . . . Dostoevsky is not sure whether Nastasya

[10] "Pis'ma Maikova," *DSiM*, 2: 345.
[11] *PSS*, 28/Bk. 2: 279–280n.12.
[12] Ibid., 278.

Filippovna will marry Rogozhin or the Prince; . . . whether Nastasya Filippovna will kill herself, be killed, or die naturally; whether Aglaya will
marry Ganya or not; whether Nastasya Filippovna and Aglaya will hate
each other or be reconciled to each other; whether Rogozhin will be a
murderer or whether he will be redeemed by the Prince's teachings. Dostoevsky's mind teems with possibilities, but the tyranny of art and the tyranny of publishing require a choice.[13]

In my view, one of the most important clarifying notes was made on March 12,
when Dostoevsky jots down: "Three kinds of love in the novel: (1) Passionate
and spontaneous love—Rogozhin. (2) Love out of vanity—Ganya. (3) Christian
love—the Prince" (9: 220). Dostoevsky had defined these various types of love
earlier as mutations in a single character, but he now assigns them to different
individuals. The love theme is central in the book, especially the tragic antinomy
implicit in the Prince's "Christian love," but Dostoevsky already had given a hint
of it in the confusion of the Swiss children over the exact nature of Myshkin's
"love" for the suffering Marie. Several times in the margin of his notes Dostoevsky puts down the phrase, "Prince Christ" (9: 246); the phrase suggests the
tension between the human and the divine that Myshkin will be forced to confront—the tension between living in the world as a prince and wishing to marry
Aglaya while being, at the same time, a seraphic visionary inspired by a self-
sacrificing Christian love for Nastasya.

Another important note indicates Dostoevsky's further reflections on the
problem broached two months earlier in his letter to his niece—"How make the
hero's personality sympathetic to the reader? . . . If Don Quixote and Pickwick
as philanthropists are sympathetic to the reader, it is because they are comical.
The hero of this novel, the Prince, is not comical but does have another sympathetic quality: he is innocent" (9: 239–240). Both Don Quixote and Pickwick
are also innocent, but become laughable because of the mocking attitude taken
toward them by others. The Prince overcomes the initial suspicions of others by
the evident sincerity of his ingenuousness—his total candor, his lack of any
normal social vanity, his impassioned sympathy with human suffering (as in his
discourses about capital punishment)—and there is as well an implicit recognition that his innocence, which discloses what others strive to keep hidden, possibly embodies a higher wisdom in the manner of the Russian "holy fools"
(*yurodivy*). And so Myshkin's bizarreries are very early endowed with a suggested
religious aura.

Well into the month of April, Dostoevsky set down one of his major difficulties, which he never did solve satisfactorily: "little by little showing *the Prince in*

[13] Fyodor Dostoevsky, *The Notebooks for* The Idiot, trans. Katherine Strelsky, ed. with intro. by
Edward Wasiolek (Chicago, 1967), 160.

a field of action. . . . But for that *the plot of the novel* is essential." The "plot" that Dostoevsky envisaged, however, was not one that he was able to incarnate artistically. "He [Myshkin] rehabilitates N. F. and exerts an ascendancy over Rogozhin. He induces humility in Aglaya, he drives the General's wife to distraction with her . . . adoration of him" (9: 252). Except for this last reference to Mme Epanchina's affection for the prince, none of these happy results of Myshkin's influence are found in the text, and the lack of such a plot in the middle sections of the novel constitutes a major structural deficiency. In addition to wrestling with the problems of theme and temporal sequence, Dostoevsky was also concerned with the technique he should use as narrator. Here we can follow the analysis of Robin Feuer Miller, who points to the following passage as a key statement: "N.B. Why not present the character of the Prince enigmatically *throughout the entire novel*, from time to time defining by means of details (more fantastically and more questioningly, arousing curiosity) and suddenly to elucidate his character at the end . . ." (9: 220).

On the basis of this passage, Miller characterizes Dostoevsky's narrative stance in *The Idiot* as a combination of "enigma with explanation," and cites other notes in which Dostoevsky indicates his wish to "balance one with the other."[14] There was to be an aura of mystery around the Prince, which the explanations of the garrulous narrator only *enhance* rather than dispel. "Write more concisely: only the facts," Dostoevsky admonishes himself, "without reasoning and without a description of feelings." But then he adds, "Write in the sense of *people say* . . ." (9: 235). In other words, the narrator would report the facts as he knew them but would not be omniscient, and many "facts" would be simply gossip and rumor—the legend, as it were—that accumulates around the prince's actions and behavior. As Miller acutely remarks, "this grouping of narrative methods has the effect of placing the facts on the side of rumor and mystery rather than on the side of description and explanation."[15]

A note sketching the final chapters in which the Prince prepares for his wedding with Nastasya reveals more about Dostoevsky's narrative stance: "(The Prince is insane—according to general rumor that is), and except for a few people they all desert him" (9: 258). This desertion of the Prince in the face of the scandal he has provoked prefigures the attitude of the narrator in these concluding pages, who relays all the various distorted and malicious explanations of the Prince's decision. Dostoevsky thus deliberately envisages in advance the abandonment of the Prince by the narrator, who continues to remain on the level of "people say," and for whom the Prince becomes an inexplicable enigma. This limitation of the narrator, however, is part of Dostoevsky's effort to present

---

[14] Robin Feuer Miller, *Dostoevsky and* The Idiot (Cambridge, MA, 1981), 79.
[15] Ibid., 81.

Myshkin's behavior as transcending *all* the categories of worldly moral-social experience.

———■———

Sometime in the latter part of April, Dostoevsky interrupted his work on the plans for the novel as a whole and managed to write the opening two chapters of Part II, which appeared in the May issue of *The Russian Messenger*, and he continued to work without interruption on the next three chapters. Meanwhile, his financial situation had worsened because of a few days of gambling at Saxon-les-Bains. Dostoevsky's luck was even worse than usual on this occasion, and he gambled away all his money in the first half-hour of play. His letters to Anna (two on the same day) are filled with the usual semihysterical apologies, this time with additional self-castigations. Referring to his wife's "troubles" in caring for Sofya, he adds, "Of whom I am not worthy. What kind of a father am I?"[16] He had intended to write Katkov and apologize for the scantiness of the chapters he had barely managed to send after a month's respite, but for obvious reasons of literary pride had put off this demeaning task. Now, however, he sketches for Anna's benefit a letter to Katkov in which he asks for a new advance to allow him to work more productively by moving his family to Vevey. "I will remain in complete solitude until I finish the novel. . . . Meanwhile, . . . we can bring up our child without fearing that she will catch cold in being exposed to the sudden local *bise* (the north wind from the mountains)."[17]

Alas for the poor Dostoevskys, the very danger they had wished to guard against was exactly what occurred. Anna's mother arrived in the early days of May, and Sofya was christened on May 4; her godparents were Mme Snitkina and Apollon Maikov. Misfortune struck just at the moment when the worst seemed over. Anna had been advised by the doctor to walk in the park with Sofya so that she could benefit from the fresh air, and when the weather turned mild and radiant in early May his counsel was zealously followed. But the hated *bise* blew in unexpectedly one day and Sofya caught a chill; it developed into an inflammation of the lungs in the course of a week, and though the worried parents were assured of recovery by the doctor just three hours before the end, she was carried off on May 12. Dostoevsky "sobbed and wept like a woman," his wife writes, "standing in front of the body of his darling as it grew cold, and covering her tiny white face and hands with burning kisses. I never again saw such paroxysms of grief."[18]

A week later, the depth of Dostoevsky's grief is revealed in a heartrending letter to Maikov. "Oh, Apollon Nikolaevich, what does it matter that my love for

---

[16] *PSS*, 28/Bk. 2: 285; March 23/April 4, 1868.

[17] Ibid., 286.

[18] *Reminiscences*, 147.

my first child may have been ridiculous, that I expressed myself ridiculously about her in letters to those congratulating me. . . . This tiny, three months old being, so pitiful, so miniscule—for me was already a person, a character. She began to recognize me, to love me, to smile when I approached, when I, with my ridiculous voice, sang to her, she liked to listen. She did not cry or wrinkle her face when I kissed her; she ceased to cry when I approached. And now they tell me, in consolation, that I will have other children. But where is Sofya? Where is that little individual for whom, I dare to say, I would have accepted crucifixion so that she might live?" [19]

All the more pathetic, and indicating the abyss of loneliness and desolation into which Dostoevsky had been plunged, is his request that Maikov say nothing as yet of Sofya's death to Dostoevsky's family. "It seems to me that not only will none of them feel sorry for my child but even, perhaps, feel the opposite, and the very thought of this fills me with bitterness. Of what is this poor little thing guilty of in their eyes? Let them hate me, let them laugh at me and my love—it makes no difference." [20] After they buried Sofya on May 24, the atmosphere of Geneva became intolerable to the Dostoevskys. They would have dearly wished to quit the country and travel to Italy, but this was impossible financially. Besides, it would take too much time from *The Idiot*, and their livelihood depended on the continuation of the novel for which Katkov was waiting. With a liberality that astonished Dostoevsky himself, Katkov again acceded to the plea of his tardy contributor and sent the requested new advance. The heartbroken pair, accompanied by Anna's mother, moved only as far as Vevey, where Dostoevsky, choking back his inconsolable sorrow, continued to toil unremittingly at his novel.

The very first letter that Dostoevsky wrote from Vevey was an answer to one received from Pasha. "Oh, Pasha, I feel so low, so bitter that I would rather be dead. If you love me, pity me." [21] Most of the letter is given over to practical matters, which could not have been worse. With the aid of Dostoevsky's friends, especially Maikov, Pasha had obtained two jobs as a clerk in various offices, but he had left both after a short time because he had felt insulted by the treatment received from his superiors. When Dostoevsky heard this news from Maikov, he could not control his anger: "What a mentality, what opinions and ideas, what braggadocio!" he exploded to Maikov. "It's typical. But then, on the other hand—how can I abandon him?" [22]

The death of little Sofya haunted him continually, and it is in his letters to Maikov that he expresses the full extent of his mourning. "Apollon Nikolaevich,

[19] *PSS*, 28/Bk. 2: 297; May 18/30, 1868.
[20] Ibid., 298.
[21] Ibid., 300; June 9/21, 1868.
[22] Ibid., 298; May 18/30, 1868.

my friend," he writes pitiably. "Never have I been as unhappy . . . as time passes, the memory and the image of the departed Sonya stands before me more and more sharply etched. There are moments that are almost impossible to bear. . . . Never will I forget, and never will I stop torturing myself!" Besides his own torment, Anna "is terribly melancholy, cries through entire nights, and this has a very bad effect on her health."[23] Coming to Vevey was a frightful mistake and was worse than Geneva, especially for Anna, who needed some cultural distraction, but given their limited resources no other alternative had been possible.

In mid-July Dostoevsky wrote to Maikov, complaining that he was sure his correspondence was being intercepted and delayed. Some well-wisher of Dostoevsky's had informed him anonymously that an order had been issued by the secret police to search him if and when he crossed the Russian border. These instructions, circulated at the end of November 1867, no doubt were the result of the following notation in the files of the Third Section: "Among the overexcitable [*eksaltirovannikh*] Russians now present in Geneva, [our] agent names Dostoevsky, who is very friendly with Ogarev."[24] Dostoevsky's frequentation of the notorious revolutionary had thus brought him under suspicion.

"The Petersburg police," he told Maikov, "open *all* my letters, and since the Orthodox priest in Geneva, according to everything known (note that these are not suspicions, but facts), works for the secret police, the post office in Geneva (with whom he has secret connections) delays letters addressed to me, and this I know full well." "This is why," Dostoevsky continues, "I am firmly convinced that my letter never reached you, and that your letter has gone astray." And then the outrageousness of the situation suddenly sweeps over him, and he cannot contain his anger: "N.B. But how can someone like myself, an honest man, a patriot, who has delivered himself into their hands to the point of betraying my previous convictions, idolizing the tsar—how can I bear to be suspected of some sort of connection with some sort of Polacks or *The Bell*! Fools, fools! . . . Really, they should know that the Nihilists, the liberals of *The Contemporary*, for three years running now have thrown mud at me because I broke with them, hate the Polacks and love my Fatherland. Oh, the scoundrels!"[25]

Maikov had already told Dostoevsky three months earlier that "among us, it is said, even in the higher circles, many do not know the difference between Katkov and Chernyshevsky, between writers devoted to Russia and the Sovereign to the marrow of their bones and the revolutionaries."[26] Now he attempted to console his friend with a story making the rounds that the letters of Katkov and Ivan Aksakov (the Slavophil editor) were also being read, and in the list of their suspicious correspondents was found the inheritor to the Russian throne. "Why should we take offense," Maikov asks jocularly, "if even he is listed in the category of suspects by the temporarily dominating party?"[27]

———■———

At the beginning of August, Dostoevsky makes clear to Maikov that "if I travel elsewhere, the main reason is to save my wife."[28] Anna was failing, and early in September, come what might, Dostoevsky decided to strike out for Italy. Their funds took them only as far as Milan, where they settled for the next two months. Dostoevsky found the climate better for his health than Vevey, but it rained a good deal, and the general atmosphere of this bustling industrial metropolis was dismal and depressing. Dostoevsky cherished some pleasant recollections of his stay in Florence in 1862, and he wished to make it the goal of his Italian journey. "Anna Grigoryevna, who is a very active and enterprising person, has nothing to do here. I can see that she is bored, and, although we love each other if anything even more than 1 1/2 years ago, it is still oppressive that she must share my sad, monastic life. It is very bad for her."[29]

Dostoevsky was somewhat heartened by Maikov's news that "in Petersburg . . . a new Russian journal," to be called *Dawn* (*Zarya*), was now being planned.[30] Maikov had asked Dostoevsky to join his name with the others (Pisemsky, Fet, and Tolstoy were mentioned) who had already agreed to collaborate. The editor in charge would be Dostoevsky's old friend Strakhov, formerly chief critic on his own journals. Dostoevsky greeted Maikov's news with enthusiasm: "it would be desirable that the review be unmistakably *Russian in soul*, as you and I understand it, although, naturally, not purely Slavophil."[31] The letter ends with a renewed expression of concern about Pasha and Emilya Feodorovna. "How much I would like to return to Russia," he confesses, and then reveals a hidden wound referred to nowhere else. "And to think, besides, that Sonya would certainly be alive if we had been in Russia!"[32]

Sometime in the early days of November the Dostoevskys moved to Florence, where they rented two rooms on the Via Guicciardini just opposite the Pitti Palace. Dostoevsky immediately inscribed his name in the register of the famed Gabinetto Scientifico-Letterario Vieusseux, which subscribed to Russian periodicals and newspapers, and where his signature joined those of Henri Beyle

[27] *PSS*, 28/Bk. 2: 482n.13.

[28] Ibid., 310n.14.

[29] Ibid., 321; October 26/November 7, 1868.

[30] A. N. Maikov, "Pis'ma k F. M. Dostoevskomu," *Pamyatniki kulturi*, ed. N. T. Ashimbaeva (Leningrad, 1984), 70.

[31] *PSS*, 28/Bk. 2: 322n.21.

[32] Ibid., 323–324; October 26/November 7, 1868.

(Stendhal), Hector Berlioz, Heinrich Heine, Lamartine, and Franz Liszt.[33] Anna, who had begun to study Italian at Vevey, was delighted with the liveliness of the streets and the wealth of treasures in the museums. Dostoevsky was tied hand and foot by *The Idiot*, but he spent some time with Anna just after arrival in visiting the sights. "The roses are still flowering in the open air in the gardens of the Boboli," he writes to Maikov in his first letter from there. "And what treasures in the galleries! My God, in 1863 I had not paid any attention to the 'Madonna of the Chair' [by Raphael]. . . . How many wonderful things there are, even aside from this painting. But I postpone everything till the end of the novel. I have closed myself off."[34]

Dostoevsky was now faced with completing the fourth and final section of *The Idiot*, which he had promised Katkov by the end of the year. Also, he had been counting on the fourth part, with its crescendo of climactic scenes and haunting finale, to induce publishers to offer substantial sums for the reprint rights, and the impact of this concluding section would be badly weakened if printed in small installments. "If there are readers of *The Idiot*," he tells Maikov, "they perhaps will be somewhat stunned by the unexpectedness of the ending; but, on reflection, they will finally agree that it had to end in this way."[35]

It was in response to Maikov's report six months later on reader reaction ("the chief criticism is in the fantasticality of the characters")[36] that Dostoevsky set down the famous declaration of his aesthetic credo of "fantastic realism." "Oh, my friend," he writes, "I have a totally different conception of reality and realism than our novelists and critics. My idealism—is more real than their realism. God! Just to narrate sensibly what we Russians have lived through in the last ten years of our spiritual development—yes, would not the realists shout that this is fantasy! And yet this is genuine, existing realism. This is realism, only deeper; while they swim in the shallow waters. . . . Their realism—cannot illuminate a hundredth part of the facts that are real and actually occurring. And with our idealism, we have predicted facts. It's happened."[37] Dostoevsky sees his own "realism" as becoming "fantastic" because it delves beneath the quotidian surface into the moral-spiritual depths of the human personality, while at the same time striving to incarnate a more-than-pedestrian or commonplace moral ideal.

This same important letter contains an exhortation to Maikov that explains how Dostoevsky wished this "ideal" to be understood—and how we should regard the ending that he thought would so surprise his readers. "In a word: 'Do you believe in the icon or not!' (My dear friend, believe more bravely and

[33] Katherine Strelsky, "Dostoevsky in Florence," *Russian Review* 23 (1964), 149–163.

[34] *PSS* 28/Bk. 2: 333; December 11/23, 1868.

[35] Ibid., 327.

[36] Maikov, "Pis'ma," 73.

[37] *PSS*, 28/Bk. 2: 329; December 11/23, 1868.

courageously)."[38] Dostoevsky's directive to Maikov refers to the experience that the Slavophil Ivan Kireevsky had described—as he stood before an icon of the mother of God—of imaginative immersion into the mystery of religious faith. As Kireevsky gazed at the icon, he was overcome by the feeling that it was not merely a wooden board painted with images. For centuries that board had soaked up all the passion and all the prayers addressed to it and had become "a living organism, a meeting place between the creator and the people." As he looked at the praying mass of sufferers and back to the icon, "I myself saw the features of the mother of God come alive; she looked on all these simple people with pity and love. . . . And I fell on my knees and humbly prayed to her."[39]

In the past, these words had filled Dostoevsky with rapture; they depicted the process of his own conversion, not from atheism, but from a semi-secularized Christian Socialism to a reverence for the people and their "childish faith." But now he found even such reverence unsatisfactory, because it accepted faith solely for its consoling and compensatory effects on human life. Such faith was not spontaneous and instinctive, not treasured for its own sake and divorced from any practical consequences it might bring about. For Dostoevsky, faith had now become completely internal, irrational, and nonutilitarian; its truth could not be impugned by a failure to effect worldly changes, nor should it be defended *rationally*, as it were, because of the moral-psychological assuagements it might offer for human misery. Myshkin's life ends tragically, but for Dostoevsky, poised to write his final pages, this in no way undermines the transcendent ideal of Christian love that he tries to bring to the world, and whose full realization is beyond the power of any earthly human to achieve.

Dostoevsky was unsuccessful in his strenuous endeavor to provide the completion of *The Idiot* with the maximum possible aesthetic power of being published as a unit. Only three chapters of the final section made the December issue, and the remainder was printed as a supplement to the second issue of 1869. On the very day that he expected his final section to have arrived in Russia, he explained to his niece, "I had two epileptic attacks, and I was ten days behind the fixed limit."[40] Once again fate had played him a nasty trick.

[38] Ibid., 333n.37.

[39] Alexander Herzen, *My Past and Thoughts*, trans. Constance Garnett, rev. Humphrey Higgins, 4 vols. (New York, 1968), 2: 539.

[40] *PSS*, 29/Bk. 1: 9–10; January 25/February 6, 1869.

CHAPTER 40

The Idiot

Writing to a correspondent more than ten years after finishing *The Idiot*, Dostoevsky remarks, "All those who have spoken of it as my best work have something special in their mental formation that has always struck and pleased me."[1] *The Idiot* is the most personal of all his major works, the book in which he embodies his most intimate, cherished, and sacred convictions. Readers who took this work to their hearts were, he must have felt, a select group of kindred souls with whom he could truly communicate. It is only in *The Idiot* that Dostoevsky includes an account of his ordeal before the firing squad—an ordeal that had given him a new apprehension of life, and Prince Myshkin struggles to bring this revelation to a world mired in the sloth of the material and quotidian. Prince Myshkin approximates the extremest incarnation of the Christian ideal of love that humanity can reach in its present form, but he is torn apart by the conflict between the contradictory imperatives of his apocalyptic aspirations and his earthly limitations.

---■---

The first part of *The Idiot*, we know, was written under the inspiration of Dostoevsky's decision to center a major work around the character of a "perfectly beautiful man," and the singular spiritual fascination of Prince Myshkin derives largely from the image of him projected in these early pages. The moral halo that surrounds the Prince is conveyed in the very first scene, where his behavior is marked by a total absence of vanity or egoism; he does not seem to possess the self-regarding feelings on which such attitudes are nourished. Even more, he displays a unique capacity to take the point of view of his interlocutor. This explains the Prince's failure to take umbrage at his reception by others, and his capacity to transcend himself in this way invariably disarms the first response of amused and superior contempt among those he encounters.

Max Scheler, in his admirable book, *The Nature and Form of Sympathy*, distinguishes what he calls "vicarious fellow feeling," which involves experiencing an understanding and sympathy for the feelings of others without being overcome

---

[1] *PSS*, 29/Bk. 2: 139; February 14, 1877.

by them emotively, from a total coalescence leading to the loss of identity and personality.[2] The underlying movement of *The Idiot* may be provisionally defined as the Prince's passage from the first kind of fellow feeling to the second, but in Part I there are no indications of such a loss of identity. Rather, all the emphasis is placed on the Prince's instinctive and undifferentiated capacity for completely lucid vicarious fellow feeling even under great stress. As an example, we may take the scene where the Prince intervenes in the bitter altercation between Ganya Ivolgin and his sister, and himself receives the blow intended for the young woman. His response is to hide his face in his hands, turn to the wall, and say to Ganya in a breaking voice, "Oh, how ashamed you will be of what you've done" (8: 99).

This quality of the Prince's character is not motivated psychologically in any way, but, in a suggestively symbolic fashion, it is linked with certain leitmotifs. On the one hand, the Prince is much possessed by the prospect of death: twice in these early pages he speaks of an execution he has recently witnessed, and he also recounts vividly the feelings and thoughts of a man first condemned to death by a firing squad and then unexpectedly reprieved. A third description stresses the immense value assumed by each moment of existence as the end approaches. Despite the obsessiveness of the death motif in these early pages, the Prince also admits to having been "happy" in the years just preceding his arrival in St. Petersburg, and the relations between these two motifs provides the deepest substratum of his values. The Prince's "happiness," we learn, began with his recovery from a state of epileptic stupor. A sudden shock of awareness woke him to the existence of the world in the form of something as humble and workaday as a donkey. The donkey, of course, has obvious Gospel overtones, which blend with the Prince's innocence and naïveté, and this patiently laborious animal also emphasizes, in accord with Christian kenoticism,[3] the absence of hierarchy in the Prince's ecstatic apprehension of the wonder of life. The same contrast is

[2] Max Scheler, *The Nature of Sympathy*, trans. Peter Heath (London, 1954), chap. 2.

[3] Kenosis is a theological term defined in *Webster's* as "Christ's action of 'emptying himself' on becoming man, humbling himself even to suffering death." One of the distinguishing aspects of the Russian religious tradition, as defined by its greatest modern historian, G. P. Fedotov, is the stress placed on the suffering and humiliated Christ, who lies at the heart of Russian spirituality. Writing of the first Russian martyred saints, the princes Boris and Gleb, Fedotov compares their meek acceptance of their fate with the teachings of the monk Theodosius, the founder of the Russian kenotic tradition. "Boris and Gleb followed Christ in their sacrificial deaths—the climax of his kenosis—as Theodosius did in His poverty and humiliations. . . . From the outside, it must give the impression of weakness as Theodosius' poverty must appear foolish to the outsider. Weak and foolish—such is Christ in his kenosis in the eyes of a Nietzsche just as he was in the eyes of the ancient pagan world." See G. P. Fedotov, *The Russian Religious Mind*, vol. 1 (New York, 1946), 130, and chap. 4 ("Russian Kenoticism"). There is good reason to believe that Nietzsche was familiar with *The Idiot,* and that Dostoevsky's novel helped to shape his whole interpretation of Christianity. See Ernst Benz, *Nietzsches Ideen zur Geschichte des Christentums und der Kirche* (Leiden, 1956), 92–103.

introduced by the Prince's remark that, in the early stages of his recovery, he had been consumed by restlessness and had thought to find "the key to the mystery of life" in his transcendent yearning to reach "that line where sky and earth meet"; but then, he adds, "I fancied that one might find a wealth of life even in prison" (8: 51).

Myshkin imaginatively reexperiences the universal and ineluctable tragedy of death with the full range of his conscious sensibilities, but this does not prevent him, at the same time, from marveling in ecstasy before the joy and wonder of existence. Indeed, the dialectic of this unity is the point of the story about the man reprieved from execution—the story that embodies the most decisive event in Dostoevsky's own life. Most dreadful of all in those last moments, Myshkin says, was the regret of the poor victim over a wasted life and his frantic desire to be given another chance. "What if I were not to die? . . . I would turn every minute into an age; . . . I would not waste one!" But on being asked what happened to this man after his reprieve, Myshkin ruefully admits that his frenzied resolution was not carried out in practice:

> "So it seems it's impossible really to live 'counting each moment,'" says Alexandra Epanchina. "For some reason it's impossible."
> "Yes, for some reason it's impossible," repeated Myshkin. "So it seemed to me also . . . and yet somehow I can't believe it." (8: 52–53)

Here is the point at which Myshkin's love of life fuses with his death-haunted imagination into the singular unity of his character. For Myshkin feels the miracle and wonder of life so strongly precisely because he lives "counting each moment" as if it were the last. Both his joyous discovery of life and his profound intuition of death combine to make him feel each moment as one of absolute and immeasurable ethical choice and responsibility. The Prince, in other words, lives in the eschatological tension that was (and is) the soul of the primitive Christian ethic, whose doctrine of totally selfless *agape* was conceived in the same perspective of the imminent end of time. [4]

There is a constant play of allusion around the Prince that places him in such a Christian context. Rogozhin, the merchant's son still close to the religious roots of Russian life, labels him a *yurodivy*, a holy fool, and though the gentlemanly and well-educated prince bears no external resemblance to these eccentric figures, he does possess their traditional gift of spiritual insight, which operates instinctively, below any level of conscious awareness or doctrinal commitment.

---

[4] Albert Schweitzer's famous book, *The Quest for the Historical Jesus* (1906), first focused attention on the importance of such eschatological expectations as the source of the Christian ethic of love. Ever since, this theory has been subjected to a flood of criticism, without being shaken as a *psychological* basis for understanding the more extreme aspects of the Christian doctrine of love (or *agape*).

The idyllic New Testament note is struck strongly in the Prince's story of the poor, abused, consumptive Swiss peasant girl Marie, who had been reviled as a fallen woman and whose last days the Prince and his band of children brighten with the light of an all-forgiving love. In this way the figure of the Prince is surrounded with a pervasive Christian penumbra that continually illuminates his character and serves to locate the exalted nature of his moral and spiritual aspirations.

The story concerning Marie also brings sharply to the foreground another leitmotif, one that may be called the "two loves"—the one Christian, compassionate, nonpossessive, and universal, the other secular, ego-gratifying, possessive, and particular. Alexandra Epanchina's suggestion that the Prince must have been "in love" prompts him to tell the story of Marie. But while the young woman was referring to the second kind of normal, worldly love, the Prince's "love," as he explains, was only of the first type. Even the children clustered around the Prince were confused by this difference and happily believed that the Prince was "in love" with Marie when they saw him kissing her. But "I kissed her," he explains, "not because I was in love with her but because I was sorry for her" (8: 60). The confusion of the children (and Myshkin is also a good bit of a child) will anticipate his own entrapment in the "two loves," whose mutually incompatible feelings and obligations will later result in the Prince's disastrous inability to choose between Nastasya and Aglaya.

———■———

The world into which the Prince is plunged upon his unexpected arrival in St. Petersburg is locked in the grip of conflicting egoisms, a world in which the desire for wealth and social advantage, for sexual satisfaction, for power over others, dominates and sweeps away all other humane feelings. All these motives are given full play in the intrigue, which in Part I revolves around the drama of Nastasya Filippovna (who, in retrospect, will survive as Dostoevsky's major female protagonist) and her fatal entanglement with Prince Myshkin.

Her appearance has been preceded by a narrative of her past as a destitute but aristocratic orphan, sequestered and violated at sixteen and kept in sexual bondage by Totsky. In contrast to the conventional literary type of the betrayed, fallen, but ultimately redeemable woman—like the heroine of *La dame aux camelias*, a novel by Dumas the Younger that Totsky naturally admired—Nastasya is cast by Dostoevsky as degraded in the eyes of society but blamelessly pure, not unlike Clarissa Harlowe. At age twenty she descends on Petersburg as a self-avenger, determined to assert herself against the terrorized Totsky's self-protective scheme to pawn her off with a dowry on the greedy Ganya Ivolgin. This would clear the way for Totsky's own marriage to one of the two older

Epanchin daughters. Facing the insurmountable contradiction of inner purity and her outward disgrace, Nastasya Filippovna as a character is irremediably doomed, and she will function to bring down "her savior," the Prince, in her own tragic end. Prince Myshkin first hears her name in the opening train scene. He is immediately spellbound by her haunting portrait displayed at the Ivolgins, which he kisses surreptitiously, and finally meets her (as does the reader) there.

Nastasya's fate is presumably to be sealed in the tumultuous birthday-party scene at her dwelling that climaxes Part I. At that time, she is supposedly to decide whether or not to marry Ganya, although her previous behavior makes it highly unlikely that she would be ready to accept Totsky's scheme. On the contrary, after indirectly exposing the ridicule and venality of her assembled guests, Nastasya is finally given full voice to evoke her past subjection and forced debauchery (quite graphic for its time, but with enough suspension points to gratify the censors) as well as her suicidal urges. Nastasya seemingly turns to the Prince to decide the question of *her* marriage to Ganya because, as she says, the Prince "believed in me at first sight and I in him" (8: 131). But when the tender-hearted smitten Prince proclaims his belief in her purity and offers her his hand in marriage, and a fortune, she rejects him as well, refusing to emulate Totsky as a violator of "innocence," and a "a cradle-snatcher," even though Myshkin is the miraculous realization of her hopeless adolescent dreams. Through her own rejection of Myshkin, she has now internalized her outward stigmata of shame and repeatedly claims a streetwalker-slut identity as she runs off with the passionate Rogozhin to certain self-destruction, after defiantly throwing the purchase money (wrapped in the *Stock Exchange News*) into the fire. The satisfaction of humiliating and thus of symbolically debasing Totsky and all her respectable "admirers" at the same time proves stronger than the Prince's appeal to her need for disinterested compassion and his recognition of her essential purity.

Although no longer an active protagonist, her half-demented, shadowy persona haunts and indirectly sets in motion all the subsequent peripeties of the plot, from Myshkin's following her to Pavlovsk to the pantomime reenactment of the aborted wedding. Finally, there is the suicidal flight with Rogozhin. A mysterious coda to her tragic destiny is provided by Myshkin's finding a copy of *Madame Bovary* in her abandoned rooms, the tale of another hopeless suicide but in this case of an adulteress betrayed by Romantic fantasies.

———■———

From the beginning of Part II, the Prince is cast in a tragic (or at least self-sacrificial) role; and the inner logic of his character now requires that the absolute of Christian love should conflict irreconcilably with the inescapable demands of normal human life. This altered projection of the Prince also leads to the introduction of a new thematic motif, which first appears in the strange dialogue between Myshkin and Rogozhin about religious faith. Somewhat improbably, a copy of Holbein's *Dead Christ* turns up in Rogozhin's living room, and, with no transition whatever, the erstwhile drunken rowdy of Part I is shown as tormented not only by Nastasya but also by a crisis of religious doubt. We learn here that "a painting of our Savior who had just been taken from the Cross" has begun to undermine Rogozhin's religious faith, and Myshkin attempts to allay Rogozhin's disquietude in a lengthy and crucial speech.

This speech consists of four anecdotes, grouped in pairs, that illustrate that the human need for faith and for the moral values of conscience based on faith transcend both the plane of rational reflection and that of empirical evidence. On the one hand, there is the learned atheist whose arguments Myshkin cannot refute; on the other, there is the murderer who utters a prayer for forgiveness before slitting his victim's throat. The point of these stories is to exhibit religious faith and moral conscience existing as an ineradicable attribute in the Russian people independent of reason, or even of any sort of conventional social morality. "The essence of religious feeling," Myshkin explains, "does not come under any sort of reasoning or atheism, and has nothing to do with any crimes or misdemeanors. . . . But the chief thing is that you will notice it more clearly and quickly in the Russian heart than anywhere else" (8: 184).

This thematic motif is of key importance for understanding the remainder of the book. For in depicting religious faith and the stirrings of conscience as the irrational and instinctive needs of "the Russian heart," whose existence shines forth in the midst of everything that seems to deny or negate its presence, Dostoevsky is surely indicating the proper interpretation of Myshkin's ultimate failure and tragic collapse. The values of Christian love and religious faith that Myshkin embodies are too deep a necessity of the Russian spirit to be negated by his practical failure, any more than they are negated by reason, murder, or sacrilege. If Holbein's picture and Myshkin's tirade are introduced so awkwardly and abruptly at this point, it is probably because Dostoevsky wished immediately to establish the framework within which the catastrophic destiny awaiting the prince would be rightly understood.

The thematic motif of religious faith is also what saves the episodes involving Myshkin's encounter with the group of so-called Young Nihilists from becoming merely an acrid satire against the radicals of the mid-1860s. Dostoevsky wisely focuses the spotlight on the dying young consumptive Ippolit Terentyev, who detaches himself from the group to rise to major heights and become the first in the remarkable gallery of metaphysical rebels that Dostoevsky created. For Ippolit is revolting not against the iniquities of a social order but, anticipating Kirillov in *Demons* and Ivan Karamazov, against a world in which death, and hence immitigable human suffering, is an inescapable reality. Ippolit is another quasi-double for Myshkin—one who shares his obsession with death and his ecstatic sense of life, yet lacks the Prince's sustaining religious faith in an ultimate world-harmony. For this reason, Ippolit cannot achieve the self-transcendence that is the secret of the prince's moral effulgence and the response he evokes in others.

Ippolit's semihysterical "Necessary Explanation" is composed to contain all the main features of Myshkin's *Weltanschauung*—the reverence for the infinite beauty and value of life—but combined with an *opposite* human attitude. His preoccupation with death does not lessen but strengthens his self-concern, and turns it into a pathetic megalomania, as can be seen from the touchingly incongruous epigraph, "*après moi le deluge!*" that he appends to his "Necessary Explanation" (8: 321). Instinctively, Ippolit's feelings are on the side of the victims of social injustice; and when he is carried on the current of such benevolent feelings, he admits "that I forgot my death sentence, or rather did not come to think of it and even did work" (8: 328). Only such concern with others can ease the tragedy of Ippolit's last days, but he finally abandons all such endeavors to brood over his own condition. Death, the universal portion, he comes to regard as a personal insult and "humiliation" aimed at him by "nature," or rather by the creator of a world that requires the individual's consent to the indignity and injustice of being destroyed.

The thematic contrast between Ippolit and the Prince is brought out most forcefully in their differing reactions to the key religious symbol of the book, Holbein's *Dead Christ*. Holbein's picture, as we have seen, had led Myshkin to affirm the irrational "essence of religious feeling" as an ineradicable component of the human spirit; but for the Young Nihilist, it is only a confirmation of his own sense of the cruel meaninglessness of life. To Ippolit, the picture conveys a sense of nature "in the form of a huge machine of the most modern construction," which "has aimlessly clutched, crushed, and swallowed up a great priceless Being, a Being worth all of nature and its laws, worth the whole earth, which was created perhaps solely for the advent of that Being" (8: 339). Ippolit simply cannot grasp how the first disciples of Christ, who witnessed in reality what he sees only at the remove of art, could still have continued to believe in the triumph over death that Christ proclaimed, but this is precisely the mystery of faith to which Ippolit is closed, and whose absence poisons his last days with bitterness and despair.

Ippolit, like the other characters, instinctively regards the Prince as the standard for his own conscience. The Prince's "humility," however, is the ideological antithesis of Ippolit's "revolt," and it is Myshkin who must bear the brunt of the Young Nihilist's vituperative shifts of feeling. "Can't I simply be devoured without being expected to praise what devours me?" Ippolit asks caustically, in rejecting the Prince's "Christian meekness" (8: 343). This question comes from such a depth of suffering in Ippolit that no offense on his part can lessen his right to an absolute claim on the indulgence of the other characters. The Prince understands that, for Ippolit, the untroubled possession of life by others is a supreme injustice, which should burden them with guilt and a sense of moral obligation.

Hence the Prince's moving reply to Ippolit's question on how best to die: "Pass by us and forgive us our happiness," says Myshkin in a low voice (8: 433). Hence, too, the macabre quality of gallows humor in several of the scenes with Ippolit, the grating callousness that some of the characters display toward his plight. No pages of Dostoevsky are more original than those in which he tries to combine the utmost sympathy for Ippolit with a pitiless portrayal of what may be called "the egoism of dying." Dostoevsky wishes to show how the egocentricity that inspired Ippolit's "revolt" also impels him to a behavior that cuts off the very sympathy and love he so desperately craves. By turns pathetic and febrilely malignant, the unfortunate boy dies offstage, unconsoled and inconsolable, "in a state of terrible agitation" (8: 508).

In addition to Ippolit, *The Idiot* is filled with all sorts of minor characters related to the main plot lines only by the most tenuous of threads. But it is not too difficult to see the thematic rationale of most of these episodes even if, structurally, they come and go with very little motivation. Many of them have the function of the comic interludes in medieval mystery plays, which parody the holy events with reverent humor and illustrate the universality of their influence. Others serve to bring out facets of the prince that Dostoevsky was unable to develop from the central romantic intrigue.

Lebedyev, General Ivolgin, and the "boxer" Keller make up a group with common characteristics—a group that affirms, sometimes in a grotesquely comic form, that the inner moral struggle precipitated by the Prince in the major figures also can be found among the smaller fry. To be sure, Dostoevsky abandons all attempts to maintain any psychological verisimilitude in the case of Lebedyev and Keller; their mechanical shuttling between devotion to the Prince and petty swindling and skullduggery sometimes reaches the point of self-parody. This is particularly true of Lebedyev, transformed from the randy scrounger of Part I into the compassionate figure who shares Myshkin's horror of capital punishment ands prays for the soul of the guillotined Mme Du Barry.

Without ceasing to be an unscrupulous scoundrel, ready to sell his soul for a ruble, Lebedyev also piously interprets the Apocalypse and rails against the "materialism" of the modern world in drunken tirades. His long mock-serious historical "anecdote" on the famines of the Middle Ages is manifestly a burlesque exemplum of the significance of his character and that of others like him. Similar to the starving medieval "cannibal"—who devoured sixty fat juicy monks in the course of his life and then, despite the prospect of the most horrible tortures, voluntarily confessed his crimes—the behavior of Lebedyev and his ilk testifies to the miraculous existence of conscience in the most unlikely places.

Another exemplum is the broken-down Falstaffian General Ivolgin, whom Dostoevsky uses very effectively in Part I to parody the "decorum" surrounding Nastasya's life, and whose colossal mythomania is a protection against the sordid reality of his moral and social decline. The general dies of a stroke brought on by his torments over having stolen Lebedyev's wallet, torments caused not so much by the theft itself—he returned the wallet untouched—but by the fear that he would henceforth be regarded as a thief in his own family. The completely fictitious narrative of how, as a young boy, the general served as a page to Napoleon and used his influence to motivate the French retreat from Moscow in 1812 is an irresistible example of Dostoevsky's too little used talent for high-flying comic extravagance.

———■———

The major action of *The Idiot* after Part I centers on the Prince's budding romance with Aglaya Epanchina. By reading Pushkin's poem "The Poor Knight" in the Prince's presence, with obvious reference to his intervention on behalf of Nastasya, Aglaya reveals to what extent her lofty imagination has become inflamed by the Prince's self-sacrificing magnanimity toward, in the eyes of society, a victimized "fallen woman." Aglaya's whole relation to the Prince is thus tainted with misunderstanding from the start. To Aglaya, Myshkin is the Poor Knight of Pushkin's poem—a poem in which she sees united "in one striking figure the grand conception of the platonic love of medieval chivalry, as it was felt by a pure and lofty knight," who was a "serious and not comic" Don Quixote (8: 207). Although these words apply to the Prince in part, their function is to bring out the illusory nature of Aglaya's image of his character. Nothing could be less characteristic of the Prince than the deeds of military valor performed during the Crusades by the Poor Knight in the service of the Christian faith:

> *Lumen coeli*, Sancta Rosa!
> Shouted he with flaming glance
> And the thunder of his menace
> Checked the Musselman's advance (8: 209).

The Poor Knight, in other words, represents the Christian ideal of the Catholic West in its days of glory and in all its corrupting confusion of spiritual faith and temporal power. The Russian Christian ideal, as Dostoevsky understood it, sharply splits off one from the other and accepts all the paradoxical and even demeaning social consequences of the Prince's humility, meekness, and all-forgiving love.

Aglaya's misconception mirrors her own character, with its combination of ardent idealism and personal arrogance and pride. Aglaya is irresistibly attracted by the purity of spirit and the selflessness that she finds in the Prince, but at the same time she wishes her ideal to be socially imposing and admired by the world. This fusion had attracted her to militant Catholicism, and she misguidedly seeks it in the Prince. By introducing the Young Nihilist scenes right after the "Poor Knight" reading, Dostoevsky forcefully dramatizes the opposition between Aglaya's image and the actual values that inspire the Prince's conduct. The combative Aglaya welcomes the intrusion of the group because, as she says, "they are trying to throw mud at you, Prince, you must defend yourself triumphantly, and I am awfully glad for you" (8: 213). Far from emerging "triumphant," though, Myshkin reacts to insult and provocation with a docility and passivity that drive Aglaya into a towering rage.

Before the party scene at which he will be presented officially as Aglaya's betrothed, she tries to have a "serious" talk with him to make sure that he will not commit any faux pas. Nonetheless, under the influence of the pre-epileptic "aura," the Prince launches into a Slavophil attack on Roman Catholicism as "unchristian" because "Roman Catholicism believes that the Church cannot exist on earth without universal political power" (8: 450). He is thus denouncing in Roman Catholicism the very confusion of the temporal and the spiritual that, on the personal level, Aglaya wishes him to incarnate. It is no hazard that this speech appears precisely at the point where his personality is shown as most hopelessly incompatible with her requirements.

Myshkin's disastrous harangue also incorporates other motifs of great importance to Dostoevsky. The Russian need for religious faith is asserted yet again as Myshkin describes the Russian proclivity to be converted to false faiths—such as Roman Catholicism or atheism. "Russian atheists and Russian Jesuits are the outcome not only of vanity," he declares, "but also of . . . spiritual thirst, a craving for something higher . . . for a faith in which they have ceased to believe because they have never known it! . . . And Russians do not merely become atheists, but they invariably *believe* in atheism, as though it were a new religion without noticing that they are putting their faith in a negation" (8: 452). Myshkin here utters some of Dostoevsky's profoundest convictions, which the author knew would be looked on by the majority of his compatriots with the same rather frightened and pitying incredulity as that displayed by the Epanchins' guests.

Despite the catastrophe of the Prince's outburst and epileptic attack at the engagement party, Aglaya still manages to overcome her dismay, since her ultimate test of Myshkin will be his relation with Nastasya. No more than Rogozhin can Aglaya view the Prince's "Christian love" for Nastasya—his boundless pity and sense of obligation—as anything but a threat to her own undisputed possession of the man she loves. In the powerful confrontation scene between the two women, Myshkin is called upon to choose and is utterly unable to do so. Nastasya's "frenzied, despairing face" causes him to reproach Aglaya for her cruelty to the "unhappy creature." Aglaya, meanwhile, looks at him with "such suffering and at the same time such boundless hatred that, with a gesture of despair, he cried out and ran to her, but it was already too late." He is stopped by Nastasya's grasp, and remains to comfort the fainting and half-demented creature whose tortured face had once "stabbed his heart forever" (8: 475).

The Prince thus finds himself helplessly caught in the rivalry of clashing egoisms, and he responds, on the spur of the moment, to the need that is most immediate and most acute. Each woman has a differing but equally powerful claim on his devotion; and his incapacity to make a choice dramatizes the profoundest level of Dostoevsky's thematic idea. For the Prince is the herald of a Christian love that is nothing if not universal; yet he is also a man, not a supernatural being—a man who has fallen in love with a woman as a creature of flesh and blood. The necessary dichotomy of these two divergent loves inevitably involves him in a tragic imbroglio from which there is no escape, an impasse in which the universal obligation of compassion fatally crosses the human love that is the Prince's morally blameless form of "egoism."

Three years earlier, sitting at the bier of his first wife, Dostoevsky had stated that Christ had given mankind only one clue to the future nature of the "final ideal goal" of humanity—a clue contained in the Gospel of Saint Matthew: "They neither marry, nor are given in marriage, but are as angels in Heaven" (20: 173). Even that "most sacred possession of man on earth" (20: 173), the family, is a manifestation of the ego, which prevents the fusion of individuals into an All of universal love. The "final ideal goal" of humanity is thus the total fusion of the individual ego with all in a mystic community literally (and not metaphorically) freed from the constraints and limits of the flesh; it is the transcendent "synthesis" that Myshkin had glimpsed in the ravishment of the pre-epileptic "aura." Hence even the most chaste and innocent of earthly love constitutes an abrogation of the universal law of love, whose realization, prefigured by Christ, is man's ultimate, supernatural goal. The closing pages of *The Idiot* strikingly present this insoluble conflict between the human and the divine that Dostoevsky felt so acutely and that could achieve its highest pitch of expressiveness and poignancy only as embodied in such a "perfectly beautiful man" as Prince Myshkin.

◆

Up until these concluding chapters, the omniscient narrator has usually been able to describe and explain what the Prince is thinking and feeling. Now, however, the narrator confesses that he is unable to understand Myshkin's behavior and must confine himself to a "bare statement of facts" (8: 475). The facts referred to are these: on the one hand, Myshkin has become the fiancé of Nastasya, and the plans for their wedding are going forward. But, on the other, the Prince still tries to visit Aglaya as if nothing had changed, and he cannot comprehend why the impending marriage should affect his relation to her. "It makes no difference that I'm going to marry her," he tells Radomsky. "That's nothing, nothing" (8: 483). The strain of the Prince's impossible position has finally caused him to lose all touch with reality. No longer able to distinguish between his vision of universal love and the necessary exclusions and limiting choices of life, he is presented as having passed altogether beyond the bounds of accepted social codes. To express this transgression, Dostoevsky adopts the guise of the baffled narrator, whose bewilderment accentuates the impossibility of measuring the Prince's comportment by any conventional standard.

The moral profundities of the Prince's conflict are thus distorted and reduced to the level of spiteful tittle-tattle and current clichés over, for example, female emancipation. The melancholy irony of the Prince's situation is now complete. Like Abraham in Kierkegaard's *Fear and Trembling*, who alone hears the secret commandment of God to sacrifice his son, the Prince has now become a knight of faith whose obedience to the divine makes his conduct appear to others, more often than not, a sign of madness. Quite appropriately, Lebedyev comes to this conclusion and tries to have the Prince committed to a mental institution before the wedding ceremony. Radomsky too shares the same conviction that the Prince "was not in his right mind"; but his thoughts come closer to Dostoevsky's thematic mark: "And how can one love two at once? With two different kinds of love? That's interesting . . . poor idiot" (8: 485).

The closing pages show us the Prince helplessly trapped between the conflicting claims of his human nature and his divine task, deprived of all comprehension and almost all sympathy, and overwhelmed by events over which he has no control. His grasp of the real world becomes weaker and weaker, and at the end his personality simply dissolves, abandoning all claims for itself and becoming a function of the needs of others. In the eerie and unforgettable death-watch scene over Nastasya's corpse, after she has deliberately chosen to submit herself to Rogozhin's knife, the Prince loses himself completely in the anguish of the half-mad murderer and sinks definitively into the mental darkness that he had long feared would be the price of his visionary illuminations. So ends the odyssey of Dostoevsky's "perfectly beautiful man," who had tried to live in the world by the divine light of the apocalyptic transfiguration of mankind into a universal harmony of love.

With an integrity that cannot be too highly praised, Dostoevsky thus fearlessly submits his *own* most hallowed convictions to the same test that he had used for those of the Nihilists—the test of what they would mean for human life if taken seriously and literally, and lived out to their full extent as guides to conduct. With exemplary honesty, he portrays the moral extremism of his own eschatological ideal, incarnated in the Prince, as being equally incompatible with the normal demands of ordinary social life, and constituting just as much of a disruptive scandal as the appearance of Christ himself among the complacently respectable Pharisees.

The last words, though, are given to Aglaya's mother, Lizaveta Prokofeyevna, the character who has always been the closest in spirit to the Prince but has managed to keep her feet successfully on the ground. Her typically explosive and matronly denunciation of Europe—"they can't make decent bread; in winter they are frozen like mice in a cellar" (8: 510)—concludes the book with a down-to-earth affirmation of the same faith in Russia that Myshkin had expressed in the messianic eloquence of his ecstatic rhapsodies. "We've had enough of being carried away by our enthusiasms," she complains. "It's high time we grew sensible." Whatever the tragedy that Prince Myshkin and those affected by him may have suffered in *this* world, however, he brings with him the unearthly illumination of a higher one that all feel and respond to; and it is this response to "the light shining in the darkness" that for Dostoevsky provided the only ray of hope for the future.

CHAPTER 41

The Pamphlet and the Poem

The termination of *The Idiot* allowed Dostoevsky, who had been writing steadily for a year and a half, to catch his breath for a moment, but it also meant the end of the monthly stipend he had been receiving from Katkov. To make matters worse, Dostoevsky calculated that the amount of copy he had furnished still left him with a debt to Katkov's journal of one thousand rubles. Dostoevsky thus begins to mention all sorts of new plans and projects, and the relation of these crisscrossing ideas to the works he then wrote is sometimes difficult to unravel.

Even before finishing the fourth part of *The Idiot*, and in the same letter to Maikov in which he defines his aesthetic of "fantastic realism," Dostoevsky had outlined the idea for a major new novel. This outline immediately precedes the statement of his aesthetic, which may have emerged not only as a response to criticisms of *The Idiot* but also as a generalization of the approach to Russian life and reality expressed in his new creative project. Dostoevsky had in mind

> a huge novel whose title will be *Atheism*. . . . The main figure is: a Russian of our society, . . . he loses faith in God. All his life he . . . did not go off the beaten path, and for forty-five years was in no way other than ordinary. . . . His loss of faith in God has a colossal effect on him. . . . He darts about among the young generation, the atheists, the Slavs and Europeans, the Russian fanatics, anchorites, the priests; he is strongly affected, among others, by a group of Jesuits, propagandizers, Poles; he slips away from them to the depths of the flagellants—and in the end finds Christ and the Russian God.[1]

Such a novel was never written, but this outline soon developed into a much longer work that also remained unwritten, *The Life of a Great Sinner* (*Zhitie velikogo greshnika*), and both then fed into *Demons*. Dostoevsky's ambition, it is clear, was to present a large fresco of Russian opinions and religious experiences,

---

[1] *PSS*, 29/Bk. 1: 58n.1; August 29/September 10, 1869.

and to dramatize his main character in terms of such competing views and ide-ologies, including those of "the young generation."

"I must absolutely return to Russia," he writes his niece from Florence; "here I will end by losing any possibility of writing for lack of my indispensable and habitual material—Russian reality (which feeds my thoughts) and the Rus-sians."[2] Dostoevsky wrote to *The Russian Messenger* again asking for an advance on a new novel that he promised to provide in about a year. Faced with tempo-rary indigence, he responded to another invitation from Strakhov at the end of January for a contribution to *Dawn*; an advance would allow him to meet his most pressing needs until the money from Katkov was forthcoming. Dostoevsky proposed that he be sent an advance of a thousand rubles with no delay, and in return he would write "a novel."

Ten days later Dostoevsky finally received an advance from Katkov, mean-while having been forced to borrow one hundred francs from some unknown benefactor and to pawn whatever he and Anna could spare for another hundred francs. (Anna recalls how they even began to joke about their unrelieved poverty and to refer to each other as Mr. and Mrs. Micawber.) Dostoevsky was relieved to receive the money, not only for obvious reasons but also because he had been worried about his status at the journal. "I don't believe," he wrote his niece, "*The Idiot* will bring them new subscribers; I am very sorry about that, and that's why I am very happy that they hold on to me despite the obvious lack of success of my novel."[3]

After much negotiating, the editors of *Dawn* finally accepted Dostoevsky's reduced demands for only three hundred rubles to be sent immediately in re-turn for "a story, rather short, about two signatures."[4] The weather in Florence was turning torrid, and the Dostoevskys had been advised to leave because Anna, now pregnant again, was expecting a child in four months. They planned to move to Dresden, where they could find a doctor and nurses "who express themselves in a comprehensible language and are competent."[5] They were await-ing the arrival of Anna's mother in a few days and planned to depart as soon as means were available.

By the time the advance arrived, however, Dostoevsky's extra expenses had eaten up what he received. Intending to quit Florence immediately, the couple had moved out of their apartment to save on rent; but the single room was more expensive for a prolonged period, and Anna's mother had by now arrived to look after her. "The heat in Florence is unbearable," he wrote to Maikov in mid-May,

[2] Ibid., 123; May 7/19, 1870.
[3] Ibid., 32; March 18/30, 1869.
[4] Ibid.
[5] Ibid.

"the city is white-hot and stifling, our nerves are overwrought—which is particularly bad for my wife; right now we are packed together (still *attendant*) in a small narrow room giving on the marketplace. I have had enough of this Florence, and now with no space and the heat, I cannot even write. In general, a terrible anguish—and worse, because of Europe; I look at everything here like a wild beast."[6] "Most of all, I felt sorry for my poor Anya," he wrote after escaping. "She, poor thing, was in her seventh or eighth month, and suffered terribly from the heat."[7]

Katkov once again came to their aid with sufficient funds to cover the cost of travel, and the suffocating Dostoevskys left Florence at the end of July, departing not for Dresden but for Prague. The abrupt change of itinerary was the result of Anna's desire to remedy Dostoevsky's dispiriting isolation from any literary or intellectual milieu, and there, too, they would be immersed in a Slavic world once again. Proceeding by way of Bologna, where a stopover was made to view Raphael's *St. Cecilia*, they stayed for several days in Venice, hardly leaving the Piazza San Marco and the cathedral, but also visiting the nearby Palazzo Ducale and the Palace of the Doges. To his niece he described how "Anna could only utter exclamations and cries of admiration in looking at the palaces and the piazza. In San Marco Cathedral (astonishing, incomparable!) she lost her sculptured Swiss fan that she adored (she had so little jewelry!). My God, how she cried!"[8] On departing from Venice, the Dostoevskys took a boat to Trieste, running into a rough sea that caused Dostoevsky a good deal of anxiety over the pregnant Anna, and then, changing to a train on shore, arrived in Prague at the beginning of August. Their plan to settle in Prague for the winter, however, was thwarted by a lack of available accommodations. Dostoevsky's hopes of living in a congenial circle outside Russia thus came to naught, and he and Anna fell back on their original Dresden goal.

———■———

The Dostoevskys arrived in Dresden in mid-August and quickly found quarters. Ten days after getting settled, Dostoevsky wrote to Maikov. "I have terrible fears about [Anna's] health. . . . She is constantly unwell, and besides this, worried, nervous, impressionable, and in the bargain seriously fears that she will die in childbirth (remembering the suffering of the first birth)."[9] In the midst of these gloomy forebodings, Dostoevsky complains that "I must begin to write, first for *Dawn*, and then begin the major work for *The Russian Messenger*. I have not written anything for eight months. . . . things have turned out for me that it

[6] Ibid., 43; May 15/27, 1869.
[7] Ibid., 56–57; August 29/September 10, 1869.
[8] Ibid., 57n.37.
[9] Ibid., 49n.2, 51; August 14/26, 1869.

would be more useful to sit in debtor's prison than remain abroad. If I remain here another year, I do not know whether I will be in a condition to write, not even well but at all, so much have I become cut off from Russia." Besides, Anna also missed Russia dearly, and both believed that Sonya had died "solely because we could not adapt ourselves to the foreign manner of nurturing and rearing a child."[10] Europe was thus to blame for this lacerating blow to their happiness, and if they were to lose the second child, both he and Anna would give way to total despair.

Happily, their second daughter, Lyubov, was born on September 26 without untoward incident, but Dostoevsky was so concerned about Anna's state of mind that he hid from her the volume of *War and Peace* depicting the death of Prince Andrey's wife in childbirth. The presence of Anna's mother was also a source of reassurance because she could look after the child in the Russian fashion considered so important. Lyubov's birth, however, brought a flood of new expenses that far surpassed the family's limited means; three days after the birth, Dostoevsky wrote Maikov that he would now be forced to sell (or pawn) his linen, his topcoat, and perhaps even his jacket, unless he received the advance he had requested from *Dawn*.

By the end of September, Dostoevsky had completed half of the still-untitled work, and in view of its increased length, had asked for a further advance of two hundred rubles. He asked Maikov to visit the editor Kashpirev and reinforce his plea that he receive an *immediate* reply. Dostoevsky had told Kashpirev that "*the time and the rapidity of the aid is almost more important than the money itself*," and that if a delay occurred, "I would be forced on the spot to sell my remaining and most necessary things, and for things worth one hundred thalers would receive twenty . . . in order to save the lives of three beings."[11] Dostoevsky added, for Maikov's eyes alone, that he was here telling an untruth; everything worth a hundred thalers had long since been pawned.

Kashpirev replied favorably within a week and dispatched a letter of credit from a Petersburg bank to one in Dresden, but Dostoevsky's financial relations with *Dawn* were dogged by misfortune. The letter of credit, by mistake, had been written in such a way as to require another document in order to be cashed, and Dostoevsky waited in vain for this paper to arrive, going to the bank every day and being told, after a while, that such letters of credit were sometimes issued *as a joke*. Desperate with fear for the well-being of Anna and the new-born Lyubov, and literally reduced to his last penny, Dostoevsky wrote a week later to Kashpirev asking him to rectify the error and send seventy-five rubles immediately. It took twelve days for him to receive a reply, even though letters from

[10] Ibid., 51.
[11] Ibid., 63; September 17/29, 1869.

Petersburg usually arrived in three days, and no seventy-five rubles were forth-coming. Noting that Kashpirev's letter, dated October 3, was postmarked as having been sent on the sixth, he dashed off a furious and frantic letter to Mai-kov asking him to intercede.

Dostoevsky's missive to Maikov is one of the most angry that he ever wrote—a letter in which he releases all his pent-up resentment at the constant humilia-tions arising from his impecunious and precarious literary situation. Dostoevsky had written to Kashpirev deferentially, almost pleadingly; and the apparent neg-ligence with which he was being treated, when he had confessed that both he and his family were being forced to pawn and sell their belongings, filled him with fury: "Doesn't he understand how much this is *insulting* for me? After all, I wrote him about the needs of *my wife* and child—and after that such careless-ness! Is this not insulting!" Dostoevsky felt that Kashpirev was behaving toward him "as only a *barin* behaves with his lackey," and he returns to this comparison again and again as the tempestuous sentences pour forth in a wave of bitterness and wounded pride. "I walk up and down and tear my hair, and at night I can't sleep! I think all the time and become furious." After enlarging on the enormity of the insult dealt both him and Anna, he exclaims defiantly: "And after that they demand artistry from me, pure poetry without strain, without tension, and refer to Turgenev, Goncharov! Just let them look under what conditions I work!"[12]

Coming to the rescue, Maikov sent one hundred rubles and another letter of credit, along with the apologies of Kashpirev and the editor's offer to reimburse Dostoevsky for all his extra expenses. Gratified by such contrition, Dostoevsky insists that he is content simply by the offer being made, and that "I don't want any compensation, I'm not a usurer!"[13] Despite his agitations, he had continued working on the novella, whose title he thought would be *The Eternal Husband* (*Vechny muzh*) and it would be even lengthier than previously reported. Dos-toevsky was also worried because Kashpirev intended to advertise the work in advance. He had promised *The Russian Messenger* the first chapters of a new novel by January 1870, a promise he knew he could not keep, and Katkov would become aware that he had been writing for *Dawn* instead.

Dostoevsky worked uninterruptedly at his novella from September through December, finishing *The Eternal Husband* in the first week of December. He was once again so badly short of funds that he could not even afford the postage re-quired for such a bulky manuscript, and he asked Maikov to urge Kashpirev to send fifty rubles immediately. By this time he was so convinced of *Dawn's* busi-ness incompetence that he preferred to approach the editors with his friend act-

---

[12] Ibid., 67, 69, 70; October 16/28, 1869.
[13] Ibid., 71–73; October 27/November 8, 1869.

ing as intermediary. He also remarked that he had so far received no further advance from *The Russian Messenger* and that *Dawn* could print his manuscript whenever it pleased.[14]

Two weeks later, having sent off his text, Dostoevsky once more pleaded with Maikov to put pressure on Kashpirev for advance payment on everything he earned. Or if not, "since it is impossible for me to remain absolutely without any money during the Christmas season," then at least to forward one hundred rubles immediately. It was necessary to buy woolens for both Lyubov and Anna, and also to christen the baby—which had not been done for lack of funds. "In three days," Dostoevsky also informs him, "I will go to work on my novel for *The Russian Messenger*. Don't think that I just write anything [the literal Russian is: that I bake *blinis*]: no matter how terrible and awful what I write may be, the idea of a novel and work on it—is yet to me, poor author, more important than anything in the world! This is not nothing [*blinis*], but the dearest and most longstanding of my ideas."[15] Dostoevsky can only be referring here to his *Atheism* plan, which by this time had metamorphosed into *The Life of a Great Sinner*. It was this novel, or one of its parts, that he was now setting out to compose.

———■———

A month later, Strakhov was able to tell Dostoevsky that the notices for *The Eternal Husband* were uniformly favorable. Dostoevsky's artistic reputation had been badly tarnished by *The Idiot*, but this new work succeeded in restoring some of its gloss. Despite this reassuring reception, so flattering for Dostoevsky's literary self-esteem, he wrote his niece after sending off the manuscript that "I have hated this story from the very start."[16] Not even the recognition that he had turned out a small masterpiece could decrease his resentment at having been deflected from a major novel that, he was convinced, would once and for all establish his claim to a place in the pantheon of major Russian writers.

Despite Dostoevsky's frustration at being distracted from the great work he was planning, this seemingly uncomplicated novella may be seen as his first artistic answer to Tolstoy's increasing fame. The most important subtext for *The Eternal Husband* is provided by Apollon Grigoryev's theory of Russian culture. Both of the main characters—Velchaninov and Trusotsky—speak of "peaceable" (*smirny*) and "predatory" (*khischny*) types of personalities. These terms were used by Grigoryev to characterize Russian literature and culture, which he viewed as a struggle between such types; and the same terms had just been revived and employed by Strakhov in his essay on Tolstoy. Types of this kind were understood

[14] Ibid., 77–78; November 23/December 5, 1869.
[15] Ibid., 81; December 7/19 1869.
[16] Ibid., 88; December 14/26, 1869.

not only as moral-psychological categories but, in addition, possessed a strong social-cultural significance. The "predatory" figures—masterful, heroic, brilliant, often glamorously Byronic—were identified with Western European culture, the "simple" or "peaceable" ones with Russia and the Russian national character. *War and Peace*, according to Strakhov, had borne out Grigoryev's views to perfection, and offered the greatest depiction so far achieved of this memorable internecine warfare taking place within the Russian national psyche.[17]

Dostoevsky, a great admirer of Grigoryev, had been deeply influenced by his typology of Russian culture, but he had never accepted all of its details. Indeed, as Grigoryev revealed in a series of articles titled "The Paradoxes of Organic Criticism"—subtitled "Letters to F. M. Dostoevsky"—the novelist had once taxed him personally with being too "theoretical." Just what Dostoevsky meant by his remark to Grigoryev may perhaps be inferred from *The Eternal Husband*, in which both the lordly Velchaninov and the docile cuckold Trusotsky momentarily exchange personalities and exhibit characteristics of each other under the stress of events. The novella may thus be taken not only as a comment on Grigoryev but also as a reply to what Dostoevsky considered Strakhov's excessive praise of Tolstoy, against whose pure personality types he was presenting his own more tangled view of the mutabilities and indeterminacies of human character.[18] Both characters turn out to contain possibilities of *either* type, the predatory and the peaceable, when a crisis occurs in their lives—a crisis that can be surmounted only by the self-transcendence of the ego. *The Eternal Husband* thus may be seen as Dostoevsky's first artistic answer to Tolstoy's increasing fame; the second would have been the great work he was planning, on as vast a scale as *War and Peace*, under the title of *The Life of a Great Sinner*.

———■———

In mid-December 1869 Dostoevsky speaks of his obligation to *The Russian Messenger* with anxiety and indicates how he will proceed. He is engaged on a vast novel, he tells his niece, "only the first part of which will be published in *The Russian Messenger*. It will not be finished sooner than in five years, and will be divided into three separate novellas. This novel is the whole hope and whole dream of my life—not only as regards money."[19] Dostoevsky, not surprisingly, voices all his qualms about taking such a decision. "In order to write this novel—I would need to be in Russia," he insists. "For instance, the second half of my

[17] N. N. Strakhov, *Kriticheskiye stati*, 2 vols. (Kiev, 1902–1908), 1: 247.

[18] The relations of Grigoryev and Dostoevsky are informatively discussed by I. Z. Serman, "Dostoevsky i Grigoryev," in *Dostoevsky i ego vremya* (Leningrad, 1971), 130–142. The polemic with Strakhov-Grigoryev in *The Eternal Husband* is analyzed in Richard Peace, "*The Eternal Husband* and Literary Polemics," *Essays in Poetics* 3 (1978), 22–49.

[19] *PSS*, 29/Bk. 1: 88; December 14/26, 1869.

first novel takes place in a monastery. I need not just see it (I have seen a lot) but to live in a monastery for a while too."[20]

The bulk of Dostoevsky's notes deal with the childhood and boyhood of the "great sinner," who is a member of an "accidental family"—as Dostoevsky liked to call households with no settled traditions of order or decorum. The central figure here is an illegitimate child, sent to live with an elderly couple in the countryside and raised in isolation from his father (a situation that will later be used for *A Raw Youth*). Dostoevsky's rivalry with Tolstoy is apparent in the definition he sets down of what he wishes his character to represent. "A type entirely contrary to the scion of that noble family of counts, degenerate to the point of swinishness, which Tolstoy had depicted in *Childhood and Boyhood*. This [Dostoevsky's new type] is simply a primitive type, subconsciously agitated by a primitive strength, a strength which is completely spontaneous" (9: 128).

The great sinner was to possess such an elemental force, symbolic of that contained in the Russian people, "an extraordinary inner power hard to bear for those who possess it, a power which demands peace out of the storms of life to the point of suffering, yet cannot help stirring up storms before it finds peace. He finally comes to rest in Christ, but his whole life is storm and disorder." Such a type "joyfully throws itself—in its period of searches and wanderings—into monstrous deviations and experiments until it comes to rest on an idea powerful enough to be fully proportionate to its own immediate primitive strength—an idea so powerful that it can at last organize this strength and calm it down to a tranquilizing stillness" (9: 128).

The great sinner is sent off to a monastery as a means of disciplining his rebellious behavior, portrayed through incidents such as the desecration of an icon. There he encounters a saintly monk named Tikhon. The character of Tikhon would be based on the figure of Saint Tikhon-Zadonsky, a Russian clergyman of the mid-eighteenth century who was elevated to sainthood in 1860 and left an abundant literary legacy (fifteen volumes). In the spring of 1870 Dostoevsky had told Maikov that "I took [him] into my heart with rapture a long time ago,"[21] perhaps when an edition of Tikhon's works was published at the time of his canonization. Father George Florovsky, the greatest modern historian of Russian theology, speaks of Saint Tikhon as undergoing what Saint John of the Cross called *la noche oscura*, the "dark night of the soul,"[22] and Dostoevsky would have been deeply moved by Saint Tikhon's open expression of moods of depression, despair, and susceptibility to temptation. Dostoevsky also found in his writings many of the moral-religious precepts that formed the basis of his own conception of Russian Orthodoxy.

[20] Ibid., 11; February 6/January 25, 1869.
[21] Ibid., 118; March 25/April 6, 1870.
[22] Georgy Florovsky, *Puti Russkogo bogoslaviya* (Paris, 1983), 123–125.

Evil, according to Saint Tikhon, was necessary to the world to bring about the birth of the good, and the chief Christian task of mankind was to conquer its own evil proclivities, to conquer "pride by humility, anger by gentleness and patience, hatred by love."[23] It is only through the experience of wrestling with the evil in itself that humankind discovers the value and meaning of human existence. Surely such ideas are the source of the famous notebook entry in which Dostoevsky defined what was for him "the Orthodox point of view" dominant in his work: "man is not born for happiness . . . because the knowledge of life and consciousness . . . is acquired by experience *pro and contra*, which one must take upon oneself. (By suffering, such is the law of our planet)" (7: 155).

For Tikhon, indeed, even crime was a way of clearing the path to such a discovery of Christian truth; in principle, the possibility of enlightenment and purification was never closed, no matter how burdensome the crime weighing down a human consciousness. "There is no kind of sin," he declared, "and there cannot be any such on earth, that God would not pardon to someone who sincerely repents." There are many references in Tikhon's works to "a great sinner," and he insists that, whatever the multitude and magnitude of sins, God would always pardon a remorseful heart. One of the best-known incidents of Saint Tikhon's life involved a quarrel with a landowner reputed to be a "Voltarian." Disputing about questions of faith with Tikhon, the irascible landowner flared up and struck the clergyman in the face. Although known for his fiery temper, Tikhon immediately kneeled and begged forgiveness for having provoked the blow. Such an incident would certainly have been taken by Dostoevsky as an early symbolic instance of that clash between the disintegrating effects of Western reason and the kenotic Russian faith that had now become the great theme of his life.

During his stay in the monastery, and under the tutelage of Tikhon, the egoism of the great sinner turns inward on itself. He is still obsessed by a need for power and domination; but he begins to believe that this need can be satisfied only by first conquering himself. Under the notebook entry titled "The Principal Idea" we read: "After the monastery and Tikhon the great sinner again goes into the world to be the *greatest of men* . . . he is the proudest of the proud and treats people with the greatest arrogance. . . . But (and this is the essential) thanks to Tikhon he had been seized by the idea (conviction): that to conquer the entire world it suffices to conquer oneself" (9: 138–139).

Self-conquest is thus the highest expression of the freedom of the will, the most exalted goal of the most powerful personality. The subsequent career of the great sinner is rapidly sketched: "Suddenly adolescence and debauchery. . . .

---

[23] For the citations from Saint Tikhon's works, see the commentary to *The Life of a Great Sinner* in *PSS*, 9: 511–514.

Insensate pride. Out of pride he becomes ascetic and pilgrim. . . . [H]e shows himself as gentle and humble toward all—precisely because he is infinitely higher than all" (9: 138). As with all the notes he made for future works, Dostoevsky is much concerned with narrative technique and form. The "tone" of his narrative was to be that of a *vita*, the hagiographic life of a saint. "N.B. *Tone* (the narrative is a *vita*, i.e., even though it comes from the author's pen, . . . The reader still ought to know at all times that the whole idea is a pious one." "The man of the future," he adds, "is to be exhibited for everyone to see, and to be placed on a pedestal" (9: 132–133). Dostoevsky would later return to these notes for both *A Raw Youth* (where the peasant "wanderer" Makar also regales an adolescent with edifying parables and apothegms) and *The Brothers Karamazov*, where Zosima's life is narrated as a *vita* and the semi-hagiographic treatment of the "man of the future" would be realized in Alyosha.

———■———

Dostoevsky did not, so far as we know, settle down to the redaction of the novel sketched in these notes. Instead, as he told Maikov just a month later, he was swept away by a new inspiration that changed all his plans. "I have tackled a rich idea," he informs his friend enthusiastically. "I am not speaking of the execution, but the idea. One of the ideas that has an undoubted resonance among the public. Like *Crime and Punishment*, but even closer to reality, more vital, and having direct relevance for the most important contemporary issue. I will finish by fall; I'm not hurrying and not rushing." [24] These words are the first reference to *Demons*, which was indeed conceived in relation to the recent discovery of a murder committed by a group of revolutionary conspirators. Dostoevsky thus sets aside his "eternal" theme, that of atheism, for one that was burningly topical because he was persuaded that such a book would solve all his problems. He would pillory the radicals once and for all, satisfy *The Russian Messenger* with a novel, reap a rich financial reward, and do all this in record time. "I hope to make at least as much money as for *Crime and Punishment*, and therefore, by the end of the year there is hope of putting all my affairs in order and of returning to Russia. . . . Never have I worked with such enjoyment and such ease." [25]

Work on the new novel began immediately and relegated *The Life of a Great Sinner*, which Dostoevsky must have given up with some relief, to a less uncertain, less economically harassed, and happily repatriated future. But his imagination could not relinquish the stately vistas it had created, and he continued to toil at their elaboration. In late March, Dostoevsky speaks of five novels to Maikov, instead of three (the size of *War and Peace*, he remarks, again disclosing the

[24] *PSS*, 29/Bk. 1: 107; February 12/24, 1870.
[25] Ibid.

competition with Tolstoy), and defines his "main question" as being "the same one that I have been tormented by consciously and unconsciously all my life—the existence of God." He also confesses how painfully he suffers from a sense of inferiority to his two great rivals, Turgenev and Tolstoy, and his hope of enhancing his status by the exalted thematic heights he would be attempting to scale. "Perhaps people will at last say," he complains sadly, "that I did not spend all my time writing trifles."[26]

More than anything else, however, and with Saint Tikhon as model, Dostoevsky wished to produce "a majestic, *positive*, holy figure."[27] His great ambition was now to provide Russian culture with an august image expressing its highest religious values. The disappointing reception of his first attempt, *The Idiot*, had not quenched his aspiration, and the historical stature of Saint Tikhon would shield his literary eulogist from the all-too-familiar accusation of giving rein to his weakness for "the fantastic." "I will not be creating anything," he assures Maikov, "I will just portray the real Tikhon." Side by side with Saint Tikhon would stand the type of character Dostoevsky had been struggling to delineate ever since the epilogue to *Crime and Punishment*—a great sinner, who would convincingly undergo a religious conversion and display the regenerative effects of Saint Tikhon's teaching and example.

Dostoevsky intended to keep his "contemporary" theme separate from his more "exalted" one of atheism, postponing the second for more propitious working conditions while quickly (and profitably) dispatching the first. In doing so, however, he was allowing his contest with Tolstoy, whose elevation of subject matter he envied and wished to emulate, to tempt him into running counter to the distinctive idiosyncrasy of his talent. Dostoevsky always found his inspiration in the most immediate and sensational events of the day—events that were often commonplace and even sordid—and then raised such material in his best work to the level of the genuinely tragic. This union of the contemporary and the tragic was the true secret of his genius, and he finally found it impossible to maintain the forced and artificial disjunction of one from the other that he thought he could impose. The great work that he called his "poem" could not be kept distinct from the social-political "pamphlet" into which he had thrown himself, and the two eventually blended together into his unprecedented novel-tragedy, *Demons*.

[26] Ibid., 117; March 25/April 6, 1870.
[27] Ibid., 118.

CHAPTER 42

Fathers, Sons, and Stavrogin

At the end of May 1869, Katkov published an article in the *Moscow Gazette* deal-ing with the recent student disorders that had broken out in St. Petersburg and Moscow, and he designated among their leaders "a certain Nechaev." He was de-scribed as a "very hardened Nihilist," an "inflamer of youth," who had been ar-rested but managed the unprecedented feat of escaping from the Peter-and-Paul Fortress and fleeing abroad. In Europe he had produced a series of incendiary proclamations calling on students to revolt, "printed them very handsomely," and sent bales of them back to Russia through the public mails.[1] In fact, Nechaev had never been arrested, much less escaped from the impregnable fortress, but this was the legend that he spread about himself in accordance with his calculated tactic of deception in the service of the revolution. Bakunin and Ogarev, who ea-gerly aided Nechaev in his proclamation campaign, at first greeted him admir-ingly in Geneva as the resurrected incarnation of the revolutionary aspirations of their youth. It was only later, when his unscrupulousness had been turned against them, that their initial enthusiasm was reversed to regretful repudiation.

Six months later, the *Moscow Gazette* carried news of the murder of a student on the grounds of the Petrovsky Agricultural Academy in Moscow, where Anna's brother, Ivan Snitkin, was a student. But it was only on December 29 that Nechaev's name was linked to the murder, and thereafter stories about him ap-peared regularly in the newspapers, with references to "some kind of wild con-spiracy with proclamations" and to Ivanov, the murdered student, as having "died because he wished to denounce the criminal scheme."[2] (What Ivanov ob-jected to, so far as can be established, was Nechaev's assertion of his right to ab-solute dictatorial control over the members of his group of five.)[3] On January 4, 1870, a leading article by Katkov, which summarized and commented on foreign newspaper reports covering the Nechaev affair, devoted a good deal of space to Bakunin, who, along with the weak-willed and compliant Ogarev, had partici-pated with Nechaev in launching his propaganda campaign. Katkov had known

[1] See the commentary to *The Devils* in *PSS*, 12: 198. I am greatly indebted in general to the ma-terial contained in pages 192–218.
[2] Ibid., 199.
[3] See Philip Pomper, *Sergei Nechaev* (New Brunswick, NJ, 1979), 112.

Bakunin all too well as a young man (he had once almost faced him in a duel), and he quoted Bakunin's anarchist call for the total destruction not only of the Russian state but of every and any existing state.[4] He also cited Bakunin's advice to the younger generation to foster in themselves that "fiercely destroying and coldly passionate fervor that freezes the mind and stops the blood in the veins of our opponents."[5]

All through the month of January, Katkov's newpaper continued to print reports about the gradually unfolding story of the Nechaev case, often using corroborating information from foreign (particularly German) newspapers, which of course Dostoevsky could read independently. It was precisely at this time—between December 1869 and February 1870—that Dostoevsky suddenly shifted his literary course, set aside the *Life of a Great Sinner*, and threw himself into a book with "direct relevance to the most important contemporary issue." The "Nechaev affair"—the murder by a secret revolutionary group led by Sergey Nechaev of a student named Ivan Ivanov—had seized Dostoevsky's imagination.

———■———

References to Nechaev, the proclamations, and the murder begin to creep into Dostoevsky's notes from this time. He was then daily poring over the flood of rumor and speculation, and the few snippets of hard fact that emerged in the various press accounts; and he must have immersed himself in such pages with a mixture of fury and gnawing despair. After all, had he not practically predicted this outcome of radical ideas when he created Raskolnikov? Nechaev and his group had merely drawn the conclusions, and taken the actions, that in *Crime and Punishment* Dostoevsky had only imagined as extreme and "fantastic" possibilities.

And who was ultimately responsible for this perversion of Russian youth, now capable of the most atrocious crimes for the sake of revolution, if not the generation of the 1840s, the generation of Dostoevsky himself and such luminaries as Belinsky, Herzen, Bakunin, and Turgenev (whose *Rudin* was well known to be an image of Bakunin in his youthful heyday)? Indeed, had not Turgenev himself, in a recent preface to a new edition of his *Fathers and Children* (1869), practically claimed such responsibility in his attempt to overcome the hostility of the radicals to his work? A "witty lady" of his acquaintance, he informed his readers, had said after perusing the novel: "You are a Nihilist yourself." And

---

[4] In 1840 Bakunin spread the word that Katkov was carrying on an affair with Ogarev's first wife (the Russian intelligentsia constituted a very small world). After a furious quarrel in Belinsky's quarters, during which Katkov called Bakunin "a eunuch" (the revolutionary firebrand appears to have been in truth sexually impotent), Bakunin challenged him to a duel. But no date was set, and Bakunin soon left for Europe in June 1840. See Aileen Kelly, *Mikhail Bakunin* (New Haven, CT, 1947), 64–65.

[5] *PSS*, 12: 200.

Turgenev adds musingly: "I will not undertake to contradict: perhaps the lady spoke the truth." In another passage he declares that, with the exception of Bazarov's views on art, "he almost shares all his convictions."[6] A shocked Strakhov, in the December issue of *Dawn*, had exclaimed in amazement: "Turgenev—a Nihilist! Turgenev shares the convictions of Bazarov!"[7]

All through the past several years, Dostoevsky's bile against his own generation had been steadily accumulating. His reminiscences of Belinsky had brought back the abusive insults to Christ made in his presence, and the bitter quarrel with the self-declared renegade Turgenev had only aggravated his animosity. The Nechaev affair reopened all these old wounds, and what he learned from the newspapers became amalgamated not only with Strakhov's ironic article on Turgenev but also with an earlier one by the same critic, whom he read so carefully and so admiringly. A biography of one of the most eminent members of the generation of the 1840s, T. N. Granovsky, was published in 1869 and reviewed by Strakhov. "He was," Strakhov wrote, "a pure Westernizer"; and Strakhov then defined this Russian type with lines from Nekrasov—lines that Dostoevsky would pick up and cite in the first chapter of *Demons*: "A living monument of reproach . . . / Thou stoodst before thy country / O liberal-idealist." Strakhov saw contemporary Russian Nihilism as a direct consequence of the influence of such "pure" Westernizers, even though the surviving members of that generation refuse to recognize their offspring in the "impure" progeny they have engendered.[8]

On the other side, the young generation had little respect for such "pure" Westernizers as Granovsky and, wrote Strakhov, "they naturally prefer Belinsky, Dobrolyubov, and Pisarev, who advanced the same position much further."[9] The battle of the generations was thus joined again in Russian culture, as it had been in *Fathers and Children*. Sometime in January or early February 1870 Dostoevsky put down in his notebook, under the heading *T. N. Granovsky*, a few sentences depicting "a pure and idealistic Westernizer in his full splendor," whose "*characteristic traits*" are sketched in as "aimlessness and lack of firmness in his views . . . which . . . used to cause him suffering before, but *have now become his second nature* (his son makes fun of this tendency)" (11: 65).

It was Strakhov's article, in all likelihood, that clarified for Dostoevsky how he might turn to creative profit his smoldering anger against his own generation and his blazing hatred of the Nechaevian avatar it had produced. Shortly after setting down his note, he dashed off a request to Strakhov for "the book of Stankevich on Granovsky. . . . I need that little book as I do the air I breathe, and

[6] *PSSiP*, 14: 103, 100–102.
[7] N. N. Strakhov, *Kriticheskiye stati*, 2 vols. (Kiev, 1902–1908), 1: 82.
[8] *Zarya* 7 (1869), 159; cited in *PSS*, 12: 170–171.
[9] *PSS*, 12: 172.

as quickly as possible, as the most necessary material for my book." [10] A month later, he wrote to Maikov: "What I am writing now is something tendentious, I want to speak out as passionately as I can. All the Nihilists and Westernizers will cry out that I am *retrograde*. To hell with them, I will speak my mind to the very last word." [11] He has high hopes for his new novel, he tells Strakhov, "but not on the artistic, rather on the tendentious side; I wish to speak out about several matters even though my artistry goes smash. What attracts me is what has piled up in my mind and heart; let it give only a pamphlet, but I shall speak out."

Once he had fixed on Granovsky as the prototype of the generation of the 1840s (though many others will be amalgamated into the type, particularly Herzen), Dostoevsky's imagination began to work rapidly. The future Stepan Verkhovensky is pinned down almost immediately and will remain unchanged throughout. "Places himself unconsciously on a pedestal, in the style of relics to be worshiped by pilgrims, and loves it. . . . Shuns Nihilism and does not understand it. . . . 'Leave me God and art, and I will let you have Christ. . . . Christ did not understand women.' Fifty years old. Literary recollections. Belinsky, Granovsky, Herzen . . . Turgenev and others" (11: 65). Dostoevsky here was manifestly summoning up all *his* memories and using them to fill out his ideological canvas.

The notes also contain a romantic intrigue between a character called the Prince and the ward of a family. This was an accessory to the initially main conflict-of-generations theme, but the Prince would evolve into Stavrogin and would no longer serve merely as an accessory. By April 1870 Stavrogin had developed to the point where he had become the hero and taken the book away from both Granovsky and Nechaev. Dostoevsky could no longer contain him within the confines of his initial idea of the novel as a tendentious "pamphlet." Indeed, at this time a process of fusion took place between the two creative projects that Dostoevsky had intended to keep separate, and it becomes difficult to distinguish one from the other.

In some May notes, the Great Sinner is said to possess "pride and immeasurable arrogance," and also to have committed "atrocious crimes." The heroes of his two novels are thus almost identical, and the barriers between the "pamphlet" and the "poem" broke down completely at this time: the Lame Girl, the future haunting Marya Lebyadkina, moves from one to the other, and Tikhon appears as well as the confessor and interlocutor of Stavrogin. It turned out to be impossible for Dostoevsky to write a novel that would be *only* a politically satiric denunciation of the Nihilist generation and its Liberal-Idealist forebears; his book had now taken on an entirely different and richer character, one that

[10] *PSS*, 29/Bk. 1: 111; February 26/March 10, 1870.
[11] Ibid., 116; March 25/April 6, 1870.

engaged Dostoevsky's deepest convictions and values. For Stavrogin has absorbed the religious thematic originally reserved for the Great Sinner's struggle with faith—a struggle that for Dostoevsky inevitably involved the theme of Russia itself and the messianic role that he believed it had been selected to fulfill in the destiny of humankind.

───■───

Dostoevsky had promised Katkov—in return for the resumption of his monthly stipend—that he would furnish the beginning of a new novel not later than June 1870. This commitment, however, was based on the rash assumption that he could dash off his pamphlet in just a few months. But the increasing complexity of his plans made this promise impossible to keep, and at the beginning of July Dostoevsky told his niece that he hoped to meet a new deadline at the end of August or early September. Five months later, he described to Strakhov some of the difficulties he had experienced even in the very early stages of composition: "All year I only tore up and made alterations. I blackened so many mounds of paper that I even lost my system of references for what I had written. I have modified the plan not less than ten times, and completely rewrote the first part each time."[12]

Short of funds as usual, and unable to obtain any further advances from Katkov before providing some manuscript, Dostoevsky had turned to *Dawn* for aid. But after receiving nine hundred rubles, nothing had appeared under his signature when *Dawn* ceased publication in 1873. During the month of July, suffering from weekly epileptic attacks, Dostoevsky found it impossible to write at all,[13] but this imposed respite gave him the opportunity, when he returned to his desk in August, to look afresh at what he had already written. He told Katkov a month later that "of the fifteen signatures already written [in the first version—J.F.], probably twelve will go into the new version of the novel."[14] He could now promise his text to Katkov, and enough copy was supplied to the journal in the next five months to ensure the beginning of publication in January 1871.

One of the most important events in the novel, he tells his editor, will be "the well-known murder of Ivanov in Moscow by Nechaev," though he hastens to add, "my Peter Verkhovensky may not at all resemble Nechaev; but it seems to me that my aroused mind has created by imagination the person, the type, that

[12] Ibid., 151; December 2/14, 1870.

[13] On January 7/19, 1870, Dostoevsky records: "NB in general, the results of an attack, that is, nervousness, weakening of the memory, a state of cloudiness, and some sort of pensiveness—now lasts longer than in previous years. Earlier, this passed in three days, now not before six. In the evening especially, by candlelight, a sick sadness without cause and as if a red coloration, bloody (not a tint) on everything. Almost impossible to work these days." E. M. Konshina, *Zapisnie tetradi F. M. Dostoevskogo* (Moscow–Leningrad, 1935), 83–84.

[14] *PSS*, 29/Bk. 1: 139–140; September 19/October 1, 1870.

really corresponds to the crime. . . . To my own surprise, this figure half turns out with me to be a comic figure." As a result, Dostoevsky continues, "even though the whole incident [the murder] forms one of the main events of the novel, it is nonetheless only accessory and a setting for the actions of another character, who could really be called the main character. . . . This other character (Nikolay Stavrogin)—is also a sinister character, also a villain. But he seems to me a tragic character. . . . I embarked on the poem about this character because for much too long I have wished to portray him. In my opinion he is Russian, and a typical character." At the same time, to balance these "somber figures," there will also be "radiant ones. . . . As the ideal of such a character I take Tikhon Zadonsky. . . . I confront the hero of my novel with him."[15]

What happened in August, then, was the recognition by Dostoevsky of what we have seen taking place in his notebooks during April and May: the transformation of the Prince into Stavrogin, whom he found more and more difficult, as he wrote, to fit into the framework originally established. As Stavrogin increased in stature, complexity, and tragic significance, he began to duplicate some of the lineaments of Nechaev as a "hero of our time" and an irresistibly attractive and powerful satanic figure. It was thus necessary to recreate Peter Verkhovensky as partly comic, and in some notes from mid-August, under the title "Something New," we find among other items: "And Nechaev's appearance on the scene as Khlestakov" (11: 202). No longer Bazarov or Pechorin, Nechaev (Peter Verkhovensky) is here reimagined as the ingratiating, fast-talking, and deceptive impostor in Gogol's *Inspector-General*, who now, like everyone else, revolves around Stavrogin and becomes an insidiously dangerous and semicomic rogue. Once this change had been made, the structural problem that had been plaguing Dostoevsky solved itself.

Dostoevsky's erstwhile political novel had now become *Demons*, a "tragic poem" about the moral-spiritual ills that had been afflicting Russian culture and had climaxed in the appearance of Nechaev and his accomplices. Writing to Maikov the day after he sent off his first chapters, Dostoevsky explains how he saw the book he was just setting out to write (or rewrite): "It is true that the facts have also proved to us that the disease that afflicted cultured Russians was much more virulent than we ourselves had imagined, and that it did not end with the Belinskys and the Kraevskys and their ilk. But at that moment what happened is attested to by Saint Luke: the devils had entered into a man and their name was legion, and they asked Him: 'suffer us to enter into the swine,' and He suffered them. The devils entered into the swine, and the whole herd ran violently down a steep place to the sea and was drowned. When the people came out to see what was done, they found the man who had been possessed now sitting at

[15] Ibid., 141–142; October 8/20, 1870.

the feet of Jesus clothed and in his right mind, and those who saw it told them by what means he that was possessed of the devils was healed." [16]

Dostoevsky dearly wished to believe that Russia too would be healed in the same way: but he knew that such hopes remained as yet only a remote possibility, visible, if at all, solely to the farseeing eyes of prophets like Maikov and himself. What he saw all around, and what he would depict in his novel, was the process of infection and self-destruction rather than the end result of purification. "Exactly the same thing," his letter continues, "happened in our country: the devils went out of the Russian man and entered into a herd of swine, that is, into the Nechaevs and Serno-Solovieviches, et al. These are drowned or will be drowned, and the healed man, from whom the devils have departed, sits at the feet of Jesus. . . . and bear this in mind, my dear friend, that a man who loses his people and his national roots also loses the faith of his fathers and his God. Well, if you really want to know—this is in essence the theme of my novel. It is called *Demons* and it describes how the devils entered into the herd of swine." [17] This self-interpretation is usually taken only as a loosely allegorical explanation of why Dostoevsky chose the passage from Luke as one of his epigraphs; but in my opinion the explanation is meant more literally, and furnishes a valuable interpretative clue to the manner in which Stavrogin is related to the other characters and to the ideological construction of the book. Just in what way, however, will be left to a later chapter.

—■—

More and more Dostoevsky felt it imperative to return to Russia, and not only for the sake of his writing. In January 1871, Dostoevsky informed his niece Sofya Ivanova, "Anna Grigoryevna has even fallen ill from missing Russia, and that torments me. . . . True, she is very exhausted physically from nursing the baby a whole year. . . . The doctors said that she has symptoms of severe exhaustion of the blood, and specifically from nursing. . . . She's been walking little, mostly sitting or lying down. I am terribly afraid." [18] Anna had become so depressed that she even refused to take the iron prescribed to her by the doctors, and Dostoevsky attributed much of her despondency to the melancholy of exile: "there's no way her inner longing, her homesickness can be chased away."

The couple thus decided to return to Russia whenever they could scrape together enough to meet the expenses of the trip; the fear of prison now took second place to their irrepressible need to regain their native soil. An advertisement had apprised him that a new edition of *Crime and Punishment* was to be published by Stellovsky, and Dostoevsky asked Maikov to collect the three thousand

[16] Ibid., 145; October 9/21, 1870.
[17] Ibid.
[18] Ibid., 163–164; January 6/18, 1871.

rubles the publisher was required by contract to pay the author. All of Dostoevsky's financial tribulations momentarily seemed at an end; this windfall would be enough to ensure a secure return. But Stellovsky, engaging in his usual delaying tactics, pleaded a poverty that Dostoevsky knew was fictitious, and even the threat of being forced to pay damages for breach of contract could not bring the wily businessman to heel. Dostoevsky was unable to obtain a single ruble when he needed it most, and it would take five years to extract his fee from Stellovsky.

Dresden harbored a large Russian colony that included some admirers of their resident author, a celebrity of sorts even if his convict past made him rather suspect. But Dostoevsky tolerated any renewal of social life solely in the hope of alleviating Anna's crippling depression. As Anna later remarked, "our Russian friends in Dresden were in his opinion not Russians but voluntary émigrés, who did not love Russia and had left it forever." [19] All the same, he was happy to lend these Russians his literary services when they appealed to him in a patriotic cause. In October 1870 the Russian government announced that it was unilaterally abrogating one of the clauses of the Treaty of Paris, which had been signed after its humiliating defeat in the Crimean War. No longer would the Russian government accept the prohibition against stationing its fleet in the Black Sea. On this occasion the Russians in Dresden sent a message of support to the Russian chancellor, and when Dostoevsky was asked to write it, he gladly complied.

The defiant action of the Russian government was one of the consequences of the quick defeat of France by Prussia, allied with the south German states, in the Franco-Prussian War. Dostoevsky's sympathies were unmistakably with the French, and he followed the campaign closely as it unfolded. He believed the Germans would win eventually, but that defeat would help to bring about a rejuvenation even of France itself. "France has grown too callous and petty. Temporary pain is of no importance; it will endure it and rise again to a new life and a new idea." [20] Presumably, the war would lead to a replacement of materialistic tendencies by more exalted values.

Like many others in France and Europe, Dostoevsky had been horrified at the uprising of the Commune and the destruction of the city that ensued (partly as the result of the desperate defense of the Communards, in whose ranks could be found Dostoevsky's erstwhile beloved Anna Korvin-Krukovskaya). Writing to Strakhov, who had objected to his scatological insults against Belinsky as "the mangy Russian liberalism preached by shitheads like the dung beetle Belinsky and the like," Dostoevsky replied by linking the critic—and thus the theme of his novel—directly to the cataclysmic events taking place in the French capital.

[19] Anna Dostoevsky, *Reminiscences*, trans. and ed. Beatrice Stillman (New York, 1975), 164.
[20] *PSS*, 29/Bk. 1: 138n.14.

"But take a look at Paris, at the Commune," he admonishes. "Can you really also be one of those who say that it again failed for lack of people, circumstances, and so on? For the whole nineteenth century that movement has . . . been dreaming of paradise on earth (beginning with the phalanstery). . . . In essence it is all the same old Rousseau and the dream of re-creating the world anew through reason and knowledge . . . (positivism). . . . The burning of Paris is a monstrosity: 'It did not succeed, so let the world perish because the Commune is higher than the happiness of the world and of France.' . . . to them (and many others) this monstrosity doesn't seem madness but, on the contrary, *beauty*. The aesthetic idea of modern humanity has become obscured."[21] True beauty for Dostoevsky had been incarnated in the world by Christ, and to equate it with violent destruction was the worst of abominations.

Dostoevsky, as we see, remained impenitent toward Belinsky, though he tries momentarily to separate the man from his ideas. "I criticized Belinsky," he explains, "more as a phenomenon of Russian life than as a person: that was the most foul-smelling, obtuse, and ignominious phenomenon of Russian life." He returns to the charge when he places Belinsky and his generation in exactly the same perspective as the one used for Stepan Trofimovich in his novel. "If Belinsky, Granovsky, and that whole bunch of scum were to take a look now, they would say: 'No, that is not what we were dreaming of, that is a deviation; let us wait a bit, and light will appear, progress will ascend to the throne, and humanity will be remade on sound principles and will be happy!' There is no way they could agree that once you have set off down that road, there is no place you can arrive at other than the Commune." Indeed, Dostoevsky even imagines Belinsky arguing that the "Commune was a failure because it was French," and that Russia could do it better because it had *no* nationality at all to impede the building of a brave new world.[22] Such bitter words indicate the unappeasable fury of Dostoevsky's indignation, and his anger leads him to deprecate Belinsky's literary judgments, once valued so highly, in ways that manifestly exaggerate their presumed wrongheadedness and dogmatism.

What Dostoevsky could never forgive was Belinsky's animadversions against Christ during their conversations in 1845. "But here is something more; you never knew him," he writes Strakhov vehemently; "but I knew him and saw him and now fully comprehend him. That man reviled Christ to me in the foulest language, but meanwhile he himself was never capable of setting all the movers and shakers of the whole world side-by-side with Christ by way of comparison. He was not able to notice how much petty vanity, spite, intolerance, irritability, vileness, and, most important, vanity, there was in him and in them. In reviling

---

[21] Ibid., 214; May 18/30, 1871.
[22] Ibid., 215.

Christ he never asked himself what we would set up in place of him—surely not ourselves, when we are so vile. No, he never pondered the fact that he himself was so vile. He was extremely satisfied with himself, and that was personal, foul-smelling, ignominious obtuseness."[23] Belinsky, to do him justice, could often be harshly self-critical and self-condemnatory, but Dostoevsky's recollection of the insults to Christ, combined with their now-evident (to him) Nechaevist consequences, now drove the novelist beyond all bounds.

All through these Dresden months, as can be seen from his comments on Russian literary and cultural matters, Dostoevsky was following closely events in his homeland. To Maikov, Dostoevsky writes, "I go through *three* Russian newspapers to the last line daily (!), and receive two journals."[24] A constant preoccupation was the fate of *Dawn*, which had failed to attract subscribers. Dostoevsky was liberal with advice on ways to increase Strakhov's feeble popularity. "Nihilists and Westernizers require an absolute whip," admonishes Dostoevsky, and should be attacked "more passionately and *coarsely*. . . . [the Nihilists] will consider you a backward old man who is still fighting with bow and arrow, while they have long since been using rifles."[25] But such combative skill and ardor was entirely foreign to Strakhov's furtive temperament and scholarly disposition.

In addition to Strakhov's article on Granovsky, another of his contributions to *Dawn*, a major series on Herzen published soon after the great man's death in Paris in January 1870, can also be linked to Dostoevsky's presentation of the character of Stepan Trofimovich. After reading the first installment, Dostoevsky wrote appreciatively, "you have done an extremely good job of establishing Herzen's main point—pessimism." Of greatest interest is Dostoevsky's own view of Herzen, whom he sees in terms not mentioned by Strakhov at all: "the main essence of all of Herzen's activity [was] that he has been, always and everywhere, *primarily a poet*. . . . The propagandist is a poet; the political activist is a poet; the socialist is a poet; the philosopher is a poet in the highest degree! That quality of his nature, I think can explain a great deal in his actions, even his flippancy and inclination to pun about the loftiest moral and philosophical questions (which, by the way, is very revolting in him).[26] The "poetic" quality of Herzen's temperament, his inability to commit himself wholeheartedly to whatever intellectual or practical activity he was involved in, will constitute one of the most engaging traits of Stepan Trofimovich's whimsically volatile character. This Herzen component of Stephan Trofimovich, as we shall see, also provides the historical background for his stormy relations with Peter Verkhovensky and the Nihilist ideas of his offspring.

[23] Ibid.
[24] Ibid., 115; March 25/April 6, 1870.
[25] Ibid., 125; May 28/June 9, 1870.
[26] Ibid., 113n.28.

Strakhov wrote a number of articles about Turgenev at this time, and Dostoevsky chided him for their lack of severity. More fuel for Dostoevsky's already red-hot animosity was added by the publication of Turgenev's article, "The Execution of Troppmann," in the journal *European Messenger* (*Vestnik Evropy*). Like Dostoevsky, Turgenev opposed capital punishment, and he had written an eyewitness account of the execution of a famous criminal as a protest. But, as Dostoevsky saw it, Turgenev had concentrated more on his own discomfiture and distaste than on the sufferings of the condemned, and his self-conscious finickiness filled Dostoevsky with a scarcely controllable rage.

"You may have a different opinion, Nikolay Nikolayevich," he fumed to Strakhov, "but that pompous and refined piece made me indignant. Why does he keep on being embarrassed and repeating that he does not have the right to be there? Yes, of course, if he only came to see a show; but no person on earth has the right to turn away and ignore what happens on earth, and there are supreme *moral* reasons for that. *Homo sum and nihil humanum*, and so on. . . . The main impression of the piece . . . is a terrible concern, to the point of extreme touchiness, for himself, for his safety and his peace of mind, and that in sight of a chopped-off head!"[27] Dostoevsky would parody this article in *Demons*, and also make use of the observation that "I consider Turgenev the most written out of all written-out Russian writers—no matter what you write 'in favor of Turgenev' Nikolay Nikolaevich." The phrase cited is the title of an article in which Strakhov gently chides Turgenev's newly announced allegiance to Nihilism, but insists that the nature of his artistic talent makes such an alliance impossible.

Strakhov continued to praise Turgenev's artistry and to maintain that his literary gifts more than compensate for his ideological vacillations. Dostoevsky could hardly believe it, and thought that perhaps he had misread Strakhov's words. "If you recognize that Turgenev has lost the point and is hedging," he objects, "and *does not know what to say* about certain phenomena of Russian life (treating them mockingly *just in case*), then you ought to have recognized that his greatest artistic ability had weakened (and this was inevitable) in his latest works." But Strakhov had not arrived at any such conclusion, much to Dostoevsky's surprise: "You recognize his former artistry even in his latest works. Is that really so? But perhaps I am mistaken (not in my opinion of Turgenev, but in your article). Perhaps you just did not state your opinion quite correctly."[28]

Dostoevsky had not been mistaken, however, and this defense of Turgenev leads him into an insight that has since become classic about the evolution of Russian literature and his own position in its ranks. Dostoevsky had once accepted the opinion that Turgenev's work had been enfeebled by his prolonged

[27] Ibid., 127–129; June 11/23, 1870.
[28] Ibid., 216n.21; December 2/14, 1870.

residence in Europe, but now he felt that "the reason is more profound" and goes far beyond Turgenev personally. "It really is all gentry-landowner literature. It has said everything that it had to say (superbly by Lev Tolstoy). But this in the highest degree gentry-landowner word was its last. There has not yet been a *new word* to replace that of the gentry-landowners, and besides, there has been no time for it."[29] Dostoevsky certainly thought of himself as capable of supplying such a *new word*—by dramatizing and combating the moral-spiritual confusion and chaos that had led to the rise of Nihilism.

Dostoevsky's reactions to Strakhov's articles about Herzen and Turgenev fed directly into the creation of his new novel; and he was also keeping a watchful eye on literary competitors dealing with the same subject. In *The Russian Messenger* he had been reading installments of a recent anti-Nihilist novel, *At Daggers Drawn* (*Na nozakh*), which N. S. Leskov was publishing under a pseudonym. Dostoevsky comments dismissively to Maikov that the book "contains a lot of nonsense . . . it is as though it takes place on the moon."[30] Dostoevsky of course is thinking of his own novel by contrast, in which he takes pains to delineate a verisimilar social framework. Dostoevsky also is careful to present his Nihilists in *Demons* not as villains acting out of dishonest or purely selfish motives but as vain, pretentious, frivolous, and simply naïve—easy prey for someone like Peter Verkhovensky who knows how to play on their human weaknesses.

■

It was in the spring of 1871, just before embarking on the return trip to Russia, that Dostoevsky took his final stab at gambling. This was the last time he ever approached a roulette table. He was laboring industriously at the first chapters of *Demons*, but in a mood of depression and anxiety. Anna had become pregnant with another child, and the expectation of an addition to the family only increased Dostoevsky's torments about their lack of means. They both desired desperately to return to Russia before the new child was born, which meant a departure by the beginning of July. It so happened that Anna had accumulated a small surplus of three hundred thalers and was willing to sacrifice one hundred of them to provide some distraction for her husband. Some subterfuge was necessary because of the presence of Dostoevsky's mother-in-law, who disapproved of gambling, and the couple concocted a little code that Dostoevsky could use in telegraphing for money from Wiesbaden. Anna writes with hindsight that she was convinced her husband would lose as usual, but perhaps even she harbored a shred of hope that he might, as had occasionally happened, bring home some winnings.

[29] Ibid.

[30] Ibid., 172; January 18/30, 1871.

But Dostoevsky lost all his money almost immediately, and, to make matters worse, also gambled away the thirty thalers sent him for the return home. Once more he writes the familiar pitifully pleading, imploring, self-castigating letters, not even asking for pardon but rather the opposite: "if you feel sorry for me at this moment, do not do so, I am not worth it." He is frantic about how the news will affect Anna, now in her final months of pregnancy, and also feels guilty when he thinks of his little daughter: "And Lyuba, Lyuba, how vile I have been!" In asking Anna to dispatch thirty more thalers, which he swears not to use for gambling, he envisions the terrible prospect of what might happen if he betrays her trust yet again. "But, my angel, try to understand, after all, I know that you will die if I were to lose again! I am not at all a madman! After all, I know that then I am done for. . . . Believe me for the last time, and you will not regret it."[31]

This last phrase refers to Dostoevsky's promise, a few sentences later, that he would never gamble again—a promise he had made often enough in the past and often enough broke. But with the benefit of hindsight, one may perhaps detect a new note of resoluteness in his vehement declarations, a desire at last to come to terms with himself once and for all. "Anya, my guardian angel! A great thing has been accomplished within me, a vile fantasy that has *tormented* me almost ten years has vanished. For ten years (or, rather since my brother's death, when I was suddenly crushed by debt) I kept dreaming of winning. I dreamed seriously, passionately. Now all that is finished. This was ABSOLUTELY the last time! Will you believe, Anya, that my hands are untied now; I had been bound by gambling." As usual, too, the letter is filled with affirmations of a desire to return to work, and he proclaims that "I will think about serious things now, and will not dream whole nights on end about gambling, as I used to. And therefore *the serious business* will move better and more quickly, and God bless it."[32] Anna, who had heard all this before, was understandably skeptical; but time would show that something decisive *had* occurred.

The specter of Anna dying from the grief brought on by his follies should be taken as more than a rhetorical flourish. Indeed, this fear had already manifested itself to him palpably in two terrifying dream images. "I dreamed of my *father* last night," Dostoevsky tells her, "but in such a horrible way as he has appeared to me only twice in my life, foretelling a terrible disaster, and twice the dream came true. (And now when I also recall my dream three days ago, that you had turned gray, my heart stops! Lord, what will happen to you when you get this letter!)"[33]

Dostoevsky not only took dream images seriously, but he also believed in signs and premonitions; in general he was superstitious and susceptible to being

[31] Ibid., 196–199; April 16/28, 1871.
[32] Ibid., 199.
[33] Ibid., 187.

influenced by any intimations of the dictates of a higher will. In Wiesbaden, after playing until 9:30 p.m. and losing everything, he ran off to seek the Russian priest. "I thought on the way," Dostoevsky explains to Anna, "running to see him, in the dark, down unfamiliar streets, that after all he is the Lord's shepherd, that I would talk to him not as with a private person, but as at a confession." Lost in the obscurity, he saw looming before him a building whose vaguely Oriental outlines seemed to mark out his destination. "When I reached the church that I had taken for a Russian one, I was told at a shop that it was . . . a Jewish one. It was as though I had had cold water poured over me. I came running home; it is now midnight, I am sitting and writing to you."[34]

Clearly, he intended to convey that he had received a shock to his entire nervous system, and this sensation he may perhaps have interpreted as an ominous sign. It could be that Dostoevsky took this error to indicate, by a signal from on high, that his gambling mania was bringing him into a degrading proximity with those people traditionally linked with the amassing of filthy lucre. Perhaps, whenever he was tempted to gamble in the future, this (for him) demeaning and chilling recollection continued to recur and acted as a barrier. A postscript to the letter confirms that he felt a decisive turning point in his life had been reached: "I *will not go to see* a priest, not for anything, not in any case. He is one of the witnesses of the old, the past, the former, the vanished! It will be painful even for me to meet him!"[35] Never again did he gamble during his several trips to Europe in the following years.

Dostoevsky came back from Wiesbaden determined, despite the loss of one hundred and eighty thalers, to return to Russia in July. He had calculated that he needed three or four thousand rubles to arrive in safety, but he now resolved to make the journey even though only a thousand might be available. "Staying in Dresden for another year," he wrote Maikov, "is the most impossible thing of all. That would mean killing Anna Grigoryevna with despair that she is unable to control. . . . It is also impossible for me not to move for a year."[36] Katkov had promised him the thousand by the end of June; but Dostoevsky wrote immediately, as he had done so often after a gambling disaster, to retail his woes and ask that the money be sent as soon as possible. Although the trip would be difficult—the Dostoevskys would be traveling without help and with Lyubov on their hands—there was no time to lose: Anna was expected to give birth at the beginning of August.

The ever-compliant Katkov agreed to send the money, and the Dostoevsky family departed on July 5. At last back in their homeland, the Dostoevskys still had a twenty-four-hour train trip ahead, but they felt as if they were living

[34] Ibid., 198.
[35] Ibid.
[36] Ibid., 205; April 21/May 3, 1871.

through the wondrous realization of a long-cherished dream. "Our consciousness of the fact that we were riding on Russian soil," Anna recalls, "that all around us were our own people, Russian people, was so comforting that it made us forget all about the troubles of our journey." [37]

[37] *Reminiscences*, 168.

CHAPTER 43

Exile's Return

On July 8, 1871, Dostoevsky and his family returned to Russia after four years of living abroad, making as unobtrusive a reentry as possible into the St. Petersburg he had quit presumably only for a summer vacation. Already published were all of Part I and two chapters of Part II of *Demons*, whose plot made spine-chilling use of the most spectacular event of the moment. Indeed, the public trial of the Nechaevtsy was taking place during Dostoevsky's arrival in the capital, and some of the essential documents, including the coldbloodedly Machiavellian *Catechism of a Revolutionary* (written by either Bakunin or Nechaev, and perhaps both), were placed in evidence and made publicly available on the very day he stepped off the train.

The Dostoevskys rented two furnished rooms near Yusupov Park, where they were soon assailed by daily visits from relatives and friends. As Dostoevsky complains in a letter to his favorite niece, Sofya Ivanova, "there was hardly any time to sleep."[1] In the midst of this overwhelming conviviality, Anna suddenly felt labor pains at dinner and gave birth to a son, Feodor, on July 16, happily without suffering the severe contractions of her earlier pregnancies. Dostoevsky was overjoyed and hastened to convey the good news to Anna's mother (then abroad) and to his family in Moscow.

A week later, at the end of July, Dostoevsky himself was in Moscow to straighten out his accounts with Katkov, receiving payment for the chapters he had supplied in recent months. The new acquisition of funds enabled the Dostoevskys to envisage moving from their furnished flat, which "was very expensive, full of comings and goings, and owned by nasty Yids."[2] The practical Anna, who had made a quick recovery after the birth of Feodor, soon turned up a suitable four-room dwelling and rented it in her own name, sparing Dostoevsky the legal formalities. Although forced to buy furniture, Anna believed she could retrieve the dinnerware and kitchen utensils, as well as the winter clothing, left in the care of relatives and friends four years earlier. But all had been lost—through careless reshufflings, or in the failure to pay insurance premiums sent

[1] *PSS*, 29/Bk. 1: 218; July 18, 1871.
[2] Ibid.

from abroad. Worst of all was the loss of Dostoevsky's library, which had been left in the care of Pasha on condition that he preserve it intact, but it had been sold piecemeal and irretrievably scattered. Anna mentions as of particular value the books inscribed by other writers, "serious works on history and on the sect of Old Believers [*raskolniki*], in which [my husband] took an immense interest."[3]

At the end of September, news of Dostoevsky's return was published, and the expected did not fail to occur: creditors immediately began to hammer at his door. One of the most importunate was the widow of a certain G. Hinterlach, who refused Dostoevsky's request, made in a personal visit, for an extension of a few months, by which time he expected to receive additional payment from Katkov. He returned home in despair, fearing that Frau Hinterlach would attach his personal property and, if this proved insufficient, send him to languish in prison.

Anna decided to take matters into her own hands and, without informing her husband, paid a visit to the implacable lady. Instead of pleading, she advised her that the household furnishings and the Dostoevsky apartment were both in her name, which meant that neither could be assigned for a debt owed by her husband. Moreover, if Dostoevsky were put in debtor's prison, Anna would insist that he remain there until the entire debt was canceled. Besides not obtaining a cent, Frau Hinterlach would also have to foot the cost of the prisoner's upkeep (as the law required of creditors using such a recourse). Anna also threatened to air the whole matter in an article for a journal: "Let everybody see what the honest Germans are capable of!"[4] Realizing that Anna was made of sterner stuff than the nervous and distraught Dostoevsky, the creditor hastened to accept the installment arrangement. After this, Anna decided to take over all the debt negotiations, and, meeting the threats with the same arguments, she succeeded in stalling demands for payment on the spot.

Busily at work on *Demons* all this while, Dostoevsky was also eager to renew relations with old friends and to make up for the cultural isolation from which he had suffered during his European sojourn. The poet Apollon Maikov, his staunchest friend and most faithful correspondent during his years abroad, introduced Dostoevsky to a literary-political circle that had gathered around Prince V. P. Meshchersky, the founder of a new publication, *The Citizen* (*Grazhdanin*), to counter the influence of the liberal and progressive press (though Meshchersky's opinion of what was "liberal" and "progressive" included journals that the radical intelligentsia regarded as pillars of reaction). Prince Meshchersky was the close friend of the heir to the Russian throne, Tsarevich Alexander,

---

[3] Anna Dostoevsky, *Reminiscences*, trans. and ed. Beatrice Stillman (New York, 1975), 176.
[4] Ibid., 178–179.

whom he had known since boyhood, and he moved freely in the very highest court circles. He gathered around him a small literary group that included Maikov, the great poet Tyutchev, Strakhov, Dostoevsky himself, and the tutor of the tsarevich, Konstantin Pobedonostsev. Pobedonostsev later acquired a sinister reputation when his former pupil succeeded to the throne as Alexander III, and the ex-tutor became known as the malevolent *éminence grise* of his oppressive regime. But in 1871 he was regarded primarily as a legal scholar and highly placed government official with a liberal past (in the Russian sense), who had supported the cause of judicial reform and the abolition of serfdom. He was also cultivated, had read widely in English, French, and German literature, and had published a translation of Thomas à Kempis in 1869. This was the literary-political environment in which Dostoevsky was to be immersed during the next three years.

Dostoevsky took great pleasure as well in reestablishing connections within his own family circle. The husband of his niece, Professor M. S. Vladislavlev, who had once been a contributor to Dostoevsky's journals, now taught philosophy at the University of St. Petersburg, and he frequently invited his eminent uncle-in-law to meet some of the luminaries of the learned world. Dostoevsky also began to entertain, and for a party on February 17, his name day, he sent invitations to close friends. Learning that N. G. Danilevsky, the author of *Russia and Europe*, was then passing through Petersburg, he asked Strakhov to bring Danilevsky along. They had known each other in the faraway days of the Petrashevsky Circle during the 1840s, when Danilevsky had earned the reputation of being the most thorough connoisseur of the Utopian Socialist doctrines of Fourier. Since then he had become a naturalist as well as a speculative historian of culture and had developed a theory of world civilization with a strong Slavophil tendency. Dostoevsky greatly admired his efforts to prove that Russian culture would soon create a new, independent phase of world history, and he employed some of these ideas for the impassionedly nationalistic speeches of Shatov in *Demons*.

In early February Dostoevsky wrote happily to his niece that, "thanks to a certain occurrence, my affairs have improved . . . I have gotten some money and satisfied the most impatient creditors."[5] His discretion can be explained by a letter addressed to A. A. Romanov, the tsarevich, which expresses Dostoevsky's embarrassment "at the boldness I exhibited." One can only assume that (probably with the help of Meshchersky and Pobedonostsev) he had been urged to explain his circumstances to the heir to the throne, who had come to his aid with a grant of money. Dostoevsky thanked the tsarevich above all "for the priceless attention . . . paid to my request. It is dearer to me than anything else,

---

[5] *PSS*, 29, Bk. 1: 226; February 4, 1872.

dearer than the very help that You gave me and which saved me from a great calamity."[6]

<hr />

The first reactions to Parts I and II of *Demons* were beginning to appear, and Dostoevsky, who had anticipated hostility from the radical critics, was not disappointed. Enough aspects of the anti-Nihilist pamphlet remained to make the book anathema to those who sympathized even remotely with Nechaev's revolutionary aims. In one of the most quoted passages of the novel, already cited earlier, a radical theoretician named Shigalev explains that, while he had begun his reflections with the idea of total freedom, he had regrettably discovered that he ended with that of total despotism. And he insists that the only logical answer to the social problem is to reduce all but one-tenth of humanity to the level of a "physiological" equality like a herd of cattle. A typical early review compares such notions to the madness of Poprishchin in Gogol's "Diary of a Madman." The novel, in the critic's view, evokes "a hospital" filled with mental patients "supposedly making up . . . a gathering of contemporary people."[7] One of the commonest charges leveled against Dostoevsky was that his characters were too mentally pathological to be taken as serious social commentary. An implicit subtext of such criticism was that the author himself, known to be epileptic, suffered from the same abnormality that filled his pages.

At the same time, welcome evidence of Dostoevsky's stature came in a letter from Pavel Tretyakov, the owner of an important art gallery in Moscow, who had commissioned the artist V. G. Perov to furnish his collection with portraits of the most eminent contemporary figures in Russian culture. Dostoevsky accepted the honor of sitting for Perov with a great deal of satisfaction, joining a group of notables that included Turgenev, Ostrovsky, Maikov, and the short-story writer and lexicographer V. I. Dal'. Perov arrived from Moscow in the spring of 1872 and visited Dostoevsky every day for a week to observe him in various moods and attitudes. The portrait is one of Perov's greatest achievements and was highly praised in all quarters, even winning the approval of Turgenev.

Despite the stimulus provided by an active social life, Dostoevsky knew that he needed solitude to complete *Demons*. He thus planned to leave Petersburg at the very beginning of the spring for a summer in the country. Dostoevsky remembered that his nephew-in-law, Vladislavlev, had praised Staraya Russa, a small watering place some hundreds of versts south of Petersburg at the confluence of several rivers. He could rent "a house with furniture, even with kitchen wares," and, as he wrote to his sister Vera, the town also contained "a station

[6] V. P. Meshchersky, *Moi vospominaniya*, 3 vols. (St. Petersburg), 2: 144.
[7] Cited in *PSS*, 12: 259.

24. Dostoevsky in 1872, by V. G. Perov

[*voksal*] with newspapers, magazines, etc."[8] Vladislavlev rented a house for the Dostoevskys from a local priest, Father Rumyantsev, and the family lived there from mid-May 1872 to the beginning of September.

To reach Staraya Russa, one took a train in St. Petersburg, transferred at a local station for Novgorod, and then boarded a boat for the trip across Lake Ilmen. Anna never forgot the view of Novgorod that greeted them as they watched the city glide by. "The sun shone bright on the river's far shore from which the crenellated walls of its kremlin rose up, the gilded cupolas of the Cathedral of St. Sophia were ablaze, and in the chilly air the bells were loudly

[8] Ibid., 235; April 20, 1872.

calling to matins. Feodor Mikhailovich, who loved and understood nature, was in a tender mood, which I unconsciously absorbed."[9] During his first stay there in 1872, these trips turned out to be far more frequent than he had anticipated. Just a few weeks before the family had planned to leave Petersburg, Lyubov fell and injured her wrist, and subsequent complications required the Dostoevskys to return to Petersburg, where Anna remained for three weeks with their daughter after the operation while Dostoevsky hastened back to Staraya Russa and his manuscript.

His letters to Anna are those of a terribly worried husband and father, upset by the disruption of his family routine. His mood was extremely irritable and querulous, and his observations on the local social scene reflected all the intemperance that so often overcame him when his nerves were frayed. "The crowd here is obviously very formal, high-toned, constantly trying to resemble high society, with the vilest French. The ladies all try to shine with their outfits, although they all must be trashy women . . . I definitely don't like the park. And in general, this whole Staraya Russa is terrible trash.[10] Worst of all, he writes Anna, "you can't help me with stenography, and I would like to send material to *The Russian Messenger*."[11] Dostoevsky tried to work, but he complains bitterly: "I'm having a horrible time writing. When will we achieve at least a month of calm, so that I wouldn't have to be worried with all my heart and could be entirely at work. . . . What a gypsy life, painful, most gloomy, without the least joy, and all there is to do is worry and worry!"[12] After a severe epileptic attack he sadly reports that "it's still dark in my head and my arms and legs ache. That has interrupted my work even more, so that I don't even know what I am going to do about *The Russian Messenger* and what they think of me there."[13]

Once Anna and Lyubov returned to Staraya Russa, life settled into its normal routine again—but not for long. Anna recalled these spring and summer months of 1872 as perhaps the most racking in her entire life. She caught a chill, developed an abscess in her throat, and ran a high fever. The doctor treating her warned Dostoevsky that her life was in danger, and "Feodor Mikhailovich fell into utter despair," retreating into another room "to put his face in his hands and sob uncontrollably." Anna believed herself to be dying and, not able to speak, "made signs first to Feodor Mikhailovich and then to the children to come over to me. I kissed them, blessed them, and wrote down for my husband my instructions as to what he was to do in the event of my death."[14] Happily, the

---

[9] *Reminiscences*, 191.
[10] *PSS*, 29/Bk. 1: 240; May 28, 1872.
[11] Ibid., 242; June 3, 1872.
[12] Ibid., 245; June 5, 1872.
[13] Ibid., 250; June 14, 1872.
[14] *Reminiscences*, 205.

abscess broke that night, and Anna began to recover, though it was weeks before she regained her full strength. At the beginning of September 1872, the sorely tried family limped back to Petersburg, scarcely having obtained the unruffled months of rustic quietude so much hoped for on their departure.

◼

The indefatigable Anna had done a bit of apartment hunting in Petersburg during her stay there, and the Dostoevskys moved into a five-room flat, owned by a general of the Izmailovsky Regiment. Dostoevsky's immediate preoccupation was the fate of his novel, on which he had been working steadily. In a remark to Maikov after the publication of the first chapters, Dostoevsky wrote: "In your comments you had a brilliant statement: 'Those are *Turgenev's heroes in their old age.*' That is brilliant! While writing, I myself was dreaming of something like that, but in these words you have designated everything, as if a formula."[15] Maikov thus confirmed Dostoevsky's own sense of the book's relation to *Fathers and Children*, but the novelist warned his friend against taking Stepan Trofimovich, to whom the comment refers, as the main character. "Stepan Trofimovich is a secondary character; the novel will not be about him at all; but his story is closely linked to other events (main ones) in the novel, and therefore I have taken him as though the cornerstone of everything. But still and all Stepan Trofimovich's star turn will be in the fourth part [actually the third]; at that point there will be a highly original conclusion to his fate."

Dostoevsky's firm grasp of the novel as a whole can be seen in what he told his niece Sofya Ivanova, to whom *The Idiot* had been dedicated in its journal text. This honor had aroused some envy in her older sister, Marya Alexandrovna, who also aspired to have her name attached to one of her uncle's novels. Dostoevsky thought, however, that it would be unseemly. "There will be passages in the novel (in the second and third parts). . . . One of the main characters . . . secretly confesses to another character a crime he has committed. The psychological influence of that crime on the character plays a large role in the novel; the crime, however, I repeat, even though it can be read about, is not suitable for a dedication. When you dedicate something, it is as though you are saying publicly to the person to whom you make that dedication: 'I thought of you as I wrote this.'"[16]

Dostoevsky is referring to a chapter of the novel that was never published during his lifetime, the chapter sometimes called "Stavrogin's Confession" or, more literally, "At Tikhon's." This chapter narrates the visit of Stavrogin to a monastery in which the monk Tikhon is living and his confession, in the form of a written document, of the violation of a twelve-year-old girl. Dostoevsky wrote this chapter in the fall of 1871 and finished it not later than November. Chapters 7 and 8 were printed in the November issue of *The Russian Messenger*, but then the serialization came to a halt. Katkov refused to accept the decidedly shocking episode, and Dostoevsky could not persuade him to change his mind; the pages thus never appeared during Dostoevsky's lifetime. The chapter was found among Dostoevsky's papers in 1921, published in 1922, and since then has been the subject of considerable critical controversy.

The text exists in two versions: one consists of the galleys Dostoevsky received from the journal before the decision was made not to publish; the second is a copy, transcribed by Anna, containing the alterations and corrections Dostoevsky undertook in an effort to meet the editors' objections. Dostoevsky was upset by the rejection of this cornerstone of his creation, which contains not only the crucial revelation of the full range and depth of Stavrogin's depravity but also his moral-philosophical motivation, his inner torments, and his longing for redemption. To test his own judgment, Dostoevsky read the galleys aloud to Maikov, Strakhov, and Pobedonostsev. When they unanimously agreed that the section containing Stavrogin's confession was "too realistic," he began to invent variations, one of which described Stavrogin's encounter with an adolescent girl who had been brought by her governess to a bathhouse to meet him. Someone had told Dostoevsky about such an incident; but his "advisers" warned against using it because it might be taken as an insult to governesses and thus ran afoul of the "woman question."[17] (This variation of the confession grew into the calumny that Dostoevsky himself, unexpectedly showing up in Turgenev's room one day when his fellow novelist was visiting Petersburg, confessed to having committed this very crime.)

Dostoevsky traveled to Moscow in January 1872 to consult with the editors about the chapter, and he informs Sofya Ivanova the next month that, after much head-breaking indecision, he has decided not to invent a new version of the crime. Instead, "remaining with the substance of the matter, I changed the text only enough to satisfy the chaste editors. And in this sense I have sent an *ultimatum*. If they do not agree, then I really do not know what to do."[18] Dostoevsky's revision left in doubt whether any violation of the young girl had actually occurred: Stavrogin refuses to give part of his manuscript to Tikhon, but affirms categorically that nothing untoward happened except for an innocent embrace. "Calm yourself," he tells Tikhon, "it is not my fault if the girl was stupid and did not understand me. There was nothing, nothing at all." To which Tikhon replies, "Thank God!" and crosses himself (12: 111). There is also an

---

[17] This is the version of events given in *Reminiscences*, 378–379. It is accepted as accurate by the editors of the commentary to the novel, *PSS*, 12: 239.

[18] Ibid., 29/Bk. 1: 227; February 4, 1872.

intervention by the narrator, speculating that the document was "a morbid work, the work of the devil who took possession of that man," and suggesting that what it recounted may be just an invention. It is compared to the scene in which Stavrogin bites the governor's ear, causing a scandal but doing no real harm. But then the narrator backtracks: "I certainly do not maintain that the document is false, that is to say, that it has been completely made up and invented. More likely, the truth is to be sought somewhere in between" (12: 108).

In March 1872, Dostoevsky wrote N. A. Lyubimov, Katkov's assistant editor, with reference to the revision: "I believe that what I have sent you . . . can now be printed. Everything scabrous has been removed. . . . I swear to you, I cannot do without the core of the matter. This is a full-fledged social type (in my opinion), *our* type, Russian, . . . having lost his ties with everything national, and, most important, his faith, depraved out of *melancholy longing*—but conscience-stricken, and making an effort through convulsive suffering, to renew himself and again begin to believe. . . . But all this will be cleared up even more in the third part." [19]

Despite such insistences and justifications, the journal still hesitated to accept the chapter. No final decision was made, however, and Dostoevsky was told that Katkov, no longer wishing to publish in small installments, would wait for the remainder of the novel before resuming publication. Dostoevsky thus forged ahead, sending in several more chapters, on the assumption that his disputed section would be included. It was only in early November 1872 that he learned there was no further hope of publishing even the revised variant of Stavrogin's confession. By this time, publication had been scheduled to begin with the November issue, and so Dostoevsky, his back to the wall, reworked as much of the manuscript as he could to cope with the new situation.

It is not necessary to detail all the differences that exist between the partly revised manuscript of Part III and its published form, but one is of particular importance. In Chapter 7, which narrates the touchingly pathetic "pilgrimage" of Stepan Trofimovich, he listens to a reading of passages from the Gospels and then takes on himself the primary responsibility for having infected the body of Russia with the devils. No such scene is found in the manuscript, which means that it was added *after* Dostoevsky had learned that his confession chapter would not be printed. The omission of this scene in the manuscript may indicate that Dostoevsky had originally intended to portray Stavrogin as having assumed this burden of guilt (which would make more thematic sense) but was unable to do so because, without the glimpse he had hoped to give into the torments of Stavrogin's conscience, a sudden display of such conscience in the final pages would have been insufficiently motivated.

[19] Ibid., 232; end March/beginning April 1872.

The remainder of *Demons* was finally published, after a year's delay, in the November and December 1872 issues of *The Russian Messenger*, arousing a fury of abuse and recrimination in the radical and progressive press. As Anna puts it mildly, serenely looking back on the turbulent past, "I must say that *Demons* had an enormous success with the reading public, but at the same time it brought my husband a great many enemies in the literary world."[20] When the novel appeared in book format the next year, it had once more been extensively revised. Several passages in Part II foreshadowing and motivating the encounter with Tikhon were eliminated, and these, along with the suppressed chapter itself, now must be taken into account in any consideration of the book. Dostoevsky himself did not include this chapter in later editions, but both internal and external reasons provide a plausible answer for his failure to reinstate it. For one thing, he had altered the published text as much as possible *before* magazine publication to meet the crisis he had not foreseen; the work thus no longer represented his original conception, and extensive rewriting would have been required to transform it once again. Also, he would then have had to face the formidable hurdle of the *official* censorship, and perhaps fail.

Dostoevsky decided to leave well enough alone, and Stavrogin remains a far more enigmatic and mysterious figure than he was initially meant to be. He lacks the clarifying moral-philosophical motivation that Dostoevsky had intended to provide, and it is remarkable that so much is still conveyed of the stature of his personality even without the both diabolic and penitential effect such motivation was meant to furnish. If Dostoevsky could not give us the book as he had originally conceived it, however, he still did nothing less than to write a symbolic history of the moral-spiritual travails of the Russian spirit in the first half of the nineteenth century.

[20] *Reminiscences*, 206.

CHAPTER 44

History and Myth in *Demons*

Dostoevsky had in the past created fictional characters who, as the embodiment of certain social-cultural ideas and attitudes, could be considered "historical" in a broad sense, but not until *Demons* (*Besy*) had he ever based himself on actual events that were a matter of public knowledge. Obviously, his novel is not limited to the actual, rather insignificant dimensions of the Nechaev affair. If this had been the case, "the facts" would have given him only a rather pitiful tale of a distressing event that had occurred among a handful of students and hangers-on in the student milieu, who had been duped by a revolutionary zealot into the useless murder of an innocent victim. Rather, this incident furnished only the nucleus of Dostoevsky's political plot, and he enlarged and magnified it, according to the technique of his "fantastic realism," into a full-blown dramatization of the far more ambitious tactics and aims set down in the writings of Nechaev and his supporters.

What happens in *Demons* is thus myth (the imaginary amplification of the real) and not history, art and not literal truth—just as Raskolnikov may be considered a "myth" engendered by the "immoderate Nihilism" of Pisarev and Zaitsev. Much of what he learned from the documents at his disposal, in any case, hardly taught him anything new, for he could draw on recollections from his own days as a revolutionary conspirator when his secret group had worked in the shadows to manipulate the larger Petrashevsky Circle. Dostoevsky thus remained faithful to the spirit, if not the letter, of what his documentation revealed about the Nechaev affair.

———■———

It may seem, at first sight, as if this monster of deviousness, Peter Verkhovensky—who resembles Shakespeare's Iago as a destructive inciter of evil in others—would be light-years removed from any conceivable image of a nineteenth-century Russian revolutionary or of the real Nechaev in particular. Yet the actions taken by Peter Verkhovensky with such masterful relish are exactly the same ones that Nechaev accomplished, or would have accomplished had it been within his power to turn desires into deeds.

An indelibly vivid portrait of Nechaev at work is sketched in a letter we are

25. A page from Dostoevsky's notebooks for *Demons*

fortunate to possess from no less a pen than that of Bakunin. He had been—
along with Dostoevsky's Geneva acquaintance, the sympathetic but weak-willed
Ogarev—one of Nechaev's most enthusiastic supporters. Many scholars have
speculated on the curious personal relations between the young revolutionary
and the passionately eloquent veteran of a hundred subversive plots, who was
crowned with the aureole of his fabulous insurrectionary past. For Bakunin soon
found himself in thrall to the young man, whom he admiringly called an *abrek*

(a pitiless Muslim warrior of the Caucasian peoples) and "a young eagle." But this was before Nechaev, after escaping to Europe in the wake of the Ivanov murder, began to use the methods they had both agreed upon against Bakunin himself and the circle of their common friends. Once Nechaev did so, Bakunin felt it necessary to write in July 1870 to a family with whom Nechaev had entered into contact. The letter is revelatory and precise in its depiction of Nechaev's limitless unscrupulosity.

My dear friend, I have just learned that N[echaev]. has called on you and that you hastened to give him the address of your friends (M. and his wife). I conclude that the two letters by which I warned you, and begged you to turn him away, arrived too late; and, without any exaggeration, I consider the result of this delay a veritable misfortune. It may seem strange to you that we advise you to turn away a man to whom we have given letters of recommendation addressed to you. . . . But . . . since then we have been obliged to admit the existence of matters so grave that they have forced us to break all our relations with N. . . .

It remains perfectly true that N is the man most persecuted by the Russian government, which has covered the continent of Europe with a cloud of spies seeking him in all countries; it has asked for his extradition both from Germany and Switzerland. It is equally true that N. is one of the most active and energetic men I have ever met. When it is a question of serving what he calls the cause, he does not hesitate; nothing stops him, and he is as merciless with himself as with all the others. This is the principal quality which attracted me, and which impelled me to seek an alliance with him for a good while. Some people assert that he is simply a crook—but this is a lie! He is a devoted fanatic; but at the same time a very dangerous fanatic whose alliance cannot but be harmful for everybody. And here is why: at first he was part of a secret committee which really existed in Russia. The Committee no longer exists; all its members have been arrested. N. remains alone, and alone he constitutes what he calls the Committee. His organization in Russia having been decimated, he is trying to create a new one abroad. All this would be perfectly natural, legitimate, very useful—but the methods he uses are detestable. . . . he has gradually succeeded in convincing himself that, to found a serious and indestructible organization, one must take as a foundation the tactics of Machiavelli and totally adopt the system of the Jesuits—violence as the body, falsehood as the soul.

Truth, mutual confidence, serious and strict solidarity only exist among a dozen individuals who form the *sanctum sanctorum* of the Society. All the rest must serve as a blind instrument, and as exploitable material. . . . It is allowed—even ordered—to deceive all the others, to compromise them, to rob them and even, if need be, to get rid of them—they are conspiratorial fodder. For example: you have received N. thanks to our letter of recommendation, you have taken him into your confidence, you have recommended him to your friends. . . . Here he is, transplanted into your world—and what will he do first? First he will tell you a pack of lies to increase your sympathy and your confidence; but he will not stop there. The tepid sympathies of men who are devoted to the revolutionary cause only in part, and who, besides this cause, have other human interests such as love, friendship, family, social relations—these sympathies are not, in his eyes, a sufficient foundation, and in the name of the cause he will try to get a hold on you completely without your knowledge. To do this, he will spy on you and try to gain possession of all your secrets; and in your absence, being alone in your room, he will open all your drawers and read all your correspondence. If a letter seems interesting to him, that is, compromising from any point of view either for yourself or one of your friends, he will steal it and preserve it very carefully as a document either against you or your friend. . . . when, at a general meeting, we accused him of this, he had the nerve to say—"Well, yes, that's our system. We consider as our enemies all those who are not with us *completely*, and we have the duty to deceive and to compromise them." This means all those who are not convinced of their system, and have not agreed to apply it to themselves.

If you have presented him to a friend, his first concern will be to sow discord between both of you by gossip and intrigue—in a word, to cause a quarrel. Your friend has a wife, a daughter; he will try to seduce them, to make them pregnant, in order to tear them away from official morality and to throw them into a forced revolutionary protest against society.

All personal ties, all friendship, all [gap in text] . . . are considered by them as an evil, which they have the right to destroy—because all this constitutes a force which, being outside the secret organization, diminishes the sole force of this latter. Don't tell me that I exaggerate: all this has been amply unraveled and proven. Seeing himself exposed, poor N. is still so naïve, so childish, despite his systematic perversity, that he thought it possible to convert me—he went so far as to implore me to develop this theory in a Russian journal that he proposed to establish. He has betrayed the confidence of us all, he has stolen our letters, compromised us terribly, in a word, behaved like a villain. His only excuse is his fanaticism! He is terribly ambitious without knowing it, because he has ended by identifying the cause of the revolution with that of himself—but he is not an egoist in the banal sense of the word because he risks his life terribly, and leads the existence of a martyr full of privations and incredible activity.

He is a fanatic, and fanaticism carries him away to the point of becoming an accomplished Jesuit—at moments, he simply becomes stupid. The majority of his lies are woven out of whole cloth. He plays at Jesuitism as others play at revolution. In spite of his relative naïveté, he is very dangerous because *each day* there are acts, abuses of confidence, treacheries, against which it is all the more difficult to guard oneself because one hardly suspects their possibility. With all this, N. is a force because of his immense energy. . . . His last project was nothing less than to set up a band of brigands and thieves in Switzerland, naturally with the aim of acquiring some revolutionary capital. I saved him by persuading him to leave Switzerland because he would certainly have been discovered, he and his gang, in a few weeks; he would have been lost, and all of us lost with him. . . .

Persuade M. that the safety of his family demands that he break with them completely. He must keep N. away from his family. Their system, their joy, is to seduce and corrupt young girls; in this way they control the whole family. I am very sorry that they learned the address of M. because *they would be capable of denouncing him.* Didn't they dare to admit to me openly, in the presence of a witness, that the denunciation of a member— devoted or only partly devoted—is one of the means whose usage they considered quite legitimate and sometimes useful? . . . I am so frightened at their knowledge of M.'s address that I beg him to change his lodgings secretly, so that they won't discover him.[1]

Ironically, the "methods" that Bakunin now castigates so severely, and from which he so fastidiously dissociates himself, are merely the application of doctrines set down in the notorious *Catechism of a Revolutionary,* written either by Nechaev and Bakunin in collaboration or by one of them alone (scholars still dispute this issue). There is no doubt that Bakunin had full knowledge of this most sinister of handbooks of revolutionary strategy and had approved of its precepts. What horrified him was only that the recommended methods were now being used against *himself* and his friends. Dostoevsky of course had no knowledge of this letter, but Bakunin's bewilderment and outrage at becoming the victim of doctrines he had originally sponsored remind one irresistibly of Stepan Trofimovich's reaction to the ideas and activities of his son Peter, whom he sees as distorting and vulgarizing the exalted ideals of *his* youth. Bakunin's letter illustrates the uncanny accuracy, *mutatis mutandis,* with which Dostoevsky had captured the essence of the historically symbolic relation between the generations.

[1] This letter has been translated in *Daughter of a Revolutionary,* ed. Michael Confino (La Salle, IL, 1973), 305–309; his translation differs somewhat in wording from my own.

Bakunin's infatuation with Nechaev survived the parting of the ways recorded in this letter, and he wrote sorrowfully to Ogarev on learning of the arrest of his erstwhile protégé by the Swiss police, who would extradite him to Russia. "I feel very sorry for him. . . . He was a man of rare energy; and when you and I first met him, there burned in him a clear flame of love for our poor and downtrodden people, he had a genuine ache for the people's age-long suffering."[2] Dostoevsky did not deprive Peter Verkhovensky of this one redeeming feature, though it is not displayed prominently. "Listen," Peter says to Stavrogin, "I've seen a child six years old leading home his drunken mother, while she swore at him with foul words. . . . When it's in our hands, maybe we'll mend things" (10: 324–325). Just as Dostoevsky remained true to Nechaev by including this one flicker of compassion, so there is not a single action of Peter Verkhovensky that Nechaev did not perform, or would not have performed if given the opportunity.

———■———

Dostoevsky's attention to factual accuracy is displayed in the entire social-political intrigue of the book. The power of Peter Verkhovensky in *Demons* is based on his claim to be the representative of a worldwide revolutionary organization, vaguely located somewhere in Europe and with which he has made contact in Switzerland. Nechaev carried credentials attesting him to be representative No. 2771 of the "Russian section of the World Revolutionary Alliance," and these credentials, signed by Bakunin, were also stamped with the seal of the "Central Committee" of the "European Revolutionary Alliance."[3] None of these bodies existed anywhere except in the vast reaches of Bakunin's conspiratorial imagination, and it is doubtful whether Nechaev placed too much faith in their power. After all, he had presented himself to Bakunin as the delegate of an equally fictitious organization of Russian students, but he was perfectly content to use the

[2] Ibid., 323. Extradited to Russia from Switzerland in 1872 as a common-law criminal accused of murder, Nechaev was tried in January of the following year and sentenced to twenty years of hard labor and exile to Siberia for life. His attitude in court was defiant, and he refused to recognize its authority. Alexander II ordered that Nechaev be secretly held for life in the Peter-and-Paul Fortress. There his rebellious attitude in solitary confinement led to further punishments, though he was provided with books he requested and apparently wrote a number of works that have disappeared. Most remarkable of all is that he gradually won over the soldiers assigned as his guard to the revolutionary cause, and they became his willing couriers. In 1879, learning through new prisoners of the existence of the underground revolutionary People's Will (Narodnaya Volya), he sent a message to the Executive Committee that they could hardly believe. Nechaev was still alive, and not in Siberia but in Petersburg! Plans were made to arrange an escape from prison, but Alexander II's assassination on March 1, 1880 put an end to a hope of escape with outside aid, though Nechaev attempted to organize one himself with the help of his allies in the prison garrison. But someone informed the authorities of his influence among the soldiers and his guard was replaced. He died of scurvy on November 21, 1882. See Franco Venturi, *Roots of Revolution* (New York, 1966), chap. 15.

[3] Yury Steklov, *Mikhail Alexandrovich Bakunin*, 4 vols. (Moscow–Leningrad, 1926–1927), 3: 489.

aura of Bakunin's prestige, and the looming shadow of these all-powerful organizations, to impress his dupes in Moscow. To reinforce his authority, he once
arrived at a meeting of his group with a stranger (an inoffensive visiting student
from Petersburg), whom he introduced as a member of the "Central Committee" in Geneva come to check on their activities. Quite appropriately, Peter
Verkhovensky instructs the glamorous Stavrogin to appear at a meeting as "one
of the founding members from abroad, who knows the most important secrets—
that's your role" (10: 299).

Nechaev's career was marked by a systematic use of falsehood and deceit,
even toward his allies and followers. Such a policy was explicitly affirmed as a
principle in the *Catechism*: "the degree of friendship, of devotion, and of other
obligations toward . . . a comrade is measured only by his degree of utility in the
practical world of revolutionary pan-destruction."[4] Peter Verkhovensky reveals
that he is acting alone only to Stavrogin, who is the key to his revolutionary
plans. All the rest of his group he considers "raw material," to be used and manipulated as he sees fit for the good of the cause. Such manipulation was foreseen in the paragraph of the *Catechism* devoted to "revolutionary chatterers" (a
perfect description of the group at Virginsky's), who were to be "pushed and involved without ceasing into political and dangerous manifestations, whose result will be to make the majority disappear while some among them will become
revolutionaries."[5] It was in accordance with this ruthless application of the principle of utility that Nechaev disposed of Ivanov, and Dostoevsky was convinced
that he wished to gain an indissoluble hold on his followers by involving them
in a common crime against a troublesome dissident.

Peter Verkhovensky arrives in the provincial town where the novel is set as the
bosom companion of the gentry scion Stavrogin and also as an intimate of the
equally wealthy Drozhdov family. Having learned the secret of Stavrogin's perverse marriage to Marya Lebyadkina, and aware of Liza Tushina's infatuation
with Stavrogin, he manifestly hopes, whether by intimidation or by catering to
Stavrogin's lusts, to gain a hold over Stavrogin and exploit him for his revolutionary purposes. Such maneuvers are completely in conformity with the doctrines of the *Catechism*: "with the aim of implacable destruction a revolutionary
may, and often must, live in the midst of society, pretending to be quite different
from what he really is."[6] The aim of this disguise, as with Peter, is to gain power
over "the great number of highly placed animals who, by their position, are rich
and have relations." Such dupes "must be exploited in every possible way, circumvented, confused, and, by acquiring their dirty secrets, be turned into our

---

[4] I cite the translation of *Catechism of a Revolutionary* given in Confino (see note 1) as the most
recent and readily available. See *Daughter of a Revolutionary*, 226.

[5] Ibid., 228.

[6] Ibid., 227.

slaves. In this manner their power, their relations, their influence, and their riches will become an inexhaustible treasure and an invaluable aid in our various enterprises."[7]

The same tactics are used by Peter Verkhovensky to gain control over the von Lembkes—the governor of the province and his wife—whom he also exploits for his revolutionary aims. Revolutionaries, the *Catechism* declares, should conspire with liberals "on the basis of their own program, pretending to follow them blindly" but actually compromising them so that they can be "used to provoke disturbances in the State."[8] Peter subverts Yulia Mikhailovna's innocent liberal fête for the benefit of the governesses of the province in exact accordance with these instructions, turning it into a riotous manifestation of protest against the authorities.

With von Lembke, Peter also plays the *agent provocateur*: he spurs this dim-witted, bewildered official to suppress signs of unrest among the Shpigulin workers and taxes him with being "too soft" and "liberal" in the performance of his gubernatorial duties. "But this has to be handled in the good old way," Peter jovially tells the hesitant von Lembke. "They ought to be flogged, every one of them; that would be the end of it" (10: 272). Peter's metamorphosis into an advocate of "the good old ways" is justified by a passage in the *Catechism* requiring the revolutionary to "aid the growth of calamity and every evil, which must, at last, exhaust the patience of the people and force them into a general uprising."[9] Two Bakunin-Nechaev pamphlets, supposedly issued by the "Descendants of Rurik and the Noble's Revolutionary Committee,"[10] preached the most outrageously reactionary sentiments and were intended to stir up right-wing opposition among the old nobility to the reforming tsar. They probably inspired Peter's friendship with the retired Colonel Gaganov, who resigned from the army partly because he "suddenly felt himself personally insulted by the proclamation" of the liberation of the serfs. Gaganov "belonged to that strange section of the nobility, still surviving in Russia, who set an extreme value on their pure and ancient lineage" (that is, "the descendants of Rurik") (10: 224).

———■———

Sources or parallels for almost every other political-ideological feature of *Demons* can be found either in the Bakunin-Nechaev propaganda or in other easily identifiable historical events. Nothing about the Bakunin-Nechaev propaganda is more striking than its total negativism, the complete absence of any specific aim or goal that would justify the horrors it wishes to bring about. It contains

[7] Ibid., 228.
[8] Ibid.
[9] Ibid., 229.
[10] Steklov, *Bakunin*, 3: 455–456.

blood-curdling exhortations and apocalyptic images of total annihilation: "We must dedicate ourselves to wholehearted destruction, continuous, unflagging, unslackening, until none of the existing social forms remains to be destroyed." Such a positive purpose is outlawed on principle as a historical impossibility and must remain wrapped in the messianic obscurity of the future. "Since the existing generation is itself exposed to the influence of those loathsome social conditions against which it is revolting, to this generation cannot belong the work of construction. This belongs to those pure forces that will be formed in the day of renovation." [11] This negativism helps to explain why Peter Verkhovensky sets himself off so sharply from "Socialists" like Shigalev, who *do* worry about the form of the future social order: "to my mind all these books, Fourier, Cabet, all this talk about the 'right to work' and Shigalev's theories—all are like novels of which one can write a hundred thousand—an aesthetic entertainment" (10: 313). As a true Bakuninist revolutionary, Peter dedicates himself only to the work of uprooting the existing moral-social norms, "but one or two generations of vice are essential now," he tells Stavrogin, "monstrous, abject vice by which a man is transformed into a loathsome, cruel, egoistic reptile. . . . I am not contradicting myself, I am only contradicting the philanthropists and Shigalevism, not myself! I am a scoundrel, not a Socialist!" (10: 325).

Marx and Engels make the same distinction, and thoroughly agreed with Dostoevsky's separation of Nechaev's tactics from Socialism as *they* understood it. Indeed, they used the Bakunin-Nechaev propaganda as one of their weapons in evicting Bakunin and his followers from the First International. "These all-destroying anarchists," they wrote sententiously, "who wish to reduce everything to amorphousness in order to replace morality by anarchy, carry bourgeois immorality to its final extreme." [12]

Nechaev's systematic Machiavellianism was alien to other radical groupings then in existence, and Peter Verkhovensky's relation to the members and sympathizers of his underground organization is one of continual struggle to overcome their opposition and mistrust. No one at the meeting really agrees with Peter, but he browbeats them into submission by playing on their vanity and curiosity: all agree to go "full speed ahead" in order to hear his mysterious "communication" from the all-powerful organization he claims to represent. Just before Shatov's murder, even the members of Peter's inner circle are panic-stricken at what has occurred—the fire, the various murders already committed, the riots and disorders—and decide that unless Peter gives them a "categorical explanation" they will "dissolve the quintet and . . . found instead a new secret society 'for the propaganda of ideas of their own and on the basis of democracy and equality'"

---

[11] Ibid., 464–465.
[12] Karl Marx and Friedrich Engels, *Werke*, 39 vols. (Berlin, 1959–), 18: 426.

(10: 415–416). Shigalev, at the last moment, refuses to have anything to do with the murder as a matter of principle; Virginsky never stops protesting even while it is taking place. However unappealing or pathetically ridiculous Dostoevsky makes them out to be, the members of the quintet do not believe in systematic amorality and universal destruction as panaceas for the ills of the social order.

To be sure, Dostoevsky's satire is not much tenderer for Shigalev than it is for Peter Verkhovensky, but he acknowledged the existing spectrum of radical opinion. Shigalev, in Dostoevsky's notes, is first called Zaitsev—the same radical critic V. A. Zaitsev who had argued in the pages of the liberal journal *The Russian Word* that without the protection of slavery, the black race would be doomed to extinction because of its inherent inferiority. Shigalev too is initially an honest democratic radical who ends up, much to his dismay, favoring the "slavery" of the masses to an omnipotent radical elite. "I am perplexed by my own data," he confesses, "and my conclusion is in direct contradiction of the original idea from which I start. Starting from unlimited freedom, I arrive at unlimited despotism" (10: 311).

The views of the radically oriented Zaitsev derived from his Social Darwinism, and this doctrine is alluded to when Shigalev asserts that all previous social thinkers "have been dreamers, tellers of fairy tales, fools who contradicted themselves, who understood nothing of natural science and the strong animal called man" (10: 311). Shigalev's own theory for attaining "the earthly Paradise" is unmistakably biological, even though it is given only in an abbreviated version. (He solemnly asks for ten meetings to expound it properly, but, alas, the revolution cannot wait!) A "lame teacher" who has read his manuscript explains the chief idea: "Shigalev suggests . . . the division of mankind into two equal parts. One-tenth enjoys absolute liberty and unbounded power over nine-tenths. The others have to give up all individuality and become, so to speak, a herd, and, through boundless submission, will by a series of regenerations attain primeval innocence, something like the original paradise. They will have to work, however. The measures the author proposes for depriving nine-tenths of humanity of their true will, and their transformation into a herd by means of the re-education of whole generations, are . . . based on the facts of nature and very logical" (10: 312).

One might imagine that Dostoevsky here has simply let his satirical fantasy run wild à la Swift, and that there could be no textual source for Shigalev's plan to create "the earthly Paradise" by selective Socialist breeding. In fact, however, such a source exists in the radical journalism of the 1860s, and Dostoevsky's familiarity with all varieties of such journalism makes it more than likely that he drew on it for his purposes. It can be found in the writings of P. N. Tkachev, one of whose first articles was published by Dostoevsky in *Time*, and who had been associated with Nechaev in agitating among Petersburg students in 1869. Together they had written a *Programme of Revolutionary Activities*, which led to

Tkachev's arrest in the roundup of Nechaev's followers after Ivanov's murder. Both Tkachev and Zaitsev developed the implications of Social Darwinism within the Russian radical context, but Tkachev drew conclusions even more extreme, and more shockingly inhumane, than the iconoclastic defender of Negro slavery.

Tkachev accepted the biological foundations of Darwinism but deplored the social-political conclusions that could be drawn from its tenets. If unchecked and uncontrolled, he argued, the struggle for existence could lead only to the eternal perpetuation of inequality and injustice. Justice could not be achieved except in a world of total equality, but this aim "must by no means be confused with political or legal or even economic equality"; rather, it meant "an organic, physiological equality conditioned by the same education and common living conditions." Such equality, Tkachev wrote, was "the final and only possible aim of human life . . . the supreme criterion of historical and social progress"; it was thus "the absolute goal and highest ideal of the coming Socialist revolution."[13] If Dostoevsky was not parodying Tkachev, it is surely a remarkable coincidence when Peter Verkhovensky exclaims that "Shigalev is a man of genius" because "he's discovered 'equality.'" "Great intellects cannot help being despots and they've always done more harm than good. . . . Cicero will have his tongue cut out, Copernicus will have his eyes put out, Shakespeare will be stoned—that's Shigalevism! Slaves must be equal: there has never been either freedom or equality without despotism, but in the herd there's bound to be equality, and that's Shigalevism!" (10: 322).

The ultimate aim of Peter Verkhovensky is to seize power by turning Stavrogin into Ivan the Tsarevich, the false pretender to the throne, and in this way to enlist the peasantry behind his revolutionary banner. Even here Dostoevsky does not depart from a verisimilar transmutation of Russian historical reality into the "myth" of his creation. Deeply rooted in the Russian folk imagination was the idea of a "tsar in hiding" who would someday appear to remedy the world's injustices. Time and again in Russian history a revolt has been justified by the claim that the reigning tsar was "false." The renegade monk Gregory Otrepeyev, who led the uprising against Boris Godunov in the early seventeenth century, claimed to be the "true" tsar and the murdered son of Ivan the Terrible. Exactly the same legend arose at the end of the eighteenth century, when the rebellious Cossack leader Pugachev claimed to be Peter III, who had been killed in a court conspiracy. Peter Verkhovensky intends to exploit the deepest historical recesses of the Russian folk imagination and use the quasi-religious status of the tsar to achieve his overthrow in the interests of social revolution.

[13] See the citation from Tkachev in Venturi, *Roots of Revolution*, 399; also B. P. Kozmin, *P. N. Tkachev i revolutsionnie dvizhenie 1860–kh godov* (Moscow, 1922), 119–120.

This is a part of the solid historical foundation on which Dostoevsky constructed what seems to be his most extravagant fictional edifice. One of the commonest charges made against *Demons* in the mostly hostile early reviews was that the book was purely a product of Dostoevsky's "psychiatric talent"—his penchant, long ago noted and harshly criticized by Belinsky, for preoccupying himself with what could only be considered abnormal and psychopathological characters. But Dostoevsky was convinced, and time has proven him right, that his "fantastic realism" cut more deeply into the problems of Russian life than the more superficially verisimilar and equally average presentation favored by his literary contemporaries. While giving free rein to his "fantasy," however, he knew that the charges of his critics might be justified unless he took great pains to anchor its flights in the "realism" we have tried to document; and we shall next show that he took the same care with Russian culture as he had done with the "myth" of Nechaev and his group.

———■———

The Nechaev affair and its ramifications is only one of the interweaving historical-ideological strands in *Demons*. Another is the satirical confrontation between Stepan Trofimovich Verkhovensky and his Nihilist son Peter. Even though this encounter became subordinate in the final text, Dostoevsky succeeded, all the same, in making *Demons* one of the two classic portrayals in Russian literature of this momentous battle between the generations.

Turgenev had depicted its opening salvos in *Fathers and Children* (1862), but Stepan Trofimovich is much closer to the central figure of an earlier Turgenev novel, *Rudin* (1856), than he is to any of the characters who speak for the past face-to-face with Bazarov. Like Stepan Trofimovich, Rudin is also a Romantic Idealist of the 1840s—a genuinely pure and noble spirit, but one too weak to live up to his lofty phrases and glowing ideals. *Demons* may thus seem as a disputation between two of Turgenev's characters at a later stage of their lives, when Rudin had sunk into a whimsically charming self-pampering *poseur* and Bazarov had stiffened into a ruthless fanatic. Dostoevsky, we know, enthusiastically agreed with Maikov's remark that Dostoevsky's characters reminded him of "Turgenev's heroes grown old."

Demons thus has an extremely important literary-cultural dimension, which includes its relation both to Turgenev's novels and to Turgenev himself (malevolently but irresistibly caricatured in the figure of Karmazinov). In addition, it also encompasses a whole range of other literary, moral-philosophical, and cultural phenomena whose richness can only be rivaled, in the nineteenth-century novel, by Balzac's *Les illusions perdues* and Flaubert's *L'Éducation sentimentale*. The book is almost a compressed encyclopedia of the Russian culture of the period it covers, filtered through a witheringly derisive and often grotesquely funny perspective, and it creates a remarkable "myth" of the main conflicts of this culture reconstructed on a firm basis of historical personages and events.

The figure of Stepan Trofimovich, as we have seen, is primarily derived from that of T. N. Granovsky, a historian from the 1840s who was already half-forgotten by 1869. Dostoevsky had cherished his image particularly because of the portrait given in Herzen's *My Past and Thoughts*. In a famous chapter, Herzen describes the end of his friendship with Granovsky in the summer of 1846. This was the fateful moment when Belinsky and Herzen had become militant atheists, but Granovsky refused to follow Herzen along this emotionally lacerating path. "I will never accept your desiccated, cold idea of the identity of the body and spirit," Herzen cites him as saying; "with that, the immortality of the soul disappears. Perhaps you don't need this, but I have had to bury far too much to give up this belief. For me personal immortality is a necessity."[14] Dostoevsky, who himself clung tenaciously to the hope of personal immortality, saw Granovsky as a kindred soul: here was a liberal Westernizer who refused to surrender the ultimate sanctuary of religious faith. It was precisely such a figure, with all its inner contradictions, oscillations, and uncertainties, that Dostoevsky wished to highlight as the precursor, as well as the shocked opponent, of the amoral Nihilism exhibited by the new breed of Bazarovs.

The sources for Stepan Trofimovich-Granovsky can be found not only in the personality and biography of the Moscow historian, who died in 1855, but also and more extensively in the controversies that began in the middle of 1858, when the tension between the generations exploded in public. The spokesmen for the newly vociferous *raznochintsy* intellectuals, Chernyshevsky and Dobrolyubov, unleashed a flood of derogatory articles against the generation of the 1840s, which was dismissed as weak and indecisive; its members were slaves to high-flown principles that only served to bolster their egoism and vanity:

> People of *that* generation were possessed by lofty but somewhat abstract strivings. They strove toward truth, longed for the good, they were captivated by everything beautiful; but highest of all for them was *principle*. . . . Withdrawing in this way from real life, and condemning themselves to the service of principle, they were not able truly to estimate their strength and took on much more than they were capable of performing. Hence their eternally false position, their eternal dissatisfaction with themselves, their eternal grandiose phrases of self-approval and self-encouragement, and their eternal failure in any practical activity. Little by little they sank into their passive role, and, of all that had gone before, they preserved only a youthful inflammability, yes, and the habit of conversing with well-

---

[14] Alexander Herzen, *My Past and Thoughts*, trans. by Constance Garnett, revised by Humphrey Higgens, 4 vols. (New York, 1968), 2: 586.

bred people about good manners and dreaming of a little bridge over the stream [that is, local, insignificant reforms and improvements—J.F.][15]

No better outline of Stepan Trofimovich's character profile could be sketched; all that remained was for Dostoevsky to fill in the traits.

Such attacks could hardly fail to elicit a reply; and one was soon forthcoming from Herzen, who had been the original inspirer and propagator of whatever radical and Socialist currents of thought existed in Russia in the 1860s. Granovsky may have furnished an external schema for Stepan Trofimovich, but the pattern of his opposition to Peter, as the horrified "father" of a Nihilist "son," is historically based on Herzen's intransigent refusal to knuckle under to the generation of the 1860s. Herzen, as we know, was much on Dostoevsky's mind exactly at the moment when he was working on the early drafts of *Demons*. His death in January 1870 immediately called forth an important series of articles by Strakhov summing up his career, and they were published almost simultaneously with Dostoevsky's decision to write a "pamphlet-novel."

Dostoevsky's reaction to these articles has already been cited; here we need only recall his remark that "the main essence of all Herzen's activity [was] that he has been, always and everywhere, *primarily a poet*." It is this aspect of his nature, Dostoevsky believed, that explains "even his flippancy and inclination to pun about the loftiest moral and philosophical questions (which, by the way, is very revolting in him)."[16] Such a comment indicates to what extent Stepan Trofimovich and Herzen blended together in Dostoevsky's imagination. For the quality that offended Dostoevsky in Herzen also offends the narrator in Stepan Trofimovich. "Why could not this week be without a Sunday—*si le miracle existe?*" exclaims the latter despairingly, anticipating a meeting with the formidable Varvara Petrovna Stavrogina on that fateful day. "What could it be to Providence to blot out one Sunday from the calendar? If only to prove His power to atheists *et que tout soit dit!*" "He wouldn't have been himself," the narrator comments acidly, "if he could have dispensed with the cheap gibing free-thought which was in vogue in his day" (10: 100).

Herzen's *The Superfluous and the Bilious* (1860) was the first reply of the generation of the 1840s to the onslaught of their detractors, and, like Stepan Trofimovich, Herzen spoke for the fathers, or at least those among them who refused to abdicate their right to paternal respect. Voicing the attitude of the "bilious" sons, their unnamed spokesman (Chernyshevsky) sarcastically remarks that the "superfluous men" of the 1840s "were educated differently, the world surrounding them was too dirty, not sufficiently wax-polished, besmirched by hands and feet. It was far pleasanter for them to moan over their unhappy lot, and meanwhile to eat

---

[15] N. A. Dobrolyubov, *Selected Philosophical Essays*, trans. J. Fineberg (Moscow, 1956), 156.
[16] *PSS*, 29/Bk. 1: 113n.28; May 28/June 9, 1870.

and drink in peace." [17] These were exactly the words, and this is unmistakably the condescendingly contemptuous tone, of Peter about his father.

Just as Stepan Trofimovich returns home in a shambles after his attempt to make a comeback in Petersburg in the early 1860s, having been discarded by the new breed of radicals as "*un vieux bonnet de coton*," so Herzen is dismissed by Chernyshevsky as similar to "the fine skeleton of a mammal . . . that had been dug up and belonged to a different world with a different sun and different trees." But Herzen, refusing to be swept so easily into the dustbin of history, stubbornly rejects an obligation to say farewell, in the name of utility and revolution, to the significance of his own past and that of humankind as a whole. For if the blinkered view of the 1860s is accepted, then, as Herzen says in eloquent words that Stepan Trofimovich will echo, "farewell not only to Thermopylae and Golgotha, but also to Sophocles and Shakespeare, and incidentally to the whole long and endless epic poem which is continually ending in frenzied tragedies and continually going on again under the title of history." [18]

Despite disagreements over tactics, particularly after Karakozov's attempt to assassinate Alexander II, which Herzen reproved in *The Bell*, Herzen insisted that the goals of the indigenous Russian radical movement, which looked to Chernyshevsky as its leader, did not differ from the ones he had advocated in exile, and he urged that the two generations should go forward hand in hand. This plea for unity only provoked a furious reply from one of the leaders of the "young emigration," Alexander Serno-Solovievich, who dismissed Herzen even more unceremoniously than Chernyshevsky had done. In words that remarkably anticipate Dostoevsky's, he proclaimed that Herzen was just another *vieux bonnet de coton*, exactly like Stepan Trofimovich:

> You are a poet, an artist . . . a storyteller, a novelist, anything you wish but not a politician. . . . Failing to perceive that you have been left behind, you flap your enfeebled wings with all your might; and then, when you see that people are only laughing at you, you go off in a rage and reproach the younger generation with ingratitude to their leader, to the founder of their school, the first high priest of Russian Socialism. . . . Come down to earth; forget that you are a great man; remember that the medals with your effigy were struck not by a grateful posterity, but by yourself out of your blood-stained wealth. . . . [Y]ou, Mr. Herzen, are a dead man. [19]

Herzen did not reply directly to this scurrilously abusive broadside. Instead, he sent the brochure, along with a letter, to Bakunin, whose indiscriminate sympathy with the younger generation would later lead to his association with

[17] Herzen, *My Past and Thoughts*, 4: 1581, 1579.

[18] Ibid., 1581, 1583.

[19] Cited in Abbott Gleason, *Young Russia* (New York, 1980), 132–133.

Nechaev. Serno-Solovievich, in Herzen's view, "is insolent and a fool; but the worst is that the majority of the young Russians *are the same* and we're the ones who have contributed to make them *like this*. . . . This isn't Nihilism. Nihilism is a great phenomenon in the evolution of Russian thought. No. These are the dispossessed noblemen, the retired officer, the village scribe, the local priest and petty landowner disguised in costumes." [20]

Dostoevsky had read the harangues of Serno-Solovievich, and the young radical is mentioned, along with Nechaev (no others are identified), as belonging in "the herd of swine" infected by "the devils" who "came out of the body of Russian man." Dostoevsky, of course, could have had no knowledge of Herzen's letter, but he was able to intuit, with remarkable percipience, exactly its mixture of consternation and guilt. "I agree that the author's fundamental idea is a true one," Stepan Trofimovich says of *What Is To Be Done?*, the "catechism" of the Nihilists, "but that only makes it more awful. It's just our idea, exactly ours; we first sowed the seed, nurtured it, prepared the way, and, indeed, what could they say new, after us? But, heavens! How it's all expressed, distorted, mutilated. . . . Were these the conclusions we were striving for? Who can understand the original idea in this?" (10: 238).

Herzen's last important work, *Letters to an Old Comrade* (1869), was written expressly to counteract the turbulent torrent of vandalism running through the Bakunin-Nechaev propaganda. These open letters addressed to Bakunin were included in a collection of Herzen's posthumous writings that Dostoevsky certainly would have hastened to procure. "The savage clamors exhorting us to close our books, to abandon science, and to engage in an absurd combat of destruction," Herzen wrote, "belong to the most uncontrollable and baneful demagoguery. They always provoke the unleashing of the worst passions. We juggle with terrible words, without thinking at all of the harm they do to the cause and to those who listen to them." [21] Herzen certainly did not believe that the Bakunin-Nechaev movement, which had led to the murder of Ivanov, was merely an isolated and aberrant episode, and he felt it his duty to raise his voice against the terrible consequences he could so clearly foresee.

One can well imagine Dostoevsky's satisfaction at reading Herzen's condemnatory words, which to him could well have sounded almost as a self-denunciation and recantation. And while Dostoevsky did not need Herzen to teach him the value of art and culture (he had defended them against Belinsky in 1849 and Dobrolyubov in 1861), he would surely have been gratified to find Herzen aligning himself so fervently against the Pisarevian iconoclasm (in the literal sense of the word) that had become endemic among the generation of the 1860s.

[20] B. P. Kozmin, *Iz istorii revolutsionnoi mysli v Rossii* (Moscow, 1961), 547.

[21] A. I. Herzen, *Sochineniya*, 10 vols. (Moscow, 1955–1958), 8: 417.

"Woe to the revolution poor in spirit and weak in a sense of art," Herzen exclaims, "which will make of all that has been acquired by time a depressing workshop, and whose sole interest would be subsistence and nothing but subsistence!" One recalls here the notorious slogan of Peter Verkhovensky: "Only the necessary is necessary, that's the motto of the whole world henceforward" (10: 323). "The force of unleashed destruction," Herzen continues, "will wipe out, along with the limits of property, the *peaks* of human endeavor that men have attained in every direction since the beginning of civilization. . . . I have often felt this keenly when, overcome by a gloomy sadness and almost shame, I have stood before some guide who showed me a bare wall, a broken sculpture, a coffin torn from its tomb, and who repeated: 'All this was destroyed during the Revolution.'"[22]

Only against this background can one fully appreciate Stepan Trofimovich's defiant "last word" in *Demons*—a last word shouted at a hooting, jeering younger generation that hounded him as unmercifully as it had hounded Herzen in his last years, and to which he replied with the voice of Herzen and that of Dostoevsky as well. "'But I maintain,' Stepan Trofimovich shrilled at the utmost pitch of excitement, 'I maintain that Shakespeare and Raphael are higher than the emancipation of the serfs, higher than Nationalism, higher than Socialism, higher than the young generation, higher than chemistry, higher than almost all humanity because they are the fruit, the real fruit of all humanity, and perhaps the highest possible fruit! A form of beauty already attained, without whose attainment I, perhaps, would not consent to live. . . . Oh, God' he cried—he clasped his hands—'ten years ago I cried exactly the same thing in Petersburg in exactly the same words, and they understood nothing in exactly the same way, they laughed and hissed as now; you pygmies, what do you need to make you understand?'" (10: 372–373). Ten years before, in *The Superfluous and the Bilious*, Herzen had anticipated these very words, and Dostoevsky's boisterously uproarious fête, which also includes other incidents and allusions taken from the stormy events of the early 1860s, is the artistic enshrinement of this momentous historical-cultural clash.

———■———

Stepan Trofimovich, to be sure, is not the only figure in the book who represents an eminent member of the generation of the 1840s. No account of *Demons* would be complete without some discussion of the malicious but masterly caricature of Turgenev in the portrait of Karmazinov (*Karmazin*, from the French *cramoisi*, means crimson in Russian and ridicules the presumed social-political sympathies of the Great Writer). Personal caricature was commonplace in Rus-

---

[22] Ibid., 405, 417.

sian fiction, and Turgenev himself had not spared Bakunin in *Rudin* or a host of well-known personalities (particularly Ogarev) in *Smoke*. But to find an equally extended lampoon of a prominent literary personage one would probably have to look to Dickens's attack on Leigh Hunt in *Bleak House* through the character of Harold Skimpole.

Karmazinov bears no physical resemblance to the handsome figure of the stately Turgenev, but otherwise Dostoevsky's target is unmistakable, and he ridicules all those aspects of his fellow novelist that had long aroused his antipathy. Turgenev's aristocratic airs and manner, his preference for residence in Europe, his demolition of Russian culture in *Smoke*, the philosophical pessimism revealed most overtly in his prose poems, the squeamish, self-protective egoism that Dostoevsky saw most blatantly manifested in the article about the execution of Troppman—nothing is spared! The first encounter between the narrator and the Great Writer is accompanied by a derisory parody of the Troppman article, transposed into an account of the wreck of a steamer off the English coast. As a young man, Turgenev had been involved in such a wreck off Lübeck (he later wrote about it in 1883, after Dostoevsky's death), and widespread rumor in literary circles attributed to him a behavior that was far from heroic.

Just as when Troppman was guillotined, Karmazinov-Turgenev is much more concerned with his own reactions than with the victims of the disaster. "All this rather long and verbose article was written solely with the object of self-display. One seemed to read between the lines: . . . 'Why look at that drowned woman with the dead child in her dead arms? Look rather at me, see how I was unable to bear the sight and turned away from it. Here I stood with my back to it, here I was horrified and could not bring myself to look; I blinked my eyes—isn't that interesting?'" "When I told Stepan Trofimovich my opinion of Karmazinov's article," the narrator adds, "he quite agreed with me" (10: 70).

Although Karmazinov's vanity and narcissism are thus displayed from the start, his role is defined more broadly by the attempts of Turgenev to worm his way back into the good graces of the generation of the 1860s. In contrast to Herzen's forthright and staunch defense of his own values, which then became embodied in Stepan Trofimovich, Turgenev had ignominiously truckled to Nihilist browbeating, implicitly giving his stamp of approval to Bazarovism and, by extension, to its latest avatar, Sergey Nechaev. Of course, the presumed approval of Nechaev was not literally true, but in the symbolic myth of Dostoevsky's creation it is perfectly defensible. Karmazinov is responsible for Peter Verkhovensky's prestige in society, just as Turgenev had been responsible for the prestige of Bazarov and his later offshoots in real life, and he acts as the young man's mentor and advocate. "When I came, I assured everyone," he tells Peter, "that you were a very intelligent man, and now I believe everyone is wild over you" (10: 286). As A. S. Dolinin has shrewdly noted, even though Stepan Trofimovich is the physical father of Peter Verkhovensky, the latter is much more the "spiritual son" of Karmazinov.[23]

The climax of Dostoevsky's ridicule of Turgenev occurs during the fête scene, when Karmazinov condescendingly agrees to read his farewell work to the hungry and fractious assemblage, having decided—or so he pretends—to put down his pen forever after his last appearance in public. Turgenev, upon receiving a letter of sympathy from a friend after the publication of this chapter, replied in a hurt tone of restrained dignity: "It is surely curious that he chose for his parody the sole work [*Phantoms*] that I placed in the journal he once edited, a work for which he showered me with grateful and flattering letters. I still have the letters. It would be amusing to publish them! But he knows that I will not do such a thing. I am only left with the regret that he employs his undoubted talent to satisfy such unsavory feelings."[24]

Phantoms is by no means the main basis for Dostoevsky's parody, which in fact takes off from another prose poem, *Enough* (*Dovol'no*). Turgenev's temperament is given free rein in these prose poems, whose dominant mood, often expressed by dreamlike events unrestrained by the limits of time and space, is a sense of world-weariness and metaphysical despair. Dostoevsky takes well-directed aim against these extremely vulnerable aspects of Turgenev's prose poems, which are easy enough to ridicule simply by introducing a note of sober prosaicism into their lugubrious fantasy. Time and again, as he does so, Dostoevsky also mocks the self-importance impelling the great genius to reduce every event and incident to a reflection of his own existential anguish. In one scene, the poet is presumably drowning after falling through the ice of the Volga in a thaw, but then "he caught sight of a tiny little ice floe, the size of a pea . . . and . . . its iridescent glitter recalled to his mind the very same tear, which you remember rolled down from your eyes when we sat beneath the emerald tree and you cried joyfully, 'There is no crime.' 'No,' I said, through my tears, 'but if that is so, there are no saints either.' We burst into sobs and parted forever" (10: 366–367). This is a hit at Turgenev's newly proclaimed adhesion to Nihilism, whose moral-metaphysical negation is here portrayed in a ridiculously burlesque register rather than, as with Stavrogin, in a tragic one.

In a similar passage, the sublime poet has dug beneath the Sukharev Tower in Moscow for three years, finds a hermit in a cave with a lamp burning before an icon, and suddenly hears a sigh. "You think it was the hermit that sighed? What does he care about your hermit? No, this sigh simply reminds him of her first sigh, thirty-seven years ago, when do you remember how we sat beneath the agate tree in Germany, and you said to me, 'Why love? Look, furze is growing

---

[23] A. S. Dolinin, "Turgenev v *Besakh*," in his *Dostoevsky i drugie* (Moscow, 1989), 173.
[24] *PSSiP*, 10: 9.

all around, and I am in love, but when the furze ceases to grow, I shall fall out of love'" (10: 367). Dostoevsky then travesties Turgenev's fondness for bestrewing his pages with learned references. "Here a mist rises again, Hoffmann appears, the water nymph whistles a tune from Chopin, and suddenly out of the mist Ancius Marcus appears over the roofs of Rome, wearing a laurel wreath. A shiver of rapture ran down our backs and we parted forever, and so on and so forth" (10: 367).

Dostoevsky's narrator finally admits that he finds it hard to make head or tail out of what Karmazinov had read, and he ends with a string of antitheses reproducing the moral-spiritual confusion engendered in such Russian geniuses after they have absorbed the sublime conquests of European thought: "There is crime, there is no crime; there is no truth, there are no truth-seekers; atheism, Darwinism, Moscow church bells. . . . But, alas, he no longer believes in the Moscow church bells; Rome, laurels. . . . But he doesn't believe in laurels. . . . Here you get a conventional attack of Byronic spleen, a grimace from Heine, something of Pechorin—and off he goes full steam ahead, with his engine emitting a shrill whistle." Behind all this, the narrator finds only the author's egoism, and he does not believe for a moment that, as Karmazinov-Turgenev promises, he will now lay down his pen forever in weariness and sorrow (10: 367). The takeoff on Turgenev's literary mannerisms and personal foibles could not have been deadlier, and it enriches *Demons* with a dazzling display of Dostoevsky's satiric virtuosity.

■

The capstone of Dostoevsky's intricate thematic construction in *Demons* is the figure of Stavrogin. No clues to any prototype for his character can be found in Dostoevsky's notes, and a debate has raged for years over whether he may not have been inspired by Bakunin. But if we are to link Stavrogin with any actual person, the likeliest candidate would be the enigmatic figure of Nikolay Speshnev, whom Dostoevsky called his Mephistopheles during the days of his involvement in the Petrashevsky Circle. This committed communist was the center of a secret revolutionary group whose seven members included Dostoevsky. This group operated *within* the larger Petrashevsky society and attempted to manipulate it for its own ends, just as Peter Verkhovensky manipulates his own little group, and society at large, for *his* ends. Speshnev was well read in the philosophy then current in progressive left-wing circles, and his moral-philosophical views are similar to those later attributed to Stavrogin. These views are expressed by Speshnev in private letters; and it is highly possible that he uttered the very same thoughts in the course of conversations with intimates such as Dostoevsky.

Speshnev closely followed the controversies that had arisen among the Left Hegelians following the publication of Feuerbach's *Essence of Christianity* (1841), and on these issues he sided with Max Stirner's totally subjective egoism.

"Anthropotheism [the position of Feuerbach] is also a religion," he wrote perceptively, "only a different one. It divinizes a new and different object [man, humanity—J.F.], but there is nothing new about the fact of divinization. . . . Is the difference between a God-man and a Man-god really so great?" Speshnev refused to accept any authority over the individual ego and concluded, as a result, that no objective criteria exist for anything. "Such categories as beauty and ugliness, good and bad, noble and base, always were and always will remain a matter of taste."[25]

These words should be set against Stavrogin's confession in the suppressed chapter "At Tikhon's," where he explains that "I formulated for the first time in my life what appeared to be the rule of my life, namely, that I neither know nor feel good and evil and that I have not only lost any sense of it, but that there is neither good nor evil (which pleased me), and that it is just a prejudice: that I can be free from any prejudice, but that once I attain that degree of freedom I am done for" (12: 113). That such a doctrine will lead to self-destruction is Dostoevsky's own conclusion; otherwise, Stavrogin's denial of any difference between good and evil remarkably coincides with Speshnev's. Indeed, the abominable violation of little Matryosha is really a terrible experiment designed to test such ideas in practice. There is thus every reason to believe that Dostoevsky recalled some of the features of Speshnev, his initiator into underground revolution and moral-metaphysical Nihilism, when the amorphous "Prince" of the early drafts began to evolve into Stavrogin.

But just as Peter Verkhovensky is not Nechaev, nor Stepan Trofimovich solely Granovsky, neither should Stavrogin be identified with Speshnev. For Dostoevsky "mythifies" this prototype into an image of the doomed and glamorous Russian Byronic dandy who haunted the literature of the 1820s and 1830s. Dostoevsky had long interpreted the immense cultural and moral-religious importance of the Russian Byronic type as a clue to the subterranean changes taking place in the national psyche. This interpretation is found most amply and explicitly in some of the articles he wrote for *Time* in 1861 arguing that Pushkin's *Evgeny Onegin* was the embodiment of a momentous crisis in the history of the Russian spirit: "Onegin precisely belongs to that epoch of our historical life marked by the very first beginnings of our agonizing consciousness and . . . our agonizing uncertainty as we look around us. . . . This was the first beginning of that epoch when our leading men sharply separated into two camps [Slavophils and Westernizers] and then violently engaged in a civil war" (19: 10). The crisis is that of the Russian spirit, which, having steeped itself in European culture, realizes that it has lost its native roots and accordingly turns back on itself with destructive

[25] The letter is published in *Proizvedeniya Petrashevtsy*, ed. V. I. Evgrafova (Moscow, 1953), 496–497.

skepticism. "The skepticism of Onegin contained something tragic in its very principle, and sometimes expressed itself with malicious irony" (19: 11).

Onegin, like the later Stavrogin, was a member of the Russian gentry, the group that "had most alienated itself from its native soil, and in which the externalities of civilization had reached their highest development (19: 11). It is proof of Onegin's moral elevation that he cannot be satisfied with the easy satisfactions of worldly pleasures or social rank; he genuinely suffers from the inner hollowness of his life. And he suffers because he does not know what to occupy himself with, "he does not even know what to respect, though he is firmly convinced that there is something that must be respected and loved. But . . . he does not respect even his own thirst for life and truth. . . . He becomes an egoist, and at the same time ridicules himself because he does not even know how to be that" (19: 11–12).

This type then enters into the consciousness of Russian society and develops new and more virulent variations with each new generation. "In the personage of [Lermontov's] Pechorin, it reached a state of insatiable, bilious malice, and of a strange contrast, in the highest degree original and Russian, of a contradiction between two heterogeneous elements: an egoism extending to the limits of self-adoration and a malicious self-contempt. And always this thirst for truth, and always the same eternal 'nothing to do!' Out of anger and as if in derision, Pechorin throws himself into outrageous, strange behavior that leads him to a stupid, ridiculous, and useless death" (19: 12). The most extreme and uncompromising development of this type, who coldly experiments with the farthest reaches of moral perversity and self-degradation, is of course Stavrogin himself.

Once Stavrogin is viewed from this perspective, it is not difficult to understand why he unexpectedly assumed such importance in Dostoevsky's early drafts. As the outlines of Stavrogin emerged from the character of the colorless Prince, Dostoevsky was seized by the temptation to extend his historical perspective backward in time and to link up the conflict of the 1840s and the 1860s with the Byronic type of the preceding years—the first manifestation of the disintegrating effects of Western influence on the Russian cultural psyche after such influence had been thoroughly absorbed. Here was the origin of the negation of Russia that had finally culminated in the abhorrent Nechaev, and since for Dostoevsky the idea of Russia was inseparable from that of the Russian Christ and the Orthodox faith, the tragedy of Stavrogin—like that of Onegin and Pechorin, as he saw it—takes the form of a moral-religious crisis. It is the search for an absolute faith that has been surrendered to the blandishments of the European Enlightenment and cannot yet be recaptured despite the torturing need for a "new truth."

This social-cultural significance of Stavrogin's Byronism suggests a more specific and concrete meaning for Dostoevsky's somewhat vague assertion that "the devils have come out of Russian man and entered into the Nechaevs and the Serno-Solovieviches." It is Stavrogin—or the type of which he is the greatest incarnation—who is "Russian man" in the fullest meaning of that phrase for Dostoevsky, and it is this type that, historically, gave birth to all the ideological "devils" that have plagued Russian culture ever since. But Stavrogin's historical role as the original fount of "the devils" became obscured because Dostoevsky retains the plot structure that makes him the pupil of Stepan Trofimovich, in effect reversing the anteriority of the Onegin type to the generation of the 1840s. It is possible that if Dostoevsky had been able to use his chapter "At Tikhon's," and thus to reveal the full ideological range of Stavrogin's supreme attempt to nullify the boundaries of good and evil, he might have allowed him to assume explicit responsibility for "the devils" despite the anachronism involved. Since the Gospel-reading scene in which Stepan Trofimovich declares *himself* to be responsible for the "devils" was *not* contained in the original manuscript, such a possibility cannot be excluded.

In any event, Stavrogin's symbolic cultural status helps to throw light on the puzzling particularities of his relationship to Kirillov and Shatov, often seen as arbitrary and enigmatic. Dostoevsky could not imagine the Byronic type without also thinking of the two competing ideologies of the Westernizers and Slavophils, who had offered divergent responses to its moral-spiritual dilemmas, and the structure of Stavrogin's linkage with these figures, as well as their own peculiar mixture of past friendship followed by antipathy, easily becomes comprehensible once seen in these historical-cultural terms. Dostoevsky dramatizes these ideologies strictly in relation to the problem of religious faith, which, as he saw it, lay at the root of the self-torments of the Byronic type. The beliefs of both Kirillov and Shatov, being derived from the tainted source of Stavrogin, are presented as secular substitutes for the genuine and spontaneous religious faith that both, like their mentor, yearn for but cannot attain.

In Kirillov, who is one of his greatest inspirations, Dostoevsky concentrates all the pathos and sublimity of the atheistic humanism inspired by Feuerbach, with its doctrine that the Man-god—that is, all of humanity—could take the place of the traditional God-man. Shatov represents Dostoevsky's view that even the Slavophils, despite their declared adherence to the Russian Orthodox faith, were still too Westernized to accept the Russian Christ with a complete inward acquiescence. This opinion of Slavophilism had recently been reinforced by the publication of Danilevsky's *Russia and Europe*, in which the ex-Fourierist and ex-Feuerbachian writer had spoken of God as the "synthetic personality" of each people, just as, for Feuerbach, God had been the "synthetic personality" of humankind—a creation of humankind itself, in other words, and not a divine truth surpassing reason. The ideas that Shatov took over from Stavrogin, and which he then repeats to his master, transcribe this Slavophil version of Feuerbachianism straight from the pages of Danilevsky's book. Dostoevsky, as we know, agreed politically with Danilevsky's glorification of Slavdom and Russia as the basis of a new world-culture, but he was troubled by the writer's failure to recognize the *universal* religious mission of Orthodoxy. Shatov thus embodies Dostoevsky's criticism of Danilevsky, and Shatov's elevation of the Russian people into a god fits very neatly into the tragic incapacity of Stavrogin, whose ideas Shatov is repeating, to attain the humility of self-surrender to a redeeming *religious* faith.

One further context, provided by the Franco-Prussian War, also helps to enrich the symbolic significance of Stavrogin. Dostoevsky had been filled with horror and rage at the flames engulfing Paris during the last days of the Commune. Of the Communards, whom he held responsible, he said, "to them (and many others) this monstrosity doesn't seem madness but, on the contrary, *beauty*. The aesthetic idea of modern humanity has become obscured." [26] These words surely bear on the scene in which Peter Verkhovensky, as he goes into raptures over Stavrogin's "beauty," finally reveals himself to be a passionately visionary fanatic and not simply a cold and ruthless tactician of terror. "'Stavrogin, you are beautiful,' cried Peter Stepanovich, almost ecstatically. 'I love beauty, I am a Nihilist, but I love beauty. Are Nihilists incapable of loving beauty? It's only idols they dislike, but I love an idol'" (10: 323). True beauty for Dostoevsky had become incarnated in the world by Christ, and to equate it with violent destruction was the height of perversity.

The calm and impassive figure of Stavrogin is thus surrounded in Dostoevsky's imagination with the infernal halo of the flames that had recently been crackling in the heart-city of Western civilization. It is he who has brought to Russia all the "beauty" of this idolatrous negation, which, if allowed to go unchallenged by the "authentic beauty" of Christ, would light the same torch of destruction in Holy Russia that was already ravaging the West. For the "beauty" of Stavrogin is that of the demonic, the beauty of Lucifer in Byron's *Cain*, who, as Herzen wrote unforgettably, "is the gloomy angel of darkness, on whose brow shines with dim lustre the star of bitter thought, full of inner discords which can never be harmonized." He lures like "still, moonlit water, that promises nothing but death in its comfortless, cold, glimmering embraces." [27]

---

[26] *PSS*, 29/Bk. 1: 214; May 18/30, 1871.
[27] Herzen, *My Past and Thoughts*, 2: 744.

CHAPTER 45

The Book of the Impostors

Demons, as we know, was initially begun as a "pamphlet-novel" in which Dostoevsky would unleash all his satirical fury against the Nihilists. It is thus not surprising that, of all his major works, it contains the greatest proportion of satirical caricature and ideological parody. This becomes immediately apparent in the rhetoric of the narrator's account of Stepan Trofimovich's career, which both exalts and deflates him at the same time. Since the narrator feels a genuine sympathy for Stepan Trofimovich, he begins by delineating the exalted and ennobling image that the eminent worthy has of *himself*. But he immediately undermines it by revealing the completely exaggerated, even illusory nature of many of the poses that his subject strikes (as a supposed "political exile," for instance, who was not an exile at all, or as a noted scholar whose "notoriety" was mainly fictitious). "Yet Stepan Trofimovich was a most intelligent and gifted man," the narrator affirms, "even, so to say, a man of science . . . well in fact he had not done such great things in science. I believe indeed that he had done nothing at all. But that's very often the case, of course, with men of science among us in Russia" (10: 8).

In fact, recalls the narrator, a famous article written by Stepan Trofimovich contained "the beginning of a very profound investigation into the causes, I believe, of the extraordinary moral nobility of certain knights at a certain epoch or something of that nature" (10: 9). This choice of subject defines the sublime elevation of Stepan Trofimovich's own ideals, which are also illustrated by the chronicler's account of Stepan Trofimovich's prose poem, written sometime in the 1830s. Described as "some sort of allegory in lyrical-dramatic form" (10:9), the poem parodies Vladimir Pecherin's *The Triumph of Death* and is the first announcement of the book's dominating symbolism:

> Then a youth of indescribable beauty rides in on a black steed, and an immense multitude of all nations follow him. The youth represents death for whom all the peoples are yearning. And finally, in the last scene we are suddenly shown the Tower of Babel, and certain athletes at last finish building it with a song of new hope, and when at length they complete the topmost pinnacle, the lord (of Olympus, let us say) takes flight in a

comic fashion, and man, grasping the situation and seizing his place, at once begins a new life with a new insight into things. (10: 10)

This parody contains the major theme of the book and foreshadows the appearance of Stavrogin. He too is of an "indescribable beauty"; he too is death and not life; he too is followed, if not by multitudes of all nations, then by the multitude of all those who look to him for inspiration. He too believes that man can take the place not of the lord of Olympus, who has nothing to do with the Tower of Babel, but of the God of the Old Testament and his Son of the New. Stavrogin is the pretender and the impostor aspiring to the throne of God, just as in the poem the youth representing death aspires to be the source of life. Everything that stems from Stavrogin is thus marked with the seal of supreme falsity and deception and leads to death. He is a counterfeit and fraudulent facsimile of truth; and this symbolism of the usurper, the pretender, the impostor runs through every aspect of the book, underlying and linking all its actions.

No one, to be sure, is more of an impostor—more of an endearing and charming old fake—than Stepan Trofimovich. Dostoevsky paints him with such an overflowing abundance of traits that it is difficult to do justice to them all, but each reinforces the comic discrepancy between his rhetorical postures and his egocentric practical performances. Nor does Dostoevsky neglect, despite his personal detestation of Nihilism, to allow Peter Verkhovensky to puncture his father's poses with deadly accuracy. But this only serves to make the fickle old Idealist even more sympathetic and appealing. Whatever the material basis of his existence, he has never exploited it basely; in yielding to his weaknesses, he always remains aware that he is unworthy of the great ideals that he proclaims and reveres. Stepan Trofimovich, in other words, has never allowed his conscience to become dulled—and this, for Dostoevsky, always leaves the path open for salvation.

■

Up to the age of sixteen, Stavrogin was the pupil of Stepan Trofimovich, and this plot structure makes a Liberal Idealist of the 1840s the spiritual progenitor of a Byronic type associated with the 1820s and 1830s. Stavrogin's Byronism loses much of its symbolic meaning when he is linked to Stepan Trofimovich as pupil to teacher, but Dostoevsky nonetheless succeeds in making their relationship humanly convincing. He underlines the tradition of metaphysical-religious Idealism that constitutes a bond between teacher and pupil, but the heritage is conveyed in a form reflecting all the velleities of Stepan Trofimovich's highly volatile character, which exercises a morbid influence on his impressionable charge. "More than once he awakened his ten- or eleven-year-old friend at night, simply to pour out his wounded feelings and weep before him, or to tell him some family secret, without noticing that this was totally impermissible" (10: 35). The tutor communicated all his own moral uncertainty and instability to his unfortunate pupil without providing anything positive to counteract their unsettling effects, and the result was to leave an aching emptiness at the center of Stavrogin's being.

"Stepan Trofimovich succeeded in reaching the deepest chords in his pupil's heart, and had aroused in him a first vague sensation of that eternal, sacred longing which some elect souls, once having tasted and discovered it, will then never exchange for a cheap gratification. (There are some connoisseurs who prize this longing more than the most complete satisfaction of it, if such were possible)" (10: 35). This passage defines Stavrogin as a personality emotionally engaged in the quest for an indeterminate absolute and also suggests the perversity springing from his lack of any positive goal. His quest is a spiritual experimentation totally preoccupied with itself, totally enclosed within the ego, and hence incapable of self-surrender to the absolute presumably being sought.

All through this first presentation of Stavrogin, Dostoevsky accentuates the pure gratuity of his scandalous behavior, the impossibility of explaining it by any commonplace motives. There is something mysterious about Stavrogin's violence, particularly about his taste for self-degradation, that challenges the norm. The sheer gratuitousness of his defiance of social convention, which so much fascinated André Gide in Dostoevsky, is stressed even more strongly in the episodes that scandalize his birthplace on his return. He suddenly pulls the nose of a harmless old gentleman who has been in the habit of asserting, "No, you can't lead me by the nose" (10: 38); on the spur of the moment he kisses Liputin's pretty wife with ardent passion; called in by his distant relative, the governor of the province, for some explanation, he surpasses himself by biting the governor's ear. All these incidents exemplify Stavrogin's rejection of any internal or external restraints on the absolute autonomy of his self-will. When he goes mad with an attack of "brain fever," the chronicler remarks that it was thought by some (and they were right) to be "neither here nor there" so far as an explanation of his actions was concerned (10: 44).

The first physical description of Stavrogin pinpoints his strange appearance of indefinable artificiality—an appearance that obviously derives from his symbolic function. "His hair was of a peculiarly intense black, his light-colored eyes were peculiarly light and calm, his complexion was peculiarly soft and white, the red in his cheeks was too bright and clear, his teeth were like pearls and his lips like coral—one would have thought the very acme of beauty, yet at the same time somehow repellent. It was said that his face suggested a mask" (10: 37). Stavrogin's masklike beauty reminds one of the vampires and ghouls of Gothic fictional mythology; like them, he is a living corpse whose unearthly beauty is the deceptive façade behind which festers the horror of evil and corruption. Several years later, however, when the chronicler observes him face-to-face again, a change has occurred. "Now—now, I don't know why he impressed me at once as absolutely incontestably beautiful, so that no one could have said that his face was like a mask." Now he seemed "to have the light of some new idea in his eyes" (10: 145).

By this time, Stavrogin has decided to overcome his past, to humiliate himself publicly by acknowledging his marriage to Marya Lebyadkina and confessing his violation of Matryosha. By seeking forgiveness, he hopes to save himself from the madness that he feels to be his impending fate. On the purely moral-personal level, Stavrogin's character is defined by his despairing struggle to triumph over the egoism of his self-will and to attain a state of genuine humility. The first overt manifestation of this "new idea" is the self-control he exhibits under the provocation of Shatov's blow; but he lies about his relation to the crippled Marya, which he wishes to reveal only under conditions of his own choosing. And this is the first justification for Tikhon's later judgment that Stavrogin's egoism, far from having been conquered by his new resolution, has taken on its subtlest form of all as a carefully staged martyrdom of contempt.

At the end of this scene the narrator attempts to define Stavrogin's character, and compares him with the well-known figure of a legendary Decembrist, L—n (Lunin). By linking Stavrogin to a member of this group and to this period—that of Russian Byronism, *Evgeny Onegin*, and Lermontov's Pechorin—Dostoevsky is attempting to compensate for the anachronism inherent in his plot structure. Consequently, Stavrogin turns out to be a *contemporary* development of the same type, its latest avatar in Russian culture, who, unlike his predecessor, is strangely afflicted by inner desiccation and emotional apathy.

In the past, such "predatory" Byronic types, as Grigoryev called them, had at least enjoyed the consciousness of their own superiority and strength. But while Stavrogin would have performed the same daring feats from which they derived pleasure, he would have done so "without the slightest thrill of enjoyment, languidly, listlessly, even with *ennui* and entirely from unpleasant necessity." Stavrogin had even more "malignancy" than such gentlemen of the past, "but his malignancy was cold, calm, and, if one may say so, *rational*—therefore, the most revolting and terrible possible" (10: 165). All the springs of human feeling have dried up in Stavrogin; his demonism is that of a total rationalism, which, once having emptied life of all significance and value, can no longer make any direct, instinctive response even to its most primitive solicitations. Byron's Manfred has different reasons for his despair with life (his crime of incest, which resembles Stavrogin's violation of innocence, is at least a crime of passion), but his self-characterization accurately applies to Stavrogin with equal force:

Good, or evil, life,
Powers, passions, all I see in other beings,

Have been to me as rain unto the sands. . . .
I have no dread,
And feel the curse to have no natural fear,
Nor fluttering throb, that beats with hopes or wishes,
Or lurking love of something on the earth.[1]

———■———

The action in the first four chapters of Part II, which concentrates on Stavrogin as he makes a round of visits to Kirillov, Shatov, and the Lebyadkins, indirectly illuminates both his historical-symbolic significance and the tragedy of his yearning for an unattainable absolution through humility. The first two figures each represent an aspect of himself that he has discarded but that has now become transformed into one or another ideological "devil" permanently obsessing his spiritual disciples. In the case of Kirillov, this devil is the temptation to self-deification logically deriving from the atheistic humanism of Feuerbach. "The necessary turning point of history," Feuerbach had written in his *Essence of Christianity*, "will be the moment when man becomes aware of and admits that his consciousness of God is nothing else but the consciousness of man as species. . . . *Homo homini Deus est*—this is the great practical principle—this is the axis on which revolves the history of the world."[2] There is a transparent echo of these famous words in the scene between Kirillov and the narrator in Part I, when Kirillov remarks that history will be divided into two parts, "from the gorilla to the annihilation of God, and from the annihilation of man ["To the gorilla?" ironically interjects the narrator—J.F.] . . . to the transformation of the earth and of man physically. Man will be God and be transformed physically" (10: 94).[3]

Kirillov is one of Dostoevsky's most remarkable creations, and, like Raskolnikov, displays Dostoevsky's intimate understanding of the moral passion inspiring many of the radical intelligentsia whose concrete politics he abhorred. Kirillov is a secular saint whose whole being is consumed by a need for self-sacrifice. Determined to take his own life for the greater glory of mankind, whom he wishes to free from the pain and fear of death, Kirillov has agreed to do so at the moment that would most aid "the cause," and Peter Verkhovensky intends to exploit this demented but great-souled resolution to cover the murder of Shatov. God, Kirillov believes, is nothing but the projected image of this pain

---

[1] Lord Byron, *Complete Poetical Works* (Cambridge, MA, 1905).

[2] Ludwig Feuerbach, *The Essence of Christianity*, trans. George Eliot (New York, 1957), 270–271.

[3] Andrzej Walicki cites a passage from the later *Lectures on the Essence of Religion* in which Feuerbach refers to "the future immortal man, differentiated from man as he exists at present in the body and flesh." See Andrzej Walicki, *A History of Russian Thought* (Stanford, 1979), 317.

and fear, and he wishes to commit suicide solely to express the highest capacity of humankind's self-will—solely to free humanity from a God who is nothing but such a fear. Kirillov is convinced that such a suicide will initiate the era of the Man-god predicted by Feuerbach, and his death will thus be a martyrdom for humankind, but a martyrdom that reverses the significance of that of Christ. Rather than testifying to the reality and existence of God and a superterrestrial world, it will mark their final elimination from human consciousness.

With a daring that has given rise to a great deal of confusion, Dostoevsky does not hesitate to endow Kirillov with many of the attributes of Prince Myshkin—his love for children, his ecstatic affirmation of life, his eschatological apprehension of the end of time. The symbolism of the book requires Stavrogin always to inspire a deformed and distorted image of the truth—but one that resembles what it imitates as closely and uncannily as Stavrogin's "mask" resembles healthy human beauty. Hence Dostoevsky gives Kirillov the "mask" of Myshkin's apocalyptic intuitions and feelings while revealing the monstrosities that result when such religious emotions, divorced from a faith in Christ, are turned into secular and subjective ideas.

Kirillov's deification of man leads to his own self-destruction as well as that of all humankind ("it will be the same to live or not to live"); his conviction that the Kingdom of God already exists, if people will only realize it, deludes him into denying the existence of evil ("everything is good"), and he sees no difference between worshipping "a spider crawling along a wall" and a sacred icon. Stavrogin's demonism is refracted in Kirillov through a religious sensibility haunted, like Ippolit Terentyev, by the loss of Christ; and Kirillov's apocalyptic yearning makes him oblivious of, and personally immune to, the horrible consequences of his own doctrines. Stavrogin, though, has lived through other experiences, and he indicates the most important of them in his question: "if anyone insults and outrages [a] little girl, is that good?" Throughout this scene he regards Kirillov "with a disdainful compassion," though, as Dostoevsky adds carefully, "there [was] no mockery in his eyes" (10: 187–189).

The dialogue with Kirillov is followed by a parallel scene with Shatov, and here again Dostoevsky uses some of his most cherished convictions to dramatize another of Stavrogin's "masks." Just as Stavrogin had inspired Kirillov with an atheistic humanism based on the supremacy of reason and the Man-god, so he has inspired Shatov, at the same time, with a Slavophilism founded on the very opposite principle. "Reason has never had the power to define good and evil," Shatov declares, repeating Stavrogin's teaching, "or even to distinguish between good and evil, even approximately; on the contrary, it has always mixed them up in a disgraceful and pitiful way; science has even given the solution by the fist." The distinction between right and wrong, as the Slavophils had argued, comes only from the irrational, only from religion and faith. "There has never been a nation without a religion, that is, without an idea of good and evil." And since, for a Russian, religion can only mean Orthodox Christianity, Stavrogin had affirmed that "a man who was not Orthodox could not be a Russian" (10: 197–199). Here, growing directly out of Stavrogin's preachments, is the metaphysical-religious essence of the two ideologies that succeeded the Russian Byronism of the 1830s.

The relation between Shatov and Stavrogin is much more complex, and much more difficult to describe accurately, than that between Stavrogin and Kirillov. Kirillov's attempt literally to incarnate the Man-god can lead only to self-destruction; he thus expresses the demonic and Luciferian side of Stavrogin's personality (but in a morally elevated form). Shatov, on the other hand, represents the need and the search for faith that is also deeply rooted in Stavrogin, the need that is impelling him to acknowledge and repent his crimes. Moreover, the effect of Stavrogin on Shatov has been the very opposite of what occurred with Kirillov; he helped Shatov to break with his radical past and imbued him with the messianic idea of the Russians as a "god-bearing" people destined to regenerate the world. Stavrogin's influence has thus led Shatov along the path that Dostoevsky certainly considered that of salvation, but the symbolic pattern of the book requires that his path also be blocked by the fatality of Stavrogin's doom.

Dostoevsky wishes to emphasize the need for convictions to be grounded in sincere religious faith. Shatov's ideas echo those of Danilevsky, who had, in Dostoevsky's view, reduced Orthodoxy simply to a national faith and thus betrayed the universal religious mission of the Russian Christ. Indeed, Dostoevsky now felt that even the old Slavophilism of Khomiakov and Kireevsky, for all its overt religiosity, was still an artificial, Western-imported substitute for the spontaneity of the people's faith. "The Slavophil," Dostoevsky wrote in his notes, identifying such a doctrine with Danilevsky, "thinks that he can manage solely thanks to the natural attributes of the Russian people, but without Orthodoxy one will not manage at all, no attributes will do anything if the world has lost faith." On the same page, in a speech not included in the text, Shatov calls Slavophilism "an aristocratic whim" and then adds: "They [the Slavophils] will never be able to believe directly" (11: 186). This idea was finally assigned to Stepan Trofimovich, who says much the same thing—and here he certainly speaks for the author—when he declares that "Shatov believes *by forcing himself to*, like a Moscow Slavophil" (10: 33). Hence Stavrogin and his pupil Shatov, for all their Slavophilism and Russian nationalism, cannot muster the simple and unquestioning faith that would infuse their ideas with the inner fire of true emotional commitment.

Stavrogin thus here again inspires a mutilated version of the truth that falls short of its grounding in religious faith, even though he knows abstractly that such faith is the only means of rescue from the chaos of his unlimited freedom. Shatov diagnoses the malady afflicting Stavrogin (and himself) in a key speech that helps to explain how Dostoevsky saw them both:

> You're an atheist [Shatov says] because you're a nobleman's son, the last nobleman's son. You've lost the distinction between good and evil because you've ceased to know your people. A new generation is coming, straight from the heart of the people, and you will know nothing of it, neither you nor the Verkhovenskys, father or son, nor I, because I am also a nobleman's son, I, the son of your serf-lackey Pashka. (10: 202–203)

On the symbolic level of the book, this can only mean that all the ideologies deriving from Stavrogin—whether liberal or radical Westernism in its political or metaphysical-religious form, or Slavophilism of whatever tint or shading—are equally tainted with the original sin of their birth among a Western-educated "aristocracy" totally divorced from the people. All are doomed to be swept away by an authentically Russian culture springing from the people's faith.

Stavrogin's personal behavior in these scenes also makes it clear that he will never be able to achieve the total abandonment of self necessary for a religious conversion. Even with Shatov, whom he comes to warn about the impending danger of his possible murder and to whom he is closer than anyone in the book except Darya Shatova, he cannot confess the truth about Matryosha. He denies that he has "outraged children," just as he had lied earlier about his marriage to Marya Lebyadkina. And he refuses to answer when Shatov poses the question that was to be clarified in his visit to Tikhon: "Is it true that you saw no distinction between some brutal obscene action and any great exploit, even the sacrifice of life for the good of humanity? Is it true that you have found identical beauty, equal enjoyment, in both extremes?" (10: 201). Shatov displays the same insight into Stavrogin that Tikhon would later exhibit when he diagnoses the motives for his marriage to Marya: "You married through a passion for martyrdom, from a craving for remorse, through moral sensuality" (10: 202). The first two impulses in Stavrogin, genuinely moral, are always crippled and distorted by the third, which stems from his enjoyment of the outrageously perverse, shocking, and sheerly gratuitous manifestations of his absolute self-will.

■

Stavrogin's next visit, to the Lebyadkins, completes the sequence unmasking Stavrogin as an "impostor." Marya Lebyadkin, Stavrogin's virginal wife, is one of Dostoevsky's most poetic and enigmatic creations. Childish and mentally feeble, unable to distinguish between objective reality and her dreams and desires, she yet pierces through the "mask" of Stavrogin with a clairvoyance that recalls Prince Myshkin and foreshadows Father Zosima. Her sense of the sacredness of the cosmos, her affirmation that "the Mother of God is the great mother, the damp earth," who brings joy to men when they "water the earth with [their] tears a foot deep" (10: 116), evokes the esoteric, heretical lore of certain sects of the *raskolniki*, who mingled their Christianity with remnants of pre-Christian paganism.

Marya represents Dostoevsky's vision of the primitive religious sensibility of the Russian people, who continued to feel a mystical union between the Russian soil and "the Mother of God." The debasement and pathos of her condition, however, reveal Dostoevsky's ambiguity about the *raskolniki* and their sectarian offshoots; he tended to see them as a precious reservoir of Old Russian values, but kept his distance from their sometimes theologically suspect extremes. At one point, Dostoevsky had thought of using Golubov, an Old Believer returned to Orthodoxy, as a positive source of moral inspiration. In this context, Marya's poignant longing for a "prince" who would not be ashamed to acknowledge her as his own takes on historical-symbolic meaning. Her false and unconsummated marriage to Stavrogin surely indicates that no true union is possible between the Christian Russian people and the embodied essence of godless Russian Europeanism.

Symbolically again, it is entirely appropriate that Marya should finally unmask Stavrogin and label him unequivocally an "impostor." Whatever confusion may exist in her mind, her demented second sight, like that traditionally possessed by a "holy fool" (*yurodivy*), has now pierced through to his ultimate incapacity for true selflessness. "As soon as I saw your mean face when I fell and you picked me up—it was as if a worm had crawled into my heart," she says; "it's not *he*, I thought to myself, not *he*! My falcon would never have been ashamed of me in front of a young society lady!" (10: 219). Stavrogin starts with rage and terror when she prophetically alludes to his "knife," that is, his lurking desire to have her murdered (on which Peter Verkhovensky hopes to capitalize). And while she reads his innermost soul, she also speaks for the Russian people in assigning him his true historical-symbolic dimension. He is not the "prince," not the genuine Lord and Ruler of Russia, but only Grishka Otrepeyev, "cursed in seven cathedrals," the impious and sacrilegious "impostor" and "false pretender"—Ivan the Tsarevich—that Peter Verkhovensky wishes to use to betray and mislead the hapless Russian people.

How justly Marya has seen into Stavrogin becomes even clearer when he throws his wallet to Fedka the convict in the solitary darkness of the storm-tossed night. By this gesture, Stavrogin silently connives at the murder of the Lebyadkins, giving way once again to the temptation of evil. His inner defeat is dramatized again in his duel with Gaganov, when he strives to achieve self-mastery and to avoid useless bloodshed, but his arrogant and contemptuous manner only enflames the uncontrollable hatred of his opponent all the more. The truly good Kirillov, ready to give his life for humankind, tries to explain to Stavrogin that moral self-conquest means a total suppression of egoism and the patient acceptance of any humiliation, even the most unjust and insupportable. "Bear your burden," he says. "Or else there's no merit" (10: 228). But Stavrogin cannot bear the burden of good, whatever his desire to do so, because his irrepressible egoism continues to stand in the way.

This crucial sequence of scenes is climaxed by Stavrogin's unexpected meeting with Darya Shatova, an episode that, in the book text, is about a page and a half shorter than the earlier magazine version. The section that Dostoevsky cut contained Stavrogin's admission that he was haunted by hallucinations and "devils," which he knew were only parts of himself; but his self-absorption indicates that he is beginning to believe in their reality. This menace of madness was meant to motivate the visit to Tikhon but became superfluous and incomprehensible without the confession chapter. One passage of the variant, however, helps to reconstruct the original historical-symbolic meaning of Dostoevsky's conception. Stavrogin tells Darya that he has begun to be obsessed with a new "devil," very different from those in the past (as represented by Kirillov and Shatov): "Yesterday he was stupid and insolent. He's a thickheaded seminarian filled with the self-satisfaction of the 1860s, with the . . . background, soul, and mentality of a lackey, fully persuaded of his irresistible beauty. . . . Nothing could be more repulsive! I was furious that my own devil could put on such a debasing mask" (12: 141). It is clear that Dostoevsky intended to make Stavrogin as much responsible for devils of the 1860s as Stepan Trofimovich, if not indeed more so, because of his disdainful collaboration with Peter.

The scene with Darya Shatova, accordingly, serves as a transition between the first and second sections of Part II. Immediately following this dialogue, Dostoevsky shifts his focus from Stavrogin to the spread of the moral and social chaos he has brought in his wake in the form of Peter Verkhovensky. Here Dostoevsky gives full play to his immense satiric verve as he sketches all the people whose stupidity and lack of principle turn them into willing dupes of Peter's intrigues. The ambitious bluestocking Yulia von Lembke, determined to impress the most exalted spheres by her influence on the young generation; her obtuse and incompetent Russo-German automaton of a husband, the governor of the province, literally driven out of his mind by the tumultuous course of events; even the normally hardheaded and domineering Mme Stavrogina—all fall under Peter Verkhovensky's spell, aided and abetted by the patronage of Karmazinov. Only poor Stepan Trofimovich, more and more lonely, isolated, and agitated, resists the general disintegration and still plans to vindicate his ideals.

Starting as the personal foible of a few foolish people, the corruption becomes a demoralization in the most literal sense. Dostoevsky introduces a whole series of incidents to illustrate it, ranging from a breakdown of standards of personal conduct and social propriety to disrespect for the dead and the desecration of a sacred icon. Just as with his general influence on society as a whole, the result of his pressure on the quintet is a collapse of their own moral-political standards and the approval of a wanton murder. There is a clear structural parallel between Stavrogin's round of visits in the first half of this section and Peter's calls in the second half on all the pawns he is engaged in maneuvering. Dostoevsky intended to bring these parallel sequences together by the two chapters of self-revelation that would conclude Part II: Verkhovensky's mad hymn to universal destruction, inspired by Stavrogin, and then a disclosure of the moral bankruptcy and despair of Verkhovensky's "idol" as he makes his confession to Tikhon.

From his first appearance in the novel, Peter Verkhovensky is depicted as the genius of duplicity. He is Stavrogin's demonism incarnated as a political will-to-power. "I invented you abroad," he cries furiously to Stavrogin. "I invented it all, looking at you. If I hadn't watched you from my corner, nothing of all this would have entered my head" (10: 326). What Peter has invented, under the spell of Stavrogin, is the plan to consecrate him as Ivan the Tsarevich—to use the very force he wishes to destroy, the faith of the Russian people in a just and righteous God-anointed ruler, as a means for their own destruction. This plan has obvious symbolic affinities with Stavrogin's effect on Kirillov and Shatov; in each of them he has inspired a "mask" of the truth shorn of its true religious foundations. This mask is "beautiful," as Peter exclaims ecstatically while gazing at Stavrogin, but, as already noted, it is the beauty of the demonic. "You are my idol!" Peter passionately proclaims to Stavrogin (10: 323). Peter's plan, however, implicitly contains its own negation, for it reveals the impotence of his godless and amoral principles to establish any basis for human life. Falsehood and idolatry must speak deceptively in the name of truth and God, thus confessing their own bankruptcy.

Following Verkhovensky's "confession" to the false god Stavrogin, Dostoevsky had planned to portray Stavrogin's confession to the true God in the person of his servitor, Tikhon. This would have dramatized all the horror and abomination of the "idol" that Peter Verkhovensky was worshiping. After a sleepless night spent in warding off his hallucinations, Stavrogin would visit Tikhon, and then the secret of his past, repeatedly hinted at up to this point, was to be finally disclosed. Like Onegin and Pechorin, Stavrogin is a victim of the famous *mal de siècle*, the all-engulfing ennui that haunts the literature of the first half of the nineteenth century and is invariably depicted as resulting from the loss of religious faith. Baudelaire, its greatest poet, called ennui the deadliest of the vices:

> Quoiqu'il ne pousse ni grands gestes ni grands cris,
> Il ferait volontiers de la terre un débris
> Et dans un baillement avalerait le monde.[4]

Ennui is a prominent symptom of that "romantic agony" whose dossier has been so industriously compiled by Mario Praz and whose usual result is some form of moral perversion.[5] Dostoevsky had depicted it as such in Prince Valkovsky (*The Insulted and Injured*), in the sudden appearance of Cleopatra in *Notes from Underground*, and in Svidrigailov (*Crime and Punishment*). With Stavrogin, it has led to the abominable violation of little Matryosha and his unspeakably vile passivity as she takes her life.

Such is the result of Stavrogin's attempt to pass beyond the limits of morality, to put into practice, with the maniacal determination of Dostoevsky's negative heroes, the conviction that there are no moral boundaries of any kind. "I formulated for the first time in my life what appeared to be the rule of my life," Stavrogin tells himself, "namely, that I neither know nor feel good and evil and that I have not only lost any sense of it, but that there is neither good nor evil (which pleased me), and that it is just a prejudice" (12: 113). For Stavrogin, these were "old familiar thoughts" that he was at last putting clearly to himself for the first time. Like Raskolnikov's crime, Stavrogin's revolting escapades had been a great moral-philosophical experiment. This is why Dostoevsky had taken such pains from the start to dissociate his conduct from any kind of banal and self-indulgent debauchery.

Yet Stavrogin's ambition to transcend the human, to arrogate for himself supreme power over life and death, nonetheless runs aground on the hidden reef of conscience. No matter what he may think, Stavrogin cannot entirely eliminate his *feeling* for the difference between good and evil. This irrepressible sentiment breaks forth from his subconscious—usually, though not invariably, the guardian of morality for Dostoevsky—in Stavrogin's famous dream of "the Golden Age," inspired by Claude Lorrain's painting *Acis and Galatea*. Stavrogin saw in his mind's eye:

> A corner of the Greek archipelago; blue, caressing waves, islands, . . . a magic vista in the distance, a spellbinding sunset. . . . Here was the cradle of European civilization, here were the first scenes from mythology, man's paradise on earth. Here a beautiful race of men had lived. They rose and

---

[4] "Without great gestures or loud cries / It would gladly turn earth into a wasteland / And swallow the world in a yawn." Charles Baudelaire, *Oeuvres*, ed. Y.-G. Le Dantec (Paris, 1954), 82.

[5] Mario Praz, *The Romantic Agony* (Oxford, 1970), 419–420.

went to sleep happy and innocent. . . . The most incredible dream that has
ever been dreamed, but to which all mankind has devoted all its powers
during the whole of its existence, for which it has died on the cross and for
which its prophets have been killed, without which nations will not live
and cannot even die. (11: 21)

This vision of a primeval earthly paradise of happiness and innocence fills
Stavrogin's heart with overflowing joy. "I woke and opened my eyes, for the first
time in my life literally wet with tears. . . . A feeling of happiness, hitherto unknown to me, pierced my heart till it ached." But then a tiny red spider, associated in Stavrogin's subconscious with Matryosha's death, replaced this blissful
vision of Eden. He sees the little girl, in his mind's eye, standing on the threshold of his room and threatening him with her tiny fist. "Pity for her stabbed
me," he writes, "a maddening pity, and I would have given my body to be torn
to pieces if that would have erased what happened" (12: 127–128). Stavrogin
finds this lacerating reminder of his own evil unbearable, but he willfully refuses
to suppress the recollection, and this insupportable need to expiate his crime,
which nothing he knows or believes in can help to absolve, is gradually driving
him mad.

Stavrogin's confession thus reveals the source of his inner torment, but this
torment has never been sufficient to overcome the supreme egoism and self-will
that originally motivated his actions. Even his confession, as Tikhon senses, is
only another and more extreme form of the "moral sensuality" that has marked
all his previous attempts at self-mastery. "This document," says Tikhon of his
manuscript, "is born of a heart wounded unto death. . . . But it is as though you
were already hating and despising in advance all those who read what you have
written, and challenging them to an encounter" (11: 24). Tikhon discerns that
Stavrogin by himself can never achieve the true humility of genuine repentance;
his need for suffering and martyrdom can thus lead only to more and more disastrous provocations. Hence Tikhon argues that Stavrogin submit his will *completely* to the secret control of a saintly *starets* and thus discipline himself, by a
total surrender to another, as the first step along the path to the acceptance of
Christ and the hope of forgiveness. But Stavrogin, irritably breaking an ivory
crucifix he has been fingering during the interview, rejects this final admonition
and goes to his self-destruction.

■

When it proved impossible to include the confession chapter in its proper place,
Dostoevsky was forced to mutilate the original symmetry of his plan. Part II was
to have exposed the origins of the chaos sown by Stavrogin and his "worshiper"
Peter Verkhovensky; Part III would then have shown the practical results of their

handiwork. Instead, Dostoevsky was forced to allow the present Chapter 9 of Part II ("Stepan Verkhovensky Is Raided") to replace the confession. From this point on, a continuous sequence unrolls the disastrous moral-social consequences of Peter Verkhovensky's intrigues, including von Lembke's madness and the weird fête for the underprivileged governesses of the province, one of the greatest comic mass scenes in the history of the novel and also containing the hilarious parody of Turgenev. These events reach dizzy heights of farce, intermingled with the shocking news of Liza Tushina's flight to Stavrogin (arranged by Peter), the destruction caused by the fires, and the discovery of the murders of Captain Lebyadkin and his sister.

Both the killing of Shatov and the suicide of Kirillov exhibit the same pattern of reversion and regression to the inhuman. The hapless conspirators are far from sharing Peter's insouciance about human life, and as the murder takes place, Lyamshin and Virginsky are overtaken by a panic return to animality. "Lyamshin gave vent to a scream more animal than human, he went on shrieking without a pause, his mouth wide open and his eyes staring out of his head. . . . Virginsky was so scared that he too screamed out like a madman, and with a ferocity, a vindictiveness that one could not have expected of Virginsky" (10: 461). Nor is Kirillov's eerie death the triumphant assertion of a total self-will; it is, rather, the demented act of a crazed and terrified subhuman creature. The annihilation of God, far from leading to a mastery over the pain and fear of death, brings on the animal frenzy with which Kirillov sinks his teeth into Peter's hand. Like Raskolnikov's crime, Kirillov's suicide is the self-negation and self-refutation of his own grandiose ideas.

If some characters may be said to sink below themselves by reverting to the level of animality, Stepan Trofimovich surprises the narrator by rising above himself and finally overcoming his eternal hesitations. His touchingly aimless peregrinations, which Dostoevsky had so much looked forward to composing, plunge him into entirely new circumstances. Nothing is finer, in this book so filled with remarkable pages, than the bewildered contact between the sheltered, pampered "liberal," who has spent his life uttering fine phrases and depreciatory remarks about the Russian people, and the dumbfounded peasants whom he finally encounters. There is mutual incomprehension on both sides, as each observes the strange ways of the other with astonishment. Above all, the inspired meeting with the ex-nurse distributing copies of the New Testament allows Dostoevsky to introduce his religious thematic in the midst of Stepan Trofimovich's perplexities.

The startled lady immediately becomes the object of his affectionate attention, and he dependently adapts himself to her as he had done for most of his life with Mme Stavrogin. "*Vous voyez, désormais nous le prêcherons* [the New Testament] *ensemble.* . . . the common people are religious, *c'est admis*, but they don't yet know the Gospel. . . . By expounding it to them verbally it is possible to correct the errors of that remarkable book, which, of course, I shall treat with the utmost respect" (10: 497). Running a high fever and near death, he attempts to persuade her of his unacknowledged genius, leaving her totally confused as she arranges for the administration of the sacraments.

From the very first pages, Stepan Trofimovich has been presented not as an atheist, to be sure, but as a species of Hegelian deist. "I believe in God," he declares importantly, "*mais distinguons*, I believe in him as a Being who is conscious of himself in me only" (10: 33). Nothing that Stepan Trofimovich says in these last pages contradicts his aversion to the naïve anthropomorphism of the popular faith, and the narrator maintains a well-justified skepticism over "whether he was really converted, or whether the stately ceremony of the administration of the sacraments impressed him and stirred the artistic responsiveness of his temperament" (10: 505). Nor does he lose his taste for risqué jests about religion even on his deathbed. It is after an imperious outburst of Mme Stavrogin, who has finally arrived to take charge, that he smiles faintly and says, "God is necessary to me if only because He is the only being whom I can love eternally" (10: 505).

Stepan Trofimovich, then, does not die a Christian in any strict meaning of the word, but a reading of the Sermon on the Mount stirs him to acknowledge: "My friend, all my life I've been lying." And after listening to the passage from Luke about "the devils" who had entered the herd of swine, he declares: "They are we, we and those . . . and Petrusha and *les autres avec lui* . . . and I perhaps at the head of them" (10: 499). Such words, though consistent with the plot structure, scarcely accord sufficient importance to Stavrogin. More convincing, and entirely in character, is Stepan Trofimovich's final statement of his credo: "The whole law of human existence is merely this, that man should always bow down before the infinitely great. If people are deprived of the infinitely great, they will not continue to live and will die in despair. The infinite and immeasurable are as necessary to man as the little planet on which he dwells. My friends, all, all: Long live the Great Idea!" (10: 506). This is not Christian in any literal sense and could hardly have been meant to be taken as such; but it contains enough of a feeling for the transcendent to constitute an answer to the hubris of the purely human.

■

Stavrogin's suicide, which terminates the novel, had been foreseen by Dostoevsky from his very first grasp of this character, but it is difficult to say how it might have been presented if the confession chapter had been included. As we have seen in the excised conversation with Darya Shatova, it is Stavrogin who feels possessed by all the ideological "devils" and ultimately sees himself as their source. As it stands, the book merely contains the somewhat feeble assertion, in Stavrogin's suicide note, that "from me nothing has come but negation, with no magnanimity and no force. Even negation has not come from me" (10: 514). This last sentence hardly jibes with Stavrogin's relations with the other characters and may have been included to strengthen the final speech of Stepan Trofimovich. Without the confession chapter, there is no doubt that the book ends somewhat lamely: the reader does not know either that Stavrogin had made a sacrilegious, proto-Nietzchean attempt to transcend the boundaries of good and evil or that his conscience has driven him to the point of madness. His suicide thus loses much of its symbolic-historical meaning as a self-condemnation of all the ideologies he has spawned.

Nevertheless, the scope of his canvas, the brilliant ferocity of his wit, the prophetic power and insight of his satire, his unrivaled capacity to bring to life and embody in characters the most profound and complex moral-philosophical issues and social ideas—all combine to make this "pamphlet-poem" perhaps Dostoevsky's most dazzling creation. It is an unprecedented historical-symbolic drama, intended to encompass all the forces of nineteenth-century Russian culture up to its time, and unlike any other work in the period in Russian or European literature. Even with the flood of such novels in the twentieth century, *Demons* remains unsurpassed as an astonishingly prescient portrayal of the moral quagmires, and the possibilities for self-betrayal of the highest principles, that have continued to dog the revolutionary ideal from Dostoevsky's day down (even more spectacularly) to our own.

PART V

The Mantle of the Prophet, 1871–1881

CHAPTER 46

The Citizen

The Dostoevskys had been living from hand to mouth on advances from Katkov, and with the conclusion of *Demons*, this source of income ceased to exist. Anna was determined to help her husband increase the family income, and the opportunity arose when Dostoevsky turned to publishers for the sale of the rights to *Demons* as an independent volume. He had hoped to net a considerable sum, but the hail of unfavorable criticism lowered the novel's value in the marketplace, and the offers he received were derisory for an important work by a famous author. He and Anna thus decided to publish the book themselves—at last realizing a dream that Dostoevsky had nourished since the mid-1840s. The project was financially risky and might sink them even further into debt, but the rewards were too enticing to resist.

With justifiable pride, Anna describes in her *Reminiscences* how she made presumably innocent inquiries of booksellers and printers about costs, discounts, and so on, carefully concealing her real purpose, and learned the secrets of the trade. The Dostoevskys then published *Demons* on their own, buying the paper, arranging for the printing and binding, and turning out an edition of thirty-five hundred copies. Anna conducted all the negotiations with the buyers, and the Dostoevskys were thus launched as a publishing firm. This was, as Anna writes with satisfaction, "the cornerstone of our joint publishing activity and, after his death, of my own work, which continued for thirty-eight years."[1] When their first edition was sold out, they had earned a profit of four thousand rubles.

Long before he even fancied that he could become a publisher, however, Dostoevsky had thought of another means of rescuing himself from his humiliating wage slavery to editors and publishers. Several times in his correspondence from abroad he had mentioned the idea of a new journalistic publication, and he even worked such a notion into the text of *Demons*. Liza Drozdova, wishing to be "useful" to her country, tells Shatov about her plan for a yearly almanac that would be a selection of facts about Russia, but all chosen in such a way as to convey "an intention, a thought, illuminating all of the whole" (10: 104). As far back as 1864–1865, Dostoevsky had also jotted down notes for a biweekly

---

[1] Anna Dostoevsky, *Reminiscences*, trans. and ed. Beatrice Stillman (New York, 1975), 220.

publication to be called *Notebooks* (*Zapisnye knizhki*). This is clearly the origin of what became his *Diary of a Writer*, and his wife tells us that he was thinking of starting such a publication just at this time. But he was afraid to begin because the economic risks were too great.

Dostoevsky's inclusion into the Meshchersky literary-political circle, though, had already led him to suggest the publication of a yearly almanac of the type mentioned by Liza Drozdova as a supplement to Meshchersky's journal, *The Citizen*, and an announcement of such a supplement appeared in October. In addition, Dostoevsky's participation in revisions of articles written by Meshchersky during the Wednesday evening gatherings at the prince's home allowed him to gradually slip into becoming a member of the journal's editorial board. When an editorial crisis arose in the winter of 1872–1873—Gradovsky, the moderately liberal editor resigned because of the prince's interference in editorial matters—it was only natural that he, the famous writer now freed from the burden of his novel, should be the person to whom all turned in their hour of need.

After obtaining the approval of the press authorities, on December 20 Dostoevsky was confirmed as editor-in-chief of *The Citizen*. A new phase in Dostoevsky's literary activity thus began, whose unexpected ideological twists and turns would surprise both his friends and his enemies during the seven years still remaining to his life. His salary was set at the modest sum of three thousand rubles a year, although he was also to be paid at space rates for all his own contributions. Anna estimates that, for the first time in his literary life, he could count on a regular income, and besides this advantage he now had the opportunity to experiment with his idea for the *Diary of a Writer*. After his long isolation from the Russian literary scene, he savored the chance to make his voice heard on all the social-cultural issues confronting his troubled country.

■

Dostoevsky's appearance in the editorial offices of *The Citizen* is recorded in one of the best memoirs written about him. Twenty-three-year-old Varvara Timofeyeva was then writing a column about social-cultural events in the radical journal *The Spark* and worked as a proofreader in the printing plant producing *The Citizen*. Setting down her recollections, based on notebook entries, in 1904, Timofeyeva gives us a striking picture of Dostoevsky in terms of what may be called his ideological physiognomy at this time of his life, and her own comments help to define the social-cultural climate to which he was then responding.

Word had spread in the printing plant that Dostoevsky was to be the next editor of *The Citizen*, and Timofeyeva could hardly contain her excitement: "At this moment, there would arrive here the famous author of *Poor Folk* and *House of the Dead*, the creator of Raskolnikov and *The Idiot*—he would arrive, and something extraordinary, new would happen to me." What she saw, however, was a middle-aged man who "seemed very tired and perhaps ill." He stood there "with a gloomy, exhausted face, covered like a net with some sort of unusually expressive shadings caused by a tightly restrained movement of the muscles. As if every muscle on this face with sunken cheeks and a broad, high forehead was alive with feeling and thought. And these feelings and thoughts were irresistibly pushing to come to the surface, but not allowed to do so by the iron will of this frail and yet at the same time thick-set, quiet and gloomy man with broad shoulders."[2] Dostoevsky shook hands with his proofreader, bowing slightly, after a formal introduction. "His hand was cold, dry, and as it were lifeless. Indeed, everything about him that day seemed lifeless . . . [his] barely audible voice and lackluster eyes that fastened on me like two immovable dots."[3] He sat silently at his table, reading proof for an hour without uttering a single word; even his pen moved silently over the proof sheets as he made corrections.

By all accounts Dostoevsky was taciturn and secretive with members of the young intelligentsia like Timofeyeva. After the denunciations of *Demons* in the radical and progressive press, he could be certain that he would be looked on with repulsion by them as a renegade from the radical ranks, and she herself bears out such a view of his suspicions. "In liberal literary circles," she writes, "and among the student youth, with whom I had some familiarity, he was unceremoniously called someone 'off his rocker,' or—more delicately—a 'mystic' or 'abnormal' (which, as understood in those days, meant the same thing). This was the time just after the din had died down of the Nechaev trial and the publication of *Demons* in the *Russian Messenger*. We, the young people, had read the speeches of the noted trial lawyers in *The Voice* and the *St. Petersburg News*, and Dostoevsky's novel seemed to us then a monstrous caricature, a nightmare of mystical ecstasies and psychopathology. . . . And after the author of *Demons* assumed the editorship of *The Citizen*, many of his friends and admirers turned against him once and for all."[4]

Even aside from such ideological undercurrents, Dostoevsky proved to be an exacting taskmaster as an editor. He made it clear that he wished his orders to be obeyed without question, even when they were unreasonable or impossible to carry out. "Neither his preemptory tone," writes Timofeyeva, "to which I was totally unaccustomed, nor his peevishly dissatisfied remarks and exasperated anxieties over a wrongly placed comma, fitted in with my image of the writer as *man*, the writer as *sufferer*, the writer as *seer of the human heart*."[5] Indeed, Timofeyeva was deeply shocked one day by an episode involving Mikhail Alexandrov, the

[2] *DVS*, 2: 139.
[3] Ibid., 141.
[4] Ibid., 140.
[5] Ibid., 142.

foreman in charge of typesetting, in which Dostoevsky, flying into a rage at this man's entirely reasonable explanation for not inserting a last-minute change in proof, shouted "like a landowner" (*pro-barski*) to make the change. "'Whether on the wall or on the ceiling, I want [this] printed,' he shrieked," according to Timofeyeva, "his face turning dead-white, his lips twitching spasmodically." Alexandrov answered that he was not capable of such miracles; and at this ironic retort, Dostoevsky thundered that he needed people who would carry out his instructions to the letter "with doglike devotion." (Timofeyeva was outraged by this phrase.) He scribbled off a note on the spot—handing it to the silent and stony-faced Timofeyeva for transmission—demanding that Alexandrov be dismissed immediately. But the insertion was dropped, the note was never passed on, and nothing more was heard about firing Alexandrov.[6] When in 1875 Dostoevsky was making preparations to publish his *Diary of a Writer* as an independent publication, he took great pains to place Alexandrov in charge of its production.

Varvara Timofeyeva only gradually overcame her hostility to Dostoevsky's chilling reserve. The ice was broken late one evening when they were going over the proofs of Dostoevsky's article about an art exhibit in Petersburg, and his analysis of a work of the artist N. N. Ge called *A Mysterious Evening*. This painting represented the Last Supper as if it had taken place in the present ("all the apostles in the picture [were shown] as if they were present-day 'Socialists,'"), and the work was a favorite of the radicals for this reason.[7] Dostoevsky's article criticized this reduction of the great Christian theme to a day in the life of a Russian radical, and Timofeyeva quotes him as writing, "Where is the Messiah, the Savior promised to the world—where is Christ?"[8] Like most of the younger radicals of the 1870s, Timofeyeva had become responsive again to the moral values of Christianity, and she was swept away by the passion of Dostoevsky's eloquence, which aroused memories of the reverence for Christ imbibed during childhood from her mother, "a woman of burning faith." "Suddenly," she recalls, "without knowing why myself, I was irresistibly drawn to look at him . . . Feodor Mikhailovich looked at me intently and point-blank, with an expression that seemed to indicate he had been observing me for some time and waiting for me to turn my glance toward him." The young woman's face must have revealed to Dostoevsky that she had been moved, though neither uttered a word, and when, long after midnight, she came to say good-bye, he stood up, clasped her hands, and spoke to her tenderly as he led her to the door. "You wore yourself out today," he said solicitously. "Hurry home and sleep well. Christ be with you!"[9] Timofeyeva walked home that night filled with joy at having finally

[6] Ibid., 163–164.
[7] Ibid., 144.
[8] Ibid.
[9] Ibid., 145–146.

encountered what she felt to be the *real* Dostoevsky, at last illuminated by the power of his thought and the depth of his feeling.

Although he was always subject to sudden shifts of mood, when he would retreat broodingly into himself, his relations with Timofeyeva became more open and friendly. She depicts him reciting some favorite verses from the poetry of Nikolay Ogarev—verses in which the poet, opening the Bible at random, hopes "That would come to me by the will of fate / The life, and grief, and death of a prophet." Timofeyeva continues: "Feodor Mikhailovich then got up, stepped into the middle of the room, and with flashing eyes and inspired gestures—exactly like a priest before an invisible sacrificial altar—recited for us "The Prophet" of Pushkin, then of Lermontov."[10] For Timofeyeva, it seemed that the poems "were Dostoevsky's own confession. To this day I still hear how he twice repeated: 'I know only—that I can endure / . . . And can endure!—'"[11]

Despite the young radical's growing affection for the seer in her midst, she found some of his pronouncements disconcerting. In the course of an impromptu attack on the danger to Russia of absorbing European influences, he said, "our people are holy in comparison with those over there. . . . [I]n Rome, in Naples, on the streets I was made the most shameful offers—youths, almost children. Disgusting, unnatural vices—and openly, before everybody, and no one even bothered about it. Try to do that amongst us! All our people would condemn it, because for *our* people that's a deadly sin, but there—it's in the customs, a simple habit, nothing more." When Timofeyeva objected that it was not *this* aspect that admirers of the West wished to emulate, he rancorously replied that "there is no other," that "Rome went to pieces because they began to transplant Greece among themselves; beginning with luxuries, fashions, and various sciences and arts, it ends with sodomy and general corruption."[12]

If Timofeyeva objected to the extremity of Dostoevsky's anti-Westernism, she found it even more difficult to accept his literal predictions of apocalyptic doom triggered by recent political events. Lifting up his head from the proofs of an article dealing with Prussia, Bismarck, and the papacy, he declared: "They [radicals] do not suspect that soon everything will come to an end—all their 'progress' and chatter! They have no inkling that the Antichrist has been born . . . and is *coming*—." Dostoevsky, she says, "pronounced this with an expression in his face and voice as if announcing to me a terrible and grandiose secret." When she gingerly expressed some skepticism, he struck the table with his fist and "proclaimed like a mullah in his minaret: 'The Antichrist is coming! It is coming! And the end of the world is closer—closer than they think!'" Timofeyeva

---

[10] The poem of Lermontov is a translation of Byron's "Farewell," first published in 1859. See *DVS*, 2: 517.

[11] *DVS*, 2: 184–185.

[12] Ibid., 179–180.

confesses, with some retrospective embarrassment, that she could not help recalling the opinion about him accepted by her Populist comrades: "ravings, epileptic hallucinations . . . the mania of one idea . . . an obsession."[13]

Timofeyeva had no such negative reaction to another of their dialogues on religious matters, when he asked, "how do you understand the Gospels?" She thought about the matter for the first time and answered, "The realization of the teachings of Christ on earth, in our life, in our conscience." When Dostoevsky expressed disillusionment ("And that's all?"), she thought harder and replied, "No. . . . Not everything finishes here, on earth . . . . All this life on earth is only a step . . . to another existence." "To other worlds!" he exclaimed triumphantly, throwing up his arm to the wide-open window, through which could be seen a bright and luminous June sky.[14]

This revelatory exchange focuses the crux of Dostoevsky's ideological-artistic preoccupations during the 1870s—the conflict between a worldly (Utopian Socialist and Populist) acceptance of Christian morality and one grounded in divine illumination. It is then followed by some poignant words: "'And what a wonderful though tragic task this is—to tell this to the people—' he continued, momentarily hiding his eyes with his hands—'wonderful and tragic because there is so much suffering here. So much suffering, but then—so much grandeur! . . . It's impossible to compare it with any well-being in the world!'"[15] Nowhere else in the Dostoevsky canon do we find another passage expressing so simply and spontaneously his conception of his own creative task and the core values of his theodicy.

———■———

These intimate conversations with Timofeyeva, combined with public expressions of Populist ideas, influenced Dostoevsky's opinion of the new radical generation and led to a softening of the harsh judgment expressed in *Demons*. Through her reactions he could see that there was no longer any *irreconcilable* opposition between the Christian moral values he had defended all through the 1860s and those of the Populists. He could still evoke some responsiveness in the new generation, and this ability was also confirmed by a letter from Vsevolod Solovyev (a son of the famous historian S. M. Solovyev), who wrote Dostoevsky the moment he learned that the novelist was again in Petersburg.

Vsevolod Solovyev, later to become a well-known historical novelist, had just embarked on a career as a journalist. He told Dostoevsky how much his novels had helped to shape his own religious convictions, upheld in arguments with school comrades mouthing the more fashionable doctrines of Nihilist atheism.

[13] Ibid., 180–181.
[14] Ibid., 161–162.
[15] Ibid.

Moreover, despite such differences of opinion, he assured him that these comrades "regard *Crime and Punishment* as one of the best works—yes, but all the same . . . Russian society still does not understand you as it should . . . and listens to your words . . . with confusion and dismay."[16] Dostoevsky was so moved by this tribute that he called on his young admirer a few days later and left his card. Returning the visit, Solovyev soon became Dostoevsky's friend and literary protégé, and no one in the future would support him more staunchly and more consistently in the Russian press. Like Timofeyeva, he helped to relieve Dostoevsky's fear that he had become isolated from the younger generation, whom he hoped to dissuade from embarking on the self-destructive path of social revolution.

Dostoevsky also exchanged letters with Vsevolod's younger brother Vladimir, destined to become the most important Russian philosopher of the turn of the century. A poet as well as a philosopher, Vladimir was a capricious, eccentric, engaging personality with a whimsical sense of humor—a highly intellectualized and spiritualized type of holy fool, which in Russian culture always implies some relation to the religious and sacred. Vladimir had sent an article to *The Citizen* in 1873, with a letter that spoke admiringly of the refusal of the journal to accept "the superstitious reverence" displayed in Russian literature for "the anti-Christian foundations of civilization," a reverence that made any "free judgment of these foundations" impossible.[17] Dostoevsky rejected Vladimir's first article but accepted another a year later after receiving a copy of his master's thesis, *The Crisis in Western Philosophy*. This talented work had caused a considerable stir for its brilliant style, its deep erudition, and its attack on the reigning acceptance of a semiscientific positivism inconsistently mingled with the profession of secularized Christian moral values. He argued that Western rationalism was now bankrupt, and he claimed that the most recent developments of Western thought—Schopenhauer and the then-fashionable Eduard Hartmann's *Philosophy of the Unconscious*—were moving in the direction of a fusion with the truths preserved in the religions of the East, specifically in Eastern Orthodox Christianity.

Like his older brother Vsevolod, Vladimir had gone through an acute radical period under the influence of reading Pisarev. Dostoevsky's novels had been one of the most effective remedies that aided both brothers to overcome their adolescent Nihilism. Vladimir once remarked that among the pages he most admired were certain passages in *Demons*, and these would have been presumably those in which Kirillov traverses the deadly dialectic of attempting to replace the God-man with the Man-god. Indeed, Dostoevsky's unmasking of the mortal

---

[16] *Pisma*, 3: 229.
[17] Cited in *LN* 83 (Moscow, 1971), 331.

26. Vladimir Solovyev

dangers of an unrestrained egoism was decisive for Solovyev's thought, which constantly stresses the importance of attaining a new reconciliation between the atomistic ego, released from the religious bonds of the past, and a revitalized source of absolute moral values.

Dostoevsky, Anna tells us, was very much taken with his young philosopher-admirer, who became a frequent visitor to their home in 1873. He reminded her husband of a friend of his youth, the innerly tormented and tempestuous poet and God-seeker Ivan Shidlovsky, who had played an important role in his own artistic-spiritual formation. "You resemble him to such a degree in appearance and character," he once told Vladimir, "that at certain moments I feel his soul to be living in you."[18] Solovyev's pale, gaunt, and angular face, with large black eyes fixed in a distant stare, was framed by locks of hair falling to his stooping shoulders. His image had been compared with the Christ figure appearing in some Russian icons, and occasionally peasants, often taking him for a priest, would kneel down to obtain his blessing. Preferring a comparison with Italian Renaissance art, Dostoevsky was reminded of the Christ image in one of his favorite pictures from the Dresden Gemäldegalerie, *The Head of the Young Christ* by Carracci.

Solovyev left Russia in June 1875 to study abroad, and there he pored over the theosophic and kabbalistic writings in the British Museum. Presumably under their inspiration, he abruptly embarked on a voyage to Egypt. A mysterious

[18] *Reminiscences*, 223.

revelation, vouchsafed to him in a vision, had assured him that in this land of ancient mystery he would encounter the Divine Sophia, the feminine incarnation of Eternal Wisdom. Learning one day about a tribe in the desert who supposedly had preserved ancient kabbalistic lore, he decided to walk to their camp wearing his usual black-hued European clothes. The local Bedouins took him for some sort of evil spirit, and the story goes that he barely escaped with his life. Solovyev returned unscathed to Russia in July 1876, and became particularly close to Dostoevsky during the very last years of the novelist's life.

———■———

Dostoevsky's duties as editor of *The Citizen* turned out to be far more demanding than he had anticipated, partly because of his own exigent literary standards and partly because the editorial interferences of Meshchersky plagued him as much as they had Gradovsky. Meshchersky was sarcastically known in radical circles as "Prince Full Stop" after having flatly declared in one of his articles that "it is necessary to bring the fundamental reforms [initiated by Alexander II with the liberation of the serfs in 1861] to a full stop." [19]

Dostoevsky's problems as editor were also compounded by the debonair carelessness of Meshchersky about the regulations governing the Russian press. At the end of January 1873, *The Citizen* published an article by the prince in which he directly quoted Alexander II asking the head of a Kirghiz delegation whether he spoke Russian. It was forbidden to cite such august utterances without special permission, and the nonchalant prince, accustomed to chatting with royalty, had neglected to abide by this formality. Legal responsibility fell not on the author but on the editor of the publication, Dostoevsky, who was condemned to pay a fine of twenty-five rubles and spend two days in the guardhouse. His lawyer told him to plead not guilty, and he later commented ironically on the legal advice he was given (and followed) when the violation of the law was perfectly obvious.

No later than the end of his first month as editor, Dostoevsky confesses to his niece Sofya Ivanova that "My time has now shaped up so awfully that I can only curse myself for the resolve with which I suddenly took upon myself the editorship of the journal." [20] He had promised Meshchersky that he would supply the weekly with a column of political commentary, and he wrote to Anna (who had taken the children to Staraya Russa for the summer) that "I have to read through newspapers by the dozens" in order to write such political articles. No wonder he says that "horribly depressing thoughts and . . . dejection . . . [have] overcome me almost to the point of illness at the thought that I have tied myself down to all this hard labor at *The Citizen* for at least another year." [21]

[19] *DVS*, 2: 512.
[20] *PSS*, 29/Bk. 1: 258–259; January 31, 1873.
[21] Ibid., 281–282; July 23, 1873.

Soliciting a contribution from the nationalist historian Mikhail Pogodin, whose staunchly patriotic writings Dostoevsky admired, he complains that the weekly had no secretary to take care of routine business matters, and even more, "my main source of distress is the mountain of topics on which I would like to write myself." "Much needs to be said," he continues, "for which reason I first joined the journal . . . here is my goal and thought: Socialism . . . has corroded an entire generation . . . . We need to fight, because everything has been infected. My idea is that Socialism and Christianity are antitheses. That is what I would like to show in a whole series of pieces, but meanwhile I haven't even started."[22]

The summer of 1873 was a particularly difficult time for Dostoevsky. His editorial duties required him to remain in Petersburg separated from his family in Staraya Russa. His letters are filled with laments about his sadness and loneliness, his (sometimes frightening) dreams about his children, his concern over Anna's health, and the difficulties of making arrangements so he could spend a few days in the country. Recounting a nightmare in which his son Fedya falls from a fourth-floor windowsill, he instructs Anna: "Write me as soon as possible about whether anything happened to Fedya . . . . I believe in second sight, the more so as it is factual, and I won't calm down until I get your letter."[23]

Provided now with an income for his own expenses, Dostoevsky was still constantly in economic straits when the time came to meet the installments for the debts of his deceased brother Mikhail. A due date fell in late July, and he was forced to pawn his watch to pay off this obligation. Some consolation, however, was provided by an evening spent with Pobedonostsev, whose invitation he accepted even though he had felt feverish for a week. He tells Anna gratefully that his host had been very solicitous: "He wrapped me in a blanket; . . . he himself saw me down three flights of stairs, with a candle in his hand, right out to the street entrance." What gratified him even more was the news that the latter had read *Crime and Punishment* with great appreciation "upon the recommendation of a certain person, an admirer of mine very well known to you, whom he accompanied to England." Pobedonostsev had just returned from vacationing on the Isle of Wight with Tsarevich Alexander, who had been the guest of the British royal family. "Consequently," Dostoevsky writes, "things are not as bad as all that. (Please don't chatter about this, darling Anechka)."[24]

Anna returned to Petersburg with the children at the end of August 1873, and Dostoevsky could once again resume the tranquil routine of family life he had so much longed for in their absence. But the anxieties and grueling routine of meeting weekly deadlines never ceased for a moment. If Meshchersky's editorial high-

[22] Ibid., 262; February 26, 1873.
[23] Ibid., 282; July 26, 1873.
[24] Ibid., 284.

handedness provided a constant source of friction, much more serious conflicts arose when they clashed on social-cultural issues. In one instance *The Citizen* became involved in a controversy with the *St. Petersburg News*, and both Dostoevsky and the prince worked on a reply. Meshchersky brought up the question of revolutionary proclamations from abroad circulating in the student milieu; and he suggested that such "distractions" might be circumvented if students lived in dormitories under the surveillance of the authorities. Dostoevsky had no objections to improving student living conditions, but explains in a note to the prince why he unceremoniously struck out seven lines "about the *task* of government surveillance." "I have my reputation as a writer," Dostoevsky states, "and in addition I have children. I do not intend to *destroy* myself." The next sentence, inked out in the original text, has been deciphered: "Besides, your idea is deeply opposed to my convictions and fills my heart with indignation."[25] This last sentence was obviously too impolitic for the rabidly reactionary Prince Full Stop, who, true to form, countered that "I presume you are not of the opinion that the students should be *without* surveillance."[26] Although no answer was given to this challenge, the odious seven lines, which would have ruined Dostoevsky's reputation forever as the partisan of a police state, remained unprinted.

His opinions were clearly not tailored to any official government line, and his independence brought on another clash with the censorship. A widespread famine afflicted several Russian provinces during 1873–1874, and he printed several articles critical of the government's response, especially in the province of Samaria. These articles brought down the wrath of the guardians of the press, who banned the sale of individual copies of *The Citizen*. Only subscribers could receive the weekly, resulting in a considerable loss of revenue. Dostoevsky wrote a fulsomely supplicating letter to a high press official, asking this dignitary to intercede with the Ministry of Internal Affairs, and the ban was lifted a month later.

By the beginning of 1874, the strains and stresses of editing *The Citizen* began to wear on Dostoevsky's health. As Anna notes sadly, "Feodor Mikhailovich, who had to leave the house in every kind of weather . . . and to sit for hours in an overheated proofreading room before each issue went to press, began to catch frequent colds." Consequently, "his slight cough became acute and a shortness of breath appeared"—the beginning of the emphysema that was eventually to cause his death. "Compressed air treatment" was prescribed by his doctor, and "Feodor Mikhailovich would sit under the bell [the apparatus placed over his head] for two hours at a time, three times a week." Even though "the treatment was very beneficial," it "made the fulfillment of his editorial duties all the more difficult."[27]

[25] Ibid., 307; November 12, 1873.
[26] Ibid., 519.
[27] *Reminiscences*, 226.

In March 1874 Dostoevsky finally served the sentence condemning him to two days' detention in a guardhouse. A. F. Koni, an official in the Ministry of Justice who was an admirer, arranged that the date be set at Dostoevsky's convenience. The guardhouse was in the center of Petersburg, and Anna brought her husband a suitcase with "overnight necessities." "He asked whether the children had missed him, and wanted me to give them some goodies for him and tell them he had gone to Moscow for toys."[28] Anna enlisted Maikov to visit Dostoevsky the next day, and he in turn contacted Vsevolod Solovyev, who also dropped in. Solovyev found the prisoner sitting at a small table in a spacious and "reasonably clean room, drinking tea, rolling and smoking cigarettes,"[29] and perusing a copy of Hugo's *Les misérables* borrowed from Timofeyeva.

The imprisonment evidently revived memories of his confinement in the Peter-and-Paul Fortress almost a quarter of a century earlier. The two men had not seen each other recently, and the younger one complained of suffering from apathy. The best treatment, Dostoevsky insisted, was the one that fate had imposed on him—a sudden change, the shock of new situations and the need to adjust to a new environment. "When I found myself in the fortress, I thought: this is the end, I thought I wouldn't hold out for three days, and—suddenly I calmed down. . . . Oh, that was a great happiness for me: Siberia and the *katorga*. People say: horror, resentment, they speak of the rightness of some sort of resentment! What awful nonsense! Only there did I have a healthy, happy life, I understood myself there, my dear fellow. . . . I understood Christ. . . . I understood Russian man and felt that I was a Russian myself, that I was one of the Russian people."[30]

Such words cannot be taken as even a remotely adequate account of Dostoevsky's experiences after his arrest and during his years in prison camp. They convey, rather, the sense of triumph over the hardships he had been forced to endure, and the transformation of his personality and convictions that had resulted from these years. He emerged from the ordeal of his mock execution with an ecstatic sense of the infinite value of life, and he recalls this epiphanic moment to Solovyev as their talk continued. "Ah, life is a wonderful thing. . . . In every incident, in every object, in every word there is so much happiness!"[31] In conclusion, asking his admirer to visit Anna and assure her that he was in the best of spirits, he cautioned him to speak softly. If the servants heard that their master was under arrest, they would conclude that he was probably guilty of theft.

This event certainly played its part in Dostoevsky's surrender of the editorship on April 1, 1874. There was as well the steady accumulation of internal rea-

[28] Ibid., 227.
[29] *DVS*, 2: 211–213.
[30] Ibid.
[31] Ibid., 213.

sons connected with editorial policy. "You ask what I've been doing," he writes to Pogodin in November 1873. "I keep being sick and flying into rages. My hands are somewhat tied. In tackling the editorship a year ago, I imagined that I would be much more independent."[32] The impossibility to write anything nonjournalistic also proved a continual torment. Early in his editorship he had told Pogodin that "the shapes of stories and novels swarm in my head and take shape in my heart. . . . I see that all my time is taken up with the journal . . . and I am driven to repentance and despair."[33] Adding to his distress was the prevailing hostility toward *The Citizen*. All the other journals of the time, Vsevolod Solovyev explains, criticized *The Citizen* harshly and even coarsely. "On the new editor, a stupid and vulgar mockery rained down from all sides. The author of *Crime and Punishment* and *House of the Dead* was called a madman, a maniac, a renegade, a traitor; the public were even invited to visit the show at the Academy of Art and contemplate the portrait of Dostoevsky painted by Perov as prime proof that here was such a madman, whose place was in a home for the feebleminded."[34] One can well understand his desire to escape from this unremitting hail of invective.

However, Dostoevsky's year-and-a-half term as editor was far from entirely negative, and a conversation relayed by Timofeyeva discloses the mutation of sensibility that occurred at this time. Telling her of his intention to resign and to begin work on a new novel, Dostoevsky suggested that she ask her Populist friends at *Notes of the Fatherland* whether they would have room for such a novel next year. For the author of *Demons* even to *think* of publishing in the most prominent of the left-wing journals of the time certainly indicated an astonishing change of front! When the question was posed by Timofeyeva to G. Z. Eliseev, the same radical publicist who had once accused Dostoevsky of slandering Russian students in *Crime and Punishment*, he replied "with the friendliest voice: 'Of course, let him send it along. We'll always find a place for him.'"[35] Dostoevsky's next novel, *A Raw Youth* (*Podrostok*), thus was serialized in the pages of *Notes of the Fatherland*—to the astonishment of all and to the dismay of his closest and oldest friends.

[32] *PSS*, 29/Bk. 1: 308; November 12, 1873.
[33] Ibid., 262; February 26, 1873.
[34] *DVS*, 2: 209.
[35] Ibid.

CHAPTER 47

Narodnichestvo: Russian Populism

Dostoevsky's surprising desire to offer his next novel to the leading Populist journal, *Notes of the Fatherland*—edited by the poet Nekrasov and the deadly satirist Saltykov-Shchedrin, who had mercilessly pilloried him in the 1860s—is a direct outcome of the young intelligentsia's shift to an ideology known as *narodnichestvo*, or Russian Populism. This new tendency in radical ideology peaked during the Nechaev trial, whose effect was to destroy the Utilitarian morality (or lack of anything that could be called morality) of the 1860s. There is ample evidence that the stirring speeches made not only by the defense attorneys but also by some of the defendants in the name of liberty and justice produced a rousing effect on the student youth who flocked to the courtroom and jammed the benches. For many, as one contemporary wrote, "those being tried appeared as fighters struggling to free the people from the oppression of the government. The youth surrendered to the fascination of the battle for the ideas of truth and justice *and tried to find a better path for bringing them into being*"[1] than had been offered by Nechaevism.

The nationwide newspaper coverage revealed the tactics of Nechaev in all their sinister details, which led to a horrified revulsion even among those who sympathized with his aims. The considerable memoir literature left by the survivors of the Populist movement returns again and again to their sense of outrage when they learned the truth. Vera Figner, for example, wrote that Nechaev's "theory—that the end justifies the means—repelled us, and the murder of Ivanov filled us with disgust."[2] (Nonetheless, she was later to become a member of the executive committee of the terrorist organization People's Will, which planned the assassination of Alexander II.)

The circles of radical youth that began to form now took the lessons of Nechaevism to heart and avoided any temptation to disregard morality in the higher interest of the revolutionary cause. Prince Peter Kropotkin—the scion of an ancient noble family destined for a distinguished career at the imperial court, who became instead both a noted scientist and an anarchist and

---

[1] Cited in B. S. Itenberg, *Dvizhenie revolyutsionnogo narodnichestvo* (Moscow, 1965), 136.
[2] Ibid., 136–137.

revolutionary—belonged to one of these circles (the Chaikovsky group) and left a portrait of its dominating ethos. "The circle of self-education of which I am speaking was constituted in opposition to the methods of Nechaev. The few friends [in the circle] had judged, quite correctly, that a morally developed individuality must be the foundation of every organization . . . whatever program of action it may adopt in the course of future events."[3] His remarks stress the new moral and ethical dimension that had now come to the fore in radical self-awareness.

The younger generation thus abandoned the Utilitarian morality preached by the dominating ideologists of the Nihilist 1860s, such as Chernyshevsky and Dobrolyubov, and especially reacted against Pisarev, who had encouraged a contemptuous elitism among the intelligentsia toward the people and envisaged the only hope of progress as lying in the self-cultivation of the educated youth through the study of science. When such ideas were combined with Pisarev's panegyric to the glories of personal self-fulfillment and rampant individualism, the *Pisarevschina* of the late 1860s opened the way for a slackening of the moral idealism that had marked the activities of the intelligentsia so notably in the earlier part of the decade.

This complex of ideas and attitudes was sharply attacked in Peter Lavrov's *Historical Letters* (1869–1870), which became a major source of inspiration for the *narodnik* (Populist) intelligentsia of the 1870s. During the student disorders at the University of St. Petersburg in 1862, Lavrov, an ex-artillary colonel who had taught mathematics at various military academies, encouraged the rebellious youth by addressing one of their turbulent meetings in full military regalia. Later arrested and stripped of his rank after the 1865 attempt on the life of Alexander II (in which he had no part), he was sent to live in a poverty-stricken village in the northern district of Vologda. There he wrote his letters and published them legally under a pseudonym. He escaped abroad after a few years and continued his career as an important, highly respected scholar and publicist who participated actively in the European radical movement. A good friend of Karl Marx, he became the editor and chief contributor of a radical Russian émigré review, *Forward* (*Vpered*), writing both as a commentator on Russian affairs and as a learned historian of social thought.

Lavrov's *Historical Letters* compose a sweeping, essayistic survey whose theme is the rise of civilization from barbarism. In the immediate Russian context, his most influential idea is contained in his fourth letter, "The Cost of Progress," which assesses the exorbitant price paid in human suffering for the advancement of civilization. He stresses the "debt" that cultivated minorities (the Russian intelligentsia) owe to the suffering millions (the Russian peasantry) who have toiled

[3] Peter Kropotkin, *Memoirs of a Revolutionist* (Garden City, NY, 1962), 201.

through the centuries to provide them with the means for their self-cultivation. How can this debt be absolved? "I shall relieve myself of responsibility for the bloody cost of my own development," writes Lavrov, "if I utilize this same development to diminish evil in the present and in the future."[4]

These words produced an electrifying effect on a whole generation of Russian youth, who were dispiritedly groping for a positive moral ideal. N. S. Rusanov, later an important publicist, experienced their galvanizing shock as a young student:

> At one time we had been attracted to Pisarev, who told us of the great utility of the natural sciences in making a "thinking realist" out of men. . . . [W]e wished to live in the name of our "cultivated egoism," rejecting all authority and making our goal a free and happy life for ourselves and for those who shared our ideas. And suddenly [Lavrov's] little book tells us that there are other things besides the natural sciences. The anatomy of frogs by itself does not take us very far [an allusion to Bazarov in Turgenev's *Fathers and Children*, who spends his time dissecting frogs]. . . . There are the people, the hungry masses, worn out by labor, working people who themselves support the whole edifice of civilization solely to make it possible for us to study frogs. . . . How ashamed we were of our miserable bourgeois plans for a happy personal life! To the devil with "rational egoism" and "thinking realism." . . . Henceforth our lives must belong wholly to the masses, and only by dedicating all our strength to the triumph of social justice could we appear anything but fraudulent bankrupts before our country and before all mankind.[5]

Such was the self-sacrificing mood in which the educated youth "went to the people" in the early 1870s, and what they expected to find in the Russian villages was not only absolution from the sin of their privileges but also a morally superior form of life, a primitive Socialist Arcadia far preferable to the supposedly more advanced countries of the West.

If Lavrov had inspired the educated youth with a sense of guilt about their own advantages, another Populist thinker, Nikolay Mikhailovsky, persuaded them that the Russian village and the Russian peasant harbored unsuspected treasures that should not be lightly surrendered to the march of "progress." Mikhailovsky, who enjoyed enormous prestige in the 1870s, was a member of the editorial board and a regular contributor to *Notes of the Fatherland*, and his monthly column was eagerly devoured. His credentials with the new generation had been established by a small book, *What Is Progress?*, which appeared shortly

---

[4] P. L. Lavrov, "The Cost of Progress," in *Russian Philosophy*, ed. J. M. Edie, J. P. Scanlan, and M. B. Zeldin, 3 vols. (Chicago, 1964), 2: 141.

[5] Cited in Itenberg, *Dvizhenie revolyutsionnogo narodnichestvo*, 83.

after Lavrov's *Letters*. These reflections are a product of that widespread disillusionment with the West, particularly France, produced among Russian progressives by the failure of the revolutions of 1848, the assumption of power by Napoleon III, and the ferocious suppression of the Paris Commune in the aftermath of the Franco-Prussian War. Taking up a refrain to which Herzen had first given voice after 1848, and which Dostoevsky had echoed in his *Winter Notes on Summer Impressions* in 1863, Mikhailovsky argued that a decadent Western civilization could no longer serve as a lodestar to the left-leaning Russians eagerly seeking the way toward a more just social-economic order.

Such disenchantment found eloquent expression in Mikhailovsky's notable critique of "progress" as this concept was understood in Europe. Employing the ideas of Charles Darwin and the then-famous Herbert Spencer, but turning them to his own purposes, Mikhailovsky maintained that progress should be measured in terms of the richness and diversity of human life that it furthered, not solely by the accumulating production of material goods. Understood only in this latter sense, as was the case in Europe, progress could well destroy the integrity of all individual life still preserved in less developed social forms (that is, the Russian village). The so-called "objective" scientific laws governing society—the laws worked out in Western social thought—offer no help in choosing between these two notions of progress, and Mikhailovsky argued that a "subjective" (moral) criterion must be introduced in favor of the protection of the individual personality.

Thus Lavrov and Mikhailovsky rejected the worship of "science"—so typical of the Nihilism of the 1860s—as the ultimate basis of human values; they firmly broke with ideas that left no independent room (at least in theory) for the human personality and hence for morality. For these thinkers, as much earlier for Kant, science determines the laws of the physical world but not of human desires and ideals. Lavrov made a direct appeal to the moral sensibility of the intelligentsia as the basis for his radicalism; and Mikhailovsky too, in his Slavophil-tinged critique of progress, used "subjective" moral criteria as the justification for his distaste of its Western avatar. Such aspects of Populist thought were much closer to Dostoevsky's own views than anything he had encountered previously among radical ideologues.

One of the dogmas of radical ideology in the 1860s, expounded most intransigently by Chernyshevsky, was a monistic materialism—supposedly the last word in "scientific" thought—that excluded the possibility of any such entity as "free will." For Dostoevsky, it was a moral-psychological *necessity* of the human personality to experience itself as free, and he now found in the key Populist texts a decisive affirmation of precisely what he had maintained all along—and what Nihilism had declared to be nonexistent. "I take as my point of departure," affirmed Lavrov, "the fact of the consciousness of freedom, and on the foundation of these facts I construct a coherent system of moral process."[6] Similarly, Mikhailovsky wrote that "society obeys certain laws in its development; but no less unquestionable is man's inherent consciousness of a free choice of action. At the moment of action I am aware that I give myself a goal freely, completely independent of the influence of historical conditions."[7]

Like Dostoevsky ten years earlier, the generation of the 1870s now explicitly rejected the incongruous attempt to extract a morality of obligation out of "rational egoism," and no one attacked it more incisively than Mikhailovsky. "Clinging to this formula," Mikhailovsky argued, "we lost sight of the fact that, in the first place, the extension of our personal ego to the point of self-sacrifice, to the possibility of identification with an alien life—is just as real as the crudest egoism. And that, in the second place, the formula that sacrifice is sheer nonsense does not at all cover our own psychic situation, for more than ever before we are ready to make the most extreme sacrifices."[8] After such a passage, it is no surprise to learn that the critic had read *Crime and Punishment* with great admiration.

This revival among the Populists of a sensitivity to the ethics of self-sacrifice, so movingly dramatized in that work, went hand in hand with a renewed respect for Christianity itself. In a speech given in 1872, Mikhailovsky explained that "the ancient world knew nothing of the idea of personality. Man as something beyond fixed castes, layers, and nationalities meant nothing to antiquity. . . . Christianity gave a completely new characteristic to history. It brought forth the thought of the absolute worth of man and human personality . . . henceforth, for all people, in spite of delays, mistakes, and wanderings, there is but one goal: the absolute recognition of man, of human personality, and of its many-sided development."[9] Such a positive view of Christianity by a spokesman for the radicals would have been inconceivable in the 1860s, but now he identifies his own social-cultural ideal—a Populist Socialism based on the supreme value of the human personality—with the emergence of Christianity as a world religion.

Such a revaluation of Christianity was typical of the mood of the entire generation for whom Mikhailovsky had become a spokesman. D. N. Ovsyaniko-Kulikovsky, the great turn-of-the-century historian of the Russian intelligentsia, accordingly stressed that what distinguished the Populists of the 1870s from the previous generation was, above all, their "psychological religiosity." "In place of the one-sided attraction for the physical sciences appeared a lively interest in social, economic, and historical questions—in particular, for the history of the movements of the people, in the *Raskol* [the religious dissenters] and the sects.

[6] Cited in V. V. Zenkovsky, *A History of Russian Philosophy*, trans. G. L. Kline, 2 vols. (London, 1953), 1: 354.

[7] Ibid., 369.

[8] N. K. Mikhailovsky, *Polnoe sobranie sochinenii*, 10 vols. (St. Petersburg, 1909), 4: 38–39.

[9] Quoted in James H. Billington, *Mikhailovsky and Russian Populism* (Oxford, 1958), 131–132.

The indifferentism and skepticism in religion, which so sharply marked the 'Pisarevist' tendency, notably declined. Unconcerned with dogmatic religion, with official religion, the new generation displayed an unmistakable interest in the Gospels, in Christian ethics, and in Christ the man."[10]

Mikhailovsky helped to infuse the Populist mentality with Proudhonian ideas, which translate the messianic hopes of the Christian faith into modern, secularized terms. N. V. Sokolov, a friend of Mikhailovsky's who was arrested and tried in the mid-1860s for a book called *The Heretics*, declared in open court that "the entire guilt of the heretic Socialists consists in the fact that they seek the Kingdom of God not in the clouds but on earth." "Silence me," he told his judges, "if you find in my words any perversion of the commandment of Christian love of neighbor. I know only that none of you loves Christ more than I."[11] Dostoevsky had accepted a similar view of Socialism in the 1840s, and a copy of Proudhon's *La célébration du dimanche* was found in his room at the time of his arrest in 1849. Whether or not he had read statements like those of Sokolov, the spirit they conveyed was familiar from his own past and was omnipresent in the Russian culture of the 1870s.

———■———

Narodnichestvo could thus hardly have failed to evoke a sympathetic response from Dostoevsky, who joined here with the Slavophils as well as the Populists. All were alarmed at the growth of capitalism in the country, and regarded the existing social-economic institutions of the peasantry (and hence the way of life and the ethos from which they sprang) as uniquely valuable and precious *in themselves and in their present form*. The most essential task of the Populists, particularly in face of the increasing pace of industrialization, was to protect peasant life from the forces leading to the disintegration of the commune. "In Russia," Mikhailovsky had declared in 1872, reversing the earlier thrust of Russian radicalism, "only the *preservation* of the means of labor in the hands of the workers is required, a guarantee to the present proprietors [the peasants] of their property."[12] As far back as 1850, Dostoevsky had agreed with the Slavophils that European conceptions of a workers' revolution had no relevance to Russian social conditions, and Mikhailovsky was now presumably agreeing with such views, in effect renouncing social-political revolution in favor of safeguarding the economic interests of the peasantry.

Even though the Populists now accepted the Christian virtue of self-sacrifice, which for Dostoevsky lay at the root of the peasant *obshchina* in a socially

[10] D. N. Ovsyaniko-Kulikovsky, "Istoria Russkoi intelligentsii," in *Sobranie sochinenii*, 10 vols. (St. Petersburg, 1910–1911), vol. 8, part 2, 197.

[11] Quoted in Billington, *Mikhailovsky*, 132.

[12] Ibid., 67–68.

modified form, they preferred to cast their ideas in more contemporary terms. Mikhailovsky thus worked out his own "sociological" variant of the pervasive myth that peasant life was valuable in its own right. The criterion of progress, he argued, should be the achievement in human life of the most harmonious and well-rounded personality. From this point of view, although Europe had reached a higher "stage" of social development than Russia, the Russian peasant represented a "higher type" of humanity than his counterpart, the European industrial worker. The Russian peasant, in accomplishing his daily tasks, employed all of his diverse physical and mental capacities and thus remained an integral individual; the European industrial worker, ever more splintered by the refinements of the division of labor, had been literally reduced to a dehumanized cog. In his still privately cherished ideology of *pochvennnichestvo*, Dostoevsky had looked forward to the Europeanized intelligentsia returning to the values embodied in their native soil to create a new and richer synthesis, and the aim of Populism was to safeguard the unique worth embodied in the superior type of life of the Russian peasant, raising it to a higher "stage" without destroying its irreplaceable virtues.

Even though *pochvennichestvo* and *narodnichestvo* cannot simply be equated, the similarity in overall perspective—particularly the quasi-Slavophil disaffection with European civilization—is nonetheless evident. Mikhailovsky had been appalled by Marx's depiction of "primitive accumulation," the process by which the English yeomen had been forced from the land in order to create an industrial proletariat dependent on wage labor. "Reason and moral feeling did not influence the economic development of Europe," he had indignantly declared to advocates of Russia's industrial expansion along European lines.[13] To exorcise the monstrous image of evil displayed in the Crystal Palace of the London World's Fair, Dostoevsky had likewise appealed to the moral values still preserved at the roots of Russian life. Mikhailovsky now wrote that "we not only do not scorn Russia, but we see in its past, and still in its present, much on which we can rely to ward off the falsities of European civilization."[14]

The activity of the Populists in the early 1870s could well have seemed to Dostoevsky a more than coincidental response to everything he had been advocating in his books. A classic description of their aims and ideals in the spring of 1874 can be found again in the memoirs of Prince Kropotkin. The primary concern of all, he writes, was to find the answer to one important question:

> In what way could they be useful to the masses? Gradually, they came to the idea that the only way was to settle among the people, and to live the people's life. Young men came to the villages as doctors, doctor's helpers,

[13] Ibid., 67.
[14] Ibid., 66.

village scribes, even as agricultural laborers, blacksmiths, woodcutters. . . . Girls passed teacher's examinations, learned midwifery or nursing, and went by the hundreds to the villages, devoting themselves to the poorest part of the population. These people went without any idea of social reconstruction in mind, or any thought of revolution. They simply wanted to teach the mass of the peasants to read, to instruct them in other things, to give them medical help, and in this way to aid in raising them from their darkness and misery, and to learn at the same time what were *their* popular ideals of a better social life.[15]

This picture is a little too idyllic, although it can be accepted as a firsthand account of the deeply altruistic mood in which the young Populists went to the people. Their aim was also to "raise the consciousness" of the people and to prepare the way for revolution. Some groups, influenced by Bakunin, were convinced that only a spark was necessary to ignite a raging fire of revolt among the descendants of Pugachev and Stenka Razin, and they were disappointed to find the Russian folk so distressingly immune to their incendiary rhetoric. The peasants on the whole would have little truck with these educated youth, who mysteriously appeared in their midst awkwardly garbed in peasant clothes, and they loyally reported them to the police. Dostoevsky had prophesied just such a reaction in the concluding pages of *Demons*, when his pathetic innocent, Stepan Verkhovensky, decided to "go to the people" about whom he had been prating all his life.

All of literate Russia was emotionally stirred by this moral crusade, which suddenly, and apparently spontaneously, moved thousands of the finest youth to "give up their riches" (many came from wealthy and highly placed families) and "go to the people." The minister of justice, Count Pahlen, noted in surprise that many respectable families helped their own children embark on this irresistible outpouring of effort to realize the Christian ideal of love, the ideal of aiding and comforting those who suffer. S. M. Kravchinsky, a participant who was scarcely a sentimentalist (a few years later he would stab to death in broad daylight the head of the Russian secret police), spoke of the movement as hardly anything "that could be called political. It was rather some sort of crusading procession, distinguished by the totally infectious and all-embracing character of a religious movement. People sought not only the attainment of a definite practical goal, but at the same time the satisfaction of a deep need for personal moral purification."[16]

Dostoevsky could well have discerned in what he heard of these events—and all of Russian society was abuzz with rumors about them—the beginning of a realization of his own social-political ideal. For the Populist youth were not only

[15] Kropotkin, *Memoirs*, 199.
[16] Quoted in V. Bogucharsky, *Aktivnoe narodnichestvo semidesyatikh godov* (Moscow, 1912), 179.

concerned to educate and arouse the people, they also wished to be educated themselves, to assimilate to them, learn about their values and beliefs. Dostoevsky had always dreamed of such a fusion between the intelligentsia and the people, and he could well have believed, during the mad spring and summer of 1874, that the longed-for day had finally dawned. But if so, a major article of Mikhailovsky's on *Demons* in *Notes of the Fatherland* revealed the gulf between the radicals and himself that would never be bridged.

Taking pains to treat Dostoevsky with respect as "one of the most talented of our contemporary writers," Mikhailovsky focuses his critique on Dostoevsky's depiction of Russian radicalism as the end product of the disintegrating European influence on Russian culture. As Dostoevsky saw it, the Russian educated classes had become detached from the Russian people and simultaneously from the people's religion, and had thus lost the capacity to distinguish between good and evil. Hence they were inevitably doomed to the destruction depicted in *Demons*. Mikhailovsky objects, however, that it is not necessary to share the religious convictions of the people in order to accept the moral values embodied in their way of life. Dostoevsky, he points out, uses the word "God" in *Demons* sometimes to mean a supreme being and sometimes as a synonym for "national particularities" and national customs, thus identifying attachment to the Russian people with religious faith. But this theory is "simply impossible," and Mikhailovsky carefully disengages the question of religion from that of the relation between the intelligentsia and the people.[17]

For the novelist, there is only the unequivocal condemnation of the intelligentsia pronounced in *Demons* or the equally unequivocal and uncritical glorification of the people in his journalistic pieces. Dostoevsky is "a happy man," Mikhailovsky writes enviously. "He knows that whatever happens with the people, in the end it will save itself and us."[18] All those who do not share this faith in the people, with all their customs and beliefs, are called *citoyens* by Dostoevsky, the French appellation stressing their alienation from their native soil. But whatever the past, Mikhailovsky goes on, it is a mistake to overlook the new group of *citoyens* (the Populists), who, while sharing his reverence for "the Russian people's truth," nonetheless find the traditions of this "truth" contradictory and confusing; they accept only that part which coincides with the general principles of "humanity" acquired from other sources (the ideals of social justice embodied in Western Socialism). Indeed, as Mikhailovsky penetratingly remarks, Dostoevsky does the very same thing himself in many instances, though refusing to acknowledge that he arbitrarily identifies his own humane values with "the Russian people's truth."

[17] *Sochineniya N. K. Mikhailovskogo*, 7 vols. (St. Petersburg, 1888), 2: 272–273.
[18] Ibid., 304.

In a passage that became famous and echoes Lavrov, Mikhailovsky writes that these *citoyens* are willing to forgo agitating for legal and political rights, which would benefit only themselves as members of the educated class, and work for social reforms of immediate benefit to the people. "Giving the preference to social reforms over political ones," Mikhailovsky explains, "we are only renouncing the strengthening of our rights and the development of our freedom as instruments for the oppression of the people and even further sin."[19] Admonishing Dostoevsky directly, he writes: "If you would stop playing with the word 'God' and become acquainted somewhat more closely with your shameful Socialism, you would be convinced that it coincides with at least some of the elements of the Russian people's truth." Rather than attack those who now share a common reverence for the people and their "truth," he urges Dostoevsky to look around and pay attention to all the new "devils" that have recently emerged to plague the country:

> Russia, that frenzied invalid you have depicted, is being girded with railroads, besprinkled with factories and banks—and in your novel there is not a single indication of this world! You focus your attention on an insignificant handful of madmen and scoundrels! There is no devil of national wealth [industrial expansion at the expense of the welfare of the people] in your novel, the most widespread devil of all and less than all the others knowing the boundaries of good and evil.[20]

Acknowledging the impact of Mikhailovsky's article in the very next issue of *The Citizen*, Dostoevsky called it "a new revelation for me" (21: 156). Dostoevsky was touched by the gravity of Mikhailovsky's tone, with its deeply felt expression of the Populists' desire to sacrifice themselves on behalf of the people. But he had no illusions concerning the major point on which he and the Populists would continue to differ, and he put his finger on the crucial bone of contention between them, no matter how much their views might otherwise coincide. "But to write and assert that Socialism is not atheistic," he admonished Mikhailovsky, "and that atheism is not its central, fundamental essence—that surprises me extremely" (21: 157).

Just about this time (1873) the antagonism between radicalism and religious faith had been resoundingly proclaimed by a resolution of the Slavic section of the First International. Under the influence of Bakunin, it had declared itself in favor of "atheism and materialism" and had pledged "to fight against any kind of divine worship, against all official religious confessions and . . . to endeavor to eradicate the idea of divinity in all its manifestations."[21] "Socialism—this is also

[19] Ibid., 306–307.
[20] Ibid.
[21] Quoted in Itenberg, *Dvizhenie revolyutsionnogo narodnichestvo*, 346.

Christianity," Dostoevsky had jotted down in his notebooks (1872–1875), "but it proposes that it can succeed with reason."[22] Such words indicate his awareness of the Christian inspiration underlying Populist Socialism, but pinpoint what he felt to be its self-contradiction.

In one of the most arresting of Dostoevsky's articles, "One of Today's False-hoods" (in which he aimed to free himself from the cloud hanging over his name as regards *Demons*), Dostoevsky focused on the atheism stemming from David Strauss for the purposes of his covert argument with the Populists. "People will tell me, perhaps . . . that, for example, even if Strauss does hate Christ and has set himself as his life's goal the mocking of Christianity, he nevertheless worships humanity as a whole and his teaching is as elevated and noble as can be." He is willing to admit that "the goals of all today's leaders of progressive European thought are philanthropic and magnificent." But he is also convinced of something else, which he expresses in a powerful peroration that now seems remarkably clairvoyant: "If you were to give all these grand, contemporary teachers full scope to destroy the old society and build it anew, the result would be such obscurity, such chaos, something so crude, blind, and inhuman that the whole structure would collapse to the sound of humanity's curses before it could even be completed. Once having rejected Christ, the human heart can go to amazing lengths. That's an axiom" (21: 132–133). Dostoevsky was thus arguing that even those who regarded Socialism as an updating of Christian ideals—as the Populists had begun to do again—were not immune from the temptations of Nechaevism, even though they had rejected the Utilitarianism basis of his tactics.

———■———

Nonetheless, because the Russian Populists no longer linked atheism to a rejection of Christian morality or the teachings of Christ *as such*, there will be a noticeable shift of accent in Dostoevsky's relation to this new brand of radicalism. He will treat it with a mildness of tone in sharp contrast with his polemics of the 1860s, and his artistic notice will no longer be on figures like the underground man (who denies the possibility of *any* kind of morality, on Nihilist principles) or like Raskolnikov and Stavrogin, who replace Christian conscience with a Utilitarian calculus or with a proto-Nietzschean theory of amoral indifferentism beyond good and evil. The Populists had now come around to accepting the Christian values of "the Russian people's truth," and so he believed he could appeal to them in terms of a morality they would not automatically reject.

Dostoevsky had always insisted that the Russian knows in his heart of hearts that he has sinned; the European, on the other hand, complacently accepts malfeasance as perfectly justified. In this context, Dostoevsky famously asserted: "I

[22] See *LN* 83 (Moscow, 1971), 290.

think that the principal and most basic spiritual need of the Russian people is the need for suffering, incessant and unslakeable suffering, everywhere and in everything. I think the Russian people have been infused with this need from time immemorial. . . . There is always an element of suffering even in the happiness of the Russian people, and without it their happiness is incomplete" (21: 36). The Russian people's imputed "love of suffering" meant a desire for moral and spiritual redemption, which in the end would gain the upper hand over the evils of the present time.

His great ambition had always been to reconcile the refractory and radicalized younger generation, if not to the existing conditions of Russian life, then to the government that, as he was convinced, offered the only possibility of changing such conditions for the better. This new basis for dialogue thus offered him an unrivaled opportunity, which he sought to utilize by publishing his next work in Mikhailovsky's own journal, *Notes of the Fatherland*. The weakest link in the Populists' ideology was their willingness to revere "the Russian people's truth" while refusing to accept the root of this "truth" in the people's inherited belief in Christ as the divine God-man. How could the Populists idolize the people without also adhering to the religious faith from which all the people's moral values sprang and which for Dostoevsky provided their only firm anchorage? The theme of the necessity for religious faith takes on a new importance and intensity in the novels of this last period and is conspicuously placed in the foreground. To be sure, it had always been present, but subordinated to a defense of the Christian ethics of love and self-sacrifice against Nihilist onslaughts.

Dostoevsky and the Populists would continue to diverge on this fateful question of religious faith, although enough points of contact remained for him to acquire a unique status as someone who, despite his loyalty to the tsar, managed to transcend a narrow factionalism. And he tried to use this eminence, as the 1870s wore on, to ward off the catastrophe that loomed closer and closer for his country as the once peaceful, apolitical Populists turned to terror out of despair.

CHAPTER 48

Bad Ems

Dostoevsky resigned from *The Citizen* in April 1874, and it was shortly afterward that an unexpected event occurred: Nekrasov called on his former friend. Anna was aware of their recent estrangement, and when her husband invited his visitor into his study she could not resist eavesdropping on their conversation. What she heard was an offer from Nekrasov for Dostoevsky to contribute a new novel to *Notes of the Fatherland* during the next year, at "a payment of two hundred and fifty rubles per folio sheet, while until this time Dostoevsky had gotten only a hundred and fifty."[1] When he went to consult Anna, she impetuously told him to accept even before he could pose the question. Dostoevsky, however, went to Moscow to first determine whether Katkov, who had supported him so loyally for so long, wished to acquire his new novel for the *Russian Messenger*. Katkov consented to the higher rate per folio sheet but demurred at a large advance, and Dostoevsky was thus released from any obligation.

Around this time, a Russian specialist, Professor Koshlakov, had advised Dostoevsky that his emphysema could be alleviated by a six-week stay at the spa of Bad Ems, whose mineral waters were famous for their curative powers. At the beginning of June he thus left Staraya Russa for Petersburg and spent a few days looking after urgent matters before undertaking his journey abroad. One such case involved the estate of his late aunt, the wealthy A. F. Kumanina, who had given Dostoevsky and his brother Mikhail ten thousand rubles each in 1864 and then excluded them from her will. Both Dostoevsky and Mikhail's widow were contesting the exclusion. In a letter a month earlier to his younger brother Nikolay, an engineer given to drink and often aided by his older brother, Dostoevsky put pressure on him to sign a statement, as one of the heirs, renouncing any claim to the money given to the brothers. "Otherwise," he writes, "don't bother to have any dealings with me at all,"[2] and Nikolay promptly complied.

Even though he was disappointed to find that only two copies of *The Idiot* had been sold at the offices of *The Citizen*, which served as a depot for the Dostoevsky publishing firm, he was heartened when he ran into a publisher named

---

[1] Anna Dostoevsky, *Reminiscences*, trans. and ed. Beatrice Stillman (New York, 1975), 228.
[2] *PSS*, 29/Bk. 1: 319; May 5, 1874.

M. P. Nadein. "Nadein," he writes Anna, "proposed to me definitely to publish a complete edition of my works . . . and all just for 5 percent, and as soon as he collects it, the whole edition will belong to me." In Dostoevsky's view, his literary stock had just risen because "the booksellers have gotten somewhat excited by Orest Miller's . . . articles about me in *Nedelya* [*The Week*], in the end very laudatory."[3] These articles form a part of the volume *Russian Literature since Gogol,* and *The Week* was a journal with both marked Populist and Slavophil sympathies. Nadein was known as a personal friend of some of the leading Populist radicals, and his offer indicates how old ideological lines were now being redrawn. As A. S. Dolinin has remarked, Miller's articles helped to remove some of the onus that had marred Dostoevsky's reputation because of his editorship of *The Citizen.*[4]

If Dostoevsky unperturbedly went his own way and allowed his readership to interpret the idiosyncrasies of his social-political position in any manner they pleased, his old comrades-in-arms were not so serenely untroubled. He tells Anna that "Maikov was a little cold somehow" when he met his old friend at the home of Strakhov, and the latter, an inveterate gossip, also conveyed the unwelcome news that "Turgenev was to stay in Russia the whole year, write a novel, and bragged that he would describe 'all the reactionaries' (that is, including me)."[5] Turgenev, as it turned out, remained in Russia for only two months, and his next novel, *Virgin Soil,* contained no such caricature. This letter also allows us to catch a glimpse of some of the intimacies of Dostoevsky's home life. It continues with lines that Anna later attempted to obliterate. "Anya, dear," her husband enjoins her, "please be attentive to them [the children]. I know that you love them. Just don't yell at them and keep them clean." There is an intimation as well that Anna ruled the servants with more of an iron hand than suited Dostoevsky's own inclinations. "And be nice to Nanny," he advised her.[6]

The overnight trip to Berlin was a grueling one, both because of the cold and because rail travel by ordinary coach meant sitting upright without sleep. From Berlin to Bad Ems was another raking ordeal ("We sat like herrings in a barrel"). Dostoevsky had arrived at the height of the tourist season, and "the prices [were] horrible"; all the careful calculations he and Anna had made bore no relation to reality. Scouring the town, he succeeded in renting two rooms, and he arranged to take his meals there as well. He hastened to see a doctor and, after being examined, was assured that there was no sign of consumption. He suffered from "a temporary catarrh" that interfered with his breathing, and he was ordered to drink water from a spring.[7]

[3] Ibid., 321; June 6, 1874.
[4] See ibid., 531.
[5] Ibid., 322; June 6, 1874.
[6] Ibid., 323–324.
[7] Ibid., 328.

Ordinarily, Dostoevsky wrote in the stillness of the late night hours, but in Ems, forced to adapt to the routine of his cure, such a schedule was impossible. "All of Ems," he explains, "wakes up at 6:00 in the morning (me too), and at 6:30 a couple of thousand patients are already crowding around two springs. It starts usually with a very boring Lutheran hymn to God: I don't know anything more sickly and artificial." His prescription was to drink one glass of curative water at 7:00, walk for an hour, drink a second glass, and then return home for coffee. He tried to work after his morning coffee, but "until now I've just been reading Pushkin and getting intoxicated with delight. Each day I find something new. But on the other hand I haven't been able to put something together for a novel." [8]

Ems was overflowing with people, among whom he often heard his native Russian, but he found the vast majority of his compatriots as intolerable as the lady—a directress of an institute in Novocherkask—that he mentions to Anna: "A fool such as the world has never produced. A cosmopolitan and an atheist, who adores the tsar but despises her native land. I came right out and told her that she was unbearable and that she didn't understand anything, laughing, of course, and in a society manner, but very seriously." [9] As his first enraptured response to the beauties of Ems wore off, his letters become one protracted litany of complaints. The unpredictable climate was trying and the epileptic attacks that he mentions in his letters also contributed to the jangled state of his nerves. "I have come to hate every building here, every bush. . . . I have become so irritable that (especially early in the morning) I view as a personal enemy every person in the slovenly crowd that throngs at the Kranchen [spring] and would perhaps be glad to be on bad terms with them." [10]

The only relief for his aching misery was the news from Anna, and he awaited her letters with eager impatience as a balm to his gnawing loneliness. She wrote faithfully, but her letters never arrived on time—not, as Dostoevsky bemoaned, because of the inefficiency of the Russian post but because, as Anna learned a year later, they were being read by the secret police. He delighted in news of the children, about whom he worried incessantly. "News about the children is essential to me," he tells Anna. "I can't look at children even here calmly, and if I hear a child crying, I give way to misery and evil premonitions." [11] The letters also reveal that the marriage, despite the twenty years' difference in age between the partners, had now become solidly rooted (for Dostoevsky at any rate) in a passionate sexual attachment. "I have seductive dreams of you," he confides to Anna. "Do you dream of me? . . . You said that I'd probably start chasing after

[8] Ibid., 331; June 16/28, 1874.
[9] Ibid.
[10] Ibid., 346; July 5/17, 1874.
[11] Ibid., 344.

other women here abroad. My friend, I have come to know by experience that I can't even imagine one other than you. . . . And besides, there's nothing better *in this regard* than my Anechka. . . . I hope you won't show this letter to any-one." [12] From a reference in this letter, one surmises that Anna too had confessed to having "indecent dreams," and he replies affectionately with a famous quote from Gogol: "Never mind, never mind—silence!" [13]

Dostoevsky gave Anna a running account of his progress on his next novel, which was coming along, if at all, only at a snail's pace. "I've prepared two plans for novels here and don't know on which one to venture . . . at the end of August I'll get down to the writing, and do you know what I'm worried about: whether I'll have the energy and health for such hard work. . . . I've finished novels, but nonetheless, *on the whole*, have ruined my health." [14] He was upset for practical, as well as artistic, reasons. "I'm terribly troubled by the daily thought of how we will arrange things for ourselves in the fall and on what funds. (I *cannot* ask Nekrasov again [for another advance], and besides, he probably *wouldn't give* me anything.) He isn't Katkov; he's a person from Yaroslavl." [15] Moreover, the flow of his inspiration was hampered by writing for a journal in which he hesitated to express himself freely. "The mere fact that *Notes of the Fatherland* will be afraid to publish certain of my opinions practically cuts off my hands." [16]

A week before returning to Russia he writes that "although there *really* is an improvement, that is . . . less dry coughing, breathing is easier, and so on . . . a certain (diseased) place remains, and that diseased place in my chest refuses to heal completely." Nonetheless, "in everything else I feel incomparably healthier than before: energy, sleep, appetite—all of this is excellent." [17] He left Bad Ems on July 27, and, according to Anna's account, "he was not able to deny himself his deep desire to visit once more the grave of our first daughter, Sonya. He went to Geneva and visited the children's cemetery of Plein Palais twice; and from Son-ya's grave he brought me a few sprigs of cypress, which in the course of six years had grown thick over our little girl's monument." [18]

Dostoevsky returned to Staraya Russa on August 1 and immediately plunged into work on the scenarios for *A Raw Youth*. By this time Anna had come to an important decision. Why return to Petersburg for the winter? They would live in the country in the spring because life there was healthier for the children, and

[12] Ibid., 333; June 16/24, 1874.
[13] Ibid., 338; June 23/July 5, 1874.
[14] Ibid., 360.
[15] Ibid., 338.
[16] Ibid., 354; July 14/26, 1874.
[17] Ibid., 352, 353.
[18] *Reminiscences*, 233–234.

they could reduce their living expenses considerably. Nor would her husband be distracted by the obligations of Petersburg's social life, where "in winter Feodor Mikhailovich hardly belonged to his family" and Anna herself had to play the burdensome role of social hostess.[19] As usual in such practical matters, she got her way. The couple immediately rented the top floor of a villa in town, with a study and separate bedroom for Dostoevsky, and it was agreed that he would go to Petersburg two or three times in the course of the winter to keep in touch with the literary scene.

Writing to Victor Putsykovich, who had taken over the editorship of *The Citizen*, Dostoevsky asks for "material on the trial of Dolgushin and company from the newspapers."[20] The public trial of this radical group (named after its leader, Alexander Dolgushin) will be partially employed in *A Raw Youth* for a fleeting portrayal of the fictional Dergachev group. Many of the Dolgushintsy had been in contact with the Nechaevsty and jailed in connection with that affair, though they took no part in any of Nechaev's activities. Indeed, they had now converted to that reverence for a Socialist Christ and for Christian moral ideals so typical of the Populists. Their propaganda was drawn from the ideas of V. V. Bervi-Flerovsky, an economist whose *Position of the Working Class in Russia* (1869) was one of the major works, along with those already mentioned by Lavrov and Mikhailovsky, that inspired the Populist movement. "Bervi-Flerovsky," writes Andrzej Walicki, "painted a vivid picture of the growing destitution of the peasantry following the introduction of capitalist social relations in agriculture; the conclusion he drew was that everything possible should be done to prevent capitalism from making further headway, and to utilize, instead, the possibility of the peasant commune."[21] A discussion of Bervi-Flerovsky's ideas had appeared in *Dawn*, which Dostoevsky read assiduously during its brief life span.

One of the three proclamations among the Dolgushintsy documents was a shortened version of a brochure written for them by Bervi-Flerovsky in a semi-liturgical style, "Of the Martyr Nikolay and How Mankind Should Live by the Laws of Nature and Justice." Another, furnished with an epigraph from Saint Matthew, was even more stylistically adapted to the sacramental language of church services. All the proclamations of the Dolgushintsy were based on moral appeal. As the commentator in the Academy of Sciences edition of *A Raw Youth* notes, "The ethical substance of the 'justice' that the Dolgushintsy desired coincided objectively . . . with the substance of the Christian teachings, even though the Dolgushintsy were opponents of Christianity. . . . '[T]he religion of

---

[19] Ibid., 235.

[20] *PSS*, 29/Bk. 1: 361; July 20/August 1, 1874.

[21] Andrzej Walicki, *A History of Russian Thought from the Enlightenment to Marxism*, trans. Hilda Andrews-Rusiecka (Stanford, 1979), 224.

equality' as the source and goal of their strivings, runs through all of their proclamations."[22]

Labors on his novel were broken only by letters from his stepson Pavel Isaev, who had married and become a father for the second time. A letter in November from Pavel's wife to Anna revealed that she had no idea of his whereabouts. Also, she requested Anna's aid in finding a foundling home where she could place their baby daughter. Locating Pavel at last, Dostoevsky sent twenty-five rubles, "because of your harsh situation," but urged him "to try and send it all to Nadezhda Nikolayevna [his wife]."[23] Anna did not mince words in expressing her disapproval of his behavior in her reply to his wife. Insulted, Pavel sent the twenty-five rubles back to his stepfather and complained that Anna had overstepped "*all the bounds of decency*" in dressing him down. Taking this rebuke to Anna badly, Dostoevsky replied, "It's impossible not to be indignant, if only from the side (and I'm not on the side for you) about how you treat your children. Do you have any notion of what a foundling home is and of the raising of the newborn by a Finnish woman, amid refuse, filth, pinches, and perhaps punches: certain death. . . . After all, I didn't send you, only a stepson, just anywhere to be taught, brought up, made into a shoemaker."[24]

It was not Dostoevsky who made the first trip to Petersburg from Staraya Russa that winter but Anna, who left in mid-December to supervise the publication of *House of the Dead* under the Dostoevsky imprint. He was gloomy about the prospects of any further demand for his prison memoirs, but Anna succeeded in selling or placing on commission seven hundred copies, returning home with a small profit. She had left him in charge of the children, aided of course by the servants and the old nanny of whom he was so appreciative, and his letters show him to be a devoted *paterfamilias*, observing his children with pleasure. "Yesterday," he writes Anna, "during the cigarettes [Dostoevsky, an inveterate smoker, rolled his own cigarettes], they started dancing, and Fedya invented a new *step*: Lilya would stand at the mirror, Fedya opposite her, and they both would go toward each other in time (moreover, Lilya was very graceful); after coming together (all the while in time), Fedya would kiss Lilya, and after kissing they would go their separate ways."[25]

Although by this time he had sent off the first chapters of *A Raw Youth* to *Notes of the Fatherland*, so far no response to them had been forthcoming. Two days later, from a story in *The Citizen*, Dostoevsky learned that Katkov had purchased *Anna Karenina* at five hundred rubles per folio sheet. "They couldn't immediately resolve to give *me* 250 rubles," he remarks ruefully, "but

[22] *PSS*, 17: 302.
[23] *PSS*, 29/Bk. 1: 364; November 4, 1874.
[24] Ibid., 366–367; December 11, 1874.
[25] Ibid., 370–371; December 20, 1874.

they paid L. Tolstoy 500 with alacrity!"[26] Even more than this blow to his literary pride, what bothered him was that "now it's quite possible that Nekrasov will cut me back if there is anything contrary to their orientation. . . . But even if we have to beg for alms, I won't compromise my orientation by so much as a line!"[27]

A month later he went to Petersburg. Nekrasov had finally written that the next installment was to be put into galleys; but he still had not proferred any opinion about the work, and Dostoevsky had begun to fret that perhaps his depiction of the Dergachev group had met with some hostility. He cheerfully informs Anna, however, that Nekrasov was "terribly happy with the novel, although he hasn't yet read the second part." Moreover, the co-editor, Saltykov-Shchedrin, with whom he had slashingly polemicized in the past, "praises [it] very highly." The opinion of the satirist, if correctly reported, drastically altered with later installments, which he spoke of as being "almost crazy."[28]

Dostoevsky read part of his proofs at Nekrasov's home and took the remainder back to his hotel, but feeling the need for company he called on the Maikovs and found Strakhov there as well. Maikov "greeted me with apparent heartiness," he writes Anna, "but . . . not a word about my novel and obviously because of not wanting to *pain* me. They also talked a little about Tolstoy's novel [*Anna Karenina*], and what they said was ridiculous in its enthusiasm. I started to speak and made the point that, if Tolstoy published in *Notes of the Fatherland*, then why were they criticizing me, but Maikov frowned and broke off the conversation and I didn't insist. In short, I see that something is going on here, and precisely what you and I talked about, that is, Maikov has spread that idea about me [that he had betrayed his former beliefs and commitments]."[29]

Dostoevsky read the first installments of *Anna Karenina* during this Petersburg visit "under a bell," that is, his compressed-air treatments for emphysema. Tolstoy's novel "is rather boring and so-so," he reports to Anna. "I can't understand what they're all so excited about."[30] He was overjoyed when Nekrasov, as he proudly told Anna, dropped in unexpectedly on the fourth day of his stay "to express *his delight* after reading the end of the first part [of *A Raw Youth*]. 'I got so carried away that I stayed up all night reading . . . And what freshness you have, my dear fellow . . . that sort of freshness doesn't happen at our age and not a single other writer had it. Lev Tolstoy's latest novel only repeats what I've read in him before, only it was better before' (Nekrasov said this)."[31]

[26] Ibid., 370; December 30, 1874.
[27] Ibid.
[28] Ibid., 2: 8; February 6, 1875. See also ibid., 194.
[29] Ibid., 9; February 4, 1875.
[30] Ibid., 11; February 1, 1875.
[31] Ibid., 13; February 9, 1875.

Dostoevsky's perturbation over the accidental competition between his novel and *Anna Karenina* was considerable. One of the warmest articles greeting the first chapters of *A Raw Youth* had appeared in the *St. Petersburg Gazette* (written under a pseudonym) by Vsevolod Solovyev. When Dostoevsky paid him a visit, Solovyev recalls the novelist was "in a highly irritable state and in the gloomiest frame of mind. 'Tell me, tell me honestly—do you think I am envious of Lev Tolstoy?' he blurted out, having greeted me and intently looking me in the eye." The startled Solovyev, hardly knowing how to respond, adroitly replied that, since the two writers were so different, he could not imagine Dostoevsky being envious of Tolstoy. "They accuse me of envy," exclaimed Dostoevsky. "And who? Old friends, who have known me for twenty years." These could only be Maikov and Strakhov. He sank into a chair, but then leaped up and, grasping Solovyev by the hand, broke out into an anguished tirade:

> You know, yes, I am in fact envious, but only not in the way, not at all in the way, that they think. I envy his circumstances, and particularly right now. . . . It's painful for me to work as I do, painful to hurry. . . . God!, and all my life! . . . Look, I recently read my *Idiot*; I had forgotten it completely . . . I read it as . . . if for the first time. . . . There are excellent chapters . . . good scenes . . . you remember the meeting between Aglaya and the prince on the bench? . . . But I also saw others, how much was unfinished, hasty. . . . And it's always so—as now, *Notes of the Fatherland* presses, it's necessary to keep up . . . you take advances . . . work them off . . . and again go ahead. . . . And there's no end! . . . And he is materially secure, never has to worry about the next day, he can polish every one of his works.[32]

Even though matters were smoothed over on the surface between Dostoevsky and Strakhov, and to all external appearances they remained friends, the rancor was never dispelled. An entry in Dostoevsky's notebook for 1876–1877 reveals the depth of his anger, and also a good deal of contempt. He ridicules Strakhov for leading a sycophantic, sybaritic life. He "loves to eat turkey, and not his own, at others' tables" (Strakhov dined regularly at the Dostoevskys'), while deriving his self-importance from holding "two public posts"—"a purely seminarian trait," Dostoevsky sneers. Even more, he accuses Strakhov of lacking any sense of "civic feeling or duty," so that "for some gross, coarsely voluptuous filth he is ready to sell everyone and everything . . . and not because he does not believe in the ideal, but because of the thick layer of fat which prevents him from feeling anything."[33] This extremely insulting characterization was never published, but

---

[32] *DVS*, 2: 214–215.
[33] *LN* 83 (Moscow, 1971), 619–620.

27. Tolstoy in 1877,
by I. N. Kramskoy

one assumes that Strakhov must have come across it in preparing Dostoevsky's biography.[34]

The estrangement from his oldest friends made him all the more eager to grasp at the chance of reviving his intimacy with Nekrasov, and perhaps establishing a new friendship with the notoriously bearlike Saltykov-Shchedrin. But he had certainly not forgotten their wounding satirical exchanges of the 1860s, which are reflected in his recently reread novel *The Idiot.* Although there is nothing to indicate that Dostoevsky was subject to any direct editorial pressure, as he had anticipated, an article by Mikhailovsky, published alongside Dostoevsky's first chapters in the January issue of *Notes of the Fatherland*, raises questions. The Populist reading public was, apparently, as much taken aback by his presence in

---

[34] Strakhov may well have taken revenge on Dostoevsky in the letter that he sent to Tolstoy in 1883, declaring that he wrote Dostoevsky's biography only in a struggle against "my own rising revulsion, trying to suppress that ugly feeling in myself." He reports having been told that Dostoevsky "had boasted of having . . . a little girl in the bathhouse, delivered over to him by her governess." See *Reminiscences*, 371–382.

the pages of their favorite journal as was his own literary circle, and Mikhailovsky felt called upon to offer some explanation. "First, Dostoevsky is one of our most talented belletrists, and second . . . the scene at Dergachev's . . . has only an episodic character. If the novel were based on this motif (as had been the case with *Demons*), *Notes of the Fatherland* would be forced to renounce the honor of seeing the creation of Dostoevsky in its pages, even if he were a writer of genius."[35] From the amount of space accorded the Dergachev motif in Dostoevsky's notes, compared with their ancillary role in the novel, it seems likely that he might have wished to avoid any editorial clash over his final text.

Dostoevsky returned to Staraya Russa after two exhausting weeks. As well as looking after his literary affairs and taking his compressed air treatments, he had dispatched the business of his publishing firm, visited the lawyer handling the litigation over the Kumanina estate as well as the dentist repairing his dentures, and made the rounds of a host of friends and relatives. He hardly had time to sleep and, to make matters worse, he suddenly received a summons from the police informing him, when he showed up, that he lacked an internal passport. On protesting that "there are twenty thousand people without passports in Petersburg, and you're detaining a person everybody knows," he was told that, even though he was "a famous person all over Russia," laws still had to be obeyed.[36] However, he was promised a certificate of residency in a few days and told not to worry. In his last letter from Petersburg, he writes: "Today I'm riding around and living as though in hell. . . . Tomorrow there are the devil only knows how many things still to take care of."[37]

———■———

Dostoevsky returned to Petersburg in mid-May to read proofs again and obtain another advance for his second trip to Ems, which produced many of the same negative reactions that had marked the first. As before, there are constant laments about the difficulty of working on the third part of *A Raw Youth* while taking the cure and in the upsetting conditions of Ems. "My darling Anya, I keep being horrified by the obligations that I've taken on myself. I see that, try as I might, there'll be almost no time to write."[38]

Echoes of his preparation for his scenarios can be found in his letters. "I'm reading about *Elijah* and *Enoch* (it's superb) and Bessonov's *Our Age*," he tells Anna. He was probably seeking inspiration for the figure of Makar Dolgoruky, the Russian peasant wanderer (*strannik*), who makes his appearance in Part III and represents an idealized image of peasant religiosity (Bessonov's book is a

[35] Cited in *PSS*, 17: 346.
[36] *PSS*, 29/Bk. 2: 10; February 7, 1875.
[37] Ibid., 20; February 14, 1875.
[38] Ibid., 36; June 4/16, 1875.

collection of Russian historical folk poetry). He also enthuses over another text of the Old Testament, and his words not only give us a glimpse into childhood memories but also look forward to the creation of *The Brothers Karamazov*. "I am reading Job and it puts me into a state of painful ecstasy: I leave off reading and I walk about the room almost crying, and if it weren't for the vile notes of the translator, I would perhaps be happy. That book, dear Anna, it's strange, it was one of the first to impress me in my life. I was still practically an infant!"[39]

He read the Russian press, and he comments on some of the recent issues of *The Citizen*, for example, "Poretsky has gone completely off his head with Tolstoy."[40] Alexander Poretsky, an old friend, had furiously defended *Anna Karenina* against a criticism of the radical publicist Peter Tkachev, who had asked whether it was worth spending so much time talking about a book with such a foolish and even corrupting theme. Dostoevsky was then himself being manhandled in some journals, and he felt acutely the lack of any defender against those who were deprecating *him*. "Absolutely everyone in literature has turned against me. . . . I won't go chasing after them," he writes defiantly, referring to criticism in the *Journal de Pétersbourg* that "il n'y a rien de saillant" (nothing stands out) in the second part of *A Raw Youth*. But Dostoevsky refuses to be discouraged: "I won't lose my energy for the future at all—you just be well, my helpmate, and we'll manage one way or another."[41]

All but one of these letters from Ems are written to his wife. The single exception is addressed to Elena Pavlovna Ivanova, to whom Dostoevsky was distantly related by marriage and with whom he had once been close. During the summer of 1868, he had asked Elena, whose husband was in the last stages of a fatal illness, whether she would consider marrying him on becoming a widow. Now he inquires after the whereabouts of the elusive Pavel and expresses regret at the hostile rumors circulating about himself because of his claim to a share in the Kumanina estate—rumors that had become even more envenomed since the suit he had filed against collateral claimants. His favorite niece, Sofya Ivanova, had ceased to write to him for this reason.[42]

Dostoevsky left Ems after a little less than five weeks of treatment, having been told by his doctor "that my chest is in excellent condition, everything has healed. But the wheezing and difficulty in breathing are left; he said that may go away on its own."[43] On arriving in Petersburg, he was so short of money that he borrowed from friends; and he hastens to explain why to Anna. "On the way I met Pisemsky and Pavel Annenkov; they were traveling to Petersburg from

[39] Ibid., 43; June 10/22, 1875.
[40] Ibid., 49; June 15/27, 1875.
[41] Ibid., 46–47; June 13/25, 1875.
[42] Ibid., 37–39; June 5/17, 1875.
[43] Ibid., 58; June 23/July 5, 1875.

Baden-Baden (where Turgenev and Saltykov are). I couldn't restrain myself and paid Annenkov (that is, to be passed on to Turgenev) fifty thalers. That's what did me in. I couldn't *possibly* have done anything else; it's a matter of honor. Both Pisemsky and Annenkov treated me superbly."[44]

[44] Ibid., 63; July 6, 1875.

CHAPTER 49

A Raw Youth

The last chapters of *A Raw Youth* were published in *Notes of the Fatherland* in the winter of 1875. Written between *Demons* and *The Brothers Karamazov*, this curious hybrid of a novel is far from attaining the artistic stature of these two works, although its severest critics may have considerably exaggerated its defects. Why should *A Raw Youth* slump so markedly when compared with Dostoevsky's other major novels? Some answers may be located in the implicit self-censorship that he here exercised on his creative faculties.

Several extended notes show that Dostoevsky had a plan for a novel about three brothers, and that he was tempted by the possibility of writing what could have become *The Brothers Karamazov*. One note contains an outline that would require only a little reshuffling to fit the later work: "one brother is an atheist. Despair. The other is a thoroughgoing fanatic. The third represents the new generation, a living force, new people . . . and the children, as the youngest generation" (16: 16). Ivan Karamazov's outraged rejection of his ticket of admission to a world of eternal harmony based on injustice and suffering is foreshadowed in the defiance of the older brother: "If the way of the world is that something disgusting always has to turn up in place of something pure, then let it all come crashing down: 'I refuse to accept such a world.'" This declaration is followed by the authorial comment: "His whole misfortune lies in the fact that He is an atheist and does not believe in resurrection"—which will be the case with Ivan as well (16: 15).

Similarly, the issue of Ivan's "Euclidean understanding," his refusal to accept the mysteries of faith, also appears in this context. "Existence must be unquestionably and in every instance superior to the mind of man. The doctrine that the mind of man is the final limit of the universe is as stupid as stupid can be, and even stupider, infinitely stupider, than a game of checkers between two shopkeepers." The relation of Versilov, a main figure in the novel, to others, and his interpretation of the love ethic of Christ, also anticipates Ivan Karamazov's Grand Inquisitor. "It is impossible to love people the way they are," he declares. "And yet one must love them, for this is what we are ordered to do (by Christ)." But "people are base, they like to love and to adore from fear," and so he believes that "without any doubt, Christ could not have loved them; he suffered them, he forgave them, but of course he also despised them. . . . Love for mankind must be understood as love for a perfected mankind, one that exists so far only as an ideal, and God only knows if it will ever become reality" (16: 156–157).

These notes also contain a jotting that supplies a first version of the plot line of *The Brothers Karamazov*: "In Tobolsk, about twenty years ago, like the Ilyinsky story" (17: 5–6). Ilyinsky, it will be recalled, had been a fellow prisoner with Dostoevsky in Siberia, convicted of the murder of his father solely on circumstantial evidence. This extended note, along with the recollection of Ilyinsky, is obviously the nucleus of *The Brothers Karamazov* (an innocent older brother sent to Siberia for a crime committed by a younger one, finally unable to endure his guilt), and indicates how close Dostoevsky came to embarking on such a novel at this point.

He was aware of this possibility and wrote about it in his *Diary of a Writer* (January 1876). "When Nikolay Alekseyevich Nekrasov asked me to write a novel for *Notes of the Fatherland*," he explained, "I almost began my *Fathers and Children*, but I held back, and thank God I did, for I was not ready. In the meantime, I wrote only *A Raw Youth*, this first attempt at my idea." Why Dostoevsky decided to confine himself to this "first attempt" is understandable. He was, after all, toiling over a book to be published in *Notes of the Fatherland*, the journal in which the influential Mikhailovsky had objected to his preference for sensational subject matter (such as murder). In addition, Dostoevsky's articles in *The Citizen* for 1873 had shown his preoccupation with the problem of the younger generation and its search for moral values. From where could these young idealists acquire those values when their fathers had become so morally bankrupt themselves? Such reasons could well have persuaded him to reserve his murder motif for a less problematic venue and to focus instead on the nonlethal but no less pernicious sins of the fathers in failing to impart any life-enhancing moral values to their sons. He therefore reduced the theme of parricide to that of parental irresponsibility and substituted a relatively innocent and boyishly illusory romantic rivalry between father and son for the merciless Oedipal clash in *The Brothers Karamazov* that so impressed Freud. He decided to write a social-psychological novel of a relatively limited range rather than to dramatize the collision of conflicting moral-spiritual absolutes that invariably inspired his best work.

If some of the defects of *A Raw Youth* may be ascribed to the decision to write for a Populist journal, the place of publication also gives a special interest to many details of the text. For *A Raw Youth* is Dostoevsky's first artistic response to the challenges posed by the new phase of Russian culture inaugurated by the ideology of Russian Populism. Indeed, while narrating the peripeties by which his youthful hero Arkady comes to manhood, he interweaves them with what he felt to be the glaring anomaly at the heart of Populist values—their recognition of the Christian moral ideals of the peasant world they idolized, and yet their refusal to accept the very foundation of this world in the divinity of Christ. *A Raw Youth*, if read in this perspective, thus becomes a kind of Trojan horse introduced into the very journalistic citadel of the former enemy to undermine its last defenses.

The novel is written as a first-person confessional memoir by the title character, Arkady Dolgoruky, the natural son of Andrey Petrovich Versilov, a once wealthy aristocrat now down on his luck (he has already run through three fortunes) and a philosophical seeker after truth. Arkady sets out, a year after the events have occurred, to recount the circumstances that have brought about a change in his life and transformed his character. These circumstances all took place in a period of six months after his arrival in Petersburg to join his family and are compressed within twelve days, leaping from September and November to December. Through the carefully arranged "disorder" of Arkady's narration (he is constantly apologizing for his lack of literary skill), all of the relevant past is included in so-called digressions. Taking full advantage of the time sequence of the memoir form, which narrates events from a point later than when they occurred, Arkady-as-narrator obviously knows the outcome of the episodes that he recounts, but his naïve determination to stick to "the facts" as they appeared to him *then* allows Dostoevsky to preserve the suspense element of his story. At the same time, Arkady-as-narrator slips in evaluations of the behavior of Arkady-as-character, and by the end he writes: "I have suddenly become aware that I have reeducated myself through the process of recalling events and writing them down" (13: 417).

A Raw Youth unquestionably contains moving scenes of childhood in Dostoevsky's best "philanthropic" manner, and his inner portrait of a rebellious adolescent is often touching and persuasive. The book is also distinguished by Dostoevsky's most modulated and sympathetic depiction of a member of the Romantic Idealist generation of the 1840s, a portrait that rises to a visionary height of lyrical pathos. However, the melodramatic plot ingredients (concealed letters, lawsuits over disputed inheritances, attempts at blackmail) whip up excitement by means that are purely superficial and external. All too much of the text relies on such a moth-eaten plot that swamps the stretches of genuine feeling and ideological elevation. The major plot-line involves Versilov and the nineteen-year-old Arkady, who has come to live with his family (his unmarried peasant mother, Sofya, and equally illegitimate sister, Liza). Arkady carries a letter entrusted to him and sewn into his jacket that compromises Katerina Akhmakova, the beautiful widow of a general and a princess in her own right. The letter asks for legal advice about committing her elderly father, Prince Sokolsky, to an institution for the mentally enfeebled, and she fears that, if he learns of this document, she will be cut out of his will. Both Katerina and Versilov are in search of this letter and rightly suspect that Arkady possesses it.

Two other subplots also run through the book, each concerning another child of Versilov's. One centers on his legitimate daughter by his deceased first wife, Anna Andreyevna, who has designs on the addlepated Prince Sokolsky. The enormously wealthy prince is an ardent but, by this time, quite harmless admirer of female pulchritude, and the helpless prince is eventually kidnapped by the much younger Anna, who plans to marry him and ensure her future. A second subplot focuses on Arkady's sister, Liza, who has an affair with the *young* Prince Sokolsky and becomes pregnant by this well-meaning but flighty and spineless aristocratic scion.

All these plots illustrate the moral chaos of Russian society, especially of its upper class; each reveals some infraction or violation of the normal family structure or of the moral code governing relations between the sexes. Also, each subplot is meant to bring out, as is typical for Dostoevsky, the significance of the main one by modulation and contrast. Arkady, who has become madly infatuated with the ravishing Katerina and is troubled by his sexual stirrings, is tempted to behave like Anna Andreyevna and to blackmail the haughty Katerina into sexual submission in exchange for the letter. Versilov and the two Princes Sokolsky are similar in their weakness for the fair sex, but Versilov, for all his personal failings, is endowed with a moral-philosophical dimension completely beyond the range of the others. He is also carelessly contemptuous about money, whereas the old prince is on the board of various stock companies and the younger one is in the clutches of the unscrupulous swindler and stock forger Stebelkov.

Dostoevsky had been criticized by Mikhailovsky for failing to include in his work "the devils" of capitalist development, and while he did not intend to expose himself to such charges again, neither did he intend to abandon his exposure of the anomaly at the heart of Populist values. Old Prince Sokolsky, writes Dostoevsky in his notes, "has . . . become an atheist himself"—in conformity with "his inbred and well-bred Westernism." One sample of his "witty" conversation on the topic of God reveals the stamp of his character: "And, finally, if it is really as you say, then prove to me, so I can see it, or as they say, have a sensation of it. All right if He (God) exists in person, and not in the form of an effusion of spirit or something (for I must admit, that is even more difficult for me to understand), then what does He wear? How tall is He? Don't be angry, my dear, naturally I have a right to ask the question, for if He is a God, a personal God, i.e., a person, then how tall is he, *et enfin*, where does he live?" (16: 25–26). Dostoevsky thus juxtaposes a comically fatuous atheist with a serious one like Versilov, emotionally torn by his inability to believe, and he also foreshadows the literal questioning of the supernatural that will be displayed more sarcastically by Feodor Karamazov.

At the center of the book is Arkady, who is left "solely to [his] own devices" and has nowhere to turn for moral guidance and support. In a note of July 23, 1874, Dostoevsky had sketched an image of the son that will remain unchanged: "The young man arrives smarting from an insult, thirsting for revenge. Colossal vanity, a plan (to become) a Rothschild (his secret)" (16: 24). The "insult" will become the irresponsible treatment of Arkady by his father all through his early life, and his vanity will take the form, which appears frequently throughout Dostoevsky's works, of "wishing to become a Rothschild."

With his mixture of justified exasperation and scarcely suppressed rage, his quasi-comical and self-glorifying aspiration toward dominance and power, Arkady is an adolescent (and much less articulate) variation of the underground man. He is a touching and sympathetic figure, not a grotesque *persona* acting out one or another dead end of Russian radical ideology. Determined to live as a self-proclaimed egoist and to isolate himself entirely from society, he hopes to amass a fortune and "to become a Rothschild." Once having scaled such a financial height, he will have gained absolute power over the whole world—or rather, the "consciousness" of such power. These self-glorifying intentions, inspired by Pushkin's "The Covetous Knight," are nothing but the pitiful, compensatory dreams of a poor, neglected schoolboy left to fend for himself emotionally and constantly humiliated because of his irregular parentage. Dostoevsky thus grounds Arkady's "underground" impulses and behavior in a "philanthropic" and social-psychological context that makes them understandable and forgivable. Arkady's love-hate dialectic with the world is presented as the twisted expression of an essentially candid and high-minded young personality shamefully thrown back on itself.

His youthful innocence is conveyed both by the naïvely enthusiastic and hyperbolic style of his narrative and, more obviously, by numerous revealing incidents. Even while determined to become a Rothschild, he spontaneously uses his savings to look after a baby girl left on the doorstep of his home. Moreover, the "ideological" expression of his egoism also has a magnanimous aspect. Arkady wishes to become a Rothschild solely for the sensation of power that his wealth would entail and imagines himself, rather like the underground man in his "sublime and beautiful" phase, donating this enormous wealth to humankind: "I shall give my millions away, let society distribute my wealth and I . . . I will mix with nothingness again" (13: 76). Dostoevsky takes care to indicate that Arkady wishes to obtain his financial goal only by "honorable" means. He would subsist only on black bread, tea, and a little soup, saving half of the small allowance he received from his guardians, submitting himself to something "like the monastic life and feats of monastic self-discipline" (13: 67). The same combination of idealism and self-centered egoism can also be seen in Arkady's father,

Versilov, though these traits manifest themselves differently in the world-weary and highly sophisticated aristocrat than in the turbulent adolescent.

———■———

Versilov is far and away the most interesting character in the book, and after Part I, Dostoevsky is unable to prevent him from taking center-stage. The events of Part I are designed to change Arkady's image of his father, who is by no means simply the scoundrelly blackguard that the youth believes him to be. However, various incidents demonstrating Versilov's rectitude are presented in such a way as to reveal his desire always "to be on a pedestal" (13: 210), that is, to believe himself to be morally elevated while, for example, seducing Arkady's mother, an attractive peasant girl married off to a much older husband. Incidents of this kind, involving Versilov in his relations with other characters, present the continuously shifting perspective from which he is viewed—one that is simply the objective correlative of his inner uncertainty and moral instability. The strongest sense of Versilov's character is given during his lengthy conversations with Arkady in Part I, which succeed in communicating the mixture of charm, intelligence, and blasé sensibility that makes him so appealing. But they also reveal an attitude of disillusionment, an ingrained inability to take himself (or anything else) with unqualified seriousness, that underlines his basic lack of moral substance.

Arkady, on closer acquaintance with his father, comments on this crippling inner disposition. "He was completely charming to me," he writes, "and jested with me, but . . . there was a strange irony on his part" (13: 18). A typical example is when Versilov first speaks of the peasant husband of Arkady's mother with great respect, but then makes a risqué allusion to his gray hairs. "Versilov had a very nasty aristocratic trick. After saying (when he could not help it) some particularly clever and fine things, he would all at once intentionally cap them with some stupid saying. . . . To hear him, one would suppose he was speaking quite seriously, and all the time he was posing to himself, or laughing" (13: 109). Dostoevsky's ability to convey both the sensitivity of Versilov's insight and the disengaging twist of his self-reflexive irony redeems a good many scenes of *A Raw Youth*.

The history of Versilov will gradually disclose his hopeless inability to master the passions that lie at the root of his self-debilitating mockery. Although he is a man of "ideas," he always regards them from a certain ironic distance; they do not penetrate his entire personality and thus become "idea-feelings." He is contrasted in this respect with the young man Kraft, whose suicide illustrates what occurs when such a powerful idea-feeling is undermined. Arkady meets Kraft when he visits the Dergachev group; a few days later, Kraft commits suicide out of what can only be called patriotic despair. He has become convinced that the "Russians are a second-rate people destined . . . not to play an independent part in the history of humanity," and this disillusionment has maimed his will to work for "the common cause" (that is, the propaganda work of the Dergachev group). The destruction of his faith in a glorious future for his people, like the destruction of Kirillov's faith in Christ as God-man in *Demons*, leads to a crisis of despair that ends in suicide (though Kirillov believed that his death would have a positive significance).

A discussion between Kraft and Arkady at Dergachev's underscores the importance of values being embedded in an idea-feeling pervading the personality to its very core, and the impossibility of replacing such an idea-feeling by any abstract notion such as a "future unknown people." Dostoevsky here is transposing his own belief in humankind's need for an irrational faith—specifically, a faith in Christ as God-man, and hence a belief in immortality and resurrection—as the sole secure buttress of moral values.

The attack on Kraft by other members of the Dergachev group also inspires Arkady to spring to his defense with a lengthy and impassioned outburst. For just as Kraft is in the grip of an idea-feeling about Russia, so Arkady has his own about becoming a Rothschild; no abstract argument can alter the resentments of his ego, in which his idea-feeling has its root. Arkady is searching for a new ideal, a new faith, that can overcome his smoldering need for revenge and power, but he sees in his interlocutors only a demand that he surrender his individuality entirely. His tirade has often been compared with that of the underground man, who expressed a similarly passionate, egoistic self-assertion against a Socialist world that Arkady imagines consisting of "barracks, communistic homes, *stricte nécessaire*, atheism, and communistic wives without children" (13: 50).

But Arkady defends his own egoism with a more relevant argument—one aimed directly at the Populist refusal to acknowledge the necessary "idea-feeling" of religious faith. "Why should it concern me what will happen to this humanity of yours in a thousand years' time, if all you allow me under your rules is no love, no life after death, and no possibility of being noble and self-sacrificing?" Returning to the charge a bit later, he invokes the doomsday vision of the earth becoming a cold planet, on which—according to the conclusions of the recently discovered and widely popularized second law of thermodynamics—human life will have vanished entirely. "And why should I be bound to love my neighbor, or your future humanity," Arkady cries, "which I shall never see, which will never know anything about me, and which will in its turn disappear and leave no trace (time counts as nothing in this) when the earth in its turn will be changed into an iceberg, and will fly off into the void with an infinite multitude of other similar icebergs?" (13: 48–49). Here Arkady addresses precisely the dedication to an ideal *without* any of the hope provided by immortality. From where would the idea-feelings necessary for its support be derived? Dostoevsky's Populist readers were thus being informed that merely secular altruistic values would not prove sufficient to sustain them indefinitely and that, like Kraft, they might reach the limit of despair.

———■———

The encounters between Arkady and Versilov in Part 1 are touching and effective because they spring from the basic father-son relationship and are not yet distorted by the complications of the intrigue. The plot begins to dominate in the second section, which takes place after a lapse of two months. Arkady, in the interval, has become transformed into a fashionable dandy-about-town, and in a series of picaresque adventures he plunges into the whirl of social life. His sponsor in this transformation is the young Prince Sokolsky, in whose apartment he lives and who furnishes him with funds. Arkady now experiences one disillusioning shock after another, and these become so severe that he is seized by the destructive impulse to set the entire world on fire.

All of Arkady's misadventures in this second part may be viewed as an exposure to what Dostoevsky calls "the common Russian fate" (13: 247), and this phrase applies to all the upper-class figures as well. They all exhibit a hopeless moral impotence, which disintegrates under extreme pressure into a pathological split personality. Young Prince Sokolsky, for example, nourishes the highest conceptions of his obligation to maintain the most rigid standards of personal honor, yet he is guilty of the most contemptible and disloyal conduct and continually violates his own principles.

None of Arkady's disillusionments is so severe as what occurs in relation to Versilov, whose elevation of spirit makes his vulnerability to "the Russian fate" all the more disturbing. At the beginning of Part 2, Versilov is presented as a propounder of the loftiest ideas, a man profoundly preoccupied with the most crucial problems of his time, but his wisdom and insight are always tinged with a feeling of impotence. Haughtily impugning the "materialism" of the modern world, he predicts to Arkady that society will finally collapse in "general bankruptcy," leading to class warfare between "the beggars" and the "bondholders and creditors." When Arkady inquires anxiously what can be done about this frightening prospect, he only replies that "to do nothing is always best. One's conscience is at rest anyway, knowing that one's had no share in anything" (13: 172).

Similarly, Arkady can derive no positive moral guidance from Versilov's general ideas about human nature and human life. "To love one's neighbor and not despise him is impossible," he informs his son, adding that "'love for humanity' must be understood as love for that humanity which you have yourself created in your soul (in other words, you have created yourself and your love is for yourself), and which, therefore, will never be reality." But such disillusioning words are counterbalanced by another dialogue, in which Versilov tells Arkady that "to turn stones into bread . . . is a great thought," but "it's not the greatest." For "men will be satisfied and forget" and then ask: "Well, I've had enough and what can I do now?" The question of the meaning of life and of the ultimate destiny of mankind transcends the issue of the satisfaction of material needs, but to the question, What shall I do now?, Versilov can provide no answer (13: 174–175). His utterances always contain this mixture of misanthropy and exalted aspiration.

As the intrigue of Part 2 unfolds, these opposing aspects of Versilov are no longer divulged through moral-philosophical dialogues but presented in dramatic action. His split personality is now depicted in terms of trivial capriciousness (such as his senseless act of challenging the young prince to a duel and then withdrawing the summons an hour later) or as dark connivance against his own son. When the young man confides the secret of his infatuation with Katerina, his father leads him to open his heart completely, but he encourages Arkady's effusions only in the hope of obtaining information about the letter to use against Katerina. Versilov finally writes Katerina an insulting letter asking her not to "seduce" an innocent lad to gain her sordid ends, and Arkady is thus humiliated and betrayed by his father in the eyes of the woman he adores.

———■———

By the end of Part 2, Arkady is ready for the major transformation of his personality that will be the reward for all his sufferings. This transformation is the result of his encounter at last with one of the three positive figures in the book (the other two being Arkady's mother and Tatyana Pavlovna, the self-sacrificing family protector who is supporting Versilov and his illegitimate family entirely from her personal savings). By far the most important is the "legal" father whose name Arkady bears, Makar Ivanovich Dolgoruky, the only peasant character of any importance in Dostoevsky's novels (excluding the peasant convicts in *House of the Dead*). His inclusion can surely be attributed to a desire to make literary capital out of the Populist idealization of the peasantry, as well as, unquestionably, an urge to compete with Tolstoy's Platon Karataev in *War and Peace*.

Where Versilov's injunctions to Arkady have been those of a man who, at bottom, entertains no belief in his own convictions, Makar possesses a tranquil certainty that Arkady has never encountered before. The religious "wanderer" is depicted as a person of great dignity and purity of heart, who bears no ill will toward either Versilov or his unfaithful wife. On the contrary, he is filled with a loving concern for her welfare and has taken steps to guarantee Sofya's financial security after his death. Nothing could contrast more strongly with the motives and machinations of the "educated" characters, who are unable to overcome the various egotistical ambitions that color all their conduct. Moreover, the words of the old man, waiting to die with a calm and joyous serenity of spirit and an untroubled faith in Christ's promise, provide Arkady with the moral inspiration he has sought in vain all his life.

Initially, Dostoevsky had seen his novel as dominated by "the idea of disintegration" that was "present everywhere, for everything is falling apart and there are no remaining ties not only in the Russian family, but even simply between people in general. Even children are apart" (16: 16). Much of the sense of dissolution was kept in the book, whose title he once thought could be *Disorder*; but with the inclusion of Makar and his legal wife, Sofya, the humble, downtrodden pair who would be firm as saints, he at last found a center of moral stability amidst the reigning chaos. Such a center was essential because of the very nature of his theme: the precipitous growth into maturity of a rebellious adolescent who has been badly bruised by the vicissitudes of his haphazard boyhood and youth as a member of "an accidental family," but who learns to accept himself and to acquire a sense of social responsibility.

In Makar, Arkady finds embodied a secure conviction of the ultimate goodness of God's creation and a profound sense of wonder and awe at the transcendent mystery both of human existence and of life after death. "Whether the tiny bird is singing, or the stars in all their multitudes shine at night in heaven, the mystery is one, ever the same. And the greatest mystery of all is what awaits the soul of man in the world beyond" (13: 287). Makar's ecstatic celebration of the beauty of life, as is usual in Dostoevsky, comes from a consciousness haunted by death, but death for him is not the stabbing anguish of despair depicted in *The Idiot* through such a character as the nonbeliever Ippolit Terentyev. It is, rather, the natural fulfillment of a life devoted to God, a life whose termination it would be "sinful" to protest against and which still keeps its contact with the world of the living. "You may forget me, dear ones," he says, "but I love you from the tomb." It is after this affirmation that the deeply impressed Arkady declares to him: "There is no 'seemliness' in them. . . . I won't follow them. I don't know where I'm going, I'll go with you" (13: 290–291). Although Arkady's resolution "to follow" Makar and presumably become "a wanderer" is obviously not meant to be taken literally, the impression left by Makar will never be forgotten.

The moral inspiration Arkady needs to surrender his ego to a higher ideal could only be offered by the "idea-feeling" of religious faith. Makar admirably fills this function, and in his notes Dostoevsky indicates his source by a line from Nekrasov's well-known poem "Vlas": "dark-visaged, tall, and straight" (16: 175). Dostoevsky thus ingeniously introduces into the pages of Nekrasov's own journal a figure based on Nekrasov's famous creation—a figure that both caters to the reverence for the peasantry nourished by the radical Populists and also strongly accentuates the religious origins of those peasant virtues they so admired.[1]

Arkady's conversations with Makar run through the first five chapters of Part 3 and provide a commentary on Versilov's discourses at the beginning of Part 2. This is evident from Makar's stories about Pyotr Valerianovich, the educated nobleman who lived in the desert with the monks but could not subdue his "understanding." These stories are meant to illuminate Versilov's inner struggle and also to refer more generally to the moral stirrings among the Russian educated class.

The scenes depicting Makar's stately descent into a dignified death alternate with the unrolling of the intrigue that presents Arkady with his greatest temptation. Arkady's old schoolfellow Lambert finally makes his appearance to serve as his Mephistopheles. Dostoevsky, in his notes, does not mince words about this character: "Lambert—flesh, matter, horror, etc." (16: 28). Lambert has always been the epitome of soulless and shameless carnality, and his arrival stirs Arkady's lascivious longings with the plan to blackmail Katerina into sexual submission by means of the letter. Torn between "seemliness" and naked lust, Arkady finds himself exposed to the full range of the conflict of opposites that constitutes "the Russian fate." "It always has been a mystery," he writes from his vantage point as narrator, "and I have marveled a thousand times at that faculty in man (and in the Russian, I believe, more especially) of cherishing in his soul the loftiest ideal side by side with the most abject baseness, and all quite sincerely" (13: 307). Arkady's situation is now similar, in its inextricable tangle of love-hate feelings for Katerina as goddess and temptress, to that of his father. The recognition of this identity allows him to understand and emotionally to master the events that climax the book in a furious cascade.

These final pages contain a lengthy confession speech by Versilov that is the high point of the novel. The death of Makar temporarily transfigures Versilov's personality, and in a sudden surge of genuine sincerity he finally divulges to Arkady the "idea" that has given inspiration to his life. To express this "idea," which is actually a "vision," Dostoevsky reaches back into his unpublished files and utilizes the myth of the Golden Age initially intended for the unpublished chapters

---

[1] Dostoevsky's notebook entries regarding this peasant world range much more widely than the more limited picture in the finished work. In one, he demonstrates his acquaintance with the theology of the Old Believers. Other notes contain extensive entries about "stinking Lizaveta," who is much more vividly developed here than she will be in *The Brothers Karamazov*. Not merely an inarticulate half-wit, she is consumed by the self-immolating fire of a passionate faith. "Stinking Lizaveta. 'Do not send me, the stinking one, to your bright paradise, but send me into utter darkness, so that even there, in fire and in pain, I could raise my voice to Thee: "Holy, holy art Thou," and I have no other love'" (16: 138).

of Stavrogin's confession. Versilov's version, however, is not moral-psychological but historical-philosophical; it illustrates Dostoevsky's own ideas about the future of European civilization and its relation to Russia. Moreover, in the ideological structure of *A Raw Youth*, Versilov's fantasy parallels that of Makar and is intended to supplement it, thus disclosing the essential unity of the Russian spirit. For Versilov projects in terms of European history what Makar expresses in terms of Russian apocalyptic religiosity.

His dream evokes "a corner of the Greek archipelago . . . blue smiling waves, isles and rocks. . . . Here was the earthly paradise of man." The innocent beauty of this vision, "when the gods came down from the skies and were of one kin with men," filled his heart with "the love of all humanity"; this was "the first day of European civilization"—a civilization whose finest flower was precisely "the love of all humanity" that brings tears of all-embracing tenderness to Versilov's eyes. "Oh, here lived a splendid race! They rose up to sleep and lay down to sleep happy and innocent. . . . Their wealth of untouched strength was spent on simple-hearted joy and love." But when sleep ends, he is jolted back into the hurly-burly of history: "The first day of European civilization which I had seen in my dream was transformed for me at once on awakening into the setting sun of the last day of civilization! One seemed to hear the death knell ringing over Europe in those days" (13: 375).

What sounded this death knell was the recent Franco-Prussian War, the temporary establishment of the Paris Commune, and the burning of the Tuileries that ensued in the struggle for control of the city. In the midst of general chaos, it was only he, as "a Russian European," who could not reconcile himself to this final collapse. Yet in a passage daring for its time, when even liberal Russian opinion regarded the destruction of the Tuileries as an abomination, Dostoevsky did not hesitate to give it a partial justification as an understandable consequence of the flagrant injustices of European society. "I alone among all the conservative reactionaries," Versilov declares, "could have told those bent on revenge that what happened at the Tuileries, though a crime, was still logical" (13: 375–376).

In compelling but ultimately sterile contrast to Makar, who had been a wanderer in Russia as a religious pilgrim, Versilov recalls having been "a solitary wanderer" in Europe. Like Makar, Versilov too was preaching the fulfillment of the reign of love and the advent of the Kingdom of God. "Among us [Russian noblemen]," he declares, "has been created by the ages a type of the highest culture, never seen before and existing nowhere else in the world—a type of worldwide compassion for all" (13: 376–377). This Russian nobleman is a prototype of "the man of the future," and his role is precisely to transcend destructive national differences. The Russian European thus fulfills the injunctions of Christian love on the level of history; the law of his being is to be most himself in total abnegation to others. The Russian peasant-pilgrim Makar and the Russian European

Versilov, each inspired by his own form of the Christian promise, are thus united in their service to this vision of a new Christian Golden Age.

What continues to separate the two, however, will be captured in Versilov's remarkable evocation of an atheistic world deprived of belief in a divine Christ—a world that is the final outcome of the inexorable European process of self-destruction. "The great idea of immortality would have vanished, and they would have to fill its place, and all the wealth of love lavished of old upon Him who was immortal would be turned upon the whole of nature, on the world, on man. . . . Men left forlorn would begin to draw together more closely and more lovingly" (13: 378–379). He thus intuits that the profane Golden Age he envisages, a world without immortality, would be pervaded by an aching sense of sadness and sorrow. This accent placed on the "sorrow" of a world without God—even a world that realizes, on its own terms, the Christian ideal of mutual love—is Dostoevsky's artistic answer to the sublimest secular ideals of Socialism.

Versilov finally breaks off his speech, acknowledging that "the whole thing is a fantasy, even one that is quite unbelievable," but "I couldn't have lived my whole life without it." He defines himself as a "deist, a philosophical deist," not an atheist, which is perhaps meant to suggest an unsatisfied religious longing that remains an abstraction rather than a vitally active personal relationship with the sacred. But Versilov cannot entirely suppress his need for a faith closer to that of Makar. "The remarkable thing," he confides, "is that I . . . could not fail to imagine Him in the last resort among the orphaned people. He would come to them and stretch out his arms to them and . . . there and then the scales would fall from their eyes and there would burst forth a great exalted hymn to the new and total resurrection" (13: 379).

This brilliant and moving portrayal of the Golden Age as a Feuerbachian world, in which mankind, rather than alienating all its love from the earthly to the supernatural, would lavish it on themselves, is one of Dostoevsky's great passages. It equals, in expressive poignancy, Raskolnikov's dream of the plague in *Crime and Punishment*, and it would be hard to find its match elsewhere. What follows is almost embarrassing, as the machinery of the plot is dutifully cranked up to display the vacillations of Versilov on the level of the intrigue.

The details of the intrigue need not concern us, except to note that the morally healing impact of Makar's death proves to be short-lived, and all the most acute symptoms of the "Russian fate" now assail Versilov. Literally, he becomes two people: one is contrite and remorseful over his eccentric and outrageous behavior, while the other continues to perform the most disgraceful actions under the uncontrollable influence of "a second self." "Do you know that I feel as though I were split in two," Versilov says. "Yes, I am really split in two mentally, and I'm horribly afraid of it." Just after uttering these words, moved by the irresistible destructive force of his "second self," he smashes the icon left him as a heritage and pledge for the future by Makar; and though he shouts, "don't take this as being allegorical, Sonya," he admits the significance a moment later: "All right, so take it as an allegory, that's how it was meant!" (13: 408–409). The Russian European "wanderer" from the intelligentsia, whatever the elevation of his spirit, is ultimately unable to take up the burden of the Cross—the "allegory" of his reunion with the Russian people. On the more prosaic level of the plot, Versilov never marries Arkady's mother, even though he is now legally free to do so.

Arkady's speculations about Versilov's demented behavior form part of the epilogue, but it was hardly to be expected that the still callow young man should give any sophisticated analysis of his father's psychological contortions. Arkady cannot draw any definite conclusions, and in refusing to go beyond the immaturity of his narrator Dostoevsky took the considerable risk of turning Versilov too obviously into a pathological case, thus furnishing fuel to the critics who had always charged him with an unhealthy concern for psychic abnormality. Elsewhere, psychic disorder is always presented as the result of a profound moral-spiritual crisis, and the attempt to "explain" it in purely psychiatric terms is satirized and ridiculed.

Versilov, the former man of the world, is now a helpless semi-invalid, entirely dependent on Sofya and Tatyana Pavlovna. "His intelligence and his moral standards have remain unchanged," remarks Arkady, "while his striving for an ideal has become even stronger." Nonetheless, the old, capricious Versilov emerges in a scaled-down replay of the superb deathbed scene of Stepan Trofimovich Verkhovensky. Versilov first expressed a desire to observe the Lenten fast of the Orthodox Church, but then, two days later, because "something had irritated him unexpectedly, something he described laughingly as 'an amusing incongruity,'" he abandons his intention. "'I do love God very much, my friends,' he said, 'but I simply have no talent for these things'"; no conversion of "the philosophical deist" to the rites of Orthodoxy takes place (13: 446–447).

Allusions to numerous writers, both Russian and European, appeared in Dostoevsky's notes for *A Raw Youth*, particularly to Pushkin and Dickens, but most frequently mentioned is Tolstoy, and these references are central to his artistic aim of going beyond what the gentry writers had accomplished. As he had written to Strakhov three years earlier, both Turgenev and Tolstoy had created only "gentry-landowner literature. It has said everything that it had to say (superbly by Lev Tolstoy) . . . but there has not yet been a *new word* to replace that of the gentry-landowners."[2] His desire to pick up the artistic gauntlet had certainly been strengthened recently by the acclaim accorded to *Anna Karenina*.

[2] *PSS*, 29/Bk. 1: 216 n.21; December 2/14, 1870.

If he had not intended to enter into a more overt rivalry with Tolstoy, he was certainly goaded into doing so while defending himself against the hostile attacks provoked by the publication of his first chapters. One critic accused him of excessive "naturalism"—a naturalism so extreme that it violated the rules of art, as if Dostoevsky wished his readers to feel that they were literally participating in the events being depicted, no matter how menacing or threatening. Two venomous articles in the *Russian Messenger*, where his own earlier novels had been published, accused him of being "immoral" and of fixing "the reader in the stinking atmosphere of the underground, [which] . . . blunts his sense of smell and accustoms him to this stinking underground."[3]

His first impulse, which he confided to his notebooks on March 22, 1875, was to answer such denigrations in a preface to be included with the novel's later publication in book form, and the notes for this preface contain the most illuminating self-definitions that he ever gave of his own artistic mission. As he saw it, his aim was to depict the moral-spiritual consequences of living in a society that "had no foundations," and which in fact "hasn't worked out any rules of life, because there really hasn't been any life either." This society has experienced "a colossal shock—and everything comes to a halt, falls down, and is negated as if it hadn't ever existed. And not just externally, as in the West, but internally, morally." Meanwhile, "our most talented writers [he mentions Tolstoy and Goncharov] have been describing the life of the upper middle class," believing they were "describing the life of the majority." But this was an illusion: the life they portray is that "of exceptions, while mine is the life of the general rule" (16: 329).

Dostoevsky speaks of "the civic feeling" that for a moment had led him to think of joining the Slavophils "with the idea of resurrecting the dreams of my childhood" (which included his reverence for Saints Sergius and Tikhon). Instead, he created the underground man, for whom he is now being insulted. "I am proud," he defiantly proclaims, "to have exposed, for the first time, the real image of the Russian majority . . . its misshapen and tragic aspects. The tragic lies in one's awareness of being misshapen." Listing characters created by other writers (including Prince Bolkonsky of *War and Peace* and Levin in *Anna Karenina*), he sees their defects as arising solely from "petty self-love," which can be adjusted according to the fixed social norms of their still unshaken moral-social order. Only *he* had brought out "the tragedy of the underground, which consists of suffering, self-laceration, an awareness of a better life coupled with the impossibility of attaining it. . . . What can sustain those who do try to improve themselves? A reward, faith? Nobody is offering any reward, and in whom could one have faith? Another step from this position, and you have extreme depravity, crime (murder). A mystery" (16: 329).

[3] Cited in *PSS*, 17: 347.

The most crucial problem of all for him was the loss of (religious) faith; and he believed that by his attempts to grapple artistically with the moral-social aftermaths of this deprivation he had probed more deeply into the Russian psyche than the gentry-landowner writers who simply accepted the values of their long-established world, with its precepts for good behavior. Far from flinching at the charges made against him, Dostoevsky glories in the validity of his moral-artistic vision: "Underground, underground, poet of the underground, our feuilleton-ists have been repeating over and over again, as if this were something deroga-tory to me. Silly fools, it is my glory, for that's where the truth lies" (16: 329).

Dostoevsky finally confided his self-defense to an epilogue, written by the character Nikolay Semyenovich, Arkady's guardian during his high school years, and his observations allow Dostoevsky to guide the reader toward a broader social-cultural comprehension of his novel. Dostoevsky's spokesman obliquely refers to Tolstoy when he affirms that a novelist aiming to leave an elegant im-pression "would only write historical novels, since there are no longer beautiful types in our time. . . . Such a novel . . . would provide an artistically finished picture of a Russian mirage, but one that really existed so long as no one guessed it was a mirage." The reference to *War and Peace* is unmistakable, but for Dos-toevsky the beauty of that world was only a mirage based on the slavery of serf-dom. This is why, as Semyenovich adds, implicitly referring to the character of Levin in *Anna Karenina*, "the grandson of the characters depicted in a picture showing a cultured, upper-class Russian family over three generations in a Rus-sian historical setting—such a descendant could not be portrayed otherwise than as misanthropic, isolated; and a sad sight to behold." Levin, in other words, was trying to carry on the tradition but was now gloomily aware that it had been "a mirage" (13: 454).

If this is true for a descendant of such a noble family, how much more would this be the case for someone like Arkady Dolgoruky, the illegitimate offspring of a peasant mother and a father belonging to the hereditary nobility! "Yes, Arkady Makarovich," he is told, "you are *a member of an accidental family*, in complete contrast to all our recent types of legitimate hero who had boyhoods and youths quite unlike yours" (those depicted in Tolstoy's trilogy, *Childhood, Boyhood, Youth*). Versilov himself is described as embodying a chaos of opposites. "He be-longs to one of the oldest families of the nobility while at the same time belong-ing to the Paris Commune. He is a genuine poet, loves Russia, and yet com-pletely denies its value. He has no religion, but he is prepared to die for almost anything vague which he cannot name but in which he can passionately believe, on the example of many, many enlightened Russian Europeanizers of the St. Pe-tersburg period of Russian history." Torn by such contradictions, what tradi-tions and moral-cultural heritage can Versilov transmit to his children? "I con-fess," confides Semyenovich, "I would not want to be a novelist trying to describe a hero from an accidental family! . . . Serious mistakes would be possible, and exaggerations and oversights. . . . But what choice does a writer have who has no wish to write historical novels but is possessed by a longing for the present scene?. . . He has to guess . . . and get it wrong"(13: 455).

Whether or not Dostoevsky believed he had "gotten it wrong," he was here implicitly answering all those critics—among them, some of his closest friends—who were measuring his world against the far more reassuring one created by Tolstoy. Even by his own standard, however, *A Raw Youth* cannot be said to hold its own against the three novels that had been its predecessors. Indeed, if the defects of *A Raw Youth* prove anything, it is that Dostoevsky could do full justice to his talent only when he allowed his eschatological imagination a free rein, and he would take this artistic lesson to heart three years later in *The Brothers Karamazov*.

CHAPTER 50

A Public Figure

With the completion of *A Raw Youth*, Dostoevsky was once again faced with the problem of what to undertake next. Although the publisher of several of his own works, he still had no regular source of income to provide for his family, recently increased to three children with the birth of a new son, Aleksey, on August 10, 1875. Now he returned to the idea of publishing a new periodical, his *Diary of a Writer*, which he had experimented with in *The Citizen*. A family decision was made to take the plunge, even though, as Anna wrote, "if the *Diary* proved to be a failure, we would be put into a hopeless position."[1]

Dostoevsky's decision to undertake his *Diary of a Writer* was an adventurous gamble that marked a new stage in his astonishing career. Although he had once more become a name to be reckoned with on the Russian literary-cultural scene, his fame was still largely confined to intelligentsia circles. With the *Diary of a Writer*, however, he reached out to a much larger and diversified reading public, to whom he spoke eloquently and passionately about matters that were uppermost in the minds of all literate Russians. No one had ever written about such matters so forcefully and vividly, with such directness, simplicity, and intimate personal commitment. It is little wonder that the public response was tremendous, and that Dostoevsky was deluged with correspondence, both pro and contra, the moment his publication appeared in the kiosks.

One of the salons he frequented in these years was that of Elena Shtakenshneider, who attracted everyone by her intelligence, sensitivity, and kindness, and by the stoic courage with which she bore her disfiguring hunchback. Noting the immense popularity of the *Diary*, she wrote in her own diary: "Dostoevsky's fame was not caused by his prison sentence, not by *House of the Dead*, and not even by his novels—at least not primarily by them—but by the *Diary of a Writer*. It was the *Diary* that made his name known in all of Russia, made him the teacher and idol of the youth, yes, and not only the youth but all those tortured by those questions that Heine called 'accursed.'"[2]

---

[1] Anna Dostoevsky, *Reminiscences*, trans. and ed. Beatrice Stillman (New York, 1975), 213.
[2] Cited in *DVS*, 2: 364–365.

His life for the next two years was intimately intertwined with the redaction of the *Diary*. Indeed, the routine necessitated by its regular appearance was so rigorous and exhausting that it left little time for anything else. The *Diary*, all of it written by Dostoevsky, appeared once a month and consisted of sixteen pages. It went on the newsstands on the last day of each month, and he was fanatic about keeping to schedule. Those close to him were aware of the exhausting pressure, both physical and mental, imposed by his *Diary*, and Mikhail Alexandrov, now employed at the printing plant, remarked that "if the expression is justified of some writers that they *write* their works *with their blood*, then this expression fits no one better than Feodor Mikhailovich Dostoevsky." Indeed, on the evidence of working so closely with him for two years, Alexandrov believed that the *Diary* "shortened his life" and that he "squandered on it his physical health, which was affected by it much more than even by his years in *katorga*."[3]

■

The Dostoevskys had lived in Staraya Russa for most of 1875, but the *Diary* required their residence in St. Petersburg once more, and they returned to the capital in mid-September, where they secured five modest rooms in an aging apartment house. Alexandrov was particularly struck by the bareness of the study, which reminded him of a monastic cell. A Turkish couch covered with oilcloth also served as a bed, and there were two tables. One was covered with a pile of magazines and newspapers; the other, larger table was garnished with an inkwell, a pen, and a thick notebook "in which Feodor Mikhailovich noted down individual ideas and facts for his future works." Above the table hung a photograph of Dostoevsky, and before it stood an armchair with a hard seat. There was no mistaking that this was the workplace of a writer, and its "strict, almost impoverished simplicity" inspired in Alexandrov "a great respect."[4]

Dostoevsky's routine now varied but little. Writing late at night and into the early morning, he slept until two in the afternoon or later. Once having risen, and donning a loose and lengthy jacket of dark broadcloth, he went to the samovar awaiting him in the dining room. Returning with his glass of tea to the study, he drank several cups as he read the newspapers and rolled cigarettes out of thick yellow paper. After tea he received visitors, and at three o'clock he ate a light meal in the dining room. Dostoevsky drank a wineglass of vodka with the meal, sipping it as he chewed on a slice of black bread, once explaining to Alexandrov that this was the healthiest way to take vodka. After finishing, he went for a walk, dropping in at the printing plant on his stroll, and returning at six o'clock to dine with the family and put the children to bed before settling down to work.

[3] Ibid., 286.
[4] Ibid., 282–283.

Such was his normal schedule and behavior, which, if nothing unexpected occurred, went smoothly and equably. But if he was unwarily aroused before his accustomed time, he became "despondently serious and silent," and in such a mood he could flare up suddenly in an outburst of irritability: "He easily got angry, and then spoke harshly," appearing to be "rude and despotic even with those close to him." But Alexandrov hastens to add that those who knew him best were aware that they represented only a momentarily unsettled state of his nerves.[5]

Concern over the future of his young children no doubt contributed to his anxiety; and it is in this context that we find Dostoevsky keeping a vigilant eye on the legal proceedings in the Kumanina estate. In November Dostoevsky assures his youngest brother Andrey that, contrary to rumors, in filing suit to exclude some collateral relatives of his aunt from any claim to a share of the estate, he was "looking after their own interests." After getting the money, he would "immediately divide it up among them and would take for myself only enough to cover the expenses of the proceedings and not a kopek more." Dostoevsky adds that, "by giving up to them [his sisters] what *by law should come to me*," he was "taking away from my children what was legally theirs."[6] (His suit proved unsuccessful.) A few months later, he writes to Andrey that he wishes "to live at least another seven years" in order to establish a firm foundation for the future of his children.[7] He had long been haunted by the fear of death because of his epilepsy, but the dread of a sudden decease had now been replaced by the conviction that he was slowly succumbing to the undermining effects of his emphysema.

A few months into publishing the *Diary*, Dostoevsky learned from a letter of Khristina Alchevskaya, a lady active in the cause of educating the people, that some considered that he was wasting his time "with trifles, with a survey of current events, little stories and suchlike." Apparently having heard the same reproach from others, he replied: "I have reached the irresistible conclusion that in addition to the original artistic inspiration, a writer of belles lettres must also know the reality portrayed down to the smallest detail (historical and current)." Far from viewing the *Diary* as a departure from his artistic task, he explained that it was an indispensable preliminary for his future works. "That is why, while preparing to write a very long novel, I in fact planned to immerse myself specifically into the study . . . of the details of contemporary life." Among such details, "one of the most important . . . is the younger generation, and with it, the contemporary Russian family."[8]

[5] Ibid., 285.
[6] *PSS*, 29/Bk. 2: 66–67; November 10, 1875.
[7] Ibid., 75–76; March 10, 1876.
[8] Ibid., 78; April 9, 1876.

The very first (January 1876) issue of his *Diary* was devoted to the theme of children, and as a preparation he asked his legal friend A. F. Koni to arrange a visit to a colony of juvenile criminals. The two men made the journey in late December 1875, and Koni mentions Dostoevsky's passionate attentiveness, "asking questions and inquiring into the smallest details in the routine of the fledglings." He was struck by Dostoevsky's ability to engage with the boys, whom he gathered together in one of the larger rooms. "He answered their questions, some searching and some naïve, but little by little this conversation turned into a lesson on his part . . . filled with the genuine love of children that shines through every page of his creations." When the two men left the room to visit the adjoining church, the boys flocked around and continued to speak with him about incidents from their lives. "One felt that . . . a spiritual bond had been created, and that they sensed in him not a *curiosity-seeking* visitor but a grieving *friend.*" [9]

On the journey home he spoke about the church they had visited. It was filled with icons, some very old and confiscated from Old Believers by the police; others, particularly those of the iconostasis guarding the priestly sanctuary, were painted in a newer, Italianate style: "I don't like that church," he muttered. "It's some sort of museum. . . . In order to act on the souls of those entering, one needs only a few images, but severe, even stern ones, just as the belief and duty of a Christian must be severe and stern." [10] Such images should accompany the boys when they fell back into the urban maelstrom from which most of them had come and recall for them the far-off days of their pure and unsullied village childhood, thus offering some moral protection against the temptation to criminal activity.

Much attention is paid in the *Diary* to criminal trials, which he always regarded as an indispensable barometer of the moral climate of the times. Although he was not in the courtroom of all the cases discussed in his *Diary* (accounts of them were carried in the daily press of the capital and provinces), he was present at some and took an active part in one, in which a young mother had been condemned to penal servitude in Siberia. Ekaterina Kornilova had pushed her six-year-old stepdaughter out of a tenement window. The girl emerged unhurt, and the stepmother immediately went to the police to denounce herself. Kornilova was in an advanced state of pregnancy and her state, Dostoevsky believed, led her to give way to a latent hostility toward her stepdaughter (as well as her husband, the father, who had beaten her that very morning). It was well known, Dostoevsky argued, that pregnant women sometimes behaved in a most peculiar fashion. On these grounds he raised the possibility

---

[9] *DVS*, 2: 242–243.
[10] Ibid.

of reversing the verdict. A reader of the *Diary*, a lawyer familiar with the process of obtaining pardons for convicted criminals, wrote Dostoevsky that he had been persuaded by his analysis. Urging Dostoevsky to visit Kornilova, he suggested advising her to ask for such a pardon and volunteered to help guide the request through the bureaucratic labyrinth. Dostoevsky did so, and his articles unquestionably played their part in the reversal of her conviction on appeal and then the dismissal of the case, though the jury was warned not to give too much weight to the opinions of "certain talented writers."[11]

The public responded not only to Dostoevsky's provocative ideas on topical issues; his very language—he addressed his readers as if he were conducting a private conversation rather than developing a thesis—produced an unusual sense of familiarity with his readers, who deluged him with letters to which he often responded both personally and in the pages of his journal. The felt need to communicate with the author of the *Diary* led to a number of unexpected encounters, such as the one recorded in Dostoevsky's letter to Alchevskaya of April 9, 1876. "Suddenly," he tells her, "the day before yesterday, in the morning, two girls, both about twenty, came to see me. . . . 'Everybody laughed at us and said you wouldn't receive us. . . . But we decided to try.'"[12] One can hardly imagine such an incident occurring earlier, when his public image had been shaped by the fearsome convicts he had portrayed in *House of the Dead*, or by the tormented protagonists of his novels. The Dostoevsky of the *Diary*, however, was a friend and counselor, and such impromptu visitors as the two girls were no longer a rarity. "They said they were students at the medical academy, that about five hundred women were there now, and that 'they enrolled in the academy so as to obtain a higher education and then do some good.'"

The humanitarian aims of those future doctors were extremely appealing, and Dostoevsky took them as an immensely encouraging sign of a new state of mind among the younger female generation, whom he contrasts favorably with earlier examples of the "new woman." "I hadn't come across this new type of woman (I knew lots of the old *female nihilists*). Would you believe that rarely have I spent time better than I did these two hours with these girls. What simplicity, naturalness, freshness of feeling, purity of mind and heart."[13] The next two issues of the *Diary* (May and June) contain strong affirmations for providing women the means to obtain a higher education.

Alchevskaya stresses in her memoirs that, "most sharply of all remains in my memory the following trait, quite outstanding in Dostoevsky . . . his fear of ceasing to understand the younger generation, of breaking with it. . . . In this

---

[11] Cited in the commentary to the letter of Maslannikov, the lawyer who offered his help, in *Dostoevsky i ego vremya* (Leningrad, 1971), 277.

[12] *PSS*, 29/Bk. 2: 79; April 9, 1876.

[13] Ibid.

28. Dostoevsky in 1876

idée fixe there was not any fear at all of ceasing to be a beloved writer or of decreasing the number of his followers and readers; no, he obviously regarded a *disagreement* with the young generation as a human *downfall*, as a moral death. He boldly and honorably defends his intimate convictions; and at the same time somehow fears not fulfilling the mission entrusted to him, and inadvertently losing his way."[14] No more penetrating remark about him at this stage of his

[14] *DVS*, 337.

career has ever been made. For he *did* feel that a mission had been entrusted to him, the mission of guiding the young generation back to the path of the Russian people's truth—which for him meant primarily the faith of the people in God. And for this reason he considered a definitive severance from younger readers to be the equivalent of a human downfall and a moral death.

In the summer of 1876 Dostoevsky made another trip to Bad Ems, where he drank the waters for a month. Such an absence, of course, involved special problems for the publication of his monthly *Diary*, and he published only a July–August combined issue. Dostoevsky's letters from Ems had always been filled with expressions of his tenderness for Anna, as well as reminders of the physical passion that united the couple. So now; and, on reading them over many years later, Anna thought it prudent to black out a number of passages that were too explicit for her decorous sensibility. These letters are among the most mutilated in the Dostoevsky canon, though one can still read his avowal that he has fallen in love with her four or five times since their marriage, and that this has now occurred again. "Anechka," he writes, "all I do is think of you. I think of you in all possible sorts of pictures and representations. . . . I love you to the point of torment." [15] This flare-up of passion may perhaps be linked to an episode occurring just before his departure, when he and Anna had quarreled because of a curious incident that she recounts in her memoirs.

A friend of theirs had written a novel that both had read, and in which an anonymous letter informed one of the characters that his wife had been unfaithful; the proof could be found in a locket that she wore. Anna decided, as a "joke," to send such a letter to Dostoevsky, assuming he would recognize the imitation of the text and that they both would enjoy a hearty laugh. Instead, he ripped her locket from her neck, drawing blood, and was furious. "'You keep on joking, Anechka,' he said, 'but just think what a terrible thing might have happened. I might have strangled you in my rage!'" Once his fury had subsided, however, the evening "passed in apologies, regrets, and the most loving tenderness"—which one suspects was the aim of the whole escapade. [16] An exchange of letters about the reappearance of one of Anna's ex-suitors also indicates that she was again attempting to stimulate his jealousy, perhaps as a means of warding off possible attractions abroad.

Dostoevsky purchased a guest register of the visitors at Ems but was unable to find the names of anyone he knew among those of rank, and he had no wish to meet the others. They were all "Russian Yids and Germans—bankers and

---

[15] *PSS*, 29/Bk. 2: 95–98; July 13/25, 1876.
[16] *Reminiscences*, 264.

pawnbrokers. Not a single acquaintance."[17] He met by chance the well-known radical publicist G. Z. Eliseev, who was also taking the cure and with whom he had rubbed elbows in St. Petersburg. It was Eliseev who had penned a bitterly hostile review of the first chapters of *Crime and Punishment*, but he had also responded generously to Timofeyeva's inquiry about publishing *A Raw Youth* in *Notes of the Fatherland*. Nevertheless, Dostoevsky's first impression of Eliseev in Ems was hardly favorable. "The old 'negator' doesn't believe in anything . . . he absolutely has a seminarian's haughty smugness."[18] Every meeting raised the hackles on both sides. "The trashy vulgar little liberals," he fumes nine days later, "have undone my nerves. They force themselves on me and greet me constantly, but treat me as though they were being careful 'so as not to get soiled by my reactionaryism.' The vainest creatures, especially her, a banal little book with liberal rules. 'Oh what he says, oh what he defends!' These two think of teaching someone like me."[19] The Eliseevs vanished henceforth from his correspondence—but not from his literary purview. For there is good reason to believe that the cynical Rakitin of *The Brothers Karamazov*, who never takes his eyes off the main chance, is based on a caricature of the career of Grigory Eliseev.

All through this period Dostoevsky doggedly continued to make preparations to write and informs Anna that "I have been rereading all the correspondence [from his readers] that I brought here. I signed up at the lending library (a pathetic library), took out Zola because I've terribly neglected European literature in recent years, and just imagine, I can scarcely read it, it's such revolting stuff. And in Russia people carry on about Zola as a celebrity, a leading light of realism."[20] Emile Zola was then writing a regular letter from Paris in the liberal *European Messenger*, having been recommended by his friend Turgenev, and he was hailed as the leading proponent and practitioner of a literary naturalism enjoying a considerable vogue. Several translations of one novel alone—*Le ventre de Paris* (*The Belly of Paris*), the book Dostoevsky borrowed from the Ems library—had been published in 1873, and there were widespread discussions of Zola's works and theories in the Russian press.

He jotted down his first reactions in his notebooks: "He will describe every nail in the heel, a quarter hour later, when the sun rises, he will again describe that nail in a different light. That is not art. Give me a single word (Pushkin), but make it the necessary word. Otherwise it . . . drags in ten thousand words, and still cannot express itself, and this with the most complete self-satisfaction, but spare me." Nor can he accept the morality that Zola contrasted with the purely materialistic ambitions and satisfactions of his shopkeeper and tradesman

---

[17] *PSS*, 29/Bk. 2: 105; July 18/30, 1876.
[18] Ibid., 104; July 21/August 2, 1876.
[19] Ibid., 117; July 30/August 11, 1876.
[20] Ibid., 99–100; July 15/27, 1876.

figures. "*Florent* [an ex-revolutionary returned from prison] dies of hunger and proudly spurned the help of an honest woman. *Zola* considers this a heroic deed, but in his heart there is no brotherhood, what sort of republican is he? Accept her help and render it to others out of the fullness of a noble heart—that will be paradise on earth" (24: 238–239). Little did he know, as he was scribbling these remarks, that ten years later his own novels would help to break the grip of Zola's naturalism on a new French literary generation.

His morose mood during these days was considerably lifted by a letter from Vsevolod Solovyev, who also sent a copy of an enthusiastic article he had written about the June issue of the *Diary*. This fascicule contained a statement of Dostoevsky's exalted conception of Russia's world-historical mission. The task of Russia, he proclaimed, was to bring about the union of all the Slavs and thus resolve the Eastern question; and this unification would be the prelude to a universal reconciliation of all peoples under the banner of the true Christ preserved only in Russian Orthodoxy. Dostoevsky was pleased with Solovyev's accolade because he felt that in this issue, for the first time, he had at last dared to allow himself "to take *certain* of my convictions to their conclusions, to say *the last word* . . . of my dreams regarding Russia's role and mission amid humanity, and I expressed the idea that this . . . was already beginning to come true." The result had been that "even the newspapers and publications friendly to me straight away started yelling that I heaped paradox on paradox."[21]

———■———

Dostoevsky's *Diary* became the most widely read of all such publications during its two-year life span, reaching audiences not only in the depths of the Russian provinces but also in the highest court circles. In the fall of 1876, Pobedonostsev requested that he send a copy regularly to Tsarevich Alexander. "I know," wrote the crown prince's tutor, "that yesterday, in the presence of his brothers, he spoke of several articles and recommended them to their attention."[22] Overjoyed, Dostoevsky wrote directly to Alexander, to whom he had presented a dedicated copy of *Demons* three years earlier, saying that "the present great energies in Russian history have elevated the spirits and hearts of the Russian people with unimaginable power to a height of understanding of much that was not earlier understood, and have illuminated in our consciousness *the sanctity of the Russian idea* more vividly than ever before. . . . I have long since thought and dreamed of the happiness of offering my modest work to your Imperial Highness." He then excuses himself for his "boldness," and asks that the crown prince "not condemn one who loves you boundlessly."[23]

[21] Ibid., 101–103; July 16/28, 1876.
[22] Ibid., 271; November 13, 1876.
[23] Ibid., 132–133; November 16, 1876.

Dostoevsky well knew that his own veneration for tsarism was hardly shared by those socially conscious members of the younger generation he was trying to influence. Indeed, there were disquieting signs that radical activity was no longer confined to "going to the people." Discouraged by their failure to arouse the countryside, the Populists in 1876 were rethinking their position and turning to political agitation to attain their aims. One of the first open manifestations of this change of tactics was a demonstration in the square leading to the Church of Our Lady of Kazan in St. Petersburg. In December 1876 a small group led by G. V. Plekhanov (later the founder of the Russian Communist Party and the mentor of Lenin) gathered to listen to a speech by their leader and unfurled a red banner bearing the words "Land and Liberty" (Zemlya i Volya), the name of their revolutionary organization. The police, as well as local workmen and shopkeepers, charged into the group, and many of the demonstrators were severely beaten before being taken into custody.

For Dostoevsky, the demonstration was simply another instance of how easily Russian youth could be misled because of the purity of their moral idealism. "The young people on December 6 in Kazan Square," he wrote in his *Diary*, "were doubtless nothing more than a 'herd' driven on by the hands of some crafty scoundrels. . . . Without a doubt there was a good deal of malicious and immoral tomfoolery here, a monkeylike aping of someone else's doings; nonetheless, it would have been possible to bring them together simply by assuring them that they were to gather in the name of something sublime and beautiful, in the name of some remarkable self-sacrifice for the greatest of purposes" (24: 52). One of the aims of Dostoevsky's *Diary* was to encourage such youthful self-sacrifice for what he considered worthier causes than those proclaimed in Kazan Square.

In May 1877, the Dostoevskys left St. Petersburg for the spring and summer months at Maly Prikol, the country estate of Anna's brother Ivan Snitkin, located in the province of Kursk. Anna's health had begun to flag under her combined responsibilities as mother, homemaker, and business manager, and Dostoevsky insisted that she take a complete rest during the summer. Russia had declared war against Turkey in April 1877, and on the journey to Maly Prikol Anna recalls the long delays at various stations, "where our train had to stand for hours because of the movement of the troops being sent off to war. At every stop Feodor Mikhailovich would go to the buffet and buy large quantities of rolls, honey cakes, cigarettes, and matches, and take them into the cars where he would give them out to the soldiers and have long talks with them."[24]

At the end of June, the family departed together from Maly Prikol and separated at the railroad junction that took Anna and the two older children on a

---

[24] *Reminiscences*, 283.

pilgrimage to Kiev, the cradle of Old Russian civilization, and Dostoevsky to Petersburg. While in the capital, he received only one letter from his wife in a two-week period and became frantic for lack of news. The four letters he wrote are also filled with exasperation at the problems encountered with issuing the *Diary* on time, as well as in supervising its printing, binding, and mailing to various distributors. The personal origin of some of his most haunting literary scenes is illuminated in a passage describing the effects of a severe epileptic attack. "At 6:30 this morning," he informs Anna, "on coming to after a seizure I headed off *to your room* and suddenly Prokhorovna told me in the parlor that the mistress wasn't home. 'Where is she?' 'Why, she's in the country at a summer house.' 'How can that be? She should be here. When did she leave?' Prokhorovna persuaded me that I had only arrived the day before yesterday myself."[25] Dostoevsky's remarkable capacity to depict such states of semiconsciousness, when a character behaves according to subliminal drives and impulses, evidently derives from such episodes in his own life. He wrote his younger brother Nikolay that the seizure "has shattered me," and he asked Nikolay, whom he saw rarely under ordinary circumstances, to come for a visit.

His seizures had apparently affected even his long-term memory. P. V. Bykov, a journalist and writer who had met Dostoevsky in the 1860s, had recently requested a biography and bibliography for a volume of essays on Russian writers that he planned to publish. But Dostoevsky confesses, "I'll tell you right out that at present I am incapable of [sending you an exact biography]. As a consequence of my epilepsy . . . I have somewhat lost my memory, and—would you believe— have forgotten (literally forgotten, without the slightest exaggeration) plots of my novels and characters portrayed, even in *Crime and Punishment*. Nonetheless, I do remember the general outlines of my life."[26] He promised Bykov that he would perhaps "put together my biography for you" in Ems, where he planned to spend the summer.

The torment of not receiving any reply to his missives was more than he could endure, and he sent off two telegrams to Maly Prikol inquiring about Anna's well-being. When a letter finally arrived on July 16, he wrote the next day to justify his harassed behavior. "I haven't been able to sleep, I worry, sort through the chances [of an accident] pace around the room, have visions of the children, worry about you, my heart pounds (I've had palpitations of the heart start up these last three days). . . . It finally begins to dawn, and I sob, pace around the room and cry, with a sort of shaking (I don't understand it myself, it's never happened before) and I just try not to let the old woman [Prokhorovna] hear it."[27] This passage can stand for many others in which he describes losing control of

[25] *PSS*, 29/Bk. 2: 163; July 7, 1877.

[26] Ibid., 80; April 15, 1876.

[27] Ibid., 170–173; July 17, 1877.

his nerves as his fertile imagination conjures up every disaster that might befall his family, especially the children.

Despite his desire to return to the sheltering warmth of the family circle, Dostoevsky felt it imperative to make a journey to Darovoe, the country property of his parents, unvisited since childhood, and now occupied by the family of his sister Varvara Karepina, who had inherited the property. He referred to this trip in his July–August 1877 *Diary*, where he reports on a conversation with "one of my old Moscow acquaintances" (probably Ivan Aksakov). "This little, unremarkable spot," he told his friend, "had left a deep and strong impression on me for my whole life." Dostoevsky emphasizes the importance for children to store up "sacred memories" (a point he will illustrate through Alyosha Karamazov), and writes that "a person cannot even live without something sacred and precious from childhood to carry into life" (25: 172). Dostoevsky's visit had unquestionably brought back recollections of his own father. A passage in Dostoevsky's text can be read as a confession of how he may have judged (and pardoned) his own progenitor.

"Today's fathers," he writes, do not possess any "great idea" that they pass on to their children, and "in their hearts" they have no great faith in such an idea. Yet, "it is only a great faith of this kind that is capable of giving birth to *something beautiful* in the memories of children, and indeed it can, even despite that same moral filth that surrounds their cradles. . . . [E]ven . . . the most fallen of fathers, who . . . has been able to transplant the seed of this great idea and great feeling into the impressionable and eager souls of his pitiable children, . . . has later been wholeheartedly forgiven by them because of this good deed alone, despite other things" (25: 180–181). Dostoevsky often uses the expression "great idea" to mean the idea of the Christian morality of love and the Christian promise of eternity. He could well have felt, after the visit to Darovoe, that his own far from blameless father had nevertheless succeeded in planting these seeds in the hearts of his children.

During the fall and winter months of 1877 Dostoevsky toiled away at the *Diary*, even though he had been *"sick in bed* for two weeks with a fever." [28] In October 1877, however, he informed readers of the *Diary* that he intended to terminate its publication at the end of the year. An old confidant, Dr. Stepan Yanovsky, wrote from Vevey in Switzerland, expressing gratitude on behalf of the Russian circle there for the patriotic support given their homeland in the *Diary*. Like many others, Yanovsky expressed regret at the cessation of the *Diary*, and Dostoevsky explains that, aside from the worsening of his epilepsy, he had decided to suspend publication because "there is a novel in my head and my heart, and it's beginning to be written." Moreover, in the future "I want to try a

---

[28] Ibid., 176–177; December 7, 1877.

new publication into which the *Diary* will enter as a part."[29] Early in 1878 he had sketched a plan for such a new monthly, no longer written exclusively by himself, that included more literary material and critical essays. "You wouldn't believe to what an extent I have enjoyed the sympathy of Russians during these two years of publication," he exultantly informs the doctor. Yanovsky had spoken disparagingly of Kraevsky's newspaper, *Voice*, which had become highly critical of the Russo-Turkish War, and Dostoevsky snaps, "These gentlemen will in fact disappear. . . . Those who do not understand the people will now undoubtedly have to join the stockbrokers and the Yids, and that's the end of the representatives of our 'progressive' thought,"[30] The "Yids" are thus automatically associated with all those non-Jewish Russians who remain skeptical about the war, and whose motives for doing so, in his extremely jaundiced eyes, can only be grossly and sordidly material.

—■—

Nekrasov died in December 1877, and the Dostoevskys attended the church services at the Novodeichy convent. Hordes of students and admirers came to pay their last respects to the poet who had given poignant expression to the social-humanitarian themes of the 1840s, and had later written so movingly of the limitless sorrows of Russian peasant life in his great cycle of poems, *Who Is Happy In Russia?* Several people spoke at the graveside, among them Dostoevsky, who improvised some remarks in response to a request, as Anna writes, from "the surrounding crowd of young people."[31] Nekrasov, Dostoevsky said, "was the last of that series of poets who came to us with their 'new word,'" and that "among such poets he should stand directly after Pushkin and Lermontov." At this, a dissenting "voice from the crowd cried out that Nekrasov was *greater* than Pushkin and Lermontov and that the latter were only 'Byronists.'" Several voices coming from a small group led by Plekhanov then took up the refrain and shouted, "Yes, greater!"[32]

This small episode may stand as a symbolic indication of the growing aggressiveness of the hitherto peaceful Populists. During 1877 the government brought three groups of them to trial: those who had demonstrated before the Cathedral of Kazan and two groups arrested for having "gone to the people" three years earlier. The second trial, known as that of "the fifty," produced a deep and lasting impression on the radical intelligentsia. The accused testified with great dignity about the intolerable conditions they had been forced to endure, and brought the more humane and educated members of the public face to face with the

[29] Ibid., 178–179; December 17, 1877.
[30] Ibid.
[31] *Reminiscences*, 288.
[32] *PSS*, 26: 112–113; 416.

grim realities of a repressive regime. This public was shocked by the unconscionable length of time these young people had been imprisoned before being brought to trial, and by the severe sentences meted out for their perfectly peaceable and often charitable "crimes."

There are numerous contemporary accounts of the religiously charged atmosphere that surrounded the trial of "the fifty," during which, according to the Populist radical writer Stepniak-Kravchinsky, the word "saints" was often heard uttered about the defendants by those in the courtroom.[33] D. N. Ovsyaniko-Kulikovsky writes:

> Not all, perhaps, but very many of those who went to the people were inspired . . . by the evangelical ideal of loving one's neighbor, and of sacrificing one's worldly goods and personal happiness. When the so-called "trial of the fifty" disclosed the activity of young women self-sacrificingly carrying the "good news" of Socialism, motifs from the Gospels, parallels with the Sermon on the Mount, involuntarily came to mind. These young women could look forward in life to happiness and satisfaction, among them were some with considerable wealth. . . . But they preferred to this the life of a saint, they exchanged their happiness for a heroic deed, and sacrificed themselves for a high ideal, which seemed to them only a new expression of this very same evangelical ideal.[34]

At the trial, in a speech that quickly became famous, one of the accused, Sophia Bardini, declared, "As regards religion [whose precepts she had been accused of violating], I may say only that I have always remained faithful to its existing principles, in that pure form in which it was preached by the founder of Christianity."[35] One of the last poems that Nekrasov wrote on his deathbed was inspired by this trial, and there is good reason to believe that it echoed in Dostoevsky's work as well. Just a year later, he began to draft *The Brothers Karamazov*; and when he came to describe his young hero, Alyosha, whose life would constitute the second (never written) volume, he wrote, "if he had decided that God and immortality did not exist, he would at once have become an atheist and Socialist (for Socialism is . . . the question of the Tower of Babel built without God, not to mount to Heaven from earth but to set up Heaven on earth" (14: 25). Alyosha's innate goodness and craving for justice led him to become a novice in a monastery once he had decided in favor of God and immortality. Both he and the Socialists look forward to the reign of goodness and charitable

[33] See Franco Venturi, *The Roots of Revolution* (New York, 1966), 586.

[34] D. N. Ovsyaniko-Kulikovsky, "Istoria Russkoi intelligentsia," *Sobranie sochinenii*, 10 vols. (St. Petersburg, 1910–1911), 8: 193–194.

[35] Quoted in V. Bogucharsky, *Aktivnoe narodnichestvo semidesyatikh godov* (Moscow, 1912), 298.

love; they differ only on whether it should be attained under the guidance of a secular or a supernatural Christ.

It was not only through his next novel, however, that Dostoevsky hoped to influence the young radicals to follow the way of Alyosha. For over two years he had attempted to do so in the *Diary of a Writer*. Let us now turn back for a closer look at this massive publication, which dominated Russian public opinion as no such journal had ever done before.

CHAPTER 51

The Diary of a Writer, 1876–1877

The ideas promulgated in the *Diary of a Writer* were already familiar from Dostoevsky's earlier journalism, as well as from the ideological flights of his novels. But they are given new life and color by the constant parade of fresh examples drawn from his omnivorous reading of the current press, from his wide knowledge of history and literature both Russian and European, and, very frequently, from the events of his own life. Such autobiographical revelations were certainly one of the main attractions of the *Diary*; readers felt they were truly being admitted into the intimacy of one of their great men. This constant interplay between the personal and the public—the incessant shift of level between the social problems of the day, the "accursed questions" that have always plagued human life, and the glimpses into the recesses of Dostoevsky's own private life and sensibility—proved an irresistible combination that gave the *Diary* its unique literary cachet.

In addition, the *Diary* served as a stimulus not only for short stories and sketches but also, as he had anticipated, for the major novel he was planning to write. Time and again motifs appear that will soon be utilized in *The Brothers Karamazov*. Even if not literally a notebook, the *Diary* lives up to this name in the exact sense of the word. It is genuinely the working tool of a writer in the early stages of creation—a writer who searches for (and finds) the inspiration for his work as, pen in hand, he surveys the passing scene and attempts to cope with its deeper import.

I. Journalism

In the 1860s, Dostoevsky's journals had advanced a doctrine of *pochvennichestvo*, advocating the return of the intelligentsia to their own native soil, to their own culture and its moral-religious roots and values. This conception of the ideal relation between the intelligentsia and the people forms the background for the treatment of this question in the *Diary*. The peasants were liberated with land, Dostoevsky writes in the June 1876 issue, "because we saw ourselves as Russians, with the Tsar at our head, exactly as the landowner Pushkin dreamed forty years ago, when . . . he cursed his European upbringing and turned to the principles of the people" (22: 120).[1] "Our demos is content," he announces with astonishing complacency, "and the further we go, the more satisfied it will become, for everything is moving toward that end via the common mood, or, to put it better, the general consensus" (22: 122). Dostoevsky was firmly persuaded that the governing class would continue to act in the name of the people's own supposedly Christian ideals. When many readers vociferously objected that the Russian demos was far from being satisfied, he took their criticisms only as additional proof of the good will of the educated class and further corroboration of his point of view ("even now no one here will stand up for the idea that we must bestialize one group of people for the welfare of another group that represents civilization, such as is the case all over Europe") (22: 31).

In a February 1876 entry dealing with Konstantin Aksakov, Dostoevsky restates the key ideas of *pochvennichestvo*. Putting the question bluntly, he asks: "Who is better, we [the intelligentsia] or the people?" And he answers: "we must bow down before the people's truth and acknowledge it as the truth, even in the awful event that some of it comes from the *Lives of the Saints*" (22: 44). "In what way," he asks, "did we, the cultured people, become *morally and essentially* superior to the people when we returned from Europe?" (22: 110). The answer that he gives is unequivocal: in no way at all, and in fact, quite the contrary.

The same point is made when he discusses the example of Foma Danilov in the January 1877 issue. This Russian soldier, captured in Turkestan, had refused under torture to convert to Islam (Smerdyakov, in *The Brothers Karamazov*, thinks he was a fool). A pension had recently been awarded his impoverished family by the tsar, and for Dostoevsky he becomes "what amounts to the portrait, the complete picture of the Russian people." It is time for the intelligentsia to ask themselves whether there is "something moral, something sublime to pass on to them [the people], to explain to them, and thus to bring light to their dark souls?" Not at all. "The people have Foma Danilovs by the thousands, while we have no faith at all in Russian strength" (25: 12–17).

The most important political event affecting the *Diary* was the outbreak of a revolt against Turkish rule in the Slavic province of Herzegovina during the summer of 1875. In mid-June 1876, the independent Slav principalities of Serbia and Montenegro also declared war against Turkey. In April 1877, Russia joined the conflict in the Russo-Turkish War of 1877–1878, whose immediate cause was the Turkish refusal to agree to Russian demands to accord more rights to Balkan

---

[1] The commentator of the Academy edition, searching for some basis for Dostoevsky's startling assertion, could only find a quotation from a letter of Pushkin written in 1824. While living in the country, the poet describes his activities, and remarks that in the evening he listens to peasant tales (*skazki*). "With these," he says, "I make up for the shortcomings of my damned education" (22: 380).

Christians living under Turkish rule. Dostoevsky was a member of the Slavic Benevolent Society, which had been in the forefront of Pan-Slavic agitation, and was a fervent supporter of both the rebellion and the war. More and more of the articles in the *Diary*, especially in 1877, proclaimed the momentous moral-spiritual consequences, for Russia and for world history, of what seemed to others merely another struggle for territory and power. Their inflammatory appeal, justifying the war on the highest moral-religious principles, helped to stir up patriotic fervor and evoked widespread response.

If Dostoevsky could brilliantly sweep aside denigrations of the people, it was still difficult for him to produce evidence to support his own contrary view of their exalted moral essence. The declaration of war by Serbia and Montenegro against Turkey was a godsend. The Russian volunteer movement, organized to support the Slavs, led to a mass outpouring not only of material aid but also of men volunteering to join the Serbian Army and women to serve as nurses. The people had embarked on "a new crusade" because they had heard that "their Slav brethren were being tortured and oppressed." No such solidarity had been expected of this "supposedly homogeneous and torpid mass." It certified for Dostoevsky that the Russian people still admired someone "who continually works for God's cause, who loves the truth, and who, when it is necessary, rises up to serve that truth, leaving his home and his family and sacrificing his life." This is why, as he informs his readers, "we can joyously allow ourselves to hope anew, our horizon has cleared, and our new sun rises with dazzling brilliance" (23: 161–162).

The final stage of Dostoevsky's apotheosis of the Russian people came after the Russian declaration of war against Turkey. Now he argues that the Russian people possess as well the capacity to create a new Christian world order. Indeed, this was the basis on which Dostoevsky believed that the people and the educated class could be brought together. The Europeanized Russian intellectuals and the people are united, with no awareness of their agreement, in the faith that Russia "will pronounce the greatest word that the world has heard," and that this word will be the mandate for the unity of all humanity in a spirit transcending "personal egoism" and "the struggle for existence" that "now unites people and nations artificially and unnaturally" (25: 19–20). Because Dostoevsky made no distinction between the Russian state and the Russian people, such lofty pronouncements also served to provide a morally attractive façade for Russian imperialism in the Balkans and Central Asia.

———————■———————

No question at this time agitated Dostoevsky more viscerally than the movement to liberate the Balkan Slavs. Even his review of Tolstoy's *Anna Karenina* focused on what the novel disclosed about the present state of Russian society and its opposing attitudes toward the Balkan Slavs. He vehemently attacks Tolstoy—already showing traces of his future pacifism and doctrine of nonresistance to evil—for having denigrated the Russian volunteer movement. Levin ridicules this military initiative as artificial and insincere, whipped up by propaganda rather than inspired by any true, spontaneous feelings of sympathy with brother Slavs. Dostoevsky took such words, with good reason, as a direct challenge to the views he had so passionately expressed in his *Diary*. And he thus mercilessly rips apart this new aspect of Levin, who is now revealed to be not really one of "the people" at all. Hence he cannot genuinely understand the national impulse that had arisen spontaneously to aid the Balkan Slavs.

The reader is invited to accept Levin as a seeker after "truth," who finally discovers it when, instructed by the casual remarks of a peasant, he suddenly realizes that he has been misled all his life by his educated ratiocinations. It is only through a direct, instinctive faith in Christ's law of love that he has finally found faith and become one with "the people." But no matter how fervently this "Moscow nobleman's son, of the middle upper-class stratum" tries to assimilate to the people—and here he is manifestly talking about Tolstoy—"it's not enough simply to think oneself one of the people or to try to become so through an act of will, and a very eccentric one at that." Indeed, he amusingly portrays the process—parodying Tolstoy's didacticism—through which Levin will in the future lose his faith.

> Kitty started to walk and stumbled. Now, why did she stumble? If she stumbled this means that she should not have stumbled for such and such a reason. It is clear that in this case everything depended upon laws which may be strictly ascertained. And if this is so, this means that science governs everything. Where, then, is Providence? What is its role? What is man's responsibility? And if there is no Providence, how can I believe in God? Take a straight line and extend it to infinity. (25: 205–206)

All these barbs, however, are merely preludes to the blistering main offensive aimed at Levin's declaration that the Russian volunteers were the usual bunch of adventurers and freebooters "who are always ready to join a Pugachev gang." In fact, Levin declares that among the Russian people "such an immediate sentiment for the oppression of the Slavs does not and cannot exist" (25: 213). Dostoevsky was particularly incensed by the argument that the Russian people, ignorant of both history and geography, could not possibly have any opinion about events in the Balkans. Such notions betrayed the usual contempt for the people among the Westernized upper class and the usual ignorance of their ideals. The imagination of the people, on the contrary, was filled with stories from the lives of the saints about the Holy Land, and they knew very well that it was now in the hands of the infidel. One of the "historical traits" of the Russian people was precisely their passion for setting off on pilgrimages to such holy places as an "act of contrition," and Dostoevsky links the upsurge of sentiment for their fellow Christians to this ingrained search for salvation (25: 214).

What the people had experienced since the liberation of the serfs was hardly inspiring. "Among other things they have seen the spread of drunkenness, the increasing number of solidly established kulaks, misery all around them, and often, the stamp of bestiality on themselves. Many—oh, very many perhaps— have been afflicted at heart by a kind of anguish, a penitent anguish, an anguish of self-accusation, and a quest for something better, something sacred." This quest was given a goal when they heard about the tortures being inflicted on fellow Christians by the hereditary Muslim enemy of Russia, and they took up the cause "*as an appeal to repentance, to prepration for a sacrament*" (25: 215–216). None of these sentiments could be understood by Levin or the old prince, his father-in-law, who refer to the volunteer movement with amused and aristocratic scorn.

Dostoevsky was outraged at Levin's declaration that he himself possessed "no immediate feeling for the oppression of the Slavs." Livid with indignation, Dostoevsky unrolls a horrifying panorama of Turkish atrocities in the Balkans, where "people are being exterminated by the thousands and tens of thousands" and "children are tossed in the air and caught on the point of a bayonet while their mothers watch," a detail close to one used in *The Brothers Karamazov*. Levin's seeming "humaneness," which recoils before the prospect of killing Turks to put an end to such barbarities, is in reality a callous indifference for everything except his own personal interests and narrowly egoistic concerns. Let us imagine Levin, he writes, reading about "a wholesale massacre, about children with crushed heads crawling around their assaulted, murdered mothers with their breasts cut off . . . and there he stands and meditates: 'Kitty is cheerful; today she ate with an appetite; the boy was bathed in the tub and he begins to recognize me: What do I care about the things that are transpiring in another hemisphere?—*No immediate sentiment for the oppression of the Slavs exists or can exist*—because I feel *nothing*.'" Dostoevsky cannot understand how Tolstoy could expect his readers to continue to take Levin "as an example of a righteous and honorable man." People like the author of *Anna Karenina*, he concludes sadly, "are the teachers of our society. . . . So what is it, then, that they are teaching us? (25: 218–223).

———■———

In Dostoevsky's first reaction to the Balkan crisis, in the April 1876 issue, he introduces a dialogue between himself as author and an interlocutor, who upholds and praises the virtues of war. Since this "paradoxicalist" merely restates, in a livelier and more elaborated fashion, much that can be read in Dostoevsky's letters to his niece Sofya Ivanova during the Franco-Prussian War, there can hardly be any doubt that he represents Dostoevsky's own point of view. To be sure, the diarist pretends to take the opposite, "Christian" side in deploring the cruelty and bloodshed that war inevitably entails, but he argues so weakly that no true dialogue takes place (unlike what occurs in Herzen's *From the Other Shore*, to which the "dialogic" pages of the *Diary* are often compared). The paradoxicalist, however, maintains that war arises because humanity could not "live without noble ideas, and I even suspect that humanity loves war precisely in order to be part of some noble idea." A lengthy period of unbroken peace inevitably leads to social decay because "the social balance always shifts to the side of all that is stupid and coarse in humanity, principally toward wealth and capital." War has "the finest and most sublime consequences" for the people themselves because war "makes everyone equal in time of battle and reconciles the master and the slave in the most sublime manifestation of human dignity—the sacrifice of life for the common cause. The landowner and the peasant were closer to each other on the battlefield of 1812 than when living on some peaceful estate in the country" (22: 122–126). War thus brings about that union of classes that Dostoevsky saw as the only hope for solving Russia's social ills, and the prospect of such a union arising (and having in fact arisen) through Russia's support for the Balkan Slavs became a leitmotif in his articles on this topic.

Launching into a discussion of Russia's role in the modern world, he outlines a staggeringly sublime image of his country's messianic destiny. Even when he envisages the first step of Russia's new policy as the unification of "all of Slavdom . . . under the wing of Russia," he specifies that this union is "not for seizing territory . . . nor for crushing the other Slavic personalities under the Russian colossus." No, its sole purpose is the restoration of these long-suffering Slavs to their place in humanity, thus "enabling them to contribute their own mite to the treasury of the human spirit." Sooner or later, he boldly asserts, Constantinople (which he also calls Tsargrad) will inevitably fall into Russian hands and become the capital city of a united Slavdom. Invoking the "Third Rome" ideology of Russian nationalism—which saw Russia as the God-appointed successor to the Byzantine Empire (the second Rome), and the inheritor of the toga of Christian world leadership—Dostoevsky argues, with incredible assurance, that Russia's "moral right" to Constantinople would be "clear and inoffensive" to other Slavs, and even to the Greeks (23: 49).

In his January 1877 issue, even before Russia entered the conflict, he viewed the events in the Balkans in apocalyptic terms. "It is evident," he writes, "that the time is at hand for the fulfillment of something eternal, something millenarian, something that has been in preparation since the very beginning of civilization" (25: 6). And he describes this climax of world history as a struggle among the three dominating ideas contending for mastery over the destiny of the world.

One was "the Catholic idea," embodied now in France and still at the heart of French Socialism. "For French Socialism is nothing other than the *compulsory* unity of humanity, an idea that derived from ancient Rome and that was subsequently preserved in Catholicism" (25: 5–9). The second was German Protestantism, which Dostoevsky, like the Slavophils, views as fundamentally a protest against Latin Catholic civilization, hence containing nothing positive of its own and ultimately leading to atheism and Nihilism.

Until recently, these two world ideas had struggled for domination, but now a third has dawned on the horizon: "the Slavic idea" contained in Eastern Orthodoxy and incarnating the true image of Christ. What will emerge from the clash of these three world ideas nobody yet knows, "though there is no doubt that it brings with it the end of all the previous histories of European humanity, the beginning of the resolution of their eventual destinies, which lie in the hands of God and which humans can scarcely foresee, even though they may have forebodings." One such prescient observer was obviously Dostoevsky; and to the mocking criticism that he anticipated—and which did not fail to arrive—he replied in advance that "ideas of such dimensions [cannot] be subordinated to petty, Yiddifying, third-rate considerations." Russia, he pronounced, had "two awesome powers that are worth all the others in the world—the intactness and spiritual indivisibility of the millions of our people, and their intimate link with the monarch" (25: 9).

By October 1876 the Serbian Army, led by the swashbuckling Russian General Chernayev, had been defeated. The Russian volunteers were ordered to leave the country, having aroused the ire of the Serbs they had come to aid by their offensive behavior. All these misfortunes, Dostoevsky believed, were the result of the intrigues of the Serbian upper class! Dostoevsky was convinced that "the Serbia of the people . . . considers the Russians alone as their saviors and brethren, and the Russian Tsar as their sun." In looking back, he in effect endows Russia with the halo of a Christ among the nations. For he regards the movement to help the southern Slavs as one "which in its self-sacrificing nature and disinterestedness, in its pious religious thirst *to suffer for a righteous cause*, is almost without precedent among other nations" (23: 150). The annals of nationalism are of course filled with similar adulatory claims for the supreme virtues of one or another people (see Fichte on the Germans and Michelet on the French).

Dostoevsky was especially bitter about the European nations, particularly England, that supported Turkey out of fear of Russian expansionism. He mentions being told about an eight-year-old southern Slav girl who suffered fainting spells because she had seen her father flayed alive before her eyes. Such barbarism is what Russia was attempting to combat, though thwarted by those European countries supposedly representing the values of "civilization." "Oh, civilization!" he exclaims. "Oh, Europe, whose interests would suffer so, were she actually to forbid the Turks to flay the skin from fathers while their children watch! These higher interests of European civilization are, of course, trade, maritime navigation, markets, factories; what can be higher than these things in European eyes?" But "let these interests of civilization, and may civilization itself, be damned," Dostoevsky cries out, "if its preservation demands the stripping of skins from living people" (25: 44). Responding to a remark made by Disraeli, who had implied that the Russian volunteers flocking to Serbia were mainly radicals and revolutionaries determined to stir up trouble, Dostoevsky accuses Disraeli of being directly responsible for the slaughter: "It was something he permitted, after all—and not just permitted—he plotted it himself; he is a novelist and this is his *chef d'oeuvre*" (23: 110).

In a letter written ten years earlier to Maikov, he had affirmed that his recognition of the union of the tsar with the people had been a major factor in converting him to tsarism.[2] Nothing like such unity, he was firmly convinced, existed in Europe, "which completely depends on the stock markets of the bourgeoisie and on the 'placidity of the proletariat.'" Russia cannot "be conquered by all the Yids of Europe taken together, nor by the millions of their gold, nor by the millions of their armies" (25: 97–98). Dostoevsky's fanaticism has reached such a pitch that Europe has now become "Yiddish"—ruled entirely by grossly material considerations—just as have all those Russian liberals and Westernizers, writing in several leading newspapers, who expressed any doubts about the sagacity of Russia's course.

The *Diary* is distressingly marred by Dostoevsky's deep-rooted xenophobia, which extended to every people not of Great Russian origin and is most obvious here in relation to the Jews. Time and again Dostoevsky hurls the direst accusations against them as ruthless exploiters of the misery of others, motivated by a greedy lust for gain, and deploying their international influence against the interests of the Russian state. By the 1870s, the liberation of the serfs had led to a period of economic transformation in which the capital of Jewish financiers played an increasingly important role, especially in the intensive spate of railway construction. It is then that Dostoevsky began belaboring the Jews in his *Diary* in the most insulting language, holding them responsible for the growing industrialization and commercialization of Russia and Russian life that he abhorred with every fiber of his being. He now never missed a chance to berate "the crowd of triumphant Jews and kikes that has thrown itself on Russia . . . kikes . . . both of the Hebraic and Orthodox persuasion" to suck the lifeblood of the liberated but hopelessly indebted peasantry (22: 81). It is all too clear that he was inclined to accept the age-old demonization of the Jews both as ruthless

[2] *PSS*, 28/Bk. 2: 281; March 21–22/April 2–3, 1868.

batteners on the misery of others and as concealed masters and manipulators of world politics.[3]

The Russian Army advanced rapidly in the early days of the campaign but was delayed for four months during the siege of the Bulgarian city of Plevna, where it sustained heavy losses. As Russian losses mounted, Dostoevsky does everything in his power to keep up the spirits of his countrymen, insisting that "the Russian people . . . all, as one man, want to achieve the great aim of the war for Christianity" (26: 44). Once Plevna had been captured, the Russian Army resumed its advance and was soon within sight of Constantinople. But when the Turks sued for peace, the war-weary Alexander II accepted. The initial treaty of San Stefano awarded the Russians a considerable amount of territory and influence in southeast Europe—so much that the united European powers demanded (and obtained) a revision of the treaty that deprived Russia of much of the fruits of victory. The war thus ended for Russia in a general sense of disappointment and frustration. The new era of world history that Dostoevsky had prophesied turned out to be a mirage.

II. Stories

The sketches and short stories in the *Diary of a Writer* contain some of the purest and most moving expressions of Dostoevsky's genius, happily free from the dubious elements of his ideology so often marring his articles. Even those critics and readers who sharply disagreed with his vehemently asserted opinions were unanimously warm in their praise of such masterpieces as "A Gentle Creature" (*Krotkaya*) and "The Dream of a Ridiculous Man" (*Son smeshnogo cheloveka*). Shortly after the publication of the first of these stories, Saltykov-Shchedrin invited Dostoevsky to contribute a story to *Notes of the Fatherland*. As he wrote to a friend, "You simply feel like crying as you read; there are very few such jewels in all of European literature."[4] These stories indeed contain the essence of the most sympathetic aspects of Dostoevsky's vision—his acute identification with human suffering, both material and spiritual, and his unswerving commitment

[3] In a special article of the March 1877 issue devoted to "The Jewish Question," Dostoevsky, in response to a Jewish reader's protests, denies using the word *zhid* (Yid) for individuals, reserving it only "to denote a well-known idea: 'Yid,' 'Yiddism,' 'the Kingdom of the Yids,' etc. These designated only a well-known concept, a tendency, a characteristic of the age" (25: 75). "We are talking," explains Dostoevsky, "about the whole and the idea; we are talking about *Yiddism* and about *the idea* of the *Yids*, which is creeping over the whole world in place of 'unsuccessful' Christianity" (25: 85). By this time, all individual and historical reality has dissolved in Dostoevsky's nightmare fantasies about Jewish-European materialism taking over the world, just as all national and political reality dissolves when he envisions the cloud-capped vistas of "the Christian idea of salvation," under the aegis of Holy Russia, leading to a new world-historical era of brotherly love and reconciliation.

[4] *PSS*, 24: 390.

to an ideal of human felicity attained through fulfilling the Christian commandment of mutual love.

The very first issue of the *Diary* contains an extremely touching sketch—"A Little Boy at Christ's Christmas Party" (*Malchik u Christa na Elke*)—that could not illustrate more clearly the organic relation between his journalism and his art. Just a month before, on December 26, 1875, Dostoevsky had taken his daughter to the annual Christmas ball for children at the Artists' Club in Petersburg, an event famous for the size of the Christmas tree in the ballroom and for the lavishness of its decorations. The next day he paid his visit, already described, to the colony for juvenile delinquents. While going to and fro in the Petersburg streets, and pondering over what to include in his first fascicule, he noticed a little boy begging for alms. These impressions, he wrote Vsevolod Solovyev, solved his problem; he decided to devote a good part of the January issue "to children— children in general, children with fathers, children without fathers . . . under Christmas trees, without Christmas trees, criminal children."[5] And so he begins with the Christmas ball and ends with the visit to the colony for delinquents; between them he inserts his fictional sketch.

The first mention of the sketch in his notebooks, dated December 30, reads: "The Christmas tree. The small boy in Rückert" (22: 322). Friedrich Rückert, a minor German poet, had composed the prose poem, *The Orphaned Child's Christmas* (*Des fremden Kindes Heiliger Christ*). Dostoevsky had lived in Germany, where its recital was a standard feature of Christmas festivities (much like Dickens's *A Christmas Carol* in English-speaking lands). The thematic similarity of Dostoevsky's story and the poem was first pointed out by G. M. Fridlender.[6] An orphaned child wanders the streets at Christmas, peering into the brightly lit windows of houses where happy children have Christmas trees. He knocks on the doors and windows of the houses, hoping that someone will take pity on his lonely misery; but all remains silent. Overcome with grief, he breaks into tears and calls on Christ to rescue him from his desolation; suddenly another child appears, carrying a torch and dressed in white. It is the Christ-child himself, who points to a huge Christmas tree shining among the stars more brightly than any in the houses. It has been lit for all the orphans of the world, and, as if in a dream, angels descend from the glittering tree. The orphan is carried up to the light, and in heavenly eternity he forgets all the travails of his life on earth.

Rückert's poem touchingly dissolves the miseries of the poor orphan into an eternity of heavenly bliss. Dostoevsky, as one might expect, gives the same theme a more somber treatment and penetrates far more deeply into the wretchedness of his little beggar-boy. The very placement of the sketch in the *Diary* brings out

[5] *PSS*, 29/Bk. 2: 72; January 11, 1876.
[6] G. M. Fridlender, *Realizm Dostoevskogo* (Moscow–Leningrad, 1964), 290–308.

the pathos of his loneliness by contrast; and because it is set between descriptions of events that actually occurred, a semblance of verisimilitude is imparted to the miraculous intervention of the Christ-child. Indeed, Dostoevsky plays effectively on the ambiguous status of the sketch as "art" and "invention," but an invention resembling "reality" so closely that it is difficult to tell the difference. "I know for certain," the sketch begins, "that I actually did invent it; yet I keep fancying that this happened somewhere, sometime, precisely on Christmas Eve, in *a certain* huge city during a terrible frost" (22: 14).

The general absence of specificity in the background detail extends the anecdote into a sort of parable. We find ourselves in an archetypal Dostoevskian milieu, characteristic of almost every work—a dark, freezing, miserable Petersburg hovel, a dying woman lying neglected and alone on a bare bed, a hungry, shivering little boy dressed in rags, uncomprehendingly watching her death agony. "How did she happen to be here?—She may have come with her little boy from some faraway town, and then suddenly had fallen ill." Everything is left in this atmosphere of vagueness, and the situation thus takes on the universal quality of a mythical exemplar. This is not an individual woman dying but one whose fate symbolizes that of thousands. By contrast, as the little boy shiveringly and futilely looks around the room for something to eat, there is a keen acuity of sensuous detail that throws the awfulness of the situation into high relief. "For a moment he stood still, resting his hand on the shoulder of the dead woman. Then he began to breathe on his tiny fingers in an attempt to warm them, and, suddenly, coming upon his little cap that lay on the bedstead, he groped along cautiously and quietly made his way out of the basement" (22: 14–15).

The remainder of the tale records the little boy's reactions as he wanders through the streets of the looming city at night, gazing into houses filled with happy children clustering around sumptuous Christmas trees, and pauses with fascination before mechanical toys in a shop window. Frightened by some older, unruly urchins, he takes refuge in a yard behind a pile of wood (a familiar Dostoevskian setting). There he falls asleep, and his frozen body is found the next morning. But before his pitiful demise, he has dreamed a wonderful dream: "Where is he now? Everything sparkles and glitters and shines, and scattered all over are tiny dolls—no, they are little boys and girls, only they are so luminous, and they all fly around him." These are the children at the party of Christ's Christmas tree, a party for all the child-victims of human sin and social injustice. Some of these children

> had frozen to death in those baskets in which they had been left at the doors of Petersburg officials; others had perished in miserable hospital wards; still others had died at the dried-up breasts of their famine-stricken mothers (during the Samara famine); these, again, had choked to death

from stench in third-class railroad cars. Now they are all here, all like little angels, and they are all with Christ, and He is in their midst holding out His hands to them and to their sinful mothers. . . . Down below, the next morning the porters found the tiny body of the runaway boy who had frozen to death behind the woodpile; they found his mother as well. . . . She had frozen to death even before him; they met in God's heaven. (22: 16–17)

In the concluding paragraph, Dostoevsky shifts back to himself as narrator and to the "imaginary" aspects of his narrative. "But the point is that I keep fancying that all this could actually have happened—I mean, the things which happened in the basement and behind the piles of kindling wood. Well, and as regards Christ's Christmas Tree—I really don't know what to tell you, and I don't know whether or not this could have happened" (22: 17). Whether or not any of these events could or did happen, the aim of this sketch is manifestly to make something approximating Christ's Christmas party happen on earth.

—■—

In the early pages of the February issue, Dostoevsky exalted the Russian people, arguing that everything of value in Russian literature originates in the assimilation by Russian writers of the people's Christian ideals. Expressing a certain weariness, however, with all these "*professions de foi,*" he decides to relate a reminiscence that, "for some reason, I am quite eager to recount precisely here and now, in conclusion of our treatise on the people" (22: 46). This reminiscence is "The Peasant Marey," and its significance far transcends its immediate purpose in the *Diary*. On one level, the episode is a supplement—and an extremely valuable one—to *House of the Dead*; on another, it is the only direct evocation of his childhood coming from his pen. This entry of the *Diary* has been discussed earlier (on pp. 207–211) in the chapter on *House of the Dead*, and is unquestionably of crucial importance, not only because of the unique childhood reminiscence but also as the only attempt by Dostoevsky to portray the inner evolution of his beliefs about the Russian peasants. Its details are worth repeating here more briefly in the context in which it was originally written.

The episode begins with a sharp and swift evocation of the Easter week celebration in the Siberian stockade, during which the prisoners could drink, carouse, and quarrel to their heart's content. Dostoevsky looked on, with a feeling of deep loathing, at the raucous turbulence and brutality of the spectacle unrolling before his eyes. "Never," he confesses, "could I stand without disgust drunken popular rakishness, and particularly in this place." Another political criminal, a cultivated Polish patriot, expressed what seemed to be their common reaction when the two met outside the barracks, where they had gone to escape the brawling and the bedlam. "He looked at me gloomily, his eyes flashing; his lips began to tremble: '*Je hais ces brigands!*'—he told me in a low voice, grinding his teeth, and passed by" (22: 46).

Returning to the barracks, Dostoevsky then lies down on the wooden boards where all the convicts slept and begins—as he did for consolation—to conjure up his past memory. And he suddenly recalls how once, at the age of nine, he had been happily exploring the forest on his father's property during a summer vacation. The one or two sentences devoted to the forest are full of feeling, evincing a sensibility rarely displayed elsewhere: "And in all my life nothing have I loved so much as the forest, with its mushrooms and wild berries, its insects and birds and little hedgehogs and squirrels; its damp odor of dead leaves, which I so adored" (22: 47). He had been warned by his mother that wolves were in the vicinity, and suddenly, in the midst of his bucolic foraging, he heard distinctly (though it turned out to be an auditory hallucination) the cry that a wolf had been spotted. Terrified, the boy ran to a peasant plowing in a nearby field.

"This was our peasant Marey. . . . He was almost fifty years old, stocky, pretty tall, with much gray hair in his bushy, flaxen beard." The peasant comforts the little boy, and blesses him. "He extended his hand and stroked me on the cheek. 'Do stop fearing! Christ be with thee. Cross thyself'" (22: 48). The consoling words calmed the agitated young Dostoevsky and convinced him that there had been no wolf. The incident had vanished from his memory for twenty years, but lay dormant there, like a seed planted in the soil, ready to blossom and flower at the moment when its reappearance would take on the stature of a revelation. Here, in his childhood experience, in one symbolic and never-to-be-forgotten instant, Dostoevsky had glimpsed all the spiritual beauty contained in the Russian peasant character. "He was our peasant serf, while I was his master's little boy; no one would learn of his kindness to me and no one would reward him . . . only God, maybe, perceived from above what a profound and enlightened human sentiment, what delicate, almost womanly tenderness may fill the heart of some coarse, bestially ignorant Russian peasant serf, who, in those days, had no intimations about his freedom" (22: 49).

The resurrection of this long-faded childhood incident brought about a complete transformation in Dostoevsky's whole relation to his previously abhorrent surroundings. No longer does he see the drunken convicts as coarse brutes, incapable of harboring any humane and generous feelings; they now have all become potential Mareys, whose natural purity of soul had been overlaid by the harshness and hopeless oppression of their lives. "I went along, gazing attentively at the faces which I encountered. This intoxicated, shaven and branded peasant, with marks on his face, bawling his hoarse, drunken song—why, he may be the very same Marey; for I have no way of peering into his heart" (22: 50). This incident furnishes a valuable paradigm for grasping how

Dostoevsky persuaded himself of the validity of his own beliefs about the Russian people. And it illustrates once more his genius for taking an isolated and commonplace personal incident and endowing it with a wide-ranging social and symbolic significance.

———■———

The first issue of the *Diary* opens on the spate of suicides among young people then disquieting Russian opinion; and this theme will be the inspiration for a number of Dostoevsky's most moving stories. "And there is not a moment," Dostoevsky comments sadly about these incidents, "of Hamlet's pondering 'that dread of something after death'" (22: 6). Indirectly, the question of immortality is thus broached, uniting an eternal "accursed question" with the dispiriting news on which he reports. Dostoevsky returned to the theme in October 1876, prompted by the recent suicide of the seventeen-year-old daughter of a "very well-known Russian émigré." Herzen's daughter Elizaveta had taken her life, and Dostoevsky cited her suicide note, written in French, requesting that, if her suicide did not succeed, her family and friends should gather "to celebrate my resurrection with Clicquot." Otherwise, she asked that her death be ascertained before burial, "because it is most unpleasant to awake in the coffin underground. *That would not be chic at all.*" He contrasts such words with those of a second suicide, "the humble [*smirennoe*] suicide," of a poor, young St. Petersburg seamstress who "jumped and fell to the ground, *holding an icon in her hands*" (23: 144–146).

Both these deaths haunted his imagination, and the second inspired one of his most beautiful stories, "A Gentle Creature." The suicide of Liza Herzen led to the composition of an imaginary suicide note, entitled "The Sentence." Devoting a few paragraphs to Liza Herzen, he compassionately senses, underneath the strained flippancy of her tone, a protest against the "stupidity" of mankind's appearance on earth and the oppressive tyranny of a meaningless causality to which humankind can never become reconciled. Without any conscious awareness of such matters, the young girl had nonetheless been affected by the "linearity" of the ideas "conveyed to her since childhood in her father's house" (23: 145). These ideas—of atheism and materialism—ultimately impelled her to take her own life. To express their disastrous effect in its most powerful form, Dostoevsky then prints his fictive suicide note.

The writer of the imaginary suicide note refuses to accept, in the name of some hypothetical paradisiacal bliss, the suffering necessarily imposed by being born a conscious human being who, as an atheist, does not believe in immortality. The inconsolable thought of her own extinction impels the writer to see in the creation of human beings, and particularly of himself, "some sort of the most profound disrespect for mankind, which, to me, is profoundly insulting, and all the more unbearable as here there is no one who is guilty" (23: 146–147). Rather than endure the humiliation of existing in a senseless universe, where mankind is merely the plaything of a cruel and sadistic nature, he chooses suicide, as the only honorable protest against the indignity of having been born.

The repercussions of this article anticipate much of the later history of Dostoevsky interpretation. So powerfully had he presented the point of view he was opposing, so penetratingly had he entered into a consciousness whose dangers he wished to expose, that he was immediately accused of supporting what he was striving to combat. "The moment my article was printed," he wrote in December 1876, "I was swamped—by letters and personal callers—with inquiries as to the meaning of 'The Sentence.'" Taking up the question publicly, he leaves no doubt that he had tried to express "the formula of a logical suicide"—the only possible conclusion about life as a whole that, in his view, could be drawn by an atheist and materialist. "I have expressed this 'last word of science' in brief terms, clearly and popularly, with the sole purpose of refuting it—not by reasoning or logic, since it cannot be refuted by logic . . . but by faith, by the deduction of the necessity of faith in the immortality of the soul" (24: 53).

It is impossible, he stresses, to give life a meaning by substituting beneficent social action for religious faith. For he insists that, where religious faith is lacking, a true "love of mankind" not only is impossible but runs the risk of being transformed into its opposite. The thought of all the unredeemed suffering that mankind has endured, and the impossibility of alleviating that suffering, cannot help but turn the initial love into hate. Addressing the Populists directly, he writes: "Those who, having deprived man of his faith in immortality, are seeking to substitute for it—as life's loftiest aim—'love of mankind,' those, I maintain, are lifting their arms against themselves, since in lieu of love of mankind they are planting in the heart of him who has lost his faith seeds of the hatred of mankind" (24: 49). Such words anticipate the creation of that despairing idealist Ivan Karamazov, who will find himself caught in exactly such a love-hate relation to mankind.

■

The image of "the humble suicide" continued to haunt Dostoevsky's imagination, and in late October he decided to use it as the subject for a story. At first he thought of making "the girl with the icon" an episode in a novel (never written) called *The Dreamer* (*Mechtatel'*). Some features of this early draft were retained in the final story, among them the monologue form and a main character who had refused to fight a duel and was convinced that he was seeking the naked truth. Work on the *Diary*, however, left no time to develop this novel project. Deciding that the theme was rich enough to deserve independent treatment, however, he turned to his old notes. What he found there was his longstanding fascination with the figure of a "usurer"—the base epitome of an egoistic selfishness excluding any concern for others.

Notes for such a figure appear in a plan for a novel in the early 1860s, and were taken up again in 1869 as an idea for a story after the completion of *The Idiot*. The character here is described as "a genuine underground type; has been insulted. Becomes embittered. Immeasurable vanity. . . . His wife cannot fail to notice that he is cultivated, but then realized, not very much; every gibe (and he takes everything as a gibe) angers him, he is suspicious. . . . For a time he endeavors to establish a loving relationship with his wife. But he had broken her heart" (24: 382). This situation already contains an outline of the later story.

Another plan for a story, set down at the same time but never written, gives a more extended description of the psychology associated with the usurer:

> Most important trait—a misanthrope, but from the underground . . . a need to confide himself [to others], which peeps out from the terrible misanthropy and the ironically insulting mistrust. . . . This need is convulsive and uncontrollable, so that with frightening naïveté (a bitter, even touching naïveté, worthy of pity) he throws himself suddenly on people and, of course, receives a rebuff, but, once receiving a rebuff, he does not forgive, forgets nothing, suffers, turns it into a tragedy. (24: 382)

These are the contours of the character whose voice will be heard as the narrator of "A Gentle Creature." Although the idea for this story first emerged in Dostoevsky's thoughts about "the girl with the icon," by the time the story took final shape she had receded into the background. Instead, her husband, the narrator, comes to the forefront, and what gives him a special stamp is the character of his self-image. He sees himself as some sort of misunderstood and neglected hero, whose life is a personal protest against an unjust society, and this self-image sustains him emotionally and motivates his behavior. It is what has made life possible for him since—in a rather stock situation in the repertoire of Russian Romanticism—he had been expelled from his regiment for having failed to defend its honor on some public occasion.

Before we learn the details of his past, however, the narrator is shown simply as the proprietor of a pawnshop; and this role again strikes a familiar Dostoevskian note. A preoccupation with money is usually the symptom of a lust for power stemming from a status of inferiority and subordination. So it is here again; but complicated by the character's need to persuade himself of his own rectitude and virtue. "You say 'pawnbroker'—everybody says it. And what of it? This means that there must, indeed, have been reasons why one of the most magnanimous of all men became a pawnbroker" (24: 16). The narrator refuses to view himself as he knows he is regarded by others—and even by some part of himself that he cannot suppress. This discrepancy is the source of the tragedy recounted in the story, which arises from the narrator's pitiless attempt, in a hopeless search for love and understanding, to impose his own self-conception on another. But because he seeks love without being willing to love (until it is too late), because he wishes to obtain love through the domination of another consciousness, the result is the very opposite of what he desires. "But here," he thinks, looking at the corpse of his dead wife, "there was something I forgot or failed to see" (24: 17).

The story traces the course of the unhappy relationship that led the child-bride to her final, despairing plunge. What attracts the narrator to the girl, when she first comes to pawn her meager belongings, is the combination of her pride and her poverty, her intelligence and her indigence. The death of her parents threw her back on two aunts, who had turned her into a virtual slave. But she is an independent character who has absorbed some of the culture and humanitarian ideals of her generation and has placed advertisements in journals in search of a position (to no avail). By no means is she ready to play a completely subservient role.

The narrator rescues her from being, in effect, sold to a much older suitor. His unexpected proposal of marriage is carefully designed to cast him in the role of a Romantic savior, but his motive is neither genuine magnanimity nor even sexual attraction (though the latter is not entirely absent). Rather, he desperately yearns for someone to recognize his outwardly demeaning life as inspired by an "idea," someone to acknowledge the inherent righteousness and dignity of the path he has chosen, someone to look beyond his ignominious profession and dishonored past into the torments of his wounded soul. "Admitting her to my house, I desired full respect. I wished that she should look at me worshipfully for all my suffering—and I deserved it! I was always proud, and I always sought either everything or nothing" (24: 14).

This overwhelming pride determines the baneful course he adopts after the marriage. Any sign of tenderness or affection on his part might be interpreted as a humiliating appeal, as an indication of remorse or self-doubt. And so the young girl's natural warmth of feeling, spontaneously expressed in the first days of their marriage, is stifled by his policy of coldness and seeming indifference. "The main thing was that from the very beginning, much as she tried to restrain herself, she threw herself at me with love. . . . But at once I threw cold water on all this ecstasy. Precisely therein was my idea. I reacted to these transports with silence—benevolent, of course" (12: 13).

This treatment leads to the reverse of what the narrator had anticipated. Rather than her accepting the inner sublimity (as he sees it) of her husband's way of life, and bowing down before him in worshipful admiration, they become locked in a secret struggle of wills. "At first she argued—how hotly!—but later she left off speaking, and, finally, she grew quite silent; only, when listening, she would open her eyes awfully wide—such big, big eyes, so attentive. . . .

And . . . and, besides, suddenly I noticed a smile—a distrustful, silent, wicked, smile. Well, it was with that smile that I brought her into my house" (12: 14).

Ultimately, however, the supposedly "gentle creature" unexpectedly erupts into outright rebellion. At the climax of their secret battle, waking from sleep, he sees her standing over him with a loaded pistol; and he waits in agony for her to pull the trigger, wondering whether she had seen him momentarily open his eyes. Despite her hatred, she is unable to take his life—her final and irreparable defeat. By later revealing his awareness of this incident, he can, at one stroke, re-move the cloud hanging over his name because of the imputation of cowardice and also reverse the moral situation. No longer will *he* be the person surrepti-tiously seeking pardon; he will now be the kindhearted, great-souled pardoner. But the private joy of this future triumph is so great that he purposely puts off its arrival. He wishes to savor the broken mortification of his wife, who falls ill with "brain fever" and never recovers her health. "Yes, at that time there oc-curred to me something strange and peculiar. . . . I grew triumphant, and the very knowledge of it proved sufficient to me. This winter passes. Oh, I was con-tent as never before—and this, all winter" (24: 23).

The dénouement occurs in the spring, after a winter spent silently sharing the same apartment but totally estranged from each other. "Of course, it was strange that not once," says the husband, "did the thought occur to me that while I liked to look stealthily at her, never throughout the whole winter did I catch even a single glance of hers at me! I thought that this was timidity on her part" (24: 25). Far from timidity, it was a deep and unconquerable aversion—as he discovers when, suddenly seized by pity for her and possessed by his own overwhelming need for love, he finally throws himself at her feet. "She shivered and shook her-self away from me in great fear, looking into my face. But, suddenly, her eyes ex-pressed *stern surprise* . . . 'So you are also after love?'—such was the question in that astonishment of hers, even though she remained silent" (24: 28). The un-controllable fervor of the narrator, who now pours out pell-mell all the psychic torment he had been suppressing in himself and concealing from others for so many years, simply throws the unhappy girl into hysterical convulsions.

The sudden breakdown and reversal of the situation precipitates the catastro-phe. The narrator is now ready to abandon everything, to give up his pawnshop and his revenge on society, if only he can recapture the love that was once within his grasp. But the sweet and gentle spirit of his wife has been irremediably es-tranged, and she is now consumed by guilt at her *own* incapacity to respond, ex-cept with profound pity, to his entreaties to begin a new life of true-hearted love. All that is left is the leap from the window, clutching to her breast the icon of the Mother of God, the symbol of the promise of eternal love. Nothing that Dostoevsky ever wrote is more poignant than the narrator's cry of despair at the end, walking up and down beside the bier of "the gentle creature," at a moment when the entire world has become for him an image of his desolation. "Oh, nature! Man on earth is alone—this is the calamity! . . . Everything is dead, and everywhere—nothing but corpses. Only men, and, around them, silence—such is earth. 'Love each other'—Who said this? Whose covenant is this?" (24: 35)

Such are among the final words of one of the finest and purest creations that ever came from Dostoevsky's pen. The subtlety and delicacy of the rendering of the narrator's consciousness (with its blend of shock, guilt, incredulity, and some last, lingering shreds of self-justification), the brilliant portrayal of the wife *through* the eyes of the narrator struggling to understand what has occurred easily overcomes the all-too-familiar plot ingredients and the touch of melodrama. "A Gentle Creature" is also Dostoevsky's best-rounded and most finely modulated portrait of his "underground man" character type. Nowhere else is he presented so fully as a sensitive and suffering human being, whose inhumanity derives from a need for love that has become perverted and distorted by egoism and vanity. What was presented only embryonically in the final episode of *Notes from Underground*, when the underground man egotistically rejects the offer of love tendered him by the suffering young prostitute Liza, is here developed with a mastery that fully justifies Saltykov-Shchedrin's enthusiastic accolade.

———■———

"The Dream of a Ridiculous Man" also emerges from Dostoevsky's preoccupation with the theme of suicide. Indeed, the story can best be seen as the second panel of a diptych, whose first is the imaginary suicide letter, "The Sentence." These two works both echo and answer each other: starting from the same point of no return as the letter, this story ends, not in despair and suicide, but in an ecstatic affirmation of the will to live. This affirmation stems from Dostoevsky's own belief in the possibility of an apocalyptic transfiguration of mankind, a moral regeneration of humanity as a whole, which first enters his work in the 1860s. The image of a Golden Age of human happiness crops up continuously in his notes for his novels. In "The Dream of a Ridiculous Man" he expresses both the moral inspiration provided by the radiant image of the Golden Age, and the loss of the instinctive human harmony that was the source of its felicity. But he also believed—or hoped—that such an instinctive harmony might perhaps be restored, if only partially, through the inspiration of Christian compassion and love for suffering humanity.

This story, which bears the subtitle "fantastic," relates a dream voyage to another earth, where the ridiculous man encounters a society living in a true Golden Age, before the fall and the existence of sin. The story is a *conte philosophique*, based on "fantasy" in the literal meaning of the word, and has often been compared to Voltaire's *Micromegas*. But the fantasy is framed by a setting taken straight from the iconography of urban shoddiness and misery favored by the Natural School of Russian writers in the 1840s. The central figure is one of those isolated and misanthropic characters estranged from everyone; but the horizon of the ridiculous man encompasses a metaphysical-religious dimension. "I suddenly felt that it made no difference to me whether the world existed or whether nothing existed anywhere at all. . . . It was then that I suddenly ceased to be angry with people and almost stopped noticing them" (25: 105).

This conviction induces a total sense of apathy toward the outside world. He is obsessed by the thought of suicide, and on one particularly gloomy and depressing evening, when even the rain seemed "full of obvious animosity toward men" (25: 105)—he decides to put a bullet through his head. On the way home, he is stopped by a little girl appealing to him to aid her dying mother. He stamps and shouts at her to leave him in peace; but sitting in his room later, with the pistol lying ready on the table, he is upset by a new sensation. Theoretically, he should have felt nothing at all shameful about having driven away the little girl; it was totally inconsistent for a man on the brink of suicide, to whom everything in the world had become meaningless, to feel pity. And yet, as with the underground man, his heart and his head refuse to act in unison. "I recall that I felt a great pity for her—to the point of some strange pain, which was quite incredible in my situation" (25: 107).

While pondering this disturbing lapse in the conclusions he has drawn about life, he suddenly falls asleep and dreams. "In a word, that little girl saved me, since, because of the questions, I postponed the shot." But the little girl also saves the ridiculous man in a deeper sense: the feelings stirred in him by this encounter are then projected into his dream and, on waking, he finds that he has been forever freed from the temptation of suicide. "It would seem," Dostoevsky surmises, "that dreams are generated not by the intellect but by desires, not by the brain but by the heart" (25: 108). In his dream, the ridiculous man reveals the desires of a heart that conjures up the panorama of the Golden Age; and in Dostoevsky's story, this opposition between head and heart, between reason and feeling, itself becomes the center of the entire spiritual history of humanity.

Dostoevsky visualizes an island in the Greek archipelago, radiant with sunlit beauty. Never before has he struck this particular note of an all-embracing harmony between man and nature. "The calm, emerald sea gently splashed against the shore embracing it with manifest, apparent, almost conscious love. Tall, beautiful trees stood there in the full luxury of their bloom, and their countless leaves—I am sure of it—welcomed me with their gentle, kind murmur, uttering, as it were, words of love" (25: 112). Love was the natural medium in which the inhabitants of this Paradise existed, or at least the aspect of their lives accessible to the comprehension of an earthling. For he realized that it was impossible for him—"a contemporaneous, progressive, and hideous Petersburg resident"— to understand them because they lived completely on the level of an intuitive feeling that was also a higher form of knowledge. Though having nothing comparable to what on earth is called science—the acme and epitome of reason—"yet their knowledge was deeper and higher than that of our science . . . I was unable to comprehend their knowledge" (25: 113). That higher knowledge is, presumably, their totally selfless and loving communion with each other and with everything.

The lives of these denizens of the Golden Age were thus completely lacking in any sort of self-consciousness, untroubled by any manifestations of egoism or vanity. "They were endowed with love and children were born to them, but never did I observe in them those impulses of *cruel* voluptuousness which affect virtually everybody on our earth—everybody—and which are the sole source of almost all sin in our human race." They had no specific religion or religious doctrines about God and eternal life, but they greeted death serenely, and "one could imagine that they continued to communicate with their dead even after death." They composed songs of praise for each other and lived in "a sort of mutual complete and universal enamoredness" (25: 113–114). To this condition of unalloyed love, which images the world before the fall of humankind into sin, the ridiculous man compares his own twisted love-hate feelings for his fellow human beings, which arose from the clash between his egoism and his longing for communion.

Somehow, the ridiculous man introduces this principle of reflexive self-consciousness and self-awareness—the ultimate psychological root of egoism—into the innocent Paradise of the Golden Age. The catastrophic result is the corruption and fall of its inhabitants. The somber emphasis is on the dialectical movement by which self-awareness engenders egoism and egoism gives rise to a world whose institutions express the loss in reality of what man becomes aware of in thought. The first step is for consciousness no longer to *live* in a loving harmony with others but to withdraw itself in a manner splitting the unconscious and instinctive acceptance and identification with the other. From this withdrawal arises an awareness of the ego as opposed to the other; and the psychological and sexual struggle begins, as well as "a struggle for self-isolation—for disjunction, for individuality, for 'mine and thine.'" The result was a growing awareness of what had been lost and the attempt to re-create it artificially by self-conscious means. "When they became wicked, they started speaking about brotherhood and humaneness and grasped the meaning of these ideas. When they grew criminal, they invented justice and enacted for themselves codes for its maintenance, and for the enforcement of their codes they used the guillotine" (25: 115–116).

A host of evils arises in this way, which compose a litany of all the ills of civilization. Slavery, the martyrdom of holy men, fratricidal warfare, the cult and doctrine of power—all came from the belief that "science will give . . . wisdom; wisdom will reveal the laws . . . and the knowledge of the laws of happiness is superior to happiness" (25: 116). But things go from bad to worse, and culminate in the growth of a cult of suffering, but the suffering does not arise from any inner conflict or feeling of remorse. Instead, it is the perverse enjoyment of suffering as an aesthetic pleasure or as the indication of intellectual superiority. The glorification of suffering for its own sake, divorced from any relation with pity, compassion, or self-examination, is for Dostoevsky one of the ultimate corruptions of the human personality.

Overwhelmed by guilt, the ridiculous man tries to introduce his perverted innocents to Christianity and its values of self-sacrifice and suffering for others ("I implored them to crucify me; I taught them how to make the cross"). But all to no avail—they simply laughed at what they could not understand. "Finally, they announced to me that I was beginning to be dangerous to them and that they would place me in an asylum if I shouldn't keep silent" (25: 117). This outcome so afflicts and oppresses the ridiculous man that at this point his sensations become too strong to be endured—and he awakens!

This extraordinary dream is a revelation, and tranforms his life. "Immeasurable ecstasy lifted my whole being"—and he instantly decides, like Nekrasov's Vlas, to become an itinerant preacher of the truth vouchsafed in his dream. What the ridiculous man will preach is a very old truth, but he has faith in it because he has *seen* and felt all the beauty of the world in which such truth had once reigned supreme. "The main thing is—love thy neighbors as thyself." And he has also seen the power of the enemy. "The consciousness of life is higher than life; knowledge of the laws of happiness is higher than happiness—this is what we have to fight against!" In the world to which he has returned, everyone sneers at his words and considers him mad, just as in the final phase of his dream; but his faith now can never be shaken because "I saw, saw it (Truth), and its *live image* filled my soul forever." His first move on his new path is to search for the little girl: "And—I did find that little girl. . . . And I shall go on! (25: 117–118).

The ridiculous man had reached the stage of personal disintegration resulting from individualism and, "being conscious of everything," had lost faith in God. But the advent of Christ on earth, according to Dostoevsky, provided humans with a new ideal, which consists of "the return to spontaneity, to the masses, but freely . . . in the highest degree willfully and consciously—and this higher willfulness is . . . a higher renunciation of the will" (20: 189–194). The ridiculous man thus devotes himself, on awakening from his dream, to preaching this return to a "higher spontaneity" through the realization on earth of the Christian law of love. He is a tragic, Russian optimist, preaching to a mocking world that he has *seen* the glories of the Golden Age and that they can be made real once again through Christ. *The Dream of a Ridiculous Man* contains Dostoevsky's most vibrant and touching depiction of his positive moral-religious ideal, expressed far more convincingly in this rhapsodic and "fantastic" form than anywhere else in his work.

CHAPTER 52

A New Novel

The Diary of a Writer for October 1877 contained the announcement that, due to illness, Dostoevsky would suspend publication for two years. When this decision brought more than a hundred letters pleading with him to continue, he told his readers that "in the forthcoming year of rest from *periodical* publication, I expect, indeed, to engage in belletristic work, which imperceptibly and involuntarily has been taking shape within me during the two years of the publication of the *Diary*" (26: 126). Both reasons certainly played their part, but perhaps the irresistible call of artistic creation was the stronger. For the next three years, Dostoevsky would be absorbed primarily with writing *The Brothers Karamazov*, whose first installment appeared in *The Russian Messenger* at the beginning of 1879. During the last two years of his life, he held all of literate Russia spellbound with monthly installments of his greatest novel. Its gripping theme placed the murder of a father in a vast religious and moral-philosophical context; and no Russian reader of the time could avoid associating its deeply probing pages with the increasingly frequent attempts then being made to assassinate the tsar.

Dostoevsky's life now took on the features of a cult figure, someone regarded with awe and unstinting admiration.[1] It became customary during these years, even among people who disagreed violently with Dostoevsky on social-political issues, to regard him with a certain reverence, and to feel that his words incarnated a prophetic vision illuminating Russia and its destiny. In the eyes of the vast majority of the literate public, he became a living symbol of all the suffering that history had imposed on the Russian people, as well as all their longing for an ideal world of (Christian) brotherly love and harmony.

Nor was Dostoevsky averse to assuming such a prophetic role, one that he could well have felt had been accorded to him by destiny itself. His life had placed him in an extraordinary position from which to understand the problems of Russian society, and his artistic-ideological evolution embodies and expresses

---

[1] One symbolic indication of this new status was his election in 1878 to membership in the Imperial Academy of Sciences, Division of Russian Language and Literature. He was pleased with such official recognition, though remarking to his wife that, compared with some of his contemporaries, his thirty-three years of literary activity made the distinction rather belated. See Anna Dostoevsky, *Reminiscences*, trans. and ed. Beatrice Stillman (New York, 1975), 297.

all the conflicts and contradictions that made up the panorama of Russian social-cultural life. At no moment was Russian public opinion more ready to seek guidance than in the crisis period the country was then living through. This stormy and unsettled time reached its climax, just a month after Dostoevsky's own death, with the assassination of Alexander II, the Tsar-Liberator whom he revered.

———■———

The period between the cessation of the *Diary* and intensive work on *The Brothers Karamazov* allowed Dostoevsky to catch up with correspondence from his readers. He disliked writing letters, he says time and again, yet he continued to reply to readers all the same, and seemed to find sustenance in doing so. An important letter came in the form of a manuscript by an unnamed writer now identified as the philosopher Nikolay Feodorov. He was a strange and enigmatic figure, the illegitimate son of a noble family who was employed as a librarian in the Rumyantsev Museum in Petersburg. He enjoyed a considerable underground reputation in his lifetime even though he never published anything under his own name, believing that all private property (in which category he included ideas) was sinful. Dostoevsky already had received an anonymous manuscript of his in 1876, a portion of which was quoted in the *Diary*. This citation argued that the absence of private organizations and associations in Russia (including labor unions) should not be judged a social deficiency. All such groups pit one part of society against another, while in Russia "there still lives, with a certain vigor, that feeling of unity without which human societies cannot exist" (22: 82). The writer who had composed Raskolnikov's final dream in *Crime and Punishment*, where such social disintegration is depicted with terrifying vividness, found Feodorov's thoughts a welcome confirmation of his own artistic vision.

This new letter dealt with the question of the resurrection of the dead and the immortality of the soul. Feodorov's doctrines, which have been labeled "a mystical positivism," enjoyed an extraordinary vogue in the 1870s, attracting the admiration not only of Dostoevsky but also of Tolstoy and Vladimir Solovyev. At the heart of his speculations was the same eschatological hope that inspired Dostoevsky and Solovyev—the vision of a total transformation of earthly life into the Kingdom of God. He believed that Christ had appeared, not simply to promise resurrection and a triumph over death in some miraculously transformed world at the Second Coming, but rather to point the way for humanity to accomplish the work of resurrection itself. He asserted that this goal could be achieved through the application of humanity's collective will, determined to turn the Christian revelation into an empirical reality.

Feodorov's ideas are an odd blend of science fiction and what he called "supramoralism." Like Fourier, who had influenced him in his youth, he indulged in cosmological fantasies that would allow for the development of new organs and convert nature from a blind, hostile, oppressive force into a realization of human desire. The ultimate aim of this development was to be a state of "multiple unity," in which everything (including nature) would exist as part of one huge, living organism. Once this condition had been attained, the natural course of human life would be reversed; instead of producing children, humanity would begin to resurrect its ancestors by reassembling the atoms and molecules of which they had been composed and which still remained scattered throughout the universe. For him, humankind's reverence for its fathers is the root of that family feeling which, empirically, points the way to the future state of humanity as a universal organism, a future in which the source of all the evils in the world—egoism and individualism—would vanish because they would be deprived of the physical basis for their perpetuation.[2]

Dostoevsky responded to this document—sent by one of Feodorov's disciples, an ex-revolutionary named Peterson—with a long and excited letter of his own. "I must say that I am essentially in complete agreement with [Feodorov's] views," he declared. "Reading them, I felt I might have written them myself." So taken was he with Feodorov's ideas that he communicated them to Vladimir Solovyev at the first opportunity. "He [Solovyev] is in profound sympathy with your thinker," he informs Peterson, "and was intending to say almost exactly the same thing in his next lecture."[3] In fact, Dostoevsky had written something similar long ago in a notebook jotting while maintaining a vigil at the bier of his first wife. He too had seen the ultimate goal of humankind as the attainment of a state in which procreation would cease, the dead would be resurrected, and all humanity would literally be united in a new physical body. Dostoevsky, however, saw this final transformation of humankind as occurring only at the end of time, not in earthly life; nor did he envisage it being achieved empirically through human effort. Hence he expresses concern over whether Feodorov's scientific fantasies had not led to a certain Utopian secularism.

Dostoevsky's epistolary relations with Feodorov, which focus on the supreme metaphysical importance of the theme of fatherhood, occurred exactly at the moment when he was mulling over his first notes for *The Brothers Karamazov*. It would appear that he thought of introducing a discussion of Feodorov's ideas into the scene in Zosima's cell. An isolated jotting reads: "*The resurrection of (our) ancestors* depends on us" (15: 204). Another reads: "The family will be enlarged: even nonkindred will enter into it, and a new organism will have been woven together" (15: 249). This last note appears among the plans for the conversations and exhortations of Zosima; and perhaps the most important influ-

[2] An introduction to Feodorov's thought can be found in George M. Young, Jr., *Nikolai Feodorov* (Belmont, MA, 1979).

[3] *PSS*, 30/Bk. 1: 13–15; March 24, 1878.

ence may be located there. For even though Dostoevsky's works are suffused with a sense of the importance of mutual moral responsibility, nowhere is this theme stated more broadly than in *The Brothers Karamazov*, where each person is declared to be responsible for all. The bold conception of a future humankind that would literally be a huge, united, and interdependent organism may well have guided Dostoevsky toward his epochal formulation.

■

Despite his intense absorption in constructing a scenario for his new novel, his recurring epilepsy, and the worsening of his emphysema, Dostoevsky maintained a wide range of social commitments. He attended the "Wednesdays" of Prince Meshchersky, often went to Pobedonostsev's home on Saturday evenings, and continued to frequent the salon of Elena Shtakenshneider. In addition to entertaining guests like Strakhov at Sunday dinners, he exchanged visits with a large family circle. He also dined once a month at a dinner organized by the Society of Writers, which included all literary factions and where, as Anna notes, "Feodor Mikhailovich met and mingled with his sworn literary enemies."[4]

In November 1878 he was introduced, at her urgent request, to Countess Sofya Andreyevna Tolstaya by their mutual friend Vladimir Solovyev. The countess was the widow of the poet and playwright Aleksey Tolstoy and, according to Anna, a woman "of great intellect, highly educated," who had established her own salon.[5] According to his wife, Dostoevsky visited her regularly, where he met not only other intellectuals and cultural luminaries but also ladies of the highest society. No fund-raiser for the needy—especially for impoverished students—was organized without inviting him to read. Such invitations were rarely refused, because nothing was more important for him than to maintain his contact with the rising generation of Russian youth.

In addition to his taxing social commitments, Dostoevsky continued to pay the closest attention to criminal and political trials, not only as reported in the newspapers but also as a spectator. Earlier in the year Dostoevsky had been present at the trial of Vera Zasulich, which, he felt, revealed the deep fissures splitting Russian society apart, and which surely filled him with gloomy forebodings. Zasulich was a determined young woman, twenty-eight years of age, who had moved in revolutionary student circles and had been arrested in connection with the Nechaev affair in 1871. She had acted as one of his couriers after he went abroad, but had no connection with the group that murdered Ivanov.

Kept imprisoned for two years, even though no charges were filed against her, she was declared innocent and emerged as a hardened revolutionary. On learning

---

[4] *Reminiscences*, 297.
[5] Ibid., 325.

that General Trepov, the governor of St. Petersburg, had illegally ordered the flogging of a Populist political prisoner for refusing to remove his cap in the general's presence, she calmly walked into his office on a false pretext and shot him, though wounding him only slightly. Her open trial, presided over by Dostoevsky's friend, A. F. Koni, was conducted with scrupulous impartiality, despite pressure from official circles. Koni, whose later career suffered as a result, allowed the defense to introduce detailed testimony about the relentless flogging. The result was a triumphant acquittal of the defendant, to the wild applause of a courtroom packed with high government functionaries and notables from the most select Petersburg society. Admission to the courtroom was limited, but Dostoevsky was present with a card falsely declaring him to be a member of the legal profession.

During the course of the trial, other Populist prisoners, called as witnesses by the defense, unanimously testified to the constant brutalities they had been forced to endure, and those frightening glimpses into the reality of the prison world produced a shattering effect. Elizaveta Naryshkin-Kurakina, a lady-in-waiting to one of the grand duchesses (and an acquaintance of Dostoevsky's), was scarcely to be suspected of revolutionary sympathies. But she wrote in her *Memoirs*, "The appearance of a number of young political prisoners created quite a stir. They had been brought into the courtroom from the Peter-and-Paul Fortress merely as witnesses to the incident in the prison. Their pale faces, their voices trembling with tears and indignation, the details of their depositions—all these statements made me lower my eyes with shame."[6] Gradovsky, whom Dostoevsky had replaced as editor of *The Citizen*, remembered feeling that, as the testimony of these youthful defense witnesses unrolled, not Zasulich but he himself and all of Russian society stood accused and were standing trial.[7]

Dostoevsky had raged against flogging in *House of the Dead*, and perhaps General Trepov's order reminded him of the savage brutalities of the sadistic Major Krivtsov of his prison camp years. Like so many others at the tribunal, he could not suppress sympathy for the vengeful Zasulich, who during her testimony had said: "It is terrible to raise one's hand against a fellow man . . . but I decided that this is what I had to do." The clash between her moral conscience and her social-political convictions made a deep impression on Dostoevsky, who felt that no formal legal judgment would be the best solution. If found guilty, she would become a martyr; if acquitted, her act would be given a legal sanction, and the authority of the Russian state would be undermined.

His prediction that Zasulich would become a heroine was soon all too dramatically borne out. On emerging from the courthouse, she was carried on the shoulders of a celebrating crowd, and this militant rejoicing led to a demonstra-

---

[6] Quoted in Samuel Kucherov, *Courts, Lawyers, and Trials under the Last Three Tsars* (New York, 1953), 217.

[7] G. K. Gradovsky, *Itogi, 1862–1907* (Kiev, 1908).

tion that ended with a splattering of gunfire and one death. When the police arrived to arrest Zasulich again, she had vanished into the throng and was later smuggled out of the country. Once abroad, she continued a notable revolutionary career in Switzerland, eventually aligning herself with Plekhanov and the Mensheviks against Lenin and the Bolshevik Revolution.

The shot fired by Zasulich echoed throughout Russia, and her example spurred on others to take up arms against tsarist officials. Indeed, in the months following her trial a wave of terrorist attacks was carried out by her hitherto peaceful comrades, formerly devoted only to propaganda among the people. High officials of the regime were killed in Kiev and Odessa, and General Mezentsev, the head of the dreaded secret police, was struck down by a dagger in broad daylight in the very heart of St. Petersburg as revenge for the death of a Populist prisoner. His assassin was Stepniak-Kravchinsky, a young Populist who had fought with the Serbs in their battle against the Turks and who, after the murder, escaped abroad. He became a noted writer whose *Underground Russia* is still an indispensable source for the Populist movement, and, while in exile in London, helped Constance Garnett improve her Russian. He is often considered one of the prototypes of Razumov in Conrad's *Under Western Eyes*.

Dostoevsky comments on the Mezentsev murder to Victor Putsykovich, an old journalist friend who was now receiving warning letters from "Odessa Socialists" threatening him with death if he did not stop printing articles against the Nihilists (he had forwarded these to Mezentsev without receiving a reply). Besides revealing the incompetence of the secret police, the reference to Odessa also occasions another display of Dostoevsky's anti-Semitic obsession. "Odessa, a city of Yids, turns out to be the center of our militant Socialism. There's the same phenomenon in Europe: the Yids are terribly active in Socialism, and I won't even mention the Lassalles and Karl Marxes. And it's understandable: for Yids the whole benefit is from any kind of radical shock or upheaval in the state, because they themselves are a *status in statu*, making up their own community that will never be shaken but will only gain from any kind of weakening of anything that is not the Yids."[8] In fact, very few of the Populists were of Jewish origin (Jewish youth would flock to the radical banner only later in the century), but Dostoevsky preferred not to accuse those purebred Russian lads whose desire for self-sacrifice he hoped to guide into other channels.

Considering the enormous prestige he enjoyed at this time, such hopes were hardly groundless. A commentator in *Voice*, referring to the termination of the *Diary*, regretted its disappearance "particularly in relation to the younger generation" and remarked that "the majority of the young, with their unspoiled intuition, were able to decipher his deep genuineness and sincerity and valued

[8] *PSS*, 30/Bk. 1: 42–44; August 29, 1878.

these very highly."[9] The oracular status he had now assumed is manifest in a letter sent to him on April 8, 1878, by a group of students at the University of Moscow.

"Dear Feodor Mikhailovich," the students wrote, "for two years now we have been accustomed to turn to your *Diary* for the solution, or for the proper posing, of the questions that loomed before us; we have been accustomed to use your decisions for the establishment of our own views, and to honor them even when we did not agree."[10] One of the six signatories was Pavel Milyukov, later a famous historian of Russian culture, leader of the Constitutional Democratic Party in the Russian Duma after 1905, and then foreign minister in an interim government before the Bolshevik takeover. The immediate occasion for this joint missive was a manifestation of popular anger directed at the activities of the young dissidents.

A number of Moscow students had gone to greet a convoy of students from the University of Kiev, who had been arrested on minor charges and were being sent to the provinces in police custody. As they proceeded together peacefully through the streets, some butchers and shopkeepers from a local food market swarmed out and, to shouts of "Beat them!" severely manhandled some of the young men. This physical attack was one of the first of its kind on such a scale, an eye-opening indication of the lack of solidarity of the urban lower-class population with student unrest. This realization caused a crisis of self-questioning in the student ranks. "What is most important for us," they told Dostoevsky, "is to resolve the question: To what extent are we, the students, guilty, and what conclusions about us should be drawn by society, and by ourselves, from this occurrence?"

To the first part of this question Dostoevsky gave an unequivocal reply: "In my view you are not guilty at all. You are only children of that very same 'society' which you are now deserting, and which is 'a lie in every sense.'" Students, he continues, "are in rightful revolt—though unfortunately still only in a European (that is, Socialist) manner . . . . Instead of going to the people so as to live their life, the young people, knowing nothing about it . . . simply despising its foundations, for example, religious faith, went not to learn from the people but . . . to instruct it arrogantly, with contempt—a purely aristocratic, leisure-class pastime!" Although he deplores the beatings, such violence was only to be expected; the people "are uncouth, they are *muzhiks*."[11]

Dostoevsky, however, refused to lose heart, despite the assassinations during the spring and summer of 1878 causing panic in the country. What he saw, or

[9] *Letopis zhizni i tvorchestvo F. M. Dostoevskogo*, ed. N. F. Budanova and G. M. Fridlender, 3 vols. (St. Petersburg, 1995), 3: 243, 247.

[10] *PSS*, 30/Bk. 1: 21–25; April 18, 1878.

[11] Ibid.

wished to see, to counterbalance a menacing reality—he writes to Leonid Grigor-yev of "the hideousness of rural district administrations and morals, vast quanti-ties of vodka, incipient pauperism and a kulak class, that is, European proletariat and bourgeoisie"—was a new consciousness that had burgeoned among the people with the Russo-Turkish War: "There has been established in them . . . a political consciousness, a precise understanding of Russia's meaning and mis-sion." But to impute such a "precise" understanding to the people was too much even for him, and he adds that this understanding was at least "*constantly becom-ing precise*. . . . In short, . . . the beginnings of higher ideas, . . . the rest will come. One must penetrate beneath the surface of the people to uncover the hid-den reality." One should not believe that "the hideous facts" reveal the essence of their ideals.[12] He was unshakably convinced that the Populists' return to the moral ideals of a secular Christianity was only the first step in their eventual ac-ceptance of the truth of a supernatural Christ, and that his mission was to sup-ply the leadership in this direction that was so woefully lacking.

During these very months, when Dostoevsky was consulted by students who, if they were not prowling the streets with revolvers themselves, sympathized with those who were, he was also asked to meet with some young men who might easily become their targets. Sometime in the first week of February 1878 he received a visit from D. S. Arsenyev, the tutor of the Grand Dukes Sergey and Paul, the younger sons of Alexander II. The purpose of the call, made in the name of the tsar himself, was to invite him to become acquainted with Arse-nyev's pupils, so that, to quote Anna, "by his conversations Feodor Mikhailovich might have a beneficial influence on the youthful grand dukes."[13]

What Dostoevsky must have felt at such a moment can well be imagined. He—who had been convicted of a crime against the state! He—who had served a prison term at hard labor in Siberia and worn the shackles and striped garment of a convict for four painful years! He—who had sunk to the lowest depths of Russian society and shared the fate of the most hardened criminals! He—now invited to enter as an honored guest into the most exalted and exclusive court circles, and to serve as guide and counselor to those in whose hands the future of Russia would eventually be entrusted!

His first appearance at court was recorded in the diary of Grand Duke Kon-stantin Konstantinovich, a cousin of Sergey and Paul and the son of the com-mander of the Russian Navy.[14] "I dined at Sergey's." he wrote. "His guests were K. N. Bestuzhev-Ryumin and Feodor Mikhailovich Dostoevsky. I was very much interested in the latter, and had read his works. . . . He speaks extremely

[12] Ibid., 40–41; July 21, 1878.

[13] *Reminiscences*, 297–298.

[14] Grand Duke Konstantin, who had serious literary interests, later published poetry and plays under a pseudonym, and a number of his poems were set to music by Peter Tchaikovsky.

well, as well as he writes." [15] This visit to his royal interlocutors was a success, and invitations to dine with them came regularly thereafter. He now found himself in the extraordinary position of being a cherished adviser not only of the young radical generation but also of the younger members of the reigning family. And if he felt that fate (or God) had entrusted him with a mission at this crucial moment of Russian history, he certainly had objective reasons for believing that such a momentous task should have fallen to his lot. Indeed, ever since returning from Siberia in 1860, he had endeavored to play precisely the role into which he had now been cast—that of arbitrator and conciliator between the dissident intelligentsia and Russian society as a whole.

Never, indeed, could Dostoevsky have felt himself in a better position to influence public opinion. Had the *Diary* not furnished ample proof of the power of his words to grip the minds and hearts of his readers? And never could he have felt it more essential to do so than in the late 1870s, when the earlier crises of Russian nineteenth-century society shrank into insignificance before the menace of the present. A fraction of the Populists, driven to despair by the relentless persecutions of the government and the lack of any response to their peaceful propaganda among the peasantry, had launched a systematic campaign of terror against tsarist officialdom and finally against the tsar himself. Both the novel Dostoevsky was now beginning and his sensational speech at the ceremonies inaugurating a monument to Pushkin two years later would mark his attempts to mediate the lethal conflict that was tearing Russian society apart.

Life proceeded for the Dostoevskys in the carefully organized routine that had enabled Dostoevsky to maintain the exacting schedule of his *Diary*—until April 30, 1878, when their three-year-old son Alyosha suffered a first epileptic convulsion of four minutes. On May 16 the boy was overcome by a major epileptic fit lasting for twelve hours and forty minutes, ending with his death. "My husband was crushed by this death," Anna writes in her *Reminiscences*. "He had loved Alyosha somehow in a special way, with an almost morbid love. . . . What racked him particularly was the fact that the child had died of epilepsy—a disease inherited from him." [16] Anna Filosofova, who rushed to see the Dostoevskys on hearing the news, was struck by their isolation, prostration, and helplessness. She was told by Anna, weeping inconsolably, that Dostoevsky had spent the entire previous night on his knees beside Alyosha's bed. [17]

"I so lost my bearings," writes Anna, "mourned and cried so much, that I was unrecognizable." Her husband, after the first shock, "to outward appearance . . .

[15] *LN* 86 (Moscow, 1973), 135.
[16] *Reminiscences*, 292.
[17] *Letopis*, 3: 273.

was calm and bore with courage the blow that fell on us; but I very much feared that this suppression of his deep grief might react fatally upon his already shaky health." Anna soon rallied from her apathetic state, responding to his entreaties "to submit to God's will" and "to take pity on him and the children, to whom I had become, in his words, 'indifferent.'" [18] Once having regained some stability, Anna thought it imperative to distract Dostoevsky from his own silent mourning by encouraging him to realize a long-cherished plan of visiting the famous monastery of Optina Pustyn. Vladimir Solovyev had called on them regularly during the period following Alyosha's death, and Anna persuaded him to convince her husband to undertake the arduous journey in his company. Dostoevsky intended to travel to Moscow in mid-June and offer his new novel to Katkov for *The Russian Messenger*, and a trip to the monastery from there would be quite feasible.

Despite the taxing pilgrimage, "My husband returned from Optina Pustyn seemingly at peace and much calmer," Anna writes, "and he told me a great deal about the customs of the hermitage, where he had passed two days. He met with the renowned elder [*starets*] Father Ambrose three times. . . . These talks had a profound and lasting effect on him." [19] Dostoevsky was not the only eminent Russian who found solace in the company of Father Ambrose. Tolstoy, who had visited Optina Pustyn a year earlier in the company of Strakhov, had written afterward, "This Father Ambrose is a true saint. I had only to speak to him, and my soul immediately felt relieved. It is when one speaks with men like him that one feels the closeness of God." [20]

Father Ambrose, revered not only as a spiritual counselor but also as a person of formidable knowledge and erudition, directed the work of translating and editing the texts of the Greek Fathers that had given the Optina cloister its reputation as a center of theological learning. He was famed for possessing the same gift of moral-psychological divination that will soon be attributed to Father Zosima; and the scene in *The Brothers Karamazov* where Zosima comforts the peasant mother mourning her little son Aleksey employs the very words that Father Ambrose told Dostoevsky to convey to his wife. The elder tells the mother to "weep and be not consoled, but weep. Only every time that you weep be sure to remember that your little son is one of the angels of God, that he looks down from there at you and sees you, and rejoices at your tears, and points at them to the Lord God. . . . but [your weeping] will turn in the end into a quiet joy, and your bitter tears will be only tears of tender sorrow that purifies the heart and delivers it from sin" (14: 46).

Dostoevsky left no firsthand account of his meetings with Father Ambrose, but Solovyev reported that he was in "a very excited state all through the visit."

---

[18] *Reminiscences*, 292, 293.
[19] Ibid., 294.
[20] Cited in John B. Dunlop, *Staretz Amvrosy* (Belmont, MA, 1972), 60–61.

There was, however, another eyewitness to this meeting, a close friend of Strakhov. He writes that Dostoevsky, instead of "obediently and with fitting humility paying attention to the edifying discourses of the elder and monk, spoke more than [Ambrose] did, became excited, heatedly raised objections, developed and explained the meaning of words pronounced by the elder, and, without being aware of it, from someone desiring to listen to an edifying discourse was transformed into a teacher." [21] However that may be, he drew a good deal of inspiration for his next novel from this visit to the monastery, although it is unlikely, as Solovyev wrote a few months later to Konstantin Leontiyev, that Dostoevsky "specifically went to Optina Pustyn . . . for the first chapters of his novel." [22]

■

Since Solovyev's friendship with the novelist had once again become close, it was only to be expected that the Dostoevskys would faithfully attend the famous series of lectures on Godmanhood that he gave in Petersburg all through the winter and early spring of 1878. These lectures were a great public as well as cultural event, and the hall was filled not only with students, normally averse to anything smacking of the religious or theological, but also with the cream of Petersburg cultivated society. Strakhov was there, and on one occasion, instead of the usual exchange of pleasantries, Dostoevsky noticed a certain evasiveness in his behavior. Strakhov later explained that "Count Leo Tolstoy came to the lecture with me. He asked me not to introduce him to anyone, and that was why I stayed away from all of you." Dostoevsky was disappointed that he had not at least been given the opportunity to scrutinize Tolstoy in the flesh: "But why didn't you whisper to me who was with you?" he asked Strakhov reproachfully. "I would have taken a look at him at least!" [23] The two giants of Russian literature, who were for the only time in their lives in the same place, were thus deliberately kept apart.

Dostoevsky's attendance at Solovyev's lectures was intimately linked with the ideas he was mulling over for his novel. No one reading the *Lectures on Godmanhood* can fail to be struck by the repeated echoes of Dostoevskian themes and preoccupations in Solovyev's text, but whether Solovyev exercised any influence on him is a more difficult question to answer. It is probable, however, that the trained philosophical mind of the young man both stimulated Dostoevsky and sharpened his awareness of some of the implications of his own convictions (Strakhov had performed much the same function in the 1860s). One challenging topic that preoccupied both was the establishment of the Kingdom of God

[21] *Letopis*, 3: 279.
[22] Ibid.
[23] *Reminiscences*, 291–292.

on earth. For Dostoevsky this notion presumably remained speculative and transcendent; it was only in a new and transfigured garb that one could imagine such a glorious fulfillment. Solovyev, however, believed in the possibility of a free Christian theocracy, in which the Christian law of love would entirely penetrate and spiritualize the workings of earthly life. His *Lectures* sketch the entrancing vision of a humanity gradually approaching such a blessed state of Godmanhood—a society in which, under the leadership of the Orthodox Christ and his Church, the divine and the human would fuse and follow the example of Christ the God-man himself so far as this was possible. Solovyev later wrote that, during their journey to Optina Pustyn, Dostoevsky had told him that "the Church as a positive social ideal must show itself to be the central idea of [his] new novel or a new series of novels, of which only the first has been written— *The Brothers Karamazov.*"[24]

There is an unmistakable resemblance between Solovyev's Utopia and Dostoevsky's hopes, but the notion of such a free Christian theocracy of love, under the exclusive hegemony of the Orthodox Church as both a social and a religious institution, is not taken with the same literality in both cases. It is Ivan Karamazov who expresses precisely such an idea and argues for the view that "the Church ought to include the whole State, and not simply occupy a corner of it, and, if this is, for some reason, impossible at present, then it ought, in reality, to be set up as the direct and chief aim of the future development of Christian society!" (14: 56–57). Ivan is accused by the Western liberal Miusov of advocating ultramontanism, that is, the Roman Catholic doctrine of the political subordination of the state to the church, which is not the same as the moral-spiritual transformation of the state into a church.

Father Zosima, while agreeing that the aim of human society should be such a transformation, takes this goal out of history and places it in an eschatological perspective. Christian society, he says, though not now ready, "will continue still unshaken in expectation of its complete transformation from a society almost heathen in character into a single, universal, all-powerful Church. So be it! So be it! Even though at the end of the ages, for it is ordained to come to pass!" (14: 61). Dostoevsky, of course, uses this argument over state and church to reveal the inner split in Ivan between his reason and his moral sensibility; but contemporaries immediately associated it with Solovyev.

Another point of contact between the philosophies of the two men may be seen in the analysis of the three temptations of Christ, which appears both in the *Lectures on Godmanhood* and then, a year later, in the Legend of the Grand Inquisitor. For Solovyev, however, Christ's subjection to these temptations is part of the gradual cosmogonic process through which God actualizes himself within

[24] V. S. Solovyev, *Sobranie sochinenii*, 10 vols. (St. Petersburg, 1911–1914), 3: 197.

the confines of time and earthly life and affirms his willingness to accept human limitations on his divine powers. There is no hint of the intense pathos of freedom expressed in Dostoevsky's treatment of this same great theme, nothing similar to the sublimity of his emphasis on Christ's rejection of the temptations in order to safeguard the liberty of human conscience and preserve humankind from enslavement to external and material forces.

To what extent the final shape of the Legend may have emerged from the intimate colloquies of the novelist and the philosopher is unknown; one should not forget the many anticipations of the Legend that had already appeared in the *Diary*. Nonetheless, there is one passage in Solovyev that is directly relevant. "Several years ago in Paris," he writes, "I heard a French Jesuit give the following reasoning: 'Of course, at present no one can believe in the greater part of the Christian dogma, for example, the divinity of Christ. But you will agree that civilized society cannot exist without a strong authority and a firmly organized hierarchy; only the Catholic Church possesses such an authority and such a hierarchy; therefore, every enlightened man who values the interest of mankind must side with the Catholic Church, that is to say, must be a Catholic.'"[25] Such a passage would not have taught Dostoevsky anything he had not long since believed and written about Roman Catholicism; but the frank affirmation of atheism from such a source, encountered exactly at this moment, may well have helped to shape the form in which the Legend finally was cast. Dostoevsky was beginning to make notes for the first chapters of *The Brothers Karamaxov* during the very months that Vladimir Solovyev was giving his lectures.

The extant notes for *The Brothers Karamazov* resemble those that Dostoevsky usually had made at a relatively late stage in composition. As we know, the essential components—including plot and narrative technique—of what became *The Brothers Karamazov* had long existed in his notebooks or in earlier works. It is thus entirely possible that Dostoevsky relied on such material without feeling the need to make a completely fresh start.

Literary works that had long fascinated Dostoevsky were also revisited now. His notes document the strong influence of Friedrich Schiller on the conception of *The Brothers Karamazov*. Schiller, we know, had produced a powerful impression on Dostoevsky in his childhood and youth, and the German playwright, poet, and philosophical essayist had been equally important in Russia for Dostoevsky's entire generation. In 1861 Dostoevsky wrote that "Schiller . . . was not only a great universal writer, but—above all—he was our national poet" (19: 17). Fifteen years later, he repeats that Schiller "soaked into the Russian soul, left an

[25] See Vladimir Solovyev, *Chteniya o bogochelovechestve* (St. Petersburg, 1994), 195–196.

impression on it, and almost marked an epoch in the history of our development" (23: 31). This conviction helps to explain why he portrays the influence of Schiller as having "soaked into" the souls of all the major characters of *The Brothers Karamazov*. Dimitry, Ivan, and even the lecherous old Feodor Pavlovich are all capable of citing Schiller by heart. Alyosha refers indirectly to Schiller's theory of art, and a few lines of Schiller are woven into the speech of the defense attorney Fetyukovich. A Schillerian atmosphere envelops *The Brothers Karamazov* from the first page to the last, and contributes a good deal to the heightening of its poetic quality.

This Schillerian ambiance is indicated in the notes only by a laconic sentence, "Karl Moor, Franz Moor, Regierender Graf von Moor" (15: 209). These words link the novel with Schiller's sensational first play, *The Robbers*, whose importance for Dostoevsky's novel is highlighted by a mocking sally of the old Karamazov. "That is my son," he says of Ivan, "flesh of my flesh, and most beloved of my flesh! He is my most respectful Karl Moor, so to say, while this one who has just come in, Dimitry Feodorovich, against whom I am seeking justice from you [Zosima], is the unrespectful Franz Moor—they are both out of Schiller's *The Robbers*, and so I am Regierender Graf von Moor. Judge us and save us!" (14: 66).

The ironic distortions contained in this speech illustrate the manner in which Dostoevsky plays his own variations on Schillerian themes. No one could be less like the tenderhearted, weak-willed, and abused Graf von Moor than the cynical, domineering, and rapacious Feodor Pavlovich, but they are structurally related as fathers involved in contentions with their sons. Karl Moor revolts against both the legal and the moral order because he believes (falsely) that his father denied him love and forgiveness; and although he resembles Ivan thematically because of his revolt against God's universe on behalf of a suffering humankind, his fiery, explosive temperament brings him much closer to Dimitry as a character type. The cold-blooded intellectual Ivan, unable to love humanity except in the abstract and from a distance, is similar to Franz Moor, Schiller's Machiavellian villain, whose rationalism causes him to doubt God and immortality and ruthlessly to order the murder of his father.

Not only does *The Robbers* depict the tragedy of a family split by deadly rivalry between father and sons, as well as between the sons themselves (Karl and Franz Moor both desire Amalia, just as Dimitry and Ivan are rivals for Katerina Ivanovna), it also poses the theme of parricide in even more lurid terms. For Schiller as for Dostoevsky, the sacredness of family ties and family feeling is the temporal reflection of the eternal moral order of the universe. It models God's relation to his creation, and since the negation of the first involves the destruction of the second, it is the atheist and blasphemer Franz Moor who pours scorn on the belief that family ties create mutual obligations of love. "I've heard so much chatter about a so-called love based on blood ties that it's enough to make the head spin . . . But even more—it is your father! He gave you life, you are his flesh, his blood—so for you he must be holy!"[26]

Franz's rationalism, like that of Ivan, dissolves these primordial ties and obligations of family love in words that are echoed in the trial scene: "I must ask you, why did he create me? Surely not out of love for me, who first had to become an I?"[27] The remainder of this speech, and a later one along the same lines, are transposed by the defense attorney Fetyukovich into the argument that "such a father as the old Karamazov cannot be called a father and does not merit the name. Filial love for an unworthy father is an absurd and impossible thing." An unworthy father impels his son to ask the questions: "Did he really love me when he begat me? Did he beget me for my sake? He did not know me . . . at the moment of passion, perhaps intensified by wine" (15: 171).

If *The Robbers* shows the morally disintegrating effects of such rationalism on the instinctive moral roots of human life, it also reveals, like *The Brothers Karamazov*, the strength of these roots in the human spirit and the inevitability of their triumph or revenge. Franz Moor's cynicism, at the last, gives way to a frenzied fear of eternal damnation for his manifold crimes; and he dies in a fit of terror, pleading for a prayer from his old servant. Karl Moor, appalled by the disastrously inhuman consequences of his revolt against the social iniquities of his time—a revolt that only unleashes the worst passions among his robber band, and includes the murder of a child—finally surrenders voluntarily as a sacrifice to the eternal moral order whose avenging instrument he had wished to become. Ivan, too, is appalled by the consequences of his own intellectual revolt as he sees his ideas put into practice by Smerdyakov, and, like Franz Moor, he is tormented by the impossibility of resolving the inner conflict between his skeptical rationalism and the religious faith supporting a moral order. Dimitry follows Karl Moor in being led through suffering to a sense of pity and compassion for others and an acceptance of the technical injustice of his conviction as a sacrifice for the temptation of parricide that he had willingly harbored in his breast.

Many references to Schiller's poetry are scattered throughout *The Brothers Karamazov* as well, and used to deepen its thematic range. A cosmic and historical-philosophical dimension is provided for Dimitry's inner conflict between the ideal of the Madonna and that of Sodom by fragments of Schiller's "Das eleusische Fest" ("The Eleusinian Feast") and the famous "An die Freude" ("To Joy"). Less overtly, Ivan's rebellion also moves within the orbit of the Schillerian lyric. When he hands back his "entrance ticket" to the promise of an ultimate eternal harmony of God's world because the price to be paid for it is too high in human

---

[26] Friedrich Schiller, *Samtliche Werke*, 16 vols. (Stuttgart, n.d.), 3: 15.
[27] Ibid., 16.

suffering, Ivan repeats the gesture and uses the same terms as the protagonist of Schiller's poem "Resignation":

Empfange meinen Vollmachtsbrief zum
    Glücke!
Ich bring' ihm unerbrochen dir zurucke;
Ich weiss nichts von Glückseligkeit.[28]

Of even greater importance are the two lines from Schiller's "Sehnsucht" ("Longing"), which, placed at the beginning of his Legend of the Grand Inquisitor, condense an important aspect of the religious theme. The Russian version, by the poet V. A. Zhukovsky, is a free translation of Schiller that fits more closely into Dostoevsky's context than does the original. The literal sense of the Russian is

Believe what the heart tells you,
Heaven does not make any pledges.

——■——

Dostoevsky's notes also contain additional traces of his reading, and two other works have plausibly been linked with *The Brothers Karamazov*. Both are by George Sand, another writer whom Dostoevsky had adored in his youth and recently recalled in the *Diary of a Writer*. The research of V. L. Komarovich has brought out convincing resemblances between George Sand's novel *Mauprat* (1837) and the plot action of *The Brothers Karamazov*. Both novels contain a crucial scene in which a young woman is on the point of being forced to sacrifice her honor, but at the last moment her presumptive ravisher renounces his villainous intentions, and this leads to an emotional entanglement between them in the future. In both, the young man is falsely accused of a murder, and tried and convicted on what seems unimpeachable circumstantial evidence. Sand's heroine, Edmée, like Katerina Ivanovna, reverses her testimony—but to exonerate rather than condemn. The surprise introduction of a letter written by the accused to the heroine, and prefiguring the crime, also plays a major role in the condemnation. A comparison of parallel passages from the trial scenes makes clear that some of the plot elements of *Mauprat* had left ineradicable traces in Dostoevsky's memory.[29]

Another work of George Sand's, her unprecedented religious-philosophical novel *Spiridion* (1839), foreshadows *The Brothers Karamazov* on a deeper thematic level. *Spiridion* takes place entirely in a monastery and consists largely of

[28] Translated literally, this reads: "Receive back my authorized permit to good fortune! / I return it to you unopened / I know nothing of happiness."

[29] V. L. Komarovich, "Dostojewski und George Sand," in *Die Urgestalt des Brüder Karamasoff* (Munich, 1928), 214–219.

conversations between a dying monk, Alexis—the inheritor of a semiheretical religious tradition handed down to him by his dead mentor, Spiridion—and a young novice named Angel. Alyosha Karamazov is also constantly called "angel," and his adoring relation to Father Zosima is similar to that of Sand's young disciple to *his* saintly teacher, also regarded with great suspicion by monks of a more orthodox persuasion. Like Zosima, Alexis is on the point of death; and he conveys his dying words to Angel, whom he calls "the son of my intelligence," exactly as Zosima confides the story of his life and his teachings to Alyosha, whom he considers the reincarnation of his brother Markel. Of course, Dostoevsky had long nourished the project of writing a work set in a monastery, and it could well be that *Spiridion*, which he had read on publication, encouraged such an intention at the very outset of his literary career.[30]

At the novel's climax the monastery is invaded by the armies of the French Revolution. Alexis is put to death, but he forgives the rampaging soldiers in his last words because he sees them acting "in the name of the *sans-culotte* Jesus," on whose behalf "they are desecrating the sanctuary of the Church." Jesus was thus for him a revolutionary figure, a *sans-culotte*, whose ideals of liberty, equality, and fraternity were being fulfilled in practice, though entirely unconsciously, by the marauding soldiers.[31] Here we have the Utopian Socialist Christ of Dostoevsky's own early manhood—the semisecularized Christ whose social ideals he had never renounced but whose aims, particularly in Russia, he had long ceased to believe could be attained through revolutionary violence.

On opening the tomb of Spiridion after Alexis's death, Angel finds buried with him the Gospel of Saint John (Dostoevsky's own favorite, from which he took the epigraph for *The Brothers Karamazov*), Jean de Parme's *Introduction to the Eternal Gospel* (a book written by a disciple of Joachim di Fiori, denounced as a heretic and burned in 1260), and Spiridion's own commentary on this latter text. He had interpreted it as a prophecy predicting the arrival of the reign of the Holy Ghost—the reign of the principles represented by the French soldiers, who were thus accomplishing God's will. His spiritual guide passes on this doctrine to Angel, who will take it into the world—just as Father Zosima passes on *his* teachings to Alyosha. Both mentors hold out the equally messianic hope (if only, for Zosima, at the end of time!) of a total transformation of earthly life into a realm of Christian felicity.

Aside from such similarities, it is impossible to read *Spiridion* without being struck by the concordance between some of Alexis's utterances and Dostoevsky's own most cherished convictions. No theme was more important for him in the

---

[30] See the excellent book of Isabelle Hoog Naginski, *George Sand* (New Brunswick, NJ, 1991), 260. An appreciative discussion of *Spiridion* is contained in chapter 6.

[31] Ibid., 146.

1870s than that of the first temptation of Christ, the turning of stones into bread. To yield to this temptation could only result in the surrender by human-kind of its freedom of conscience; and Sand expressed the same thought forty years earlier. "This gigantic task of the French Revolution was not, it could not be," Alexis declares, "only a question of bread and shelter for the poor; it was something much loftier. . . . [I]t had to, it still must . . . fully accomplish the task of giving freedom of conscience to the entire human race. This soul that torments me, this thirst for the infinite which devours me, will they be satisfied and appeased because the body is safe from want?"[32]

Nor was anything of greater moment for Dostoevsky than to emphasize the supreme significance for human life of the prospect of eternity, and to combat the atheistic confinement of existence to the limits of life on earth. Here too we find Alexis eloquently expressing the same longing, the same innate human need to transcend terrestrial boundaries. "And . . . when all the duties of men among themselves are established through a system of mutual interest, will this suffice for human happiness? . . . No matter how peaceful, how sweet one supposes life on earth to be, will it suffice for the desires of mankind and will the world be vast enough to encompass human thought?" Alexis also proclaims one of Zosi-ma's most sublime moral principles: the universal responsibility of each for all.[33] One can well understand why Dostoevsky felt no hesitation in stretching the literal, historical truth when, in his obituary of her in the *Diary*, he spoke of George Sand as "one of the most perfect confessors of Christ."

—■—

On returning to Petersburg on October 3, the Dostoevskys moved into a new apartment for reasons that Anna poignantly explains: "We could not bring our-selves to go on living in that apartment, filled with memories of our dead child." Anna also dwells on the shadow that continued to hang over their lives because of Alyosha's death. "No matter how my husband and I strove to submit to God's will and not grieve, we could not forget our darling Alyosha. All that autumn and the following winter were darkened by desolate memories. Our loss had the ef-fect on my husband (who had always been passionately attached to his children) of making him love them even more intensely and fear for them even more."[34] All this time Dostoevsky was working on *The Brothers Karamazov*, and the very problems raised in the impassioned declamations of Ivan—the unmerited suffer-ing of little children and the difficulty of reconciling oneself to God's will because of their torments—lay at the very center of his own life and feelings.

[32] Quoted in ibid., 149–150.
[33] Ibid., 150, 143.
[34] *Reminiscences*, 294.

In the beginning of November 1878, with the first two books of *The Brothers Karamazov* completed, he traveled to Moscow to make the financial arrangements for publication. Dostoevsky called on Lyubimov, who was co-editor now of the *Russian Messenger* and would be in charge of publishing the novel. Katkov had fallen ill and could not receive Dostoevsky, who then felt obliged to assure Anna, who might be suspicious, that "of course he is not making excuses. He is really sick." He himself was suffering from constipation and censoriously declares that "everything is vile." "I am terribly lonely here," he complains, "unbearably so."[35]

Visits to his relatives provided the only bright spots in his unending catalogue of woes, though even with them the talk turned on Alyosha's death. Nor was his temper improved by visits to the lawyers who were haggling over the details of the never-ending litigation concerning the Kumanina estate. Katkov's cashier at long last came to the hotel with Dostoevsky's advance, and he was able to leave Moscow two days later after tidying up his other affairs. The strain of this trip probably took its toll on Dostoevsky's health. At the end of the month he visited his physician, Dr. von Bretsall, who advised him not to leave the house for several days.

[35] *PSS*, 30/Bk. 1: 48–49; November 9, 1878.

CHAPTER 53

The Great Debate

The first installment of *The Brothers Karamazov* was published on February 1, 1879. A few days later the governor-general of Kharkov—a cousin of the anarchist revolutionary Peter Kropotkin—was killed, and in March an unsuccessful attempt was made on the life of the new head of the secret police, the successor of General Mezentsev, as he was driving his carriage through the center of Petersburg. In April, a revolutionary acting on his own, but with the knowledge of the Populist Land and Liberty, attempted to assassinate the tsar as he was taking his morning walk in the Winter Palace grounds. The would-be assassin, Alexander Solovyev, missed his mark and was publicly hanged in May. It was in this atmosphere of murder and mayhem that Dostoevsky's novel was being written and read. It was also the atmosphere in which he and Turgenev appeared together at benefit readings and banquets to represent the two extremes of the great debate that was taking place in the minds and hearts of all educated Russians—the debate between a despotic tsarism, unwilling to yield an inch of its authority, and the longing for a liberal, Western-style constitution that would allow for greater participation of the public in government affairs.

■

Just how intensely Dostoevsky was working at this time may be judged from the dispatch of Chapters 6–11 of *The Brothers Karamazov* on January 31, even before the first installment had been published. The galleys of the first two chapters had just arrived, and he enlisted the help of Elena Shtakenshneider with the proofreading. She returned the proofs along with a request to send back a borrowed copy of Zola's *L'Assomoir*. Dostoevsky evidently wished to keep up to date, and *The Brothers Karamazov* contains ironic references to the physiologist and psychologist Claude Bernard, the main source of Zola's theories about heredity and environment. The literary prominence given by Zola to Bernard's deterministic theories of human character imparted to the French novel an ideological as well as a literary significance. Dostoevsky was writing his own family novel, with its defense of the freedom of the human personality, in direct competition with Zola's deterministic Rougon-Macquart series.

Just about this time, a young woman named E. P. Letkova-Sultanova (a *kursistka* in the higher education courses for women) wrote in her diary about a meeting with Dostoevsky at one of the famous Fridays of the poet Yakov Polonsky. Advancing into the drawing room, she saw everyone, dignified gentlemen and smartly dressed ladies, clustered around one of the three windows and intently listening to someone talking. Suddenly she recognized the voice of Dostoevsky and caught a glimpse of the speaker, whom she had never seen before. Her first impression did not correspond at all to the imperious image she had formed in her mind; he was shriveled, rather short, and struck her as someone who looked *vinovaty*, that is, as if he felt guilty about something. The window before which he stood gave onto Semenovsky Square; and he was holding the other guests spellbound as he relived the past. It was Polonsky who had led him to the window and asked if he recognized what he saw. "Yes!.. Yes! . . . Really! . . . How could I not recognize it," he had replied.[1]

Dostoevsky's words came tumbling out in a stream of spasmodic sentences. He evoked the freezing coldness of the morning, and the horror that overcame him and the other Petrashevtsy as they heard the death sentence being pronounced. "It could not be that I, amidst all the thousands who were alive—in something like five to six minutes would no longer exist!" The appearance of a priest holding a cross convinced them that death was inevitable. "They could not joke even with the cross! . . . They could not stage such a tragicomedy!" Dostoevsky remembered that a feeling of numbness and torpor overcame him: "Everything seemed insignificant compared to this last terrible minute of transition to somewhere, . . . to the unknown, to darkness"; and this numbness did not lift even after he learned that their lives had been spared. Polonsky approached him to break the tension and said consolingly, "Well, all this is past and gone," inviting him to drink tea with their hostess. "Is it really gone?" Dostoevsky whispered.[2] The indelible impact of this confrontation with death had exercised a decisive effect on the remainder of his days.

Letkova was deeply moved by Dostoevsky's words, uttered in breathless bursts, and she describes him, when he finished, standing "as if a waxen figure: sallow and pale, eyes sunken, lips bloodless, smiling but with a look of suffering."[3] Her opinion of Dostoevsky up to that moment had been anything but favorable, and she tells of the heated discussions in her student group caused by each issue of the *Diary*. It was generally agreed that his anti-Semitism was intolerable; nor could they endorse the warmongering chauvinism of his articles about the Russo-Turkish War, whose sacrifice in human lives now seemed so vain and futile. Letkova and her fellow students had unanimously detested

[1] *DVS*, 2: 444–445.
[2] Ibid.
[3] Ibid., 445.

Demons, and felt light-years removed from Dostoevsky's political tendency and ideas.

All this was forgotten, however, in the aftermath of what she had just heard. What now emerged before her mind's eye was "his entire sacrificial path: the torture of awaiting death, its replacement by *katorga*, the 'House of the Dead' with all its horrors: and all this had been borne by this puny man, who suddenly appeared to me greater than everyone surrounding him." Everything else vanished into oblivion before this vision, and "a feeling of unbelievable happiness, the happiness one can only feel when young, took hold of me. And I wanted to throw myself on my knees and bow down to his sufferings."[4]

Everyone had read *House of the Dead*, and the emotion she experienced was widely shared by all those who, at one public event or another, had listened to him read. Her reaction thus helps to explain some of the astonishing responses called forth by Dostoevsky's presence on the platform before a mass audience— an audience that, in the majority and at a more sober moment, could well have been antagonistic to his politics. If it was true, as he untiringly maintained, that the Russian peasants particularly revered the suffering of their Christian saints who had endured martyrdom for their faith, then some of this reverence appears to have been transferred—by the new generation who once again accepted the value of suffering and self-sacrifice—to Dostoevsky himself.

———■———

A dinner invitation from Grand Duke Sergey for March 5, conveyed through Arsenyev, informed him that the grand duke had perused *House of the Dead*, *Crime and Punishment*, and the first part of *The Brothers Karamazov*. Hence he was even more eager to enjoy the benefits of Dostoevsky's conversation, of which he retained "a pleasant memory." At the table were also Pobedonostsev and Grand Duke Konstantin Konstantinovich, who commented about the evening in his diary, "Feodor Mikhailovich pleases me very much, not only because of his writings but simply because of himself." Several days later he again noted in his diary, "I have obtained *The Idiot* of Dostoevsky. When you read his works, it's enough to drive you out of your mind."[5]

Even though he had been invited to dine with younger members of the royal family for the purpose of broadening their minds and shaping their sensibilities, the anomalies of Russian imperial society were such that Dostoevsky was still, as an ex-convict, under the surveillance of the secret police. To end this exasperating situation, he decided to use the considerable influence he could now muster. On March 10 he received a letter from Lieutenant-General A. A. Kireyev,

---

[4] Ibid., 446.

[5] *Letopis zhizni i tvorchestvo F. M. Dostoevskogo*, ed. N. F. Budanova and G. M. Fridlender, 3 vols. (St. Petersburg, 1995), 3: 303–306.

an aide-de-camp of Grand Duke Konstantin Nikolaevich, the brother of the tsar, obviously in response to efforts to acquaint some important personages with his plight. Kireyev informed Dostoevsky that it would be necessary to make the demand himself to the proper authorities. The document, written the same day, outlines the facts of the restoration of his civil rights. Dostoevsky concludes: "On hundreds of pages I have spoken . . . of my political and religious convictions. I hope that these convictions are such that they cannot give cause to suspect my political morality."[6] His name was thus finally stricken from the list of those on whom the Third Section was keeping a watchful eye.

Social obligations continued to pile up. On March 8 he received a visit from Anna Filosofova, ever busy with charitable endeavors and now arranging a reading for the Literary Fund. Turgenev, just returned to Russia, had already accepted an invitation the day before, and she now solicited Dostoevsky's participation. Turgenev's return to Russia amounted to a rehabilitation of his reputation among the radicals who had mercilessly repudiated him after *Fathers and Children*. His next novel, *Smoke*, had aroused even more hostility among all sections of the reading public because of the speeches of one character, who caustically denied that Russia had contributed anything of value to world culture except the samovar. *Virgin Soil*, his most recent work, presented a not unsympathetic yet disabused view of the Populist "going to the people" movement, and was generally considered a failure. Few champions had come forward to defend these later novels, and Turgenev's self-imposed exile was in part a means of escaping the implacable hostilities of Russian literary life. This absence from Russia had also injured his reputation. Even Anna Filosofova, surely more sympathetic to his reformist liberalism than to Dostoevsky's instransigent tsarism, remarked: "I respect him less than Dostoevsky. Feodor Mikhailovich bears the traces of all the miseries of Russia on his skin, he has suffered through them and was tortured by all his convictions, while Ivan Sergeyevich became frightened and fled, and all his life he criticized us from the beautiful beyond."[7]

By the spring of 1879, however, the social-political situation in Russia had become intolerably tortuous because of the continuing assassinations. As a result, the return of the Europeanized liberal Turgenev, which led to public banquets and celebrations in his honor, assumed a special significance. The festivities in which he took part became symbols of the longing, which could not be expressed openly, for some concessions on the part of the iron-fisted, despotic government to the increasingly desperate radical youth. Annenkov, Turgenev's alter ego, commenting on the enthusiasm aroused by his appearance in Russia, wrote in April that a "complete rehabilitation has been occurring of the repre-

---

[6] *PSS*, 30/Bk. 1: 247.
[7] *DVS*, 2: 377.

sentatives of the 1840s, a public recognition of their services, and they are accorded a deep, classless, and typically Russian bow, even to the earth and to the point of prostration. It may be that the exploits of Nechaev, Tkachev, and tutti quanti have moved society to the side of the old development, beginning under the banner of art, philosophy, and morality; but however that may be—the present moment in Russia may be the most important of all that it has lived through these last twenty-five years."[8]

What Anna Filosofova tells us of Turgenev's reception by the audience at this reading amply confirms Annenkov's words. "The hall was filled to overflowing. Suddenly Turgenev appeared. . . . [E]verybody rose as one and bowed to the king of the [enlightened] mind. I recalled the episode of Victor Hugo when he returned from exile to Paris and the whole city poured into the streets to greet him."[9] Other writers participated, but all eyes were fixed on Turgenev and Dostoevsky. Their juxtaposed presence on the stage brought together the opposing poles of Russian culture. As the writer B. M. Markevich put it: "What is there in common, I asked myself . . . between such an 'incurable Westernizer,' to use Turgenev's own words about himself, and that eternal seeker of the *genuine* Russian truth—whose name is Dostoevsky?"[10] Both were competing, on these nominally apolitical occasions, for the minds and hearts of the public on whom would depend the future; and everyone felt, like Annenkov, that their country was facing its greatest social-political crisis since the Crimean War.

Turgenev read early in the program, and chose a story, "The Bailiff," from his classic *A Sportsman's Sketches*. Dostoevsky always preferred to read in the second half, and then he produced the as yet unpublished "Confession of a Passionate Heart," which elicited a sensational response. As Anna Filosofova wrote, "He read that part where Katerina Ivanovna takes the money to Mitya Karamazov, to a beast who wishes to show his superiority over her and to dishonor her because of her pride. But then the beast calmed down and the human being triumphed. . . . Good God! How my heart beat . . . is it possible to convey the impression left by the reading of Feodor Mikhailovich? We all sobbed, everyone was filled to overflowing with some sort of moral ecstasy." And she continues: "For me, that evening, Turgenev somehow vanished, and I almost did not hear him."[11]

Also present in the audience was Varvara Timofeyeva, Dostoevsky's one-time assistant and confidante at the time he was editing *The Citizen*. She had not met him since, and memories came surging back when she heard his voice again. For her "it was something like the revelation of our destiny. . . . It was the anatomical dissection of our ailing, gangrenous corpse—a dissection of the abscesses and

[8] Ibid., 553.
[9] Ibid., 377–378.
[10] *Letopis*, 3: 306.
[11] *DVS*, 2: 178.

illnesses of our stultified conscience, our unhealthy, rotten, still serflike life." [12] The whole audience was stirred to its depths, and Timofeyeva depicts an unknown young man sitting next to her who "shivered and sighed" and "blushed and turned pale, convulsively shaking his head and clenching his fists, as if restraining himself with difficulty from breaking into applause." When the applause finally came, it was deafening, lasting for fifteen minutes and calling him back to the stage five times. "We suddenly felt," writes Timofeyeva, "that . . . it was impossible to hesitate for a single moment . . . because each moment brings us closer to eternal darkness or to eternal light—to the evangelical ideals or to bestiality." [13]

Dostoevsky's apocalyptic sensibility could not have been better attuned to the tension-ridden mood of his audience, torn by conflicting emotions over the desperate duel between the ever-more oppressive regime of the Tsar-Liberator, now fighting for his life, and the revolutionaries who had begun by invoking the example of Christ and were now committing murder. When Dostoevsky visited Filosofova the next day, even before he could ask her, in a trembling voice, whether the evening "had gone well," she threw her arms around his neck and began to weep with deep feeling. [14]

While Turgenev and Dostoevsky had thus far managed to observe the proprieties in public, hostilities between the two writers came out into the open on March 13 at a banquet organized in Turgenev's honor by a group of Petersburg literati. Some of the speeches, which came to more than twelve, were embarrassingly fulsome. Grigorovich, for example, said that if one were to place Turgenev against a window, light would shine through him as through a piece of crystal, "so pure is he morally among us." At last Turgenev rose and greeted what he saw as the new reconciliation of the generations, whose separation he had once depicted in *Fathers and Children*. The moment had come, he affirmed, when the split could at last be healed because both generations now accepted "an ideal that . . . perhaps is quite close, and in which they are unanimously united." [15] Everybody knew that he was referring to the possibility of "crowning the edifice" (as the Russians liked to call it), that is, the granting of a Western-style constitution by Alexander II that would, by creating a representative democracy, complete the process begun with the liberation of the serfs.

This speech elicited a thunderous ovation, and when others flocked to congratulate the speaker, Dostoevsky chose this moment to precipitate a scandal

[12] Ibid., 192–193.
[13] Ibid., 193.
[14] Ibid., 378.
[15] *PSS*, 25: 60.

enshrined in the annals of Russian literary history—a scandal that may well have been caused by his dismay at the news of the latest assassination attempt earlier that day. He too approached Turgenev and defiantly shot out the question: "Tell me now, what is your ideal? Speak!" Instead of replying, Turgenev merely lowered his head and waved his arms helplessly, but others present said loudly: "Don't speak! We know!" Dostoevsky's unseemly behavior, which, as one journal put it, broke "the general tone of veneration accorded to Turgenev," was more than an outburst of ill humor or envy.[16] He had always been an unrelenting opponent of a Russian constitution, on the ground that it would benefit only the educated portion of the population.

Turgenev left Russia shortly afterward, encouraged to do so by the authorities, who had become upset over the social-political implications of the public demonstrations in his honor. He and Dostoevsky met again, however, just a day after the second Literary Fund evening, in the salon of Countess Sofya Tolstaya. Whether they exchanged anything more than a few perfunctory words is not known, but present also was Vicomte Eugène Melchior de Vogüé, an aspiring young French *homme de lettres* then in the diplomatic service and stationed in the French embassy in St. Petersburg. He had laboriously acquired a fluent command of Russian during his first two years there, married into the highly placed Annenkov family (his wife was a lady-in-waiting to the tsarina), and moved assuredly in the cultivated circles of the capital. Having immersed himself in Russian literature, the Vicomte was of course familiar with the works of Dostoevsky, and he has left observations of their meetings, especially valuable because they come from a neutral foreign observer. Dostoevsky's face "was that of a Russian peasant, a true *muzhik* of Moscow: the flattened nose, small eyes blinking under the arched eyebrows, burning with a fire sometimes gloomy, sometimes gentle; a large brow, mottled with indentations and protuberances, the temples receding as if shaped by hammer blows; and all these features drawn, contorted, collapsed into a painful mouth. Never have I seen on a human face such an expression of accumulated suffering. . . . His eyelids, his lips, all the fibers of his face trembled with nervous tics."[17]

Some of their conversations are preserved in de Vogüé's pathbreaking study, *Le roman Russe*, which introduced the great Russian writers to the Western world. "Literary discussions with Dostoevsky," he remarks with quiet irony, "ended very quickly; he stopped me with a word of prideful compassion: 'We possess the genius of all the peoples and also have our own; thus we can understand you and you cannot understand us.'" Much the same opinion, if less laconically, had been expressed in the *Diary*. The worldly Frenchman was also entertained by his

[16] I. Volgin, *Posledny god Dostoevskogo* (Moscow, 1986), 75–76; also, *Letopis*, 3: 308.
[17] E. M. de Vogüé, *Le roman Russe* (Paris, 1910), 269.

opinions about Western Europe, which he found to be "of an amusing naïveté." One evening he spoke of Paris "as Jonah must have spoken of Nineveh, with biblical fire." He said: "A prophet will appear one night at the Café Anglais and will write three flaming words on the wall; and that will be the signal of the end of the old world and Paris will collapse in blood and fire with everything of which it is proud, its theaters and its Café Anglais." De Vogüé could only raise his eyebrows at this tirade against the Café Anglais, "that inoffensive establishment," which Dostoevsky seemed to consider "the umbilical cord of Satan."[18] Little did Dostoevsky know that the elegant French diplomat he was hectoring would, six years later, be primarily responsible for making his name familiar among cultivated European readers.

In mid-March, *Voice* contained an account of the trial of two foreigners, a couple named Brunst, who were accused of mistreating their five-year-old daughter in a monstrous fashion, and Dostoevsky used some of its details (the smearing of the child's face with excrement) in Ivan Karamazov's rebellious vituperation against God for creating a world in which such outrages were possible. Unfortunately, another trial at the time also attracted his attention, that of nine Georgian Jews accused of murdering a young girl in the Kutais district of that region. The girl had disappeared on the eve of Passover, and although the blood libel was not mentioned in the indictment, there had been much discussion in the Russian press, including *The Citizen*, as to whether "fanatical [Jewish] sectarians" kidnapped and killed Christian children to obtain their blood for ritual purposes at this time of year. Everyone thus knew what the charges involved, and it says much in honor of the reformed Russian judicial system that the Kutais Jews, against whom there was no evidence, were acquitted on March 17. An appeal to a higher court a year later met with no more success. Reading the newspaper accounts, Dostoevsky came to an opposite conclusion. Writing to Olga Novikova, whose contributions to the English press earned her the title of "the M. P. from Russia," he said, "How disgusting that the Kutais Jews are acquitted. They are beyond doubt guilty. I'm persuaded by the trial and by everything, including the vile defense by Alexandrov, who is here a remarkable scoundrel—'a lawyer is a hired conscience.'"[19] This tidbit of news too, alas, becomes part of *The Brothers Karamazov*, whose pages were then causing a furor among the Russian reading public.

Not only was Dostoevsky's artistic mastery self-evident, but the thematic issue that that the book posed—whether a murder to destroy a monstrous evil could morally be justified—was placed before the same readers practically every time they opened their newspapers. One official after another fell victim to the

[18] Ibid., 270–271.
[19] *PSS*, 30/Bk. 1: 59; March 28, 1879.

revenge of the Populists, who had declared war on the tsarist regime; and on April 2 an attempt was made on the life of the tsar himself. In 1866, when Alexander had escaped assassination, there had been a huge outpouring of national support for the government and widespread rejoicing at the tsar's good fortune. Nothing even remotely similar occurred this time. As a government commission noted two months later, "especially noteworthy of attention is the almost complete failure of the educated classes to support the government in its fight against a relatively small band of evildoers. . . . They [the educated classes] are . . . waiting for the results of the battle."[20] Dostoevsky had been almost hysterical on hearing of the failed assassination in 1866, and we may presume that he was also upset this time as well. One episode in the memoir literature has been plausibly linked to this event.

M. V. Kametskaya, the daughter of Anna Filosofova, recalls hearing the doorbell of their apartment ring one day, and when she went to greet the visitor, there was Dostoevsky, "embarrassed, apologetic, [who] suddenly understood that all this was not necessary. He stood before me, his face drained of color, wiping the perspiration from his brow and breathing heavily from having hurried up the stairs. 'Is Mama home? Well, God be praised!' Then he took my head in his hands and kissed me on the brow: 'Well, God be praised! I was just told that you had both been arrested!'"[21] A rumor had spread in the city that both mother and daughter had been taken into custody. Although Kametskaya does not specify the date of this visit, it has credibly been placed on the day of the assassination attempt.[22] Indeed, it would not be long before the authorities decided to put a stop altogether to the activities of Filosofova. In November 1879 she was politely but firmly requested to go to Wiesbaden, where she often vacationed, and not to return. Alexander II told her husband that it was only in gratitude for his services that she had not been sent to a much less pleasant place of exile.

Work on *The Brothers Karamazov* continued without a pause, and on April 17 Dostoevsky left for Staraya Russa, where he could continue writing in relative tranquility. The immense success of the sections already published convinced him that his book was touching an acutely aching nerve in the public. If Dostoevsky had any doubts on this score, they would have been dissipated by a letter he received from the influential editor Sergey Yuriev, who had just acquired permission to launch his new journal, *Russian Thought* (*Russkaya Mysl'*). In urging Dostoevsky once more to contribute a novel, he wrote that it would not only "embellish his pages" but also serve to drain "the moral abscess which is eating up our life."[23]

---

[20] Franco Venturi, *Roots of Revolution* (New York, 1966), 633.

[21] *DVS*, 2: 380.

[22] *Letopis*, 3: 312.

[23] Ibid., 314.

CHAPTER 54

Rebellion and the Grand Inquisitor

Dostoevsky would remain at Staraya Russa until July 17, hard at work on his novel. He was then writing Book 5 of Part 2, "Pro and Contra," which contains Ivan's rebellion against God's world and the Legend of the Grand Inquisitor. His life during this period was spent entirely tied to his desk, turning out chapter after chapter of his final masterpiece. To avoid misunderstandings that might lead to objections, and perhaps censorship, each section sent to his editor Lyubimov was accompanied by a letter of explanation. These provide a running self-commentary on his ideological and artistic aims that are unique in the corpus of his work.

On May 7, Dostoevsky sent off the first half of Book 5. He describes his intention as "the portrayal of the uttermost blasphemy and the seed of the idea of destruction in our time in Russia among the young people uprooted from reality, and, along with the blasphemy and anarchy—the refutation of them, which is now being prepared by me in the last words of the dying elder Zosima." He characterizes these convictions of Ivan "as a synthesis of contemporary Russian anarchism. The rejection not of God, but of the meaning of His creation. All of Socialism has sprung from and began with the denial of the meaning of historical reality and ended in a program of destruction and anarchism." [1]

Dostoevsky reserved a separate book for Zosima's preachments; "Pro and Contra" thus refers only to the inner debate taking place in Ivan between his recognition of the moral sublimity of the Christian ideal and his outrage against a universe of pain and suffering (and on a world-historical scale, by his questioning of the moral foundations of both Christianity and Socialism in the Legend of the Grand Inquisitor). The Populists had restored the morality of the Christian God (independently of their own opinions about his divinity) that had been negated in the previous decade; and they were now applying it to his own creation. Indeed, they were rejecting "the meaning of historical reality" that he had presumably established in order to correct his work in light of the very Christian principles he had proclaimed. Ivan's protest against God's world is thus couched in terms of the Christian value of compassion—the very value that Dostoevsky

---

[1] *PSS*, 30/Bk. 1: 63; May 10, 1879.

himself (or Myshkin in *The Idiot*) had once called "the chief and perhaps the only law of all human existence" (8: 192). "My heroes take up the theme," Dostoevsky continues in his letter to Lyubimov, "that I think irrefutable—the senselessness of the suffering of children—and derive from it the absurdity of all historical reality."[2] Reason or rationality cannot cope with the senselessness of such suffering, and Zosima will respond to it only with a leap of faith in God's ultimate goodness and mercy.

Invoking the considerable authority of Pobedonostsev, Dostoevsky attempts to counter in advance the usual charges made against him. He informs Lyubimov that, while some of the characters in *Demons* had been criticized as pathological fantasies, they "were all vindicated by reality and therefore had been discerned accurately. I have been told by [Pobedonostsev] about two or three cases of arrested anarchists who were amazingly similar to the ones depicted by me." All the tortures that Dostoevsky portrays through Ivan's feverish words were taken from newspaper accounts or from historical sources for which he was ready to give the exact reference. He also assures the editor that his pages do not contain "a single indecent word," but worries that some of his details might be softened. He "beg[s] and implore[s]" that the expression used in describing the punishment inflicted on a child—"the tormentors who are raising her *smear her with excrement* for not being able to ask to go to the bathroom at night"—be retained. "You mustn't soften it . . . that would be very, very sad! We are not writing for ten-year-old children." (The wording was not changed.) And then, turning to a larger issue, Dostoevsky reassures the editor that "my protagonist's blasphemy . . . will be solemnly refuted in the following (June) issue, on which I am now working with fear, trepidation, and reverence, since I consider my task (the rout of anarchism) a civic feat."[3]

There were ample precedents in Dostoevsky's work for his thematic focus on the problem of theodicy raised by Ivan—the problem of the existence of evil and suffering in a world presumably created by a God of love. No Judeo-Christian reader can help but think of the book of Job in this connection, and Dostoevsky's creation is one of the few whose voice rings out with an equal eloquence and an equal anguish. Although there is no explicit reference to Job in the notes for these chapters, his name appears three times in other sections, and Zosima will narrate the story of Job, stressing its consolatory conclusion, in his departing words. Dostoevsky, we know, had written to his wife in 1875 that "I am reading Job and it puts me into a state of painful ecstasy; I leave off reading and I walk about the room almost crying. . . . This book, dear Anna, it's strange, it was one of the first to impress me in my life. I was still practically

[2] Ibid.
[3] Ibid., 64.

an infant."[4] This recollection is then attributed to Zosima, who recalls hearing the book of Job read aloud in church at the age of eight, "and I feel as I did then, awe and wonder and gladness. . . . Ever since then . . . I've never been able to read that sacred tale without tears" (14: 264–265). Nourished by Dostoevsky's own grief over the loss of his son Alyosha, this magnificent chapter drew as well on feelings that had been stirring within him throughout his life.[5]

In mid-May, Dostoevsky provides another explanation for producing such a troubling and powerful condemnation of God. Repeating that Book 5 "in my novel is the culminating one," he defines "the point of the book" as being "blasphemy and the refutation of blasphemy." "The blasphemy I have taken as I myself sensed and realized it, in its strongest form, that is, precisely as it occurs among us now in Russia with the whole (almost) upper stratum, and primarily with the young people, that is, the scientific and philosophical rejection of God's existence has been abandoned now, today's practical Socialists don't bother with it at all (as people did the whole last century and the first half of the present one). But on the other hand God's creation, God's world, and *its* meaning are *negated* as strongly as possible. That's the only thing that contemporary civilization finds nonsensical."[6]

Dostoevsky had always argued that characters like Stavrogin and Kirillov, who were hardly "realistic" in the sense of being recognizably typical, nonetheless revealed the essence of Russian life, and he now maintains that this presentation of Ivan Karamazov is far from being only an artistic invention. "Thus I flatter myself," he insists, "that even in such an abstract theme [the rejection of God's world], I have not betrayed realism. The refutation of this (not direct, that is, not from one person to another) will appear in the last words of the dying elder. Many critics have reproached me for generally taking up in my novels themes that are allegedly wrong, unreal, and so forth. I, on the contrary, don't

---

[4] *PSS*, 29/Bk. 2: 43; June 10/22, 1875.

[5] Russian scholarship has also located a more contemporary source that may have had some effect on Dostoevsky's text. A. N. Pypin published a biography of Belinsky in 1875 that included extensive abstracts from his letters of the early 1840s. At this time Belinsky was breaking free from an erroneous interpretation of Hegel propagated by Bakunin. Bakunin insisted that Hegel was advocating "a reconciliation with reality" (the terrible reality of the Russia of Nicholas I!) because Hegel had proclaimed that "the real is the rational." Finding this doctrine intolerable, Belinsky exploded in letters denouncing, very much as does Ivan, the apologia for evil contained in the notion that the immolation of some is necessary for the harmony of the whole. "Even if I attained to the actual top of the ladder of human development," he wrote, "I should at that point still have to ask [Hegel] to account for all the victims of life and history, all the victims of accident and superstition, of the Inquisition and Philip II, and so on and so forth; otherwise I will throw myself head-downwards" (cited in *PSS*, 15: 470). One may assume that Dostoevsky would have read Pypin's book, and this letter was also quoted in an article by Mikhailovsky on "Proudhon and Belinsky" in the November 1875 issue of *Notes of the Fatherland*.

[6] *PSS*, 30/Bk. 1: 66; May 19, 1879.

know anything more real than precisely these themes."[7] His technique had always been to refute the ideas he was combating "indirectly," by dramatizing their consequences on the fate of his characters.

Dostoevsky also offers pointed instructions on how to read his works, and indicates how carefully he created the closely woven texture of his characters. In the *Diary*, he was writing in his own name and voice, whereas

> now, here, in the novel *it is not I who am* speaking in distressing colors, exaggerations, and hyperboles (although there is no exaggeration concerning the reality), but a character of my novel, Ivan Karamazov. This is *his* language, *his* style, *his* pathos, and not mine. He is a gloomily irritable person who keeps silent about a good deal. He would not have spoken out for anything in the world if not for the accidental sympathy for his brother Aleksey that suddenly flares up. Besides, he is a very young man. How else could he speak out on what he had kept silent for so long without this particular transport of feeling, without foaming at the mouth. He had strained his heart to the utmost so as not to break forth. But I precisely wanted his character to stand out, and that the reader notice this particular passion, this leap, this literary, impulsively sudden behavior.[8]

In response to another criticism by the editor of "a needless particularity," a euphemism for an indecent detail about the child whose face had been smeared with excrement, Dostoevsky insists that this observation of Ivan's character is crucial for communicating the complexity he wishes to convey about Ivan's personality. "If a twenty-three-year-old notices, that means he took it to heart. It means that he turned [the details] over in his mind, that he was an advocate of children, and no matter how heartless he is presented there later, compassion and the most sincere love of children remain in him still."[9] Ivan's deep-rooted trait of character should influence the manner in which the reader regards him: "This Ivan then obliquely commits a crime . . . in the name of an idea, with which then he was not able to cope; and he gives himself up precisely because, it may be, that once, at some time, his heart, dwelling on the suffering of children, did not overlook such a seemingly insignificant circumstance."[10]

In mid-June Dostoevsky sent off to Lyubimov "The Grand Inquisitor," accompanied by a commentary. "It finishes up," he explained, "*what the mouth*

---

[7] Ibid., 67.
[8] Ibid., 2: 45–46.
[9] Ibid.
[10] Ibid.

speaking great things and blasphemies says."[11] "A contemporary negator," Dostoevsky goes on,

> one of the most ardent, comes right out and declares himself in favor of what the devil advocates, and asserts this is truer for people's happiness than is Christ. To our Russian Socialism, which is so stupid (but also dangerous, because the young generation is with it), the lesson, it would seem, is very forceful—one's daily bread, the Tower of Babel (i.e., the future reign of Socialism), and the complete enslavement of freedom of conscience—that is the ultimate goal of this desperate denier and atheist!
>
> The difference is that our Socialists (and they are not just underground Nihilist scum—you know that) are conscious Jesuits and liars who do not admit that their idol consists of violence to man's conscience and the leveling of mankind to a herd of cattle, while my Socialist (Ivan Karamazov) is a sincere person who comes right out and admits that he agrees with the Inquisitor's view of humanity and that Christ's faith (allegedly) elevated man to a much higher level than where he actually stands. The question is stated in its boldest form: 'Do you despise humanity or admire it, its future saviors?' And all of this for them is allegedly in the name of love of humanity: Christ's law, they claim, is burdensome and abstract, and too heavy for weak people to bear—and instead of the law of Freedom and Enlightenment, they offer them the law of chains and enslavement through bread.[12]

Once more Dostoevsky does everything in his power to allay the fears of his editors. "In the next book the elder Zosima's death and deathbed conversations with his friends will occur. . . . If I succeed, I'll have . . . forced people to recognize that a pure, ideal Christian is not an abstract matter but one graphically real, possible, standing before our eyes, and that Christianity is the only refuge of the Russian land from its evils. I pray God I'll succeed; the piece will be moving, if only my inspiration holds out. . . . The whole novel is being written for its sake, but only let it succeed, that's what worries me now!"[13]

Writing to his journalist friend Putsykovich on the same day, Dostoevsky voices all his trepidation over the reception of his recent chapters: "in my novel I've had to present several ideas and positions that, as I feared, would not be much to their liking, since until the conclusion of the novel these ideas and positions really can be misinterpreted; and now, just as I feared, it has happened;

---

[11] The italicized phrase is the King James translation of the passage in the book of Revelation that Dostoevsky cites. The Russian version of the same text reads: "the mouth proud and blasphemous."

[12] *PSS*, 30/Bk. 1: 68; June 11, 1879.

[13] Ibid.

they're caviling at me; Lyubimov sends the proofs and makes notes and puts question marks in the margins. I've prevailed, with difficulty, so far, but I very much fear for yesterday's mailing for June, that they'll rear up and tell me they can't print it."[14]

The notes for Book 5 contain passages concerning the Inquisitor that are much more provocative than those eventually used. One of the bluntest challenges to Christ, for example, is the Inquisitor's charge: "I have only one word to say to thee, that thou hast been disgorged from Hell and art a heretic" (15: 232), but none of this imagery was kept. As Edward Wasiolek has written, these notes contain a much clearer assertion that "it is Christ who is guilty and cruel, and it is the Grand Inquisitor who is kind and innocent. It is Christ who demands that men suffer for Him, whereas the Grand Inquisitor suffers for men."[15]

Dostoevsky's notes contain no reference to sources for the Legend, though central of course are the New Testament accounts of the three temptations of Christ by Satan. As for the character of the Inquisitor, the incarnation of spiritual despotism over the conscience of mankind, his prototype can be found in Schiller's *Don Carlos*, translated by Mikhail Dostoevsky in the 1840s. The play shares the same justification for the existence of evil in the world, the same answer to the problem of theodicy, that is at the heart of Dostoevsky's Legend— and indeed, at the heart of his religious worldview. This answer is given in the great scene in which the Marquis of Posa tries to persuade King Philip of Spain to grant freedom of conscience to his Protestant subjects in the Netherlands. Turning to the examples of nature and of the world for his argument, the marquis urges Philip to recognize that God himself allows evil to exist rather than interfere with the moral-spiritual freedom of mankind—the freedom to choose between good and evil:

> . . . Look about you
> At the splendors of nature! On freedom
> Is it founded—and how rich it is
> Through Freedom—He, the great Creator—
> —He—. . . So as not to disturb the enchanting
> Appearance of Freedom—
> He leaves the dreadful army of evils
> To rage in his universe—He, the artist,
> Remains invisible, modestly He
> Hides himself in eternal laws.[16]

[14] Ibid., 70.
[15] *The Notebooks for* The Brothers Karamazov, ed. and trans. Edward Wasiolek (Chicago, 1971), 63.
[16] Schiller, *Samtliche Werke*, 4: 161.

This is the fundamental idea that Dostoevsky had already expressed when interpreting the first temptation, "turning stones into bread," and explaining why God had not provided mankind with *both* beauty and bread.

With the Legend, Dostoevsky told his editor he "had achieved the culminating height of his literary activity." When his friend Putsykovich asked why he gave such importance to the Legend, Dostoevsky replied that he "had carried the theme of the Legend in his soul, so to speak, during the whole course of his life, and wished particularly now to place it in circulation since he did not know if he would ever again succeed in printing something important." The Legend, he added, was directed "against Catholicism and the papacy, and particularly . . . the period of the Inquisition, which had such awful effects on Christianity and on all of humanity." [17] Even though Dostoevsky said nothing about Socialism in these remarks, both Socialism and Catholicism had become identical for him as embodiments of the first and third temptations of Christ, the betrayal of Christ's message of spiritual freedom in exchange for bread, and the aspiration toward earthly power.

———■———

Dostoevsky's schedule required him to send off a text on the tenth of each month, and he tried to snatch some time between installments to keep in touch with friends. A consoling letter to Anna Filosofova, not yet in exile, responds to her truly agonizing situation. "I was," she wrote, "between two fires: on the one hand, my husband received proclamations from the nihilists that they would kill him; on the other, the government sent my son into exile, and threatens me with the same." As for herself, she had written to her husband: "You know very well that I hate our present government . . . that band of brigands, who are bringing Russia to ruin." [18] Even while trying to raise her spirits, Dostoevsky confesses that he is "depressed" himself. "The main thing is that my health has gotten worse, the children have all been ill—the weather is horrible, impossible, it rains buckets from morning to night . . . it's cold, damp, . . . In that state of mind . . . I was writing the whole time, working nights, listening to the high wind howling and breaking hundred-year-old trees." [19]

By this time, he had decided to travel to Bad Ems once again and told his editors that it was impossible for him to complete the work in one year. In addition to his health, he wrote, "I want it to be finished off well, and there's an idea in it that I would like to put forth as clearly as possible. It contains the trial and pun-

---

[17] *Letopis zhizni i tvorchestvo F. M. Dostoevskogo*, ed. N. F. Budanova and G. M. Fridlender, 3 vols. (St. Petersburg, 1995), 3: 332.

[18] *PSS*, 30/Bk. 1: 301; July 11, 1879.

[19] Ibid., 77–79.

ishment of . . . Ivan Karamazov."[20] His trial and punishment are of course moral-psychological; and Dostoevsky gives them so much importance because, through the depiction of Ivan's inner torments, he was attempting to undermine from within the intense humanitarian pathos of the Populist ethic. On July 17, having abandoned his previous deadline, Dostoevsky left Staraya Russa for Petersburg, Berlin, and Bad Ems.

He arrived in Petersburg on July 18, after a grueling trip that left him, as he wrote to Anna, "collapsing from exhaustion . . . my head is spinning, and I can see spots before my eyes." Despite feeling that "I've grown as weak as a five-year-old child,"[21] he staunchly went about completing the preparations for his journey. First collecting the money for the recent chapters of his novel, he then went off to the Blockhead embassy (as he called the Germans) to obtain a visa. The trip to Berlin was equally exhausting; nor did he particularly wish to see the awaiting Putsykovich, who was attempting to establish another version of *The Citizen* on German soil. The two men went to visit the aquarium, the museum, and the Tiergarten, and Dostoevsky found himself, despite his prior determination, "paying for his beer, at the restaurant, the cabby, and so on." Moreover, "he borrowed forty-five marks from me for paper and stamps (postage) for the first issue, which will come out in a week."[22] Dostoevsky's liberality, one assumes, was prompted by his willingness to support the new journal.

He reached Ems on July 24 and immediately went to see Dr. Orth. "He found," Dostoevsky reports to Anna, "that a part of my lung had moved from the spot and changed position, just as my *heart* also has changed from its former position and is now located in another one—all as a consequence of the emphysema, although he added by way of consolation the heart is absolutely healthy, and all these changes don't mean very much either and are no special threat." Far from being reassured, he adds that "if the emphysema, still just at the outset, has already produced such effects, what's going to happen later?" A program of gargling and drinking the two types of curative waters (Kranchen and Kesselbrunnen) was prescribed, and he writes with hope that "I'm relying on the waters greatly and began drinking them today."[23]

Dostoevsky's final stay in Bad Ems was marked by the loneliness and isolation he had anticipated before departing, and his reaction to the environment of the fashionable spa, already quite atrabilious, reached a new pitch of irascibility. His anti-Semitism came into full play as well, though he exhibited a fine impartiality in scattering his abuse right and left. It is somewhat ironic that, concurrently,

[20] Ibid., 75–77; July 8, 1879.
[21] Ibid., 79–80; July 19, 1879.
[22] Ibid., 83–84; July 24/August 5, 1879.
[23] Ibid., 85–87; July 25/August 6, 1879.

he was working to complete his chapters on the teachings of Zosima, whose message of love and universal reconciliation he hoped would answer the anathemas of Ivan Karamazov. One can hardly imagine a writer whose everyday feelings and emotions were more at odds with the sentiments he was pouring into his artistic work.

If Putsykovich had one virtue it was that of persistence, and he knew that Dostoevsky's name would provide a much-needed luster to his proposed journal. Reminding Dostoevsky of his promise to support the launch of the journal, he received on July 28 a letter for publication testifying that the journal's orientation "is sincere and incorruptible."[24] This official letter was accompanied by a private one in which once again Dostoevsky gives rein to his dislike of "the polyglot crowd, almost half of them rich Yids from all over the globe." In this connection, he calls Putsykovich's attention to an article he had read in Katkov's newspaper, *Moscow News* (*Moskovskie Vedomosti*), which summarized "a German tract that has just appeared: *Where Is the Jew Here?* Interestingly, it coincides with my own thought just as soon as I entered Germany: that the Germans will become completely Judaized and are losing their old national spirit."[25] The brochure mentioned in this article was a reply to another, from the pen of an ex-Socialist turned anti-Semite, which had attacked the growing Jewish influence on German life. As Dostoevsky wrote to Pobedonostsev, he took this controversy as confirmation of his own opinion that in Germany "there's the influence of the Jew everywhere."[26]

In a letter to Pobedonostsev, he describes himself as "being sick and over-anxious in my soul," attributing his lamentable state of mind "to the depressing impression from observing what has been going on in the 'Madhouse' of the Russian press and the intelligentsia too. . . . 'Pan-European' ideas of learning and enlightenment stand despotically over everyone, and no one dares state his opinion." These issues had worked up Dostoevsky to the point of "being tormented by the desire to continue the *Diary*, since I really do have things to say . . . without fruitless, uncouth polemic, but instead with firm, fearless words."[27]

He then strikes off a passage accurately defining the unique place he had managed to carve out for himself amidst the deadly rivalries of Russian social-cultural life—a position that allowed him alone to speak out fearlessly:

I consider my literary position . . . almost phenomenal: how has a person who writes at the same time against European principles, who has com-

[24] Ibid., 91; July 28/August 9, 1879.
[25] Ibid., 90–91.
[26] Ibid., 104–105; August 9/21, 1879.
[27] Ibid., 120–122; August 24/September 5, 1879.

promised himself forever with *Demons*, that is, with reaction and obscurantism, how is it that this person, without the help of all their Europeanizing journals, newspapers, and critics, has nonetheless been recognized by our young people, by those very same young Nihilists who have lost their moorings and so on? . . . They have announced to me that they await a sincere and sympathetic word from me *alone* and they consider me alone as a *guiding writer*. These declarations by the young are known to our literary leaders, brigands of the pen and swindlers of print, and they are all struck by that, otherwise they wouldn't allow me to write freely! They would eat me alive, like dogs, but they're afraid and watching in perplexity to see what happens next.[28]

Such words reveal the burning sense of mission that inspired him, and led him to believe he could participate in saving his country from the catastrophe so clearly, as he felt, looming ahead.

◼

What occupied Dostoevsky most during his stay in Bad Ems was, of course, his novel. At the beginning of August he sent off his manuscript, as usual, with an explanatory letter. "I have entitled this book 'The Russian Monk'—a daring and provocative title, since all the critics who do not like us will scream: 'Is that what a Russian monk is like? How can you dare to put him on such a pedestal?' But so much the better if they scream, isn't it? . . . it's correct, not only as an ideal but as an actuality too."[29] "I took the character and figure," Dostoevsky explains, "from ancient Russian monks and saints: along with profound humility—boundless, naïve hopes about the future of Russia, about her moral and even political mission. Didn't Saint Sergius and the metropolitans Pyotr and Aleksey always have Russia in mind in this sense?" He pleads with Lyubimov to assign a reliable proofreader to this text because the language is not ordinary Russian. Of the chapter entitled "About the Holy Scriptures in the Life of Father Zosima," he writes, "That chapter is exalted and poetic: the prototype is taken from certain of Tikhon Zadonsky's teachings, and the naïveté of style from the monk Parfeny's book of wanderings. Look through them yourself, dear Nikolay Alekseyevich, be like a father!"[30]

Dostoevsky thus indicates the stylistic models he was imitating, which differ considerably from the tonal register of the remainder of the novel. V. L. Komarovich has given a description of the style that Dostoevsky borrowed from *The Story of the Monk Parfeny about the Holy Mountain Athos, of His Pilgrimage and*

---

[28] Ibid.
[29] Ibid., 102–103; August 7/19, 1879.
[30] Ibid.

Voyages through Russia, Moldavia, Turkey and the Holy Land.[31] This work, long a favorite of Dostoevsky's (it was one of the few books he took along on his European travels between 1866 and 1870), was also greatly appreciated by Westernizers such as Saltykov-Shchedrin and Turgenev for its touching images of Old Russian piety. Parfeny's own book is filled with such a moving spirit of kindness and benevolence, even toward those with whom he argued about questions of faith, that it attracted not only a reader like Dostoevsky but also many whose relation to Christianity was more cultural than religious.

In the stories and preachments of Zosima, as Komarovich notes, one finds "even in the arrangement of their parts, and the whole of their syntax, a rhythm entirely strange to Russian literary speech. It appears as a departure from all the norms of modern syntax, and at the same time imparts to the entire narration a special, emotional coloring of ceremonial and ideal tranquility. The frequent repetition of the same words and even the same word combinations in successive sentences . . . the alternation between long, rhythmically united sentences and introductory sentences in indirect speech; finally, the pleonasms, the tendency to pile up epithets that describe one and the same picture, as if words failed the narrator to attain the desired richness of expression—all this gives to the meaning of the teachings a certain shading of inexpressibility."[32] The influence of the monk Parfeny's book extends to many aspects of the depiction of monastic life as well.

The influence of Saint Tikhon Zadonsky, a mid-eighteenth-century Russian monk elevated to sainthood in 1860, goes back a long way in Dostoevsky's moral-spiritual evolution. He may well have come across Saint Tihkon's abundant literary legacy in the early 1860s when he was editing *Time* and beginning to work out his own social-political ideal of *pochvennichestvo*. Saint Tikhon was one of the few Russian saints who underwent an intense inner struggle to attain his religious ideal—the conquest of "pride by humility, anger by gentleness and patience, hatred by love."[33] As Komarovich has suggested, Dostoevsky might well have seen a relation between his own personal character and that of Tikhon. "The bishop always displayed a tendency to nervous ailments and hypochondriacal onsets," wrote one of his cell servants. These episodes included accesses of anger and displeasure, and at the end of his life he "fell into a completely hypochondriacal state."[34] It was by no means easy for him to attain the state of self-mastery that would enable him to dominate his hostile reactions to others. In addition, he was often the butt of mockery and derision in the monastery, and here again Dostoevsky might have felt some similarity with his own situation as a writer.

[31] *Die Urgestalt des Brüder Karamasoff,* ed. V. L. Komarovich (Munich, 1928), 127–128.
[32] Ibid.
[33] Georgy Florovsky, *Puti Russkogo bogosloviya* (Paris, 1983), 123–125.
[34] Quoted in Komarovich, *Die Urgestalt,* 78.

The clergyman intervened, whenever he could, on behalf of peasants who were mistreated—and this during the darkest days of serfdom!—attempting to put into practice, on the level of social life, the ideas of Christian love that he was preaching. Several times he was struck by irate landowners, influenced by the prevalent antireligious Voltairianism then all the rage (and still reflected in the speeches of the totally unprincipled father of the Karamazov family). In each case, though not without an inner conflict, Tikhon finally begged the pardon of his assailants for having provoked them to rage; and such humility led to a complete change of heart on the part of his offenders. Dostoevsky probably saw in such episodes not only the clash of two opposing moral-religious principles— Old Russian piety and the new, destructive spirit of atheism—but also the power of humility to produce a moral transformation even in those who, under the influence of rationalism, thought themselves immune to the effect of its redeeming force.

The issue of immortality had become the foundation of Dostoevsky's own moral-religious convictions, and this Christian hope, including the Resurrection, was a recurrent preoccupation for Tikhon as well. "It is this churchly doctrine," writes Komarovich, "to which his spiritual ear is especially attuned, and like Dostoevsky, the saint attributes the spread of disbelief in his own day to the oblivion into which this conviction had fallen." Saint Tikhon hardly ever mentions the Last Judgment when he evokes the Resurrection (nor does Dostoevsky); this event was "never connected with the idea of retribution and punishment for sins, but always with the glory and ultimate bliss of 'God's children.'"[35] The Resurrection is also almost invariably linked by Tikhon with the image of the glory of "the Son of God," and he celebrates the eventuality of humankind attaining such glory in ecstatic words: "The flesh of our abasement will be transformed. . . . The chosen of God [the Christians] will be clothed in such exalted, wonderful glory that they will shine like the sun."[36]

Dostoevsky would also have found in Tikhon's work rhapsodic depictions, similar to those he would pen himself, of the Christian Utopia of love that glimmered before his enraptured eyes as his ultimate earthly ideal. "Oh, how wonderful everything would be," Tikhon wrote, "if everyone would love one another! Then there would be no theft, no robbery, no deceit, no murder . . . the jails would not be overflowing with prisoners, locked up because of crimes, moneylending, failures to pay debts; there would finally be no poor and needy any longer, but all would be equal."[37] Dostoevsky's own apocalyptic intimations of the earthly paradise could not have been expressed more vividly. Over and over again in his notes, Dostoevsky plays variations on his key motif: all are

[35] Ibid., 107.
[36] Quoted in ibid., 108.
[37] Quoted in ibid., 114.

responsible for all, and "everyone is guilty before all and for everything, and *therefore* everyone is strong enough also to forgive everything for others, and all will then become the work of Christ, and He Himself will appear among them, and they will see Him and become united with Him" (15: 249). None of these reflections, however, which would hardly have been permitted by the censorship, were retained in the text.

In response to Pobedonostsev's remark that he was eagerly awaiting "the repulse, the retort, and elucidation"[38] to the powerful Grand Inquisitor, Dostoevsky expresses his trepidation over whether his reply to this "*negative side*" of his work will be "a *sufficient* reply." "The more so," he goes on, "as the reply, after all, is . . . only an indirect one . . . an artistic picture. . . . [T]here are a few of the monk's precepts in response to which people will absolutely yell that they're absurd in the everyday sense, but in another, inner sense I think they [Zosima's precepts] are right."[39]

After completing Book 6, Dostoevsky immediately began work on the next installment, promised for the September issue. But his departure from Ems on August 29, and the ensuing break of six days required for the journey, slowed down work on his next installment. The trip from Bad Ems to Staraya Russa had been so exhausting that it took him a week to recover. On September 16 he sent off the first three chapters of Book 7, which narrate the burial of Zosima and the scandal caused by the odor of corruption emanating from his corpse. Dostoevsky feared this might give offense because of his use of the word "stink," but insisted it was suitable coming from Father Ferapont. He also requests Lyubimov "to do a good job" of proofing the legend about the "onion" narrated by Grushenka. "It's a gem," Dostoevsky declares, "written down by me from the words of a peasant woman, and, of course, *is recorded for the first time*."[40] A Russian folklorist had printed a similar legend in 1859, but this only illustrates the authenticity of Dostoevsky's own use of the moral-religious creations of the folk tradition.

On October 8, Dostoevsky informed Lyubimov that "I am again *forced to be late*" with the next installment.[41] The first chapters of this installment contain the scene in which Dimitry, lurking in his father's garden, gives the signal that brings the old man to the window. Dostoevsky stops the action after Dimitry "suddenly pulled the brass pestle out of his pocket" by inserting a few lines of dots, leaving his readers in suspense; but the sentence immediately following the hiatus was meant to suggest what had *not* occurred: "'God was watching over me then,' Mitya himself said afterwards" (14: 355). However, Dostoevsky perhaps relied too much on the perspicacity of his readers to decipher this reference to

[38] *LN* 15 (Moscow, 1934), 139.
[39] *PSS*, 30/Bk. 1: 121–122; August 24/September 5, 1879.
[40] Ibid., 125–126; September 16, 1879.
[41] Ibid., 127; October 8, 1879.

divine protection. These chapters appeared on November 1, and on November 8 he replied to a letter from a troubled reader unable to wait for further clarification: "The old man Karamazov was killed by his servant Smerdyakov. All the details will be clarified as the novel progresses. . . . Ivan Karamazov participated in the murder only obliquely and remotely, only by (intentionally) keeping from bringing Smerdyakov to his senses during the conversation with him before his departure for Moscow and stating to him clearly and categorically his repugnance for the crime conceived by him (which Ivan Feodorovich clearly saw and had a premonition of) and thus *seemed to permit* Smerdyakov to commit the crime. The *permission* was essential for Smerdyakov. . . . Dimitry Feodorovich is completely innocent of the murder of his father."[42]

Dostoevsky evidently had a clear grasp of his murder plot and its thematic significance. He also includes in his reply a lesson on how he should be read. "Not just the plot is important for the reader," he tells her, "but in addition a certain knowledge of the human soul (psychology), which an author has the right to expect from a reader." When Dimitry, instead of continuing his flight, leaps down from the fence to examine Grigory's wound and wipe the blood on his forehead, "he seemed to say to the reader already that he was *not* the parricide." His behavior shows compassion, not the cruelty of a murderer, and "if he had killed his father he wouldn't have stood over the servant's body with words of pity."[43] Certain types of behavior are simply incompatible with killing another human being.

———■———

October 30 was Dostoevsky's fifty-eighth birthday, and it was marked by a gift from his wife obtained with the help of Countess Tolstaya. He had long expressed admiration for Raphael's *Sistine Madonna*, a painting that had enthralled him during his visits to the Gemäldegalerie while residing in Dresden. The countess arranged for a large photographic reproduction to be made and presented to Anna by Vladimir Solovyev. When Dostoevsky went to his study that day, much to his surprise and delight he found the picture, framed in wood by Anna, hanging above the couch. "How many times," Anna recalls, "I found him in his study in front of that great picture in such deep contemplation that he did not hear me come in."[44] At such moments, she left him undisturbed.

On November 16, he dispatched the remaining chapters of Book 8 and informs Lyubimov of an alteration of his initial plan. Instead of limiting himself to the judicial investigation, he would include a chapter on "the sore spot in our criminal procedure," the preliminary investigation, "with the old routine and

[42] Ibid., 129; November 8, 1879.
[43] Ibid.
[44] Anna Dostoevsky, *Reminiscences*, trans. and ed. Beatrice Stillman (New York, 1975), 326.

the most modern abstract impersonality embodied in the young lawyers, judicial investigators, and so on."[45] All this material would constitute the new Book 9, promised for the December issue. Aside from allowing him to dramatize on a larger scale the shortcomings of the abstract notions of law imported from the West, whose human limitations he had already railed against through Razumikhin in *Crime and Punishment*, he informs Lyubimov that "I'll outline Mitya Karamazov's character even more strongly: he experiences a purification of his heart and conscience under the storm of misfortune and false accusation. He accepts with his soul punishment not for what he did but for the fact that he was so hideous that he could and did want to commit the crime of which he will be falsely accused through a judicial error. It's a thoroughly Russian personality: if the thunder doesn't rumble, the peasant won't cross himself. His moral purification begins during the several hours of preliminary investigation to which I intend to devote Book 9."[46]

On December 8 he wrote Lyubimov that "I worked so hard that I fell ill, [and] the book's theme (the preliminary investigation) has grown longer and more complicated." Aside from his own desire to produce as polished a work as possible, his novel, as he also stresses, "is being read everywhere, people write me letters, it's being read by young people, it's being read in high society, it's being criticized or praised in the press, and never before, with regard to the impression produced all around, have I had such a success."[47] Dostoevsky assures Lyubimov that Book 9 will be sent for the January issue.

At the end of the month Dostoevsky took part in a benefit organized on behalf of the students at the University of St. Petersburg, where he read the Legend of the Grand Inquisitor. The organizers had submitted the text to the theological authorities for permission. In reply, Archimandrite Iosif declared that "certain monuments of religious literature and even to the lives of Orthodox saints" lacked "the respect deserved" and could not be approved.[48] He was finally permitted to read the Legend, but was forced to omit the introductory section with its references to Dante and Victor Hugo. This clerical interdiction probably motivated him to supply some prefatory remarks to replace what had been prohibited. He began the reading with his own explanation of the Legend, saying, in part:

> The fundamental thought is that if you distort the truth of Christ by identifying it with the aims of this world, you instantly lose the meaning of Christianity; your reason must undoubtedly fall prey to disbelief; instead of the true ideal of Christ, a new Tower of Babel is constructed.[49]

[45] *PSS*, 30/Bk. 1: 130; November 16, 1879.
[46] Ibid.
[47] Ibid., 132; December 8, 1879.
[48] *Letopis*, 3: 360.
[49] *PSS*, 15: 198.

The audience reaction may be gathered indirectly from a letter Dostoevsky wrote later in response to an invitation by the Literary Fund to present the Legend again. He replied regretfully that it was impossible. "The supervisor [of the St. Petersburg schools, Prince M. S. Volkonsky] . . . told me that, judging by the impression it had made, he would not allow me to read it from now on."[50] The wary prince thought it unwise to allow so much excitement to be stirred up once more.

[50] *PSS*, 30/Bk. 1: 143; March 21, 1880.

CHAPTER 55

Terror and Martial Law

The new year 1880 began auspiciously for the Dostoevskys. On February 3, the members of the Slavic Benevolent Society selected him to write a congratulatory address to be presented to Alexander II on February 19, the twenty-fifth anniversary of his accession to the throne. Two weeks before the festivities, however, Russia was shaken by an event that cast a gloomy pall over the prospective festivities.

On February 5, at twenty-two minutes past six in the evening, a bomb exploded in the Winter Palace just under the dining room of the tsar. A diplomatic dinner had been scheduled for that hour in honor of Prince Alexander von Battenburg, the newly elected ruler of Bulgaria, and the party was just about to enter the banquet chamber when the explosion occurred. Neither the tsar nor his guests were injured, but the blast killed ten soldiers on guard duty and wounded fifty-six others. Responsible for the carnage was the People's Will (Narodnaya Volya), a group of formerly Populist radicals who had decided that the assassination of Alexander II was an indispensable first step toward any social-economic improvement. One of their members, Stepan Khalturin, a skilled cabinetmaker and carpenter, had obtained employment in the palace under a pseudonym and lived in a room in the basement. He smuggled in small quantities of dynamite, storing it at his bedside until he believed he had enough to accomplish his purpose, but the explosion, though powerful, had not been strong enough to collapse the dining room floor.

This was the fourth unsuccessful attempt by the People's Will to kill the tsar. Previously they had made elaborate plans to blow up the railroad carriage on which he traveled but were thwarted by a series of accidents, although in one case a baggage car was blown to smithereens. Despite this new failure, Khalturin's defiant invasion of the tsar's own residence succeeded in creating an awesome image of the power of the hidden revolutionaries, who were apparently able to penetrate anywhere they pleased. The authorities were impotent to cope with their activities, and the terrified state of mind overwhelming the ruling circles can be caught in the diary of Dostoevsky's admirer, Grand Duke Konstantin Konstantinovich. "We are living through a time of terror," he wrote on February 7, "with this one difference. The Parisians during the revolution saw their enemies face-to-face, and we not only do not see them or know them, but have not the faintest idea of their number . . . general panic."[1]

On February 7, the People's Will published a statement taking responsibility for the explosion and expressing "deep distress" at the death of the soldiers, but declaring that such efforts would continue unless the tsar handed over his powers to a constituent assembly. The educated upper classes remained as disaffected from the throne as they had been during the earlier assassination attempt by Alexander Solovyev. In response to this new threat, erupting at the very moment when the tsar's loyal subjects were scheduled to offer their expressions of fidelity and devotion, Alexander II decided that drastic measures had to be taken. Count Mikhail Loris-Melikov, an army officer who had been ennobled in recognition of his victories in the Russo-Turkish War, had successfully suppressed terrorist radicals as governor-general of Kharkov while understanding the necessity of placating moderately liberal opinion. The tsar now appointed him dictator in charge of the entire country, empowered "to make all dispositions and to take all measures" necessary to ensure public tranquility anywhere in the empire.[2] The period of his rule, which began on February 12, has been called "the dictatorship of the heart" because of some slight easing of government controls. Dostoevsky reacted favorably to Loris-Melikov's assumption of power, although he complained to the journalist Suvorin that Loris-Melikov's declarations to Russian society (which meant its educated upper class) to cooperate in reestablishing a basis for civic order were "badly written."[3]

On February 14, Dostoevsky presented a draft of his jubilee address to the members of the Slavic Benevolent Society, and, according to the historian Bestuzhev-Ryumin, "he electrified the meeting in reading his confession of faith."[4] The first paragraphs contain the obligatory conventional phrases expressing the devotion of the members of the society, along with all the Russian people, to their beneficent and loving ruler. Dostoevsky then eulogizes the reign of a tsar who had liberated the serfs and instituted a far-reaching series of other praiseworthy reforms. All the same, other passages transform this text into one of the most unusual documents ever written for such an occasion.[5]

The document informs the tsar—as if he did not already know it!—that, among the vast majority of fervent and devoted servants of the fatherland, there had long since appeared, in "the cultural [*intelligentny*] stratum of society," people "not believing in either the Russian people or its truth, nor even in God."

---

[1] Quoted in P. Zaionchkovsky, *Krisis samoderzhaviya na rubezhe 1870–1880–kh godov* (Moscow, 1964), 148.

[2] *Letopis, zhizni i tvorchestvo F. M. Dostoevskogo*, ed. N. F. Budanova and G. M. Fridlender, 3 vols. (St. Petersburg, 1995), 3: 379.

[3] Ibid., 379.

[4] Ibid.

[5] The text of this address can be found in *PSS*, 30/Bk. 2: 47–48.

On the heels of such people came "impatient destroyers, ignorant even in their convictions . . . sincere evildoers, proclaiming the idea of total destruction and anarchy" but genuinely believing that whatever remained after destruction had done its work would be preferable to what exists. Now "the young Russian energies, alas, so sincerely deluding themselves, have at last fallen under the power of dark, underground forces, under the power of enemies of the Russian land and consequently of all Christendom." These were the forces that, "with unexampled audacity," not long ago "committed unheard-of evil deeds in our country, which caused shudders of outrage in our upright and mighty people and in the entire world." (Whether it was diplomatic to have referred, even obliquely, to the Winter Palace explosion or to the earlier attempts on the tsar's life may well be questioned.)

Nor does Dostoevsky denounce the perpetrators of these outrages with any of the condemnatory epithets that might have been expected. For him they are "young Russian energies" whose motives, whatever their "evil deeds," could hardly be considered *entirely* criminal or wicked because they had been misguided in their *sincerity* and gone astray. The nefariousness of their actions begins to dissolve when these young people are viewed as the products of the entire course of Russian social-cultural development, the end result of what had begun with those who did not believe in the Russian people, in its truth, and in God (presumably the generation of the 1840s). Dostoevsky assures the tsar that the Slavic Benevolent Society "stands, so far as their opinions are concerned, firmly opposed—both to the faintheartedness of so many fathers, and the wild madness of their children, *who believe in villainy and sincerely bow down before it.*" This repeated emphasis on the "sincerity" of the radicals was hardly the language that the tsar was accustomed to hear about those attempting to destroy him and his regime.

Dostoevsky highlights the contrasting convictions held by the Slavic Benevolent Society—but of course voicing his own views—concerning the relations between the tsar and his people. This relation is purely patriarchal and derives from "the ancient truth, which from time immemorial has penetrated into the soul of the Russian people: that their Tsar is also their father, and that children always will come to their father without fear so that he hears from them, with love, of their needs and wishes; that the children love their father and the father trusts their love; and that the relation of the Russian people to their Tsar-Father is lovingly free and without fear, not lifelessly formal and contractual." This last phrase is a thrust at the idea of "crowning the edifice" by a Western-style constitution. Rumors had been widely circulating that, to celebrate the anniversary, the granting of such a constitution would be announced on that day.

Dostoevsky knew that this familial image of the relation between the tsar and his people was more a longed-for ideal than a reality. Whatever the people might feel about their Tsar-Father, their approach to him, if it took place at all, could occur only by means of a tightly controlled ritual, and was hardly one of free and easy access. By twice emphasizing the importance of being able to appeal to the tsar "without fear," he distinctly implies the absence of such a desirable state of affairs. Indeed, in a notebook entry made during the last year of his life, he states his view: "I am a servant of the Tsar like Pushkin, because his children, the people, do not disdain to be servants of the Tsar. They would be his servants even more when he actually believes that the people are his children. Something that, for a very long time, he has not believed."[6]

Like the radicals who had called for a constituent assembly, Dostoevsky was also admonishing the tsar to consult the people. Moreover, instead of emphasizing the immutability of the reign that he was presumably glorifying, he looks forward (though of course discreetly) to its eventual modification in the public interest. For it is on the "unshakable" foundation of this father-child relation, he affirms, "that perhaps may be accomplished and completed the structure of every future transformation of our state, to the extent that these will be recognized as necessary." He too looked forward to a "crowning of the edifice," but not by the granting of a constitution; what he desired was the distribution of more land to the peasantry by the will of the tsar.

This document, presented to the tsar on February 19 by the minister of the interior, L. S. Makov, was read carefully by its recipient, who perhaps understood its underlying drift more clearly than its official sponsors. For the tsar remarked to his minister (his words were reported to Anna after Dostoevsky's death), "I never suspected the Slavic Benevolent Society of solidarity with the Nihilists."[7] The tsar could only have been speaking ironically, which means he had grasped those aspects of the address betraying not only a latent sympathy with the *sincere* radicals but also a desire that the tsar allow the people to make their wishes known "without fear."

Dostoevsky visited Suvorin on the same day his address was given to the tsar, and, in a two-hour conversation, the journalist found Dostoevsky in an extremely good mood, "very lively" and full of hope about a change for the better under Loris-Melikov. "You will see," he told Suvorin, "something new is beginning. I'm not a prophet, but you'll see. Now everything looks different."[8]

———————■———————

On the day following the tsar's anniversary celebration, an extraordinary conversation took place between Dostoevsky and Suvorin. The former had just suffered another epileptic attack, and Suvorin found him in a gloomy and depressed

[6] *Biografiya*, 366; cited in I. Volgin, *Posledny god Dostoevskogo* (Moscow, 1986), 84.
[7] *Letopis*, 3: 381.
[8] Ibid.

state of mind. The talk turned to the wave of political crimes, and to the explosion in the Winter Palace. "Deliberating on these events," Suvorin recalled, "Dostoevsky dwelt on the strange relation of society to these crimes. Society sympathized with them, as it were, or, closer to the truth, did not really know what to think about them." Then he invented a dramatic situation, as he had so often done for the characters in his novels, in which he himself would be confronted with having to choose a course of action that would define his moral attitude. What if he and Surovin had overheard a conversation between two terrorists about imminent plans to blow up the Winter Palace. Would they turn to the police to arrest the conspirators?. When Surovin replied in the negative, Dostoevsky concurred, "Nor would I. . . . Why? . . . I turned over all the reasons that would cause me to do it. Well-founded reasons . . . then considered all the reasons that would hold me back. These reasons are—simply insignificant. Simply the fear of being reputed to be an informer."[9]

Nothing shows more glaringly the moral discredit into which the tsarist regime had fallen by this time and the torturing moral-political dilemma that confronted all thinking Russians as they observed from the sidelines the attempts to kill the Tsar-Father. No wonder that every installment of *The Brothers Karamazov* was snapped up and read with such passionate intensity, as if the literate classes were hoping the novel would help them find some answer to their quandary. There can be no doubt, in any case, that Dostoevsky felt the dilemma he and Suvorin were contemplating to have the most intimate connection with the thematics of the novel. For it was at the conclusion of this dialogue, and under its stimulation, that he outlined for his listener one of the possible continuations envisaged for his second volume. In this version, Alyosha Karamazov prepared himself "to pass through the monastery and become a revolutionary. He would commit a political crime. He would be executed. He would have searched for truth, and in these searches, naturally, he would have become a revolutionary."[10] Such words surely indicate the affinity between his morally positive hero Alyosha and the radicals. They also help us to understand why, despite all the "solid" reasons he could muster, Dostoevsky flinched at the prospect of turning the terrorists over to the police.

On the very day of this conversation, an attempt was made on the life of Loris-Melikov. A young Jewish radical, Ippolit Mlodetsky, fired at the newly appointed plenipotentiary point-blank but missed. Mlodetsky was captured, tried by court-martial, and condemned to death. Soon afterward, Suvorin writes that "the attempt on the life of Count Loris-Melikov agitated Dostoevsky, [who] was afraid of a reaction." "God forbid that we turn back to the old road," he is

---

[9] Ibid., 381–382.
[10] Ibid.

quoted as having said. Suvorin also notes that "during the period of our political crimes he was in terrible fear of a massacre, a massacre of the educated class by the people, who would surge up as the avengers. 'You haven't seen what I saw,' he would say, 'you don't know what the people are capable of when they are enraged. I have seen terrible, terrible instances.'"[11]

The public hanging of Mlodetsky took place on February 22, at the same Semenovsky Square where, thirty years before, Dostoevsky had stood as a condemned man. Now he took his place in the crowd of onlookers, which he estimated to be about fifty thousand. He was still under the unhappy effect of the execution two days later when visited by Countess A. I. Tolstaya, who describes him in a letter to her daughter Ekaterina Yunge as "disturbed, sickly, terribly pale"; knowing him quite well, she attributes his condition to the Mlodetsky hanging.[12] To cheer him up, she asked Anna to read a laudatory letter from Mme Yunge containing perceptive remarks about the published portions of *The Brothers Karamazov.* "Involuntarily," she tells her mother, "you compare Dostoevsky with European novelists—I pick only the best of them—the French: Zola, Goncourts, Daudet—they are all honorable, desire improvement; but, my God! how they paddle in shallow water! But he . . . [is] also a . . . realist, a precise investigator, a psychologist, an idealist, a philosopher."[13]

In conclusion, expressing a sentiment aroused in many others as well, she writes that, after reading about the suffering of the children and the Legend of the Grand Inquisitor, she was unable to continue and felt a desire "to make her confession before [Dostoevsky] and hear from him some sort of necessary, helpful . . . word."[14] As Dostoevsky listened to the young woman's encomium, his face gradually "lit up, acquired some living color, his eyes sparkled with satisfaction, often with tears. . . . It seemed that he suddenly became younger." He asked the countess to convey his thanks for such a comprehension of his novel, which "nobody has yet read so thoughtfully."[15]

The letter from Ekaterina Yunge to her mother was followed by another addressed to him directly. A month later he replied, complaining that he had wished to answer her perceptive missives sooner, but "honest to God, my life goes on at such a disorderly boil and even in such a bustle that I rarely belong to myself." Dostoevsky knew that Mme Yunge was a painter and (from her mother) that she was personally unhappy, "living in solitude and embittering [her] soul with recollections." He urges her to have recourse "to a single medicine: art and creative work." She had described for Dostoevsky the troubling "duality" that

[11] Cited from the *Diary* of A. S. Suvorin in Volgin, *Posledny god Dostoevskogo,* 141.
[12] *Letopis,* 384.
[13] *LN* 86 (Moscow, 1973), 496.
[14] Ibid.
[15] *Letopis,* 3: 384.

she felt in her personality, and his reassuring comments on this problem touch on one of the major leitmotifs of his own work. Such a personality trait, he tells her, "is peculiar to human nature in general," but not everyone suffers from it to the same degree as Mme Yunge—or himself. "That's precisely why you are so kindred to me, because that *split* in you is exactly the same as my own and has been so all my life. It's a great torment, but at the same time a great delight too. It's a powerful consciousness, a need for self-evaluation, and the presence in your nature of the need for moral obligation toward yourself and toward humanity. That's what that duality means."[16]

Such words offer insight into his psyche, and also into the *moral* significance of all the so-called "schizophrenic" characters that he portrays. "If you were less developed in intellect," he writes, "if you were limited, you would be less conscience-stricken and there wouldn't be that duality. On the contrary, very great vanity would result. But the duality is nevertheless a great torment." The positive moral value assigned to "suffering" in Dostoevsky's work is always such an inner wrestling with the self; and the only source of comfort is to turn to Christ. As he advises Mme Yunge, "If you believe (or very much want to believe), then give yourself over to Him completely and the torment from that split will be greatly assuaged and you will receive an emotionally spiritual answer, and that's the main thing."[17]

■

Despite a social and public life that would have proved taxing even for a younger man, work on *The Brothers Karamazov* proceeded apace. Dostoevsky had sent Book 9 to Lyubimov in early January, and he sent Book 10 sometime between the end of March and early April. At the same time, whatever the status that Dostoevsky had now attained in Russian literary life, he was reminded of some of the embarrassments of his youthful literary début by a reference in the April issue of the liberal Westernizing journal *European Messenger*. This influential publication had been running a series of reminiscences of the 1840s by Annenkov, later published as *The Extraordinary Decade*—a book that takes its place just behind Herzen's *My Past and Thoughts* as the most penetrating and insightful portrait of the period. Many pages are devoted to Belinsky, the central figure of that day, and the critic's enthusiastic response to Dostoevsky's first novel, *Poor Folk*, provides part of the story. But Annenkov, who was the closest Russian confidant of Turgenev and served as his literary factotum, could not resist paying back Dostoevsky for the deadly caricature of Turgenev in *Demons* and for the recent incident at the banquet. According to Annenkov, the young Dos-

[16] *PSS*, 30/Bk. 1: 147–149; April 11, 1880.
[17] Ibid.

toevsky became so inflated with his newly acquired fame that he asked Nekrasov, the editor of the *Petersburg Almanac*, "to separate [*Poor Folk*] from all the other works by a special typographical sign, for example—borders. The novel was actually surrounded by such borders in the almanac."[18]

Incensed by this charge, Dostoevsky dashed off a letter to Suvorin, who a few days later printed a denial in his conservative Petersburg newspaper *New Time* (*Novoe Vremya*). After several other publicists joined in the fray, Dostoevsky ended the controversy by requesting Suvorin to print the following: "We have received a formal declaration from F. M. Dostoevsky that nothing similar to what was stated in the *European Messsenger* ever happened, nor could it have."[19] Dostoevsky intended to reply at length in his *Diary* for 1881 since the gossip about "borders" had cast doubt on his account of his relations with Belinsky, and "if I do not object, they would say that [Annenkov's version] was the correct one."[20] Dostoevsky "was so infuriated by Annenkov's slander," Anna writes, "that he resolved not to recognize him if he met him at the Pushkin festivities, and if Annenkov should approach him he would refuse to shake hands."[21]

The Pushkin festivities mentioned by Anna refer to the planned unveiling of a monument to Pushkin in Moscow and to a series of public receptions, speeches, and banquets celebrating Russia's national poet. The prestige of the romantic and aristocratic Pushkin had been considerably damaged by the campaign carried on against him, and against art in general, by the radical publicists of the 1860s. Nonetheless, a large majority of educated Russians read and admired Pushkin, whose poems formed part of the school curriculum, and the idea of erecting a monument to him in Moscow had long been making the rounds. A subscription to raise funds became serious in 1871. After several competitions, the sculptor A. M. Opekushin was chosen to create the full-scale statue; its unveiling, along with the other planned events, was finally scheduled for June 5–9, 1880. Dostoevsky had set down a few thoughts for an article about Pushkin when, on April 5, he received a letter from Sergey Yuriev, chairman of the Society of Lovers of Russian Literature (in charge of the preparations for the festivities). Yuriev had earlier asked Dostoevsky to contribute a new novel to his journal *Russian Thought*; this time he was approaching him for a contribution about Pushkin. Dostoevsky doubted that he would "be able to find the time to write anything," but promised to keep *Russian Thought* in mind.[22]

---

[18] Ibid., 335. A satirical poem about Dostoevsky, written jointly by Turgenev and Nekrasov, had circulated among the members of the Belinsky Pléiade of young writers during 1845–1846. It contained a jesting reference to a story of his that had been framed "with borders," and the anecdote resuscitated by Annenkov turns the jeering thrust into fact.

[19] Ibid., 155; May 14, 1880.

[20] *PSS*, 27: 198.

[21] Anna Dostoevsky, *Reminiscences*, trans. and ed. Beatrice Stillman (New York, 1975), 330.

[22] *PSS*, 30/Bk. 1: 147; April 9, 1880.

The month of April was so crowded with social engagements that he found it impossible to supply *The Russian Messenger* with a new installment. "I am really prevented from writing here," he wrote apologetically to Lyubimov. *The Karamazovs* are again to blame for that. So many people come to see me every day apropos of them, so many people . . . invite me to their homes—that I'm absolutely at my wit's end and am now fleeing Petersburg!" Dostoevsky planned to leave for Staraya Russa "in a week, and in three weeks I will have the whole novel finished."[23]

If he had been able to work uninterruptedly in Staraya Russa, he might have come closer to meeting the sanguine schedule outlined for his editor. On May 1, however, he received another letter from Yuriev, written on behalf of the Society of Lovers of Russian Literature, asking him "to honor the memory of the great poet" by speaking at one of the public sessions to take place after the unveiling of the monument.[24] A private letter from Yuriev urged him to prefer the Moscow celebration to the one that would also take place in Petersburg, and he lists the names of other participants who would be present: Ivan Aksakov, Pisemsky, Ostrovsky, Turgenev. On May 4, at a meeting of the Slavic Benevolent Society, Dostoevsky (who had recently been elected vice president) was appointed the society's representative to the Moscow festivities, and he accepted Yuriev's invitation the very next day.[25]

On May 8, he was again the guest of Grand Duke Konstantin and read fragments from *The Brothers Karamazov*, including, at the request of his host, the confession of Zosima, which the grand duke considered one of the best pieces Dostoevsky had ever written. The tsarevna, all through the evening, "listened very attentively and was in ecstasy"; one of the ladies openly wept.[26] Once this highly gratifying obligation had been fulfilled, the family left for Staraya Russa sometime between May 9 and 11.

[23] Ibid., 151–152; April 29, 1880.
[24] *LN* 86 (Moscow, 1973), 509.
[25] Ibid., 153–154; May 5, 1880.
[26] *LN*, 137.

CHAPTER 56

The Pushkin Festival

The Moscow Pushkin festival in the spring of 1880 has been remembered by posterity largely because of the sensation created by Dostoevsky's impassioned apotheosis of the great poet. At the time, however, the event assumed considerable importance because of the tense and ominous social-political climate in the country, which imparted a political coloring to any large manifestation of public opinion. In this instance, the cream of the Russian intelligentsia gathered in the ancient capital (as well as in other major cities) to eulogize a poet who had incurred the displeasure of Nicholas I, had been sent into exile, and had close friends among the revolutionary Decembrists of 1825. Such a celebration was in itself unprecedented and, indeed, was felt as an implicit demand for a liberty of expression still lacking in Russian literature and society.

Even more, the initiative for this enterprise had come from private individuals (a group of Pushkin's surviving classmates from the lycée in Tsarskoe Selo), and funds for the statue had been raised by private subscription. Eventually the project was approved and even patronized by the crown, and the Moscow Duma agreed to pay the expenses of all the invited guests; but participants did not feel they were taking part in any official function. Instead, as one observer put it, here "for the first time a social longing was displayed by us with such broad-ranging freedom. Those who attended felt themselves to be citizens enjoying a fullness of rights."[1]

Moreover, the official acceptance of this independent endeavor was seen positively as the augury of a new era in the relations between the tsar and the intelligentsia. Indeed, as a testimony to the influence that the educated class had begun to exercise, Count Loris-Melikov instructed the government of Moscow not to require preliminary approval of the speeches to be given after the unveiling. "Here in Petersburg," Dostoevsky complains to Yuriev, "at the most innocent literary reading . . . every line, even one written twenty years ago, [has to be] submitted . . . for advance permission for reading. . . . Will they really allow one to read something newly written without *someone's* advance censorship?"[2]

---

[1] *PSS*, 26: 442.
[2] Ibid., 30/Bk. 1: 153–154; May 5, 1880.

An atmosphere of expectation was created; perhaps even more concessions by the government would be forthcoming! What seemed to be a purely cultural event thus took on—as was usually the case in Russia, where no unfettered political discussion of any kind was possible—an important social-political subtext. On a more personal level, this subtext was dramatized by the culmination of the ideological duel that Turgenev and Dostoevsky had been carrying on ever since the mid-1860s.

On May 19, Dostoevsky wrote to convey name day greetings to Pobedonostsev, and also to wish him "every wonderful success in your new labors" as head procurator of the Holy Synod, the council supervising the Russian Orthodox Church. Informing him of the impending trip to Moscow, Dostoevsky reveals some of the ideological dissensions that had begun to surface in the preparations for the great event. As it happens, he writes, "I've already heard in passing even in Petersburg that there is a clique raging there in Moscow . . . and that they are afraid of certain *reactionary* words that could be spoken by *certain people* at the sessions of the Lovers of Russian Literature."[3] Dostoevsky, however, firmly declares: "I have prepared my speech about Pushkin, and precisely in the most *extreme* spirit of my (that is *our*, I make bold to thus express myself) convictions, and therefore I expect, perhaps, a certain amount of abuse . . . but I'm not afraid, and one should serve one's cause, and I will speak without fear. The professors there are paying court to Turgenev, who is absolutely turning into a personal enemy of mine."

In the background of these remarks is the attempt by the Society of Lovers of Russian Literature to ban Katkov from speaking. The committee of the society in charge of organizing the festivities was ideologically in league with the moderately liberal Westernizer orientation of influential professors at the University of Moscow, who felt reinforced by the presence of Turgenev. He had returned to Russia for the celebration and had been appointed an honorary member of the society. Turgenev and Katkov had long been enemies, and the latter had recently attacked the novelist for being in sympathy with the revolutionaries. In addition, Katkov had offended the intelligentsia as a whole by objecting to Loris-Melikov's appeal for their collaboration, which he regarded as a first step toward a weakening of the autocrat's power. "There is no need to seek support and aid from society," he had written after the explosion in the Winter Palace. "Only discipline in state ranks, which will make everyone in them fear deviating from their duty and deceiving the supreme power, and patriotism in the educated spheres of society—that's what's needed."[4] It was thus a simple matter for Turgenev to persuade the committee to blacklist Katkov, even though the latter was

---

[3] Ibid., 155–156; May 19, 1880.

[4] Cited in Marcus C. Levitt, *Russian Literary Politics and the Pushkin Celebration of 1880* (Ithaca, NY, 1989), 62. My account of the Pushkin celebration is greatly indebted to this excellent book.

a member of the society and had defended the value of Pushkin's art against the attacks of the radical critics in the 1860s. An attempt was also made to blacklist Dostoevsky because of the disruptive incident at the dinner for Turgenev the previous year, but Dostoevsky had too many admirers, including the chairman of the society, Yuriev, for this effort to succeed.

■

Dostoevsky left Staraya Russa on May 22, seen off by Anna, the children, and his mother-in-law. Anna had desired to travel to Moscow herself with the children, but such an expedition was beyond their means. Worried about Dostoevsky's health, in view of the anticipated strain, Anna made him promise to write every day, and he faithfully kept his word—often writing not once but twice. A full, firsthand account thus exists of the swirling round of activities in which he became engulfed during a stay that was expected to be no more than a week, but lasted twenty-two days.

This prolongation was partly due to the death of Tsarina Marya Alexandrovna on the very day of Dostoevsky's departure. He heard about it from fellow passengers, and his first thought was that the festivities would be cancelled, but he decided to continue his trip nonetheless. Arriving in Moscow, he spent his morning returning visits from various notables, including Ivan Aksakov, and then went to call on Yuriev. "An enthusiastic meeting with kisses," he reports with an edge of irony. He was not at all impressed with the editor, whom he compares with the scatterbrained Repetilov in Griboyedov's *Woe from Wit*. "He's a fibbertigibbet as a person, a Repetilov in a new form." That evening he went to see Lyubimov and Katkov, who received him cordially, but were anxiously awaiting a new installment of his novel for June ("when I get home I'll have to work like the devil").[5]

A dinner had been arranged in Dostoevsky's honor at the Hermitage on the twenty-fifth because "all the young Moscow writers are wildly anxious to meet me." Twenty-two guests attended, among them Ivan Aksakov and Nikolay Rubinshtein, founder and director of the Moscow Conservatory, who had been placed in charge of the musical arrangements for the festival; there were also four university professors. He was impressed with the lavishness of the meal: "quail, amazing asparagus, ice cream, a river of fine wines and champagne . . . after dinner, over coffee and liqueur, two hundred magnificent and expensive cigars appeared." Six laudatory speeches were given, and "mention was made of my 'great significance as an artist of worldwide sensitivity,' as a journalist, and as a Russian. . . . Everyone was in an enthusiastic state. . . . I replied to everyone with a quite successful speech that produced a great effect; moreover, I made Pushkin the topic of the speech."[6]

[5] *PSS*, 30, Bk. 1: 158–159; May 25, 1880.
[6] Ibid., 160–161; May 26, 1880.

During the dinner, Dostoevsky announced that he was planning to leave on the twenty-seventh and, he tells Anna, "an absolute din arose: 'We won't let you go.'" Earlier in the day, Prince Dolgoruky had told representatives of the society that the festivities *would* take place sometime between June 1 and 5, and Dostoevsky was admonished: "All of Moscow will be grieved and indignant if you leave."[7] When he pleaded that he had to work on *The Karamazovs*, it was instantly proposed that a deputation be sent to Katkov to demand a revision of the publication schedule. Under this pressure, he wavered and said he would come to a decision the next day.

On May 27, he learned that the Moscow Duma would be covering the room and board of all the invited delegates. Far from being pleased, he objected strenuously but was told he would insult all of Moscow if he persisted in refusing. Why, even the surviving members of Pushkin's family, all residing in the same hotel, had accepted the hospitality of the Duma! In view of Dostoevsky's concern about expenses, one might think that his resistance was feigned, but a writer known to have accepted *any* kind of official support was assumed to have lost his independence, and Dostoevsky wished to avoid such an imputation at all costs. He thus tells Anna that he will "purposely go to restaurants for dinner so as to reduce as much as possible the bill that will be presented to the Duma by the hotel."[8] He did not want any gossip to spread that he was exploiting the situation unduly for his own advantage.

On the afternoon of May 26 it was learned that the ceremonies would take place on June 4, and most of the deputations, from all parts of Russia, decided to remain. Preparations for the great event were in full swing; "the windows of the buildings surrounding the square are being rented out for fifty rubles a window."[9] Dostoevsky explained again to Anna that "*I should* stay . . . it's not just [the Society] who need me, but our whole party, our whole idea, for which we have been struggling thirty years now because the hostile party (Turgenev, Kovalevsky, and almost the entire university) definitely want to play down Pushkin's significance as a spokesman for the Russian national character, denying that very national character. . . . I have fought for this my whole life and can't flee the field of battle now."[10] Moreover, as he had told the more practical Anna just the day before, "if my speech at the gala meeting is a success, then in Moscow (and therefore in Russia too) from then on I will be better known as a writer (that is, in the sense of the eminence already won by Turgenev and Tolstoy). Goncharov, for instance, who doesn't leave Petersburg, is known here, but from afar and coldly."[11]

[7] Ibid.
[8] Ibid., 165; May 27, 1880.
[9] Ibid., 169; May 28/29, 1880.
[10] Ibid.
[11] Ibid., 168; May 27/28, 1880.

Turgenev had been assigned the delicate, unenviable task of journeying to Yasnaya Polyana to persuade Tolstoy to attend the Pushkin celebration, even though Tolstoy by this time had renounced literature for reasons comparable to those of the radical critics who had denounced Pushkin in the 1860s. Just what occurred during their meeting on May 2–3 is not known, but Grigorovich, an inveterate gossip, told Dostoevsky that "Turgenev, who has come back from seeing Lev Tolstoy, is ill, while Tolstoy has nearly lost his mind, and has perhaps quite lost it."[12] A day later Tolstoy informs Strakhov: "I had many interesting conversations with Turgenev. Up to now . . . people have said: 'What's Tolstoy doing, working away at some nonsense or other. He ought to be told to stop that nonsense.' And every time it's been the case that the people giving advice have become ashamed and frightened about themselves. I think it was the same with Turgenev too. I found it both painful and comforting to be with him. And we parted amicably."[13] Another report, however, claims that Turgenev was "hurt and offended" by the encounter. In a succeeding letter, Dostoevsky writes: "Katkov also confirmed about Lev Tolstoy that he has quite lost his mind. Yuriev has been trying to get me to see him. . . . But I won't go, even though it would be very interesting."[14]

On May 31, he finally received a letter from Anna and was greatly relieved: "An oppression seems to have lifted from my heart." The provident Anna had charged him with the task of inscribing the name of their son Feodor in the register of the nobility in Moscow; but after several reminders, he replied that "in the first place, even if it were possible, I don't have the time, and most important it needs to be done from Petersburg, *through people*."[15] A meeting had been held at Turgenev's lodgings that day to make the final arrangements, and two days later Dostoevsky complains to Anna about having been excluded. On the morning of June 1, he learned that instead of the readings that had been initially assigned to him, he had been given Pushkin's "The Prophet," which of course he knew by heart. "I probably won't refuse 'The Prophet,' but how could they not notify me officially?"[16]

Such offhand treatment was as nothing compared with the blow dealt to Katkov on the same day. Visiting him that evening, Dostoevsky met Lyubimov, who told him that Yuriev, in the name of the society, had *withdrawn* an invitation to Katkov as editor of *Moscow News*, where Katkov's attacks on the intelligentsia had appeared, on the ground that it had been sent through an error. Dostoevsky was outraged at this display of ideological partisanship, even more

[12] Ibid., 165; May 27, 1880.
[13] The quotations are from Levitt, *Russian Literary Politics*, 101.
[14] *PSS*, 30/Bk. 1: 168; May 27/28, 1880.
[15] Ibid., 173–174; May 31, 1880.
[16] Ibid., 175–176; June 2/3, 1880.

so when he learned from the irrepressible tattler Grigorovich that "Yuriev was made to sign it, mainly by Kovalevsky but by Turgenev too." "It's vileness," Dostoevsky fumed, "and if I weren't so involved in these festivities I would perhaps break off relations with them."[17]

On June 3, Dostoevsky went to a meeting of the executive committee of the society, where—in spite of his previous suspicions—the final dispositions were made. "Everything was arranged to everyone's general satisfaction," he tells Anna contentedly. "Turgenev was rather nice to me, while Kovalevsky (a big fat hulk and enemy of our tendency) kept staring at me intently." He would read his Pushkin speech "on the second day of the morning meeting, and on the evening of the sixth I'm reading Pimen's scene from *Boris Godunov*. . . . on the eighth, I'll read three poems by Pushkin (two from 'Songs of the Western Slavs'), and at the finale, for the *conclusion* of the celebrations, Pushkin's 'The Prophet.'" His public renditions of this poem had always created a sensation and become deservedly famous. "I was purposely put into the finale so as to produce an effect."[18]

On returning to his hotel at ten o'clock, he found a card from Suvorin and hastened to the hotel where this Petersburg ally was staying with his wife. "I was terribly glad. Because of his articles he's in disgrace with the 'Lovers [Society]' just like Katkov."[19] Suvorin had written several pieces attacking Yuriev's *Russian Thought* and, though not defending Katkov directly, had assailed his enemies. These opinions had been enough for him to fall out of the good graces of the society. "They didn't even give him a ticket for a morning meeting." Dostoevsky and Grigorovich planned to visit the Kremlin Museum of Antiquities the next day, and Suvorin begged that they "take him and his wife." "Poor fellow," Dostoevsky remarks, "he seems bored with his wife"—an attitude very far from his own sentiments. Replying to Anna's teasing accusation that "I don't love you," he confesses, "I keep having terrible dreams, nightmares every night, about your betraying me with others."[20]

---■---

The official opening ceremonies of "the Pushkin days" began on June 5. In the afternoon all one hundred and six delegations were received in the hall of the Duma by Prince Oldenburgsky, head of the commission for the Pushkin monument, and Governor-General Dolgoruky. "The fussing around, the chaos—it's impossible to describe," Dostoevsky writes. Each delegation advanced in turn to a stage covered with luxuriant greenery and dominated by a large bust of Pushkin, at the foot of which they deposited their wreaths. (Dostoevsky had been

[17] Ibid., 179; June 3/4, 1880.
[18] Ibid., 177–179; June 3/4, 1880.
[19] Ibid.
[20] Ibid.

tormented by the problem of acquiring such a wreath and paying for it out of his own pocket.) The delegates then read speeches, and the press comments on the merits of these oratorical efforts were hardly complimentary. The Populist writer Gleb Uspensky, who covered the festival for *Notes of the Fatherland*, remarked that "there were speeches so strange that even if one wanted to, one could not track down precisely where the main clause was located."[21] Dostoevsky says nothing about the oratory but mentions that he managed to speak to Pushkin's daughter while standing in line, and that "Turgenev ran up courteously," as did the playwright Ostrovsky, "the local Jupiter."[22]

For June 7, he begins his letter to Anna with an account of the events of the day preceding, when the Pushkin monument had been unveiled and dedicated. His pen faltered, however, at depicting this epochal event. "You couldn't describe it even in twenty pages, and besides, I don't have even a moment's time. For three nights I've slept only five hours each, and tonight too."[23] As a prelude to the unveiling, a mass had been held at the Strastnoi Monastery just across the square from the monument, and Metropolitan Makary—a member of the society—solemnly wished "eternal memory" to Pushkin's shade. The plan had been for Metropolitan Makary to lead a solemn procession from the church to the statue, which he would sprinkle with holy water, but the clergy remained within the church and the statue did not receive the expected blessing. Protests had been raised that such a blessing would be sacrilege. Thus, without benefit of clergy, the processions marched to the strains of "four orchestras and several choruses and groups of schoolchildren" led by Rubinshtein. "Delegates wore badges and carried wreaths; some waved flags of red, white, and blue with their delegation's name stamped in gold";[24] other banners bore the names of Pushkin's poems.

The unveiling produced an explosion of joyful hysteria, and all accounts agree that "people were 'crazed with happiness'; many wept, and even the most hard-nosed of newspapermen admitted afterward to shedding a few tears." A columnist in *Voice* wrote of "How many sincere handshakes, how many good, honest kisses people exchanged—often people who weren't even acquainted."[25] One should keep this generally ecstatic mood in mind in gauging what Dostoevsky tells us about the fervent testimonies of admiration lavished on him even before his speech. Once the unveiling had taken place, the delegations, marching to the music of Meyerbeer's "The Prophet," paraded to the monument and laid their wreaths at its foot.

[21] *DVS*, 2: 396.
[22] *PSS*, 30/Bk. 1: 180; June 5, 1880.
[23] Ibid., 182; June 7, 1880.
[24] Levitt, *Russian Literary Politics*, 83–85.
[25] Ibid., 85.

That evening, a dinner held under the auspices of the Moscow Duma was to be followed by the first of the readings by the important authors present. Also, despite the maneuvers of the Society, Katkov had been invited to speak as a member of the Duma. Gaideburov, editor of the semi-Populist *Week*, who called on Dostoevsky just before dinner, noted his agitation. "I dropped by Dostoevsky's, and see that he is in a most horrible state; he is somehow twitching all over, in his eyes—anxiety, in his movements—irritation and alarm. I knew he was a highly nervous and impressionable person, who passionately gave himself up to every emotion, but I had never seen him in such a state before." When Gaideburov asked what was wrong. "'Ah, what will happen, what will happen?' he exclaimed in answer with despair."[26] Gaideburov understood him as referring to the impending dinner and Katkov's speech. The pariah would now be able to speak his mind, and the result might be, as Dostoevsky had feared a day earlier, that people would come to blows.

When Katkov took the floor, however, he spoke of the celebration as a "holiday of peace" and hoped that "perhaps this passing rapprochement will serve us as a pledge for a more durable unity in the future that will lead to the dying out, or at least the mitigation, of hostilities." He concluded with the famous poetic toast of Pushkin: "Let the sun shine forth, let the darkness cease!" These pacifying words were generally well received and evoked some applause (just how much depended on what newspaper one read). Both Aksakov and Gaideburov rose to congratulate the speaker, but when Katkov extended his arm to clink glasses with Turgenev, the latter turned away. According to Kovalevsky, Dostoevsky and Turgenev spoke about it later in the evening. "There are some things it is impossible to forget," Turgenev maintained. "How could I extend my hand to a person whom I consider a renegade?"[27]

During the dinner on June 6, which began at five o'clock in the afternoon, "two ladies," as he tells Anna, "brought me flowers," but this tribute could not overcome his disappointment at what occurred that evening, when he read his assigned pieces, along with Pisemsky, Ostrovsky, Grigorovich, and, of course, the only other participant he cared about—Turgenev. "I read Pimen's scene," he writes Anna the next day. "They say I read superbly, but they say they couldn't hear me very well." Although he "was greeted wonderfully" and called back three times, he still felt that he had been bested: "Turgenev, who read very badly, was called back more than I was."[28]

Turgenev had been greeted clamorously by the audience, and one of the poems he read, "Again in the Homeland," had a particular resonance because of

[26] Ibid., 86.

[27] *Letopis, zhizni i tvorchestvo F. M. Dostoevskogo*, ed. N. F. Budanova and G. M. Fridlender, 3 vols. (St. Petersburg, 1995), 2: 429.

[28] *PSS*, 30/Bk. 1: 182; June 7, 1880.

his own self-exile. Dostoevsky, however, suspiciously persisted in believing that Kovalevsky had planted a claque ("a hundred young people shouted in a frenzy when Turgenev came out") and that its purpose, besides applauding Turgenev, "was to humiliate us [the nonliberals] if we were to go against them." For all that, he could not complain of any lack of adulation on the part of the public. "The reception offered me yesterday was amazing. During the intermission I went through the hall, and a horde of people, young people, gray-haired people, and ladies, rushed up to me, saying, 'You are our prophet. You have made us better since we read *The Karamazovs*.' In short, I am convinced that *The Karamazovs* has colossal significance."[29] All this appreciation was only a foretaste of what would occur the very next day.

———■———

The two most important literary figures at the Pushkin festival were Turgenev and Dostoevsky, and their barely concealed rivalry underlay all the solemn rituals of the occasion. Each gave entirely different readings of Pushkin—Turgenev viewing him in the context of European literature, Dostoevsky proclaiming his genius to be equal to, if not surpassing, anything that European genius had produced. Each presented not only a literary-critical view of Pushkin but also, implicitly, an evaluation of Russian achievement in relation to Europe. The argument, as the audience well understood, was thus only nominally about a literary figure; it was also a replay of the longstanding Westernizer-Slavophil debate carried on in Russian culture all through the nineteenth century. On this occasion, the historical record is clear: Dostoevsky emerged triumphant! He gave the public what it had been waiting to hear, and achieved a victory that astonished even himself.

June 7, the first session of the Pushkin festivities, opened with some words about Pushkin from the only foreign delegate to make the journey, the French Slavist Louis Léger. Telegrams were read from Victor Hugo, Berthold Auerbach, and Alfred Tennyson, but the main event, eagerly awaited by all—if for differing reasons—was Turgenev's speech. In composing it, Turgenev drew on two lectures he had given on Pushkin in the 1860s and on his famous article, "Recollections of Belinsky," which had paid tribute to the great critic who had first defined Pushkin's place in Russian literature. Indeed, much of what Turgenev says about Pushkin's historical position, compared with that of Lermontov and Gogol, is derived from Belinsky's famous series of essays on the poet.

He begins by declaring Pushkin to be "the first Russian artist-poet," and praises him profusely as the founding father of modern Russian literature. Declaring art to be "the embodiment of the ideals lying at the foundation of a people's [*narodnoi*] life, defining its spiritual and moral physiognomy," he quickly moves on to some of the well-known facts of Pushkin's artistic career.[30] At first imitating foreign models (Voltaire and Byron are mentioned), Pushkin rapidly freed himself from such tutelage and found his own voice. But then, to an audience inflamed by patriotic fervor, Turgenev rather maladroitly equates Pushkin's rejection of foreign models in his poetry with an equal rejection of Russian folk poetry itself: "The independent genius of Pushkin quickly . . . freed itself from the imitation of foreign forms and from the temptation of the counterfeiting of a folk [*narodnoi*] tonality." When he yielded to this temptation, as in "Ruslan and Ludmilla," he produced "the weakest of all his works." In Russia, "the simple people" (*prostoi narod*) do not read Pushkin any more than the German people read Goethe, the French Molière, or the English Shakespeare. For "every art is the elevating of life based on an ideal, those remaining on the level of ordinary, everyday life remain lower than this ideal level."[31]

All the same, Goethe, Molière, and Shakespeare are *narodnoi* poets in the true sense of that word, which Turgenev defines in his own way. For him it means imparting to the values of one's own culture a national significance, thus attaining a level of universality that transcends mere class or regional boundaries. Such poets unquestionably represent their people, but they have so absorbed its values that they raise those values to the universal level of the ideal. To drive home this point, Turgenev disparages the slogan of "folk-character [*narodnost'*] in art" as the sign of weak, inferior, and enslaved peoples struggling to preserve their existence and identity.[32] Russia, happily, is not such a country, and there is thus no reason for it to have recourse to such a palliative. At a moment when Populism (*narodnichestvo*) was the dominating social-political, as well as artistic, ideal of the Russian intelligentsia both on the right and on the left, Turgenev was completely at odds with the reigning mood of the vast majority of his audience.

He then raises the crucial question of whether Pushkin can be considered a "national" poet in this sense, equal to Shakespeare, Molière, and Goethe, and replies evasively: "For the moment we shall leave this open." There is no question, however, that Pushkin "gave us our poetic, our literary language, even though some argue that no such language exists even yet because it can only come from 'the simple people,' along with other tradition-preserving institutions" (a passing jab at the virtues attributed to the Russian peasant commune). Pushkin's language, all the same, expresses the best elements of the Russian character—its "virile charm, strength, and clarity, its straightforward truth, absence of deceit and pose, [its] simplicity, the openness and honesty of its feelings."[33] But then, to support such claims, Turgenev invokes remarks made to him by

[30] *PSSiP*, 15: 66.
[31] Ibid., 68.
[32] Ibid., 69.
[33] Ibid., 69–70.

Victor Hugo and Prosper Merimée, as if his Russian audience were likely to be impressed by the approbation of such eminent foreign authorities. Turgenev also cites Merimée as approving "the absence of any explanations and moral conclusions" in Pushkin's poetry.[34] What Turgenev offered as artistic praise could well be seen by his audience as a denial that Pushkin's poetry had any moral significance whatever!

Referring to the radical rejection of Pushkin in the 1860s, which merely developed the critique initiated by Belinsky in the late 1840s, he explains it as a result of "the historical development of society under conditions that gave birth to a new life, which stepped from a literary epoch into a political one." The adoration of art and Pushkin ceased, and he was replaced by the wrathful Lermontov, the satirical Gogol, and "the poet of revenge and sorrow" (Nekrasov). They won the adherence of succeeding generations and created a different kind of literature more responsive to the moral-social needs of the times.[35]

Turgenev thus refuses to condemn the assault on Pushkin by the radicals, which reflected the new realities of Russian life, but he rejoices that this period of artistic inconoclasm appears to be reaching its end. In Pushkin's day, belles lettres had served as the unique expression of Russian society, but then a time came when the aims of art as such were entirely swept aside. "The previous sphere was too large; the second shrunk it to nothing; finding its natural limits, poetry will be firmly established forever." And then, perhaps, a poet will appear "who will fully deserve the title of a national-universal poet, which we cannot make up our mind to give to Pushkin, although we do not dare deprive him of it either."[36]

A concluding paragraph of panegyric follows, but the damage had been done. As Dostoevsky wrote to Anna, Turgenev "had denigrated Pushkin by refusing him the title of national poet."[37] And this was the sentiment of a large part of the audience as well. Turgenev had finally balked, no matter how hesitantly and reluctantly, at placing the Russian among the very first rank of the European poets with whom he had been compared. The exhilaration of the ceremony was badly deflated by this embarrassing denial, which seemed to indicate the continued inferiority of Russian culture, supposedly being celebrated, vis-à-vis Europe.

Turgenev's talk left his audience with a sense of "dissatisfaction and indistinct vexation," to quote Strakhov.[38] His subtly balanced considerations tried to unite a eulogy of Pushkin with an apologia for his rejection by the radical critics of the 1860s, and he had also expressed his own opposition, as a liberal Westernizer, to the Slavophil and Populist idolization of "the people." All these opinions were

---

[34] Ibid., 70.
[35] Ibid., 73–74.
[36] Ibid.
[37] *PSS*, 30/Bk. 1: 182; June 7, 1880.
[38] Quoted in *PSSiP*, 15: 827.

hardly in accord with the overheated emotional temperature of the moment, and he was well aware of his failure to stir his audience.

Turgenev's speech, delivered in the afternoon, was followed by a dinner that evening. "The young people," Dostoevsky reports to Anna "greeted me at my arrival, treated me, waited on me, made frenzied speeches to me—and that was still before dinner." Toasts were offered, one by the playwright Ostrovsky to Russian literature, and Dostoevsky was prevailed upon to speak. "I only said a few words—and there was a roar of enthusiasm—literally a roar." He proposed a toast to Pushkin as one of the greatest poets, "the purest, the most honorable, the most intelligent of all Russian men," thus giving a foretaste of what he would proclaim the following afternoon.[39] As the party broke up, he was surrounded by a group of young people. In conversation with them, Dostoevsky complained about his illness, which prevented him from working and then, pausing in silence for a moment, he continued: "'I will write my *Children* and die.' The novel *Children*, according to him, would be the continuation of *The Brothers Karamazov*. In it, the *children* of the preceding novel would come forward as the main heroes."[40]

Dostoevsky continues to describe the adulation he received on the night before his speech: "At 9:30 when I got up to go home, they raised a hurrah for me in which even people not in sympathy with me were forced to take part. Then this whole crowd rushed down the stairs with me, and without coats, without hats, followed me onto the street and put me in a cab. And then they suddenly started kissing my hands—and not one, but tens of people, and not just young people, but gray-haired old folks. No, Turgenev just has members of a claque, while mine have true enthusiasm." "Tomorrow, the eighth, is my most fateful day," he goes on. "In the morning I read my piece."[41]

———————■———————

The session of June 8 opened with some introductory remarks and a poem, "To the Memory of Pushkin," written and read by Dostoevsky's old companion in the Petrashevsky circle, Aleksey Pleshcheev. Then it was Dostoevsky's turn, and, to use the words of Marcus Levitt, he advanced to the podium "to hijack the festival."[42] Even though many accounts exist of what became an epochal event, none takes us so directly to its heart as his own, written on the night of his astonishing triumph. "No, Anya, no," he writes, "you can never conceive of and imagine the effect it produced! What are my Petersburg successes! Nothing, *zero*, compared to this! When I came out, the hall thundered with applause and it was a very long time before they let me read. I waved, made gestures, begging to be allowed to

[39] *PSS*, 30/Bk. 1: 183; June 7, 1880. See also ibid., 354.
[40] *Letopis*, 3: 430.
[41] *PSS*, 30/Bk. 1: 183; June 7, 1880.
[42] Levitt, *Russian Literary Politics*, 122.

read—nothing helped: rapture, enthusiasm (all because of *The Karamazovs*). I finally began reading: I was stopped by thunderous applause on absolutely every page, and sometimes even at every sentence. I read loudly, with fire."[43]

From Gleb Uspensky, we obtain the view of an outside observer who, at the beginning of the session, noticed Dostoevsky sitting "as quietly as a mouse" (*smirnekhonko*) at the back of the stage as if in hiding, "scribbling something in a notebook."

> When his turn came, he *smirnekhonko* stepped up to the speaker's stand, and not five minutes had elapsed before everyone without exception present in the assemblage, all hearts, all thoughts, all souls, were in his power. He spoke to them simply, absolutely as if he were conversing with an acquaintance, not declaiming weighty phrases in a loud voice or tossing his head. Simply and distinctly, without the slightest digression or unnecessary embellishment, he told the public that he thought of Pushkin as someone who expressed the strivings, hopes, and wishes of that very public—the one listening to him at that moment, in that hall. He found it possible, so to speak, to bring Pushkin into that hall, and with his words clarify for all those gathered there something about their own present anxieties, their present anguish. Until Dostoevsky, no one had done that, and this was the major reason for the extraordinary success of his speech.[44]

How was Dostoevsky able to accomplish this remarkable feat? Drawing on a lifetime of observations about Pushkin scattered through his work,[45] and employing his most brilliant critical style, he unites these ideas into a powerful synthesis hailing Pushkin as the poetic herald of the glorious mission that Russia has been called upon to accomplish on behalf of humanity. Dostoevsky usually interprets literary works not in terms of the author's personality or the historical and social-cultural problems with which he or he may have been engaged, but always in the light of some larger issue. His criticism is thus an example of what Nietzsche called the "monumental" style of historical writing, in which the subject becomes a symbolic expression of some much greater theme, whether psychological, moral-metaphysical, or religious. In this instance, he turns Pushkin into a symbol of his own Russian messianism and his exalted conception of "the people," which now harmonized so perfectly with the emotions of the vast majority of his audience.

He begins by citing Gogol—"Pushkin is an extraordinary and, perhaps, unique manifestation of the Russian spirit"—a citation that wipes out at the very start Turgenev's reference to the replacement of the artistic Pushkin by the satirical

[43] *PSS*, 30/Bk. 1: 184; June 8, 1880.

[44] *DVS*, 2: 398.

[45] An account is given in the commentary to the speech contained in *PSS*, 26: 445–451.

Gogol. For Dostoevsky, Pushkin was not only "extraordinary" but above all "prophetic," and it is the essence of this prophecy that he intends to illuminate. He divides Pushkin's work into three periods, though stressing that no hard-and-fast boundaries can be drawn. "The accepted view is that during this first period of his work Pushkin imitated the European poets . . . particularly Byron." Dostoevsky, however, insists that "even [his imitations] expressed the extraordinary independence of his genius. Imitations never contain the kind of personal suffering and depth of self-consciousness that Pushkin displayed" (26: 136–137).

As an example, he takes Pushkin's early poem, "The Gypsies" (1824), in which a Russian nobleman named Aleko leaves civilization to live with his gypsy mistress and joins her wandering tribe. Dostoevsky interprets this scenario as already emblematic of a fundamental Russian dilemma, which gave birth to a new character type. "In Aleko, Pushkin had already found and brilliantly rendered that unhappy wanderer in his native land, that historical suffering Russian who appeared with such historical inevitability in our educated society after it had broken away from the people."

As he enlarges on Pushkin's creation of this type, he manages, in Uspensky's words, to bring Pushkin into that very hall. The "Russian wanderer" has become "a permanent fixture" of the culture, and Dostoevsky now imagines his successors "running off to Socialism, which did not yet exist in Aleko's time." Pushkin's "wanderer" thus becomes identical with the Socialist youth who were hanging from the rafters of the auditorium and drinking in Dostoevsky's every word—not to mention a Populist Socialist like Uspensky himself. And then, alluding to those who now "take this new faith in a different field and work it zealously" (those who "went to the people"), Dostoevsky sees them as adding an additional trait to the character of the "Russian wanderer." What he needs is no longer something purely personal but something universal: he needs "the happiness of the whole world in order to find his own peace of mind" (26: 137).

Dostoevsky steps back to glance at the historical roots of this character type, dating it from "just at the beginning of the second century after the great Petrine reforms"; it was then that educated Russian society became totally "detached from the people and the people's strength." Of course, an awareness of this detachment did not affect the vast majority of Russians, but "it is enough if it happens merely to 'the chosen few' . . . since through them the remaining vast majority will be deprived of their peace of mind." Aleko was seeking something but did not know what, but in fact he and those like him were seeking "for the truth which someone, somewhere had lost, and which he simply cannot find." Later Russian generations, instead of turning to nature, went to Europe's "stable historical order and well-established civic and social life" in search of this lost truth. This quest was a self-deception, however, because "the wanderer" must find the truth "first of all, within himself"; but how could he understand this necessity when he has become a stranger in his own native land, "no more than a blade of grass, torn from its stem and carried off by the wind. And he can sense that and suffer for it, and often suffer so painfully!" (26: 138).

Aleko was called "a disdainful man" by the gypsies, who drive him away after he commits a murder out of jealousy; and while Dostoevsky acknowledges this Romantic climax to be "far-fetched," he nonetheless accepts the characterization of Aleko as "real, and Pushkin's perception here [as] apt." Aleko is still a Russian nobleman who takes full advantage of his station and "angrily attacks his opponent and punishes him" when he is offended. But Dostoevsky also detects in the poem a suggestion of "the Russian solution" to Aleko's rage, "in accordance with the people's faith and truth." This solution is: "Humble yourself, O haughty man; first curb thy pride; Humble yourself, O idle man; first labor on thy native soil." [46] Proclaimed here is Dostoevsky's statement of his positive ideal, which he identifies with the people's "truth." Urging "the Russian wanderer"—and all those like him in the audience—to accomplish such a self-conquest, Dostoevsky assures them "you will embark on a great task and make others free . . . you will find happiness . . . and you will at last understand your people and their sacred truth" (26: 138–139). No passage in the speech aroused more commentary, both positive and negative, than this call for humility and submission.

If "this solution . . . is already strongly suggested" in "The Gypsies," Dostoevsky finds it even more clearly expressed in *Evgeny Onegin* (1833), whose first chapters were composed during the writing of "The Gypsies." The main figure again "wanders in anguish through his native land and through foreign parts" and is everywhere a stranger. "It's true that he loves his native land, but he has no faith in it" and looks down "with sad mockery" on those who do have faith. Onegin kills Lensky "simply out of spleen," and such spleen "may have been caused by his longing for some universal ideal." He compares Onegin with Tatyana, whom he sees as the embodiment of the Russian ideal, and he regrets that the poet did not use her name for his title; it is she, after all, who is the positive protagonist of the work. "One might even say that a positive type of Russian woman of such beauty has almost never been repeated in our literature except, perhaps, in the character of Liza in Turgenev's *Nest of Gentlefolk*" (26: 140). This tribute to Turgenev was unexpected and much appreciated; he was sitting on the stage, and everyone could see that he blew a kiss in Dostoevsky's direction when the flattering reference was made. [47]

---

[46] Dostoevsky is not so much citing Pushkin as rewriting him. In the poem, the elder of the Gypsy tribe simply says to Aleko after the murder: "*Ostav nac, gordy chelovek*" ("Leave us, proud man"). There is nothing about humbling oneself or toiling on thy native soil. A. S. Pushkin, *Polnoe sobranie sochinenii*, 6 vols. (Moscow, 1949), 2: 240.

[47] The reference to Liza was followed by one to Natasha Rostov of *War and Peace*, but it was drowned out by the storm of applause for Liza. See *PSS*, 26: 496.

In comparing Onegin to Tatyana, Dostoevsky turns her into someone "who stands solidly on her own native soil" and is the incarnation of true Russian folk values (though in fact she is no more a member of "the people" than Onegin himself). Onegin's rejection of the love she offers him at the beginning of this novel in verse is transformed into an exemplum of his contempt for the treasures to be found in his native land. While Dostoevsky concedes that "he treated her honorably . . . Onegin's manner of looking down on people caused him to disregard Tatyana entirely when he met her for the first time, in a provincial backwater, and in the humble image of a pure, innocent girl so timid in his presence." He could not appreciate her sterling moral qualities because "he is a man of abstractions, he is a restless dreamer and has been so all his life." Onegin did not understand Tatyana, but, after the famous stanzas describing her visit to his room (Dostoevsky speaks of "their matchless beauty and profundity"), where she examines his foreign books and trinkets, she finally understands his essential hollowness: "*Uzh ne parodiya li?*" ("Is he not a parody?") (26: 140–141).

It is only later, when he meets her again as the queen of Petersburg society, "married to a worthy old general whom she cannot love because she loves Onegin," that he is suddenly overcome by her charms. But when he throws himself at her feet in adoration, she turns him away: "*No ya drugomu otdana / Ya budu vek emu verna*" (But I have been given to another / And will be true to him for life). Dostoevsky exalts this decision as Tatyana's "apotheosis"; here she speaks specifically "as a Russian woman" and as the embodiment of Russian moral values—at least as Dostoevsky understood them. And here too, as everyone in the audience knew, he was taking issue with a famous passage of Belinsky's in which the critic, under the influence of French Utopian Socialism and George Sand, had refused to recognize any moral sublimity in Tatyana's conduct. Belinsky considered her loyalty to a marriage bond not based on love as immoral rather than praiseworthy. (Kolya Krasotkin, inspired by Belinsky, had recently parroted this criticism of Tatyana as he paraded his adolescent braggadacio in the pages of *The Brothers Karamazov*.)

For Dostoevsky, however, Tatyana's faithfulness stems from her deep-rootedness in the values of the Russian folk soul. She refused to evade the moral responsibility for her own earlier decision. She knew that the abandonment of her husband "would cast shame and disgrace upon him and would mean his death. And can one found happiness on the unhappiness of another?" Dostoevsky here speaks in the very accents of Ivan Karamazov as he poses the question of whether an "edifice" of happiness could be built "if its foundations rested on the suffering of, say, even one insignificant creature, but one who had been mercilessly and unjustly tortured?" This query demonstrates the impossibility for Tatyana, as "a pure Russian soul," to do anything but sacrifice *herself*, rather than to construct her own happiness on the destruction of her innocent husband. What surprises

Dostoevsky "is that for such a long time we cast doubt on the moral solution to this question" (26: 142).

Carrying his analysis of this imbroglio one step further, he insists that Tatyana, even if she were free, would still have rejected Onegin. She would have understood that his character had no substance, that he had become bedazzled by her position in society; his infatuation is no proof that he has come to any better understanding of the values of her soul, of "the Tatyana who was as humble as before." What he loves is "his fantasy; indeed, he himself is a fantasy." But she, on the other hand, "still has something solid and unshakable on which her soul can rely. These are her memories of childhood, her memories of her native home deep in the provinces where her humble, pure life began; it is 'the cross and the shade of boughs o'er the grave of her poor nurse.'" All these evocations "represent contact with her native land, her native people and their sacred values." Onegin completely lacks any such sustenance: "he has no soil under his feet, this blade of grass borne by the wind" (26: 143).

He thus concludes that, with Onegin, Pushkin proved himself to be "a great national [*narodny*] writer" who had "identified the innermost essence of the upper class of our society that stood above the people" and also "identified the type of Russian wanderer, who continues his wandering even in our days." But as well as depicting such negative images of Russian life, Pushkin also "showed us a whole series of positively beautiful Russian types he found among the Russian people." In addition to Tatyana, Dostoevsky adduces "the type of Russian chronicler-monk" (Pimen in *Boris Godunov*) and somewhat later "The Tale of the Bear" and a peasant drinking song. Unlike other writers, who came from a different world and whose work "shows a wish to raise the people to their own level and make them happy by doing so," there was something in Pushkin "that *truly* makes him akin to the people, something that reaches the level of simple-hearted tenderness." From Pushkin, as a result, Russians derive "faith in our Russian individuality, our now conscious hope in the strength of our people, and with it our faith in our future independent mission in the family of European peoples" (26: 144).

The last part of the speech is devoted to "the third period" of Pushkin's work, in which "our poet stands forth as an almost miraculous and unprecedented phenomenon," with a universality surpassing even the greatest creators of European literature—Shakespeare, Cervantes, Schiller. In this period, Pushkin began to write works that "reflect the poetic images of other nations and incarnate their genius." Dostoevsky expressively characterizes an array of such poems, but unlike Turgenev, who had praised such works rather halfheartedly, he gives them fundamental importance. No other poet or writer in world literature has this capacity to enter into and reproduce the spirit of other cultures to the same degree because no other people except the Russian possess such universal empathy.

"This we find only in Pushkin, and in this sense, I repeat, he is unprecedented and, in my view, prophetic." He was "prophetic" because this feature of his work, "his ability to infuse his spirit into the spirit of other nations," is precisely indicative of the great future mission of the Russian people (26: 145).

Dostoevsky's messianism is here given a new power and resonance by being prefigured in Pushkin, and this linkage responded perfectly to the need for some uplifting vision felt by his agitatedly expectant audience. Russia's mission, Dostoevsky proclaimed, was "the general unification of all people of all tribes of the great Aryan race." (This was the first time he had employed the word "Aryan," which reveals the influence of the anti-Semitic literature of the period, and it provoked a great deal of criticism.) He then declared that "all our Slavophilism and Westernizing" had been nothing but a great misunderstanding, because "to become a real Russian, to become completely Russian, perhaps, means just (in the final analysis—please bear that in mind) to become a brother to all peoples, a *pan-human*, if you like" (26: 147). Dostoevsky then repeats his assertion that Russian foreign policy, even in the past, had served Europe much more than Russia itself.

Admitting that "my words may seem ecstatic, exaggerated, and fantastic," Dostoevsky is yet willing to let them stand as such. And at this point he makes his most masterly move by identifying Pushkin and Russia with the kenotic essence of Russian religious feeling, the reverence for the suffering and humiliated Christ. The claims he had made for Russia may, after all, seem merely pretentious; indeed, how could such "an impoverished, crude land" as Russia claim such an exalted destiny? "Can it be we who are ordained to utter a new word to humanity?" But he reminds his listeners that he is not making any claim to "economic prominence . . . the glory of the sword or science." Paraphrasing and quoting a poem of Tyutchev's, he intones: "'Our Land may be impoverished, but Christ Himself in slavish garb traversed this impoverished land and gave [it] His blessing!' Why may we not contain His ultimate word?" "If my idea is a fantasy," he concludes, "then in Pushkin, at least, there is something on which this fantasy can be founded." But Pushkin died young, "and unquestionably he took some great secret with him to the grave. And so we must puzzle out his secret without him"—a secret that, as Dostoevsky must have surely believed, his speech had already done a good deal to disclose (26: 148–149).

———■———

The effect of this speech on the audience was absolutely overwhelming, and the emotions it unleashed may be compared with the hysterical effusions typical of religious revival meetings. The memoirs of the period are full of its description, and we may begin with the image given by D. A. Lyubimov—the son of Dostoevsky's editor and then still a young student—of its finale. "Dostoevsky pronounced the last words of his speech in a sort of inspired whisper, lowered his head, and in a deathly silence, began rather hurriedly to leave the podium. The hall seemed to hold its breath, as if expecting something more. Suddenly from the back rows rang out a hysterical shriek, 'You have solved it!' [the secret of Pushkin], which was taken up by several feminine voices in chorus. The entire auditorium began to stir. You could hear the shrieks, 'You solved it! You solved it!' a storm of applause, some sort of rumbling, stamping, feminine screeches. I do not think that the walls of the Hall of the Moscow Nobility either before or since had ever resounded with such a tempest of ecstasy." [48]

Dostoevsky's account to Anna of his spectacular success cannot be equaled in communicating the excitement of the moment:

Everything that I said about Tatyana was received with enthusiasm. (This is the great triumph of our idea over twenty-five years of delusions.) When I spoke at the end, however, of the *universal unity* of people, the hall was as though in hysteria. When I concluded—I won't tell you about the roar, the outcry of rapture, strangers among the audience wept, sobbed, embraced each other, and *swore to one another to be better, not to hate one another from now on, but instead to love one another.* The order of the meeting was violated; everyone rushed toward the platform to see me, highborn ladies, female students, state secretaries, students—they all hugged me and kissed me. All the members of our society [the Society] who were on the platform hugged me and kissed me. All of them, literally all of them wept from delight. The calls continued for half an hour; people waved handkerchiefs; suddenly, for instance, two old men whom I don't know stopped me: "We had been enemies to one another for twenty years, hadn't spoken to one another, but now we have embraced and been reconciled. It's you who reconciled us, you, our saint, you, our prophet!" "Prophet, prophet" people in the crowd shouted.

  Turgenev . . . rushed to embrace me with tears. Annenkov ran up to shake my hand and kiss my shoulder. "You're a genius, you're more than a genius!" they both told me. Aksakov (Ivan) ran up onto the platform and declared to the audience that my speech *was not just a speech, but a historic event!* A thundercloud had been covering the horizon, and now Dostoevsky's speech, like the sun coming out, had dissipated everything, illuminated everything. Beginning now, brotherhood had arrived and there would no longer be any perplexity. "Yes, yes!" everyone cried and again embraced and again there were tears. The meeting was broken up. I rushed to the wings to escape, but everyone from the hall burst in there, and mainly women. They kissed my hands, tormented me. Students came

[48] *DVS,* 2: 418.

running in. One of them, in tears, fell to the floor before me in convulsions and lost consciousness. A complete, absolutely complete victory![49]

With the exception of the reconciliation of the two old enemies, every other detail of this account can be confirmed from independent sources. The young man who collapsed at his feet was the most conspicuous among those so overcome, but the *kursistka* Letkova-Sultanova, who had met Dostoevsky at the poet Polonsky's, also refers to a female friend who lost consciousness at its conclusion.[50] As for Annenkov, in addition to embracing Dostoevsky, he buttonholed Strakhov and said excitedly, "There, that's an example of a literary characterization made by a genius! It settles the affair in one stroke!"[51]

It took an entire hour for the session to resume again. Despite Aksakov's reluctance to take the floor, he was prevailed upon to do so by Dostoevsky and all the others. He wisely improvised some remarks, focusing on the agreement with Dostoevsky's words manifested both by a representative of the Slavophils like himself and by the most important of the Westernizers, Turgenev. Henceforth all misunderstanding had been eliminated, and a new era of harmony in Russian culture was about to dawn. By this time, Dostoevsky "had grown weak and wished to leave, but was forcibly kept from going."[52]

During the hour that had elapsed after his speech, a large laurel wreath had been procured by a group of *kursistki*, who invaded the platform (Dostoevsky said they were more than a hundred) and crowned him with this weighty tribute. It bore the inscription in gold letters, "On behalf of Russian women, about whom you said so many good things." Again, "everyone wept, again there was enthusiasm." The head of the Moscow Duma thanked Dostoevsky on behalf of the city, and the session then came to an end. His letter was written at eight that evening, but for him the day was not yet finished. "In an hour," he tells Anna, "I'll go read at the second literary celebration. I'll read 'The Prophet.'"[53]

At this final session, he read from "Songs of the Western Slavs" and "The Tale of the Bear" in the first part of the program; in the second, he declaimed "The Prophet." Strakhov recalled this latter performance as "the most remarkable" of the evening, which also included readings by Turgenev. "Dostoevsky recited it twice [he was called back by the audience], and each time with such intense passion that his listeners felt uncanny. . . . His right hand, tremblingly pointing out guilt, clearly refrained from any overwrought gestures; the voice was strained to an outcry."[54]

[49] *PSS*, 30/Bk. 1: 184–185; June 8, 1880.
[50] *DVS*, 2: 453.
[51] *PSS*, 26: 461.
[52] *PSS*, 30/Bk. 1: 185; June 8, 1880.
[53] Ibid.
[54] Ibid., 358.

These events did not end the evening, which continued with a repetition of the public "apotheosis" of the bust of Pushkin that had begun the ceremonies. Wreaths were again placed there by all the writers present, and this time it was Dostoevsky, not Turgenev, who crowned Pushkin's head; Turgenev laid his tribute at the foot of the pedestal. This arrangement could well have been made at the start to give the two most prominent writers these alternating roles, but it now seemed to be a symbolic gesture, objectifying what many in the audience had come to feel—that Dostoevsky had emerged victorious, and that it was he, not Turgenev, who had inherited the mantle of Pushkin. He was at last allowed to return to his hotel and obtain some much-needed rest, but was too excited and happy to remain quiet for very long. As Anna tells it, "late at night he went to the Pushkin monument once again. The night was warm, but there was almost no one in the street. Arriving at Strastnaya Square, he lifted with difficulty an enormous laurel wreath which had been presented to him at the morning session after his speech, laid it at the foot of the monument to his 'great teacher,' and bowed down to the ground before it."[55]

———■———

Dostoevsky remained in Moscow for two more days, finding little respite from the round of activities in which he had been caught since his arrival. On the morning of the ninth, he sat for his portrait at the request of the best photographer in Moscow, M. M. Panov. He had already decided to give his Pushkin piece to Katkov, for publication in the *Moscow News*, where it would appear more rapidly and reach a larger reading public than it would in Yuriev's journal.

Later in the afternoon, while he was making his round of obligatory visits before departing, he by chance ran into an acquaintance from Petersburg, Evgeny Opochinin, who worked in the library and museum of the Society of the Lovers of Old (Russian) Literature. The two strolled along until Dostoevsky became weary. Sitting down on a bench to continue their conversation, they suddenly heard "a cheerful voice" behind them hailing Dostoevsky—a voice that turned out to be Turgenev's. Joining the two men, Turgenev engaged Dostoevsky in a conversation to which, regrettably (though this is difficult to believe), Opochinin paid no attention. His thoughts were interrupted when Dostoevsky suddenly rose from the bench, "his face pallid and with trembling lips." "'Moscow is very big,' he angrily threw out at his interlocutor. 'but there is nowhere to hide in it from you!' And waving his arms, he strode away down the boulevard."[56]

Whatever was said in this encounter may have been caused by Turgenev's upset over the accounts of Dostoevsky's speech in the newspapers, which had

[55] Anna Dostoevsky, *Reminiscences*, trans. and ed. Beatrice Stillman (New York, 1975), 235.
[56] Quoted in I. Volgin, *Posledny god Dostoevskogo* (Moscow, 1986), 300–301.

reported on his participation in the general enthusiasm. The words of Aksakov about the Westernizer-Slavophil reconciliation accomplished by Dostoevsky also troubled him deeply. And since he had said nothing at the moment to disrupt the rapturous jubilation, he feared his silence might be taken as agreement. On June 11 he wrote to M. M. Stasyulevich, editor of the *European Messenger*, requesting that he include in an article about the Pushkin celebration a denial that "he [Turgenev] had been completely subjugated" by Dostoevsky's speech and accepted it completely. "No, that's not so," Turgenev insisted. "It was a very clever, brilliant, and cunningly skillful speech, [and] while full of passion, its foundation was entirely false. But it was a falseness that was extremely appealing to Russian self-love."[57]

The next morning, while waiting for his train at the railroad station, Dostoevsky wrote the *Moscow News* requesting that his speech be printed "as soon as possible" and that the editors not make "any editorial corrections (that is, in sense and content)."[58] With that, he departed for home. In the next few months, the last remaining in his life, buoyed by the enthusiasm and the reverence he had encountered from the adoring crowds at the festival, he threw himself with renewed vigor into completing *The Brothers Karamazov* and then into reviving his *Diary of a Writer*.

[57] *PSSiP*, 12/Bk. 2: 272.
[58] *PSS*, 30/Bk. 1: 186; June 10, 1880.

CHAPTER 57

Controversies and Conclusions

Back in Staraya Russa, Dostoevsky dispatched a letter to Countess Sofya Tolstaya, who, along with Vladimir Solovyev and the singer and composer Yulia Abaza, had signed a collective telegram congratulating him on his Pushkin success. He repeats in brief much of what we already know, including the glowing spontaneous responses of Turgenev and Annenkov ("the latter absolutely an *enemy* to me"), and adds an extra detail: "'I'm not saying that because you praised my Liza,' Turgenev told me." Apologizing for "talking so much about myself," Dostoevsky insists, "I swear it isn't vanity: one lives for such moments, it's for them that you in fact come into this world. My heart is full—how can I help telling my friends. I'm still stunned."[1]

As a veteran campaigner in the Russian social-cultural wars, Dostoevsky was under no illusions that he would emerge unscathed or that battle would not rapidly be joined. "Don't worry—I'll soon hear 'the laughter of the crowd'" (a citation from Pushkin), he assures the countess. "I won't be forgiven this in various literary dark alleys and tendencies." From the summaries of his speech in the newspapers, he already saw that two of his main points were being overlooked. One is Pushkin's "universal responsiveness," which "comes completely from our national spirit." Hence Pushkin "is in fact our most national poet." The second point was that "I gave a formula, a word of reconciliation for all our parties, and showed the way out to a new era. That's what everyone in fact felt, but the newspaper correspondents either didn't understand that or refused to."[2] He was convinced that he had been understood by the public, regardless of what the newspapers were saying or what the monthly journals would print in their next issues.

On June 15 Dostoevsky wrote to Yulia Abaza, responding to a story of hers on which she asked him to comment. Dostoevsky's criticism furnishes him an occasion to release the anti-Semitic animus that now more and more dominated his thoughts. The idea of Abaza's story, as Dostoevsky defines it, is "that races of people who have received their original idea from their founders, and *who subordinate themselves* to it exclusively over several generations, subsequently

---

[1] *PSS*, 30/Bk. 1: 187–188; June 13, 1880.
[2] Ibid.

must necessarily degenerate into something separate from humanity as a whole, and even, in the best conditions, into something inimical to humanity *as a whole*—that idea is true and profound." Whether Abaza presented this idea as being embodied in the Jewish people is not clear, but Dostoevsky interprets Jewish history as an instance of this general law. "Such, for instance, are the Jews [*evrei*] beginning with Abraham, and continuing to the present when they have turned into Yids [*zhidy*]. Christ (besides the rest of his significance) was the correction of this idea, expanding into pan-humanness [*vsechelovechnost'*—a key term in the Pushkin speech]. But the Jews refused the correction and remained in all their former narrowness and inflexibility, and therefore instead of pan-humanness have turned into the enemies of humanity, denying everyone except themselves, and now really remain the bearers of the Antichrist and, of course, will be triumphant for a while."[3]

Dostoevsky had always claimed that neither he nor the Russian people nurtured any hostility toward the Jewish religion, but his previous identification of "Yiddism" with the materialism of the modern world had by now hardened into dogma. The Jews had become the agents of the Antichrist who would dominate the world for a time—as predicted in Dostoevsky's favorite book of Revelation—before the world would be redeemed by the Russian Christ and the *vsechelovechnost'* of the Russian people. But meanwhile, the reign of darkness was at hand, and the Jews "are coming, they have filled all of Europe, everything self-ish, everything inimical to humanity, all of mankind's evil passions are for them—how could they not triumph, to the world's ruination!"[4] Such a passage shows him at the very worst of his anti-Semitic animosity.

On July 6, a letter to Lyubimov accompanied the first chapters of Book 11 of *The Brothers Karamazov*, the completion being promised for the August issue. "The final twelfth book," he writes, would be published in September, and then, "for the October issue there will follow . . . a short 'Epilogue.'" Meanwhile, however, he has "been held up a bit by the publication of the *Diary*," which now, besides his Pushkin speech, will include "a rather long foreword and, I think, an afterword, in which I want to say a few words in reply to my dear critics."[5] The Russian press was filled with commentaries on Dostoevsky's speech, as well as reprints of it in whole or in part.

"I undertook to read everything written about me and my Moscow speech in the newspapers," Dostoevsky explains to Elena Shtakenshneider, "and I decided to reply to Gradovsky, that is, not so much to Gradovsky as to write our whole *profession de foi* [profession of faith] for all of Russia." G. K. Gradovsky, a professor of civil law at the University of Moscow, had published a respectful but criti-

---

[3] Ibid., 191; June 15, 1880.
[4] Ibid., 192.
[5] Ibid., 196–197; July 6, 1880.

cal article on Dostoevsky's speech, entitled "Dreams and Reality," in *Voice*. Dostoevsky probably chose Gradovsky's article as the target of his reply because it was such a well-reasoned statement of the liberal Westernizing position, free from the acerbities of critics influenced by radical ideas. He felt it essential to take up the polemical cudgels because, as he told his correspondent, a positive attitude toward Russia had disturbed the Petersburg press and thus "has to be sullied, destroyed, distorted, and everyone has to be dissuaded: ultimately nothing new happened, they say, it was just the good humor of kindly hearts after Moscow dinners." But something new *had* happened, in Dostoevsky's view, and he considered the task of asserting it so important that he wrote his afterword about Gradovsky on his son's birthday. "Guests came, and I sat to the side and finished up the work."[6]

His irate words hardly do justice to the temperate tone of Gradovsky's article. Still, while praising Dostoevsky's comprehension of Pushkin as a poet, Gradovsky refuses to accept the social-historical implications that are drawn from Pushkin's work. Driven to a fury, Dostoevsky counterattacked with all the considerable rhetorical resources at his command. Written as an afterword to an explanatory introduction and the reprinting of his speech, Dostoevsky's answer is indeed a *profession de foi*, a declaration of principles rather than an attempt to reason with his opponent so as to convince him to alter his ideas. "You and I will never come to an agreement," he rightly says, "and so I have no intention whatsoever of trying to persuade or dissuade you." Indeed, Dostoevsky asserts that he is not addressing himself to Gradovsky at all but rather to his own readers. "I hear, I sense, I even see the rise of new elements who are longing for a new word, who have grown weary of the old liberal snickering over any word of hope for Russia" (26: 149). His article contains a summary of his beliefs and convictions as they had already been expressed in the *Diary of a Writer*, but these ideas had previously been set down with reference to one or another topical subject. Here they are stated boldly and unequivocally, asserted in their own right, and often supported by the same autobiographical anecdotes already used to illustrate the personal roots of his convictions.

First he deals with Gradovsky's charge that, if Russians wished to "enlighten" themselves, they must draw such "enlightenment" from Western European sources. But what does Gradovsky mean, Dostoevsky inquires, when he speaks of enlightenment? Does he mean "the sciences of the West, practical knowledge, trade, or spiritual enlightenment? If the first, then all such ideas could come from Europe, "and we truly have no way to escape them, and no reason to try." But if he means "spiritual enlightenment that illuminates the soul, enlightens the heart, guides the mind, and shows it a path in life," then Russians have no

---

[6] Ibid., 197–198; July 17, 1880.

need to appeal to Western European sources. "I maintain that our people were enlightened long ago, when they took Christ and His teachings as their very essence." He then sketches, in vivid images, the endless sufferings endured by the Russian people throughout their history—years during which they had nothing but Christ to cling to as consolation. But he knows very well that "my words will seem childish babble" to those of Gradovsky's persuasion, indeed, "almost indecent" (26: 150–151).

Dostoevsky's denunciation of the West, with all its "enlightenment," reduces the entire social-political situation of that part of the world to an illustration of the two slogans that presumably define the European moral horizon: *Chacun pour soi et Dieu pour tous* (Everyone for himself, and God for all), and *Après moi, le déluge!* (After me, the flood!). These are the slogans of the most arrant and egoistic individualism, and they rule all of Western social-political life. These sayings "*everyone* there serves and believes in. At least all those who stand above the people, who keep them in check, who own the land and the proletariat, and who stand on guard for 'European enlightenment.' Why do we need that kind of enlightenment? We will find another sort here at home" (26: 152–153).

The Russian "wanderers," Gradovsky had argued, were fleeing from the intolerable realities of Russian social life as represented by the characters of Gogol. The only *solution* Dostoevsky offers, as Gradovsky righly charges, is in terms whose tacit social dimension was a submission to the existing social-polical order, with vaguely hopeful intimations of some impending tsarist benevolence. Dostoevsky picks up this challenge by arguing that such Gogolian types, even though seemingly rooted in Russian life, had really become as alienated from the people as "the wanderers." In truth, according to Dostoevsky, Aleko, Onegin, and others like them were the products of a European education, and "their relation to the people was that of a master to a serf." If they had not been so haughty, if they had not begun "to marvel at their own nobility and superiority," they might "have seen that they themselves were also Derzhimordas [a policeman in Gogol's *Inspector-General*] . . . [and] they might have found a path toward reconciliation" (26: 157).

Gradovsky regarded "the wanderers" as "normal and admirable, admirable by the very fact that they fled from the Derzhimordas." Indeed, Gradovsky had praised them "for their hatred of the slavery that oppressed the people," adding that "they loved the people in their own way, 'in a European way,' if you like. But who, if not they, prepared our society for the abolition of serfdom?" Dostoevsky refuses such a claim outright, retorting that those who fled from Russia in "civic sorrow" did not hate serfdom "for the sake of the Russian peasant who worked for them and fed them and who, accordingly, was oppressed by them, as well as by the others." Why, if "the wanderers" were "so overcome by civic sorrow that they had to run off to the gypsies or the barricades of Paris" (an allusion to Turgenev's *Rudin*, a character based on Bakunin), had they not "simply liberated their serfs with land"? Of course they would have had no income, and "one still needs money to live in 'gay Paree'" (26: 157–158).

With a sideswipe at Herzen that all his readers would understand, Dostoevsky speaks of those who "mortgaged, sold, or exchanged (is there any difference?) their peasants and, taking the money thus raised, went off to Paris to support the publication of radical French newspapers and magazines for the salvation of humanity." (Herzen had helped Proudhon finance the publication of his newspaper.) Dostoevsky accuses "the wanderers" of having such a low opinion of the Russian peasantry that they thought flogging them was still necessary. (Indeed, in a lengthy tirade against Turgenev in 1879 to Evgeny Opochinin, he asserted that all those Russian peasants Turgenev treats so poetically were flogged by his mother, adding, in an unworthy taunt, that Turgenev "would not renounce this pleasure" if it had still been allowed.)[7] He refers to all the scabrous anecdotes circulating about peasant family life among "those whose own family lives were frequently houses of ill repute," and who accepted "the latest European ideas in the fashion of Lucrezia Floriani" (26: 159).[8] This gibe is again aimed at Herzen, who had written about the affair of his own wife with the radical German poet Georg Herwegh, and who himself fathered several children with the wife of his best friend Nikolay Ogarev.

To illustrate the contempt with which such "enlightened" Russians looked down upon the people, he then recounts an incident recently made public in Annenkov's *The Extraordinary Decade*. After dinner "at a lovely Moscow dacha" in 1845, a party of "most humane professors, celebrated lovers and connoisseurs of the arts, . . . renowned democrats who subsequently became prominent figures of worldwide importance, critics, writers, and charmingly learned ladies" all went for a stroll. Catching sight of a group of peasants who had been working all day gathering the harvest, which caused the women partially to undress because of the discomfort of laboring all day in the burning sunlight, one wag remarked that "the Russian woman is the only one in the world who feels no shame in front of anyone!" Another added that "it is only the Russian [woman] before whom no one feels ashamed about anything!" Others objected, but Dostoevsky was convinced that even they would not have seen the point. "Why, it was for you, the universal wanderers, that she was working; it was her labor that let you eat your fill!" (26: 159–160)

Once again, quite unjustifiably, Dostoevsky declines to accord "the wanderers" any credit for having helped to prepare the way for the abolition of serfdom, "though naturally, all this entered into the overall total and was of use." Of far

---

[7] *DVS*, 2: 381–382.
[8] Lucrezia Floriani, the main character in a novel by George Sand, bears a number of illegitimate children to various lovers while searching for an ideal mate.

more weight, in his opinion, was the work of someone like the Slavophil Yury Samarin, who took an active part in the preparation of the reform and was a member of the commission that wrote the final statutes. Gradovsky, he notes, makes no reference at all to such people, "who were utterly unlike the wanderers." These latter became "quickly bored . . . and once more they began to sulk squeamishly." On receiving the "redemption" payments for their former serfs, "they began selling their lands and forests to merchants and kulaks to be cut down and destroyed; the wanderers settled abroad, beginning our practice of absenteeism." As a result, Dostoevsky "simply cannot consent to accept this image, so dear to you [Gradovsky], of the superior and liberal person as the ideal of the real, normal Russian" (26: 160–161).

Extremely effective as a polemicist when drawing on such concrete examples of Russian life, Dostoevsky is much less so when forced to cope with more general ideas, such as, for example, Gradovsky's sally that "personal betterment in the spirit of Christian love" is not sufficient to bring about a fundamental moral improvement in society. Even if such landowners as Korobochka and Sobakevich (characters in *Dead Souls*) had been "perfect Christians," their faith, according to Gradovsky, would not have abolished serfdom. Although Dostoevsky cleverly seizes on this notion of "perfection" to advance his own case, the argument he propounds is far from being persuasive. No genuine, perfect Christian, he insists, could possibly own slaves, even though there will continue to be masters and servants; and Dostoevsky cites St. Paul's epistles to his servant Timothy to prove that with perfect Christian love "there will no longer be masters, nor will servants be slaves." Father Zosima had already preached this inner Christian transformation of the master-servant relationship from one of dominance to that of mutual affection, and Dostoevsky now holds up the image of "a future perfect society" in which people like Kepler, Kant, and Shakespeare would be freely served by persons recognizing their importance for humanity. By serving such geniuses voluntarily, the person doing so would demonstrate that "I am in no way beneath thee in moral worth and that, *as a person*, I am equal to thee" (26: 163–164).

Dostoevsky asserts his belief in the Christian ideal as an act of faith. "If I believe that the truth is here, in those very things in which I put my faith, then what does it matter to me if the whole world rejects my faith, mocks me, and travels a different road?" The value of such an ideal cannot "be measured in terms of immediate benefit, but is directed toward the future, toward eternal ends and absolute joy" (26: 164). This is the vision that Dostoevsky upholds as the Russian answer to Western "enlightenment."

■

The single issue of the *Diary of a Writer* for 1880 was published on August 1, and both the Pushkin speech and Dostoevsky's article evoked a new flood of commentary from the unrelentingly hostile liberal and radical journals. Turgenev remained extremely upset at his role in the controversy, and V. V. Stasov, who met him in Paris in mid-July, reports him referring to the Pushkin speech as "abhorrent," even though "almost the whole intelligentsia, and thousands of people, had gone out of their minds about it." He "found unbearable all the lies and falsifications of [Dostoevsky's] preachment," his "mystical verbiage" about "the Russian all-man," the Russian "all-woman Tatyana."[9]

Even some of Dostoevsky's friends and political allies were unable to accept the full implications of his views. Writing to O. F. Miller, who was composing an article on the festival for *Russian Thought*, Yuriev remarked ironically that "it is necessary to cancel out all questions about political freedom because Zosima feels free in chains." Miller's article, which defended Dostoevsky, nonetheless concedes gingerly that "to quarrel with Dostoevsky . . . is of course quite possible if one does so on particular points; his strength is not in these, but in . . . his thought *as a whole*."[10] The most penetrating critique of this kind, which raised fundamental questions about his social-religious ideas, came from the intransigent reactionary pen of Konstantin Leontiyev.

In mid-July Dostoevsky had complained about his embattled situation to Pobedonostsev, the secular head of the Orthodox Church, and his confidant consoled him in a curiously ambiguous manner. "If only your thought is anchored in yourself clearly and firmly, *in faith*, and not in vacillation—there is then no need to pay attention to how it is reflected in broken mirrors—such as are our journals and newspapers."[11] Pobedonostsev then sent Dostoevsky articles about the Pushkin speech published by Konstantin Leontiyev in three issues of the *Warsaw Diary*. Their dispatch would certainly have raised some questions in Dostoevsky's mind. For Leontiyev deals critically with the social-religious questions raised by the Pushkin speech, contrasting its equivocations with the firmness expressed by Pobedonostsev himself in a recent graduation address, praised by Dostoevsky, to students of a school for the daughters of clergymen. Why should Pobedonostsev have called attention to Leontiyev's article if not to indicate what he too found suspect in Dostoevsky's convictions?

Leontiyev's article, "On Universal Brotherhood," contains a probing analysis of the wider implications of Dostoevsky's views as well as of his literary work as a whole. Often called the Russian Nietzsche, Leontiyev occupies a unique place in the social-cultural spectrum of his homeland. Educated as a doctor, he was a novelist as well as a brilliant, slashing, highly original essayist, writing from an arch-reactionary position. He hated bourgeois Western civilization in all its aspects,

[9] *Letopis zhizni i tvorchestvo F. M. Dostoevskogo*, ed. N. F. Budanova and G. M. Fridlender, 3 vols. (St. Petersburg, 1995), 2: 449.

[10] *PSS*, 26: 487.

[11] *LN* 15 (Moscow, 1934), 145.

preferring that of the Ottoman Empire, where he had served as a diplomat; and he advocated a reign of tyranny and despotism in Russia as a defense against the infiltration of Western ideals of progress and universal human betterment. During his later years, he underwent an intense religious phase, spending 1871 in the severely ascetic ambiance of the Greek Orthodox monastery on Mount Athos. Later, he lived in the Optina Pustyn sanctuary and took monastic vows shortly before his death. Leontiyev thus wrote from a point of view that was hostile not only to Gradovsky's liberalism but also to Dostoevsky's inconsistency—at least so he charged—in offering essentially Western ideals as the fulfillment of those of Orthodox Christianity.[12]

Leontiyev well understood why those who had listened to Dostoevsky's impassioned declamation at the Pushkin festival should have been swept away by his eloquence. Reading his words in print, however, and at a remove allowing for sober consideration, he finds them incompatible with Christianity as he understands it. True, he recognizes Dostoevsky to be one of the few Russian writers who has "not lost faith in man himself," since he attributes moral responsibility to the individual rather than shifting it to society. In this respect, he has remained faithful to a truly Christian demand on the personality. Nonetheless, Christianity does not believe "unconditionally . . . either in a better autonomous personal morality, or in the wisdom of humankind as a whole, which must sooner or later create an earthly paradise." It is this latter hope, so central to Dostoevsky's sensibility, that Leontiyev rejects as contrary to Orthodox Christianity; he equates it, rather, with "the doctrines of antinational eudaemonism in which there is nothing new so far as Europe is concerned. All these hopes of earthly love and earthly peace can be found in the verses of Béranger, and even more in George Sand and many others."[13] Leontiyev here discerns quite accurately the continuing influence of the Utopian Socialist Christianity of Dostoevsky's youth—the Christianity that defined itself as the application of the love-ethic of Christ to earthly social life.

Leontiyev's own position, on the contrary, is that of a "Christian pessimism," which confronts the "irremediable tragedy of earthly life" with an unflinching realism. "Suffering, loss, the disillusionment of injustice *must be*," he wrote. "They are even useful to us for our repentance and the salvation of our souls beyond the grave." He identifies his own position with that of Pobedonostsev's speech, which had not advocated any unconditional love for humanity at all. The most important love, the procurator had proclaimed, was love for the Orthodox Church and a strict, unswerving adherence to its dogmas. "Christ," as

[12] For a brief but cogent introduction to Leontiyev's ideas, see Andrzej Walicki, *A History of Russian Thought from the Enlightenment to Marxism*, trans. Hilda Andrews-Rusiecka (Stanford, 1979), 300–308.

[13] Konstantin Leontiev, *Sobranie sochinenii*, 9 vols. (St. Petersburg, 1912), 8: 188–189, 199.

Leontiyev declared, "is not known otherwise than through the Church," but in Dostoevsky's speech the Saviour "is to such an extent available to all of us outside the Church [that] we allow ourselves the right to ascribe to him a promise he never uttered" (that is, the earthly paradise).[14]

Dostoevsky's immediate response to Pobedonostsev was to remark that "in the final analysis Leontiyev is a bit of a heretic . . . [though] there is much of interest in his opinions."[15] But since Pobedonostsev, as the official head of the Orthodox Church, approved of Leontiyev's article (which cited his own words), Dostoevsky was in effect imputing a bit of "heresy" to him as well. One wonders what the procurator of the Holy Synod might have thought of the entry that Dostoevsky made in his notebook for a future (but never written) reply to his critic. "*Leontiyev (it is not worth doing good in the world, for it is said, it will be destroyed).* There's something foolhardy and dishonest in this idea. Most of all, it's a very convenient idea for ordinary behavior: since everything is doomed, why exert oneself, why love to do good? Live for your paunch" (27: 51–52). He thus refused, on moral-social grounds, to adopt the fatalistic, exclusively otherworldly perspective of his critic, who saw the existence of evil as necessary for salvation and thus hardly to be combated or opposed. For Dostoevsky, humanity was endowed with the freedom to struggle against evil, and Christian love would ultimately triumph, although his predictions of a transformation of human life appear to be reserved for a miraculous heavenly upheaval.

■

On August 10, Dostoevsky sent off the concluding chapters of Book 11, and told Lyubimov that Chapters 6, 7, and 8, depicting Ivan's visits to Smerdyakov, had "turned out well." "But I don't know," he adds, "how you'll view Chapter 9." Dostoevsky was concerned that the masterly depiction of Ivan's hallucination and encounter with the devil might not be accepted as written, and he assures Lyubimov that its details had been "checked with the opinion of doctors" and explains that "it's not just a physical (diseased) trait here, when a person begins at times to lose the distinction between the real and the unreal (which has happened to almost every person at least once in his life), but a spiritual trait as well, which coincides with the hero's character: in denying the reality of the phantom, he defends its reality when the phantom disappears. *Tormented by lack of faith, he (unconsciously) wishes at the same time that the phantom were not imaginary, but something real.*"[16]

For Dostoevsky, "the fantastic" was created by the oscillation between the real and the supernatural and the difficulty of deciding between the two. In his notes for Ivan's encounter with the devil, he thus reminds himself several times to

[14] Ibid., 203, 207.
[15] *PSS*, 30/Bk. 1: 210; August 16, 1880.
[16] Ibid., 205; August 10, 1880.

depict the rather grubby materiality of Ivan's supernatural visitor. "Satan enters and sits down (a gray old man, warty)" (15: 320). Satan is also greatly concerned about his health, fearing that he has caught a cold on his journey to earth through the glacial realms of interstellar space; and there are several references to "Hoffmann's Malt Extract" as a remedy, as well as to "honey and salt" (15: 336). All these anchor Satan firmly in the quotidian reality of ordinary existence, while he remains a supernatural Satan at the same time. Surely with Dante and Milton in mind, Dostoevsky humorously apologizes for having portrayed the devil in such an inglorious guise—"he's only a devil, a petty devil, and not Satan 'with scorched wings.'"[17]

Dostoevsky's stroke of genius was to provide this thematic topos with a religious-philosophical dimension by transforming Ivan's doubts about the reality of the devil into the question of whether or not he believes in the existence of a supernatural realm, and hence of God. He wishes to believe in what he sees in order to convince himself, on the purely psychological level, that he is not losing his mind; but he also wishes Satan to be only a hallucination so as to preserve his conviction that God does not exist. Thus, the oscillation of "the fantastic" here receives perhaps its greatest literary expression as Dostoevsky turns its ambiguities into a probing of the question of religious faith.

Although irritated at the lack of notice accorded the appearance of the *Diary* ("if Goncharov hiccuped, all the newspapers would immediately start crying: 'Our venerable novelist has hiccuped'—while they ignore me"),[18] Dostoevsky was now totally absorbed in writing the final chapters of *The Brothers Karamazov*. By September 30, Dostoevsky had completed Book 12, which terminates with the conviction of Dimitry Karamazov for the murder of his father. Work on these chapters had been interrupted on September 2 by "a terrible epileptic attack" that incapacitated him for eight days, but on the eleventh he resumed work, and these pages were sent to Lyubimov on October 6, the same day that the Dostoevsky family returned to Petersburg from Staraya Russa. Only the epilogue, containing the funeral of little Ilyusha and Alyosha's graveside speech to the assembled boys, remained to be written.

Meanwhile, on October 15, he penned a long letter to Pelagaya Guseva, a novelist whom he had met in Bad Ems in 1875. Guseva had reprimanded him in several letters for not replying to her missives, which asked him not only to retrieve a manuscript of hers from the journal *Light* (*Ogonka*) but also to aid her in placing it elsewhere. Dostoevsky acceded to her request, even though "I wouldn't lift a finger for anyone else," but "this is for you, in memory of Ems; I remember you *too well*."[19] In one of her letters Guseva confesses that, while not

[17] Ibid.

[18] Ibid., 206–207; August 11, 1880.

[19] Ibid., 216–218; October 15, 1880.

"indifferent" to Dostoevsky in Bad Ems, she had "heroically concealed" from him "her sinful feelings." Possibly she had not succeeded as well as she imagined, and it was for this reason that Dostoevsky still felt a certain obligation to a lady who had found him so powerfully attractive.

Before acceding to her request, however, he details all the woes by which he is presently afflicted. He has worked so intensively at finishing his novel that "if there is a person at hard labor, it's me. I was at hard labor in Siberia, for four years, but the work and life there were more bearable than the present one." He has no time at all to read a single book, or even to talk to his children ("and I don't"). His emphysema is so bad that "my days are numbered. Because of my hard work my epilepsy also has gotten worse." Moreover, he is assailed by people asking him for answers to all their personal problems, and unless "I resolve some insoluble 'accursed' question," the petitioner says he will "be driven to shoot himself. (And I'm seeing him for the first time.)" Overwhelmed by invitations to participate in every benefit reading, Dostoevsky wails, "When am I to think, when am I to work, when am I to read, when am I to live?"[20]

Four days later, he felt free to attend one of the regular Tuesday salons at the home of Elena Shtakenshneider. The gathering lasted until three in the morning, much later than customary, and the evening was so unusually animated that the hostess wrote a lengthy entry in her diary. Poems were read, songs were sung by guests accompanied at the piano by accomplished musicians, and "no one noticed how time was passing." Dostoevsky read "The Prophet" again (since the Pushkin festival it had more and more become identified with his own personality), as well as some other poems from Pushkin, Dante, and one from John Bunyan's *Pilgrim's Progress*. "What a fantastic and devious old man!" she writes. "[Dostoevsky] is himself a magical tale, with its miracles, unexpected surprises, transformations, with its enormous terrors and its trifles."[21]

She describes him as often sitting in her living room morose and silent, brooding over some imagined slight, his eyes sunken, his head hanging, his lower lip twisted in a crooked half-smile. At such moments he spoke to no one, or if he did so, only in abrupt outbursts; but if he managed to say something "with a drop of malice," then his ill mood vanished, "as if a spell had been lifted," and he would smile and join in the general conversation. "To those who knew him," she adds, "he is very kind, genuinely kind, despite all his malice; he may give way to the wretched disposition of his soul, but then he repents and wishes to compensate with amiability."[22]

Another entry in Elena Shtakenshneider's diary comments on a visit to her home by Anna and the children early on the day Dostoevsky was scheduled to

[20] Ibid.
[21] *DVS*, 2: 360.
[22] Ibid.

read at an afternoon benefit for the Literary Fund. "Really, her husband is a curious fellow, judging from her words," she writes. "He does not sleep at night, thinking over ways to provide for his children, works like a convict, denies himself everything, never even taking a carriage to go anywhere, and he, without saying a word about it, supports his brother and stepson [somewhat an exaggeration—J. F.] . . . [and] still concerns himself with the first person he meets if this is requested." Anna went on in this vein with examples of his charities, complaining that he could not go anywhere, for a walk or a journey, without an open pocketbook, ready to scatter largesse to all who appealed to his kindness. "'That's how we live,' she concluded, 'And if something happens, where do we turn? How will we live? We are poor! No pension will be coming our way.'"[23]

His reading for the Literary Fund, which included "The Prophet," was an enormous success, and she marveled that Dostoevsky, "ill, with a sickly chest and emphysema," seemed "to grow in size and become healthier" as he read. In ordinary conversation he coughed continually, but his cough vanished when he declaimed, "as if it did not dare" to manifest itself.[24] Such triumphs on the platform no doubt served to reassure him about the "prophetic" mission he had assumed, but it is likely that nothing at this time brought him greater satisfaction than a few lines in a letter that Tolstoy wrote to his faithful correspondent Strakhov on September 26: "Just recently I was feeling unwell and read *House of the Dead*. I had forgotten a good bit, read it over again, and I do not know a better book in all our new literature, including Pushkin. It's not the *tone* but the wonderful point of view—genuine, natural, and Christian. A splendid, instructive book. I enjoyed myself the whole day as I have not done for a long time. If you see Dostoevsky, tell him that I love him."[25] Dostoevsky was then living in Staraya Russa, and it was only on November 2 that Strakhov conveyed Tolstoy's praise to him.

"I saw Dostoevsky," Strakhov informs the recluse of Yasnaya Polyana, "and transmitted to him your praise and love. He was greatly overjoyed, and I had to leave with him the page of your letter containing such precious words. He was a little annoyed at your derogation of Pushkin which is expressed there. . . . 'How including [Pushkin]?' he asked. I said that you had been even earlier, and now had particularly become, a hardened freethinker."[26]

On November 7, Dostoevsky completed work on *The Brothers Karamazov* and sent the final section to Lyubimov. "Well, and so the novel is finished," he wrote elegiacally. "I have worked on it for three years, spent two publishing it—this is a significant moment for me. . . . Allow me not to say farewell to you.

[23] Ibid., 363.
[24] Ibid.
[25] *Letopis*, 3: 478.
[26] Ibid., 493.

After all, I intend to live and write for another twenty years." [27] The completion of the manuscript of his greatest work had no doubt filled him with a happy sense of renewed vigor, which overshadowed his previous comments about the dangerous state of his health. Alas, the more pessimistic prediction in so many of his letters turned out to be all too justified.

[27] *PSS*, 30/Bk. 1: 227–228; November 8, 1880.

The Brothers Karamazov: Books 1–4

The Brothers Karamazov (*Brat'ya Karamazovy*) achieves a classic expression of the great theme that had preoccupied Dostoevsky since *Notes from Underground*: the conflict between reason and Christian faith. The controlled and measured grandeur of the novel spontaneously evokes comparison with the greatest creations of Western literature. *The Divine Comedy, Paradise Lost, King Lear, Faust*—these are the titles that come to mind as one tries to measure the stature of *The Brothers Karamazov*, for these too grapple with the never-ending and never-to-be-ended argument aroused by the "accursed questions" of mankind's destiny. By enlarging the scale of his habitual poetics of subjectivity and dramatic conflict, Dostoevsky imparts a monumental power of self-expression to his characters that rivals Dante's sinners and saints, Shakespeare's titanic heroes and villains, and Milton's gods and archangels. Dostoevsky's personages seem to dwarf their surroundings with the same superhuman majesty as the figures of Michelangelo's Sistine Chapel.

The characters of *The Brothers Karamazov* are not only contemporary social types, they are linked with vast, age-old cultural-historical forces and moral-spiritual conflicts. The internal struggle in Ivan Karamazov's psyche, for example, is expressed through the legends and mystery plays of the Middle Ages in Europe, the autos-da-fé of the Spanish Inquisition, the eschatological myth of the returning Christ, and the New Testament narrative of Christ's temptations by Satan. Dimitry is surrounded with the atmosphere of Schiller's Hellenism and the struggle between the Olympian gods and the dark, bestial forces that had subjugated humankind before their coming. Zosima is the direct inheritor of the thousand-year-old rituals and traditions of the Eastern Church and a representative of the recently revived institution of *starchestvo*, both of which are evoked so solemnly in the early chapters. Alyosha is situated in this same religious context, and his crisis of doubt, which, like those of King Lear and Hamlet, calls into question the entire order of the universe, is resolved only by a cosmic intuition of the secret harmony linking the earth with the starry heavens and other worlds.

Feodor Pavlovich's anecdotes about Diderot and Catherine the Great, as well as his quotations from Voltaire, tinge his grossness and cynicism with a distinct eighteenth-century flavor. He is also placed much farther back in time when he takes pride in possessing "the countenance of an ancient Roman patrician of the decadent period" (14: 22). Dostoevsky always associated these later years of the declining Roman Empire with rampant licentiousness and moral break-down, and in 1861 he wrote that this period was the world "to which our divine redeemer descended. And you understand much more clearly the meaning of the word redeemer" (19: 137). Nor should one forget the rich network of biblical and literary allusions and parallels that interweave with the action throughout the book.[1] This symbolic amplification thickens and enriches the texture of the work, and gives its conflicts the range and resonance we are accustomed to find-ing in poetic tragedy rather than in the more quotidian precincts of the novel.

All these factors contribute to the impression of classic grandeur made by the book, but most important of all is the weight and dignity of its theme. With *The Brothers Karamazov* Dostoevsky takes up the subject of the breakdown of the Rus-sian family that had begun to preoccupy him in the early 1870s and had fur-nished the starting point for *A Raw Youth*. But if that novel had shown him any-thing, it was that he could not confine this subject to a social-psychological level. For Dostoevsky, the breakdown of the family was only the symptom of a deeper, underlying malaise: the loss of firmly rooted moral values among edu-cated Russians stemming from their loss of faith in Christ and God. The moral-ity deriving from these values had once again become accepted—but not their linkage to the supernatural presuppositions of the Christian faith, which for Dostoevsky offered their only secure support. Concurrently, therefore, there is also, for the first time, the extensive presentation of another world of true faith, love, and hope in the monastery, as well as in the evolution of the relations be-tween Dimitry and Grushenka and among the children.

The conflict between reason and faith—faith now being understood as the irrational core of the Christian commitment—was thus, as Dostoevsky saw it, posed more centrally in current Russian culture than in the 1860s. And its new prominence gave him his long-cherished opportunity to place this conflict, grasped at its highest moral-philosophical level, at the center of a major work. In his last novel, he thus brought all the resources of his sensibility, his intelli-gence, his culture, and his art to cope with this new version of radical ideas—just as he had done earlier with Chernyshevsky's materialism and Utilitarianism in *Notes from Underground*, with Pisarev's Nihilism in *Crime and Punishment*, and with the revolutionary amorality of the Bakunin-Nechaev ideology in *Demons*.

This opposition between reason and faith is dramatized with incomparable force and sublimity in Books 5 and 6, the famous ideological center of *The*

---

[1] For an impressive "poetic" reading of the novel, which tries to do justice to this dense web of references, parallels, and figural anticipations, see Diane O. Thompson, *The Brothers Karamazov and the Poetics of Memory* (Cambridge, UK, 1991).

Brothers Karamazov. It contains Ivan's revolt against a Judeo-Chrisitan God in the name of an anguished pity for a suffering humanity, and the indictment of Christ himself in the Legend of the Grand Inquisitor for having imposed a burden of free will on humankind too heavy for it to bear. In reply, there is Zosima's preachment of the necessity for a faith in God and immortality as the sole guarantee for the active love for one's fellow man demanded by Christ. Here this conflict is expressed in overt religious terms and in relation to the age-old problem of theodicy, which, ever since the book of Job, has furnished the inspiration for so much of the religious problematic in the Western tradition. But it is not enough to focus attention solely on these magnificent set pieces. For the same theme of reason and faith appears in all the multiplicity of action in the book, and its specifically religious form serves as a symbolic center from which it radiates analogically through all the situations in which the major characters are involved.

Dostoevsky rather incautiously spoke of the utterances of Zosima in Book 6 as having been designed specifically to answer the accusations of Ivan against God, but he did so partly to pacify the fears of Pobedonostsev that the reply would not be as powerful as the attack. Later, however, in an entry in his notebook set down *after* the work had been completed, he wrote that "the whole book" was a reply to the Legend of the Grand Inquisitor (27: 48). This remark indicates much more accurately the linkages that exist among the various parts and levels—a linkage based on the analogy between the dominant situation reflected in Ivan's poem and the conflicts of all but the most accessory and secondary characters.

For an intellectual like Ivan, his anguish at the sufferings of humankind opposes any surrender to the Christian hope—a hope justified by nothing but what Kierkegaard called a "leap of faith" in the radiant image of Christ the God-man. Similarly, all the other major characters are confronted with the same necessity to make a leap of faith in something or someone beyond themselves, to transcend the bounds of personal egoism in an act of spiritual self-surrender. For these characters, this conflict is not presented in terms of a specific religious choice but rather in relation to their own dominating drives and impulses, their own particular forms of egoism. They too are called upon to accomplish an act of self-transcendence, an act "irrational" in the sense that it denies or overcomes immediate ego-centered self-interest. The identification between "reason" (which on the moral level amounted to Utilitarianism) and egocentrism was deeply rooted in the radical Russian thought of the period, and this convergence enables Dostoevsky to present all these conflicts as part of one pervasive and interweaving pattern. Indeed, the continuing power of the novel derives from its superb depiction of the moral-psychological struggle of each of the main characters to heed the voice of his or her own conscience, a struggle that will always remain humanly valid and artistically persuasive whether or not one accepts the theological premises without which, as Dostoevsky believed, moral conscience would simply cease to exist.

Such a pattern, indeed, may be found not only in the thematic involvements of the book but even in the organization of the plot action. The central plot is carefully constructed so as to lead, with irresistible logic, to the conclusion of Dimitry's guilt; the accumulated mass of circumstantial evidence pointing to him as the murderer is literally overwhelming. The fact remains, however, that he is innocent of the crime (though implicated in it by his parricidal impulses), and the reader is thus constantly confronted with the discrepancy between what reason might conclude and the intangible mystery of the human personality, capable even at the very last moment of conquering the drives of hatred and loathing. The entire arrangement of the plot action thus compels the reader to participate in the experience of discovering the limitations of reason. Only those among the characters who are willing to believe *against* all the evidence—only those whose love for Dimitry and whose faith, deriving from this love, are stronger than the concatenation of facts—only they are able to pierce through to the reality of moral-spiritual, as well as legal, truth in its most literal sense, and this motif illustrates why Dostoevsky could legitimately maintain that "the whole book" is a reply to the "Euclidean understanding" that created the Legend of the Grand Inquisitor.

The Brothers Karamazov begins with a preface labeled "From the Author," and some question has arisen as to whether this "author" is Dostoevsky himself or the fictional narrator of his story. This question raises the more general issue of his fictional narrator as such, who determines the perspective from which a good deal of the novel will be read. In fact, two narrators are provided: one who comes to the foreground and is indirectly characterized as a resident of the town personally acquainted with the Karamazov story, another who allows the characters to express themselves in lengthy monologues or in dramatic confrontations with hardly any commentary. Dostoevsky was well aware of this problem of narrative perspective, and the solution he adopts here is similar to his earlier choice for *Demons*. There we find the same two types of narration, one expository and the other dramatic; but while the expository narrator in that novel participated in the dramatic action, in *The Brothers Karamazov* he is totally detached from the events. Since these took place thirteen years earlier, he serves only as a historian or chronicler, but one who indicates some personal acquaintance with the events at the time they occurred. Although he may disappear as a presence in the dramatic scenes, he is nonetheless important otherwise and exhibits a distinct physiognomy.

The Russian scholar V. E. Vetlovskaya writes that Dostoevsky deliberately blurred the lines between himself as author and his fictional narrator because this indistinction allowed him to express his own opinions in a veiled and seemingly naïve fashion.[2] He was writing what she calls a "philosophical-publicistic" work, which advanced a definite tendency and advocated a specific moral-religious point of view—and one to which, as he well knew, many of his readers would be opposed. He thus tried to defuse negative reactions by creating a figure that evokes a "modernized" version of the tone and attitude typical of the pious narrators of the hagiographical lives of Russian saints. His language constantly plays on associations that would recall such saints' lives to the reader, and other attributes of the narrator's style, such as syntactical inversions that would be felt as archaisms, can also be traced to such an intent. The fumbling, tentative quality of his assertions, his uncertainty about details, his moralistic judgments and evaluations, his emotional involvement in the lives of the characters, his lack of literary sophistication, and the heavy-handedness of his expository technique— all can be seen as an up-to-date version of the pious, reverent, hesitant, hagiographical style of the Russian religious tradition. Such a narrator would be apt to produce a sense of trust in the reader by his very awkwardness and simplicity, and his constant appeal to the opinion of the community also imparts a chorus-like quality to the testimony that he offers. Dostoevsky thus uses him to insinuate his own point of view without arousing an instantly hostile response.[3]

The preface, however, contains remarks about Russian criticism and critics that would come more naturally from the pen of a professional writer. It is more the author than the provincial chronicler who explains that from the outset he wished to focus attention on Alyosha, even though he is still "a vague and undefined protagonist" (14: 5) who will become more important in a second volume. Because Dostoevsky wished to indicate the future importance of Alyosha, he felt it necessary to say a few words about him outside the framework of this first story.

Dostoevsky sets out immediately to counter the prejudices that he knew would be stirred by Alyosha's Christian commitment and the other peculiarities of his character. Alyosha, he writes, is "an original" (*chudak*), but his singularity does not mean that his strangeness and eccentricity have nothing to teach others. "For not only is an eccentric 'not always' a particularity and a separate element, but on the contrary, it happens sometimes that such a person . . . carries within himself the heart of the whole, and the rest of the men of his epoch have for some reason been temporarily torn from it, as if by a gust of wind" (14: 5). Alyosha and his teacher, Zosima, were certainly the heart of the Russian "whole"

[2] V. E. Vetlovskaya, *Poetika romana "Brat'ya Karamazovy"* (Leningrad, 1977), chap. 1.
[3] Ibid.

for Dostoevsky, and one aim of the book was to drive this point home to those who rejected the divinity of Christ while revering the values of the Russian people who came to adore him through the person of Zosima.

———■———

Book 1 opens with a series of short background chapters devoted to the history of the Karamazov family in which Dostoevsky touches on all the main characters and thematic motifs that he will develop so luxuriantly later. Dostoevsky's characters, always portrayed in a relatively brief time span, obviously cannot undergo a long process of maturation. Instead, they appear to grow in size and stature because, even if a change occurs, it is accomplished through developing latent aspects of the personality already present from the start. This is probably why, as the characters visibly amplify before our eyes, the reader receives so strong an impression of their monumentality.

No such change takes place in the elder Karamazov, who incarnates personal and social viciousness on a grand scale. He totally neglects his three children by his two wives, who grow up as members of the kind of "accidental family" that Dostoevsky increasingly felt to be typical of educated Russian society. His presumed bastard, Smerdyakov, is treated with a contempt that only increases the latter's resentment and hidden rage. Feodor Pavlovich, however, is not simply a monster of wickedness existing solely on the level of his insatiable appetites; he is clever and cynical, educated enough to sprinkle his talk with French phrases, to be familiar with Schiller's *The Robbers*, and he is shown to have strange velleities that suggest some concealed modicum of inner life. On receiving the news of the death of his domineering first wife—the mother of Dimitry—he both shouts with joy and weeps. Years later, though continuing to abuse the monks, he donates a thousand rubles to the monastery to pay for requiems for her soul. This leitmotif of the "broad" Russian nature, swinging between competing moral-psychological extremes, characterizes both Feodor Pavlovich and his eldest son Dimitry, and its symbolic significance will be highlighted toward the end of the book.

The narrator sketches Dimitry's recklessly dissipated army career, and his expectations that he would inherit money from his mother on coming of age, before moving on to the second brother, Ivan, who possesses the familiar traits of Dostoevsky's young intellectuals. He is a reserved and morose nature thrown back on itself and brooding over the injustices of the world. The ideas that absorb him now express the core of the Populist problematic. Is it possible to transform the world into a realization of the Christian ideal without a belief in Christ? Ivan's inner conflict is suggested by the ambiguity surrounding his article on the ecclesiastical courts, which had been applauded both by the Church party and the secularists. The issue was whether such courts should be subordinate to the state (and hence secular) authorities, or whether state courts should ultimately be absorbed by ecclesiastical ones, whose decisions would be made according to the law of Christ. Ivan had presented both extreme positions with equal force, and each party thought it could claim him as an advocate. In reality, his apparent refusal to choose already presents the inner conflict that will ultimately lead to his mental breakdown.

It is to Alyosha that, after Feodor Pavlovich, the narrator devotes the most attention. Dostoevsky endeavors to persuade the reader that, unlike the previous incarnation of his moral ideal in Myshkin, such a figure was not "a fanatic . . . and not even a mystic" (14: 17); on the contrary, he was "a well-grown, red-cheeked, clear-eyed lad of nineteen, radiant with health" (14: 24). He is immediately associated with Christian values by his earliest memory, that of his mother, partially deranged by her suffering at the hands of Feodor Pavlovich, who prays for him before the image of the Mother of God, "as though to put him under the Mother's protection." Alyosha's moral sensibility is thus shaped by the all-forgiving love traditionally associated with the Mother of God in Russian Orthodoxy. "There was something about [Alyosha] which made one feel at once . . . that he did not care to be a judge of others—that he would never take it upon himself to criticize and would never condemn anyone for anything" (14: 18).

The depiction of Alyosha's character and behavior, which the narrator makes no attempt to explain psychologically, conforms to the hagiographical pattern; the moral purity of his nature, and the love that he inspires in everyone despite his "eccentricity," are traditional saintly attributes. The forces that move him, which are left deliberately vague so as to suggest a possibly otherwordly inspiration, come from the childhood impressions just mentioned, and from the nature of the religious vocation they have inspired. Alyosha was instinctively religious, and until his faith is tested later, he has had no doubts about God or immortality, or even about the truth of the miraculous legends connected with the institution of elders (*startsy*). Novices who entrusted themselves to an elder committed their will to his guidance in "the hope of self-conquest, of self-mastery" (14: 28), and Alyosha had decided to submit himself to Zosima in this way. He fully shared the Russian peasantry's adoration of the ideals of holiness embodied in the saintly monk, whom he also believed to possess the gift of a spiritual force—the force of Christian love—capable of redeeming the world.

This submission to Zosima does not mean that Alyosha is detached from the questions posed by the modern world. Indeed, Dostoevsky brings Alyosha into immediate relation with the social-political situation by describing him as "an early lover of humanity," as "a youth of our last epoch" (14: 17) passionately seeking truth and justice and ready to sacrifice himself for these ideals on the spot. These phrases unmistakably associate Alyosha with the discontent and moral idealism of the generation of the 1870s; and he is clearly intended, at least in this initial volume, to offer an alternative form of "action" and "sacrifice" to that prevalent among the radical youth. For if Alyosha, we are told, "had decided that God and immortality did not exist, he would at once have become an atheist and Socialist (for Socialism is not merely the labor question or that of the fourth estate, it is the question of atheism in its contemporary incarnation, the question of the Tower of Babel built without God, not to mount to Heaven from earth but to bring down Heaven on earth)" (14: 25). The same ideals and feelings that had led Alyosha to Zosima might have led him to atheism and Socialism since both offer divergent paths leading to the same goal of the transformation of earthly life into a society closer to the Kingdom of God; but the first would be guided by Christ, while the second is deprived of the moral compass that he provides.

It is also in relation to Alyosha that the main theme of the novel—the conflict between reason and faith—receives its first exemplification. When the narrator touches on Alyosha's belief in miracles, he immediately explains that this did not prevent him from being "more of a realist than anyone" (14: 24). Alyosha's "realism" does not counteract his faith because the latter is defined as an inner state or disposition anterior to (or at least independent of) anything external, visible, tangible, empirical. Alyosha's faith thus colors and conditions all his apprehension of the empirical world; it is not the evidence from the world that inspires or discourages faith. Alyosha's spiritual crisis will be caused by the decay of Zosima's body, a crisis that is only one instance of Dostoevsky's major theme—that true faith must be detached from anything external, any search for, or reliance on, a confirmation or justification of what should be a pure inner affirmation of the emotive will.

Dostoevsky plays endless variations on this irreconcilable opposition between faith, on the one hand, and the empirical and rational on the other—an opposition initially dramatized in a brief dialogue between Alyosha and his father. Feodor Pavlovich's jeering words foreshadow Ivan's soaring speculations, and they link the two in more than merely a father-son relation; but what will be noble and elevated in Ivan becomes vulgarly cynical in the corrupt old scoundrel. Agreeing to let Alyosha enter the monastery, the half-drunken Feodor explains the reason: "You'll pray for us sinners; . . . I've always been thinking who would pray for me, and whether there's anyone in the world to do it." But this implicit admission of moral awareness and of a faith in an afterlife is immediately canceled by a scoffing inability to imagine the physical paraphernalia of hell. If there are hooks in hell that will drag Feodor down, where did they come from? Were they attached to a ceiling? "If there's no ceiling there can be no hooks, and if there are no hooks it all breaks down, which is unlikely again, for then there would be none to drag me down to Hell, and if they don't drag me down what justice is there in the world? *Il faudrait les inventer*, those hooks, on purpose for me alone" (14: 23–24). This is the debased and niggling form of "realism"—a parody of Russian Voltairianism—in which Ivan's "Euclidean understanding" becomes manifest in his father, in Mme Khokhlakova, in Smerdyakov, and finally in the hallucinatory devil, whom Ivan will accuse of representing "the nastiest and stupidest" of his blasphemous thoughts and feelings.

The action begins in Book 2 with the gathering of the Karamazovs in the monastery, and the threads of the main plot and subplots are skillfully exposed as the father and son shout furious insults at each other. The reader is also brought into the secluded world of the monastery, which Dostoevsky had never depicted before, and he contrasts the dignity and serenity of its inhabitants with the various types of egoistic self-concern exhibited by the secular characters. The grouping and succession of chapters is a part of Dostoevsky's technique of conveying thematic motifs without direct authorial intervention. And so, after "the old buffoon" (Feodor plays his role to the hilt) has begun his sacrilegious antics in the cell of Zosima, the narrative shifts to the profoundly moving faith of the peasants assembled to receive the elder's spiritual counsel and blessing. The chapter ends on a comforting note of Christian love and solidarity operating among the Russian people.

The tonality of reverence is then replaced by amusing satirical comedy. Zosima turns from the suffering peasantry to the spoiled and wealthy Mme Khokhlakova and her cripped daughter Liza. This giddy lady is Dostoevsky's diverting portrait of an affluent society matron with intellectual pretensions, who swings like a weather vane in response to every fashionable ideological gust. Perhaps because she is in no position to cause any harm, she is treated with affectionate condescension. The tone is given by Zosima's reply when she protests her overflowing "love for humanity" and her occasional dreams of becoming a sister of mercy. "Sometimes, unawares," he observes, "you may do a good deed in reality" (14: 52). Not only do the self-indulgent lucubrations of Mme Khokhlakova provide an obvious antithesis to the devotion of the peasants, the exchange between Zosima and the burbling lady also prefigures one of the book's deepest motifs.

For her chatterings anticipate, in a seriocomic version, Ivan Karamazov's doubts concerning God and immortality, and Zosima's response condenses the essence of what will soon be dramatized more seriously and powerfully. Mme Khokhlakova has picked up at second hand some of the fashionable atheism of the period, and wonders whether faith does not simply come from terror. What if, she asks with charming illogic, she discovers when she dies that "there's nothing but burdocks growing on my grave" (as Turgenev had written in *Fathers and Children*)? "How, how," she asks despairingly, "is one to prove it?" To which Zosima replies that no proof is possible, but "If you attain to perfect self-forgetfulness in the love of your neighbor, then . . . no doubt can possibly enter your soul" (14: 52). The difference between such Christian love and a "rational love for humanity," which leaves the emotive roots of egoism untouched, is stressed in Zosima's story of the doctor who confessed—as Ivan will—that "the more I detest men individually, the more ardent becomes my love for humanity" (14: 53).

No other novelist can rival Dostoevsky's ability to develop his themes, and reveal the moral-psychological sensibility of his characters, through discussions of seemingly abstract ideas. When Zosima returns to the fractious Karamazov assemblage, a discussion arises out of Ivan's article on Church jurisdiction, already referred to, which enlarges on the hints already given about his character. Ivan had argued that the Christian Church should aspire to transform and absorb the state into itself, and should not be satisfied with a limited area of power; but this does not mean that the Church should assume the prerogatives of a state, as in Roman Catholicism, which claims temporal power over humanity. Rather, the law of Christian love that rules in the Church should penetrate every area of secular existence, and the principles governing the relations among people would be based not on external force, but on the free and voluntary operation of the Christian moral conscience. Such a world would truly be the establishment of the Kingdom of God on earth, the total triumph of religious faith over secular reason, and Ivan's eloquent exposition of this goal indicates how deeply he responds to this Christian ideal in its loftiest form.

Ivan's emotive receptivity to this Orthodox-Slavophil Christian ideal is only one aspect of his character; another—equally rigorous and uncompromising—is exhibited by his public declaration that the Christian law of love could not be detached from the Christian faith and that, without a belief in God and immortality, "the moral law of nature must immediately be changed into the exact contrary of the former religious law, and that egoism, even extending unto crime, must become not only lawful but recognized as the inevitable, the most rational, even honorable outcome of [this] position" (14: 64). Only Christian faith supports the application of the law of love in the world; otherwise, there is nothing to oppose selfishness and the depredations of vainglory. Ivan refuses to stop at any halfway house here, anymore than he had done on the issue of church and state, and his own inner conflict is mirrored by the absolute incompatibility between these alternatives. His rationalism prevents him from believing in Christ and immortality, but his moral sensibility will make it impossible for him to accept the appalling consequences that logically flow from such a lack of faith.

Zosima, the experienced reader of souls, sees through to the anguish of Ivan's spiritual condition, and the dialogue between them highlights both the genuineness and the agonizing uncertainty of Ivan's plight. When Zosima accuses him of believing neither in immortality nor in what he had written in defense of the supremacy of the Church, Ivan acknowledges the accusation, but adds,

"I wasn't altogether joking." Zosima pierces to the quick by warning Ivan that he is playing with the martyrdom of his own indecision and despair. Completely discomfited, Ivan fully exposes himself by asking Zosima "strangely, looking at the elder with [an] inexplicable smile," whether the question of God "can be answered by him in the affirmative." Zosima's response may be taken as an expression of Dostoevsky's own attitude toward the whole generation of young Russians whom Ivan was meant to represent:

> If it can't be decided in the affirmative, it will never be decided in the negative. You know that is the peculiarity of your heart, and all its suffering is due to it. But thank the Creator who has given you a lofty heart capable of such suffering, "of thinking and seeking higher things, for our dwelling is in the heavens." God grant that your heart will attain the answer on earth, and may God bless your path. (14: 65–66)

Ivan now reverently kisses the elder's hand.

The presentation of Dimitry in Book 2 is less directly revelatory, but the outlines of his character come through nonetheless. For all his rowdiness and dissipation, there is a longing in him for "seemliness." He is the only "educated" character who kisses Zosima's hand as a matter of course, and he is capable, even in the midst of the furious altercation with his father, of sincerely acknowledging guilt. "Father, I don't justify my action," he says of his assault on the pathetic Captain Snegiryov. "Yes, I confess it publicly, I behaved like a brute to the captain, and I regret it now, and I'm disgusted with myself for that brutal rage" (14: 67). Whipped up, however, by his father's falsely pathetic taunts and reproaches about Katerina and Grushenka, Dimitry's rage becomes uncontrollable. "Tell me," he thunders to the assembled audience, "can he be allowed to go on defiling the earth?" (14: 69). It is immediately after this suggestion of parricide that Zosima—having noted both the terrible violence of Dimitry's nature and his displays of conscience—bows down at his feet.

Alyosha is scarcely developed in this section and, after the opening page, remains in the background until a later stage. As Robin Feuer Miller has remarked, he functions as what Henry James called a *ficelle*, that is, a string tying together the action of the other characters as he goes from one to the other.[4] Book 2 is thematically rounded out by the one chapter devoted to Alyosha and his negative counterpart, the envious and self-serving Rakitin, a young novice in the monastery who has secretly and painlessly converted to atheism, science, and positivism. Rakitin is "a young man bent on a career," ready to sell his soul—in which he does not believe—for material success and social advancement (14: 71). If Ivan represents the aspect of Populist youth that Dostoevsky saw as genuinely

---

[4] Robin Feuer Miller, *The Brothers Karamazov* (New York, 1992), 23.

inspired by Christian ideals, Rakitin indicates how easily these ideals, when divorced from even a modicum of feeling for their original source, can be converted into a mask for meanness and mendacity.

Setting himself up as Ivan's intellectual opponent, Rakitin declares that "humanity will find in itself the power to live for virtue even without believing in immortality. It will find in it love for freedom, for equality, for fraternity." But Rakitin is incapable of imagining that anyone can truly "live for virtue" or act except from the most shamelessly selfish motives (14: 71). Dostoevsky uses Rakitin's disabused perspective as a foil to contrast the gross materialism of his "progressive" point of view with the actual human and moral complexity of the situation in which his characters have become embroiled.

—————■—————

Books 3 and 4 consist externally of a round of visits that Alyosha makes to various personages. This device allows Dostoevsky to develop more fully such characters as Grushenka, Katerina, and Snegiryov, who have been seen so far only in the distorted and partial images provided by the furious exchanges between Dimitry and his father. With Alyosha as the pivot of these sections, Dostoevsky frames the multiplicity of events, with their abundant displays of human folly, passion, and suffering, within the overarching shadow of the monastery and the impending death of Zosima.

We are first introduced to the history of Smerdyakov, who may, according to rumor, be the illegitimate son of Feodor. His mother was "stinking Lizaveta," who roamed the town as a "holy fool" and was treated kindly in accordance with Russian religious tradition. She gave birth to Smerdyakov in the garden of the Karamazov dwelling, and her choice of this locale was taken as an indirect suggestion of Feodor's paternity. The question of how Lizaveta managed, in her condition, to climb over the "high, strong fence" (14: 92) to get into the garden is referred to twice in the crucial scene on the night of the murder of Feodor, and although it is shrugged off by the narrator, the suggestion of an "uncanny" dimension nonetheless imparts a symbolic overtone to this detail.

This question, along with naturalistic details of the Karamazov dwelling, accompanies the presentation of Feodor's relation with his servant Grigory, who is intensely religious in a fanatic and semiliterate peasant fashion; and this attachment offers the first dramatic analogue for the central thematic conflict between reason and faith. Dostoevsky's aim is to suggest the moral-psychological difficulty of a totally amoral reason to sustain itself, not only on the level of Ivan's sophisticated ratiocinations, but even on the lowest and most primitive plane of the subconscious psyche. "Corrupt and often cruel in his lust, like some noxious insect, Feodor Pavlovich was sometimes, in moments of drunkenness, overcome by superstitious terror and a moral convulsion which almost, so to speak, physically shook his soul." In such moments, "he could not have explained the extraordinary craving for someone faithful and devoted, which sometimes unaccountably came upon him all in a moment" (14: 86). The old scoundrel, relying on the solace of Grigory's slavishly faithful presence, makes an irrational leap of faith in his loyalty and devotion. The relation between the two mimics, in a semiparodistic fashion, the challenge that all the characters are called upon to confront.

These sections are followed by Alyosha's encounter with Dimitry in three memorable chapters of feverish monologue. Dostoevsky here poetically elevates both sides of Dimitry's personality—an unbridled nature and dissolute life with a lurking sense of guilt at having given free rein to his sensuality and his rages—to a mythical stature. The snatches of poetry that he quotes from Nekrasov, Goethe, and Schiller interweave with his feverish narrative and constantly expand and amplify its range. The irresistible drive of his passions, as well as the deep disgust at his own degradation, now rise above the purely private and the personal; they become the struggle of humankind from the earliest ages to sublimate and purify its animal lusts and instincts. Dimitry sees himself in the guise of "the naked troglodyte" of Schiller's "The Eleusinian Feast," who appears, in the eyes of the Olympian goddess Ceres, as living in a state of hideous savagery:

> From the fields and from the vineyards
> Came no fruit to deck the feasts,
> Only flesh of blood-stained victims
> Smoldered in the altar-fires,
> And wher'er the grieving goddess
> Turns her melancholy gaze,
> Sunk in vilest degradation
> Man his loathsomeness displays. (14: 98)

The forces at work in him are those of natural man, who can all too easily become a slave to his instincts and his passions. But Dimitry has an obscure sense of nature as God's handiwork, which cannot be totally evil, and he feels in his own uncontrollable exuberance some of the overflowing joy that Schiller called "the soul of all creation." Even though Dimitry is incapable of curbing his elemental sensuality, unlike his shameless father, who glories in his depravity, Dimitry longs for some alteration *within* his own nature that will enable him to attain self-respect. His longing and his dilemma are summed up by Schiller again:

> Would he purge his soul from vileness
> And attain to light and worth,
> He must turn and cling forever
> To his ancient mother Earth.

29. A page from the manuscript of *The Brothers Karamazov*

"But the difficulty is," Dimitry exclaims piteously, "how am I to cling forever to Mother Earth. . . . I don't cleave to her bosom. . . . I go on and I don't know whether I'm going to shame or to light and joy." Varying the imagery as the passage continues, and turning from Schiller's Hellenism to Christianity and the Bible, Dimitry rises to heights of inspired eloquence in the famous passage on humankind's disquieting capacity to harbor both the ideal of the Madonna and the ideal of Sodom in its breast. "Beauty is a terrible thing. . . . Here all the boundaries meet and all contradictions exist side by side. . . . The awful thing is that beauty is mysterious as well as terrible. God and the devil are fighting there and the battlefield is the heart of man" (14: 100).

It is against this vast cultural-historical background, and the eternal struggle of humankind with the contradictions of its own nature, that the story of Dimitry's involvement with Katerina unfolds. Only when he is seen as this sort of Antaeus, irrevocably bound to the earth, can the calamity of their engagement be rightly understood. Dimitry had set out to seduce Katerina solely out of wounded vanity at her contemptuous indifference. The very means he chose to bend her to his will, offering to save her father from disgrace as the price of her surrender, was a profound insult; his refusal to take advantage of her when she complied was an even deadlier blow to her pride and gave him the psychological advantage in their relations. Katerina's only weapon in this struggle of wills was a magnanimity that, in constantly reminding Dimitry of his moral inferiority, would allow her to maintain the upper hand. Life has thus become intolerable for Dimitry under the burden of Katerina's "gratitude," which at the same time deprives him of any cause for grievance.

— ∎ —

Attention shifts to Smerdyakov in the next four chapters, this haunting and enigmatic character who inspires pity and repulsion at the same time. Smerdyakov had been sadistic and blasphemously scornful of religion even in childhood, someone completely devoid of any natural feeling of gratitude or obligation. These personal traits are ideologically transposed in the discussion that he carries on with Feodor, Ivan, and Grigory. Here he is revealed as another of the "rationalists" who people the book; and like Feodor's obscene jests and scoffing sacrileges, Smerdyakov's "rationalism" is another caricature, in the form of crafty logical sophistry, of Ivan's tortured moral ratiocinations. Debating the heroism of Foma Danilov, the Russian soldier who had been tortured and put to death by Muslim enemies for refusing to renounce his Christian faith, Smerdyakov argues that the heroic martyr had really been a fool. The mere thought of renouncing Christianity to save his life would have immediately separated him from God and Christ, and he would thus not have committed any sin as a Christian. Weakness of faith is in any case the most ordinary and venial kind of sin, because nobody any longer can command nature to perform such miracles as moving mountains—except perhaps, as he concedes, much to the delight of Feodor, one or two hermits in the desert. And do not the Scriptures, Smerdyakov asks triumphantly, promise such powers to *all* those who have faith?

His arguments are those of a petty and calculating nature, which seeks to rationalize its own inclinations for treachery and uses "reason" to undermine and dissolve any firm moral commitment. At the same time, though, Smerdyakov is enough of a credulous Russian peasant to believe in the wonder-working powers of one or two hermits in the desert. The importance of this point is stressed when Feodor asks Alyosha, "That's the Russian faith all over, isn't it?" and Alyosha agrees, "that's purely Russian" (14: 120–121). Smerdyakov's casuistry cannot entirely destroy his belief in the sanctity of those two hermits.

Smerdyakov serves as Ivan's alter ego in the same fashion as Svidrigailov had done for Raskolnikov; he carries Ivan's theories to their logical and repugnant extreme, and exhibits their distorted and dangerous refraction in a more uncouth and less high-minded nature. But Smerdyakov is also meant to convey more than mere thematic extrapolation. For he is a well-marked social type— the peasant who has been uprooted from his community and his group values, who has acquired a smattering of urban culture and manners, and who feels immeasurably superior to his benighted fellow peasants and resentful at his inferior social status. It is among such peasants, Dostoevsky is suggesting, that the destruction of the Christian faith by the "rationalism" of the Ivans is most likely to be greeted with admiration and to have the most explosive consequences.

Indeed, he evokes such possibilities in Aesopian imagery when his fictional narrator compares Smerdyakov with a type of peasant "contemplative" depicted in a painting by I. N. Kramskoy. "There is a forest in winter, and on a roadway through the forest, in absolute solitude, stands a wandering peasant in a torn caftan and bark shoes." He is not thinking but brooding inwardly, "contemplating." If asked about what was passing through his mind, he would not be able to reply; but "probably he had hidden within himself the impression which had dominated him during the period of contemplation." And then he "may suddenly . . . abandon everything and go off to Jerusalem on a pilgrimage for his soul's salvation, or perhaps he will suddenly set fire to his native village, and perhaps do both" (another instance of the "broad" Russian nature) (14: 116–117).

Every contemporary reader would know that such a "contemplative" contained a threat of revolution, or at least of a *jacquerie,* and this suggestion is reinforced a few pages later in the conversation about Smerdyakov between Feodor and Ivan. Noting that the lackey is enthralled by Ivan, his father asks, "What have you done to fascinate him?" Ivan answers, "Nothing whatsoever," but then adds, "He's a lackey and a mean soul. A prime candidate, however, when the time comes."[5] From the context, it is understood that this means "a prime candidate" for some sort of uprising, though Ivan also adds, "There will be others and better ones. . . . His kind comes first, and better ones after." But it is also possible, he continues, that "the rocket will go off and fizzle out, perhaps. The peasants are not very fond of listening to these soup makers, so far" (14: 22). (Smerdyakov had been sent to Petersburg to learn cooking, and his speciality was soup.) Elsewhere, Ivan directly calls Smerdyakov "raw material for revolution," thereby providing a distinct social-political subtext to their relation.

Just as Smerdyakov, in ridiculing Danilov, is shown as advocating a betrayal of moral principle, so we see Ivan in the next scene also justifying such a betrayal, though with much less complacency. The discussion with Smerdyakov ends when Dimitry, frantically in search of Grushenka, suddenly invades the room in which the three—Feodor, Ivan, and Grigory—have been talking. Flinging his father to the floor, Dimitry "kick[s] him two or three times with his heel in the face." Ivan wrestles Dimitry away, helped by Alyosha, and later remarks that "if I hadn't pulled him away, perhaps he'd have murdered him."

---

[5] The "prime candidate" here (Garnett-Matlaw translation) renders *peredovoe myaso* in the Russian text, which Victor Terras translates literally as "progressive flesh" in his indispensable, almost line-by-line commentary on *The Brothers Karamazov.* Terras also offers "cannonfodder of progress" as an alternative. The adjective *peredovoe* (progressive) is what gives the phrase a specific social-political meaning. See Victor Terras, *A Karamazov Companion* (Madison, WI, 1984), 181.

Alyosha exclaims: "God forbid!" To which Ivan replies, "with a malignant grimace, 'One viper will devour the other. And serves both of them right, too.'" Ivan declares that, although he would always act to defend the father he hates, "in my wishes I reserve myself full latitude in this case" (14: 128, 129, 132). He instinctively behaved according to the accepted moral code, but nothing in his thoughts ("wishes") would cause him to oppose such a murder; his moral sensibility and his external behavior are thus totally at odds. This scission in his personality will deepen and intensify as the book proceeds, and his statement about "the vipers" will come back to haunt him.

■

The scene between Katerina and Grushenka in the next chapter echoes Katerina's relations with Dimitry. Just as with him, she tries to gain control over Grushenka with her condescending "magnanimity." But she is herself humiliated in the presence of Alyosha by Grushenka's refusal to be dominated. Grushenka's turning of the tables nakedly reveals the egoistic roots of Katerina's "kindness" and "generosity"; these are merely the means she uses to attain moral-psychological mastery over others.

In Book 4, Dostoevsky keeps the spotlight focused on Katerina and devotes another chapter to her—"Laceration in the Drawing Room"—in which the supremely intelligent Ivan analyzes her behavior with exemplary acuity, and explains why she is incapable of any but a "lacerated" love. "You need [Dimitry] so as to contemplate continually your heroic fidelity and to reproach him for infidelity. And it all comes from your pride. Oh, there's a great deal of humiliation and self-abasement about it, but it all comes from pride" (14: 175). Ivan's insight springs from a thematically relevant source since the character traits of both are fundamentally the same: Ivan has only to look into himself to understand the motives of his tormentress.

The parallels between the two are an example of Dostoevsky's carefully wrought thematic texture. All the attitudes exhibited by Katerina vis-à-vis the other characters are the exact replica, on the moral-psychological level, of Ivan's ideological dilemma. Katerina thus expands and rounds out the human qualities of Ivan's character, presented mainly in the transposed form of theological argument and poetic symbol. Ivan's intellectual arrogance and spiritual egoism will prevent him from surrendering to the mystery of faith and the reality of God's love; and Katerina's inability to love anyone but herself exhibits the same qualities in terms that are social and personal; her "painful brooding" will only serve to reinforce and strengthen the rampant egoism concealed under the elegant surface of her civilized manners. Just as Katerina needs Dimitry's betrayals to reinforce her own virtue, so Ivan tortures himself with the horrors of the sufferings of the innocent to nourish the pride of his own rejection of God's world and its inhabitants. When Katerina hysterically cries in a frenzy, "I will be a god to whom [Dimitry] can pray" (14: 172), she reveals the deepest symbolic meaning of Ivan's Legend.

Another important thematic motif in Book 4 is seen in the chapter devoted to Zosima's enemy, the old ascetic Father Ferapont. His unbalanced fanaticism allowed Dostoevsky to dissociate himself from the harsher and more repellent forms of Russian asceticism, and to stress, on the contrary, the humane and enlightened features of Zosima's Christianity, which did not fear to open itself to the influences of the modern world. Ferapont is more than a caricatural figure intended to bring Zosima's virtues into higher relief; he also takes on a symbolic importance as part of the great theme of reason and faith. For the ascetic, in his own fashion, is also a literalist of the supernatural like Feodor. There is a concealed "rationalism" in his reduction of spiritual life to the observance of external rules about fasting and in the naïvely materialistic fashion in which, concretizing the mysteries of faith, he claims to see devils with his own eyes and to have killed one by catching its tail in a door. For both the cynically Voltairian Feodor and the superstitiously pious Ferapont, religious faith depends on such physical evidence of its reality; and they are thus thematically united in this manner despite their evident divergences otherwise. Nor should one overlook Ferapont's fierce pride—he is convinced that Christ will come to carry him away like the Prophet Elijah—a claim that again is counterpointed against Zosima's profound meekness and humility. The treatment of Ferapont illustrates the subtlety and delicacy of Dostoevsky's handling of his theme of faith and the profundity of his intuition, rivaling that of Kierkegaard, of its total irrationality and subjectivity.

———■———

Two chapters of Book 4 are devoted to the Snegiryovs, a family that, after the disappearance of the monastery world from the novel upon the death of Father Zosima, will provide Dostoevsky with his major contrast to the world of the Karamazovs. The Snegiryov family is familiar to all readers of Dostoevsky. They are the equivalent of the Marmeladovs in *Crime and Punishment* and of all the insulted and injured he had depicted since the beginning of his literary career. Captain Snegiryov is a buffoon type like Feodor, but one whose masochistic ironies conceal a deeply wounded sensibility that has not turned resentful or revengeful. Far from having neglected his family, the cashiered captain has done his best, under impossible conditions, to provide them with love and care. His little son Ilyusha, who bites Alyosha's finger to revenge his father's public humiliation by Dimitry, also sturdily defends his father against the insults of his jeering classmates, and even Ilyusha's sister Varvara—a "progressive" student with "rational" ideas, home from her Petersburg studies—sacrifices herself unselfishly, if resentfully, to care for her hapless kinfolk.

The adolescent Ilyusha will later, along with his classmates, allow Dostoevsky to fulfill his long-cherished desire to depict the relation between a charismatic Christian figure and a group of children. The scene in which Alyosha visits the miserable hovel of the Snegiryovs, entitled "Laceration in the Cottage," is placed immediately after Katerina Ivanovna's "Laceration in the Drawing-Room." The laceration in the drawing room is the result of self-will and pride, which perverts suffering into an instrument of domination; the laceration in the cottage, when the captain hysterically tramples on the badly needed money offered by Alyosha, is a pathetic effort to maintain a last, remaining shred of self-respect and to justify Ilyusha's desperate faith in his father's honor and dignity.

By the time he completed Book 4, Dostoevsky had presented all his characters, clearly indicated the future course of the main plot action, and raised his primary ideological issue of reason and faith in a fascinating variety of scenes and characters. In Books 5, 6, and 7, this theme comes to the foreground and is treated directly in some of the greatest pages in the history of the novel.

CHAPTER 59

The Brothers Karamazov: Books 5–6

The two set pieces of Book 5, Ivan's "rebellion" and the Legend of the Grand Inquisitor, reach ideological heights for which there are few equals. In the nineteenth century one can think only perhaps of Balzac's *Seraphita* and *Louis Lambert*, George Sand's *Spiridion*, or possibly Flaubert's *La tentation de Saint Antoine*. These inspired pages take their place in a Western literary tradition that begins with Aeschylus's *Prometheus Bound* and the book of Job. They also continue the Romantic titanism of the first half of the nineteenth century, represented by such writers as Goethe, Leopardi, Byron, and Shelley. The Czech critic Vaclav Cerny, in a penetrating book, saw Dostoevsky (along with Nietzsche) as the culmination of this Romantic tradition of protest against God on behalf of a suffering humanity.[1]

Formally, the three chapters devoted to Ivan illustrate again that sudden vertical expansion of a character that enlarges his symbolic status and poetic power. Now the coldly conceptual Ivan is consumed by the same passionate thirst for life as Dimitry. Alyosha tells him affectionately during their conversation in the tavern, "You are just a young and fresh nice boy, green in fact!" "It's a feature of the Karamazovs, it's true," Ivan replies, "that thirst for life regardless of everything, you have it no doubt too, but why is it base?" Of course it can become so, as in old Feodor or Dimitry's escapades, but it can be a life-sustaining force as well. As Ivan acknowledges, "even if I . . . lost faith in the order of things, were convinced in fact that everything is a disorderly, damnable and perhaps devil-ridden chaos, if I were struck by every horror of man's disillusionment—still I would want to live, and, having once tasted of the cup, I would not turn away from it till I had drained it." This loss of faith "in the order of things" is exactly what torments Ivan, but his primordial love for life is powerful enough to counteract the dispiriting conclusions of his reason: "I have a longing for life, and I go on living in spite of logic" (14: 209).

Enumerating all the endearments that still link him to life, he lists not only nature ("I love the sticky little leaves as they open in spring, I love the blue sky")

[1] Vaclav Cerny, *Essai sur le titanisme dans la poésie romantique occidentale entre 1815 et 1850* (Prague, 1935).

867

but also "the previous graveyard" of European civilization, filled with the glories of the past, before which he "shall fall to the ground and kiss those stones and weep over them." Such thoughts and actions may be totally irrational, but "it's not a matter of intellect or logic, it's loving with one's insides, with one's guts." This capacity for an irrational love, whether of nature or the monuments of culture, is the first step toward an understanding of the meaning of life; for such understanding is possible only when the ego is taken beyond itself. To Ivan's question whether we should "love life more than the meaning of it," Alyosha replies: "Certainly, love it regardless of logic as you say, . . . and it's only then one can understand the meaning of it." But because Ivan's "logic" had already concluded that life has no meaning, he predicts that when "I am thirty . . . I shall begin to turn aside from the cup, even if I have not emptied it" (14: 209–210). Such words raise the specter of a suicide out of despair, but the emphasis on Ivan's youthfulness and his "longing for life" hold out hope of other possibilities.

This friendly encounter of the two brothers is placed in the foreground of Chapter 3, but the shadow of an archetypal murder lurks in the background and has already been suggested. Questioned about Dimitry's whereabouts, Smerdyakov had answered "superciliously": "How am I to know. . . . It's not as if I were his keeper." A few pages later, after learning about Ivan's imminent departure, Alyosha anxiously asks about the quarrel between Dimitry and their father: "How will it end?" And Ivan irritably snaps back, "What have I to do with it? Am I my brother Dimitry's keeper?" Then he suddenly smiles "bitterly": "Cain's answer to God about his murdered brother—wasn't it. Perhaps that's what you're thinking at this moment?" (14: 206, 211). Both Ivan and Smerdyakov, who echo each other's thoughts, are thus linked with the murder motif by this biblical reference, which also intimates their subterranean connection.

As the conversation between the two brothers continues, Ivan vehemently challenges Alyosha's devotion to Zosima's world of all-embracing forgiveness and overflowing, selfless love. Ivan is struggling inwardly against his own yearning to accept the very worldview he is attacking with such passion. He half admits to himself, "quite like a little gentle child," that he does not "want to corrupt you [Alyosha], or to turn you from your stronghold, perhaps I want to be healed by you," but this moment of reassuring tenderness is soon swept away (14: 215). Ivan introduces his famous distinction between "Euclidean" (earthly) and "non-Euclidean" (supernatural) understanding, insisting that, although he is perfectly willing to accept the existence of this non-Euclidean world (and hence of God), his Euclidean understanding refuses to reconcile itself to all the moral horrors of the world created by such a divinity.

Since Ivan does not believe in God as more than a hypothesis, his opinion on this point reflects the same ambiguity that marked his article on church jurisdiction. "As for me," he says, "I've long resolved not to think of whether man created God or God man." Such a question is "utterly inappropriate for a mind created with an idea of only three dimensions" (and hence Euclidean). Ivan remains neutral on this issue, though perfectly willing to accept all the sublime consequences that flow from postulating the existence of God. Paraphrasing the Gospel of Saint John, he declares, both with deep feeling and a touch of irony: "I believe in the underlying order and the meaning of life; I believe in the eternal harmony in which they say we shall one day be blended. I believe in the Word to Which the entire universe is striving, and Which Itself was 'with God,' and Which Itself is God, and so on, and so on, to infinity" (14: 214). But to profess these beliefs as more than hypotheses would mean possessing a faith that transcends reason—a faith that Ivan is not only unable but also morally unwilling to muster even if he could manage to do so. What he desires is that such ecstatic expectations should justify themselves before the bar of his Euclidean understanding, of his earthly reason—and this, obviously, they cannot do.

■

The dialogue between Ivan and Alyosha serves as a prelude to the chapter "Rebellion," an attack on God and the world he created so powerful that many critics have doubted whether the book as a whole succeeds in overcoming its subversive impact. Dostoevsky made some effort, however, to moderate the disquieting effects of his deeply moving jeremiad even before composing its "refutation" in Book 6. For Ivan begins by exhibiting his emotional incapacity to experience the fundamental act of Christian fellow-feeling, that of loving one's neighbor. "I could never understand," he says, "how one could love one's neighbors . . . though one might love them at a distance." Citing an extreme and repulsive example of self-sacrificial Christian love from Flaubert's *La légende de Saint Julien l'hospitalier* (the embrace by the saint of a frozen beggar with some loathsome disease), Ivan sees it only as "a love imposed by duty, as a penance," similar to Katerina's "love" for Dimitry. It is an act accomplished "from the laceration of falsity" rather than from a sincerely spontaneous response to human suffering (14: 215–216). For Ivan, the precepts of Christianity thus become transformed into a duty and obligation contrary to human nature. Ivan's feverishly overstrained compassion for humanity that follows is thus undermined by the suspicion that he may also be experiencing only a "laceration of falsity."

The details of Ivan's searing indictment of God unroll a catalogue of atrocities that Dostoevsky drew from many sources—court cases, barbarities reported about the Russo-Turkish War, a pamphlet distributed by an aristocratic Christian sect describing the edifying conversion of a criminal in Geneva just before his execution—which did not for a moment stop his being put to death. Ivan dwells particularly on the torture inflicted on helpless and innocent children, and does so with a morbid delectation that makes Alyosha distinctly uneasy;

there are indications that Ivan's fascination with human evil has begun to unbalance his mental equilibrium (he speaks "as though in delirium"). Humanity has become for Ivan nothing but a creator of destruction and darkness, an image not of God but of the devil. "I think if the devil doesn't exist," he tells Alyosha, "and therefore was created by man, he has created him in his own image and likeness" (14: 215–218).

It is the existence of all this suffering and misery in the world that Ivan finds emotionally unendurable and intellectually incomprehensible. At the very least, sinful adults might be made to pay a price. But how is one to accept the idea of original sin—the idea that children must suffer for the sins of their fathers? For Ivan, "such a truth . . . is incomprehensible for the heart of man here on earth. The innocent must not suffer for another's sins, and especially such innocents!" Dostoevsky even allows Ivan to reject in advance the position from which he will be opposed. "Do you understand why this infamy must be permitted?" he shouts at Alyosha. "Without it, I am told, man could not have existed on earth for he could not have known good and evil. Why should he have known that diabolical good and evil when it costs so much?" (14: 218–220). The force of Ivan's argument is adroitly countered by the adjective "diabolical," which reveals the implicitly Manichean premise of his indignation, his conviction that humans can use freedom *only* to accomplish evil.

Ivan's tortured cogitations reject the very idea of "a universal harmony" in the future as something monstrous and unjust. With bitter irony, he declares that he can well envisage how glorious it would be "when the mother embraces the fiend who threw her child to the dogs, and all three cry aloud with tears, 'Thou art just, O Lord.'" He can understand this sublime apotheosis, but he cannot accept it: "It's not worth the tears of that one tortured child who . . . prayed in the stinking outhouse, with its unexpiated tears, to 'dear, kind God!'" Nobody, Ivan argues, has the right to forgive her torturer. "I don't want harmony. From love for humanity, I don't want it. I would rather be left with unavenged suffering . . . *even if I were wrong*" (14: 223). The intensity of Ivan's conflict between his desire for "rational" retributive justice, on the one hand, and the sublimity of universal forgiveness, on the other, is revealed by Dostoevsky's underlining. Nonetheless, Ivan is unyielding in his refusal, which culminates in his famous declaration: "And so I hasten to give back my entrance ticket, and if I am an honest man I must give it back as soon as possible. . . . It's not God that I don't accept, Alyosha, only I most respectfully return Him my ticket" (the ticket to a world of non-Euclidean eternal harmony that would redeem all suffering in the Euclidean realm) (14: 223).

Ivan has set out to unsettle Alyosha's faith, and he succeeds momentarily. When he asks Alyosha whether a general who had unleashed his dogs on a peasant boy should be shot "for the satisfaction of our moral feelings," Alyosha cannot help replying, "To be shot!" Delighted at this reply, Ivan exclaims, "Bravo! . . . so there is a little devil sitting in your heart, Alyosha Karamazov!" (to agree with Ivan is to surrender to the temptation of the devil) (14: 221). Ivan then challenges Alyosha to answer whether he would consent to found the fabric of human destiny—"that would bring future happiness to mankind"—on the unavenged torture of an innocent child. Alyosha again replies in the negative, but then, recovering himself, he recalls that the fabric of human destiny (at least in their moral universe) is founded on another principle—that of *self*-sacrificial Christian love. In response to Ivan's other question—whether there is "in the whole world a being who would have the right to forgive and could forgive" the terrible tapestry of human suffering he has just unrolled—Alyosha replies with a passionate affirmation. "But there is a Being and He can forgive everything, all *and for all*, because He gave His innocent blood for all and everything . . . and on Him is built the edifice, and it is to Him they cry aloud, 'Thou are just, O Lord, for Thy ways are revealed'" (14: 223–224).

These pages are among the most justly famous in all of Dostoevsky's work, and they reveal once again his boldness in giving the most powerful expression to the very attitudes he was attempting to combat. Aside from Alyosha's final invocation of Christ, there has been no attempt up to this point to counter Ivan's implacable attack on God's world. Nor would any such effort have been consistent with Dostoevsky's artistic strategy. The ideas he opposed are invariably combated by portraying their effects on the lives of his characters, not by attempting to demonstrate their lack of theoretical persuasiveness or rational coherence. Ivan's sense of despair and inner desolation, his disabused cynicism about his own youthful love of life, the contempt for mankind that has corrupted his feelings despite all his supposed "love for humanity"—all these are meant to illuminate indirectly the hopelessly self-destructive nature of his convictions. Alyosha's sudden appeal to the image of the God-man lights up in a flash the narrowness and vindictiveness of Ivan's "love of humanity." His insistence on justice—and hence on punishment and retribution—glaringly contrasts with Christ's gospel of all-reconciling and all-forgiving love and the hope of infinite mercy for the sinner who repents.

Numerous commentators have understandably stressed the moving pathos of Ivan's humanitarianism; it has even been suggested, as Blake said of Milton, that Dostoevsky was really of the devil's party and could not suppress his emotional agreement with Ivan. There is no question that Dostoevsky poured into these passages all his own anguish over the abominations he was recording. However, Ivan represents, on the highest level of intellectual and moral sensibility, the supreme and most poignant dramatization of the conflict between reason and faith at the heart of the book, and it would have been inconsistent with his thematic aim to have softened or weakened his utterances. Faith, as Dostoevsky wishes it to be felt in *The Brothers Karamazov*, must be totally pure, a commitment supported by nothing except a devotion to the image and example of Christ, and the opposing arguments of reason must thus be given at their fullest strength.

——■——

What provides Ivan's overwhelming monologue with its still undiminished power is the relentless rejection of God's world in the name of the very morality of love and compassion that Christ himself had brought to it. Ivan is expressing what Dostoevsky saw as the deepest challenge of the Populist mentality to a genuine acceptance of the Christian faith of the Russian people. To combat this challenge, Alyosha had called the image of Christ to his aid, the true source of Ivan's own morality. He accuses his brother of having "forgotten" Christ, and in reply Ivan narrates a prose poem of his own composition, the renowned Legend of the Grand Inquisitor. A complex narrative, it encompasses three levels: that of Dostoevsky the author, that of the fictional narrator, who vanishes during Ivan's majestic monologue, and that of Ivan himself, the presumed creator, whose moral-social psychology it symbolically dramatizes in all the tangle of its oppositions.

As a preface, the erudite Ivan indulges in a brief survey of the universal popularity of similar poems and plays in the past, when "it was customary . . . to bring down heavenly powers on earth." Most important of all was a Byzantine apocryphal tale, "The Wanderings of Our Lady in Hell," which depicts the Mother of God being led through hell by the archangel Michael. Horrified by the suffering of the damned, she falls before God "and begs for mercy for all in Hell . . . indiscriminately." God points to the crucified Christ and asks how "His tormentors" can be forgiven, but he relents when Our Lady summons "all the saints, all the martyrs, all the angels and archangels" to join her in pleading for mercy. When God finally agrees to "a respite of suffering" for those in hell every year from Good Friday until Trinity Day (eight weeks after Easter), the sinners chant, "Thou art just, O Lord, in this judgment" (14: 224–225).

Ivan's poem is placed in sixteenth-century Spain, where Christ appears again. Humankind awaited him with "greater faith" than ever because "it is fifteen centuries since man had ceased to see signs from Heaven." It is into a world filled with such yearning and such faith that Ivan imagines Christ returning—to southern Spain, in the darkest days of the Inquisition. Ivan paints the scene in a few suggestive strokes, calling to his aid both poetry and the New Testament. The reader is taken to Seville the day after a hundred heretics have been burned in a magnificent auto-da-fé. At this juncture, "Christ suddenly appears softly, unobserved, and yet, strange to say, everyone recognized Him. . . . The sun of love burns in His heart. Light, Enlightenment, and Power shine from His eyes, and their radiance, shed on the people, stirs their hearts with responsive love."

Out of the fullness of his overflowing love, Christ brings back the sight of a blind man and raises a little girl from the dead on the steps of the cathedral; "the crowd weeps and kisses the earth" (14: 226–227).

The Grand Inquisitor orders Christ arrested, and comes to the prison that night. Throughout their encounter, Christ does not utter a word; and his mute presence serves as a goad to the conscience of the Grand Inquisitor, who, while pretending to carry out Christ's wishes on earth, knows that he is doing the opposite. The monologue of the Inquisitor, swinging between his accusations against Christ and self-exculpation, betrays the tension gnawing at his conscience, a conscience that has led him, out of pity for the suffering of a weak and unhappy humanity, to "correct" Christ's work by relieving humankind of the source of its misery: the burden of free will. Ivan had refused to accept God's world in the previous chapter, and now he indicates how he would reconstruct it according to more "humane" specifications.

His narrative is a free variation of the Gospel version of the temptations of Christ included in Saints Mark, Matthew, and Luke. According to the sacred text, Christ spent forty days in the desert being tempted by Satan before embarking on his mission to humanity. Like Milton in *Paradise Regained*, Ivan elaborates this account into a magnificent historiosophical panorama of the future course of human history, which he sees as prefigured in this temptation episode of the New Testament. Indeed, the Grand Inquisitor is certainly speaking for Dostoevsky when he rapturously praises the three questions put to Christ in the desert by "the wise and dread spirit, the spirit of self-destruction and nonexistence." He is certain that these questions must be the product not of "the fleeting human intelligence . . . but [of] the absolute and eternal," because the mind of man could not possibly have invented by itself the grandeur of this prophetic vision (14: 229–230).

Why, Christ is asked, had he come to man "with empty hands, with some promise of freedom," when he could have performed the miracle of turning "these stones in this parched and barren wilderness" into bread? "Turn them into bread," the devil had advised in the first temptation, "and mankind will run after Thee like a flock, grateful and obedient." Christ refused because "Thou would not deprive man of freedom," but the Grand Inquisitor, prophesying the victory of what, from the terminology, can only be Socialism, foresees that "ages will pass, and humanity will proclaim by the lips of their sages that there is no crime, and no sin, there is only hunger." And then, "for the sake of that earthly bread . . . all will follow him, crying: 'Who can compare with that beast? He has given us fire from heaven!'" (a citation that combines the book of Revelation with the myth of Prometheus) (14: 230).

As we know from the *Diary*, Dostoevsky believed in the possibility of Roman Catholicism joining forces with the Socialists to lead the impending revolution that would destroy the West. Both, in his eyes, had surrendered to the first temptation of Christ by subordinating his message—freedom of conscience—to earthly aims and ambitions, and were thus united in his imagination. "The spirit of the earth" will thus achieve a temporary victory because humanity will lay its disastrous freedom at their feet. For "freedom and bread enough for all are inconceivable together, for never, never will they be able to share between them." The moral principle of "sharing" cannot originate from any source other than the true Christ, who calls for the free sacrifice for others out of love; and humankind will finally be forced to return to him as the sole fount of morality. In this instance, however, it will return to a false Christ, the Roman Catholic one of the Grand Inquisitor, who believes that "nothing has ever been more insupportable for a man and human society than freedom," and that humanity "can never be free, for it is weak, vicious, worthless, and rebellious" (14: 230–231).

Despite this disparaging view of human nature, Ivan's Grand Inquisitor makes the same appeal to pity that Ivan made in the chapter "Rebellion." He acknowledges that although the doctrine of "the bread of Heaven," the freedom of human conscience, may appeal to thousands, millions more "will not have the strength to forgo the earthly bread for the heavenly"; and it is for these millions, "who are weak, but love," that the Grand Inquisitor is speaking (14: 231). This "care," however, will not be accepted unless offered in the name of the *true* Christ preaching freedom and love while his ideal is being distorted and betrayed.

The Grand Inquisitor now turns from the first temptation to the more properly religious issue of whether humanity possesses the moral strength to support the freedom proclaimed by Christ. For the Grand Inquisitor is willing to agree with Christ—the only time he does so!—"that if someone gains possession of [humankind's] conscience—Oh! then [it] will cast away Thy bread and follow after him who has ensnared [its] conscience. In that Thou wast right. For the secret of man's being is not only to live but to have something to live for." In other words, man does not live by bread alone; but Christ refused to take command over the conscience of humanity, thus denying it the tranquility of certitude and obedience. "Didst Thou forget that man prefers peace, and even death, to freedom of choice in the knowledge of good and evil?" Far from providing a new and immutable guide for human conscience, Christ, the Grand Inquisitor charges, only increases its plight. "Nothing is more seductive for man than his freedom of conscience, but nothing is a greater source of suffering. . . . In place of the rigid ancient law, man must hereafter with free heart decide for himself what is good and what evil, having only Thy image before him as a guide" (14: 232).

To guarantee such freedom, Christ had rejected the second temptation, that of offering proof of his divinity. And finally, he had turned away from the third temptation, that of assuming power over "all the kingdoms of the earth," not wishing like the Grand Inquisitor to enforce faith with temporal power. Christ had thus repudiated what the Grand Inquisitor declares to be "the three powers . . . able to conquer and to hold captive forever the conscience of the impotent rebels for their own happiness—these forces are miracle, mystery, and authority" (14: 232).

No segment of the Legend poses a knottier problem or is more difficult to unravel than this charge leveled against Christ. Interpreters of the stature of Berdyaev have taken it as Dostoevsky's own definitive declaration—made *a contrario* through Ivan—that mankind's freedom of conscience, the freedom defended by Christ in the Legend, is totally incompatible with magic, mystery, and authority. Such a reading, however, can hardly be reconciled with the description earlier given of the reappearance of Christ. As Roger Cox has pointed out, when the Grand Inquisitor accuses Christ of having abandoned miracle, mystery, and authority, "the Inquisitor's most characteristic language and imagery come directly from the Book of Revelation, where it is associated with the 'false prophet.'"[2] We should not neglect this earlier image in endeavoring to grasp Dostoevsky's thematic aim.

Earlier, when Alyosha had submitted himself to the *starets* Zosima, the narrator warns "that this instrument . . . may be a two-edged weapon. . . . [I]t may lead some not to humility and complete self-control but to the most Satanic pride, that is, to bondage and not freedom" (14: 27). The forces of legitimate miracle, mystery, and authority are thus open to perversion, as we see in the case of the Grand Inquisitor, but the text clearly indicates that they are far from having been repudiated by Christ in their authentic manifestation. For him, however, they derive their legitimate power only from a genuinely unconditional faith, only in that interpenetration of the earthly and the heavenly proclaimed by Zosima. When the Grand Inquisitor berates Christ for having abandoned such powerful instruments of control, the imperious prelate is speaking of them only as a means of coercion and domination. But they can exercise their influence by means of "responsive love," and Dostoevsky hardly desired them to be viewed only through the distorted lens that the Grand Inquisitor provides. As Cox cogently puts it, the Grand Inquisitor has debased the authentic forms of miracle, mystery, and authority into magic, mystification, and tyranny.

Under the challenge of Christ's silent gaze, the Inquisitor confesses the secret he has not yet openly declared. "We are not with Thee, but with *him*—that is our mystery." The Roman Church had treacherously accepted the third temptation of the devil in Christ's name and had "accomplished all that man seeks on earth—someone to worship, someone to keep his conscience, and some means of uniting all in one unanimous and harmonious ant-heap." (The word "ant-heap" is

[2] Roger L. Cox, *Between Earth and Heaven* (New York, 1969), 194.

frequently used by Dostoevsky to characterize a social order where no free will exists.) Having taken up the sword of the Caesars, the Inquisitor is certain that "we [the Roman Church] shall triumph and be Caesars, and then we shall plan the universal happiness of man." But this ultimate state will not be achieved before the interregnum of "the ages . . . yet to come of the confusion of free thought, of their science and cannibalism," when humans will try to construct the Tower of Babel solely on the basis of reason and science and will end in devouring each other in a Darwinian struggle for life (14: 234–235).

By this time, even those who had initially served the true Christ ("the elect") will have "grown weary of waiting for Thee," and "they will transfer the powers of their spirit and the warmth of their heart to the other camp, and end by raising their *free* banner against Thee." The very banner of Christ himself now will be transformed into its delusory opposite. "Oh, we shall persuade them that they will become free only when they renounce their freedom to us and submit to us." Humankind will then be reduced to the level of children and will be given "the quiet humble happiness of weak creatures such as they are by nature." Even sin will be allowed to these will-less creatures, "because we love them, and the punishment for these sins we take upon ourselves." Every detail of their existence, including the most intimate sexual and family matters, "the most powerful secrets of their conscience," will be under the Grand Inquisitor's control.[3] Here is the earthly paradise of the Grand Inquisitor, the fraudulent facsimile of the freedom proclaimed by Christ. "Peacefully they will die, peacefully they will expire in Thy name, but beyond the grave they will find nothing but death." Immortality does not exist, but "for their happiness we shall entice them with the reward of heaven and eternity" (14: 235–236).

The Legend is Ivan's creation, and is therefore meant to objectify dramatically the struggle in his own consciousness between reason and faith. This struggle suddenly comes to the fore when the Grand Inquisitor reveals himself to be someone who has only reluctantly abandoned the true Christ, and who still feels the lofty beauty of the Christian faith and its image of humanity as free and morally responsible. "I too have been in the wilderness," he confesses to Christ, "I too was striving to stand among Thy elect. . . . But I awakened and would not serve madness." If Christ were to return again one day, he defiantly asserts, in the thunderclap of the Second Coming, then the Grand Inquisitor and his fellows could say, "pointing out to Thee the thousand of millions of happy children who have known no sin . . . 'Judge us if Thou canst and darest.'" He concludes

---

[3] No part of the Legend has been more influential and important than this prediction of what is the world of twentieth-century totalitarianism. Dostoevsky's nightmare vision of the surrender of inner freedom for untroubled security was also a predecessor of the literary genre of Dystopia, represented by such works as Evgeny Zamiatin's *We*, Aldous Huxley's *Brave New World*, and George Orwell's *1984*.

by declaring that he will order Christ to be burned at the stake as a heretic the following day "for coming to hinder us" (14: 236–237).

Alyosha now interjects, "Your poem is in praise of Jesus, not in blame of Him," and surely Alyosha's interpretation may be taken as Dostoevsky's own. To rebuke Christ for insisting on humanity's right to choose between good and evil solely according to the dictates of their hearts was in effect to praise him for protecting the very foundation of man's humanity as Dostoevsky conceived it. Ivan does not reply to this first exclamation of Alyosha's, but he responds when Alyosha heatedly affirms that the Grand Inquisitor and his Romish army of Jesuits represent "a simple lust for power, . . . something like a universal serfdom with them as masters." Refusing to accept such a reductive accusation, Ivan enlarges on the image of the Grand Inquisitor as a tragic figure, genuinely suffering because he "has wasted his whole life in the desert and yet could not shake off his incurable love for humanity" and is obligated to "lead men consciously to death and destruction and yet deceive them all the way . . . in the name of Him in whose ideal the old man had so fervently believed all his life long" (14: 237–239). The Grand Inquisitor is a grandiose extrapolation of his own inner conflict; and the tragic nature of the Inquisitor's dilemma—the tragedy of having accepted the morality of Christ the Son and of acting in his name while no longer believing in God the Father—is also a preparation for the dénouement of the Legend.

Ivan proposes the following conclusion to his narrative. The prisoner's unbroken muteness "weighed down" on his jailer, but "He suddenly approached the old man in silence and softly kissed him on his bloodless, aged lips." The Grand Inquisitor shuddered and opened the cell door. "'Go,' he said, 'and . . . come not at all, never, never.'" As for the now solitary Grand Inquisitor, Ivan says that "the kiss glows in his heart, but the old man adheres to his idea." Alyosha immediately recognizes this last sentence to be applicable to Ivan himself, torn between his sensitivity to the Christian ideal and his "idea" that "everything is lawful" once faith in God and immortality has been lost. To Alyosha's anguished question, "How will you live? . . . With such a hell in your heart and your head, how can you?" Ivan reasserts his former "rebellious" declaration: the "Karamazov baseness" will see him through until age thirty, and then he will dash the cup to the ground (14: 240).

At the end of their conversation, when Alyosha looks at him in silence, Ivan expresses sadness because "now I see that there is no place for me in your heart, my dear hermit." This sentiment motivates Alyosha to kiss Ivan on the lips, and he is then jokingly accused of "plagarism" by an Ivan "highly delighted" at this symbol-laden reenactment. Presented here in his most humanly appealing side, Ivan is shown as fully aware of the grief gnawing at his brother's heart at this moment. Dostoevsky, however, did not wish to end on such a sympathetic image of Ivan, who had succeeded in provoking Alyosha to approve of an act of revenge. And so the narrator introduces a subtly discordant note in the final paragraphs as Ivan walks away after directing his brother, "and now you go to the right and I to the left." Alyosha "notices that Ivan swayed as he walked and that the right shoulder looked lower than the left" (14: 241). Traditionally, the devil is associated with the left side, and because he limps when he walks, the left shoulder seems higher than the right. The narrator thus uses folk beliefs to associate Ivan with the dread spirit the latter had just evoked so approvingly in his Legend.

■

Ivan's rebellion and his Legend are framed between two encounters with Smerdyakov. He returns home to encounter the obsequiously insinuating but also vaguely sinister presence of his father's cook and manservant, and the subconscious expectation of meeting Smerdyakov plunges him, though he is not fully aware of this reason himself, into a state of intense depression. The relation between the two—only hinted at previously—is now developed more fully. Ivan had initially "taken an interest in Smerdyakov, and had even thought him very original." They discussed questions such as the literal accuracy and truthfulness of some of the statements in the Old Testament, and Smerdyakov had begun to see himself as Ivan's disciple. Indeed, when Smerdyakov was ridiculing the heroism of Foma Danilov in refusing to renounce his faith, Feodor had said to Ivan, "He's got this all up for your benefit. He wants you to praise him" (14: 118).

Ivan soon comes to feel an "aversion" to Smerdyakov because the lackey "began to betray a boundless vanity, and a wounded vanity," that Ivan finds intolerable. The irony of this observation is obvious: Smerdyakov's "vanity" is a parody of his admired model, who in the person of the Grand Inquisitor had imagined himself capable of "correcting" the work of God. Worst of all, from Ivan's point of view, is that Smerdyakov now acts as if they "had some kind of compact, some secret between them," unknown to everyone else, which created a bond (14: 242–243). Such a bond exists whether Ivan desired it or not because Smerdyakov has assimilated the amoral nihilism of Ivan's ideas, which had begun to ferment within a mind and heart lacking his own sensitivity to human suffering. The dialogue that ensues is portrayed on two levels—the exchange of words between them, accompanied by the dialogue of Ivan with himself. In this second dialogue, the loathing Ivan has come to feel for Smerdyakov is dominated by his subconscious sense that both are linked by a secret, subliminal compact—one that he resents but cannot resist or shake off. Ivan's clash of feelings about Smerdyakov dramatizes, on the moral-psychological level, the same conflict between reason and faith (the source of moral conscience for Dostoevsky) that forms the basis of Ivan's character.

Even though Ivan does not wish to speak to Smerdyakov, he finds himself involuntarily addressing Smerdyakov in a tone inviting conversation. Ivan behaves under a compulsion, almost a fascination, that can only arise from the tormenting paralysis resulting from his inner conflict. In the course of their exchange, Smerdyakov insinuates in veiled terms all the events that will leave the way clear, if Ivan goes to Chermashnaya, for Dimitry to invade the house again and carry out the threat to kill his father. As he listens, Ivan becomes incensed by Smerdyakov's allusive words, which seemingly provide purposeless information but in fact hint at the likelihood of murder. Almost throwing himself upon the servant in a paroxysm of rage, he then quietly announces instead that he will leave for Moscow the next day. Ivan's contradictory behavior has been foreshadowed by his words to Alyosha, after they both pulled Dimitry away from their bloodied father. "One viper will devour the other," he had said. "And serves both of them right, too." Nonetheless, while insisting to Alyosha that he would always defend his father, Ivan had also added: "But in my wishes I reserve myself full latitude in this case."

Ivan's "wishes" prove stronger than his asserted obedience to the moral code, and he decides to leave even after becoming aware that his absence might bring on the crime. The narrator reports objectively on the turmoil in Ivan's spirit that night, "fretted by all sorts of strange and almost surprising desires," such as wishing to go to the lodge and beat Smerdyakov. He could not explain why, "except perhaps that he loathed the lackey as one who had insulted him more gravely than anyone in the world." Smerdyakov's "insult" consisted in his perfectly justified assumption that Ivan had no deeply rooted objection to the murder of his loathsome father, though he himself refused to face up to this truth. That night, hearing his father stirring downstairs, Ivan went out on the staircase and listened "with a sort of strange curiosity, holding his breath while his heart throbbed," and he never forgot the memory of that brief span of time. "That 'action,' all his life afterward he called 'infamous,' and at the bottom of his heart, he thought of it as the basest action of his life" (14: 251). It was the moment when he decided to let the two vipers devour each other—or so he believed.

Ivan tells his father the next morning that he will go to Chermashnaya, as the old man had requested, to sell a copse for him. Feodor is delighted, "because you are a clever man," but Ivan avoids kissing him on departure (14: 253). This repeated designation echoes Ivan's remark to Alyosha that the Grand Inquisitor, after losing his faith in Christ, had joined "the clever people." As Ivan rolls through the countryside, he at first feels a sense of relief, but then recalls the lackey's parting words, whose implications he pretends not to understand. Changing his plans, Ivan travels to Moscow, but his gloom and anguish do not vanish, and on arriving in Moscow he has a moment of truth: "'I am a scoundrel,' he said to himself" (14: 255). It is only much later, however, that he will experience the full implications of this recognition.

———————■———————

Book 6, "The Russian Monk," is an account of Zosima's life and teachings cast in the form of a *zhitie*, the hagiographical biography of the life of a saint as composed by his disciple, Alyosha. It is perhaps the most artistically daring section of the work—in the sense that it is almost unprecedented to include in a novel, except perhaps for purposes of parody, an extended example of a text imitative of a purely religious genre. While *The Brothers Karamazov* is filled with violent movement, strong passions, and intense psychological dramatics, the *zhitie* lacks (quite intentionally) the powerful vehemence to which it is meant to respond, and most modern readers have considered it ineffectual in countering the brunt of Ivan's unbridled assault. However that may be, there is no doubt that Zosima conveys the essence of Dostoevsky's own moral-social views, and the account of Zosima's life also plays an important part in the structure of the novel.

Through Zosima Dostoevsky was trying to present an alternative attitude toward life and toward the problem of human suffering—an attitude of serene acceptance of human destiny deriving from a conviction in the all-forgiving mercy of a loving God. Figures embodying states of virtuous beatitude have always been more difficult to make interesting and convincing than those struggling to confront the problems of human existence. Nonetheless, Dostoevsky took the risk of couching the response to Ivan in the genre of a saint's life, written in a highly poetic style full of Church Slavonic expressions and the pious language of Saint Tikhon Zadonsky's eighteenth-century clerical sentimentalism. Since no attempt is made to ground such a narrative in realistic particularities or verisimilar psychological analyses, events occur according to the laws of the moral lesson to be illustrated, not by the causality of mundane existence. There is a timeless quality about such narratives precisely because they are related to the real world only in an ancillary fashion, and the moral they exemplify remains valuable for any time and any place.

Book 6 has not fared very well in critical opinion because it is viewed primarily as a direct answer to the Legend of the Grand Inquisitor. Commentators have not paid sufficient attention to Dostoevsky's remark that "*the whole novel* is an answer" to Ivan and his Legend. Such a definitive assertion makes us aware that Dostoevsky was not depending *only* on these stories and utterances to accomplish his artistic task. This will be achieved through the interweaving of Zosima's experiences with the remainder of the plot-action, which reveals the salutary effect of his own life, and of the values he practiced, on the lives of others. It will illustrate as well that the image delineated by the Grand Inquisitor of a weak, debased humanity, incapable of fulfilling Christ's law of love, is delusory and pernicious.

The stories of Book 6 are narrated, as in a *zhitie*, in a style intended to awaken pious and reverential responses, and to communicate a sense of serenity opposed to the agitations and passions depicted elsewhere. It begins with the life of Zosima's elder brother Markel, who had converted to atheism as a youth but then, after being suddenly taken ill, his spirit is transformed by the immanence of death. Attempting to comfort his grieving mother, he tells her that "we are all in paradise, but we won't see it; if we would, we should have heaven on earth the next day" (14: 262). Feeling unworthy of the love lavished on him, he desires to change places with the servants. He tells his mother that "every one of us has sinned against all men, and I more than any." Like Saint Francis, he asks pardon from the birds and from nature because "there was such a glory of God all about me, birds, trees, meadows, sky, only I lived in shame and dishonored it all and did not notice the beauty and glory" (14: 263). Not understanding this act of self-surrender to "the glory of God," the family doctor, a man of science, declares that Markel's "disease is affecting his brain" (14: 262). But the afflicted young man is only rejoicing in that ecstatic apprehension of life as an ultimate good that even Ivan had experienced, and he embodies this crucial epiphanic sentiment—that Dostoevsky himself had once voiced in the shadow of death.

Zosima confides details of his own early years that fill out the picture of his spiritual formation, and here again Dostoevsky draws on particularities from his own life, recalling the deep impression made on him by the book of Job during a pre-Easter mass. The ancient biblical cry of anguish against a presumably merciful God, who submits His faithful servitor to the worst torments in order to test his loyalty, bears the closest connection with Dostoevsky's thematics, and Zosima is still deeply moved by it: "I've never been able to read that sacred book without tears." Some have been incited by it to mock and blame God because of the terrible fate so unjustly meted out to the righteous Job; but the greatness of the work "lies just in the fact that it is a mystery—that the passing earthly scene and the eternal verity are brought together in it" (14: 265). Zosima says nothing about Job's anguished outcries and accusations. The "mystery" of the tale for him is that, despite his "earthly" sufferings, Job still proclaims his faith in God and in the goodness of God's creation.

If Zosima's first narrative is associatively linked to Alyosha, then the second, dealing with his own life as a young man, is related to Dimitry. Sent by his mother to a school for military cadets in Petersburg, Zinovy (his secular name) had, by the time he graduated, been "transformed into a cruel, absurd, almost savage creature" (14: 268). The calamitous events that follow, precipitated by a blow to his vanity and pride, lead to a crisis during which, implicitly, the lessons of Markel begin to work in his soul (14: 270). He participates in a duel but refuses to fire, apologizes to his servant for having beaten him, and resigns his

Army commission, announcing that he was entering a monastery. Here is a foreshadowing of Dimitry's future self-discovery and moral transformation.

The third story, "The Mysterious Visitor," is clearly connected with Ivan. A respected citizen, well known for his charitable activities, visits Zinovy, who has become known for acting in accordance with *his* moral conscience rather than submitting to the non-Christian code of his position and rank. The older man's interest was inspired by "a secret motive"—he himself is a murderer! (14: 274). As a young man, out of jealousy, he had killed a girl who refused his suit, and he had successfully made it appear as a robbery. He had hoped that family life would help him escape brooding over his past; but the presence of his wife and children only made the memory of his crime more oppressively painful, and he became haunted by the idea of ending his torments with a full confession.

Like Ivan, the visitor was concerned with the general moral situation of society and human life. He reiterates one of the favorite ideas expressed in the *Diary*, that the modern world is living through a period of "isolation" in which the solidarity of humans with each other has been replaced by separation and division. Change can come only through "a spiritual, psychological process. . . . Until you have become really, in actual fact, a brother to everyone, brotherhood will not come to pass. No sort of scientific teaching, no kind of common interest, will ever teach us to share property and privileges with equal consideration for all." Eventually, "this terrible individualism must indubitably have an end. . . . And then the sign of the Son of Man will be seen in the heavens," the sign presumably announcing the Second Coming of Christ (14: 274).

Despite all the torments that the visitor knows will ensue, he follows Zinovy's advice to confess. Nobody believes the confession of this model citizen, who has led such an exemplary life (any more than Ivan will be believed in the courtroom scene later). And when the mysterious visitor, producing evidence of his crime, is declared insane, the parallel with Ivan could not be clearer. A few days later the penitent murderer is taken ill and dies; before his death he admits to Zinovy that, on his last visit, he had come back to kill him. But "the Lord vanquished the devil in my heart" and stayed his hand (exactly as will occur with Dimitry) (14: 283). All three stories are a *mise en abyme*, that is, a relatively subordinate narrative element either reproducing *in nuce* the main theme of the work, or presenting it as here in a form somewhat altered but still recognizable. Zosima's *zhitie* is not his alone but that of the three Karamazov brothers as well. Each story indicates the paths that all (including Ivan) will take in the remainder of the book to refute his Legend of the Grand Inquisitor.

———■———

Zosima's narratives are followed by a chapter of his "conversations and exhortations," in which Dostoevsky, without concern for their didacticism, develops some of his own most cherished ideas. Monasticism and the Russian monks are defended against their numerous critics. Zosima replies in terms of Dostoevsky's religious messianism, which views the Russian monks as those who "keep the image of Christ pure and undefiled." By contrast, those worldly people who criticize the monks "have science, but in science there is nothing but what is the object of sense. The spiritual world, the higher part of man's being is rejected altogether, dismissed with a sort of triumph, even hatred." The modern world has proclaimed "the reign of freedom" and "the multiplication of desires," but such an unregulated existence can only lead among the rich to "isolation and spiritual suicide; in the poor, [to] envy and murder; for they have been given rights, but have not been shown the means of satisfying their wants" (14: 284).

Zosima plays variations on this contrast between the life of the worldly, who sacrifice everything to their ever-increasing desires, and the regime of the monks, which consists of "obedience, fasting, and prayer." For Dostoevsky, "freedom" meant mastery and suppression of one's desires, not liberation from all constraints on their satisfaction; such a life of self-control was for him the only "way to real, true freedom." But the humble, believing Russian people were not immune to the new forces of disintegration undermining society, and Zosima utters a horrified castigation of "the fire of corruption" spreading through the peasantry itself, here touching on the actual problems of Russian society, including drunkenness and child labor (14: 286). But what will ultimately save the Russians, Zosima affirms, is the consciousness of their iniquity—one of the extremely dubious linchpins of Dostoevsky's ideology since the early 1860s.

Zosima launches into an encomium of the Russian peasantry, and he dreams of a halcyon social future, one that "will come to pass when even the most corrupt of our rich will end by being ashamed of his riches before the poor, and the poor, seeing his humility, will understand and give way before him, and will respond joyfully and kindly to his honorable shame" (14: 286). Here, unquestionably, is Dostoevsky's own dream-world of the Russian future, expressed with all the naïveté suitable for Zosima. Of course, all these ingenuous expectations will be met with mockery, but Zosima thinks that those who rely on reason alone to reach the same goal of unity and solidarity (the Socialists) "have more fantastic dreams than we. They aim at justice, but, denying Christ, they will end flooding the earth with blood." Indeed, "were it not for Christ's covenant, they would slaughter one another down to the last two men on earth," and even those two would kill each other "in their pride" (14: 287–288).

In his most overtly theological preachment, he tells them to pray every day for all those whose souls were appearing before God at that moment. Such prayer is only one expression of the universality of love that is the leitmotif of Zosima's admonitions. "For all is like an ocean, all is flowing and bending; a touch in one place sets up movement at the other end of the earth." He also insists that it is necessary "to love a man even in his sin, for that is the semblance of the Divine love and is the highest love on earth." Love "all God's creation, the whole and every grain of sand in it . . . every ray of God's light, love the animals, love the plants, love everything" (14: 288–289).

Because sin is omnipresent, a good deal of effort is required to achieve the state of mind that he recommends. As a remedy, "there is only one means of salvation": "Take yourself and make yourself responsible for everything and for all men, you will see at once that it is really so, and that you are to blame for everyone and for all things." To take on oneself the burden of universal guilt thus becomes the only antidote to despair at the existence of evil. Only by taking responsibility for *all* sin could they avoid "sharing the pride of Satan and murmuring against God" (as Ivan had done). Even a judge appointed by law should "act in the same spirit so far as possible, for [the criminal] will go away and condemn himself more bitterly than you have done" (14: 290–291). Such would be the ideal situation, already mentioned by Zosima in discussing Ivan's article, when the state would be transformed into a church and the punishment of a criminal would be exclusively the work of his own moral conscience. If the criminal should go away unredeemed, however, "mocking at you," his self-chastisement will eventually occur. Nothing that happens can thus infirm such a faith.

Faith does not require confirmation by miracles, nor should failure in combating evil lead to discouragement. Zosima urges his listeners to subdue any "desire for vengeance on the evildoers" by seeking suffering and blaming only themselves. "If you had been a light, you would have lighted the path for others too. . . . And even though your light was shining, yet you see men were not saved by it, hold firm and doubt not the power of the heavenly light. . . . Men are always saved after the death of the deliverer" (14: 292). This later redemption is what occurred in the case of Christ, and we will see it repeated after Zosima's death as well.

Dostoevsky well knew that these injunctions are difficult for human reason to understand, and as a last resort Zosima falls back on the mystery of human life itself. Much is concealed in the earthly life of humankind, and "many of the strongest feelings and movements of our nature we cannot comprehend. . . . On earth, indeed, we are as it were astray, and if it were not for the precious image of Christ before us, we should be undone and altogether lost, as was the human race before the flood." Dostoevsky then sets down Zosima's often-quoted words of the link between earthly life and other worlds: "God took seeds from different worlds and sowed them on the earth, . . . but what grows . . . is alive only through the feeling of its contact with other mysterious worlds." Once "such contact is lost, then you will be indifferent to life and even grow to hate it." Zosima returns to the Franciscan note of cosmic mysticism in affirming the beauty and goodness of all God's creation: "Love to throw yourself on the earth and kiss it.

Kiss the earth and love it with an unceasing, consuming love. Love all men, love everything. . . . Water the earth with the tears of your joy and love those tears" (14: 290–292).

After such an ecstatic summation, Zosima shifts back to the problem of the human condition. Hell contains no scenario of hooks and grappling irons, à la Feodor. Rather, according to Zosima, hell is this eternal torment, "the suffering of no longer being able to love." So far as "hellfire in the material sense" is concerned, he declares that "I don't go into that mystery and I shun it" (14: 293). Hell is purely a spiritual torment, not to be depicted, *pace* Dante and Milton, in physical imagery at all. Dostoevsky thus remains faithful to his poetics of subjectivity by transforming even hell into an attribute of the human psyche. Milton had preceded him when Satan declares in *Paradise Lost*, "The mind is its own place, and in itself / Can make a Heaven of Hell, a Hell of Heaven,"[4] but this is not accompanied in Milton by a rejection of the traditional imagery.[5]

So ends Alyosha's rendition of Zosima's *zhitie*, and the thread of the story is then taken up again by the narrator. We return to the cell where Zosima was speaking to his intimates, "so cheerful and talkative" that he seemed to have undergone a temporary recovery, but he dies on this very day, his peacefully solemn demise fully in accord with the sanctity of his life since becoming a priest, and with the teachings that Alyosha had recorded.

[4] John Milton, *Paradise Lost*, ed. Merritt Y. Hughes (New York, 1933), 235.

[5] Dostoevsky's depiction of the monastic milieu and the *zhitie* of Zosima was subjected to severe censure by Konstantin Leontiyev, who also reported that it had displeased the community of Optyna Pustin. He found that "*a genuine mystical* sentiment was . . . expressed rather weakly, but the sentiment of *humanitarian idealization* even in the speeches of the monks was expressed very ardently and at length" (*PSS*, 15: 497). Indeed, in the assertion made by Markel that it is entirely within man's will to make paradise come true, nothing is said about any cooperation of man with God in effectuating such a transformation, and it thus appears to be an entirely secular event, only requiring, as the Utopian Socialists had once preached, the unconditional application of the Christian law of love to earthly life. Nor does the cosmic mysticism indigenous to Eastern Orthodoxy, as Zosima expresses it, require any supernatural grace to be experienced.

CHAPTER 60

The Brothers Karamazov: Books 7–12

Ivan's Legend and Zosima's *zhitie* have established the polarities of the conflict between reason and faith, and each of the main characters will be confronted by a crisis that requires choosing between them. Faith of some kind will prevail in all of these climactic moments—not necessarily faith in a specifically moral-religious form, as will occur with Alyosha, but a faith that incarnates some aspect of the morality of love and the self-transcendence of egoism represented and preached by Zosima. Alyosha is the first of the three brothers whose life experiences have been foreshadowed by those of Zosima, and there is a structural parallel between the unrolling of the crisis situations and the order of the linkage of the brothers with Zosima's life. It is thus with Alyosha that the first conflict between reason and faith is posed and resolved.

Alyosha's disaccord occurs on the moral-religious level and arises as a result of Zosima's death and the accompanying expectation throughout the monastic community and the town that God would provide some external reward for the sanctity of his life. The monks were filled with excitement and expectation to such a degree that the learned Father Paissy, versed in Church doctrine and history, considered it "unseemly" and "an evil temptation." And so it was: a version of the second temptation of Christ, who had refused to demonstrate his immunity to the laws of nature by leaping unharmed from the pinnacle of the temple. Yet even Paissy "secretly, at the bottom of his heart, cherished almost the same hopes and could not but be aware of it" (14: 296).

At the very least, the sanctity of Zosima's life might have guaranteed a respite from the normal laws of earthly decay; and so the unexpected "odor of corruption" emitted by the corpse was immediately seized on by those unfriendly to him as a sign of heavenly disapproval, unleashing a malevolent chorus of criticism. "I feel it almost repulsive to recall that event," says the narrator, and he would not have done so "if it had not exerted a very strong influence on the heart and soul of the chief, though *future*, hero of my story" (14: 297). Ivan's powerful attack on God for having created a world of suffering and injustice had continued to undermine Alyosha's faith; and the death of Zosima, coupled with this seeming disgrace, had dealt a staggering blow to the tranquil stability of Alyosha's convictions. But his faith will reemerge strengthened from the trial and this reaffirmation is already foreshadowed by his encounters with Grushenka, who is struggling between feelings of resentment and rage against the Polish officer who had seduced and abandoned her and the desire to forgive.

The narrator insists that "it was not miracles [Alyosha] needed but only 'the higher justice' which had been in his belief outraged by the blow that had so suddenly and so cruelly wounded his heart." Because such "higher justice" presumably would have meant displaying a certain immunity to "the pitiless laws of nature," all the narrator's apologetic efforts cannot conceal that, even if inspired by the greatness of his love, Alyosha has yielded like the others to the second temptation of the devil. And at this moment, quite appropriately, Alyosha also recalls the "vague but tormenting impression left by his conversation with Ivan the day before," who had also found intolerable this lack of any "higher justice" in a creation that allowed the suffering of innocent children (14: 306–307).

Most likely this is why, for the first and only time, the narrator allows himself to criticize the character he had taken under his wing: "All the love that lay concealed in his pure heart for 'everyone and everything' had, for the past year, been concentrated—and perhaps wrongly so—primarily . . . on his beloved elder, now dead" (14: 306). As a result, the shock of the event led him to neglect his obligations to "everyone and everything"—for example, to his brother Dimitry, whom he had been told to watch over, and to the utterly destitute Snegiryov family, for whom he had been entrusted with two hundred rubles by Katerina. Alyosha's situation is similar to that of Ivan, whose "rebellion" allowed him to stifle any resistance to a possible murder. The parallel is clearly drawn in his conversation with the cynical and disabused Rakitin. Observing Alyosha's disillusionment, the latter scoffs at his dismay "because your old man had begun to stink," amusedly accusing him of "being in a temper with your God, you are rebelling against him." Alyosha's reply—"I am not rebelling against my God; I simply 'don't accept his world'"—quotes Ivan's very words (14: 308).

A characteristic of Dostoevsky's mature technique is to refract a thematic motif through a succession of characters, each of whom expresses a different aspect of its meaning. The totally unprincipled Rakitin is thus another version of Ivan, completely lacking those moral-religious yearnings that Zosima had instantly detected in the young, controversial publicist. The narrator exhibits no mercy whatever toward Rakitin, who is now shown tempting the weakened Alyosha on another level by leading the innocent to Grushenka, who wished to obtain revenge by seducing the religious novice, her presumed despiser. But hearing of Zosima's death, everything is transformed, and memories of her unsullied childhood resurface as she retells the folktale of the onion, heard long ago from a peasant woman.

This tale embodies that condemnation of a totally self-centered egoism that, according to Dostoevsky, was typical of the morality of the Russian folk character, and it is narrated by Grushenka in a style imitative of folk poetry. A wicked old woman, submerged in the fiery lake of hell, had once given an onion to a beggarwoman, and her guardian angel endeavors to save her because of this one good deed. The angel lowers an onion to pull her up, but when other sinners cling to her as she rises, she cries back at them, "It's my onion, not yours." At this expression of selfishness the stem snaps, she falls back into hell, and the angel sadly departs (14: 319).

This childhood recollection provokes an even stronger crisis of conscience in Grushenka, and Alyosha is so moved by her confession and repentance, as well as the strength of her desire to forgive her Polish betrayer, that he tells Rakitin, "She is more loving than we" (14: 321). When the disgruntled cynic asks what Alyosha has said that stirs Grushenka so profoundly, she falls on her knees before the "cherub" and answers, "I've been waiting all my life for someone like you. I knew that someone like you would come and forgive me . . . would really love me, not only with a shameful love" (14: 323). The scene recalls the first meeting between Myshkin and Nastasya Filippovna in *The Idiot*, when the Prince recognizes the purity of her spirit despite her past degradation.

Just as in *The Idiot*, where Nastasya asks Myshkin to decide whether she should marry, Grushenka asks Alyosha to make the fateful decision whether she should now forgive her seducer. Alyosha replies, "You have forgiven him already." Having hoped to debauch Alyosha, Rakitin spitefully refers instead to his intended victim as having "turned the Magdalene onto the true path." The sarcasm of his embittered words nonetheless reluctantly recognizes the truth: "So you see that the miracles you were looking for just now have come to pass" (14: 322). Genuine miracles occur when faith succeeds in aiding the morality of love to conquer egoistic resentment, hatred, and revenge.

Alyosha's encounter with Grushenka restores him to himself and reveals the depths of unselfish love hidden in the human conscience. Men and women are not as weak and selfish as Ivan's Grand Inquisitor had claimed; they are capable of putting into practice the morality of love stemming from a faith in Christ. The meeting thus serves as a transition to the resolution of Alyosha's crisis, which begins when he reenters the cell where Paissy, holding a vigil beside Zosima's corpse, is reading aloud from the Gospel of Saint John. His state of mind had entirely changed, and "the odor of corruption . . . no longer made him feel miserable and indignant." Instead, "there was a sweetness in his heart . . . and joy, joy was glowing in his mind and in his heart" (14: 325).

Such joy, a leitmotif of this chapter, indicates the first effect of his meeting with Grushenka, and it continues to dominate his subconscious. After dozing off, his thoughts mingle with what he hears being read—the account of the wedding feast in "Cana of Galilee"—it's "the first miracle," he tells himself, the miracle in which Christ changed water into wine at the wedding feast of a poor, humble couple. The Mother of Christ was present at the feast, and Alyosha muses that she "knew that He had come not only to make His great, terrible sacrifice" but also to bring joy to humankind. By now asleep and dreaming, Alyosha suddenly sees Zosima, no longer lying in his coffin but moving among the guests, inviting him to join the feast, explaining his presence at the joyous occasion by saying, "I gave an onion to a beggar. And many here have given only an onion each—only one little onion." Alyosha too had "known how to give an onion to a famished woman today," and Zosima tells him, "Begin your work, dear one, begin it, gentle one," in effect instructing Alyosha to continue the "work" he had instinctively begun with Grushenka. Christ, also among the guests, is not named but referred to as "our Sun," and when Alyosha is too overcome even to cast a glance in Christ's direction, Zosima urges him to do so. "He is terrible in His greatness, awful in His sublimity, but infinitely merciful"; he "had made Himself like unto us from love and rejoices with us." *His* Christ did not view earthly life only as "a vale of tears" but rather as the venue for the happiness and joy of mutual love and forgiveness. With this resurrected image of Zosima still before his mind's eye, and as "tears of rapture rose from his soul," Alyosha awakens (14: 325–327).

Alyosha's awakening is the prelude to the great scene in which, symbolically, the spirit of Zosima becomes reembodied in the young novice. After gazing at the corpse lying in state, whose voice he had just heard in his dream, Alyosha walks out into the night, where "the vault of heaven, full of soft, shining stars stretched vast and fathomless above him." Dostoevsky exerts all his poetic powers to evoke the beauty of the spectacle, and to infuse it with a sense of religious awe. "The white towers and golden domes of the cathedral gleamed out against the sapphire sky," and Alyosha, invaded by a feeling that "the mystery of the earth was one with the mystery of the stars," throws himself down, following the injunctions of his teacher, to embrace the earth and water it with his tears. "There seemed to be threads from all those innumerable worlds of God, linking his soul to them, and it was trembling all over 'in contact with other worlds.' He longed to forgive everyone and for everything, and to beg forgiveness" (14: 328). The climax of this scene is a famous and oft-quoted passage:

> With every instant, [Alyosha] felt clearly and, as it were, palpably, that something firm and unshakable as that vault of heaven had entered into his soul. It was as though some idea had seized the sovereignty of his mind—and it was for all his life forever and ever. He had fallen to earth a weak youth, but he rose up a resolute champion. . . . 'Someone visited my soul in that moment,' he used to say afterward, with firm belief in his words. (14: 328)

During these hours, Alyosha recovered not so much a faith in God that he had never lost as a faith in the ultimate beauty and goodness of God's universe.

The confluence of the earthly and the heavenly that Zosima had proclaimed cannot be mistaken, and it is reinforced by Alyosha's decision to leave the monastery three days later, obeying Zosima's command to "sojourn in the world."

———■———

In the same time interval during which Alyosha was undergoing his spiritual awakening, Dimitry was frantically watching to see whether Grushenka would visit his father, and searching desperately for the means of obtaining the money that might allow him to begin a new life with her. These semi-comic episodes culminate in the fateful moment when "'God,' as Mitya himself later said, 'watched over me then'" (14: 355). Earlier, Dimitry had declared the ideal of the Madonna and the ideal of Sodom were battling in the heart of man, and his own character is an embodiment of this conflict. Despite his tumultuous passions, the ideal of the Madonna, the all-merciful Mother of God, had exerted her power again in staying his hand against his father. It is this same ideal that now affects his feelings for Grushenka, and his new "normal" love relation with her lifts their mutual love above sensuality to a level that Kierkegaard would have called "ethical."

Dimitry too thus undergoes a decisive moral transformation, and his "spiritual purification" is completed during the several hours of the preliminary investigation to which Book 9 is devoted. The titles of the chapters (3, 4, and 5) devoted to the questioning of Dimitry are "A Soul's Journey through Torments," and three such torments (*mitarstva*) are enumerated. A Russian reader would recognize this structure as an allusion to the Orthodox belief that the soul after death, as it ascends from earth to heaven, is subject to trials by various evil spirits. In a notebook entry of 1877, Dostoevsky mentions wishing to write about the *sorokovina* (a memorial service held on the fortieth day after death) in the form of "a book of pilgrimages" that would describe the trials of such a soul. This idea is now secularized and applied to the "torments" that Dimitry experiences as, in effect, he bares his soul under the pressure of the pitiless questioning. But the ordeal leads him to a much more severe self-examination than he had ever known before, and culminates not only in an overwhelming feeling of pity for human suffering as a whole, but also a desire to suffer himself for all his past misdeeds.

Dimitry had dealt a near-fatal blow to Grigory when the faithful servant had attempted to stop him from fleeing his father's garden on the night the old man was murdered. Learning that Grigory is still alive, Dimitry is overjoyed, and because he knows he did not kill his father, he assumes at first that the whole matter can easily be settled. Time and again, though, he candidly acknowledges all the overpowering impulses that might have led him to commit such a murder and, under the calculated questioning of the investigators, unwittingly builds the case against himself. Dimitry has now begun that process of self-scrutiny and self-judgment that will lead to his moral metamorphosis. "I'm not very beautiful," he says, "so that I had no right to consider him [his father] repulsive." None of these responses is taken into account, any more than his statement that he is "a man who has done a lot of nasty things, but has always been, and still is, honorable at bottom, in his inner being" (14: 416).

As the circumstantial evidence piles up against Dimitry, and the rashness and intemperance of his earlier statements and actions against his father are thrown back in his face, he sees himself at last through the eyes of those he calls "blind moles and scoffers," and struggles to define himself against the image they have been constructing (14: 437–438). At the core of his character are concern and anguish over others—over Grushenka, to be sure, but also a terrible sense of remorse over Grigory. It is this realization that now pierces through, even as he flares up against his questioners and displays all the storminess and irascibility of his temperament. The climax of this development comes after Dimitry has been reduced to despair and is at the end of his considerable physical tether: "His eyes were closing with fatigue." He had declared publicly to Grushenka once more that he was innocent, and she had accepted his word after crossing herself before the icon. "He'll never deceive you against his conscience," she affirms to his questioners. "He's telling the whole truth, you may believe it" (14: 455). But such utterances of faith are futile, and Dimitry finally sinks into a deep sleep on a chest in the room. Like Alyosha, he then dreams a dream crystallizing the moral conversion that has taken place within him as a result of all his "torments."

Dimitry's dream, "utterly out of keeping with the place and time," visualizes him driving somewhere in the steppes during a snowstorm. In the distance he could see the ruins of a burned-down village, and as his carriage approaches he meets a line of women standing along the road, "all thin and wan," and especially one, "a tall, bony woman" looking much older than her years and carrying a crying baby. "Her breasts must have been so dry that there was not a drop of milk in them." Dimitry asks the driver why the baby was crying, and the peasant assumes he is referring to the immediate situation: "They're poor people burned out. They have no bread." But Dimitry is really asking the same question that had been posed so vehemently by Ivan and led to his attack on God. "Why are people poor?" Dimitry queries. "Why is the babe poor? Why is the steppe barren? . . . Why don't they sing songs of joy? Why are they dark from black misery? Why don't they feed the babe?" (14: 455–456).

No answer is given to *these* questions, which Dimitry himself felt "were unreasonable and senseless," but his response is a sudden upsurge of emotion that marks the completion of his moral-spiritual transformation. "And he felt that a passion of pity, such as he had never known before, was rising in his heart, and he wanted to cry that he wanted to do something for them all . . . that no one should shed tears from that moment, and he wanted to do it at once, regardless of all obstacles, with all the Karamazov recklessness." Quite appropriately, he also hears "the voice of Grushenka," full of emotion, saying, "I won't leave you now for the rest of your life." On waking, he finds that someone had put a pillow under his head, and he is moved "with a sort of ecstatic gratitude" by this little gesture of concern (14: 456–457).

Dimitry's dream objectifies the transformation that has taken place in his conscience as a result of his own suffering, bringing on a new awareness of the wretchedness of others. Such human distress, though of a different nature, had led to Ivan's upsurge of rebellion against God, but with Dimitry it leads to a passionate desire to throw himself into alleviating the world's miseries instead of, as in the past, increasing their number by giving free rein to all his impulses and appetites. Just before departing under escort back to the town, he describes the new realization to which he has come. In the past, "I've sworn to amend every day of my life, beating my breast, and every day I've done the same filthy things." But now, under the blows of fate, he has undergone a decisive change: "I accept the torment of accusation, and my public shame, and I want to suffer and by suffering I shall be purified." Once more he declares himself not guilty of his father's blood, but adds: "I accept my punishment, not because I killed him, but because I meant to kill him and perhaps I really might have killed him" (14: 458).

The preliminary investigation thus ends with Dimitry acknowledging his moral guilt but insisting, so far as legal guilt is concerned, that "I'll fight it out with you to the end, and then God will decide" (14: 458). Both Alyosha and Dimitry have chosen to follow Zosima's path of love and Christian faith, each in his own way. It will be the turn of Ivan to follow the same route, but one that, in his case, leads to a tormenting, brilliantly depicted, more severe inner struggle and total mental breakdown.

———— ■ ————

Dostoevsky interrupts the narrative course of Dimitry's fate after his arrest and shifts to a thematic motif introduced earlier, realizing one of his long-held literary ambitions—to present, on a larger canvas than in *The Idiot*, the interaction between an idealistic Christian character and a group of children. Alyosha becomes the spiritual guide of the boys introduced earlier as the classmates of Ilyusha Snegiryov. The chapters of Book 10 center on the relations of the gravely ill Ilyusha, Alyosha, and the group of boys.

Kolya Krasotkin is the most daring and independent of the lot, a future leader, who in the past had taken Ilyusha under his wing. Kolya is portrayed as a prideful youth, haughtily insisting on his independence from the others, intelligent and self-assured, ready to take unusual risks to prove his superiority—he lies between the railroad tracks while a train passes over him—and scornful of any sort of "sheepish sentimentality." His poor, widowed mother, who slavishly devotes her life to him, would tearfully "reproach him with his coldness"; but he was not really cold-hearted, only resistant to displays of emotion that might suggest any weakness, any loss of self-control (14: 463). Despite this assumed façade of strength, he breaks down when his mother goes into hysterics on learning of the train episode, and he "sobbed like a boy of six" (14: 465).

Rakitin has also been busy among the schoolchildren, in competition with Alyosha, and he is cited by Kolya as an authority who has converted him into being a "Socialist" (14: 474). Critics have long recognized Kolya as an embryonic Ivan, through whom Dostoevsky brilliantly transposes some of the dominating motifs of his book into an adolescent register. Kolya, for example, tells Alyosha that "God is only a hypothesis" (exactly Ivan's position) and that "it's possible for one who doesn't believe in God to love mankind" (as does, in his perversely pitying fashion, Ivan's Grand Inquisitor). Dostoevsky amuses himself when he has Kolya repeat what he has picked up from Rakitin: "I am not opposed to Christ . . . , He was a most humane person, and if He were alive today, He would be found in the ranks of the revolutionaries, and would perhaps play a conspicuous part" (14: 499–500). When asked for the source of this claim, Kolya can only reply that "they say he [Belinsky] said it"—and of course it was Dostoevsky himself who had made public this utterance of Belinsky's in the *Diary of a Writer*.

Dostoevsky uses Kolya not only to parody the already familiar image of Ivan but also to anticipate the drama soon to be played out. One of Kolya's escapades was to induce a peasant lad, "a stupid, round-mugged fellow of twenty," to see what would occur if a cart was moved just as a goose was nibbling at a bag of oats with its neck under the wheel. A slight displacement of the cart then breaks the neck of the goose. When the two are hauled into court by the infuriated owner of the goose, "the errand boy" blubbered that Kolya had egged him on. But "I answered," he explains to Alyosha, "with the utmost composure that I hadn't egged him on, that I simply stated the general proposition, had spoken hypothetically" (14: 495–496). Ivan had assumed exactly the same role with Smerdyakov, stating the general proposition that "everything was permitted" and, at least for the moment, refusing like Kolya to accept any responsibility for what might occur as a result. The justice of the peace, amused by Kolya's sophistry, lets him off with only a warning; but Ivan's conscience will not allow him to escape so lightly.

Kolya harmed no one except the goose in this particular exhibition of egoistic playfulness, but the same is not the case with his treatment of poor, suffering Ilyusha. Even though Kolya knew that Ilyusha wished to see him most of all, he failed to join the other boys in visiting the bedside of their stricken comrade. Kolya's need to dominate others and to control every situation in which he becomes involved mimics the aim of Ivan's creation, the Grand Inquisitor, to relieve humankind of the burden of freedom. Indeed, Kolya's relation to Ilyusha in the past may well be seen as a callow facsimile of Ivan's poetic invention. Ilyusha "was proud," Kolya tells Alyosha, "but he was slavishly devoted to me, and yet all at once his eyes would flash, and he'd refuse to agree with me, fly into a rage." Ilyusha seemed to be developing, as Kolya puts it, "a little free spirit of his own." The reason was that "I was cold in responding to his endearments," and "the tenderer he became, the colder I became" (14: 480, 482). Kolya's aversion to "sheepish sentimentality" excludes any reciprocity of feeling, just as Ivan's rationalism excludes (or represses) any emotions stemming from his moral conscience. But when Kolya comes face-to-face with the wasted, fever-ridden visage of the dying Ilyusha, his posture of commanding self-control breaks down, and he gives way to his feelings of pity and compassion.

Dostoevsky uses the long-suffering Snegiryov family, and the poignant love that exists beween Ilyusha and his father, as a foil to set off the rankling hatreds of the Karamazovs. The family's condition has improved because the captain has accepted the charity of Katerina. But nothing can relieve his wrenching agony as he watches his doomed son expire before his eyes. Kolya had scornfully called the captain "a mountebank, a buffoon," but Alyosha's analysis presents Dostoevsky's own understanding of this particular character-type. "These are people of deep feeling," Alyosha says, "who have been somehow crushed. Buffoonery in them is a sort of resentful irony against those to whom they daren't speak the truth, from having been for years humiliated and intimidated by them. Believe me, Krasotkin, that sort of buffoonery is sometimes tragic in the extreme" (14: 483). By such observations, Alyosha brings the boy to an awareness of how badly his pride had misled him in his treatment of Ilyusha and his contempt for the captain.

Zosima had sent Alyosha into the world to do his work there, and the scene with Kolya and the boys is the first illustration of how such work might be accomplished. Alyosha listens patiently to all of Kolya's prattle about "Socialism" and the various other "subversive" notions that he has picked up from Rakitin about Voltaire, God, and so on, all of which ape Ivan. Alyosha answers him "quietly, gently, and quite naturally, as though he were talking to someone of his own age, or even older." Kolya thus undergoes a miniature conversion experience, similar to that of Alyosha and Dimitry, and confesses, "I am profoundly unhappy, I sometimes fancy . . . that everyone is laughing at me, the whole world, and that I feel ready to overturn the whole order of things." He realizes now that "what kept me from coming [to see Ilyusha earlier] was my conceit, my egoistic vanity, and the beastly willfulness which I can never get rid of, though I have been struggling with it all my life." After this avowal, he asks Alyosha if he does not find him "ridiculous," and Alyosha admonishes him to overcome any fear of confessing his faults. Indeed, such vanity is now "almost a sort of insanity," Alyosha declares. "The devil has taken the form of that vanity and entered into a whole generation." "'It's simply the devil,' added Alyosha, without a trace of the smile that Kolya, staring at him, expected to see" (14: 503). Alyosha takes the devil seriously, refusing amusedly to dismiss such an antiquated superstition. Ivan will soon find himself oscillating between Kolya's incredulity and Alyosha's gravity as he struggles to determine whether the devil he sees is (or is not) a hallucination.

Book 10 ends with a variation on the Job motif that runs throughout the novel, and Dostoevsky now makes no effort to soften its emotionally devastating impact. The captain gives way to abject despair when the doctor from the capital fails to hold out any hope, and Kolya poignantly tells his father to "get a good boy" when he dies and "love him instead of me." But the grief-stricken father, on leaving the room, tells Kolya and Alyosha "in a wild whisper": "I don't want a good boy, I don't want another boy. . . . 'If I forget thee, Jerusalem, may my tongue. . . .'"—a biblical allusion that Kolya does not understand and asks Alyosha to explain (14: 507). Such a scene could well have been maudlin, but from Dostoevsky's pen it conveys an overpowering purity and intensity of emotion. The death of his son Aleksey just two years before certainly contributed its share to the moving pathos of these pages. And he had written, in an anguished letter in 1868 on the death of his two-month-old daughter, Sofya, expressing the same inconsolable grief as the captain's: "And now they tell me in consolation that I will have other children. But where . . . is that little individual for whom, I dare to say, I would have accepted crucifixion so that she might live?"[1]

———■———

In Book 11 the focus returns to the main characters and events in the two-month interval since Dimitry's arrest. When Alyosha goes to visit Grushenka, she reports that Ivan has also been to see Dimitry secretly in prison, and the two appear to be involved in some private plan. The mystery of Ivan's behavior and motivation thus begins to move into the foreground.

Dostoevsky, as we know, often introduces a serious theme by first giving it a comic or scandalous form. As Alyosha goes from Grushenka to visit Liza Khokhlakova he is, as usual, waylaid by her garrulous mother, who rambles on about the impending trial, and the satire becomes more serious as the loquacious lady chatters on about the possibility of a plea of temporary insanity, which Dimitry had insisted he would not accept because it implied his guilt. But Mme Khokhlakova is enchanted by the notion that crime could be just an "aberration" for which Dimitry was not really responsible. "They found out

[1] *PSS*, 28/Bk. 2: 297; May 18/30. 1868.

about aberrations," she tells Alyosha happily, "as soon as the law courts were re-formed." Indeed, for her no one can be guilty of anything, because "who isn't suffering from aberration nowadays?—you, I, all are in a state of aberration and there are ever so many examples of it" (15: 18–19). This universal malady thus be-comes a parodistic reversal of Zosima's universal guilt, in which all are responsi-ble for all. Mme Khokhlakova's mindless volubility also brings into view the motif of mental instability and madness that will soon be illustrated by Ivan.

Mental imbalance, specifically linked with the devil, appears both frighten-ingly and pathetically in the next chapter. On visiting Liza, who is now able to walk again, Alyosha notices a change for the worse in her mental state. She has begun to revel in sadomasochistic fantasies of destroying both others and herself—and hence has become "the little demon" of the chapter's title. "Yes, I want disorder," she tells Alyosha, affirming her desire that "everything might be destroyed." Alyosha admonishes her that "you take evil for good," though he cannot simply negate one of her provocative taunts: "Listen, your brother is being tried now for murdering his father, and everyone loves his having killed his father." Then she tells him of a dream in which devils assailing her withdraw when she crosses herself, but return when she begins to revile God out loud. "It's awful fun," she says, "it takes your breath away" (15: 22–23).

Liza has also been visited by Ivan, who, instead of attempting, like Alyosha, to counter her sadomasochistic inclinations, had reinforced them by his complicity. When she tells him of how "nice" it would be to eat pineapple compote (an ex-treme luxury) while watching the prolonged agonies of a crucified child, "he laughed and said it really was nice" (15: 24). (Unfortunately, Dostoevsky could not resist the anti-Semitic implication that the child had been crucified by fanati-cal Jews to obtain Christian blood, and Alyosha refuses to deny that possibility.) Ivan, as we shall soon learn, is now being visited by a devil himself, and the im-plication is that he has brought his own illness with him to aggravate Liza's. But she is not yet completely possessed by the evil spirit, and she appeals to Alyosha as her only rescuer, crying "Alyosha save me!" Liza still struggles against her worst impulses, and at the conclusion of this scene she puts her finger in the crack of the doorjamb, slams the door shut, and mutilates herself as punishment. "I am a wretch, a wretch, wretch, wretch!" she whispers, duplicating Ivan's self-castigation as "a scoundrel" after he had departed on the day of the murder (15: 25).

When Alyosha next visits Dimitry in prison, he finds his brother upset be-cause Rakitin has been attempting to undermine his faith in God. The revela-tory effect of Dimitry's dream about the burned-out village and the crying baby has permanently altered his own character and sense of values. Rakitin intended to write an article about the crime "to prove some theory," namely, that Dimitry "couldn't help murdering his father, he was corrupted by his environment, etc." In a seriocomic recitation of Rakitin's physiological determinism, Dimitry expresses his dismay. "I'm sorry to lose God," he says. God has been replaced by "sorts of little tails, the little tails of those nerves, and as soon as they begin quivering—then an image appears. . . . That's why I see and think, because of those tails, and not at all because I've got a soul and that I am some sort of image and likeness" (that is, of God) (15: 28). When Dimitry had objected to this explanation, paraphrasing Ivan's thesis that "without God and immortal life all things are lawful," Rakitin laughingly agreed that "a clever man can do what he likes." This reiteration of Ivan's doctrine by the unscrupulous Rakitin lays the groundwork for the upcoming depiction of Ivan's struggle with *his* conscience in the chapters that immediately follow. All the same, as Dostoevsky makes clear, the despicable Rakitin and the tormented Ivan are not comparable. "Brother Ivan is not Rakitin," says Dimitry explicitly. "There is an idea in him" (15: 29).

Dimitry's faith remains unshaken by Rakitin's scornful sallies. Innocent though he knows himself to be, Dimitry is ready to go to Siberia "for all the babes . . . [and] because we are all responsible for all," echoing again the doctrine of Zosima and implying the analogy with Christ ("I go for all") (15: 10). Dostoevsky then probably draws on memories of his own imprisonment when Dimitry exclaims: "One cannot exist in prison without God, it's even more impossible than out of prison. And then we men underground will sing from the bowels of the earth a tragic hymn to God, with Whom is joy. Hail to God and His joy! I love Him!" Dimitry's rapturous affirmations rise to a climax when he declares: "I think I could stand any suffering, only to be able to say and to repeat to myself every moment: 'I exist'" (15: 31).

The five remaining chapters of Book 11 focus on Ivan, who has been constantly alluded to in the preceding four. Ivan finally appears in person during Alyosha's visit to Katerina. Aware of his own increasing mental instability, oscillating as he does between states of lucidity and what he fears to be hallucinations (such as being visited by the devil), he asks Alyosha if it is possible to know that one is going mad.

On the surface, Ivan refuses to accept "the myth about that crazy idiot, the epileptic Smerdyakov" (15: 39) having committed the murder. Nonetheless, Alyosha possesses Zosima's intuitive gift of moral-psychological penetration, and realizes that Ivan has been brooding these last two months over his own possible responsibility. When Ivan calls Dimitry a "murderer" and a "monster," Alyosha objects; and when challenged to name someone else, he replies: "I know only one thing . . . *it wasn't you* who killed father." Ivan is so taken aback by this reply touching on all his own hidden fears that he thinks Alyosha must know of his hallucinatory conversations with the devil on the same subject (15: 40). The haughty Ivan suddenly decides to visit Smerdyakov—not for the first but for the third time, the two earlier encounters having already led to the demented condition in which we find him.

A violent snowstorm begins as Ivan makes his way through the unlit streets on his way to Smerdyakov's cottage, and he stumbles into a drunken peasant singing the first two lines of a popular ditty: "Ach, Vanka's gone to Petersburg / I won't wait till he comes back." This song recalls to Ivan his own departure for Moscow, and what had occurred before *he* returned; and although such a connection is not made explicitly, no doubt this is why "Ivan felt an intense hatred for [the peasant]" (15: 57). When the peasant lurches against him, Ivan knocks him down and leaves him lying in the snow, although the thought crosses his mind that the peasant will freeze to death.

Smerdyakov had become ill again, and each immediately remarks on how sickly the other looks; both are being undermined by the same moral-psychic anguish. Smerdyakov, however, now has the upper hand. As he has come to understand, Ivan is fearful that his implicit consent to the crime would be exposed. Disgusted by Ivan's unwillingness to face the truth, Smerdyakov admits his own guilt while refusing to assume it alone. "You murdered him," he tells Ivan, "you are the real murderer. I was only your instrument, your faithful servant . . . and it was following your words that I did it" (15: 57). Under Ivan's persistent questioning—he is avid to learn all the details—Smerdyakov explains how the crime had been committed just after Dimitry had struck Grigory and leaped over the fence, fleeing his father's house.

There is an aspect of this dialogue that should not be overlooked. Just after Smerdyakov has made his confession and his interlocutor has "shuddered all over with a cold shiver," Ivan mutters that "I'm afraid you're a dream, a phantom sitting there before me." Smerdyakov replies that there "are only us two and one other," immediately adding: "No doubt that he is here, that third, between us." This reference to "a third" terrifies Ivan, who takes it as a mention of the devil and looks around, with "his eyes hastily searching for someone in all the corners." Smerydakov, however, explains "that this third one is God, sir, Providence itself, sir, it's right here with us now, sir, only don't look for it, you won't find it" (15: 60). While the devil has been appearing to Ivan's tormented and demented consciousness, Smerdyakov apparently has been returning to the sources of his own faith since losing his respect for Ivan's ideas. That he has been seeking moral comfort in such a return is indicated by a small detail: he covers the money he obtained from the murder, and which he now displays to Ivan, with a copy of *The Sayings of the Holy Father Isaac the Syrian*, a collection of popular religious texts by a sixth-century ascetic. Father Isaac has replaced the French grammar Smerdyakov had been studying at the time of the second visit, and we may recall that, even at the height of his fascination with Ivan and his ideas, this offspring of stinking Lizaveta had still readily accepted the existence of the two or three hermits in the desert who could move mountains.

Smerdyakov is filled with contempt for Ivan's dismay at the recognition of his own share of guilt, and his struggle to diminish it as much as possible. "'God sees,' Ivan raised his hand, 'perhaps I, too, was guilty, perhaps I really had a secret desire for my father's . . . death, but I swear I was not as guilty as you think and I didn't urge you on at all.'" Nonetheless, he assures Smerdyakov that he will disclose the truth at the trial the next day, including his own share of responsibility; but Smerydakov refuses to believe that he will have the courage to perform what would, in any case, be only a futile gesture. Smerdyakov would simply deny Ivan's testimony and argue that he was trying to save his brother. Most wounding of all, he taunts Ivan with the inconsistency between his sentiments and his ideas: "You used to say yourself that everything is lawful, so now why are you so upset, too?" (15: 66–67). Smerdyakov, however, is caught in a similar inner conflict: denying that he again believes in God, he no longer has any faith in what had replaced God for him, namely, Ivan's ideas. His peasant conscience has made him ill, just as Ivan's educated sense of guilt has been undermining *him*, and the suicide of Smerdyakov will coincide exactly with Ivan's mental breakdown in the next chapter.

The scene ends with Ivan, as he walks out into the snowstorm, firmly deciding to meet Smerdyakov's challenge. Stumbling against the inert body of the peasant, Ivan now brings him to a police station, arranges for a doctor, and saves his life. This is the first effect of his new resoluteness, which overcomes all the contempt for erring and sinful humankind that he had previously exhibited, and which perhaps foreshadows his role in the envisaged second volume. Although he is now capable of such a spontaneous gesture of personal human solidarity, it is a different matter when he thinks of going to the prosecutor at once to denounce Smerdyakov as the murderer and reveal his own share of the responsibility.

Choosing to put off this ordeal until morning, his determination to act decisively thus wavers; once again he is caught in the toils of his moral-psychological dilemma—the dilemma of intending to follow the dictates of a conscience whose precepts his reason cannot justify. Entering his room and, trying to keep from falling asleep, he "got up uneasily and walked across the room to shake off his drowsiness" (15: 66–67). This last phrase, conveying Ivan's own awareness, turns out to be entirely illusory; he is now in fact asleep and only dreaming that he walked across the room. "I have dreams now," Ivan tells Alyosha in the next chapter, "yet they are no dreams but reality. I walk about, talk, and see" (15: 86). Ivan has become incapable of distinguishing between his dreams and the objective world; and when he looks uneasily at a sofa in his room, he observes someone sitting there "who had not been in the room when Ivan Feodorovich came into it" (15: 70).

No scene testifies so abundantly to the brilliance and bite of Dostoevsky's satirical talent as the chapter devoted to Ivan's dialogue with the devil. It is customary to allude to the inspiration of Goethe's *Faust*, and several references to it are contained in this scene as well as elsewhere in the text; but the relation between Ivan (who has been called "the Russian Faust") and his devil is quite different from that of Faust and Mephistopheles. There is no question in Goethe about the reality of Mephistopheles's existence or of the supernatural world from which he sprang. This is precisely the issue, however, that is posed to Ivan by the obsequiously ingratiating patter of his amiable visitor. Nowhere is Dostoevsky's theme—the antagonism between reason and faith—dramatized with more subtlety and finesse than in these mocking pages, which illustrate Dostoevsky's extraordinary ability to play with his own most deeply held convictions.

The portrait of the devil, as Victor Terras has remarked, contains more descriptive detail than that of any other character.[2] Dostoevsky takes great pains to present him in entirely earthly terms as a Russian social type. Because Ivan keeps insisting that the devil is just a figment of his imagination, Dostoevsky ironically gives him a solid embodiment. He shows up as a rather down-at-heels member of the landed gentry, a gentleman no longer able to support himself because the income from his estate has vanished since the abolition of serfdom, but he still exhibits all the social graces of his former position, such as embroidering his conversation with French phrases. His clothes were good, but now somewhat out of fashion: "in brief, there was every appearance of gentility on straitened means" (15: 70). He lives as what the Russians call a *prizhivalchik*, a sponger on more affluent relatives and friends, who continue to offer him hospitality because he is, after all, a gentleman; his manners are good, he can be presented in society, and he is agreeable, accommodating, and amusing. Such an image carries a symbolic meaning. Religion itself, from Dostoevsky's point of view, was now a hanger-on in Russian educated society, accepted as a respectable relic of the past but hardly exercising its old power and influence. As the devil remarks himself, "it's an axiom generally accepted in society that I am a fallen angel. . . . If I ever was, it must have been so long ago that there's no harm in forgetting it" (15: 73).

Ivan's dialogue with the devil plays on the continual fluctuation between the stirrings of his conscience and the amorally Nihilistic conclusions that he has drawn from his refusal to accept God and immortality. The devil had first appeared to Ivan once he began to brood over his possible part in the murder, and in this sense the devil represents paradoxically (unlike any other treatment of this *topos* known to me) the voice of Ivan's conscience revolting against his reason. Dostoevsky's devil, however, does not preach moral sermons but ridicules the inconsistency between Ivan's pangs of conscience and the ideas he has ac-

---

[2] Victor Terras, *A Karamazov Companion* (Madison, WI, 1984), 385.

cepted and expounded. "Everything is permitted" for those who do not believe in God and immortality, and Ivan has rejected both. Why, then, should he be tormented by feelings of moral guilt that derive from such principles? The devil arrives to personify Ivan's self-mockery of his own moral-psychic contradictions, which have driven him into what Dostoevsky called brain fever and we now diagnose as schizophrenia. Ivan will finally break down completely—but not before the devil has exhibited both Ivan's longing for faith and the difficulty of attaining it for someone who refuses to accept any non-Euclidean world.

The involutions of Ivan's conversation with the devil are so intricate that it is impossible to give in brief any adequate account of their complexities. Essentially, however, its aim is to dramatize the antinomies in which Ivan is trapped once his conscience comes into clashing opposition with those rational convictions that give rise to his rebellion against God and Christ. The supreme irony, of course, is that it should be the devil who apparently leads him along the path to faith; and Ivan (who is of course speaking to himself *through* the devil) realizes all the incongruity of such a situation. As the devil remarks, "if you come to that, does proving there is a devil prove that there is a God?" Ivan insists all through the dialogue that the devil is only his hallucination and has no independent reality. "'You are a lie, you are my illness, you are a phantom . . . you are my hallucination,' he cries out" (15: 71–72). So long as Ivan believes this, he does not have to accept that the devil emanates from some non-Euclidean, irrational world of Christian faith; but the upsurge of moral conscience from which he has begun to suffer makes it impossible for him to dismiss such a possibility entirely.

The devil himself both asserts his ontological reality, which Ivan vehemently denies, and then helps Ivan to reinforce such a denial. When Ivan accuses the devil of lying (!), the latter obligingly agrees: "Just so. But hesitation, suspense, conflict between belief and disbelief—is sometimes such a torture to a conscientious man, such as you are, that it's better to hang oneself at once." For Ivan's benefit, the devil explains, he is using a "new method," no longer the old one in which belief and disbelief were presented as polar opposites; now he is employing homeopathic medicine, in which small doses of a drug that augment the disease can result in a cure.[3] "I lead you to belief and disbelief by turns," the devil says; "as soon as you disbelieve in me completely, you'll begin assuring me to my face that I cannot be a dream but a reality." Reason may prevent Ivan from believing, but the moment he refuses, his moral conscience will drive him to the opposite pole despite all the conclusions of his logic. By this method the devil will sow in Ivan "only a tiny grain of faith and it will grow into an oak tree—and such an oak tree that, sitting on it, you will try to enter into the ranks of 'the

---

[3] I am indebted to Robin Feuer Miller for her analysis of the devil as a practitioner of metaphysical homeopathy. See *The Brothers Karamazov: Worlds of the Novel* (New Haven, CT, 2008), 123–125, and *Dostoevsky's Unfinished Journey* (New Haven, CT, 2008), 150, 166–170.

hermit monks and chaste women' [a quote from Pushkin] for that is what you are secretly longing for. You'll dine on locusts, you'll wander in the wilderness to save your soul" (15: 80). Ivan's devil knows him very well: this is precisely the path the Grand Inquisitor had followed before he lost his faith.

The devil lives up to his reputation as an amiable and entertaining interlocutor, and several of his amusing, debonair anecdotes contain that combination of a scoffing skepticism with a yearning desire for faith that typify Ivan, though he is enraged at being confronted with himself in this guise through the devil's repartee. Many of the devil's sallies include parodies of one or another idea expressed by Ivan earlier, either in the chapter "Rebellion" or in his Legend of the Grand Inquisitor, and they are written with a satirical brio for which it would be hard to find any equal since Swift.

One of the most expressive of these parodies manifestly takes off from Ivan's indignant refusal to join in the "hosannahs" of the universal harmony, of the final reconciliation. It is contained in a legend that the devil recounts even though it is now out of date in *his* world (which he does not want Ivan to confuse with the earthly one, though he then immediately adds that there is no difference between the two). This legend could not be more explicit in depicting Ivan's quandary, and its resolution ends on an ironic note that can be taken as a self-reflexive allusion to Dostoevsky himself. It involves "a thinker and philosopher" who on earth "rejected everything, 'laws, conscience, faith' [a citation from Griboyedov] and, above all, the future life." Indignant at finding himself living such a future life after his death, he protested and was punished by being told that he would have to walk a quadrillion kilometers before reaching the gates of heaven and being forgiven.

Combining "the soul of an enlightened Russian atheist . . . with the soul of the prophet Jonah, who sulked for three days and nights in the belly of the whale," he lay there for a thousand years, but he finally picked himself up and went on. Ivan then interjects that the philospher behaved stupidly by agreeing to move at all because, by Euclidean reckoning, it would take him a billion years to reach his goal. But in fact, as the devil explains, "he got there long ago," because all such mathematical reckonings refer to the present earth, and "our present earth may have been repeated a billion times . . . [disintegrating] into its elements, again 'the water above the firmament' [a quotation from Genesis in Church Slavonic], then again a comet," and so on. Dostoevsky here appeals to the same idea of eternal recurrence, a commonplace in classical antiquity, that Nietzsche would employ for his own purposes, and like his German counterpart, Ivan also finds this cyclical prospect "insufferably tedious." The lexical admixture of the scientific terminology of the period with biblical references is typical of the devil's narrative style and conveys the quandary in which Ivan is trapped.

Reaching his goal at last, the philosopher had not been there for two seconds (though the devil doubts that he still had a watch) when "he cried out that those two seconds were worth walking not a quadrillion kilometers but a quadrillion of quadrillions, raised to the quadrillionth power." In fact, he was so carried away that "he sang 'hosannah' and overdid it so that some persons there of lofty ideas wouldn't shake hands with him at first—he'd become too rapidly reactionary, they said" (15: 78–79). Is this not Dostoevsky sarcastically referring to the criticisms he so often encountered of being a turncoat? And although Ivan then recalls having written this anecdote to ridicule religion when he was still a schoolboy, it also reveals, underneath the jesting, his subliminal longing for faith, a longing equally expressed in the devil's desire to leave the realm of non-Euclidean "indeterminate equations" and become incarnate "once for all and irrevocably in the form of some merchant's wife, weighing two hundred fifty pounds and . . . believing all she believes" (15: 73–74). This yearning is disclosed directly by Ivan when, after asserting that "not for a minute" did he believe in the reality of the devil, he adds "strangely": "But I should like to believe in you" (15: 19).

The full implication of Ivan's ideas becomes clear when the devil reminds him of one of his earlier compositions—not the "Grand Inquisitor," whose mention causes Ivan to become "crimson with shame"—but a work called "The Geological Cataclysm." This title refers to a future when men will have lost all notion of God, and human life will be as much transformed as if the earth had undergone a geological mutation. Dostoevsky here employs his familiar symbolism of the Golden Age; this would again be a Feuerbachian universe, where "love will be sufficient only for a moment of life, but the very consciousness of its momentariness will intensify its fire, which now is dissipated in dreams of an eternal love beyond the grave." This would be a world in which "man will be lifted up with a spirit of divine titanic pride and the Man-god would appear." And by "extending his conquest of nature infinitely by his will and his science, man will feel such lofty joy . . . that it will make up for all his old dreams of the joys of heaven" (15: 83).

Such had been Ivan's vision, which draws on imagery recalling Kirillov in *Demons* as well as that of the Golden Age. But because of "man's inherent stupidity," of which Ivan is only too well aware, the devil understands that it may take a thousand years or more before such a world can come into being; and perhaps it may never be born at all. Ivan and those who share his ideas will therefore become impatient, like those "elect" who finally joined the Grand Inquisitor, and decide that "everyone who recognizes the truth even now may legitimately order his life as he pleases, on the new principles. In that sense 'all things are lawful for him' . . . and since there is no God and no immortality anyway, the new man may well become the Man-god . . . who may lightheartedly overstep all the barriers of the old morality of the old slave-man, if necessary."

(The proto-Nietzschean term "slave-man," *rab-chelovek*, is quite literal.) As the devil cynically comments, all this theorizing "is very charming, but if you want to swindle why do you want a moral sanction for doing it?" (15: 83–84). Idealistic dreams of a transformed humanity can lead not only to swindling but also, as Ivan has now become aware, to a justification for murder. It is impossible here not to think again of Dostoevsky's actual social-political position, in which those whom he was willing to accept as misguided "idealists" were bent on murdering the Tsar-Father.

All through this chapter, the violence of Ivan's reaction to the devil's words is turned back against himself. For if the devil is nothing but his hallucination, why respond so furiously? When Ivan threatens to kick the devil, the latter responds, "I won't be altogether sorry, for then my object will be attained. If you kick me, you must believe in my reality, for people don't kick ghosts" (15: 73). At the climax of the scene, as the devil runs on about "The Geological Cataclysm," Ivan "suddenly snatched a glass from the table and flung it at the orator," who leaps up, brushes off the drops of tea, and comments, "He remembers Luther's inkstand [which Luther had flung at the devil]! He takes me for a dream and throws glasses at a dream!" (15: 84). The devil has thus succeeded in convincing Ivan that he is "real," though the latter continues to insist that the visitation is still only part of himself. But Ivan can no longer refuse to understand what he has been telling himself through the devil—that reason cannot eradicate the torments of his moral conscience.

At this point, the outside world begins to intrude on the sleeping Ivan, and waking, he finds that the physical events he had dreamed of had never taken place. No wet towel lay on his feverish brow, no glass of tea had moved from its place on the table, nor was there any nagging visitor sitting on the sofa facing him. Ivan's first reaction is then to affirm the "reality" of what he had earlier insisted had been only an apparition. "It was not a dream!" he cried out to himself, thus trying to preserve the safeguard of his sanity. When he opens the window, Alyosha (who has been tapping on the window), informs him that "an hour ago Smerdyakov had hanged himself" (15: 85).

Ivan insists "I knew Smerdyakov hanged himself," affirming that "*he* [the devil] had told me so just now." This is not literally true, but the devil had indeed warned Ivan that the conflict between belief and disbelief was such torture that "it could be enough to make you hang yourself" (15: 80). And in Ivan's disordered frame of mind, such words applied to himself could well have been shifted to Smerdyakov, similarly tormented by the same uncertainties. Alyosha's arrival causes the devil to vanish from Ivan's psyche, if not as a recollection then as a presence, but Ivan's inner debate with himself continues. Completely bewildered, he insists that the devil had been in his rooms, but then acknowledges that "*he* is myself . . . All that's base in me." Still, Ivan admits that "he told me a good deal that was true about myself. . . . I would never have owned it to my-self." Most of all, the devil understood the source of Ivan's mortification: "You are going to perform an act of heroic virtue," he had told Ivan, "and you don't believe in virtue; that's what tortures you and makes you angry, that's why you are so vindictive." Now that Smerdyakov is dead, any hope of saving Dimitry has vanished, and yet, the devil sneers, Ivan will go anyway. "And it would be all right if you believed in virtue. . . . But you are a little pig like Feodor Pavlovich and what do you want with virtue?" (15: 87–88).

The devil had had no doubt about how Ivan would act: "you'll go because you won't dare not to go," though why this should be so "is a riddle for you" (15: 88). But it is not a riddle for Alyosha, who finally puts Ivan to bed when he collapses. Alyosha "began to understand Ivan's illness. The anguish of a proud determination. A deep conscience! God, in Whom he disbelieved, and His Truth were gaining mastery in his heart." Alyosha naturally imagines that "God will conquer," and we shall soon see that Ivan will indeed obey the voice of his con-science. But Alyosha's fears also leave open the possibility, not resolved by the time the novel ends, that Ivan will "perish in hate, revenging himself on himself and on everyone for having served the cause he does not believe in" (15: 89).

Indeed, during the trial of Dimitry for the murder of their father, all of Ivan's contempt for humanity—the contempt underlying the Legend of the Grand Inquisitor, despite its humanitarian pathos—comes to the fore as he turns on the judges and all the spectators in the courtroom, none of whom is shown as especially concerned with moral questions. When the startled president asks if Ivan is in his right mind, he replies, "I should think I am in my right mind . . . in the same nasty mind as you . . . and all those . . . ugly faces." Humankind now becomes identified with himself: "They all desire the death of their fathers. One reptile devours another." Alyosha cries out that Ivan has "brain fever," but Ivan continues, "I am not mad, I am only a murderer." When asked for proof of his accusation against Smerdyakov, he replies that he has no witnesses—except possibly the devil—and then rambles on, as if confiding a secret, in a stream-of-consciousness monologue composed of fragments taken from earlier scenes. "I told him I don't want to keep quiet and he talked about the geological cata-clysm . . . idiocy! Come . . . release the monster [Dimitry] . . . he's been singing a hymn. . . . That's because his heart is light. . . . It's like a drunken man in the street howling how 'Vanka went to Petersburg,' and I would give a quadrillion quadrillions for two seconds of joy" (15: 117–118). The poignancy of these last words requires no comment.

———■———

The final section of the novel contains the extensive speeches of both the prose-cuting attorney and the defense, and Dostoevsky uses them not only to provide the proper climax to the plot-action involving Dimitry and Ivan but also as a means of internal commentary on the novel itself. The two lawyers argue about a case of murder, but their orations also illuminate the larger moral-spiritual (and hence implicitly social and political) problems that the novel has presented with such majestic amplitude.

According to the prosecuting attorney Ippolit Kirillovich, Russians are no longer horrified by the crime of murder, and his indictment would certainly have been read, in the context of the time, as a condemnation of those who, if not in sympathy with terrorism, then at least remained neutrally indifferent to its ravages. He argues that the Karamazov family presents a picture of contemporary educated Russia, and Feodor Pavlovich certainly represents—in the extreme, symbolically expressive form that only Dostoevsky knew how to create—the older generation of Russians among whom stable moral-social standards had entirely disappeared. Moreover, Ivan's loss of faith and his theory, as Ippolit Kirillovich puts it, that "everything in the world is lawful," that "nothing must be forbidden in future," has driven Smerdyakov "out of his mind" (15: 126–127); and Dostoevsky here raises the possibility that the intelligentsia's atheism will undermine the still devout Russian people.

Dimitry is seen as a symbol of Russia itself. He, argues the prosecutor, "represents Russia directly. . . . Yes, here she is, our Mother Russia, the very scent and smell of her. Oh, we are spontaneous, we are a marvelous mingling of good and bad, we are lovers of culture and Schiller, yet we brawl in taverns and pluck the beards of our boon companions" (15: 128). Both are part of the Karamazov character, which is "capable of containing the most incongruous contradictions and simultaneously contemplating both abysses, . . . the hightest ideals, and . . . the lowest and foulest degradations" (15: 129). These words echo Dimitry's about the ceaseless conflict between the ideal of Sodom and that of the Madonna, but the entire book has shown his struggle to wrench himself free from the temptations of Sodom and commit himself to the Mother of God.

In conclusion, the prosecutor returns to the image of the Russian troika made famous in Gogol's *Dead Souls*, where Russia is compared with a troika, furiously galloping to some distant destination and before which all the other nations give way. The jurors represent, he tells them, all "of our holy Russia, . . . her principles, her family, everything that she holds sacred!" The whole country awaits their verdict, as "our fatal troika dashes on in headlong flight, perhaps to destruction, and for a long time past men have stretched out imploring hands and called a halt to its furious, reckless course." Other nations stand aside, "not from respect . . . but simply from horror," and he warns that some day they may "form a firm wall confronting the hurrying apparition . . . for the sake of their own safety, enlightenment, and civilization." The jury, Ippolit Kirillovich warns, must not increase "their growing hatred by a sentence justifying the murder of a father by his son" (15: 150).

The famous defense attorney Fetyukovich, the star of the Petersburg bar, now offers a masterly defense of Dimitry in terms that the reader recognizes as accurate. His defense not only discredits the psychological inferences drawn by Ippolit Kirillovich, he also understands that Dimitry could act under the influence of love, honor, and pity, as well as out of the rage and jealousy considered his sole motivations by the prosecutor. Dostoevsky's main criticism of the legal profession in his journalism, however, had been that defense lawyers, carried away by their task, often lost sight of the larger moral implications of their arguments, and this is exactly what occurs here. Fetyukovich goes too far, swept beyond the bounds of the morally legitimate by the desire to defend his client (who in this case at least was innocent).

Fetyukovich treads on dangerous ground when he raises the question of whether the murder of such a reprehensible father as Feodor Pavlovich could be condemned. While insisting that Dimitry is innocent, he nonetheless argues that such a murder could well be justified, driving home the point with examples taken from a tirade of the villainous Karl Moor in Schiller's *The Robbers*. The indignant narrator now labels him "an adulterer of thought" (the chapter's title); and it is here that the defense plea intersects with the novel's deepest moral-philosophical motifs. "Filial love for an unworthy father," Fetyukovich insists, "is an absurdity, an impossibility. Love cannot be created from nothing: only God can create something from nothing" (15: 169). If fathers wish to be loved by their children, they should earn such love by their deeds. Love for a father should rest on a rational, responsible, and strictly humanitarian basis"; it should not derive from a "mystical meaning which I cannot comprehend with my intellect, but only accept by faith, or better, *on faith*, like many other things which I do not understand, but which religion leads me to believe" (15: 170). The courtroom audience, as the narrator notes sarcastically, went wild over this denunciation of a filial love based solely on faith. "Even persons of high position, old men with stars on their breasts, sitting on specially reserved seats behind the judges, applauded the orator and waved their handkerchiefs" (15: 171). The bitter irony of this comment is certainly reminiscent of what had occurred in the Zasulich courtroom, when high government officials had frenziedly applauded her acquittal.

Fetyukovich is here making the same argument against unconditional filial love, based only on faith, that Ivan had made against a God-father who incomprehensibly permits the undeserved suffering of his children. But the lawyer goes still further when he suggests that, even if Dimitry had entered the house—which he denied having done—with no intent to kill, he might have struck

Feodor Pavlovich precisely *because* "The mere sight of the father who hated him from his childhood, had been his enemy, his persecutor, and now his unnatural rival, was enough." His feeling of hatred would have become so strong that he might have dealt him a blow, "not knowing that he would kill him" and not intending at all to do so. But if he *had* killed him, "the murder of such a father," Fetyukovich insists, "cannot be considered parricide . . . can only be reckoned a parricide by prejudice" (15: 172).

Fetyukovich undermines his own case, however, by raising doubts as to whether he himself believed in the innocence of his client. And we know that the terms of Fetyukovich's argument recall those that Ivan had made against the God-father. But in asking the reader to accept Ivan's attack on God and Dimitry's hatred of Feodor Pavlovich as equally impious assaults on the sacrosanct principle of fatherhood, Dostoevsky was taking a considerable artistic-ideological risk. Indeed, if there is some question among interpreters as to whether Dostoevsky ever truly succeeded in blunting the force of Ivan's rebellion, an even stronger doubt arises over his effort to merge the levels of this same thematic motif. God, after all, bestowed on man the immense gift of freedom, however badly this gift may have been abused and misused, and while he can be held implicitly responsible for all the horrors that have ensued, they occurred, as even Ivan conceded in his Legend, because he refused to enslave the dignity of the human conscience.

It is entirely different, however, to substitute Feodor Pavlovich for God and to ask readers to accept a refusal to love *him* unconditionally as an equivalent violation of the sacred principle of fatherhood. The stark realism with which his cynicism and debauchery are displayed, and his complete lack of any redeeming features, undermine the parallel that Dostoevsky was trying to establish. Readers, in this case, are likely to ally themselves with Fetyukovich's insistence that mundane filial-paternal love should involve reciprocity and mutual responsibility. Nonetheless, just as Dostoevsky had not softened the asperities of Ivan's attack on the shortcomings of both God and Christ, so here too he dares to proffer the protection of the sacrosanct principle of fatherhood, unassailable by reason and justified by faith alone, even to so odious a specimen as Feodor Pavlovich. One cannot help wondering whether the extremity of this effort was not a forlorn response to the nerve-racking situation that all of Russia was then living through, as one attempt after another was made on the life of the Tsar-Father.

After appealing to reason to defend a crime that Dimitry had not committed, Fetyukovich then concludes by evoking a totally opposite principle—that of Christian mercy. As he goes on, Fetyukovich's eloquent words continue to ask for mercy in a manner implying Dimitry's guilt. "Let other nations think of retribution and the letter of the law, we will cling to the spirit and the meaning—the salvation and reformation of the lost" (15: 172). The argument is thus a tissue of contradictions, more an apologia for the crime than a clear-cut defense of Dimitry's innocence.

These concluding words excite a demonstration from the audience that was like "an irresistible storm." Everyone wept, and even "two important personages shed tears" at this combination of rationalism and an appeal to a sentimental humanitarianism deriving from Christian principles. When Ippolit Kirillovich rose to protest, "shaking with emotion . . . people positively looked at him with hatred." In his articles, Dostoevsky had often criticized the abuse of the Gospels by defense lawyers, and Ippolit Kirillovich charges Fetyukovich with such malpractice by his reference to Christ as "the crucified lover of humanity . . . in opposition to all of orthodox Russia, which calls to Him, 'for thou art our God.'" "Religion and the Gospels," Ippolit Kirillovich cries, "are corrected—that's all mysticism, we are told, and ours is the only true Christianity which has been subjected to the analysis of reason and common sense" (15: 173–175).

The jury retires, and while the courtroom waits for its decision, the narrator sets down snatches of conversation among the public. Everyone, it seems, was convinced of an acquittal despite the weight of the evidence. Many believed he would get off because, as one official said, "suppose he did murder him—there are fathers and there are fathers!" (15: 177). These choral voices seem to justify Ippolit Kirillovich's opening statement that murder is now taken as a matter of course in Russia. Like the public, Fetyukovich too was convinced that he had won the case, but after an hour's deliberation the jury returned to find Dimitry guilty on all counts and, even worse, made no recommendation for mercy. During the indescribable hubbub in the courtroom, the narrator recalls one exclamation: "Well, our peasants have stood firm!" (15: 178).

The culmination of this central plot action thus creates a mixed impression—one both negative and positive. An obvious "miscarriage of justice" (the title of Book 12) has occurred on the legal level, though Dimitry has inwardly accepted the justice of suffering for his parricidal impulses. But "the peasants have stood firm" against justifying the murder of a father for *any* reason, thus upholding the "mystic" sanctity of the moral-religious law that Dimitry had violated in thought if not in deed.

———■———

The epilogue is composed of two episodes, one detailing the relations between Ivan, Katerina, and Dimitry, the other between Alyosha and the group of boys who had clustered around the bedside of the ailing Ilyusha. Ivan's future remains unknown, though he is left in the care of Katerina, and this uncertainty was no doubt intended to sustain interest for the next volume. Dimitry has fallen ill with "a nervous fever" and is waiting to be sent to Siberia; whether he will escape along the way is left in doubt. Dimitry has concluded that he is too weak to bear the burden that, in a moment of rapture, he had believed he could assume: "I am not able to resign myself. I wanted to sing a 'hymn'; but if a guard speaks to me, I haven't the strength to bear it." Alyosha agrees that "you are not ready, and such a cross is not for you," that is, the cross of an *imitatio Christi*, the acceptance of punishment by an innocent as expiation for the sins and injustices of others. Dimitry had wished to make himself "another man by suffering" and had in fact gone a long way toward becoming that "other man" spiritually. Alyosha assures him that if "you only remember that other man always, all your life and wherever you escape to . . . that will be enough for you" (15: 185). The disciple of Zosima is prepared to break the letter of the law by conniving in Dimitry's possible escape so as to avert an obvious injustice and a human tragedy.

The book ends with the funeral of little Ilyusha. No one but Dickens can rival Dostoevsky's well-known "philanthropic" manner here, as he depicts the anguish and despair of the desolate Captain Snegiryov and his afflicted family. Twelve of Ilyusha's schoolmates, gathered around his bier, were soon joined by Alyosha, and this symbolic number provides a Christological aura to the pathos of the scene. Kolya, foremost among the boys as usual, exclaims about Dimitry: "So he will perish an innocent victim for the truth—though ruined he is happy!" Astonished at this reaction, Alyosha objects, "but not in such a cause, and with such disgrace and such horror." Kolya agrees, but then continues, "I would like to die for all humanity, and as for disgrace, I don't care about that. . . . I respect your brother!" (15: 190). Dostoevsky had emphasized this desire to "die for humanity," to sacrifice oneself for "the truth," as typical of the new generation of the 1870s, and perhaps we catch a glimpse here of what he intended the future to hold for both Kolya and Alyosha.

The boys pass the stone under which Ilyusha had wished to be buried and here Alyosha, addressing them as "my dear, dear children," explains that he will soon part from them. But he asks them to make a pact never to forget Ilyusha or one another, "whatever happens to us later in life." He urges them to remember "how good it was once here when we were all together united by a good and kind feeling." Alyosha then proclaims, "there is nothing higher and stronger and more wholesome and good for life in the future than some good memory, especially a memory of childhood and home" (15: 195). A "good and sacred memory" of this kind is the best protection against the evil that may arrive, and will remain so no matter how badly some among them may go astray.

Alyosha's words grip the hearts of his young listeners, and when the boys promise to remember, shouting at the same time, "Karamazov, we love you," Alyosha adds: "And may the dear boy's memory live eternally!" The mention of eternity impels Kolya to ask whether "It is true what's taught us in religion," that a bodily resurrection will occur and we "shall live and see each other again, all, Ilyushechka too?" Alyosha answers, "half laughing, half ecstatic": "Certainly we shall all arise again, certainly we shall all see each other" (15: 196). The tragedy of the Snegiryovs thus vanishes into "a sacred memory" that will guard against evil in the future; and death is overcome by the Christian hope of resurrection—when, as Alyosha promises, "we shall tell each other with joy and gladness all that has happened" (15: 197). The book ends on this boyish note of innocence and optimisim, providing a welcome relief, similar to the epilogues of eighteenth-century plays, to all the tragic tensions that have gone before. And just as those earlier examples pointed to the moral of the story, so Dostoevsky reaffirms, in a naïvely acceptable and touching form, the basic beliefs and moral-religious convictions he has sought to champion so peerlessly all through his greatest novel.

CHAPTER 61

Death and Transfiguration

After the intense pressure under which he had been laboring for the past three years, Dostoevsky might well have felt a need to relax, rest, and recoup his strength. But now that the first volume of *The Brothers Karamazov* had been completed he threw himself, with his usual assiduity, into gathering material for his revived *Diary of a Writer*. Well aware of the severe demands this renewal would make on his gradually deteriorating health, he was driven by economic need—other sources of income were quite insufficient—and also by the mission he had assumed to speak out against the forces disintegrating the fabric of Russian society.

Two memories portray Dostoevsky at this time as aged, feeble, and sickly. I. I. Popov, a student at the Pedagogical Institute and later a member of the terrorist organization People's Will, lived close to the Dostoevsky residence and often saw the writer sitting in the park of the nearby church, watching the children at play. "Hunched up, emaciated, with a yellowish-colored face, hollow cheeks, sunken eyes. . . . He gave the impression of a person seriously ill."[1] Popov once saw him walking with his old friend and fellow author Grigorovich, dragging himself along and leaning heavily on an umbrella, and he thought that Grigorovich would surely outlive his companion. A similar image is given by Letkova-Sultanova, who saw Dostoevsky at the home of the marquis Paulucci, where he took part in a benefit evening. In the stately and brilliantly lit reception room, filled with fashionably dressed society, he was attired in an ill-fitting formal evening suit too large for his frame and appeared "even more shrunken, more emaciated, more pallid than ever," and she was struck by "his look of suffering."[2]

Whatever the state of his physical health, and perhaps because he knew that his days were numbered, Dostoevsky felt it imperative to speak out in defense of his ideas that were now under attack by both liberals and radicals. Many entries in the notebooks rebut K. D. Kavelin, an important liberal Westernizer and university professor who had been tutored by Belinsky as a young student. Kavelin had attacked Dostoevsky's belief that personal and moral betterment could

[1] *DVS*, 2: 475.

[2] *Letopis zhizni i tvorchestvo F. M. Dostoevskogo*, ed. N. F. Budanova and G. M. Fridlender, 3 vols. (St. Petersburg, 1995), 3: 503.

provide the basis for an improved (indeed, for an "ideal") society. Society, he argued, could be changed for the better only by social-political action, not by that Christian self-perfecting of individuals advocated by Dostoevsky as an infallible remedy for Russia's social ills.

Dostoevsky's notes reaffirm, in the very last month of his life, one of the basic beliefs that had sustained him ever since emerging from the Siberian prison camp in 1854. At that time, he had written the famous letter declaring that, "if someone proved to me that Christ is outside the truth, and that *in reality*, the truth were outside of Christ, then I would prefer to remain with Christ rather than with the truth."[3] The same type of choice is posed more than twenty years later with reference to the Christian commandment of selfless love: "Turn the other cheek, love more than yourself, not because it is useful, but because it is pleasing, to the point of a burning feeling, to the point of passion. Christ made mistakes—it has been proven! This burning feeling says: It is better for me to stay with a mistake, with Christ, rather than with you" (27: 57). Another passage recasts the idea of the *extreme* nature of the demands made by Christ on the human personality and stresses its opposition to Utilitarian reasoning. "All of Christ's ideas," he writes, "can be debated by the human mind and seem impossible to fulfill. To turn the other cheek, to love more than yourself. For goodness sake, now why should that be? I am here for an instant, there is no immortality, I will live in my [obscenity]" (27: 56).

Kavelin's tone of lofty professorial self-assurance also provoked Dostoevsky to an extremely rare outburst of self-praise. "The Inquisitor and the chapter about children," he confides to his notebook. "In view of these chapters, you [Kavelin] could regard me from a scientific point of view; but not so arrogantly when it concerns philosophy, although philosophy is not my specialty. Even in Europe, such a force of atheistic *expression* does not exist, *nor did it ever*. Therefore, it is not like a child that I believe in Christ and profess faith in him, but rather, my *hosanna* has come through the great *crucible of doubt*, as the devil says in that same novel of mine" (27: 86). Kavelin's criticisms prompted Dostoevsky to probe and clarify his own convictions carefully, and it is unfortunate that his response remains only fragmentary.

Another note returns to the same point. "The scoundrels [his critics] provoke me with *an ignorant* and retrograde faith in God. These asses could not even dream of such a powerful negation of God as is depicted in the Inquisitor and in the preceding chapter, to which the entire novel serves as an answer. It is not like a fool or a fanatic that I believe in God. And they want to teach me, and sneer at my backwardness. Yes, their stupidity could not dream of as strong a negation as I went through. They teach me! . . . Ivan Feodorovich is profound,

---

[3] *PSS*, 28/Bk. 1: 176; February 20, 1854.

not one of the contemporary atheists, who demonstrate in their disbelief only the paltriest narrowness of their stupid abilities" (27: 48).

On December 3, Dostoevsky replied to a letter that Ivan Aksakov had sent a month earlier. "The main reason for the delay," he writes, is "my very bad health . . . my emphysema has worsened."[4] The letter is devoted to the cultural-ideological issues that were in the forefront for both Dostoevsky and his correspondent, and Dostoevsky now expresses an unqualified hostility to the historical legacy of Peter the Great. He finds that Aksakov, having written that Peter "moved us into Europe and gave us European civilization," had not sufficiently stressed the unhappy consequences of this presumably beneficial feat. Peter's reforms, Dostoevsky insists, had divided Russian society into layers—"the authorities, the enserfed masses, and the city dwellers, with fourteen classes among them. That's Peter's work. Liberate the people and it would seem that Peter's work was undone. But the belt, the zone between the authorities and the masses won't retreat for anything and won't give up its privilege of ruling the broad masses." The social transformation, begun with the liberation of the serfs, had ground to a halt, and Aksakov should have made clear that as a result of the European civilization imported by Peter, "what in fact lies between the authorities and the people like a fatal belt [is] made up of the 'best people' from the fourteen classes."[5]

His notes at this time echo the same antagonism to Peter the Great. One reads, "Nihilism appeared in our country because we are *all Nihilists*. . . . (All are Feodor Pavloviches right down to the last man.)" Dostoevsky ridicules "the wise men" who wonder where the Nihilists came from: "No, . . . we are not Nihilists, we simply want to save Russia by rejecting her (i.e., form *a layer* of aristocrats above the people, raising the people up to our own nothingness)" (27: 54). In the only issue of the *Diary* that Dostoevsky was able to complete before his death, he proposes that this "fatal belt" be swept away entirely.

------◼------

By December 9, the two-volume edition of *The Brothers Karamazov* was ready. Dostoevsky began to distribute gift copies among his friends and family, and one was sent to Pobedonostsev, who advised him to present the book in person to Tsarevich Alexander. The heir to the throne and his consort, Marya Feodorovna, received him a week later at the Anichkov Palace. The only account of this presentation was left by Lyubov Dostoevskaya, then still a child, who probably relays what her mother had been told by Pobedonostsev. Her father behaved in

[4] Ibid., 30/Bk. 1: 232; December 3, 1880.
[5] Ibid., 232–233.

the presence of royalty exactly "as he was accustomed to behave in the salons of his friends. He spoke first, rose when he found that the conversation had gone on sufficiently long, and, taking leave of the Tsarevich and his wife, quitted the room as he had always done, turning his back" to his hosts. The tsarevich reportedly "was not offended by this, and later spoke of my father with esteem."[6]

An informative account of Dostoevsky at this time has been left by Dimitry Merezhkovsky, one of the most important Russian novelists and critics of the twentieth century (his two-volume study, *Tolstoy and Dostoevsky*, did much to shape later critical opinion about both writers). The fifteen-year-old Merezhkovsky had begun to write poetry, and his father seized the opportunity to obtain a professional opinion about his son's adolescent scribblings after meeting Dostoevsky by chance in the salon of Countess Sofya Tolstaya. "I remember," Merezhkovsky wrote in an autobiographical fragment, "the diminutive apartment in Kuznechny Alley with its low ceiling and cramped living room, piled with copies of *The Brothers Karamazov*, and the study, almost as narrow, in which Feodor Mikhailovich sat over galleys. Blushing, turning pale, stuttering, I read my childish, paltry verses. He listened silently, with impatient annoyance. We must have been disturbing him. 'Weak, bad, worth nothing,' he said at last. 'In order to write well, one must suffer, suffer!' 'No,' said my father, 'let him not write any better, only let him not suffer.' I recall the pellucid and penetrating look of the pale blue eyes when Dostoevsky shook my hand. I never saw him again, and then very shortly learned that he had died."[7]

On December 27, Dostoevsky wrote a note to Countess Anna Komarovskaya, accepting her invitation to come to the Winter Palace at five on the afternoon of December 30. This titled lady was a member of the intimate court circle with which he had become acquainted, and at her request he read from his works for the guests she had assembled. Among them was Countess Alexandra Andreyevna Tolstaya, a distant relative of the novelist, who had spent her life as lady-in-waiting to one or another grand duchess but whose cultivation and intelligence were valued so highly by Tolstoy that she became one of his epistolary confidantes. Dostoevsky was eager to meet and speak with her about the enigmatic sage of Yasnaya Polyana, and she, on whom *Crime and Punishment* had produced an ineffaceable impression ("no other novel had ever stirred me so strongly"), had been impatient to make his acquaintance. Once the introduction was over, he immediately posed a question about Tolstoy, in whom, the countess notes, he took "a passionate interest." "Can you explain his new tendency?" he asked. The countess admitted that it was "mysterious" to her as well,

[6] *Letopis*, 3: 513.

[7] Cited in G. M. Fridlender, "D. S. Merezhkovsky i Dostoevsky," in *Dostoevsky—materialy i issledovaniya*, vol. 10 (St. Petersburg, 1992), 4.

but she promised to produce Tolstoy's letter, where he spoke about all this—on the condition that he come to visit her for its transmission.[8]

He set January 11 as the date, and we shall abandon chronology a bit to round out this episode. "This enchanting and unique evening has remained fixed in my memory forever," the countess continues. "I heard Dostoevsky with reverence: he spoke, like a true Christian, about the fate of Russia and the whole world; his eyes burned, and I felt in him a prophet." The countess, a devout Christian, had broken into tears when her cousin Lev had announced to her in 1878 that he no longer accepted the divinity of Christ or regarded him as the Saviour, and the letter she read to Dostoevsky contained many of the same sentiments. "I can see Dostoevsky before me now, as he clutched his head and in a despairing voice repeated: 'Not that! Not that!' He did not sympathize with a single thought of Lev Nikolaevich; despite which he gathered up all the writing lying on the table: the original and the copy of Lev's letter. From some of his words I concluded that the desire was stirring within him to dispute the false ideas of Lev Nikolaevich."[9] Countess Tolstaya's intuition was quite accurate, and although he did not live to carry out this intention, his last notebook contains the entry: "To what extent man has *worshipped* himself (Lev Tolstoy)" (27: 43).

———■———

The new year 1881 found Dostoevsky in a buoyant mood, despite the occasionally gloomy predictions in his letters and conversations. To Grigorovich, sometime in the early part of January, he said that he doubted whether he would live out the winter months,[10] but Anna wrote that "in the first half of January Feodor Mikhailovich was in excellent spirits. He frequented his friends, and even agreed to take part in some private theatrics that the Countess S. A. Tolstaya intended to stage. He wished to play the part of the ascetic recluse in the play *The Death of Ivan the Terrible* by A. K. Tolstoy, the countess's deceased husband."[11] His emotions probably wavered constantly, depending on his mood; and since he understood so well the importance of hope in resisting despair, he would have struggled against the occasional onslaughts of dejection brought on by his increasingly physical debility.

One catches a glimpse of Dostoevsky in the memoirs of his former proofreader, Varvara Timofeyeva, on which we have already drawn so extensively. When she passed him in the street at the beginning of 1881, he failed to recognize her, and she was too timid to approach him; but her words indicate the change of sentiment about him on the part of her generation. "I so much wished

[8] *DVS*, 2: 363–364.
[9] Ibid.
[10] *Letopis*, 3: 529.
[11] Anna Dostoevsky, *Reminiscences*, trans. and ed. Beatrice Stillman (New York, 1975), 341.

to go to him, hear his voice again, tell him *how deeply* I now understood him, and how much that was good he had brought to me. . . . I felt myself to be his disciple, indebted to him for my moral world, my spiritual freedom."[12] Such emotions were not the result only of personal acquaintance, as can be seen from the memoirs of a writer now fallen into oblivion, A. V. Kruglov. "I was walking along the Nevsky Prospect with a medical student. Dostoevsky happened to come past us in a carriage. The medical student quickly, before I could do so myself, raised his hat. 'Do you perhaps know Dostoevsky?' I asked. 'No, but what does that matter? I did not bow to him, but bared my head as I did in Moscow when I walked past the statue of Pushkin.'"[13]

He had become a revered, symbolic figure who stood above the merciless battle of ideologies. His works had raised all the burning issues of the day far beyond the limits of a narrow partisanship. While Dostoevsky was being pilloried by the liberal and radical press, the presumably left-wing students were receiving him with open arms; and the reason, as his friend Orest Miller wrote in the January issue of the Populist Slavophil journal *The Week*, was that he always spoke "openly and boldly in all directions, not worrying what would be said about him. The youth welcome, with the discernment of the heart, everything straightforward and unservile."[14]

While he was organizing the notes for the January issue of his *Diary*, others for February and March piled up. Several articles written by Suvorin shortly after Dostoevsky's decease provide information about what the future *Diary* might have contained. One comment reveals the astonishing paradox of Dostoevsky's social-political position—the dream of an ideal Russia coming to birth in a state embodying the very opposite of what such a dream was striving to attain. "In his opinion," Suvorin writes, "it is possible for us to attain complete freedom, a freedom existing nowhere else, and all this without any revolution, any restrictions, any controls."[15] In a conversation about the continuation of *The Brothers Karamazov*, Suvorin heard from the author that "Alyosha Karamazov would emerge as the hero of the novel's continuation, a hero from whom [Dostoevsky] wished to create a type of Russian Socialist, not the usual type that we know and which sprouted entirely out of European soil."[16] Grand Duke Alexander Mikhailovich recalls Suvorin as having also quoted these words: "It seems to you [Suvorin—J. F.] that in my last novel, *The Brothers Karamazov*, there was much that was prophetic. But wait for the continuation. In it Alyosha will leave the monastery and become an anarchist. And my pure Alyosha will

---

[12] *DVS*, 2: 195.
[13] Cited in I. Volgin, *Posledny god Dostoevskogo* (Moscow, 1986), 387.
[14] *Letopis*, 3: 526–527.
[15] *DVS*, 2: 469–470.
[16] *Letopis*, 3: 536.

kill the Tsar."[17] If there is any mistake in the testimony of the grand duke, it would be in characterizing Alyosha as an "anarchist" rather than as the much more plausible "Russian Socialist," a term that receives some support from the *Diary*.

On January 22, Anna records in her notebook that, in speaking of their plans for the summer, they had discussed a long-cherished ambition to purchase a country estate. "In the evening," she writes, "we talked about where to go, and he spoke of his dreams."[18] With the money still owed him by *The Russian Messenger* and the subscriptions pouring in for the new *Diary*, he thought it possible. On the twenty-fourth, he was a dinner guest of Countess Tolstaya and borrowed a copy of her late husband's play about Ivan the Terrible to prepare for the theatrics, and he also made the final corrections to the *Diary*. The next day, January 25, he went to the printing plant with these pages and asked that galleys be sent the day following. He also wrote to Countess Komarovskaya, accepting her invitation to the Winter Palace on the first day he thought he would be free, January 29.

———◼———

At times, in these pages for the *Diary*, he comes dangerously close not only to criticizing government policy but also to impugning its very basis. "I believe as a matter of economics," he writes in a passage that could well be considered subversive, "that the land is *possessed*, not by railway magnates, not by the industrialists, not by the millionaires, not by the banks, and not by the Yids, but only by those who cultivate it . . . the tillers of the soil are themselves the state, its nucleus, its vital core." But the financing of railways, which were built at a speed much greater than in Europe, was done "when the land was most in need of [capital]" (27: 10). No wonder he was so concerned about getting this issue of the *Diary* through the censorship! It was impossible for him to expatiate any further on the question of "possession" without implying that the peasants should not be required to buy back their own land from those who had no right to its ownership.

Naturally, the government had always been concerned with the peasants; numerous commissions had been appointed over the years to study their "economic health" and every aspect of their way of life (27: 13). Dostoevsky insists, however, that the people have become totally alienated from all the social institutions of Russia because the *zemstvos* and the courts are all under the control of the bureaucracy. Even the *obshchina*, that bastion of Russian peasant democracy, "seems to be moving toward becoming a kind of authority" because its elections are now overseen by "some government official or other" (27: 17).

[17] Ibid., 3: 535–536; *DVS*, 2: 473.
[18] *Letopis*, 3: 539.

Indeed, the more the authorities try to aid the people, the worse the situation becomes. Their total misunderstanding of the people derives from a failure to grasp the importance of Orthodoxy, which constitutes the very essence of the people's being. Dostoevsky writes: "I am speaking now not about church buildings and not about sermons; I am speaking about our Russian Socialism (and . . . I am taking this word, which is quite the opposite of all that the church represents, to explain my idea)" (27: 18). In daring to apply the phrase "Russian Socialism" to his own messianic hope, he employs a term first coined by Herzen to predict that the peasant-based cooperative social institutions of Russia, such as the *obshchina* and the *artel,* would take the lead over Europe in creating the Socialist world of the future. Dostoevsky thus stresses, as he had already done with Alyosha Karamazov, the similarity between his own ultimate aims and those of the Russian radicals. But for him, this aim had now become identified with "the establishment of the universal church on earth, insofar as the earth is capable of containing it"; and he believed that such an aim was shared, even if only inchoately and unconsciously, by the vast multitude of the Russian peasantry (27: 18–19).

The people trust only in God and the tsar, and for Dostoevsky the first step toward relieving their malaise is to sweep away everything that stands between them and their revered ruler. "Summon the gray peasant coats," he admonishes, "and ask them what they lack and what they need and they will tell the truth, and all of us, for the first time perhaps, will hear the real truth!" (27: 21). Today we can hardly imagine just how daring such a Populist suggestion was in a totally despotic state, all of whose policy and decisions were determined in secret by the tsar and his advisers, and in which the democratic notion of consulting the people was considered nothing less than lèse-majesté. Nor was Dostoevsky suggesting what the Russians call a *zemsky sobor,* an assembly of all classes in the land, which had been convoked during the Time of Troubles and established the Romanov family as the ruling house. No, only the peasantry should be consulted. "[A]nd we, 'the people's intelligentsia,' shall stand meekly aside for the moment and at first merely look on while they speak and we listen" (27: 24). Dostoevsky explains that he is asking the intelligentsia to step aside not for "political" but for pedagogical reasons. This image of the people was either scornfully dismissed, or more charitably regarded as just another flight of Dostoevsky's artistic-poetic imagination.

Dostoevsky concludes this issue of the *Diary* with reflections on Russian foreign policy, prompted by the advance of a Russian expeditionary force into Central Asia. The liberal St. Petersburg journals were highly critical of this imperialist adventure, particularly in view of the financial difficulties with which the country was struggling. Dostoevsky took up the cudgels not only to praise the victorious General Skobelev and his troops, but also to expound again the thematic leitmotif of this first issue—Russia was not Europe, and hence should not determine its foreign policy with European interests and concerns in mind.

For Dostoevsky, the spread of Russian power in Central Asia will shake the prestige of England and convince all the peoples "up to the very borders of India ... of the invincibility of the white Tsar and the omnipotence of his sword" (27: 32). The time is now ripe for Russia to think of Asia, which could play the same role for it as the discovery of America had done for Europe. All of Russia would be rejuvenated by this acquisition, the country would free itself from its inertia and sense of dependence on Europe, and a brave new world would come to birth. "In Europe we were hangers-on and slaves, while in Asia we shall be the masters." Like other advocates of imperialism, Dostoevsky argues that Russia will perform "a civilizing mission" in Asia, but he is perhaps more straightforward in pointing to all the riches that could be exploited—"the metals, the minerals, the countless coal fields." And Asiatic expansion would also revitalize the Russians themselves. "Our mission will elevate our spirits, it will help give us dignity and self-awareness" (27: 36–37).

Dostoevsky had always relished predicting the downfall of European civilization, and he now adds some new touches to the usual evocation of merciless class warfare. "Let people understand that when Europe, because of overcrowding alone, establishes the inevitable and humiliating communism, which she herself will loathe, when whole crowds of people will have to press around a single hearth and, little by little, individual households will be destroyed and families will abandon their own homes and start living collectively in communes, when children (three-quarters of them foundlings) are raised in institutions, then—then we shall still have broad expanses, fields, and forests, and our children will grow up with their own fathers, not in cramped stone prisons, but amid orchards and cultivated fields, seeing the pure, blue sky above them" (27: 38). Presumably, Asiatic expansion will drain off enough of the Russian population to avoid the "overcrowding" that will stifle Europe. And so he concludes: "Long live Skobelev and his good lads, and eternal memory to the heroes who were 'struck off the rolls'" (27: 40). Three days after editing this celebratory elegy, Dostoevsky's name itself vanished from the rolls of the living.

It is regrettable that the last words from his pen should glorify imperial conquest, and perhaps we can alleviate their dispiriting effect by citing some others, written at approximately the same time, that provide a more adequate picture of the full scope of his complex and self-conflicted personality. In his last notebooks, he wrote: "With total realism, to find the man in mankind. This is primarily a Russian trait, and in this sense I am really in the last analysis of the people [*naroden*] (for my tendency flows from the depths of the Christian soul of the people)—although I am unknown to the Russian people at present, I will be known in the future" (27: 65). This is the Dostoevsky who has become an important part of the patrimony of world culture, not the misguided patriot waving the banner of imperial domination, though it is part of the mystery of the human personality with which he struggled that both could coexist in his breast.

———■———

On the twenty-fifth of January, Dostoevsky was visited by two of his oldest friends, Apollon Maikov and Nikolay Strakhov. Conversation turned on the January issue of the *Diary*, as well as his plans for the February number, and then Orest Miller arrived. Miller had his own business to transact about the Pushkin evening. Posters for the event listing Dostoevsky were already on display, but Dostoevsky decided against his first choice and wished to read some of Pushkin's shorter poems. Miller, understandably, became quite exasperated. Aside from the problem of the posters, it could lead to endless bother with the censorship and the other authorities whose consent would be required for any alteration. Dostoevsky's annoyance in turn changed to genuine anger. Matters were settled when Miller agreed to the change, but there is no doubt that, on the afternoon of January 25, Dostoevsky had been subjected to severe nervous strain.

After the unfortunate disaccord, Dostoevsky departed for the printing plant to hand in the final corrections for the last pages of the *Diary*. Returning home at 7:30, the usual time for the family dinner, he joined Anna and the children, who had been to the theater and seen a play taken from *The Pickwick Papers*. "And all through the dinner," Anna writes, "we spoke of the Pickwick club, recalling every particularity, telling him about them, and then I asked who that actor was. 'Mr. Jingle,' answered Feodor Mikhailovich."[19] There is something extremely touching about this image of Dostoevsky, on one of the last days of his life, talking lightheartedly with his wife and children about Dickens, an author whom he loved both for his gaiety and for his Christian compassion—a compassion so much less tortured and tormented than his own. Extremely touching, but, as it turns out, entirely fictional.

In a letter written in 1883 to Strakhov, who shared with Miller the task of putting together the first biography of her husband, Anna tells the truth. "During the day," she wrote, "it happened that [Dostoevsky] had an angry exchange and almost a quarrel with his sister Vera Mikhailovna, who had arrived from Moscow (of course this should not be mentioned in print)." The quarrel, whose details we learn from Lyubov, concerned the Kumanina estate and took place at the dinner table. The issue of the estate arose because, despite having renounced his claims to a share in 1844, Dostoevsky had succeeded in being reinstated and now owed money to his sisters. Vera Mikhailovna, speaking for her

---

[19] Volgin, *Posledny god Dostoevskogo*, 414. My chapter on Dostoevsky's last days is greatly indebted to Volgin's book.

sister Alexandra as well, thought his reinstatement had been unfair. Tempers rose as these matters came to the fore, with Vera finally breaking into tears. "Dostoevsky lost patience," his daughter writes, "and in order to cut short these painful recriminations, rose from the table before the meal was finished. At the same time as my mother tried to detain her sister-in-law, continuing to weep and preparing to return home as quickly as possible, my father shut himself in his room." Sitting down at his writing table, he passed his hand over his mouth and moustaches, and then withdrew it in a fright—it was covered with blood! There are some discrepancies of detail in these two versions ("during the day"; "at dinner"), but the main facts are clear enough, and Lyubov's account is more extensive.[20]

At six that evening Anna sent an imploring letter to Dr. von Bretsall, who finally arrived. After he had auscultated the patient, a strong new flow of blood began that caused Dostoevsky to lose consciousness for a brief time. Dr. von Bretsall thought it wise to send for a noted specialist, Professor Koshlakov, who did not disturb the patient with another examination. Since the flow of blood had diminished, he speculated that perhaps a "clot" had developed and that "the case was going in the direction of recovery."[21] After recommending that Dostoevsky speak and move as little as possible, the specialist left, but von Bretzell was less sanguine and advised Anna to send for a priest. One came from the nearby Vladimirsky church to administer communion to Dostoevsky and listen to his confession.

———■———

On the night of the twenty-fifth—the night his nosebleed occurred—other events were also taking place in the very building where the Dostoevskys occupied apartment 10. Apartment 11 was actually a small rooming house where individuals could rent single accommodations. Sometime before midnight on the twenty-fifth, the police entered that apartment and carried out a search of one of the rooms in the presence of witnesses. Its inhabitant, Alexander Barannikov, had been arrested elsewhere earlier that day, and, although he carried a false passport, there was a well-founded suspicion that he was a member of the executive committee of the terrorist People's Will. Barannikov enjoyed a considerable reputation with the police as one of the most dangerous of their opponents, having been involved in all the attempts so far made to assassinate Alexander II. He was best known as the accomplice of Kravchinsky in the murder of General Mezentsev, having distracted attention from the assassination by firing a shot and then driving the carriage in which both men escaped. That Dostoevsky had

[20] Ibid., 416–418.
[21] Ibid.

been living side-by-side, for two and a half months, with one of the most sought-after terrorists in his country was noticed by Victor Shklovsky, who made their neighborliness the subject of a short story in 1933, and he also discussed the incident in his short book on Dostoevsky years later.[22]

The name of Dostoevsky is not mentioned in any of the police reports, but there is a suggestive remark in the memoirs of another revolutionary, M. F. Frolenko, one of Barannikov's comrades. He remembers Barannikov's surprising calm in face of the possibility of capture, and attributes this both to the quietness of the neighborhood in which he resided and to the fact that he lived in "the apartment" of Dostoevsky (presumably meaning "apartment house").[23] The writer's presence was thus far from being unknown to his neighbor; and he felt it to be an additional protection against suspicion and discovery. Whether Dostoevsky, who liked to chat with people in the street, and especially with young men, ever exchanged a word with the well-mannered Barannikov can only remain a matter for conjecture.

As we know from the unpleasant incidents at Bad Ems, Dostoevsky needed absolute silence while writing, and would not hesitate to attempt to end any disturbing commotion. Is it possible that he was upset by the disruptive noises next door and, on going out to inquire, became terribly upset when he discovered what was taking place? Or might the police, still trying to establish the identity of their prisoner, have come to his flat and questioned him about his next-door neighbor? None of these speculations is beyond the realm of possibility, and if they had occurred, they could well have contributed to Dostoevsky's fatal illness.

———■———

On the evening of January 26, Dostoevsky had taken confession and communion from the priest of the nearby church. At two in the morning of January 27, Anna wrote a note to Miller, explaining that her husband had become "seriously ill" the night before and could not fulfill his obligation to read on the Pushkin evening. Anna also wrote to Countess Komarovskaya, explaining why Dostoevsky could not come to the Marble Palace on January 29.[24]

On the morning of the twenty-seventh, after sleeping soundly, Dostoevsky awoke feeling "cheerful and healthy." The flow of blood had ceased, and hope thus revived that the worst was over. Suvorin describes him as being "jovial and calm, joking, speaking of the future, of his work, of his children, soothing those

---

[22] See Victor Shklovsky, *Za i protiv* (Moscow, 1957), 254–255. Even though the official documents give the number of Barannikov's apartment as 11, Shklovsky continues to maintain, without offering evidence, that the number was changed in the official documents.

[23] Volgin, *Posledny god Dostoevskogo*, 436.

[24] *Letopis*, 3: 543.

around him. 'Why are you reading my funeral service? I will outlive all of you.'" [25] Miller and Elena Shtakenshneider came to call, and letters and telegrams began to pile up as friends and acquaintances passed on the word of his illness. Dostoevsky decided to dictate a "bulletin" about his health to Anna, and a draft of a similar one, addressed to Countess Elizaveta Geyden, appears as the last letter in his correspondence. Here Dostoevsky objectively describes what has occurred and the temporary betterment of his condition. "But since the burst vein has not healed, a hemorrhage may start again. And then, of course, death is likely. Now, however, he is fully conscious and vigorous, but afraid that the artery will again burst." [26] He was indeed "fully conscious," and when the typesetter arrived with the galleys of the *Diary* for final approval, he was able to participate in a correction.

Professor Koshlakov, returning about seven in the evening, found the patient much improved, predicting that he would be up and about in a week. Vera Mikhailovna and Dostoevsky's stepson, Pavel Isaev, also showed up, though Anna hardly welcomed his presence. Dostoevsky slept soundly through most of the night, but when Anna awoke at seven and looked over at him, she found him staring at her fixedly. Speaking in a half-whisper, he said: "You know, Anna, I have not been sleeping for three hours now, and have been thinking all that time; and only now have I clearly realized that I shall die today." [27]

Sweeping aside whatever she may have hastily uttered in reply, he continued: "Light a candle, Anna, and hand me the New Testament." This was the volume given to him by the Decembrist wives in Siberia, and throughout his life it had never left his possession. Opening its pages at random, as he had often done in the past to divine what the future might hold, he asked Anna to read the first passage he had come across. This was from Saint Matthew, chapter 13, verses 14–15, in which Jesus asks John the Baptist to baptize him, and John replies: "I have need to be baptized of thee, and comest thou to me?" The Russian text, translated literally, then reads: "And Jesus said to him: 'Delay not, for thus it becomes us to fulfill the great truth.'" As Anna was reciting this passage in a trembling voice, and with tears in her eyes, he said: "you hear—delay not—that means I will die." [28]

Anna never forgot the next few hours during which her husband tried to console her, "uttering tender and affectionate words, thanking me for the happy life that he had spent with me. He entrusted the children to my care, said that he believed in me, and hoped I would always love and protect them." One utterance above all was cherished, which, as she writes, not many other husbands

[25] Volgin, *Posledny god Dostoevskogo*, 420.
[26] *PSS*, 30/Bk. 1: 242–243; January 28, 1881.
[27] *Reminiscences*, 345–346.
[28] Ibid.

could proffer to their wives after fourteen years of marriage: "Remember, Anya, I have always loved you passionately, and never betrayed you once, not even in thought."[29] Clutching her hand, he fell asleep about ten o'clock, but woke suddenly at eleven, sank back on the pillow, and blood began to flow again. He recovered somewhat from this attack, but when Anna tried to console him, "he only sadly shook his head, as if fully convinced that the prediction of his death today would not be gainsaid."[30]

New Time published the first announcement of Dostoevsky's illness on January 28, and a flood of visitors immediately began to besiege the grief-stricken Anna. Only Maikov, at Dostoevsky's request, was allowed to come to his bedside. The newspaper story pronounced, in a mixture of sarcasm and eulogy, "Those people who, not long since, reproached him for too often seeking ovations at public readings, may now quiet down: the public will not listen to him again very soon. If only the precious life be preserved for the Russian people of the most profound of our contemporary writers, the direct inheritor of our literary geniuses!"[31] When this passage was read to Dostoevsky, who was curious ("What are they saying about me?"), he asked Anna to read it again. In his very last hours he thus had the satisfaction of hearing his enemies mocked, and his own genius celebrated as the continuator of the Russian literary tradition. It is possible that he took communion and confession again, and at five o'clock he dictated the bulletin to Countess Geyden already mentioned.

Dostoevsky then asked that the children be summoned, and they kissed him while he gave them his final blessing, enjoining them always to love and obey their mother. He requested that his copy of the New Testament be given to his son Fedya and that the parable of the Prodigal Son be read to the children. Lyubov later recalled him telling them that, if they should ever commit a crime (*prestuplenie*, which has a wider meaning than merely a legal offense) to trust God as their Father, plead with him for forgiveness, and be certain that he would rejoice in their repentance, just as the father had done on the return of the Prodigal Son. It was this parable of transgression, repentance, and forgiveness that he wished to leave as a last heritage to his children, and it may well be seen as his own ultimate understanding of the meaning of his life and the message of his work.

There was again a copious flow of blood at about 6:30, and he fell into a coma from which he never awoke. During the final death throes, which lasted for approximately two hours, he was mercifully unconscious. Anna and the children were "kneeling and crying" all the while, but trying to choke back their sobs because they had been told that the auditory sense was the last to go and that any

[29] Ibid., 346.
[30] Volgin, *Posledny god*, 422.
[31] *Letopis*, 3: 545–546.

sound might prolong the suffering of the dying. "I held the hand of my husband in my own," Anna writes, "and felt the pulse becoming feebler and feebler."[32]

Maikov had sent for another doctor, and when the writer Boleslav Markevich came to the door (he had been dispatched by Countess Tolstaya to inquire after Dostoevsky's condition), he was mistaken for this personage. With a "heartrending shriek," the eleven-year-old Lyubov rushed to meet him, shouting: "Doctor, Doctor, for God's sake, save my father [*papashy*], he is wheezing." This was the last death rattle, and when the doctor arrived a few moments later, he could do nothing but certify the decease. Markevich, whose writing was known for its melodramatic effects, pictures Anna and Lyubov in hysterics, with Anna exclaiming, "Oh, whom have I lost! Whom have I lost!" as she sank into a chair. "'Whom has Russia lost' involuntarily, and at the same time, broke out of Maikov and myself."[33] This final sentence could not have more feelingly expressed the sentiment of all of literate Russia.

Anna's brother arrived that evening, two hours after Dostoevsky's death, and "thanks to [him], I was relieved of all practical problems, and was spared much that was difficult and unpleasant in these sorrowful days."[34] The next morning, the twenty-ninth, Suvorin was in the apartment early and, in an article the next day, described with a shudder how the corpse had been washed and prepared for burial. He dashed off a note to the artist Kramskoy, asking him to come round immediately because Anna had spoken of "photographs and masks" being made.[35] Kramskoy did produce a famous drawing of the dead Dostoevsky, with his head lying on a pillow and with what seems to be the beginning of a faint half-smile on his face. All of the many memoirists confirm that Kramskoy had caught the unusual expression they had seen themselves. The sculptor Bernshtam, instead of beginning on the planned bust of Dostoevsky, took the plaster cast for a death mask.

Dostoevsky's friends in high places began to do what they could on behalf of the family. Pobedonostsev informed Loris-Melikov of the death and requested that he inform Alexander II. He also wrote the tsarevich to enlist his aid in obtaining some financial help for the family, urging him to speak to Loris-Melikov as well. An official of the Ministry of Internal Affairs soon arrived to inform Anna that the expenses of the funeral would be borne by the government, but Anna claimed to have proudly refused: "I considered it my moral obligation to bury my husband with the money he had earned."[36] No such refusal is mentioned in the official report, and she is described as having expressed gratitude for the aid.

[32] *Reminiscences*, 348.
[33] Volgin, *Posledny god*, 429–430.
[34] *Reminiscences*, 351.
[35] *Letopis*, 3: 547–548.
[36] *Reminiscences*, 352.

30. Dostoevsky on his bier, by I. N. Kramskoy

The first service for the dead (*panikhida*) began at one o'clock in the afternoon. It had been announced in the newspapers, and Anna observed that "known and unknown arrived to pray at his coffin, and there were so many that very quickly all the five rooms were filled with a dense crowd, and when the office for the dead was recited the children and I had a hard time pushing through the crowd to stand near the coffin."[37] Pobedonostsev wrote to Katkov the same day, requesting that the money owed Dostoevsky be sent to Anna as speedily as possible, along with the authority to collect it in her name. "Today was the first *panikhida*," he added. "He seems as if still alive, with a face of total quietude, as in the best moments of his life."[38] Anna's brother then went to the Novodeichy

[37] Ibid.
[38] *Letopis*, 3: 550.

monastery, where, at the time of Nekrasov's funeral, Dostoevsky had expressed a desire to be buried. But the price demanded for a gravesite seemed so exorbitant that it was decided to seek elsewhere. Anna suggested the Okhtinsky monastery, which contained the graves of their son Alyosha and of Anna's father, and they planned to go there the next morning to buy a plot.

Meanwhile, however, others had heard of the Dostoevskys' difficulties, and an important editor and publisher, prompted by the wife of a general, approached Metropolitan Isidor of the Alexander Nevsky *lavra* (a religious compound containing a cemetery) to suggest that it would be fitting for Dostoevsky to be buried there free of charge. Their request was met with a flat refusal: the worthy and learned metropolitan said that he was nothing but "a simple novelist, who never wrote anything serious," and that in addition his funeral might cause a "disorder undesirable within the walls of the *lavra*."[39] When Pobedonostsev, now the highest secular official in charge of the Russian Church, heard of this retort at the evening *panikhida*, he responded, "We will allocate the money for the burial of Dostoevsky." Metropolitan Isidor was no doubt read a thorough lesson in private, and the next day the newspapers announced that the place of burial would be the Alexander Nevsky *lavra*.

At the evening *panikhida*, the cramped apartment of the Dostoevskys was even more filled to overflowing; a newspaper correspondent wrote that those arriving at eight could not reach the coffin until at least ten. Saltykov-Shchedrin was there, and so was Countess Komarovskaya, accompanied by Baroness Feleisen. In a letter to Grand Duke Konstantin Konstantinovich, the countess described how the two titled ladies were unable to approach the coffin all through the service—no doubt a new experience for those before whom everyone made way. When the countess finally saw Dostoevsky, she too was struck by his expression: "As if alive, a bright, peaceful face . . . like a man who has done his duty, borne everything, not at all embittered." The children were busy around the coffin, lighting candles that had been snuffed out by the lack of air and "asking visitors not to kiss the forehead [of the corpse] but the icon."[40]

Ever since his return from Siberia in 1860, Dostoevsky had dreamed of uniting Russian society into one harmonious whole linked by faith and love. The closest this sublime chimera ever came to being realized was during the days when his body lay in its bier. All—literally all—of those who made up the cultural-political life of St. Petersburg, the nerve center of the Russian Empire, came to pay him homage. Saltykov-Shchedrin rubbed elbows with Countess Komarovskaya; Mikhailovsky, who had just begun to write under a pseudonym for the underground newspaper of the terrorist People's Will, found himself in

[39] Ibid., 551.
[40] Ibid.

the same rooms with Pobedonostsev and Grand Duke Dimitry, who was there accompanied by his tutor. Contemporaries themselves could not help marveling at the unanimity of grief and of reverence suddenly exhibited by all sections of a society otherwise torn apart by unceasing conflict—a conflict that, just a month later, would culminate in the assassination of Alexander II. Anna later remarked that, if her husband had not died on January 28, he would have had only a month longer to live—the news about Alexander would certainly have brought on an arterial rupture.

It is not surprising that those who had known him personally, or had taken part either for or against him in the literary polemics of the day, should have felt it obligatory to participate in the funeral ceremonies. More remarkable is the astonishingly widespread response that the news of his death aroused in the community at large, especially among the student youth. Koni recalls one of his young lawyers, whom he had asked to read a legal brief aloud, hesitating and stumbling while doing so. When asked if he were ill, he blurted out the news (which Koni had not yet heard) that Dostoevsky was dead, and then dissolved into tears.[41] As the word spread in the *gymnasiums* and the schools of higher learning in the capital, groups immediately began to organize, to assign delegates to attend the *panikhida*, and to collect funds to buy wreaths so that they could participate en masse in the burial ceremonies.

Dostoevsky's appeal to the student youth was never more apparent than on this final occasion. I. F. Tyumenev, a student at the Academy of Fine Arts, has left a classic account of the funeral and the procession in which he and his comrades took part. He remarked that if Turgenev, Goncharov, or Ostrovsky had died, their loss would not have been as "painful" as that of Dostoevsky, "who had just begun to attract the attention of society, just begun to interest everyone with his 'Karamazovs,' and just getting ready to continue narrating the fate of Alyosha, this (according to his intention) new Russian evangelical Socialist."[42] Tyumenev is obviously in sympathy with what he accurately calls Alyosha's "evangelical Socialism," and he also speaks as if his work had just come to public attention and gained a widespread readership. Although far from being true, this error helps us to understand why a new generation had become so receptive to his influence; they had grown up absorbing Populist (not Nihilist) ideas, and thus would not turn away from the Christian implications of Dostoevsky's moral ideal. The remainder of this entry describes the instantaneous decision of the students in the academy to collect funds. When those assigned to the task were met occasionally by the question, "And who is this Dostoevsky?" no answer was given; some of the collectors even spat to show their contempt for such ignorance.

[41] *DVS*, 2: 246.
[42] Ibid., 479.

On the afternoon of January 30, the head of the censorship, N. S. Abaza, presented Anna with a letter from the Ministry of Finance informing her that the tsar had deigned to grant her a lifetime pension of two thousand rubles a year "because of [her husband's] services to Russian literature."[43] This was, apparently, the first pension of its kind ever awarded in Russia to a writer as such. (Those given to Pushkin and Karamzin, who had occupied official government positions as sinecures, were for their services to the state.) Two vacancies, one in the prestigious Corps of Pages and the other in the Smolny Institute (a school for daughters of the nobility), also were to be reserved for the Dostoevsky children, and while Anna accepted all these offers gratefully, she later sent both children to other educational institutions.

Meanwhile, on the evening of the same day, Grigorovich made a list of all the groups who wanted to march in the funeral procession and established an order of the places where the delegates should assemble. The student representatives were told to help maintain order; older Dostoevsky friends were also appointed to oversee various groupings. The procession would begin at 10:30 the next morning (it started at 11:00) and proceed from the apartment to the Alexander Nevsky *lavra* along the Nevsky Prospect.

—■—

January 31, a Saturday, dawned bright and clear. *The Diary of a Writer* appeared on that very day. A numberless crowd had gathered around the apartment at Kuznechny Alley by nine o'clock that morning, all bearing wreaths and banners inscribed with the names of their institutions and societies, including journals and newspapers. A count made came to sixty-seven such groups, with fifteen choirs accompanying the cortège. Tyumenev described the moment when the coffin emerged from the house and appeared to the crowd. "From the belfry of the Vladimirsky church sounded the bell, and just right after the first impact a solemn 'Holy God' rang out. . . . At the first sound of the prayer all heads were bared . . . and to many of us, sobs rose in our throats. At that moment everyone, whether believer or not, felt something like the breath of godliness."[44] The procession wound its way through the streets, the coffin being carried by alternating bearers; among the first were Dostoevsky's surviving fellow Petrashevtsy, A. I. Palm and A. N. Pleshcheev. They were followed by mourners stretching for almost a mile, with banners and wreaths. "It can boldly be said," wrote Strakhov, "that, up until then, there had never before been such a funeral in Russia."[45]

Observers were struck by the orderliness of the crowd. The police kept their distance, except for one episode not reported in the newspapers but appearing

[43] *Letopis*, 3: 554.
[44] *DVS*, 2: 480.
[45] Cited in Volgin, *Posledny god*, 495.

in two private memoirs. One delegation of women students, instead of a wreath, displayed a pair of the convict shackles that Dostoevsky had worn and about which he had written in *House of the Dead*. When the police came to appropriate them, they were surrendered peacefully so as not to disturb the solemnity of the occasion. Dostoevsky's prison past was one of his badges of honor, and when an elderly passer-by asked a member of the delegation who was receiving such a majestic funeral, the answer came back, "A *katorzhnik*" (an exiled convict). The mass of the population assumed that such an imposing cortège must be that of some important general.

It took two hours for the coffin to reach the portals of the Alexander Nevsky *lavra*, where it was met at the gateway by the students of the Theological Seminary and the clergy in their ceremonial robes. The clergy were led by the head of the *lavra*, Archimandrite Simeon, and the rector of the Theological Seminary, Dostoevsky's old friend Father Yanishev. After the coffin was carried into the Church of the Holy Spirit within the *lavra*, the doors of the entry were closed and only delegations with wreaths were admitted. The crowd was told that the church would hold at most fifteen hundred mourners, and the procession began to disperse until about four the next day, when the burial would take place. At eight o'clock that evening the night service for the dead began, attended by Anna and the children (Lyubov had almost been crushed in the crowd around the gates earlier in the day). "The church," Anna wrote, "was filled with those in prayer; many were . . . students of various higher educational institutions, the Theological Academy and *kursistki*. The majority of them stayed in the church for the entire night, relaying each other in reading the psalms over Dostoevsky's coffin."[46]

On February 1, the day of the burial, a second edition of the *Diary* was published, its first page rimmed with a black border. At ten o'clock, a mass was performed in the church in the presence of Pobedonostsev and other high officials of the government, and this was followed by the *otpevanie*, the service for the dead. Father Yanishev then spoke a few words about his friend, all of whose work as a novelist, he said quite acutely, was an echo of Christ's Sermon on the Mount. The coffin, which remained closed on Pobedonostsev's order so as to spare Anna and the children, was then carried to a plot in the cemetery adjoining the grave of the poet Zhukovsky. Lyubov gave a heartrending cry, which moved all those present to their depths when she exclaimed: "Good-bye [*proshchai*, which can also mean forgive], dear, kind, good papa, good-bye."[47] Various people spoke at the grave, and Popov, who climbed a tree to get a better view above the crowd, recalled "the apostolic figure of V. S. Solovyev

[46] *Reminiscences*, 359.
[47] *Letopis*, 3: 561.

[with his] curls falling on his forehead," "who spoke with great pathos and expressiveness."[48]

Let us end with some of Solovyev's words, ones not spoken at the grave site but days earlier (January 30) in the lectures he was giving both at the University of St. Petersburg and at the Bestuzhev Higher Courses for Women, whose students were among Dostoevsky's most fervent admirers. To the first, he said, "last year, at the Pushkin festival, Dostoevsky called Pushkin a prophet, but Dostoevsky himself deserves this title to an even greater degree." To the female students, he declared: "Just as the highest worldly power somehow or other becomes concentrated in one person, who represents a state, similarly the highest spiritual power in each epoch usually belongs in every people to one man, who more clearly than all grasps the spiritual ideals of mankind, more consciously than all strives to attain them, more strongly than all affects others by his preachments. Such a spiritual leader of the Russian people in recent times was Dostoevsky."[49]

[48] *DVS*, 2: 478.
[49] *Letopis*, 3: 548, 553.

EDITOR'S NOTE

I was delighted when Joseph Frank asked if I would compose the one-volume edition of his monumental five-volume work on Dostoevsky. As I reread the volumes to formulate some principles for editing, it became clear that the rich detail (of biography, literary culture, ideology) is employed in a singular manner—namely, to bring out the full power of Dostoevsky's work. All of the stories and novels are then analyzed, as literary texts, in separate, self-contained chapters. Frank doesn't analyze the literary work as a window into Dostoevsky's life and times, quite the reverse; and what he achieves in the process is a literary criticism that gives the reader the most intense and clearest possible impression of the fiction.

My aim as I set to work was to maintain that brilliant balance of biography, literary criticism, and intellectual history that Joseph Frank originated; and to keep as well the "novelistic" narrative style so appropriate to the life of Dostoevsky. The challenge was to do this while cutting nearly two-thirds of the original material. I therefore went through several editing rounds carefully, cutting more each round, summarizing more each round, reorganizing or rewriting passages as needed for narrative cohesion. I frequently combined two, three, or even four chapters of the original volumes into one chapter. For the major novels, I maintained a separate chapter or chapters for the analysis of the literary text, as in the original volumes, though condensing as necessary. For some of the early minor works, however, I was forced to weave Frank's analysis of the literary text into the narrative; and I did this by cutting much of the plot summary and focusing on the key ideas of the work and its significance for Dostoevsky's development as a writer, or for the development of important themes in Dostoevsky's greatest novels. Despite the cuts, the essential material of the original is preserved.

My warmest thanks to Robin Feuer Miller for reading the first draft of the condensation side by side with the original and for her suggestions for restoring text; to Joseph Frank for his meticulous review of the condensation in its final stages; and to Hanne Winarsky, whose idea it was to bring out this edition, for her generous and steadfast support.

Mary Petrusewicz is an independent scholar, writer, and translator who lectures in Russian literature and history at Stanford University.

INDEX

Page numbers in italics refer to illustrations. Mentions of Dostoevsky in subheadings and qualifiers are abbreviated "FMD."